P9-CSG-827

The Holt Foreign Film Guide

The Holt Foreign Film Guide

Ronald Bergan and Robyn Karney

HENRY HOLT AND COMPANY
NEW YORK

First published in the United States in 1989 by
Henry Holt and Company, Inc.,
115 West 18th Street, New York,
New York 10011.

Originally published in Great Britain under the title
Bloomsbury Foreign Film Guide.

Library of Congress Catalog Card Number:

88 - 45750

ISBN 0-8050-0991-4
First American Edition
Printed in Great Britain
10 9 8 7 6 5 4 3 2 1

Introduction

As ever-increasing numbers of travellers love to visit the Taj Mahal, the Kremlin, the Eiffel Tower, the castles of the Rhine, Mount Fujiyama, the Sistine Chapel and the pyramids, so growing numbers of movie lovers have come to relish Indian, Russian, French, German, Japanese, Italian or Arabic films—not to mention the riches that are coming our way from China, Argentina, Spain, Brazil, Turkey, the Philippines, West Africa, and indeed, almost every country in the world. For, in an age of internationalism, the cinema has proved itself the most international of arts.

However, as there are some people who prefer never to venture out of their own country and feel, like the Nancy Mitford character, that 'abroad is unutterably bloody and foreigners are fiends,' so there are cinema-goers who seldom take a journey into the world of non-English language films. Still residing in the minds of many is the idea that foreign-language films are somehow elitist, representing the 'serious', the 'heavy' and the 'intellectual' branch of the cinema industry. There is an element of truth in this, but it is secondary to the fact that foreign film cannot be categorized.

We hope and believe that this book will prove a valuable reference for students, buffs and committed foreign-film enthusiasts in that it collates a wealth of factual information in one volume. However, our major purpose has been to open an Aladdin's cave for those movie-lovers who are still intimidated by the challenge of the foreign film. In browsing through our pages, in using the book as a guide and a reference, it should become clear that the vast range of films from over 50 countries is as multifarious as the cultures that produced them. Here, you will find the best (and occasionally, the worst) of gangster movies, horror pics, whodunnits, Westerns, melodramas, musicals, war epics, love stories, comedies and tragedies, and realize that entertainment and escapism are not the preserve of Hollywood. Where the foreign film *does* often differ is in transcending formula, using experiment and innovation to amuse, shock, or provoke us into a new awareness and understanding of issues and of the medium.

Most of the greatest films ever made come from outside the English-speaking world. Many European, African and Asian governments are generous in subsidizing their film industries, treating them as part of their country's essential culture and allowing directors and producers the freedom to work without the commercial constraints that bedevil their British and American counterparts. The films are not, on the whole, products of big studios where decisions, at every stage, are taken by the front office. As a result, they tend to be personal and individual in their artistic expression, thus enabling us to enter into an alien culture even more easily than travel might do, since they illuminate the character of the people and the psychology of a nation.

More and more countries are producing films that are entering the international bloodstream. African nations like Mali, Burkino Faso (formerly Upper Volta), Mauritania and Senegal have given birth to directors of unique imagination such as Ousmane Sembène, Souleymane Cissé and Med Hondo; China is sending films of spectacular visual quality, as well as absorbing content, to a Western world ever more eager to receive them; and Denmark, neglected as a film-making country since the days of Carl Dreyer, is experiencing a renaissance which won it a prestigious double in 1988 when *Babette's Feast* took the Best Foreign Film Oscar, and *Pelle The Conqueror* carried off the Palme D'Or at Cannes. Foreign films have become an integral part of our cultural landscape and the barriers between the worlds of English-speaking cinema and the rest are disappearing daily. Over the last few decades we have grown used to seeing 'our' stars—Burt Lancaster, Donald Sutherland, Robert De Niro, John Gielgud—acting for Luchino Visconti, Federico Fellini, Bernardo Bertolucci and Andrzej Wajda; Nastassia Kinski, Christopher Lambert, Isabella Rossellini and Charlotte Rampling move with ease between English-speaking and foreign films; Louis Malle can make *Atlantic City* in the United States and return to his native France a few years later for *Au Revoir Les Enfants*.

Of course, this cultural cross-fertilization is not new. From its earliest days, Hollywood has benefited from the influx of gifted Europeans. From Sweden came Greta Gustafsson (Garbo) and Ingrid Bergman (mother of Isabella Rossellini), from Germany Maria Magdalena Dietrich Von Losch (Marlene Dietrich) and from Austria Hedy Kiesler (Hedy Lamarr). Italy gave America Sofia Sciccolone (Sophia Loren), Egypt supplied Michael Shalhoub (Omar Sharif), from France came Charles Boyer and Maurice Chevalier. All of these, and many more stars familiar to us, began their careers in their native lands, appearing in many of the films which are dealt with in the following pages. Also under scrutiny here is a generous selection of the pre-Hollywood work of directors such as Ernst Lubitsch, Fritz Lang, Douglas Sirk (Detlef Sierck), Robert Siodmak, Billy Wilder, Roman Polanski, Milos Forman and Andrei Konchalovsky.

Hollywood has drawn inspiration from the foreign cinema, as a glance at the long list of Hollywood remakes will confirm: Akira Kurosawa's *Seven Samurai* became *The Magnificent Seven*; Julie Andrews starred in the remake of Germany's 1933 *Viktor Und Viktoria*, while the French *Three Men And A Cradle* took only two years to become *Three Men And A Baby*. René Clair's *À Nous La Liberté* furnished Chaplin with the basis for his *Modern Times* and, more recently, the bath scene in *Fatal Attraction* was clearly lifted from Clouzot's classic thriller, *Les Diaboliques*. Woody Allen, who idolizes Ingmar Bergman ('The greatest artist that ever pointed a camera at anything') and Fellini, has paid his own tribute to them with *Interiors, A Midsummer Night's Sex Comedy*, and *Stardust Memories*.

Although, in the 1920s, the general public in Britain and America flocked to see silent masterpieces such as Eisenstein's *Battleship Potemkin*, Clair's *The Italian Straw Hat*, and Abel Gance's *Napoleon*, a wider appreciation of foreign films began to spread after World War II, when Italian, Japanese, German and French motion pictures were once more available in the Allied countries. The increasing awareness of the quality of these films was aided by the recognition given each year by the Academy of Motion Pictures, Arts and Sciences. Vittorio De Sica's *Shoeshine* was the first to receive a special award from the Academy in 1947 and, since 1956, with Fellini's *La Strada* the first winner, the Academy has given an Oscar, in competition, to the Best Foreign-Language Film.

Nowadays, there are few regular movie-goers who are not familiar with the names of directors such as Buñuel, Bergman, Truffaut, Kurosawa, Fassbinder, Malle and Fellini; or unacquainted with performers such as Brigitte Bardot, Jean Gabin, Jean-Paul Belmondo, Catherine Deneuve, Alain Delon, Marcello Mastroianni, Stéphane Audran, Toshiro Mifune, Klaus Kinski, Gérard Depardieu, Monica Vitti, Max Von Sydow, Isabelle Adjani and Karl-Maria Brandauer. With the mushrooming of small cinemas that show foreign films, the plentiful showings on British and American television, the proliferation of, and growing interest in, festivals all over the world, including Sydney, Toronto and Hong Kong, we can look forward to larger audiences than ever for foreign film.

We feel, therefore, that it is now appropriate to offer movie-goers an accessible guide for quick—and, we hope, entertaining and illuminating—consultation on plot, critical opinion, general context and credits. We have not attempted to suppress our personal likes and dislikes, our prejudices and blind spots, or our enthusiasms, but we have tried to give the reader enough objective information to be able to assess the type, quality, content and style of each work under discussion.

Selection of titles

Our book contains over 2,000 entries. As tens of thousands of foreign films have been made since the dawn of the cinema, our list is necessarily selective, but we set out to be as wide-ranging and far-reaching as possible. We hope that not only do we have almost every significant film—classics which have stood the test of time or works that are integral to cinema history—but big box-office successes and movies which, irrespective of quality or current appeal, are representative of trends, fashions, styles and developments.

Although we have included some films that are difficult to see for various reasons, our choice has been dictated, to a large extent, by films that have been publicly released or shown on television in Britain and/or the United States; those included in retrospectives at the National Film Theatre and other repertory cinemas in Britain, or the Museum of Modern Art and similar establishments in the USA; films with a reputation; films that are significant in the understanding of a film-maker's work as a whole, or of a specific country's film history; a large number of winners from the three major festivals at Cannes, Venice and Berlin; experimental, *avant-garde* and underground films; the purely commercial, and a small selection of opera films (as opposed to filmed opera) and documentaries.

In the case of several directors of exceptional stature and reputation—among them Jean Renoir, Fellini, Eisenstein, Robert Bresson, Buñuel and Kurosawa—we have dealt with their complete, or almost complete *oeuvres*. With others, such as Kenji Mizoguchi and Yasujiro Ozu, who were phenomenally prolific, we have included most of their mature extant works, together with examples of their early works of quality.

On the whole, we have omitted movies that are virtually impossible to see in their original foreign language versions, many of which were specifically shot in English for release in Britain and the USA or are only ever screened with an execrably dubbed sound track. These include 'Spaghetti' Westerns, Italian muscle epics; films, such as *The Young Girls Of Rochefort* and *Daughters Of Darkness*, released exclusively in English, or Jean-Pierre Melville's *The Red Circle*, shown only in a dubbed and mutilated version. On the other hand, a film such as Visconti's *The Leopard*, made simultaneously in English, can be seen in Italian and is, in any case, a major example of its director's work and is therefore included. Eisenstein's unfinished *Que Viva Mexico* has been omitted because it exists in so many forms, all mutilated, and is generally shown as *Time In The Sun* with a specially written English commentary. Others with an English commentary, however, such as the Russian *Tchaikowsky* or the Dutch documentary, *The Voice Of The Water*, are included because, commentary or no, the dialogue within the films is in its original language.

Names and accents

We have tried to be as accurate as possible in the spelling of names, standardizing where there are discrepancies in source material. These occur very often when actors change the way their names are spelled; where Italians in French films or vice versa are billed with a variation in spelling; or, most significantly, when names are transcribed from languages with a different alphabet. The difficulty can be summarized by the case of the Russian director, Josef Heifits. In the course of our researches, we have come across Mr Heifits billed in the following forms: Iosif and Yosif Heifitz (National Film Theatre programmes), Josif Heifits (*Oxford Companion To Film*), Josef and Joseph Heifits (Leslie Halliwell's *Film Guide*), Iosif Kheyfits (Scheuer's *TV Film Guide*), Jozef Heifitz (Katz's *International Film Ecyclopaedia*) and Josef Heifets (Richard Roud's *The Cinema: A Critical Dictionary*). None of these gentlemen is wrong, and the Heifits saga has been the least of our problems!

Accents have presented a major difficulty. In deference to the cultures whose work we discuss and in the interests of reference, we elected to use accents. Having done so, however, it became clear why so many English-language publications now omit them. Source material is contradictory and incomplete and often without the accents, while even the screen credits themselves vary in usage, non-usage or conflicting usage. Consequently, we have had to do our incomplete best and beg indulgence—particularly from the Czechs, Poles, Hungarians, Yugoslavs, Bulgarians and Scandinavians—towards errors and omissions.

Explanatory notes

TITLES: Films are filed alphabetically, ignoring the article. Thus *The Story Of A Cheat* will be found under S. We have used the English-language title as known in Britain, but, when the American title differs, we have listed this beneath, as well as any *aka* (also known as) titles. All US and aka titles are cross-referred. Thus, if you look up Louis Malle's *Murmur Of The Heart*, you will be instructed to see *Dearest Love* for the entry, since that is the British release title.

There are exceptions to the English-language rule where the title of a film has never been translated or the film is best known under its original foreign title eg *La Dolce Vita* (filed under D). The original foreign title is given beneath the English-language title or titles. This, too, is cross-referred as described above.

COUNTRY OF ORIGIN: This generally relates to the original language of the movie, regardless of how many countries were involved in the production process financially and/or creatively, or in terms of locations. That French money, for example, helped to finance films by Youssef Chahine doesn't alter the fact that these films are Egyptian. There are exceptions—Helma Sanders-Brahms' *The Future Of Emily*, for example. Here we have combined French and German money financing a German director, a French cinematographer, a combined French and German cast, and locations in both countries, to justify the shared credit for country of origin.

DATE: This refers, wherever possible, to the date of the film's first release, generally in the country of origin. Sometimes this coincides with the foreign release date, but there are often gaps of some years.

RUNNING TIME: This is always a contentious subject. Pictures are often cut after festival showings or initial release, or on reaching the USA or Britain, or for television. There are distributor's cuts and/or censor's cuts and, on occasion, replacement of cut material. Needless to say, this can cause a deal of confusion and we have opted, as far as possible, to give the original running time. Silent films, shot at a different speed and with their running times originally given in metres, pose a different problem. All silent film times are, therefore, approximate.

COLOUR: The abbreviations bw and col are used to indicate black-and-white or colour.

PRODUCTION COMPANY: As we have indicated in our notes on country of origin, films are very often co-productions, largely for financial reasons. We have tried to indicate the involvement of different countries where relevant eg MK2 Productions (Paris)/Austra(Brazil).

TECHNICAL CREDITS: These are given in the following order: director (d), screenplay (sc), cinematographer (ph) and composer (m). The music credit generally refers to the soundtrack composer, although the use of classical music is identified and, on occasion, pop music is identified by its performers. Silent films are denoted as such under the music credit. Where there *is* no music credit, the film had no music or, more rarely, there is no credit listed anywhere. In no more than two or three instances, a photography or writing credit may be missing because it is totally unavailable.

CAST: All leading players are named, as well as significant supporting cast.

TEXT: Each piece opens with a plot summary. We have tried to keep the surprises—not give away the murderer and so forth. We have generally matched players to leading roles except where role attributions have proved contradictory or unavailable. Plot is followed by critical comment and any information of special interest.

AWARDS: We have confined awards, given at the bottom of an entry, to the Best Film, Best Director, Best Actor and Best Actress as given at Cannes, Venice and Berlin, and to the Oscar winners for Best Foreign Film. The date given is the date of the award presentation.

Authors' Acknowledgements

It only remains to thank those who have helped to make this undertaking possible.

Clive Hirschhorn's assistance has been of immeasurable value. Not only did he offer advice and encouragement but, with astounding generosity, gave us unlimited use of his remarkable collection of reference books.

Joel Finler has been on hand throughout with advice, erudition, the loan of research material and an eagle eye on the manuscript. He has also made specific specialist contributions: the synopsis of *Une Vie Sans Joie*, for example, almost always given incorrectly, is accurate here, thanks to Joel's supplying it from his reservoir of personal work on Renoir.

Musicologist and critic Max Loppert guided us in the selection of opera films and answered queries on musical detail, while Tony Coghan's knowledge solved a few thorny problems.

Hillel Tryster brought unswerving dedication, enthusiasm and long hours to the arduous research problems, helped in setting up our master list of titles and contributed much of practical value from his own knowledge. When circumstances forced Hillel to leave before completion of the book, Richard Chatten graciously stepped into his shoes, bringing *his* knowledge and remarkable energy to the final hurdles.

The documentation and resources of the British Film Institute have been indispensable. To the staff at the BFI, whose patience was sorely tried, our sincere appreciation for their help and courtesy. To all these we owe a debt of gratitude.

Our heartfelt thanks also to Gilbert Adair, Brian Baxter, Helen Bourne, Catriona MacGregor and Deborah Sharp for their generous assistance; to our editor Linda Doeser for the expertise she applied to an exceptionally onerous task; and to Kathy Rooney at Bloomsbury and our agent, Tony Peake of London Management, for their encouragement and their understanding.

Ronald Bergan
Robyn Karney
London 1988

EDITOR	Linda Doeser
EDITORIAL ASSISTANT	Leone Edwards
CONSULTANT & HISTORIAN	Joel W. Finler
RESEARCH	Hillel Tryster Richard Chatten

a

Aan

aka Savage Princess

India 1952 190 mins col

All India Film Corporation/Mehboob Productions

d **Mehboob**
sc **Chaudary, Ali Raza**
ph **Faredoon, A. Irani**
m **Naushad Dilip**
Dilip Kumar, Nimmi, Premnath, Nadira

Jai (Kumar), an heroic peasant, and his girlfriend, Mangala (Nimmi), help unseat a usurping prince and his savage sister, Aan (Nadira). The first Indian feature in Technicolor, it was also one of the very few Indian films to reach the West before the advent of Satyajit Ray. Its exotic music, costumes, and spectacle, as much as the swashbuckling tale made it an immediate hit abroad where it was shown in a 130-minute version. Doubtless, the strong Western influence apparent in the film also added to its popular appeal.

Aanslag, De see Assault, The

Abenteuer Des Prinzen Achmed, Die see Adventures Of Prince Achmed, The

---

Abenteuer Des Werner Holt, Die see Adventures of Werner Holt, The

---

Abhijan see Expedition, The

Abismos De Pasión see Wuthering Heights

A Bout De Souffle see Breathless

Abschied see Farewell

Abschied Von Gestern see Yesterday Girl

Abus De Confiance see Abuse Of Confidence

Abuse Of Confidence

Abus De Confiance

France 1938 82 mins bw

Compagnie Commerciale Française Cinématographique

d **Henri Decoin**
sc **Henri Decoin, Jean Boyer**
ph **L.H. Burel**
m **Georges Van Parys**
Danielle Darrieux, Charles Vanel, Valentine Jessie, Pierre Mingand

A poor law student (Darrieux) gets a prominent historian (Vanel) to adopt her by pretending to be his long-lost daughter, and later has to defend a girl who committed a similar breach of confidence. One of a number of run-of-the-mill films that director Decoin made starring his wife Darrieux during their marriage from 1934 to 1940. The early scenes between her and Vanel, until the plot creaks to its court-room conclusion, are the best.

Abwärts see Out Of Order

The Abyss

L'Oeuvre Au Noir

Belgium 1988 110 mins col

La Sept/Films A2(Paris)/La Nouvelle Imagerie(Brussels)

d **André Delvaux**
sc **André Delvaux**

ph **Charlie Van Damme**
m **Frédéric Devreese**
Gian Maria Volonté, Jean Bouise, Philippe Léotard, Sami Frey, Anna Karina, Marie-Christine Barrault, Marie-France Pisier

Zenon (Volonté), a 16th-century Flanders physician and alchemist, spends some years wandering Europe to escape the Inquisition, which is after him for dissident writings, devilish medical practices (he actually cures the sick) and his bisexuality. He eventually returns, incognito, to his native Bruges, but is discovered and arrested. Delvaux's most expensive project (and his first in period) is a meticulous but somewhat stodgy adaptation of the last section of a 1976 novel by Marguerite Yourcenar, who died shortly before the film's completion. It's difficult to fault the acting of the large cast, led by the always splendid Volonté—here sporting a handsome head of white hair—and Van Damme's lighting photography is outstanding in helping to capture the brooding medieval atmosphere. However, for all its virtues, the work is episodic, lacks rigour, and remains uninvolving.

Accatone

Italy 1961 120 mins bw
Cino Del Duca/Arco

d **Pier Paolo Pasolini**
sc **Pier Paolo Pasolini**
ph **Tonino Delli Colli**
m **J.S. Bach**
Franco Citti, Silvana Corsini, Franca Pasut, Roberto Scaringella, Adele Cambria

Accatone (Citti), a young pimp from the Roman slums, after trying to make an honest living, takes to thieving and is killed while escaping arrest. Pasolini, already a well-known novelist, poet, short-story writer and screenwriter, based his first feature on one of his novels. It drew on his intimate knowledge of sub-proletarian Rome and revealed his fatal attraction to the social outcast. It is brutal, realistic, unsentimental, and bustling with life, despite some rough edges. Particularly effective is the use of Bach on the soundtrack ironically counterpointing the world of pimps, prostitutes and street fighters. Citti, leading the cast of non-professionals, plays Accatone with a mixture of lethargy and vigour, seeking no sympathy. The director was to be murdered in 1975 by a young man from the same milieu.

Action Man

aka Leather And Nylon

Le Soleil Des Voyous

France 1966 95 mins col
Les Films Copernic-Fida

d **Jean Delannoy**
sc **Jean Delannoy, Alphonse Boudard**
ph **Walter Wottitz**
m **Francis Lai**
Jean Gabin, Robert Stack, Margaret Lee, Suzanne Flon

A former crook (Gabin), now an aging, bored tycoon, links up with an American adventurer (Stack) to organize one last crime, the seizure of an army payroll. A run-of-the-mill gangster movie is almost saved by Gabin as his usual crusty, watchable self. In contrast, Stack, popular in Europe through TV's *The Untouchables*, is extremely wooden.

Act Of Aggression

L'Agression

France 1975 102 mins col
SNE Gaumont/Les Films Du Jeudi/Les Films De La Seine

d **Gérard Pirés**
sc **Gérard Pirés, Jean-Patrick Manchette**
ph **Silvano Ippoliti**
m **Robert Charlebois**
Jean-Louis Trintignant, Catherine Deneuve, Claude Brasseur, Milena Vukotić

While driving off on holiday, a woman and her daughter are raped and murdered by a group of motorcyclists. So the husband and father decides to take the law into his own hands. Another French attempt to rival American crime thrillers of the 1970s, it contains unpleasant characters, a violent and sour screenplay, and is glibly directed. One remembers that the lovely blonde Deneuve, as the bitchy sister-in-law, used to make superior films.

An Actor's Revenge

Yukinojo Henge

Japan 1963 113 mins col
Daiei

d **Kon Ichikawa**
sc **Daisuke Ito, Teinosuke Kinugasa, Natto Wada**

ph **Setsuo Kobayashi**
m **Yasushi Akutagawa**
Kazuo Hasegawa, Fujiko Yamamoto, Ayako Wakao, Ganjiro Nakamura

In the early 19th century, an *onnagata* (female impersonator) of the Kabuki theatre takes revenge on the three men who caused the death of his parents. The veteran screen actor, Hasegawa, not only gives an extraordinary performance as the hero/heroine, but also plays a daring bandit in the complex sub-plot. The Daieiscope screen is brilliantly used to create the impression of Japanese prints, the theatre stage and comic strips in this fascinating study of opposites—love/hate, illusion/reality, masculinity/femininity.

Actors, The see Players, The

Adalen Riots, The see Adalen 31

Adalen 31

aka The Adalen Riots
Sweden 1969 115 mins col
Svensk Filmindustri

d **Bo Widerberg**
sc **Bo Widerberg**
ph **Jörgen Persson**
m **Duke Ellington and other composers**
Peter Schildt, Kerstin Tidelius, Roland Hedlund, Stefan Feierbach, Anita Björk

In 1931, a working-class family suffers during a lengthy strike at a paper mill in a small town in the north of Sweden, which ends with five workers being killed by soldiers. With its heart in the right place, the film is a colour-supplement socialist view of a tragic episode in modern Swedish history. The action takes place in sun-kissed, dappled surroundings, the camera even lingering on the beauty of blood on a white sheet covering a dead body.

Special Jury Prize Cannes 1969

Adam And Eve

Adam Y Eva
Mexico 1956 78 mins col
Costelaçion

d **Alberto Gout**
sc **Alberto Gout**
ph **Alex Phillips**
m **Gustave Cesar Carreon**
Carlos Baena, Christiane Martel

In the Garden of Eden, Adam and Eve are happy until she is tempted to eat the forbidden fruit. Despite some good camerawork, this feeble and ludicrous version of Genesis created an exodus of audiences. Eve, played by Miss Universe 1953 with eye shadow and plucked eyebrows, had only a scream to utter.

Adam Y Eva see Adam And Eve

L'Addition

aka The Patsy
France 1983 87 mins col
Swanie/TF1/UGT-Top 1

d **Denis Amar**
sc **Denis Amar, Jean-Pierre Bastid, Jean Curtelin**
ph **Robert Fraisse**
m **Jean-Claude Petit**
Richard Berry, Richard Bohringer, Victoria Abril, Farid Chopel

A young actor (Berry), after coming to the aid of a woman shoplifter, finds himself in prison where his sentence is increased following his supposed part in a break-out. A proficient and slick contemporary variation on the fatalistic pre-war French thrillers, but distinctly lacking their atmosphere and style.

Adeus Português, Um see Portuguese Goodbye, A

Adieu Bonaparte

Al-Wedaa Ya Bonaparte
Egypt 1984 120 mins col
Misr International/Lyric International/TF1 Films/Renn (Paris)

d **Youssef Chahine**
sc **Youssef Chahine**
ph **Mohsen Nasr**
m **Gabriel Yared**
Michel Piccoli, Mohsen Mohiedine, Mohsena Tewfik, Patrice Chereau

The experiences of an Egyptian family during the occupation of Alexandria by Napoleon and his army, and the uneasy friendship between a young Egyptian poet and one of Bonaparte's advisers. The exigencies of a big budget co-production might have accounted for a diminution in the great Chahine's poetry and power, but there are some spectacular scenes and excellent performances, notably from Chereau as a fanatical Bonaparte.

Adieu Léonard

France 1943 90 mins bw
Essor

d **Pierre Prévert**
sc **Pierre and Jacques Prévert**
ph **André Thomas**
m **Joseph Kosma (billed as Georges Mouqué)**

Pierre Brasseur, Charles Trenet, Julien Carette, Jacqueline Bouvier

A crook (Carette) is blackmailed by a man (Brasseur) into murdering a wealthy imbecile (Trenet), but the would-be killer and victim escape together into the country. This whimsical farce, the second of the three features Pierre Prévert directed and co-scripted with his elder brother, was twice as long as the others and half as funny. Yet there is much to enjoy in the performances, though there was tension between Trenet and the director, because the latter had the popular singer imposed on him by the producer.

Adieu Les Beaux Jours

Germany 1933 95 mins bw
UFA

d **André Beaucler**
sc **Pierre France**
ph **Friedl Behn-Grund**
m **E.E. Buder, Raoul Ploquin**

Brigitte Helm, Jean Gabin, Henri Bosc, Lucien Dayle, Henri Vilbert, Ginette Leclerc

A high class crook (Helm) steals a valuable necklace. While escaping to Spain, she gets involved with an innocent young advertising man (Gabin) who unwittingly helps her. Similar in plot to the later Dietrich-Gary Cooper film *Desire*, this German-made comedy-romance was a pleasant diversion, which gave audiences a chance to see the statuesque German star opposite the up-and-coming Gabin. Made in two languages, it was released in the USA and England in French versions for political as well as artistic reasons (most of the cast were French).

Adieu Philippine

France 1962 106 mins bw
Unitec/Alpha/Rome-Paris

d **Jacques Rozier**
sc **Michèle O'Glor, Jacques Rozier**
ph **René Mathelin**
m **Jacques Denjean, Maxime Saury, Paul Mattei**

Jean-Claude Aimini, Yveline Céry, Stefania Sabatini, Vittorio Caprioli

In his last few months before military service, a young TV technician, on holiday, is torn between two girls. Rozier's first feature, using improvisation, amateur performers, hidden microphones and cameras in real locations, had a rough spontaneity very much in line with the aesthetics of the *Nouvelle Vague*. Disputes with the producer, delays in editing and its failure at the box office, prevented Rozier from making another film for 11 years.

The Adolescent

aka An Adolescent Girl

L'Adolescente

France 1978 90 mins col
Janus

d **Jeanne Moreau**
sc **Jeanne Moreau, Henriette Jelinek**
ph **Pierre Gautard**
m **Philippe Sarde**

Simone Signoret, Laetitia Chauveau, Francis Huster, Hugues Quester

A 12-year-old Parisian girl (Chauveau), spending the summer of 1939 in the country with her grandmother (Signoret), falls for a young Jewish doctor (Huster), causing much heartache. Moreau's second venture behind the camera (her debut film, *Lumière*, was made in 1975) is an old-fashioned and conventional tale of a sentimental education, overlaid with soppy lyricism. However, the playing of the innocent, confused girl and the wise old grandmother gives some dimension to the stock characters, and something of pre-war rural life is evoked.

Adolescente, L' see Adolescent, The

Adolescent Girl, An see Adolescent, The

Adolphe Or The Awkward Age see Tender Age, The

Adolphe Ou L'Âge Tendre see Tender Age, The

Adoption

Orökbefogadás

Hungary 1975 89 mins bw
Hunnia

d **Márta Mészáros**
sc **Márta Mészáros, Gyula Hernádi, Ferenc Grunwalsky**
ph **Lajos Koltai**
m **György Kovács**
Kati Berek, László Szabó, Gyon Gyver Vigh, Dr Arpad Perlaky, Péter Fried

When her married lover (Szabó) refuses to give her a child, a 42-year- old widowed factory worker (Berek) strikes up an intense friendship with an adolescent girl (Vigh). Well played as the leading character is, it is difficult to find her demands on others very sympathetic. Everyday sounds—factory noises, an alarm clock—add to the sense of alienation in this penetrating, intimist, uncomfortable film.

Best Film Berlin 1975

Adorable Creatures

Adorables Créatures

France 1952 105 mins bw
Jacques Roitfeld/Sirius

d **Christian-Jaque**
sc **Charles Spaak, Jacques Companeez**
ph **Christian Matras**
m **Georges Van Parys**
Daniel Gélin, Danielle Darrieux, Edwige Feuillère, Antonella Lualdi, Martine Carol

A Paris fashion executive (Gélin) remembers his past love affairs with four very lovely but very different women. This light-weight quartet of sex sketches, played with some class, provided the naughtiness lacking in English and American products at the time. Yet Gélin still ends up with a 'good' girl.

Adorable Julia

aka The Seduction Of Julia

Julia, Du Bist Zauberhaft

Austria 1962 97 mins bw
Wiener Mundus/Étoile(France)

d **Alfred Weidenmann**
sc **Johanna Sibelius, Eberhard Keindorff**
ph **Werner Krein**
m **Rolf A. Wilhelm**
Lilli Palmer, Charles Boyer, Jean Sorel, Thomas Fritsch, Jeanne Valérie

Glamorous middle-aged Julia (Palmer), an actress on the London stage, embarks on one last fling with a younger man (Sorel), but finally realizes that her patient, adoring husband (Boyer) is the only man she really wants. Somerset Maugham's novel *Theatre* was the basis for this sugary, old-fashioned film, made with an eye on the international market. The charm of Palmer and Boyer can't disguise the faded air that hangs over the enterprise.

Adorable Liar

Adorable Menteuse

France 1961 110 mins bw
Elefilm/Art Et Réalisation

d **Michel Deville**
sc **Michel Deville, Nina Companeez**
ph **Claude Lecompte**
m **Jean Dalve**
Marina Vlady, Macha Meril, Michel Vitold, Jean-Marc Bory

A pretty 18-year-old girl is a compulsive liar, but when she genuinely falls for her 40-year-old neighbour (Vitold) her reputation makes him doubt her sincerity. A fairly breezy comedy which runs out of steam before the happy end, but Vlady makes a fetching fibber. The director, almost the same age as Godard and Chabrol, eschewed the *Nouvelle Vague* for commercial movies until the 1980s when he attempted to enter less conventional territory with films like *Death In A French Garden*.

Adorable Menteuse see Adorable Liar

Adorables Créatures see Adorable Creatures

À Double Tour see Web Of Passion

Adrienne Lecouvreur

France 1938 110 mins bw
Georges Lampin/UFA

d **Marcel L'Herbier**
sc **Madame Simone**
ph **Fritz Arno Wagner**
m **Maurice Thiriet**
Pierre Fresnay, Yvonne Printemps, Junie Astor, André Lefaur

Adrienne Lecouvreur, the famous 18th-century actress, loves Maurice De Saxe, son of the King of Poland, but when he goes off to war, she is poisoned by a rival for his love. The popular husband-and-wife team of Fresnay and Printemps tenderly acted out this tragic love story against a well-created background of theatre and aristocracy. The subject of four minor operas, it makes an attractive if minor film.

Adrift

Hrst Plna Vody

Czechoslovakia 1969 108 mins col
Studio Barrandov-MPO

d **Jan Kadar**
sc **Jan Kadar, Elmar Klos, Imre Gyöngyössy**
ph **Vladimir Novotny**
m **Zdeněk Liška**
Rade Marković, Milena Dravić, Paula Pritchett, Jožef Kroner

A happily married fisherman (Marković) becomes obsessed with a girl suffering from amnesia whom he rescued from the river but, after rejecting his love, she disappears again into the water. Freely adapted from Lajos Zilahy's best seller, *Something Is Adrift In The Water*, the film was being shot on the banks of the Danube in the summer of 1968 when it was interrupted by the arrival of Russian tanks. A year later, the cast and crew were reassembled to make this simple but intense tale, told in a rather complex manner, mixing past and present, real and imagined. It was helped considerably by the acting of Dravić as the wife and the striking looks of American fashion model Paula Pritchett as the river nymph.

Adua E Le Compagne see Hungry For Love

Adulteress, The see Thérèse Raquin

Adulterio All'Italiana see Adultery Italian Style

Adultery Italian Style

Adulterio All'Italiana

Italy 1966 93 mins col
Fair Film

d **Pasquale Festa Campanile**
sc **Ottavio Alessi, Luigi Malerba, Pasquale Festa Campanile**
ph **Roberto Gerardi**
m **Armando Trovaioli**
Catherine Spaak, Nino Manfredi, Maria Grazia Buccella, Vittorio Caprioli, Akim Tamiroff

When Marta (Spaak) learns that her husband Franco (Manfredi) has been dallying with her friend (Buccella), she decides to make him pay for it by inventing a fictitious lover. Franco falls for the ploy with unexpected, complicated and chaotic results. This is a wild farrago of largely coarse and repetitive farce in which credibility plays no part whatsoever. However, it is relieved by occasional scenes which, in degenerating into desperate parody, become extremely funny.

An Adventure Of Salvator Rosa

Un Avventura Di Salvator Rosa

Italy 1939 97 mins bw
Stella

d **Alessandro Blasetti**
sc **Ugo Scotti Berni**
ph **Ugo Scotti Berni**
m **Alessandro Cicognini**
Gino Cervi, Luisa Ferida, Rina Morelli, Osvaldo Valenti

In the 17th century, a masked knight (Cervi) aids the peasants against the landed gentry, breaks up an unhappy marriage between a young duchess (Morelli) and a money-seeking count (Valenti), and woos a peasant beauty (Ferida). This is a typical spectacular costume drama from the leading director in Fascist Italy, who nevertheless managed some social insights. Although Blasetti made his name with this kind of escapist fare, his realist *Four Steps In The Clouds* (1942) was a great influence on post-war Italian cinema.

The Adventures Of Arsène Lupin

Les Aventures D'Arsène Lupin

France 1956 103 mins col
Chavane/SNE-Gaumont/Lambor-Costel Lazione

d **Jacques Becker**
sc **Jacques Becker, Albert Simonin**
ph **Edmond Séchan**
m **Jean-Jacques Grünewald**
Robert Lamoureux, Liselotte Pulver, O.E. Hasse, Henri Rolland

Arsène Lupin (Lamoureux), man-about-town and gentleman thief in the Paris of 1912, is involved in several robberies, falls for a beautiful Baroness (Pulver) and is kidnapped by the Kaiser (Hasse). Lamoureux makes a stylish light-fingered job of Maurice Leblanc's famous character (the subject of a number of films), but it is the evocation of the last days of the *Belle Époque* that gives the film its appeal. Undemanding, commercial entertainment from a director capable of far better.

The Adventures Of Baron Münchhausen

Münchhausen

Germany 1943 134 mins col
UFA

d **Josef Von Baky**
sc **Berthold Bürger (pseudonym for Erich Kästner)**
ph **Werner Krien**
m **Georg Haentzschel**
Hans Albers, Wilhelm Bendow, Michael Bohnen, Marina Von Ditmar, Hans Brausewetter

At a costume ball in 1943, the Baron Münchhausen (Albers) recounts the story of his life to a young woman who thinks she's in love with him. He tells of his encounter with a magician in the 18th century who gave him the ability to make his wishes come true, one of them being never to age. The magic helps him get out of all kinds of scrapes, including one on the moon. The story of the extraordinary exploits of the mendacious Baron was ideally suited to the lavish production which matched anything from Hollywood at the time. The instigator of this extravagant German fantasy was Nazi propaganda minister Josef Goebbels (no mean liar himself) who wanted an international success to celebrate the 25th anniversary of UFA studios. Superbly photographed in Agfacolor, with breathtaking art direction by Emil Hasler and Otto Gulstorff, this enjoyable film took three years to make.

Adventures Of Don Quixote see Don Quixote

The Adventures Of Goopy And Bagha

aka Goopy And Bagha

Goopy Gyne Bagha Byne

India 1968 132 mins bw/col
Purnima

d **Satyajit Ray**
sc **Satyajit Ray**
ph **Soumendu Roy**
m **Satyajit Ray**
Tapan Chatterjee (Goopy), Robi Ghosh (Bagha), Santosh Dutta, Harindranath Chattopadhyay

Two wandering musicians encounter the King of Ghosts who offers them three wishes and a pair of magic slippers. Ray's first film to be made principally with children in mind, was adapted from a tale by his writer- artist grandfather. Its mixture of music, broad comedy, fantasy and romance, in the tradition of popular Indian cinema, made it Ray's biggest success in his own country. Westerners found the lengthy, whimsical picaresque tale less palatable, despite magic moments and an ending in bright colour in an otherwise black-and-white film.

The Adventures Of Prince Achmed

Die Abenteuer Des Prinzen Achmed

Germany 1926 65 mins bw (Restored print tinted)
Comenius Film

d **Lotte Reiniger**
sc **Lotte Reiniger**
ph **Animated film**
m **Silent**

Prince Achmed rescues a princess from the clutches of assorted monsters and witches and is helped to a happy ending by Aladdin's lamp. The best-known work of animator Lotte Reiniger, who filmed it in the special silhouette technique which she invented herself, *Achmed* has the distinction of being the world's first feature-length animated film. Made over a three-year period in Potsdam, with the director's husband, Carl Koch, supervising the photography, it enjoyed world-wide success, although today's post-Disney audiences might find it a little limited. By 1954 only one print survived (held by the British Film Institute). From this, a new negative was made and, in the early 1970s, the original tinting instructions were found and applied under Reiniger's personal supervision. (She died in 1981, having settled in Britain).

The Adventures Of Rabbi Jacob

aka The Mad Adventures Of Rabbi Jacob

Les Aventures De Rabbi Jacob

France 1973 96 mins col
Films Pomereu/Horse Films

d **Gérard Oury**
sc **Gérard Oury, Danielle Thompson, Josy Eisenberg**
ph **Henri Decaë**
m **Vladimir Cosma**

Louis De Funès, Suzy Delair, Marcel Dalio, Claude Giraud

An anti-Semitic French businessman (De Funès), on his way to his daughter's wedding, unwittingly becomes involved with an Arab terrorist, disguises himself as a rabbi, and ends up at a barmitzvah. A broad comedy with a serious intent—an anti-Semite comes to like Jews—it has its amusing moments, although two men falling into a vat of chewing gum is not one of them. One of the few of the irascible De Funès' vehicles to make its appeal to a wider audience than his home fans.

The Adventures Of Rémi

Sans Famille

France 1958 100 mins col
Societé De Productions Cinématographique/Européennes/Francinex SA- Rizzoli

d **André Michel**
sc **Pierre Véry**
ph **Robert Juillard**
m **Paul Misraki**

Pierre Brasseur, Gino Cervi, Bernard Blier, Joël Flateau

Rémi (Flateau), a little boy from a wealthy background, is sold to a wandering player (Cervi) by his foster parents, but is sought by an Englishman (Brasseur) acting for a wicked uncle. This adaptation of Hector Malot's 19th-century children's classic, is colourful and incident-packed enough to appeal to sub-teenagers, but the many moments of excessive sentimentality might make hardier kids blow raspberries.

The Adventures Of Till Eulenspiegel

(US: The Bold Adventure)

Les Aventures De Till L'Espiègle

France 1956 90 mins col
Les Films Ariane/Defa

d **Gérard Philipe, Joris Ivens**
sc **Gérard Philipe, René Wheeler**
ph **Christian Matras**
m **Georges Auric**

Gérard Philipe, Jean Vilar, Nicole Berger, Fernand Ledoux

Till, a 16th-century Flemish folk-hero, organizes a liberation army and drives the occupying Spaniards from his country. Philipe enjoyed co- directing and starring in this lavish knockabout swashbuckler, but the genre was better served by Fairbanks in the 1920s, and by himself in *Fanfan The Tulip* (1951).

The Adventures Of Werner Holt

Die Abenteuer Des Werner Holt

E. Germany 1963 164 mins bw
DEFA/VEB

d **Joachim Kunert**
sc **Joachim Kunert, Claus Kuechenmeister**
ph **Rolf Sohre**
m **Gerhard Wohigemuth**
Klause-Peter Thiele, Arno Wyzniewski, Manfred Karge, Gunter Junghans

Two young Nazi soldiers (Thiele and Wyzniewski) former schoolfriends, go different ways during the last days of the war, one questioning the cause, the other determined to defend Hitler to the end. Two years in the making, this anti-war, anti-Nazi epic impresses with its ambition and sincerity. Rather cluttered with flashbacks and characters, it contains some spectacular battle sequences and the potent atmosphere of 1945.

Adventure Starts Here

Här Börjar Äventyret

Sweden 1965 90 mins bw
Sandrew/Fennada

d **Jörn Donner**
sc **Jörn Donner**
ph **Jean Badal**
m **Bo Nilsson**
Harriet Andersson, Matti Oravisto, Claude Titre, Göran Cederberg

A Swedish fashion-buyer (Andersson) on a trip to Berlin meets a Finnish architect (Oravisto) and her French ex-lover (Titre) but hesitates to fall in love again. Donner's third feature, and third film with his lover and future wife Harriet Andersson, is a personal tale consisting of a series of meetings, musings on language barriers, and fragmented memories with an indeterminate ending. Reviled at the time, this uneven film did show that there was a way to get out of the large shadow of Ingmar Bergman that hung over Swedish cinema.

The Adversary

aka Siddharta And The City

Pratidwandi

India 1970 100 mins bw
Priya

d **Satyajit Ray**
sc **Satyajit Ray**
ph **Soumendu Roy**
m **Satyajit Ray**
Dhritiman Chatterjee, Jayashree Roy, Krishna Bose, Kalyan Chatterjee

A young man (Dhritiman Chatterjee), on the death of his father, is forced to give up his studies and look for a job in order to support his mother, sister and younger brother, but he is unable to compete in the rat race. Ray paints a perceptive portrait of a lethargic, rather insufferable, educated man trying to cope with life in the vast and teeming city of Calcutta. The other characters are also beautifully observed in this funny, sad and bitter tale.

Aelita

USSR 1924 70 mins bw
Mezhrabpom

d **Yakov Protazanov**
sc **Fedor Ozep, Alexei Faiko**
ph **Yuri Zhelabuzhsky**
m **Silent**
Julia Solntseva, Nikolai Batalov, Igor Ilinsky

Two Russian soldiers land on Mars and organize a revolution on the Soviet model against the autocratic ruler Queen Aelita (Solntseva). The Soviet cinema's first venture into science fiction is a delightful didactic comedy with futuristic set designs by Sergei Kozlovsky and interesting footage of 1920s Moscow. The screenplay (from a novel by Alexei Tolstoy) optimistically views the future from the standpoint of the USSR's New Economic Policy. Solntseva, making her screen debut, would soon become the wife of Dovzhenko and a remarkable director herself.

Aerograd

aka Frontier

aka Air City

USSR 1935 81 mins bw
Mosfilm-Ukrainfilm

d **Alexander Dovzhenko**
sc **Alexander Dovzhenko**
ph **Edouard Tissé, Mikhail Gindin**
m **Dmitri Kabalevsky**
Semyon Shagaida, Stepan Shkurat, Sergei Stolyarov

A new city under construction in Siberia is almost destroyed by eight Japanese saboteurs smuggling dynamite across the border. Although rhetorical and overly patriotic, the rhythmic cutting and lyrical images make it one of the most unforgettable of Soviet films of the 1930s. Among the memorable scenes are a plane fight, a priest confronting a group of war widows, and the villain dying with the word 'Mama' on his lips.

L'Affaire Est Dans Le Sac

aka It's In The Bag

France 1932 47 mins bw

Pathé/Nathan

d **Pierre Prévert**

sc **Jacques Prévert**

ph **Alphonse Gibory, Eli Lotar**

m **Maurice Jaubert**

Lora Hays, Julien Carette, Jacques Brunius, Etienne Decroux, Jacques Prévert, J.P. Dreyfus, Gildes

A bored millionaire wishes his daughter only to marry a man who can amuse him. As his future son-in-law turns out to be a kidnapper, he gets more than he bargained for. The surreal humour of the first and best of the three features made by the Prévert brothers outraged the general public at the time. No-one could be shocked today by this delightful, irreverent, medium-length burlesque. It marked the first screen appearance of Carette, one of the French cinema's greatest comic character actors.

The Affair Lafont

Conflit

France 1939 85 mins bw

Transatlantic

d **Leonid Moguy**

sc **Hans Wilhelm, Gina Kaus**

ph **Ted Pahle**

m **Wal-Berg**

Corinne Luchaire, Annie Ducaux, Raymond Rouleau, Armand Bernard

A girl gives her illegitimate child to her barren married sister to bring up as her own, but tries to reclaim the child some years later. Similar to the superior Bette Davis weepie of the same year, *The Old Maid*, this reasonably diverting melodrama shifts the sympathy in favour of the sister fighting to keep the child she has nurtured, even to resorting to murder. This bias is further emphasized by the deeper characterization from Ducaux as opposed to the mediocre Luchaire as the real mother.

Affair Of The Heart, An see Switchboard Operator, The

The Affairs Of Dr Holl

aka Angelika

Doktor Holl

W. Germany 1952 99 mins bw

Friedrich Mainz-Sama

d **Rolf Hansen**

sc **Thea Von Harbou**

ph **Franz Weihmayr**

m **Mark Lothar**

Maria Schell, Dieter Borsche, Heidemarie Hatheyer

The doctor (Borsche) who cures the invalid daughter of a wealthy industrialist marries her out of pity, believing she might not have long to live. Although Maria Schell as the suffering heroine smiles a lot through her tears, there is little for audiences to smile at in this cloying, clichéd concoction. The script was by Fritz Lang's former wife who had been an official screenwriter under the Nazis.

Afraid To Live

(US: The Confession Of Ina Kahr)

Das Bekenntis Der Ina Kahr

W. Germany 1954 102 mins bw

Omega

d **G.W. Pabst**

sc **Erna Fentsch**

ph **Günther Anders**

m **Erwin Haletz**

Curt Jurgens, Elisabeth Müller, Vera Molnar, Albert Lieven

A much-betrayed wife (Müller) plans to poison both herself and her husband (Jurgens), and when he dies and she lives, she is accused of murder. A low point in Pabst's career, this routine battle-of-the-sexes melodrama has little substance or style. The wife gets off lightly, the film does not.

Africa Addio

Italy 1965 138 mins col

Rizzoli

d **Gualtiero Jacopetti, Franco Prosperi**
sc **Gualtiero Jacopetti, Franco Prosperi**
ph **Antonio Climati**
m **Riz Ortolani**

With scenes, mainly of cruelty, perpetrated in different parts of Africa, this is another lurid, so-called documentary from Jacopetti, without even the humour that some might see in *Mondo Cane* to redeem it. It took over three years (according to the publicity) to photograph and collect these pictures of the bloody slaughter of wild life, the execution of people in the Congo, and barbaric tribal rituals. Under the guise of making anthropological points, the film obviously revelled in its material.

L'Âge D'Or

(US: The Golden Age)

France 1930 60 mins bw
Vicomte De Noailles

d **Luis Buñuel**
sc **Luis Buñuel, Salvador Dali**
ph **Albert Dubergen**
m **Wagner, Mendelssohn, Beethoven, Debussy**
Gaston Modot, Lya Lys, Max Ernst, Pierre Prévert, Jacques Brunius, Luis Buñuel

Two lovers (Modot and Lys) constantly have their sexual desires thwarted by *bourgeois* society. With the logic of a dream, Buñuel's second film contains all the themes that would reappear in his future work. Owing much to Freud and to the Surrealist Manifesto, it set out to shock with anti-clerical images: a blind man being kicked, a cow on a bed and fellatio with the toe of a statue. As a result, it was banned for some years after the screen was splattered with ink by a Fascist group. What Henry Miller called 'a divine orgy' is still pretty potent today.

The Age Of Indiscretion

L'Eta Dell'Amore

Italy 1953 85 mins bw
I.C.S./Cormoran

d **Lionello De Felice**
sc **Lionello De Felice, Franco Brusati, Vittorio Novarese**
ph **Mario Montuori**
m **Mario Nascimbene**
Marina Vlady, Pierre-Michel Beck, Aldo Fabrizi, Fernand Gravey

Two 15-year-olds, one the son of a well-to-do lawyer, the other the daughter of a widowed jailbird, fall in love, but suffer great pressure from the adults when the girl becomes pregnant. A well-meaning, uninspiring drama presenting all the adults as heavies. The young couple (Vlady and Beck) come off best in the acting department.

Age Of Infidelity see Death Of A Cyclist

Age Of The Earth

Idade Da Terra

Brazil 1980 158 mins col
Glauber Rocha Prod. Artisticas

d **Glauber Rocha**
sc **Glauber Rocha**
ph **Roberto Pires**
m **Rogerio Duarte**
Ana Maria Magalhaes, Mauricio Do Valle, Jece Valadao, Norma Benguel

A visionary argument between Marxism, Catholicism and African-derived beliefs, with scenes of folk rituals, the Mardi Gras, disputing political demogogues, and a historian in Brasilia. Rocha's first film shot in Brazil on his return from 10 years' exile and his last film before his death in 1981, aged 43, contains many of the elements of his past films: the ferment of juxtaposed images, the complex structure, the loud diatribes and repetitions. However, the numbing effect of it all is to make *Cinema Novo*, which Rocha helped to found in the early 1960s—and of which this is an example—seem very old hat.

Agnus Dei

Égi Bárány

Hungary 1970 90 mins col
Mafilm Studio 1

d **Miklós Jancsó**
sc **Miklós Jancsó, Gyula Hernádi**
ph **János Kende**
m **National songs**
József Madaras, Márk Zala, Lajos Balázsovits, Daniel Olbrychski, Anna Széles, András Kozák

Agonia

In a small religious peasant community in 1919, the Whites and Reds struggle for power, until an inspired Red leader emerges triumphant. A hymn of both despair and celebration in song, dance, and dialogue taken mainly from the Bible and Hungarian folk literature, orchestrated by the laterally-tracking camera and long takes that marked Jancsó's intensely personal style before it became self-parodic.

Agonia see Agony

Agony
Agonia
USSR 1975 148 mins col
Mosfilm

d **Elem Klimov**
sc **Semyon Lungin, Ilya Nusinov**
ph **Leonid Kalashnikov**
m **Alfred Shnitke**
Alexei Petrenko, Anatoly Romashin, Velta Linei, Alisa Freindtlich

In the final days of the Romanov regime, the 'mad monk' Rasputin wields power at court. This forceful epic took nine years to make, then spent 10 more on the shelf, because the pre-*glasnost* Soviet authorities baulked at the orgies and at what they saw as a sympathetic portrayal of the doomed Tsar (Romashin). However, the latter is seen as a man completely out of touch with the people and political reality. To demonstrate this, the action is cleverly intercut with contemporary newsreels. Although the direction is sometimes a little feverish, it befits the character of Rasputin, a startling performance by Petrenko.

Agostino
Italy 1962 90 mins bw
Baltea/Dino De Laurentiis

d **Mauro Bolognini**
sc **Mauro Bolognini, Goffredo Parise**
ph **Aldo Tonti**
m **Carlo Rustichelli**
Ingrid Thulin, John Saxon, Paolo Colombo

An attractive widow (Thulin) and her small son are enjoying their holiday at the Venice Lido, until a man (Saxon) begins to court the mother, alienating the child, who runs off and joins a street gang where he learns the brutal facts of life. One of Alberto Moravia's best stories, turned into a rather shallow film with an unnecessary narration to explain the boy's emotions. The Venetian locales, as usual, look good on the wide screen.

Agression, L' see Act Of Aggression

Aguirre, Der Zorn Gottes see Aguirre, Wrath Of God

Aguirre, Wrath Of God
Aguirre, Der Zorn Gottes
W. Germany 1972 95 mins col
Werner Herzog/Hessicher Rundfunk

d **Werner Herzog**
sc **Werner Herzog**
ph **Thomas Mauch**
m **Popol Vuh**
Klaus Kinski, Ruy Guerra, Helena Rojo, Cecilia Rivera

In the 16th century, a Spanish conquistador leads a hazardous expedition through the wilds of Peru in search of El Dorado. The fascination of this ponderous morality tale derives from the jungle atmosphere and pictorial flair, as well the intense performance of Kinski as Aguirre, the role that brought him international fame. Like his hero, the director had to overcome difficult conditions while filming in the Peruvian Andes. The final shot, an aerial view of the lone survivor on a raft, is masterful.

Ahdat Sanawouach El-Djamr see Chronicle Of The Burning Years

Ah! Les Belles Bacchantes see Femmes De Paris

Aida
Italy 1953 96 mins col
Oscar Film

d **Clemente Fracassi**
sc **G. Castilli, A. Gobbi, V. Salvucci**

ph **Piero Portalupi**
m **Verdi**
Sophia Loren (Aida, dubbed by Renata Tebaldi), Lois Maxwell (Amneris, dubbed by Ebe Stignani), Luciano Della Marra (Radames, dubbed by Giuseppe Campora), Afro Poli (Amonasro, dubbed by Gino Bechi)

Aida, an Ethiopian slave girl to Amneris, the King of Egypt's daughter, is torn between her love for Radames, an Egyptian army officer, and for her own defeated people. Without causing DeMille any loss of sleep, this colourful, faithful rendition of Verdi's grand opera was well served by the unseen singers and their embodiments. In the role turned down by Gina Lollobrigida, Sophia Loren, painted chocolate and striking in an Afro wig, came to the attention of the English-speaking world.

Aien Kyo see Straits Of Love And Hate

Aigle A Deux Têtes, L' see Eagle Has Two Heads, The

Ai No Borei see Empire Of Passion

Ai No Corrida see In The Realm Of The Senses

Ai No Kawaki see Longing For Love

Air City see Aerograd

Ajantrik see Mechanical Man

A. K.

France 1985 75 mins col
Greenwich Film Productions/Herald Ace

d **Chris Marker**
sc **Chris Marker**
ph **Frans-Yves Marescot**
m **Tohru Takemitsu**
Akira Kurosawa and the cast and crew of *Ran*

A documentary on the location shooting of *Ran* in late 1984 on the slopes of Mount Fuji, including an interview with its 75-year-old director. This often too reverential impression of the Japanese master at work is nonetheless revealing about his methods and his relations with his crew. Marker also uses the subject for his own brand of poetic-philosophical celluloid essay on the Japanese and the filming of a film.

Akahige see Red Beard

Akasen Chitai see Street Of Shame

Åke And His World

Åke Och Hans Värld

Sweden 1984 103 mins col
Sandrew Film

d **Allan Edwall**
sc **Allan Edwall**
ph **Jörgen Persson**
m **Thomas Lindahl**
Martin Lindström, Loa Falkman, Gunnel Fred, Katja Blomquist, Ulla Sjöblom, Suzanne Ernrup, Allan Edwall

Six-year-old Åke (Lindström), the son of a country doctor, commits a small misdemeanour and imagines that all sorts of punishments will befall him, from being struck down by the local pastor to being eaten by wolves. The film operates in the same delightful territory as *My Life As A Dog*, giving a child's eye view of quirky Swedish village life. It only falls short of the later film in that its scope is a little narrower. Åke, pronounced 'O-keh', is played by an exceptional nine-year-old, and the rest of the characters, seen through his eyes, ring true. Åke's world is beautifully captured by the photography of Persson (best known abroad for *Elvira Madigan*), and the director of this touching and funny film manages to avoid sentimentality.

Åke Och Hans Värld see **Åke And His World**

Akibiyori see Late Autumn

Al Asfour see Sparrow, The

Albatros, L' see Albatross, The

The Albatross
aka Love Hate
L'Albatros
France 1971 90 mins col
Balzac Films/Profilms/Bestar Productions

d **Jean-Pierre Mocky**
sc **Jean-Pierre Mocky, Claude Veillot, Raphael Delpard**
ph **Marcel Weiss**
m **Léo Ferré**
Jean-Pierre Mocky, André Le Gall, Paul Muller, Marion Game

A criminal (Mocky), escaping from jail, forces a woman (Game) to drive him to the German border, but political intrigue enmeshes them and tragedy ensues. This sometimes powerful political thriller is undermined by implausible plotting, uncertain shifts from melodrama to satire, and an attempt to be all things to all parties.

Albero Degli Zoccoli see Tree Of Wooden Clogs, The

Albert - Warum? see Albert - Why?

Albert - Why?
Albert - Warum?
W. Germany 1978 115 mins bw
HFF

d **Josef Rödl**
sc **Josef Rödl**
ph **Karlheinz Gschwind**
Fritz Binner, Michael Eichenseer, George Schiessl, Elfriede Bleisteiner

Albert is a simple-minded gentle giant, considered an idiot by the Bavarian villagers because he stutters and has spent a while in a mental home. He loses control of the family farm to a cousin. Young director Rödl's graduation piece from the Munich Film School brings a small community brilliantly to life, while avoiding making judgements about ignorant attitudes. However, what makes the film memorable, is the remarkable performance of Fritz Binner, on whose own life Rödl based his screenplay.

Aleko
USSR 1953 60 mins col
Lenfilm

d **Sidelov**
sc **A. Abramov, G. Roshal**
ph **A. Nazarov**
m **Rachmaninov**
A. Ognivtsev, I. Zubkovskay, M. Reizen

A gypsy youth loves a married girl whose husband finally kills them both. The chance to see this rarely performed Rachmaninov opera, based on Pushkin's poem *The Gypsies*, is ruined by static direction, bad colour, and the lack of passion demanded by the sweeping music. However, this was a first attempt by the USSR to shoot an opera away from the confines of the stage against natural landscapes, foreshadowing more successful opera films.

Aler Sandhane see In Search Of Famine

Alerte En Méditeranée see Hell's Cargo

Alexander Nevsky
USSR 1938 112 mins bw
Mosfilm

d **Sergei Eisenstein**
sc **Sergei Eisenstein, Piotr Pavlenko**
ph **Edouard Tissé**
m **Prokofiev**
Nikolai Cherkassov, Nikolai Okhlopov, Alexander Abrikosov, Dmitri Orlov

Prince Alexander Nevsky (Cherkassov) forms a people's army to drive brutal Teutonic invaders from the soil of Holy Russia in 1242. Although less experimental stylistically than Eisenstein's previous work (he had been charged with 'formalism' by the authorities), it has what the great Russian director called a 'symphonic structure' because of his close collaboration with Prokofiev. The result is an operatic, patriotic pageant offering stirring images and a dramatic use of music, particularly in the brilliant Battle of the Ice sequence. Eisenstein's most enjoyable film was withdrawn at the time of the German-

Soviet Pact in 1939, and only re-shown, appropriately, when the Nazis invaded the Soviet Union.

Alexander The Great

O Megalexandros

Greece 1980 210 mins col
RAI/ZDF/Angelopoulos Prod.

d **Theo Angelopoulos**
sc **Theo Angelopoulos**
ph **Ghiorgos Arvanitis**
m **Christodoulos Halaris**
Omero Antonutti, Eva Kotamanidu, Grigoris Evangelatos, Michalis Yannatos

The bandit Alexander (Antonutti) takes a party of English aristocrats hostage, leading them to a mountain village where the peasants have overthrown the landowners and established a commune. Angelopoulos certainly takes his time in the telling of this allegory of Greek socialism, using slow pans, long takes and pauses, but it is superb to look at and often intriguing and mentally stimulating.

Alexandre

(US: Very Happy Alexandre)

Alexandre Le Bienheureux

France 1967 96 mins col
Les Productions De la Guéville/Madeleine Films/Les Films De la Colombe

d **Yves Robert**
sc **Yves Robert, Pierre Levy Corti**
ph **René Mathelin**
m **Vladimir Cosma**
Philippe Noiret, Françoise Brion, Marlène Jobert, Paul Le Person, Jean Carmet, Pierre Richard

After the death of his wife (Brion), Alexandre (Noiret) decides to lock himself up in his house with his dog and stay in bed all day, every day. After two months, he gets up and leads a holiday existence, until he is almost trapped into remarriage. As is the hero, so is the film—likeable, leisurely, unambitious. Both Noiret and Kaly, the dog, are perfectly cast, the colour photography attractive, and the philosophy of sloth seductive. It's also rather misogynistic and forgettable.

Alexandre Le Bienheureux see Alexandre

Alexandria - Why?

Iskindirya - Leh?

Egypt 1978 125 mins col
Misr International Films (Cairo)/Oncic (Algeria)

d **Youssef Chahine**
sc **Youssef Chahine, Mohsen Zayed**
ph **Mohsen Nasr**
m **Fouad El Zaheri**
Mohsen Mohiedine, Naglaa Fathi, Farid Shawki, Ezzat El Alayli, Gerry Sundquist

In the Alexandria of 1942, while the Allied troops await Rommel, a film- mad schoolboy's hopes of becoming a star seem dashed when things go wrong at the end of a school play. The vitality and humour of the film is influenced by the Hollywood movies (particularly MGM musicals) into which the well-drawn characters escape from the wartime situation. This is the most immediately accessible of the great Egyptian director's works.

Best Director Berlin 1979

Alfredo Alfredo

Italy 1971 98 mins col
Rizzoli/Francoriz RPA

d **Pietro Germi**
sc **Leo Benvenuti, Tullio Pinelli, Piero De Bernardi**
ph **Aiace Parolin**
m **Carlo Rustichelli**
Dustin Hoffman, Stefania Sandrelli, Carla Gravina, Saro Urzi

A timid bank clerk (Hoffman) discovers after marriage that his wife (Sandrelli) is an over-sexed bore, so he takes up with another girl (Gravina) only to find he can't get a divorce. Top Hollywood star Dustin Hoffman studiously learned his part in Italian before leaving for Rome, but Germi shot it in English and then dubbed it. Hoffman's talent was also wasted in this frenzied, intermittently funny, misogynistic satire on Italian customs and the divorce laws.

Al Grito De Este Pueblo see Cry Of The People, The

Ali see Fear Eats The Soul

Ali Baba And The Forty Thieves
Ali Baba Et Les Quarante Voleurs

France 1954 90 mins col
Films Du Cyclope

d **Jacques Becker**
sc **Jacques Becker, Marc Maurette, Maurice Griffe, Jean Manse**
ph **Robert Le Fèbvre**
m **Paul Misraki**
Fernandel, Samia Gamal, Dieter Borsche, Henri Vilbert

Ali Baba (Fernandel), sent to buy a new wife for his brutal master, comes across a cave full of treasures and is discovered by the thieves. He returns to his village a changed man. Adapted from a Cesare Zavattini treatment of the Arabian Nights tale, this rather rambling, lacklustre vehicle for the popular horse-faced French comic, tries to bring in elements of social comment about the poor. Its main appeal lies in the handsome Moroccan locations shot in Eastman Colour.

Ali Baba Et Les Quarante Voleurs see Ali Baba And The Forty Thieves

Alibi, L' see Alibi, The

The Alibi
L'Alibi

France 1937 82 mins bw
Tellus Films

d **Pierre Chenal**
sc **Marcel Achard**
ph **Ted Pahle, Jacques Mercanton**
m **Georges Auric, Jacques Dallin**
Erich Von Stroheim, Albert Préjean, Louis Jouvet, Jany Holt

A Parisian dance hostess (Holt), blackmailed into providing an alibi for a murderer (Stroheim), falls in love with a secret police agent (Préjean) sent to win her confidence. Other thrillers of the period were as sharply directed and written, but few had the inestimable advantage of the sparks set up between Stroheim's killer and Jouvet's police chief. The film was slightly spoiled by the dragged-in love interest and an insipid happy ending imposed by the producers.

Alice In Den Städten see Alice In The Cities

Alice In The Cities
Alice In Den Städten

W. Germany 1974 110 mins bw
Filmverlag Der Autoren

d **Wim Wenders**
sc **Wim Wenders**
ph **Robby Müller**
m **Pop songs, Mahler**
Rüdiger Vogler, Yella Rottländer, Liza Kreuzer

An almost wordless German photo-journalist (Vogler), numbed by recent assignments, travels down the east coast of America with a nine-year-old girl (Rottländer) in search of her grandmother. This gently amusing and melancholy road movie that foreshadows themes more deeply explored in *Paris Texas* (1984), was the first of four leisurely-paced, odd odysseys featuring Vogler. Wenders was much more comfortable with this low budget movie over which he had complete control, than on the international co-production of *The Scarlet Letter* from which he emerged as numbed as his photo-journalist character.

Alice Or The Last Escapade
Alice Ou La Dernière Fugue

France 1977 93 mins col
Filmel/PHPG

d **Claude Chabrol**
ph **Jean Rabier**
m **Pierre Jansen**
Sylvia Kristel, Charles Vanel, Jean Carmet, André Dussollier, Thomas Chabrol, Marcel Dalio

Alice Carrol (Kristel) suddenly gets into her car and leaves her husband, but a huge storm forces her to take refuge in a mysterious old house where an old man (Vanel) and his valet (Carmet) seem to expect her. A surprising departure into fantasy for Chabrol which doesn't really come off. In this half-hearted homage to Lewis Carroll, there are psychological clues, an 'old dark house' movie pastiche and the beautiful Sylvia 'Emmanuelle' Kristel looking as confused as her audience.

Alice Ou La Dernière Fugue see Alice Or The Last Escapade

Alienista, O see Alienist, The

The Alienist

O Alienista

Brazil 1970 82 mins col
Dos Santos/Barreto/Farias

d **Nelson Pereira Dos Santos**
sc **Nelson Pereira Dos Santos**
ph **Dib Lutfi**
m **Guilherme Maga'haes Vaz**
Nildo Parente, Isabel Ribeiro, Arduino Colasanti, Irene Stafnaia

A new priest (Parente) comes to a small town and builds an insane asylum for people who do not agree with his ways and religion, but the many homeless poor seek shelter within its walls. Dos Santos, the doyen of the *Cinema Novo* movement, used a famous 17th-century tale to make a rather confused political parable on contemporary Brazil. However, there is enough visual flair and caustic humour to make it watchable.

Ali: Fear Eats The Soul see Fear Eats The Soul

All About Loving

De L'Amour

France 1964 90 mins bw
Films De La Pleiade/Cocinor Marceau (Paris)/Cinesocolo (Rome)

d **Jean Aurel**
sc **Cecil Saint-Laurent, Jean Aurel**
ph **Edmond Richard**
m **André Hodeir**
Elsa Martinelli, Michel Piccoli, Martine Carol, Anna Karina, Joanna Shimkus, Philippe Avron, Jean Sorel, Bernard Garnier

Serge (Avron) pursues Hélène in a busy Paris street and successfully seduces her; Werther (Garnier) takes Sophie (Shimkus) to the dentist, Raoul (Piccoli), who seduces her; Sophie deceives Raoul with her ex-husband (Sorel); Raoul drops Sophie in favour of Mathilde (Martinelli) to whom he shows films of his conquests in which Sophie and Hélène—remember Hélène?—appear. A sort of mini *La Ronde*, 1960s style, which, aside from a very tedious commentary read from the work of Stendhal (which inspired the screenplay), is not as crass as it sounds. Documentary maker Aurel directs his first fiction film with the lightest of touches, some inventive situations and an ironic edge, while the actors are delightfully in command of themselves. Footnote: Aurel was born aboard the Orient Express as it passed through Romania one day in 1925.

Allegro Non Troppo

Italy 1976 85 mins col/bw
Bruno Bozzetto Film

d **Bruno Bozzetto**
sc **Bruno Bozzetto, Guido Manuli, Maurizio Nichetti**
m **Debussy, Dvořák, Ravel, Sibelius, Vivaldi, Stravinsky**
Maurizio Nichetti, Nestor Garay, Maurizio Micheli, Maria Luisa Giovannini

Various animated sequences in colour set to classical music are linked with live-action scenes involving the producer, the conductor, an orchestra of old ladies and a reluctant animator (in monochrome). Not a patch on Disney's *Fantasia*, the inspiration behind this uneven pot-pourri, but there is some imaginative animation to be enjoyed between the ponderously unfunny live-action sections.

Allez France

(US: The Counterfeit Constable)

France 1964 86 mins col
Le Film D'Art/Les Films Arthur Lesser/Films Borderie

d **Robert Dhéry**
sc **Robert Dhéry, Pierre Tchernia**
ph **Jean Tournier**
m **Gérard Calvi**
Robert Dhéry, Colette Brosset, Diana Dors, Jean Lefèbvre

All Good Citizens

A French rugby supporter crosses the Channel for the England-France match, gets lost, finds himself at a dentist's and in a policeman's uniform. Dhéry's comedy here is as subtle as a rugby scrum, and the joke of French-English misunderstandings wears pretty thin before the stock-shot finale of the match.

All Good Citizens see All My Good Countrymen

All In Order

Ordnung

W. Germany 1980 96 mins bw
Marten Taege Film/ZDF

d **Sohrab Shahid Saless**
sc **Sohrab Shahid Saless, Dieter Reifarth, Bert Schmidt**
ph **Ramin Molai**
m **Rolf Bauer**
Heinz Lieven, Dorothea Moritz, Ingrid Domann, Dagmar Hessenland

A prosperous Frankfurt engineer (Lieven), who suddenly decides to stop going to work, gets up early in the mornings, goes into the streets and shouts 'Wake up!'. He is eventually put into a mental clinic by his wife (Moritz) and friends. This powerful, low-budget, socio-political parable excellently directed by an Iranian exile in West Germany, effectively puts into question the notion of sanity and German values. The protagonist's provocative cry to Germans to wake up, becomes, in the end 'Auschwitz!' (a German play on words).

All My Good Countrymen

(US: All Good Citizens)

Všichni Dobří Rodaci

Czechoslovakia 1968 126 mins col
Filmove Studio Barrandov

d **Vojtěch Jasný**
sc **Vojtěch Jasný**
ph **Jaroslav Kučera**
m **Svatopluk Havelka**
Radoslav Brozobohaty, Vlastimil Brodsky, Vladimír Menšík, Drahoslava Hofman, Pavel Pavlovsky

The life in a small Moldavian village from the summer of 1945 to early 1968, punctuated by significant deaths. These include the shooting of a postman (Pavlovsky), a young member of the local Communist Party, the death from blood poisoning of Joe the Lip (Menšík), a likeable thief, and that of František (Brozobohaty), a farmer who refuses to give up his land to the collective. Jasný, who first emerged as leader of the Czech 'New Wave' in 1957 with *September Nights*, a critique of Stalinist abuses in his country, won acclaim with this lyrical epic. But soon after its award at Cannes, the film was banned in Czechoslovakia, and Jasny left the country for Germany. Its brilliant blend of satire, drama and comedy, dream and reality, make it one of the finest features to emerge during the short 'Prague Spring'.

Best Director Cannes 1969

All Night Long

Toute Une Nuit

Belgium 1982 89 mins col
Avidia/Paradise/Gerick/Lyric/Partners/Centre Bruxelles De L'Audiovisuel/Film International/Cine 360

d **Chantal Akerman**
sc **Chantal Akerman**
ph **Caroline Champetier**
m **Mahler and a variety of songs**
Angelo Abazoglou, Frank Aendenboom, Natalia Akerman, Véronique Alain, Paul Allio, Aurore Clément, Gabrielle Claes, Nicole Colchat

In Brussels on a hot summer's night, a number of couples meet, make love, part, dance, drink, eat, telephone each other and sleep. Although there is no plot and little dialogue, this series of amorous fragments, some sad, some happy, is a unique and strangely riveting experiment in narrative to which audiences must be prepared to bring their own imagination.

All Night Through

aka Restless Night

Unruhige Nacht

W. Germany 1958 100 mins bw
Realfilm

d **Falk Harnack**
sc **Hurst Bud Juhn**
ph **Friedl Behn-Grund**

m **Hans-Martin Majewski**
Bernhard Wicki, Ulla Jacobsson, Hansjörg Felmy, Ann Savo

A Protestant pastor (Wicki) called to administer the last rites to a German soldier (Felmy) about to be shot for desertion, discovers that the man deserted to help the Russian girl (Jacobsson) he loved. This dreary, badly shot 'good German' World War II drama has only Wicki's pastor to give it some depth. It was in the same year that Wicki directed *The Bridge*, one of the best German films on World War II.

All Nudity Shall Be Punished
Toda Nudez Sera Castigada

Brazil 1973 102 mins col
R.F. Faria

d **Arnaldo Jabor**
sc **Arnaldo Jabor**
ph **Lauro Escorel**
m **Paulo Santos**
Darlene Glória, Paulo Porto, Paulo Sacks, Paulo César Pereio

When a widower (Porto) marries a prostitute, his teenage son (Sacks), supposedly ready to die defending the memory of his mother, is attracted to his new step- mother and a *ménage-à-trois* is set up. Banned in Brazil at the time, this baroque satire on middle-class hypocrisy is as unsubtle as its title. However, it is biting, exuberant and funny, with Darlene Glória standing out amidst the overplaying as a variation on the tart with a heart of gold.

Allonsanfan

Italy 1974 100 mins col
Una Cooperativa Cinematografica

d **Paolo and Vittorio Taviani**
sc **Paolo and Vittorio Taviani**
ph **Giuseppe Ruzzolini**
m **Ennio Morricone**
Marcello Mastroianni, Lea Massari, Mimsy Farmer, Laura Betti

A middle-aged Italian nobleman (Mastroianni) disillusioned by the 1816 Restoration in France, betrays the leader of a secret, revolutionary, Republican society to which he belongs. The Taviani brothers said that the film evoked 'the splendour of regression,' an equivocal statement on an equivocal film. It is never clear whose side the directors are on—the weak and regressive Mastroianni's or the bungling revolutionaries'—none of which is helped by some gimmicky camerawork and overemphatic direction. There is some splendour, however, in the more spectacular scenes.

All Screwed Up
aka Everything's Ready Nothing Works
Tutto A Posto

Italy 1973 105 mins col
Euro Intern Films

d **Lina Wertmüller**
sc **Lina Wertmüller**
ph **Giuseppe Rotunno**
m **Piero Piccioni**
Luigi Diberti, Nino Bignamini, Lina Polito, Sara Rapisarda

A group of young people from the country come to Milan and form a commune to enable them to survive the economic evils of the big city. Any social or political points Wertmüller wants to make are blunted by her alienating self-indulgent style. Ham-fisted cutting and camerawork, and a deliberate attempt at bad taste—a ballet motif in an abattoir, for example—dull even the satire inherent in her subject. It was one of a series of her films that unaccountably gained a following in America during the 1970s.

All The Gold In The World
Tout L'Or Du Monde

France 1961 100 mins bw
Seca/Filmsonor/Cinériz/Royal Film

d **René Clair**
sc **René Clair**
ph **Pierre Petit**
m **Georges Van Parys**
Bourvil, Philippe Noiret, Claude Rich, Colette Castel, Annie Fratellini, Françoise Dorléac

An obstinate peasant, his son and his cousin (all Bourvil) refuse to sell their land with its health-giving spring to property developers anxious to turn the place into a fashionable spa. Shot in natural locations (unusually for Clair) in rural France, this traditional, rather plodding bucolic comedy lacks the director's customary gentle touch. Some of the yokels vs city slickers satire—in which Clair ingenuously disclaimed taking any one side—and Bourvil in three roles provide some amusement.

All These Women see Now About These Women

All The Youthful Days see Boys From Fengkuei, The

Almost a Man

Un Uomo A Meta

Italy 1966 100 mins bw
Vittorio De Seta

d **Vittorio De Seta**
sc **Vittorio De Seta, Vera Gherarducci, Fabio Carpi**
ph **Dario Di Palma**
m **Ennio Morricone**
Jacques Perrin, Lea Padovani, Gianni Garko, Ilaria Occhini, Pier Paolo Capponi, Francesca De Seta

A young writer in the grip of a personal and artistic crisis, retreats further and further from the real world, contemplates suicide, and is committed to a clinic for shock treatment. He escapes, returning to the home of his youth where he recollects the traumas of his past. A study of guilt and neurosis, told in a combination of flashback and flash forward, that is stronger on mood than on plot. An intelligent performance from Perrin helps to hold it together but Lea Padovani is wasted in a small part as his mother.

Best Actor (Jacques Perrin) Venice 1966

Alone On The Pacific

Taiheiyo Hitoribochi

Japan 1963 104 mins col
Ishihara/Nikkatsu

d **Kon Ichikawa**
sc **Natto Wada**
ph **Yoshihiro Yamazaki**
m **Yasushi Akatagawa, Tohru Takemitsu**
Yujiro Ishihara, Masayuki Mori, Kinuyo Tanaka, Ruriko Asaoko

A young yachtsman takes three months to sail from Osaka to San Francisco on a 19-foot craft. Based on the 1962 true adventure of Kenichi Horie (Ishihara), it seemed an intractable filmic subject. But Ichikawa, using the wide screen to magnificent effect and integrating flashbacks to the sailor's life on shore, makes even the boring bits of the voyage interesting. The climactic scene, as the Golden Gate looms out of the mist, is genuinely moving.

Aloïse

France 1975 120 mins col
Unité Trois

d **Liliane De Kermadec**
sc **Liliane De Kermadec, André Téchiné**
ph **Jean Penzer**
Isabelle Huppert, Delphine Seyrig, Marc Eyraud, Valérie Schoeller, François Chatelet

The life of Aloïse, the Swiss primitive painter whose work was accomplished during 40 years in a mental hospital to which she was committed after her emotional protests against World War I. A slow, detailed but absorbing look at an extraordinary woman and, in general, at the oppression of women in society. Both Huppert and Seyrig, who play Aloïse in youth and maturity respectively, give poignant performances.

Alphaville

Alphaville, Une Étrange Aventure De Lemmy Caution

France 1965 98 mins bw
Chaumiane/Filmstudio

d **Jean-Luc Godard**
sc **Jean-Luc Godard**
ph **Raoul Coutard**
m **Paul Misraki**
Eddie Constantine, Anna Karina, Akim Tamiroff, Howard Vernon, László Szabó

Private-eye Lemmy Caution (Constantine) is rocketed through space into a city run by dictator scientist Von Braun (Vernon), where individuality and love have been suppressed. Although actually filmed in contemporary Paris, an eerie futurist world has been superbly well created, and Godard's use of the trappings of American pulp fiction to make political statements is again telling. Constantine, the American in Paris, who made his name as Peter Cheyney's Caution in a number of cheap French thrillers, is perfect, as is Godard's then wife, the Danish-born Karina, as Von Braun's daughter.

Best Film Berlin 1965

Alphaville, Une Étrange Aventure see Alphaville

Alpine Fire

Hohenfeuer

Switzerland 1985 117 mins col
Bernard Lang/SRG/WDR/Rex

d **Fredi Murer**
sc **Fredi Murer**
ph **Pio Corradi**
m **Mario Beretta**
Thomas Nock, Johanna Lier, Dorothea Moritz, Rolf Illig

An adolescent girl has an incestuous relationship with her deaf-mute, younger brother on an isolated farm in the Alps, where the only other people they see are their strict parents and grandparents. Based on the director's own novel (originally set in Iceland), the film skilfully creates an atmosphere of Alpine mysticism, and never sensationalizes the subject. In what is virtually a four-hander, Thomas Nock, a moody boy tormented by his desires, and Johanna Lier, maternal and sexually provocative, are superb as the incestuous siblings.

Alraune

aka A Daughter Of Destiny

aka Unholy Love

Germany 1928 105 mins bw
Ama

d **Henrik Galeen**
sc **Henrik Galeen**
ph **Günther Krampf**
m **Silent**
Brigitte Helm, Paul Wegener, John Loder, Ivan Petrovich

Alraune (Helm), born by artificial insemination from a hanged man and a prostitute, acquires a series of lovers, and takes revenge on the scientist (Wegener) who brought her up. Galeen, who contributed as screenwriter to the chilling *Nosferatu* and *Waxworks*, brought a similar menace to bear on this first screen version of H. Ewers' classic novel of 1900. As the perverse seductress, Brigitte Helm sometimes seems unsuitably to be repeating her role as the robotic woman in *Metropolis*, and there are some unintentional laughs. Yet the 'shocking' theme and the late Expressionist atmosphere make it superior to the 1930 sound remake (with Helm again), the 1952 version starring Hildegard Knef, and the rapidly vanished 1981 attempt featuring Nastassja Kinski.

Alsino And The Condor

Nicaragua 1982 89 mins col
Nicaraguan Film Institute/Cuban Film Institute/Latin American Producers of Mexico/Costa Rican Film Cooperative

d **Miguel Littin**
sc **Miguel Littin, Isidora Aguirre, Tomás Turrent Pérez**
ph **Jorge Herrera, Pablo Martínez**
m **Leo Brouwer**
Alan Esquivel, Dean Stockwell, Carmen Bunster, Alejandro Parodi

A 12-year-old peasant boy (Esquivel) from a jungle village in Nicaragua during the struggle against the Somoza dictatorship, dreams of flying like the helicopters he sees. Littin, a Chilean director, managed to combine 'magic realism' and a powerful depiction of war into a charming political allegory. This impressive first fiction film produced in Nicaragua after the Sandinista revolution, gained an Oscar nomination.

Alsino Y El Cóndor see Alsino And The Condor

Älskande Pär see Loving Couples

Älskar Innan see Swedish Mistress, The

Alte Gesetz, Das see Ancient Law, The

Al-Wedaa Ya Bonaparte see Adieu Bonaparte

Amant De Cinq Jours, L' see Infidelity

Amant De Poche, L' see Lover Boy

Amants, Les see Lovers, The

Amants De Teruel, Les see Lovers Of Teruel, The

Amants De Verone, Les see Lovers Of Verona, The

Amants Du Tage, Les see Lovers Of Lisbon, The

Amarcord

Italy 1973 123 mins col
FC Produzione/PECF

d **Federico Fellini**
sc **Federico Fellini, Tonino Guerra**
ph **Giuseppe Rotunno**
m **Nino Rota**
Puppela Maggio, Magali Noël, Armando Brancia, Ciccio Ingrassia

Memories of the seaside town of Rimini during the Fascist regime, particularly of one family with a sex-obsessed teenage son, an irascible anti-Fascist father, and an insane uncle. One of Fellini's most affectionate semi-autobiographical films, it is an often dreamlike vision of the past (the title means 'I remember' in Roman dialect), as well as exaggerated, bawdy, funny and melancholy. Nino Rota's jaunty music and Danilo Donati's impressionistic art direction add to the special Fellini flavour, and the set-piece of the townspeople meeting a luxury liner is an inspired moment among many.

Best Foreign Film Oscar 1974

Amator see Camera Buff

Amelia Or The Time For Love

aka A Time To Die
Amélie Ou Le Temps D'Aimer

France 1961 111 mins bw
Port Royal Films/Indusfilms/Prima Film

d **Michel Drach**
sc **Michel Drach**
ph **Jean Tournier**
m **Bach**
Jean Sorel, Marie-José Nat, Sophie Daumier, Clotilde Joano

An orphan girl (Nat) living on a small island off the Breton coast is in love with her cousin (Sorel), but he is more interested in the sea and a glamorous actress. Michel Drach's first major film is unashamedly romantic with a fine feel for the turn of the century. The dark-eyed Marie-José Nat, soon after to be the director's wife, made a heroine worth piping the eye for.

Amélie Ou Le Temps D'Aimer see Amelia Or The Time For Love

Américain, L' see American, The

The American

L'Américain

France 1969 80 mins col
Films 13/Les Films Ariane

d **Marcel Bozzuffi**
sc **Marcel Bozzuffi**
ph **Pierre Willemin**
Jean-Louis Trintignant, Simone Signoret, Marcel Bozzuffi, Bernard Fresson, Françoise Fabian

A Frenchman (Trintignant), who has lived in America for 11 years, returns to his native town to settle down, but after meeting old friends and having a brief fling with an attractive middle-aged woman (Fabian), he leaves. The first film directed by Bozzuffi, the actor who was to gain international fame in *The French Connection* (1971), is a well-observed, bitter-sweet, small-scale, small-town drama with only a tenuous American connection. This minor stuff has a major cast, including Simone Signoret as a bar owner.

The American Friend

Der Amerikanische Freund

W. Germany 1977 123 mins col
Road Movies/Wim Wenders-Westdeutschen Rundfunk/Films Du Losange

d **Wim Wenders**
sc **Wim Wenders**
ph **Robby Müller**
m **Jürgen Knieper**
Bruno Ganz, Dennis Hopper, Gérard Blain, Liza Kreuzer, Nicholas Ray, Sam Fuller, Daniel Schmid, Jean Eustache, Lou Castel, Peter Lilienthal

A dying man (Ganz) unwillingly takes a job as a hit man in order to have money to leave to his widow. Wenders' first real success in the USA (the dialogue is partly in English) is an extremely loose adaptation from the Patricia Highsmith thriller *Ripley's Game*. But the flashy camerawork and too-conscious myth-making act against the story through which the director's real-life heroes Fuller, Ray and Hopper distractingly wend their way.

The American Soldier

Der Amerikanische Soldat

W. Germany 1970 80 mins bw
Antiteater

d **Rainer Werner Fassbinder**
sc **Rainer Werner Fassbinder**
ph **Dietrich Lohmann, Herbert Pajzold**
m **Peer Raben**
Karl Scheydt, Elga Sorbas, Jan George, Margarethe Von Trotta, Kurt Raab, Rainer Werner Fassbinder

After serving in Vietnam, Ricky (Scheydt) returns from the USA to the Munich of his childhood, and carries out a series of murders for the police. Described by Fassbinder as 'what's left in the minds of the German people who see a lot of American gangster films,' this film is peopled by unsmiling, sadistic men in 1950s hats who make their women suffer. What matters is not so much the impenetrable plot or the self-conscious references, but the finely controlled visual style which expertly creates a desolate, absurdist world in the shadows.

Amerikanische Freund, Der see American Friend, The

Amerikanische Soldat, Der see American Soldier, The

Amiche, Le see Girl Friends, The

Amici Per La Pelle see Friends For Life

Ami De Mon Amie, L' see My Girlfriend's Boyfriend

Amitiés Particulières, Les see This Special Friendship

Un Ami Viendra Ce Soir

(US: A Friend Will Come Tonight)

France 1946 120 mins bw
Francinex

d **Raymond Bernard**
sc **Yvan Noë, Jacques Companeez**
ph **Robert Le Fèbvre**
m **Arthur Honegger**
Michel Simon, Madeleine Solange, Louis Salou, Saturnin Fabre, Marcel André, Daniel Gélin

A group of French Resistance fighters pose as inmates in a lunatic asylum in occupied France in order to carry on sabotage undetected. One of the first films about the Resistance to come out of liberated France, the idea behind it was better than the execution. The director, the son of playwright Tristan Bernard, who had not shot a film for six years, made the plot seem rather implausible and paced it poorly. But there are some fine character performances, especially by Simon, top-billed in a smallish role.

Among People see My Apprenticeship

Amor Brujo, El see Love Bewitched, A

Amore E Rabbia see Love And Anger

Amore In Città see Love In The City

L'Amore

(US: Woman aka Ways Of Love)

Italy 1948 79 mins bw
Tevere Film

d **Roberto Rossellini**
sc **Roberto Rossellini, Tullio Pinelli, Federico Fellini**
ph **Robert Juillard, Aldo Tonti**
m **Renzo Rossellini**
Anna Magnani, Federico Fellini

A film composed of two separate episodes: in *The Human Voice*, a woman on the phone tries to persuade her lover not to desert her; and in *The Miracle*, a peasant woman is seduced by a man she believes to be St Joseph and thinks she will give birth to the New Messiah. Rossellini's departure from Neo-Realism was a homage to the awesome art of actress Anna Magnani, first as a society woman in an adaptation of Jean Cocteau's monodrama, and then as a simple devout peasant opposite Fellini who plays a man who may or may not be St Joseph. The rather theatrical and spurious film, only worth seeing for Magnani, was banned in New York as blasphemous.

Amorosa

Sweden 1986 113 mins col
Swedish Film Institute/Sandrew/Film Sveriges TV-SVT 1

d **Mai Zetterling**
sc **Mai Zetterling**
ph **Rune Ericson**
m **Roger Wallis**
Stina Ekblad, Erland Josephson, Philip Zanden, Catherine De Seynes, Olof Thunberg

The story of Swedish novelist Agnes Von Krusentjerna's strict upbringing, her controversial marriage, her scandalous writings, her sexual fantasies and her mental breakdown. Zetterling's first feature, *Loving Couples* (1964), was based on a novel by the subject of this one—her first Swedish film for 17 years. Ekblad has an intensity that makes her series of tantrums and grotesque nightmares (effectively rendered by the excellent camerawork) less monotonous than they might have been. As these seem to take up most of her time, it is difficult to know when she got around to writing.

L'Amour À Mort

France 1984 93 mins col
Dussart/Les Films Ariane/Films A2

d **Alain Resnais**
sc **Jean Gruault**
ph **Sacha Vierny**
m **Hans Werner Henze**
Sabine Azéma, Pierre Arditi, Fanny Ardant, André Dussollier, Jean Dasté

An archaeologist (Arditi) is pronounced dead but recovers. The experience gives greater intensity to his life and to his love for the woman he lives with (Azéma). Resnais has always ventured into areas where few film-makers have dared go, this time depicting resurrection as a fact. This leads to some stylishly acted and filmed but rather stony-faced debates on the subject, frequently punctuated by shots of snowflakes (or feathers?) which are accompanied by Henze's haunting music.

Amour À Vingt Ans, L' see Love At Twenty

Amour De Pluie, Un see Loving In The Rain

Amour De Swann, Un see Swann In Love

Amour En Fuite, L' see Love On The Run

Amour En Question, L' see Love In Question

L'Amour Fou

France 1968 256 mins bw
Marceau/Cocinor/Sogexport

d **Jacques Rivette**
sc **Jacques Rivette, Marilu Tonilini**
ph **Alain Levent**
m **Jean-Claude Eloy**
Jean-Pierre Kalfon, Bulle Ogier, André Labarthe, Denis Berry, Michele Moretti, Josée Destoop

A theatre group prepares to stage Racine's *Andromaque* while being filmed by a TV team. During the rehearsal, the director (Kalfon) replaces his wife (Ogier) in the lead with his former mistress (Destoop). The film, shot in both 35mm and 16mm, was developed from ideas of the cast and technicians, and improvised during filming. Its extreme length is integral to its meaning and texture, but the producers initially distributed it in a condensed two-hour version, disowned by Rivette. This led the director to follow up with *Out One* (1971) which originally ran 12 hours and 40 minutes, but was cut down to *Out One: Spectre* (1973) of four hours and 20 minutes. As they don't attempt to reach any conclusion, these intensely personal, cerebral and sensual films could have gone on for ever. For adventurous filmgoers with time on their hands.

Amour L'Après-Midi, L' see Love In The Afternoon

Amour Par Terre, L' see Love On The Ground

Amour Violé, L' see Violated Love

Amphitryon
Aus Den Wolken Kommt Das Glück

Germany 1935 93 mins bw
UFA/Alliance Cenenat

d **Reinhold Schünzel**
sc **Reinhold Schünzel**
ph **Fritz Arno Wagner, Werner Böhne**
m **Franz Doelle**
Willy Fritsch, Käthe Gold, Paul Kemp, Adele Sandrock, Aribert Wäscher

Jupiter (Fritsch) disguises himself as the mortal Amphitryon in order to make love to Alkmene (Gold), Amphitryon's faithful wife. The popular myth makes a charming and tuneful operetta with a minimum of spoken dialogue. Amusing anachronisms (Mercury on roller skates) and characterizations make one forget that musicals were an important part of Dr Goebbels' film programme.

Ana And The Wolves
Ana Y Los Lobos

Spain 1972 100 mins col
Elias Querejeta

d **Carlos Saura**
sc **Carlos Saura**
ph **Luis Cuadrado**
m **Luis De Pablo**
Geraldine Chaplin, Fernando Fernan-Gomez, José Maria Prada, José Vivó

Ana (Chaplin), an English governess, arrives at an old mansion in Spain where she becomes the object of the ravenous sexual desires of the three sons of a monstrous mother. One of Saura's least oblique attacks on the Franco regime, it is easy to read the three sons as representing aspects of Francoism. The film was passed by the censors only because they found it 'nonsense'. The mixture of farce, fantasy and melodrama may be a little disconcerting, but it is trenchant.

Anatomy Of A Marriage
La Vie Conjugale

France 1963 193 mins bw
Films Borderie/Jolly Film/Terra Arco

d **André Cayatte**
sc **André Cayatte**
ph **Roger Fellous**
m **Louguy**
Marie-José Nat, Jacques Charrier, Georges Rivière, Macha Meril

The same events that lead to the breakdown of the marriage of a young couple (Nat and Charrier) are seen from two opposite points of view. Originally two separate full-length features (later shown in one 112-minute version), under the titles *My Days With Jean Marc* and *My Nights With Françoise*, they contained the seed of a good idea which grew out of all proportion. Like many a marriage, it lasts too long, becoming flat and repetitious.

Ana Y Los Lobos see Ana And The Wolves

The Ancient Law
aka Baruch
Das Alte Gesetz
Germany 1923 110 mins bw
UFA

d **E.A. Dupont**
sc **Paul Reno**
ph **Théodor Sparkühl**
m **Silent**
Ernst Deutsch, Henny Porten, Ruth Weyher, Hermann Vallentin

A Rabbi's son (Deutsch) goes against his father's wishes and becomes a famous actor, adored by the aristocracy. The first film by Dupont to gain international attention, it is psychologically perceptive and uses a more realist technique than earlier German expressionist works. The glimpses of contemporary German theatre in the mid-19th century (the film's period), though silent, are fascinating.

Andalusian Dog, An see Chien Andalou, Un

And God Created Woman
aka And Woman Was Created
Et Dieu Créa La Femme
France 1956 92 mins col
Iena/UCIL/Cocinor

d **Roger Vadim**
sc **Roger Vadmi, Raoul Lévy**
ph **Armand Thirard**
m **Paul Misraki**
Brigitte Bardot, Curt Jurgens, Jean-Louis Trintignant, Christian Marquand

An 18-year-old girl (Bardot), shortly after her marriage (to a wimpish Trintignant), finds she is attracted to other men, particularly her brother-in-law (Marquand). This was the film in which a new sex symbol reared her pretty, pouting, kittenish head, put St Tropez on the map, and brought French films out of the art house ghetto into mainstream cinema. (It earned $4 million in the USA alone.) Mostly shot on location, the rather silly, but certainly sensual, tale was a good excuse for Vadim (in his first feature) to display the amoral charms of his wife in various forms of dress (mainly jeans) and undress.

And Now My Love
Toute Une Vie
France 1974 150 mins col
Les Films 13/Rizzoli

d **Claude Lelouch**
sc **Claude Lelouch, Pierre Uytterhoeven**
ph **Jean Collomb**
m **Gilbert Bécaud**
Marthe Keller, André Dussollier, Charles Denner, Carla Gravina, Charles Gérard, Gilbert Bécaud

A wealthy Jewish girl (Keller), whose grandfather (Denner) was a cameraman in the early days of cinema, and whose father (also Denner) survived a concentration camp, falls in love with a petty thief (Dussollier). Three generations of a family treated in a glossy, superficial fashion, decked out with tear-jerking 'philosophical' songs performed by Bécaud. La schmaltz!

And Quiet Flows The Don
Tikhi Don
USSR 1958 107 mins col
Gorki Film Studio

d **Sergei Gerasimov**
sc **Sergei Gerasimov**
ph **Vladimir Rapoport**
m **Yuri Revitnin**
Ellina Bystritskaya, Pyotr Glebov, Zinaida Kirienko, Danilo Ilchenko

The lives and events in and around a small village during and after World War I. This adaptation of Sholokov's lengthy novel (made in two parts, but reduced to one in Britain and the USA) flows slowly and quietly in a pleasing but academic manner, lacking the lyrical intensity of the great classics of the Soviet cinema in previous decades. There are some effective character vignettes and action scenes, such as the charge of the Cossacks, and good location shooting. In 1949, Gerasimov made a famous speech at the Cultural and Scientific Conference for World Peace in New York, in which he criticized the low moral standards of American films.

And Quiet Rolls The Dawn
Ek Din Prati Din
India 1979 94 mins col
Mrinal Sen

d **Mrinal Sen**
sc **Mrinal Sen**
ph **K.K. Mahajan**
m **B.V. Karanth**
Mamata Shankar, Gita Sen, Satya Banerjee, Sreela Majumdar

A night in the Calcutta tenement of a lower middle-class family, who are waiting anxiously for news of their daughter, also their breadwinner, who has failed to return home at the usual time. Sen's mordant, rigorous attack on social convention, shot in 21 days, is mainly confined to the house of the family who are trying to keep up appearances. 'I wanted to piss in the face of such decency,' commented the forthright director.

Andrei Rublev
USSR 1966 185 mins bw
Mosfilm

d **Andrei Tarkovsky**
sc **Andrei Tarkovsky, Andrei Mikhalkov-Konchalovsky**
ph **Vadim Yusov**
m **Vyacheslav Tcherniaiev**
Anatoly Solonitsin, Ivan Lapikov, Nikolai Grinko, Nikolai Sergeyev

Eight imaginary episodes in the life of the great 15th-century icon painter Rublev (Solonitsin) as he journeys through feudal Russia, gradually abandoning speech, his art and his faith, because of the cruelty he witnesses, but finally regains them. This slow, powerful, impressive epic was shelved for some years by the Soviet authorities, who felt it was too 'dark' for the 50th anniversary of the October Revolution, before being released in a cut version (GB: 146 mins, US: 165 mins). This parable of the artist's position in society ends with a sequence in which colour and the CinemaScope screen do justice to the paintings.

And So To Bed
Das Grosse Liebespiel
Austria/W. Germany 1963 133 mins bw
Team Film/Stadthallen Prod.

d **Aldred Weidenmann**
sc **Herbert Reinecker**
ph **Georg Bruckbauer**
m **Charly Niessen**
Lilli Palmer, Hildegard Knef, Nadja Tiller, Daliah Lavi, Alexandra Stewart, Peter Van Eyck, Thomas Fritsch, Martin Held

A call girl teaches the ways of love to a student who then seduces his teacher's wife, whose husband has an erotic escapade with his secretary who ... Another change rung on the *La Ronde* theme, with a bed at the film's centre, but a movie more likely to promote thoughts of slumber than sex. Passing through this monotonous, mechanical film, are a number of star performers who should have stayed in their own beds.

And The Ship Sails On
E La Nave Va
Italy 1983 132 mins col
RAI/Vides/Gaumont

d **Federico Fellini**
sc **Federico Fellini, Tonino Guerra**
ph **Giuseppe Rotunno**
m **Gianfranco Plenizio, Giuseppe Verdi**
Freddie Jones, Barbara Jefford, Victor Poletti, Peter Cellier, Elisa Mainardi, Norma West, Janet Suzman

In 1914, a luxury liner, full of statesmen, opera singers, aristocrats and a rhinoceros, sails from Naples to an island where the ashes of the world's greatest soprano (Suzman) are to be scattered. Bordering on the precious at times, it is a loving, critical, comic and moving evocation of an era, coloured by the coming war which is symbolized by Serbian refugees boarding the ship. Fellini and art director Dante Ferretti successfully celebrate artifice, allied to Italian romantic opera and the crumbling pre-war society, with a dazzling ship, a painted sky and plastic sea in a Cinecitta studio.

And The Wild Wild Women see Caged

And Woman Was Created see And God Created Woman

Angel see Angelos

Angel Dust

Poussière D'Ange

France 1987 94 mins col
Président Films-U.G.C./Film De La Saga/FR3 Films /La Sofica

d **Edouard Niermans**
sc **Edouard Niermans, Jacques Audiard, Alain Le Henry**
ph **Bernard Lutic**
m **Leon Senza, Vincent-Marie Bouvot**
Bernard Giraudeau, Fanny Bastien, Fanny Cottençon, Jean-Pierre Sentier, Michel Aumont, Gérard Blain

Police inspector Simon Blount (Giraudeau) is shattered when he discovers that his estranged wife (Cottençon) is living with another man. The man turns out to be a pimp implicated in the murder of a prostitute who was the mother of a bizarre girl (Bastien) whom Blount has befriended. Although the film's title might suggest something magical or romantic, it is a cold, calculating, and contrived thriller very much modelled on American lines. Its strengths lie in Giraudeau's unshaven, dishevelled, baggy-eyed lush of a cop, and the sharp photography of night scenes and deserted locations.

Angèle

France 1934 162 mins bw
Films Marcel Pagnol

d **Marcel Pagnol**
sc **Marcel Pagnol**
ph **Willy**
m **Vincent Scotto**
Orane Demazis, Henri Poupon, Annie Toinon, Fernandel, Jean Servais, Edouard Delmont

Seduced and abandoned, Angèle, (Demazis) a young, naive peasant girl, goes to Marseilles where she has a child and becomes a prostitute. The beautifully crafted script (from a Jean Giono short story) and the realistic Provençal background transcend the melodramatic plot of the fallen woman redeemed. By installing his troupe on a farm and using direct sound, Pagnol not only made the first important French talkie shot on location, but the first Neo-Realist film, as acknowledged by De Sica and Rossellini. In addition, Fernandel, as the simple-minded farm hand, emerged as a great tragicomic actor.

Angel Exterminador, El see Exterminating Angel, The

Angelina

L'Onorevole Angelina

Italy 1947 90 mins bw
Lux/Ora

d **Luigi Zampa**
sc **Luigi Zampa, Suso Cecchi D'Amico, Piero Tellini, Anna Magnani**
ph **Mario Craveri**
m **Enzio Masetti**
Anna Magnani, Nando Bruno, Ave Ninchi, Agnese Dubbini, Gianni Glori

Angelina (Magnani), a housewife, fights heroically to improve the living conditions of her neighbours in post-war Italy. Although made at the height of the Italian Neo-Realist movement by one of its minor members, this is really a star vehicle for the earthy, humorous and passionate Magnani, who appears in almost every scene.

Best Actress (Anna Magnani) Venice 1947

Angélique

Angélique, Marquise Des Anges

France 1964 116 mins col
Francos/Films Borderie/Gloria/Fono

d **Bernard Borderie**
sc **Bernard Borderie, Claude Brûlé**
ph **Henri Pérsin**
m **Michel Magne**
Michèle Mercier, Robert Hossein, Jean Rochefort, Giuliano Gemma

Angélique, the comely daughter of a penniless nobleman at the court of Louis XIV, is married off to a man who is later imprisoned for witchcraft. The first in a widely popular series of bodice-rippers, based on the books of Serge and Anne Golon which feature the adventures of a Forever Amber- like heroine, it is less fun than it should have been. The settings and costumes are colourful, and Mlle Mercier in the title role pouts prettily.

Angélique, Marquise Des Anges see Angélique

Angelos

aka Angel

Greece 1982 126 mins col
Greek Film Centre

d **George Katakouzinos**
sc **George Katakouzinos**
ph **Tassos Alexakis**
m **Stamatis Spanoudakis**

Michael Maniatis, Maria Alkeou, Dionyssis Xanthos, Katerina Helmi

A young homosexual (Maniatis) falls in love with a sailor (Xanthos) and leaves home to live with him. However, his lover soon persuades him into a life of degrading transvestite prostitution to earn them extra money. Not as melodramatic or sensationalist as it sounds, this debut film from a man who had worked as assistant on 60 previous films, is a sensitive and realistic portrait of a subculture. Based on a real-life case, it is a painful tale, containing some brutally explicit love scenes. Big box-office in Greece, it was also lauded at various festivals.

Angels Of The Streets see Anges Du Péché, Les

Angemaeul see Village In The Mist

Les Anges Du Péché

(US: Angels Of The Streets)

France 1943 73 mins bw
Synops

d **Robert Bresson**
sc **Robert Bresson, Jean Giraudoux, R. Bruckberger**
ph **Philippe Agostini**
m **Jean-Jacques Grünewald**

Jany Holt, Renée Fauré, Sylvie, Mila Parély, Marie-Hélène Dasté

A young novice (Fauré) devotes herself to the redemption of an ex- prisoner and murderer (Holt) even though it means sacrificing herself. Bresson's first feature, made when he was 36, has a religious intensity and rigour that overcomes some of its more melodramatic aspects. Although the film uses professional performers and was shot in a studio, the theme and images prefigure his later work.

Angi Vera

Hungary 1978 96 mins col
Mafilm Studio/Hungarofilm

d **Pál Gábor**
sc **Pál Gábor**
ph **Lajos Koltai**
m **György Selmeczi**

Veronika Papp, Erszi Pásztor, Éva Szabó, Tamás Dunai, László Horváth

When naive, 18-year-old Vera (Papp) criticizes management methods at the hospital where she works, she is sent for institutionalized training in the ways of the Party. Gradually corrupted by the system, she betrays a colleague and, in the process, her integrity. Her conversion to an honoured senior Party member is chilling in a sombre and gripping film that eloquently conveys the repressive climate of Stalinist Hungary in 1948. Coming from the Soviet bloc, the film's portrayal of the regime surprised and impressed critics in the West.

Angst see Fear

Angst Des Tormanns Beim Elfmeter, Die see Anxiety Of The Goalie At The Penalty, The

Angst Essen Seele Auf see Fear Eats The Soul

Aniki-Bobo

Portugal 1942 70 mins bw
Tobis

d **Manoel De Oliveira**
sc **Manoel De Oliveira, Manuel Matos, António Lopes Ribeiro, Nascimento Fernandes**
ph **António Mendes**
m **Jaime Silva**

Nascimento Fernandes, Vital Dos Santos, Antonio Palma, Armando Pedro

The adventures of street urchins growing up in the slums of Oporto and on the banks of the river. This first feature by Portugal's only renowned director is, in style, much simpler than his later films, and gained some recognition abroad for its excellent location shooting and natural performances by the actual children of the area.

Ani Ohev Otach Rosa see I Love You Rosa

Ani To Song Imoto see Brother And His Younger Sister, A

Ankur see Seedling, The

Anna

Italy 1951 95 mins bw
Dino De Laurentiis/Lux

d **Alberto Lattuada**
sc **Giuseppe Berto, Dino Risi, Ivo Perilli, Franco Brusati, Rodolfo Sonego**
ph **Otello Martelli**
m **Nino Rota**
Silvana Mangano, Raf Vallone, Vittorio Gassman, Gaby Morlay

Anna (Mangano), a nightclub singer, enters a convent to avoid making a choice between two men. The presence of three of Italy's biggest stars of the 1950s, and the heady mixture of the sacred and profane, ensured a healthy box-office success at home and abroad. However, the gaggle of screenwriters and Lattuada's stolid direction only resulted in a risible melodrama.

Anna

Finland 1970 83 mins col
Jörn Donner Productions

d **Jörn Donner**
sc **Jörn Donner, Elija-Elina Bergholm**
ph **Heikki Katajisto**
m **Claes Af Geïjerstam**
Harriet Andersson, Marjatta Packalen, Tapio Rautavaara, Tapani Perttu

A 38-year-old woman becomes aware of the passage of time during a holiday trip to the Finnish archipelago, accompanied by her young daughter and teenage maid. Andersson's expressive performance under her husband's direction and some attractive locations make this psychological mood piece more watchable than it might have been. However, the film is still rather enclosed and self-consciously arty.

Anna Boleyn

(US: Deception)
Germany 1920 100 mins bw
Messter/GMBH

d **Ernst Lubitsch**
sc **Norbert Falk (billed as Fred Orbing)**
ph **Théodor Spärkuhl**
m **Silent**
Emil Jannings, Henny Porten, Aud Egede Nissen

Henry VIII (Jannings) is disappointed that Anne (Porten) has not given him a son and has her executed after he decides to marry Jane Seymour (Nissen). Jannings, looking as though he had stepped out of a Holbein portrait, set the prototype for the lusty king taken up by Charles Laughton in *The Private Life Of Henry VIII* (1933), which displayed a similar ironic approach to history. More inventive and historically accurate than the later film, this one had sets of Hampton Court etc built at the UFA studios by architects Kurt Richter and Poelzig.

Anna Di Brooklyn see Anna Of Brooklyn

Anna Karenina

USSR 1967 135 mins col
Mosfilm

d **Alexander Zarkhi**
sc **Alexander Zarkhi, V. Katanian**
ph **Leonid Kalachnikov**
m **Rodion Chtchedrine**
Tatiana Samoilova, Vassily Lanovoi, Nikolai Gritzenko, Anastasia Vertinskaya, Boris Goldaiev

Anna (Samoilova), married to an older man (Gritzenko), falls in love with Vronsky (Lanovoi), a dashing officer, for whom she forsakes her social position and even her beloved little boy. Old-time director Zarkhi, using the 70mm screen effectively, comes closer to Tolstoy's romance than previous versions which tended to ignore many of the important subsidiary characters and relationships. Samoilova, following such luminaries as Garbo and Vivien Leigh, had her best role since *The Cranes Are Flying* 10 years previously.

Anna Of Brooklyn
(US: Fast And Sexy)
Anna Di Brooklyn

Italy 1958 106 mins col
Circeo Cinematografica/France Cinema/RKO

d **Reginald Denham, Carlo Lasticati**
sc **Ettore Margadonna, Luciana Corda, Joseph Stefano**
ph **Giuseppe Rotunno**
m **Alessandro Cicognini, Vittorio De Sica**
Gina Lollobrigida, Dale Robertson, Vittorio De Sica, Peppino De Felippo, Amedeo Nazzari

A wealthy and attractive widow (Lollobrigida), returning from New York to her native Italian village in search of a husband, charms all the eligible bachelors except the handsome blacksmith (Robertson). This predictable, resistible romp at least had an eye-catching La Lollo and a witty performance by De Sica (who also 'supervised' the direction) as a gossiping priest.

Anne And Muriel
(US: Two English Girls)
Les Deux Anglaises Et Le Continent

France 1971 108 mins col
Films Du Carrosse/Cinétel/Simar

d **François Truffaut**
sc **François Truffaut, Jean Gruault**
ph **Nestor Almendros**
m **Georges Delerue**
Jean-Pierre Léaud, Kika Markham, Stacey Tendeter, Sylvia Marriott, Philippe Léotard, Marie Mansart

At the turn of the century, an aspiring young French writer (Léaud) spends a holiday on the Welsh coast with two English sisters (Markham and Marriott) and falls in love with both of them. Truffaut's second adaptation of a novel by Henri- Pierre Roché is less successful than *Jules And Jim*, the first. This triangle, despite much delicacy and wit, is weighed down by the rather irritatingly over-sensitive characters. The desaturated colour was an attempt to recreate early two-tone Technicolor.

Année Dernière À Marienbad, L' see Last Year At Marienbad

Anne Trister

Canada 1986 115 mins col
Société Générale Du Cinéma Du Québec/Téléfilm Canada/ Société De Radio-Télévision Du Québec

d **Léa Pool**
sc **Marcel Beaulieu, Léa Pool**
ph **Pierre Mignot**
m **René Dupéré**
Albane Guilhe, Louise Marleau, Lucie Laurier, Guy Thauvette, Hugues Quester, Nuvit Ozdogru

Anne Trister (Guilhe) is a 25-year-old Jewish painter living in Israel. The death of her father triggers an emotional crisis and, abandoning her lover (Quester), her mother and her studies, she goes to Canada to stay with her older female friend Alix (Marleau), a psychologist. Anne falls in love with Alix, plunging the latter's life into confusion, and their relationship is both enriched and further complicated by Alix's special bond with Sarah (Laurier), a rebellious, love-starved 10-year-old patient. An official entry at Berlin, this second feature by a maker of documentary and short films is an ambitious work that sets out to explore the voids created by bereavement, loss of self and change. Pool utilizes Anne's calling as an artist with originality, and treats the Lesbian theme intelligently, but the movie suffers from an overload of metaphor and unrelieved emotional intensity.

Anonimo Veneziano see Anonymous Venetian, The

The Anonymous Venetian
Anonimo Veneziano

Italy 1970 93 mins col
Ultra Film

d **Enrico Maria Salerno**
sc **Enrico Maria Salerno, Giuseppe Berto**
ph **Marcello Gatto**
m **Stelvio Cirpriani**
Tony Musante, Florinda Bolkan, Toti Del Monte

An estranged couple spend a day together in Venice remembering the high and low moments of their marriage, but the reconciliation is short-lived because the man is dying of an incurable disease. The debut film of Salerno, an established actor and theatre director, is a rather tedious tear-jerker with virtually only three protagonists—the constantly promenading couple and the wonderfully photogenic Venice. Naturally, the latter steals almost every scene.

À Nos Amours see To Our Loves

Another Man, Another Chance

aka Another Man, Another Woman

Un Autre Homme, Une Autre Chance

France 1977 128 mins col
Les Films Ariane/UA/Les Films 13

d **Claude Lelouch**
sc **Claude Lelouch**
ph **Jacques Lefrançois**
m **Francis Lai**
Geneviève Bujold, James Caan, Jennifer Warren, Susan Tyrrell, Francis Huster

The French widow (Bujold) of a murdered photographer meets and falls in love with an American veterinary surgeon (Caan), whose wife was raped and slain in the Far West in the 1870s. A vain attempt by the ever-romantic Lelouch to remake his first success, *A Man And A Woman* (1966) into a Western. The muddled plot and unconvincing leads are not helped by the show-off style and pretentious use of the first bars of Beethoven's Fifth Symphony.

Another Man, Another Woman see Another Man, Another Chance

Another Way

Egymásra Nézve

Hungary 1982 109 mins col
Mafilm

d **Károly Makk**
sc **Károly Makk, Erzsébet Galgóczi**
ph **Tamás Andor**
m **László Dés**
Jadwiga Jankowska-Cieslak, Grazyna Szapolowska, Jožef Kroner, Gábor Reviczky

The Lesbian love affair between two journalists in the period following the 1956 Hungarian uprising leads to the attempted murder of one by her husband and the death of the other. Hungary's senior director returned to his best form with this politically courageous, touching and intelligent plea for tolerance, based on the semi-autobiographical bestseller by his co-scriptwriter. The two Polish actresses as the doomed lovers, give remarkably perceptive performances.

Best Actress (Jadwiga Jankowska-Cieslak) Cannes 1982

À Nous La Liberté

(US: Freedom For Us)

France 1931 97 mins bw
Tobis

d **René Clair**
sc **René Clair**
ph **Georges Périnal**
m **Georges Auric**
Raymond Cordy, Henri Marchand, Rolla France, Paul Olivier, Jacques Shelly, André Michaud

Two convicts, Louis (Cordy) and Emile (Marchand), escape from prison, but Emile is recaptured. Louis advances from gramophone salesman to owner of a huge, modern gramophone factory. Emile is released, finds work at the plant, rediscovers his old cell-mate and, after things go wrong, they take to the road together as tramps. Making clever use of songs, sound effects, a horizontally panning camera, rhythmic dialogue and choreographed movements, Clair has created a sublime musical comedy satire on the work ethic and the dehumanizing effects of mass-production techniques. In a light-hearted manner, an analogy is made between prison and the factory, underlined by Lazare Meerson's striking Bauhaus sets dwarfing the workers. The film inspired Chaplin's *Modern Times*, in which there are similar sequences on the assembly line. Tobis, the production company, wanted to sue Chaplin, but Clair took it as the highest form of flattery, just as he, in his silent period, had doffed his beret to the great comic.

À Nous Les Petites Anglaises!

France 1976 112 mins col
Irene Silberman

d **Michel Lang**

sc **Michel Lang**
ph **Daniel Gaudry**
m **Mort Shuman**
Rémy Laurent, Stéphane Hillel, Véronique Delbourg, Sophie Barjac, Brigitte Bellac

Because he has failed his English exam a middle-class, Parisian schoolboy (Laurent) is sent to England for his summer vacation instead of to St Tropez. What was intended as a punishment turns out to be the best time he has ever had. A certain freshness and authenticity among the youthful players, an air of improvisation, and holiday situations that many French and English teenagers could recognize, led to the success of this debut film from a young director. Not for anyone past the acne stage, though.

Ansikte Mot Ansikte see Face To Face

Ansiktet see Face, The

Answer To Violence

Zamach

Poland 1958 83 mins bw
Illuzion Film Unit

d **Jerzy Passendorfer**
sc **Jerzy Stefan Stawinski**
ph **Jerzy Lipman**
m **Adam Walacinski**
Bozena Kurowska, Grazyna Staniszewska, Zbigniew Cyncutis, Andrzej Kostenko, Roman Klosowski, Tadeusz Lomnicki, Andrzej May, Jerzy Pichelski, Wojciech Siemion

In Warsaw during the winter of 1943-44, Polish hostages are executed by German firing squads. The Resistance decides to kill the man responsible, the General in command of the Warsaw SS, and the task is entrusted to a group of medical students. Few countries lost more lives in World War II than Poland, so it is perhaps not surprising that those years were still an obsession in 1958. A former member of the Cracow Resistance, Passendorfer has reconstructed a factual incident with an impressive concern for authenticity, ending up with a film with the flavour of a documentary. However, this approach works against the film because the action is far too slow and drawn out and characterization is almost non-existent. Worthy, and occasionally affecting, but a failure.

Anthracite

France 1980 90 mins col
Rush/Antenne 2

d **Edouard Niermans**
sc **Edouard Niermans**
ph **Bernard Lutic**
m **Alain Jomy**
Jean-Pol Dubois, Jérôme Zucca, Bruno Cremer, Jean Bouise

At a Jesuit college for boys, one of the priest-teachers (Dubois), nicknamed 'Anthracite', is despised by colleagues and pupils alike for trying to teach by love rather than force. At the same time, Pierre (Zucca) suffers derision from his fellow pupils. The first feature by 37-year-old Jesuit-educated Niermans presents a bleak but realistic picture of the tensions and cruelty of school life, while avoiding many of the clichés of the genre. His second film, the very different *Angel Dust*, appeared seven years later.

Antigone

Greece 1960 93 mins bw
Norma Film Prod.

d **George Tzavellas**
sc **George Tzavellas**
ph **Dinos Katsourdis**
m **Arghyris Kounadis**
Irene Papas, Manos Katrakis, Maro Kontou, Nikos Kazis

Antigone (Papas) is condemned to death for defying King Creon (Katrakis) by burying her two brothers killed in a quarrel over their succession to the throne of Thebes. Greek tragedy made filmic with no tricks so that Sophocles' poetic parable comes across with lucidity. Flashback and voice-over unobtrusively overcome the problem of long speeches by the chorus and messenger, thus giving more impact to the images, dominated by the excellent Irene Papas' dramatic beauty.

Antoine And Antoinette

Antoine Et Antoinette

France 1947 95 mins bw
SNEG

d **Jacques Becker**

sc **Jacques Becker, Françoise Giroud, Maurice Griffe**
ph **Pierre Montazel**
m **Jean-Jacques Grünewald**
Roger Pigaut, Claire Maffei, Noël Roquevert

The everyday life of a young couple—he works for a printing firm, she is a shop assistant—is disrupted when they find they have won a lottery but lost the ticket. With a nod to René Clair's *Le Million* (1931), this beguiling romantic comedy, the first of Becker's Parisian 'loving couples' trilogy (including *Rendezvous De Juillet*, 1949 and *Edward And Caroline*, 1951), is interested less in plot than in the depiction of relationships and in affectionately filmed Paris locations.

Antoine Et Antoinette see Antoine And Antoinette

Antonieta

Mexico 1981 104 mins col
Gaumont/Conacine/Nuevo Cine

d **Carlos Saura**
sc **Carlos Saura, Jean-Claude Carrière**
ph **Teo Escamilla**
m **José Antonio Zavala**
Isabelle Adjani, Hanna Schygulla, Ignacio Lopez Tarso, Carlos Bracho

A French author (Schygulla) goes to Mexico to research the life of Antonieta Rivas Mecadé (Adjani), Mexican patroness of the arts and liberal, who committed suicide in Notre Dame Cathedral in Paris in the 1920s. Denounced and hounded by the Spanish after *Sweet Hours* (1981), Saura fled to Central America where he made this big budget co-production, one of his least personal films. Although jumping back and forth between the present day and the past, it remains fairly static, with rather lifeless performances from the two female leads.

Antonio Das Mortes

Dragao Da Maldade Contra O Santo Guerreiro

Brazil 1969 95 mins col
Glauber Rocha/Mapa

d **Glauber Rocha**
ph **Glauber Rocha**
m **Marlos Nobre, Walter Queiroz, Sergio Ricardo**
Mauricio Do Valle, Odete Lara, Othon Bastos, Hugo Carvana

A hired killer ends up siding with the peasants in their fight against the brutal landowners. Like *Black God, White Devil* (1962), this political allegory was set in the arid north-east of Brazil, and contains similar characters and characteristics: ritualized techniques drawing on the mystic cultural traditions of the country. Made under repressive conditions, it was Rocha's last radical cry from Brazil before almost 10 years' exile.

Best Director Cannes 1969

The Anxiety Of The Goalie At The Penalty

aka The Goalkeeper's Fear Of The Penalty Kick

(US: The Goalie's Anxiety At The Penalty Kick)

Die Angst Des Tormanns Beim Elfmeter

W. Germany 1972 101 mins col
Filmverlag Der Autoren

d **Wim Wenders**
sc **Wim Wenders, Peter Handke**
ph **Robby Müller**
m **Jürgen Knieper, Roy Orbison, and several pop groups**
Arthur Brauss, Kai Fischer, Maria Bardischewski, Erika Pluhar

A veteran goalkeeper (Brauss), who lets in a penalty without moving a muscle, meets up with a cinema cashier, goes to bed with her, and calmly strangles her in the morning. The film, based on Handke's first novel, uses the sporting metaphor to express the *angst* of modern life. Like the goalkeeper, the camera hardly moves. Each scene is separated by slow fades creating an atmosphere midway between the hypnotic and the soporific.

Any Number Can Win see Big Snatch, The

Anyone Can Play

Le Dolci Signore

Italy 1967 102 mins col
Documento Films

d **Luigi Zampa**
sc **Ruggero Maccari, Ettore Scola**
ph **Romano Dandi**
m **Armando Trovaioli**
Ursula Andress, Virna Lisi, Marisa Mell, Claudine Auger, Jean-Pierre Cassel

Four contrasting married women each solve their sex problems by committing adultery. The 1960s saw an interminable string of Italian sex comedies that only slightly rib-tickled and titillated. This loosely scripted portmanteau picture was no exception.

Apa see Father

Aparajito

aka The Unvanquished
India 1956 127 mins bw
Epic Films

d **Satyajit Ray**
sc **Satyajit Ray**
ph **Subrata Mitra**
m **Ravi Shankar**
Pinaki Sen Gupta, Karuna Bannerjee, Kanu Bannerjee, Sumiran Ghosjal

Apu (played by two boy actors, Gupta and Ghosjal) goes to Benares with his mother, then returns to his village where he begins his education. In the second part of Ray's great 'Apu trilogy' (the linking episode between the childhood in *Pather Panchali*, 1955 and the manhood in *The World of Apu*, 1959), we see Apu growing away from his mother (Karuna Bannerjee) and the village. The mother-son relationship is delicately observed, as are the contrasting scenes between the country and the city.

Best Film Venice 1957

... A Paty Jezdec Je Strach see Fifth Horseman Is Fear, The

The Ape Woman

La Donna Scimmia
Italy 1964 97 mins bw
Compagnia Cinematografica Champion/Les Films Marceau/Cocinor

d **Marco Ferreri**
sc **Marco Ferreri, Rafael Azcona**
ph **Aldo Tonti**
m **Teo Usuelli**
Annie Girardot, Ugo Tognazzi, Achille Majeroni, Filippo Pompa

A man (Tognazzi) discovers a monstrous woman (Girardot) covered with hair, marries her to exploit her at a funfair, falls in love with her and, after her death, travels with her embalmed body. No one could ever accuse Ferreri of good taste, but this cynical comedy has much vigour, and a hirsute Girardot brings some poignancy to the title role. Two endings were shot: a softened one terminating with the wife's death, and the other starker one. The latter, better, ending is more frequently shown.

A Porte Chiuse see Behind Closed Doors

The Apple Game

Hra O Jablko
Czechoslovakia 1976 101 mins col
Krátky

d **Véra Chytilová**
sc **Véra Chytilová, Kristina Vlachová**
ph **František Ulček**
m **Miroslav Kořinek**
Jiří Menzel, Dagmar Bláhová, Evelyna Steimarová, Jiří Kodet, Nina Popeliková

A country girl (Bláhová), who works as a midwife at a maternity clinic, becomes pregnant by one of the doctors (Menzel). In her first film for 10 years in her native land, having been at odds with the Czech authorities, Chytilová continued in much the same anarchic vein. But the joky, jumpy, jazzy style had staled over the years, despite some funny moments and striking images (mostly of babies).

À Propos De Nice

France 1930 45 mins bw
Lozinski

d **Jean Vigo**
sc **Jean Vigo**
ph **Boris Kaufman**
m **Silent**

A satirical documentary on the famous Riviera resort. Under the influence of the experiments in montage of the Russian director Dziga

Vertov, Vigo and Kaufman (Vertov's younger brother) brilliantly elaborated the simple contrast between the rich tourists and the poorer inhabitants of Nice. A woman suns herself until she becomes a skeleton, people walking along the promenade are compared with animals, a croupier rakes up passengers just arrived by train, and a girl at a café is stripped nude in a series of dissolves. The latter scene was cut from the 35 mm version shown in Britain, but remained in the 16 mm print which was not subject to censorship.

Apu Sansar see World Of Apu, The

The Arabian Nights

aka A Thousand And One Nights

Il Fiore Delle Mille E Una Notte

Italy 1974 155 mins col
PEA/Artistes Associés

d **Pier Paolo Pasolini**
sc **Pier Paolo Pasolini**
ph **Giuseppe Ruzzolini**
m **Ennio Morricone**

Ninetto Davoli, Franco Citti, Franco Merli, Ines Pellegrini

Ten interspliced tales of love and love-making, potions and betrayal, linked by the story of Mur-El-Din searching for his kidnapped slave girl. Pasolini took almost two years to complete this final and best segment of his trilogy of great story cycles, the others being *The Decameron* (1971) and *The Canterbury Tales* (1972). Filmed in Yemen, Eritrea, Iran and Nepal, it captures the beauties (landscape, buildings and people) of those countries, and the bawdy spirit of the original tales remains untramelled by Freudian or religious guilt.

Aranyer Din Ratri see Days And Nights In The Forest

Archimède Le Clochard see Archimède The Tramp

Archimède The Tramp

(US: The Magnificent Tramp)

Archimède Le Clochard

France 1958 91 mins bw
Filmsonor/Intermondia

d **Gilles Grangier**
sc **Albert Valentin, Michel Audiard**
ph **Louis Page**
m **Jean Prodromidès**

Jean Gabin, Darry Cowl, Bernard Blier, Dora Doll, Julien Carette

Archimède (Gabin), a crusty old tramp, wrecks a bar in order to be able to spend the winter in jail, gets involved with a dog-stealing tramp and has various altercations with the rich. The script, based on an idea by Gabin, was a sketchy affair but it allowed the star at the end of his third decade in films, to display the full range of his mature mannerisms. He is as forceful as the film is feeble—it was the start of a decline in the material Gabin was to choose for the next two decades.

Best Actor (Jean Gabin) Berlin 1959

Ard, El see Land, The

Ardh Satya see Half-Truth

Aren't We Wonderful?

Wir Wunderkinder

W. Germany 1958 120 mins bw
Filmaufbau

d **Kurt Hoffmann**
sc **Heinz Pauck, Günter Neumann**
ph **Richard Angst**
m **Franz Gröthe**

Johanna Von Koczian, Hansjörg Felmy, Wera Frydtberg, Robert Graf

An ex-Nazi, who has become a respected captain of industry in modern Germany, has his past exposed by a campaigning journalist, but is nonetheless honoured at his funeral. As the general level of West German films was lamentably low in the 1950s, this light satirical comedy came as a pleasant surprise. A pianist and a narrator in front of a small screen comment in a Brechtian manner on the rise and literal fall (down a lift shaft) of a Nazi, while at the same time finding room for a tender love story.

Are We All Murderers?

(US: We Are All Murderers)

Nous Sommes Tous Les Assassins

France 1952 95 mins bw
UGC

d **André Cayatte**
sc **André Cayatte, Charles Spaak**
ph **Jean Bourgoin**
m **Raymond Legrand**
Mouloudji, Raymond Pellegrin, Antoine Balpêtre, Paul Frankeur, Georges Poujouly

A former Resistance fighter (Mouloudji) is condemned to death for killing a policeman after the war, and awaits the guillotine with two other prisoners. Former lawyers Cayatte and Spaak followed up their previous success, *Justice Is Done* (1950) about mercy killing, with this heavy-handed and wordy, but nevertheless effective, condemnation of the death penalty. Audiences are left in ignorance as to whether the young killer is reprieved or not.

Special Jury Prize Cannes 1952

Argent De Poche, L' see Small Change

L'Argent

France 1928 195 mins bw
Cinémondial/Pathé

d **Marcel L'Herbier**
sc **Marcel L'Herbier**
ph **Jules Kruger**
m **Silent**
Pierre Alcover, Alfred Abel, Mary Glory, Brigitte Helm, Raymond Rouleau, Antonin Artaud

A tale of the constant rivalry between two business tycoons (Alcover and Abel), unscrupulously crushing anyone in their way, including friends and relations. The last and most ambitious of L'Herbier's great silent films was an expansive, updated adaptation of Zola's novel condemning big business. Unequivocally indicting the possession of vast wealth, the film had an enormous budget. A strong cast move through the huge, luminously photographed Art Deco sets. The mobility of the camera was another exciting element in a film that was known for many years only by reputation until it reappeared in the 1960s to general acclaim. Among the many bravura sequences is the camera skimming over the floor of the Stock Exchange, cross-cut with an aircraft taking off.

L'Argent

France 1983 84 mins col
EOS/Marion's Films/FR3

d **Robert Bresson**
sc **Robert Bresson**
ph **Emmanuel Machuel, Pasqualino De Santis**
m **Bach**
Christian Patey, Sylvie Van Den Elsen, Michel Briguet, Caroline Lang

A young man passes a forged note in a photographer's shop, an action that leads him into theft and murder. Whatever one's views on Bresson's use of non-actors manipulated like expressionless puppets, his sparse editing, austere images, and severe Jansenist beliefs, the 76-year-old director remained true to his constant vision in this updating of a Tolstoy story. Non-Bressonians should abstain.

Best Director Cannes 1983

Ariane see Loves Of Ariane

Les Aristocrates

aka The Aristocrats

France 1955 105 mins bw
Gaumont

d **Denys De La Patellière**
sc **Roland Laudenbach, Denys De La Patellière**
ph **Pierre Petit**
m **René Cloërec**
Pierre Fresnay, Brigitte Auber, Jacques Dacqmine, François Guérin, Léo Joannon

An aging French aristocrat (Fresnay), locked into the style and habits of his past, comes into bitter conflict with his now grown-up children who try to push him into adapting to their modern way of life. This is the director's debut film and his inexperience shows in the lack of properly paced dramatic climaxes and a generally loose and choppy style. The acting, particularly from Fresnay, however, just about keeps the tale going. As the almost pathetically outmoded nobleman, living on dreams in his crumbling mansion which he refuses to modernize and clinging on to the last vestiges of dignity, he is a moving figure.

Aristocrats, The see Aristocrates, Les

Armée Des Ombres, L' see Army In The Shadows, The

Arms And The Man

Helden

W. Germany 1958 96 mins col
Casino Films

d **Franz Peter Wirth**
sc **Johanna Sibelius, Eberhard Keindorff**
ph **Klaus Von Rautenfeld**
m **Franz Gröthe**
O.W. Fischer, Lilo Pulver, Ellen Schwiers, Ljuba Welitsch, Kurt Kasznar

Bluntschli (Fischer), a Swiss mercenary fleeing the enemy, takes refuge in the bedroom of Raina (Pulver), engaged to the Bulgarian officer who put him to flight. Shaw's famous anti-romantic comedy is given handsome settings and some good acting, but the film is as talky as the play, which the stiff direction does nothing to alleviate.

The Army In The Shadows

L'Armée Des Ombres

France 1969 143 mins col
Corona/Fono Roma

d **Jean-Pierre Melville**
sc **Jean-Pierre Melville**
ph **Pierre Lhomme**
m **Eric De Marsan**
Lino Ventura, Simone Signoret, Jean-Pierre Cassel, Paul Meurisse, Claude Mann, Christian Barbier, Serge Reggiani, Alain Libolt, Paul Crauchet

Resistance fighter Philippe Gerbier (Ventura) is arrested in Vichy France and sent to a prison camp before being handed over to the Gestapo. He is determined to track down the informer who betrayed him and his group. This is the main strand that weaves through the bleakly atmospheric portrayal of the daring and complex workings of the French Resistance in German-occupied Lyons during World War II. Melville's third film on the subject (he was himself in the *maquis*), based on Joseph Kessel's novel, is a moving, truthful and ultimately tragic view of the Resistance, while not being afraid to glorify the heroism of its members. These are given powerful performances from a superb cast able to express the moral ambiguities of the characters. Using the format of his gangster movies—cool, classical images and a commanding use of flashback—Melville turns the underworld into the underground.

Arohan see Ascending Scale

Arsenal

USSR 1929 99 mins bw
VUFKU

d **Alexander Dovzhenko**
sc **Alexander Dovzhenko**
ph **Danylo Demutsky**
m **Silent**
Semyon Svashenko, A. Buchma, Mikola Nademsky

The Bolsheviks' revolutionary struggles against opposing forces and the problems of collectivization in the Ukraine of 1918. The Ukrainian Dovzhenko's highly symbolic and lyrical account of his homeland's emergence from feudalism expertly blends folklore, agit-prop, drama, comedy and caricature. This was the sort of plotless Soviet film (where a tractor plays a leading role) that caused much sniggering from some Western critics, but nevertheless became a strong influence, notably on documentary movements, in other countries including Britain.

Artisten In Der Zirkuskuppel: Ratlos, Die see Artists At The Top Of The Big Top: Disorientated

---

Artists At The Top Of The Big Top: Disorientated

Die Artisten In Der Zirkuskuppel: Ratlos

W. Germany 1968 103 mins col
Kairos Film

d **Alexander Kluge**
sc **Alexander Kluge**
ph **Günther Hörmann, Thomas Mauch**
Hannelore Hoger, Siegfried Graue, Alfred Edel, Bernd Höltz

A young circus director (Hoger), whose father was killed in a trapeze accident, wants to create the ideal circus, but gives it up and goes into TV. Kluge's second and best-known feature attempts to create an allegory of modern day Germany using four narrators, including the director, newsreel footage, interviews, stills and acted scenes around the tired old symbol of the circus as life. Influenced by early Godard, much of it is wittily cerebral, but seemed fresher at the time when the new German cinema was emerging.

Best Film Venice 1968

Artist With The Ladies see Coiffeur Pour Dames

Arturo's Island

L'Isola Di Arturo

Italy 1962 102 mins bw
Champion Cinematografica/Titanus/Metro

d **Damiano Damiani**
sc **Damiano Damiani, Ugo Liberatore, Enrico Ribulzi**
ph **Roberto Gerardi**
m **Carlo Rustichelli**
Reginald Kernan, Key Meersman, Vanni De Maigret, Luigi Giuliani, Gabriella Giorcelli

Sixteen-year-old Arturo (De Maigret), whose mother is dead and whose strange and taciturn father, Wilhelm (Kernan), travels much of the time, lives a quiet life on an island in the Bay of Naples. One day Wilhelm returns, bringing a new young wife (Meersman) with him and, when he goes away again, Arturo falls hopelessly in love with his stepmother. Damiani has placed a story of adolescent turbulence in a beautiful and strongly atmospheric setting. However, in adapting a highly romantic novel (by Elsa Morante), character development has been neglected so that the protagonists drown in a sea of melodramatic plot. The casting, too, lets the piece down since the principals—with the exception of Key Meersman—don't have the expertise to overcome the weaknesses of the script.

Ascending Scale

Arohan

India 1982 147 mins col
West Bengal Government

d **Shyam Benegal**
sc **Shama Zaidi**
ph **Govind Nihalani**
m **Purna Das Baul**
Om Puri, Victor Banerjee, Noni Ganguly, Rajen Tarafdar, Gita Sen

A share-cropper, who is refused his rights, spends 10 years fighting for them in the courts. Benegal paints a horrifying picture of corruption and exploitation in modern India, based on an actual case history. Yet the film never sentimentalizes, but rather analyses the system that produces oppression of the individual.

Ascenseur Pour L'Echafaud see Lift To The Scaffold

The Ascent

Voskhozhdenie

USSR 1976 105 mins bw
Mosfilm

d **Larisa Shepitko**
sc **Larisa Shepitko, Juri Klepikov**
ph **V. Chuhnov**
m **Alfred Shnitke**
Boris Plotkinov, Ludmila Poliakova, Vladimir Gostjuhin, Sergei Jakovlev, Anatoly Solonitsin

A small group of Soviet partisans during World War II escapes from the Germans across the snow and ice, but tragedy occurs when two of them leave the unit to forage for food. Far from the days of Socialist realism, the film depicts cowards and collaborators as well as heroes. Small figures in a brutal white landscape, suffering faces in close-up, and an incomparably powerful hanging scene, make a triumphant climax to Shepitko's four-feature film career. She was killed in a car crash in 1979 while preparing *Farewell*, later made by her widower, Elem Klimov.

Best Film Berlin 1976

Ascent to Heaven see Mexican Bus Ride

Ashanti Sanket see Distant Thunder

Ashes
aka The Lost Army
Popioly

Poland 1965 233 mins bw
Film Polski

d **Andrzej Wajda**
sc **Aleksander Scibor-Rylski**
ph **Jerzy Lipman**
m **Andrzej Markowski**
Daniel Olbrychski, Pola Raksa, Boguslaw Kierc, Beata Tyszkiewicz, Piotr Wysocki

A Polish legion under General Dombrowski fights on the side of Napoleon, hoping to free their own country but, in reality, actually helping to destroy the freedom of other nations. Costing $3 million, a huge sum by Polish standards, and running nearly four hours (cut by 73 minutes in the USA), Wajda's ambitious CinemaScope epic, based on the classic neo-romantic novel by Stefan Zeromski, hoped for a wide international audience. However, impressive as much of it is, particularly the battle scenes, it was too excessive and meandering to realize its box-office ambitions outside Poland.

Ashes And Diamonds
Popiol I Diament

Poland 1958 104 mins bw
Film Polski

d **Andrej Wajda**
sc **Andrej Wajda, Jerzy Andrzejewski**
ph **Jerzy Wojcik**
m **Jan Krenz, Michal Kleotas Oginski**
Zbigniew Cybulski, Ewa Krzyzanowska, Adam Pawlikowski, Bogumil Kobiela

On the last day of the war in 1945, Maciek (Cybulski), the youngest member of a Nationalist underground movement in a provincial Polish town, is ordered to kill the new Communist district secretary. As he waits in a hotel during the night, he meets and falls in love with a girl (Krzyzanowska) and learns that there is something other to life than killing. More mature and ironic than the two preceding films in the trilogy (*A Generation*, 1954 and *Kanal*, 1957) about the resistance in Warsaw as carried out by the young, this is perhaps Wajda's finest work. The assassination scene, Maciek's death and the slow motion polonaise climax are stunningly realized. The brilliant Cybulski embodied the sceptical new generation in a complex characterization, and the film's enigmatic twilight world communicated the 'Polish experience' far beyond the country's frontiers.

As Long As You're Healthy
Tant Qu'on A La Santé

France 1965 78 mins bw
Films De La Colombe

d **Pierre Etaix**
sc **Pierre Etaix, Jean-Claude Carrière**
ph **Jean Boffety**
m **Jean Paillaud**
Pierre Etaix, Alain Janey, Denise Peronne

A little man (Etaix) is harassed wherever he goes—in the city crowds and traffic, at the doctor's surgery, on a camping site, and even on a desert island. The invention of Etaix, the dapper little French visual gagman, seems to be below his norm in his third feature. Chuckles there are, but he is best over a shorter distance. In fact, it was his 'shorts', including the Oscar-winning *Happy Anniversary* (1962), co-directed by Carrière, which made his reputation.

Aspern

France 1981 96 mins col
VO/Oxala

d **Eduardo De Gregorio**
sc **Michael Graham**
ph **Acácio De Almeida**
m **Mozart**
Alida Valli, Jean Sorel, Bulle Ogier, Ana Marta

The biographer (Sorel) of the long-dead writer Jeffrey Aspern, visits the rambling villa in Lisbon where Aspern's aged mistress (Valli) and her niece (Ogier) live, in order to obtain some unpublished papers. De Gregorio, an Argentinian exile in Paris, relocated the well-known Henry James novella from 19th-century Venice to present-day Lisbon, mainly because the film was made with Portuguese money and was cheaper to shoot there. The updating and transplanting neither damaged the tale significantly nor enhanced it much in this solid, atmospheric drama.

Asphalt

Germany 1929 114 mins bw
UFA

d **Joe May**
sc **Rolf Vanloo, Fred Majo, Hans Szekely**
ph **Günther Rittau**
m **Silent**
Gustav Fröhlich, Betty Amann, Else Heller

A prostitute-thief (Amann) seduces a young policeman (Fröhlich) to avoid arrest and leads him accidentally to kill his rival for her love. This expressionistic drama holds a certain morbid fascination from the brilliant opening sequence of the lights in the big city to the inevitable tragic climax. The film came at the end of a series of what influential German critic Siegfried Kracauer termed 'Street Films', in which middle class characters, bored by their homes, are enticed by the forbidden attractions of the streets. One of the most famous examples is G.W. Pabst's *Joyless Street*.

The Assassin
(US: The Ladykiller Of Rome)
L'Assassino

Italy 1961 105 mins bw
Titanus/Vidas/SGC

d **Elio Petri**
sc **Elio Petri**
ph **Carlo Di Palma**
m **Piero Piccioni**
Marcello Mastroianni, Salvo Randone, Micheline Presle, Andrea Checci

A day in the life of a prosperous antique dealer wrongly accused of murder, a situation which reveals and changes his personality. Told mostly in short, wry flashbacks, sometimes unrelated to each other or to the plot, the film relies heavily on Mastroianni who provides humour and pathos. Petri's debut feature was one of his more achieved Kafkaesque investigations into crime and a corrupt police force.

Assassin Habite Au 21, L' see Murderer Lives At No. 21, The

Assassino, L' see Assassin, The

Assassins Et Voleurs see Lovers And Thieves

The Assault
De Aanslag

Netherlands 1986 148 mins col
Cannon Netherlands

d **Fons Rademakers**
sc **Gerard Soeteman**
ph **Theo Van Der Sande**
m **Jurriaan Andriessen**
Derek De Lint, Mac Van Uchelen, Monique Van De Ven, Huub Van Der Lubbe, John Kraaykamp

Anton, who as a 12-year-old in Haarlem in January 1945, saw his whole family and 40 hostages killed by the Nazis, many years later encounters three people from that period who reopen his mental scars. The veteran Dutch director's fascinating examination of the changing political background of Europe works not only on the public and personal level, but as an exciting thriller. Its episodic structure, rather heavy symbolism, and many coincidences, do not hinder the illumination of moral questions or its ability to move.

Best Foreign Film Oscar 1986

Assault In Broad Daylight
(US: It Happened In Broad Daylight)
Es Geschah Am Hellichten Tag

Switzerland 1958 102 mins bw
Praesens Film

d **Ladislao Vajda**
sc **Ladislao Vajda, Hans Jacoby, Friedrich Dürrenmatt**
ph **Heinrich Gaertner**
m **Bruno Canfora**

Heinz Rühmann, Sigfrit Steiner, Siegfrier Löwitz, Michel Simon, Gert Fröbe

A police inspector gets on to the case of a child sex murder after an old pedlar has been forced into a false confession. What could have been a salacious melodrama is handled with intelligence and care, though it lacks pace. Rühmann as the cop and Simon, in the short part of the pedlar, both make an impact.

L'Astragale

France 1968 102 mins col
Films De La Pleiade/C.C.C. Filmkunst

d **Guy Casaril**
sc **Guy Casaril**
ph **Edmond Richard**
m **Joss Baselli**
Horst Buchholz, Marlène Jobert, Magali Noël, Claude Génia, Georges Géret

While escaping from prison to be with her Lesbian friend, a 19-year-old girl fractures her ankle bone (*l'astragale*) and is picked up by an ex-con (Buchholz) with whom she has a passionate affair and for whom she becomes a prostitute and thief. Albertine Sarrazin's best-selling autobiographical novel was given a shallow, showy treatment with plenty of nude love scenes. The freckled Marlène Jobert almost makes the heroine an object of contempt thanks to her self-indulgent performance coupled with the character's compliance in her own destiny.

Asymvivastos see Easy Road

L'Atalante

France 1934 89 mins bw
Nounez-Gaumont

d **Jean Vigo**
sc **Jean Vigo, Jean Guinée, Albert Riera**
ph **Boris Kaufman, Louis Berger**
m **Maurice Jaubert**
Jean Dasté, Dita Parlo, Michel Simon, Gilles Margarites

A young barge captain (Dasté) takes his bride (Parlo) to live on his boat that plies the canals around Paris. Any telling of the simple story cannot do justice to the richness of Vigo's only full-length feature. The everyday life is filled with magical moments such as the mate (Simon) telling fantastic stories of his travels, a waltz on a phonograph, and Dasté searching for his sweetheart under water. Much of it was shot on location in severe weather conditions, contributing to Vigo's death of TB at the age of 29, just before completing the picture. Poorly received on first showing, it was badly cut and a popular song imposed upon it. Happily, it has since been restored to its original form.

At First Sight
(US: Entre Nous)
Coup De Foudre

France 1983 110 mins col
Partner's Productions/Alexandre Films/Hachette Première/Films A2/SFPC

d **Diane Kurys**
sc **Diane Kurys, Alain Le Henry**
ph **Bernard Lutic**
m **Luis Bacalov**
Miou-Miou, Isabelle Huppert, Guy Marchand, Robin Renucci, Jean-Pierre Bacri, Patrick Bauchau

Two women's passionate friendship leads them to leave their husbands and set up a dress shop together. The true story of the director's mother and friend, most of it takes place in the Lyons of the 1950s, and is filled with the familiar nostalgic bric-à-brac of the period. The men are ineffectual creatures, and any suggestion of Lesbianism is dealt with somewhat coyly. But there is a throb of genuine feeling beneath the glossy surface, due largely to the performances of the four principals. The green- eyed Huppert and the dark-eyed Miou-Miou are elegantly framed on the CinemaScope screen.

Atithi see Runaway, The

L'Atlantide

France 1921 125 mins bw
Thalman

d **Jacques Feyder**
sc **Jacques Feyder**
ph **Georges Specht, Victor Morin**
m **Silent**
Stacia Napierkowska, Jean Angelo, Georges Melchior, Marie-Louise Iribe, Mohammed Ben Nuri

Two soldiers serving in North Africa rediscover the lost city of Atlantis where the queen has the power to make all men fall in love with her. Shot on location in the Algerian desert at a cost of two million francs, making it the most expensive French film to date, its exoticism and extravagance drew the crowds. In his first major film, Feyder's effective use of the spectacular sands could not overcome the miscasting of the plumpish Napierkowska as the supposedly seductive queen. This was the first of four versions of Pierre Benoît's novel.

L'Atlantide

aka Queen Of Atlantis

Die Herrin Von Atlantis

Germany 1932 90 mins bw
Nero

d **G.W. Pabst**
sc **Ladislaus Vajda, Hermann Oberländer**
ph **Eugen Schüfftan, Ernst Koerner**
m **Wolfgang Zeller**
Brigitte Helm, Gustav Diessl, Tela Tschai, Heinz Klingenberg/(French version) Brigitte Helm, Jean Angelo, Pierre Blanchar, Florelle

Two soldiers, who have come across the lost city of Atlantis, fall under the hypnotic spell of its queen. Pabst's last film before the Nazis came to power, was made simultaneously in German, French and English (with the French cast), all three versions dominated by the statuesque presence of Brigitte Helm. Unlike Feyder's *L'Atlantide* (1921), with its genuine desert location, this campy, exotic fantasy takes place in a decor of dazzling white buildings, studio sand, and artificial pools.

The Atonement Of Gösta Berling

(US: The Legend Of Gosta Berling)

Gösta Berlings Saga

Sweden 1924 190 mins bw
Svensk Filmindustri

d **Mauritz Stiller**
sc **Mauritz Stiller, Ragnar Hylten-Cavallius**
ph **J. Julius Jaenzon**
m **Silent**
Lars Hanson, Gerda Lundeqvist, Greta Garbo, Sixten Malmerfeldt

Gösta Berling (Hanson), a defrocked priest, becomes tutor to a well- off provincial family, and then returns to a dissipated life. This rambling family saga, almost a series of historical tableaux, is notable mainly for bringing Garbo to the world's attention. It was Stiller who discovered Greta Gustafson, renamed her, and got her to shed 10 kilos. The film lost about 45 minutes on foreign release, and much of its coherence. Garbo, however, stood out enough in the role of an Italian countess to catch the eye of Louis B. Mayer. The rest is history.

Att Älska see To Love

Attentat, L' see Plot

At The Meeting With Joyous Death

Au Rendez-vous De La Mort Joyeuse

France 1972 82 mins col
Telecip/Artistes Associés

d **Juan Buñuel**
sc **Juan Buñuel, Pierre Maintigneux**
ph **Ghislain Cloquet**
m **Beethoven**
Françoise Fabian, Jean-Marc Bory, Yasmine Dahm, Jean-Pierre Darras, André Weber

After seeing her parents (Fabian and Bory) making love, an adolescent girl (Dahm) starts strange things happening in the Gothic house where she lives. These include the shattering of windows and making the refrigerator and washing-machine move about wildly. The son of Luis Buñuel, making his first picture, seems to be a chip off the old block with his mischievous sense of the surreal. However, as social satire it lacks the bite of Buñuel Sr's work, although there is a feeling for suspense, and the mayhem unleashed at the end is well staged.

Auberge Rouge, L' see Red Inn, The

Auch Zwerge Haben Klein Angefangen see Even Dwarfs Started Small

---

Au Dela Des Grilles see Walls Of Malapaga, The

The Audience
L'Udienza

Italy 1971 114 mins col
Vides

d **Marco Ferreri**
sc **Marco Ferreri, Rafael Azcona**
ph **Mario Vulpiani**
m **Teo Usuelli**
Enzo Jannacci, Ugo Tognazzi, Claudia Cardinale, Vittorio Gassman, Michel Piccoli, Alain Cuny

A young provincial (Jannacci) comes to Rome determined to communicate a personal message to the Pope but is constantly frustrated by Vatican officialdom. Ferreri's usual tendency to over-caricature and underline is held in check in this sardonic, Kafkaesque, anti-clerical tale, well acted by an experienced cast. Jannacci, a pop singer who had seldom acted, is excellent as the bewildered youth.

Aufstand, Der see Uprising, The

Augen Der Mummie Ma, Die see Eyes Of The Mummy, The

Au Hasard Balthazar see Balthazar

Au Rendez-vous De La Mort Joyeuse see At The Meeting With Joyous Death

Au Revoir Les Enfants

France 1987 104 mins col
Nouvelles Éditions De Films/MK2 Productions/Stella Film(Munich)/NEF(Munich)

d **Louis Malle**
sc **Louis Malle**
ph **Renato Berta**
m **Schubert, Saint-Saëns**
Gaspard Manesse, Raphaël Fejtö, Francine Racette, François Negret, Philippe Morier-Genoud, Peter Fitz

Towards the end of World War II, Jean Bonnet (Fejtö) arrives as a new student at a French provincial Catholic boarding school where he becomes friendly with Julien (Manesse) who gradually discovers that Jean is Jewish, and his real name Kippelstein. He is one of three Jewish boys given refuge by the sympathetic staff but, acting on an informer's tip, a Gestapo officer appears ... Based on Malle's own childhood experiences and directed with the finesse expected of the director, this is a remarkably clear-eyed, unsentimental yet moving evocation both of a period and, more particularly, the anarchic and sometimes brutal world of schoolboys as evoked by Vigo's *Zéro De Conduite* and Truffaut's *The Four Hundred Blows.*

Best Film Venice 1987

Aus Dem Leben Der Marionetten see From The Life Of The Marionettes

Aus Den Wolken Kommt Das Glück see Amphitryon

Aus Einem Deutschen Leben see Death Is My Trade

Au Service De La France see Marthe Richard

Aussi Longue Absence, Une see Long Absence, The

Austeria

Poland 1982 110 mins col
Film Polski(Kadr Unit)

d **Jerzy Kawalerowicz**
sc **Tadeusz Konwicki, Jerzy Kawalerowicz, Julian Stryjkowski**
ph **Zygmunt Samosiuk**

m **Leopold Kozlowski**
Franciszek Pieczka, Wojciech Pszoniak, Jan Szurmiej, Ewa Domanska

On the first day of World War I, a group of Jews flees from a Cossack army in Polish Galicia and finds itself trapped overnight in a border inn. Relationships develop, love affairs are snatched, the religious pray, hopes and fears are aired—both within the beleaguered band and between them and the innkeeper's family. Making his first film in five years, the distinguished director combines his gifts for intimate psychological drama with his penchant for history to re-create a vivid picture of a recently vanished world. Full of warmth and vitality, it captures the Jewish sense of humour which seems, uniquely, to draw inspiration from disaster.

Austerlitz

(US: The Battle Of Austerlitz)
France 1959 166 mins col
CFPI/SCLF/Galatea/Michael Arthur/Dubrava

d **Abel Gance**
sc **Abel Gance, Roger Richebe**
ph **Henri Alekan, Robert Juillard**
m **Jean Ledrut**
Pierre Mondy (Napoleon), Jean Mercure (Talleyrand), Martine Carol (Josephine), Jack Palance, Orson Welles, Michel Simon, Jean-Louis Trintignant, Leslie Caron, Claudia Cardinale, Rossano Brazzi, Jean Marais, Ettore Manni, Anna Moffo, Vittorio De Sica

Napoleon's strategy against, and subsequent defeat of, the Austro- Russian army at Austerlitz. Thirty years after making his silent masterpiece *Napoleon*, the 70-year-old director returned to his hero in a long, talky, academic and stilted pageant, made watchable by the familiar faces of the cast. It was cut by over an hour on release in the USA.

Austernprinzessin, Die see Oyster Princess, The

Autre Homme, Une Autre Chance, Un see Another Man, Another Chance

---

An Autumn Afternoon

Samma No Aji
Japan 1962 115 mins col
Shochiku/Ofuna

d **Yasujiro Ozu**
sc **Yasujiro Ozu, Kogo Noda**
ph **Yushun Atsuta**
m **Kojun Saito**
Chishu Ryu, Shima Iwashita, Shinichiro Mikami, Keiji Sada

A widowed and aging company auditor (Ryu) arranges a marriage for his daughter (Iwashita), then finds himself alone except for his drinking cronies. During the shooting, Ozu's mother, with whom he had lived all his life, died. He was to follow her the next year. His valedictory film has a simplicity, mellowness and nostalgia that makes it a fitting finale to one of the most consistent and rewarding *oeuvres* in cinema.

Autumn Marathon

Osenny Marafon
USSR 1979 90 mins col
Mosfilm

d **Georgy Danelia**
sc **Alexander Volodin**
ph **Sergei Vronski**
m **Andrei Petrov**
Oleg Basilashvili, Natalia Gundareva, Marina Neyelova, Evgeni Leonov

A mild-mannered English-language teacher (Basilashvili) in Leningrad has a problem running between his wife (Gundareva) and mistress (Neyelova), as well as coping with his students, and prying neighbours. A wry comedy, from the Georgian satirist, Danelia, manages to combine humour with social comment on urban intellectual life in an adept manner. Its lack of bite is compensated for by the nicely observed gallery of obsessive characters, the droll playing and the Leningrad background.

Autumn Sonata

Hostsonaten
Sweden 1978 97 mins col
Personafilm/ITC

d **Ingmar Bergman**
sc **Ingmar Bergman**
ph **Sven Nykvist**
m **Chopin, Bach, Handel**
Ingrid Bergman, Liv Ullmann, Halvar Bjork, Erland Josephson, Gunnar Björnstrand

A world-renowned concert pianist (Bergman) returns to Sweden to visit the married daughter (Ullmann) she has not seen for many years, and has to face up to her feelings of guilt for having put her career above her family. As he did in *Persona*, Bergman places two women face to face with each other and their own inadequacies and, as in *Wild Strawberries*, there is the painful recognition that the past cannot be changed. With his masterly use of the close-up, and the flashback utilized as the subconscious, he creates a chamber work of almost Strinbergian intensity. This long night's journey into day, allows the director's namesake to give a remarkable performance, displaying every aspect of her screen personality over the years—naïvety, sophistication, gaiety, and tragedy. It was Ingrid Bergman's first Swedish film for almost 40 years and, sadly, her last feature before her death.

Avenir D'Emilie, L' see Future Of Emily, The

Aventures D'Arsène Lupin, Les see Adventures Of Arsène Lupin, The

---

Aventures De Casanova see Loves Of Casanova

Aventures De Rabbi Jacob, Les see Adventures Of Rabbi Jacob, The

---

Aventures De Till L'Espiègle, Les see Adventures Of Till Eulenspiegel, The

---

Aveu, L' see Confession, The

The Aviator's Wife
La Femme De L'Aviateur

France 1980 106 mins col
Les Films Du Losange

d **Eric Rohmer**
sc **Eric Rohmer**
ph **Bernard Lutic**
m **Jean-Louis Valero**
Philippe Marlaud, Marie Rivière, Anne-Laure Meury, Matthieu Carrière

A boy (Marlaud) meets a girl (Rivière) in a park and agrees to help her spy on her pilot lover (Carrière) who is seeing another woman (Meury). The first of Rohmer's series called 'Comedies and Proverbs', is a delightful comedy of errors concerned with the illusions of love and the indiscretions of youth. In fact, the young dominate the sequence, in contrast to the more adult concerns of the previous 'Six Moral Tales'. It also introduces the figure of the exacting and spoiled young woman (here, as in *The Green Ray*, played by Rivière) who exasperates those around her, and some audiences too. Shot in Paris, using direct sound, the film provides a ravishing centrepiece in a verdant park.

Avrianos Polemistis see Tomorrow's Warrior

L'Avventura

Italy 1960 145 mins bw
Cino Del Duca/PCE/Lyre

d **Michelangelo Antonioni**
sc **Michelangelo Antonioni, Elio Bartolini, Tonino Guerra**
ph **Aldo Scavarda**
m **Giovanni Fusco**
Monica Vitti, Lea Massari, Gabriele Ferzetti, Dominique Blanchar

Anna (Massari) disappears when a group of wealthy people visit a Sicilian island by yacht, resulting in her architect fiancé (Ferzetti) and friend (Vitti) gradually coming together. This was the film in which, after five features in 10 years, Antonioni's style reached its maturity, redefining our views of time and space in the cinema. The long tracking shots, the limited dialogue and the strong relationship between the characters and their environment disconcerted some at the time, but average filmgoers should now take these in their stride. What matters in the plot is not the unsolved mystery story (as in *Blow Up* 1967, and *The Passenger* 1975), but the effect it has on the characters, especially the ravishing Vitti in her first role for the director whose lover she would become.

Special Jury Prize Cannes 1960

Avventura Di Salvator Rosa, Un see An Adventure Of Salvator Rosa

---

Away From It All

USSR 1981 90 mins col
Mosfilm

d **Nikolai Gubenko**
sc **Nikolai Gubenko**
ph **Alexander Kniazhinski**
m **Isaak Shvarts**
Zhanna Bolotova, Regimantas Adomaitis, Georgy Burkov, Rolan Bykov, Anatoly Solonitsin, Lydia Fedoseeva-Shukshina

An assorted group of late holiday-makers are thrown together at a Crimean seaside resort where they gossip, flirt, play cards, and eat. Here, also, a love affair blossoms between an educated woman and a taciturn man. The film is a beautifully observed, amiable, wry, Chekhovian satire on the Russians at play. A pinch of Tati and a soupçon of Fellini add to the pleasant dish which climaxes with a delightful farewell party. Only the rather too-leisurely central love story slows the film down.

Aziza

Tunisia 1980 90 mins col
SATPEC (Tunisia)/Radio Television Algeria/LATIF

d **Abdel-Latif Ben Ammar**
sc **Abdel-Latif Ben Ammar, Toufik Jebali**
ph **Youssef Sharaqui**
m **Ahmed Malek**
Yasmine Khlat, Raouf Ben Amor, Dalila Ramez, Mohammed Zinet

Aziza (Khlat), a young, obedient orphan girl, moves with her old uncle and irresponsible cousin (Amor) from the country to the big city. When her uncle dies, she gets a job in a textile factory and becomes, for the first time in her life, economically independent. The theme of the role of women in Arab society, something that has concerned many of the younger Arab directors, is here presented in a direct, economical and affecting way in Ben Ammar's third film. Its frankness on sensitive issues and its compassionate portrayal of a woman who finds her own worth (beautifully played by the Lebanese Khlat) marked the coming of age of Tunisian cinema.

Až Příjde Kocour see When The Cat Comes

---

b

Baara

Mali 1978 93 mins col
Souleymane Cissé Productions

d **Souleymane Cissé**
sc **Souleymane Cissé**
ph **Etienne Carton De Grammont**
m **Lamine Konté**
Balla Moussa Keita, Baba Niaré, Bubakar Keita, Oumou Diarra, Ismaïla Sarr

The investigations into the murder of a young engineer (Balla Moussa Keita) who encouraged union activities at a local factory, opens up a web of intrigue and corruption. Cissé sets his superbly accomplished drama in Bamako, the capital of Mali, thus moving away from the folklore and tribal customs central to many of his other films and to black African films in general. It concentrates on 'baara', translated as 'the world of work', in a country just beginning to industrialize and the problems that have derived from it. The thriller storyline provides a base on which Cissé builds a rich tapestry of African urban life, pulsating with its particular rhythms and colours.

Bab El Hadid see Cairo Station

Babette Goes To War

Babette S'En Va-T'En Guerre

France 1959 106 mins col
Iena

d **Christian-Jaque**
sc **Raoul Lévy, Gérard Oury**
ph **Armand Thirard**
m **Gilbert Bécaud**
Brigitte Bardot, Jacques Charrier, Hannes Messemer, Ronald Howard, Francis Blanche

In 1940, a French refugee girl is sent by British intelligence from England to France to use her feminine charms in a plot to kidnap a Nazi general and delay the German invasion of England. Bardot was at the height of her fame when she embarked on this weary, witless war comedy, so it still made money. During the shooting, she fell in love with her handsome 22-year-old co-star Jacques Charrier, and they were married the same year, a short-lived affair which was a kind of war in itself.

Babette S'En Va-T'En Guerre see Babette Goes To War

Babette's Feast

Babettes Gaestebud

Denmark 1987 105 mins col
Panorama Film International/Nordisk Film/Danish Film Institute

d **Gabriel Axel**
sc **Gabriel Axel**
ph **Henning Kristiansen**
m **Per Norgaard**
Stéphane Audran, Bodil Kjer, Brigitte Federspiel, Jean-Philippe Lafont, Jarl Kulle, Bibi Andersson

On the bleak Jutland Peninsula in the 1870s live two spinster sisters (Kjer and Federspiel), daughters of the former pastor and founder of an austere religious sect, who devote themselves to keeping alive his memory and his teachings in the tiny, remote community. Subtle changes occur when Babette, a Frenchwoman who has fled the war-torn Paris of 1871, turns up on their doorstep seeking refuge and becomes their cook-housekeeper. Fourteen years elapse before it is revealed that Babette is a *cordon bleu* cook—a fact which leads to a cathartic event for her, her employers and the community. This superb adaptation of the Karen Blixen (Isak Dinesen) novella remains true to its literary source with no loss to cinematic quality. Axel shifts from past to present and between voice-over narrative and dialogue with considerable skill, casting a spell over the spectator with an entrancingly bitter-sweet mix of comedy and deep poignancy. Audran, no stranger to meals in the films of her husband, Claude Chabrol, stands out among a large and flawless cast. A deserving winner in a particularly strong list of Foreign Oscar contenders.

Best Foreign Film Oscar 1987

Babettes Gaestebud see Babette's Feast

Backstairs

Hintertreppe

Germany 1921 60 mins bw
UFA

d **Leopold Jessner, Paul Leni**
sc **Carl Mayer**
ph **Karl Hasselmann, Willy Hameister**
m **Silent**
Henny Porten, Wilhelm Dieterle, Fritz Kortner

Failing to hear from her distant lover (Dieterle), a servant girl (Porten) goes on a visit to the postman (Kortner). Unbeknown to her, the latter—handicapped mentally as well as physically—is morbidly infatuated with her and has been intercepting her lover's letters. This intimate piece, steeped in gloom and with a miscast leading lady, was not well-received by audiences of the day, but its Expressionistic style is interesting, as is writer Mayer's allegorical approach to character. Co-directed by Leni, who had a hand in the sets, it is mainly Jessner's work—a stage director known for his stylized use of staircases, the term *Jessnertreppe* was already part of the vocabulary of the German theatre before this film was made.

Bad Girls Don't Cry see Night Heat

Bad Luck

Zezowate Szczescie

Poland 1960 158 mins bw
WFF

d **Andrzej Munk**
sc **Jerzy Stefan Stawinski**
ph **Jerzy Lipman, Krzysztof Winiewicz**
m **Jan Krenz**
Bogumil Kobiela, Maria Ciesielska, Barbara Kwiatkowska, Aleksander Dzwonkowski, Bronislaw Pawlik

Piszczyk (Kobiela), a middle-aged prisoner, relates the story of his unfortunate life to the warden: his failures as a boy scout, student, lover, soldier, prisoner-of-war, underground fighter and Stalinist bureaucrat. Munk's last completed work before his untimely death is a harsh satire on political and social conformity as represented by his pathetic hero. Naturally, the conformists in the Polish government at the time strongly criticized the film. Most movie critics, however, were more favourable and, despite its excessive length, the picaresque, poignant and humourous tale is a timely reflection of the painful history of Poland from the 1930s to the 1950s.

The Bad Sleep Well

Warui Yatsu Yoku Nemuru

Japan 1960 151 mins bw
Tomoyuki Tanaka/Kurosawa

d **Akira Kurosawa**
sc **Akira Kurosawa, Hideo Oguni, Eijiro Kusaka, Ryuzo Kikushima, Shinobu Hashimoto**
ph **Yuzuru Aizawa**
m **Sasaru Sato**
Toshiro Mifune, Masayuki Mori, Takashi Shimura, Chishu Ryu

The private secretary (Mifune) to a corrupt government official (Mori) marries his superior's daughter as part of a scheme to avenge his father's murder, for which he holds his father-in-law responsible. For his first independent production Kurosawa, leaning Westwards again, took an Ed McBain novel as the basis for this contemporary thriller. Although the Japanese style sits rather awkwardly on the American model, the use of the large 'Scope screen and the accomplished performances keep alive the interest in the rather complicated proceedings.

A Bad Son

Un Mauvais Fils

France 1980 110 mins col
Sara Films/Antenne 2/SFP

d **Claude Sautet**
sc **Claude Sautet, Daniel Biasini, Jean-Paul Torok**

ph **Jean Boffety**
m **Philippe Sarde**
Patrick Dewaere, Yves Robert, Brigitte Fossey, Jacques Dufilho, Claire Maurier

Bruno (Dewaere), a young Frenchman, returns to Paris after serving five years in an American prison for drug trafficking. Readjustment proves difficult as he searches for work, faces his working-class father (Robert), who holds his past behaviour responsible for his mother's death, and has an affair with another ex-addict (Fossey), whose drug problems are not fully resolved. An excellent film from Sautet, who brings restraint to his usually glossy professionalism in this story of ordinary people in ordinary settings. It's a sympathetic, straightforward treatment, with Dewaere excellent, Fossey exhibiting the right degree of emotional fragility and actor-director Robert effective as the lonely and embittered father.

Baghe Sangui see Garden Of Stones

Baie Des Anges, La see Bay Of Angels

Baisers Volés see Stolen Kisses

Báječni Muži S Klikou see Those Wonderful Movie Cranks

Baker's Bread

Das Brot Des Bäckers

W. Germany 1976 122 mins col
Artus Film/ZDF

d **Erwin Keusch**
sc **Erwin Keusch, Karl Saurer**
ph **Dietrich Lohmann**
m **Condor**
Günther Lamprecht, Bernd Tauber, Maria Lucca, Silvia Reize, Anita Lochner

Werner Wild (Tauber), apprentice to a small-town traditional baker Georg Baum (Lamprecht), moves to a bread factory in another town where his girlfriend (Lochnar) works. Georg's old-fashioned methods fail to meet the increased demand, until Werner returns to help him and he agrees to put his business on a co-operative basis. The first feature by Keusch, himself the son of a baker, is absorbing enough merely in the loving and detailed demonstration of the making of bread, rolls and cake. A lot more arises in this gentle, observant Brechtian tale (it is divided into captioned chapters) of the place of an 'artist' in a society where money is more important than dough.

The Baker's Wife

La Femme Du Boulanger

France 1938 117 mins bw
Marcel Pagnol Films

d **Marcel Pagnol**
sc **Marcel Pagnol**
ph **G. Benoit, R. Lendruz, N. Daries**
m **Vincent Scotto**
Raimu, Ginette Leclerc, Charles Moulin, Charpin

A village baker (Raimu) refuses to bake bread when his attractive young wife (Leclerc) runs off with a handsome shepherd (Moulin), a situation which forces the breadless villagers to take action. Pagnol, combining the best of his humour with sympathetic characterizations of Provençal life, gives an individual drama of infidelity a collective dimension. The great Raimu is at his peak as the cuckold who welcomes back his errant wife warmly but reviles her cat for having been away—the kind of masterstroke seen throughout Pagnol's films.

Bakushu see Early Summer

Le Bal

France 1984 112 mins col
S.A./A2/Massfil/Oncic

d **Ettore Scola**
sc **Ruggero Maccari**
ph **Ricardo Aronovich**
m **Vladimir Cosma**
Jean-François Perrier, Marc Berman, Nani Noël, Danielle Rochard, Liliane Delval, Monica Scattini

Events in France from 1936 to the present day are reflected inside a ballroom by the changing music and the characters who have frequented the place over the years. A sort of

'La-Vie-En-Roseland' view of modern French history, drawing much of its imagery from movie mythology. But behind this and the caricature performances, one senses the pain of real events underlined with the potency of cheap music. Films speak in many ways. *Le Bal* manages to say a lot without a single line of dialogue.

Best Director Berlin 1984

La Balance

France 1981 102 mins col
Les Films Ariane/Films 42

d **Bob Swaim**
sc **Bob Swaim, M. Fabiani**
ph **Bernard Zitzermann**
m **Roland Bocquet**
Nathalie Baye, Philippe Léotard, Richard Berry, Maurice Ronet

In order to nail a gang boss (Ronet), the Brigades Territoriales (élite French plainclothes police) coerce a petty crook (Léotard) into turning informer—'la balance' in underworld parlance—using his relationship with a prostitute (Baye). Swaim is an American director resident in Paris, and this tough and exciting police thriller, set in the Casbah-like district of Belleville, was a huge commercial and critical success in France. But atmosphere and some brilliant set-pieces, such as a shoot-out in a traffic jam, don't quite compensate for the unsympathetic characters on both sides of the law.

Ballad

Sweden 1968 82 mins bw
Sandrew/Svenska Filminstitutet/Gösta Ågren

d **Gösta Ågren**
sc **Gösta Ågren**
ph **Per-Åke Dahlberg**
m **Bach and others**
Vivian Gude, Stig Torstensson, Stefan Ekman, Jarl Lindblad, Lennart Snickars

An anti-Fascist journalist writing in Finland in the 1930s becomes aware that his neighbour and one-time friend, now recruited to the Fascist cause, is about to betray him. He goes into hiding, later joined by two friends, a man and a woman, and by using their logic they escape assassination. In spite of some plot points that are difficult to swallow, this is a stylish, serious-minded piece, with an underlying theme that examines the nature and possibilities of pacifism in the face of violence. It does so within a framework of a tense story, lyrically filmed against a summer landscape, and is an absorbing small film.

Ballada O Soldate see Ballad Of A Soldier

Ballad Of A Soldier

Ballada O Soldate

USSR 1959 89 mins bw
Mosfilm

d **Grigori Chukrai**
sc **Grigori Chukrai, Valentin Yoshov**
ph **Vladimir Nikolayev, Era Saveleya**
m **Mikhail Ziv**
Vladimir Ivashev, Sharma Prokhorenko, Antonina Maximova, Nikolai Kryuchkov

A young soldier (Ivashev) on four days leave from the front travels by train, truck and on foot to visit his mother (Maximova). *En route* he meets various people affected by the war, and a girl (Prokhorenko) with whom he falls in love. This simple, sentimental and unrhetorical view of everyday life in wartime Russia continued the trickle of Soviet films welcomed in the West in the late 1950s. In fact, it was the first film from the USSR to enter an American film festival—the San Francisco—which it won.

Special Jury Prize Cannes 1960

Ballad Of Berlin

(US: The Berliner)

Berliner Ballade

W.Germany 1948 77 mins bw
Comedia Film

d **Robert Stemmle**
sc **Günter Neumann**
ph **Georg Krause**
m **Günter Neumann, Werner Eisbrenner**
Gert Fröbe, Anton Zeithammer, Tatjana Sais, O.E. Hasse

The film starts 100 years in the future in a peaceful, prosperous and rebuilt Germany. Then, as though going back in time, it focuses on the contemporary, immediate post-war world. Otto Nobody (Fröbe), a reluctant soldier, returns from the front to a Berlin in ruins, where he becomes prey to bureaucrats and black marketeers. Like *Film Without A Title*, this film with a title added a sense of irony to the *Trümmerfilm*—works indulging in the mood of resignation and self-pity experienced by a defeated people. An awkward but interesting mixture of satire, songs, and sentiment, it was one of the first post-war German productions to be shown abroad. Gert Fröbe, the future 'Goldfinger', made his screen debut as the skinny hero.

The Ballad Of Narayama

Narayama-Bushi-Ko

Japan 1958 98 mins col
Shochiku

d **Keisuke Kinoshita**
sc **Keisuke Kinoshita**
ph **Hiroyuki Kusuda**
m **Rokuzaemon Kineya, Matsunosuke Nozawa**

Kinuyo Tanaka, Teiji Takahashi, Yuko Mochizuki, Eijiro Tono

The custom in a small, impoverished village is for the elderly, on reaching the age of 70, to be abandoned on a mountain top. Sixty-nine-year-old Orin (Tanaka), living with her son (Takahashi) and three grandchildren, prepares for her departure. When the day arrives, the son carries his mother up the mountain and tearfully leaves her. Less violent and explicit than the later Imamura version of the famous legend, it is also far more stylized, echoing Kabuki theatre, and shot almost entirely in studio settings. This makes the barbaric customs more palatable, giving the film an air of fantasy. Kinuyo Tanaka is as wonderful as ever and the use of colour and wide screen is superb.

The Ballad Of Narayama

Narayama Bushi-Ko

Japan 1983 130 mins col
Toei

d **Shohei Imamura**
sc **Shohei Imamura**
ph **Masao Tochizawa**
m **Shinichiro Ikebe**

Ken Ogata, Sumiko Sakamoto, Tonpei Hidari, Takejo Aki

During the last century, an old woman prepares for death in a remote mountain village in North Japan where the customs include premature burial for theft, and the abandonment of anyone over 70 on the top of Mount Narayama. Imamura neither condemns nor condones this imaginary primitive society, derived from a novel by Shichiro Fukazawa (also filmed by Keisuke Kinoshita in 1958), but plainly seeks comparisons with the cruelty of our own time. The point is rammed home somewhat repetitiously, but the ritual sex and violence, and the long final sequence when a dutiful son carries his old mother up the mountain slopes, cannot fail to impress and shock.

Best Film Cannes 1983

Ballon Rouge, Le see Red Balloon, The

Balthazar

Au Hasard Balthazar

France 1966 95 mins bw
Parc/Athos/Ardos/Svensk Industri

d **Robert Bresson**
sc **Robert Bresson**
ph **Ghislain Cloquet**
m **Jean Wiener, Schubert**

Anne Wiazemsky, François Lafarge, Philippe Asselin, Nathalie Joyaut

The birth, life and death of a donkey which passes from drawing a carriage to pulling a plough, is ridden by children, becomes a circus attraction, and turns a miller's grindstone before being shot by a customs officer during a smuggling escapade. One of Bresson's more lyrical and accessible films, this Christian parable sometimes edges into the territory of children's animal movies. The death of the donkey on the hillside surrounded by sheep, is a stunning sequence, and it is not too frivolous to note that the quadruped gives one of the best Bressonian performances.

Special Jury Prize Venice 1966

Baltic Deputy

USSR 1937 107 mins bw
Lenfilm/Amkino

d **Alexander Zarkhi, Joseph Heifits**
sc **Alexander Zarkhi, Joseph Heifits, David Dell, Leonid Rakhmanov**
ph **Hoissaye Kaplan**
m **Nikolai Tomofeev**

Nikolai Cherkassov, Marta Domasheva, Boris Livanov, Otto Zhakov

Incidents in the life of the distinguished Russian scientist and former Oxford professor Klement Timiriazev (renamed in the film) who, despite ostracism by colleagues, joined the Bolsheviks in 1918 and became a hero of the revolution. The 32-year-old Cherkassov gives a remarkable portrayal, especially as a 70-year-old, in a film which ably balances propaganda, action, humour and pathos.

Bambini Ci Guardano, I see Children Are Watching Us, The

Bande A Part see Outsiders, The

Band Of Outsiders see Outsiders, The

The Bandit

O Cangaceiro

Brazil 1953 119 mins bw
Vera Cruz

d **Lima Barreto**
sc **Lima Barreto, Rachel De Queiroz**
ph **Chick Fowle**
m **Gabriel Migliori**
Alberto Ruschel, Marisa Prado, Milton Ribeiro, Vanja Orico

A rift develops between the leader (Ribeiro) of a gang of *cangaceiros*, Brazilian bandits of the Robin Hood type, and his young lieutenant (Ruschel), when the latter falls for a schoolmistress captured by the group. The first Brazilian film to become internationally known is a poetic adventure played and directed with gusto. Particularly striking was the pulsating music, derived from folk themes.

The Bandit

La Cucaracha

Mexico 1959 90 mins col
Ismael Rodriguez Productions

d **Ismael Rodriguez**
sc **José Balanos Prado, Ismael Rodriguez, José Luis Celis, Ricardo Garibay**
ph **Gabriel Figueroa**
m **Raúl Lavista**
Emilio Fernández, Maria Felix, Dolores Del Rio, Pedro Armendáriz, Antonio Aguilar

A thoroughly battle-weary and demoralized group of conscripts to Pancho Villa's cause is given a new lease of life and courage by a woman soldier, known as 'La Cucaracha' (Felix), who falls in love with their leader, Colonel Zeta (Fernández). He abandons her for another woman (Del Rio) and is subsequently killed. Both women, La Cucaracha now pregnant with his child, trek to the mountains with the army. A brash, commercial exploitation of the Mexican Revolution, exhibiting little flair or originality, but it's highly entertaining to watch some of Hollywood's best-known native Mexicans going through their paces, and Fernández, better-known as a director, is superior to the overstated script and garish photography.

Banditi A Orgosolo see Bandits at Orgosolo, The

The Bandits At Orgosolo

Banditi A Orgosolo

Italy 1961 98 mins bw
Titanus

d **Vittorio De Seta**
sc **Vittorio De Seta, Vera Gherarducci**
ph **Vittorio De Seta**
m **Valentino Bucchi**
Michele Cossu, Peppeddu Cuccu, Vittorina Pisano

A young Sardinian shepherd (Cossu), unjustly accused of a crime, flees with his flock, but becomes a bandit when his sheep die. This first feature by a documentary film-maker, played entirely by Sardinian peasants and made with minimum financial and technical facilities, impressed by its honesty and splendid photography. Its only compromise was the dubbing of the Sardinian argot into standard Italian.

Bangiku see Late Chrysanthemums

Banshun see Late Spring

Barefoot Savage see Sensualita

Bariera see Barrier

Barocco

France 1976 102 mins col
Films La Boétie/Sara

d **André Téchiné**
sc **André Téchiné, Marilyn Goldin**
ph **Bruno Nuytten**
m **Philippe Sarde**
Isabelle Adjani, Marie-France Pisier, Gérard Depardieu, Jean-Claude Brialy

A crook (Depardieu) kills his double, and takes his place and his girlfriend (Adjani). Together, the couple blackmail a politician and escape with the money to start a new life. The title gives some idea of what Téchiné was aiming for in this flamboyant parodic thriller. Unfortunately, the self-conscious and pretentious references to German Expressionism and *film noir* are inept, despite some atmospheric sets such as a red-light district where Pisier's seductive prostitute hangs out. Depardieu seems constrained and Adjani pouts.

Le Baron De L'Écluse

France 1959 94 mins bw
Filmsonor/Intermondia/Cinétel(Paris)/Vides (Rome)

d **Jean Delannoy**
sc **Maurice Druon**
ph **Louis Page**
m **Jean Prodromidès**
Jean Gabin, Micheline Presle, Blanchette Brunoy, Jacques Castelot, Jean Desailly

Baron Jérôme Napoléon Antoine (Gabin), who lives on chance opportunities in Deauville, makes a killing at the casino and buys a yacht he has been commissioned to sell. He takes his former mistress Perle (Presle), an adventuress, cruising on the canals, but is stranded at a lock waiting for his commission to arrive from the yacht's former owner. He marries off the now petulant Perle to the local wine millionaire, while he himself... This film is a casually thrown together series of good-natured episodes, elevated by Gabin's superb performance as the monocled Baron who retains his optimism despite the knowledge that love has passed him by. The rest of the acting is also at par, but it is the star's magic presence which makes this a thoroughly pleasing and funny excursion.

Baron Fantôme, Le see Phantom Baron, The

Baron Munchausen

Baron Prásil

Czechoslovakia 1962 81 mins col
Ceskoslovensky Film

d **Karel Zeman**
sc **Karel Zeman**
ph **Jiří Tarantik**
m **Zdeněk Liška**
Miloš Kopecký, Hana Brejchová, Rudolf Jelinek, Jan Werich

On the moon, an astronaut meets the famous liar Baron Munchausen (Kopecky) who returns to earth with him to enact a number of fantastic adventures. Using puppets, cartoons, special effects, and live-action against painted backdrops, Czech animator Zeman succeeded in creating a magical world, enticing to both children and adults. His inspiration sprang from the 1862 edition of G.A. Burger's novel with drawings by Gustav Doré, and the turn-of-the-century films of conjurer and cinema pioneer, Georges Méliès.

Baron Prásil see Baron Munchausen

Barren Lives

Vidãs Sêcas

Brazil 1963 135 mins bw
Richers/Barreto/Trelles

d **Nelson Pereira Dos Santos**
sc **Nelson Pereira Dos Santos**
ph **Luiz Carlos Barreto, José Rosa**
m **Leonardo Alencar**
Átila Iório, Maria Ribeiro, Orlando Macedo, Jofre Soãres, Gilvan and Genivaldo Lima

Around 1940, a poverty-stricken family—an itinerant herdsman (Iório), his wife (Ribeiro) and two young sons (Gilvan and Genivaldo Lima)—are forced to wander the barren *sertao* of Brazil, scratching out an existence. A film of quiet dignity and compassion, it recalls the best of the Italian Neo-Realists, while the photography portrays the dry, harsh Brazilian landscape exposed in a particular light. By the use of subjective shots, Dos Santos allows more identification with the characters, but avoids self-pity. A landmark in Latin-American cinema.

Barrier

Bariera

Poland 1966 83 mins bw
Film Polski

d **Jerzy Skolimowski**
sc **Jerzy Skolimowski**
ph **Jan Laskowski**
m **Krzysztof Komeda**
Jan Nowicki, Joanna Szczerbic, Tadeusz Lomnicki, Zygmunt Malonowicz

A disillusioned young medical student (Nowicki) travelling through modern Poland in quest of the meaning of life, meets only bureaucracy and materialism, but finally finds satisfaction in a relationship with a young woman tram driver (Szczerbic). Only in his twenties at the time, Skolimowski became a mouthpiece for the cynical new Polish generation. This assured surreal satire presents a grim picture of his homeland, yet with an underlying quirky humour.

The Bartered Bride

Die Verkaufte Braut

Germany 1932 80 mins bw
Reichaliga

d **Max Ophüls**
sc **Kurt Alexander, Jaroslav Kvapil, Max Ophüls**
ph **Reimar Kuntze, Franz Koch, Herbert Illing**
m **Smetana**
Jarmila Novotná, Willy Domgraf-Fassbaender, Paul Kemp, Karl Valentin, Liesl Karlstad, Max Nadler

In a village in Bohemia in the mid-19th century, Mařenka (Novotná), the mayor's daughter, promised to a rich nitwit, tricks the marriage broker and her parents by marrying Jeník (Domgraf-Fassbaender). Not content merely to record a wonderfully sung performance of Smetana's delightful Czech opera (given here in German), Ophüls manages, by complex camera angles, to present his own comment on the filming of opera. Rarely seen, Ophüls' second feature-length film shows a master in the making.

Baruch see Ancient Law, The

Barwy Ochronne see Camouflage

Bas Fonds, Les see Lower Depths, The

Basilischi, I see Lizards, The

Bas Ya Bahar see Cruel Sea, The

Battaglia Di Algeri, La see Battle of Algiers, The

Bataille Du Rail, La see Battle Of The Rails

Batalla De Chile, La see Battle Of Chile, The

The Battle Of Algiers

La Battaglia Di Algeri

Italy 1965 135 mins bw
Casbah/Igor

d **Gillo Pontecorvo**
sc **Franco Solinas**
ph **Marcello Gatti**
m **Ennio Morricone, Gillo Pontecorvo**
Brahim Haggiag, Jean Martin, Yacef Saadi, Tommaso Neri

The guerrilla war for Algerian independence from the French in 1954 as seen through the eyes of some of the participants. Shot in the actual locations, mixing actors with those who fought in the battle and without recourse to any newsreel footage, the film probably comes closer to the truth and the complexities of the situation than any documentary could have. Although banned in France for some years, its main strength lies in its scrupulous attention to the views and problems on both sides.

Best Film Venice 1966

Battle Of Austerlitz, The see Austerlitz

The Battle Of Chile

La Batalla De Chile

Cuba/Chile 1977 287 mins bw
Equipe Tercer Ano Productions—in collaboration with Chris Marker

d **Patricio Guzman**
sc **Patricio Guzman**
ph **Jorge Mueller**

A documentary on the 10 weeks in 1973 leading up to and including the overthrow of the Allende government by the CIA and the forces of General Pinochet. It is presented in three parts: 1) The Insurrection Of The Bourgeoisie 2) The Coup D'État 3) The Power Of The People. This remarkable record of a turbulent and tragic time in Chile was smuggled out of the country into Cuba where Guzman, with a group of Cuban film-makers, took over four years to edit it. Stating its Marxist credentials, the film does not pretend to be objective, yet it is analytical and not uncritical of the Left. Apart from supporters of the Chilean dictatorship, it would be hard for any spectator not to be moved and informed by the movie.

Battle Of The Rails

La Bataille Du Rail

France 1946 87 mins bw
CGCF

d **René Clément**
sc **René Clément**
ph **Henri Alekan**
m **Yves Baudrier**
Salina, Daurand, Lozach, Tony Laurent

A reconstruction of the resistance work, including sabotage of the railway link between the Occupied and Free Zones by French railwaymen during World War II. Clément brought the stark realism of his documentary shorts to bear on his first feature, a paean to the courage of the railway workers, with the men themselves re-enacting their exploits.

Best Film Cannes 1946
Best Director Cannes 1946

The Battleship Potemkin

(US: Potemkin)

Bronenosets Potemkin

USSR 1925 75 mins bw
Goskino

d **Sergei Eisenstein**
sc **Sergei Eisenstein**
ph **Edouard Tissé**
m **Silent**
A. Antonov, Vladimir Barski, Grigori Alexandrov, M. Gomorov

An incident during the 1905 revolution when the crew of the battleship *Prince Potemkin* mutinied rather than eat rotting food, an action supported by some of the civilian population who were mown down by government troops. Made as part of the 20th anniversary of the Revolution, the film contains—in the massacre on the Odessa Steps (an invention of Eisenstein's)—one of the most memorable and exciting sequences in all cinema. Down a seemingly endless flight of steps march soldiers advancing on the fleeing citizens. A nurse is shot and the pram and baby bounce down the steps to destruction. The rapid montage, and the effects devised by using a trolley and a camera strapped to the waist of an acrobat, still take the breath away. The film that put Soviet cinema and Eisenstein on the international map.

Bayan Ko: My Own Country

Bayan Ko—Kapit Sa Patalim

Philippines 1984 108 mins col
Malaya Films (Manila)/Stephan Films (Paris)

d **Lino Brocka**
sc **José F. Lacaba**
ph **Conrado Baltazar**
m **Jess Santiago**
Phillip Salvador, Gina Alajar, Claudia Zobel, Carmi Martin, Raoul Aragonn, Rez Cortez

Turing (Salvador), a worker at the Jefferson Printing Press, is given a loan by his boss on condition he doesn't join a trade union. During a strike, he becomes a scab but loses his job when he goes to the aid of pickets being attacked by hired thugs. Unable to pay his wife's hospital bill, he attempts to rob the plant, a decision which has tragic consequences. It is very much in line with those Hollywood films of doomed couples such as Fritz Lang's *You Only Live Once*, but given a political context. In fact, Lino Brocka is far more explicit in his condemnation of the system than he had been hitherto (the film got him charged with subversion by the Marcos regime), while still creating a hero who fails to embody any direct commitment to a cause.

Despite some crudities of narrative, the film's force is undeniable.

Bayan Ko—Kapit Sa Patalim see Bayan Ko: My Own Country

Bay Of Angels
La Baie Des Anges
France 1962 90 mins bw
Sud-Pacifique

d **Jacques Demy**
sc **Jacques Demy**
ph **Jean Rabier**
m **Michel Legrand**
Jeanne Moreau, Claude Mann, Paul Guers, Henri Nassiet

An ordinary bank clerk (Mann), who has had a streak of good luck at the Nice Casino, falls in love with a compulsive gambler (Moreau), who has left a husband and child to satisfy her craving. Shot very quickly on the French Riviera, this love story with a roulette wheel as the motif and the motive, is one of the most vivid evocations of gambling fever on film. The luminous photography and the hypnotic music add to the film's attraction.

The Beads Of One Rosary
Paciorki Jednego Rózańca
Poland 1979 111 mins col
PRF Zespoly Filmowe-Zespol Kadr

d **Kazimierz Kutz**
sc **Kazimierz Kutz**
ph **Wieslaw Zdort**
m **Wojciech Kilar**
Marta Straszna, Augustyn Halotta, Jan Bógdol, Ewa Wiśniewska

In a provincial Polish town, a retired miner and his wife refuse to leave the small cottage the family has occupied for over 50 years when property developers want to destroy it in order to erect high-rise buildings on the site. The picture of individuals taking on large corporations always provides pleasure, and this likeable but soft-centred film is no exception. Non-professionals Straszna and Halotta as the elderly couple give the tale an authentic ring, but they are too often seen as eccentrics to be pitied rather than people fighting for their rights.

The Beast
La Bête
France 1975 102 mins col
Argos

d **Walerian Borowczyk**
sc **Walerian Borowczyk**
ph **Bernard Daillencourt, Marcel Grignon**
m **Scarlatti**
Sirpa Lane, Pierre Benedetti, Guy Tréjean, Lisbeth Hummel, Elisabeth Kahson

An American heiress (Hummel), staying at the château of a marquis (Tréjean) whose son (Benedetti) she is about to marry, comes across the 18th-century diary of Romilda. She dreams of Romilda's sexual arousal by a mythological beast, half bear, half wolf. Another erotic fairy tale by Borowczyck became a *succès de scandale* because of the taboo subject of bestiality. But although it is never as shocking or as amusing as it sets out to be, the film provides a host of Freudian sexual symbols scattered throughout a story observed with the eye of a painter.

Beau Mariage, Le see Good Marriage, A

Beau-Père see Stepfather

Le Beau Serge
(US: Bitter Reunion)
France 1958 97 mins bw
AYJM

d **Claude Chabrol**
sc **Claude Chabrol**
ph **Henri Decaë**
m **Emile Delpierre**
Gérard Blain, Jean-Claude Brialy, Bernadette Lafont, Michèle Meritz

A theology student (Brialy), suffering from TB, returns to his native village to discover his talented childhood friend, Serge (Blain), has become a hopeless drunk and is estranged from his pregnant wife. An inheritance from his first wife enabled the 28-year-old critic Chabrol to finance his debut feature, considered the first film of the *Nouvelle Vague*. This well-drawn view of a grey, unattractive small town— actually Sardent where the director spent the war years—is encased in a rather stiff Christian metaphor of salvation, ending with a death and a birth. Chabrol's personal style only emerged in his second film, *The Cousins* (1958) with the same two young male leads.

Beauté Du Diable, La see Beauty And The Devil

Beauties Of The Night see Night Beauties

The Beautiful Swindlers

Les Plus Belles Escroqueries Du Monde

France/Italy/Holland/Japan 1963
90 mins bw
Ulysse/Primex/Lux/Vides/Toho/Cesar

d **1) Roman Polanski (Amsterdam)**
2) Ugo Gregoretti (Naples)
3) Claude Chabrol (Paris)
4) Hiromichi Horikawa (Tokyo)
sc **Roman Polanski, Gérard Brach Paul Gégauff**
ph **1) Jerzy Lipman 2) Tonino Delli Colli 3) Jean Rabier 4) Asakazu Nakai**
m **1) Krzysztof Komeda 2) Piero Umiliani 3) Pierre Jansen 4) Keitaro Miho**
1) Nicole Karen, Jan Teulings 2) Gabriella Giorgelli, Guido Giuseppone 3) Jean-Pierre Cassel, Catherine Deneuve, Francis Blanche 4) Mie Hama, Ken Mitsuda

1) A young French woman, a compulsive thief, cons a wealthy, middle-aged and married Dutchman into lending her his apartment, where she cons some jewellers out of a diamond necklace. 2) A pimp plans to marry off his girls to doddering old men. 3) A stupid German tourist buys the Eiffel Tower. 4) A bar girl goes home with a rich old musician who dies while eating noodles. A fifth episode, shot by Jean-Luc Godard with Jean Seberg, was dropped and released as a short. The biggest con of all was that perpetrated on the audience. Only Chabrol's contribution was mildly amusing in the whole tame enterprise.

Beauty And The Beast

La Belle Et La Bête

France 1946 95 mins bw
André Paulve

d **Jean Cocteau**
sc **Jean Cocteau**
ph **Henri Alekan**
m **Georges Auric**
Jean Marais, Josette Day, Mila Parély, Michel Auclair, Marcel André, Nane Germon

Beauty (Day) goes to the Beast's castle to take the place of her father whom the Beast has threatened to kill, but he falls hopelessly in love with her, proposing to her nightly. Finally, when she reciprocates, the Beast turns into a handsome Prince. Cocteau stated that he discouraged his photographer, and the brilliant art director Christian Berard, from virtuosity in order to show unreality in realistic terms. But thankfully virtuosity is everywhere evident in the magical scenes in the Beast's castle. Jean Marais, behind extraordinary make-up, is touching, and Beauty is slightly disappointed when he turns into his romantic self. A fairy tale for children and intelligent adults.

The Beauty And The Beast

Skønheden Og Udyret

Denmark 1983 90 mins col
Per Holst Filmproduktion/Danish Film Institute

d **Nils Malmros**
sc **Nils Malmros**
ph **Jan Weincke, Søren Berthelin**
m **Gunner Moller Pedersen, Purcell**
Line Arlien Søborg, Jesper Klein, Carsten Jørgensen, Eva Schjoldager, Brian Theibel

Sixteen-year-old Mette (Søborg) and her father (Klein) enjoy a close relationship built on love, mutual understanding and his pride in her. Left alone with her at Christmas while his wife is in hospital, he becomes aware that Mette has been concealing her romantic interest in Jonne (Jørgensen), a photographer, whom he considers a bad influence. Father feels that daughter has betrayed his trust, and his distress increases when Jonne becomes a constant visitor in his house. A stylish film in which the difficulties of a father-daughter relationship are well-delineated but, intrinsically, Malmros probes the individual psyches of his protagonists to reveal that the father is suffering from fear of losing his youth and needs to keep his daughter a little girl, while she is experiencing the growth of sexual awareness. Avoiding cliché, the director combines humour and pain, lending the story the weight of truth.

Beauty And The Devil

La Beauté Du Diable

France 1949 96 mins bw
AYJM/Franco London

d **René Clair**
sc **René Clair, Armand Salacrou**
ph **Michel Kelber**
m **Roman Vlad**

Michel Simon, Gérard Philipe, Simone Valère, Raymond Cordy, Nicole Besnard, Gaston Modot, Paolo Stoppa

Old Doctor Faust (Simon) is willing to sell his soul to Mephistopheles (Philipe), an agent of the Devil so that he can, in fact, look as young and handsome as the Prince of Darkness, and win the heart of the woman (Valère) he loves. Clair's clever conceit, therefore, is to allow Simon and Philipe to exchange roles midway. There is plenty of intelligence and wit in this ambitious version of the Faust legend, shot entirely among Léon Barsacq's splendid Baroque sets at Cinecittà in Rome, but it lacks delicacy and charm. However, the two great French actors are hard to resist.

Bébert And The Train

aka The Holy Terror

Bébert Et L'Omnibus

France 1963 90 mins bw
Les Productions De La Guéville

d **Yves Robert**
sc **François Boyer**
ph **André Bac**
m **Philippe-Gérard**

Petit Gibus, Jacques Higelin, Jean Richard, Blanchette Brunoy, Michel Serrault, Pierre Mondy

Five-year-old Bébert (Gibus) gets lost on a train while travelling with his big brother (Higelin) and a frantic search ensues. Meanwhile, the brat causes a great deal of chaos. A pleasant, well-observed little film made by an actor who made his name as a director the year before with *War Of The Buttons*. Unlike the previous film, with its hordes of kids, in this one Robert was able to concentrate on the delightful performance of Petit Gibus.

Bébert Et L'Omnibus see Bébert And The Train

Bebo's Girl

La Ragazza Di Bube

Italy 1963 110 mins bw
Lux/Ultra/Vides

d **Luigi Comencini**
sc **Luigi Comencini, Marcello Fondato**
ph **Gianni Di Venanzo**
m **Carlo Rustichelli**

Claudia Cardinale, George Chakiris, Marc Michel, Dany Paris, Emilio Esposito

A country girl (Cardinale) falls in love with a man (Chakiris) she hardly knows. When he is imprisoned for 14 years for killing a Fascist policeman during the war, she prefers to wait for his release, despite an offer of marriage from a writer (Michel). Cardinale gives one of her best performances (opposite a wooden, unconvincing Chakiris) in a gentle film that excellently re-creates the 1940s atmosphere of an Italian village. Shot on location, it is a throwback to the Neo-Realist period, well understated until the mawkish ending.

Bed And Board

Domicile Conjugale

France 1970 97 mins col
Films Du Carrosse/Valoria/Fida

d **François Truffaut**
sc **François Truffaut, Claude De Givray, Bernard Revon**
ph **Nestor Almendros**
m **Antoine Duhamel**

Jean-Pierre Léaud, Claude Jade, Hiroko Berghauer, Daniel Ceccaldi, Barbara Laage

Antoine Doinel (Léaud) marries his sweetheart, does a variety of jobs, writes a novel, becomes a father, takes up with a Japanese girl, and returns to his wife, ready to face the responsibilities of adulthood. The fourth and penultimate film in the semi-autobiographical Doinel cycle has, like its hero, some difficulty in retaining its youth and innocence. Truffaut retreats into the past cinematic Paris of René Clair, Jacques Becker, and Jean Renoir—charming enough in itself.

Bed And Sofa
Tretia Mecht Chanskaya
USSR 1927 115 mins bw
Sovkino
d **Abram Room**
sc **Victor Shklovsky**
ph **Gregori Giber**
m **Silent**
Nikolai Batalov, Ludmila Semenova, Vladimir Fogel

A married couple (Batalov and Semenova) have a small flat in Moscow. When an old friend (Fogel) of the husband's turns up in the city and is unable to find lodgings due to the housing shortage, he moves in with them. While the husband is away on business, sensual wife and attractive friend fall in love and have an affair but, after his initial outrage, the husband calms down and the three settle into a cosy, domesticated *ménage-à-trois* in which the wife virtually comes to assume the role of mother to her two boys... Rediscovered in the 1970s, Room's film has come to be regarded as a little masterpiece of the silent cinema. Aside from the extraordinary fluidity of his camera in a confined set and the splendidly natural performances of his cast, he deals with his subject in an almost casual, matter-of-fact way. Unusually frank for its period, it tells its tale with warmth, humour and absolute psychological truth, free of any trauma or sensationalism.

The Beekeeper
O Melissokomos
Greece 1986 112 mins col
Greek Film Centre/Marin Karmitz Productions/ERT 1/ Theo Angelopoulos
d **Theo Angelopoulos**
sc **Theo Angelopoulos, Dimitris Nollas**
ph **Giorgos Arvanitis**
m **Helen Karaindrou**
Marcello Mastroianni, Nadia Mourouzi, Serge Reggiani, Jenny Roussea, Dinos Iliopoulous

Spyros (Mastroianni), a morose retired schoolteacher, sets off on a trip around the beehive sites of Greece, taking his treasured beehives with him, and picks up an enigmatic young woman hitchhiker (Mourouzi) *en route*. 'A film on the silence of history, of love and of God,' is how the director describes his compelling metaphysical road movie. Set against the vividly caught landscape and small towns of Greece in winter, it sustains an atmosphere and even tempo throughout. Mastroianni's stoic performance proved that he had entered, in his sixties, the greatest period of acting in his career.

Before The Revolution
Prima Della Rivoluzione
Italy 1964 115 mins bw
Cineriz/Iride
d **Bernardo Bertolucci**
sc **Bernardo Bertolucci**
ph **Aldo Scavarda**
m **Gino Paoli, Ennio Morricone**
Francesco Barilli, Adriana Asti, Alain Midgette, Morando Morandini

A middle-class youth (Barilli) in Parma is torn between radical politics and conformism, and between a passionate affair with his young aunt (Asti) and *bourgeois* marriage. He opts for respectability on both counts. Favourite themes such as father/son relationships and political/personal conflicts are already apparent in this richly textured and technically impressive second film by Bertolucci, still in his early twenties. But, like his hero, there is an element of the dilettante in the director's use of references to Marx, Freud and Stendhal, and the works of Verdi.

The Beggar Student
Der Bettel Student
Germany 1936 75 mins bw
UFA
d **Georg Jacoby**
sc **Walter Wasserman, H. Dilber**
ph **Ewald Daub**
m **Carl Millöcker**
Marike Rökk, Carola Höhn, Ida Wüst, Johannes Heesters, Fritz Kampers

In German-occupied Cracow in 1704, as a practical joke, a revolutionary student (Heesters) is introduced as a duke to an aristocratic woman (Höhn), who falls in love with him. In the end, he turns out to be the nephew of the king. A typically light and lavish period operetta from UFA studios, by then under Nazi-government control. Full of pretty blondes, handsome soldiers, and plenty of anachronistic but pleasing melodies, the film appealed to audiences at home and abroad. It was remade in Germany in 1958 starring the Kessler twins.

The Beginning

aka The Debut

Nachalo

USSR 1970 90 mins bw
Lenfilm

d **Gleb Panfilov**
sc **Yevgeni Gabrilovich, Gleb Panfilov**
ph **Dmitri Dolynin**
m **Vadim Bibergan**
Inna Churikova, Leonid Kuravlev, Valentina Telichkina, Yuri Klepikov, Mikhail Kononov

Pasha (Churikova), a lively working girl in a small town, is spotted performing in an amateur play and is offered the role of Joan of Arc in a forthcoming film. She goes to the city, leaving behind Arkady (Kuravlev), the married man she loves who has decided to go back to his wife. When the film is over, so is Pasha's new career, and she returns home to a welcome from her factory workmates, having gained a measure of maturity. Panfilov, making his second film, is adroit in inter-cutting his narrative with scenes from the film-within-a-film, even before Pasha is involved in the latter. *The Beginning* is a charming comedy, laced with pathos, made with exceptional lightness of touch, and offering an accomplished leading lady of extraordinary range.

Beguines, The see Rempart Des Béguines, Le

Behind Closed Doors

A Porte Chiuse

Italy 1960 130 mins bw
Fair Film/Rire Cinematografica/SGC

d **Dino Risi**
sc **Marcello Coscia, Dino Di Palma, Sandro Continenza**
ph **Mario Montuori**
m **Piero Umiliani**
Anita Ekberg, Claudio Gora, Fred Clark, Ettore Manni, Gianni Bonagua

Olga Dubovich (Ekberg) is being tried for the murder of her wealthy lover from whose death she benefits. The evidence is so confusing that the prosecutor transfers the trial to the island where the crime took place and where Olga, back in familiar surroundings, is able to use her not inconsiderable charms as a trade-in for an acquittal—although that's not the end of the story. The plot belies the nature of Risi's film which is, in fact, a wild comic caper at the expense of Italian justice. It is very funny and Ekberg is a delight as the amoral enchantress, but the appeal is somewhat dissipated by the over-extended courtroom scenes in which the jokes wear a little thin.

Behold Thy Son

Kiiroi Karasu

Japan 1957 104 mins col
Shochiku

d **Heinosuke Gosho**
sc **Kennosuke Tateoka, Keije Hasebo**
ph **Yoshio Miyajima**
m **Yasushi Akutagawa**
Chikage Awashima, Yunosuke Ito, Koji Shitara, Kinuyo Tanaka, Masako Yasumura

When his father, whom he has never seen, returns home from an enforced 10-year sojourn in China, a young boy suffers intense feelings of resentment at the intrusion of a 'stranger', which increase when a baby sister is born. This is a moving and truthful exploration of a difficult father-son relationship, but it lets itself down in its latter stages with a melodramatic runaway sequence and a sentimental *rapprochement* between father and son.

Bekenntis Der Ina Kahr, Das see Afraid To Live

Beliye Nochi see White Nights

Bell'Antonio, Il see Handsome Antonio

Belle

Belgium 1973 93 mins col
Albina/La Nouvelle Imagerie

d André Delvaux
sc André Delvaux
ph Ghislain Cloquet
m Frédéric Devreese
Jean Luc Bideau, Danièle Delorme, Adriana Bogdan, Roger Coggio

A middle-aged married professor (Bideau) who has an almost incestuous desire for his daughter, meets a mysterious woman (Delorme) in the woods and has an affair with her.The professor lectures on obscure writers, and director Delvaux is obscure in another sense. One is seldom sure what is dream and what is reality—is the woman in the woods real or imaginary? As the director himself stated, 'The imaginary can introduce things that haven't yet taken place but will happen in reality later on'. As always, his work is visually arresting, but tends to hover between the poetic and the arty.

La Belle Américaine

France 1961 101 mins bw/col
CCFC/Film D'Art/Panorama/Corflor

d **Robert Dhéry**
sc **Robert Dhéry, Pierre Tchernia, Alfred Adam**
ph **Ghislain Cloquet**
m **Gérard Calvi**
Robert Dhéry, Louis De Funès, Colette Brosset, Alfred Adam, Bernard Lavalette, Annie Ducaux

When a Parisian factory worker (Dhéry) manages to buy a huge Cadillac (the 'beautiful American' of the title) at a bargain price, he gets into all kinds of trouble. Robert Dhéry became famous for his brilliant clowning in the London and Broadway hit review *La Plume De Ma Tante*. In his films, of which this was the most widely seen, he retains his zany comic skills, but only in short bursts. Unlike the supercar (seen in colour at the finale), Dhéry is not built for long distances.

Belle De Jour

France 1967 100 mins col
Paris Film/Five Film

d **Luis Buñuel**
sc **Luis Buñuel, Jean-Claude Carrière**
ph **Sacha Vierny**
Catherine Deneuve, Jean Sorel, Michel Piccoli, Geneviève Page, Pierre Clémenti

The respectable wife of a doctor finds herself spending her afternoons working in a high-class brothel with kinky clients ... and enjoying it. This witty, erotic, elegant and subversive film, obviously encouraging sexual fantasies, began Buñuel's fertile last period of French works, pointedly aimed at *bourgeois* hypocrisy. 'My biggest commercial success ... I attribute more to the marvellous whores than to my direction,' said the 67-year-old Buñuel modestly. As chief whore, in an excellent cast, Deneuve grows more beautiful with each perversion, imagined or otherwise.

Best Film Venice 1967

La Belle Équipe
(US: They Were Five)

France 1936 94 mins bw
Arys/Ciné Arts

d **Julien Duvivier**
sc **Julien Duvivier, Charles Spaak**
ph **Jules Kruger, Marc Fessard**
m **Maurice Yvain**
Jean Gabin, Charles Vanel, Viviane Romance, Aimos, Raphael Medina

Five unemployed workers win a lottery and buy a country inn on the banks of the Marne, but their friendship is threatened by the vampish wife of one of them. A perfect example of French cinema of the Popular Front— believable working-class characters, their simple pleasures, lilting music, sunny open-air camerawork . . . and Gabin, the icon of the age. It loses its way a little when melodrama intervenes, but Duvivier shot alternative tragic and happy endings, the latter being more widely shown.

Belle Et La Bête, La see Beauty And The Beast

Belle Fille Comme Moi, Une see Gorgeous Bird Like Me, A

Belles De Nuit, Les see Night Beauties

Bellissima

Italy 1951 113 mins bw
Bellissima Films

d **Luchino Visconti**
sc **Luchino Visconti, Suso Cecchi D'Amico, Francesco Rosi**
ph **Piero Portalupi, Paul Ronald**
m **Franco Mannino**
Anna Magnani, Walter Chiari, Tina Apicella, Alessandro Blasetti

A woman from the slums determines to get her pretty seven-year-old daughter into films, but becomes disillusioned with Cinecitta, and refuses a screen test for her. Visconti's third feature already saw him moving into the realms of the 'woman's picture', and any attempt at Neo-Realism is blown away by Magnani's noisy larger-than-life performance. Alessandro Blasetti, an early Neo-Realist, is cast as a director, and there are some interesting glimpses of Cinecitta, one of Europe's biggest studios, contrasted with the steaming tenements of Rome.

Benjamin Or The Diary Of An Innocent Young Man

Benjamin Ou Les Mémoirs D'Un Puceau

France 1966 104 mins col
Parc/Marianne/Paramount

d **Michel Deville**
sc **Nina Companeez**
ph **Ghislain Cloquet**
m **Boccherini, Haydn, Mozart, Rameau**
Pierre Clémenti, Michèle Morgan, Catherine Deneuve, Michel Piccoli, Francine Bergé, Anna Gäel, Odile Versois

In the 18th century, a handsome 17-year-old orphan boy (Clémenti) is taken to live at the château of his wealthy aunt (Morgan) where he happily learns about sex from a variety of women of all ages and classes. The sort of film generally termed a 'romp', it has gorgeous costumes and settings, and a pleasant cast in becoming wigs that includes old hands Morgan and Piccoli, and Clémenti and Deneuve as attractive virgins. But its rococo ribaldry lacks sufficient charm and wit to sustain it. It was a huge success in France, presumably with those for whom Marivaux and Beaumarchais are closed books.

Benjamin Ou Les Mémoirs D'Un Puceau see Benjamin Or The Diary Of An Innocent Young Man

Benvenuta

Belgium 1983 106 mins col
La Nouvelle Imagerie (Brussels)/UGC/Europe 1/FR3 (Paris)/Opera-Film (Rome)

d **André Delvaux**
sc **André Delvaux**
ph **Charlie Van Damme**
m **Frédéric Devreese and extracts from, Mozart, Schumann, Brahms**
Fanny Ardant, Vittorio Gassman, Françoise Fabian, Matthieu Carrière, Claire Wauthion

François (Carrière), a writer from Alsace, has been commissioned to script a film from a novel which was something of a *cause célèbre* 20 years previously, and visits Jeanne (Fabian), the author, now living reclusively in Ghent, to discuss the material—how much is autobiographical, how much invention—and to plunder her memories of the story's several locales. True to his form, Delvaux plays an elaborate game with fantasy and reality, moving between the two, as between time and place, with consummate ease in a series of painterly images. François' vision of the story forms most of the action, with Benvenuta (Ardant, poker-faced) locked in an *amour fou* with Livio (Gassman, aging but attractive). But how much of it is Benvenuta's story, and how much is Jeanne's? For all its skill, this brew of eroticism, spiritual self- flagellation and quasi-poetic philosophizing, relentlessly ambiguous and indulgent, may strike some viewers as pretentious rather than intriguing.

Berg-Ejvind Och Hans Hustru see Outlaw And His Wife, The

Berget Pa Manens Baksida see Hill On The Dark Side Of The Moon, A

Bergkatze, Die see Mountain Cat, The

Berlin: Die Sinfonie Einer Gross-stadt see Berlin: Symphony Of A Great City

Berlin: Symphony Of A Great City

Berlin: Die Sinfonie Einer Gross-stadt

Germany 1927 70 mins bw
Fox Europa

d **Walter Ruttmann**
sc **Karl Freund, Walter Ruttmann**
ph **Reimar Kuntze, Robert Baberske, Laszlo Shäffer**
m **Silent**

An impressionistic view of life in Berlin on a Spring day from dawn to midnight, the film took 18 months to make. Most of it was shot using cameras concealed in a removal van or in suitcases to catch people unawares. Edmund Meisel, who composed a jazzy score (since lost) for a 75-piece orchestra to accompany the film, worked with Ruttman on the editing to give it a rhythmic effect. Influenced by the montage developments of Eisenstein and Vertov, it led to further 'abstract' documentaries in the same style.

Berlin-Alexanderplatz

Germany 1931 121 mins bw
Allianz Tonfilm/Capital

d **Phil Jutzi**
sc **Alfred Döblin, Hans Wilhelm**
ph **Erich Giese**
m **Allan Gray, Artur Guttman**

Heinrich George, Bernhard Minetti, Margarete Schlegel, Albert Florath

Franz Biberkopf (George), a simple-minded ex-con, desperately tries to go straight, but his sexual obsession with Mieze (Schlegel) and his economic dependency on unsavoury characters lead to tragedy. Although Döblin himself collaborated on the screenplay of his great novel, which did for Berlin what Joyce's *Ulysses* did for Dublin (a direct influence), the structure and psychology of the tale were somewhat flattened out. It took Fassbinder, in his overwhelming 13-episode made-for-TV version (made in 1980 and running altogether 975 minutes), to do it full justice. But Jutzi gets strong performances from his cast, and the atmosphere of period Berlin is vividly captured.

Berliner, The see Ballad Of Berlin

Berliner Ballade see Ballad Of Berlin

Bernadette

France 1988 118 mins col
Les Films De L'Étoile D'Or/Bernadette Association International S.A.

d **Jean Delannoy**
sc **Jean Delannoy, Robert Arnaut**
ph **Jean-Bernard Penzer**
m **Francis Lai**

Sydney Penny, Jean-Marc Bory, Roland Lesaffre, Michèle Simonnet, Bernard Dhéran, Michel Duchaussoy, François Dalou, Arlette Didier

While collecting firewood in a grotto near Lourdes, Bernadette (Penny), the seriously asthmatic 15-year-old daughter of the near-destitute Soubirous family, has a spiritual vision of 'a beautiful lady in white'. Further visions follow, earning the girl the devotion of the poor, the derision of the *bourgeoisie* and the opprobrium of the State, the officers of which attempt to have her certified insane until the cynical Father Peyramale (Bory) comes to believe in her. The distinguished director, 79 when he made the film that he spent spent three years researching, brings unmistakable sincerity to the enterprise. Setting out to recount the facts—and Delannoy insists that not a single incident is his invention—of a very short and specific period in Bernadette's life, he does so with technical proficiency and a solid cast. The tone of the film is spiritual but not narrowly religious, and its stance neutral. The young American Sydney Penny, speaking excellent French and glowing with inappropriate health and beauty, convinces with the right quality of innocence, yet the film is simplistic, sometimes dull and suffers from an air of old-fashioned, clichéd unreality.

Bernadette Of Lourdes
Il Suffit D'Aimer

France 1960 102 mins bw
EDIC-Films/S.E.N/Tamara(Paris)/Zebra Film/Cineriz(Rome)

d **Robert Darène**
sc **Gilbert Cesbron, Robert Darène**
ph **Marcel Weiss**
m **Maurice Thiriet**
Danièle Ajoret, Madeleine Sologne, Bernard Lajarrige, Blanchette Brunoy, Lise Delamare, Henri Nassiet

Bernadette Soubirous (Ajoret), the sick daughter of a poverty-stricken family, sees a vision of the Virgin Mary. Her faith finally overcomes the disbelief and opposition of Church and State and, as thousands flock to the healing waters at Lourdes, she enters a convent where she dies, aged 35, from continued ill-health. It is interesting to compare this with Delannoy's large-scale colour movie almost 30 years later. Like its successor, this version is restrained, but covers Bernadette's entire life. The later scenes in the convent, contrasting the simple girl with the more educated nuns who continue to view her with a mixture of resentment, curiosity and awe, are the most interesting, and Ajoret, whose girlish qualities earlier on are a little synthetic, comes into her own. What emerges clearly from both films is that the undeniably absorbing subject seems to limit directorial imagination.

Berührte, Die see No Mercy No Future

The Best Age
Nejkrasnejsí Vek

Czechoslovakia 1968 80 mins bw
Barrandov Studio

d **Jaroslav Papoušek**
sc **Jaroslav Papoušek**
ph **Josef Ort-Snep**
m **Karel Mares**
Hana Brejchová, Věra Křesadlová, Jan Stöckl, Josef Sebánek, Jiří Sykora

An art school selects models for the sculpture class from a daily queue of hopefuls, who include a group of pensioners. An elderly gentleman is chosen for his head but keeps dozing off; a young married woman with a baby agrees to pose in the nude whereupon her jealous husband smashes up the statues; a middle-aged coalman, recently injured, represents a wounded soldier . . . Papoušek's film is the work of a gentle miniaturist, wryly and affectionately recording day-to-day human absurdity. What he is really examining is the tendency to believe that one's best age is either past, or yet to come, as exemplified by the students' fascination with the old man's face, stamped with the marks of experience and impending death, while he envies them their youth. A charming piece, marred only by some moments of overstatement.

Best Way, The see Best Way To Walk, The

The Best Way To Walk
(US: The Best Way)
La Meilleure Façon De Marcher

France 1976 90 mins col
Contrechamp/Speciality

d **Claude Miller**
sc **Claude Miller, Luc Béraud**
ph **Bruno Nuytten**
m **Alain Jomy**
Patrick Dewaere, Patrick Bouchitey, Christine Pascal, Claude Piéplu

When an instructor at a summer camp for boys accidentally discovers the son of the camp-owner in make-up and drag, he bullies him unmercifully, but it's the victim who gets the girl. The first film by the former assistant to Truffaut and Godard is a neatly made, sardonic but too pat tale of sexual identity. Dewaere as the bully, and Bouchitey as the camp camp counsellor, set up sexually ambiguous sparks leading to the rather embarrassing farewell party scene.

Bête Humaine, La see Human Beast, The

Bête, La see Beast, The

Betrayer, The see Vanina Vanini

Bettel Student, Der see Beggar Student, The

Betty Blue
37°2 Le Matin
France 1986 121 mins col
Claudie Ossard - Jean-Jacques Beineix

d **Jean-Jacques Beineix**
sc **Jean-Jacques Beineix**
ph **Jean-François Robin**
m **Gabriel Yared**
Béatrice Dalle, Jean-Hugues Anglade, Consuela De Haviland, Gérard Darmon

Betty (Dalle), a young, disgruntled waitress, discovers a novel written by 35-year-old handyman, Zorg (Anglade), sets fire to his beach shack and takes off with him to Paris and then a provincial town where, disillusioned and on drugs, she goes mad. After the spectacular failure of *Moon In The Gutter*, Beineix recovered his reputation somewhat with this more realistic character study and narrative, but without sacrificing too much of his flamboyance. The torrid ephemeral affair of the central couple is depicted with frankness, and the playing, especially by new discovery Dalle, avoids the histrionics that the roles might have encouraged.

Between Time And Eternity
Zwischen Zeit Und Ewigkeit
W. Germany 1956 97 mins col
Neue Terra

d **Arthur Maria Rabenalt**
sc **Robert Thoeren**
ph **Georg Bruckbauer**
m **Bert Grund**
Lilli Palmer, Carlos Thompson, Willy Birgel, Ellen Schwiers

Nina (Palmer) is dying of a brain disease and, although her doctor husband has concealed the truth from her, she senses that she hasn't much time and goes off alone to a Mediterranean island where she falls in love with Manuel (Thompson), a handsome and carefree fisherman. There is absolutely nothing original or profound about this three-handkerchief weepie but, within its genre, it is entirely competent. The lovely Lilli Palmer (co-starring with her future husband after Rex Harrison) gives a sensitive and controlled performance, played out amid enticing Majorcan locations.

Between Two Wars
Zwischen Zwei Kriegen
W. Germany 1977 83 mins bw
Harun Farocki

d **Harun Farocki**
sc **Harun Farocki**
ph **Axel Block, Melanie Walz, Ingo Kratisch**
m **Mahler**
Jürgen Ebert, Michael Klier, Ingemo Engström, Hartmut Bitomsky

A series of six episodes and dialogues from 1917 to 1933 which set out a Marxist analysis of the causes of World War II and how it could have been avoided. Farocki took almost seven years to put together this film, which asks of the audience a certain political frame of reference and an ability to reflect on the arguments presented. With minimal means (it was made on a budget of less than $8,000), Farocki reconstructs the past by using visual synecdoche (the part for the whole) such as a bicycle toolbag and a shiny Horch automobile to stand for class differences. Although self-restrained and intellectual, there is a dramatic thread. The young hero (Ebert) hopes that 'science could blend with the dreams of the workers', joins the Communist party, sees the inevitability of the German industrial *bourgeoisie* supporting Hitler and commits suicide.

Between Two Worlds see Destiny

Beware Of A Holy Whore
Warnung Vor Einer Heiligen Nutte
W. Germany 1970 103 mins col
Antiteater-X Film/Nova International

d **Rainer Werner Fassbinder**
sc **Rainer Werner Fassbinder**
ph **Michael Ballhaus**
m **Peer Raben and extracts from Donizetti, Elvis Presley, Ray Charles, Leonard Cohen, Spooky Tooth**
Lou Castel, Eddie Constantine, Hanna Schygulla, Marquard Böhm, Rainer Werner Fassbinder, Ulli Lommel, Margarethe Von Trotta, Kurt Raab, Ingrid Caven, Werner Schroeter

A German film crew sits around an old hotel at a Spanish seaside resort arguing, griping, drinking and making love, as they wait for the director (Castel), the star (Constantine) and money from Bonn. Fassbinder's bitter critique of himself and his own group of friends and hangers-on is also one of the most devastatingly honest views of film-makers and film-making ever put on screen. Apparently, much of the film reflected the actual shooting (in Sorrento, Italy) and the uglier side of the real people involved. Self-indulgent, self-righteous and self-pitying, it is also funny, provocative and well made. It ends with a quotation from Thomas Mann which was Fassbinder's own *cri de coeur* at the time: 'I tell you that I am often weary to death of portraying humanity without participating in what is human'.

Beyond Good And Evil

Oltre Il Bene E Il Male

Italy 1977 127 mins col
Clesi Cinematografica/Lotar/Artemis/Artistes Associés

d **Liliana Cavani**
sc **Liliana Cavani, Franco Arcalli, Italo Moscati**
ph **Armando Nanuzzi**
m **Danièle Paris, Mahler, Schumann, Gounod, Schönberg**
Dominique Sanda, Erland Josephson, Robert Powell, Virna Lisi, Philippe Leroy

In turn-of-the-century Rome, the German philosopher Nietzsche (Josephson) and his Jewish friend Paul Rée (Powell) meet a beautiful 20-year-old Russian girl, Lou Von Salomé (Sanda). They decide to set up an 'intellectual' *ménage-à-trois*. This is broken up through Nietzsche's jealousy and because anti-semitism causes Paul to try to poison himself. This fictionalized, febrile account of three people who defied convention is by a director with pretensions to do the same. To succeed it needed a little more intellect, less emotion, and a closer look at the truth. The performances range from the passive (Sanda) to the strident (Powell). There is even a lurid ballet depicting the struggle between Good and Evil, supposed to be Nietzsche's hallucination brought about by drugs. The result is neither Good nor Evil but Bad.

Beyond The Wall see Destiny

Beyond The Walls

Me'Achorei Hasoragim

Israel 1984 103 mins col
April Films

d **Uri Barbash**
sc **Benny Barbash, Eran Preis**
ph **Amnon Salomon**
m **Ilan Virtzberg**
Arnon Zadok, Muhamad Bakri, Hilel Ne'eman, Assi Dayan, Boaz Sharaabi, Jacob Ayali, Iris Kanner, David Kedem

In an Israeli prison, Jewish criminals are housed with a number of Arabs being held on political charges. Their natural hostility is fuelled by the guards who pursue a divide and rule policy, and feelings are further inflamed by the arrival of an Israeli who sought contact with the PLO. Jewish Uri (Zadok) and Arab Issam (Bakri) find mutual respect when confined together away from the other prisoners, and unite to lead a prison strike. Barbash sets up an intelligent situation which he uses to examine the Arab-Israeli conflict but the metaphor of the title is not pursued. What we have is a prison drama, visually authentic and atmospheric, but peopled with every stereotype and offering the obligatory homosexual rape. It might just as well be the State Penitentiary, courtesy of Hollywood, but lacking the narrative tightness of the American genre.

Bez Konca see No End

Bez Svidetelei see Private Conversation, A

Bez Znieczulenia see Rough Treatment

Bhumika see Role, The

Les Biches

aka The Does

France 1968 99 mins col
La Boetie/Alexandra

d **Claude Chabrol**
sc **Claude Chabrol, Paul Gégauff**
ph **Jean Rabier**
m **Pierre Jansen**
Stéphane Audran, Jacqueline Sassard, Jean-Louis Trintignant

A rich and beautiful woman (Audran) picks up a student (Sassard) in Paris and takes her off to her villa in St Tropez, but the local architect (Trintignant) causes a rift in their Lesbian relationship. After seven years of rather paltry stuff, Chabrol re-established his reputation with this elegantly enacted, cool, callous and witty bisexual *ménage-à-trois*. It was also the first film in which Audran (Mrs Chabrol since 1964) was given a role worthy of her subtle expressiveness. The character Sassard plays is called Why. You might well ask.

Best Actress (Stéphane Audran) Berlin 1968

Bicycle Thief, The see Bicycle Thieves

Bicycle Thieves

(US: The Bicycle Thief)

Ladri Di Biciclette

Italy 1948 90 mins bw
PDS/ENIC

d **Vittorio De Sica**
sc **Vittorio De Sica, Cesare Zavattini, Oreste Biancoli, Suso Cecchi D'Amico, Adolfo Franci**
ph **Carlo Montuori**
m **Alessandro Cicognini**
Lamberto Maggiorani, Lianella Carell, Enzo Staiola, Gino Saltamarenda

An unemployed man (Maggiorani) is offered a job as a bill-sticker provided he has a bicycle. He retrieves his own from the pawnbroker but it is stolen on his first day at work, and he spends a day with his small son (Staiola) desperately searching for it. After De Sica's success in the USA with *Shoeshine* (1946), David O. Selznick offered to produce his next film with a star like Cary Grant, but De Sica refused, raised the money himself, and continued his policy of working with non-actors in real locations. It paid off because it was this very un-Hollywood quality—the simplicity and underlying social criticism—that gave it wide appeal. At the time it seemed fragmentary and naturalistic, but it has a highly organized script, and is very moving.

Best Foreign Film Oscar 1949

Bidone, Il see Swindlers, The

Bienvenido, Mr Marshall see Welcome, Mr Marshall

The Big City

Mahanagar

India 1963 131 mins bw
R.D. Bansal

d **Satyajit Ray**
sc **Satyajit Ray**
ph **Subrata Mitra**
m **Satyajit Ray**
Anil Chatterjee, Madhabi Mukherjee, Vicky Redwood, Haren Chatterjee

The wife of an impoverished bank clerk takes a door-to-door job selling knitting machines to rich housewives in Calcutta, and thus becomes emancipated. Ray's warmth, humour, depth, and scrupulous attention to social detail—witness the scene in the home of an Anglo-Indian—are much in evidence in the first of his films to be given a contemporary urban setting. The convincing progress of the appealing Madhabi Mukherjee from timid housewife to sole breadwinner, is extremely satisfying, particularly in an Indian context.

Best Director Berlin 1964

Big Deal On Madonna Street see Persons Unknown

A Big Family

Bolchaia Semia

USSR 1955 105 mins col
Lenfilm

d **Josef Heifits**
sc **V. Kochetov, S.Kara**
ph **S. Ivanov**
m **Venedikt Pushkov**
Serge Lukyanov, Boris Andreyev, Vera Kuznetsova, Andrei Batalov, S. Kurilov, Vadim Medvedev, B. Bityukov, I. Arepina, Katya Luchko, Elena Savinova

Events in the lives of the Zhurbin family, all 10 of them, who make up three generations of dedicated shipyard workers, all living together under the eye of papa Zhurbin (Lukyanov). An old-fashioned, leisurely, heart-warming domestic portrait that Louis B. Mayer would have been pleased to call his own, were it not for the fact that Alexei's fiancée becomes pregnant by somebody else, and Viktor's wife leaves him rather than endure an unhappy marriage. Incidents such as these, emerging from 1950s Russia, caused the film to be rapturously received on release; if it's less impressive now, the reasons for the acting accolade remain apparent.

Best Acting Award (Complete Cast Ensemble) Cannes 1955

The Big Parade

Da Yuebing

China 1986 103 mins col
Guangxi Film Studio

d **Chen Kaige**
sc **Gao Lili**
ph **Zhang Yimou**
m **Qu Xiaosong**
Wang Xueqi, Sun Chun, Lu Lei, Wu Ruofu, Guan Qiang, Kang Hua, Members of the Airborne Division of the People's Liberation Army

In China in 1984, 400 recruits, most of them in their teens and still raw, commence a year of gruellingly intensive training that will win some of them places in the National Day Parade in Peking's Tiananmen Square. Focusing on the hopes and fears of six central characters of contrasting ages and abilities, the film observes and records the relationship between the individual and the group, culminating in the immense parade itself. In the West, this movie has been received as a high-quality Chinese answer to the familiar American rookie-authority-patriotism genre. In China, however, the authorities regarded it as unacceptably critical of the People's Army and only allowed its release when Chen (*Yellow Earth*) Kaige made some adjustments, including, notably, the addition of the climactic Parade where he had intended only the empty square. To a Western viewer, it is a realistic drama with unmistakable elements of irony but no hint of subversion. A little dour, perhaps, and at times relentless in its portrayal of difficulties, but the compellingly naturalistic performances and strikingly sophisticated visual composition absorb and entertain.

The Big Snatch

(US: Any Number Can Win)

Mélodie En Sous-Sol

France 1963 112 mins bw
Cipra-Cité Film/C.C.M.

d **Henri Verneuil**
sc **Henri Verneuil, Albert Simonin, Michel Audiard**
ph **Louis Page**
m **Michel Magne**
Jean Gabin, Alain Delon, Viviane Romance, Dora Doll, José De Villalonga

An ex-con (Gabin) sets up one last job and enlists the help of a younger crook (Delon) to rob the casino at Cannes. Everything goes according to plan right up to the last minute until... The main interest in this competently-staged but conventional heist movie with a clever twist, is the coming together of the biggest star of the 1930s and the rising star of the 1960s. Also noteworthy is the appearance of Viviane Romance, who had played 'the vamp' opposite Gabin 27 years previously in *La Belle Equipe*.

Bijoutiers Du Claire De Lune, Les see Heaven Fell That Night

Bilans Kwartalny see Woman's Decision, A

The Birch Wood

Brzezina

Poland 1970 99 mins col
Tor/Zespoly Filmowe

d **Andrzej Wajda**
sc **Jaroslaw Iwaszkiewicz**
ph **Zygmunt Samosiuk**
m **Andrzej Korzyński**
Olgierd Lukaszewicz, Daniel Olbrychski, Emilia Krakowska, Marek Perepeczko, Jan Domański

In the early 1930s, the tubercular Stanislaw (Lukaszewicz) returns from Switzerland to Poland to stay with his healthy, but bitter, forest warden brother (Olbrychski). Here, he experiences a new lease of life and, in the process, wins the love of the country girl (Krakowska) whom his brother secretly covets. Driven by 'censorship behind closed doors', Wajda turned to non-political literature for his material. Like the later *The Young Ladies Of Wilko*, this bitter-sweet drama was based on a book by Jaroslaw Iwaszkiewicz (who also wrote the screenplay). The general look of the film derives from Polish *art nouveau* paintings, while Wajda's direction is simple, slow, and understated. Like the contrasting brothers, the film moves between the pallid and the robust.

The Birds Come To Die In Peru

(US: Birds In Peru)

Les Oiseaux Vont Mourir Au Pérou

France 1968 98 mins col
Universal France

d **Romain Gary**
sc **Romain Gary**
ph **Christian Matras**
m **Kenton Coe**
Jean Seberg, Maurice Ronet, Danielle Darrieux, Pierre Brasseur, Jean-Pierre Kalfon

An insecure woman (Seberg), craving sexual excitement, leaves her husband (Brasseur) on his own almost every night to search for sex in a seaside brothel or on the beaches. This was undoubtedly one of the lowest points in Jean Seberg's sad life and career (she killed herself in 1979) and it was the first film directed by novelist-diplomat Romain Gary, her second husband. Like the birds of the title, this pretentious, salacious picture landed with a deadening thud.

Birds In Peru see Birds Come To Die In Peru, The

Birds Of A Feather see Cage Aux Folles, La

The Birds, The Bees And The Italians

Signore E Signori

Italy 1965 115 mins bw
Dear/RPA/Les Films Du Siècle

d **Pietro Germi**
sc **Pietro Germi, Luciano Vincenzoni, Age, Scarpelli**
ph **Aiace Parolin**
m **Carlo Rustichelli**
Virna Lisi, Nora Ricci, Gastone Moschin, Alberto Lionello, Patrizia Valturri, Beba Loncar

Three separate short tales of illicit sex in a small Italian town. 1) A man feigns impotence so that he can cuckold a husband without arousing suspicion 2) A henpecked husband leaves home and lives openly with a bar cashier 3) A young girl is seduced by most of the village men until her father reveals that she is under age. The Italian way with sex (at least in the movies) continued to provide endless amusement at home and abroad in the 1960s. This had more edge than most, and even managed to supply the occasional belly-laugh.

Best Film Cannes 1966

Biruma No Tategoto see Burmese Harp, The

Bitteren Tränen Der Petra Von Kant, Die see Bitter Tears Of Petra Von Kant, The

---

Bitter Reunion see Beau Serge, Le

Bitter Rice

Riso Amaro

Italy 1950 107 mins bw
Lux/De Laurentiis

d **Giuseppe De Santis**
sc **Giuseppe De Santis, Carlo Lizzani, Gianni Puccini**
ph **Otello Martelli**
m **Goffredo Petrassi**
Silvana Mangano, Doris Dowling, Vittorio Gassman, Raf Vallone

One of the many city women who come each year to work in the rice fields of the Po valley, falls for a petty crook who hopes to steal the rice crop. To most of the public, *Bitter Rice* means the voluptuous Mangano in thigh-revealing shorts and torn nylons, her sizeable breasts thrust forward, her seductive head held high, standing in a rice paddy. The huge success of the steamy film and of the 19-year-old actress, who married producer De Laurentiis the same year, paved the way for other Italian sexpots to join the international scene. Ostensibly a Neo-Realist exposé of the exploitation of women workers the film, in reality, it exposes only La Mangano and exploits the subject.

Bitter Spirit, The see Eternal Love

The Bitter Tears Of Petra Von Kant

Die Bitteren Tränen Der Petra Von Kant

W. Germany 1972 124 mins col
Tango

d **Rainer Werner Fassbinder**
sc **Rainer Werner Fassbinder**
ph **Michael Ballhaus**
m **Verdi, and a selection of pop records**
Margit Carstensen, Hanna Schygulla, Irm Hermann, Katrin Schaake, Eva Mattes

Petra Von Kant (Carstensen), a successful fashion designer, conducts a sado-masochistic relationship with her assistant Marlene (Hermann), until the arrival of Karin (Schygulla), with whom Petra has a tempestuous love affair. Fassbinder wrote the screenplay for Carstensen, giving her plenty of scope to emote and to change her wigs and gowns frequently. This hermetic all-female chamber piece, confined to the heroine's apartment which is dominated by a brass bed, recalls an old-fashioned melodrama of the 1920s despite the Lesbianism—something the director might have taken as a compliment.

Bizalom see Confidence

Bizarre, Bizarre

Drôle De Drame

France 1937 95 mins bw
Corniglion Molinier

d **Marcel Carné**
sc **Jacques Prévert**
ph **Eugen Schüfftan**
m **Maurice Jaubert**
Françoise Rosay, Michel Simon, Louis Jouvet, Jean-Louis Barrault, Jean-Pierre Aumont

In Edwardian London, a bizarre chain of events is set in motion when an English mystery writer (Simon) has to pretend to a visiting Bishop (Jouvet) that his wife (Rosay) has been called away. A witty and anarchic farce, played to perfection by the superb cast and filmed in a cardboard London imagined by art director Alexander Trauner. Among the delights are Jouvet in a kilt and Barrault as a vegetarian who murders butchers.

Black And White In Colour

La Victoire En Chantant

France 1976 100 mins col
Reggance/SEP/Artco/Société Ivorienne De Production

d **Jean-Jacques Annaud**
sc **Jean-Jacques Annaud, Georges Conchon**
ph **Claude Agostini, Eduardo Serra, Nanamoudou Magassouda**
m **Pierre Bachelet, Mat Camison**
Jean Carmet, Jacques Dufilho, Catherine Rouvel, Jacques Spiesser, Dora Doll

When war is declared in Europe in 1914, a group of self-satisfied French colonials at a remote trading post in West Africa decide to attack a nearby German fort and confusion ensues. This first feature by a former TV-commercial director, is a mildly amusing but strained satire on colonialism. Nicely shot in the Ivory Coast, and co-produced by the former French colony, it was the Oscar-winner from a particularly poor bunch of nominations.

Best Foreign Film Oscar 1976

Black Brood

Camada Negra

Spain 1977 85 mins col
El Iman

d **Manuel Gutiérrez Aragón**
sc **José Luis Borau, Manuel Gutiérrez Aragón**
ph **Magi Torruella**
m **José Nieta**
José Luis Alonso, Maria Luisa Ponte, Angela Molina, Joaquín Hinojosa, Manuel Fadon, Emilio Fornet

Tatin (Alonso), aged 15 and too young to join the Right wing terrorist group run by his mother in memory of her late Falangist husband, privately vows to live by its three sacred principles: revenge, secrecy and willingness to sacrifice loved ones to the cause. The consequences of the decision are appalling, culminating in his brutal killing of his girlfriend (Molina). Set in Madrid and directed and acted with conviction, this obvious critique of Franco's Spain makes connections between gangsterism and political fanaticism, but constantly surprises with shifts of mood, sympathy and action. The title refers both to the fanatical mother and her stepsons (one of whom admits to being a former policeman) and to a litter of black puppies that conceals the hatch under which the gang's weapons are hidden.

Best Director Berlin 1977

The Black Cannon Incident

Hei Pao Shi Jian

China 1985 102 mins col
Xi'an Film Studio

d **Huang Jianxin**
sc **Li Wei**
ph **Wang Xinsheng, Feng Wei**
m **Zhu Shirui**
Liu Zifeng, Gerhard Olschewski, Gao Ming, Wang Yi, Yang Yazhou, Ge Hui

A technical consultant-interpreter (Zifeng) on a major Sino-German civil engineering project is also a chess buff. One day, Party members intercept a cryptic telegram he sent to a friend about a lost chess piece (the black cannon). Believing it to be a coded message, they relieve him of his post. His replacement, with little knowledge of German, makes a terrible mess of the project. Huang Jianxin, a young graduate of the Beijing Film Academy, made the wittiest and cheekiest satire on bureaucracy to have come out of China to date. It targets stupid and corrupt Party hacks, avaricious workers and noisy teenagers, and portrays a fine friendship between the hapless hero and a rather overbearing German engineer (Olschewski). The use of bold colours and clever camera effects adds to the pleasure.

Black God White Devil

Deus E O Diabo Na Terra Do Sol

Brazil 1964 120 mins bw
Luiz Augusto Mendes/Copacabana

d **Glauber Rocha**
sc **Glauber Rocha**
ph **Waldemar Lima**
m **Bach, Villa-Lobos, folk songs**
Yona Magalhaes, Geraldo Del Rey, Othon Bastos, Mauricio De Valle, Lidio Silva

When his boss tries to rob him, an impoverished cowman kills him, becomes an outlaw and a follower of a self-styled black saint who preaches bloodshed. The first of

25-year-old Rocha's essays on the *sertão*, the parched lands of north-east Brazil, is less fragmented and hysterical than his later work, and is an intoxicating synthesis of symbolism, realism and popular culture, often evoking directors as diverse as John Ford, Buñuel and Eisenstein.

Black On White

Mustaa Valkoisella

Finland 1968 85 mins col
F. J. Filmi

d **Jörn Donner**
sc **Jörn Donner**
ph **Esko Nevalainen**
m **Georg Riedel**
Jörn Donner, Liisamaija Laaksonen, Kristina Halkola, Lasse Martenson

A young businessman (Donner) leaves his wife (Halkola) and his perfect marriage to pursue an affair with a flighty secretary (Laaksonen) who wants no ties. Donner's first film in his homeland after making four features in Sweden is a gentle satire on the affluent society with a simple love triangle (and explicit sex scenes) at its centre. Without moralizing or melodrama, the director (himself excellent in the lead) calmly records the man's impossible quest for happiness. Despite the title, it is in eye-catching colour.

Black Orpheus

Orfeu Negro

France 1958 106 mins col
Dispatfilm/Gemma/Tupan

d **Marcel Camus**
sc **Vinitius De Moraes, Jacques Viot**
ph **Jean Bourgoin**
m **Luis Bonfa, Antonio Carlos Jobim**
Breno Mello, Marpessa Dawn, Ademar Da Silva, Lourdes De Oliviera

During carnival time in Rio, a philandering tram driver (Mello) accidentally kills his girlfriend (Dawn) and goes to seek her in the Underworld. The wide appeal of this crude transposition of the Orpheus myth to modern Rio lies in its exoticism, vigorous dancing, exciting music and the frenetic atmosphere of the Rio carnival, not in the veiled social comment or the naive acting. Marpessa Dawn, the lovely Eurydice, was the director's wife.

Best Foreign Film Oscar 1959
Best Film Cannes 1959

Black Peter see Peter And Pavla

Black Shack Alley

Rue Cases Nègres

France 1983 106 mins col
Su Ma Fa Productions/Orca Productions/NEF Diffusion

d **Euzhan Palcy**
sc **Euzhan Palcy**
ph **Dominique Chapuis**
m **Groupe Malavoi**
Garry Cadenat, Darling Legitimus, Douta Seck, Joby Bernabe, Francisco Charles, Marie-Jo Descas

Young José (Cadenat), an orphan, lives with his grandmother (Legitimus) in Black Shack Alley, a collection of shacks attached to a cane plantation in Martinique. Grandma's ambition is to see the boy properly educated and thus able to escape the servitude of the plantation—an ambition which is finally realized, but at the cost of her life through overwork. The first full-length feature from documentary-maker Palcy is an extremely moving evocation of poverty, dreams and black struggle during the 1930s, as well as a beguiling and funny tale of childhood and of loving relationships. The director draws outstanding performances from her cast, notably the full-blooded and entrancing Darling Legitimus, and her handling of the children on the plantation and in José's school is first class.

Best Actress (Darling Legitimus) Venice 1983

Black Thursday see Gates Of The Louvre, The

The Black Tulip

La Tulipe Noir

France 1963 115 mins col
Mediterranée/Mizar/Agatha

d **Christian-Jaque**
sc **Christian-Jaque, Henri Jeanson, Paul Andreota, Marcello Ciorciolini**

ph **Henri Decaë**
m **Gerard Calvi**
Alain Delon, Virna Lisi, Akim Tamiroff, Dawn Addams, Francis Blanche, Adolfo Marsillach

In 1789, Guillaume De Saint-Preux, seemingly cynical and corrupt, is in reality the legendary Black Tulip, masked scourge of the monarchy. When he receives a savage gash across his cheek—a mark which will identify him as a wanted outlaw—he sends for Julien, his idealistic twin brother to continue his exploits. Alain Delon, whose blank pretty-boy features had been used effectively by directors such as Clément, Visconti and Antonioni, here attempts to take on the mantle and buckle on the sword of Gérard Philipe. He looks rather than feels the twin parts, in this overlong but reasonably diverting version of the Alexandre Dumas novel. Delon has the classic line in the dubbed version, 'The horse tossed me off!'.

Blade Of Satans Bog see Leaves From Satan's Book

Blanche

France 1971 92 mins col
Telepresses/Abel Et Charton

d **Walerian Borowczyk**
sc **Walerian Borowczyk**
ph **Guy Durban, André Dubreuil**
m **13th-century music**
Ligia Branice, Michel Simon, Jacques Perrin, Georges Wilson, Lawrence Trimble

Blanche (Branice), beautiful, young and innocent, is married off to an aged nobleman (Simon) who keeps her heavily guarded, but her stepson (Trimble), a page (Perrin) and the King (Wilson) manage to penetrate the castle. The Paris-based Polish animator's second live-action film began a series of erotic and decorative period pieces, usually set in the middle ages. Here, his pictorial sense—a two-dimensional design that gives the film the look of a tapestry or medieval painting—overcomes much of the tiresome tushery. Branice, the director's wife, compared to a white dove throughout, flutters gently and beautifully as the aptly named Blanche.

Blaue Engel, Der see Blue Angel, The

Blaue Licht, Das see Blue Light, The

Bláznova Kronika see Jester's Tale, A

Blechtrommel, Die see Tin Drum, The

Le Bled

France 1929 87 mins bw
Société Des Films Historiques

d **Jean Renoir**
sc **Henri Dupuy-Mazuel, André Jaeger-Schmidt**
ph **Marcel Lucien, Morizet**
m **Silent**
Enrique Rivero, Jackie Monnier, Arquillière, Diana Hart, Manuel Raaby

Pierre (Rivera), a young Frenchman, sailing to Algeria to join his prosperous farmer uncle, meets a young woman on the boat (Monnier). Once in his new country, he becomes romantically involved with her and, when she is abducted, he manages to rescue her, paving the way for 'happily-ever-after'. Made to celebrate the centenary of the first French colonists who settled in Algeria in 1830, this blatantly commercial film demonstrates that Renoir, quite early in his career, had the gift of breathing life into run-of-the-mill material. There is a dramatically staged climactic chase and the location photography is picturesque. This film marked the end of the great director's silent output.

Blé En Herbe, Le see Ripening Seed, The

Bleierne Zeit, Die see German Sisters, The

A Blonde Dream

Ein Blonder Traum

Germany 1932 87 mins bw
UFA

d **Paul Martin**
sc **Walter Reisch, Billy Wilder**
ph **Günther Rittau, Otto Baecker**
m **Werner R. Heymann**

Willy Fritsch, Lilian Harvey, Willi Forst, Paul Hörbiger

A young girl with film ambitions is cheated and robbed by a man pretending to be an American agent. Two window cleaners, both in love with her, come to her assistance. An effervescent comedy in which the doll-like Harvey sang and danced delightfully, and appeared in a mock-Expressionistic dream sequence of Hollywood. It was made at the same time in English in Germany with Jack Hulbert and Sonnie Hale replacing Fritsch and Forst, and retitled *Happy Ever After*.

A Blonde In Love

(US: Loves Of A Blonde)

Lásky Jedné Plavovlásky

Czechoslovakia 1965 82 mins bw
Barrandov Studios

d **Miloš Forman**
sc **Miloš Forman, Jaroslav Papoušek, Ivan Passer**
ph **Miroslav Ondřiček**
m **Evzen Illin**
Hana Brejchová, Vladimir Pucholt, Joseph Sebánek, Milada Jezkova

A shy, romantic factory girl (Brejchová) in a small town depleted of men, falls in love with a visiting young pianist (Pucholt), but is made unwelcome by his parents when she pursues him to Prague. Following up the success of his first feature, *Peter And Pavla* (1963), Forman again used a simple plot to show young people in conflict with their elders in this Oscar-nominated movie. His gently mocking humour and keen eye for the minutiae of human behaviour is best demonstrated in the delightful sequence when a group of middle-aged army reservists cause a flutter among the sex-starved girls at a dance.

Blonder Traum, Ein see Blonde Dream, A

Blood Of The Beasts

Le Sang Des Bêtes

France 1949 20 mins bw
Forces Et Voix De La France

d **Georges Franju**
sc **Georges Franju**
ph **Marcel Fradetal**
m **Joseph Kosma**

The daily slaughter of animals in an abattoir is juxtaposed with images of everyday life in Paris not long after the carnage of World War II. Franju's first film since he co-directed a short with Henri Langlois in 1934, shows in cold and vivid detail, as never before or since, 'the bleeding flesh dripping down the screen,' as Godard described it. Those who have managed to keep their eyes on the screen find it a powerful and moving statement. Franju, a non-vegetarian himself, forces carnivores to face the reality in which they are participants.

Blood Of The Condor

Yawar Mallku

Bolivia 1969 74 mins bw
Ukamau Limitada

d **Jorge Sanjines**
sc **Jorge Sanjines, Oscar Soria**
ph **Antonio Eguino**
m **Alberto Villalpando, Alfredo Dominguez, Gregorio Yana, Ignacio Quispe**
Marcelino Yanahuaya, Benedicta Mendoza Huanca, Vicente Salinas, and the people of the Kaata rural community

Ignacio (Yanahuaya), head of a small community of Quechua Indians, and his wife Paulina (Huanca), having lost their children through illness, are anxious to have more, but Paulina seems unable to conceive. Hearing that others have the same problem, Ignacio visits the American Progress Corps clinic where, to his horror, he learns that the Americans are sterilizing Indian women to keep the population down. The villagers' reaction to this discovery leads to bloodshed. Not surprisingly, the Bolivian government banned this film, releasing it only when forced to do so by vociferous protest campaigns. Simple, honest and direct, this account of the gap between cultures, classes and ideologies both grips and appals. Everybody portrayed here is victim of a system, and Sanjines, in making the movie, both exposed political corruption and revealed the dawning of a wider political consciousness in his country.

The Blood Of The Poet

Le Sang D'Un Poète

France 1930 58 mins bw
Vicomte De Noailles

d **Jean Cocteau**
sc **Jean Cocteau**
ph **Georges Périnal**
m **Georges Auric**
Lee Miller, Pauline Carton, Odette Talazac, Enrique Rivero, Jean Desbordes

A young poet passes through a mirror into a world where he sees a Mexican revolutionary executed and restored to life, opium smoking, a hermaphrodite, a boy killed in a snowball fight and living statues. Cocteau's first film, made when he was 41 and already famous, contains all the signs and symbols of his personal mythology evident in his poems, plays, novels and drawings. Thanks to the patronage of the Vicomte De Noailles, Cocteau was free to experiment with the new medium, exploring the creative process in arresting, dream-like images. Lacking the mastery of his later films, it nevertheless had a great influence; particularly on the American *avant-garde.*

Blood On The Land

To Homa Vaftike Kokkino

Greece 1965 120 mins bw
Finos Films

d **Vassilis Georgiades**
sc **Nicos Foscolos**
ph **Nicos Dimopoulos**
m **Mimis Plessas**
Nicos Courcoulos, Mary Chronopoulos, Yannis Voglis, Manos Katrakis

Peasants and landowners fight over land partition in the Greece of the early 1900s, and two enemy brothers fight over a woman. Despite some hair-tearing passions, and rather one-dimensional characterizations, this Oscar-nominated drama gets by on sincerity and some injection of genuine social consciousness. It was one of the last Greek films to be released before the military take-over in 1967 which led to a decline in creative film-making.

Blood Wedding

aka Red Wedding
(US: Wedding In Blood)
Les Noces Rouges

France 1973 90 mins col
La Boétie/Canaria

d **Claude Chabrol**
sc **Claude Chabrol**
ph **Jean Rabier**
m **Pierre Jansen**
Stéphane Audran, Michel Piccoli, Claude Piéplu, Eliana De Santis, Clotilde Joano

The mayor (Piéplu) of a small town in the Loire valley discovers that his wife (Audran) is having an affair with his deputy (Piccoli), and decides to blackmail the latter into going along with a crooked property deal. Another variation on Chabrol's pet theme of infidelity leading to murder is as elegant, cool and blackly humorous as one expects from a director secure in his subject.

Blood Wedding

Bodas De Sangre

Spain 1981 72 mins col
Emiliano Piedra

d **Carlos Saura**
sc **Carlos Saura, Antonio Gades**
ph **Teo Escamilla**
m **Emillo De Diego**
Antonio Gades, Cristina Joyas, Juan Antonio Jiminez, Pilar Cardenas

Antonio Gades and his troupe rehearse and perform a flamenco ballet version of Lorca's tragedy in a empty dance studio. Forget the Lorca play, as Gades has done, and thrill to the Andalusian passion expressed in the eloquent movements of the heel-tapping dance and soulful song of the flamenco, seen through the eye of a rhythmic camera.

Blow-Out

La Grande Bouffe

France 1973 130 mins col
Mara/Capitolina

d **Marco Ferreri**
sc **Marco Ferreri, Rafael Azcona**
ph **Mario Vulpiani**
m **Philippe Sarde**
Marcello Mastroianni, Philippe Noiret, Ugo Tognazzi, Michel Piccoli, Andréa Ferréol

Four middle-aged men—a pilot (Mastroianni), a judge (Noiret), a master chef (Tognazzi) and a TV personality (Piccoli)—bored with life, meet at a secluded villa in order literally to eat themselves to death. Only Buñuel might have brought off this attempt to demonstrate that men (and women, here represented by the statuesque Andréa Ferréol) are victims of their appetites. Ferreri uses shock tactics and excremental schoolboy humour to make a wearisome, excessive movie about excess. It did no harm at the box-office though.

Blow To The Heart

Colpire Al Cuore

Italy 1982 105 mins col
RAI/Antea Cinematografica

d **Gianni Amelio**
sc **Gianni Amelio, Vincenzo Cerami**
ph **Tonino Nardi**
m **Franco Piersanti**
Jean-Louis Trintignant, Laura Morante, Fausto Rossi, Sonia Gessner, Vanni Corbellini, Laura Nucci

Camera-mad teenager Emilio (Rossi), son of Dario (Trintignant), meets two young acquaintances of his father's, Sandro (Corbellini) and unmarried mother Giulia (Morante). Having photographed the pair and formed an attachment to Giulia, Emilio sees Sandro dead in the street after a terrorist shooting, which leads to his keeping his father and Giulia under surveillance... Amelio's film, fluent and beautifully judged, has the issue of terrorism hovering over it like a miasma, but does not explore it. The director is essentially concerned with family relationships, examining the consequences on an only child of parents who keep themselves at a distance. (His mother, perfectly played by Morante, is forever typing while wearing earphones that effectively isolate her.) If certain questions are left unanswered, this is nevertheless a gripping and intelligent movie.

The Blue Angel

Der Blaue Engel

Germany 1930 98 mins bw
UFA

d **Josef Von Sternberg**
sc **Robert Liebmann, Karl Zückmayer, Karl Vollmüller**
ph **Günther Rittau, Hans Schneeberger**
m **Friedrich Holländer**
Emil Jannings, Marlene Dietrich, Kurt Gerron, Hans Albers

Professor Unrath (Jannings), an aging and puritanical schoolteacher, becomes infatuated by and marries Lola-Lola (Dietrich), a nightclub singer who deceives and humiliates him. Commonly supposed to be Dietrich's first film, it was, in fact, the 28-year-old's seventeenth screen appearance. She had been a leading lady in B films and on stage when Sternberg, invited to Germany by Jannings to direct him in a screen version of Heinrich Mann's novel, saw potential sensuous, mysterious, glamorous star qualities in her. These qualities were fully exploited in the following six films he made with her in Hollywood. Her Lola-Lola, sitting on a chair huskily singing 'Falling In Love Again', in top hat, black stockings, bare thighs, clutching her knee, encapsulates an age and an impulse of German cinema. Beside her, Jannings, in his first talkie, seems out of date, though his crowing like a cock is a startling moment.

Bluebeard see Landru

The Blue Light

Das Blaue Licht

Germany 1932 77 mins bw
Sokal/Leni Riefestahl Film

d **Leni Riefenstahl**
sc **Leni Riefenstahl, Béla Balázs**
ph **Hans Schneeberger**
m **Giuseppe Becce**
Leni Riefenstahl, Max Holzboer, Mathias Wieman, Beni Führer

A painter (Wieman) falls in love with a young girl (Riefenstahl) thought to be a witch because she alone in the Dolomite village can reach the top of a dangerous peak. When he discovers her secret route, she jumps to her death. Riefenstahl had appeared in four of Arnold Fanck's mountain films, and her first venture as a director was in a similar romantic vein, shot on location and emphasizing a Germanic mystical union with nature. It impressed Hitler so much that he asked her to make films for the Nazi party.

Blue Mountains

Golubye Gory Ely Nepravdopodobnaya Istoria

USSR 1983 97 mins col
Gruziafilm Studios

d **Eldar Shengalaya**
sc **Rezo Cheishvili**
ph **Levan Paatashvili**
m **Giya Kancheli**
R. Giorgobiani, V. Kakhniashvili, T. Chirgadze, D. Sumbatashvili, I. Sakvarelidze

Soso (Giorgobiani) arrives at a publishing company in a Georgian town to submit the manuscript of his new novel. It is autumn. Everybody appears interested, but their other concerns—will, for example, a picture fall off the wall on to an elderly editor's head?—prevent them from reading it. Winter comes, then Spring, then Summer. Still Soso haunts the offices, still nobody reads the book... The joke starts wearing thin around summmer time and the ending is a little weak, but *Blue Mountains* is an anarchic and witty satire about the plight of the artist as victim. The decaying publishing house, which eventually crumbles away, is a splendid metaphor for bureaucracy, the movie is alive with dotty action, and the characterizations are splendidly detailed.

The Blue Veil

Le Voile Bleu

France 1942 90 mins bw
CGC

d **Jean Stelli**
sc **François Camaux**
ph **René Caveau**
m **A. Theurer**
Gaby Morlay, Elvire Popesco, Marcelle Géniat, Charpin, Larquey

A World War I widow (Morlay), whose child dies at birth, becomes a governess and devotes her life to the care of other people's children, even to the point of giving up a lover to be near her charges. Popular French star Gaby Morlay had them crying in the aisles with this unashamedly sentimental story. Although soppy, it does contain scenes of real pathos, and it is beautifully played. Hollywood didn't have to alter much in its 1951 remake starring Jane Wyman. The title refers to the head-dress of the governess.

Blushing Charlie

Lyckliga Skitar

Sweden 1970 96 mins col
Sandrew

d **Vilgot Sjöman**
sc **Vilgot Sjöman, Bernt Lundquist, Solveig Ternström**
ph **Rune Ericson**
m **Christer Boustedt, Lasse Werner, Gösta Wälivaara, Jan Carlsson**
Bernt Lundquist, Solveig Ternström, Lilian Johansson, Janet Petterson, Tomas Bolme

Charlie (Lundquist), a confirmed bachelor, lives on a barge, drives a lorry for a living and, at weekends, drinks with jazz musician friends and chases after bunny girls. However, when pregnant Pia (Ternström) arrives to stay, Charlie, now involved in Left-wing politics, decides he'd like to marry her. Sjöman, following the recipe of his passingly notorious *I Am Curious-Yellow*, again makes a bid to combine frank sexual exploration and politics, resulting in a film which, although photographed with an excess of lyricism, is convincingly acted and directed until the hard-to-swallow dénouement.

The Boat

Das Boot

W. Germany 1981 150 mins col
Bavaria Atelier/Radiant Film

d **Wolfgang Petersen**
sc **Wolfgang Petersen**
ph **Jöst Vacano**
m **Klaus Doldinger**
Jürgen Prochnow (The Captain), Herbert Grönemeyer, Klaus Wennemann, Hubertus Bengsch

In 1941, a German U-Boat goes on a dangerous mission from La Rochelle to Spain and back, hunted by Allied depth charges and air raids. At $12 million, the most expensive German film to date is a compendium of every submarine movie ever made, with all the expected claustrophobic horrors. Its main interest is not in the flat characterizations of the 'good' German crew—there is only one despised Nazi on board—but in the spectacular handheld camerawork, accurately depicting conditions under water. It was nominated for six Academy Awards.

The Boat Is Full

Das Boot Ist Voll

Switzerland 1981 100 mins col
Limbo Film/SRG/ZDF/ORF

d **Markus Imhoof**
sc **Markus Imhoof**
ph **Hans Liechti**
Tina Engel, Curt Bois, Hans Diehl, Martin Walz, Ilse Bahis, Gerd David

A group of Jewish refugees of all ages struggle to escape the Nazis across the Swiss border. They make it, only to be sent back to the waiting Germans by the Swiss in the village where they fetch up. Stylistically muted and unadorned, but with the camera picking up a complexity of small, telling detail, Imhoof's film is totally absorbing and quite chilling. What is different from other films of similar plot is that this is not so much an escape story or a memoir of victims of Nazi persecution, as an exposé of ordinary people's attitudes—bewilderment, suspicion, neutrality, hostility—to refugees whose plight they simply fail to comprehend. The acting is superb, notably from Tina Engel of Peter Stein's theatre company, and the 80-year-old veteran star, Curt Bois.

Bob Le Flambeur see Bob The Gambler

Bob The Gambler

Bob Le Flambeur

France 1955 100 mins bw
Jenner/Cyme/Play Art/OGC

d **Jean-Pierre Melville**
sc **Jean-Pierre Melville, Auguste Le Breton**
ph **Henri Decaë**
m **Eddie Barclay, Jean Boyer**
Roger Duchesne, Isabelle Corey, Daniel Cauchy, Howard Vernon, Gérard Buhr, André Garret, Guy Decomble

Bob (Duchesne), a retired bank robber and inveterate gambler, has an unlucky streak, so he decides to mastermind a raid on the casino at Deauville. Melville's first original script and first entry into the world of *film noir* is an ironical variation on the plot of his favourite picture, John Huston's *The Asphalt Jungle* (1950). What is astonishing is how much its gritty, free-wheeling camera style and location shooting predates the French New Wave. Everything is already here, the jump cuts, the jazzy score, and the visual quotes. At the film's centre is Bob, the 'aging young man', played soulfully by Duchesne, masterfully expressing the man's moral code. Narrated by the director (billed merely as Melville), it reverberates with the atmosphere of the mean streets and brash nightclubs around Place Pigalle between dusk and dawn.

Boccaccio 70

Italy 1962 210 mins col
CCC/Cineriz/Francinex/TCF

d **1) Federico Fellini 2) Luchino Visconti 3) Vittorio De Sica**
sc **1)Federico Fellini, Tullio Pinelli, Ennio Flaiano 2) Luchino Visconti, Suso Cecchi D'Amico 3) Cesare Zavattini**
ph **1) and 3) Otello Martelli 2) Giuseppe Rotunno**
m **1) and 2) Nino Rota 3) Armando Trovaioli**
1) Anita Ekberg, Peppino De Filippo 2) Romy Schneider, Tomas Milian 3) Sophia Loren, Luigi Gillianni

1) A large, sexy model comes down from her billboard advertising milk to pursue a little puritan who campaigned against it. 2) A wife, on learning that her husband visits brothels, decides to charge him massive fees for her services. 3) A desirable woman offers herself as a prize in a raffle at a funfair, fixing the draw so a country bumpkin can win. Three of Italy's major directors (a fourth episode by Mario Monicelli was cut from most foreign prints) provided three minor stories for a modern Decameron. They are respectively broad, dull and vulgar, but with Ekberg and Loren in the cast there are, to paraphrase Howard Hughes, four good reasons to see the picture.

Bodas De Sangre see Blood Wedding

Bokhandlaren Som Slutade Bada see Bookseller Who Gave Up Bathing, The

---

Bokser see Boxer, The

Bolchaia Semia see Big Family, A

Bold Adventure, The see Adventures Of Till Eulenspiegel, The

Bombay Our City

Hamara Shaher

India 1985 82 mins col
Anand Patwardhan

d **Anand Patwardhan**
ph **Ranjan Palit, Anand Patwardhan**
m **Aavhan Natya Manch**

Called by the *Times of India* 'quite clearly the best documentary ever made' in that country, Patwardhan's film allows the city and its people to speak for themselves in both words and pictures, without formal scripting or narration. The result is an intelligent and sympathetic examination of frailty, injustice, greed and complacency that has the unmistakable ring of truth. The camera catches several haunting images, such as that of people cooking their evening meal on the pavements against the glittering backdrop of the city at night, while a street voice sings of why 'we left our villages and came here'.

Bona

Philippines 1981 83 mins col
G.N.V. Productions

d **Lino Brocka**
sc **Cenen Reamones**
ph **Conrado Baltazar**
m **Max Jocson**
Nora Aunor, Phillip Salvador, Rustica Carpio, Venchito Galvez, Nanding Josef

Eighteen-year-old Bona (Aunor) is infatuated with Gardo (Salvador), a bit player in movies, a womanizer and a violent lout. When she sees him set upon by some youths with a grudge, she goes home with him and stays overnight to tend his wounds. As a consequence her father beats her up, so she moves in with Gardo, caring for him with absolute devotion while his treatment of her becomes increasingly appalling. That the credibility of this film is not shaken when Bona, after an inordinately long time suddenly comes to grips with her self-imposed ordeal and shows a bit of mettle, is a tribute to the Philippines' foremost film-maker. Working from a tight script, Brocka makes the most of the highly dramatic moments and offers a vivid portrayal of community life in the poorer quarters of Manila. The film was financed by leading lady Aunor, the Philippines' most popular actress.

Le Bonheur

aka Happiness

France 1965 79 mins col
Parc

d **Agnès Varda**
sc **Agnès Varda**
ph **Jean Rabier, Claude Beausoleil**
m **Mozart**
Jean-Claude Drouot, Marie-France Boyer, Claire Drouot, Sandrine and Olivier Drouot

A young carpenter wants his wife to accept that he can be happily married and, at the same time, love his mistress. When his wife drowns herself, he lives happily ever after with his mistress and his two children. The idyllic colour landscapes, advertisement-style prettiness, and Mozart's music created an ambiguity and ironic reflection on the film's title, but also swamped its statement about an extended family. Its amorality provoked controversy, added to which the male lead's real-life family played his wife and children.

Special Jury Prize Berlin 1965

La Bonne Année

(US: Happy New Year)

France 1973 115 mins col
Les Films 13(Paris)/Rizzoli Film(Rome)

d **Claude Lelouch**
sc **Claude Lelouch, Pierre Uytterhoeven**
ph **Claude Lelouch**
m **Francis Lai**
Lino Ventura, Françoise Fabian, Charles Gérard, Michou, André Falcon, Mireille Mathieu, Silvano Tranquilli

Paroled from prison, jewel thief Simon (Ventura) who robbed the Cannes branch of Van Cleef and Arpels, arranges a reunion with his mistress, Françoise (Fabian). Meanwhile, he sets out to look for his accomplice, which leads him to recall the past events. Lelouch provides both a heist movie in which he nicely maintains the tension, and a love story about the attraction of opposites—Simon earthy, monogamous and uneducated, Françoise fashionable, liberated and intellectual. An entertaining movie, which begins with the convicts watching *A Man And A Woman*: partly the director's joke at his own expense, partly his comment on a changed social climate.

Les Bonnes Femmes

aka The Girls

France 1960 102 mins bw
Paris/Panitalia/Hakim

d **Claude Chabrol**
sc **Paul Gégauff**
ph **Henri Decaë**
m **Paul Misraki, Pierre Jansen**
Bernadette Lafont, Stéphane Audran, Clothilde Joano, Lucile Saint-Simon, Claude Berri, Mario David

Four shop girls long to escape their monotonous existence: Ginette (Audran) sings at a tatty music hall, Jane (Lafont) simply wants a good time, Rita (Saint-Simon) drifts into a *bourgeois* marriage, and Jacqueline (Joano) yearns for romantic love, but is strangled by a sex murderer in the woods. Chabrol's early masterpiece offers a gallery of grotesques, macabre and farcical humour, but also poetry and tenderness. The mixture of compassion for the girls and contempt for their dreams created an ironic structure that disturbed the majority of critics when it first appeared, forcing Chabrol into making a series of potboilers.

La Bonne Soupe

(US: Careless Love)

France 1963 100 mins bw
Belstar/Dear/Du Siècle

d **Robert Thomas**
sc **Robert Thomas**
ph **Roger Hubert**
m **Raymond Le Sénéchal**
Marie Bell, Annie Girardot, Claude Dauphin, Jean-Claude Brialy, Raymond Pellegrin, Franchot Tone, Christian Marquand, Bernard Blier, Daniel Gélin, Gérard Blain, Sacha Distel

An aging woman tells the story of how she was seduced as a girl by a salesman, became a kept woman, married for money, made love to her son-in- law, and ended up a high-class prostitute. Felicien Marceau's hit boulevard comedy provided the source for this old-hat frolic, allowing a number of leading French actors (and Franchot Tone) to make passes at Marie Bell and Annie Girardot (as Bell's younger self). A sort of sexy version of *Un Carnet De Bal* in which Madame Bell had starred 26 years previously.

The Bookseller Who Gave Up Bathing

Bokhandlaren Som Slutade Bada

Sweden 1968 99 mins col
Sandrew

d **Jarl Kulle**
sc **Jarl Kulle**
ph **Rune Ericson**
m **Ulf Björlin**
Allan Edwall, Margaretha Krook, Jarl Kulle, Nils Eklund, Ingvar Kjellson

Middle-aged bachelor bookseller Jacob (Edwall) falls in love with sexy, sophisticated Amélie (Krook), a widow who has been living in France. They marry, Jacob gives up his Sunday afternoons at the river with his friends and the couple is blissfully happy until Amélie's brother reveals her past as a whore. Actor Jarl Kulle, well-known to followers of the Swedish cinema, made his directing debut with this bitter-sweet film in which tranquillity and nostalgia rub shoulders with sensual passion and farcical comedy. Jacob and his friend Krakow (Kulle), desperately trying to preserve life as a set of dreams and illusions, are poignantly realized in a beautifully controlled film, well acted and splendid to look at.

Boomerang

Bulgaria 1979 90 mins col
Bulgarofilm, Sofia

d **Ivan Nichev**
sc **Svoboda Bucharova, Jenny Radeva**
ph **Victor Chichov**
m **Kiril Tsiboulka**
Lyuben Chatalov, Yavov Spassov, Nikolai Binev, Katya Paskaleva, Krassimira Damyanova

Mihail (Chatalov), recently graduated from Sofia University's journalism school, is determined to break into the highest professional and social echelons with a minimum of sacrifice, avoiding the usual period of probation in the provinces. How he cons his way into relationships that can advance him—notably with a clapped-out but influential novelist (Binev)—forms the substance of the plot. A sharp screenplay and perceptive direction give an inside view of the rat race in Bulgaria, surprisingly similar to our own, and probes the weaknesses of the political regime. Well- delineated characters are portrayed by an extremely accomplished cast, notably Chatalov as the handsome, arrogant Mihail, who becomes increasingly enmeshed in his own moral turpitude, causing his schemes to 'boomerang'.

Boot, Das see Boat, The

Boot Ist Voll, Das see Boat Is Full, The

Border Street
Ulica Graniczna

Poland 1948 110 mins bw
Film Polski

d **Alexsander Ford**
sc **Ludwik Starski, Alexsander Ford, Jan Fethke**
ph **Jaroslav Tuzar**
m **Roman Palester**
Maria Broniewska, Mieczyslawa Ćwiklińska, Jerzy Lesczyński, Wladyslaw Godik, Wladyslaw Walter

The lives of several families from different social classes in a neighbourhood of pre-war Warsaw are changed by the tragic events of the period. The respected doctor's family has to move into the Jewish ghetto, the father of an upper-class family joins the Resistance, and another family becomes pro-Nazi. The film climaxes with the Warsaw ghetto uprising. One of the first of a cluster of Polish films that emerged from the rubble of the war, it was made by an established pre-war director and a founder of Film Polski in 1945. In 1936, his *Street Of Youth*, which tried to reconcile Polish and Jewish youth, was banned. This one, returning to the theme with far more passion and anger, is marred by rather broad characterizations and rhetorical gestures, but the final sequences are well staged and the message got through to a wide audience in and outside Poland.

Borsalino

France 1970 128 mins col
Adel/Marianne/Mars

d **Jacques Deray**
sc **Jacques Deray, Jean-Claude Carrière, Claude Sautet, Jean Cau**
ph **Jean-Jacques Tarbes**
m **Claude Bolling**
Jean-Paul Belmondo, Alain Delon, Michel Bouquet, Catherine Rouvel, Corinne Marchand

In the Marseilles of the 1930s, two petty crooks join up and rise in the underworld until they control all meat supplies. The teaming of two of France's biggest box-office stars was a good commercial bet (Delon was the producer), and pre-dated buddy-buddy gangster movies like *The Sting* (1973). The two leads with tongues-in-cheek and borsalino hats on heads, the jazz score, and the period detail, passed most of the time agreeably enough. There was a less popular sequel, *Borsalino And Co* (1974).

Boucher, Le see Butcher, The

Boudu Sauvé Des Eaux see Boudu Saved From Drowning

Boudu Saved From Drowning
Boudu Sauvé Des Eaux

France 1932 87 mins bw
Haik/CCF

d **Jean Renoir**
sc **Jean Renoir**
ph **Marcel Lucien**
m **Raphael, Johann Strauss**
Michel Simon, Charles Grandval, Marcelle Hainia, Jean Dasté, Severine Lerczinska, Jacques Becker

A tramp, saved from drowning by a bookseller and taken into the latter's home, sets about seducing his rescuer's wife and mistress (the maid), before retreating thankfully to the banks of the Marne. The last and best of the four films that Renoir made with the extraordinary simian-faced Michel Simon, it is an exhilarating mixture of farce and drama through which runs the spirit of anarchy fighting *bourgeois* convention. The sense of Paris in the summer is heightened by the deep focus photography and direct sound.

Boule De Suif

Pyshka

USSR 1934 65 mins bw
Mosfilm

d **Mikhail Romm**
sc **Mikhail Romm**
ph **Boris Volchok**
m **Silent**
Galina Sergeyeva, Anatoli Goryunov, P. Repnin, Faina Ranevskaya, Andrei Fait

A Russian-made version of De Maupassant's famous short story attacking hypocrisy and selfishness, as demonstrated by the fate that befalls a brave and good-hearted prostitute known as Boule De Suif (Sergeyeva). During the Franco-Prussian War of 1870 she travels on a stagecoach with a group of aristocrats, merchants and their wives, and saves them from the threats of a Prussian officer by bestowing her favours on him. For this act, which the group was happy to encourage and accept, she is scorned and disdained. Sticking to the letter of the original, Romm also comes admirably close to capturing the French spirit in a compact, straightforward adaptation. Stylishly made and with a well-cast leading lady, it was the director's first film as well as the last of the Russian silents.

Boule De Suif

France 1945 105 mins bw
Artis Film

d **Christian-Jaque**
sc **Henri Jeanson**
ph **Lucienne Chevert**
m **Maurice Paul Guillot**
Micheline Presle, Louis Salou, Alfred Adam, Suzet Mais, Roger Karl, Marcel Simon, Brochard

This is a workmanlike adaptation of De Maupassant's story of a prostitute in the Franco-Prussian war (see above), with a sympathetic and dignified Micheline Presle impressive in the title role. In this version, however, writer and director have cleverly combined plot elements from De Maupassant's other well-known work of the period, *Mademoiselle Fifi*, thus giving Boule De Suif an opportunity to take some audience-satisfying revenge on the Prussian officer to whom she is forced to give herself. The film had a strong impact at the time of its release because of its unmistakable resonances of World War II and the Nazi occupation of France.

Boxer see Boxer, The

The Boxer

Bokser

Poland 1967 96 mins bw
Polski Film/Start

d **Julian Dziedzina**
sc **Bohdan Tomaszewski**
ph **Mikolaj Sprudin**
Daniel Olbrychski, Leszek Drogosz, Tadeusz Kalinowski, Malgorzata Wlodarska

A young blacksmith (Olbrychski), who has gained early recognition as an amateur boxer of outstanding talent, looks back over his tempestuous career as he waits in the dressing room for his Olympic final. Like his compatriot, Jerzy Skolimowski, who made *Walkover* two years previously, Dziedzina deals with the amateur side of the pet sport of the movies, showing it as far more skilful than brutal but no less exciting. The atmosphere of the arena at the Mexican Olympics is well caught, and 22-year-old Olbrychski (soon to become the favourite actor of Andrzej Wajda), using no stand-ins, is convincing as the boxer.

The Boxer

Boxer

Japan 1977 95 mins col
Toei

d **Shuji Terayama**
sc **Shuji Terayama, Shiro Ishimori, Rio Kishida**
ph **Tatsuo Susuki**
m **J.A. Seazer**
Kentaro Shimizu, Bunta Sugawara

A retired boxer (Sugawara) leaves his wife and child in order to train a young featherweight (Shimizu) for the title. The experience Terayama gained as a sports writer before he became a theatre and film director came in useful for this drama of the ring, made to capitalize on the huge success of *Rocky* the year before. However, despite its surface resemblance to the Stallone hit—it also builds up to a big fight finale—the film has far more psychological insight, and there are also inserted tributes to great Japanese champions of the past. Pop singer Shimizu is dynamic in the lead, while most other roles are taken by members of Terayama's theatre group.

Boy
Shonen

Japan 1969 97 mins col
Sozosha/ATG

d **Nagisa Oshima**
sc **Tsutomu Tamura**
ph **Yasuhiro Yoshioka**
m **Hikaru Hayashi**
Tetsuo Abe, Fumio Watanabe, Akiko Koyama

A 10-year-old boy is trained by his parents to be knocked down by cars so that they can demand money from the frightened drivers before moving on to the next town. Structurally more conventional than Oshima's previous films, it is, nevertheless, an unusual story, taken from an actual case and told with remarkable social and psychological insight. The acting, the colour and the CinemaScope screen are all handled in a masterly manner.

Boy Meets Girl

France 1984 100 mins bw
Abilene

d **Leos Carax**
sc **Leos Carax**
ph **Jean-Yves Éscoffier**
m **Jacques Pinault**
Denis Lavant, Mireille Périer, Carroll Brooks, Elie Poicard, Anna Baldaccini

After breaking up with Florence (Baldaccini), the rootless Alex (Lavant), obsessed with a need for romantic fulfilment, falls in love with Mireille (Périer), but their attachment is doomed to fail. With his first feature, 22-year-old Carax joined Jean-Jacques Beineix, another precocious director, as one of France's brightest hopes. Shot in dazzling black and white in nocturnal Paris, and with the strange brooding personality of Denis Lavant (he plays the same role in Carax's second film *The Night Is Young*, 1986), the film, though hugely derivative—especially of early Godard—shows great promise. The appropriately simple title (the original given in English) reveals both the lack of plot and a nice sense of irony.

The Boys From Fengkuei
aka All The Youthful Days
Feng-Kuei-Lai-Te jen

Taiwan 1983 104 mins col
Evergreen Film Company

d **Hou Hsiao-hsien**
sc **Zhu Tianwen**
ph **Chen Kunhou**
m **Bach, Vivaldi**
Niu Cheng-tse, Lin Xiuling, To Tsung-hua, Chang Shih

Three youths leave the small fishing village of Fengkuei, where they have grown up, to look for a more exciting life in the city of Kaohsiung. With no idea of what to expect and no sense of responsibility, they embrace all the experiences, both joyful and painful, that come their way, earning a living doing menial jobs in an export processing plant. This film, which would automatically be referred to as a rites-of-passage piece in the West, demonstrates a coming of age in the Taiwanese film industry. The exuberant and sincere central performances convince and involve, and the piece has an altogether more modern and universal approach than Taiwanese movies of a few years before. It is enjoyable, interesting and directed with sophistication by a director making his fourth feature.

Boys' School see Disparus De St Agil, Les

Božská Ema see Divine Emma, The

Bratya Karamazovy see Brothers Karamazov, The

Brave Soldat Schwejk, Der see Good Soldier Schweik, The

Bread And Chocolate
Pane E Cioccolata
Italy 1974 112 mins col
Verona Cinematografica

d **Franco Brusati**
sc **Franco Brusati, Iaia Fiastri, Nino Manfredi**
ph **Luciano Tovoli**
m **Daniele Patrucchi**
Nino Manfredi, Anna Karina, Johnny Dorelli, Paolo Turco

An uneducated working man (Manfredi) from Naples gets a job as a waiter at a smart hotel in Switzerland, but is arrested as an illegal immigrant, and accused of indecent exposure and murder. An amusing and touching illustration of a culture clash, and a graphic depiction of a complacent and condescending Switzerland, occasionally ruined by too much sugar in the mixture.

Bread, Love, And Dreams
Pane, Amore, E Fantasia
Italy 1953 90 mins bw
Titanus

d **Luigi Comencini**
sc **Luigi Comencini**
ph **Arturo Gallea**
m **Alessandro Cicognini**
Vittorio De Sica, Gina Lollobrigida, Marisa Merlini, Roberto Risso

In a small rural village, the new sergeant of police (De Sica), hoping to get married, chases the midwife (Merlini) and the local spitfire (Lollobrigida), who is in love with his deputy (Risso). In the early 1950s this fast-moving comedy seemed awfully saucy and elemental, but now comes across as tame and artificial. De Sica is amusing enough though, and the film brought La Lollo to the world's attention. Being the top Italian money-maker up to that time, it naturally engendered a sequel, *Bread, Love And Jealousy* (1954), with the same director and cast.

Bread, Love And Jealousy
Pane, Amore E Gelosia
Italy 1954 98 mins bw
Titanus

d **Luigi Comencini**
sc **Luigi Comencini, Vincenzo Talarico, Ettore Margadonna**
ph **Carlo Montuori**
m **Alessandro Cicognini**
Gina Lollobrigida, Vittorio De Sica, Marisa Merlini Roberto Risso

In a mountain village, the engagement of the police sergeant (De Sica) to the midwife (Merlini), and that of the local beauty (Lollobrigida) to the sergeant's deputy (Risso) are endangered by gossiping and suspicious neighbours. Partners are switched, an unknown father turns up, and one of the women lands in jail. A mildly amusing, likeable and well-observed follow-up to *Bread, Love, And Dreams* has some lively playing by 'La Lollo' and De Sica. More *Bread, Love...* films ensued, but they got less and less nourishing.

Breakup, The see Rupture, La

Breathless
À Bout De Souffle
France 1960 90 mins bw
SNC

d **Jean-Luc Godard**
sc **Jean-Luc Godard**
ph **Raoul Coutard**
m **Martial Solal**
Jean-Paul Belmondo, Jean Seberg, Daniel Boulanger, Jean-Pierre Melville

A young car thief kills a policeman and goes on the run with his American girlfriend. Godard's first feature, from an idea by François Truffaut and dedicated to Monogram Pictures (Hollywood's all-B movie studio), attempted to recapture the directness and economy of the American gangster movie. This was superbly achieved by the use of a handheld camera, often with the cameraman in a wheelchair, location shooting, and jump cuts which eliminated the usual establishing shots so that the film lives up to its title. This greatly influential picture made the anarchic Belmondo a star, revitalized Seberg's career, and established Godard as a leading member of the *Nouvelle Vague*.

Der Brennende Acker

Best Director Berlin 1960

Brennende Acker, Der see Burning Earth, The

Breve Vacanza, Una see Brief Vacation, A

The Bride Wore Black

La Mariée Était En Noir

France 1967 107 mins col

Films Du Carrosse/Artistes Associés/De Laurentiis

d **François Truffaut**
sc **François Truffaut, Jean-Louis Richard**
ph **Raoul Coutard**
m **Bernard Herrmann**
Jeanne Moreau, Jean-Claude Brialy, Michel Bouquet, Charles Denner, Claude Rich, Michel Lonsdale, Daniel Boulanger

After a bridegroom is shot on the steps of the church on his wedding day, his widow (Moreau) traces the group of men responsible and eliminates them one by one. Truffaut's most direct homage to Hitchcock was based, like *Rear Window*, on a novel by William Irish (Cornell Woolrich), and uses Hitch's frequent and distinctive composer, Bernard Herrmann. The result is slacker, more episodic and far more implausible than the Master would have allowed but still highly entertaining in itself. The glossy locales and splendid cameos from the victims give sturdy support to Moreau's intelligent performance as a meticulous avenging angel.

The Bridge

Die Brücke

W. Germany 1959 106 mins bw

Fono/Jochen Severin

d **Bernhard Wicki**
sc **Michael Mansfield, Karl-Wilhelm Vivier**
ph **Gerd Von Bönen**
m **Hans-Martin Majewski**
Volker Bohnet, Fritz Wepper, Franz Glaubrecht, Karl Michael Balzer, Günther Hoffman

In 1945, two days before the end of the war, seven schoolboys are drafted into the dregs of Hitler's army to defend an unimportant bridge against American tanks, which they do to the death. This powerful anti-war film, made in a semi-documentary style, was based on a true episode. One of the few good movies to come out of Germany in the 1950s, it was nominated for an Oscar.

Brief Encounters see Short Encounters

A Brief Vacation

Una Breve Vacanza

Italy 1973 106 mins col

Verona/Azor

d **Vittorio De Sica**
sc **Cesare Zavattini**
ph **Giulio Battiferri**
m **Manuel De Sica**
Florinda Bolkan, Renato Salvatori, Daniel Quenaud, José Maria Prada, Teresa Gimpera

A Milanese factory worker (Bolkan), leading a squalid life with her macho husband (Salvatori) and children, contracts a lung disease and is sent to a sanatorium in the Alps. There she leads a happier life and discovers her true worth. Based on Apollinaire's epigram that 'sickness is the vacation of the poor,' De Sica's penultimate film reveals the deep humanist values which permeate most of his work. With Zavattini, his collaborator from way back, a gorgeous alpine setting and fine performances, especially from Bolkan, and allowing for some soap operatics, it is an appealing film with an effective feminist message.

Brightness

Yeelen

Mali 1987 105 mins col

Les Films Cissé/Government of Mali

d **Souleymane Cissé**
sc **Souleymane Cissé**
ph **Jean-Noël Ferragut, Jean-Michel Humeau**
m **Michel Portal, Salif Keita**
Issiaka Kané, Aova Sangere, Niamanto Sanogo, Soumba Traoré, Ismaïla Sarr, Balla Moussa Keïta

A young man (Kané), granted special magical powers, flees his jealous father (Sanogo) who plans to kill him. During the journey, the boy gains the wisdom with which to confront his father. A remarkably strange and beautiful film which draws us into the world of African ritual and legend. Some of the symbols might be obscure for those outside the culture, but there's no discounting their visual power. The performances, particularly that of the extremely handsome hero, are uniformly mesmeric.

Brink Of Life see So Close To Life

Broken Commandment, The see Sin, The

Broken Mirrors

Gebroken Spiegels

Netherlands 1984 116 mins col
Sigma Films

d **Marleen Gorris**
sc **Marleen Gorris**
ph **Frans Bromet**
m **Lodewijk De Boer, and an extract from Haydn's *Stabat Mater***
Lineke Rijxman, Henriette Tol, Edda Barends, Coby Stunnenberg, Anke Van't Hoff, Eddy Brugman

A sadistic killer kidnaps women and dumps their corpses on waste ground. In the Happy House brothel, presided over by a madame who keeps a gun, the women are united in their dislike of their work and their low opinion of men. This is, of necessity, a summary of the bare bones of a complex plot which focuses on certain relationships with absolute clarity, and whose parallel strands meet for the denouement. Using some of the same cast and the cameraman from *A Question Of Silence* made two years previously, writer-director Gorris here displays the same gifts of control and commitment, developed with intelligence and efficiency to create an absorbing and disturbing film. However, unlike its predecessor, this one is strident in its feminist message, transmitting violent and indiscriminate anti-male attitudes which, ultimately, undermine its own case and leave the viewer depressed rather than encouraged.

Bronenosets Potemkin see Battleship Potemkin, The

The Brontë Sisters

Les Soeurs Brontë

France 1979 115 mins col
Gaumont

d **André Téchiné**
sc **André Téchiné, Pascal Bonitzer, Jean Gruault**
ph **Bruno Nuytten**
m **Philippe Sarde**
Isabelle Adjani, Isabelle Huppert, Marie-France Pisier, Pascal Greggory, Patrick Magee

Emily (Adjani), Charlotte (Pisier) and Anne (Huppert) lead an isolated, claustrophobic life at the Haworth rectory in Yorkshire with their father (Magee) and brother Branwell (Greggory). Tragedy occurs when the latter, after a doomed affair with an older woman, turns to drink and drugs before dying at the age of 31. The decision to concentrate the plot around the sisters' relationship with their spoiled-genius brother would seem one way of avoiding the difficulties of presenting the tormented trio of writers on screen. Not so. The sluggish direction, and the almost caricature notion of what the Brontës were about—Emily spends her time stalking the moors in drag—cancel out the careful re-creation of period. The only interest comes from seeing three of France's most talented young actresses together. Lovers of kitsch are better advised to see the Hollywood version of 1946 called *Devotion*.

Brot Des Bäckers, Das see Baker's Bread

A Brother And His Younger Sister

Ani To Song Imoto

Japan 1939 100 mins bw
Shochiku

d **Yasujiro Shimazu**
sc **Yasujiro Shimazu**
ph **Toshio Ubukata**
m **Hikaru Saotome**

Shin Saburi, Michiko Kuwano, Kuniko Miyake, Ken Uehara

The unmarried sister (Kuwano) of an office worker (Saburi) turns down a marriage proposal from the nephew (Uehara) of her brother's boss. She thinks that acceptance might damage her brother's prospects of promotion as the company is opposed to nepotism. Shimazu is considered the father of the 'home dramas' perfected by Ozu, Naruse and his pupil Gosho, and this typical drama of ordinary people is one of the best—and last—examples of his work in the genre. The rigidly conventional characters are not given much depth, but the small details of their domestic lives are carefully and lovingly drawn and the subtle shifts in mood give the narrative variety.

The Brothers Karamazov

aka The Murder Of Dmitri Karamazov

Bratya Karamazovy

USSR 1968 220 mins col
Mosfilm

d **Ivan Pyriev**
sc **Ivan Pyriev**
ph **Sergei Vronsky**
m **Isaac Schwartz**
Mikhail Ulianov, Lionella Pyrieva, Kirill Lavrov, Andrei Myahkov, Marc Prudkin

The effect of the murder of a dominating father on the lives of his three sons: the hedonistic Dmitri (Ulianov), the sceptical intellectual Ivan (Lavrov) and the devout Alyosha (Myahkov). Pyriev did not live to see the completion of his Dostoyevsky trilogy after *The Idiot* and *White Nights*, because he died during the making of this handsomely-mounted, extremely faithful (almost too much so) wide-screen adaptation of the great 19th-century novel, which had been filmed rather broadly 10 years before in Hollywood. It was completed by Ulianov and Lavrov, who both gave powerful performances. The film, released in the USA, was Oscar-nominated.

Brücke, Die see Bridge, The

Bruhaban see Sunday Romance, A

Bruno, L'Enfant Du Dimanche see Bruno - Sunday's Child

Bruno - Sunday's Child

Bruno, L'Enfant Du Dimanche

France 1968 90 mins col
Pro-Gé-Fi/Consortium Pathé/ Sirius (Paris)/Arthur Mathonet (Brussels)

d **Louis Grospierre**
sc **Alain Quercy, Louis Grospierre**
ph **Quinto Albicocco**
m **Jean-Pierre Bourtayre**
Christian Mesnier, Roger Hanin, Lena Skerla, Francine Bergé, Mary Marquet

Thirteen-year-old Bruno (Mesnier), whose parents' divorce is about to come through, sees his father (Hanin), whom he adores, one Sunday in each month but, during the August holidays, they spend a long weekend together in Belgium. This is a very slight but touching film about a father-son relationship which sensitively delineates the problems each faces in their difficult situation. Careful direction avoids the pitfall of cloying sentiment, Hanin's performance is beautifully judged, and the Bruges locations are pleasing.

Brussels-Transit

Bruxelles-Transit

Belgium 1980 90 mins bw
Paradise Films

d **Samy Szlingerbaum**
sc **Samy Szlingerbaum**
ph **Michel Houssiau**
Hélène Lapiower, Boris Lehman, Jeremy and Micha Wald

Malka Szlingerbaum (Lapiower), the director's mother, tells the story of her post-war journey from Poland to Belgium with her husband (Lehman) and of the struggles to make a new life for themselves. The first Yiddish feature since 1961 is also probably the first Yiddish experimental film. Samy Szlingerbaum commented that 'the film has two themes—on the one hand the way my mother remembers it, and on the other hand the way I remember my mother's stories'. Using voice-over narration, still photographs and long takes, set against a series of static compositions, this restrained and economical work, manages to re-create the pain of displacement.

The Brute

El Bruto

Mexico 1952 93 mins bw
Internacione Cinematografica

d **Luis Buñuel**
sc **Luis Buñuel, Luis Alcoriza**
ph **Agustín Jiménez**
m **Raúl Lavista**
Pedro Armendáriz, Katy Jurado, Andrés Soler, Rosita Arenas

A simple-minded slaughterhouse worker (Armendáriz), employed by a decadent landowner (Soler) to scare his tenants, becomes the lover of his boss's wife (Jurado). Her jealousy is aroused when she finds out he has seduced the daughter (Arenas) of one of his victims. Shot in just 18 days, it 'could have been a good film..., but I was forced to change it completely'. Despite Buñuel's stricture, the film has a smouldering power and stifling atmosphere, and the theme of sexual passion balanced by gentle love breaks through the conventions of the plot.

Bruto, El see Brute, The

Brutti, Sporchi E Cattivi see Down And Dirty

Bruxelles-Transit see Brussels-Transit

Brzezina see Birch Wood, The

Büchse Der Pandora, Die see Pandora's Box

Budapesti Mesĕk see Budapest Tales

Budapest Tales

Budapesti Mesĕk

Hungary 1976 91 mins col
Hunnia Studio

d **István Szabó**
sc **István Szabó**
ph **Sándor Sára**
m **Zdenkó Tamássy**
Maja Komorowska, Agi Mészáros, Ildiko Bánsági, András Bálint, Franciszek Piecza, Karoly Kovάks

In the last days of World War II, a group of soldiers, civilians, and refugees take shelter in an abandoned streetcar by a riverbank. They decide to put it in working order and set off together to Budapest. Friendships, love affairs, and conflicts develop along the way. Szabó's fifth film in 12 years is plainly (but not so simply) an allegory of modern Hungarian history. The passengers on this streetcar named Hungary are representatives of a variety of opinions and obsessions, which they express in monologues to camera from time to time. Overloaded with symbols as the vehicle is while moving on its ponderous way, the film does raise some important questions and there are moments of genuine emotion and amusement.

Buffet Froid

(US: Cold Cuts)

France 1979 93 mins col
Sara/Antenne 2

d **Bertrand Blier**
sc **Bertrand Blier**
ph **Jean Penzer**
m **Brahms**
Bernard Blier, Gérard Depardieu, Michel Serrault, Geneviève Page, Jean Carmet

A layabout (Depardieu) who lives in a deserted tower block is suspected by a crooked police inspector (Blier) of being the killer of an unknown man (Serrault)—only the first in a number of murder victims. Blier *fils* puts his father through his paces in this buffet of leftovers from better black comedies and droppings from Buñuel. None of the characters is convincing, even within the artificial conventions of the genre, and the director's notorious bad taste fails to shock this time.

Buraikan see Scandalous Adventures Of Buraikan, The

Burglar

Vzlomshchik

USSR 1987 89 mins col
Lenfilm

d **Valery Ogorodnikov**
sc **Valery Priyomykhov**
ph **Valery Mironov**
m **Viktor Kisin**
Oleg Elykomov, Konstantin Kinchev, Yuri Tsapnik, Svetlana Gaitan, Polina Petrenko

Senka (Elykomov), who plays in a classical boys' band, lives with his heavy-drinking widowed father and his brother Kostya (Kinchev) who is a rock band singer. When Kostya and his friends plan to steal a synthesizer from the community centre where they perform, Senka warns the organizers of the place. They take no notice, so he steals it himself, but confesses when the police appear. This is director Ogorodnikov's first feature, but it is technically and visually sure of itself. The focus on youth in the *glasnost* era adds to the increasingly varied subject matter of Russian films that are being shown in the West, although this one doesn't seem too sure of its themes which seem to muddle private and public issues. Not great, but certainly interesting.

The Burmese Harp

(US: Harp Of Burma)

Biruma No Tategoto

Japan 1956 116 mins bw
Nikkatsu

d **Kon Ichikawa**
sc **Natto Wada**
ph **Minoru Yokoyama**
m **Akira Ifukube**
Shoji Yasui, Rentaro Mikuni, Tatsuya Mihashi

A young soldier-musician (Yasui), in Burma at the time of the Japanese capitulation, takes on the role of a Buddhist priest and tries to bury as many bodies as he can. Ichikawa's first film to explore what he termed 'the pain of the age', is a non-naturalistic odyssey in visionary black and white images throbbing with the anguish that war brings. Scripted by the director's wife, it was one of the first Japanese films concerned with pacifist themes related to the defeat of Japan in 1945.

Burning Angel

Palava Enkeli

Finland 1984 105 mins col
Skandia Filmi

d **Lauri Törhönen**
sc **Claes Andersson, Hannele Törrönen, Lauri Törhönen**
ph **Esa Vuorinen**
m **Hector**
Riita Viiperi, Tom Wentzel, Eeva Eloranta, Juuso Hirvikangas, Elina Hurme

Tuulikki (Viiperi), a newly graduated nurse, takes up her first post which is in a mental hospital. Inexperienced and shocked at what she sees, she is nonetheless assigned the special care of a violent and pyromaniac patient (Eloranta) to whom she dedicates herself. It is a losing battle, fought while having to cope with staff tensions and the sexual advances of the doctors, with one of whom (Wentzel) she has an unhappy affair. Apparently based on the true case of a young Finnish psychiatric nurse who cracked up, Törhönen's film is a skilful and quite horrifying dissection of prevailing attitudes in Finnish mental asylums which, alas, do not seem too different from those elsewhere. Although depressing and critical, the piece is leavened with humour, thus managing to entertain, much as *One Flew Over The Cuckoo's Nest* did. Viiperi, making her debut, is impressive and, if the film is a little over the top at times, it is nevertheless compelling.

The Burning Earth

Der Brennende Acker

Germany 1922 80 mins bw
Goron-Deulig Exklusiv Film

d **F.W. Murnau**
sc **Willy Haas, Thea Von Harbou, Arthur Rosen**
ph **Karl Freund, Fritz Arno Wagner**
m **Silent**
Werner Krauss, Eugen Klöpfer, Wladimir Gaidarow, Eduard Von Winterstein, Stella Arbenina, Lya De Putti

An old peasant dies, leaving his farm to his two sons. One of them, Johannes (Gaidarow), determined to rise in the world, obtains a post as secretary to a Count whose young wife,

Helga (Arbenina), and daughter by a previous marriage (De Putti) both fall in love with him. When the Count dies Johannes, in order to get his hands on a piece of oil-rich land, marries Helga, thus setting in motion a train of misery, destruction and death. Murnau directs with a subtle and penetrating observation of human behaviour but it is, above all, for its visual quality that the film was acclaimed as a masterpiece by critics at the time: the brilliantly well-utilized deep-focus photography that captures the rustic harmony of the peasant farm interiors contrasted with the airy and elegant castle; the bleak snowbound winter landscape in opposition to the dramatic burning of the oil well. Alas and alack, much of the film is lost and the surviving reels have deteriorated in quality and are seldom shown. They are worth looking out for, however, since they belong to the *oeuvre* of a cinematic genius.

Bushido

Bushido Zankoku Monogatari

Japan 1963 123 mins bw
Toei

d **Tadashi Imai**
sc **Naoyuki Suzuki**
ph **Makoto Tsuboi**
m **Toshiro Mayuzumi**
Kinnosuke Nakamura, Masayuki Mori, Kyoko Kishida, Yoshiko Mita, Ineko Arima

An episodic tale, ranging over 300 years of history and demonstrating the consequences of 'bushido', the code of obedience to the feudal lord, as it affected one family. Imai's notion of exposing the brutal underbelly of honorable tradition is a fascinating departure for the Japanese cinema. Unfortunately, he fails to probe the history and moral conflicts of his subject, presenting instead an almost unrelieved excess of cruelty horrible to behold—beheadings, disembowellings, and the like. The film lacks narrative fluency and emotional drive, but is very well made and obviously seriously intentioned.

Best Film Berlin 1963

Bushido Zankoku Monogatari see Bushido

Bus Number Three

Xiaozi Bei

China 1980 90 mins col
Changchun Film Studio

d **Wang Jiayi, Luo Tai**
sc **Si Minsan, Zhou Yang, Wu Benwu, Sun Xionfei**
ph **Wu Guojiang**
m **Lei Zhengbang**
Chen Yixin, Chi Zhiqiang, Wang Weiping, Yu Yangping

The events that take place on a city bus taken daily by workers, students, intellectuals, housewives and schoolchildren are depicted, and the lives of the two conductors, a hard-working young woman (Yixin) and an impatient and lazy man (Zhiqiang) are contrasted. The film's quirky humour, gentle romance and youthful vitality have plenty of appeal for the 'younger generation', the meaning of the Chinese title. This charming, episodic comedy, a departure for this country's film-makers in that it stresses individual achievement, gives a detailed picture of everyday life in modern China.

Buta To Gunkan see Pigs And Battleships

The Butcher

Le Boucher

France 1969 94 mins col
La Boetie/Euro International

d **Claude Chabrol**
sc **Claude Chabrol**
ph **Jean Rabier**
m **Pierre Jansen**
Stéphane Audran, Jean Yanne, Antonio Passalia, Mario Beccaria

Hélène (Audran), a schoolmistress in a small Périgord town, is courted by Popaul (Yanne), the shy local butcher who turns out to be a sex murderer. On the surface a thriller in the Hitchcock mode—the discovery of a mutilated body by a group of schoolchildren, and Hélène's awareness of Popaul's guilt while alone with him—the film is more of a subtle, compassionate psychological study of sexual frustration. The two leads are superb, supported by local people playing themselves.

Bwana Toshi

aka The Song of Bwana Toshi

Bwana Toshi No Uta

Japan 1965 115 mins col
Toho

d **Susumu Hani**
sc **Susumu Hani, Kunio Shimizu**
ph **Manji Kanau**
m **Tohru Takemitsu**
Kivoshi Atsumi, Hamisi Salehe, Tsutomu Shimomoto

A large firm sends one of its employees (Atsumi) to the wilds of Tanzania to prepare for the arrival of his company by getting houses built. At first wary and uncomprehending of each other, the Japanese and the Africans eventually come to understand each other's cultures and to learn from them. Hani, who made documentaries of African wildlife for Japanese TV, approaches the serio-comic tale without any condescension or sentimentality. The film is unusual, entertaining and doubly exotic (for Western audiences), while serving its humanistic message.

Bwana Toshi No Uta see Bwana Toshi

Bye Bye Brazil

Brazil 1979 110 mins col
Carnaval Films/Aries Cinematografica/Gaumont (France)

d **Carlos Diegues**
sc **Carlos Diegues**
ph **Lauro Escorel Filho**
m **Chico Buarque, Roberto Menescal, Dominguinhos**
José Wilker, Betty Faria, Fabio Junior, Zaira Zambelli, Principe Nabor

The adventures of a tatty group of travelling players as they cross the vast North of Brazil. The troupe consists of a black strongman (Nabor), Salome (Faria) 'Queen of the Rhumba', and her lover Lord Cigano (Wilker), a magician. But wherever they go, even in the Amazon jungle, they find people prefer to watch TV rather than come to see them. Diegues, one of the leading lights in the *Cinema Novo* movement, uses the flamboyant performers and their garish show to comment, in a witty and equally flamboyant and garish manner, on what 'progress' has done to his country. The use of popular music from the States and an eye for the vulgar fetishes of the population—nightclubs, discos, portable radios and TV—give the film a satiric edge, as well as making a sad and pointed statement on the destruction of the culture of the Indians.

Byeleyet Parus Odinoky see Lone White Sail

By Rocket To The Moon see Woman In The Moon, The

By The Blood Of Others

Par Le Sang Des Autres

France 1973 95 mins col
Kangourou Films/Les Films La Boétie(Paris)/Merona Produzione(Rome)/Cinévideo(Montreal)

d **Marc Simenon**
sc **Jean Max**
ph **René Verzier**
m **Francis Lai**
Mariangela Melato, Yves Beneyton, Bernard Blier, Charles Vanel, Mylène Demongeot, Claude Piéplu

A young mental patient (Beneyton) in rural France brutally kidnaps a woman and her daughter and holds them hostage, demanding as his price for their release the company of the most beautiful girl in the nearby village. The local mayor, the prefect, the police chief, the doctor and the priest become involved in seeking a solution. Simenon, son of Maigret's creator Georges, delivers a proficient film dealing in a subject appropriate to the late 20th century. Sadly, however, neither the excellent cast (an incidental pleasure is a brief appearance by Demongeot, who co-produced the film) nor the basically interesting situation can triumph over a screenplay that quickly slides into predictability.

By The Bluest Of Seas

U Samovo Sinyevo Morya

USSR 1936 1309 metres bw
Mezhrabpomfilm/Azerfilm

d **Boris Barnet**
sc **K. Mints**
ph **M. Kirillov**
m **S. Pototski**

Elena Kouzmina, Lev Sverdline, Nikolai Krioutchkov, S. Svachenko, V. Sateieva

Two young Caspian fisherman (Sverdline and Krioutchkov) are shipwrecked on an island where they fall in love with the same bouncy girl (Kouzmina), who rejects them both. The blithest of Barnet comedies blissfully breaks the bonds of the studio by being filmed at a marine location. The players, particularly the delicious Kouzmina, and the director communicate the enjoyment they obviously had making it. Sadly, Barnet never again recaptured the spontaneity and joy of his pre-war films. He committed suicide in 1965.

By The Law

aka Dura Lex

Po Zakonu

USSR 1926 83 mins bw
Goskino

d **Lev Kuleshov**
sc **Lev Kuleshov, Viktor Shklovsky**
ph **Konstantin Kuznetsov**
m **Silent**

Sergei Komarov, Alexandra Khokhlova, Vladimir Fogel, Pyotr Galadzhev, Porfiri Podobed

Five gold prospectors in the Yukon are isolated in a hut by storms and floods. One of them, an Irishman, goes berserk and kills two of the men. The remaining man is prevented by his wife from exacting instant retribution. 'It must be done by the law,' she says. They conduct a trial, find the Irishman guilty and hang him from a solitary tree. Based on Jack London's story *The Unexpected*, this strangely hypnotic work is divided into five 'acts', moving through a range of moods to the tense and bitter climax. At the centre is the riveting, stylized performance from Kuleshov's wife, Alexandra Khokhlova.

C

The Cabinet Of Dr Caligari

Das Kabinett Des Dr Caligari

Germany 1919 73 mins bw
Decla-Bioskop

d **Robert Wiene**
sc **Carl Mayer, Hans Janowitz**
ph **Willy Hameister**
m **Silent**
Werner Krauss, Conrad Veidt, Friedrich Fehér, Lil Dagover, Hans Heinz Von Twardowski, Rudolf Lettinger

Caligari (Krauss), a fairground showman, hypnotizes his servant (Veidt) into committing murder at night and carrying off the girlfriend (Dagover) of the young hero (Fehér). The surprise ending enters the mind of a madman. Considered to be the first true example of Expressionism in the cinema, it was a great influence on German films for the next decade and on horror films in general. It has its risible moments today, but the weird and distorted sets (Walter Röhrig, Hermann Warm and Walter Reimann) and grotesquely angled photography still create a potent nightmarish atmosphere. In 1985, a print was shown that restored the colour tinting, original German intertitles and additional scenes.

Cabiria

Italy 1914 180 mins bw
Itala

d **Giovanni Pastrone**
sc **Giovanni Pastrone**
ph **Segundo De Chomon, Giovanni Tomatis, Augusto Batagliotti, Natale Chiusano**
m **Silent**
Italia Almirante Manzini, Lidia Quaranta, Umberto Mozzato, Bartolomeo Pagano

The many adventures of the Sicilian slave girl Cabiria (Quaranta) with Maciste (Pagano), her strongman companion, and her love for Fulvio (Mozzato), a Roman, during the Second Punic War. The most expensive, the most spectacular and the longest film up to that date (even when generally shown less 32 mins), took over six months to shoot and contained technical innovations, such as dolly and crane shots and lighting from below. It was the first motion picture to merit a complete review in the Italian press, and its great success in America, where it opened the new Astor theatre, inspired D.W. Griffith to embark on his large-scale productions and influenced the Babylonian sequence in *Intolerance*. Yet Pastrone (working under the pseudonym of Piero Fosco) remained unknown for many years because the film publicized the name of Gabriele D'Annunzio, the most famous Italian writer of the day, who only wrote the intertitles.

Caccia Tragica see Tragic Pursuit, The

Cadaveri Eccellenti see Illustrious Corpses

Caduta Degli Dei, La see Damned, The

La Cage Aux Folles

aka Birds Of A Feather

France 1978 109 mins col
Les Productions Artistes Associés/DaMa Produzione

d **Edouard Molinaro**
sc **Marcello Danon, Edouard Molinaro, Francis Véber, Jean Poiret**
ph **Armando Nannuzzi**
m **Ennio Morricone**
Ugo Tognazzi, Michel Serrault, Rémy Laurent, Claire Maurier, Benny Luke

Renato (Tognazzi) and Albin (Serrault) own

'La Cage Aux Folles', a nightclub where Albin is the star drag queen. The two men, lovers for 20 years, have brought up Renato's son, the product of a fleeting heterosexual liaison. The boy now wishes to marry, and all hell breaks loose in the attempts to conceal his background from his strait-laced future in-laws. An old-fashioned bedroom farce with a new angle, the movie is extremely funny, and the relationship between Renato and Albin is touching, thanks largely to the accomplished acting of the two leads, particularly an outrageous Serrault. Originally a long-running French play and, later, a successful Broadway musical, the film grossed a fortune and gathered three Oscar nominations. However, the rush to cash in on its success led to two progressively awful sequels, *La Cage Aux Folles II* (1980) and *La Cage Aux Folles III* (1985), with the same stars.

Cage Aux Rossignols, La see Cage Of Nightingales, A

Caged
(US: And The Wild Wild Women)
Nella Citta L'Inferno
Italy 1958 110 mins bw
Riama Prod/Francinex

d **Renato Castellani**
sc **Renato Castellani**
ph **Leonida Barboni**
m **Roman Vlad**
Anna Magnani, Giulietta Masina, Myriam Bru, Cristina Gajoni

The relationship in prison between an old timer and a younger, inexperienced woman is soon corrupted by their *milieu.* A film that brings Magnani and Masina together in a small space cannot be all bad, but this comes close. They give good imitations of themselves and then swop roles in this aimless and false prison drama, punctuated by plenty of shouting and hysterics.

A Cage Of Nightingales
La Cage Aux Rossignols
France 1947 78 mins bw
Gaumont

d **Jean Dréville**
sc **Noël-Noël, René Wheeler**
ph **Paul Cotteret**
m **Paul Cloërec**
Noël-Noël, Micheline Francey, Georges Biscot, René Genin, Marguerite Ducouret

A drama with music in which an ex-reform school boy (Noël-Noël) writes a novel based on his experiences, and earns a living working for a toy manufacturer while doing so. When the novel is published, his girlfriend reads it and, through her eyes, we see his story in flashback. An unusual little film which offers an adept mixture of past and present, together with a realistic and sympathetic view of delinquent youth.

Caida, La see Fall, The

Cairo: Central Station see Cairo Station

Cairo Station
aka Cairo: Central Station
Bab El Hadid
Egypt 1958 95 mins bw
Gabriel Talhamy

d **Youssef Chahine**
sc **Abdel Hay Adib, Mohamad Abou Youssef**
ph **Alvise**
m **Fouad El Zahiry**
Farid Chawki, Hind Rostom, Youssef Chahine, El Baroudy, Sofia Sarwat, Naima Wasfy

Life in, on and around Cairo's teeming central station, focusing on Quinawi, a poverty-stricken, crippled newspaper vendor, obsessively and hopelessly in love with the prettiest lemonade seller. His jealousies and fantasies fuel his descent into madness and violence. This early film from Egypt's most distinguished director is bursting with ideas and themes—worker exploitation, the corrupting influence of the Coca-Cola culture, the dangers of sexual repression. And that's the trouble. A Neo-Realist approach encloses what is essentially a melodrama, leaving no room to explore these themes and presenting characters drawn in broad, simplistic brush strokes. However, Chahine himself is marvellous as the doomed Quinawi.

Calle Mayor
aka Grande Rue
(US: The Love Maker)

Spain 1956 95 mins bw
Play Art Iberia/Cesario Gonzales

d **Juan Antonio Bardem**
sc **Juan Antonio Bardem**.
ph **Michel Kelber**
m **Joseph Kosma**
Betsy Blair, Yves Massard, René Blancard, Lila Kedrova, José Suarez

In a small Spanish town, a group of gamblers persuades a young stud (Suarez) from Madrid to make love and propose to a plain spinster (Blair) for a bet. But things aren't as simple as they seem. It was during the filming of this uncomfortable comedy-drama that Bardem was arrested and imprisoned on political grounds. He was released after two weeks as a result of an international outcry. The atmosphere of the stultifying town is well caught and so is the portrayal of *machismo*. The problem is the now rather dated view of an unmarried woman, not helped by Betsy Blair's repetition of her Oscar-nominated role in *Marty* the year before.

Camada Negra see Black Brood

Camera Buff
Amator

Poland 1979 112 mins col
Zespoly Filmowe-Film Polski

d **Krzysztof Kieslowski**
sc **Krzysztof Kieslowski, Jerzy Stuhr**
ph **Jacek Petrycki**
m **Krzysztof Knittel**
Jerzy Stuhr, Malgorzata Zajaczkowska, Ewa Pokas, Krzysztof Zanussi (as himself)

A factory worker (Stuhr) buys a home-movie camera to film his baby, but he becomes the official film-maker to his factory, wins a contest, and comes into conflict with his bosses. This wry satire explored the role and limits of the artist in Polish society, but was slightly blunted by the leading character's almost pathological obsession with his camera.

Camila

Argentina 1984 97 mins col
GEA Cinematografica(Buenos Aires)/Impala(Madrid)

d **Maria Luisa Bemberg**
sc **Maria Luisa Bemberg, Beda Docampo Feijo, Juan Batista Stagnaro**
ph **Fernando Arribas**
m **Luis Maria Serra**
Susu Pecoraro, Imanol Arias, Héctor Alterio, Elena Tasisto, Carlos Munoz

Camila (Pecoraro), an upper middle-class Catholic from a strict family, falls in love with Ladislao (Arias), a priest, who fights his feelings until he falls ill. The couple run away, outraging family, Church and state, and settle as husband and wife under assumed names in a distant village, but with a warrant out for their arrest. A bare outline fails to do justice to this powerful indictment of repression, set during the vicious dictatorship of De Rosas in 1847. Bemberg exposes the political complicity between Church and state—their cruel destruction of individual freedom —while making a strong feminist case: the ultimate tragedy occurs because Ladislao, not Camila, lacks the strength to defy the rules. Technically, the film is of a high order in all departments, and the director's incisive intelligence neatly avoids the conventions of period melodrama. Bemberg was denied permission to make the film (based on actual events) for several years because of its implied critique of contemporary regimes.

Camille Without Camellias see Lady Without Camellias, The

Camminacammina
aka Keep Walking
aka Walking, Walking

Italy 1983 165 mins col
RAI

d **Ermanno Olmi**
sc **Ermanno Olmi**
ph **Ermanno Olmi**
m **Bruno Nicolai**
Alberto Fumagalli, Antonio Cucciarre, Eligio Martel Lacci, Renzo Samminiatesi, Marco Bartolini

A vast caravan of pilgrims goes on a long trek, following the light in the East in order to welcome the birth of Christ. This humorous, moving, magical and irreverent re-enactment of the Journey of The Magi is seen as if through the eyes of children. In fact, it is they who seem to have a stronger faith than the querulous and squabbling adults (all played by non-professionals). The caravan is made up of Italian peasants with all their strengths and weaknesses, giving the event a believable reality. Olmi, who also designed the costumes and sets, sees it like a Western wagon train moving to the promised land.

Camorra: The Naples Connection

Un Complicato Intrigo Di Donne, Vicoli E Delitti

Italy 1985 106 mins col
Cannon Productions/Italian International

d **Lina Wertmüller**
sc **Lina Wertmüller, Elvio Porta**
ph **Giuseppe Lanci**
m **Tony Esposito**
Angela Molina, Francisco Rabal, Harvey Keitel, Daniel Ezralow, Vittorio Squillante

A member of the notorious Rocco Family is shot dead while assaulting Annunziata (Molina), an ex-whore turned Neapolitan hotelier. The incident implicates Annunziata in a series of violent happenings involving sex, drugs, abduction and death. The film is a hodge-podge of crime and plot complication in the typically overheated style of this director, who offers much gratuitous sensationalism before finally revealing her moral focus— the fight of mothers against drug pushers who exploit and destroy their children. A long title for a long film with little depth.

Camouflage

Barwy Ochronne

Poland 1977 100 mins col
Tor Film Unit

d **Krzysztof Zanussi**
sc **Tadeusz Wybult, Krzysztof Zanussi,**
ph **Edward Klosínski**
m **Wojciech Kilar**
Zbigniew Zapasiewicz, Piotr Garlicki, Christine Paul, Marius Dmochowski, Magdalena Zawadska

At a summer seminar for linguistic students held at a country palace, a young, liberal-minded professor (Garlicki) finds himself at odds with an older, cynical colleague (Zapasiewicz) in particular and the whole university establishment in general. As in several previous Zanussi films, the plot unravels against an academic background, but it is really more about bureaucratic pettiness and the crushing of idealism. With his characteristic understatement and intelligence, Zanussi marks out his territory by showing the clash between two generations in a series of penetrating duologues. However, non-Polish speakers will miss certain important nuances.

Cangaceiro, O see Bandit, The

The Canterbury Tales

I Racconti Di Canterbury

Italy 1971 109 mins col
UA/PEA/PAA

d **Pier Paolo Pasolini**
sc **Pier Paolo Pasolini**
ph **Tonino Delli Colli**
m **Ennio Morricone**
Pier Paolo Pasolini, Hugh Griffith, Laura Betti, Tom Baker, Ninetto Davoli, Franco Citti, Josephine Chaplin, Jenny Runacre

Chaucer (Pasolini) is among the group of medieval pilgrims on their way to Canterbury who pass the time by telling each other stories. The presence of a number of English actors in the cast does not prevent the eight tales (including those of the Merchant, the Wife of Bath, and the Pardoner) from being filtered through Pasolini's Italian sensibility and, as the English classic was itself derived from *The Decameron* (the first in Pasolini's story-cycle trilogy), it hardly mattered. However, even non- purists might object tò the coarsening of some of the episodes and the broad performances, while acknowledging the exuberance of the enterprise.

Best Film Berlin 1972

Caporal Épinglé, Le see Vanishing Corporal, The

Capricious Summer

Rozmarné Léto

Czechoslovakia 1968 75 mins col
Barrandov

d **Jiří Menzel**
sc **Jiří Menzel, Vaclau Nyult**
ph **Jaromír Šofr**
m **Jiří Šust**
Rudolf Hrušinsky, Vlastimil Brodsky, František Rehák, Jana Drchalová, Jiří Menzel, Mila Myslíková

The beautiful assistant (Drchalová) of an itinerant circus tightrope walker (Menzel) creates sexual tension among three middle-aged men (Hrušínsky, Brodsky and Rehák), who while away their time beside the lake of a sleepy provincial town. The film's gentle pace, seemingly uneventful plot and the soft colours reflect the season and the setting, but Menzel has packed it with a myriad of small comic incidents that add up to a more substantial whole. It is the sort of amusing, affectionate and observant bitter-sweet comedy that one expects from the minor master Menzel, who learnt to walk a tightrope for his own role in the film.

The Captain From Kopenick

Der Hauptmann Von Köpenick

W. Germany 1956 93 mins col
Real Film

d **Helmut Käutner**
sc **Karl Zuckmayer, Helmut Käutner**
ph **Albert Benitz**
m **Bernhard Eichhorn**
Heinz Rühmann, Hannelore Schroth, Martin Held, Erich Schellow

While in prison, Wilhelm Voigt (Rühmann) learns the regulations and procedures of the Prussian army from a handbook. On his release, unable to find work, he impersonates an army captain, commandeers soldiers on the streets of Berlin and takes over the city hall of the suburb of Köpenick in order to get himself a passport. This third screen version of Zuckmayer's 1931 play (filmed in the same year, and again in Hollywood in 1941, both by Richard Oswald) updated the action to that of the complacent Adenauer era, and shares some of the defects of the German cinema of the 1950s, namely a lack of style and teeth. The film, basically about the dangers of militarism, plays too much on the audience's sympathy for the imposter, and some clever satire and visual juxtapositions only make one wish it had taken more risks.

Les Carabiniers

aka The Soldiers

(US: The Riflemen)

France 1963 80 mins bw
Rome-Paris Films/Laetitia

d **Jean-Luc Godard**
sc **Jean-Luc Godard, Jean Gruault, Roberto Rossellini**
ph **Raoul Coutard**
m **Philippe Arthuys**
Marino Masè, Albert Juross, Geneviève Galéa, Catherine Ribero

Two young peasants, lured by promises of booty, leave home to fight for King and Country only to be betrayed when a peace treaty is signed. The violent critical reaction in France to this seemingly dispassionate view of the horrors of war caused the film to be withdrawn after its initial release. But Godard's achievement was to create a powerful anti-war, anti-imperialist statement, using Brechtian distancing techniques, and literary devices, shooting in the grainy images of old newsreels in an unspecified time and place.

Careless Love see Bonne Soupe, La

The Carmelites

Le Dialogue Des Carmelites

France/Italy 1959 113 mins bw
Champs-Elysées/Titanus

d **R. Bruckberger, Philippe Agostini**
sc **R. Bruckberger, Philippe Agostini**
ph **André Bac**
m **Jean Françaix**
Jeanne Moreau, Alida Valli, Pascale Audret, Madeleine Renaud, Pierre Brasseur, Georges Wilson

Two young Carmelite novices take the veil almost on the eve of the French Revolution, and find themselves, their sister nuns and the convent itself caught up in the political events and violence that follow. This rather unwieldy film version of the Georges Bernanos novel is an interesting showcase for Moreau and Valli, but it fails to come to grips either with history or religion and is thus rather dull. The ending, when several nuns sacrifice themselves voluntarily to the guillotine, is moving and dramatic, but it's a long time to wait.

Carmen

Spain 1983 101 mins col
Emiliano Piedra Productions

d **Carlos Saura**
sc **Carlos Saura, Antonio Gades (inspired by Merimée & Bizet)**
ph **Teo Escamilla**
m **Paco De Lucia, Bizet**
Antonio Gades, Laura Del Sol, Paco De Lucia, Cristina Hoyos, Juan Antonio Jimenez, Sebastian Moreno, José Yepes

Choreographer Antonio (Gades) casts an unknown girl (Del Sol) to dance the title role in his new ballet set to Bizet's *Carmen.* During the rehearsal period, he falls in love with her and they have an affair, although she has a husband, currently in jail on a drugs charge. She proves incapable of fidelity to either of them and, when he surprises her making love with a boy from the chorus in the dressing room, he stabs her in a fit of jealousy. Saura's film, using the well-tried but effective device of life mirroring art, tells the Carmen story twice—offstage and on. The edges tend, occasionally, to blur, but since the enterprise is really the foundation for a display of brilliant choreographic pyrotechnics, danced with breathtaking expertise and filmed with pulsating energy, no matter. A treat for lovers of the genre, with the added bonus of Bizet's music, some of it sung, using voices of the calibre of Regina Resnik and Mario Del Monaco.

Carmen

France/Italy 1984 152 mins col
Gaumont/Production Marcel Dassault/Opera Film Produzione

d **Francesco Rosi**
sc **Francesco Rosi, Tonino Guerra (libretto by Meilhac & Halévy)**
ph **Pasqualino De Santis**
m **Georges Bizet (conducted by Lorin Maazel)**
Julia Migenes-Johnson (Carmen), Placido Domingo (Don Jose), Ruggero Raimondi (Escamillo), Faith Esham (Micaela)

The narrative of Bizet's popular opera—a simple soldier's passion for a wayward and tempestuous gypsy leads to jealousy and murder—is followed exactly by Rosi's film, which uses the full *opéra comique* version (i.e. with spoken dialogue). The director opted for realism, filming on location in Andalucia, which achieves authenticity on the one hand, but creates disruption on another: a vegetable cart, for example, rumbles into the midst of Jose and Micaela's duet to farcical effect, and too many big musical moments are diminished by long-shot cameras. The opening credit sequence, however, using slow-motion in the bullring, followed by a dramatic Corpus Christi procession, sets the tone for the events to come, rooting them firmly in the dark mystique of Spanish ritual. Julia Migenes- Johnson lights up the screen with a smoulderingly sexy Carmen, Domingo convinces as her victim, and Raimondi delivers a polished toreador. Purists will notice a musical excision in Act III, but this is a handsome, intelligent and entertaining opera film rather than a filmed opera.

Carmen Comes Home

Karumen Kokyo Ni Kaeru

Japan 1951 87 mins col
Shochiku

d **Keisuke Kinoshita**
sc **Keisuke Kinoshita**
ph **Hiroyuki Kusuda**
m **Chuji Kinoshita, Toshio Uzumi**
Hideko Takamine, Toshiko Kobayashi, Takeshi Sakamoto, Shuji Sano, Chishu Ryu

A pretty Tokyo stripper (Takamine) pays a visit home to the little country village where she grew up and scandalizes the community, especially her father (Sakamoto), with her city ways. She learns the lesson that to return to one's past can be a dreadful mistake but, before she and her friend (Kobayashi) depart, they stage a strip show in an old barn and donate the proceeds to local charities. The first Japanese film to have been made and released in colour is a charming and light weight comedy on the surface, but it does have an underlying seriousness as we watch the tragicomic villagers falling victim to the worst aspects of the Coca-Cola culture. Takamine is effective as the flighty but likeable heroine. The following year saw a sequel, *Carmen's Pure Love*, also shot in colour, but the process was thought unsatisfacory and it was released in black and white.

Un Carnet De Bal

aka Life Dances On

aka The Dance Programme

France 1937 135 mins bw
Lévy Strauss/Sigma

d **Julien Duvivier**
sc **Julien Duvivier, Jean Sarment, Pierre Wolff, Bernard Zimmer, Henri Jeanson**
ph **Michel Kelber, Philippe Agostini**
m **Maurice Jaubert**
Marie Bell, Françoise Rosay, Louis Jouvet, Raimu, Harry Baur, Fernandel, Pierre Blanchar, Pierre-Richard Willm

A rich, middle-aged widow (Bell) finds an old dance card and decides to find out what happened to the men whose names are on it. She discovers an epileptic doctor (Blanchar), a monk (Baur), a hairdresser (Fernandel), a crooked nightclub owner (Jouvet), a skiing instructor (Willm) and a small town mayor (Raimu). A haunting waltz theme accompanies this elegant but patchy sketch-film which allows a galaxy of French stars each to do a short turn. The film was so successful that Duvivier was invited to Hollywood to make *The Great Waltz*. He repeated the multi-story formula in four further films with variable results.

Best Foreign Film Venice 1937

Carnival In Flanders

La Kermesse Héroïque

France 1935 115 mins bw
Tobis/Regina

d **Jacques Feyder**
sc **Jacques Feyder, Charles Spaak**
ph **Harry Stradling**
m **Louis Beydts**
Françoise Rosay, Louis Jouvet, Jean Murat, Alfred Adam, Bernard Lancret, André Alerme

When Spanish troops enter a small town in 17th-century Flanders, the male inhabitants disappear, leaving the women, including the burgomaster's wife (Rosay), to enjoy the attentions of their conquerors. Lazare Meerson's sets and costumes conjure up the period with the eye of Jan Breughel (a character in the film) and the witty script and performances have made this mock-heroic farce a continual favourite. But it caused great offence in Belgium for its presentation of the Flemings in a less than heroic light, and was liked by the Nazis for its sympathetic attitude towards collaboration.

Best Director Venice 1936

Caroline Chérie

France 1951 135 mins bw
SNEG/Cinéphonie

d **Richard Pottier**
sc **Jean Anouilh**
ph **Maurice Barry**
m **Georges Auric**
Martine Carol, Jacques Dacqmine, Marie Déa, Pierre Cressoy

Caroline and a young count (Dacqmine) are in love, but the upheavals of the French Revolution separate them. After a series of affairs with others, they are reunited. Martine Carol's appearance in the title role rocketed her to stardom, the only fact of importance to note about this slightly prurient, somewhat tedious, run-of-the-mill costume drama, the script of which does not do justice to its writer's reputation.

Caroline Chérie

France 1967 105 mins col
Cineurop/Nordeutsche/Mancori

d **Denys De La Patellière**
sc **Cecil Saint-Laurent**
ph **Sacha Vierny**
m **Georges Garvarentz**
France Anglade, Jean-Claude Brialy, Vittorio De Sica, Bernard Blier, Isa Miranda

A beautifully photographed but otherwise very poor colour remake of the French Revolution romance with Anglade in the role that made Martine Carol famous. This version offers a more *angst*-ridden and sexually explicit account of Caroline's tribulations, including rape and an enforced marriage before she is finally reunited with her true love (Brialy).

Caro Michele see Dear Michael

Carrosse D'Or, Le see Golden Coach, The

Carrozza D'Oro, La see Golden Coach, The

Cartouche

aka Swords Of Blood

France 1961 114 mins col
Les Films Ariane/Filmsonor/Vides

d **Philippe De Broca**
sc **Philippe De Broca, Daniel Boulanger**
ph **Christian Matras**
m **Georges Delerue**
Jean-Paul Belmondo, Claudia Cardinale, Odile Versois, Marcel Dalio, Philippe Lemaire, Jean Rochefort

In the 18th century, Cartouche (Belmondo) and Vénus (Cardinale) take over a Paris crime syndicate in order to rob the rich and succeed in antagonizing the foppish Chief of Police (Lemaire).After his first four films, featuring Jean-Pierre Cassel, De Broca switched to Belmondo, an equally animated hero, for this snappy, swashbuckling spoof. The film also manages, with some expertise, to encompass an element of drama and even tragedy.

Casa Del Angel, La see House Of The Angel, The

Casanova

aka Fellini Casanova

Italy 1976 163 mins col
PEA/TCF

d **Federico Fellini**
sc **Federico Fellini, Bernadino Zapponi**
ph **Giuseppe Rotunno**
m **Nino Rota**
Donald Sutherland, Tina Aumont, Cicely Browne, Carmen Scarpitta

Episodes from the life of Giacomo Casanova (Sutherland), the 18th- century Venetian author, scientist and libertine who fornicates mechanically with one girl after another until, in this version, he has sex with an actual automaton. After the warmth of Fellini's three previous autobiographical films, this is a cold, empty, repetitious study of a sexual obsessive. There are, of course, a number of eye-catching scenes, enhanced by Danilo Donati's Oscar-winning costume design. Nino Rota's music is as haunting as ever, and Sutherland does his best behind extraordinary make-up.

Cas Du Docteur Laurent, Le see Case Of Dr Laurent, The

The Case Of Dr Laurent

Le Cas Du Docteur Laurent

France 1957 93 mins bw
Cocinor

d **Jean-Paul Le Chanois**
sc **Jean-Paul Le Chanois, René Barjavel**
ph **Henri Alekan**
m **Joseph Kosma**
Jean Gabin, Nicole Courcel, Sylvia Montfort, Arius Daxely

A Paris doctor (Gabin) moves to the countryside to pioneer natural childbirth methods. He meets with hostility from the locals and opposition from the medical establishment but, when an unwed mother gives birth without difficulty under his care, he wins over his critics. An intelligent film, authenticated by actual scenes of birth that are well-presented and sensitively handled, and with an excellent performance from Gabin.

Caso Mattei, Il see Mattei Affair, The

Casque D'Or see Golden Marie

Castle Of The Spider's Web see Throne Of Blood

Castle Vogelöd see Haunted Castle, The

Cat, The see Chat, Le

Cat And Mouse

Le Chat Et La Souris

France 1975 108 mins col

Les Films 13

d **Claude Lelouch**
sc **Claude Lelouch**
ph **Jean Collomb**
m **Francis Lai**

Michèle Morgan, Serge Reggiani, Jean-Pierre Aumont, Philippe Léotard, Valérie Lagrange

The wife (Morgan) of a wealthy husband (Aumont), humiliated by his continual philandering, is tempted to push him off a skyscraper that he is in the process of having built, but does not. When he is later found shot, the detective investigating the case—named, in a delightfully improbable pun, Inspector Lechat (Reggiani)—suspects the widow of the crime. Lelouch has delivered a slick and glossy cop thriller, using flashbacks with skill, but it is all rather superficial and lacking in suspense or true drama. A disappointing vehicle for the lovely Michèle Morgan's return to films after an absence of eight years.

Catherine see Vie Sans Joie, Une

Cathy Tippel see Keetje Tippel

The Cat In The Bag

(US: The Cat In The Sack)

Le Chat Dans Le Sac

Canada 1964 74 mins bw

National Film Board Of Canada

d **Gilles Groulx**
sc **Gilles Groulx**
ph **Jean-Claude Labrecque**
m **John Coltrane, Couperin, Vivaldi**

Claude Godbout, Barbara Ulrich, Manon Blain, Véronique Vilbert, André Leblanc

Barbara (Ulrich), an actress, and Claude (Godbout), a journalist, are a young couple living out 'the last days of their intimacy' during a winter in Montreal. Their estrangement personifies the dilemmas of a bilingual, bicultural country— she is Anglo-Canadian, and he Québecois. The film that marked the beginning of Quebec cinema, and was the first feature of 33-year-old Groulx, a maker of short films, manages to be a personal history as well as an expression of the aspirations of French-speaking Canada. This is carried off by improvised techniques heavily influenced by Godard's early films, particularly *It's My Life*, with its monologues to camera, interviews, jump cuts and quotations, but it incorporates them into the freshly viewed Canadian experience.

Cat In The Sack, The see Cat In The Bag, The

The Cat Shows Her Claws

La Chatte Sort Ses Griffes

France 1959 102 mins bw

Paris-Elysée Films/Metzger & Woog/Films Balar

d **Henri Decoin**
sc **Jacques Rémy**
ph **Pierre Montazel**
m **Joseph Kosma**

Françoise Arnoul, Horst Frank, Harold Kay, François Guérin, Bernard Lajarrige

Cora (Arnoul) is a French Resistance worker known as The Cat. Suspecting, erroneously, that she has betrayed them, a group of her colleagues shoot her and leave her for dead, but she is rescued by the Germans. Major Von Hollwitz (Frank) makes her the subject of a brainwashing experiment and sends her back to the Resistance as a spy, but his plans come unstuck. Good locations, good photography and good acting, notably from Frank as the Nazi doctor who starts falling in love with his victim. Decoin directs with confident efficiency, but it is rather difficult to swallow the story, which has Arnoul performing some Pearl White-style heroics at the final fade.

Cats' Play

Macskajaték

Hungary 1974 115 mins col

Hunnia Studio

d **Károly Makk**
sc **Károly Makk, János Tóth**
ph **János Tóth**
m **Péter Eötvös**

Margit Dayka, Elma Bulla, Margit Makay, Samu Balász

Mrs Orbán (Dayka), an elderly, widowed music teacher living in Budapest, focuses her life on her wealthy but paralyzed sister (Bulla) in Germany, with whom she communicates by letter and telephone, and on her old flame, Viktor (Balász), a retired opera singer who comes to dine every Thursday evening. When a friend from the past (Makay) appears and falls in love with Viktor, the balance and security of her existence are badly disturbed. As in his previous film, the award- winning *Love*, Károly Makk concentrates on the frailty, foibles and survival mechanisms of the old. The piece demands concentration, but is poignant, fragile and unsentimental, displaying fine judgement in direction and performance. Beautifully photographed, it effectively utilizes flashbacks to summon up the heroine's memories of youth.

Cave Se Rebiffe, Le see Counterfeiters, The

Caza, La see Hunt, The

Ceddo

Senegal 1976 117 mins bw
Filmi Doomireev

d **Ousmane Sembène**
sc **Ousmane Sembène**
ph **Georges Caristan**
m **Manu Dibango**
Ismaila Diagne, Tabara N'Diaye, Moustapha Yade, Ousmane Camara, Mamadou Dioum

An Imam from the North tries forcibly to convert the population to Islam, using the king as his puppet. The king's daughter is kidnapped by a group that refuses conversion. Though their leader is slain and his followers defeated, his spirit lives on in the captive princess who returns to kill the Imam. As 70 per cent of the population of Senegal is Muslim, Black Africa's leading director again courted controversy in his own country, where the film was banned. It was his most daring and mature work in style and substance. Deeply rooted in African culture, it is a powerful allegory confounding European expectations of narrative.

Cela S'Appelle L'Aurore

France 1955 108 mins bw
Marceau/Laetitia

d **Luis Buñuel**
sc **Luis Buñuel, Jules Ferry**
ph **Robert Le Fèbvre**
m **Joseph Kosma**
Georges Marchal, Lucia Bosé, Gianni Esposito, Julien Bertheau, Henri Nassiet

In Corsica, a doctor (Marchal) falls in love with a widow (Bosé) when his wife is away on holiday, while his befriending of a peasant (Esposito) leads to murder. For his first film in Europe for 23 years, Buñuel chose to adapt an Emmanuel Roblès novel which he found to be 'a story so perfectly pure'. The film might have been perfectly pure melodrama, except for the director's spicing it with social consciousness. It was merely a sturdy stepping stone towards better works in his long career. Georges Marchal, the stony-faced male lead, unaccountably appeared in three further Buñuel films.

Céleste

W. Germany 1981 106 mins col
Pelemele/Bayerische Rundfunk

d **Percy Adlon**
sc **Percy Adlon**
ph **Jürgen Martin**
m **Franck**
Eva Mattes, Jürgen Arndt, Norbert Wartha, Wolf Euba, Joseph Manoth

The day-to-day existence of Céleste Albaret (Mattes), a young, uneducated country girl, who came to work as housekeeper to the ailing author Marcel Proust (Arndt) in his Paris apartment in 1913 and stayed with him until his death nine years later. Though made in German, Adlon's adaptation is extremely faithful to Céleste's memoirs, and marvellously evokes the closed world in which Proust lived. Although offering no plot to speak of, the film is a subtle, humorous and touching study of the loyal relationship between a middle-aged homosexual intellectual and a simple, caring girl.

Celine And Julie Go Boating

Céline Et Julie Vont En Bateau

France 1974 192 mins col

Céline Et Julie Vont En Bateau

Les Films Du Losange/Christian Fletcher/Les Films 7/Rennes/Saga/Simar/Vincent Malle

d **Jacques Rivette**
sc **Jacques Rivette, Eduardo Di Gregorio, Juliet Berto, Dominique Labourier**
ph **Jacques Renard**
m **Jean-Marie Senia**
Dominique Labourier, Juliet Berto, Bulle Ogier, Marie-France Pisier, Barbet Schroeder, Nathalie Asnar, Philippe Clevenot

Celine (Berto), a magician in a cheap nightclub, meets librarian Julie (Labourier) in Montmartre and tells her how she sometimes works as governess to a little girl who lives in a strange suburban house with her widower father and two women. Celine and Julie enter the house and become involved in the repeated drama being played out within. Suggested by two Henry James stories, this brilliantly allusive comic meditation on the nature of fantasy manages to take in Lewis Carroll, Cocteau, Borges, Kafka, Proust, cartoons and Vincente Minnelli on the way. Although lengthy, it is the most approachable and accomplished of Rivette's films, and led critic David Thomson to call it 'the most important film made since Citizen Kane'.

Céline Et Julie Vont En Bateau see Celine And Julie Go Boating

---

Celui Qui Doit Mourir see He Who Must Die

C'Era Una Volta see Cinderella—Italian Style

C'Eravamo Tanto Amati see We All Loved Each Other So Much

The Ceremony

Gishiki

Japan 1971 123 mins col
ATG/Argos

d **Nagisa Oshima**
sc **Tsutomu Tamura, Mamoru Sasaki, Nagisa Oshima**
ph **Toichiro Narushima**
m **Tohru Takemitsu**
Kenzo Kawarazaki, Atsuko Kaku, Kei Sato, Nobuko Otowa, Maki Takayama

The history of Japan from the end of World War II to the present day is represented by the large and influential Sakurada family. Each stage is marked by a specific ceremony when the entire family gathers for an anniversary, a wedding or a funeral. 'Ceremonies are a time when the special characteristics of the Japanese spirit are revealed. It is this spirit that concerns and worries me,' commented Oshima on his most ambitious film to that date. It not only gave him the opportunity for some stunning stylistic devices and bizarre humour, but it also displayed a deeply ambivalent and revealing attitude to Japanese society.

Cerny Petr see Peter And Pavla

Certo Giorno, Un see One Fine Day

César

France 1936 117 mins bw
Marcel Pagnol

d **Marcel Pagnol**
sc **Marcel Pagnol**
ph **Willy**
m **Vincent Scotto**
Raimu, Orane Demazis, Pierre Fresnay, Charpin, André Fouché, Alida Rouffe

After his years in the merchant navy, Marius (Fresnay) runs a garage in Toulon. On the death of Panisse (Charpin), Fanny (Demazis) reveals to her adult son Césariot (Fouché) that he is really Marius's son. With much manoeuvring from grandfather César (Raimu), the lovers of 20 years before are reunited. The last part of Pagnol's trilogy (four years after the second, *Fanny*) was the only one he directed himself. Less fluent cinematically, the plot more predictable and the limited Demazis unable to suggest the passage of time, it still has Pagnol's delicious dialogue and Raimu's all-enveloping performance. Starting with *Marius*, the three films are fictionalized portraits of Marseilles life and characters described by a wonderful storyteller, a humorist who created pathos without sentimentality.

César And Rosalie

César Et Rosalie
France 1972 105 mins col
Fildebroc/U.P.F./Mega Film

d **Claude Sautet**
sc **Claude Sautet, Jean-Loup Dabadie**
ph **Jean Boffety**
m **Philippe Sarde**
Yves Montand, Romy Schneider, Sami Frey, Umberto Orsini

Rosalie (Schneider), the divorced mother of a little girl and mistress of César (Montand), runs off with an old flame (Frey). After various comings and goings, the two men become devoted friends and a *ménage- à-trois* is set up until Rosalie leaves. This see-sawing diversion, meandering along to a deliberately inconclusive ending, is a pleasant, amusing and polished—if somewhat rambling—offering, elevated by Montand's superb portrayal of a rough but kind self-made man.

César Et Rosalie see César And Rosalie

Cet Obscur Objet Du Désir see That Obscure Object Of Desire

Chacal De Nahueltoro, El see Jackal Of Nahueltoro, The

Chagrin Et La Pitié, Le see Sorrow And The Pity, The

Chaika see Seagull, The

Chained see Mikaël

Chamade, La see Heartbeat

Chambre Verte, La see Green Room, The

The Champagne Murders

Le Scandale
France 1967 110 mins col
Universal (France)

d **Claude Chabrol**
sc **Claude Brûlé, Derek Prouse, Paul Gégauff**
ph **Jean Rabier**
m **Pierre Jansen**
Anthony Perkins, Maurice Ronet, Stéphane Audran, Yvonne Furneaux, Suzanne Lloyd

The wealthy owner (Furneaux) of a champagne company, her former-gigolo husband (Perkins) and her secretary (Audran) plot to make an eccentric playboy (Ronet), who holds the key to a profitable takeover bid, believe himself to be a murderer. Chabrol flounders around in this grotesque and unpleasant thriller, using some clever contrivances and achieving a showy overhead final shot. Happily, he would soon return from the wilderness in which films like this had placed him.

Chapayev

USSR 1934 99 mins bw
Lenfilm

d **Sergei Vasiliev, Georgi Vasiliev**
sc **Sergei Vasiliev, Georgi Vasiliev**
ph **Alexander Sigayev**
m **Gavril Popov**
Boris Babochkin, B. Blinov, Leonid Kmit, Vavara Myasnikova

Red Army commander Chapayev (Babochkin), fighting against Czech and Kolchak forces during the Civil War of 1919, has to resist the attempts of a commissar to tame his impulsive and heroic nature. Shown to the public as the highlight of the fifteenth anniversary of Soviet cinema, the film was hailed at home and abroad as the first great Soviet success in the sound era. Although the directors (unrelated despite their shared surname) lacked the invention and genius of an Eisenstein or a Dovzhenko, the humanity of this modern folk tale makes it a good example of socialist realism.

Chapeau De Paille D'Italie, Un see Italian Straw Hat, The

Charles And Lucie

Charles Et Lucie

Charles Dead Or Alive

France 1979 98 mins col
Cythère Films/Les Films De La Chouette/Antenne 2

d **Nelly Kaplan**
sc **Jean Chapot**
ph **Gilbert Sandoz**
m **Pierre Perret**
Daniel Ceccaldi, Ginette Garcin, Jean-Marie Proslier, Samson Fainsilber, Georges Claisse

Misfortune has reduced antique dealer Charles (Ceccaldi) to selling bric-à-brac, while former chanteuse Lucie (Garcin), her looks gone, is a charwoman. They fall victim to an elaborate con-trick which lands them in the South of France, penniless and pursued by gangsters and police alike, but it all ends happily. Firmly in the tradition of picaresque fantasy, Kaplan's film is charming, poignant, and sometimes witty, but remains little more than a light-weight divertissement.

Charles Dead Or Alive

Charles Mort Ou Vif
Switzerland 1969 93 mins col
Le Group 5

d **Alain Tanner**
sc **Alain Tanner**
ph **Renato Berta**
François Simon, Marcel Robert, Marie-Claire Dufour, André Schmidt

Charles, a middle-aged watchmaker (played by François, Michel Simon's son), opts out of the rat-race, abandoning business and family and moving in with an artist and his mistress. He retreats further and further from reality and ends as a willing accomplice to his son's decision to send him to an asylum. Switzerland's best-known and most accomplished director made an assured and intelligent debut with this film, suggesting the left-wing and sociological themes he would develop in later works.

Charles Et Lucie see Charles And Lucie

Charles Mort Ou Vif see Charles Dead Or Alive

Charme Discret De La Bourgeoisie, Le see Discreet Charm Of The Bourgeoisie, The

---

Charulata

aka The Lonely Wife
India 1964 124 mins bw
R.D. Bansal

d **Satyajit Ray**
sc **Satyajit Ray**
ph **Subrata Mitra**
m **Satyajit Ray**
Sailen Mukherjee, Madhabi Mukherjee, Soumitra Chatterjee, Shyamal Ghoshal, Geetali Roy

Towards the end of the 19th century, Charulata (Madhabi Mukherjee), the bored and neglected wife of a Calcutta intellectual (Sailen Mukherjee) deeply involved with his English-language political journal, falls in love with Amal (Chatterjee), a young poet and her husband's cousin. She sees in Amal a man who would appreciate her for herself and encourage her own writing, but it is an illusion. This subtle masterpiece of Ray's middle period, based on a story by his beloved Rabindranath Tagore, is a warm, wry and rounded picture of the breaking up of a middle-class marriage. The garden scene where the wife (a delicately beautiful performance) swings higher and higher as Amal sits writing, is equal to similar outdoor moments in the work of Renoir and suggest a sexuality that is unusual in the context of Indian cinema.

Best Director Berlin 1965

Chasers, The see Young Have No Morals, The

Chastnaya Zhizn see Private Life

Le Chat

aka The Cat
France 1971 88 mins col
Lira Films/Cinétel

d **Pierre Granier-Deferre**

sc **Pascal Jardin, Pierre Granier-Deferre**
ph **Walter Wottitz**
m **Philippe Sarde**
Jean Gabin, Simone Signoret, Annie Cordy, Jacques Rispal

Julien and Clemence (Gabin and Signoret), an aging married couple, spend their days in their shabby house on the edge of Paris, locked in mutual hatred and contempt. They barely ever speak, are intent on causing each other misery and Julien has transferred the love he once had for his wife to his cat. Adapted from a novel by Georges Simenon, this is unlikely film material since the action is minimal, the environment hermetically sealed and the dialogue almost non-existent. However, by dint of inspired casting and a sensitivity in imparting meaning to objects and small gestures, Granier-Deferre almost manages to sustain our interest. It is a little drawn out and the flashbacks that remind us of the couple's youth are superfluous—particularly as we are left in the dark as to why their love turned to hate—but the leads' wholehearted double act is marvellous to watch.
Best Actor (Jean Gabin) Berlin 1971
Best Actress (Simone Signoret) Berlin 1971

Chat Dans Le Sac, Le see Cat In The Bag, The

Chat Et La Souris, Le see Cat And Mouse

Chatte Sort Ses Griffes, La see Cat Shows Her Claws, The

Cheat, The see Wanton, The

Cheats, The see Youthful Sinners

Chelovek S Kinoapparatom see Man With The Movie Camera, The

Chère Louise see Louise

The Chess Players

Shatranj Ke Khilari
India 1977 135 mins col
Devki Chitra

d **Satyajit Ray**
sc **Satyajit Ray**
ph **Soumendou Roy**
m **Satyajit Ray**
Sanjeev Kumar, Saeed Jaffrey, Richard Attenborough, Amjad Khan

In Lucknow in 1856, two indolent chess-obsessed noblemen, neglecting their families, continue to play while the Maharajah, an effete poet- musician, is being dethroned by the British East India Company. Ray's first film in Hindi (and English delivered by Attenborough's Scots accent) is quietly humorous and sharply-observed, as well as being acute about Anglo- Indian relations in Victorian times. The attempt to link the chess playing to the wider political games is less successful.

Cheval D'Orgueil, Le see Proud Ones, The

Chichi Ariki see There Was A Father

Chieko-Sho see Portrait Of Chieko

Un Chien Andalou

(US: An Andalusian Dog)
France 1928 17 mins bw
Luis Buñuel-Salvador Dali

d **Luis Buñuel**
sc **Luis Buñuel, Salvador Dali**
ph **Albert Dubergen**
m **Silent**
Simone Mareuil, Pierre Batcheff, Jaime Miravilles, Salvador Dali, Luis Buñuel

An open eye is slashed in half with a razor, ants emerge from the palm of a hand, breasts dissolve into buttocks, priests are pulled along the ground, dead donkeys lie on two pianos ... Made under the influence of André Breton's Surrealist Manifesto, this series of unconnected incidents designed to have the logic of a dream, was the cinematic equivalent of the surrealist's automatic writing. And so

Buñuel's career as a director began with one of the most startling and most famous images in all cinema—the cutting of the eye. The film is still, as Jean Vigo stated in 1930, 'a work of major importance in every respect'. It was financed by Buñuel's mother, as well as the Vicomte de Noailles and 'money won by a friend on the lottery'. The music of Wagner, Beethoven, and a tango was added as a sound track in 1960.

La Chienne

France 1931 100 mins bw
Braunberger-Richebé

d **Jean Renoir**
sc **Jean Renoir**
ph **Théodor Sparkühl, Roger Hubert**
Michel Simon, Janie Marèze, Georges Flament, Jean Gehret

An unhappily married clerk (Simon) falls for a prostitute (Marèze), steals from his employer to satisfy her demands, and kills her out of jealousy of her pimp (Flament). Renoir demonstrates his ability to turn an amoral little melodrama into a work of unsentimental naturalism, creating characters rather than types. By filming in the noisy streets of Montmartre, without using any dubbed sound, a real, habitable world is created. But if the film imitated life, so life imitated the film. During the shooting, Simon became infatuated with Marèze who fell for Flament. The film completed, Flament drove along the Riviera with Marèze in his new American car and had an accident in which she was killed. *La Chienne*—an English translation of the title (The Bitch) was deemed unfit—was remade by Fritz Lang as *Scarlet Street* (1945).

Chikamatsu Monogatari see Crucified Lovers, The

Chikuzan Hitori Tabi see Life Of Chikuzan, The

Chikuzan Travels Alone see Life Of Chikuzan, The

The Childhood Of Maxim Gorky

Detstvo Gorkovo

USSR 1938 101 mins bw
Soyezdetfilm

d **Mark Donskoi**
sc **Mark Donskoi, I. Grudzev**
ph **Pyotr Yermolov**
m **Lev Schwartz**
Alexei Lyarsky (Maxim Gorky), Y. Valbert, M. Troyanovski, Valeria Massalitinova

Young Alexei Pyeshkov (later Maxim Gorky) arrives to live with his struggling grandparents in a small riverside town. With his eccentric bickering relations, the peasants and the workmen, the boy experiences early joys and sorrows, and learns to love the people and landscape of his country suffering under the Tsar. The first film in the Gorky trilogy, on which Donskoi's fame rests, is rich in humour, character and period detail, faithful to the vision of the great Marxist proletarian writer. Outstanding is Massalitinova's old grandmother.

The Children Are Watching Us

I Bambini Ci Guardano

Italy 1943 85 mins bw
Scalera/Invicta

d **Vittorio De Sica**
sc **Cesare Zavattini, Vittorio De Sica, Cesare Giulio Viola, Adolfo Franci, Margherita Maglione, Gherardo Gherardi**
ph **Giuseppe Caracciolo**
m **Renzo Rossellini**
Isa Pola, Luciano De Ambrosis, Adriano Rimoldi, Giovanna Cigoli

A four-year-old boy (De Ambrosis) watches the break-up of the marriage of his middle-class parents, an unfaithful mother (Pola) and a suicidal father (Rimoldi). After directing and acting in four sentimental comedies, De Sica suddenly made a breakthrough with a dramatic, humane and sharply realistic work. It was also his first important collaboration with the writer Cesare Zavattini, who was to contribute to virtually all his following films. Here, with the recently orphaned De Ambrosis, De Sica showed himself a sensitive director of children as he was to prove still further in *Shoeshine* and *Bicycle Thieves*. One of the first Neo-Realist films, it was influential in changing the face of Italian cinema, although financially unsuccessful.

Children In Uniform see Mädchen In Uniform

Children Of Hiroshima

Genbaku No Ko

Japan 1952 97 mins bw
Kendai Eiga Kyokai/Gekidan Mingei

d **Kaneto Shindo**
sc **Kaneto Shindo**
ph **Takeo Itoh**
m **Akira Ifukube**
Nobuko Otowa, Chikako Hoshawa, Niwa Saito

In 1952, seven years after the dropping of the first atomic bomb, a schoolteacher returns to Hiroshima to visit her parents' grave and to discover how her friends and ex-pupils have lived since that horrendous day. The brief but harrowing flashback reconstruction of the bombing clouds the rest of the humanist tale of the aftermath. The film is surprisingly free from bitterness, although it cannot disguise the revulsion most people feel about the event.

Children Of Paradise see Enfants Du Paradis, Les

China Is Near

La Cina E Vicina

Italy 1967 95 mins bw
Vides Cinematografica

d **Marco Bellocchio**
sc **Marco Bellocchio, Elda Tattoli**
ph **Tonino Delli Colli**
m **Ennio Morricone**
Paulo Graziosi, Glauco Mauri, Elda Tattoli, Daniela Surina, Pierluigi Apra

When Vittorio (Mauri), the elder brother of a wealthy land-owning family, becomes a Socialist candidate, his younger brother (Apra), who has become a Maoist, does everything he can to disrupt his campaign. Their sister (Tattoli) is indifferent until she meets and falls in love with Vittorio's Party manager (Graziosi). Bellochio, who made an impressive debut with *Fists In The Pocket*, which dealt with family oppression, again uses the metaphor of the family to analyse the way revolutionary activity is absorbed into the *bourgeois* state. With a controlled camera style, the film is sharply ironic about Italian politics, casting its net of mockery far and wide. The performers successfully take on the tone of the picture.

Special Jury Prize Venice 1967

Chinese Girl, The see Chinoise, La

Chinese Roulette

Chinesisches Roulette

W. Germany 1976 86 mins col
Albatros/Films Du Losange

d **Rainer Werner Fassbinder**
sc **Rainer Werner Fassbinder**
ph **Michael Ballhaus**
m **Peer Raben**
Margit Carstensen, Ulli Lommel, Anna Karina, Macha Meril, Brigitte Mira, Andrea Schober, Volker Spengler

A crippled girl (Schober) tricks her businessman father (Lommel) and her mother (Carstensen) into going to their country house with their lovers (Karina and Spengler) on the same weekend. There they play a series of games culminating in Chinese Roulette, a truth game that reveals more than they bargained for. It was during the shooting (at photographer Ballhaus's *schloss*) of this bizarre and bitter comedy of bad manners that Fassbinder started on the hard drugs that were to lead to his premature death only six years later. Yet, the roaming camera movements, the aesthetic framing and colour photography make it one of the most controlled and formalistic of his films. Some of the more melodramatic elements of the screenplay are acceptable due to the exemplary ensemble playing.

Chinesisches Roulette see Chinese Roulette

La Chinoise

aka The Chinese Girl

France 1967 95 mins col

Production De La Guéville/Parc/Simar/Anouchka/Athos

d **Jean-Luc Godard**
sc **Jean-Luc Godard**
ph **Raoul Coutard**
m **Stockhausen**
Anne Wiazemsky, Francis Jeanson, Jean-Pierre Léaud, Juliet Berto

One summer vacation in Paris, a group of young people, including an actor, a painter, a student, an economist and a philosopher, set up a Maoist cell to try to put their theories into revolutionary practice. With this lively, polemical comedy thriller, Godard moved more directly towards the Maoist commitment, which only crystallized with the events of 1968, so prophetically set out here. Many of the debates about *bourgeois* ideology that would take place on the streets of Paris less than a year later are already being expounded by his characters. But it's certainly not only a film of words; there are actions and relationships revolving around Wiazemsky (Godard's new wife) as a student at Nanterre trying to balance her personal and political life. Appropriately, red is the dominant colour of the photography.

Special Jury Prize Venice 1967

Chips Are Down, The see Jeux Sont Faits, Les

Chistoye Nebo see Clear Sky

Chloë In The Afternoon see Love In The Afternoon

Choses De La Vie, Les see Things Of Life, The

Christiane F.

Christiane F. Wir Kinder Vom Bahnhof Zoo

W. Germany 1981 131 mins col
Solaris Film/Maran Film/Popular Film/CLV

d **Ulrich Edel**
sc **Herman Weigel**
ph **Justus Pankau, Jürgen Jürges**
m **David Bowie, Jürgen Knieper**
Natja Brunckhorst, Thomas Haustein, Jens Kuphal, Rainer Wölk

Thirteen-year-old Christiane (Brunckhorst) gets involved with the teenage drug scene in Berlin, and has an affair with Detlef (Haustein) who works as a male prostitute in order to pay for the dope. Their cold-turkey attempt goes for naught when they visit friends at the Zoo station, main hangout for addicts, pushers and hustlers. Edel, a TV director making his first feature, based it on a bestseller, itself written up from Christiane's confessions to two *Stern* reporters. First-time actors and a semi-documentary style contribute to a bleak and harrowing film in which the director has eliminated any suggestion of glamour by using bleached out colour and close-ups to convey the full physical horrors of heroin addiction. Salutary, and not a pleasant way to pass the time.

Christiane F. Wir Kinder Vom Bahnhof Zoo see Christiane F.

Christ Stopped At Eboli

Cristo Si E Fermato A Eboli

Italy 1979 155 mins col
Vides/RAI/Action/Gaumont

d **Francesco Rosi**
sc **Francesco Rosi, Tonino Guerra, Raffaele La Capria**
ph **Pasqualino De Santis**
m **Piero Piccioni**
Gian Maria Volonté, Alain Cuny, Paolo Bonacelli, Lea Massari, Irene Papas, François Simon

In 1935, doctor-painter-writer Carlo Levi (Volonté) is exiled from Turin to a primitive southern village because of his anti-Fascist views. There he learns to understand the national character which he finds amusing, irritating and sympathetic. Like Levi's reactions in Volonté's brilliantly nuanced performance, one might react to Rosi's leisurely, often too literary film in the same way. The authentic mountain village background and characters offer an interesting insight into the place and period. A television version runs 240 minutes.

Ta Chromata Tis Iridas see Colours Of Iris, The

Chronicle Of A Death Foretold

Cronaca Di Una Morte Annunciata

Italy 1987 110 mins col
Italmedia/Soprofilms/Les Films Ariane/FR3 Films

d **Francesco Rosi**
sc **Francesco Rosi, Tonino Guerra**
ph **Pasqualino De Santis**
m **Piero Piccioni**
Rupert Everett, Gian Maria Volonté, Ornella Muti, Anthony Delon, Irene Papas, Lucia Bosé

Twenty years after a handsome youth (Delon) was murdered for supposedly deflowering a beautiful virgin (Muti), leading to the ruin of her glittering marriage to a wealthy man (Everett) who abandons her, the community's doctor (Volonté) returns to investigate the circumstances of the death. Set in a small and steamy Colombian town, Rosi's adaptation of Gabriel Garcia Marquez' novel concentrates on the misplaced codes of honour, *machismo* and revenge which led the girl's twin brothers to commit the brutal crime, and exposes the hypocritical conspiracy of silence which made possible the killing of an almost certainly innocent man. Told in flashback, the film has epic sweep and visual power, but is somewhat slow and static, and lacking in a strong authorial voice.

Chronicle of A Love

(US: Story Of A Love Affair)

Cronaca Di Un Amore

Italy 1950 96 mins bw
Villani Films

d **Michelangelo Antonioni**
sc **Michelangelo Antonioni, Danièle D'Anza, Silvio Giovaninetti, Francesco Maselli, Piero Tellini**
ph **Enzo Serafin**
m **Giovanni Fusco**
Lucia Bosé, Massimo Girotti, Ferdinando Sarmi, Gino Rossi, Marika Rowsky

An adulterous wife (Bosé) and her impoverished lover (Girotti) consider the murder of her rich husband, but he dies—by accident or suicide—and they have to live with the guilt of their intention. Antonioni was 38 years old before he found 'a man from Turin who was willing to finance a film for me'. Already his personal stamp is noticeable in the cool, elegant style in contrast to the Neo-Realist manner of many of his Italian contemporaries, and to his own documentaries. Foreshadowing his later work are the intricate camera movements, the use of an urban landscape and an unsolved mystery. The plot was in the tradition of American thrillers such as *The Postman Always Rings Twice* which had inspired Visconti's *Ossessione* (1942) also featuring Girotti.

The Chronicle Of Anna Magdalena Bach

Chronik Der Anna Magdalena Bach

W. Germany 1967 93 mins bw
IDI/RAI/Franz Seitz/Kuatorium Junger Deutscher Film/ Straub-Huillet/Filmfonds/Tele Pool

d **Jean-Marie Straub**
sc **Jean-Marie Straub, Danièle Huillet**
ph **Ugo Piccone**
m **Johann Sebastian Bach**
Gustav Leonhardt, Christiane Lang, Paolo Carlini, Katrin Leonhardt, Rainer Kirchner, Ernst Castelli

The daily life of Johann Sebastian Bach (Leonhardt)— his conflicts with his patrons, his work as a composer and musician, his relationships with his family—as seen through the eyes of his second wife (Lang). Straub's second feature, which took 10 years to prepare, is totally convincing in its historical accuracy and musical authenticity, with most of the roles taken by professional musicians. Thus Leonhardt, playing Bach, both the man and the music, contributes to making this an almost documentary account of instrumentalists at work during the 18th century. The chronicle is interspersed with concerts and landscape scenes, and the use of direct sound and extremely long takes helps the frozen images to supplement, rather than distract from, the music.

Chronicle Of A Summer

Chronique D'Un Été

France 1961 90 mins bw
Argos Films

d **Jean Rouch, Edgar Morin**

sc **Jean Rouch, Edgar Morin,**
ph **Roger Morillers, Raoul Coutard, Jean-Jacques Tarbes, Michel Brault**

One summer, a cross-section of Parisians are asked by anthropologist film-maker Rouch and sociologist Morin to respond to the question 'Are You Happy?'. Edited down from 25 hours of interviews, the film takes a fascinating ethnological approach to the French. The development of light-weight sound and ciné equipment helped create the style which was called for the first time *cinéma-vérité* (a translation of Dziga Vertov's *Kino Pravda*) to publicize the film. The ambitious document ends with the interviewees reacting to themselves on screen.

Chronicle Of The Burning Years

aka Chronicle Of The Years Of The Brazier
aka Chronicle Of The Years Of Embers
Ahdat Sanawouach El-Djamr
aka Chronique Des Années De Braises
Algeria 1975 175 mins col
ONCIC

d **Mohammed Lakhdar-Hamina**
sc **Mohammed Lakhdar-Hamina, Rachid Boujedra**
ph **Marcello Gatti**
m **Philippe Arthuys**
Mohammed Lakhdar-Hamina, Jorge Voyagis, Leila Shenna, Cheik Nourredine

The history of Algeria from 1939 to 1954, the year of the beginning of the revolution, is reflected in the lives of the people in two impoverished villages who rise up against the French colonial presence. One of the most ambitious and expensive productions ever to come out of the Third World, it has the look of a Hollywood epic woven through with Arab culture. Spectacular though it is, Lakhdar-Hamina, one of the pioneers of Algerian cinema, and Boujedra, the great Algerian novelist, still succeed in presenting a personal view of events. Still, a smaller film might have created deeper characters.

Best Film Cannes 1975

Chronicle Of The Years Of Embers see Chronicle Of The Burning Years

---

Chronicle Of The Years Of The Brazier see Chronicle Of The Burning Years

---

The Chronicles Of The Grey House

Zur Chronik Von Grieshuus
Germany 1925 172 mins bw
UFA

d **Arthur Von Gerlach**
sc **Thea Von Harbou**
ph **Fritz Arno Wagner**
m **Silent**
Arthur Kraussneck, Paul Hartmann, Lil Dagover, Rudolf Forster, Gertrud Welcker

In the Middle Ages, Hinrich (Hartmann), heir to the Castle Grieshuus, marries Greta (Dagover), a commoner. Hinrich kills his brother (Forster) in a duel over his inheritance and Greta dies in childbirth. After eight years of wandering, Hinrich returns to be reunited with his son. A film known more by reputation than by experience, it has been difficult to see at its original length, and a 42-minute condensed version is the only evidence most critics have of its quality. Influenced more by Swedish melodramas than the German *Caligari* tradition, it is striking for its location shooting—the castle overlooking a melancholy moor is particularly effective—and its atmospheric lighting. Von Gerlach, a shadowy figure in the German cinema, died of apoplexy soon after completing this, his fourth film. Of the others only *Vanina* (1922) is extant.

Chronik Der Anna Magdalena Bach see Chronicle Of Anna Magdalena Bach, The

---

Chronique Des Années De Braises see Chronicle Of The Burning Years

---

Chronique D'Un Été see Chronicle Of A Summer

Chuquiago

Bolivia 1977 87 mins col
Grupo Ukamau

d **Antonio Eguino**
sc **Oscar Soria**
ph **Antonio Eguina, Julio Lencina, Juan Miranda**
m **Alberto Villalpando**
Nestor Yujra, Edmundo Villaroel, David Santalla, Tatiana Aponta, Alejandra Quispe

Four stories about four people from different social strata in La Paz, the capital of Bolivia: an Indian boy (Yujra) working for a drink vendor, a restless teenage son (Villaroel) of workers, a middle-aged lower middle-class functionary and playboy (Santalla) and a university student and spoiled daughter (Aponta) of the *haute bourgeoisie.* Antonio Eguino, the photographer on the once-banned *Blood Of The Condor*, reached a wider audience with this movie, the most expensive to be made in Bolivia by Bolivians, which became the country's biggest box-office success ever, at home and abroad. Made under the military regime, it naturally lacks a political dimension, yet audiences may come to their own conclusions on the lives so skilfully depicted.

The Churning

Manthan

India 1976 133 mins col
Gujarat Co-operative Milk Marketing Federation

d **Shyam Benegal**
sc **Vijay Tendulkar**
ph **Govind Nihalani**
m **Vanraj Bhatia**
Girish Karnad, Smita Patil, Naseeruddin Shah, Anant Nag, Amrish Puri

A government team, headed by veterinary surgeon Dr Rao (Karnad) and his assistant (Nag), arrive in the village of Gujarat to help set up a milk co-operative. They encounter many obstacles, not least from the local moneylender (Puri), who also owns the local dairy. Consolidating the reputation established earlier with his debut film, *The Seedling*, Benegal offers another and even more assured study of rural life. Ostensibly about the virtues of the co-operative movement, the film can be taken on many levels—as a tale of class intrigue and hostilities, a view of women's emancipation or as a series of humorous, sharply observed and, superbly photographed studies of village life. The only weakness comes in some of the romantic scenes. Benegal's films, which carry a powerful plea for equality and justice, usually manage to pay for themselves, and, being in Hindi, they reach a wider audience in India than many other fine films in regional languages.

Chute De La Maison Usher, La see Fall Of The House Of Usher, The

---

Le Ciel Est À Vous

(US: The Woman Who Dared)

France 1944 105 mins bw
Raoul Ploquin

d **Jean Grémillon**
sc **Albert Valentin, Charles Spaak**
ph **Louis Page**
m **Roland Manuel**
Madeleine Renaud, Charles Vanel, Jean Debucourt, Anne Vandenne, Raymonde Vernay

Thérèse and Pierre Gauthier (Renaud and Vanel), a *bourgeois* couple with two children, suddenly develop a passion for flying. Thérèse becomes a pilot and, after many crises, breaks the women's non-stop, long distance flight record. A film about flying that has few aerial sequences, doesn't show the heroine at the controls of the plane or a pilot's subjective view, is quite an achievement. Although not overtly political, it was also a brave film to make in Vichy France which stressed that a woman's place is in the home. With his customary tenderness and restraint, Grémillon, a most under-rated director outside France, charts the movements of the marriage and the obsession, in one brilliant passage using a parallel between music and flying. Renaud's and Vanel's performances also take flight.

Cielo Sulla Palude see Heaven Over The Marshes

Cigalon

France 1935 70 mins bw
Les Films Marcel Pagnol

La Cina E Vicina

d **Marcel Pagnol**
sc **Marcel Pagnol**
ph **A. Assouad**
m **Vincent Scotto**
Arnaudy, Henri Poupon, Madame Chabert, Alida Rouffe, Jean Castan, Léon Brouzet, Charles Blavette

Cigalon (Arnaudy), once a grand chef in the best hotels, runs the only restaurant in a village in Provence until Madame Toffi (Chabert), ex-laundress, opens a rival restaurant just opposite. War is declared, culminating in a battle over a 'rich' client, followed by a merger i.e. marriage. A comedy as delicious as the 200-franc meal served in the film, and played with the verve usual in Pagnol's *oeuvre*. However, as with *Merlusse*, he was dissatisfied with the first shooting and refilmed it a few weeks later. In the premier attempt, Poupon played the title role, but was more at ease here as The Client.

Cina E Vicina, La see China Is Near

Cinderella—Italian Style
(US: More Than A Miracle)
C'Era Una Volta

Italy 1967 103 mins col
Champion Films/Concordia

d **Francesco Rosi**
sc **Tonino Guerra, Raffaele La Capria, Giuseppe Patroni Griffi, Francesco Rosi**
ph **Pasquale De Santis**
m **Piero Piccione**
Sophia Loren, Omar Sharif, Dolores Del Rio, Georges Wilson, Leslie French, Carlo Pisacane

A Spanish nobleman (Sharif), under family pressure to marry which he does his best to ignore, falls in love with a beautiful peasant girl (Loren). Misunderstandings and the deceits practised by others keep them apart until the intervention of a priest, now become an angel, helps them to a happy ending. This curious confection from Rosi, concocted from several Italian fairy tales, is photographed to recall the look of storybook illustrations. Acted with a light touch, the film is charming and sometimes funny, but is hampered by being overlong for its content.

Ciociara, La see Two Women

Circle Of Deceit
Die Fälschung

W. Germany 1981 109 mins col
Bioskop-Film/Artemis-Film (Munich)/Argos Films (Paris)

d **Volker Schlöndorff**
sc **Volker Schlöndorff, Jean-Claude Carrière, Margarethe Von Trotta, Kai Hermann**
ph **Igor Luther**
m **Maurice Jarre**
Bruno Ganz, Hanna Schygulla, Jerzy Skolimowski, Gila Von Weitershausen, Jean Carmet

A West German journalist (Ganz) in the throes of marital conflict is sent to the Lebanon with his photographer (Skolimowski). Once there, he gets caught up in events that compromise his professional integrity, has an affair with an old friend (Schygulla), now the widow of an Arab, and stabs an Arab civilian in panic, all the while undergoing a crisis of conscience, until he finally returns home to his wife. Schlöndorff's film is an uneasy mix of personal and political concerns. Actually filmed in war-torn Lebanon, the scenes of civil strife and daily atrocities have a terrifying and dramatic immediacy, but the hero's indulgent preoccupation with self, his political confusion and his half-baked opportunism, as well as his clichéd domestic situation, amount to an irritating character who fails to serve any deeper political purpose the director might have had.

The Citizen
Nagarik

India 1952 120 mins bw
Film Guild

d **Ritwick Ghatak**
sc **Ritwick Ghatak**
ph **Ramananda Sengupta**
m **Hariprasanna Das**
Satindra Bhattacharya, Prabha Devi, Shobha Sen, Ajit Banerjee, Ketaki Devi

In the teeming city of Calcutta, a young college graduate (Bhattacharya) is unable to get a job that would allow him to marry the girl (Ketaki

Devi) he loves. When his father dies, things go from bad to worse and he, his mother (Prabha Devi) and unmarried sister (Sen) move from a middle-class neighbourhood into the working-class slums. Ghatak's first feature, made three years before Satyajit Ray's watershed *Pather Panchali*, was only released in 1977, two years after the director's death. The main strength of the film is its neo-realist depiction of the city which forms the background to a *petit-bourgeois* family with illusions of upward social mobility. The weaknesses come in some of the theatrical acting, some erratic editing and lighting (not surprising as it was made with little money under difficult circumstances) and a belief that the use of the 'Communist Internationale' on the sound track at the end is sufficient to make a Marxist point.

Città Delle Donne, La see City Of Women

City Of Pirates

La Ville Des Pirates

France 1983 121 mins col
Les Films Du Passage (Paris)/Metro Films (Lisbon)

d **Râúl Ruiz**
sc **Râúl Ruiz**
ph **Acácio De Almeida**
m **Jorge Arriagada**
Hugues Quester, Anne Alvaro, Melvil Poupaud, André Engel, Duarte De Almeida

A surrealist fantasy involving a murderous child (Poupaud), a dreamy girl (Alvaro), who might be his mother, a schizophrenic pirate (Quester) who keeps her prisoner on a rocky island, incestuous relationships, a castration and a rape. It is impossible to give a synopsis of Ruiz's delirious baroque tale and even more difficult to compare it to anything else in contemporary cinema. Elusive and allusive as the film is, defying definitive interpretation, the surprising imagery and the bizarre humour hold the interest in this *reductio ad absurdum* of storytelling.

City Of Women

La Città Delle Donne

Italy 1980 140 mins col
Opera Film/Gaumont(France)

d **Federico Fellini**
sc **Federico Fellini, Bernardino Zapponi**
ph **Giuseppe Rotunno**
m **Luis Bacalov**
Marcello Mastroianni, Anna Prucnal, Bernice Stegers, Ettore Manni, Donatella Damiani

Snàporaz (Mastroianni), a middle-aged businessman, is enticed off a train and finds himself in a world completely dominated by women. As more and more bizarre adventures overtake him, it is clear that he is moving through his own fears and fantasies about women. This rather simple-minded and self-indulgent anti-feminist allegory has the advantage of Fellini's visual and emotional mastery and for much of its excessive length, there is a great deal to wonder at. But it lacks Nino Rota's essential musical collaboration, as well as any recognizable characters, although Mastroianni makes what he can of the pathetic and ridiculous hero.

Ciulinii Baraganului see Thistles Of Baragan, The

Claire's Knee

Le Genou De Claire

France 1970 106 mins col
Films Du Losange

d **Eric Rohmer**
sc **Eric Rohmer**
ph **Nestor Almendros**
Jean-Claude Brialy, Aurora Cornu, Laurence De Monaghan, Béatrice Romand, Gérard Falconetti

Prior to his marriage to a Swedish woman, a diplomat in his thirties (Brialy) takes a brief summer holiday at the lake resort of Annecy. Encouraged by his Romanian novelist friend (Cornu), he flirts with two sisters, but is only satisfied when he gets to fondle the knee of the elder one (De Monaghan), a sensuous beauty. Rohmer's lucid prose and witty observation delights as much as the shimmering background to his film. The actual moment when Brialy fulfils his desire is as erotic as any heavy- breathing bed play.

Clan Des Siciliens, Le see Sicilian Clan, The

Classe Operaia Va In Paradiso, La see Working Class Go To Heaven, The

Class Relations

Klassenverhältnisse

W. Germany 1984 127 mins bw
Janus Film/Hessischer Rundfunk

d **Jean-Marie Straub, Danièle Huillet**
sc **Jean-Marie Straub, Danièle Huillet**
ph **William Lubtchansky**
Christian Heinisch, Mario Adorf, Manfred Blank, Harun Farocki, Kathrin Bold, Libgart Schwarz, Laura Betti, Anne Bold, Alfred Edel, Andi Engel

Sixteen-year-old Karl Rossmann (Heinisch), sent from Prague to America, is unexpectedly welcomed by a rich uncle (Adorf). After failing in business, Karl sets out across country with two tramps, gets a job as an elevator-boy in a hotel and becomes a servant to an ex-opera singer (Betti). Wherever he goes, he feels he has been unjustly treated, but his goodness and integrity remain intact. Much of the original dialogue has been retained in Straub and Huillet's adaptation of Kafka's *Amerika*, as has the irony and moments of slapstick comedy; only the unfinished novel's final chapter in Oklahoma has been omitted. The America that Kafka never saw was created by filming surroundings in Germany that could be anywhere. The directors' most approachable film, it demonstrates their characteristic 'minimalist' style of paring down each scene to its essentials (usually only one actor on screen at a time), restraining any expression and, as the title suggests, bringing out more social than psychological elements of the picaresque tale.

Clean Slate

Coup De Torchon

France 1981 128 mins col
Les Films De La Tour/Les Films A2/Little Bear

d **Bertrand Tavernier**
sc **Jean Aurenche, Bertrand Tavernier**
ph **Pierre William Glenn**
m **Philippe Sarde**
Philippe Noiret, Isabelle Huppert, Jean-Pierre Marielle, Stéphane Audran, Guy Marchand

Lucien Cordier (Noiret), lackadaisical law officer and general laughing stock of a West African township in 1938, undergoes a complete transformation of character when, after shooting a pair of pimps, he sets out to get rid of everybody who is a thorn in his side, including his wife whose death he contrives, and his mistress whom he frames. Noiret is excellent in a film which offers some quirky humour and a good sense of atmosphere, and some entertainment is to be had from this portrait of a man seized by a form of mania, provided one doesn't look for any coherency of motivation. Tavernier has translated, adapted and distorted a novel by Jim Thompson set in the Deep South, and, in so doing, has muddied its motivations.

Clear Sky

Chistoye Nebo

USSR 1961 109 mins col
Mosfilm

d **Grigori Chukrai**
sc **Daniel Khrabrovitsky**
ph **Sergei Poluyanov**
m **Mikhail Ziv**
Nina Drobysheva, Yevgeny Urbansky, N. Kuzmina, Vitali Konyayev

A young woman (Drobysheva) meets and falls in love with a famous test pilot (Urbansky). She has his child and waits for him to come back from the war. When he returns, he is unjustly accused of treachery and stripped of his membership of the Party but, after Stalin's death, he is recognized as a 'Hero of the Soviet Union'. Watching this competently directed romantic drama, it is difficult to imagine its impact in the USSR at the time. When the ex-hero is told he cannot rejoin the Party, a huge effigy of Stalin looks down on him. The film ends with a symbolic shot of an iced-over river beginning to thaw. Aside from the historical interest of the piece, the acting of the leads is extremely good and many of the scenes have a ring of truth, despite the sprinkling of clichés throughout.

Cléo De 5 À 7 see Cleo From 5 To 7

Cleo From 5 To 7

Cléo De 5 À 7

France 1961 90 mins bw-col
Rome-Paris Films

d **Agnès Varda**
sc **Agnès Varda**
ph **Jean Rabier**
m **Michel Legrand**
Corinne Marchand, Antoine Bourseiller, Dorothée Blanck, Michel Legrand, José-Luis Villalonga

Two hours in the life of a spoiled nightclub singer as she waits for the medical verdict on whether she is to live or die. Rabier's camera captures the sheen of Paris where every trivial incident takes on a new significance for the heroine. In fact, everything is seen in such *Nouvelle Vague* brilliance that the anxiety of the protagonist (the coolly beautiful ex- model Marchand) gets somewhat buried. The silent comedy Cleo watches shows Varda's colleagues Jean-Luc Godard, Anna Karina, Eddie Constantine and Jean-Claude Brialy enjoying themselves.

Cloak, The see Overcoat, The

Clochemerle

aka The Scandals Of Clochemerle
France 1947 93 mins bw
Cinéma Productions

d **Pierre Chenal**
sc **Gabriel Chevallier**
ph **Robert Le Fèbvre**
m **Henri Sauguet**
Brochard, Maximilienne, Simone Michels, Jane Marken, Paul Demange, Félix Oudart, Saturnin Fabre

The progressive mayor (Brochard) of a small, conservative French village decides to build a public convenience in the town square, much to the horror of the inhabitants. As nobody in British or American films ever went to the lavatory or even possessed one until the 1960s, this mildly amusing comedy which revolved round a latrine, was a big hit abroad. But Chevallier seemed to have coarsened the satire in the adaptation from his own bestseller.

Closely Observed Trains

(US: Closely Watched Trains)
Ostře Sledované Vlaky
Czechoslovakia 1966 92 mins col
Ceskoslovensky Film

d **Jiří Menzel**
sc **Jiří Menzel, Bohumil Hrabal**
ph **Jaromír Šofr**
m **Jiří Pavlik**
Václav Neckár, Jitka Bendová, Libuše Havelková, Vladimir Valenta, Josef Somr, Jiří Menzel

During the German Occupation, a young trainee railway guard (Neckár) at a remote country station desperately tries to lose his virginity. He finally succeeds with the station master's wife (Havelková). Menzel's first solo-directed film is closely observed, satiric, touching, anti-heroic and humorous, very much in the Czech new wave tradition of the 1960s. It is also perfectly balanced between comedy and tragedy. The director wanted a happy ending, but co-writer Hrabal, on whose novel the film was based, persuaded him to retain the tragic conclusion.

Best Foreign Film Oscar 1967

Closely Watched Trains see Closely Observed Trains

Close To The Wind

Oss Emellan
Sweden 1969 110 mins col
Omega Film/Filmmakarna/'Oss Emellan' Inc

d **Stellan Olsson**
sc **Stellan Olsson, Per Oscarsson**
ph **Jesper Höm, Lasse Dahlqvist**
m **Joe Hill, Tage Sivén**
Per Oscarsson, Bärbel Oscarsson, Lina Oscarsson, Boman Oscarsson, Maria Oscarsson, Beppe Wolgers, Christina Johansson

Per (Oscarsson), an unsuccessful artist with three children, devotes his energies to attempting a life of individualistic non-conformism, while his wife Bärbel teaches at the local school to support them. Per's excesses of behaviour are infinite and include the unveiling of pornographic designs to the board that has commissioned a mural. In his debut film, Olsson retains control of a tricky subject by recognizing the contradictions inherent in opposing a social system without having a coherent alternative to offer, and by creating an impressively naturalistic world for his protagonist. Per Oscarsson's close involvement in the project includes the casting of his wife and children, called by their own names in the film and thus helping to blur the lines between fiction and reality. The movie, which analyses the artist's role in society, does so in tones of parody and deploys some wonderfully contrary images: episodes of marital discord are set against lyrical backgrounds, while Per's idyllic outing on the beach with his mistress is accompanied by grey skies and blustery wind.

Clothes Make The Man

Kleider Machen Leute

Germany 1940 102 mins bw
Terra-Filmkunst

d **Helmut Käutner**
sc **Helmut Käutner**
ph **Ewald Daub**
m **Bernhard Eichhorn**
Heinz Rühmann, Hertha Feiler, Hilde Sessak, Hans Sternberg, Fritz Odemar, Rudolf Schündler, Erich Ponto

Wenzel (Rühmann), a daydreaming tailor's apprentice in a small Tyrolean town, gives in to fantasy and cuts the Mayor's new dress suit to fit himself. Sacked for this action, he leaves town with only the suit to his name and is everywhere mistaken for a nobleman. Encouraged by a puppet master (Ponto), he goes to Goldbach, pretending to be Stroganov (Odemar), a Russian Count who is expected there by Fräulein Von Serafin (Sessak), who falls in love with him. To complicate matters further, the real Stroganov turns up... Basing his third film on a novella by the 19th-century Swiss-German Romantic, Gottfried Keller, Käutner has made a thoroughly entertaining film from a well-constructed screenplay. Aside from its obvious merits of directorial quality, and a story in which romance and humour is the veneer applied to an ironic comment on the hypocritical surface of *bourgeois* values—all show and no substance—the film offers other pleasures. These spring from Käutner's exceptional eye for incidental but telling visual detail that contribute to his loving and critical evocation of period folksiness, from which the deceiver emerges as worthier than the deceived.

Clowns, Il see Clowns, The

The Clowns

Il Clowns

Italy 1970 92 mins col
RAI/Leone/O.R.T.F./Bavaria Film (Munich)

d **Federico Fellini**
sc **Federico Fellini, Bernardino Zapponi**
ph **Dario Di Palma**
m **Nino Rota**
Riccardo Billi, Tino Scotti, Fanfulla, Carlo Rizzo, Freddo Pistoni (and other Italian and French clowns), Pierre Etaix, Annie Fratellini, Anita Ekberg, Victoria Chaplin, Maya Morin

Fellini and a comically clumsy film crew investigate the art of the circus clown by watching and talking to still active, as well as former, exponents of the profession. He also remembers the Rimini of his childhood when the circus came to town. 'My films owe an enormous amount to the circus. For me the clowns were always a traumatic visual experience, ambassadors of a vocation of a showman,' Fellini has stated. Here the great Italian ringmaster of the cinema affectionately returns to the root of his inspiration, absorbing it masterfully into his own personal vision.

Coach To Vienna

Kocár Do Vidne

Czechoslovakia 1966 80 mins bw
Ceskoslovensky Film, Barrandov Studio

d **Karel Kachyna**
sc **Jan Procházka, Karel Kachyna**
ph **Josef Illík**
m **Jan Novák**
Iva Janzurová, Jaromír Hanzlík, Ludek Munzar

In 1944 in Czechoslovakia, a young peasant woman Christa (Janzurová) watches the Germans hang her husband for stealing two bags of cement. She buries him and then her farm wagon is commandeered by an Austrian soldier and his seriously wounded German colleague who order her to drive them to the frontier. Appearing to comply, she plans her revenge..... Centring on Janzurová's almost silent and compellingly strong performance, this tightly constructed film eloquently describes the brutalizing effects of war and the tragic pointlessness of revenge. It is unfortunate that a work of grim horror, made with clear-sighted intelligence and irony, should have an English title that so misleadingly evokes a period romance.

Cobra Verde

W. Germany 1988 111 mins col
Concorde Film/Werner Herzog Film Production, in co-operation with ZDF & the Ghana Film Industry Corp.

d **Werner Herzog**
sc **Werner Herzog**
ph **Viktor Ruzicka**
m **Popol Vuh**
Klaus Kinski, King Ampaw, José Lewgoy, Salvatore Basile, Peter Berling

Francisco Manoel Da Silva (Kinski), an abused and exploited Brazilian peasant, becomes the notorious bandit Cobra Verde. He is sent off to revive the Brazilian slave trade in West Africa, where he confronts the mad King of Dahomey. Another manic trip by Herzog and Kinski into the more untamed territories of the world (this was made under difficult conditions in Ghana) has plenty of stunning photography of exotic locations. But the narrative, based loosely on Bruce Chatwin's novel *The Viceroy Of Ouidah*, is shapeless and halting, and the flaxen-haired Kinski is a more ludicrous and unsympathetic figure than any of his previous incarnations of obsessive heroes have been. The putative theme of slavery and colonialism is also dubiously expounded.

Cobweb Castle see Throne Of Blood

Cochecito, El see Wheelchair, The

Coeurs Verts, Les see Naked Hearts

Coiffeur Pour Dames

(US: Artist With The Ladies)

France 1932 71 mins bw
Joinville

d **René Guissart**
sc **Paul Armont, Marcel Garbidon**
ph **Enzo Riccioni**
m **Claude Pigault, Fernand Vimont**
Fernand Gravey, Mona Goya, Irene Brilliant, Nina Miral

An ordinary barber (Gravey) from the country makes a great hit in Paris as a fashionable hairdresser and ends up with a string of beautiful women getting in his hair. Also busy with their scissors were the American censors who snipped about five 'lewd' minutes of the film. Nonetheless, much of Gravey's charm and the light comedy with songs survived. It was remade 20 years later with Fernandel.

Cold Cuts see Buffet Froid

Cold Days

Hideg Napok

Hungary 1966 101 mins col
Mafilm Studio

d **András Kovács**
sc **András Kovács**
ph **Ferenc Szécsényi**
Zoltán Latinovits, Iván Darvas, Adám Szirtes, Tibor Szilágyi, Margit Bara, Eva Vas, Mari Szémes

In 1946, four ex-soldiers await trial in a Hungarian prison cell for their involvement in the army's massacre of over 3,000 people in the Yugoslav town of Novi Sad in 1942. Their conversation reveals the part each played in the event, their attitudes towards it, and the concerns which now preoccupy them. Kovács tells his tale in the form of a jigsaw puzzle, his visual approach linking the cold white cell walls with the snow that covered Novi Sad, and evoking the gruesome details of mass murder in swift, subtle images: a pile of discarded clothes, a distant huddle of figures, the echo of shots. A superb exercise in tension building and a penetrating, horrifying exposé of the processes which blunt man's humanity.

La Collectionneuse

France 1967 90 mins col
Films Du Losange/Rome-Paris

d **Eric Rohmer**
sc **Eric Rohmer**

ph **Nestor Almendros**
m **Blossom Toes, Giorgio Gomelsky**
Patrick Bachau, Daniel Pommereulle, Haydée Politoff, Alain Jouffroy

An artist (Bachau) and an antique dealer (Pommereulle) share a friend's villa in St Tropez with a bikini-clad nymphette (Politoff) who sleeps with a different boy each night. The two older men try to resist being added to her collection. The third of Rohmer's Six Moral Tales (and the first of feature length), made just before *My Night With Maud*, is, in the director's words, 'less concerned with what people do than with what is going on in their minds while they are doing it'. As in most of his films, the main action is in the witty analytical dialogue spoken among hedonistic settings, although it never becomes static, and Rohmer establishes the theme of resistance to sexual temptation, making sure that the lure is tantalizingly erotic.

Special Jury Prize Berlin 1967

Colonel Redl

Redl Ezredes

Hungary/W. Germany/Austria 1984
149 mins col
Mafilm Studio Objectiv/Mokep/Film Und Fersehen/ZDF/ORF

d **István Szabó**
sc **István Szabó, Peter Dobai**
ph **Lajos Koltai**
m **Extracts from Schumann, Chopin, Liszt and others**
Klaus Maria Brandauer, Hans-Christian Blech, Armin Müller-Stahl, Gudrun Landgrebe, Jan Niklas, László Mensáros, Eva Szabó and 50 further featured players

Alfred Redl (Brandauer), a humble railwayman's son, is fiercely patriotic and ambitious. He earns a place at the military academy and eventually becomes head of military intelligence to the Austro-Hungarian Empire in its dying days. He is both bisexual and Jewish and, in seeking to conceal these facts, he betrays his fellow officers, becomes a spy, and ends up shooting himself in one last act of honour. There are many complex and interweaving strands of plot and character examination present in this work which Szabó based on John Osborne's play, *A Patriot For Me*. The director has composed a very handsome film of epic sweep, but never loses sight of his central concern—the ambiguity of Redl's nature and the ease with which he tells the lies that destroy him. Brandauer, as in Szabó's *Mephisto*, is magnificent.

Special Jury Prize Cannes 1986

The Colour Of Pomegranates

Tsvet Granata

aka Sayat Nova

USSR 1969 73 mins col
Armenfilm

d **Sergo Paradjanov**
sc **Sergo Paradjanov**
ph **Suren and M. Shakhbazian**
m **Tigran Mansurian**
Sofico Chiaureli, M. Aleksanian, V. Galstian, G. Gegechkori, O. Minassian

Imagined and actual episodes from the life of the 18th-century Armenian poet Arutiun Sayadin, known as Sayat Nova, in which he rises from carpet weaver's apprentice to court minstrel and then to archbishop. Paradjanov was imprisoned for various 'crimes' in 1974 and released in 1977, the year a faded 16mm copy of this extraordinary film was smuggled into the West. Six years later, with the full co-operation of the Soviet authorities, it was shown widely and to acclaim in its original condition. A visual experience that defies description, its eloquent imagery and often obscure symbols are derived from Armenian paintings, poetry and history. As a friend of the director remarked, 'Paradjanov makes films not about how things are, but how they would have been had he been God'.

The Colours Of Iris

Ta Chromata Tis Iridas

Greece 1974 100 mins col
George Papalios

d **Nikos Panayotopoulos**
sc **Nikos Panayotopoulos**
ph **Nikos Kavoukidis**
m **Stamatis Spanoudakis**
Nikitis Tsakiroglou, George Dialegmenos, Vangelis Kazan, George Moschides

During the shooting of a commercial on a beach, a portly middle-aged man, wearing a brown suit and carrying an umbrella, walks into the sea and is not seen again. Nico (Tsakiroglou), a composer, carries out his own investigation into the incident when the police drop the case. With the fall of the repressive regime of the Colonels, there was naturally a sudden burgeoning of liberated works of art, of which this striking, *avant-garde*, absurdist comedy is a good example. Homages are made to Godard, to French and American *policiers*, and to Greece's most distinguished director, Theo Angelopoulos. Political satire is also strongly present in the depiction of the police as both sinister and comic. Much of the film is rather too self-regarding and clever for its own good, but there is a lot to admire and to be surprised at.

Colpire Al Cuore see Blow To The Heart

Come And See

Idi I Smotri

USSR 1985 142 mins col/bw
Byelarusfilm/Mosfilm

d **Elem Klimov**
sc **Ales Adamovich, Elem Klimov**
ph **Alexei Rodionov**
m **Oleg Yanchenko, Mozart**
Alexei Kravchenko, Olga Mironova, Liubomiras Laucevicius, Vladas Bagdonas

Teenaged Florya (Kravchenko) is taken on by a group of anti-German partisans, fighting in the woods of Byelorussia in 1943. They disappear and he is left to wander, gun in hand, until he rejoins them at the end as an active and hardened participant. Klimov's film is a product of mixed merits. Florya's ordeal, which turns his hair grey and wrinkles his young face, is undeniably moving, and there are some striking visual set-pieces. However, from the moment early on when the boy discovers his village is destroyed and his family dead, the viewer joins him in witnessing an unbroken series of Nazi atrocities, until the assault of deranged images on the senses leads to numbed detachment.

Comédie Du Bonheur, Le see Comedy Of Happiness, The

The Comedy Of Happiness

Le Comédie Du Bonheur

France 1940 108 mins bw
Paulvé/Scaleta

d **Marcel L'Herbier**
sc **Marcel L'Herbier**
ph **Massimo Terzano**
m **Jacques Ibert**
Michel Simon, Ramon Novarro, Louis Jourdan, Micheline Presle, Alermé, Doumel

A banker (Simon), whose altruistic tendencies have led his family to put him in a mental institution, escapes and ends up in a boarding house full of sad residents. He hires a troupe of carnival players to give them the illusion of happiness. Subtle, whimsical and witty (with additional dialogue by Jean Cocteau), this made-in-Rome picture was an excellent vehicle for the ebullient anarchic talents of Michel Simon. It also has an interestingly diverse cast, including former silent star Ramon 'Ben Hur' Novarro, and 21-year-old Louis Jourdan in one of his first films. L'Herbier's aesthetic sense is evident in the costumes and decoration of the carnival scenes.

Comic Strip Hero

(US: The Killing Game)

Jeu De Massacre

France 1967 95 mins col
Francinor/Coficitel/AJ Films/Films Modernes

d **Alain Jessua**
sc **Alain Jessua**
ph **Jacques Robin**
m **Jacques Loussier**
Jean-Pierre Cassel, Claudine Auger, Michel Duchaussoy, Eléonore Hirt, Guy Saint-Jean

Pierre (Cassel) is a creator and writer of comic strips which his wife Jacqueline (Auger) illustrates. The couple's routine is disrupted by the visit of Bob (Duchaussoy), a young stranger who claims to live the experiences of Pierre's heroes and says that he is being pursued by a gang after his life. In dealing with the clashing and merging of imagination and reality, Jessua is traversing territory similar to that of his *Life Upside Down*, this time resolving his situation with inventiveness that is rooted nearer to sanity than madness.

It's a good-natured film, full of incidents to hold the attention, well acted, cleverly designed and with the comic strips (drawn by Guy Peellaert) used to enhance the tale.

Commare Secca, La see Grim Reaper, The

Communicants, The see Winter Light

Compagni, I see Organizer, The

Company Limited
Seemabaddha

India 1971 112 mins bw
Barat Shumshere Rana

d **Satyajit Ray**
sc **Satyajit Ray**
ph **Soumendu Roy**
m **Satyajit Ray**
Barun Chanda, Sharmila Tagore, Parumita Chowdhary, Harindranath Chattopadhyaya, Haradhan Banerjee

Shyamal Chatterjee (Chanda) has, via a university education, worked his way up in industry. He lives in privileged circumstances in Calcutta, aping a middle-class English life-style, and is angling for a seat on the company board. This he achieves by politically questionable contrivance. The social and moral distance which Chatterjee has travelled from his roots is subtly unveiled in the guided tour of his haunts which he proudly gives his visiting sister-in-law (Chowdhary). Completing the trilogy begun with *Days And Nights In The Forest*, followed by *The Adversary*, this film continues Ray's examination of trends in urban Indian life, concentrating on a young man caught between ambition and his natural integrity. The work bears all the hallmarks of Ray's style and concerns, and displays his sense of irony at both its most charming and its most pointed.

Compartiment Tueurs see Sleeping Car Murders, The

Complicato Intrigo Di Donne, Vicoli E Delitti, Un see Camorra: The Naples Connection

Comrades Of 1918 see Westfront 1918

Condamné À Mort S'est Échappé, Ou Le Vent Souffle Où Il Vent, Un see Man Escaped, Or The Wind Bloweth Where It Listeth, A

Condé, Un see Cop, The

The Conductor
Dyrygent

Poland 1979 110 mins col
PRF/Film Polski—Group X

d **Andrzej Wajda**
sc **Andrzej Kijowski**
ph **Slawomir Idziak**
m **Beethoven**
John Gielgud, Krystyna Janda, Andrzej Seweryn, Jan Ciercierski, Tadeusz Czechowski

A famous Polish-born conductor (Gielgud) returns to his birthplace after 50 years in the USA. Although old and dying, he is able to electrify the struggling provincial orchestra, something their own conductor (Seweryn) has never been able to do. The younger man's feeling of inadequacy puts a strain on his marriage. One of John Gielgud's most distinguished and distinguishing features is his mellifluous voice, but here we are deprived of it by the Polish dubbing. Yet even with a borrowed voice and his obvious inexperience as a conductor, he gives a fine performance of a character that is not fully realized in the writing. The screenplay keeps hinting at deeper meaning without actually revealing it, leaving us with neither a significant parable nor a realistic look at the failures of provincial culture.

The Confession
L'Aveu

France 1970 160 mins col
Corona/Pomereu/Selena

d **Costa-Gavras**
sc **Jorge Semprun**
ph **Raoul Coutard**
Yves Montand, Simone Signoret, Gabriele Ferzetti, Michel Vitold, Jean Bouise

In 1951, Czech foreign minister Artur London (Montand) was arrested, imprisoned and tortured during a political purge. After attacking the far Right with enormous success in *Z*, Costa-Gavras turned his attention to the Stalinist Left. Based on London's book about his experiences, the screenplay's static and wordy nature is not sufficiently tempered by the direction or the playing. However, some of the interrogation scenes which lead to the false confession of the title cannot fail to have an impact.

Confession Of Ina Kahr, The see Afraid To Live

The Confessions Of Winifred Wagner

Winifred Wagner Und Die Geschichte Des Hauses Wahnfried 1914-1975

W. Germany 1976 104 mins bw
Syberberg Film/ORF

d **Hans-Jürgen Syberberg**
ph **Dietrich Lohmann**
m **Wagner**

An interview with the 78-year-old, English-born wife of Richard Wagner's son Siegfried in which she recounts her life at Wahnfried, the Wagners' house at Bayreuth, and talks about their family squabbles, her running of the Festival, her relationship with Hitler, and her views on the conductors and the artists she worked with. This fascinating interview with a formidable woman exists in a five-hour form, but is no less riveting in the released shorter version. Almost the entire film is made up of medium close-ups or head shots of Winifred, who addresses Syberberg and the camera unselfconsciously, hardly ever needing to be prompted. She stares out at us without a qualm and describes Hitler as 'a kindly uncle ... absolutely sweet with the children,' and 'if Hitler walked through the door today, I should be just as pleased and happy to see him as I ever was'.

Confidence

Bizalom

Hungary 1979 117 mins col
Mafilm/Objectiv Studio

d **István Szabó**
sc **István Szabó**
ph **Lajos Koltai**
Ildikó Bánsági, Peter Andorai, O. Gombick, Karoly Csaki

Two fugitives (Bánsági and Andorai), hiding from the Fascists in 1944, are thrown together and forced to pose as man and wife in a small room in the suburbs of Budapest. Although both are married, they find some sexual gratification with each other but lack mutual confidence. A chamber work in both senses, the film is as muted and as subtle as the colours used. It stands or falls on the performances of the two leads, as it is virtually a two-hander. They are as convincing as the often irritating and irrational roles allow them to be, and the threat from the world outside is made palpable.

Confidentially Yours see Finally Sunday

Conflagration

aka The Flame Of Torment

Enjo

Japan 1958 96 mins bw
Daiei

d **Kon Ichikawa**
sc **Keiji Hasebe, Natto Wada**
ph **Kazuo Miyagawa**
m **Toshiro Mayazumi**
Raizo Ichikawa, Ganjiro Nakamura, Tatsuya Nakadai

A young acolyte (Ichikawa) comes to study at the Golden Pavilion in Kyoto, where he sees tourists violating its beauty. Disillusioned by the post-war world, he despairingly sets fire to the holy temple in order to preserve it from contamination. As in all of Ichikawa's major films, this superb adaptation of Mishima's novel, *Temple Of The Golden Pavilion*, is a study of a man pushed to extremes. Beautifully photographed—witness the final shot of the burning temple as seen from the mountain—and deeply disturbing, it remains the director's own favourite.

Conflit see Affair Lafont, The

Conformista, Il see Conformist, The

The Conformist
Il Conformista

Italy 1969 115 mins col
Mars/Marianne/Maran

d **Bernardo Bertolucci**
sc **Bernardo Bertolucci**
ph **Vittorio Storaro**
m **Georges Delerue**
Jean-Louis Trintignant, Stefania Sandrelli, Dominique Sanda, Gastone Moschin, Pierre Clémenti, Enzo Taroscio

The childhood trauma of having shot a chauffeur who tried to seduce him, together with his own repressed homosexuality, is a strong factor in making Marcello (Trintignant) contract a *bourgeois* marriage and offer his services to the Fascist party for whom he is asked to assassinate his former professor. Bertolucci's most successful combining of his Freudian and political preoccupations is an ironic and stylish study of pre-war Italy, hauntingly evoked by Storaro's camera. Trintignant brings great conviction to the title role, and there are enticing performances from Sandrelli and Sanda who get to dance a tango together.

The Confrontation
aka Sparkling Winds
Fenyes Szelek

Hungary 1969 85 mins col
Mafilm Studio

d **Miklós Jancsó**
sc **Gyula Hernádi**
ph **Tamás Somló**
m **Paul Arma**
Lajos Balázsovits, Andrea Drahota, András Bálint, Kati Kovács, András Kozák, Benedek Tóth

In 1947, after the Communist Party has come to power in Hungary, a group of revolutionary students set out on a glorious summer's day to win over a nearby Catholic school to their cause, but they are manipulated by higher Party officials. Jancsó's first film in colour, of which he makes dazzling symbolic use, is conceived in choreographic and folk-opera terms. The film echoes the 1968 student movements in the West (the girls anachronistically wear mini-skirts) with an understanding of the Hungarian context of which Jancsó is such a singular and invigorating observer.

Congress Dances
Der Kongress Tanzt

Germany 1931 92 mins bw
UFA

d **Erik Charrell**
sc **Norbert Falk, Robert Liebmann**
ph **Carl Hoffmann**
m **Werner Heymann**
Conrad Veidt, Willy Fritsch, Lilian Harvey, Lil Dagover, Gibb McLaughlin

A shopgirl (Harvey) wins the affections of Tsar Alexander (Fritsch) during the 1814 Congress of Vienna. Complications occur, stirred up by a scheming Prince Metternich (Veidt) and a vampish countess (Dagover), when he returns to Russia leaving a double in his place. Made in Germany in three different language versions (Henri Garat replaced Fritsch in the French one), this frothy musical comedy was more concerned with romantic than political intrigues, and sets them in ornate drawing rooms, beer- gardens, and at grand balls. The feather-light script was directed with equivalent weight, and the film helped set a style for early screen musicals in Europe and Hollywood.

Conjugal Bed, The see Queen Bee

The Consequence
Die Konsequenz

W. Germany 1977 100 mins bw
Solaris Film/WDR

d **Wolfgang Petersen**
sc **Alexander Ziegler, Wolfgang Petersen**
ph **Jörg Michael Baldenius**
m **Nils Sustrate**

Jürgen Prochnow, Ernst Hannawald, Walo Lüond, Edith Volmann, Erwin Kohlund

Martin (Prochnow), a homosexual actor imprisoned for a relationship with a minor, falls reciprocally in love with a warder's young son. When they try to make a life together, family pressures and interference lead them to tragedy. Petersen's film, shot in monochrome tones appropriate to the pall of oppression that hangs over it, is an excellent drama that is both a plea for tolerance and an indictment of the prejudice that leads to using prisons as instruments of persecution.

Constans see Constant Factor, The

The Constant Factor

Constans

Poland 1980 96 mins col
PRF-Zespol Filmowy

d **Krzysztof Zanussi**
sc **Krzysztof Zanussi**
ph **Slawomir Idziak**
m **Wojciech Kilar**
Tadeusz Bradecki, Zofia Mrozowska, Malgorzata Zajaczkowska, Cezary Morawski

Witold (Bradecki) travels the world for his job in Polish international exhibitions, trapped by his complex nature which believes that life can be ordered by mathematical equations, and incapable of accommodating to petty corruption. His mother dies as a result of his inept handling of a bribe to a doctor, and he ends up as a window cleaner. Although cold and polemical, this outspoken tale is told with a good deal of visual flair, and the characters are analysed with precision.

Contempt

Le Mépris

France 1963 103 mins col
Rome-Paris Films

d **Jean-Luc Godard**
sc **Jean-Luc Godard**
ph **Raoul Coutard**
m **Georges Delerue**
Brigitte Bardot, Michel Piccoli, Jack Palance, Fritz Lang, Giorgia Moll

A scriptwriter (Piccoli) is increasingly despised by his wife (Bardot) as he tries to set up a film in Rome of *The Odyssey* with an American producer (Palance), to be directed by Fritz Lang. Godard has slyly used Alberto Moravia's novel *Il Disprezzo* to make his own sharp comment on international film-making, using colour, wide screen and a multilingual cast. The first third of the movie, however, is concerned with the breakdown of a marriage in a remarkable flowing sequence set in the apartment of the couple (Bardot and Piccoli are superb). Palance ('When I hear the word culture I reach for my chequebook') brings an imposing presence to bear on the fascinating proceedings.

Contes Immoraux see Immoral Tales

The Contract

Kontrakt

Poland 1980 111 mins col
PRF-Zespol Filmowy

d **Krzysztof Zanussi**
sc **Krzysztof Zanussi**
ph **Slawomir Idziak**
m **Wojciech Kilar, with extracts from Schubert, Strauss, Debussy**
Maja Komorowska, Tadeusz Lomnicki, Magda Jaroszowna, Krzysztof Kolberger, Ignacy Machowski, Leslie Caron

A Warsaw physician arranges the civil marriage of his son, (Lomnicki), but the new young wife (Komorowska) refuses to go through with the subsequent church ceremony. Unperturbed, her father-in-law proceeds with the wedding party. It is a day of both wild carousal and unpleasant events, at the end of which the groom sets the house on fire. This is Zanussi at his least metaphorical, making an ironic, even comic, film that examines a sector of well-to-do Polish society which is, inevitably, on the brink of collapse. Interesting and entertaining, the film has an authentic cosmopolitan flavour, with dialogue moving easily between Polish, French, English and German.

Conversation Piece

Gruppo Di Famiglia In Un Interno

Italy 1974 121 mins col
Rusconi/Gaumont

d **Luchino Visconti**
sc **Luchino Visconti, Suso Cecchi D'Amico, Enrico Medioli**
ph **Pasqualino De Santis**
m **Franco Mannino**
Burt Lancaster, Helmut Berger, Silvana Mangano, Claudia Cardinale, Claudia Marsani

A reclusive professor (Lancaster), living a well-ordered existence among his 18th-century art collection in his Rome apartment, has his tranquillity disturbed and his latent homosexuality aroused after reluctantly agreeing to let his top flat to a Countess (Mangano), her 'kept boy' (Berger) and her daughter (Marsani). Visconti's penultimate film was directed after a serious illness, which may account for some of its weaknesses. But the plot, although treated as drama, resembles a 1940s Hollywood screwball comedy in which an egghead learns to let his hair down, and is nothing short of ludicrous. Lancaster seems bemused throughout, and if one can believe Berger as a revolutionary student then one can believe anything.

Le Cop
Les Ripoux

France 1985 106 mins col
Film 7

d **Claude Zidi**
sc **Claude Zidi, Didier Kaminka**
ph **Jean-Jacques Tarbes**
m **Francis Lai**
Philippe Noiret, Thierry Lhermitte, Régine, Grace De Capitani, Julien Guiomar

A veteran plain clothes policeman (Noiret), who happily turns a blind eye to all crime as long as he's paid off, has to educate his priggish new partner (Lhermitte) in his ways. The subject of police corruption and brutality could have been treated as a cynical satire, but it has been turned into an extremely amiable, often very funny, soft-hearted cop comedy. Noiret is such a lovable old rogue that one can't help being on his side.

The Cop
Un Condé

France 1970 98 mins col
Stephen Films(Paris)/Empire Films(Rome)

d **Yves Boisset**
sc **Claude Veillot, Yves Boisset**
ph **Jean-Marc Ripert**
m **Antoine Duhamel**
Michel Bouquet, Françoise Fabian, Gianni Garko, Michel Constantin, Rufus, Bernard Fresson, Henri Garcin

A nightclub owner is murdered and his sister Hélène (Fabian) beaten up by members of a gang whose leader has police and political connections. Hélène's friend Dan (Garko) shoots the gang leader and unleashes a vendetta with the police, led by Inspector Favenin (Bouquet). Controversial in 1970, when its release was delayed because of ministerial objections to the portrayal of the police as corrupt thugs, this film now is no more than a violent crime thriller. It is directed and played (notably by Bouquet) with maximum efficiency, using techniques reminiscent of Jean-Pierre Melville's *policiers*, but the characters are largely two-dimensional and the excessive brutality becomes a bit much to take.

Cop Au Vin
Poulet Au Vinaigre

France 1984 109 mins col
MK2

d **Claude Chabrol**
sc **Claude Chabrol, Dominique Roulet**
ph **Jean Rabier**
m **Matthieu Chabrol**
Jean Poiret, Stéphane Audran, Michel Bouquet, Lucas Belvaux, Jean Topart, Josephine Chaplin, Pauline Lafont

A crippled woman (Audran), living with her teenage postman son (Belvaux) in a small provincial town, is determined not to sell her house to a local cartel. When one of the members of the cartel is killed, Inspector Lavardin (Poiret) arrives to investigate. This mordant view of the nastiness of the provincial *bourgeoisie*, in Chabrol's commercial thriller mode, only really comes alive some way into the film with the arrival of the sardonic cop of the title. Basically sympathetic, in Poiret's clever performance, his 'lively methods' give the movie a moral ambiguity. The rest of the characters are one-dimensional, but it's done with style, and there are at least two Chabrolian meals to relish. Poiret and Chabrol recreated the cop character in *Inspector Lavardin* in 1986.

Coquille Et Le Clergyman, La see Seashell And The Clergyman, The

---

Corbeau, Le see Raven, The

Corde Raide, La see Lovers On A Tightrope

Counterfeit Constable, The see Allez France

The Counterfeiters

Le Cave Se Rebiffe

France 1961 98 mins bw

Cité Films/Compagnia Cinematografica Mondiale (Rome)

d **Gilles Grangier**
sc **Albert Simonin, Gilles Grangier, Michel Audiard**
ph **Louis Page**
m **Francis Lemarque, Michel Legrand**
Jean Gabin, Martine Carol, Bernard Blier, Ginette Leclerc, Frank Villard, Maurice Biraud, Françoise Rosay

A small-time crook (Villard), together with a couple of friends, plans a forgery operation using the skills of Robert (Biraud), an engraver and the husband of his mistress (Carol). A professional mastermind (Gabin) is persuaded out of retirement to run the racket, and he and Robert double- cross the others and make off with the loot. A compact, small-scale comedy- thriller, marred by a somewhat limp and repetitive screenplay, but kept entertaining by crisp direction and its superior casting.

Coup De Foudre see At First Sight

Coup De Grâce

Der Fangschuss

W. Germany 1976 95 mins bw

Bioskop Film/HR/Argos Films

d **Volker Schlöndorff**
sc **Genevieve Dorman, Margarethe Von Trotta, Jutta Bruckner**
ph **Igor Luther**
m **Stanley Myers**
Margarethe Von Trotta, Matthias Habich, Rudiger Kirschstein, Matthieu Carrière, Valeska Gert

A German army unit, sent to keep Communism at bay in the Baltic during 1919-1920, is billeted on the now war-ravaged estate of a once wealthy family. Their commander, Erich (Habich), obsessed with all aspects of soldiering, attracts the unwelcome love of Sophie (Von Trotta), daughter of the mansion who, spurned by him, finally devotes herself to the Bolshevik cause. A complicated work, dealing in ideologies, the film nonetheless focuses largely on the nature and consequences of Sophia's hopeless passion. The bleak winter landscape is realistically evoked in the black and white photography but, while the film intrigues, it fails to come to grips with the dark undersides of human emotion at which it continually hints.

Coup De Torchon see Clean Slate

Couple, Un see Love Trap, The

Courage Fuyons see Courage - Let's Run

Courage - Let's Run

Courage Fuyons

France 1978 98 mins col

Productions De La Guéville/Gaumont

d **Yves Robert**
sc **Jean-Loup Dabadie, Yves Robert**
ph **Yves Lafaye**
m **Vladimir Cosma**
Jean Rochefort, Catherine Deneuve, Philippe Leroy-Beaulieu, Robert Webber, Dominique Lavanant

Middle-aged Martin (Rochefort), the insignificant proprietor of a small Paris chemist shop, gets involved in the 1968 riots and ends up in Amsterdam with glamorous singer Eva (Deneuve). Later reunited with his wife, he longs for Eva, and gets her after his wife leaves him for her lover. Robert's handsomely filmed comedy begins with Martin and Eva in Amsterdam and flashes back, via Martin's reflections, to the events that brought them there, then moves back into present time. This device, plus Rochefort essaying two other roles as members of his family, keeps things moving, but does little to elevate what is, in the end, a rather old-fashioned and silly story, jam-packed with ill-assorted characters and plot complications.

Cousin Angelica

La Prima Angelica

Spain 1973 105 mins col
Elias Querejeta

d **Carlos Saura**
sc **Carlos Saura**
ph **Luis Cuadrado**
m **Spanish popular melodies**
José Luis López Vázques, Lina Canalejas, Maria Clara Fernández De Loayza, Fernando Delgado

A shy, balding, 45-year-old bachelor (Vázquez) returns from Barcelona to his home town of Segovia after many years. There, he finds his cousin Angelica (Canalejas), whom he had loved as a child, now married to a Fascist (Delgado). He relives his childhood days at the time of the Civil War. What gives this plaintive 'remembrance of things past' drama a certain interest is that the middle-aged actor plays his nine-year-old self, rather in the manner of the old man's childhood memories in Bergman's *Wild Strawberries*. 'For years I have been studying how memory, imagination and close reality form a complex and fascinating whole,' Saura says. The film achieves its aims within its rather rigid structure.

Cousin Cousine

France 1975 95 mins col
Les Films Pomereu

d **Jean-Charles Tacchella**
sc **Jean-Charles Tacchella, with Danièle Thompson**
ph **Georges Lendi, Eric Faucherre, Michel Thiriet**
m **Gérard Anfosso**
Marie-Christine Barrault, Victor Lanoux, Marie-France Pisier, Guy Marchand, Ginette Garcin

Two married couples, who meet at a wedding which makes them in-laws, become entangled with each other's spouses. In the case of Marthe (Barrault) and Ludovic (Lanoux), they hold on to their virtue in the face of their partner's adultery until they decide they love each other and must go away together. A big hit in the US, this polished and sometimes charming comedy, with elements of satire directed at the hypocrisy of the French *bourgeoisie*, is ultimately a little tedious in its superficiality—the ingredient which frequently appears as the limiting factor in Tacchella's work.

Cousins, Les see Cousins, The

The Cousins

Les Cousins

France 1959 110 mins bw
AJYM

d **Claude Chabrol**
sc **Claude Chabrol**
ph **Henri Decaë**
m **Paul Misraki**
Jean-Claude Brialy, Gérard Blain, Juliette Mayniel, Claude Cerval

Simple, good-hearted country cousin Charles (Blain) comes to study at the Sorbonne in Paris where he stays at the luxury apartment of Paul (Brialy), his cynical town cousin. Charles works hard but fails his exams, Paul doesn't but passes and gets Charles's girl (Mayniel). Chabrol's second film is a riveting and perverse study of decadent Parisian student life, with a touch of Cocteau's *Les Enfants Terribles*. The City of Light is captured by Decaë's camera as if seen through the amazed eyes of Blain.

Best Film Berlin 1959

Čovek Nije Tica see Man Is Not A Bird

The Cow

Gav

Iran 1968 101 mins bw

Caspain Studios

d **Daryush Mehrjui**
sc **Daryush Mehrjui, Golam Hossein Suedi**
ph **Fereydun Ghovanlu**
m **Hormoz Farhat**
Ezat Entezami, Ali Nasirian, Jamshid Mashayekhi, Shojazedeh, Jafar Vali

Mashdi Hassan (Entezami) owns the only cow in his little village and cherishes it to the point of mania. While he is absent on business the cow dies and, to protect him, the villagers tell him it strayed. Paralyzed with both grief and disbelief, Hassan gradually assumes the cow's identity and slides into madness. Mehrjui's film is carefully structured to capture the detail and atmosphere of life and landscape in his chosen milieu, moving to a minutely observed study of the processes of madness. The images are well-judged and the editing is imaginative but, alas, once Hassan's madness is total and a resolution has to be found, the piece loses its focus and gives way to chaos and frenzy.

The Cow And I

La Vache Et Le Prisonnier

France 1959 119 mins bw
Cyclope/Omnia

d **Henri Verneuil**
sc **Henri Verneuil, Henri Jeanson, Jean Manse**
ph **Roger Hubert**
m **Paul Durand**
Fernandel, René Havard, Albert Rémy, Bernard Musson

A French prisoner-of-war (Fernandel) escapes from a German labour farm, taking with him his favourite cow, Marguerite, to avoid suspicion. Among his various adventures on his way to the French border, he encounters other escapees disguised as Germans, has a skirmish with an amorous bull, and gets involved in military manoeuvres. A charming and quite touching comedy-drama in which the equine-faced French comic vies for the acting honours with his bovine co-star.

Crainquebille

France 1922 70 mins bw
Trarieux Films

d **Jacques Feyder**
sc **Jacques Feyder**
ph **L.H. Burel**
m **Silent**
Maurice De Féraudy, Françoise Rosay, Félix Oudart, Jean Forest

Crainquebille (De Féraudy), a poor but honest Parisian vegetable seller, is arrested and tried for telling a policeman to go to hell. Anatole France's story (the basis for two further film versions in 1933 and 1954) provided Feyder with one of his most experimental and brilliant works. It combines realistic location shooting with extraordinary dream sequences. Apart from the splendid De Féraudy in the title role, it gave Feyder's wife, Rosay, her first chance to shine on screen.

The Cranes Are Flying

Letyat Zhuravli

USSR 1957 94 mins bw
Mosfilm

d **Mikhail Kalatozov**
sc **Victor Rosov**
ph **Sergei Urusevski**
m **M. Vainberg**
Tatiana Samoilova, Alexei Batalov, Vasili Merkuriev, Alexander Shvorin

When a young hospital worker (Samoilova) hears that her fiancé (Batalov) has been killed in the war, she refuses to believe it, yet she marries a man (Shvorin) she does not love. It has a happy ending. One of the first films after the 'thaw' which seemed to usher in a new liberty in Soviet cinema, is an unpretentious, lyrical love story that benefits from some sweeping camerawork and a touching performance from Samoilova (the great-niece of Stanislavsky). It was shown to acclaim in America in 1959 under a USA-USSR cultural exchange programme.

Best Film Cannes 1958 and Special Award to Samoilova

The Crazy Family

Gyakufunsha Kazoku

Japan 1984 107 mins col
Art Theatre Guild/Directors Company/Kokusai Hoei

d **Sogo Ishii**

sc **Yoshinori Kobayashi, Fumio Konami, Sogo Ishii**
ph **Masaki Tamura**
m **1984**
Katsuyo Kobayashi, Mitsuko Baisho, Yoshiki Arizono, Yuki Kudo, Hitoshi Ueki

The Kobayashi family moves into a spacious urban house. It is a dream come true—until grandfather's visit disturbs the balance of Kobayashi *père*'s mind. He becomes obsessed with digging a cellar for the old man to live in, his excavations become wilder and wilder, the family falls apart, the house is destroyed, and they all end up living happily in a space between two motorway flyovers! Played loud and fast, Ishii's third feature treats the theme—of crisis in a nuclear family with urban ambition—in a series of painful and ugly episodes presented in the style of a comic strip. Satire and slapstick rain blows on their targets in a film beautifully photographed by one of Japan's best cinematographers, and with a bizarre final sequence of special effects designed by *avant-garde* structuralist Takashi Ito.

Creeps see Dreszcze

Cria! see Raise Ravens

Cria Cuervos see Raise Ravens

Cries And Whispers

Viskingar Och Rop

Sweden 1972 95 mins col
Svensk Filminstituten

d **Ingmar Bergman**
sc **Ingmar Bergman**
ph **Sven Nykvist**
m **Chopin, Bach**
Harriet Andersson, Ingrid Thulin, Liv Ullmann, Kari Sylwan, Erland Josephson, George Arlin, Henning Moritzen

Agnes (Andersson), riddled with cancer, is dying in the family mansion, cared for by the faithful old retainer. Her two sisters (Thulin, frigid and suicidal and Ullmann, earthy and reckless) return home to give her comfort. Only the most extravagant superlatives could hope to convey the visual, aural and acting artistry of this film, the action of which occurs mostly in an agony of suffering silence, punctuated by the cries and whispers of the title. Unremittingly bleak and harrowing, it is a powerful document about dying, and reactions to dying, made by a master. Nykvist won the cinematography Oscar but, for all its beauty and emotionally charged use of blood colours, it needs a strong stomach to watch it.

Crime And Punishment

Crime Et Châtiment

France 1935 110 mins bw
CGPC

d **Pierre Chenal**
sc **Marcel Aymé, Pierre Chenal, Christian Stengel, Wladimir Strijewski**
ph **Colas, Joseph-Louis Mundwiller**
m **Arthur Honegger**
Pierre Blanchar, Harry Baur, Marcelle Géniat, Madeleine Ozeray

Raskolnikov (Blanchar), a tormented student, kills a pawnbroker, and then plays mouse to the cat of Police Inspector Porfiry (Baur). Pierre Chenal, recently rediscovered in his eighties after years of neglect, had established his reputation as a leading French director of the 1930s with this taut, atmospheric adaptation of the Dostoevsky classic. Against the claustrophobic studio sets, Blanchar and Baur display their brilliant acting skills. The film looks even better when compared with Sternberg's stilted Hollywood version which appeared in the same year.

Best Actor (Pierre Blanchar) Venice 1935

Crime And Punishment

Crime Et Châtiment

France 1956 110 mins bw
Champs Elysée Productions

d **Georges Lampin**
sc **Charles Spaak**
ph **Claude Renoir**
m **Maurice Thiriet**
Robert Hossein, Jean Gabin, Ulla Jacobsson, Bernard Blier, Marina Vlady, Gaby Morlay

René Brunel (Hossein), a Left Bank student, commits murder and robbery, to prevent his sister (Jacobsson) from having to marry a wealthy suitor (Blier), but is drawn to confess by the psychological wiles of a police inspector (Gabin). Dostoevsky's great complex novel has here been updated to modern Paris, and turned into just another *policier*. The idea of making the student Raskolnikov a young Parisian Existentialist in a duffle coat might have seemed a good one but, as morosely and flatly played by Hossein, it fails to generate any sense of the inner torment or tragedy of the character. Gabin and Blier, however, keep the botched enterprise from sinking completely into the Seine.

Crime And Punishment

Prestupleniye I Nakazaniye

USSR 1970 200 mins bw
Gorky Studio

d **Lev Kulidzhanov**
sc **Lev Kulidzhanov, Nikolai Figurovsky**
ph **Vyacheslav Shumsky**
m **Piotr Pakevich**
Georgi Taratorkin, Viktoria Fyodorova, Irina Gosheva, Innokenti Smoktunovsky, Yevgeni Lebedev

Raskolnikov (Taratorkin), a former student living in poverty in St Petersburg, murders a pawnbroker and her daughter. Gradually, through his relationship with various characters, and his confrontation with Porfiry (Smoktunovsky), the prosecutor, Raskolnikov confesses to the murder. The ninth version of Dostoevsky's most-filmed novel follows the plot and sub-plot more closely than any of its predecessors. Yet the director has opted to stress the insane streak in Raskolinov at the expense of the intellectual, so that Taratorkin rolls his eyes and gesticulates for most of the film's rather tedious 200 minutes. The most impressive scenes are those with Smoktunovsky, and the period atmosphere is well caught.

Crime De Monsieur Lange, Le see Crime Of Monsieur Lange, The

Crime Et Châtiment see Crime And Punishment

Crimen De Cuenca, El see Crime Of Cuenca, The

The Crime Of Cuenca

El Crimen De Cuenca

Spain 1980 92 mins col
Incine/Jet Films

d **Pilar Miró**
sc **Pilar Miró, Salvador Maldonado**
ph **Hans Burmann**
m **Antón García Abril**
José Manuel Cervino, Daniel Dicenta, Amparo Soler Leal, Fernando Rey, José Vivó, Héctor Alterio

After a quarrel with two farmers, an illiterate shepherd disappears. His parents insist that the local police charge the two men (Cervino and Dicenta) with his murder. A priest (Vivó), a politician (Rey) and a magistrate (Alterio) collude, for their own purposes, to have the innocent men convicted...Miró, one of Spain's few female film directors, has also become one of the most controversial. Her first film *The Engagement Party* (1976) was banned for a time because of its explicit sex scenes, and this stark exposé of a legal conspiracy and of torture inflicted on prisoners, caused a storm of protest from the Civil Guard. Naturally, when it was released in Spain a year later, it packed in the public.

The Crime Of Monsieur Lange

Le Crime De Monsieur Lange

France 1935 85 mins bw
Obéron

d **Jean Renoir**
sc **Jacques Prévert, Jean Renoir, Jean Castanier**
ph **Jean Bachelet**
m **Jean Wiener, Joseph Kosma**
Jules Berry, René Lefèvre, Florelle, Nadia Sibirskaïa, Sylvie Bataille, Henri Guisol

A group of exploited workers take over a publishing house when its crooked boss Batala (Berry) absconds, making them believe he is dead. After they have made a success of the co-operative, Batala returns to regain control, but Lange (Lefèvre), a writer of pulp Westerns, kills him. Shot in 25 days, this classic film of working-class solidarity, presented in the language of ironic black comedy, expressed the optimism of the Popular Front better than more didactic efforts. The two contrasting central actors—evil Berry and good Lefèvre—are superb, as is Renoir's use of the courtyard setting, and the famous 360-degree pan when Lange murders Batala is a *tour de force*.

The Criminal Life Of Archibaldo De La Cruz

aka Rehearsal For A Crime

Ensayo De Un Crimen

Mexico 1955 91 mins bw
Alianza Cinematografica

d **Luis Buñuel**
sc **Luis Buñuel, E. Ugarte**
ph **Augustín Jiménez**
m **Jorge Perez**
Ernesto Alonso, Ariadna Welter, Miroslava Stern, Rita Macedo

Because of a childhood experience of the death of a maid in erotic circumstances, Archibaldo (Alonso) grows up into a psychopathic woman- killer, although he is constantly thwarted in his efforts to carry out a murder. Still working within the budget and style limitations of Mexican cinema, Buñuel came up with one of his best black comedies of the period. It not only pokes wicked fun at the decadent *bourgeoisie* and at the Latin male, but at some of the director's own obsessions—foot fetishism, *l'amour fou*, and surrealism.

The Crimson Curtain

Le Rideau Cramoisi

France 1952 43 mins bw
Argos

d **Alexandre Astruc**
sc **Alexandre Astruc**
ph **Eugen Schüfftan**
m **Jean-Jacques Grünewald**
Jean-Claude Pascal, Anouk Aimée, Madeleine Garcia, Jim Gérald

A young officer (Pascal), is billetted on a *bourgeois* couple (Gérald and Garcia) with a beautiful daughter (Aimée). To his astonishment, the girl makes advances to him and they embark on a silent nocturnal affair, carried out with some difficulty since her bedroom leads off that of her parents. The intrigue culminates in a surprise tragic ending. Astruc, novelist and film critic, who coined the phrase *camera-stylo*, wrote that cinema should be 'a means of writing as supple and as subtle as that of written language'. In this, his first film, the director practised what he preached, achieving a stylish, unusual and moving work in which narrative takes the place of dialogue and the camera and silent presences of the actors convey the drama. This little gem of a short feature, demonstrating the maxim that less is more, remains the best work of Astruc, whose later, longer films tend towards the turgid and lack clarity of purpose.

Cristo Proibito, Il see Forbidden Christ, The

Cristo Si E Fermato A Eboli see Christ Stopped At Eboli

Cronaca Di Un Amore see Chronicle of A Love

Cronaca Di Una Morte Annunciata see Chronicle Of A Death Foretold

Cronaca Familiare see Family Diary

Crook, The see Simon The Swiss

The Crossing Of the Rhine

(US: Tomorrow Is My Turn)

Le Passage Du Rhin

France 1960 125 mins bw
Franco-London/Gibe/Jonia/UFA

d **André Cayatte**
sc **André Cayatte, Armand Jammot**
ph **Roger Fellous**
m **Louiguy**
Charles Aznavour, Nicole Courcel, Georges Rivière, Cordula Trantow

Two French POWs, a baker (Aznavour) and a journalist (Rivière), escape separately from the German farms where they have been forced to work, but meet up again in Paris after various adventures. This plodding, conventional, but well-intentioned escape story has the advantage of a sympathetic portrayal by Aznavour, and the disadvantage (for English- speaking audiences) of a moronic American commentary. Judges at Venice might have been swayed by its depiction of the Germans also suffering during the war.

Best Film Venice 1960

Crossroads see Crossways

Crossways

aka Crossroads

aka The Shadows Of The Yoshiwara

Jujiro

Japan 1928 80 mins bw
Shochiku

d **Teinosuke Kinugasa**
sc **Teinosuke Kinugasa**
ph **Kohei Sugiyama**
m **Silent**

J. Bandoha, A. Tschihaya, Yujiko Ogawa, I. Sohma

A young man, tormented by thinking he has killed a rival on an archery ground, takes refuge with his sister who has killed her seducer. This was one of the few Japanese silents to be distributed in the West and critics spoke of German Expressionist influence: fragmentary close-ups, a claustrophobic atmosphere of *angst* and dark impressionistic décor. However, it is said that Kinugasa had not seen any German films at that time. Even more like *Caligari* and the like, is his long-lost *A Page Of Madness* (1926), the major cinematic rediscovery of the early 1970s.

Crows And Sparrows

Wuya Yu Maque

China 1949 113 mins bw
Kunlun

d **Zheng Junli**
sc **Chen Baichen, Shen Fu, Wang Lingu, Xu Tao, Zheng Junli, Zhao Dan**
ph **Miao Zhenhua, Hu Zhenhua**
m **Wang Yunjie**

Zhao Dan, Wu Yin, Wei Heling, Sun Daolin, Li Tianji, Ouyang Yunzhu

When the corrupt landlord (Tianji) of a Shanghai boarding house decides to sell up and move to Taiwan, the tenants must find another home and therefore suffer hardship. They include a teacher (Daolin) and his family, a pedlar (Dan), a clerk (Heling), students and workers. As the Red Army approaches, the tenants gain their rights. One of the last fruits of a fertile period in the cinema of pre-revolutionary China, it was also a landmark in its move towards a style not far removed from Italian Neo-Realism. Both the dialogue and the acting are vibrant and authentic, and the principal location (the boarding house) teems with life. At first, Junli's first solo directorial effort was subject to censorship from the Nationalist Kuomintang government, but when the Communists came to power during post-production, much of the cut dialogue was restored and more anti-KMT slogans were added with relish.

Crucible, The see Witches of Salem, The

The Crucified Lovers

Chikamatsu Monogatari

Japan 1954 110 mins bw
Daiei

d **Kenji Mizoguchi**
sc **Yoshitaka Yoda**
ph **Kazuo Miyagawa**
m **Fumio Hayasaka**

Kazuo Hasegawa, Kyoko Kagawa, Eitaro Shindo, Sakae Ozawa, Yoko Minamida

In late 17th-century Kyoto, a merchant's wife (Kagawa) and a young clerk (Hasegawa) take flight from the powerful influence of the Shoguns, and find themselves at the mercy of an avaricious society. Although based on a play by the 18th-century playwright Chikamatsu, there is little in the fluid filmic narrative to suggest its theatrical origins. Mizoguchi gives us a vivid picture of a complex mercenary system, as well as a love story which builds in emotion. The gleaming photography of Miyagawa—the camera keeping a discreet distance where necessary—and the performances, contribute to the impact of one of the best films of the director's great last phase.

The Cruel Sea
Bas Ya Bahar

Kuwait 1971 107 mins bw
Falcon Productions

d **Khalid Siddik**
sc **Abdel-Rahman Saleh, Saad Faraj, Walaa' Salah El-Din, Khalid Siddik**
ph **Tewfik El-Amir**
m **Bo Tarik**
Saad Faraj, Hayat El-Fahad, Mohammed Mansour, Amal Bakr

A young man (Mansour), whose father (Faraj) was maimed by a shark in his days as a pearl diver, is determined to make enough money so that he can marry a rich merchant's daughter (Bakr). But he also has to pay the price for extracting pearls from the cruel sea. The first feature to be made in the tiny Gulf state of Kuwait is a pearl in itself. Not only does Siddik's debut film authentically and atmospherically re-create the harsh pre-oil boom society, but it points an accusatory finger at mercantile exploitation, the inferior position of women and the negative effect of religion.

The Cry Of The People
Al Grito De Este Pueblo

Argentina 1972 65 mins col/bw
Grupo Tercer Cine

d **Humberto Rios**
sc **Humberto Rios**
ph **Mario Diez**
m **Folk music**

A documentary on Bolivia from the disastrous Chaco war with Paraguay in 1932 to the present-day military dictatorship, using newsreels, commentary and interviews. Although angry at the appalling exploitation and conditions of the majority of the population, the film is rooted in hard facts and statistics that examine the reasons for the oppression and avoids being a mere salve to the liberal conscience. The images of mine workers, or of Indians trying to survive on the land, eloquently show suffering, while the commentary explains how the old tin barons have been replaced by even worse exploiters such as Standard Oil and Shell. The film stands with the short documentaries of the Cuban, Santiago Alvarez, and Fernando E Solanas's *The Hour Of The Furnaces*, which use the cinema as a powerful weapon for change.

The Cry
(US: The Outcry)
Il Grido

Italy 1957 102 mins bw
SPA/Robert Alexander

d **Michelangelo Antonioni**
sc **Michelangelo Antonioni, Elio Bartolini, Ennio De Concini**
ph **Gianni Di Venanzo**
m **Giovanni Fusco**
Steve Cochran, Alida Valli, Dorian Gray, Betsy Blair, Lynn Shaw, Gabriella Pallotta

A worker (Cochran) in a sugar refinery in the Po valley wanders with his little daughter from place to place in search of love after the mother (Valli) of his child has deserted him for another man. The film directed just before *L'Avventura* made Antonioni an international name is morose and meandering with unconvincing performances from an international cast including Hollywood stalwart Cochran as an Italian worker. The desolate landscapes, rather obviously reflecting the hero's mental state, are well captured by Di Venanzo's camera.

The Cry
Krik

Czechoslovakia 1963 80 mins bw
Ceskoslovensky Film, Barrandov Studio

d **Jaromil Jires**
sc **Ludvik Askenázy, Jaromil Jires**
ph **Jaroslav Kučera**
m **Jan Klusák**
Eva Limánová, Josef Abrhám, Eva Kopecká, Dr J. Kvapil

When Ivana (Limánová) goes to hospital for the birth of her first baby, both she and her husband Slavek (Abrhám), a young TV repair man, reflect on their lives as a couple. Meanwhile, Slavek goes about his usual business and finds that his world and his daily encounters assume a new significance. This feature by a young and talented director overloads its message—a plea for a better world, put across by the unrealistic device of Slavek's encountering every kind of intolerance and threat in a single day—but it is choc-full of charm and youthful vitality, adding up to a well-wrapped package of small pleasures.

Csend Es Kiáltás see Silence And Cry

Csillagosok, Katonák see Red And The White, The

Cuba Si!

France 1961 58 mins bw
Films De La Pléiade

d **Chris Marker**
sc **Chris Marker**
ph **Chris Marker**
m **E.G. Mantici, J. Calzada**

An account of the early days of the Cuban Revolution and the building of the new nation, including two interviews with Castro. It ends with the Bay of Pigs fiasco, which took place in April 1961 during the cutting of the film which had been shot a few months previously. Castro is the star of this personal, passionate and influential documentary which Marker made to celebrate the second anniversary of the Revolution. The anti-American tone of the ending caused the French government to ban the film until 1963, but Marker published the text and stills. However, these couldn't amply communicate his expert use of sound, image and text that makes his films so special.

Cucaracha, La see Bandit, The

Current

Sodrásban

Hungary 1963 86 mins bw
Hunnia Studio

d **István Gaál**
sc **István Gaál**
ph **Sándor Sára**
m **András Szöllösy, Vivaldi, Frescobaldi**
Andrea Drahota, Marianne Moór, Sándor Csikós, János Harkányi, András Kozák

A group of teenage friends, between school and college, hang around the streets of a small town, play soccer, flirt, joke and go swimming. When one of their number is drowned, everything changes. After starting off as a Hungarian 'teen movie about kids on a summer vacation, the film's moral purpose soon becomes clear. The death of the boy makes the young people come to terms for the first time with their own mortality, and to realize how shallow and immature they have been. Gaál, in his debut feature, copes skilfully with the shift in mood, while fine visual use is made of the setting, dominated by the river. However, the theme is slighly overstressed and some of the acting is a little rough edged.

Curse, The see Xala

Curtain Rises, The see Entrée Des Artistes

Cybèle Ou Les Dimanches De Ville D'Avray see Sundays And Cybèle

The Cycle

Dayereh Mina

Iran 1974 102 mins col
Telfilm

d **Daryush Mehrjui**
sc **Daryush Mehrjui, Golam Hossein Saedi**
ph **Houshang Beharlou**
Esmail Mohammadi, Ezat Entezami, Frouzan, Said Kangarani, Ali Nasirian

A father (Mohammadi) and his son (Kangarani) come to Teheran for the old man to be treated for a persistent illness. The innocent boy, in an effort to pay for his father's cure, succumbs to the corruption around him, becoming a shrewd and unscrupulous middle-man in the city. 'I wanted to reveal this drama in all its absurdity and painfulness, before which I can express nothing but a feeling of profound horror,' stated Mehrjui, who made his name in 1968 with *The Cow*, which took a less virulent view of society. Banned for three years, this remarkable and dark look at the Shah's Iran, manages to get many of its points across with black and bitter humour, and a striking visual quality. The central theme of the trafficking in contaminated blood is even more powerful today in a world confronting AIDS.

Cyrano Et D'Artagnan

France 1963 145 mins col
Circe-Astarte Productions(Paris)/G.E.S.I. Ciné/Agata Film(Rome)

d **Abel Gance**
sc **Abel Gance, Nelly Kaplan**
ph **Otello Martelli**
m **Michel Magne**
José Ferrer, Jean-Pierre Cassel, Sylva Koscina, Daliah Lavi, Michel Simon, Philippe Noiret

The musketeer D'Artagnan (Cassel) and the long-nosed poet Cyrano De Bergerac (Ferrer, reprising his Oscar- winning Hollywood role), join forces in trying to prevent revolution in Paris, and become involved in complicated *amours* with two attractive ladies of the court (Koscina and Lavi). This is an out-and-out swashbuckling romance, done with a modicum of dash, style and humour, much heroic swordplay and a handsome sense of period. However, the plot, drawn from both Edmond Rostand and Dumas *père*, is a somewhat rambling affair and the triviality of the exercise belies the then 75-year-old Gance's well-deserved reputation and achievements as a pioneer of the cinema.

Czlowiek Z Marmur see Man Of Marble

Czlowiek Z Zelaza see Man Of Iron

d

Daisies

Sedmikrásky

Czechoslovakia 1966 76 mins col
Bohumil Smida-Ladislav Fikar

d **Věra Chytilová**
sc **Ester Krumbachová, Věra Chytilová**
ph **Jaroslav Kučera**
m **Jiří Šlitr, Jiří Šust**
Jitka Cerhová, Ivana Karbonavá, Julius Albert

Brunette Marie I (Cerhová) and blonde Marie II (Karbonová) are two bored girls who decide to respond to the consumer-orientated society by playing a number of outrageous pranks on those who belong to it, and by destroying material goods. Chytilová's first collaboration with leading Czech screenwriter Krumbachová (who also designed the film), and her second with her cameraman husband Kučera was the most adventurous and anarchic Czech movie of the 1960s. Its bold use of colour and range of visual effects perfectly underline the sardonic comedy, which ends in a slapstick orgy of destruction at a banquet. It shocked Czech government officials who withheld its release for a year. It was then welcomed enthusiastically at home and abroad.

Dama S Sobachkoi see Lady With The Little Dog, The

Dame Aux Camélias, La see Lady Of The Camellias, The

Les Dames Du Bois De Boulogne

(US: Ladies Of The Park)

France 1946 90 mins bw
Films Raoul Ploquin

d **Robert Bresson**
sc **Jean Cocteau, Robert Bresson**
ph **Philippe Agostini**
m **Jean-Jacques Grünewald**
Maria Casarès, Elina Labourdette, Lucienne Bogaërt, Paul Bernard

When Jean (Bernard) confesses to Hélène (Casarès) that he no longer loves her, she vows revenge. Hélène contrives a meeting between Jean and Agnès (Labourdette), a woman of 'easy virtue' whom he thinks to be devout and chaste. They fall in love and marry. After the wedding ceremony, Hélène reveals the truth. Bresson's second feature film was his last to use professional performers and to be shot in a studio. The transposition of an interpolated story in Diderot's *Jacques Le Fatalist* to a 20th-century *haute bourgeois* setting with few plot changes, plus the cold abstraction of the images might have been the cause of its commercial failure, but it brilliantly lays bare the ethical issues of the fable, and dramatic tension is created between the verbal flights of Cocteau and Bresson's natural austerity.

The Damned

Les Maudits

France 1947 105 mins bw
Spéva Films

d **René Clément**
sc **René Clément, Jacques Rémy**
ph **Henri Alekan**
m **Yves Baudrier**
Henri Vidal, Florence Marly, Kurt Kronefeld, Jo Dest, Anne Campion, Michel Auclair

A group of Nazi officials and assorted hangers-on, realizing their days are numbered as the end of the war approaches, take a U-boat from Oslo and head for South America. One of the women is seriously hurt in an attack by a destroyer, so they land on the French coast and kidnap a doctor (Vidal) who becomes the hero of the piece. Clément offers a thriller-style entertainment, topical when it was made, combined with some satisfying anti-Nazi propaganda. A strong cast convinces as the group of desperate nasties, and the director does well to keep things interesting within the claustrophobic confines of the submarine.

Best Film Cannes 1947

The Damned

aka Götterdämmerung

La Caduta Degli Dei

Italy/W. Germany 1969 164 mins col
Praesidens/Pegaso

d **Luchino Visconti**
sc **Nicola Badalucco, Enrico Medioli, Luchino Visconti**
ph **Armando Nannuzzi, Pasquale De Santis**
m **Maurice Jarre**
Dirk Bogarde, Ingrid Thulin, Helmut Berger, Renaud Verley, Helmut Griem, René Kolldehoff, Umberto Orsini, Charlotte Rampling

The conflicts within the powerful Essenbeck family of munitions manufacturers, operating in Germany during the growth of Nazism. The first of Visconti's 'German decadence' trilogy (followed by *Death In Venice* and *Ludwig*) is a ludicrously baroque and garish caricature of the 20th century's most tragic era. It sets out to examine the ideological and economic link between the Nazis and the capitalist *bourgeoisie*, but gets hypnotized by the Nazi regalia. The jackboot- kissing Helmut Berger in Dietrich drag romps with the Boys in the Bund, while the rest of the British, Swedish, French, Italian and German cast mouth banalities in whichever of the languages the film is shown in.

Dance Programme, The see Carnet De Bal, Un

Dangerous Moves

La Diagonale Du Fou

Switzerland 1983 110 mins col
Arthur Cohn

d **Richard Dembo**
sc **Richard Dembo**
ph **Raoul Coutard**
m **Gabriel Yared (based on César Franck)**
Michel Piccoli, Alexandre Arbatt, Leslie Caron, Liv Ullmann, Daniel Olbrychski, Michel Aumont

The World Chess Championship is played in Geneva between the Soviet Grand Master (Piccoli)—suffering a heart condition but supported by all the accoutrements of the blessing of the Kremlin—and the former world champion (Arbatt) who defected five years previously. This film, which can be read as a metaphor for the Cold War, offers a great deal for chess lovers, and first-time director Dembo builds up a certain amount of suspense in the moves and countermoves which are echoed by the offstage strategies of the opposing camps. However, there is little character development, the personalities are rather shallow and two-dimensional, and the Hollywood honour comes as something of a surprise.

Best Foreign Film Oscar 1984

Daniel Takes A Train

Szerencsés Daniel

Hungary 1983 92 mins col
Mafilm (Hunnia Studio)

d **Pál Sándor**
sc **Zsuzsa Tóth**
ph **Elemér Ragályi**
m **György Selmeczi**
Péter Rudolf, Sándor Zsótér, Kati Szerb, Mari Töröcsik, Dezsö Garás, Gyula Bodrogi

After the 1956 Hungarian uprising, Daniel (Rudolf) and his friend Gyuri (Zsótér)—a soldier on the run—travel to a small town on the Austrian border. Gyuri knows he must leave Hungary but Daniel, looking for his girlfriend, is trapped in conflict and uncertainty. As a political drama, the film hedges its bets by taking an even-handed look at the options on offer to the protagonists; as a piece of film-making, it is constantly absorbing. Sándor draws marvellous performances from his cast, the camera is inventive (notice the tracking shot at the railway station), and the storyline is full of surprises, both wry and tragic.

Dans La Ville Blanche see In The White City

Danton

France 1982 136 mins col
Films Du Losange/Groupe X/Gaumont/TF1/SFPC/TM

d **Andrzej Wajda**
sc **Jean-Claude Carrière**
ph **Igor Luther**
m **Jean Prodromidès**
Gérard Depardieu, Wojciech Pszoniak, Anne Alvaro, Roland Blanche, Patrice Chéreau, Angela Winkler, Roger Planchon

The clash between the warmly idealistic Danton (Depardieu) and the coldly pragmatic Robespierre (Pszoniak) over the way the French Revolution should go, ends with Danton on the guillotine. At the time of its release, most critics made an analogy between the central ideological conflict and that of General Jaruzelski and Lech Waleska in contemporary Poland, although the film was based on a 1931 play by Stanlislawa Przybyszewska. Perhaps their theories added interest to this long-winded, visually conventional film with a posturing central performance by Depardieu.

Daoma Zei see Horse Thief

Dark Eyes
Oci Ciornie

Italy 1987 117 mins col
Excelsior Film/RAI 1

d **Nikita Mikhalkov**
sc **Alexander Adabakhian, Nikita Mikhalkov (with the collaboration of Suso Cecchi D'Amico)**
ph **Franco Di Giacomo**
m **Francis Lai**
Marcello Mastroianni, Silvana Mangano, Marthe Keller, Elena Sofonova, Vsevolod Larionov, Innokenti Smoktunovsky

On board ship, Romano (Mastroianni), an aging Italian *roué*, tells his story to an amiable Russian (Larionov). When a poverty-stricken student, Romano had married a beautiful heiress (Mangano) and had lived in indolent luxury, taking refuge in buffoonery, mistresses and lone visits to spas. At one such, he met and seduced the married Anna (Sofonova) who fell in love with him and fled, whereupon he pursued her to her home in the Russian provinces... Working from several short stories by Chekhov, of which the most evident is *The Lady With The Little Dog* (the 'lady' here is Anna, the 'dark eyes' of the title), Mikhalkov has made what the American critic Pauline Kael termed 'a massive hunk of Italo-Russian kitsch'. The material encompasses a range of mood from poignant to farcical, dominated by Mastroianni, every inch the star, moving back and forth between youth and age. Unfortunately, it's an uncomfortably exhibitionistic performance, and the film as a whole is crowded with overstated stereotypes and insistent close-ups. The women are fine, the clothes stunning and the sense of period convincing.

Best Actor (Marcello Mastroianni) Cannes 1987

The Dark Side Of The Moon
aka The Man In The Moon
Manden I Maanen

Denmark 1986 94 mins col
Film-Cooperative Denmark

d **Erik Clausen**
sc **Erik Clausen**
ph **Morten Bruus, Jens Schlosser**
m **John Høybe**
Peter Thiel, Catherine Poul Dupont, Christina Bergtsson, Kim Jansson, Tavuzer Cetinkaya

A prisoner (Thiel) is released 16 years after being jailed for killing his wife. Reticent and introspective, he adjusts slowly to society, steeling himself to approach his daughter (Bergtsson) who views him only as her mother's murderer. Dark it certainly is (there is not one daylight setting), and bleak, with Denmark presented as a loveless place, where people speak slowly and monosyllabically. But a ponderous and pretentious tendency is offset by the intense film debut of Peter Thiel who is strangely watchable, as unattractive as he is, and the almost expressionistic photography and lighting.

Daughter Of Destiny, A see Alraune

Daughter Of The Nile

Nilouhe, Nuer

Taiwan 1988 91 mins col
Fu Film Productions

d **Hou Hsiao-hsien**
sc **Zhu Tianwen**
ph **Ch'en Huai-en**
m **Ch'en Cihyuan, Chang Hung-yi**
Yang Lin, Kao Jai, Yang Fan, Li Tien-lu

A schoolgirl (Lin), washing, cooking and doing the housework for her father, grandfather, elder brother and younger sister, as well as working at a Kentucky Fried Chicken fast food joint after school, can only escape by reading the comic strip *Daughter Of The Nile*. Brisker, and more substantial than Hsiao-hsien's first big international success *A Summer At Grandpa's*, the film has as much warmth and gentle observation as that picture. Yang Lin, a popular singer in Taiwan, Kao Jai, an owner of fashion boutiques, and Li Tien-lu are perfect as the drudge, her ne'er-do-well brother and loving grandfather respectively. Only some of the tenuous allusions to the comic strip may escape the Western spectator.

Daughters Of China

Zhonghua Nuer

China 1949 92 mins bw
Northeast Film Studios

d **Ling Zhifeng, Zhai Jiang**
sc **Yan Yiyan**
ph **Qian Jiang**
m **Tung Yeng Orchestra**
Zhang Zheng, Yueh Shen, Bo Li, Tai Pu-hua, Chou-Su-Fei, Xie Yan

During the Japanese invasion of North-east China in 1936, a peasant woman (Zheng) joins the resistance and finds herself in a guerilla group with seven other women, headed by Commissar Yun (Shen). After liberating an important town, they run into a large Japanese force with tragic but heroic consequences. The film, which can claim to be the first production under the new government of the People's Republic of China, was based on a real incident—the martrydom of eight women fighting the Japanese. It was a perfect subject to inspire national unity and point the way towards the New China style of films. Although the women are pictured as superheroines and symbols, much of the life in the army, as well as the relationships among the characters, is invested with an affecting naturalism.

David

W. Germany 1979 125 mins col
Vietinghof Filmproduktion/Pro-ject Film Produktion/ Filmverlag Der Autoren/ZDF/Dedra Pictures

d **Peter Lilienthal**
sc **Jurek Becker,Ulla Zieman, Peter Lilienthal**
ph **Al Ruban**
m **Wojciech Kilar**
Mario Fische, Torsten Henties, Walter Taub, Irena Vrkljan, Eva Mattes

When Rabbi Singer (Taub) has his synagogue burnt down and his bald head scarred with a swastika by the Nazi persecutors, his daughter (Mattes) and teenage son David (Fische) go into hiding. The girl is given refuge by a shoemaker in return for money, but David goes on the run alone, taking odd jobs, and finally acquiring false papers to get to Israel. A small tale about a major chapter in history, the film is overlong and attempts no new insights into or comments on the Holocaust. However, although no more than competent in all departments, it is nonetheless a moving, and occasionally powerful, document.

Best Film Berlin 1979

Daybreak

Le Jour Se Lève

France 1939 95 mins bw
Vog/Sigma

d **Marcel Carné**
sc **Jacques Prévert, Jacques Viot**
ph **Curt Courant, Philippe Agostini**
m **Maurice Jaubert**
Jean Gabin, Jules Berry, Arletty, Jacqueline Laurent, René Génin, Mady Berry, Bernard Blier

A worker (Gabin) gets involved with the mistress (Arletty) of a shady showman (Berry) and kills him in a jealous confrontation over an innocent flower-seller (Laurent). He then barricades himself in his small room during the night as the police and crowds wait below. The most celebrated of the pessimistic poetic realist films of the Carné-Prévert partnership makes memorable atmospheric use of the dark tenement set (designed by Alexandre Trauner) and of Gabin's tragic stature almost, matched by the hypnotically suave villainy of Berry. Although most of the film is told in flashback as Gabin thinks back over the past, it is the image of the oppressively small room in which he is trapped, that lingers in the mind. When RKO bought the rights for an inferior 1947 remake called *The Long Night* with Henry Fonda, it shamelessly tried to destroy all prints. Happily it failed to do so.

Dayereh Mina see Cycle, The

Day For Night

La Nuit Americaine

France 1973 116 mins col
Films Du Carrosse/PECF/PIC

d **François Truffaut**
sc **François Truffaut, Jean-Louis Richard, Suzanne Schiffman**
ph **Pierre-William Glenn**
m **Georges Delerue**
Jacqueline Bisset, Valentina Cortese, Jean-Pierre Aumont, Jean-Pierre Léaud, Alexandra Stewart, François Truffaut, Dani, Jean Champion, David Markham

During the filming of a melodrama called *Meet Pamela*, the juvenile lead (Léaud) falls hopelessly in love with the married international star (Bisset), an actress (Cortese) keeps forgetting her lines, the male lead (Aumont) is killed in a crash, time and money begin to run out, and someone has a baby. 'Are films more important than life?' asks Léaud at one stage. Truffaut, himself playing the director, answers in the affirmative with this exuberant celebration of movie-making, even if the plainly lousy film being shot seems hardly worth the trouble. But the enthusiasm he feels comes across forcefully and so does the involved process of creating a film. Incidentally, novelist Graham Greene appears in an uncredited bit part.

Best Foreign Film Oscar 1973

A Day In The Country

Une Partie De Campagne

France 1936 45 mins bw
Panthéon/Films De La Pléiade/Pierre Braunberger

d **Jean Renoir**
sc **Jean Renoir**
ph **Claude Renoir, Jean Bourgoin**
m **Joseph Kosma**
Sylvie Bataille, Georges Darnoux, Jane Marken, Paul Temps, Jacques Brunius, Gabriello, Gabrielle Fontan, Jean Renoir

A tradesman, his wife, daughter and future son-in-law take a rare Sunday trip to the country where they picnic, go boating and fishing, and where the daughter falls in love with a young holiday-maker. The idyll ends on a regretful note. Originally Renoir only intended to make an hour-long film based on Guy De Maupassant's short story, shot on location in the countryside of the Île De France. However, the summer of 1936 was particularly rainy so the project was abandoned with only two sequences to shoot. In 1946, two intertitles were added to explain the missing passages, and it has been delighting audiences ever since. Renoir's glowing, witty, sensuous tribute to the countryside through which a river runs has seldom been surpassed.

Day Of Wrath

Vredens Dag

Denmark 1943 105 mins bw
Palladium

d **Carl Dreyer**
sc **Carl Dreyer, Poul Knudsen, Mogens Skot-Hansen**
ph **Karl Andersson**
m **Poul Schierbeck**
Thorkild Roose, Lisbeth Movin, Sigrid Neiiendam, Preben Lerdoff Rye, Anna Svierkier

In 17th-century Denmark, a pastor (Roose) is cursed by a dying witch (Svierkier). His wife (Movin) then commits adultery with a younger man (Rye), the discovery of which kills the pastor, and she in turn is burned as a witch. Dreyer's 10 years of silence after *Vampyr* was broken with this rather ponderous, measured and academic study of people caught in a web of superstition. One cannot deny the splendid interior compositions or fail to recognize the glimmerings of Dreyer's austere genius. The film, one of his most famous, was taken as an allegory for occupied Denmark, so Dreyer took refuge in Sweden until after the war to avoid reprisals.

Days And Nights In The Forest

Aranyer Din Ratri

India 1969 115 mins bw
Priya

d **Satyajit Ray**
sc **Satyajit Ray**
ph **Soumendu Roy**
m **Satyajit Ray**
Soumitra Chatterjee, Sharmilia Tagore, Shubhendu Chatterjee, Samit Bhanja

Four young men spend their country holiday in an unused bungalow where they come into contact with the villagers, meet a rich family, and develop relationships with women, before returning to their urban existence. Chekhov and Jean Renoir (with whom Ray worked) come to mind, especially in the magical picnic scene, but the subtle revelation of character through the purposefully slow tempo and the deceptively simple cinematic effects are all the master Indian director's own.

Days Of Hope see Man's Hope

Days Of 36

Imeres Tou 36

Greece 1972 120 mins col
Finos Film

d **Theo Angelopoulos**
sc **Theo Angelopoulos**
ph **Georges Arvanitis**
Georges Kiritsis, Thanos Grammenos, Yannis Kandilas, Christoforos Chimara, Takis Dukakos

A man (Grammenos) is arrested for the assassination of a politician. He protests his innocence and holds a deputy (Kiritsis) hostage in his cell, threatening to kill the man and himself unless he is released. The first of Angelopoulos' triptych about recent Greek history (*The Travelling Players* and *The Huntsmen* followed), is based on actual events in 1936. Made during the reign of the Colonels, the film subtly undermines that regime in its portrayal of official incompetence. The prison governors and politicians are struck by a paralysis of indecision, finally breaking the deadlock by violent means in which justice has no place. The film is brilliantly photographed and, given its physical confines, its acreage of silence and the fact that the prisoner keeps himself out of sight for a good deal of the time, the high level of tensión is a real achievement, especially considering the director's penchant for drawing things out.

Da Yuebing see Big Parade, The

Deadlier Than The Male see Murder À La Carte

Dear Detective see Dear Inspector

Dearest Love

(US: Murmur Of The Heart)

Le Souffle Au Coeur

France 1971 118 mins col
Nouvelles Éditions/Marianne/Vides Cinematografica/Franz Seitz

d **Louis Malle**
sc **Louis Malle**
ph **Ricardo Aronovich**
m **Charlie Parker, Sidney Bechet, Gaston Freche, Henri Renaud**
Lea Massari, Benoít Ferreux, Daniel Gélin, Fabien Ferreux, Jacqueline Chauveau, Michel Lonsdale

Fifteen-year-old Laurent (Benoit Ferreux) is wrestling with the ache of adolescent sexual longings while his mother (Massari), though successfully married, has a lover with whom she is undergoing a crisis. After an illness leaves Laurent with a heart murmur, his mother takes him to a health spa where they each meet with sexual rejection, and their mutual sympathy and love culminates in bed. Malle treats incest with subtlety and sensitivity but the film is fundamentally about the pains and pleasures of adolescence and, as the mother makes clear, theirs is a one-off encounter, appropriate to that moment only. Played out in the context of 1950s middle-class family life, this truthful, funny, observant and affectionate work is served by first- class performances, notably from Massari who handles her task with exquisite finesse.

Dear Inspector
(US: Dear Detective)
Tendre Poulet

France 1977 105 mins col
Les Films Ariane/Mondex Films

d **Philippe De Broca**
sc **Michel Audiard, Philippe De Broca**
ph **Jean-Paul Schwartz**
m **Georges Delerue**
Annie Girardot, Philippe Noiret, Catherine Alric, Guy Marchand, Roger Dumas, Simone Renant

Lise (Girardot), divorcée and mother, is also a police inspector. While engaged on an important murder investigation, she romances with a professor of Greek (Noiret), an old acquaintance whom she met again through accidentally knocking him down in the street. The leads—Noiret confused, pompous and endearing, Girardot confused, madcap and endearing—shine in this charming comedy thriller, full of inventive gags, serious *policier* undertones and touching romance. Although De Broca's taste for the eccentric here degenerates on occasion into uncomfortable contrivance, there is much to enjoy in a light-hearted fashion.

Dear Irene
Kaere Irene

Denmark 1971 102 mins bw
Kollektiv Film

d **Christian Braad Thomsen**
sc **Christian Braad Thomsen, Mette Knudsen**
ph **Dirk Brüel**
m **Blue Sun**
Mette Knudsen, Sten Kaalø, Ebbe Kløvedal, Agneta Ekmanner, Erik Nørgaard, Katrine Behrendt

Irene (Knudsen), who married Claus (Kløvedal) some years ago because she could not get an abortion, is locked into an affair with Ebbe (Kaalø), who is very much in love with her. He leaves his journalist's job on a conventional newspaper in order to express his revolutionary views, while she, obsessed with asserting her independence, is cruelly unfaithful to him. The debut feature of the Marxist critic Thomsen is impressive. Shot in *cinéma vérité* style, it achieves a casual and convincing realism, while the events of the plot mask complex layers of social and political argument. A film about commitment and contradiction, about difficulties of choice, loneliness and isolation, and the political versus the personal, it grips on the surface level, too—especially as played by Knudsen, whose destructive and confused Irene is nonetheless sympathetic.

Dear John
Kare John

Sweden 1964 111 mins bw
Sandrew

d **Lars Magnus Lindgren**
sc **Lars Magnus Lindgren**
ph **Rune Ericson**
m **Bengt-Arne Wallin**
Jarl Kulle, Christina Schollin, Helena Nilsson, Morgan Andersson, Synnove Liljeback

Anita (Schollin), an unmarried mother, works as a waitress in a small coastal town. John (Kulle) is a sailor whose barge anchors there for a weekend which they spend together. When he has to leave, she thinks she will never see him again. A skilfully constructed love story, tender but sensual, about two young people fearful of being hurt, but irresistibly drawn together. Lindgren uses flashback techniques with control, his stars act with sensitivity and conviction, and the photography makes palpable the clear light of a Swedish summer.

Dear Michael
Caro Michele

Italy 1976 108 mins col
FLAG Production

d **Mario Monicelli**
sc **Suso Cecchi D'Amico, Tonino Guerra**
ph **Tonino Delli Colli**
m **Nino Rota**
Mariangela Melato, Delphine Seyrig, Aurore Clément, Marcella Michelangeli, Lou Castel, Fabio Carpi

A middle-class Roman family finds its long-standing traditions and ideals challenged by the changing climate of the times, culminating in the free-thinking, free-living zany Mara (Melato) giving birth to the child of their rebellious son, Michael. When Michael, who is abroad fighting for some unspecified revolution, is killed, Mara, mother of the family's sole male heir, finds the problems of choice between individualism and conformity devolving on her. Working from a novel by the distinguished Russian, Natalia Ginzburg, Monicelli has made a literate and good-spirited film in which he strikes a convincing balance between sympathy for, and criticism of, his characters. Standing out in a first-rate cast is the accomplished and deliciously uninhibited Melato. Michael, to whom everyone writes letters and who serves to link the action, remains offscreen.

Best Director Berlin 1976

Death By Hanging
Koshikei

Japan 1968 117 mins bw
Sozosha

d **Nagisa Oshima**
sc **Tsutomu Tamura**
ph **Yasuhiro Yoshioka**
m **Hikaru Hayashi**
Yun-Do Yun, Kei Sato, Fumio Watanabe, Toshiro Ishido, Masao Adachi

An intelligent young Korean (Yun) is being hanged for the rape and murder of two Japanese girls, but his body refuses to die. The characters act out the man's story in seven chapters. Oshima's startling, angry and blackly humorous film begins like a documentary on the death penalty, becoming more and more unreal as the arguments are pursued. The main subject that emerges is the shameful treatment by the Japanese of the Korean minority, a fact of crucial importance to an understanding of the film.

Death In A French Garden
Péril En La Demeure

France 1985 101 mins col
Gaumont/Elefilm/TFI Films

d **Michel Deville**
sc **Michel Deville, Rosalinde Damamme**
ph **Martial Thury**
m **Extracts from Brahms, Schubert, Enrique Granados**
Michel Piccoli, Nicole Garcia, Anemone, Christophe Malavoy, Richard Bohringer, Anaïs Jeanneret

David (Malavoy) arrives to teach music to Viviane (Jeanneret), the young and sexually precocious daughter of a wealthy industrialist (Piccoli) and his wife, Julia (Garcia). Seduced by Julia, he finds himself entangled in a web of deception, voyeurism and murder, with a hired homosexual killer who is after his affections. Deville has delivered a stylish and accomplished film, beautiful to look at. However, its manipulative mix of thriller, sophisticated critique of *bourgeois* mores and suggested allegory, alternately dark and playful in tone, adds up to a superficial exercise which is sometimes tedious, sometimes engrossing.

Death In Venice
Morte A Venezia

Italy 1971 128 mins col
Alfa Cinematografica

d **Luchino Visconti**
sc **Luchino Visconti, Nicola Badalucco**
ph **Pasquale De Santis**
m **Mahler**
Dirk Bogarde, Bjorn Andresen, Silvana Mangano, Marisa Berenson, Mark Burns

Von Aschenbach, an aging and celebrated composer in poor health and suffering a crisis of his creative powers, visits Venice. There he becomes possessed by the beauty of a young Polish boy, Tadzio (Andresen), to whom he never speaks but who appears to embody his ideals of physical beauty and spiritual purity. He remains in Venice, in spite of a cholera epidemic, until ill health and his obsession combine to kill him. Visconti's transposition of Thomas Mann's novel is intelligent and sensitive, and evokes *fin-de-siècle* Venice to breathtaking perfection. The flashbacks examining Von Aschenbach's crisis are clumsy, and the intellectual heart of the novel is, perhaps, ultimately impossible to film. The transformation of Mann's writer into a composer is doubtless an attempt to overcome the difficulties and, although the device works well, the suggestion that

Aschenbach—in the slightly too English, too young guise of Bogarde—composed the works of Gustav Mahler is a little unsettling. The Cannes Festival jury awarded its special twenty-fifth anniversary prize to Visconti for this film in particular, and his *oeuvre* in general.

Death Is My Trade

Aus Einem Deutschen Leben

W. Germany 1977 145 mins col
WDR (Cologne)/Iduna-Film (Munich)

d **Theodor Kotulla**
sc **Theodor Kotulla**
ph **Dieter Naujeck**
m **Eberhard Weber**
Götz George, Elisabeth Schwarz, Kurt Hübner, Kai Taschner, Sigurd Fitzek, Peter Franke, Hans Korte, Walter Czaschke

The life, from 1922 until 1946, of Franz Lang (George), a German working-class patriot who joins the Nazi Party in 1924 and distinguishes himself by dedicated hard work and application. Himmler appoints him to an important post at Dachau and, seven years later, he is commandant at Auschwitz, responsible for carrying out the Final Solution. After the war, he writes his memoirs and dies without exhibiting a hint of remorse. Although given a fictitious name here, Lang is actually the notorious Rudolph Höss (not to be confused with Hess), portrayed here as a rather ordinary man, unquestioningly committed to his duty. If this is, in itself, a comment on the German high command's skill in securing faith in its ideology, Kotulla's film actually offers no comment and no apology. A detached, ordered account of events makes for a historical document, all the more chilling for its lack of emotion and the seeming normality of its protagonists.

Death Occurred Last Night

La Morte Risale A Ieri Sera

Italy 1970 98 mins col
Lombard Film/Filmes/C.C.C. (Berlin)

d **Duccio Tessari**
sc **Biagio Proietti, Duccio Tessari, Arthur Brauner**
ph **Lamberto Caimi**
m **Gianni Ferrio**
Raf Vallone, Frank Wolff, Gabriele Tinti, Gillian Bray, Eva Renzi

When 25-year-old Donatella Berzhagi disappears, the police are offhand with her desperate father (Vallone), until he explains that she has a mental age of three and suffers from a tendency to nymphomania. To find her abductor, Inspector Lambert (Wolff) institutes a manhunt throughout a world inhabited by participants in every kind of call-girl racket. On the surface this is a slick thriller, trading in the currency of sleaze, but don't be fooled—Tessari has made an intelligent study of a milieu, using his plot to carry a series of observant character studies and pointing to a society composed of lonely and unhappy people, conveyed in some powerful and inventive images.

Death Of A Bureaucrat

La Muerte De Un Burocrata

Cuba 1966 84 mins bw
I.C.A.I.C.

d **Tomás Gutiérrez Alea**
sc **Alfredo Del Cueto, Ramón Suárez, Tomás Gutiérrez Alea**
ph **Ramón Suárez**
m **Leo Brouwer**
Salvador Wood, Silvia Planas, Manuel Estanillo, Gaspar De Santelices, Carlos Ruiz De La Tejera, Omar Alfonso

After an exemplary worker is buried, clutching his union card, his widow (Planas) finds she needs it to claim her pension. The fruitless attempts of her nephew (Wood) to obtain an exhumation order lead to his visit to the cemetery at night and a series of further complications. This amusing satire not only takes a swipe at Red red-tape, but pays tribute to a whole range of other films on the way. Laurel and Hardy, Harold Lloyd, Buñuel and Bergman are all evoked, but it is to Alea's credit that they become integral to this inventive narrative.

Death Of A Cyclist

(US: Age Of Infidelity)

Muerte De Un Ciclista

Spain 1955 85 mins bw
Guion/Suevia/Trionfalcine

d **Juan Antonio Bardem**

sc **Juan Antonio Bardem**
ph **Alfredo Fraile**
m **Isrido Maiztegui**
Lucia Bosé, Alberto Closas, Carlos Casaravilla, Otello Toso, Bruna Corra

A university professor (Closas), driving with his mistress (Bosé) who is married to an important man, knocks down a worker on a bicycle. Fearing their affair will be discovered, they leave the man to die in the road. Their subsequent guilt leads to a further tragedy. Bardem's most famous work was a decent attempt to make a socially critical film under Franco's regime. The milieu of the rich and the contrasting poor districts of Madrid are well caught in this bitter comment on contemporary Spain. Unfortunately, censorship forced Bardem to punish the adulterous woman in a melodramatic ending.

Death Of A Friend

Morte Di Un Amico

Italy 1959 87 mins bw
Universalcine

d **Franco Rossi**
sc **Giuseppe Berto, Oreste Biancoli, Pier Paolo Pasolini, Franco Riganti**
ph **Toni Secchi**
m **Mario Nascimbene**
Gianni Garko, Spiros Focas, Didi Perego, Angela Luce, Anna Mazzucchelli, Fanfulla

Bruno (Focas), a delinquent layabout who lives with and is kept by a prostitute (Luce), succeeds in persuading quiet, respectable Aldo (Garko), his best friend since childhood, to join him in his own way of life. The ensuing catastrophes end in Aldo's tragic death. Rossi exercises commendable restraint and subtlety in dealing with a storyline and characters tailormade for overheated treatment. Focas and Garko convince and, although compassion tips over into sentimentality, this essentially small film is nonetheless affecting.

The Death Of Maria Malibran

Der Tod Der Maria Malibran

W. Germany 1971 104 mins col
Werner Schroeter

d **Werner Schroeter**
sc **Werner Schroeter**
ph **Werner Schroeter**
m **Brahms, Beethoven, Thomas, Stravinsky, Mozart, Cherubini, Handel, Puccini, Rossini, and various popular standards**
Magdalena Montezuma, Candy Darling, Annette Tirier, Christine Kaufmann, Ingrid Caven

A series of unrealistic tableaux enact the short life of Maria Malibran (Montezuma), the 19th-century Spanish prima donna, who died during a performance, at the age of 28 in 1836, from injuries received in a riding accident. High camp has to be the description of this perverse but curiously hypnotic and beautiful 'biopic', with no discernible plot, no direct dialogue (there are Shakespearian soliloquies etc), or direct singing (the voices are mostly disembodied) and a vast range of anachronistic melodies including 'St Louis Blues'. 'Mad genius' Schroeter was the only man Rainer Werner Fassbinder considered his artistic equal.

The Death Of Mario Ricci

La Mort De Mario Ricci

Switzerland 1983 101 mins col
Pegase Fils/Television Suisse Romande/Swanie Productions/FR3 (Paris)/Tele München

d **Claude Goretta**
sc **Claude Goretta, Georges Haldas**
ph **Hans Liechti**
m **Arié Dzierlatka, Christian Bonneau, and extracts from Vivaldi and Monteverdi**
Gian Maria Volonté, Heinz Bennent, Mimsy Farmer, Magali Noël, Jean-Michel Dupuis

Having been partly crippled in the course of duty in South America, a Swiss TV journalist (Volonté) returns home to interview a world-famous expert on famine who lives in an Alpine village. He discovers that the man is on the verge of a nervous breakdown, and learns that mystery surrounds the death of Mario Ricci, an Italian worker killed in a motorcycle smash. Compelling visual images hint at the dark secrets harboured by a community, but the film lets itself down with too many sub-plots, red herrings and existential meanderings. A worthy, but finally unsatisfying piece, held together by its technical expertise and excellent casting.

Best Actor (Gian Maria Volonté) Cannes 1983

The Death Ray

Luch Smerti

USSR 1925 125 mins bw
Goskino

d **Lev Kuleshov**
sc **Vsevolod Pudovkin**
ph **A. Levitski**
m **Silent**
Porfiry Podobed, Sergei Komarov, Vsevolod Pudovkin, Alexandra Khokhlova, Vladimir Fogel, Lev Kuleshov

A group of Fascist spies tries to steal the Death Ray, an invention of a Soviet scientist (Podobed), but they are eventually foiled by a series of subterfuges. Mysterious masked men, women brandishing guns and sinister figures in black tights prowling across rooftops are all elements reminiscent of the Feuillade serials, but the film is original in its use of mobile cameras, quick cutting and breathless pacing. (Pudovkin was nearly killed performing a stunt, when he fell from a three-storey building.) All great fun, accidents apart, but it failed to amuse Soviet officialdom who thought it lacked 'meaningful' content and stripped Kuleshov of much of his company's budget. What the po-faced commissars did not see was its prediction of the growth of Fascism.

Debut, The see Beginning, The

Decamerone, Il see Decameron, The

The Decameron

Il Decamerone

Italy 1971 111 mins col
PEA/Artemis/UA

d **Pier Paolo Pasolini**
sc **Pier Paolo Pasolini**
ph **Tonino Delli Colli**
m **Pier Paolo Pasolini, Ennio Morricone**
Franco Citti, Ninetto Davoli, Angela Luce, Patrizia Capparelli, Pier Paolo Pasolini, Jovan Jovanovic, Gianni Rizzo

Eight of Boccaccio's tales, set mostly around 14th-century Naples, including those of the seducing nuns, the three jealous brothers who murder their sister's lover, a false saint, a deceiving husband, and the man who travels to buy horses but finds himself caught up in a series of disasters. The first in Pasolini's lively and colourful trilogy based on famous story cycles (*The Canterbury Tales* and *The Arabian Nights* followed) included the director as Giotto working on a fresco as the pivot around which Boccaccio's tales of sexual deception revolved. Pasolini chose many ordinary Neapolitans to appear among the cast of 54 to populate this re- creation of the teeming Naples of the Middle Ages.

Special Jury Prize Berlin 1971

Deception see Anna Boleyn

De Cierta Manera see One Way Or Another

Déclin De L'Empire Américain, Le see Decline Of The American Empire, The

---

The Decline Of The American Empire

Le Déclin De L'Empire Américain

Canada 1986 101 mins col
Corporation Image M&M/National Film Board Of Canada/Téléfilm Canada/Société Générale Du Cinéma Du Québec

d **Denys Arcand**
sc **Denys Arcand**
ph **Guy Dufaux**
m **F. Compierre**
Dominique Michel, Dorothée Berryman, Louise Portal, Geneviève Rioux, Pierre Curzy, Rémy Girard, Yves Jacques, Daniel Brière

Four history professors discuss their contrasting sex lives while preparing a gourmet dinner in a country mansion. Meanwhile, their four female guests conduct a similar discussion in a sauna. Later, at the dinner, talk consists of fashionable and wide-ranging intellectual exchange until one of the women (Michel) announces that she has slept with two of her hosts, including the married Rémy (Girard) whose wife (Berryman) is present. Arcand's film is a cynical and observant conversation piece in which the protagonists' attitudes to sex serve to unmask their personalities, their deeper political concerns and their positions in the battle of the sexes. Dense, perhaps, but intelligent and interesting.

Dédée

Woman Of Antwerp

Dédée D'Anvers

France 1948 95 mins bw

Sacha Gordine/André Paulvé

d **Yves Allégret**

sc **Yves Allégret, Jacques Sigurd**

ph **Jean Bourgoin**

m **Jacques Besse**

Simone Signoret, Marcel Pagliero, Bernard Blier, Marcel Dalio, Jane Marken

When Dédée (Signoret), a prostitute around the docks at Antwerp, falls for a sailor (Pagliero), her pimp (Blier) causes trouble that leads to tragedy. The first of three doom-laden melodramas that Allégret made with his then wife Signoret, was filmed in the kind of poetic realism which Marcel Carné made popular before the war. Without approaching the quality of such films as *Quai Des Brumes* (1938), it depicts the dockside low life with conviction. Above all, there is 27-year-old Signoret, shining in her first important role.

Dédée D'Anvers see Dédée

Le Defroqué

aka The Renegade Priest

France 1953 111 mins bw

SFC/SNEG

d **Léo Joannon**

sc **Léo Joannon, Denys De La Patellière**

ph **Nicolas Torporkoff**

m **Jean-Jacques Grünewald**

Pierre Fresnay, Pierre Trabaud, Nicole Stéphane, Marcelle Géniat, René Blancard

In a German prison camp, a defrocked priest (Fresnay) rails against the Church and religion, but his unselfish acts inspire a young fellow prisoner (Trabaud) to take up the priesthood after the war. In addition, it takes two deaths on his conscience to bring the heretic back to God. The Protestant Fresnay followed up his convincing portrayals of Catholic holy men in *Monsieur Vincent* and *Isle of Sinners* with another brilliant performance in the devotional mode. While in no way competing with the two true religious artists of the cinema—Dreyer and Bresson—Joannon manages in a modest manner to make a telling drama with a highly emotional ending that only an actor of Fresnay's calibre could carry off.

Best Director Berlin 1954

A Degree Of Murder

Mord Und Totschlag

W. Germany 1967 87 mins col

Rob Houwer Films

d **Volker Schlöndorff**

sc **Gregor Von Rezzori, Niklas Franz, Arne Boyer**

ph **Franz Rath**

m **Brian Jones**

Anita Pallenberg, Hans P. Hallwachs, Manfred Fischbeck, Werner Enke, Angela Hillebrecht

A girl (Pallenberg) accidentally kills her boyfriend in a quarrel over a revolver. She persuades a stranger (Hallwachs), in exchange for some money, to help her dispose of the body which, via a sexual encounter with her, he does. They place it in a hole in a construction site and, as the bulldozers are about to dig it up, she is planning a trip to Greece with another young man whom she has just met. In his second film, Schlöndorff confirms the competence he displayed in his first, *Young Torless.* It is a naturalistic and convincing piece, but so determinedly neutral in its examination of a bunch of drifters that the point is not altogether clear. While it is happening, though, this rather amoral but well-paced tale is fairly absorbing. The acting is fine, but Pallenberg's claim to fame would remain her liaison with Keith Richard of The Rolling Stones rather than her thespian abilities. Ex-Stones guitarist Jones composed the music shortly before his death.

Déjeuner Sur L'Herbe, Le see Lunch On The Grass

De L'Amour see All About Loving

De Mayerling À Sarajevo see Sarajevo

Demise Of Father Mouret, The see Sin Of Father Mouret, The

Il Demonio

Italy 1963 100 mins bw
Titanus/Vox Film (Rome)/Cocinor/Marceau (Paris)

d **Brunello Rondi**
sc **Ugo Guerra, Brunello Rondi, Luciano Martino**
ph **Carlo Bellero**
m **Piero Piccioni**
Daliah Lavi, Frank Wolff, Giovanni Cristofanelli, Luca Pascarella, Lea Eusso, Giuseppe Macaluso

Purif (short for Purification), who lives in an isolated mountain village with her family and is passionately in love with Antonio (Wolff), is plagued by voices and visions, and is believed to be possessed by the devil. Attempts to exorcise her fail, she is driven out of the village, and meets Antonio, now married to someone else, who succumbs to his desire for her then kills her. An unexpectedly convincing performance from international Israeli glamour girl Dahlia Lavi lends credence to this first feature from Rondi, which he based on a documented anthropological study. He is clearly committed to the material and handles the cast and atmosphere well, but falls into the trap of concentrating his narrative in episodes of abnormal behaviour, bypassing daily life rather than placing Purif's story in opposition to it.

Demonios En El Jardin see Demons In The Garden

Demonio Y Carne see Susana

Demons In The Garden
Demonios En El Jardin

Spain 1982 105 mins col
Producciones Cinematograficas/Luis Megino

d **Manuel Gutiérrez Aragón**
sc **Manuel Gutiérrez Aragón, Luis Megino**
ph **José Luis Alcaine**
m **Javier Iturralde**
Angela Molina, Ana Belen, Eusebio Lazáro, Imanol Arias, Alvaro Sanchez-Prieto

Two brothers, Oscar and Juan (Lázaro and Arias), living in a provincial Spanish town in 1942, both love Ana (Belen). She marries Oscar but loves Juan who has made her rival, Angela (Molina), pregnant. Juan abandons Angela, who gives birth to his illegitimate son. Ten years later the family, spearheaded by the grandmother, decide that 10-year-old Juanito (Sanchez-Prieto), whose nature combines the opposing temperaments of his father and uncle, must be raised in their midst. This complex study of sexual mores, political attitudes and family relationships, by one of Spain's most accomplished directors, unfolds against the background of Franco's regime. Aragón employs subtle symbolism and a poetical style, but sweetens the pill of weighty themes and fiery emotions with some well-judged irony and black humour.

Den Røde Rubin see Song Of The Red Ruby, The

Dentellière, La see Lacemaker, The

Le Départ

Belgium 1966 91 mins bw
Elisabeth

d **Jerzy Skolimowski**
sc **Jerzy Skolimowski, Andrzej Kostenko**
ph **Willy Kurant**
m **Krzysztof Komeda**
Jean-Pierre Léaud, Catherine Duport, Jacqueline Bir, Paul Roland

A young ladies' hairdresser (Léaud), crazy about racing cars, dreams of driving his employer's Porsche in a rally, but all his machinations and dreams come to nothing. When the Polish authorities banned *Hands Up!* (1967), Skolimowski left the country to become, like his friend Roman Polanski, an international itinerant film-maker, carrying his vision and acid humour with him. The playful irony, the freewheeling, sharp photography, and the presence of Jean-Pierre Léaud (the darling of directors François Truffaut and Jean-Luc Godard), cloaked it in the French New Wave influence. But the fact that it was shot in Brussels, that surreal city of surrealists, gave it a different visual edge, and a more maniacal quality.

Deprisa, Deprisa

aka Fast, Fast

Spain 1981 98 mins col
Elias Querejeta/Les Films Molière/Consortium Pathé

d **Carlos Saura**
sc **Carlos Saura**
ph **Teo Escamilla**
m **Spanish songs**

José Antonio Valdelomar, José Maria Hervas Roldan, Jesus Arias Aranzeque, Berta Socuellamos Zarco

Three young criminals are joined by Angela (Zarco), a waitress who can shoot with the best of them and who has an affair with one of the boys (Valdelomar). When a man is killed during a robbery, spiralling disaster follows, leaving Angela the sole survivor of the gang. Saura's film, sharp and—like its title—fast, takes a non-moralistic look at the punks from Madrid's urban waste land who spend their ill-gotten gains on drugs and fast cars. The director recruited his actors from the milieu he portrays and, ironically, Valdelomar was arrested for a bank robbery shortly before the film's Spanish première, while Aranzeque was caught by the police making a getaway from a raid a few months later. Saura was apparently upset by these developments, as well as by the sensationalist press coverage given to them.

Best Film Berlin 1981

Deputat Baltiki see Baltic Deputy

Derman see Remedy

Dernier Combat, Le see Last Battle, The

Dernière Femme, La see Last Woman, The

Dernière Milliardaire, La see Last Millionaire, The

Les Dernières Vacances

(US: The Last Vacation)

France 1948 95 mins bw
Productions Cinématique/Les Films Constellation

d **Roger Leenhardt**
sc **Roger Breuil, Roger Leenhardt**
ph **Philippe Agostini**
m **Guy Bernard**

Roger Leenhardt, Michel François, Renée Devillers, Pierre Dux, Odile Versois, Jean D'Yd

Jacques (François) and Juliette (Versois) are 16-year-old cousins who have spent many summer holidays together with their families at the ancestral estate in Southern France. But when the family, fallen on hard times, must sell the property, the children plot to drive potential buyers away. Made up mainly of two long flashbacks—the daydreams of Jacques while in the classroom—the film is bathed in an impressionistic glow that represents a memory of summer holidays. Yet, it avoids sentimentality and clichés of nostalgia, the tone being reminiscent of Renoir's *A Day In The Country*. Leenhardt, whose only other feature was *Le Rendez-vous De Minuit* (1962), though he made various shorts of interest, was much admired by the *Nouvelle Vague* directors for his independent qualities and intelligence. Godard and Truffaut gave him roles in *A Married Woman* and *The Man Who Loved Women*, respectively.

Dernier Métro, Le see Last Metro, The

Dernier Tournant, Le see Last Bend, The

Derzu Uzala

USSR-Japan 1975 140 mins col
Mosfilm/Toho

d **Akira Kurosawa**
sc **Akira Kurosawa, Yuri Nagibin**
ph **Asakazu Nakai, Yuri Gantman, Fyodor Dobronravov**
m **Isaak Shvartz**

Maxim Munzuk, Yuri Solomin, M. Bichkov, V. Khrulev, V. Lastochin

A Russian scientist (Solomin) is sent with a party of soldiers to make a topographical survey of the wilds of Siberia at the turn of the century. He relies greatly on his hunter-guide Derzu Uzala (Munzuk), whose knowledge of nature saves his life more than once. Based on the journals of Vladimir Arseniev, the film contains a splendid performance from Munzuk as a wily, noble savage. There is also one memorable set-piece of the building of a shelter during a storm, rendered magnificently on the 70mm screen with its six-track stereo sound, but most of the lengthy film is of the undemanding Disney real-life adventure sort.

Best Foreign Film Oscar 1975

The Deserter And The Nomads

Zbehovia A Poutníci

Czechoslovakia 1968 102 mins col
Koliba Film Studio (Bratislava)/Ultra Film (Rome)

d **Juro Jakubisko**
sc **Juro Jakubisko, Karol Sidon**
ph **Juro Jakubisko**
m **Štepan Koníček**

Štefan Ladižinský, August Kubán, Gejza Ferenc, Jana Stehnová, Helena Grodová

Death (Kubán) is personified in three stories set in World Wars I, II and III. In the first, a gypsy soldier (Ferenc), deserting the battlefield, meets Death at a wedding in his own village. In the second, a Russian army captain (Ladižinský) orders an itinerant egg seller to be shot for spying for the Germans. In the future, after a nuclear holocaust, a young girl (Stehnová) and an old man try to find other survivors. This three- part fresco reveals an original but undisciplined talent in Jakubisko. The first episode, taking its imagery from peasant art, becomes excessive in its colour distortions and camera movements; the second is more restrained stylistically, but more familiar thematically; the third lacks the shock element necessary, while making a tenuous attempt to link it to the first episode. Yet much of it is involving and the film is an example of the last experimental gasp of film-makers just before the Prague Spring ended.

Deserto Rosso, Il see Red Desert, The

Destiny

(US: Between Two Worlds aka Beyond The Wall)

Der Müde Tod

Germany 1921 79 mins bw
Decla-Bioscop

d **Fritz Lang**
sc **Fritz Lang, Thea Von Harbou**
ph **Erich Nietzschmann, Fritz Arno Wagner, Hermann Salfrank**
m **Silent**

Lil Dagover, Walter Janssen, Bernhard Goetzke, Eduard Von Winterstein, Rudolph Klein-Rogge, Karl Huszar

A honeymoon is destroyed when the husband (Janssen) disappears with a sinister stranger (Goetzke), who turns out to be Death. The wife (Dagover) pleads with him for her husband's life and he strikes a series of bargains with her, which she ultimately loses, but which project her into several different situations of love and death in Arabia, Venice and China. The plotting of this film is far too intricate to recount here, but it's an intricacy which applies equally to its themes, switches of style, details of character and incident, and extravagant settings. A dark and mystical allegory, *Destiny* was Lang's first notable critical success, and remains impressive for its range of mood and the mastery of its visual composition.

Destiny Of A Man

aka Fate Of A Man

Sudba Cheloveka

USSR 1959 98 mins bw
Sovexportfilm/Mosfilm

d **Sergei Bondarchuk**
sc **Y. Lukin, F. Shakhmagonov**

ph **Vladimir Monakhov**
m **V. Basnov**
Sergei Bondarchuk, Zinaida Kirienkova, Pavlik Boriskin, V. Markin, P. Volkov

During World War II, Andrei Sokolov (Bondarchuk) leaves his young wife (Kirienkova) and children for the front. He is captured and sent to a concentration camp from which he escapes. On returning home, Andrei learns of the death of his family. 'In the beginning I led a very ordinary life...' is how the hero of the film, based on the novel by Mikhail Sholokhov, begins his story. The distinguished Soviet actor Bondarchuk, in his first film as director, takes on the task of interpreting this life of an 'ordinary' Russian man, who has to dig deep into his resources for physical and mental survival. As both director and actor Bondarchuk succeeds to a great extent, even if at times he treads rather heavily. The realism of the fighting, of the camps and of the bitter aftermath of war is powerfully captured, and the optimistic ending, though predictable, is still moving. The film won the best film award at the first Moscow Film Festival.

Détective

France 1985 95 mins col
Sara Films/JLG Films

d **Jean-Luc Godard**
sc **Alain Sarde, Philippe Setbon**
ph **Bruno Nuytten**
m **Schubert, Wagner, Chopin, Liszt, Honegger, Chabrier, Ornette Coleman, Jean Schwarz**
Nathalie Baye, Claude Brasseur, Johnny Hallyday, Laurent Terzieff, Jean-Pierre Léaud, Alain Cuny, Stéphane Ferrara

Various people investigate various suspects in a murder that was committed in a Paris hotel two years previously. Dedicated to John Cassavetes, Clint Eastwood and Poverty Row director Edgar G. Ulmer, Godard's film is a wordy, witty, banal and stimulating set of variations on a B-movie theme. The joky murder mystery plot goes out the window as Godard's camera prowls around the hotel, more interested in the antics of his accomplished cast.

Detenuto In Attesa Di Giudizio see Why?

Detstvo Gorkovo see Childhood Of Maxim Gorky, The

Deus E O Diabo Na Terra Do Sol see Black God White Devil

Deutschland, Bleiche Mutter see Germany, Pale Mother

Deutschland Im Herbst see Germany In Autumn

Deux Anglaises Et Le Continent, Les see Anne And Muriel

Deuxième Souffle, Le see Second Breath

Deux Lions Au Soleil see Two Lions In The Sun

Deux Ou Trois Choses Que Je Sais D'Elle see Two Or Three Things I Know About Her

---

Les Deux Timides

France 1928 66 mins bw
Albatros/Sequana

d **René Clair**
sc **René Clair**
ph **Robert Batton, Nicolas Roudakoff**
m **Silent**
Maurice De Féraudy, Pierre Batcheff, Vera Flory, Jim Gérald, Françoise Rosay

A mouse running across a courtroom causes a shy young lawyer (Batcheff) to lose a case and almost to lose his fiancée (Flory) to a rival suitor (Gérald). His prospective father-in-law (De Féraudy) is the other timid character of the title. Clair's last silent film was, like *The Italian Straw Hat* immediately preceding it, based on a wordy Labiche-Michel farce. It is funny and gentle, and seems to have no need for dialogue (the sign of a good silent film?) as the images speak volumes. The acting, particularly of De Féraudy and Rosay, the latter as a dragon aunt, helps it along.

Deveti Krug see Ninth Circle, The

Devi

aka The Goddess

India 1960 93 mins bw

Satyajit Ray Productions

d **Satyajit Ray**
sc **Satyajit Ray**
ph **Subrata Mitra**
m **Ali Akbar Khan**

Chabi Biswas, Sharmila Tagore, Soumitra Chatterjee, Karuna Bannerjee

A young woman (Tagore) is persuaded by her fanatical father-in-law (Biswas) that she is the reincarnation of the goddess Kali. She becomes an object of mystical reverence much to the despair of her educated husband (Chatterjee). Ray emerged from his great 'Apu Trilogy' to make a less expansive work, its theme even more strongly illustrative of the clash between ancient and modern beliefs. The well-organized plot has a less universal appeal, and the more dramatic style leans on occasion towards melodrama. However, the visual images are striking and there are intriguing glimpses into religious fervour on the sub-continent.

The Devil

(US: To Bed... Or Not To Bed)

Il Diavolo

Italy 1963 103 mins bw

Dino De Laurentiis

d **Gian Luigi Polidoro**
sc **Rodolfo Sonego**
ph **Aldo Tonti**
m **Piero Piccioni**

Alberto Sordi, Inge Sjorstrand, Ulf Palme, Ulla Smidje, Barbo Wastenson

When Amadeo Ferretti (Sordi), a small-town Italian, takes a trip to Sweden without his wife, his imagination takes flight with fantasies of possible romantic encounters. However, reality turns out quite differently. The girls he meets view him as no more than a kindly soul and a good friend, while he himself withdraws from the voracious demands of more mature women. The thick-set, lovable and comically gifted Sordi is very engaging in this efficiently made, funny film which, though clearly to the taste of the jury at Berlin, is no more than an engaging piece of fluff.

Best Film Berlin 1963

Devil And The Flesh, The see Susana

The Devil And The Nun

aka Mother Joan Of The Angels

Matka Joanna Od Aniolów

Poland 1960 108 mins bw

Film Polski

d **Jerzy Kawalerowicz**
sc **Jerzy Kawalerowicz, Tadeusz Konwicki**
ph **Jerzy Wójcik**
m **Adam Walacinski**

Lucyna Winnicka, Mieczyslaw Voit, Anna Ciepielewska, Maria Chwalibóg

In a 17th-century Polish convent a priest (Voit), investigating demonic possession among the nuns, becomes the object of desire of the Mother Superior (Winnicka). Based on actual events at Loudun, also the subject of an Aldous Huxley novel, a John Whiting play, a Ken Russell film and a Krzysztof Penderecki opera, it was one of the first post-war Polish films not dealing with the theme of war to be seen in the West. The stylized narrative, design and performances make for a powerful allegory of Good vs Evil, Chastity vs Eroticism.

Special Jury Prize Cannes 1961

The Devil By The Tail

Le Diable Par La Queue

France 1969 93 mins col

Fildebroc/Les Productions Artistes Associés/Produzioni Européé Associate Films

d **Philippe De Broca**
sc **Philippe De Broca, Daniel Boulanger**
ph **Jean Penzer**
m **Georges Delerue**

Yves Montand, Maria Schell, Jean Rochefort, Jean- Pierre Marielle, Madeleine Renaud, Marthe Keller, Xavier Gélin

In order to entice guests to her château, now turned into a hotel to make ends meet, the Marquise (Renaud) gets a young mechanic (Gélin) to sabotage the cars of motorists who stop at his garage and to convey them to the hotel while the 'repairs' are being carried out. One such guest turns out to be a bank robber (Montand) on the run. Much of De Broca's efforts to make a light, escapist, crazy comedy are helped by a pretty setting, Delerue's cod classical music and old hands, Montand, Rochefort and Renaud, who blissfully sail through it all. The balloon is weighed down occasionally by some unfunny slapstick and overdrawn caricatures.

Devil In The Flesh

Le Diable Au Corps

France 1947 110 mins bw
Transcontinental

d **Claude Autant-Lara**
sc **Jean Aurenche, Pierre Bost**
ph **Michel Kelber**
m **René Cloërec**
Micheline Presle, Gérard Philipe, Jean Debucourt, Denise Grey, Jacques Tati

During the last months of World War I, a young married woman (Presle) has an affair with a 17-year-old schoolboy (Philipe) while her husband is at the front. The film of Raymond Radiguet's precocious semi- autobiographical novel caused outrage in some quarters for its non-condemnatory and sympathetic portrayal of lovers cuckolding a soldier away at war. The controversial aspect now diminished, the film can be seen as a sensuous and romantic love story, framing two touching performances, notably from 25-year-old Philipe (the same age as Presle), who shot to international stardom on the strength of it.

The Devil, Probably

Le Diable, Probablement

France 1977 95 mins col
Sunchold/GMF

d **Robert Bresson**
sc **Robert Bresson**
ph **Pasqualino De Santis**
m **Philippe Sarde**
Antoine Monnier, Tina Irissari, Henri De Maublanc

A young man (Monnier), horrified by the physical and spiritual pollution in the world, rejects politics, religion and psychoanalysis and pays a junkie friend to shoot him in Père Lachaise cemetery. Bresson's most didactic film, probably. Different groups offering a panacea for the world's ills are rather simply taken off, while smoke fills the sky and large trees are felled. It is all very earnest and schematic, but the uncluttered images and autumnal photography give it a touch of grace.

Special Jury Prize Berlin 1977

Devil's Envoys, The see Visiteurs Du Soir, Les

The Devil's Eye

Djävulens Öga

Sweden 1960 90 mins bw
Svensk Filmindustri

d **Ingmar Bergman**
sc **Ingmar Bergman**
ph **Gunnar Fischer**
m **Scarlatti**
Jarl Kulle, Bibi Andersson, Nils Poppe, Stig Järrel, Gunnar Björnstrand

Because, as the proverb says, 'a woman's chastity is a sty in the devil's eye', the devil (Järrel) sends Don Juan (Kulle) to earth to deflower Virtue (Andersson), the daughter of a naive country parson (Poppe). Although demonstrating Bergman's metaphysical preoccupations, this rather heavy-handed comedy that shifts uneasily between an extremely theatrical Hell and the realism of the pastor's household, has been justifiably dismissed as a minor aberration by the great director. Perhaps he deserved a divertissement between the starkness of *The Virgin Spring* and *Through A Glass Darkly*.

The Devil's General

Des Teufel's General

W. Germany 1955 124 mins bw
Real Film

d **Helmut Käutner**

sc **Georg Hurdalek, Helmut Käutner**
ph **Albert Benitz**
m **Archive music**
Curt Jurgens, Victor De Kowa, Karl John, Marianne Koch, Werner Fuetterer

Caught between patriotism and loyalty to his comrades on the one hand, and revulsion against the Nazi regime on the other, General Harras (Jurgens) of the Luftwaffe deliberately crashes his new bomber rather than be a party to the continuance of the war. Ironically, he is honoured as a martyred hero of the Reich. Käutner's film is based on a play by Carl Zuckmayer which is, in turn, loosely based on the life of Ernst Udets, the highest-ranking German air ace to have survived World War I, who committed suicide on the eve of World War II because of his horror of Hitler's regime. Jurgens is excellent, and the movie, although overlong, is well made and engrossing.

Best Actor (Curt Jurgens) Venice 1955

The Devil Strikes At Night
aka Nazi Terror At Night
aka Nights When The Devil Came
Nachts Wenn Der Teufel Kamm
W. Germany 1957 105 mins bw
Divina

d **Robert Siodmak**
sc **Werner Jörg Lüddecke**
ph **George Krause**
m **Siegfried Franz**
Claus Holm, Mario Adorf, Hannes Messemer, Anne Marie Düringer, Werner Peters

In 1944 the German authorities are baffled by the murders of 80 women, all strangled. An outside investigator finds the killer, a Gestapo member, but the Gestapo covers up and pins the crime on an innocent minor official. Siodmak's third film in Germany after his long and successful sojourn in Hollywood is a model of tasteful restraint, as well as a demonstration of the director's expertise in handling suspense. The screenplay was based on the true case, found documented in Gestapo files, of the mentally deranged Bruno Luedtke, who was secretly liquidated. The film gives a chilling glimpse into the ruthlessness, solidarity and complete moral rot which characterized the Nazi edifice.

The Devil's Wanton
Fängelse
Sweden 1949 80 mins bw
Terrafilm

d **Ingmar Bergman**
sc **Ingmar Bergman**
ph **Göran Strindberg**
m **Erland Von Koch**
Doris Svedlund, Birger Malmsten, Eva Henning, Hasse Ekman, Stig Olin, Irma Christenson, Anders Henriksson

A director (Ekman) discusses an idea with an alcoholic writer friend (Malmsten) who suggests that they film the true story of a prostitute (Svedlund) he once knew who eventually killed herself. The appalling details of her wretched life then take over the action. Another of those early Bergman's only released abroad when his fame had travelled, this film points the way to the director's later explorations of unhappiness, but, while long on *angst*, it is short on conviction. It is more amusing to read some reviews of yesteryear which find one critic stating that the film 'finds Bergman in bleak mood'. Little did he guess what was yet to come!

Devyat Dnei Odnogo Goda see Nine Days Of One Year

Devuchka S Korobkoi see Girl With The Hatbox

Diable Par La Queue, Le see Devil By The Tail, The

Diable Au Corps, Le see Devil In The Flesh

Diable, Probablement, Le see Devil, Probably, The

Diabolique see Diaboliques, Les

Les Diaboliques
aka The Fiends
(US: Diabolique)
France 1954 114 mins bw
Filmsonor/Vera Films

d **Henri-Georges Clouzot**
sc **Henri-Georges Clouzot, Jérôme Géronimi, Frédéric Grendel, René Masson**
ph **Armand Thirard**
m **Georges Van Parys**
Simone Signoret, Vera Clouzot, Paul Meurisse, Charles Vanel

Nicole and Christina (Signoret, and the director's wife, Vera Clouzot) join forces to murder Christina's sadistic husband (Meurisse). They dump his corpse in the swimming pool of the seedy and unpleasant school where he is the headmaster but, by the next day, it has disappeared. He keeps turning up in the most unlikely places. Is he dead or alive? The answers are revealed only in the last terrifying moments of this masterpiece of suspense from the director of *The Wages of Fear*. Original, and very well made, this much-acclaimed film is a must for all fans of the genre.

Diabolo Menthe see Peppermint Soda

Diagonale Du Fou, La see Dangerous Moves

Dialogue Des Carmelites, Le see Carmelites, The

Diary For My Children
Napló Gyermekeimnek
Hungary 1982 107 mins bw
Mafilm Studio/Hungarofilm

d **Márta Mészáros**
sc **Márta Mészáros, Balázs Fakan, András Szeredás**
ph **Miklós Jancsó Jr**
m **Zsolt Döme**
Zsuzsa Czinkóczi, Anna Polony, Jan Nowicki, Tamás Tóth, Mari Szémes, Pál Zolnay

In 1947 orphaned Juli (Czinkóczi) returns with her grandparents to Budapest from the USSR where members of the Hungarian underground had fled. The family find the country greatly changed, the old-style Communism replaced by a rigid bureaucratic regime in which Juli's aunt Magda (Polony), in whose luxury flat they stay, is a high flyer. Disliking both Magda and her politics, Juli begins her quest for freedom and independence. Mészáros brings her fine intelligence and a penetrating eye for detail to an analytical critique of recent Hungarian history. Utilizing the past—Juli's memories lyrically filmed —she brings her heroine to terms with the present in an engrossing story that embraces the individual, the family and the state, making the political personal and vice versa. The Hungarian authorities withheld this film from the West for two years after its completion.

Special Jury Prize Cannes 1984

Diary Of A Chambermaid
Journal D'Une Femme De Chambre
France 1964 98 mins bw
Speva/Ciné Alliance/Filmsonor/Dear

d **Luis Buñuel**
sc **Luis Buñuel, Jean-Claude Carrière**
ph **Roger Fellous**
Jeanne Moreau, Georges Géret, Michel Piccoli, Françoise Lugagne, Daniel Ivernel, Jean-Claude Carrière

Célestine (Moreau) takes up a post as chambermaid to a middle-class, provincial family, and becomes the catalyst that reveals their sexual, religious and social repressions. Both she and the sadistic valet Joseph (Géret) achieve their *petit bourgeois* ambitions. More acid and less lightweight than Renoir's 1945 Hollywood version of Mirbeau's novel, the film, foot fetishism and all, is pure Buñuel. By updating the story and making Joseph a member of the French Fascist party, Buñuel brings the social satire into sharper focus. Moreau—sexy, cruel and cool—is wonderful.

Diary Of A Country Priest
Journal D'Un Curé De Campagne
France 1950 120 mins bw
UGC

d **Robert Bresson**
sc **Robert Bresson**
ph **L.H. Burel**
m **Jean-Jacques Grünewald**
Claude Laydu, Jean Riveyre, Armand Guibert, Nicole Ladmiral, Nicole Maurey

A young priest (Laydu) unable to resolve the problems of his small parish and assailed by self-doubt, dies alone of stomach cancer murmuring 'All is Grace'. The first truly Bressonian film in which he used non- actors, natural sound, pared down images and real locations to tell a spiritual tale. Bernanos' book published in 1936 seemed a most unlikely subject for the cinema, but Bresson managed to convey the solitude and inner anguish of the characters by their external behaviour and by shots of them in isolation while using the literary device of the first person narrative.

Diary Of A Lost Girl

Tagenbuch Einer Verloren

Germany 1929 110 mins bw
G.W. Pabst

d **G.W. Pabst**
sc **Rudolf Leonhardt**
ph **Sepp Allgeier**
m **Silent**
Louise Brooks, Fritz Rasp, Josef Rovensky, Edith Meinhard, Vera Pawlowa

A girl (Brooks) from a wealthy family is seduced by her pharmicist father's assistant (Rasp), becomes pregnant, is placed in a reform school, and ends up in a brothel. Adapted from a cheap contemporary novel, Pabst's film is a vivid exploration of a corrupt society in which sex and money dominate social relationships, despite the heavy cutting by the censors. (Apparently the film ends about half-way through the original script.) The eloquent faces in close-up have no need for dialogue, nor do sequences such as that when the headmistress of the reform school makes the girls march like puppets to the rhythm of her cane. However, what lingers in the mind is the exquisite bob-haired Louise Brooks exerting her *femme fatale* fascination, continuing the impact she made in Pabst's *Pandora's Box* of the same year.

Diary Of A Shinjuku Burglar see Diary Of A Shinjuku Thief

Diary Of A Shinjuku Thief

(US: Diary Of A Shinjuku Burglar)

Shinjuko Dorobo Nikki

Japan 1968 94 mins col/bw
Sozosha

d **Nagisa Oshima**
sc **Nagisa Oshima, Tsutomu Tamura, Mamoru Sasaki, Masao Adachi**
ph **Yasuhiro Yoshioka, Seizo Sengen**
Tadanori Yokoo, Rie Yokoyama, Moichi Tanabe, Tetsu Takahashi, Kei Sato

A young student (Yokoo) is caught shoplifting in a bookshop by a girl (Yokoyama), masquerading as an assistant, with whom he goes on to have a sexually unfulfilled affair. After seeking sexual advice, they finally find ecstasy while a street riot is breaking out. Using black and white with colour inserts and mixing realistic and theatrical acting, *cinéma vérité* techniques and Brechtian intertitles, Oshima has made an explosive agit-prop movie equating sexual liberation with revolution. Coming hot on the heels of the student riots of 1968, its impact has cooled only marginally.

Diavolo, Il see Devil, The

Dieu A Besoin Des Hommes see Isle Of Sinners

Dillinger E Morto see Dillinger Is Dead

Dillinger Is Dead

Dillinger E Morto

Italy 1969 90 mins col
Pegaso Film

d **Marco Ferreri**
sc **Marco Ferreri, Sergio Bazzini**
ph **Mario Vulpiani**

m **Teo Usuelli**
Michel Piccoli, Anita Pallenberg, Annie Girardot

While his wife (Pallenberg) is in bed with a headache, an industrial designer (Piccoli) spends an evening at home, making himself a meal, watching TV and seducing the maid (Girardot). He finds a package containing an old 45-calibre revolver and decides to kill his wife and go off to Tahiti. This bleak study of alienation allows a man's life to be laid bare in one evening and one setting, using a cast of only three. The objects in the protagonist's house take on a significance (he manufactures masks) by means of the careful camerawork, compositions and colour and the film reveals Ferreri at his most controlled.

Dimanche À La Campagne, Un see Sunday In The Country

Dimanche De La Vie, Le see Sunday Of Life, The

Dimenticare Venezia see Forget Venice

Dirty Hands see Mains Sales, Les

Dirty Mary

(US: A Very Curious Girl)
La Fiancée Du Pirate
France 1969 106 mins col
Cythère

d **Nelly Kaplan**
sc **Nelly Kaplan, Claude Makovski**
ph **Jean Badal**
m **Georges Moustaki**
Bernadette Lafont, Georges Géret, Michel Constantin, Julien Guiomar, Jean Paredes, Claire Maurier

Marie (Lafont) lives with her mother in a small shack on the outskirts of a village. When her mother is killed in a hit-and-run accident and disputes arise over burial expenses, she decides to organize the funeral herself. She then takes revenge on the leading citizens of the village, who have treated her with scorn. Extrovert Lafont was perfect in this extrovert social satire, first as a sloppy despised servant girl, then as a seductive woman. Kaplan's film has verve, some good gags, and lively music, but it leans too far towards stereotypes, including that of a Lesbian.

Dirty Money

Un Flic
France 1972 98 mins col
Corona (Paris)/Oceania/Euro (Rome)

d **Jean-Pierre Melville**
sc **Jean-Pierre Melville**
ph **Walter Wottitz**
m **Michel Colombier**
Alain Delon, Richard Crenna, Catherine Deneuve, Ricardo Cucciolla, André Pousse

An overworked Paris police commissioner, intent on smashing a drug- smuggling operation, gets a fortuitous lead through a bank robbery in a distant seaside town. He also has an affair with a girl (Deneuve) who turns out to be the gang leader's mistress. The last feature from Melville, chief purveyor of the gangster genre in France, is a study of disenchantment and betrayal, juxtaposing time and locations in an almost experimental form to create a disjunctive mood. The set-piece in which a load of heroin is lifted off a moving train by helicopter is terrific, and Delon's embittered cop is effective.

The Discreet Charm Of The Bourgeoisie

Le Charme Discret De La Bourgeoisie
France 1972 105 mins col
Greenwich

d **Luis Buñuel**
sc **Luis Buñuel, Jean-Claude Carrière**
ph **Edmond Richard**
m **Galaxie Musique**
Fernando Rey, Delphine Seyrig, Stéphane Audran, Bulle Ogier, Jean-Pierre Cassel, Paul Frankeur, Michel Piccoli, Julien Bertheau

A small group of friends, members of the wealthy middle class, gather at a house for dinner only to find their host absent. Further attempts to take a meal together are continually frustrated by a series of bizarre events, mostly dreamed by the participants. This best and most assured of the four anecdotal surrealist satires of Buñuel's final years is a blistering but witty assault on the director's constant targets—the church, the state and the army. The masterful shifting of different levels of consciousness, the depiction of collective phobias and the ensemble playing of the impeccable cast are sophisticated joys.

Best Foreign Film Oscar 1972

Les Disparus De St Agil

(US: Boys' School)

France 1938 103 mins bw
Francinex/Vog

m **Christian-Jaque**
sc **J.H. Blanchon**
ph **Marcel Lucien**
m **Henri Verdun**

Michel Simon, Erich Von Stroheim, Aimé Clariond, Armand Bernard, Mouloudji

At St Agil, a boys' boarding school, pupils mysteriously disappear. A group of boys decides to take action and discovers a forger and murderer on the premises. Christian-Jaque made his name with this atmospheric and enjoyable black comedy. In the school building, with its sliding doors and secret underground rooms, lurk Simon as a drunken art master and Stroheim as an eccentric language teacher, both having a fair old time.

Distant Thunder

Ashanti Sanket

India 1973 101 mins col
Palaka Movies

d **Satyajit Ray**
sc **Satyajit Ray**
ph **Soumendu Roy**
m **Satyajit Ray**

Soumitra Chatterjee, Babita, Sandhya Roy

In a small Bengali village in 1943, the schoolteacher-priest-doctor and his wife begin to see the causes—and the horrifying effects—of famine on their community. Often criticized for ignoring the bitter realities of his country, Ray here takes a more political line while retaining his gentle wit and humanism. The village movingly becomes a microcosm for the wider sufferings of India, giving more weight to the statistic (seen at the end) that over five million people died at the time.

Best Film Berlin 1973

Dîtes-Lui Que Je L'Aime see This Sweet Sickness

Diva

France 1981 117 mins col
Les Films Galaxie/Greenwich Film Production

d **Jean-Jacques Beneix**
sc **Jean-Jacques Beneix, Jean Van Hamme**
ph **Philippe Rousselot**
m **Vladimir Cosma, and arias by Catalani and Gounod**

Frédéric Andrei, Roland Bertin, Wilhelminia Wiggins Fernandez, Thuy An Luu, Dominique Piñon, Anny Romand, Richard Böhringer

A young postal messenger (Andrei) illicitly records a recital by his opera idol (Fernandez), but the possession of the cassette unwittingly leads him into a complicated quagmire of corruption and murder. Beneix's debut feature begins promisingly enough with an intriguing idea and some startlingly adventurous camerawork. Alas, it soon becomes an overlong confusion of both style and content, mixing fact and fantasy, violence and romance—with a nod to Feuillade in its hallucinatory quality—to degenerate into a flashy package of ultra-chic designer images and punk aesthetics of little meaning and less coherence. Nonetheless, there is evidence of a stylish talent looking for a home, and the movie is not without a modicum of entertainment value.

Divine

France 1935 80 mins bw
Eden

d **Max Ophüls**
sc **Colette, Jean-Georges Auriol, Max Ophüls**
ph **Roger Hubert**
m **Albert Wolff**

Simone Berriau, Georges Rigaud, Gina Manès, Philippe Heriat, Catherine Fonteney

A country girl (Berriau) goes to Paris where she becomes a chorus girl, gets involved with a dope-peddling snake charmer (Heriat) and his girlfriend (Manès), falls in love with a handsome milkman (Rigaud) and returns to the country with him. 'My biggest flop,' was Ophüls comment, and most critics, except François Truffaut who called it 'a little masterpiece', agree with him. Its weakness lies in the miscasting of the female lead and the sentimental view of the superiority of the country over the wicked city. Actually, the director is defeated by his own expertise in re-creating the delightful and exciting atmosphere of the music-hall—including a 360-degree pan when 'Divine' first arrives at the theatre—so that the alternative espoused by the film can only seem dull.

The Divine Emma

Božská Ema

Czechoslovakia 1979 111 mins col
Filmove Studiu Barrandov

d **Jiří Krejčík**
sc **Zdeněk Mahler, Jiří Krejčík**
ph **Miroslav Ondříček**
m **Zdeněk Liška, Svatopluk Havelka, and operatic extracts from Bizet, Mozart, Verdi, Wagner, Puccini, Ponchielli, Richard Strauss, Dvořák, Smetana and Leoncavallo**

Božidara Turzonovová (singing dubbed by Gabriela Beňačková), Juraj Kukura, Miloš Kopecký, Jiří Adamíra, Cestmír Randa

The world-famous soprano Emma Destinn (well-played by Turzonovová) returns to her native Czechoslovakia when World War I breaks out. Suspected (correctly) of being a Czech sympathizer and (incorrectly) a spy, she is confined to her estate and forbidden to sing. The simple-minded mix of fact and fiction will be immediately recognizable to all followers of the Hollywood biopic, who will also relish the appearances of other 'real-life' characters such as Caruso and Toscanini. Opera-lovers will revel in the arias, beautifully sung by the soprano generally regarded as the nearest thing to the great Diva herself, although Emma's propensity to burst into song on any and every occasion (Hollywood again) grows a little tiresome. Ondříček's camera does justice to the period settings.

Divorce Italian Style

Divorzio All'Italiana

Italy 1961 108 mins bw
Lux/Vides/Galatea

d **Pietro Germi**
sc **Pietro Germi, Ennio De Concini, Alfredo Giannetti**
ph **Leonida Barboni**
m **Carlo Rustichelli**

Marcello Mastroianni, Daniela Rocca, Stefania Sandrelli, Leopoldo Trieste

An indolent Sicilian nobleman (Mastroianni) can only marry his pretty cousin (Sandrelli) by arranging for his stupid wife (Rocca) to be seduced, so that he can kill her with impunity as a jealous husband defending his honour. The first, and best, of a number of 'Italian style' sex comedies of the 1960s delightfully satirizes the Italian male and the country's laws on divorce and *crime passionnel* in its Oscar-winning script. Mastroianni, with sleeked-down hair and waxed moustache, is just the right side of caricature, and there are a number of hilarious visual jokes.

Divorzio All'Italiana see Divorce Italian Style

Djävulens Öga see Devil's Eye, The

Doctor In The Village

Dorp Aan De Rivier

Netherlands 1958 92 mins bw
N.V. Nationale Filmproductie Maatschappij

d **Fons Rademakers**
sc **Hugo Claus**
ph **Eduard Van Der Enden**
m **Jurriaan Andriessen**

Max Croiset, Mary Dresselhuys, Bernhard Droog, Jan Teulings, Hetty Beck, Fritz Butselaar

The eccentric Doctor Van Taeke (Croiset) settles in a little village on the banks of the River Meuse early in the century. He dedicates himself to caring for the poor in the community and to puncturing the pomposity of the local authorities, of whom he eventually falls foul, and has to leave. This was the debut feature of Holland's best-known director, and one can only feel grateful that his later films had more appeal. The doctor's story is told in flashback as the reminiscences of the local poacher, known as Deaf Cis (Droog)—a device which, on this occasion, deflates the narrative energy. Rademakers appears to emulate Pagnol in his anecdotal treatment of village life, but the characterization is superficial, sometimes to the point of parody, and most of the major incidents are either bizarre or cloying. The lead performance is the saving grace and the director, who started his career in the theatre, does exhibit a certain technical command of the medium.

Doctor Mabuse, The Gambler

Doktor Mabuse, Der Spieler

Germany 1922 265 mins (Part I 153 mins; Part II 112 mins) bw
UFA

d **Fritz Lang**
sc **Fritz Lang, Thea Von Harbou**
ph **Carl Hoffman**
m **Silent**
Rudolph Klein-Rogge, Alfred Abel, Gertrud Welcker, Lil Dagover, Paul Richter, Bernhard Goetzke

Master criminal Dr Mabuse (Klein-Rogge), a man of many disguises, builds an underworld empire with the intention of taking over the world, but is finally foiled by the forces of good. Made at a time of political turmoil in Germany, Lang's early masterpiece is a superb study of a decadent society, foreshadowing the coming of Hitler. Unfortunately, it is still mainly known in its pared down 101-minute version, which lost its essential serial-type form. The evil genius Mabuse, of course, did not die. Lang brought him back in two sequels, *The Testament Of Dr Mabuse* (1933), and *The Thousand Eyes Of Dr Mabuse* (1961).

Dodes'kaden

Japan 1970 140 mins col
Yonki No Kai/Toho

d **Akira Kurosawa**
sc **Akira Kurosawa, Hideo Oguni, Shinobu Hashimoto**
ph **Takao Saito**
m **Tohru Takemitsu**
Yoshitaka Zushi, Kin Sugai, Junzaburo Ban, Kiyoko Tange, Michiko Hino

Life in a shanty town in which people live with their fantasies—an old man and a boy build an imaginary dream house, a silent man is obsessed by the idea of his wife's infidelity and a mentally retarded adolescent thinks he is a tram, repeating the sound 'dodes'kaden, dodes'kaden'. Kurosawa's first film in colour is a sporadically interesting but uninvolving and rather indigestible mixture of realism, social comment, melodrama and fantasy. The director himself painted the poster-style walls which make an impression as oddball as the characters.

Does, The see Biches, Les

Dog's Life, A see Mondo Cane

Doktor Holl see Affairs Of Dr Holl, The

Doktor Mabuse, Der Spieler see Doctor Mabuse, The Gambler

Dolce Corpo Di Deborah, Il see Sweet Body Of Deborah, The

La Dolce Vita

aka The Sweet Life

Italy 1960 174 mins bw
Riama/Pathé

d **Federico Fellini**
sc **Federico Fellini, Ennio Flaiano, Tullio Pinelli, Brunello Rondi**
ph **Otello Martelli**
m **Nino Rota**
Marcello Mastroianni, Anouk Aimée, Yvonne Furneaux, Magali Noël, Alain Cuny, Anita Ekberg, Nadia Gray, Valeria Ciangottini, Annibale Ninchi, Lex Barker

Gossip columnist and would-be serious writer Marcello (Mastroianni), is caught in the morass of decadent Roman society in which he rootlessly and amorally wanders in search of himself. Perhaps Fellini's most famous film,

La Dolce Vita was given a re-release in a new print in 1987, thus allowing re-appraisal. Its notorious set-pieces (a vast statue of Christ is flown over Rome; Marcello and a bored heiress pick up a prostitute for a *ménage-à-trois*; Nadia Gray hosts an orgy at which she performs an immortal striptease) have lost their capacity to shock, but the imaginative brilliance and periodic wit of their construction is now clearly evident. The director places his study of crippling *ennui*, loss of self and the pursuit of false values in a contrived world of shoddy pleasures. It is photographed with striking attention to heightened images and atmosphere on the large screen, which brings excitement and lends cohesion to the episodic nature of the work.

Best Film Cannes 1960

Dolci Signore, Le see Anyone Can Play

The Doll

Lalka

Poland 1968 159 mins col
Kamera Film Unit

d **Wojciech Has**
sc **Wojciech Has, Kazimierz Brandys**
ph **Stefan Matyaskiewicz**
m **Wojciech Kilar**
Beata Tyszkiewicz, Marius Dmochowski, Jan Kreczmar, Tadeusz Kondrat, Tadeusz Fijewski, Janina Romanówna

Stanislaw Wokulski (Dmochowski), a middle-aged man who failed to realize his youthful dreams of becoming an inventor, is now a wealthy merchant, a liberal and a philanthropist. He falls in love with Isabela (Tyszkiewicz), the remote and beautiful daughter of a Count, but is looked down upon because of his humble origins. She, however, marries him to save her father from financial ruin and brings him only pain. A film which combines a straightforward tale of unrequited love with a sharply satirical observation of Polish society during the turbulence of the mid-19th century, exposing snobbery and greed and charting all manner of frustrations. It is a visually rich evocation, but it wanders off into curious enigmatical distractions which remain puzzling, making it sometimes difficult to follow but worth the trouble.

The Doll With Millions

Kukla S Millionami

USSR 1928 83 mins bw
Mezhrabpom

d **Sergei Komarov**
sc **Fedor Ozep, Oleg Leonidov**
ph **Konstantin Kuznetsov, Evgeni Alexeyev**
m **Silent**
Vladimir Fogel, Igor Ilinsky, G. Grauvhenko, A. Voytsik, Sergei Komarov

A rich widow dies leaving the key to her fortune hidden inside a doll. But which doll? Two of her greedy relatives, a penniless dandy (Fogel) and his maladroit brother (Ilinsky), both living in Paris, hurry back to Moscow in rival pursuit of the doll with millions. This chaotic comedy combines elements of the slapstick of Mack Sennett, the witty sophistication of Komarov's earlier *The Kiss Of Mary Pickford*, and an episodic narrative resembling the much-filmed Russian novel *The Twelve Chairs* by Il'f and Petrov. Most of the fun is derived from the brilliant comic playing of Fogel and Ilinsky.

Domenica D'Agosto see Sunday In August

Domicile Conjugale see Bed And Board

Dom Na Trubnoi see House On Trubnaya Square, The

Dona Flor And Her Two Husbands

Dona Flor E Seus Dois Maridos

Brazil 1976 110 mins col
Carnaval Films

d **Bruno Barreto**
sc **Bruno Barreto**
ph **Maurilo Salles**
m **Chico Buarque De Holanda**
Sonia Braga (Dona Flor), Jose Wilker, Mauro Mendonca, Dinorah Brillanti, Nelson Xavier

Shortly after the profligate and sexually accomplished Vadinho drops dead at a carnival, his widow remarries a respectable but sexually dull man. On the anniversary of her first husband's death, he reappears to her in tangible form and shares her bed. This Brazilian cousin to Noel Coward's *Blithe Spirit* provides some fun, and Braga is both attractive and sexy. However, it's a one-joke movie which veers unmistakably in the direction of soft porn rather than romantic charm.

Dona Flor E Seus Dois Maridos see Dona Flor And Her Two Husbands

---

Dona Herlinda And Her Son

Dona Herlinda Y Su Hijo

Mexico 1986 90 mins col

Clasa Films Mundiales

d **Jaime Humberto Hermosillo**

sc **Jaime Humberto Hermosillo**

ph **Miguel Erhenberg**

m **Popular Mexican songs**

Arturo Meza, Marco Antonio Trevino, Leticia Lupersio, Guadalupe Del Toro, Angelica Guerrero

A young music student (Meza) and a doctor (Trevino) have a homosexual relationship, but the latter's mother (Del Toro) wants him to marry. Everyone is satisfied when he marries and his mother, wife (Lupersio), child and boyfriend live together under one roof. Hermosillo, an openly gay Latin-American film-maker, has used his insider's knowledge to make a deliciously alert social comedy about a macho-dominated culture and sexual hypocrisy. The film's sustained joke is that everyone pretends not to know about the heroes' gayness. It was the first of the director's low-budget films to gain a wide and appreciative audience.

Dona Herlinda Y Su Hijo see Dona Herlinda And Her Son

Donatella

Italy 1956 101 mins col

Sudfilm

d **Mario Monicelli**

sc **Roberto Amoroso, Mario Monicelli, Piero Tellini, Sandro Continenza, Ruggero Maccari**

ph **Tonino Delli Colli**

m **Xavier Cugat**

Elsa Martinelli, Gabriele Ferzetti, Walter Chiari, Aldo Fabrizi, Xavier Cugat, Abbe Lane

Donatella (Martinelli), humble secretary to a wealthy household, is mistaken for the heiress to the family fortune by a visiting lawyer who, accordingly, pays court to her. Reminiscent of those Hollywood romantic comedies based on the mistaken identity idea that were popular a decade or two earlier, this is a disappointing flim-flam and its dated air and American flavour is emphasized by the appearance of Latin American music king Cugat, and his vocalist wife Lane. However, the luscious Martinelli, (discovered by Kirk Douglas), returning to Italy from Hollywood made an impression.

Best Actress (Elsa Martinelli) Berlin 1956

Dongdong De Jiaqui see A Summer At Grandpa's

Don Giovanni

France-Italy-Germany 1979 184 mins col

Opera Film Produzione (Rome)/ Gaumont/Caméra One/Antenne-2 (Paris)/Janus Films (Frankfurt)

d **Joseph Losey**

sc **Joseph Losey, Patricia Losey, Frantz Salieri (libretto by Lorenzo Da Ponte)**

ph **Gerry Fisher**

m **Mozart (conducted by Lorin Maazel)**

Ruggero Raimondi (Giovanni), Kiri Te Kanawa (Elvira), Edda Moser (Anna), Jose Van Dam (Leporello), Kenneth Riegel (Ottavio), Teresa Berganza (Zerlina), John Macurdy (the Commendatore), Malcolm King (Masetto)

Don Giovanni, the object of vengeance by Donna Anna whose father he killed, the object of the affection of Donna Elvira whom he has abandoned, and the seducer of peasant girl Zerlina on her wedding day, is finally dragged down to Hell. Although superbly sung by singers who, for the most part, look right in the roles, and shot in and around handsome Palladian villas in northern Italy, Losey's attempts to make the conventions of opera 'filmic' have an air of desperation about them. For example, the two static arias of Ottavio have him standing up in a boat being rowed along and walking over sleeping peasants. During the 'Catalogue' aria, a vulgar parade of nubile young women is displayed. Other perversions include the introduction of a young man in black (Isabelle Adjani's brother), and the fact that Giovanni seems to fall into a glass-blower's vat rather than journey to the depths of Hell.

Don Juan 73 Or If Don Juan Were A Woman

Don Juan 73 Ou Si Don Juan Etait Une Femme

France 1973 94 mins col
Filmsonor/Marceau/Paradox/Filmes(Rome)

d **Roger Vadim**
sc **Roger Vadim, Jean Cau, Jean Pierre Petrolacci**
ph **Henri Decaë, Andréas Winding**
m **Michel Magne**
Brigitte Bardot, Jane Birkin, Maurice Ronet, Mathieu Carrière, Robert Hossein, Robert Walker Jr

Jeanne (Bardot) confesses to her cousin, a young priest (Carrière), that she has committed a murder and tells him of the men she has driven to destruction. Eleven years after their last film together, B.B. and the director who made and married her (they were divorced amicably in 1957), concocted this modernized, distaff version of the Don Juan legend. It was as arty as it was salacious, and also proved that the 39-year-old former sex kitten no longer had the power to create a stir. The film caused her to decide to retire from the screen after 21 years. Vadim continued unabashed.

Don Juan 73 Ou Si Don Juan Etait Une Femme see Don Juan 73 Or If Don Juan Were A Woman

Donkey Skin see Magic Donkey, The

Donna Del Fiume, La see Woman Of The River

Donna Scimmia, La see Ape Woman, The

Don Quichotte see Don Quixote

Don Quixote

aka Adventures Of Don Quixote
Don Quichotte

France 1933 82 mins bw
Vandor/Nelson/Wester

d **G. W. Pabst**
sc **Paul Morand, Alexandre Arnoux**
ph **Nikolas Farkas**
m **Jacques Ibert**
Feodor Chaliapin, Dorville, Renée Valliers, Mady Berry, Mireille Balin, Vladimir Sokoloff

Don Quixote (Chaliapin), whose mind is full of tales of chivalry, fancies himself as a knight errant, and sets out on many adventures with his squire Sancho Panza (Dorville). Realizing that it would be almost impossible to reproduce the vastness and depth of Cervantes' novel, Pabst, in the first film of his five-year sojourn in France, opted for episodes from the tale punctuated by songs. As these were rendered by the great Russian bass Chaliapin (in one of the rare surviving film records of him), there were few complaints. It was simultaneously shot in English, with George Robey replacing Dorville. Eerily, considering the contemporary rise of Nazism in Germany, the film ends with a book-burning in which a copy of *Don Quixote* seems to survive the flames.

Don't Let It Kill You

(US: No Good To Die For That)
Il Ne Faut Pas Mourir Pour Ça

Canada 1967 75 mins bw
Cinak

d **Jean-Pierre Lefèbvre**
sc **Jean-Pierre Lefèbvre, Marcel Sabourin**
ph **Jacques Leduc**
m **Andrée Paul**
Marcel Sabourin, Monique Champagne, Suzanne Grossman, Claudine Monfette

Abel (Sabourin) is a bizarre, child-like young man who collects insects and who keeps model airplanes in cages and books in the fridge. His life is divided into three by his relationships with his dying mother (Champagne) and his girlfriends, the blonde, English-speaking Mary (Grossman) and the dark Quebécoise Madeleine (Monfette). Lefèbvre, the most prolific and original of French Canadian film-makers, made his name with this, his third movie (and first in 35 mm) the title of which comes from a Georges Brassens song that states that 'no idea is worth dying for'. The central character is alienated and detached from society, something the film's minimalist style conveys through a sparsity of close-ups and cuts and by the use of selective sound effects. Though without any strong narrative line and teetering on the whimsical, it forces one into a reappraisal of received ideas of society and commitment.

Don't Look Now . . . We're Being Shot At!

La Grande Vadrouille

France 1966 130 mins col
Les Films Corona

d **Gérard Oury**
sc **Gérard Oury, Georges and André Tabet**
ph **Claude Renoir**
m **Georges Auric**
Terry-Thomas, Bourvil, Louis De Funès, Claudio Brook, Marie Dubois, Benno Sterzenbach

A British bomber crew, forced to bale out over Paris, land in some odd places—the conductor's dressing room at the Opera, for example—and have to make their escape to the Free Zone. How they do so, together with a couple of Frenchmen and a nun, forms the content of a wild, protracted and only occasionally amusing farce. Some eye-catching locations and photography bring relief to a film where Bourvil and De Funès (neither at his best) speak fractured English on a flimsy plot pretext.

Donzoko see Lower Depths, The

Doomed see Living

Doro No Kawa see Muddy River

Dorp Aan De Rivier see Doctor In The Village

Dossier 51

France 1978 108 mins col
Elefilm/Société Française De Production/Maran Film

d **Michel Deville**
sc **Michel Deville, Gilles Perrault**
ph **Claude Lecompte**
m **Jean Schwarz, Schubert**
François Marthouret, Claude Marcault, Jenny Clève, Roger Planchon, Françoise Lugagne

A rising French diplomat (Marthouret) is the target of a secret agency that wishes to control him. Using a variety of bugging and tracking devices, they try to find out everything about him and trap him into an indiscretion. Deville's cold and complex thriller stands out among spy stories by the way the spectator becomes the eavesdropper and agent, watching the development of plot through video screens and overhearing conversations on tape. The hero, or target, is seen almost exclusively in long shot, and the process rather than the character becomes the focus of attention. It was said that the Soviet embassy in Paris asked for a print of this expertly made adaptation of Gilles Perrault's best seller.

Double Suicide

Shinjo Ten No Amijima

Japan 1969 106 mins bw
Hyogensha/Nippon Art Theatre Guild

d **Masahiro Shinoda**
sc **Taeko Tomioka, Masahiro Shinoda**
ph **Toshiro Narushima**
m **Tohru Takemitsu**
Shima Iwashita, Kichiemon Nakamura, Hosei Komatsu, Yasuke Takita

Social and moral restraints lead a married newspaper seller (Nakamura) and the prostitute with whom he is having a passionate affair to kill themselves in a love-in-death pact. The formalized playing and the painted backdrops betray the film's origin—a 1720 puppet play by Chikamatsu. However, within the stylization, Shinoda has injected realistic sex scenes and a bloody ending. An added interest is that both the plain wife and the beautiful prostitute are played by the splendid Shima Iwashita.

Douce

(US: Love Story)

France 1943 106 mins bw
Société Parisienne De L'Industrie Cinématographique

d **Claude Autant-Lara**
sc **Jean Aurenche, Pierre Bost**
ph **Gaston Thonnart**
m **René Cloërec**
Odette Joyeux, Jean Debucourt, Marguerite Moreno, Roger Pigaut, Madeleine Robinson

There are tragic consequences when Douce (Joyeux), the young daughter of an aristocratic family, falls for a manservant (Pigaud) in their large Parisian house around Christmas 1887. This is one of four light and elegant films that Autant-Lara made during the war from Aurenche-Bost scripts and starring the charming Joyeux. It makes for slightly musty but civilized entertainment.

Doulos, Le see Doulos—The Finger Man

Doulos—The Finger Man

Le Doulos

France 1962 108 mins bw
Rome-Paris Films/CCC

d **Jean-Pierre Melville**
sc **Jean-Pierre Melville**
ph **Nicolas Hayer**
m **Paul Misraki**
Serge Reggiani, Jean-Paul Belmondo, Monique Hennessy, Michel Piccoli, Jean Desailly, Fabienne Dali

Maurice (Reggiani), just out of jail, takes refuge with a girlfriend (Hennessy) and seeks out Silien (Belmondo) to help him organize a safe-cracking job. Silien obtains the tools for Maurice then informs on him, sending him back to jail, and has his girlfriend killed. He then organizes Maurice's escape, but... Cast and shot with all Melville's usual command, this is nonetheless a disappointment. There is much violence and gun-play and cops'n'robbers action, but the characterization lacks depth, and the particular loyalties and treacheries of the underworld which so fascinate this director and which would coalesce so brilliantly in *Second Breath* are here ambiguous and incoherent—in spite of the 9-minute 38-second take of which Melville was especially proud. Belmondo portrays a brutal and unsympathetic meanie whose constant changes of heart and behaviour are hard to fathom.

Do Widzenia Do Jutra see See You Tomorrow

Down And Dirty

aka Ugly, Dirty and Mean
Brutti, Sporchi E Cattivi

Italy 1976 115 mins col
Compagnia Cinematografica Champion

d **Ettore Scola**
sc **Ettore Scola, Ruggero Maccari**
ph **Dario Di Palma**
m **Armando Trovaioli**
Nino Manfredi, Maria Luisa Santella, Francesco Anniballi, Maria Bosco, Giselda Castrini

A large family, headed by the aging, one-eyed Giacinto (Manfredi), lives in squalor in one rat- infested room in a shanty town on the outskirts of Rome. He lavishes his attention on an obese prostitute (Santella) who causes problems when she moves in with his abused wife, sons and daughters. Scola treats his poverty-stricken characters far less kindly than the directors of the Neo-Realist movement to whom he considers himself an heir, who saw the poor as innocent victims of a brutal system. No less critical of a system that breeds poverty, he does show its degrading effects in graphic, grotesque, scatological detail. Although much of the film is Ugly, Dirty and Mean, Scola establishes an ironic, often comic distance, and the cast—non-professionals apart from Manfredi—are as repulsively watchable as required.

Best Director Cannes 1976

Down The Ancient Stairs

Per Le Antiche Scale

Italy 1975 102 mins col
Italian International Film/Les Productions Fox Europa

d **Mauro Bolognini**
sc **Raffaele Andreassi, Mario Arosio, Tullio Pinelli, Bernardino Zapponi, Sinko Solleville Marie**
ph **Ennio Guarnieri**
m **Ennio Morricone**
Marcello Mastroianni, Françoise Fabian, Marthe Keller, Barbara Bouchet, Lucia Bosé

In an insane asylum in Tuscany in 1930, Dr Bonnacorsi (Mastroianni) pursues a chemical cure for schizophrenia while conducting affairs with the asylum director's wife, the wife of another doctor, and a nurse. He has not been outside the walls for eight years, but when his new assistant (Fabian) arrives, rebuffs his sexual advances, and discredits his research, he leaves. At the station he encounters a new form of madness—Fascism. Bolognini's attempt at a political allegory is strained, obtuse and unconvincing, while his glamorous leads contrast unpleasantly with scenes of risibly caricatured lunatics. The talents wasted included those of Pierre Blaise (*Lacombe Lucien*), who was killed in an accident shortly after this film.

Do You Remember Dolly Bell?

Sjecas Li Se Dolly Bell

Yugoslavia 1981 90 mins col
Sutjeska Film/TV Sarajevo

d **Emir Kusturica**
sc **Abdulah Sidran**
ph **Vilko Filač**
m **Zoran Simjanović**
Slavko Štimac, Ljiljana Blagojević, Slobodan Aligrudić, Borislav Stjepanović

Sixteen-year-old Dino (Štimac), son of a Muslim-Marxist father (Aligrudić) in Sarajevo in the early 1960s, loses his virginity to teenage prostitute 'Dolly Bell' (Blogojević) and acquires maturity. This is the first feature by 26-year-old Kusturica, who would win the Cannes Grand Prix with his second, *When Father Was Away On Business*, also written by the Muslim Sidran. As can be expected from someone who studied under Jiří Menzel in Prague, the film is a beautifully perceptive, bitter-sweet comedy full of delightful eccentric touches. The background details and the natural performances blow like a breath of fresh air through some of the more conventional 'rites of passage' moments.

Drachenfutter see Spicy Rice

Dragao Da Maldade Contra O Santo Guerreiro see Antonio Das Mortes

Drageurs, Les see Young Have No Morals, The

Dragon's Food see Spicy Rice

Drama Of The Rich

Fatti Di Gente Perbene

Italy 1974 115 mins col
Filmarpa(Rome)/Lira Films(Paris)

d **Mauro Bolognini**
sc **Sergio Bazzini, Mauro Bolognini**
ph **Ennio Guarnieri**
m **Ennio Morricone**
Giancarlo Giannini, Catherine Deneuve, Fernando Rey, Marcel Bozzuffi, Corrado Pani, Tina Aumont, Laura Betti, Ettore Manni, Paolo Bonacelli

Linda (Deneuve), daughter of the distinguished Professor Murri (Rey), confesses to her brother Tullio (Giannini) that her marriage to Count Bonmartini (Bonacelli) is unhappy and that she fears for her life. Tullio takes matters into his own hands and the family becomes enmeshed in scandal and murder. Bolognini has exhumed the records of the actual Murri case that shook Italy early in the century, but has long been forgotten. It is likely to remain so because the director has, alas, failed to bring it to life, merely glancing off the surface of the known facts without examining character or motive and failing to engender suspense. It looks splendid, but the almost operatic visual grandeur doesn't help. Acting honours go to Bozzuffi's relentless magistrate.

Drame De Shanghai, Le see Shanghai Drama, The

Dramma Della Gelosia—Tutti see Jealousy, Italian Style

Dream Flights

Polioty Vo Sne Naiavou
USSR 1983 90 mins col
Aleksandr Dovzhenko Kiev Film Studios

d **Roman Balayan**
sc **Victor Merezhko**
ph **Vilen Kaliuta**
m **Vadim Khrapachev**
Oleg Yankovsky, Ludmila Gurchenko, Oleg Tabakov, Ludmila Ivanova, Ludmila Zorina, Elena Kostina

About to turn 40, Sergei (Yankovsky) rebels against the responsibilities of work and family, only to find that his girlfriend (Kostina) has lost interest in him, while his wife (Zorina), unable to tolerate his infidelities, throws him out. Several adventures later, he ends up alone in a haystack after his birthday party. Light in tone and splendidly acted by Yankovsky as the male-menopausal philanderer, the film is somewhat ambiguous. On the one hand it deals in the attractive notion of individualism defying convention; on the other, it exposes its protagonist as an immature man who lets everybody down and deserves his rejection. Some efficient set-pieces and an in-joke or two—Sergei wanders into a film location where Mikhalkov is directing—make for a pleasing but forgettable film.

Dreams see Journey Into Autumn

Dreigroschenoper, Die see Threepenny Opera, The

Drei Von Der Tankstelle, Die see Three Men And Lilian

Dreszcze

aka Creeps
(US: Shivers)
Poland 1981 106 mins col
Film Polski

d **Wojciech Marczewski**
sc **Wojciech Marczewski**
ph **Jerzy Zielinski**
m **Andrzej Trzaskowski**
Teresa Sawicka, Wladyslaw Kowalski, Teresa Marczewski, Tomas Hudziec, Jerzy Binczycki, Marek Kindrat

In 1950s Poland, Stalinism takes over. Young Tomek (Hudziec) is sent to a youth indoctrination camp after his father (Kowalski) has been arrested, a neighbour has committed suicide and religion condemned. When father and son meet again, the boy is a changed being. A chilling account of one of Poland's many recent dark periods as it affected children. An autobiographical excursion for Marczewski, who uses some telling images to reflect his theme: a recurring shot of a leaking roof seems to echo the slow seep of poison into young minds. Made just after the Gdansk riots, the film played for a successful three weeks in Poland before being banned and withdrawn as the country's official Oscar entry.

Special Jury Prize Berlin 1982

Drevo Zhelanya see Wishing Tree, The

Dritte Generation, Die see Third Generation, The

Drôle De Drame see Bizarre, Bizarre

Drôle De Paroissien, Un see Heaven Sent

Drunken Angel

Yoidore Tenshi
Japan 1948 102 mins bw
Toho

d **Akira Kurosawa**
sc **Akira Kurosawa, Keinosuke Vegusa**

ph **Takeo Ito**
m **Fumio Hayasaka**
Takashi Shimura, Toshiro Mifune, Reisaburo Yamamoto, Chieko Nakakita, Michiyo Kogure, Norika Sengoku

When a young gangster (Mifune) comes to a doctor's surgery one night to have a bullet removed, the alcoholic doctor (Shimura) discovers his patient has tuberculosis, and finds himself involved in the man's world and destiny. Although Kurosawa's first important film has been compared with the Italian Neo-Realists for its evocation of post-war misery, it comes closer to a Warner Bros. gangster film of the 1930s, the James Cagney role being taken by Mifune. It made the latter a star, and it marked the first of his invaluable performances in all but one of Kurosawa's films until the mid-1960s.

Dry Summer see Waterless Summer

Dubarry Von Heute, Eine see Modern Dubarry, A

Du Bist Die Welt Für Mich see You Are The World For Me

Due Soldi Di Speranza see Two Pennyworth Of Hope

Dulces Horas see Sweet Hours

Dura Lex see By The Law

Durante L'Estate see During The Summer

Du Rififi Chez Les Hommes see Rififi

During The Summer

Durante L'Estate

Italy 1971 105 mins col
Palumbo Film/RAI

d **Ermanno Olmi**
sc **Fortunato Pasqualino, Ermanno Olmi**
ph **Ermanno Olmi**
m **Bruno Lanzi**
Renato Parracchi, Rosanna Callegari, and a cast of unbilled non-professionals

A solitary, materially poor, and idealistic self-styled professor weaves a fantasy universe in which his fellow creatures are ennobled by the realization of their potential and the discovery of their dignity. He gives substance to his vision by conferring honours on ordinary mortals of his choice. One summer, he meets and falls in love with a girl whom he sees as a sort of madonna princess, but he is arrested for fraudulently awarding titles. Although overlong and sometimes too leisurely, Olmi's film, originally made for Italian television, is full of imagination and sensitivity. The 'professor' is a Christ figure, whose positive qualities are a beacon of light in a world dark with cynicism, violence and destruction, and the absolute simplicity with which the piece is played and directed lends it conviction.

Dusman see Enemy, The

Duty Free Marriage

Vámmentes Házasság
(Finnish: Tullivapaa Avioliittor)

Hungary/Finland 1980 101 mins col
Mafilm Hunnia Studio/Finnish Film Foundation

d **János Zsombolyai**
sc **Ákos Kertész, Matti Ijäs, János Zsombolyai, Ildikó Kóródy, K.K. Suosalmi, Olli Soinio**
ph **Elemér Ragályi**
m **Omega Group**
Mari Kiss, Tom Wentzel, Cecilia Esztergályos, Ági Margittay, Juha Hyppönen, Päävo Piskonen

Mari (Kiss) is anxious to join her boyfriend who has defected to Finland, but is reluctant to lose her Hungarian passport. She persuades Pekka (Wentzel), a Finnish businessman, to agree to a marriage of convenience. Set partly in Budapest, partly in Helsinki, and enacted by an attractive cast, this movie successfully combines carefree comedy with a more serious consideration of moral dilemmas. There are some very funny sequences as Mari and her friends scheme to get out of Hungary; once gone, she and Pekka have to face the attraction that has grown between them and deal with the guilt of deceiving his family who gives the couple a warm welcome and a large wedding—the dramatic high-point of an interesting and enjoyable film.

Duvar see Wall, The

Dvadtsat Dnei Bez Voini see Twenty Days Without War

Dvorianskoe Gnezdo see Nest Of Gentlefolk, A

Dwadzat Schest Dnej Is Shisni Dostojewskogo see Twenty Six Days In The Life Of Dostoevsky

Dybbuk see Dybbuk, The

The Dybbuk
Dybbuk

Poland 1938 128 mins bw
Fencke Films

d **Michael Wasynski**
sc **Al Kacyzna, Marek Arenstein**
ph **Albert Wywerka**
m **Henryk Kon**
Abraham Morevski, R. Samberg, Moishe Lipman, Lili Liliana, Leon Liebgold, Dina Halpern

In a Jewish *shtetl* in mid-19th century Poland, a young man (Liebgold), wishing to marry the daughter (Liliana) of his father's friend (Lipman), calls up the Devil to help him, and dies. The girl then becomes possessed by a *dybbuk*, the soul of a dead person that enters the body of a living one, until the rabbi (Morevski) exorcises it. One of the last, and most celebrated, examples of Yiddish films made in Europe before the war, it was adapted from a play by S. Anski, steeped in the folklore and traditions understood by Jewish audiences. Wasynski's well-crafted, technically proficient film expanded the plot, explaining certain aspects of the story to make it more widely appreciated.

Dyrygent see Conductor, The

Dzieje Grezechu see Story Of Sin, The

e

The Eagle Has Two Heads
(US: Eagle With Two Heads)
L'Aigle A Deux Têtes

France 1948 93 mins bw
Les Films Ariane/Sirius

d **Jean Cocteau**
sc **Jean Cocteau**
ph **Christian Matras**
m **Georges Auric**
Edwige Feuillère, Jean Marais, Sylvia Monfort, Edouard Dermithe, Yvonne De Bray

In a small mid-European kingdom in the 19th century, a young anarchist (Marais), who happens to be the double of the dead king, breaks into the palace in order to kill the queen (Feuillère), but falls in love with her. The consequences are, nonetheless, tragic. Cocteau's high-flown romantic melodrama, an international stage success, was brought to the screen by its author with the same two leads as in the Paris production. Feuillère is majestic, vulnerable and tragic, but 35-year-old Marais in *Lederhosen* is difficult to accept as the fiery young revolutionary. Although Cocteau's cinematic sense is too great to make the film look stagey, the screenplay smacks too much of the theatre. It is thus the most minor of his own directed films.

Eagle With Two Heads see Eagle Has Two Heads, The

Early Autumn see End Of Summer, The

Early Spring
Soshun

Japan 1956 108 mins bw
Shochiku

d **Yasujiro Ozu**
sc **Yasujiro Ozu, Kogo Noda**
ph **Yushun Atsuta**
m **Takayori Saito**
Ryo Ikebe, Chikage Awashima, Keiko Kishi, Chishu Ryu

A young clerk (Ikebe), bored with his office work and his wife (Awashima), has a brief affair with the firm's flirt (Kishi) during an office outing. When his wife hears about it, she leaves him. The characteristically slight plot, involving a modern Japanese couple, unravels slowly with great formal beauty, economy, lucidity and humour. The film opens with the start of a working day in Tokyo, thereafter limiting the outdoor scenes to brief glimpses or to pauses in the action.

Early Summer
Bakushu

Japan 1951 135 mins bw
Shochiku

d **Yasujiro Ozu**
sc **Kogo Noda, Yasujiro Ozu**
ph **Yuharu Atsuta**
m **Senji Ito**
Setsuko Hara, Chishu Ryu, Kuniko Miyake, Chikage Awashima, Chiyeko Higashiyama, Ichiro Sugai

Twenty-eight-year-old Noriko (Hara), who lives with her aged parents (Higashiyama and Sugai), her older brother (Ryu) and his wife (Miyake) and their two small sons, is under pressure to marry. But she rejects the suitors acceptable to the family and marries a man of her choice. The simple plot gives no indication of the meticulous observation, humour and pain, nor the delicacy of the playing of some 19 characters. Ozu's unique use of the spatial and the temporal is totally assured and those encountering his art for the first time should soon find themselves in tune with his rhythm and elliptical narrative technique.

Earrings Of Madame De ..., The see Madame De ...

Earth
Zemlya
USSR 1930 90 mins bw
VUFKU

d **Alexander Dovzhenko**
sc **Alexander Dovzhenko**
ph **Danylo Demutsky**
m **Silent**

Semyon Svashenko, Stepan Shkurat, Mikola Nademsky, Yelena Maximova

Collectivization in the Ukraine is implemented in the face of opposition from the Kulaks (landowners). After the leader of the village committee is shot by a resentful Kulak, the peasants become more united than ever. One of the supreme masterpieces of the Soviet cinema, it was not seen in its entirety until 1958. The authorities censored those scenes where the dead man's betrothed mourns him, naked and hysterical, and where the peasants urinate in the tractor's radiator. Even truncated, this political poem made an enormous impact in the West. Using choreographed images, counterpoints, juxtapositions and a final long elaborate parallel montage, Dovzhenko has created an indelible image of a rural paradise earned by the blood of the peasants.

Earth, The see Land, The

Earth Entranced see Land In Anguish

Eastern Wind
Hamsin
Israel 1982 88 mins col
Nachsoh Films

d **Daniel Wachsman**
sc **Daniel Wachsman, Danny Verete, Jacob Lifshin**
ph **David Gurfinkel**
m **Raviv Gazit**

Shlomo Tarshish, Hemda Levy, Ruth Geler, Shawaf Yassin, Daou Selim, Zvika Cornfeld, Shmuel Shilo

Gedalia Birmann (Tarshish) is a Jewish farmer in Galilee whose family has been closely connected with that of his chief Arab labourer Khaled (Yassin) for two generations. Further, Gedalia's sister (Levy) and Khaled are involved in an illicit love affair. Now the Israeli authorities are to appropriate the Arab land, thus destroying the established order with tragic results. Wachsman's film is well made and very well acted, skilfully drawing together themes of class conflict, racial tension, and eroticism. A rare and uncompromising Israeli excursion into liberal argument, it is thought provoking and disturbing and caused much controversy at home.

Easy Road
Asymvivastos
Greece 1979 110 mins col
Greca Film

d **Andreas Thomopoulos**
sc **Andreas Thomopoulos**
ph **Dimitris Vernikos**
m **Mikis Theodorakis, George Theodorakis, Andreas Thomopoulos**

Paul Sideropoulos, Betty Levanon, Elen Manyiati, Vera Kruzka, Stavros Xenidis, Kostas Vrettas

Paul (Sideropoulos), a composer of ballads and a street troubador, is a former postgraduate medical student who dropped out in order to seek a new, freewheeling life and avoid commitment. Things change when he falls in love with a divorced mother of two children, assumes responsibility for the family and returns to his studies, only to be disillusioned by the corruption of the medical profession. This movie—it's title an echo of *Easy Rider*— is a commercially cunning little package, combining, as it does, a sharp look at the realities of modern day life, while offering something for the youth market in its hero's attitudes and its generous dose of music. These latter elements come off best, thanks largely to Sideropoulos' relaxed, attractive style of acting and singing.

Ebreo Errante, L' see Wandering Jew, The

The Eclipse
L'Eclisse

Italy 1962 125 mins bw
Cineriz/Iteropa/Paris Film

d **Michelangelo Antonioni**
sc **Michelangelo Antonioni, Tonino Guerra, Elio Bartolini, Ottiero Ottieri**
ph **Gianni De Venanzo**
m **Giovanni Fusco**
Monica Vitti, Alain Delon, Francisco Rabal, Lilla Brignone, Louis Seigner

Vittoria (Vitti) leaves her lover (Rabal) of four years and begins an affair with Piero (Delon), a stockbroker, but finally opts for solitude rather than marriage or a failing relationship. *The Eclipse*—the title refers to the wiping out of emotions between men and women in modern industrial society—completes what is now seen as Antonioni's trilogy of alienation begun with *L'Avventura* and continuing with *La Notte* (both 1960). The film centres on the superb Vitti, through whose eyes we see the buildings and landscape echoing her emptiness. Perhaps the symbolic intentions are too plain, but nobody could deny the bravura of the stock exchange sequence or the haunting beauty of the final shots—52 of them— of a city bereft of living creatures.

Special Jury Prize Cannes 1962

Eclisse, L' see Eclipse, The

École Buissonière, L' see Passion For Life

Écoute Voir... see See Here My Love

Ecstasy
Extase

Czechoslovakia 1933 90 mins bw
Elektra

d **Gustav Machaty**
sc **Gustav Machaty, Franz Horky, Vitezslav Nezval, Jacques A. Koerpel**
ph **Jan Stallich, Hans Androschin**
m **Giuseppe Becce**
Hedy Kiesler (later Lamarr), Aribert Mog, Jaromír Rogoz, Leopold Kramer

A child bride whose husband is impotent, has an affair with a roadway engineer and is granted a divorce, but declines to go away with her lover when her ex-husband commits suicide. Because of the teenage Hedy's one or two demure nude scenes in an idyllic pastoral setting, the film caused a rumpus; Pope Pius XII denounced it, Hitler banned it, and the offending scenes were excised from most European and American versions. The gorgeous star's husband, German munitions magnate Fritz Mandl, spent millions trying to buy up all the prints. It was much ado about nothing on, but it helped win Hedy a Hollywood contract. (Louis B. Mayer changed her name to Lamarr because he thought Kiesler sounded too much like a slang word for buttocks.) The film itself, shot partly on location, is full of lyrical beauty and stylish eroticism, and Hedy's kiesler is hardly seen.

Edipo Re see Oedipus Rex

Edith And Marcel
Edith Et Marcel

France 1983 162 mins col
Les Films 13/Parafrance

d **Claude Lelouch**
sc **Claude Lelouch**
ph **Jean Boffety**
m **Francis Lai**
Evelyne Bouix, Jacques Villeret, Francis Huster, Marcel Cerdan Jr, Jean-Claude Brialy, Jean Bouise, Charles Gérard, Charles Aznavour

The love affair between singer Edith Piaf and champion boxer Marcel Cerdan, idols of France in the 1940s, ending with his death in a plane crash, is parallelled with the romance between an ordinary plump army private (Villeret) and a wealthy woman (Bouix) with whom he corresponds. Lelouch, known for seeing 'la vie en rose', made a superficial and artificial entertainment out of a passionate and exciting story, adding a completely pointless and dull sub- plot. Evelyne Bouix struggled vainly to suggest 'the little sparrow', with some of her songs actually sung by Piaf and others by Mama Bea. When Patrick Dewaere, originally chosen to play Cerdan, committed suicide just before shooting, Cerdan's son switched from his role as technical advisor to take that of portraying his father.

Edith Et Marcel see Edith And Marcel

Edouard Et Caroline see Edward And Caroline

Edvard Munch

Norway 1974 210 mins col
Norsk Rikskringkasting/Sveriges Radio

d **Peter Watkins**
sc **Peter Watkins**
ph **Odd Geir Saether**
Geir Westby (Munch), Gro Fraas, Eli Ryg, Knut Khristiansen, Nils-Eger Pettersen, Morten Eid

A portrait of the great Norwegian Expressionist painter Edvard Munch (1863-1944) and the hypocritical, puritanical society of Christiana (later Oslo), where he lived his tormented life. The English director Watkins concentrates mainly on the artist's early years (derived mainly from Munch's memoirs), his mother's and younger sister's deaths, his brother's suicide, his own ill-fated affair with a married woman (Fraas) and his struggle to maintain his sanity. This is done with a controlled intensity that reflects the visual world of Munch, as well as getting to grips with the artistic process itself. Although too long and repetitive (even in the 167-minute version released in the USA), it is one of the most remarkable film biographies to date and the antithesis of Ken Russell's vulgar efforts. The non-professional cast, particularly Westby, is wonderful.

Edward And Caroline

Edouard Et Caroline

France 1951 99 mins bw
UGC/CICC

d **Jacques Becker**
sc **Jacques Becker, Annette Wademant**
ph **Robert Lefèbvre**
m **Jean-Jacques Grünewald**
Daniel Gélin, Anne Vernon, Jacques François, William Tubbs, Jean Galland

A struggling young pianist and his wife (Gélin and Vernon) quarrel on the evening he is to play at her rich uncle's fancy soirée to help launch his career. The best of Becker's comedies with a contemporary Paris setting, it is as light as a feather and twice as rib-tickling. Without much plot, the action, taking place in just a few hours, bubbles along towards the cheerful reconciliation of its appealing young couple.

Eeny Meeny Miny Moe see Who Saw Him Die?

Effi Briest

Fontane Effi Briest

W. Germany 1974 140 mins bw
Tango/Filmverlag Der Autoren

d **Rainer Werner Fassbinder**
sc **Rainer Werner Fassbinder**
ph **Jürgen Jürges, Dietrich Lohmann**
m **Saint-Saëns**
Hanna Schygulla, Wolfgang Schenck, Ulli Lommel, Karl-Heinz Böhm, Ursula Stratz

Seventeen-year-old Effi (Schygulla), forced into marriage with an aristocrat (Schenck) twice her age, has a brief affair with a young officer (Lommel). Six years later, the husband discovers love letters and challenges the ex-lover to a duel. Fassbinder has been as faithful as possible to Theodor Fontane's famous 1895 novel on the restraints of a hidebound society, complete with narration and printed extracts, but this is no academic transposition. The elegant monochrome photography (bright fades punctuate the short scenes), the stylized framing (many a mirror image), and the finely shaded performances put it among the director's finest achievements. The radiant Schygulla, having appeared in almost all of Fassbinder's films since 1965, then went her own way for four years after a row about money.

Effrontée, L' see Impudent Girl, An

Égi Bárány see Agnus Dei

Egy Erkölcsös Éjsz see Very Moral Night, A

Egymásra Nézve see Another Way

An Egyptian Story
Hadduta Misriya

Egypt 1982 130 mins col
Misr International

d **Youssef Chahine**
sc **Youssef Chahine, Fakhry El-Leithy**
ph **Mohsen Nasr**
m **Gamal Karraze**
Mohiel Dine, Ussama Nadir, Magda-I-Khatib, Leila Hamada, Haman

An Egyptian film director (Dine) goes to London for open-heart surgery. While on the operating table, hovering between life and death, he reviews his life and the events in his country that affected it. Like Bob Fosse's *All That Jazz*, which this film coincidentally and superficially resembles in theme and structure, this is also a personal recollection of the director's own open-heart operation not long before. But unlike the show-bizzy American film's director, Chahine's hero is part of the political process. In this rich, energetic, rather meandering memoir, scenes from Chahine's own films are replayed against their autobiographical and historical context—the end of the war, the fall of Farouk and the Suez crisis.

Ehe Der Maria Braun, Die see Marriage Of Maria Braun, The

Eien No Hito see Eternal Love

8½
Otto E Mezzo

Italy 1963 188 mins bw
Cineriz

d **Federico Fellini**
sc **Federico Fellini, Ennio Flaiano, Tullio Pinelli, Brunello Rondi**
ph **Gianni De Venanzo**
m **Nino Rota**
Marcello Mastroianni, Claudia Cardinale, Anouk Aimée, Sandra Milo, Rosella Falk, Barbara Steele

A famous movie director, unable to find the inspiration to start his new film and harried by people in the industry, his wife and his mistress, retreats into personal recollections, dreams and fantasies. Fellini's seventh solo effort (plus three collaborations counting a half each) is one of the most celebrated creations about the inability to create. The problem is that no matter how visually stunning, exhilarating, and surprising the film was on first viewing, it cannot avoid being self-indulgent, satirically shallow, and as spiritually bankrupt as the director—played by Mastroianni as a calculated self-portrait of Fellini. It remains, however, a compendium of every Fellini theme and stylistic device, good and bad.

Best Foreign Film Oscar 1963

1860

Italy 1934 75 mins bw
Cines

d **Alessandro Blasetti**
sc **Alessandro Blasetti, Gino Mazzucchi, Emilio Cecchi**
ph **Anchise Brizzi, Giulio De Luca**
m **Nino Medin**
Giuseppe Gulino, Aida Bellia, Gianfranco Giachetti, Mario Ferrari

The events surrounding the battle of Calatafimi in May 1860 when the Sicilians rose up and defeated the troops of the King of Naples. Among the rebels is a young shepherd (Gulino) who carries a message to Garibaldi in Genoa requesting support. The use of non-professional actors, actual landscapes and regional dialects makes Blasetti's intimate epic a precursor of Neo-Realism, and a direct influence on Visconti. The main difference is that the film presents the peasants, whose faces are seen being inspired by an unseen Garibaldi, as part of the historical process and not as individual victims. But rhetorical postures are avoided and Blasetti succeeded in creating a restrained, elegant and poetic work in the midst of the many pretentiously grandiose films being made in Fascist Italy at the time.

Eijanaika see Why Not?

Einmal Ku'damm Und Zurück see Girl In A Boot

Ek Din Prati Din see And Quiet Rolls The Dawn

Ekti Jiban see Portrait Of A Life

El

(US: This Strange Passion)
Mexico 1952 100 mins bw
Nacional Film/Tepeyac

d **Luis Buñuel**
sc **Luis Buñuel, Luis Alcoriza**
ph **Gabriel Figueroa**
m **Hernandez Breton**
Arturo De Cordova, Delia Garces, Luis Beristain, Aurora Walker

A 40-year-old male virgin (De Cordova) marries a beautiful young girl (Garces) and then falls victim to paranoid jealousy which leads him to attempted murder and a monastery. One of Buñuel's finest black comedies from his Mexican period continues the theme of *l'amour fou* first dealt with in *L'Âge D'Or* (1930). He transforms a basic Latin-American melodrama into a biting anti-clerical satire, full of bizarre touches such as having his protagonist jab a knitting needle through a keyhole when he thinks he is being spied upon.

E La Nave Va see And The Ship Sails On

El Dorado

Spain 1988 151 mins col
Iberio-Americana TV/Chrysalide Films/Canal Plus/FR 3

d **Carlos Saura**
sc **Carlos Saura**
ph **Teo Escamilla**
m **Alejandro Masso**
Omero Antonutti, Lambert Wilson, Eusebio Poncela, Gabriela Roel, Inés Sastre, José Sancho, Féodor Atkine

In 1560, Pedro De Ursúa, accompanied by his mistress, 300 Spanish soldiers and 300 natives, set out from Peru to search for the legendary land of El Dorado. As the expedition travelled ever deeper into the jungle, it met with increasing disaster, and Ursúa's position was forcibly usurped by the conquistador Lope De Aguirre, who went mad and was killed by his few surviving soldiers. Excavating the same ground as Werner Herzog's *Aguirre, The Wrath Of God*, Carlos Saura has made a lavish and beautiful epic, reported to be the most expensive Spanish production to date ($8million). A faithful account of history, the film features some startling set-pieces (the graphic carving up of the horses for food, for example) but, alas, it simply fails to ignite. It drags its heavy load with insufficient action to hold the interest and does so for rather too long. Antonutti and Wilson, Aguirre and Ursúa respectively, are highly competent, but lack the necessary bite.

Electra

Elektra
Greece 1962 113 mins bw
Finos

d **Michael Cacoyannis**
sc **Michael Cacoyannis**
ph **Walter Lassally**
m **Mikis Theodorakis**
Irene Papas, Aleka Katselli, Yannis Fertis, Phoebus Rhazis

Electra (Papas) and Orestes (Fertis) plot the death of their mother Clytemnestra (Katselli), whom they believe to have been responsible for their father's murder. Because of political and financial pressures, Cacoyannis turned from modern to Ancient Greece with the first and best of his rather uninspiring Euripides trilogy, (*The Trojan Women*, 1971 and *Iphigenia*, 1976 followed), all featuring Irene Papas chewing the scenery—in this case the barren landscape around Mycenae. The old story still grips despite unnecessary flashbacks and overpowering close-ups.

Electra, My Love see Elektreia

Elektra see Electra

Elektreia

aka Electra, My Love
Szerelmem, Elektra
Hungary 1974 76 mins col
Hunnia Film

d **Miklós Jancsó**
sc **Gyula Hernádi, L. Gyurkó**
ph **János Kende**
m **Popular Hungarian songs**
Mari Töröcsik, György Cserhalmi, Jószef Madaras, Lajos Balázsovits

On the Hungarian plains, Elektra (Töröcsik) and her brother Orestes (Cserhalmi) fight against the tyranny of Egisto (Madaras). Through one of Jancsó's most stylized and choreographed narratives can just be discerned the Electra myth. All the elements of the director's personal visual vocabulary are rather too densely packed in—the horsemen, the whips, the nudes, the dances, the folk songs, the extraordinary tracking shots and extremely long takes. But there are comical scenes, such as Egisto perched on a gigantic ball, and the surprising and optimistic ending when a red helicopter called *Revolution*, flying from East to West, comes down from the sky to rescue the hero and heroine. The message may be simple, but the symbols are strong.

Eléna Et Les Hommes

(US: Paris Does Strange Things)
France 1956 95 mins col
Franco London/Les Films Gibé/Electra Compania Cinematographica

d **Jean Renoir**
sc **Jean Renoir**
ph **Claude Renoir**
m **Joseph Kosma**
Ingrid Bergman, Mel Ferrer, Jean Marais, Magali Noël, Juliette Greco, Jean Richard

An impoverished Polish princess (Bergman) sets out to find herself a rich husband among her many admirers in the Paris of the 1880s. She is finally faced with three choices—an elderly but wealthy boot magnate (Richard), a conquering soldier-hero (Marais) and an aristocratic dilettante (Ferrer). 'For a long time I had been dying to make a film with Ingrid Bergman. I wanted to see her laughing and smiling on the screen,' said Renoir, who rescued the Swedish star from the gloom of her four Rossellini films and restored her popularity. Bergman has seldom been more beguiling than in this, one of Renoir's most artificial films. Love is at the centre of a Paris of parades, ballad singers, salons and street carnivals, captured by Claude Renoir's camera as a series of popular prints. It sets out to prove, rather ingenuously, that 'Dictatorship has no chance in a country where affairs of the heart are so important'.

Eléphant Ça Trompe Enormément, Un
see Pardon Mon Affaire

The Elephant God

Joi Baba Felunath
India 1978 112 mins col
RDB

d **Satyajit Ray**
sc **Satyajit Ray**
ph **Soumendu Roy**
m **Satyajit Ray**
Soumitra Chatterjee, Siddartha Chatterjee, Santosh Dutta, Utpal Dutta

Private detective Feluda (Soumitra Chatterjee), on holiday in Benares with his teenage cousin (Siddartha Chatterjee), gets involved in the mysterious theft of a valuable gold statuette, the Elephant God. This follow-up to *The Golden Fortress* reintroduces the Indian Sherlock Holmes and his young Dr Watson in an enjoyable tale, told with all of Ray's affection and artistry. A range of picturesque characters, including a phoney holy man, and a wonderful use of the Benares setting puts it in the Feuillade serial tradition.

Eles Nao Usam Black Tie see They Don't Wear Black Tie

Elippathayam see Rat-Trap

Elisa, My Life

aka Elisa, My Love
Elisa, Vida Mía
Spain 1977 125 mins col
Elias Querejeta

d **Carlos Saura**
sc **Carlos Saura**
ph **Teo Escamilla**
m **Erik Satie**
Geraldine Chaplin, Fernando Rey, Norman Brisky, Isabel Mestres, Joaquín Hinojosa

Elisa (Chaplin), estranged from her husband (Brisky), visits her father (Rey), whom she has not seen for many years, at his cottage in the Segovian hills. He is writing a biography from her point of view and, gradually she begins to see things with his perspective. Saura's interest in memory, shifting chronology and different narrative devices is at its most complex in this drama of identity. 'The things that bother me are less clear than under Franco,' Saura said in 1976, and the film seems to express this opaque state. Yet the ambiguity—it seldom separates memory from imagination—and the subtle performances of Chaplin and Rey, pay some dividends.

Best Actor (Fernando Rey) Cannes 1977

Elisa, My Love see Elisa, My Life

Elisa, Vida Mía see Elisa, My Life

El Topo see Topo, El

Elvira Madigan

Sweden 1967 95 mins col
Europa/Janco

d **Bo Widerberg**
sc **Bo Widerberg**
ph **Jörgen Persson**
m **Mozart**
Pia Degermark, Thommy Berggren, Lennart Malmer

Elvira (Degermark), a tightrope artist, and Sixten (Berggren), a married army officer, fall in love, run away together, and enjoy an idyll in the countryside. Totally shunned by the 19th-century Swedish society whose moral code they have outraged, their passion ends in death. Widerberg's film version of a true story is lyrically photographed in soft focus and slow motion, and well acted—largely to the strains of Mozart's Piano Concerto No 21 (2nd movement). Some regard the film as an overblown and sentimental cigarette commercial; others find the lover's unrealistic and tragic quest for happiness almost unbearably moving.

Best Actress (Pia Degermark) Cannes 1967

The Emigrants

Utvandrarna

Sweden 1971 190 mins col
Svensk Filmindustri

d **Jan Troell**
sc **Jan Troell, Bengt Forslund**
ph **Jan Troell**
m **Erik Nordgren**
Max Von Sydow, Liv Ullmann, Eddie Axberg, Svenolof Bern, Allan Edwall, Alina Alfredsson

A group of poor Swedish peasants, forced to emigrate to the USA because of hardship at home, survive a cramped voyage before optimistically settling down in Minnesota. Based on the novels of Vilhelm Moberg, this slushy, slow, solemn saga and its sequel *The New Land* (1973) did well in the New World but failed dismally in the Old. One almost forgets that Von Sydow and Ullmann, as the loving couple surviving disasters against beautiful landscapes, were the linchpins of many a Bergman film

---

Emil And The Detectives

Emil Und Die Detektive

Germany 1931 73 mins bw
UFA

d **Gerhard Lamprecht**
sc **Billy Wilder**
ph **Werner Brandes**
m **Schmidt-Boelke**
Rolf Wenkhaus, Fritz Rasp, Kaethe Haack, Olga Engl, Inge Landgut

Young Emil (Wenkhaus) becomes a hero when he tracks down a notorious thief with the help of the child population of Berlin. This first of five film versions of Erich Kastner's children's novel outstrips all the rest, including one from Walt Disney Studios in 1964. Lively and amusing, with good location photography, it never condescends to a youthful audience, allowing adults to enjoy it, too.

Emil Und Die Detektive see Emil And The Detectives

Emitai

Senegal 1972 103 mins col
Films Domirev

d **Ousmane Sembène**
sc **Ousmane Sembène**
ph **Michel Remaudeau**
Robert Fontaine, Michel Remaudeau, Pierre Blanchard, Ibou Camara, Ousmane Camara

The French arrive in a small West African village to recruit soldiers for their World War II armies, but meet with resistance. However, the colonized community's attempt to protect its traditional values and way of life has a tragic outcome. Leading Senegalese director Sembène's film, made on a tiny budget, is no less exemplary in its choices and judgement than a more expensive venture. The story, told from the point of view of the oppressed with a stoical regard for the truth that informs much as a documentary might, is poignant and salutary.

Emmanuelle

France 1974 94 mins col
Trinacra/Orphée

d **Just Jaeckin**
sc **Jean-Louis Richard**
ph **Richard Suzuki, Marie Saunier**
m **Pierre Bachelet**
Sylvia Kristel, Marika Green, Daniel Sarky, Alain Cuny

The bored wife of a French embassy official in Bangkok, urged by her libertine husband to explore all the possibilities of sex, finds herself in bed with, among others, a Lesbian archaeologist and an elderly *roué*. This glossy soft porn package dressed up (or undressed) as art, with Kristel on display, was a huge international hit and spawned a mulitude of Emmanuelle sequels (and derivative copies) even worse than their begetter.

The Emperor Of California
Der Kaiser Von Kalifornien

Germany 1936 100 mins bw
Luis Trenker Film

d **Luis Trenker**
sc **Luis Trenker**
ph **Albert Benitz, Heinz Von Jaworsky**
m **Giuseppe Becce**
Luis Trenker, Viktoria Von Ballasko, Werner Kunig, Karl Zwingmann, Bernhard Minetti, Luis Gerold

In 1834, John Sutter (Trenker), a revolutionary, has to flee from Switzerland to America. In California, he becomes the leader of an immigrant community and later gains power as a Senator and a US Army General, until he is finally brought down. Blaise Cendrars' novel *L'Or* was originally to have been a Hollywood project for Sergei Eisenstein, but when that fell through Trenker applied to Universal to direct it. After they gave *Sutter's Gold* to James Cruze, Trenker made his own rival version in the same year. Some locations were filmed in America, but many others were shot in North Italy and Berlin. In fact, the film's splendid camerawork, clever montage and imaginative use of sets give it more of a feeling for the grandeur of the Old West than the second-rate Hollywood edition. Because Trenker made films under the Third Reich, the work was banned by both the Americans and Russians after the war.

Best Film Venice 1936

Empire Of Passion
(US: Phantom Love)
Ai No Borei

Japan 1978 105 mins col
Argos/Oshima

d **Nagisa Oshima**
sc **Nagisa Oshima**
ph **Yoshio Miyajima**
m **Tohru Takemitsu**
Kazuko Yoshiyuki, Tatsuya Fuji, Takahiro Tamura, Takuzo Kawatani, Akiko Koyama

In a village in 1895, an old rickshaw man is murdered by his wife (Yoshiyuki) and her young lover (Fuji). Three years later, the old man's ghost appears, reawakening their guilt and leading to the exposure of their crime. This companion piece to *In The Realm Of The Senses* is less sexually explicit but equally steamy and cruel. Oshima's control of the medium is evident in this ghost story with an *amour fou* at its centre, but the social conviction and complexity of his earlier films seems to have evaporated. This has one keen eye on the audience's emotions and the other on the box-office.

Best Director Cannes 1978

The Empress Yang Kwei Fei

aka Princess Yang Kwei Fei

Yokihi

Japan 1955 125 mins col
Daiei-Shaw Brothers

d **Kenji Mizoguchi**
sc **Yoda Yoshikata**
ph **Kohei Sugiyama**
m **Hayasaka Fumio**
Masayuki Mori, Machiko Kyo, So Yamamura, Sakae Ozawa

When the emperor of China marries a scullery maid on the death of his wife, the new empress is destroyed by jealousies and intrigue around her. Undeterred by the big budget spectacle requirements of the Shaw Brothers of Hong Kong, Mizoguchi triumphantly retains his reputation. The exquisite colour, costumes and decor are used almost as *leitmotifs* to counterpoint the emotions of the characters, especially the glowing Kyo in the title role. Sadly, the director would not live long enough (he died a year later) to experiment in colour on the wide screen.

The Empty Canvas

La Noia

Italy 1964 118 mins bw
CC Champion/Concordia

d **Damiano Damiani**
sc **Damiano Damiani, Tonino Guerra, Ugo Liberatore**
ph **Roberto Gerardi**
m **Luis Bacalov**
Bette Davis, Horst Buchholz, Catherine Spaak, Isa Miranda, Lea Padovani, Georges Wilson

A young painter (Buchholz), obsessed by his deficiencies as an artist, falls in love with a model (Spaak) whom he brings home to the family estate to meet his mother (Davis). When she refuses to remain faithful to him, he becomes insanely jealous. The novels and stories of Alberto Moravia have seldom made good movies and this plodding, pompous film is no exception. Consolation comes (as always) from Bette Davis, amusing to watch as an Italian matriarch in her first foreign language film. But as for the rest...an empty screen might have been preferable.

The Empty Table

Shokutaku No Nai Ie

Japan 1985 142 mins col
Marugen Building Group/Haiyu-za Film Production/ Herald Ace

d **Masaki Kobayashi**
sc **Masaki Kobayashi**
ph **Kozo Okazaki**
m **Tohru Takemitsu**
Tatsuya Nakadai, Mayumi Ogawa, Kie Nakai, Kiichi Nakai, Takeyuki Takemoto, Shima Iwashita, Mikijiro Hira

Kidoji (Nakadai), a high-powered electronics academic is the head of a family which is disintegrating as a result of the arrest of his eldest son (Kiichi Nakai) for terrorist activities. Public disgrace walks hand-in-hand with private grief; he refuses to visit the boy in jail, and his wife loses her sanity. Kobayashi tells his story—primarily one of family relationships—in a series of shifting time blocks, and fills it with hints of political argument and examinations of moral responsibility. However, the dilemmas are presented rather than explored, and done so with a disciplined restraint that suggests something weightier than is actually present. It's a well-made, interesting film that never rises to the level of one's expectation.

En Cas De Malheur see Love Is My Profession

The Enchanted Desna

Zacharovannaya Desna

USSR 1964 81 mins col
Mosfilm

d **Juiia Solntseva**
sc **Alexander Dovzhenko**
ph **A. Temerine**
m **Gavril Popov**
Yevgeni Samoilov, Volodya Gontcharov, E. Bondarenko, Zinaida Kirienkova, V. Orlovsky

During World War II, a soldier (Samoilov) on retreat finds strength in his memories, both sad and happy, of the Ukraine of his youth and in the beauty of his homeland. 'If Dovzhenko had lived, I would never have become a director; all that I do I consider as propaganda, defence and illustration of Dovzhenko,' stated Solntseva on the filming of her husband's three unrealized scenarios. The third and best (after *Poem Of The Sea* and *The Flaming Years*) astonishes with its eye-boggling rhetorical images in 70mm and stereophonic sound. Perhaps it lacks Dovzhenko's unique lyricism, but its amalgam of illusion and reality, legend and Ukrainian nationalism is very much in the tradition of *Zvenigora*. For what it's worth, *The Enchanted Desna* is one of Godard's favourite films.

The Endless Land Of Alexis Droeven

Le Grand Paysage D'Alexis Droeven

Belgium 1981 88 mins col
Les Films De La Drève(Brussels)/ RTBF(Liège)/Radio-Cinés SA(France)

d **Jean-Jacques Andrien**
sc **Jean-Jacques Andrien, Franck Venaille**
ph **Georges Barsky**
m **Monteverdi, Wagner**
Jerzy Radziwilowicz, Nicole Garcia, Maurice Garrel, Jan Decleir, the inhabitants of the Aubel district

When dairy farmer Alexis Van Droeven (Garrel) dies, his son Jean-Pierre (Radziwilowicz) returns to bury him. It is only from the speeches at Alexis' graveside that the young man learns of his father's struggles for political rights and, from his aunt (Garcia), that Alexis wanted to save him from inheriting a life of isolation and hardship. Jean-Pierre must now decide whether to sell the farm or carry it on. Andrien spent three years in the Aubel district, living among the farming community of his ancestry to gather his material. The result is a complex story of family relationships and socio-political problems, using flashback to portray key incidents in the late Alexis' life. Spare and intelligent, the film is outstandingly beautiful in its evocation of landscape and won the best cinematography prize at Berlin.

The End Of A Day

La Fin Du Jour

France 1939 108 mins bw
Regina/Filmsonor

d **Julien Duvivier**
sc **Julien Duvivier, Charles Spaak**
ph **Christian Matras**
m **Maurice Jaubert**
Victor Francen, Louis Jouvet, Michel Simon, Madeleine Ozeray, Arthur Devere, Gabrielle Dorziat, Sylvie

The feuds, friendships, loves and hates of a group of elderly actors and actresses in a retirement home threatened with closure. The film offers a feast of French ensemble acting with Michel Simon standing out as a pathetic prankster who hides the fact that he had only ever been an understudy in his career. Duvivier ably balances comedy and sentiment in virtually one setting.

End Of Innocence see House Of The Angel, The

The End Of St Petersburg

Konyets Sankt-Peterburga

USSR 1927 122 mins bw
Mezhrabpom

d **Vsevolod Pudovkin**
sc **Nathan Zarkhi**
ph **Anatoli Golovnya**
m **Silent**
Ivan Chuvelov, Vera Baranovskaya, A.P. Khristiakov, V. Obolenski

In 1917, an uneducated peasant boy (Chuvelov) arrives in St Petersburg in time to witness the October Revolution, including the storming of the Winter Palace and the fall of Kerensky. Commissioned, like Eisenstein's *October*, as part of the tenth anniversary celebrations of the Revolution, and shot concurrently using the same sites and events, Pudovkin's was the more popular film with the public and officialdom— perhaps because it was made more human by having a central figure with whom audiences could identify, and was rather less stylized. Nevertheless, it also contained its share of marvellous montage sequences, such as the high- angle shot of the top hats of businessmen contrasted with the faces of dead soldiers in the trenches.

The End Of Summer
aka Early Autumn
Kohayagawa-Ke No Aki
Japan 1961 103 mins col
Toho

d **Yasujiro Ozu**
sc **Yasujiro Ozu, Kogo Noda**
ph **Asakazu Nakai**
m **Toshiro Mayuzumi**
Ganjiro Nakamura, Setsuko Hara, Yoko Tsukasa, Michiyo Aratama, Yumi Shirakawa

When an elderly man (Nakamura) decides to take up with his former mistress, his three daughters—one a widow about to remarry, another engaged and the third married—become extremely upset. The father dies of a heart attack. One of Ozu's bleakest films starts out in a light, anecdotal manner, gradually getting harsher, but all the time enriching our knowledge of family relationships. The film also contains one of Ozu's greatest characters in the wily old father.

Endstation Freiheit see Slow Attack

The Enemy
Dusman
Turkey 1979 160 mins col
Guney Filmcilik

d **Zeki Ökten**
sc **Yilmaz Güney**
ph **Cetin Tunca**
m **Yavuz Top**
Aytac Arman, Gungor Bayrak, Guven Sengil, Kamil Sonmez, Sevket Altug

A poor uneducated labourer, with a discontented wife, can find no work until he gets a job poisoning stray dogs. One of the four extraordinary films directed by proxy from a detailed script by Yilmaz Güney, serving a long prison sentence in Turkey, it is a powerful, passionate plea for social justice. What puts it beyond a tract is the gritty, sometimes quirky depiction of everyday life as lived by the disinherited.

Enfance Nue, L' see Naked Childhood

Enfant Sauvage, L' see Wild Child, The

Les Enfants Du Paradis
(US: Children Of Paradise)
France 1945 195 mins bw
Pathé

d **Marcel Carné**
sc **Jacques Prévert**
ph **Roger Hubert**
m **Joseph Kosma, Maurice Thiriet**
Arletty, Jean-Louis Barrault, Pierre Brasseur, Marcel Herrand, Maria Casarès, Louis Salou, Pierre Renoir, Gaston Modot, Jane Marken

In the 19th-century Paris of Louis Philippe, among the crowds that throng the boulevards, are the classical actor Frédéric Lemaître (Brasseur), the mime Debureau (Barrault), the criminal Lacenaire (Herrand), the aristocrat Comte Montray (Salou), the elusive courtesan Garance (Arletty), and the simple Nathalie (Casarès), all of whose fates are intertwined. This richly entertaining and intensely romantic evocation of an epoch, with vivid sets by Alexandre Trauner, came about because the Occupation forced Carné and Prévert to make 'escapist' films. The larger-than-life characters and performers, the ironic dialogue, the narrative skill and sweep of the whole production has placed this on many critics' lists as one of the greatest films ever made.

Des Enfants Gâtés see Spoiled Children

Enfants Terribles, Les see Strange Ones, The

The Engagement
(US: The Fiancés)
I Fidanzati
Italy 1963 84 mins bw
Titanus Sicilia/Ventidue Dicembre/SEC

d **Ermanno Olmi**
sc **Ermanno Olmi**
ph **Lamberto Caimi**
m **Gianni Ferrio**
Carlo Cabrini, Anna Canzi

A young man gladly accepts a welding job in Sicily which will take him away from his fiancée in Milan for 18 months, because he thinks the separation will be good for their relationship. However, loneliness and an unfamiliar environment make him long to see her again. Olmi's strength lies in the depiction of humble people (played here by a pair of non- professionals), whose problems he highlights without condescension or preaching. The film's use of natural sounds and actual locations creates an alienating environment in which there are pockets of warmth and humanity.

The Enigma Of Kaspar Hauser

(US: Every Man For Himself And God Against All aka The Mystery Of Kaspar Hauser)

Jeder Für Sich Und Gott Gegen Alle

W. Germany 1974 110 mins col
ZDF

d **Werner Herzog**
sc **Werner Herzog**
ph **Jorge Schmidt-Reitwein**
m **Albinoni, Pachelbel, Di Lasso**
Bruno S, Walter Ladengast, Brigitte Mira, Hans Musaus, Willy Semmelrogge

In the early 19th century, a strange young man, who seemed to have had no contact with human beings since his childhood, appeared in the town square at Nuremburg. He became an attraction in society until killed one day by an unknown assailant. Herzog's fascination with the outsider fixes itself on Kaspar Hauser, the ultimate misfit. The mysterious side of the true tale is, however, mainly ignored in favour of a stilted examination of the confrontation between innocence and corruption, and some obvious satire on social conventions. What makes the film riveting is the disturbing and remarkable presence of Bruno S, a man who spent 22 years in various institutions, including prison, before Herzog discovered him.

Special Jury Prize Berlin 1975

Enjo see Conflagration

Ensayo De Un Crimen see Criminal Life Of Archibaldo De La Cruz, The

---

Enthusiasm

aka Symphony Of The Don Basin

Entuziazm

USSR 1931 96 mins bw
Kiev Film Studio/ Ukrainfilm

d **Dziga Vertov**
sc **Dziga Vertov**
ph **Zeitlin**
m **N. Timofeyev**

A documentary on the industrial and agricultural workers in the Donets Coal Basin in the Eastern Ukraine, and their efforts to fulfil the Five Year Plan. No, it is not as boring as it sounds. In fact, this 'symphony of noise', this 'futuristic visual poem', much admired by Chaplin, not only celebrates workers in the building of the Soviet Union but the art of cinema. Enthusiasm for both his subject and his style permeates Vertov's first sound film, contrasting the old order and the new through didactic, dynamic montage. As in *The Man With The Movie Camera*, one's attention is drawn to the making of the film itself as a contribution to the modernization programme, epitomizing Lenin's statement, 'Of all the arts, for us cinema is the most important'.

Entotsu No Mieru Basho see Where Chimneys Are Seen

Entr'acte

France 1924 22 mins bw
Ballets Suédois

d **René Clair**
sc **Francis Picabia**
ph **Jimmy Berliet**
m **Silent**
Jean Borlin, Inge Fries, Francis Picabia, Man Ray, Georges Auric, Marcel Achard, Marcel Duchamp, Erik Satie, Georges Charensol, Rolf De Maré

A number of crazy characters rush around Paris where they end up at a funeral chasing a runaway hearse. This Dada joke was conceived by the painter and poet Picabia in order to be shown during the interval between the two acts of his ballet *Relâche* (music by Satie). Clair shot it in three weeks at various well-known locations in the city, intending it as a tribute to the pioneers of screen comedy, including Chaplin. An exercise in pure cinema—no plot, visual surrealism such as speeded-up motion and balletic slow motion—it is more interesting than funny, as it features many members of the French *avant-garde* of the day, and shows the emergence of a new genius of the cinema.

Entrée Des Artistes

(US: The Curtain Rises)

France 1938 90 mins bw
Regina

d **Marc Allégret**
sc **Henri Jeanson, André Cayatte**
ph **Christian Matras**
m **Georges Auric**

Louis Jouvet, Odette Joyeux, Claude Dauphin, Bernard Blier, Janine Darcey, Dalio, Carette, Sylvie

At the Paris Conservatory, two drama students (Joyeux and Darcey) fight over a fellow student (Dauphin), who is later accused of murdering one of them. Far more interesting than the melodramatic plot is the background of the cafés, the school and, particularly, the lessons with Jouvet—delightfully himself as a drama teacher. The film also proved to be a springboard for the careers of the young Joyeux, Dauphin and Blier.

Entre Nous see At First Sight

Entuziazm see Enthusiasm

Equinox Flower

Higan-Bana

Japan 1958 118 mins col
Shochiku

d **Yasujiro Ozu**
sc **Kogo Noda, Yasujiro Ozu**
ph **Yuharu Atsuta**
m **Takanobu Saito**

Shin Saburi, Fujiko Yamamoto, Kinuyo Tanaka, Ineko Arima, Keiji Sada

A young woman (Yamamoto) wishes to marry the man of her choice, but her obstinate father (Saburi) objects. although her mother (Tanaka) understands. Eventually he is won round. 'Colour is all right once in a while, but if you see it all the time, it's like eating *tendon* (seafood on rice). You get fed up with it,' said Ozu on the making of his first colour film. Actually, it was the producers who wanted it in colour to show off Yamamoto's beauty. Not only did it give the film a more modern look, but also showed the director becoming more interested in the younger generation, although he doesn't take sides. Here, the whole family is subjected to his gentle irony and loving detail. An example of Ozu's meticulous working methods on the film was recalled by Tanaka who, in a very short scene, had to say the line 'Yes, that's so' over 40 times before the director was satisfied.

Eredità Ferramonti, L' see Inheritance, The

Erendira

Mexico 1982 105 mins col
Les Films Du Triangle/Films A2/Ministère De La Culture(France)/Cine Qua Non(Mexico)/Atlas Saskia Film/Austra(W. Berlin)

d **Ruy Guerra**
sc **Gabriel García Márquez**
ph **Denys Clerval**
m **Maurice Lecoeur**

Irene Papas, Claudia Ohana, Michel Lonsdale, Oliver Wehe, Rufus, Blanca Guerra, Ernesto Gomez Cruz

For accidentally burning down the mansion of her tyrannical grandmother (Papas), Erendira (Ohana) is forced to sell her virginity to the highest bidder. After seeking refuge in a convent and then escaping to marry Ulysses (Wehe), the son of the police chief, she and her lover plan to kill her grandmother. Márquez's screenplay (from two of his own stories) is a cruel fairytale of an ogrish woman, an innocent maiden and an ineffectual Prince Charming. The director goes in for the most bizarre images of Latin Grand Guignol, shot amid grotesque surreal settings. Eccentric, funny and often plain silly, the film has some memorable nightmarish sequences. The performances of the baddies are suitably over the top.

Ernesto

Italy 1979 98 mins col
Clesi Cinematografica/José Frade Productions/ Albatros Produktion

d **Salvatore Samperi**
sc **Barbara Alberti, Amadeo Paganini, Salvatore Samperi**
ph **Camillo Bazzoni**
m **Carmelo Bernaola**
Martin Halm, Michele Placido, Virna Lisi, Turri Ferro, Lara Wendel

Ernesto (Halm), a young Jewish boy in Trieste at the turn of the century, has his sexual initiation via a male worker at his uncle's factory whom he subjugates then discards. He visits a female prostitute successfully, then finds himself attracted to a twin brother and sister. He settles for heterosexuality with the girl. Samperi's promising debut with *Grazie Zia* (1968) rather fizzled out as his attempts at serious analysis of social and sexual problems became blurred by the dominance of his gift for soft porn. *Ernesto* exemplifies the problem, although it is a handsome film and not unenjoyable.

Eroica

aka Heroism
Poland 1957 83 mins bw
Kadr/WFF/WFD

d **Andrzej Munk**
sc **Jerzy Stefan Stawinski**
ph **Jerzy Wojcik**
m **Jan Krenz**
Barbara Polomska, Leon Niemszyk, Edward Dziewonski, K. Rudzki, Roman Klosowski

Subtitled *A Heroic Symphony In Two Movements*. 1) *Scherzo Alla Polacca* tells of a black marketeer during the Nazi occupation who accidentally becomes involved with the Polish underground movement. 2) *Ostinato Lugubre* explains how the morale of the inmates of a concentration camp was kept high by making them believe one of their number had escaped. Munk's second feature, an ironic and ambivalent study of heroism during the war, disconcerted audiences accustomed to the romantic and passionate treatment of the subject by his contemporaries.

Erotikon

Sweden 1920 85 mins bw
Svensk Filmindustri

d **Mauritz Stiller**
sc **Rellits and Nedron (pseudonym for Stiller and Arthur Nordren)**
ph **Henrik Jaenzon**
m **Silent**
Lars Hanson, Karin Molander, Tora Teje, Anders De Wahl

An entomologist (De Wahl), who lectures on the sex life of beetles, is happy to give up his sophisticated wife (Teje) to his sculptor friend (Hanson) because he has fallen for a simple girl (Molander) who wins his affections with her delicious stuffed cabbage. The most celebrated of Stiller's comedies, but not the best, it was his last before moving on to more sombre works, and anticipates Bergman's *Smiles Of A Summer's Night* in its sexual manoeuvres and graceful wit. The highlight is the performance of Karin Molander, who starred in all the director's early comedies and was his most favoured incarnation of the 'modern' heroine. Renowned for his successful promotion of the liberated woman on screen, nonetheless, it is for discovering Garbo that Stiller will be best remembered.

Erotissimo

France 1968 100 mins col
Les Films De La Pléiade/Les Films Des Deux-Mondes (Paris)/Kinesis (Rome)

d **Gérard Pirès**
sc **Nicole De Buron, Gérard Pirès, Pierre Sisser**
ph **Jean-Marc Ripert**
m **William Sheller**
Annie Girardot, Jean Yanne, Francis Blanche, Dominique Maurin, Venantino Venantini

Philippe (Yanne) is preoccupied with a tax inspector's investigations into his business, leading his wife (Girardot) to believe he has lost interest in her. She embarks on a series of seductive ploys to reawaken his flagging desires, but to no avail, and her decision to take a lover collapses through lack of courage. All, however, ends happily, but not before this derivative and frenzied farce degenerates into tedium. Filmed in the style of an extended commercial, Pirès appears to be taking a sideswipe at consumerism and advertising (the film's misleading title refers to a brand of cooking oil), but he has nothing new to say.

Escalier C

France 1985 101 mins col
Films 7/FR3 Films

d **Jean-Charles Tacchella**
sc **Jean-Charles Tacchella, Elvire Murail**
ph **Jacques Assuérus**
m **Raymond Alessandrini**
Robin Renucci, Jean-Pierre Bacri, Catherine Leprince, Jacques Bonaffé, Jacques Weber, Mony-Rey

Lafont (Renucci), a rarefied, egocentric, malicious art critic, and a ruthless womanizer, is jolted by a series of encounters and experiences into reconsidering his character. The film's title refers to the floor of the apartment block where Lafont lives and periodically crosses paths with his neighbours, who include a gay artist whose affection he does nothing to discourage. What begins as an intriguing character study eventually degenerates into a superficial, uninspiring and soft-centred film, largely populated by a selection of stereotypes, and of no particular distinguishing features.

Escape To Nowhere see Silent One, The

Es Geschah Am Hellichten Tag see Assault In Broad Daylight

Es Geschah Am 20 Juli see Jackboot Mutiny

Espions, Les see Spies, The

Espiritu De La Colmene, El see Spirit Of The Beehive, The

Espoir see Man's Hope

Eta Dell'Amore, L' see Age Of Indiscretion, The

État De Siège see State Of Siege

Et Dieu Créa La Femme see And God Created Woman

Été Meurtrier, L' see One Deadly Summer

Eternal Love

aka The Bitter Spirit

Eien No Hito

Japan 1961 107 mins bw
Shochiku

d **Keisuke Kinoshita**
sc **Keisuke Kinoshita**
ph **Hiroshi Kusuda**
m **Chuji Kinoshita**
Hideko Takamine, Yoshi Kato, Keiji Sada, Kiyoshi Nonmura, Tatsuya Nakadai, Yasushi Nagata, Nobuko Otowa

Sharecropper's daughter Sadako (Takamine) awaits the return of her sweetheart, Takashi (Sada) from the war. Meanwhile, Heibei (Nakadai), son of the wealthy local landowner is invalided out of the army and forces himself on Sadako who is left with no choice but to marry him. For almost three decades, until the death of Takashi which releases Sadako from her bitter memories and longings, the couple live through a miserable marriage, leavened only by occasional affection. With a cast led by the accomplished Hideko Takamine, always a sympathetic heroine, Kinoshita manages to stay just this side of melodrama in his portrait of an ill-conceived marriage. The film is compassionate as well as sentimental and lyrical, and its most notable and imaginative feature is the music: a startlingly un-Japanese score for Flamenco guitar, with vocal interpolations used as a linking commentary. After the initial shock, it proves surprisingly effective.

The Eternal Mask
Die Ewige Maske

Austria/Switzerland 1935 88 mins bw
Progress Films

d **Werner Hochbaum**
sc **Leo Lapaire**
ph **Oscar Schnirch**
m **Anton Profes**
Peter Petersen, Mathias Wieman, Olga Tschechowa, Tom Kraa, Thekla Ahrens

A young doctor (Wieman) suffers an acute nervous breakdown following the death of a patient whom he injected with a new serum contrary to the orders of his superior (Petersen). The only film for which director Hochbaum is remembered is a vivid and eerie depiction of a psychotic state, realized through Expressionistic devices reminiscent of *The Cabinet Of Dr Caligari* (1919).

Eternal Return, The see Love Eternal

Eternel Retour, L' see Love Eternal

Étoile Du Nord, L' see Northern Star, The

Europa 51
(US: The Greatest Love)

Italy 1952 118 mins bw
Ponti/De Laurentiis/Lux

d **Roberto Rossellini**
sc **Roberto Rossellini, Sandro De Leo, Mario Pannunzio, Ivo Perilli, Brunello Rondi**
ph **Aldo Tonti**
m **Renzo Rossellini**
Ingrid Bergman, Alexander Knox, Giulietta Masina, Ettore Giannini

A frivolous American society woman living in Rome causes the death of her son. She seeks redemption by giving her life up to helping the underprivileged, but is certified insane. The second collaboration between Bergman and her director husband was an improvement on the first, *Stromboli* (1950), mainly because she was more at ease among professional actors. Although equally as naive and melodramatic as its predecessor, the film carries through it a genuine feeling of spirituality, especially from the moment Bergman's face in shadow comes into the light when she sees the hope of salvation.

Even Dwarfs Started Small
Auch Zwerge Haben Klein Angefangen

W. Germany 1970 96 mins bw
Herzog

d **Werner Herzog**
sc **Werner Herzog**
ph **Thomas Mauch**
m **Florian Fricke, Spanish folk music**
Helmut Döring, Gerd Gickel, Paul Glauer, Gisela Hertwig

A group of dwarfs living in a penal institution on a bleak island take advantage of the Prison Governor's absence to indulge in an escalating series of acts of rebellion and destruction. Already taking giant strides down the unbeaten track in his second feature, Herzog cast dwarfs in all the roles. Although it produced the desired bizarre and blackly comic effect, the film is too systematic and forced to provide a distorted mirror-image of society. At least it gave more roles to 'small people' than even *The Wizard Of Oz*, and was happily free from any pity or easy solutions.

Evening Dress
Tenue De Soirée

France 1986 85 mins col
Hachette Première/DD Productions/Ciné Valse

d **Bertrand Blier**
sc **Bertrand Blier**
ph **Jean Penzer**
m **Serge Gainsbourg**
Gérard Depardieu, Michel Blanc, Miou-Miou, Michel Creton, Mylène Demongeot

A macho homosexual criminal (Depardieu) accosts a couple in a bar one night and persuades them into burglary and a *ménage-à-trois*, but he turns out to have designs on the nondescript little husband rather than the gorgeous wife, with surprising consequences. Blier's predilection to shock is here let loose on an outrageous black comedy which up-ends conventional *bourgeois* notions of morality. Depardieu is superb, but it is Michel

Blanc's conversion into a camp queen that is the highlight of the fun.

Best Actor (Michel Blanc) Cannes 1986

Every Man For Himself see Slow Motion

Every Man For Himself And God Against All see Enigma Of Kaspar Hauser, The

---

Everything For Sale

Wszystko Na Sprzedaz

Poland 1968 105 mins bw
Film Polski

d **Andrzej Wajda**
sc **Andrzej Wajda**
ph **Witold Sobociński**
m **Andrzej Korzyński**
Andrzej Lapícki, Beata Tyszkiewicz, Daniel Olbrychski, Elzbieta Czyżewska

During the making of a film the leading man, who leads a complicated personal and professional life, is killed while trying to jump on to a moving train. In 1967, aged 40, the short-sighted actor Zbigniew Cybulski, who starred several times for Wajda, died in the manner depicted in this ambiguous and earnest tribute, although his name is never mentioned here. The less charismatic Olbrychski plays the actor, and Lapicki is good as the Wajda surrogate.

Everything's Ready Nothing Works see All Screwed Up

Eve Wants To Sleep

Ewa Chce Spac

Poland 1957 98 mins bw
Syrena Film Unit/Film Polski

d **Tadeusz Chmielewski**
sc **Tadeusz Chmielewski, Andrzej Czekalski**
ph **Stefan Matyjaszkiewicz, Josef Stawiski**
m **Henryk Czyz**
Barbara Lass, Stanislaw Mikulski, Ludwik Benoit, Zygmunt Zintel

Sixteen-year-old Eve (Lass) arrives at technical school a day too soon and, in her attempts to find somewhere to sleep, encounters thieves and police helping each other plan a jewel robbery. A crazy comedy, in which even the film crew gets involved in the end, blew like a gust of fresh air from Poland in the late 1950s.

Evil Eden

La Mort En Ce Jardin

aka La Muerte En Esta Jardin

France/Mexico 1956 105 mins col
Dismage Producciones Tepeyac

d **Luis Buñuel**
sc **Luis Alcoriza, Luis Buñuel, Raymond Queneau, Gabriel Arout**
ph **Jorge Stahl Jr**
m **Paul Misraki**
Georges Marchal, Simone Signoret, Charles Vanel, Michel Piccoli, Michèle Girardon, Tito Junco

When anti-military rebellion erupts in a remote Central American tin- mining settlement, a group of French people led by Chark (Marchal), an escaped prisoner, make for Brazil via the river. The party consists of the town prostitute (Signoret), a compromised priest (Piccoli), an old innkeeper (Vanel) who goes mad, and the latter's deaf-mute daughter (Girardon). Forced to abandon their boat, the fugitives trek through the jungle, enduring all manner of hardship and deprivation. This is a straightforward adventure yarn, indeed, a potboiler, populated by a colourful mix of goodies and baddies, but Buñuel's familiar targets—greed and hypocrisy—are still in evidence. The cast doesn't quite live up to its promise, but the film boasts richly textured photography and lighting which make the locations tangibly real.

Ewa Chce Spac see Eve Wants To Sleep

Ewige Maske, Die see Eternal Mask, The

The Executioner

(US: Not On Your Life)

El Verdugo

Spain 1963 110 mins bw
Naga/Zebra

d **Luis Berlanga**
sc **Luis Berlanga, Rafael Azcona, Ennio Flaiano**
ph **Tonino Delli Colli**
m **Miguel Asins Arbó**
Nino Manfredi, Emma Penella, José Isbert, José Luis Lopez Vázquez

An undertaker's assistant (Manfredi), who marries an executioner's daughter (Penella), agrees to take over his father-in-law's job but finds he can't go through with it. Despite cuts by Franco's censor, the film is not only a condemnation of capital punishment but contains social criticism spiked with gallows humour. Typical is the scene where the executioner is reluctantly dragged along to perform his macabre duty on a calm and dignified political prisoner.

The Expedition
Abhijan
India 1962 150 mins bw
Abhijatrik Calcutta

d **Satyajit Ray**
sc **Satyajit Ray**
ph **Soumendu Roy**
m **Satyajit Ray**
Soumitra Chatterjee, Waheeda Rehman, Robi Ghosh, Ruma Guha Thakurta

A taxi driver (Chatterjee) gets involved with a variety of characters including drug smugglers, white-slavers, and a prostitute. The film is closer in style and in its picaresque plot to commercial Indian cinema (it even borrows Hindi star Waheeda Rehman) than to the best of Ray's work, but there is enough of the director's humanity and humour to make it more than run of the mill.

Experiment In Evil see Testament Of Dr Cordelier, The

Extase see Ecstasy

The Exterminating Angel
El Angel Exterminador
Mexico 1962 95 mins bw
Ininci/Films 59

d **Luis Buñuel**
sc **Luis Buñuel, Luis Alcoriza**
ph **Gabriel Figueroa**
m **Alessandro Scarlatti, Paradisi, Gregorian Chants**
Silvia Pinal, Enrique Rambal, Jacqueline Andere, Claudio Brook, José Baviera, Rosa Elena Durgel

The guests at a high-society party find themselves unable to leave the room where they are gathered. As days pass without food, water or servants (who have all managed to leave), their social façade crumbles, revealing bestial qualities beneath. One of Buñuel's most effective parables is a savage attack on the *bourgeoisie*, launched in his mature blackly humorous and surreal manner. 'Basically I simply see a group of people who couldn't do what they want to . . . that kind of dilemma, the impossibility of satisfying a simple desire, often occurs in my movies.' Typical moments such as the introduction of a bear and a flock of sheep into the manor are reminders of *L'Âge D'Or.* After *Viridiana* the year before, the director himself proved he had entered his golden age.

The Extraordinary Adventures Of Mr West In The Land Of The Bolsheviks
Neobychainiye Priklucheniya Mistera Vesta V Stranya Bolshevikov
USSR 1924 2600 m bw
Goskino

d **Lev Kuleshov**
sc **N. Asseiev**
ph **A. Levitski**
m **Silent**
Porfiry Podobed, Boris Barnet, Alexandra Khokhlova, Vsevolod Pudovkin

Accompanied by Jed (Barnet), his faithful cowboy aide, Mr J. West (Podobed), president of the YMCA, leaves the USA for a tour of the Soviet Union, his head full of images of leering evil Bolsheviks. When he gets to the USSR, a petty gang exploits his prejudices, but he soon gets to know the real Russian people. Kuleshov, who wrote the first theoretical studies of montage, put his researches at the service of this gag-filled satire. Using mobile cameras, quick cutting and sequences derived from American chase films, the film manages to deride the West's stereotyped view of 'mad, savage, Russians', while creating its own stereotyped Americans—the Harold Lloyd-type Mr West, clutching an American flag, and Jed firing six-guns and roping motorcyclists like steers from the top of a Moscow taxi.

The Eyes Of The Mummy

Die Augen Der Mummie Ma

Germany 1918 55 mins bw
Projektions - AG

d **Ernst Lubitsch**
sc **Hans Kräly, Emil Rameau**
ph **Alfred Hansen**
m **Silent**
Pola Negri, Emil Jannings, Harry Liedtke, Max Laurence

A young English painter (Liedtke) rescues a girl (Negri) from an Egyptian tomb where she is being kept prisoner by a resurrected mummy (Jannings) who then pursues her to London. The first of six films that the alluring, dark-eyed, black-haired Negri made with Lubitsch in Germany, it was also the director's first important picture. Curiously, he received no credit on screen in the USA. Lubitsch used tracking shots to create horror, while Jannings was chilling in the leading role.

Eyes Without A Face

(US: The Horror Chamber Of Doctor Faustus)

Les Yeux Sans Visage

France 1959 90 mins bw
Champs Elysées/Lux

d **Georges Franju**
sc **Jean Redon**
ph **Eugen Schüfftan**
m **Maurice Jarre**
Pierre Brasseur, Alida Valli, Edith Scob, Juliette Mayniel

A plastic surgeon (Brasseur), responsible for the car crash in which his daughter (Scob) is hideously disfigured, gets his assistant (Valli) to kidnap and murder beautiful girls so that their facial tissue may be grafted on to his daughter's face. Unlike Hollywood's approach to this sort of material, Franju attempted to film this horror movie in a realistic and, above all, frightening manner, although it remains often poetic and haunting. However, it is too conscious of elevating the sordid tale and of its debts to Cocteau and early German cinema.

Fabian

W. Germany 1980 116 mins col
Regina Ziegler/UA

d **Wolf Gremm**
sc **Wolf Gremm, Hans Borgalt**
ph **Jürgen Wagner**
m **Charles Kalman**
Hans P. Hallwach, Silvia Janisch, Brigitte Mira, Hermann Lause, Ivan Desny

Although Fabian (Hallwach), who works in an advertising agency in pre-war Berlin, sees the injustices around him, he spends his nights prowling the bars, brothels and nightclubs and enjoying the easy women. Eventually, reality intrudes when a friend (Lause) commits suicide, and he finds himself in love with a woman (Janisch) who becomes a film star. We're in the familiar *Cabaret* territory of decadent Berlin in the late 1920s, but Gremm brings some new insights to his serio-comic view of the era. He also manages to recapture the look of German movies of the time, but the sex scenes are more realistic.

The Face
(US: The Magician)
Ansiktet

Sweden 1958 103 mins bw
Svensk Filmindustri

d **Ingmar Bergman**
sc **Ingmar Bergman**
ph **Gunnar Fischer**
m **Erik Nordgren**
Max Von Sydow, Ingrid Thulin, Gunnar Björnstrand, Naima Wifstrand, Åke Fridell, Bibi Andersson

Vogler (Von Sydow), a 19th-century mesmerist and magician, is stopped, with his troupe by officials at the gates of Stockholm and subjected to severe questioning in an attempt to reveal him as a fraud. A favourite Bergman theme, that of the duality of the artist, is forcefully expounded in this tragicomic Gothic study of a man, part charlatan part Messiah, which Von Sydow's mask/face expresses admirably. The character is, figuratively, a cousin to the wordless actress in *Persona* (1966), also called Vogler (Elizabeth).

Special Jury Prize Venice 1959

The Face Of Another
Tanin No Kao

Japan 1966 121 mins bw
Hiroshi Teshigahara Productions

d **Hiroshi Teshigahara**
sc **Kobo Abe**
ph **Hiroshi Segawa**
m **Tohru Takemitsu**
Tatsuya Nakadai, Machiko Kyo, Mikijiro Hira, Miki Irie

A scientist (Nakadai), whose face was disfigured in an industrial explosion, hides behind a handsome mask. In this disguise he seduces his wife (Kyo), and then accuses her of adultery. Like Teshigahara's most celebrated film, *Woman Of The Dunes*, this is an allegorical drama, also scripted by Kobo Abe from his own novel, but with a deeper interest in the psychology of the characters. Bizarre it certainly is, and a little distasteful, especially in the depiction of the parallel story of a beautiful woman (Irie, a half- Japanese model), with a hideously scarred left profile, in love with her brother. A lot of heavy significance is placed on questions of identity that remain unresolved, but it does work as a sombre study in alienation.

Face To Face
Ansikte Mot Ansikte

Sweden 1975 136 mins col
Dino De Laurentiis/Cinematograph

Fadern

d **Ingmar Bergman**
sc **Ingmar Bergman**
ph **Sven Nykvist**
m **Mozart**
Liv Ullmann, Erland Josephson, Gunnar Björnstrand, Aino Taube-Henrikson, Kari Sylwan

A psychiatrist has a nervous breakdown while staying with her grandparents when her husband and daughter are away. Originally made as a four-part series for Swedish TV, this painful, obsessive and airless psycho-drama has the doleful, expressive and lovely face of Liv Ullmann in close-up as the main field of vision. The audience often feels awkwardly excluded from the intimacy created between the Norwegian actress and the director with whom she had lived for five years.

Fadern see Father, The

Falbalas

(US: Paris Frills)
France 1945 112 mins bw
Essor

d **Jacques Becker**
sc **Jacques Becker,**
ph **Nicolas Hayer**
m **Jean-Jacques Grünewald**
Raymond Rouleau, Micheline Presle, Jean Chevrier, Gabrielle Dorziat

A top Parisian fashion designer (Rouleau), a highly successful seducer of women, falls genuinely in love with the fiancée (Presle) of a friend (Chevrier), thus triggering a situation which finally leads to tragedy. Becker's dazzling but withering look at the world of *haute couture* shows him to be a master stylist in his own right. But the characters and situations don't have the freshness and appeal typical of his next three Parisian romantic comedies, *Antoine And Antoinette* (1947), *Edward And Caroline* (1951) and *Rendezvous De Juillet* (1949).

The Falcons

Magasiskola
Hungary 1970 90 mins col
Mafilm

d **István Gaál**
sc **István Gaál**
ph **Elemér Ragályi**
m **András Szöllösy**
Ivan Andonov, György Bánffy, Judit Meszléri

A visitor (Andonov) to a falcon-training camp ruled by an iron disciplinarian (Bánffy) finally flees in horror. The film draws an impressive analogy between the taming of birds and a way of life which requires blind obedience. An atmosphere of menace is carefully built up, ending with the hero in a hostile landscape among vibrating telephone wires. A sensitive director of meagre output, Gaál gained international recognition with this picture.

The Fall

La Caida
Argentina 1958 86 mins bw
Argentine Sono

d **Leopoldo Torre-Nilsson**
sc **Beatriz Guido, Leopoldo Torre-Nilsson**
ph **Alberto Etchebehere**
m **Juan Carlos Paz**
Elsa Daniel, Duilio Marzia, Lydia Lamaison, Carlos Lopez Monet

A strictly brought-up young girl (Daniel), on the verge of womanhood, lodges with an eccentric family. Her relations with the parents, their precocious children and a young lawyer, give her a new perspective on life. Torre-Nillsson and his wife Beatriz Guido consolidated the international success of *The House Of The Angel* with a further claustrophobic exploration into Argentinian family structures, seen through the eyes of a virginal girl, played perfectly in both cases by Elsa Daniel.

The Fall

A Queda
Brazil 1978 120 mins col
Zoom Cinematográfica/Daga/Nelson Xavier

d **Ruy Guerra, Nelson Xavier**
sc **Ruy Guerra, Nelson Xavier**
ph **Edgar Moura**
m **Milton Nascimento, Ruy Guerra**
Nelson Xavier, Lima Duarte, Isabel Ribeiro, Maria Sílva, Hugo Carvana

When José (Carvana) is killed in an accident

on a building site where he worked, his friend Mario (Xavier) attempts to gain compensation for his widow (Sílva). Although the management refuses to accept responsibility, Mario, at the cost of his marriage and his job, fights on. A sequel to Guerra's acclaimed *The Guns* from which sequences are quoted, it follows the lives of three of the soldiers from the earlier film. However, during the 15 years between the two films, *Cinema Novo* had shifted its attention from the peasants to the urban working class. Guerra directs his powerful attack on Brazilian capitalism from different stylistic angles—using still photos, *cinéma vérité* techniques and genuine interviews with workers—all combining in a complex and successful aesthetic whole.

Best Film Berlin 1978

The Fall Of The House Of Usher

La Chute De La Maison Usher

France 1928 48 mins bw
Les Films Jean Epstein

d **Jean Epstein**
sc **Jean Epstein**
ph **Georges Lucas, J.A. Lucas**
m **Silent**

Marguerite Gance, Jean Debucourt, Charles Lamy, Pierre Hot, Halma

Roderick Usher (Debucourt) buries his sister (Gance) alive in the large family mansion, but she returns after death to take her revenge. Coming out of the French *avant-garde* movement, Epstein recreated the eerie lyricism of the Edgar Allan Poe story by the device of slow motion (one of the first times the technique was used in a fictional film) and surreal sets. Despite a certain over-stylization, there is much impressive imagery—long, windswept corridors, the mist-shrouded trees, the burial with four men carrying a white coffin—and the macabre features of Marguerite Gance (wife of Abel Gance) as the *revenant.* Luis Buñuel was the assistant director.

Falsche Bewegung see Wrong Movement

Fall Jägerstätter, Der see Refusal, The

Fälschung, Die see Circle Of Deceit

Family Diary

Cronaca Familiare

Italy 1962 122 mins col
Titanus/Metro

d **Valerio Zurlini**
sc **Valerio Zurlini, Mario Missiroli**
ph **Giuseppe Rotunno**
m **Goffredo Petrassi**

Marcello Mastroianni, Jacques Perrin, Salvo Randone, Sylvie, Valeria Ciangottini

When his younger brother Lorenzo (Perrin) dies from an untreatable disease, Enrico (Mastroianni) is grief-stricken. He leaves the newspaper office where he works to sit in his lodgings and reflect on Lorenzo's short and unhappy life, the circumstances which separated them in childhood, and those that later brought them together in a close and loving relationship in which he tried to act as protector. This leisurely, elegaic and intolerably sad film, played with sensitivity and absolute conviction, is directed with well-gauged fidelity to the semi-autobiographical novel by Vasco Pratolini on which it is based. Zurlini is a superb visual artist, and he evokes feelings, events and atmosphere by use of an Impressionist- painter style to moving and memorable effect, displaying a subtle eye for the significance of small moments.

Family Game

Kazoku Geemu

Japan 1983 107 mins col
ATG/New Century Producers/Nikkatsu

d **Yoshimitsu Morita**
sc **Yoshimitsu Morita**
ph **Yonezo Maeda**

Yusaku Matsuda, Ichirota Miyagawa, Junichi Tsujita, Juzo Itami, Saori Yuki

The Numatas are the perfect Japanese nuclear family: submissive wife, hardworking, self-important husband who drinks too much and limits his communication with his two boys to anxiety over their school marks. When yet another in a long line of tutors is hired to coach the bored and recalcitrant younger son, the outcome is surprising. This absurdist satire—a funny, intriguing, ambiguous critique of the aspirations and lifestyle of modern industrial society—is set largely inside the family's high rise apartment with its panoramic view of factories. Morita, a leading director of what is loosely termed the New Japanese cinema, owes a clear debt to the old: clean, crystalline images are framed with a formalism and breathtaking sense of composition somewhat reminiscent of Ozu, but his sense of the ridiculous is very much his own. Alas, the latter tends to the coarse-grained and lets him down in the undisciplined closing sequences of a beautifully played movie that is full of unexpected tenderness.

Family Life

Zycie Rodzinne

Poland 1971 93 mins col
Tor Unit Film Polski

d **Krzysztof Zanussi**
sc **Krzysztof Zanussi**
ph **Witold Sobociński**
m **Wojciech Kilar**
Daniel Olbrychski, Jan Nowicki, Jan Kreczmar, Maja Komorowska, Halina Mikolajska

After six years in Warsaw, a design engineer (Olbrychski) reluctantly returns to his family home, a dilapidated mansion in the country. There he has to come to terms with his alcoholic father and slightly deranged sister, as well as with his own life. Zanussi's second film is more traditional than his first, *The Structure Of Crystals*, although it has the same questioning intelligence. A controlled, melancholy mood piece, sustained by good acting and careful lighting, it is lacking in emotion.

The Fanatics

Les Fanatiques

France 1957 92 mins bw
Cinégraph/Coopérative Générale Du Cinéma/Les Films Régent

d **Alex Joffé**
sc **Alex Joffé, Jean Levitte**
ph **L.H. Burel**
m **Paul Misraki**
Pierre Fresnay, Michel Auclair, Grégoire Aslan, Françoise Fabian, Tilda Thamar

A political hit-man (Fresnay) is detailed to blow up the private plane carrying a South American dictator (Aslan) home from France. When, at the eleventh hour, the General changes his flight to a regular airline carrying 50 other passengers, the hit-man's assistant (Auclair) balks at carrying out the assassination. This French approach to the kind of high-tension thriller popular in Hollywood was made with formula expertise and acted, notably by Fresnay, with cold, mechanical efficiency. Although offering some excitement, the film was already rather old hat by the time of its release abroad in 1960. Today, in the age of the hijack, it is more interesting, with its moral argument about the killing of innocent civilians no longer the preserve of commercial film-makers.

Fanatiques, Les see Fanatics, The

Fanfan La Tulipe see Fanfan The Tulip

Fanfan The Tulip

Fanfan La Tulipe

France 1951 104 mins bw
Filmsonor/Les Films Ariane/Amato

d **Christian-Jaque**
sc **René Wheeler, Jean Fallet**
ph **Christian Matras**
m **Georges Van Parys, Maurice Thiriet**
Gérard Philipe, Gina Lollobrigida, Noël Roquevert, Marcel Herrand, Geneviève Page

Fanfan (Philipe), a soldier in the army of Louis XV, rescues the king's daughter (Lollobrigida) from coach robbers, defeats the Austrian army single-handed and returns to win the princess's hand. The last of three films made by the dashing Philipe for Christian-Jaque, it merrily swashbuckled its way into the international hit category. However, some of the comedy is a little too self-consciously facetious.

Best Director Cannes 1952

Fängelse see Devil's Wanton, The

Fangschuss, Der see Coup De Grâce

Fanny

France 1932 128 mins bw
Marcel Pagnol/Braunberger-Richebe

d **Marc Allégret**
sc **Marcel Pagnol**
ph **Nicolas Toporkoff**
m **Vincent Scotto**
Raimu, Orane Demazis, Pierre Fresnay, Charpin, Alida Rouffe, Robert Vattier

Fanny (Demazis), expecting the child of Marius (Fresnay) who left her to go to sea, marries Panisse (Charpin), an elderly widower. When Marius returns, his father César (Raimu) persuades him to renounce any claim on the child. The second and best-directed of the so-called *Pagnol Trilogy* picks up exactly where *Marius* ended, retaining the latter's vitality, warm humour and depth of character. The performances (excepting the pudding-faced Demazis, Pagnol's then wife) are a joy to behold—witness Raimu's feigned indifference at not hearing from his son—and Pagnol's dialogue displays supreme comic skill. The film's success enabled him to build his own studio near Marseilles.

Fanny And Alexander

Fanny Och Alexander

Sweden 1982 188 mins col
AB Cinematograph/Svensk Filminstituten/Swedish TV One/Gaumont

d **Ingmar Bergman**
sc **Ingmar Bergman**
ph **Sven Nykvist**
m **Daniel Bell**
Gunn Wallgren, Börje Ahlstedt, Christina Schollin, Bertil Guve, Pernilla Alwin, Gunnar Björnstrand, Jan Malmsjö, Ewa Froeling, Erland Josephson, Harriet Andersson

The well-to-do, loving and ebullient Ekdahl family gathers to celebrate Christmas. After the actor-father of 10-year-old Alexander (Guve) and eight-year-old Fanny (Alwin) dies, their mother marries a sadistic minister whose cruelty leads Grandmother Ekdahl's Jewish friend and lover to rescue them. Happiness and balance is restored as new babies are born and the family gathers once more to celebrate. Bergman's most optimistic film creates pure enchantment as comedy, tragedy, romance, realism and fantasy blend into a perfect evocation of childhood, place and period (turn-of-the-century Sweden), caught in glowing images by Sven Nykvist. Announced as Bergman's final film, it offers a superlative culmination of his 37 years as one of the cinema's greatest artists.

Best Foreign Film Oscar 1983

Fanny Och Alexander see Fanny And Alexander

The Fantastic Night

La Nuit Fantastique

France 1942 89 mins bw
U.T.C.

d **Marcel L'Herbier**
sc **Louis Chavance**
ph **Pierre Montazel**
m **Maurice Thiriet**
Fernand Gravey, Micheline Presle, Saturnin Fabre, Charles Granval

A student (Gravey), who works as a night porter, continually dreams of a mysterious woman in white (Presle). When he meets her in reality, he finds she has a father (Fabre) and a fiancé (Granval), both of them unpleasant. He and the woman have a series of fantastic adventures, so that he is still not sure whether he's dreaming or not. The most widely-known of L'Herbier's sound films is a comedy-fantasy tinged with pessimism. Although restricted by certain conventions of commercial French cinema, the former *avant-garde* director created a palpable enough dream world for the audience to identify with the dreamer-hero.

Fantômas

France 1913 75 mins bw
Gaumont

d **Louis Feuillade**
sc **Louis Feuillade**
ph **Guérin**
m **Silent**
René Navarre, Bréon, Georges Melchior, Renée Carl, Jane Faber

Fantômas (Navarre), arch-criminal and master of disguise, continues to defeat Inspector Juve (Bréon) and ace-reporter Fandor (Melchior). Feuillade's first great success was a serial in three episodes based on an extremely popular series of detective novels by Pierre Souvestre and Marcel Allain. While they are unread (and unreadable) today, the film, with its chases, robberies, and kidnappings, brilliantly mixing real locations with studio settings, can still be enjoyed. The director's genius for location is best seen in the shoot-out on the Quai De Bercy between Fantômas and Juve, using wine barrels as shields. Feuillade went on to make four further Fantômas serials, and the character has been revived in later films.

Fantômas

France 1964 105 mins col
P.A.C./S.N.E.G.(Paris)/P.C.M.(Rome)

d **André Hunebelle**
sc **Jean Halain, Pierre Foucaud**
ph **Marcel Grignon**
m **Michel Magne**
Jean Marais, Louis De Funès, Mylène Demongeot, Marie-Hélène Arnaud, Robert Dalban

Fandor, a journalist, invents a sensational interview with the infamous criminal Fantômas and publishes it as the real thing. A displeased Fantômas kidnaps the newspaperman, demanding a follow-up article telling the truth but, on his release, Fandor is held for police questioning. His editor writes another hoax piece and Fandor is again seized by Fantômas. This ham-fisted dreary and feeble film is a travesty of Feuillade's famous silent serial. There are one or two striking set-pieces and the short-lived novelty of Jean Marais essaying a double role as journalist and villain, but De Funès' hammy performance as the police inspector is dreadful and, as the film is often released with excrutiating dubbing, it is best avoided.

Fantôme De La Liberté, Le see Phantom Of Liberty, The

Fantômes Du Chapelier, Les see Hatter's Ghosts, The

Faraon see Pharaoh

Farceur, Le see Joker, The

Farewell
Abschied

Germany 1930 71 mins bw
UFA

d **Robert Siodmak**
sc **Emeric Pressburger, Irma Von Cube**
ph **Eugen Schüfftan**
m **Erwin Bootz**
Aribert Mog, Brigitte Horney, Vladimir Sokoloff, Emilia Unda, Konstantin Mic

Life in a boarding house in West Berlin populated by a range of characters, including a ruined baron (Sokoloff), a skirt-chasing Russian emigré (Mic), a young salesman (Mog) and the girlfriend (Horney) he must leave. After his debut co-directing the silent *People On Sunday*, Siodmak made his first solo feature, a kind of anti-*Grand Hotel* comedy-drama. The film's imaginative manipulation of sound, the fluent use of the enclosed area of the *pension*, and the vivid character sketches, launched the director into his often neglected but excellent German period (necessarily brief, thanks to Hitler).

Farewell
Proshchanie

USSR 1981 126 mins col
Mosfilm

d **Elem Klimov**
sc **Larisa Shepitko, Rudolf Tyurin, German Klimov**
ph **Alexei Rodionov, Yuri Skhirtladze, Sergei Taraskin**
m **V. Artyomov, A. Shnitke**
Stefaniya Stayuta, Lev Durov, Alexei Petrenko, Leonid Kryuk, Vadim Yakovenko

An old village in Siberia is to be destroyed and its peasant community, locked into ancient ritual, resettled in a development of faceless apartment blocks. Darya (Stayuta) opposes the move, preferring to die rather than acquiesce, while her son works as foreman of the operation. The whole period, from the announcement of the scheme to its completion, is covered, presenting a conflict between the old order and the new, and a record of the price that has to be paid for progress. Klimov's film unfolds in a controlled, schematic style, focusing on the landscape as the centre of its debate. The result is a finely composed work which reflects a dilemma only too familiar in the West. Larisa Shepitko, Klimov's wife, was to direct *Farewell*, but was killed in a motor smash in 1980.

The Farewell

Jaahyvaiset

Finland 1982 90 mins col
Oy Mainos TV Raklam/Swedish Film Institute/Sveriges TV2

d **Tuija-Maija Niskanen**
sc **Eija-Elina Bergholm**
ph **Esa Vuorinen, Lasse Karlsson**
Carl-Axel Heiknert, Sanna Hultman, Pirkko Nurmi, Kerstin Tidelius, Gunnar Björnstrand

A child grows to womanhood in an upper-class family at the time of World War II, and clashes with her stern father over many matters, including her right to live as a Lesbian. This first feature by one of Finland's few women directors, succeeds in creating a claustrophobic atmosphere by confining most of the action to the old family mansion. However, though the psychology of the heroine is well explored, the theme is familiar from many other films about oppressive Scandinavian families.

Far From Vietnam

Loin De Vietnam

France 1967 115 mins bw/col
SLON

d **Jacques Demy, Jean-Luc Godard, Claude Lelouch, Alain Resnais, Joris Ivens, Agnès Varda, Chris Marker, William Klein, Ruy Guerra**
sc **Over 38 writers,**
ph **photographers,**
m **musicians,**
and performers in a co-operative effort

Thirteen reflections on the war in Vietnam, including newsreel shots of American bombing, demonstrations in the USA, a speech by Fidel Castro, a North Vietnamese travelling theatre, an anti-war song from folk-singer Tom Paxton, and Jean-Luc Godard behind a 35 mm camera explaining why he found it impossible to make a film on Vietnam. The question he asks is 'What possible help can a film-maker contribute to the Vietnamese struggle?' The rest of the film tries to answer it in various ways, some more satisfactorily than others. Alain Resnais and his writer Jacques Sternberg offer another interesting self-enquiry by showing an intellectual trying to justify his reluctance to take a moral stand on the war. On the whole, it was a timely propaganda piece, financed by Chris Marker's SLON independent company. It may still have lessons for us today.

Fårö—Dokument 1979 see Fårö 1979

Fårö 1979

Fårö—Dokument 1979

Sweden 1979 103 mins col
Cinematograph

d **Ingmar Bergman**
sc **Ingmar Bergman**
ph **Arne Carlsson**
m **Svante Pettersson, Sigvard Huldt, Dag and Lena, Ingmar Nordströms, Strix Q, Rock De Luxe, Ola And The Janglers**
Richard Östman, Ulla Silvergren, Annelie Nyström, Per Broman, Irene Broman

Ingmar Bergman (off-camera) conducts a series of interviews with the inhabitants of the small Baltic island of Fårö where he lives and where he has set a number of his films. Ten years earlier, Bergman had made *The Fårö Document*, when he felt the central government was killing the life and traditions of the island. Many of the same people he spoke to a decade earlier talk eloquently about the place, and Bergman narrates and watches them go about their work, which includes the gruesome slaughter of a pig. It makes for a fascinating, affectionate and rather melancholy home movie by one of the world's greatest directors.

Farrebique

France 1947 85 mins bw
L'Écran Français/Les Films Etienne Lallier

Fast And Sexy

d **Georges Rouquier**
sc **Georges Rouquier**
ph **André Dantan**
m **Henri Sauguet**

The life of a peasant family in a remote area of South-west France from December 1944 to November 1945, including the struggles in work, the harvesting, an engagement, a death, and baking of bread. Rouquier's first feature was made in his native Massif Central, using a family known to him. This personal involvement, the affectionate and detailed rendering of the people's lives and the lyricism of the cutting and camerawork make it one of the finest of documentaries. The stunning time-lapse photography on the coming of spring was actually shot by Daniel Sarrade and Maurice Delille in the Jardin Des Plantes in Paris.

Fast And Sexy see Anna Of Brooklyn

Fast, Fast see Deprisa, Deprisa

Fate Of A Man see Destiny Of A Man

Father
Apa
Hungary 1966 95 mins bw
Hungarofilm/Mafilm Studio 3

d **István Szabó**
sc **István Szabó**
ph **Sándor Sára**
m **János Gonda, Mahler**
András Bálint, Miklós Gábor, Kati Solyom, Klari Tolnay, Dani Erdélyi

A growing boy (Bálint) attempts to come to terms with truths about his dead father (Gábor) whom he remembers only as a hero who helped the Jews during the war. He has a Jewish girlfriend (Solyom) and, after the 1956 uprising, they both begin to question their parents' generation. Szabó's second film, told in a technically assured fragmentary style, explores a subject that forms the basis for most of his work—the relationship of Hungary's post-war generation to the past. Here it is symbolized by a sensitively and humorously observed personal history, acted with great conviction, especially by Bálint.

The Father
Fadern
Sweden 1969 100 mins col
Svenska Filminstitutet

d **Alf Sjöberg**
sc **Alf Sjöberg**
ph **Lars Björne**
m **Torbjörn Lundquist**
Georg Rydeberg, Gunnel Lindblom, Lena Nyman, Jan-Olaf Strandberg, Tord Stal

A retired army captain (Rydeberg) and his wife (Lindblom) continually fight over Berta (Nyman), their beloved daughter. Because the father plans for Berta to board out, and the mother is determined to keep her at home, the latter schemes to destroy her husband mentally. 'The border between theatre and film is as flexible as the people in Strindberg's work—there is no set form saying how a film should be made. *In absurdum*—everything in film is really theatre.' So said Sjöberg about the transposition of his acclaimed Royal Dramatic Theatre of Stockholm production to the screen, using the same cast. It was managed without much loss or any real gain. What we have been given is the chance to see some wonderful acting in Strindberg's powerful play, in its original language, directed by a specialist in his work. Sjöberg's most famous film remains the excellent *Miss Julie* (1950).

Father And Son
Fuzi Qing
Hong Kong 1981 96 mins col
Feng Huang Motion Picture Company

d **Allen Fong (aka Fong Yuk-Ping)**
sc **Chan Chiu, Lee Bik-Wah, Cheung Kin-Ting**
ph **Patrick Wong**
m **Violet Lam**
Shek Lui, Lee Yu-Tin, Cheng Yu-Or, Chan Sung, Yan Sin-Mei, Cheung Kwok-Ming, Kung Yee

After graduating with a degree in film in America, Law Ka-Hing (Yu-Or) returns to Hong Kong for his father's funeral. He reflects on his childhood and adolescence in a hillside shanty town, pursuing a fantasy world through comic books, magic lantern shows and attempts to make home movies—all of which causes conflict with his father and leads him into trouble at school. This first independent feature from a Hong Kong television director is clearly an autobiographical piece, reflecting the struggles of a would-be film-maker and confirmed fantasist to realize his ambitions in the face of his father's desire to push him into more traditional pursuits. Fong draws a vivid picture of the squalid environment and depicts the complex father-son relationship with truth. This is an entertaining film and refreshing in its departure from the all-pervasive martial arts genre from Hong Kong.

Father Master see Padre Padrone

Fatti Di Gente Perbene see Drama Of The Rich

Faust

Germany 1926 136 mins bw
UFA

d **F. W. Murnau**
sc **Hans Kyser**
ph **Carl Hoffmann**
m **Silent**
Gösta Ekman, Emil Jannings, Camilla Horn, Wilhelm Dieterle, Yvette Guilbert

Faust (Ekman), an elderly professor, sells his soul to the devil in exchange for a return to his youth. Murnau's last film in Germany prior to going to Hollywood was a lavish studio production, with the masterly sets, constructed by the leading German designers Robert Herlth and Walter Röhrig, related to the camera set-ups to avoid any staginess. The chiaroscuro, the imagery derived from Romantic painters such as Caspar David Friedrich, and the magical photography, all cast a spell. There are imposing performances too from Ekman, Jannings (Mephistopholes), and Horn (Marguerite) in a part intended for Lillian Gish.

Faustrecht Der Freiheit see Fox

Faute De L'Abbé Mouret, La see Sin Of Father Mouret, The

Favoris De La Lune, Les see Favourites Of The Moon

Favourites Of The Moon

Les Favoris De La Lune

France 1984 101 mins col
Philippe Dussart Co/FR3/Ministère De La Culture/RAI TV

d **Otar Iosseliani**
sc **Otar Iosseliani, Gérard Brach**
ph **Philippe Theaudière**
m **Nicolas Zourabichvili**
Katja Rupé, Jean-Pierre Beauviala, Christiane Bailly, Mathieu Amalric, Alix De Montaigu, Pascal Aubier

The separate paths of dozens of Parisian thieves constantly criss-cross as money, paintings and *objets d'art* are passed from one to another. For a good while the film seems to be a series of incoherent incidents concerning inexplicable characters. But Iosselliani, a Georgian in Paris, has a scheme which becomes clearer if not more involving. What the kaleidoscopic method reveals is the greed and emptiness of Western *bourgeois* society. The tiny details begin to add up, but the camera never lingers long enough for us to get to know any of the characters, mostly played by the director's friends. There are rewards, but they are few and far between.

Special Jury Prize Venice 1984

Fear

Angst

aka La Paura

W. Germany-Italy 1954 91 mins bw
Minerva/Ariston/Aniene

d **Roberto Rossellini**
sc **Roberto Rossellini, Sergio Amedei, Franz Graf Treuberg**
ph **Peter Heller**
m **Renzo Rossellini**
Ingrid Bergman, Mathias Wieman, Kurt Kreuger, Elsie Aulinger

The wife of a German factory owner is blackmailed by the mistress of the man she had an affair with while her husband was in a POW camp. The final film Rossellini made with his then-wife Bergman was an unwieldy psychological thriller about a marriage in crisis, the theme of four of their six uneven collaborations. (The Rossellinis' own marriage was nearing its end.) Based on a story by Stefan Zweig, the picture displayed many of the faults and the virtues of that curious teaming of Hollywood Swede with Neo-Realist Italian.

Fear Eats The Soul

(US: Ali: Fear Eats The Soul
aka Ali)

Angst Essen Seele Auf

W. Germany 1973 94 mins col
Tango Film

d **Rainer Werner Fassbinder**
sc **Rainer Werner Fassbinder**
ph **Jürgen Jürges**
m **Selections from archive material**
Brigitte Mira, El Hedi Ben Salem, Barbara Valentin, Irm Hermann, Peter Gauhe, Rainer Werner Fassbinder

Emmi (Mira), a lonely, widowed charlady, strikes up a friendship with Ali (Ben Salem), a Moroccan mechanic who is equally lonely and half her age. Their relationship meets with outraged disapproval and hostility, particularly when they marry. A serious and realistic articulation of its milieu, this film explores racism (and other prejudices), doing so through a fairly straightforward use of narrative, modelled on Hollywood melodramas of the 1950s, particularly Douglas Sirk's *All That Heaven Allows.*

Feine Gesellschaft Beschränkte Haftung see High Society Limited

---

Fellini Casanova see Casanova

Fellini Satyricon

aka Satyricon

Italy 1969 129 mins col
PAA/UA/PEA

d **Federico Fellini**
sc **Federico Fellini, Bernadino Zapponi, Brunello Rondi**
ph **Giuseppe Rotunno**
m **Nino Rota, Ilhan Mimaroglu, Tod Dockstader, Andrew Rudin**
Martin Potter, Hiram Keller, Max Börn, Capucine, Magali Noël, Alain Cuny, Salvo Randone, Lucia Bosé, Tanya Lopert

In Rome *circa* 500 AD, two students (Potter and Keller) go their different ways after fighting over a pretty boy (Börn). They have many adventures before meeting up again, some of which include a drunken orgy, imprisonment on a galley ship and a duel with the Minotaur. This adaptation of Petronius' witty fragment is overblown and over-indulgent, but with one or two moments of the director at his grotesque best. It is really *La Dolce Vita* in Ancient Rome with Fellini looking ponderously and with assumed disapproval at the immoral goings-on of a pre-Christian society (and by implication today's), and the 'spiritual' episode is not far from Cecil B. DeMille territory.

Fellini's Roma

aka Roma

Italy 1972 128 mins col
Ultra/UA

d **Federico Fellini**
sc **Federico Fellini**
ph **Giuseppe Rotunno**
m **Nino Rota**
Peter Gonzales, Stefano Majore, Britta Barnes, Pia De Doses, Fiona Florence, Renato Giovannoli, Federico Fellini, Gore Vidal

Fellini, making a documentary on Rome, recalls his arrival in the city in his early twenties, the seedy pre-war music halls and the brothels. In present day Rome there is a gigantic traffic jam, the discovery of ancient Roman murals underground and an ecumenical fashion show. On the same lines as *The Clowns, Amarcord,* and *Intervista*, this blend of fantasy, autobiography and documentary is orchestrated by Fellini into a 'nostalgic carefree diary,' as the *maestro* called it. Some of the brew gives off a bad odour, but there are many delicious moments such as the young man's first night in Rome (a splendid bustling set), the very funny music hall scene, the traffic jam (mostly filmed at Cinecittá) and the last screen appearance of Anna Magnani, caught unawares late at night.

Female Prisoner, The see Woman In Chains

Femme D'Á Côté, La see Woman Next Door, The

Femme De L'Aviateur, La see Aviator's Wife, The

Femme De Mon Pote, La see My Best Friend's Girl

La Femme De Nulle Part

aka The Woman From Nowhere

France 1922 70 mins bw
Cosmograph

d **Louis Delluc**
sc **Louis Delluc**
ph **Alphonse Gibory, Georges Lucas**
m **Silent**
Eve Francis, Roger Karl, Michel Duran, Gine Avril, André Daven

A woman (Francis), who sacrificed everything for love, returns to the house from which she had fled with her lover years before. An air of disillusionment pervades the penultimate of Delluc's few films (he died of tuberculosis, aged 33, in 1924), a fantasy expertly intermingling memory and sensations. Eve Francis, the director's wife, gives a poignant portrayal in the title role. The Prix Louis Delluc (instigated in 1937) is awarded annually to the best French film of the year.

Femme Douce, Une see Gentle Creature, A

Femme Du Boulanger, La see Baker's Wife, The

Femme Est Une Femme, Une see Woman Is A Woman, A

La Femme Infidèle

aka The Unfaithful Wife

France 1968 98 mins col
Films De La Boétie/Cinégai

d **Claude Chabrol**
sc **Claude Chabrol**
ph **Jean Rabier**
m **Pierre Jansen**
Stéphane Audran, Michel Bouquet, Maurice Ronet, Stephen Di Napolo, Michel Duchaussoy

A respectable middle-class husband (Bouquet), complacently happy in his marriage, discovers that his wife (Audran) has been having an affair with another man (Ronet). He confronts the lover, suddenly strikes him dead and attempts to get rid of the body. The marriage is saved. Chabrol followed his return to form in *Les Biches* with the even superior 'Hélène cycle'—films in which his wife Audran played Hélène in variations on the theme of marital infidelity leading to murder. Here, in the first and best, his sharp scalpel is applied brilliantly to the *bourgeois* marriage. He is particularly good in showing that, although passions seethe beneath the surface, the niceties of life (such as family meals) must continue. The three performers at each corner of the triangle match the director's skill and subtlety.

Femme Mariée, Une see Married Woman, A

Femme Ou Deux, Une see Woman Or Two, A

Femmes De Paris

(US: Peek-A-Boo)

Ah! Les Belles Bacchantes

France 1954 85 mins col
Optimax/Lux

d **Jean Loubignac**
sc **Robert Dhéry**
ph **René Colas**
m **Gérard Calvi**
Robert Dhéry, Colette Brosset, Louis De Funès, Raymond Bussières, Rosine Luguet, The Bluebell Girls

Feng-Kuei-Lai-Tejen

With the arrival of a variety show in his town, Inspector Leboeuf (De Funès) goes to the rehearsals to make sure it accords with standards of decency and ends up taking part in the show. This is a more or less straightforward record of Robert Dhéry's Crazy Show, a stage hit of its time, enveloped by a tenuous plot. Neither the revue—a series of comedy sketches, performed mostly by Dhéry and his wife Brosset and spiced with plenty of 'tasteful' nude scenes—nor the narrative have enough amusing moments to commend them.

Feng-Kuei-Lai-Tejen see Boys From Fengkuei, The

Fenyes Szelek see Confrontation, The

Ferestadeh see Mission, The

Ferroviere, Il see Railroad Man, The

Fête À Henriette, La see Holiday For Henrietta

Les Fêtes Galantes

France 1965 90 mins col
S.N.E.G.(Paris)/Studio Bucuresti(Bucharest)

d **René Clair**
sc **René Clair**
ph **Christian Matras**
m **Georges Van Parys**
Jean-Pierre Cassel, Geneviève Casile, Philippe Avron, Jean Richard, György Kovács, Alfred Adam

The army of the Prince De Beaulieu (Richard) lays siege to that of the Maréchal D'Allenberg. Inside the fortress, provisions dwindle while, without, Beaulieu and his lot pass the time in gourmandizing. Joli-Coeur (Cassel), a soldier on the losing end, is sent by the Princess (Casile) to fetch her lover, and has to survive several dangerous hurdles before the siege ends. So does the viewer. Set in the 18th century and pleasing to look at, Clair's film is a knockabout farce that cocks a snook at aristocratic leadership and sympathizes with peasant soldiery. Alas, the jokes are so repetitious and overworked, the characterization so thin and the entire enterprise so heavy- handed that there's little to enjoy in what was, sadly, Clair's last film.

Feu De Paille, Le see Fire In The Straw

Le Feu Follet

aka Will O' The Wisp
aka A Time To Live And A Time To Die
(US: The Fire Within)

France 1963 121 mins bw
Nouvelles Editions/Arco

d **Louis Malle**
sc **Louis Malle**
ph **Ghislain Cloquet**
m **Erik Satie**
Maurice Ronet, Lena Skerla, Yvonne Clech, Hubert Deschamps, Jeanne Moreau, Alexandra Stewart

An alcoholic writer (Ronet) leaves a clinic determined to kill himself, but decides to find out first if any of his friends can give him a reason to change his mind. They can't and he calmly shoots himself through the heart. Commenting on the commercial failure of the critically well-received film, Malle said, 'It is such a harsh subject and it's such a depressing movie'. But this poignant, unsentimental study of a spoiled and selfish man still deserving of pity, transcends the merely depressing because of the director's perception and authority, and Ronet's superb performance. Pierre Drieu La Rochelle, the author of the 1931 novel on which the film was based, killed himself in 1945 after having collaborated with the Nazis.

Special Jury Prize Venice 1963

Feu Mathias Pascal see Late Mathias Pascal, The

Fever

Goracza

Poland 1981 122 mins col
Film Polski, Warsaw Unit

d **Agnieszka Holland**
sc **Krzysztof Teodor Toeplitz**
ph **Jacek Petrycki**
m **Jan Kanty Pawluskiewicz**
Olgierd Lukaszewicz, Barbara Grabowska, Adam Ferency, Tomasz Miedzik, Boguslaw Linda, Ryszard Sobolewski

In 1905, Poland is a troubled country, partitioned between Tsarist Russia, Germany and the Hapsburg Empire. The Russian sector suffers most from oppression, and it is there that a group of anarchists manufactures a bomb and plots to assassinate the Tsar's governor. This is Polish film-making at its best, with a strong and well-controlled narrative line, first-class photography and acting, and a sensitive, in-depth script that subtly reveals the motives and the temperaments of the individual anarchists as the bomb is passed from one to the other. Leon (Lukaszewicz), son of a rich industrialist, is the cold and objective leader; Kielza (Ferency), a simple peasant, is easily betrayed; Kama (Grabowska), the only woman, suffers a breakdown after she fails to carry out the assassination and ends up insane. A salutary political drama, it engenders the tension of a gripping thriller.

Best Actress (Barbara Grabowska) Berlin 1981

Fiancée Du Pirate, La see Dirty Mary

Fiancés, The see Engagement, The

Fidanzati, I see Engagement, The

Fiends, The see Diaboliques, Les

Fièvre Monte À El Pao, La see Republic Of Sin

Fifi La Plume

France 1964 80 mins bw
Les Films Montsouris

d **Albert Lamorisse**
sc **Albert Lamorisse**
ph **Pierre Petit, Maurice Fellous**
m **Jean-Michel Defaye**
Philippe Avron, Mireille Nègre, Henri Lambert, Raoul Delfosse, Michel De Ré

Fifi (Avron), a burglar specializing in the theft of clocks and watches, escapes from a raid into a circus arena. One thing leads to another, with Fifi becoming the circus birdman and discovering that he can actually fly. He does, across France, before settling down in Brittany with the pretty bareback rider (Nègre). Albert (*Red Balloon*) Lamorisse takes to the skies again with a piece of whimsy that offers some imaginative comic touches and a certain charm. However, the enterprise is too artificial, too sprawling and too unsure of its purpose to hold much appeal for adults.

The Fifth Horseman Is Fear

... A Paty Jezdec Je Strach

Czechoslovakia 1965 100 mins bw
Barrandov Film Studio

d **Zbyněk Brynych**
sc **Zbyněk Brynych, Jan Kališ, Milan Nejedlý, Ester Krumbachová, Ota Koval**
ph **Jan Kališ**
m **Jiří Sternwald**
Miroslav Macháček, Olga Scheinpflugová, Ilja Prachař, Josef Vinklář

During the Nazi occupation of Czechoslovakia, the Jewish Dr Braun (Macháček) is asked to remove a bullet from a wounded Resistance fighter. After the operation, he begins a nightmarish search for morphine through the streets of Prague. Begun as a realistic portrait of the life of Czech Jews under the Nazis, the script was reconceived (by Krumbachová) as an expressionist Orwellian fable that transcended the specific (there are some shots of contemporary Prague). The ominous atmosphere is created by acute camera angles, shock editing and harsh lighting, in contrast to the understated nature of the performances. It is an impressive attempt to show, in the director's words, that 'Fascism is an international disease capable of emerging in many contexts'.

Fille Aux Yeux D'Or, La see Girl With The Golden Eyes, The

Fille Du Puisatier, La see Well-Digger's Daughter, The

Film D'Amore E D'Anarchia see Love And Anarchy

Film Ohne Titel see Film Without A Title

Film Without A Name see Film Without A Title

Film Without A Title

(US: Film Without A Name)

Film Ohne Titel

W. Germany 1947 100 mins bw
Camera Film

d **Rudolf Jügert**
sc **Helmut Käutner, Ellen Fechner, Rudolf Jügert**
ph **Igor Oberberg**
m **Bernard Eichhorn**
Hans Söhnker, Hildegard Knef, Irene Von Meyendorff, Willy Fritsch, Fritz Odemar

A screenwriter (Odemar) and an actor (Fritsch) imagine a story of an employer (Söhnker) who falls in love with his maid (Knef), told from different points of view and with alternative endings. One of the very first post-war German film exports was an expertly witty piece, not only on human relationships but on the problems of making a comedy in that war-torn country. These problems were not solved in the German cinema for many years.

Fimpen see Stubby

Final Accord see Final Chord

Final Chord

(US: Final Accord)

Schlussakkord

Germany 1936 100 mins bw
UFA

d **Detlef Sierck**
sc **Kurt Heuser, Detlef Sierck**
ph **Robert Baberske**
m **Kurt Schröder, excerpts from Beethoven, Handel, Tchaikovsky**
Willy Birgel, Lil Dagover, Maria Von Tasnady, Theodor Loos, Maria Koppenhöfer, Albert Lippert, Kurt Meisel

When her husband, an embezzler who fled to New York, commits suicide, Hanna (Von Tasnady) returns to Germany to find her small son. The boy is now in the care of an orchestral conductor (Birgel) and his faithless wife Charlotte (Dagover), who is locked into an affair with a villainous clairvoyant (Lippert). Hanna takes a job as governess to her son and, after many highly charged complications, a harmonious resolution is found. Sierck (Douglas Sirk) claimed here to have consciously attempted, for the first time, to divest himself of theatrical and literary influences on his work. In fact, it is highly theatrical—literally so, with productions of Handel's *Judas Maccabaeus* and a children's theatre performance of *Snow White And The Seven Dwarfs* featured, while Beethoven's *Ninth Symphony* in concert lends both the 'chord' and 'accord' implicit in the title. Though highly schematic, this is, above all, an out-and-out melodrama, rich in visual and emotional resonances which signal the style for which the director became universally regarded. Over the top, but absorbing.

Finally Sunday

(US: Confidentially Yours)

Vivement Dimanche

France 1983 117 mins bw
Les Films Du Carrosse/A2/Soprofilms

d **François Truffaut**
sc **François Truffaut, Suzanne Schiffman, Jean Aurel**
ph **Nestor Almendros**
m **Georges Delerue**
Fanny Ardant, Jean-Louis Trintignant, Philippe Laudenbach, Caroline Sihol, Philippe Morier-Genoud

A real-estate agent (Trintignant), accused of the murder of his wife and her lover, goes into hiding while his secretary (Ardant) attempts to prove his innocence. As he had done in several other films, and with far more aplomb,

Truffaut took an American pulp novel (this time *The Long Saturday Night* by Charles Williams) as the basis for a comedy thriller. Shot in monochrome in a strained effort to capture the style of 1940s Hollywood, it is a self-regarding, hollow, mildly amusing cinéphile's game. However, Fanny Ardant proves to be the most attractive and versatile of French actresses.

The Finances Of The Grand Duke

Die Finanzen Des Grossherzogs

Germany 1923 80 mins bw
Pagu

d **F.W. Murnau**
sc **Thea Von Harbou**
ph **Karl Freund, Franz Planer**
m **Silent**
Mady Christians, Harry Liedtke, Alfred Abel, Robert Scholz

The Grand Duchess Olga (Christians), in love with an insolvent Grand Duke (Liedtke), decides to bail him out of his financial difficulties. She writes him an embarrassing letter which is stolen, giving rise to mirth as it is passed from hand to hand among several people. The chief attraction of this film is Mady Christians' delightful performance, its chief interest the novelty of Murnau tackling such frivolous fare. (It was based on an anti-Semitic novel but the racial slant was removed.) Sadly, only incomplete prints of this film survive, depriving modern audiences of the beautiful landscape photography shot in Yugoslavia.

Finanzen Des Grossherzogs, Die see Finances Of The Grand Duke, The

---

Fin Du Jour, La see End Of A Day, The

Finis Terrae

France 1929 90 mins bw
Société Générale Des Films

d **Jean Epstein**
sc **Jean Epstein**
ph **Joseph Barth, Joseph Kottula**
m **Silent**
Fishermen of the islands of Ouessant and Bannec

The everyday lives of the fisherfolk on remote islands off the coast of Brittany. A precursor of Neo-Realism and very much in the tradition of the ecological documentaries of Robert Flaherty, the film was a strange departure for a director who had just astonished audiences with *The Fall Of The House Of Usher*. Although his aesthetic style kept the human dimension at a distance, the film showed Epstein's expert handling of non-professional actors.

Finyé see Wind, The

Fiore Delle Mille E Una Notte, Il see Arabian Nights, The

Fire Festival

Himatsuri

Japan 1985 120 mins col
Gunro/Seibu Group/Ciné Saison

d **Mitsuo Yanagimachi**
sc **Kanji Nakagami**
ph **Masaki Tamura**
m **Tohru Takemitsu**
Kinya Kitaoji, Kiwako Taichi, Ryota Nakamoto, Norihei Miki, Rikiya Yasuoka

In a coastal village in South-west Japan, a lumberjack in his forties (Kitaoji) has a mystical relationship with the goddess of the mountains. Seeing the fishing grounds polluted, speculators moving in and traditions being eroded, he turns a gun on his family and himself. Yanagimachi has used an actual event to create a mysterious parable of change—the young replacing the old, the modern encroaching upon the ancient. Some of the symbolism might confuse Western audiences, but the imagery of the sea and forest, the startling moments in the narrative and the visuals, and the pyrotechnics of the festival of the title make a deep impression.

Fire In The Straw

Le Feu De Paille

France 1939 89 mins bw
Véga

d **Jean-Benoît Lévy**
sc **Jean-Benoît Lévy, Henri Troyat**
ph **Marcel Lucien**
m **Marcel Lattès**
Lucien Baroux, Orane Demazis, Jean Fuller, Jeanne Helbling, Aimos

A once-famous actor (Baroux) sees his son (Fuller) rise to fame in the movies while his own career fades. But the son's popularity does not last, and he discovers what his father has long known—acting is a precarious career. This well-characterized serio-comic story takes place against a somewhat unconvincing show business background and the leads, while competent, are hardly charismatic. The film was advertised in the US as the last picture to be exported from France before the Nazi occupation.

The Firemen's Ball

Hoří, Má Panenko

Czechoslovakia 1967 73 mins col
Barrandov/Carlo Ponti

d **Miloš Forman**
sc **Miloš Forman, Ivan Passer, Jaroslav Papoušek**
ph **Miroslav Ondřiček**
m **Karel Mares**
Vaclav Stockel, Josef Svet, Josef Kolb, Jan Vostřcil, František Debelka

During a small-town firemen's ball, a beauty contest fizzles out when the contestants refuse to leave the cloakrooms, the raffle prizes are stolen, someone has a heart attack, and a house burns down. After his more gently ironic previous films, Forman's rather gross satire on simple people with some sharp side swipes at petty bureaucracy caused 40,000 Czech firemen to resign in protest until it was explained that the picture was merely allegorical. Very popular in the West, the film was the last Forman made in his homeland before his self-imposed exile in America.

Fires On The Plain

Nobi

Japan 1959 108 mins bw
Daiei

d **Kon Ichikawa**
sc **Natto Wada**
ph **Setsuo Kobayashi**
m **Yasushi Akutagawa**
Eiji Funakoshi, Osamu Takizawa, Micky Curtis, Mantaro Ushio

On an island in the Philippines a soldier (Funakoshi), part of the retreating Japanese army, is forced to hide in the jungle where he encounters death, disease, starvation and cannibalism. This grim and gruesome, but dignified, film is a worthy companion piece to Ichikawa's other anti-war masterpiece, *The Burmese Harp* (1956). Its visual intensity is increased by keeping the dialogue to a minimum.

Fire Within, The see Feu Follet, Le

First Name Carmen

Prénom Carmen

France 1983 85 mins col
Sara/A2/Jean-Luc Godard Films

d **Jean-Luc Godard**
sc **Jean-Luc Godard, Anne-Marie Miéville**
ph **Raoul Coutard**
m **Beethoven, Tom Waits**
Maruschka Detmers, Jacques Bonnaffé, Myriem Roussel, Christophe Odent, Jean-Luc Godard

Carmen (Detmers), a member of a gang of thieves and the lover of a security guard she met during a bank hold-up, uses the making of a film by her director uncle as a cover for a kidnapping. This is Godard at his most mischievous, playing wittily with Mérimée's *Carmen* (no Bizet, but a Beethoven string quartet rehearsed and played), a B-film plot—it ends wih the dedication 'In Memoriam Small Pictures'—and notions of cinema. Above all, it offers Godard in a hilarious and mocking self-portrait.

Best Film Venice 1983

The First Teacher

Pervy Uchitel

USSR 1965 98 mins bw
Kirghizfilm/Mosfilm

d **Andrei Mikhalkov-Konchalovsky**
sc **Chingiz Aytmatov, Boris Dobrodeyev**
ph **Georgy Rerberg**

m **Vyacheslav Ovchinnikov**
Bolot Beishenaliev, Natalia Arinbasarova, Idris Nogaibayev, D. Kouioukova, M. Kychtobaiev

In 1923, an ex-Red Army Officer (Beishenaliev) opens a new school in a Kirghiz village, gradually winning over the hostile community, but when he falls in love with a beautiful 16-year-old girl (Arinbasarova) whom the local Kulak demands to marry, conflict and violence erupt. Set against an inhospitable landscape, Konchalovsky's first feature is partly a folk tale, replete with gnarled peasants and primitive customs, and partly a realistic account of genuine hurdles to progress. Technically, too, it combines cliché with some imaginative and persuasive images, and conveys a sense of menace that is controlled and convincing.

Best Actress (Natalia Arinbasarova) Venice 1966

Fist In His Pocket see Fists In The Pocket

Fists In The Pocket
(US: Fist In His Pocket)
I Pugni In Tasca

Italy 1965 113 mins bw
Doria

d **Marco Bellocchio**
sc **Marco Bellocchio**
ph **Alberto Marrama**
m **Ennio Morricone**
Lou Castel, Paola Pitagora, Liliona Gerace, Marino Masè, Pier Luigi Troglio

In a middle-class family consisting of a blind widow (Gerace) and her children—three brothers, two of whom are epileptics, and their half- crazed sister (Pitagora)—the eldest son (Masè), breadwinner and only normal member is prevented from marrying and living a full life. His younger brother (Castel) decides to free him by killing off the rest of the family. Twenty-five-year-old Bellocchio borrowed £28,000 from his family to make this searing critique of repressive Italian *bourgeois* family life, based on a script he wrote while following a film course at the Slade school in London under Thorold Dickinson. A remarkable first feature, it is notable for its intensity, claustrophobic atmosphere, and a powerful performance from Castel as the *deus ex machina.*

Fitzcarraldo

W. Germany 1982 158 mins col
Werner Herzog/Pro-ject Filmproduktion/Zweite Deutsches Fernsehen/Wildlife Films

d **Werner Herzog**
sc **Werner Herzog**
ph **Thomas Mauch**
m **Popol Vuh**
Klaus Kinski, Claudia Cardinale, José Lewgoy, Paul Hittscher, Miguel Angel Fuentes

In an attempt to realize his dream of establishing an opera house in the Peruvian jungle at the turn of the century, an eccentric Irish rubber baron called Fitzgerald (Fitzcarraldo to the natives), has to have a massive steamship hauled over a mountain. 'If I should abandon this film I should be a man without dreams . . . I live my life or end my life with this project,' Herzog stated characteristically. Whether one thinks that this grandiose screwball epic might have been no worse with less effort, one can't help but admire the tenacity and daring of the director's determination to live his films. More interesting than this long haul is *Burden Of Dreams*, Les Blank's documentary on the hazardous making of the film, which originally cast Jason Robards (who fell ill with jungle fever) in the role taken here by the grimacing Kinski.

Best Director Cannes 1982

Five Boys From Barska Street
Piatka Z Ulicy Barskiej

Poland 1953 115 mins col
Film Polski

d **Aleksander Ford**
sc **Aleksander Ford, Kazimierz Kozniewski**
ph **Jaroslav Tuzar, Karel Chodura**
m **Kazimierz Serocki**
Tadeusz Janczar, Aleksandra Slaska, Andrzej Kozák, Mieczyslaw Stoor

A gang of five boys are put on probation for robbery with violence in post-war Warsaw. Their kindly probation officer gets them jobs and helps them reject their old values and come to terms with society. Poland's leading director of the 1950s was entrusted with his country's first major production in colour. What emerged was a propagandist piece that parallels the rehabilitation of the delinquents with the reconstruction of Poland. In fact, it is not dissimilar to preachy American or British models of the genre. Ford was a sympathetic director of young people, as he had already proved in earlier 'street' films—*The Legion Of The Street* (1932) and *Border Street* (1948). The assistant on this film was Andrzej Wajda, whose first feature, *A Generation*, the following year was to give a very different view of Polish youth.

Five-Day Lover, The see Infidelity

Five Evenings

Pyat' Vecherov

USSR 1980 101 mins bw/col
Mosfilm

d **Nikita Mikhalkov**
sc **Aleksander Adabashyan, Nikita Mikhalkov**
ph **Pavel Lebeshev**
m **Yu. Mikhailov**
Ludmila Gurchenko, Stanislav Liubshin, Valentina Telichkina, Larisa Kuznetsova, Igor Nefedov, Aleksander Adabashyan

Sasha (Liubshin), who claims to be the chief engineer of the Soviet Union's largest chemical plant, has arrived in Moscow on leave. A man of volatile temperament, he impulsively visits Tamara (Gurchenko) with whom he was romantically involved when the war broke out. She has never married and, over the course of five evenings characterized by revelations and vicissitudes, they resolve their relationship. This adaptation of a play by Alexander Volodin is only partially successful. It retains the running gags and act breaks that belong in the theatre, while an attempt to be cinematically adventurous in the closing sequences (black and white gives way to colour) is sentimental and contrived. However, as in his other films, Mikhalkov displays a pronounced gift for handling actors and it is the presence of his performers, notably the accomplished Gurchenko, that holds it together. The period, too, is interesting: 1957, when Khruschev was beginning to loosen the bonds of Stalinist austerity, conveyed in a series of images that signal the change.

Five Women Around Utamaro

(US: Utamaro And His Five Women)

Utamaro O Meguru Gonin No Onna

Japan 1946 94 mins bw
Shochiku

d **Kenji Mizoguchi**
sc **Yoshitaka Yoda**
ph **Shigeto Miki**
m **Hisato Osawa, Tamezo Mochizuki**
Minosuke Bando, Kinuyo Tanaka, Kotaro Bando, Hiroko Kawasaki

Utamaro (Minosuke Bando), the legendary 18th-century Edo artist, gains his inspiration from the many courtesans who surround him. Jealousies and intrigues, however, are rife among the female entourage, as well as among his other friends. Although scenarist Yoda stated that the film was, unconsciously, a portrait of the director, it is consciously about the problems of artists in general and Utamaro in particular. It also suggests the link between erotic and creative impulses, and exquisitely evokes the period. One of Mizoguchi's most stylized works, *Utamaro* is also somewhat confusing in its treatment of complex relationships.

A Flame In My Heart

Une Flamme Dans Mon Coeur

France 1987 110 mins bw
Garance/La Sept(Paris)/Filmograph(Geneva)

d **Alain Tanner**
sc **Myriam Mézières, Alain Tanner**
ph **Acácio De Almeida**
m **Bach**
Myriam Mézières, Benoît Régent, Aziz Kabouche, André Marcon, Jean-Gabriel Nordman, Biana

Mercedes (Mézières), a Parisian actress, decides to break up with her uneducated Arab lover (Kabouche), which proves easier said than done due to his unbalanced persistence and their mutual sexual attraction. She finally escapes him by holing up in a hotel, then picks up Pierre (Régent), a journalist, on the Métro and goes to live with him. During his absence on an assignment, she disintegrates and, on his return, he takes her to Cairo although their relationship is by now very shaky. Although Tanner is still dealing with the alienation of the individual, familiar from his better films, he does so here with a mixture of pretentious attitudinizing and soft porn that manages to be at once tasteless and boring. The technique of the piece appears as a sort of retarded excursion into the New Wave, while the content, similarly, is a sketchy and incoherent nod to the 'permissive' past.

Flame Of My Love see My Love Has Been Burning

Flame Of Torment, The see Conflagration

Flame Top

Tulipää

Finland 1980 135 mins col
P-Kino Oy/Finnish Film Foundation

d **Pirjo Honkasalo, Pekka Lehto**
sc **Pirjo Honkasalo, Pekka Lehto**
ph **Kari Sohlberg, Pertti Mutanen, Raimo Paananen**
m **Heikki Valpola**
Åsko Sarkola, Rea Mauranen, Kari Franck, Esko Salminen, Åri Suonsuu

An account of the adult life of Maiju Lassila (Sarkola), the prolific Russian-Finnish writer who began as a successful businessman in Russia at the turn of the century, made a glittering marriage which soon collapsed, and became a Socialist revolutionary forced to flee to Finland. There, he led a mysterious existence and an unusual love-life, practising politics through his pen under several pseudonyms. The directors, concentrating largely on Lassila's affair with the failed actress, Olga (Maurinen), and his life during the German occupation of Finland have found a visionary, almost epic approach to an unpromising subject and have re-created a period of upheaval in a series of gripping images. The film, very controversial in Finland, took eight years to make.

The Flaming Years

aka History Of The Burning Years
aka The Turbulent Years
Povest' Plamennykh Let

USSR 1961 105 mins col
Mosfilm

d **Julia Solntseva**
sc **Alexander Dovzhenko**
ph **Fyodor Provorov, Alexei Temerine**
m **Gavril Popov**
Nikolai Vingranovsky, Boris Andreyev, Svetlana Zhgun, Zinaidi Kirienko, Sergei Loukianov, Vassili Merkouriev

Ivan Orlyuk (Vingranovsky), a soldier of infinite courage and patriotism, fights in World War II, overcoming continual wounding in battle, and survives to marry his brave schoolteacher sweetheart (Zhgun). Continuing her homage to her late husband, the great Dovzhenko, Solntseva has achieved a memorable use of 70mm, creating a series of skilful, fluid, imaginative and affecting images. Alas, the content is rather less impressive, being an overt piece of flag waving to the indomitable spirit of Russia, symbolized by the ever-smiling Ivan. The simplistic story grows tedious and the director lacks her husband's conspicuous gifts that might have served to enliven his script. Nonetheless, it is a landmark in the use of the 70mm screen, its photography beautifully controlled by the experienced Provorov.

Best Director Cannes 1962

Flamme Dans Mon Coeur, Une see Flame In My Heart, A

The Flavour Of Green Tea Over Rice

Ochazuke No Aji

Japan 1952 115 mins bw
Shochiku/Ofuna

d **Yasujiro Ozu**
sc **Yasujiro Ozu, Kogo Noda**
ph **Yuharu Atsuta**
m **Ichiro Saito**
Shin Saburi, Michiyo Kogure, Koji Tsuruta, Keiko Tsushima, Kuniko Miyake

A middle-aged, middle-class couple find that their childless marriage has gone stale. The husband (Saburi) is a creature of habit with simple tastes, and the snobbish wife (Kogure) goes off on jaunts with other wives. They finally come together again in the kitchen when they share a bowl of *ochazuke* (green tea over rice). The delicate flavour of Ozu is seen in the subtle playing and camerawork. One of his brightest and funniest films, full of sly little surprises, it was considered by the director to be 'not very well made'.

Les Fleurs Sauvages

aka Wild Flowers

Canada 1982 153 mins col/bw
Cinak

d **Jean Pierre Lefèbvre**
sc **Jean Pierre Lefèbvre**
ph **Guy Dufaux**
m **Raoul Duguay**
Marthe Nadeau, Michèle Magny, Pierre Curzi, Claudia Aubin, Eric Beausejour

Seventy-year-old Simone (Nadeau) arrives for her annual visit to her daughter's family in rural Quebec. Michèle (Magny), her photographer husband (Curzi) and the two children are happy to see her. The week passes in carefree summer pursuits in which Simone, rooted in a more restrained and less loving past, does her best to join with equanimity. Originally shot on 16mm with the lowest of budgets, Lefèbvre's film is technically accomplished, sensitive and beautifully acted. This is a perceptive and naturalistic tale of family life, which initially reveals the barriers and tensions beneath the surface of the mother-daughter relationship when Michèle presents her mother with a welcoming vase of wild flowers—a gift that is subtly disparaged. Michèle's quiet acknowledgement of a gap in understanding between them remains private, while Simone, too, keeps her criticisms and resentments to herself. Unfortunately, the film is far too long and is disrupted by the ill-judged use of voice-overs and black-and-white sequences to express private thoughts.

Flickorna see Girls, The

Flic, Un see Dirty Money

Floating Clouds

Ukigumo

Japan 1955 123 mins bw
Toho

d **Mikio Naruse**
sc **Yoko Mizuki**
ph **Masao Tamai**
m **Ichiro Saito**
Hideko Takamine, Masayuki Mori, Mariko Okada, Daisuke Kato

A solitary woman (Takamine), returning to Japan after serving as a nurse at the front in South-east Asia, seeks out a soldier (Mori) she fell in love with there. But they have no control over their destiny because he cannot leave his invalid wife and she must suffer degradation. One of the most popular of Naruse's subtle, pessimistic melodramas flows relentlessly towards the heartfelt conclusion. Naruse has remarked of his characters that 'If they try to move forward even a little, they quickly hit a wall'. But they struggle on bravely, especially the women, played here (as in 16 other Naruse films) by the remarkable Hideko Takamine.

Floating Weeds

Ukigusa

Japan 1959 119 mins col
Daiei

d **Yasujiro Ozu**
sc **Yasujiro Ozu, Kogo Noda**
ph **Kazuo Miyagawa**
m **Takanobu Saito**
Ganjiro Nakamura, Haruko Sugimura, Machiko Kyo, Ayako Wakao, Hiroshi Kawaguchi

A troupe of travelling players visits a remote island town where lives the ex-mistress (Sugimara) of the leading actor (Nakamura) with whom she had had a son. Complications arise when the actor's present lover (Kyo) becomes jealous. This close remake of Ozu's silent 1934 film, *A Story Of Floating Weeds*, has a mellowness lacking in the bitterer earlier film, but retains much of the comedy of the theatre scenes. It also has glowing colour photography by the great Miyagawa, who had worked for Kurosawa (*Rashomon*) and Mizoguchi (*Ugetsu Monogatari*), but only this once with Ozu.

Fontane Effi Briest see Effi Briest

För Att Inte Tala Om Alla Dessa Kvinnor see Now About These Women

The Forbidden Christ
Il Cristo Proibito

Italy 1950 100 mins bw
Excelsa

d **Curzio Malaparte**
sc **Curzio Malaparte**
ph **Gabor Pogany**
m **Curzio Malaparte**
Raf Vallone, Elena Varzi, Gino Cervi, Alain Cuny, Rina Morelli, Philippe Lemaire, Anna Maria Ferrero

Bruno (Vallone), a soldier, returns to Tuscany after 10 years of war and captivity to learn that his young Partisan brother was betrayed to the Nazis. Bent on revenge, he receives no help from the war- weary villagers; even his family refuses to tell what it knows. Events spiral and he is led into killing the wrong man. The only film made by writer Malaparte is an allegory on themes of guilt and expiation which, while not always coherent and sometimes heavy-handed, is nonetheless powerful. It is redolent with striking images of death and encounters of telling irony, caught by an adventurous camera and given stylized playing (very successful from Vallone, less so elsewhere). Well-known for shifting his allegiances between Communism and Fascism, Malaparte claimed to have renounced politics with this gripping film, inspired by accounts of an actual incident. It was a box-office disaster, causing him to abandon future film plans and return to journalism.

Forbidden Fruit
Le Fruit Défendu

France 1952 103 mins bw
Gray Films

d **Henri Verneuil**
sc **Henri Verneuil, Jacques Companeez, Jean Manse**
ph **Henri Alekan**
m **Paul Durand**
Fernandel, Françoise Arnoul, Claude Nollier, Sylvie, Jacques Castelot

A respectable doctor (Fernandel), a widower living with his mother (Sylvie), takes a second wife (Nollier), but gets involved with a young prostitute (Arnoul). Georges Simenon's novel *Lettre À Mon Juge* was the basis for this absorbing little drama. The Belgian author's favourite theme—the deep passions that lie beneath the surface of stifling middle-class respectability—is well articulated by the film, which seemed terribly daring to English-speaking audiences in the early 1950s (Arnoul reveals a breast). Fernandel, not just a funny face, gives one of his rare serious performances.

Forbidden Games
aka The Secret Game
Jeux Interdits

France 1952 102 mins bw
Robert Dorfmann

d **René Clément**
sc **Jean Aurenche, Pierre Bost**
ph **Robert Juillard**
m **Narcisco Yepes**
Brigitte Fossey, Georges Poujouly, Amedée, Laurence Badie, Jacques Marin

In 1940, as refugees flee the Germans, an orphaned five-year-old girl and the young son of a peasant family who takes her in, build a cemetery for animals, stealing crosses from the churchyard to do so. Clément's direct and simple approach and the wonderfully natural performances he obtained from the young Poujouly (discovered at a camp for deprived children) and Fossey (who returned to films as an adult) make for a moving document on the effects of war on children. It is topped and tailed by two justly famous sequences—the column of refugees being strafed by Nazi planes and the final crane shot revealing the little girl in a sea of displaced persons.

Best Foreign Film Oscar 1952
Best Film Venice 1952

Forbidden Relations

Visszaesök

Hungary 1983 90 mins col
Mafilm

d **Zsolt Kézdi-Kovács**
sc **Zsolt Kézdi-Kovács**
ph **János Kende**
Lili Monori, Miklós B. Székely, Mari Töröcsik, József Horváth, József Tóth

In a remote farming community, a widow (Monori) finds solace in the arms of a man (Székely) whom she then discovers is, in fact, her half-brother. Despite the inevitable social ostracism and a term of imprisonment, they decide to live as a married couple and have children. This tale of brother-sister incest is directed in a measured, objective manner, eschewing melodramatics and presenting a love affair that seems as natural as the beautifully caught surroundings. (Although making them half siblings takes away half the shock.) The couple play with touching honesty and there is a splendidly strong performance from Töröcsik as their mother, literally trying to wash her feelings of guilt away.

The Forest

Kaadu

India 1973 123 mins col
LN Combines

d **Girish Karnad**
sc **Girish Karnad**
ph **Govind Nihalani**
m **B.V. Karanth**
G.S. Nataraj, Amrish Puri, Nandini, Lokesh, Kalpana Sirur, Uma Shivakumar

Kitti (Nataraj), a 10-year-old boy, accompanies his aunt (Nandini) on a nocturnal visit to the witchdoctor in the forest. There, they hope to obtain a spell to stop his uncle (Puri) spending his nights with a widow (Shivakumar). After a number of adventures in and around the same forest, he watches helplessly as his aunt is raped on her way to visit the witchdoctor for a second time. The first film directed by the writer-actor Karnad is, like Satyajit Ray's *Pather Panchali*, a tale told through the eyes of a child. But the haunting, lucid, and finally tragic drama stands on its own considerable merits. Karnad's story, based on an autobiographical novel, with its underlying violence, superstition and rigid sexual codes, reveals a darker side to Indian rural life than Ray's film.

Forest of Hanged Men see Lost Forest, The

Forest Of The Hanged, The see Lost Forest, The

Forever My Love

Sissi/Sissi-Die Junge Kaiserin/ Sissi-Schicksalsjahre Einer Kaiserin

Austria 1955/1956/1957 317 mins col
Erma-Film

d **Ernst Marischka**
sc **Ernst Marischka**
ph **Bruno Mondi**
m **Anton Profes**
Romy Schneider, Karl-Heinz Böhm, Gustav Knuth, Walther Reyer, Magda Schneider, Vilma Degischer

Young Franz Joseph, the Hapsburg Emperor (Böhm), falls in love with Elizabeth (Sissi), the sister of the Bavarian princess whom his mother has arranged for him to marry. He marries Sissi instead, much to his mother's chagrin, but she brings a breath of fresh air to the Court, wins the slavish devotion of the formerly unhappy Hungarians, falls dangerously ill but recovers, and tours Austria's Italian states with her husband, once again captivating a hostile populace. Such is the plot of this laboured marathon, comprising three consecutive films, but generally shown as one— substantially cut but still interminable. Part-operetta, part Hollywood-style biopic, the tone is cloying, the technique uneven, and the leading lady (Romy Schneider) too lightweight. Nonetheless, this film proved massively successful, attracting large lines at the box-office. Perhaps its appeal lay in satisfying a world hungry for nostalgia?

Forfolgelsen see Witch Hunt

Forget Venice

Dimenticare Venezia

Italy 1979 107 mins col
Rizzoli Film/Action Film

d **Franco Brusati**
sc **Franco Brusati, Jaj Fiastri**
ph **Romano Albani**
m **Benedetto Ghiglia, Saverio Mercadante, Gluck**
Erland Josephson, Mariangela Melato, Eleonora Giorgi, David Pontremoli, Hella Petri, Fred Personne

Middle-aged Nicky (Josephson) and his male lover arrive to stay with Marta, Nicky's widowed and ailing sister, in her country house near Venice. Marta's adopted niece, Anna, lives with her, and the visit of the men sets in motion a series of childhood memories—played in flashback—for Nicky (happy recollections) and Anna (desperately miserable). Dealing, presumably, with the potency and the healing effects of memory, Brusati's film is stylish and elegant, but amounts to little more than a languid and superficial examination of his theme. Worse, his characters are rather boring. Forget it.

Fort Saganne

France 1984 190 mins col
Albina Productions/Films A2/SFPC

d **Alain Corneau**
sc **Henri De Turenne, Alain Corneau, Louis Gardel**
ph **Bruno Nuytten**
m **Philippe Sarde**
Gérard Depardieu, Philippe Noiret, Catherine Deneuve, Sophie Marceau, Michel Duchaussoy, Salah Teskouk

Charles Saganne (Depardieu), a young man of simple peasant stock, joins the military and is posted to a garrison in the French Sahara. Overcoming initial setbacks, he develops into a heroic leader of men until his flame is extinguished by World War I. Along the way and among other things, he joins issue with the aggressive colonel (Noiret), enjoys a fling with a sophisticated Parisian journalist (Deneuve), marries the innocent daughter (Marceau) of a superior *bourgeois* family and performs an amputation on a tribal chieftain with the contents of a tool box. Adapted from a prizewinning novel by Louis Gardel, based on the real-life exploits of his grandfather, and filmed on location in France, Tunisia and Mauritania, this saga of Empire-building cost upwards of $6,000,000, making it one of France's most expensive films ever. A starry cast, led by the virile Depardieu, go through their expert paces, enhanced by superb CinemaScope photography, and directed by Corneau with enough style and sense of period to overcome most of the clichés. This is the epic adventure movie revisited and it works.

Fortunella

Italy 1958 96 mins bw
Dino de Laurentiis/Les Films Marceau (Paris)

d **Eduardo De Filippo**
sc **Federico Fellini, Tullio Pinelli, Ennio Flaiano**
ph **Aldo Tonti**
m **Nino Rota**
Giulietta Masina, Paul Douglas, Alberto Sordi, Franca Marzi

The homeless Fortunella (Masina) works for (and sleeps with) Peppino (Sordi), a weak-willed junk merchant, and is protected by a raffish professor (Douglas). But she imagines that she is the illegitimate daughter of a Prince who will someday claim her. Whimsical it sounds, and whimsical it is, with Masina repeating her repertoire of Chaplinesque mannerisms from *La Strada* and *Cabiria*, but without the controlling vision of her husband behind the camera. De Filippo had a good crack at making a Fellini film out of a Fellini script. Apart from the presence of Masina, and Nino Rota's music, there is the realistic setting on the banks of the Tiber intruded upon by the fantasy of wandering players, and a pleasing mixture of comedy and pathos.

The Forty First

Sorok Pervyi

USSR 1927 80 mins bw
Mezhrabpom

d **Yakov Protazanov**
sc **Boris Lavryenov, Boris Leondinov**
ph **Pyotr Yermolov**
m **Silent**
Ada Voitsik, Ivan Koval-Samborski, I. Strauch

During the civil war in Turkestan, a Red

woman soldier takes prisoner a member of the retreating White army. They find themselves alone on an island where they fall in love, but she remembers her duty to the cause and kills him—her forty-first victim. Skilfully shot in desert locations in two months, the film's wide popularity was probably due more to the romantic than the political or visual aspects of the action tale, although the romance was the weakest element. It was remade in colour by Grigori Chukhrai in 1956.

Four Adventures Of Reinette And Mirabelle

Quatre Aventures De Reinette Et Mirabelle

France 1986 95 mins col
CER/Les Films Du Losange

d **Eric Rohmer**
sc **Eric Rohmer**
ph **Sophie Maintigneux**
m **Ronan Girre, Jean-Louis Valero**
Joëlle Miquel, Jessica Forde, Philippe Laudenbaum Yasmine Haury, Marie Rivière, Béatrice Romand, Fabrice Luchini

Four adventures lived by Mirabelle (Forde), a student of ethnology at the Sorbonne, and Reinette (Miquel), an art student. The first takes place in the country, where Reinette lives and they initially meet, later becoming flatmates in Paris. Here they find themselves having to cope with an obnoxious waiter, a kleptomaniac and an art dealer. Rohmer, with a small crew, very little money, a screenplay that was improvised as he went along and two unknown teenage actresses among a few of his regulars, has worked a tiny miracle. The performances of the girls are beguilingly natural as Rohmer contrasts their attitudes—country girl Reinette with rigorous principles, the city girl more pragmatic. It does not stand up to Rohmer's more ambitious work, but he shows in his 66th year that 'youth is not a question of age'.

Four Bags Full see Pig Across Paris, A

Four Chimneys see Where Chimneys Are Seen

The Four Days Of Naples

Le Quattro Giornate Di Napoli

Italy 1962 119 mins bw
Titanus/MGM

d **Nanni Loy**
sc **Nanni Loy, Pasquale Festa Campanile, Massimo Franciosa, Carlo Bernardi**
ph **Marcello Gatti**
m **Carlo Rustichelli**
Regina Bianchi, Aldo Giuffre, Lea Massari, Jean Sorel, Franco Sportelli, Charles Belmont, Gian Maria Volonté

In 1943, when the occupying Germans rounded up all males aged from five to 50 to send to Nazi camps, the people of Naples rose up and drove them out after an epic battle in the streets. This grim and powerful cinematic reconstruction of an heroic event was nominated for an Oscar in 1962, losing out to the inferior *Sundays And Cybèle*.

The Four Hundred Blows

Les Quatre Cents Coups

France 1959 94 mins bw
Films Du Carrosse/SEDIF

d **François Truffaut**
sc **François Truffaut**
ph **Henri Decaë**
m **Jean Constantin**
Jean-Pierre Léaud, Claire Maurier, Albert Rémy, Patrick Auffray, Robert Beauvais

A 12-year-old Parisian boy, Antoine Doinel (Léaud), neglected by his mother and stepfather, plays truant and takes to petty crime. He is placed in a reform school, but escapes to the coast. Truffaut, a harsh critic on the influential magazine *Cahiers Du Cinéma*, was challenged by his movie producer father-in-law to make a film himself. His first feature, based on his own deprived childhood, was an immediate success which helped to launch the *Nouvelle Vague*, and started a series of films following Doinel through adolescence, marriage, fatherhood and divorce. From the start there was an extraordinary rapport between the director and his alter-ego, and much of the film's freewheeling quality is due to Léaud's spontaneous performance. The freeze of the child's face as he runs towards the sea, is one of cinema's most celebrated endings. Incidentally, both Truffaut and Jeanne Moreau can be glimpsed briefly.

Best Director Cannes 1959

Four Nights Of A Dreamer

Quatre Nuits D'Un Reveur

France 1971 87 mins col
Albina/Del Orso

d **Robert Bresson**
sc **Robert Bresson**
ph **Pierre Lhomme**
m **Brazilian folk songs**
Isabelle Weingarten, Guillaume Des Forêts, Maurice Monnoyer, Jérôme Massart

One night a young artist (Des Forêts)) sees a girl (Weingarten) on the Pont Neuf trying to commit suicide. They talk, and meet on subsequent nights until her lover returns and she leaves the artist. Like his previous picture, *A Gentle Creature* (1969), Bresson's second colour film was based on Dostoevsky, this time the oft-lensed *White Nights*. The strength of the film lies in the enchanting nocturnal background of the bridges of Paris and the *bateaux mouches* gliding up the Seine, rather than in the blank and enigmatic young characters that drift around in the foreground unaware of the surrounding beauty. The intrusion of hippies into the Bressonian world seems curiously false.

Four Steps In The Clouds

Quattro Passi Fra Le Nuvole

Italy 1942 90 mins bw
Cines

d **Alessandro Blasetti**
sc **Cesare Zavattini, Giuseppe Amato, Piero Tellini, Aldo De Benedetti**
ph **Vaclav Vich**
m **Alessandro Cicognini**
Gino Cervi, Adriana Benetti, Giuditta Rissone

A dull, unhappily married, travelling confectionery salesman (Cervi) meets a pregnant girl on a bus who begs him to pretend to be her husband for one night for the sake of her family. Anticipating the Neo-Realists by using humble characters and backgrounds, the film helped cheer up audiences in war-torn Italy. Since then non-Italians have been able to appreciate its genuine wit and charm. It was remade in France in 1957 as *The Virtuous Bigamist* starring Fernandel.

The Fourteenth of July

(US: July 14)

Quatorze Juillet

France 1932 98 mins bw
Tobis

d **René Clair**
sc **René Clair**
ph **Georges Périnal, Louis Page**
m **Maurice Jaubert**
Annabella, Georges Rigaud, Pola Illery, Paul Olivier, Raymond Cordy

On Bastille Day in Paris, a flower-girl (Annabella) and her taxi-driver boyfriend (Rigaud) meet various people. A child is born, a woman dies, there is a hold-up, and a drunkard (Olivier) is blissfully unaware of his surroundings. Clair's films have the same reputation for gaiety as Paris, the city he loved. This light, inconsequential comedy is quintessentially Clair, and the last of his pre-war 'Paris' pictures. Actually, the city is more the wittily artificial creation of Russian emigré set designer Lazare Meerson, who created the ideal space for Clair's choreographed characters.

The Fourth Man

Die Vierde Man

Netherlands 1983 102 mins col
De Verenigde Nederlandsche Filmcompagnie

d **Paul Verhoeven**
sc **Gerard Soeteman**
ph **Jan De Bont**
m **Loek Dikker**
Jeroen Krabbé, Renée Soutendijk, Thom Hoffman, Dolf De Vries, Geert De Jong

Amsterdam novelist Gerard (Krabbé) gives a lecture in another town and sleeps with the mysteriously thrice- widowed Christine (Soutendijk), treasurer of the literary society. He discovers that she is engaged to Herman (Hoffman), a young man he spied at the station who has entered his quasi-religious visions. Finally, Gerard has sex with Herman and tries to warn him that Christine spells destruction.... A novel by Gerard Reve—gay, Catholic and a best-selling Dutch author—has become a wonderfully overwrought film, combining Christian guilt, homo-erotic imagery, black humour and high Gothic camp. Verhoeven's direction is assured, his actors expert.

Fox

aka Fox And His Friends

Faustrecht Der Freiheit

W. Germany 1975 123 mins col
Tango

d **Rainer Werner Fassbinder**
sc **Rainer Werner Fassbinder, Christian Hohoff**
ph **Michael Ballhaus**
m **Peer Raben**
Rainer Werner Fassbinder, Peter Chatel, Harry Baer, Ulla Jacobsson, Adrian Hoven, Karl-Heinz Böhm

A carnival barker (Fassbinder) who wins a fortune in a lottery, is manipulated into investing in his upper-class boyfriend's family business with disastrous consequences. Although an honest and lucid look at homosexual relationships, *Fox* is even more concerned with class exploitation, as conveyed in Fassbinder's no-nonsense narrative. He himself makes a sympathetic but weak central figure, especially in the cruellest scene when the snobbish family humiliates him at the dinner table.

Fox And His Friends see Fox

Fragment Of An Empire

Oblomok Imperii

USSR 1929 81 mins bw
Sovkino

d **Friedrich Ermler**
sc **Friedrich Ermler, Katerina Vinogradskaya**
ph **Yevgeni Schneider**
m **Silent**
Fyodor Nikitin, Yakov Gudkin, Ludmila Semyonova

A young man (Nikitin), who lost his memory in World War I and regained it ten years later, takes a trip to Leningrad where he is reunited with his lost wife (Semyonova) and where he finds everything has changed under the new Soviet order—customs, the landscape and even the name of the city (from St Petersburg). Ermler's most celebrated film combines political parable with social satire most effectively. Its humanity and the splendid location photography give the piece its well-earned reputation.

The Fragrance Of Wild Flowers

Miris Poljs Kog Sveca

Yugoslavia 1977 93 mins col
Centar Film

d **Srdjan Karanović**
sc **Rajko Grlić, Srdjan Karanović**
ph **Živko Zalar**
m **Zoran Simjanović**
Ljuba Tadić, Sonja Divać, Nemanja Zivić, Rastislava Gacić, Olga Spiridonović

Ivan Vasiljevic (Tadić), a famous actor, suddenly leaves a play rehearsal, walks out on his career and his wife (Spiridonović), and decides to sail down the Danube on an old barge operated by his friend Stinky (Zivić). But escape is not as simple as it seems. After the Black Cinema (the sombre Yugoslavian movement in the cinema of the 1960s), a new wave of film-makers emerged, more concerned with individual than national identity. Kranović described his second feature as a 'kind of documentary fairy tale', by which he presumably meant that fantastic elements grow out of a realistic situation. It is at its best when it ironically and warmly observes the many characters (mostly played by non- professionals) that Tadić, himself a well-known stage and screen actor, meets on his journey.

Française Et L'Amour, La see Love And The Frenchwoman

Francisca

Portugal 1981 166 mins col
V.O. Filme

d **Manoel De Oliveira**
sc **Manoel De Oliveira**
ph **Elso Roque**
m **João Paes**
Teresa Meneses, Diogo Dória, Mário Barroso, Rui Mendes, Glória De Matos, Lia Gama

Camilo Castelo Branco (Barroso) and José Augusto (Dória) are both in love with the exquisite Fanny (Meneses), who finally marries José. Meanwhile, the two men are close friends and spend much time in philosophical conversation. De Oliveira, Portugal's most distinguished director, was already 73 when he made this film, based on a romantic novel by Agustina Bessa Luís. She, in turn, drew her material from the real-life triangular story, recorded in a novel by Camilo and the diaries of José and Fanny. It is a highly formal work, creating climaxes of unhappiness and self-destruction through slowly unfolding dialogue that reveals the pride, sadism, spite, vanity and despair of the characters, and building atmosphere through richly-detailed Velasquez-like compositions. An unusual, complex and rewarding piece.

Françoise Steps Out

Rue De L'Estrapade

France 1953 95 mins bw
Cinéphonic/SGGC/Filmsonor

d **Jacques Becker**
sc **Annette Wademant**
ph **Marcel Grignon**
m **Georges Van Parys**
Louis Jourdan, Anne Vernon, Daniel Gélin, Jean Servais, Micheline Dax

When Françoise (Vernon) discovers that her racing driver husband (Jourdan) has been unfaithful, she moves into a small flat in Paris, only to be pestered by a Left Bank crooner (Gélin). The last of Becker's enchanting modern Parisian comedies has all his characteristic warmth and observation. It summed up the director's credo: 'I believe in the possibility of entertaining friendship and in the difficulty of maintaining love...And I believe above all in Paris'. Vernon and Gélin are as charming as they were in Becker's *Edward And Caroline*, and Jourdan makes an effective return to a French film in between his less than inspired work in Hollywood movies.

Frantic see Lift To The Scaffold

Frau Im Mond, Die see Woman In The Moon, The

Freedom For Us see À Nous La Liberté

French Cancan

(US: Only The French Can)

France 1955 105 mins col
Franco London/Jolly

d **Jean Renoir**
sc **André-Paul Antoine**
ph **Michel Kelber**
m **Georges Van Parys**
Jean Gabin, Françoise Arnoul, Maria Felix, Jean-Roger Caussimon, Gianni Esposito

The impresario (Gabin) who opened the Moulin Rouge in Montmartre in 1880, falls for a young laundress (Arnoul) whom he tries to make into a star—much to the annoyance of his fiery mistress (Felix). Renoir's return to film-making in France after 15 years' absence is an exuberant, colourful homage to the theatre of *La Belle Epoque*. (Edith Piaf and Patachou appear briefly as stars of the day.) The hackneyed story, based on the life of Ziegler, founder of the Moulin Rouge, is the stuff of many a Hollywood biopic, but expounded with delicate period taste and affection. It also gave Renoir the opportunity to work with Gabin again, having made three films with him in the 1930s.

Frenzy

(US: Torment)

Hets

Sweden 1944 101 mins bw
Svensk Filmindustri

d **Alf Sjöberg**
sc **Ingmar Bergman**
ph **Martin Bodin**
m **Hilding Rosenberg**
Stig Järrel, Alf Kjellin, Mai Zetterling, Olof Winnerstrand, Märta Arbin, Gunnar Björnstrand

A sensitive schoolboy (Kjellin), victimized by a sadistic Latin teacher (Järrel) and misunderstood at home, turns for love to a young alcoholic prostitute (Zetterling). Twenty-six-year-old Ingmar Bergman's first screenplay, based on a recollection of one of his schoolmasters, prefigured some of the themes of his early films as director—young lovers at odds with society, the humiliation of the weak by the strong. Sjöberg's highly-charged Expressionist picture, rather too close to its title for comfort, not only launched Bergman, but the teenage Zetterling, and instigated the renaissance of Swedish cinema.

Freudlose Gasse, Die see Joyless Street

Fric-Frac

France 1939 120 mins bw
Maurice Lehmann

d **Claude Autant-Lara, Maurice Lehmann**
sc **Michel Duran**
ph **Armand Thirard**
m **Casimir Oberfeld**
Fernandel, Michel Simon, Arletty, Hélène Robert, Andrex

A gullible jeweller's assistant (Fernandel), through his infatuation with a jewel thief (Arletty), becomes unwittingly involved in a plan to rob his employer's shop. A film to defeat any sub-title writer since it was conceived almost entirely in (now dated) slang with the language an essential part of the humour. But the trio of top performers and the jolly plot are enough to keep non-French speakers content. Autant-Lara was virtually the sole director, but his producer boss claimed a co-credit.

Frida

Frida Naturaleza Viva

Mexico 1984 108 mins col
Cooperativa Buten

d **Paul Leduc**
sc **José Joaquín Blanco, Paul Leduc**
ph **Angel Goded**
m **Saint-Saëns, popular Spanish music**
Ofelia Medina, Juan José Gurrola, Max Kerlow, Salvador Sánchez, Claudio Brook, Cecilia Toussaint

The gifted Mexican painter Frida Kahlo (Medina), wife of Diego Rivera (Gurrola), committed Communist and close friend of Leon Trotsky (Kerlow), is on her deathbed. She reflects on her life and art, and on her many physical afflictions that began with polio in childhood and culminated in the amputation of a leg. This is an impressionistic view of a remarkable woman that slowly comes together, like an emotional jigsaw puzzle, in a series of haunting images, some moving, some painful and ugly, others enchanting, but all dominated by the dramatically powerful presence of Medina. Every frame exhibits a depth and range of colour, light and texture appropriate to its subject and its setting, be it the watermelons of Diego, the surrealist portraits by Frida, Mexican Indians singing by firelight or the bullet-scarred pillars of an imposing public building. However, it must be acknowledged that, with its lack of narrative, its minimal dialogue and sequences of excruciating slowness, the film initially requires much patience and concentration.

Frida Naturaleza Viva see Frida

Friends And Husbands

Heller Wahn

W. Germany 1982 106 mins col
Bioskop-Film(Munich)/Les Films Du Losange(Paris)

d **Margarethe Von Trotta**
sc **Margarethe Von Trotta**
ph **Michael Ballhaus**
m **Nicolas Economou**
Hanna Schygulla, Angela Winkler, Peter Striebeck, Christine Fersen, Franz Buchriese

Olga (Schygulla), strong, confident and an expert in Classical Romantic literature, is the emotional mainstay of her husband, her lover and her son. Ruth (Winkler), a gifted but unfulfilled and suicidally depressive artist, is married to Franz (Striebeck), a university colleague of Olga's, on whom she is utterly dependent but who undermines her. The women meet and develop a close friendship which initially helps Ruth, but finally destroys both of them and Franz. Continuing her exploration of bonds between women begun with *Sisters, Or The Balance Of Happiness* and perfected in *The German Sisters*, Germany's most formidable woman director now takes it a step further in exposing the destructive potential of such relationships. Magnificently played by Schygulla and Winkler, and emotionally charged beneath its leisurely surface, this complex and intelligent film touches on many thorny issues and is distinctly devoid of comfort.

Friends For Life

Amici Per La Pelle

Italy 1955 100 mins bw
Cines

d **Franco Rossi**
sc **Franco Rossi, Leo Benvenuti, Piero De Bernardi, Ugo Guerra, Giandomenico Giagli**
ph **Gabor Pogany**
Geronimo Meynier, Andrea Scire, Luigi Tosi, Paolo Ferrari, Dina Perbellini

A motherless schoolboy goes to stay in the stable environment of his friend's family. However, when the two youngsters quarrel, the boy leaves for the Middle East with his businessman father, a decision which proves to be a painful wrench for both youngsters. This compassionate and sensitive study of the closed world of childhood, tinged with an adult's sentimentality, has two remarkable juvenile leads.

Friend Will Come Tonight, A see Ami Viendra Ce Soir, Un

Fröken Julie see Miss Julie

From The Life Of The Marionettes

Aus Dem Leben Der Marionetten

W. Germany 1980 104 mins col/bw
ITC

d **Ingmar Bergman**
sc **Ingmar Bergman**
ph **Sven Nykvist**
m **Rolf Wilhelm**
Robert Atzorn, Christine Buchegger, Martin Benrath, Rita Russek, Lola Muethel, Walter Schmidinger

A rich, youngish businessman (Atzorn), going through a marriage crisis with his independent dress-designer wife (Buchegger), murders a prostitute in the back room of a nightclub. Bergman's second film made during his short tax exile in Germany is superior to the misconceived *The Serpent's Egg* (1977). Opening with a murder in a blood red room, most of the film is shot in stark monochrome with an intense whiteness in the dream sequences. Balanced between the distancing device of Brechtian titles and the use of large close-ups, Bergman has created a tightly controlled case history in the German idiom. Outstanding is a deeply depressing monologue by an aging gay man (Schmidinger), who is one of the rare male homosexuals in Bergman's *oeuvre*.

Frontier see Aerograd

Frühlingssinfonie see Spring Symphony

Fruit Défendu, Le see Forbidden Fruit

Fruits De La Passion, Les see Fruits Of Passion, The

The Fruits Of Passion

Shina Ningyo

aka Les Fruits De La Passion

France/Japan 1981 83 mins col
Argos(Paris)/Terayama(Tokyo)

d **Shuji Terayama**
sc **Shuji Terayama, Pauline Réage**
ph **Tatsuo Susuki**
m **J.A. Seazer**
Klaus Kinski, Isabelle Illiers, Arielle Dombasle, Peter, Kenichi Nakamura, Takeshi Wakamatsu

In the 1920s, English aristocrat Sir Stephen (Kinski) takes his willing slave 'O' (Illiers) to Hong Kong, where he installs her in a brothel while he takes his pleasure elsewhere. But Sir Stephen becomes jealous of one of her clients (Nakamura) and shoots him dead. The film was meant as a sado-masochistic follow-up to Oshima's *In The Realm Of The Senses* and *Empire Of Passion*, and French producer Anatole Dauman got Terayama to adapt the pseudonymous Pauline Réage's sequel to the erotic novel *The Story Of O*. In French, Japanese and some 'English', the film, when trying for some narrative coherence, is a badly acted, badly scripted disaster. When Terayama is left to explore his own fantasies, echoing earlier works, the picture has some morbid fascination. The brothel Madam is played effectively by the transvestite Peter, the Fool in Kurosawa's *Ran*.

Frustration see Ship Bound For India, A

Full Moon In Paris

Les Nuits De La Pleine Lune

France 1984 102 mins col
Les Films Du Losange/Les Films Ariane

d **Eric Rohmer**
sc **Eric Rohmer**
ph **Renato Berta**
m **Elli and Jacno**
Pascale Ogier, Tcheky Karyo, Fabrice Luchini, Christian Vadim, Virginie Thevenet

A young trainee textile designer (Ogier), working in the centre of Paris but living with her boyfriend in the suburbs, gains some independence by finding a small apartment for herself in the capital. Rohmer, master of the minutiae of relationships, captures the way people, whatever their level of articulacy, talk things through. Here, however, he just manages to skate on the right side of the thin line that separates an interesting film from a trivial one about trivial young people. Pascale Ogier (daughter of Bulle Ogier), who also designed the sets, died prematurely in October 1984 aged 24.

Best Actress (Pascale Ogier) Venice 1984

The Funeral

Ososhiki

Japan 1985 123 mins col
Itami/N.C.P

d **Juzo Itami**
sc **Juzo Itami**
ph **Yonezo Maeda**
m **Joji Yuasa**
Tsutomu Yamazaki, Nobuko Miyamoto, Kin Sugai, Shuji Otaki, Ichiro Zaitsu, Nekohachi Edoya, Chishu Ryu

When elderly Mr Amamiya dies suddenly, it falls to Wabisuke (Yamazaki), the actor husband of the dead man's actress daughter (Miyamoto, director Itami's wife), to assume the role of chief mourner. The bereaved couple hurry off a film set to their country house where the three-day wake is to be held, and where Wabisuke swots up his duties from a video called 'The ABC Of Funerals'. Such is the tone of Itami's black comedy, peopled with a gallery of richly drawn supporting characters ranging from the pompous undertaker, through the Rolls Royce-owning, money grubbing priest (Ryu), to the deceased's fussy brother obsessed with the comfort of the corpse. The director cruelly satirizes the breach in the observance, but rescues his irreverence from tastelessness with the sincerity of the widow's address and the solemnity of the cremation. Actor Itami's first comedy as director is somewhat heavy-handed (the more accomplished *Tampopo* would follow), but it is inventive and amusing.

A Funny Dirty Little War

No Habra Mas Penas Ni Olvido

Argentina 1983 79 mins col
Aries Cinematografica Argentina

d **Hector Olivera**
sc **Roberto Cossa, Hector Olivera**
ph **Leonardo Rodriguez Solis**
m **Oscar Cardoza Ocampo**
Federico Luppi, Hector Bidonde, Victor Laplace, Miguel Angel Sola, Graciela Dufau, Angel Sola

In 1974, after Peron has returned to power following 18 years in exile, a wave of violence erupts as different factions, all professing loyalty to the president, fight among themselves. In the sleepy town of Colonia Vela, administrator Fuentes (Luppi), together with a small motley band, occupies the town hall in an act of resistance against the army. Complications proliferate, as does the cold-blooded murder of defenceless civilians, for Olivera is much concerned with the role of essentially innocent folk rebelling against a messy regime. The film is fast, furious and funny—a penetrating political satire which hits its targets with a mixture of broad comedy and brutal images.

Special Jury Prize Berlin 1984

Furia

Italy 1946 90 mins bw
Franchini/AGIC

d **Goffredo Alessandrini**
sc **Goffredo Alessandrini**

ph **Pierot Portalupy**
Isa Pola, Rossano Brazzi, Gino Cervi, Adriana Bennetti, Umberto Spadaro

Pola, bored with her marriage to wealthy horse breeder Cervi, has a steamy affair with stud keeper Brazzi who then marries Cervi's daughter. But he and Pola still can't keep their hands off each other, while stable-hand Spardaro lusts after her with violent consequences. Neo-Realist Alessandrini tended to utilize his style in the service of the box-office and this uncompromising portrait of lust, acted and directed with conviction, was no exception. Don't search for meaning.

Fussgänger, Der see Pedestrian, The

The Future Is Woman
Il Futuro È Donna

Italy 1984 100 mins col
Faso Film(Rome)/UGC-Top No 1(Paris)/Ascot Film(West Berlin)

d **Marco Ferreri**
sc **Marco Ferreri, Dacia Maraini, Piera Degli Esposito**
ph **Tonino Delli Colli**
m **Carlo Savina, plus 12 Italian pop songs**
Ornella Muti, Hanna Schygulla, Niels Arestrup, Maurizio Donadoni, Michèle Bovenzi, Ute Cremer

Gordon (Arestrup) and his wife Anna (Schygulla) have decided against having children because of the nuclear threat. At a disco one evening, Anna rescues Malvina (Muti), a young woman who is being harassed by some youths. Learning that Malvina is pregnant and homeless, Anna takes her back with them, thus beginning a cycle of tensions, jealousies, reconciliations, leave-takings and returns. Although strongly cast (Schygulla and Muti are as sexy a pair as ever there was) and offering several dramatic and threatening images, Ferreri's film degenerates into an incoherent triangle that promises much but delivers little. As suggested by the title, there is a message about the expendability of men lurking somewhere in the script (Maraini and Esposito are well-known Feminists), together with the idea that parental instincts cannot be dictated by intellectual argument, but the themes are expressed with dreary pretension.

The Future Of Emily
L'Avenir D'Emilie

France/W. Germany 1984 116 mins col
Les Films Du Losange(Paris)/Helma Sanders Filmproduktion/Literarisches Colloquium(Berlin)

d **Helma Sanders-Brahms**
sc **Helma Sanders-Brahms**
ph **Sacha Vierny**
m **Jürgen Knieper**
Brigitte Fossey, Hildegarde Knef, Ivan Desny, Herman Treusch, Camille Raymond, and the voice of Mathieu Carrière

Movie star Isabelle (Fossey) completes a film in Berlin and leaves for Normandy to see her parents (Knef and Desny) and her young daughter Emily (Raymond) who lives with them during her frequent absences. Her arrival is complicated by a call from her leading man (Treusch) who is romantically pursuing her. Mother and daughter spend a long night exchanging their innermost thoughts, and Isabelle makes plans with Emily which both know will not materialize. With sensitivity, imagination, control and razor-sharp insight, Sanders-Brahms has delivered a multi-layered essay on life, art, parenthood and the patterns of generations. She is brilliantly well-served by her actresses, including young Camille Raymond, and the result is a powerful, if more loving, cousin to Bergman's *Autumn Sonata*, exploring similar territory about life versus art and mother-daughter relationships.

Futuro È Donna, Il see Future Is Woman, The

Fuzi Qing see Father And Son

Le Gai Savoir

aka The Joyful Wisdom

France 1969 95 mins col
ORTF/Anouchka/Batavia Atelier

d **Jean-Luc Godard**
sc **Jean-Luc Godard**
ph **Georges Leclerc**
m **Revolutionary Cuban hymn**
Jean-Pierre Léaud, Juliette Berto

Patricia Lumumba and Emile Rousseau sit in an empty TV studio and talk about the media, education and language, occasionally interrupted by street scenes. Godard was commissioned by French TV to make an adaptation of fellow Swiss Jean-Jacques Rousseau's classic *Emile*, but it became very much his own treatise on 'progressive' education. Cut during and after the events of May 1968, this stimulating two-character conversation piece was a key film in Godard's career. At one stage Léaud says, 'We must start again from zero,' and Godard's own return to zero resulted in a break from all commercial film-making until 1972. With Jean-Pierre Gorin, he shot a series of cinétracts in 16mm and later video. They include *Pravda*, *Vent D'Est*, and *Vladimir And Rosa*.

Galia

aka I And My Lovers

France 1965 105 mins bw
Speva/Ciné Alliance/Variety

d **Georges Lautner**
sc **Georges Lautner, Vahe Katcha**
ph **Maurice Fellous**
m **Michel Magne, Bach (The Swingle Singers)**
Mireille Darc, Venantino Venantini, Françoise Prévost, Jacques Riberolles

A badly-treated wife (Prévost) is rescued from a suicidal leap into the Seine by a passer-by (Darc). The latter visits the husband (Venantini), who believes his wife dead after seeing the suicide note and they carry on an affair. However, the wife decides to save her rescuer by killing her husband. The only reason for this absurd melodrama having had a fairly profitable release in Britain and the USA must have been the sexy disrobed presence of ex-model Darc. The film also had a veneer of chic and cheek.

The Gambler

Le Joueur

France 1958 105 mins col
Franco-London

d **Claude Autant-Lara**
sc **Jean Aurenche, Pierre Bost, François Boyer**
ph **Jacques Natteau**
m **René Cloërec**
Gérard Philipe, Liselotte Pulver, Nadine Alari, Bernard Blier, Jean Danet, Françoise Rosay, Carette

While waiting for his aunt to die and leave him her fortune, an aging general (Blier) lives and gambles in Baden-Baden at the expense of an adventurer who is the lover of his daughter (Pulver). Her tutor (Philipe), who is in love with her, arrives intending to rescue her from her sordid lot but is defeated by the consequences of the gambling fever that affects everybody. A somewhat overblown and melodramatic adaptation of the 1866 novella by Dostoevsky, the showy and garish colour and design actually suit the milieu. The dashing hero of the French cinema, Philipe, is as beguiling as usual, while Pulver is touching as the tragic victim of her father's dissolute habits. Among the many screen versions of this subject was a 1949 Hollywood contribution, titled *The Great Sinner* and starring Gregory Peck.

Game Of Love, The see Ripening Seed, The

Gamlet see Hamlet

Le Gang

France 1976 103 mins col
Adel Productions(Paris)/Mondial Ti-Fi(Rome)

d **Jacques Deray**
sc **Alphonse Boudard, Jean-Claude Carrière**
ph **Silvano Ippoliti**
m **Carlo Rustichelli**
Alain Delon, Maurice Barrier, Roland Bertin, Laura Betti, Giampiero Albertini, Nicole Calfan

It is 1945 and the French police, busy weeding out Nazi collaborators from their ranks, are somewhat disorganized. Taking advantage of this, Robert (Delon) assembles a gang which embarks on a series of daring robberies, commencing with the interception of a bullion consignment. Finally cornered by the law, Robert escapes, only to meet his end in ironic circumstances. Deray's film, full of imaginative, almost quaint characters and situations, tells its tale in flashback from the point of view of Robert's mistress (Calfan) as his mournful gang gathers round his deathbed. However, although not evidently intended as a parody of the genre, it is so amiable and free from violence that it's good for little more than lazy family entertainment. Delon, sporting cheeriness, reckless bravado and a curly wig, sums up the tone.

Garde À Vue see Inquisitor, The

Garden Of Stones

Baghe Sangui

Iran 1976 84 mins col
N.I.R.T.

d **Parviz Kimiavi**
sc **Parviz Kimiavi**
ph **Freydoun Ghovaniou**
Darvich Khan, his family, and villagers of Balvarad

An elderly shepherd (Khan), living in the semi-desert of the Iranian hinterland, has a mystic vision which leads him to construct an elaborate garden of stones attached to dry tree branches. The garden is dedicated to an unknown god and he worships there daily. The word spreads, however, and soon other villagers come to join him in his strange and private shrine, thus destroying the spell. Using a non-professional cast who project simplicity and convinction, Kimiavi has constructed a spare and beguiling mixture of fable and reality. He manages some gently ironic digs at established values, but dialogue is kept to a minimum, leaving the tale best told by its attractive and well-judged images.

Special Jury Prize Berlin 1976

The Garden Of The Finzi-Continis

Il Giardino Dei Finzi-Contini

Italy 1970 95 mins col
Documento Film/CCC Filmkunst

d **Vittorio De Sica**
sc **Tullio Pinelli, Valerio Zurlini, Franco Brusati, Vittorio Bonicelli, Ugo Pirro, Alain Katz**
ph **Ennio Guarnieri**
m **Manuel De Sica**
Dominique Sanda, Lino Capolicchio, Helmut Berger, Romolo Valli, Fabio Testi, Inna Alexeiff, Camillo Angelini-Rota

The opulent Ferrara mansion inhabited by the cultivated, Jewish Finzi- Contini family is already a ghetto created by their wealth, when the coming of Fascism forces them to retreat further behind its walls. The younger members, Micol and Alberto (Sanda and Capolicchio) open up the tennis courts when Jews are barred from the club, and spend the summer caught in ambiguous relationships complicated by the intrusion of politics and war, and the need to define allegiances. The film, famously, ends with the Finzi-Contini dynasty assembled in the schoolroom awaiting deportation. This tragic testament to Italy's involvement in the Holocaust brought De Sica out of the directorial wilderness in which he had languished for some years. His august reputation was deservedly restored by this hauntingly beautiful, intelligent and tasteful film.

Best Foreign Film Oscar 1971
Best Film Berlin 1971

Garm Hava see Hot Winds

Gate of Hell

Jigokumon

Japan 1953 90 mins col
Daiei

d **Teinosuke Kinugasa**
sc **Teinosuke Kinugasa**
ph **Kohei Sugiyama**
m **Yasushi Akutagawa**
Machiko Kyo, Kazuo Hasegawa, Isao Yamagata, Koreya Senda

A 12th-century feudal warlord (Hasegawa) desires a married woman (Kyo), but she kills herself rather than submit to him. Filled with remorse, he becomes a monk. One of the few Kinugasa films known in the West, its director studied with Eisenstein and this was the first Japanese picture to use a western colour process (Eastmancolor). Although it makes a strong visual impact—it won the Oscar for costume design—and Kyo and Hasegawa are outstanding, the simple tale nonetheless conforms to the strict conventions of the *Jidai-Geki*, the popular Japanese period films.

Best Foreign Film Oscar 1954
Best Film Cannes 1954

Gate Of Lilacs see Gates Of Paris

Gates Of Paris

aka Gate Of Lilacs

Porte Des Lilas

France 1957 95 mins bw
Filmsonor/Rizzoli

d **René Clair**
sc **René Clair, Jean Aurel**
ph **Robert Le Fèbvre**
m **Georges Brassens**
Pierre Brasseur, Georges Brassens, Henri Vidal, Dany Carrel, Raymond Bussières, Amedée

Juju (Brasseur), a drunken drifter, and his troubadour friend (Brassens) offer refuge to a gangster (Vidal), who repays them by making a play for Juju's girlfriend (Carrel). However, Juju accidentally kills the gangster. This is the sort of dark-toned film not usually associated with its director. Perhaps the critics who attacked the picture on first release, failed to see that, beneath the shadows of the underworld setting, it contains a modicum of wit, charm and poetry. However, the stylized sets and the somewhat stilted script surround it with an aura of faded artificiality that might have worked two decades previously in the hands of Marcel Carné and Jacques Prévert.

The Gates Of The Louvre

(US: Black Thursday)

Les Guichets Du Louvre

France 1974 92 mins col
Les Films Du Parnasse/Saga/ORTF/Les Films Du Limon

d **Michel Mitrani**
sc **Michel Mitrani, Albert Cossery**
ph **Jean Tournier**
m **Mort Shuman**
Christine Pascal, Christian Rist, Judith Magre, Alice Sapritch, Michel Auclair, Michel Robin

It is 'Black Thursday', a July day in 1942 when 13,000 Parisian Jews were rounded up and taken to a stadium before deportation and eventual extermination. Paul (Rist), a non-Jewish student, helps to rescue Jeanne (Pascal), a girl whose family has been arrested. They fall in love, but she decides to return to her people. With the breakthrough of Marcel Ophüls' *The Sorrow And The Pity*, after over 25 years of silence about the complicity of the French in the Final Solution, this shameful period began to be aired in fictional films. This notable example overcomes many of the pitfalls in the plot that could have become mawkish and moralistic—Jewish families being split, the love affair and the parting—because Mitrani handles them with taste and restraint. The characters, whether victims or oppressors, are never stereotyped, only the young lovers lack depth.

Gates Of The Night

Les Portes De La Nuit

France 1946 106 mins bw
Pathé

d **Marcel Carné**
sc **Jacques Prévert**
ph **Philippe Agostini**
m **Joseph Kosma**

Pierre Brasseur, Yves Montand, Nathalie Nattier, Serge Reggiani, Jean Vilar, Saturnin Fabre, Raymond Bussières, Julien Carette

Among various doomed lovers in a *quartier* in immediate post-war Paris are a Resistance hero (Montand) and a young woman (Nattier) whose husband was a black-marketeer and brother a collaborator. The film marked the end of the great Carné-Prévert partnership and the sombre poetic- realist tradition of which they formed such an important part. Since the film-makers failed to take account of the optimistic post-war mood in France, it was reviled on its release and failed miserably at the box- office. Today, the gloomy, rather pretentious fable is of interest for its heady 1940s atmosphere, the expensive studio sets by Alexander Trauner and the famous theme song, called 'Autumn Leaves' in English. Twenty-five-year- old Montand and the insipid Nattier replaced Jean Gabin and Marlene Dietrich, who both turned down the lead roles at the last moment.

Gattopardo, Il see Leopard, The

Gav see Cow, The

Gebroken Spiegels see Broken Mirrors

Geheimnisse Einer Seele see Secrets Of A Soul

Gehenu Lamai see Girls, The

Geisha see Gion Festival Music

Genbaku No Ko see Children Of Hiroshima

General Della Rovere

Il Generale Della Rovere

Italy 1959 137 mins bw
Zebra/Gaumont

d **Roberto Rossellini**
sc **Roberto Rossellini, Sergio Amedei, Diego Fabbri, Indro Montanelli**
ph **Carlo Carlini**
m **Renzo Rossellini**

Vittorio De Sica, Hannes Messemer, Sandra Milo, Giovanna Ralli, Anne Vernon

A con man (De Sica), persuaded by the Nazis to pose as an Italian general and Resistance leader to discover who the partisans are, begins to identify with his role and dies a martyr. After some years in disfavour, Rossellini regained some of his prestige by returning to the subject of war and resistance with which he made his name in the 1940s. Rather stodgily directed, and with an unconvincing patriotic ending, it nevertheless has a fine performance from De Sica and poses some important questions.

Best Film Venice 1959

Generale Della Rovere, Il see General Della Rovere

The General Line

aka Old And New

Generalnaya Linya

aka Staroye I Novoye

USSR 1929 90 mins bw
Sovkino

d **Sergei Eisenstein**
sc **Sergei Eisenstein**
ph **Edouard Tissé**
m **Silent**

Marfa Lapkina, Vasya Buzenkov, Kostya Vasiliev, Chukhamarev

A peasant woman (Lapkina) is converted to the socialist principles of agriculture and fights to maintain collective farming in her community. After *October* (1927) displeased the powers that were, Eisenstein tried to toe the Party line with his last silent film, but got into hot water again. Apparently the satirically humorous treatment of some of the peasants was not to its liking, and neither were the advanced editing techniques. However, the film, centred around identifiable human characters, works equally as art and propaganda. The 'tonal montage', as the director called it, is at its best in the demonstration of the cream separator and the courtship of a bull and cow.

Generalnaya Linya see General Line, The

A Generation

Pokolenie

Poland 1954 85 mins bw
Film Polski

d **Andrzej Wajda**
sc **Bohdan Czeszko**
ph **Jerzy Lipman**
m **Andrzej Markowski**
Tadeusz Lomnicki, Urszula Modrzynska, Roman Polanski, Zbigniew Cybulski

A young man (Lomnicki) involved with the Resistance, who helps fighters from the Warsaw Ghetto uprising in 1942 to escape, and who falls in love with a girl (Modrzynska) who leads a youth group, grows in maturity and acquires qualities of leadership from his experiences. The title refers to Poland's 'lost generation', that of most of the people in their twenties whose first feature film this was—the director, the screenwriter, the photographer, the composer and many of the actors. It formed the realistic first part of an (unplanned) war trilogy that made Wajda's name and put Polish cinema firmly on the map. Compared with *Kanal* (1957) and *Ashes And Diamonds* (1958) it is over-simplistic, but the youthful fervour carries it off.

Genesis

India 1986 109 mins col
Scarabée Films (Paris)/Mrinal Sen Productions (Calcutta)/Les Films De La Drève (Brussels)/Cactus Film (Zurich)

d **Mrinal Sen**
sc **Mrinal Sen, with Mohit Chattopadhya**
ph **Carlo Varini**
m **Ravi Shankar**
Shabana Azmi, Naseeruddin Shah, Om Puri, M.K. Raina

The Farmer and The Weaver eke out a bare existence in a ruined and deserted village. The Woman arrives, disturbing the balance between the two men who both desire her. She becomes pregnant and leaves, they fight, and the Trader's machines come to rebuild the village. Heavy with symbolism, the film's message is nonetheless explicitly simple: the poor will remain poor, being always at the mercy of the powerful and prosperous. Beautifully photographed—often in images that seem too contrived and manicured for the landscape they represent—*Genesis* is, for all its virtues of intelligence and social conscience, a somewhat alienating and passionless piece that keeps the viewer distanced from its nameless protagonists.

Genou De Claire, Le see Claire's Knee

Genroku Chushingura see Loyal 47 Ronin, The

Les Gens Du Voyage

aka The Wanderers

France 1938 123 mins bw
Tobis

d **Jacques Feyder**
sc **Jacques Feyder, Jacques Viol**
ph **Franz Koch**
m **Wolfgang Zilzer**
Françoise Rosay, André Brûlé, Fabien Loris, Mary Glory, Sylvie Bataille

A lady lion tamer (Rosay) gives refuge to her husband (Brûlé), a fugitive from justice, in the circus where she performs. Meanwhile their son (Loris) is having an affair with the bareback rider (Glory) and there are jealousies and intrigues among the circus folk. One of Feyder's last films, it isn't exactly the greatest show on earth, but it skillfully juggles the variegated elements of the plot. Rosay, of course, can make any cliché seem new-minted. The film was simultaneously made in a German version, entitled *Fahrendes Volk*, with Hans Albers in the role of the husband.

A Gentle Creature

Une Femme Douce

France 1969 87 mins col
Parc/Marianne

d **Robert Bresson**
sc **Robert Bresson**
ph **Ghislain Cloquet**
m **Jean Wiener**
Dominique Sanda, Guy Frangin, Jane Lobre

A young woman (Sanda) marries a pawnbroker (Frangin) but finds she cannot adapt her life to his. She toys with murdering him, but kills herself instead. Using colour for the first time, Bresson brought a more overt sensuality and 'modernity' to his work than hitherto. Visually composed almost entirely of blue and green tones, the plot (a Dostoevsky story transposed to contemporary Paris) and acting are mainly grey. By eschewing all psychology, the film never begins to explain the miserable girl's motives. It was the screen debut of 20-year-old fashion model Dominique Sanda, one of the rare Bresson discoveries who went on to make a career in acting.

Germania, Anno Zero see Germany, Year Zero

The German Sisters

Die Bleierne Zeit

W. Germany 1981 107 mins col
Bioskop

d **Margarethe Von Trotta**
sc **Margarethe Von Trotta**
ph **Franz Rath**
m **Nicolas Economou**
Jutta Lampe, Barbara Sukowa, Rüdiger Vogler, Doris Schade, Verenice Rudolph

Two contrasting sisters—a feminist journalist (Lampe) and a Baader Meinhof activist (Sukowa)—are brought closer when the latter is imprisoned, goes on hunger strike and dies, although the official version of 'suicide' is refuted by the remaining sister. Inspired by real-life sisters Christiane and Gudrun Ensslin, the film never really answers the interesting questions it raises: how much does our upbringing affect our political beliefs and what is the best way to combat the injustices in Western society? However, it does have the force to unsettle, and is beautifully acted.

Best Film Venice 1959

Germany In Autumn

Deutschland Im Herbst

W. Germany 1978 134 mins col
Filmverlag Der Autoren/Hallelujah/Kairos

d **Alf Brustellin, Alexander Kluge, Maximiliane Mainka, Edgar Reitz, Katja Rupé, Hans Peter Cloos, Volker Schlöndorff, Rainer Werner Fassbinder, Bernhard Sinkel, Beate Mainka-Jellinghaus, Peter Schubert, Heinrich Böll**
sc **Heinrich Böll, Peter Steinbach**
ph **Jürgen Jürges, Bodo Kessler, Dietrich Lohmann, Michael Ballhaus, Colin Mounier, Jörg Schmidt-Reitwein**
m **Ennio Morricone, Tchaikowsky, Mozart**
Hannelore Hoger, Katja Rupé, Hans Peter Cloos, Angela Winkler, Franziska Walser, Vadim Glowna, Helmut Griem, Mario Adorf, Rainer Werner Fassbinder, Armin Meier

A dozen West German film-makers contribute their reportage, political statements and artistic comments on the political situation in their country after the kidnap and murder of the industrialist, Hans Martin Schleyer. Two episodes in particular stand out in this illuminating anatomy of West Germany seen principally from the Left: Böll on the subject of German TV's refusal to air Sophocles' *Antigone* on the grounds of its being too provocative; and Fassbinder's brave and painful piece of autobiographical film, in which he is seen trying to drop his lover and talk politics to his mother while on drink and drugs.

Germany, Pale Mother

Deutschland, Bleiche Mutter

W. Germany 1980 109 mins col
Literarisches Colloquium/WDR

d **Helma Sanders-Brahms**
sc **Helma Sanders-Brahms**
ph **Jürgen Jürges**
m **Jürgen Knieper**
Eva Mattes, Ernst Jacobi, Elisabeth Stepanek, Angelika Thomas

Just after her marriage, on the eve of the German invasion of Poland, a young woman (Mattes) sees her husband (Jacobi) go off to join the German army. She and her daughter (Stepanek) struggle for survival during the long war years until the husband returns, an embittered and brutal man. Sanders-Brahms (born 1940) based her most celebrated film on her own mother's experiences during and after the war. It works as a harrowing personal document of a woman's courage, but the director weighs the character down with the symbolic burden suggested by the title. As such it becomes spurious, melodramatic and over-extended. The splendid Eva Mattes makes us suffer with the mother in more ways than one.

Germany, Year Zero

Germania, Anno Zero

Italy 1947 78 mins bw
Tevere/Sadfilm

d **Roberto Rossellini**
sc **Roberto Rossellini, Carlo Lizzani, Max Kolpet**
ph **Robert Juillard**
m **Renzo Rossellini**
Edmund Moeschka, Franz Kruger, Barbara Hintz, Werner Pittschau, Erich Gühne

In Occupied Berlin, a 12-year-old boy (Moeschka), trying to feed his family, poisons his sickly father to lessen the burden but, unable to live with the deed, he throws himself off a ruined building. For his last Neo- Realist film, Rossellini took his cameras to a destitute post-war Berlin, using only one professional actor (Kruger), as the father. Despite the weaknesses in exposition and execution, the director's compassion shines through, and the documentary material is fascinating. The final section when the child, isolated from others and society, finds a moment to play before dying, is Rossellini at his poignant best.

Germinal

France 1963 110 mins bw
Marceau/Cocinor/Metzger & Woog/Laetitia

d **Yves Allégret**
sc **Charles Spaak**
ph **Jean Bourgoin**
m **Michel Magne**
Jean Sorel, Berthe Grandval, Claude Brasseur, Bernard Blier, Lea Padovani, Simon Valère

Etienne (Sorel) gets a job in a French coal-mining town during the 1860s, and leads the exploited miners in a strike for better conditions. Emile Zola's monumental novel about social and economic conditions in 19th-century industrial France has been robbed of its power by a dull screenplay, a subdued leading man, and direction that is generally underpowered, apart from the excellent handling of the strike scenes. Although it was filmed in Hungary, both place and period convince, but the film emerges as little more than a period melodrama that fails to capitalize on the opportunities offered by Zola's rich tapestry.

Gertrud

Denmark 1964 116 mins bw
Palladium

d **Carl Dreyer**
sc **Carl Dreyer**
ph **Henning Bendtsen, Arne Abrahamsen**
m **Jørgen Jersild**
Nina Pens Røde, Bendt Rothe, Ebbe Røde, Baard Owe, Axel Strøbye

Gertrud (Pens Røde) leaves her husband for a young musician only to find he cannot give her his total love. Later she rejects the marriage proposals of three men in succession, finally accepting that her ideal will never be realized. Made after a 10-year gap, Dreyer's final film takes the form of a series of duologues photographed with an almost immobile camera and immensely long takes, and given stylized performances. It was critically ill-received on its release by those whose definition of action in the cinema is severely limited. The action here is in the dialogue and emotions which create a film of exceptional intensity and warmth and a serenity achieved in the best of chamber music.

Gervaise

France 1956 116 mins bw
Agnes Delahaye/Silver/CLCC

d **René Clement**
sc **Jean Aurenche, Pierre Bost**
ph **Robert Juillard**
Maria Schell, François Périer, Suzy Delair, Mathilde Casadeus, Armand Mestral

In the Montmartre of 1850, washerwoman Gervaise (Schell) is left with two children by her lover. She marries a roof repairer (Périer) and opens her own laundry, but difficult circumstances lead her and her husband to drink. The fifth screen adaptation of Zola's *L'Assommoir* was the most lavish and convincing portrait of the bustling place and harsh period. Despite the severe limitations of her superficial performance, Maria Schell impressed the Venice Film Festival jury.

Best Actress (Maria Schell) Venice 1956

Get Out Your Handkerchiefs

Préparez Vos Mouchoirs

France 1978 108 mins col
Les Films Ariane/CAPAC/Belga/SODEP

d **Bertrand Blier**
sc **Bertrand Blier**
ph **Jean Penzer**
m **Georges Delerue, Mozart, Schubert**
Gérard Depardieu, Patrick Dewaere, Carole Laure, Riton, Michel Serrault

Raoul (Depardieu), finding his wife (Laure) sexually unresponsive, decides to present her with a lover (Dewaere) but he has no luck either. It takes a 13-year-old boy (Riton) to solve her problem and make her pregnant. Neither as ribald nor as funny as it sets out to be, the film has a great deal of old-fashioned charm. Depardieu and Dewaere, the leads in Blier's *Going Places* (1974), play with a lightness reminiscent of the New Wave days of Belmondo and Brialy.

Best Foreign Film Oscar 1978

Ghare-Baire see Home And The World, The

Gharibeh-Va-Meh see Stranger And The Fog, The

Giardino Dei Finzi-Contini, Il see Garden Of The Finzi-Continis, The

---

Gift see Poison

The Gift Of God

Wend Kuuni

Upper Volta 1982 70 mins col
National Cinema Centre

d **Gaston J.M. Kaboré**
sc **Gaston J.M. Kaboré**
ph **Sekou Ouedraogo, Issaka Thiombiano**
m **René B. Guirma**
Serge Yanago, Rosine Yanago, Joseph Nikiema, Colette Kaboré

In pre-colonial days, a small boy (Serge Yanago), found wandering lost in the bush and unable to speak, is adopted by a young couple (Nikiema and Kaboré). The boy spends his days silently tending their goats in the fields, sometimes with their young daughter (Rosine Yanago) who dreams that his speech will come back and he will be able to tell her what happened to him and where he comes from. Kaboré's concise first feature shows sensitivity and a simplicity of expression in a beautifully photographed story of an African childhood. The two children appear wonderfully natural under his careful direction.

Gigi

France 1948 109 mins bw
Codo-Cinéma

d **Jacqueline Audry**
sc **Pierre Laroche**
ph **Gérard Perrin**
m **Marcel Landowski**
Danièle Delorme, Gaby Morlay, Yvonne De Bray, Frank Villard, Jean Tissier

In turn-of-the century Paris, Gigi (Delorme), a young girl trained to be a courtesan by her aunt (Morlay), opts for true love and marriage to a rake (Villard) whom she reforms. This charming, faithful adaptation of Colette's novel had the advantage of a close collaboration between the director, her screenwriter husband and the novelist herself. It was the first of a successful trilogy of films based on Colette stories, all directed by Audry and all starring the delicate Danièle Delorme, and, of course, was the subject of the award-winning Hollywood musical, starring Leslie Caron.

Ginger And Fred

Ginger E Fred

Italy 1986 127 mins col
PEA(Rome)/Revcom Films/Les Films Ariane/FR3 Films (Paris)/Stella Films/Anthea(Munich)

d **Federico Fellini**
sc **Federico Fellini, Tonino Guerra, Tullio Pinelli**
ph **Tonino Delli Colli, Ennio Guarnieri**
m **Nicola Piovani**
Giulietta Masina, Marcello Mastroianni, Franco Fabrizi, Frederick Von Ledebur,

Augusto Poderosi, Martin Maria Blau, Toto Mignone

Before the war, dancers Amelia Bonetti (Masina) and Pippo Botticella (Mastroianni) performed a cabaret as Ginger and Fred in homage to the great Hollywood duo. Many years have passed since they went their separate ways; now they are reunited by an invitation to resurrect their act for a popular TV programme. A simple story in which Fellini simultaneously pays a nostalgic and affectionate tribute to old troupers and digs the knife into the crass commercialism of Italian television—at whose hands he has suffered with the indiscriminate mangling of his films. Masina, serene without being coy, and a flabby, balding Mastroianni are a delight as the couple, now past it but able to relive their former glory for a few magical moments. This is the director at his most warmly accessible.

Ginger E Fred see Ginger And Fred

Gion Bayashi see Gion Festival Music

Gion Festival Music

(US: Geisha)

Gion Bayashi

Japan 1953 100 mins bw
Daiei

d **Kenji Mizoguchi**
sc **Yoshikata Yoda**
ph **Kazuo Miyagawa**
m **Ichiro Saito**
Michiyo Kogure, Ayako Wakao, Seizaburo Kawazy, Cheiko Naniwa, Eitaro Shindo

An elderly geisha (Kogure) trains a young girl (Wakao) in the ancient art, but the novice soon realizes that her romantic vision of her role is a far cry from the sordid reality. Almost a remake of *Sisters Of The Gion* (1936), it is one of Mizoguchi's finest chamber works, being a sensitive and thoughful study of two contrasting geishas (superbly played) and of the reduced status of their calling after World War II.

Gion No Shimai see Sisters Of The Gion

Giornata Particolare, Una see Special Day, A

Gioventu Perduta see Lost Youth

Girasoli, I see Sunflower

The Girl Friends

Le Amiche

Italy 1955 90 mins bw
Trionfalcine

d **Michelangelo Antonioni**
sc **Suso Cecchi D'Amico, Alba De Cespedes, Michelangelo Antonioni**
ph **Gianni Di Venanzo**
m **Giovanni Fusco**
Eleanora Rossi Drago, Valentina Cortese, Yvonne Furneaux, Gabriele Ferzetti, Franco Fabrizi, Madeleine Fischer, Annamaria Pancani

Clelia (Drago), who has done well in Rome as a fashion designer, returns to her native Turin where she becomes involved in the affairs of four of her *haute bourgeois* girl friends. Adapted from a Cesare Pavese story, the film manages to hold 10 characters in balance, giving almost equal weight to their individuality and the shifting pattern of relationships. The elaborate social groupings and Antonioni's ability to set people meaningfully against landscapes is best illustrated by the extended sequence of an afternoon on the beach. The film, which won a prize at Venice, proves that Antonioni's greatness did not begin with *L'Avventura* (1960).

A Girl From Lorraine

La Provinciale

France 1980 112 mins col
Phoenix/Gaumont/FR3/SSR

d **Claude Goretta**
sc **Claude Goretta, Jacques Kirsner, Rosina Rochette**
ph **Philippe Rousselot**
m **Arié Dzierlatka**
Nathalie Baye, Bruno Ganz, Angela Winkler, Patrick Chesnais, Pierre Vernier

With great expectations, 30-year-old Christine (Baye) leaves her friends, local choir and dog in her small home town in Lorraine to find work in Paris. After having an affair with a married Swiss businessman (Ganz), struggling to make a living and avoiding temptation, she returns home disillusioned. Goretta followed *The Lacemaker* with another fable about a 'typical ordinary Frenchwoman', as Christine is described. To go by the film, this means priggish, humourless and rather dull. Like the life in Paris, the screenplay is too obviously loaded against her in order to prove the contentious point that existence in the provinces, no matter how hard, tedious and unrewarding, is morally superior to that in the big bad city.

The Girl From Stormycroft

(US: A Girl From The Marsh Croft)

Tosen Fran Stormytorpet

Sweden 1917 96 mins bw
Svenska Biografteatern

d **Victor Sjöström**
sc **Victor Sjöström, Esther Julin**
ph **Henrik Jaenzon**
m **Silent**
Greta Almroth, Lars Hanson, Karin Molander, Georg Blomstedt

Helga (Almroth) becomes a social outcast when she gives birth to an illegitimate baby, but eventually wins the respect of the remote rustic community in which she lives by refusing to let the father (Hanson) of her child court eternal damnation by taking a false oath on the Bible denying responsibility. She eventually wins the love of a young man (Blomstedt) who has also faced unjust opprobrium. With 32 films already behind him, Sjöström became an international figure with *The Girl From Stormycroft*, the first of several adaptations from novels by Selma Lagerlöf. The plot has its inconsistencies and crudities, but the superb underplaying and the director's ability to create a believable community make it one of his finest films. It was remade by Detlef Sierck (Douglas Sirk) in Germany in 1935.

Girl From The Marsh Croft, A see Girl From Stormycroft, The

Girl In A Boot

Einmal Ku'damm Und Zurück

W. Germany 1983 96 mins col
Cinecom/Neue Filmproduktion/Sender Freies

d **Herbert Ballmann**
sc **Jürgen Engert**
ph **Ingo Hamer**
m **Jürgen Knieper**
Ursela Monn, Christian Kohlund, Evelyn Meyka, Peter Schiff, Peter Seum

East Berliner Ulla (Monn), whose father (Schiff) is a hard-line Party member, has a clandestine affair with Thomas (Kohlund), the cook at the Swiss Embassy. (Food is a nicely used recurring image.) Hiding Ulla in the boot of Thomas's car, the couple make a series of visits to the Western sector until a car accident in which Ulla is injured exposes them. Ballmann, who lived in East Berlin and made documentaries there, captures the details of daily life behind the wall, contrasting the struggles of the inhabitants with the cavalier consumerism of their privileged neighbours. The film is not, however, a didactic piece, being more concerned with Ulla who opts to sacrifice Thomas and stay at home, not for political reasons but because her roots are there.

The Girl In Black

To Koritsi Me Ta Mavra

Greece 1955 93 mins bw
Hermes

d **Michael Cacoyannis**
sc **Michael Cacoyannis**
ph **Walter Lassally**
m **Argyris Kounadis, Manos Hadjidakis**
Ellie Lambetti, Georges Foundas, Dimitri Horne, Eleni Zafiriou, Stefanos Stratigos

On the remote fishing island of Hydra, Marina (Lambetti) is persecuted by her neighbours for her widowed mother's indiscretions. A visiting Athenian writer (Foundas) tries to take her back to the mainland, but his attempts to save her end in near tragedy. Ellie Lambetti, the beautiful star of Cacoyannis' first film, the comedy *Windfall In Athens*, impressed even more as an actress of tragic stature in this controlled but passionate story. The German-born British Lassally gave it the keen-edged black and white photography it needed.

The Girl Rosemarie
(US: Rosemary)
Das Mädchen Rosemarie
W. Germany 1958 100 mins bw
Roxy

d **Rolf Thiele**
sc **Rolf Thiele, Erich Kuby, Jo Herbst, Rolf Ulrich**
ph **Klaus Von Rautenfeld**
m **Norbert Schultze**
Nadja Tiller, Peter Van Eyck, Carl Raddatz, Gert Fröbe, Mario Adorf, Horst Frank

The diary of a murdered Frankfurt prostitute reveals that she was blackmailing her wealthy and powerful clients, some of them the investigators of the crime itself. This biting satire on Adenauer's Germany was based on a real case that opened up a cesspool of corruption within the Establishment. The slickly-made film had more impact in pre-Fassbinder days, but it's still a good exposé and Tiller, a former Miss Austria, is seductive in the title role.

Girls, The see Bonnes Femmes, Les

The Girls
Flickorna
Sweden 1968 100 mins bw
Sandrew

d **Mai Zetterling**
sc **Mai Zetterling, David Hughes**
ph **Rune Ericson**
m **Michael Hurd**
Bibi Andersson, Harriet Andersson, Gunnel Lindblom, Gunnar Björnstrand, Erland Josephson, Frank Sundström

Three actresses—Liz (Bibi Andersson), Marianne (Harriet Andersson), Gunilla (Lindblom)—are in a production of Aristophanes' *Lysistrata*. Each has an unhappy personal life, suffering boorish husbands, married lovers, and so forth, and the play begins to influence them. Led by Liz, they begin to stand up for their rights as women. Casting some of the leading lights of Swedish film, Mai Zetterling brings her not inconsiderable experience to bear on a feminist plea, usefully intercutting the action with the Aristophanes classic. Unfortunately, she overstates her case, making all the men either ineffectual or unpleasant and the women visibly militant, and so loses the argument.

The Girls
Gehenu Lamai
Sri Lanka 1977 110 mins bw
Lester James Peries Productions

d **Sumitra Peries**
sc **Sumitra Peries**
ph **M.S. Anandan**
m **Nimal Mendis**
Vasanthi Chaturani, Ajith Jinadasa, Jenita Samaraweera, Trilicia Gunawardana, Chitra Wakista

Kusum (Chaturani), daughter of a poor village family, wins a scholarship to boarding school. On her visits home she looks after her crippled father, acts as mentor to her younger sister Soma (Samaraweera) and has a secret love affair with her cousin (Jinadasa) to which her aunt puts a stop. Soma wins a beauty contest and goes off to a movie career, but becomes pregnant, and Kusum, unhappy, fails her exams and must face a bleak future. This first feature is the work of Sri Lanka's first woman director—an achievement in itself. It's a modest, straightforward film in both style and content and, by Western standards, somewhat old-fashioned in its particular brand of simplicity. As a glimpse of Sinhalese rural values it's interesting and rather sad, but the director has missed opportunities to develop both her characters and her subject.

Girls In Uniform see Mädchen In Uniform

The Girl With A Suitcase
La Ragazza Con La Valigia
Italy 1960 135 mins bw
Titanus (Rome)/S.G.C. (Paris)

d **Valerio Zurlini**
sc **Leo Benvenuti, Piero De Bernardi, Enrico Medioli, Giuseppe Patroni Griffi, Valerio Zurlini**
ph **Tito Santoni**
m **Mario Nascimbene**
Claudio Cardinale, Jacques Perrin, Luciana

Angelillo, Corrado Pani, Romolo Valli, Gian Maria Volonté

Aida (Cardinale), a nightclub singer, is seduced by, and leaves her job for, Marcello (Pani), a rich idler who then abandons her. When she follows him to his family home in Parma, he instructs his 16-year-old brother Lorenzo (Perrin) to get rid of her, but the couple fall in love before circumstances force them to part. Zurlini, one of the most sensitive, economical and visually aware of Italian directors of the period, has made a poignant film of some depth, at the centre of which is a lost soul ill- equipped to find redemption. Cardinale and Perrin are excellent, but beware of badly cut versions: the film's original British release lost 39 minutes, and was thus severely distorted.

The Girl With The Golden Eyes

La Fille Aux Yeux D'Or

France 1961 105 mins bw
Madeleine

d **Jean-Gabriel Albicocco**
sc **Jean-Gabriel Albicocco, Pierre Pelégri, Philippe Dumarçay**
ph **Quinto Albicocco**
m **Narcisco Yepes, Arcangelo Corelli**
Marie Laforêt, Paul Guers, Françoise Prévost, Jacques Verlier, Françoise Dorléac

A man (Guers) working in the world of *haute couture* falls for a girl (Laforêt) of whom he knows nothing. He soon discovers that she is the lover of a female colleague (Prévost), and becomes a threat to their relationship. It would be hard to guess that this chic, arty, stylized Lesbian tale, set in and around the Paris fashion houses of the 1960s, was based on a Balzac story. Albicocco in his first feature, strains too hard to be stylish and provocative, attributes which come naturally to his wife, Laforêt.

Girl With The Hatbox

(US: When Moscow Laughs)

Devuchka S Korobkoi

USSR 1927 61 mins bw
Mezhrabpom

d **Boris Barnet**
sc **V. Tourkine, V. Cherchenievitch**
ph **B. Frantzisson, B. Filshin**
m **Silent**
Anna Sten, Vladimir Fogel, I. Koval-Samborski, V. Milhailov

While travelling on a train, Natasha (Sten), a Moscow milliner, meets a homeless student (Koval-Samborski) from the provinces. In order to get accomodation, he pretends to be married. After getting mixed up in a lottery squabble and stringing him along, she finally obliges him by marrying him. Barnet's first solo effort is a charming satirical comedy in the American style, that also owes much to Lev Kuleshov's experimental workshop. A model of cinematic storytelling, it includes some splendid location scenes in the wintry countryside and in Moscow's busy streets. Making her screen debut in the lead was the irresistible Anna Sten who, seven years later, was to have a disastrous Hollywood career.

The Girl With The Red Hair

Het Meisje Met Het Rode Haar

Netherlands 1981 114 mins col
Movies Filmproductions

d **Ben Verbong**
sc **Ben Verbong, Pieter De Vos**
ph **Theo Van Der Sande**
m **Nicola Piovani**
Renée Soutendijk, Peter Tuinman, Ada Bouwman, Loes Luca, Robert Delhez, Lineke Rijxman

The wartime experiences of Hannie (Soutendijk), a Dutch Resistance worker who overcomes her reluctance to use a gun, has an affair with her colleague Hugo (Tuinman) and is caught and shot by the Germans when her distinctive red hair, dyed for protection, begins to grow out. The tale is told as a flashback recollection by An (Luca), the girl who trained Hannie, but is used as the basis for a feminist examination of Hannie's situation. This is an intriguing idea, but Verbong's message is a dreadful muddle, appearing to blame Hannie's tragedies on her impulsive temperament, 'typical' of redheads. Even the well-worn path of Resistance activities is retrod without imagination or sufficient tension.

Gishiki see Ceremony, The

Giulietta Degli Spiriti see Juliet Of The Spirits

Giuseppe Verdi see Life And Music Of Giuseppe Verdi, The

The Given Word

O Pagador De Promessas

Brazil 1962 98 mins bw
Oswaldo Massaini

d **Anselmo Duarte**
sc **Anselmo Duarte**
ph **Chick Fowle**
m **Gabriel Migliori**
Leonardo Vilar, Dionizio Azevedo, Gloria Menezes, Geraldo Del Rey, Carlos Torres

A poor farmer (Vilar) drags a huge cross to the village church as an offering to Santa Barbara for saving his injured donkey. The priest (Azevedo) learns that he made his vow to do this at a voodoo ceremony, refuses him entry, and a battle of wills is fought, ending in the farmer's death. Adapted from a successful Brazilian play, Duarte's film retains its stage origins in confining the action largely to the steps of the church. A simple folk drama, brought to life with plenty of convincing atmosphere, but the central conflict becomes boring because the protagonists—both as written and played—are two-dimensional stereotypes.

Best Film Cannes 1962

Gläserne Himmel, Der see Glass Heaven, The

The Glass Heaven

Der Gläserne Himmel

W. Germany 1988 87 mins col
Avista Film/Voissfilm/Nina Grosse Film

d **Nina Grosse**
sc **Nina Grosse**
ph **Hans Bücking**
m **Flora St Loup**
Helmut Berger, Silvie Orcier, Agnes Fink, Maria Harmann, Tobias Engel, Circe

Businessman Julien (Berger) lives an uneventful life with his wife (Harmann) and his bedridden mother (Fink) until he becomes haunted by a nightmare in which he sees a woman strangled in an aquarium. On his way to work one day, he sees the woman from his dreams and follows her into a bar. She disappears, but he recognizes a customer as the killer from his dream. and becomes involved with Bichette (Orcier), a prostitute who is friendly with the man... This is an exceptionally stylish debut film, boasting several imaginative ideas and unusual images. The resolution is a touch predictable but, until then, Grosse keeps up the momentum of her mysterious events, creating some nail-biting tension. She is helped by solid performances and excellent camerawork.

Goalie's Anxiety At The Penalty Kick, The see Anxiety Of The Goalie At The Penalty, The

Goalkeeper's Fear Of The Penalty Kick, The see Anxiety Of The Goalie At The Penalty, The

Gobbo, Il see Hunchback Of Rome, The

Godard's Passion see Passion

Goddess, The see Devi

God Needs Men see Isle Of Sinners

Gods Of The Plague

Götter Der Pest

W. Germany 1970 91 mins bw
Antiteater-X Film

d **Rainer Werner Fassbinder**
sc **Rainer Werner Fassbinder**
ph **Dietrich Lohmann**
m **Peer Raben**
Harry Baer, Hanna Schygulla, Margarethe Von Trotta, Günter Kaufmann, Ingrid Caven

Franz (Baer) comes out of jail and meets an old pal (Kaufmann) with whom he plans to rob a supermarket. The men are betrayed by two girls (Schygulla and Van Trotta) who both love Franz. Like Fassbinder's first feature, *Love Is Colder Than Death*, his third was influenced by Hollywood *film noir* as filtered through the French New Wave. Far too cool and self-conscious to work as a crime movie or even as pastiche, it does make an impact as a melancholy study of characters trapped in an unfriendly milieu, including the gloomy 'Lola Montes' nightclub. Except for a spectacular long- take helicopter shot, it is Fassbinder at his most austere. Günter Kaufmann, who dies beautifully at the end, was the illegitimate son of a black GI and a Bavarian woman. Fassbinder met him in 1969, fell in love and put him in his next few films.

Goha

France/Tunisia 1957 90 mins col
Films Franco Africains

d **Jacques Baratier**
sc **Georges Schéhadé**
ph **Jean Bourgoin**
m **Maurice Ohana**
Omar Chérif (later Sharif), Zina Bouzaiane, Lauro Gazzolo, Gabriel Jabbour

A clever young man (Chérif), under the guise of stupidity, woos the bride of the town's wise man and helps a blind musician. Lovely colour, exotic locations and handsome 25-year-old Omar Sharif, still five years away from international stardom, make this Arab folk tale extremely pleasing. Baratier, in his debut feature, manages to switch from humour to drama with maturity.

Going Places see Making It

Gold

Germany 1934 120 mins bw
UFA

d **Karl Hartl**
sc **Rolf Vanloo**
ph **Günther Rittau, Otto Baecker, Werner Böhne**
m **Hans-Otto Borgman**
Hans Albers, Brigitte Helm, Friedrich Kayssler, Lien Deyers, Michael Bohnen

A scientist (Albers) creates an atomic reactor able to change lead into gold, but destroys the machine rather than have it used for evil ends. It is now difficult to believe that after World War II the US government had this plodding but atmospheric science fiction drama screened for scientists to see whether it showed the Germans capable of producing nuclear power. It did not, but it was a tribute to the film's prescience. Hollywood re-used the underwater lab scenes for *The Magnetic Monster* (1953).

Golden Age, The see Âge D'Or, L'

The Golden Coach
La Carrozza D'Oro
aka Le Carrosse D'Or

Italy 1952 100 mins col
Panaria/Hoche

d **Jean Renoir**
sc **Jean Renoir, Renzo Avanzo, Jack Kirkland, Giulio Macchi, Ginette Doynel**
ph **Claude Renoir**
m **Vivaldi**
Anna Magnani, Odoardo Spadaro, Duncan Lamont, Nada Fiorelli, Ralph Truman, Ricardo Rioli, Paul Campbell

In 18th-century Peru, an actress (Magnani) with a touring Commedia Dell'Arte troupe is wooed by a bullfighter (Rioli), a soldier (Campbell) and the Viceroy (Lamont). When the latter presents her with a golden coach from Europe, she donates it to the church and opts for her first love—the theatre. Renoir conceived the *opera-buffa* type script while listening to Vivaldi, and the film contains much of the exuberance, and the dark undertones, of the Italian baroque composer. Based on a one-act play by Mérimée, it is a rich illustration of the theme of the tension between life and theatre. Only the casting of the somewhat coarse-grained Magnani as the centre of attraction seems a little perverse. It was a favourite film of Truffaut, who named his production company Les Films Du Carrosse after it.

Golden Eighties

France/Belgium 1986 96 mins col

La Cecilia (Paris)/Paradise Films (Brussels)/Limbo-Films (Zurich)

d **Chantal Akerman**
sc **Chantal Akerman, Leora Barish, Henry Bean, Pascal Bonitzer, Jean Gruault**
ph **Gilberto Azevedo, Luc Benhamou**
m **Marc Herouet**
Delphine Seyrig, Myriam Boyer, Fanny Cottençon, Lio, Charles Denner, Jean-François Balmer, John Berry, Nicolas Tronc

Jeanne Schwartz (Seyrig) and her husband own a clothes boutique in a shopping mall where their son Robert (Tronc) works. He, along with several other men, is infatuated with Lili (Cottençon), manageress of the hairdressing salon, whose assistant Mado (Lio) loves Robert. Everybody's lives are complicated by the arrival of Eli (Berry), Jeanne's pre-war lover, who tries to persuade her to go away with him. Akerman, feminist director of often minimalist and low-key films, has turned her hand to a musical in which the themes of love, sex and commerce are closely linked. If the undertones are bitter-sweet and sometimes cynical, the surface glints diamond-bright as the characters play out their destinies to the accompaniment of a lively score and witty, sometimes raunchy, lyrics, with a stylistic nod towards Jacques Demy (*The Umbrellas Of Cherbourg*). An original and intelligent film, with the graceful Seyrig glowing at its centre.

Golden Marie
Casque D'Or
France 1952 96 mins bw
Speva/Paris

d **Jacques Becker**
sc **Jacques Becker, Jacques Companeez**
ph **Robert Le Fèbvre**
m **Georges Van Parys**
Simone Signoret, Serge Reggiani, Claude Dauphin, Raymond Bussières, Gaston Modot

In turn-of-the-century Paris, an honest carpenter (Reggiani), drawn into a world of pimps, prostitutes and petty crooks because of his passion for gangster's moll Marie (Signoret), is driven to murder. Becker's lovingly re-created Paris of the past almost equals the radiance of Renoir *père et fils*. Despite the *crime passionnel* plot, the film throbs with the affirmation of love and friendship. The glowing sensuality of Signoret is reflected in the wonderful open air scenes and the warm morning sunshine as the lovers awake together.

Gold Of Naples
L'Oro Di Napoli
Italy 1955 135 mins bw
Gala/Ponti-De Laurentiis

d **Vittorio De Sica**
sc **Vittorio De Sica, Cesare Zavattini, Giuseppe Marotta**
ph **Otello Martelli**
m **Alessandro Cicognini**
Vittorio De Sica, Sophia Loren, Totò, Paolo Stoppa, Silvana Mangano, Pasquale Cennamo, Lianella Carrell, Giacomo Furia, Alberto Farnese, Erno Crisa

Four Neapolitan sketches. 'The Racketeer': a little man (Totò) outwits a bullying racketeer (Cennamo) who has imposed upon him and his wife (Carrell); 'Pizza On Credit': a wife (Loren) loses her wedding ring during a rendezvous with a lover (Farnese), arousing the suspicions of her husband (Furia); 'The Gambler': an inveterate gambler (De Sica) continues to believe himself lucky even after squandering his family's fortune; 'Theresa': a prostitute (Mangano) marries a mentally unbalanced young man (Crisa) and uses sexual therapy to help him. One of the better portmanteau films, with some good jokes and good performances from Mangano, Totò, 20-year-old Loren and De Sica, although the film could be seen as the beginning of De Sica's decline as a director. Perhaps it was just as well that only four of the original six sketches survived for import, because it might have overstayed its welcome.

Gold, Silver, Bad Luck
Oro, Plata, Mata
Philippines 1982 194 mins col
Experimental Cinema of the Philippines

d **Peque Gallaga**
sc **José Javier Reyes**
ph **Rody Lacap**
m **José Gentica V**
Manny Ojeda, Liza Lorena, Sandy Andolong, Cherie Gil, Fides Cuyugan Asensio

Two aristocratic families are gathered together to celebrate the birthday and coming-out of debutante Maggie (Andolong), but the gaiety is dispelled by the possibility of a Japanese invasion. The families, with their servants, flee to a primitive hunting lodge in the mountains where they live a precarious and fraught existence. One of the most ambitious and epic films to be made in the Philippines has a fine sweep and vigour, especially astonishing as it is former production designer Gallaga's solo directorial debut. Yet it is too diffuse, derivative (Visconti comes to mind), exceptionally bloody (tongues cut out, fingers chopped off, knives plunged into chests) and, despite some implied social criticism, rather suspect politically.

Golem: Wie Er In Die Welt Kam, Der see Golem, The

Golem, Le see Golem, The

The Golem

Der Golem: Wie Er In Die Welt Kam

Germany 1920 75 mins bw
UFA

d **Paul Wegener, Carl Boese**
sc **Paul Wegener, Henrik Galeen**
ph **Karl Freund, Guido Seeber**
m **Silent**

Paul Wegener, Albert Steinruck, Ernst Deutsch, Lyda Salmonova

In 16th-century Prague, a rabbi (Steinruck) creates a monster (Wegener) out of clay to help his people fight against the Emperor's expulsion of the Jews from the ghetto. The most eye-catching of the various versions of the ancient Jewish legend, mainly because of the Expressionistic sets by Hans Poelzig, and the use of chiaroscuro to create a Gothic effect. Wegener's lumbering gait was imitated by Boris Karloff in *Frankenstein* (1931).

The Golem

aka The Legend Of Prague
Le Golem

France 1936 95 mins bw
AB

d **Julien Duvivier**
sc **Julien Duvivier, André-Paul Antoine**
ph **Jan Stallich, Vaclav Vich**
m **Joseph Kumok**

Harry Baur, Roger Karl, Ferdinand Hart, Charles Dorat, Germaine Aussey

A rabbi (Dorat) brings the Golem (Hart) back to life in order to frighten the Emperor Rudolf II (Baur) into freeing the Jews from the slavery to which they have been reduced. The first sound version of the Jewish folk legend, almost a sequel to the 1920 remake, had the advantage of actually being shot in Prague. But despite good special effects and Baur's strong presence, it lacked the atmosphere and narrative drive of the earlier film.

Golfos, Los see Hooligans, The

Golgotha

France 1935 100 mins bw
Ichtys Film

d **Julien Duvivier**
sc **Joseph Reymond**
ph **Jules Kruger, René Ribault, Marie Fossard, Robert Juillard**
m **Jacques Ibert**

Harry Baur, Robert Le Vigan, Jean Gabin, Charles Grandval, André Bacque, Edwige Feuillère

The Passion and the Crucixion of Christ. Duvivier's straightforward, well-crafted account of the life of Christ was the first sound film to be made on the subject tackled earlier in Cecil B. DeMille's superior *The King Of Kings* (1927). The cast was a curious one with Gabin as Pontius Pilate and Le Vigan as Christ. (Le Vigan, who became a Nazi collaborator, killed himself after the war.) Harry Baur made an imposing Herod.

Golubye Gory Ely Nepravdopodobnaya Istoria see Blue Mountains

---

A Good Marriage

Le Beau Mariage

France 1981 97 mins col
Les Films Du Losange/Les Films Du Carrosse

d **Eric Rohmer**

sc **Eric Rohmer**
ph **Bernard Lutic**
m **Roman Girre, Simon Des Innocents**
Béatrice Romand, André Dussollier, Feodor Atkine, Arielle Dombasle, Huguette Faget

A 25-year-old art student (Romand) breaks off an affair with a married man (Atkine) and determines to get a husband of her own. Unfortunately, she decides on a handsome, well-to-do lawyer (Dussollier) who has no intention of marrying. The title of Rohmer's elegant, witty and touching 'Comedy and Proverb' refers to an ideal rather than an actual event. The film is also a wry comment on the contradictions that exist in a liberated woman with some old-fashioned ideas. As usual the backgrounds are meticulously observed— this time Le Mans is the principal setting.

Best Actress (Béatrice Romand) Venice 1981

Good Morning
Ohayo

Japan 1959 97 mins col
Shochiku

d **Yasujiro Ozu**
sc **Yasujiro Ozu, Kogo Noda**
ph **Yuharu Atsuta**
m **Toshiro Mayuzumi**
Chishu Ryu, Kuniko Miyake, Yoshiko Kuga, Keiji Sada, Masahiko Shimazu, Koji Shidara

Two young boys (Shimazu and Shidara), living with their parents (Ryu and Miyake) in suburban Tokyo, are refused a TV set. Told to shut up by their father, they take a vow of silence, refusing even to say 'good morning' to a neighbour. Returning to the theme of juvenile rebellion he had dealt with in *I Was Born But...* 28 years previously, Ozu here treats it with less depth but with the gentle, mocking affection and mastery of his late works. A sensitive use of colour and fine performances make the film an all-round pleasure.

The Good Soldier Schweik
Der Brave Soldat Schwejk

W. Germany 1960 96 mins bw
CCC/Filmkunst-Weinfilm/Lionex

d **Axel Von Ambesser**
sc **Hans Jacoby**
ph **Richard Angst**
m **Bernhard Eichhorn**
Heinz Rühmann, Ernst Stankowski, Ursula Borsodi, Senta Berger, Erika Von Thellmann

Schweik (Rühmann), a good-hearted, garrulous dog salesman, is reluctantly drafted into the Austrian army of 1914. Emeshed in red tape and harassed by police, doctors, priests and officers, he makes his eventful way towards the moment when he is captured by his own troops. Jaroslav Hasek's classic novel brilliantly conveys both the obscenity of war and its absurdity through one of the greatest comic characters in all literature. Unfortunately, this pedestrian adaptation never begins to approach the glories of the novel, although there are glimmerings of what might have been in Rühmann's performance if only he had been surrounded by artists with more vision.

Goopy And Bagha see Adventures Of Goopy And Bagha, The

Goopy Gyne Bagha Byne see Adventures Of Goopy And Bagha, The

Goracza see Fever

A Gorgeous Bird Like Me
(US: Such A Gorgeous Kid Like Me)
Une Belle Fille Comme Moi

France 1972 98 mins col
Films Du Carrosse/Columbia

d **François Truffaut**
sc **François Truffaut, Jean-Loup Dabadie**
ph **Pierre William Glenn**
m **Georges Delerue**
Bernadette Lafont, Claude Brasseur, Charles Denner, Guy Marchand, André Dussollier, Philippe Léotard

Camille Bliss (Lafont), a woman convicted of murder, tells a criminologist (Dussollier) the tale of her involvement with a singer (Marchand), a rat catcher (Denner), and a lawyer (Brasseur). An uncomfortable blend of French and American farce (it was based on an American novel by Henry Farrell), social document and black comedy, the film is not one of Truffaut's most accomplished works. The 'gorgeous' Lafont may wield immense power over the men in the film, but her strident performance might not seduce audiences quite so easily.

The Gospel According To Saint Matthew

Il Vangelo Secondo Matteo

Italy 1964 142 mins bw
Arco/Lux

d **Pier Paolo Pasolini**
sc **Pier Paolo Pasolini**
ph **Tonino Delli Colli**
m **Bach, Mozart, Prokofiev, Webern, Negro Spirituals**

Enrique Irazoqui (Christ), Susanna Pasolini (Mary), Mario Socrate (John the Baptist), Marcello Morante (Joseph)

The birth, life, teachings and death on the cross of Jesus Christ. Pasolini's second feature seemed a strange choice for a Marxist, but it is an attempt to take Christ out of the opulent church and present him as an outcast Italian peasant. Applying Neo-Realist methods, the director shot the film in Calabria, using the expressive faces of non-professionals including that of his mother as the Virgin Mary. Although considered by some critics as the greatest screen version of the 'greatest story ever told', it might have been more adventurous had not the Church helped to finance it.

Special Jury Prize Venice 1964

Gösta Berlings Saga see Atonement Of Gösta Berling, The

Goto, Island Of Love

Goto, L'Ile D'Amour

France 1968 93 mins bw
Euro-Images/Les Productions René Thévenet

d **Walerian Borowczyk**
sc **Walerian Borowczyk, Dominique Duvergé**
ph **Guy Durban, Paul Cotteret**
m **Handel**

Pierre Brasseur, Ligia Branice, Ginette Leclerc, René Dany, Jean-Pierre Andréani

Goto III (Brasseur) is a cruel dictator who rules over a small island, cut off from the world, where most of the population toil in the stone quarries. Goto's wife, Glossia (Branice), loves Gono (Andréani) with whom she hopes to flee. But things take a nasty turn. The Polish-born Borowczyck, in France since 1959, pursued the bitterly ironic surrealist vein of his animated films into his first live-action feature. Despite claims by the director that 'it is a realistic film', it creates an absurd and nightmarish world, full of nostalgic paraphernalia like music-boxes, phonographs and ancient instruments of torture. Given his truly surreal vision, it's not surprising that Borowczyk received the Max Ernst prize in 1967.

Goto, L'Ile D'Amour see Goto, Island Of Love

Götterdämmerung see Damned, The

Götter Der Pest see Gods Of The Plague

Goupi-Mains-Rouges

(US: It Happened At The Inn)

France 1943 95 mins bw
Minerva

d **Jacques Becker**
sc **Jacques Becker, Pierre Véry**
ph **Pierre Montazel, Jean Bourgoin**
m **Jean Alfaro**

Fernand Ledoux, Georges Rollin, Blanchette Brunoy, Robert Le Vigan

When a member of the powerful but bickering Goupi family is killed and another suspected of the crime, the patriarch (Ledoux) decides to take the law into his own hands. Shot on location in the Charente, this outrageous black comedy with extravagant characters is nevertheless rooted in the reality of rural life. Owing much to Pagnol and Renoir, Becker's second feature (based on a novel by Pierre Véry) was a great success in Occupied France because of its affirmation of national identity.

Graal, Le see Lancelot Of The Lake

Graduate First see Passe Ton Bac D'Abord

Grail, The see Lancelot Of The Lake

Le Grand Amour

France 1969 col 85 mins
CAPAC

d **Pierre Etaix**
sc **Pierre Etaix, Jean-Claude Carrière**
ph **Christian Guillouet**
m **Claude Stieremans**
Pierre Etaix, Annie Fratellini, Nicole Calfan, Ketty France, Louis Mais

Pierre (Etaix) and Florence (Fratellini, Etaix's real-life wife) are a reasonably happy married couple. One day, Pierre falls madly in love with his new young secretary (Calfan). While his wife is away on vacation, he tries to change his personality and woo her, but finds he is no Don Juan. There are many good visual gags running through this amiable comedy, and Etaix, working for the first time in colour, times most of them reasonably well. The problem lies in the fact that greater comedians, such as Max Linder and Buster Keaton, did the same sort of thing much better.

Grand Amour De Beethoven, Un see Life And Loves Of Beethoven, The

Grand Blond Avec Une Chaussure Noire, Le see Tall Blond Man With One Black Shoe, The

Grande Bouffe, La see Blow-Out

Grande Guerra, La see Great War, The

La Grande Illusion

aka Grand Illusion
France 1937 117 mins bw
Cinedis

d **Jean Renoir**
sc **Jean Renoir, Charles Spaak**
ph **Christian Matras, Claude Renoir**
m **Joseph Kosma**
Pierre Fresnay, Erich Von Stroheim, Jean Gabin, Marcel Dalio, Julien Carette, Gaston Modot, Dita Parlo, Jean Dasté

Three French soldiers, the working-class Maréchal (Gabin), the middle- class Rosenthal (Dalio) and the aristocrat Boïeldieu (Fresnay), are held prisoner in a fortress run by Commandant Von Rauffenstein (Von Stroheim). Boïeldieu dies so that his fellow POWs can escape. The script of Renoir's most popular film was touted around for three years before Gabin finally got it produced. Based on a true story of World War I told to the director by a friend, it is not only a moving anti-war statement but a rich exploration of class loyalties and transcending friendships. The fluid, deep-focus camerawork, the set pieces such as the singing of the 'Marseillaise' during theatricals, and the extraordinary performances make it one of the cinema's most enduring masterpieces, and it was awarded a prize at Venice for the best artistic ensemble.

Grande Rue see Calle Mayor

Les Grandes Familles

(US: The Possessors)
France 1958 93 mins bw
Filmsonor/Intermondia

d **Denys De La Patellière**
sc **Michel Audiard, Denys De La Patellière**
ph **Louis Page**
m **Maurice Thiriet**
Jean Gabin, Jean Desailly, Bernard Blier, Pierre Brasseur, Jean Murat, Louis Seigner, Emmanuele Riva

The patriarch (Gabin) of a rich and powerful family with controlling interests in banking, the press and the arts, has doubts about the fitness of his weak son (Desailly) to succeed him, while trying to do down his rivals and keep the large family together. Gabin's imposing presence as an actor keeps the whole film together—an enjoyable, literate, old-fashioned entertainment. Based on the first third of Maurice Druon's 1948 three-part novel, the film's solid virtues and its veteran star made it popular at home and abroad.

Grandes Manoeuvres, Les see Summer Manoeuvres

Grandeur Nature see Life Size

Grande Vadrouille, La see Don't Look Now . . . We're Being Shot At!

Grand Illusion see Grande Illusion, La

Le Grand Jeu

France 1934 115 mins bw
Films De France

d **Jacques Feyder**
sc **Jacques Feyder, Charles Spaak**
ph **Harry Stradling, Maurice Forster**
m **Hanns Eisler**
Pierre-Richard Willm, Marie Bell, Françoise Rosay, Charles Vanel

A Foreign Legionnaire (Willm) goes to Morocco to forget a coquettish Parisian society woman, only to find her double in the person of a cabaret singer. In order to create a strange ambiguity, Marie Bell, in a dual role, was dubbed by another actress for the Moroccan scenes. After a short sojourn in Hollywood where he directed Garbo in *The Kiss* (1929), Feyder returned to France and solidified his reputation with three successful films featuring his wife Françoise Rosay, beginning with this exotic, erotic romance.

Grand Maneuver, The see Summer Manoeuvres

Grand Meaulnes, Le see Wanderer, The

Grand Paysage D'Alexis Droeven, Le see Endless Land Of Alexis Droeven, The

---

Grands Chemins, Les see Of Flesh And Blood

Grazie Zia

aka Thank You, Aunt
Italy 1968 96 mins bw
Doria Film

d **Salvatore Samperi**
sc **Sergio Bazzini, Salvatore Samperi, Pier Luigi Murgia**
ph **Aldo Scavarda**
m **Ennio Morricone**
Lou Castel, Lisa Gastoni, Gabriele Ferzetti, Luisa De Santis, Massimo Sarghielli

Alvise (Castel), seeking release from the world that awaits him as heir to a wealthy industrialist, develops a psychosomatic paralysis that confines him to a wheelchair. Placed in the care of his brilliant, beautiful and liberated doctor aunt (Gastoni), he draws her into a series of elaborate and increasingly erotic fantasies and games which lead to the loss of her independence. Samperi, admitting to the obvious influence of Bellocchio, Losey, Polanski and Buñuel, made this first feature at the age of 24. He fails to explore the drives behind Alvise's vicious behaviour, but succeeds in creating a suffocatingly enclosed world, evoked by accurate and intelligent images. The leads are first-class and, if the piece is derivative and lacking in cohesion, it is nonetheless undeniably talented.

The Great Adventure

Det Stora Aventyret
Sweden 1953 80 mins bw
Sandrew/Bauman

d **Arne Sucksdorff**
sc **Arne Sucksdorff**
ph **Arne Sucksdorff**
m **Lars Erik Larsson**
Anders Norberg, Kjell Sucksdorff, Arne Sucksdorff

Two young boys (Norberg and Kjell Sucksdorff) in north Sweden attempt to tame a wild otter but the animal longs to return to the forests and lakes. What struck most adult spectators was the brilliant photography of wintry landscapes and wildlife, while children, the main audience worldwide, identified with the young heroes' adventures among the animals in this charming and beautiful little film.

The Great Consoler
Velikii Uteshitel

USSR 1933 97 mins bw
Mosfilm

d **Lev Kuleshov**
sc **Lev Kuleshov, Alexander Kurs**
ph **Konstantin Kuznetsov, G. Kabalov**
m **Zinovi Feldman**
Konstantin Khokhlov, I. Novoseltsev, Alexandra Khokhlova, Andrei Fayt

While serving a three-year prison sentence, Bill Porter (Khokhlov), who wrote under the name of O. Henry, sees the suffering of safecracker Jimmy Valentine (Novoseltsev). In a story, the writer transforms Jimmy into a hero who rescues a girl trapped in a bank vault. Reading it is Dulcy (Khokhlova), a naive shop assistant, who has to wake up to reality when she loses her job. Kuleshov, a great admirer of American films and literature (*By The Law* was based on a story by Jack London), presents his 'interrogation' of O. Henry's short story, *A Retrieved Reform*, in three different narratives and styles—realistic, burlesque and symbolic. This daring, novel, but rather heartless film, which includes a Western pastiche, was accused of 'intellectualism' and American influences by officialdom, and it was the last work of interest that Kuleshov directed.

Greatest Love, The see Europa 51

The Great War
La Grande Guerra

Italy 1959 bw
DD/Gray

d **Mario Monicelli**
sc **Mario Monicelli, Luciano Vincenzoni, Age, Furio Scarpelli**
ph **Giuseppe Rotunno, Roberto Gerardi**
m **Nino Rota**
Vittorio Gassman, Alberto Sordi, Silvana Mangano, Folco Lulli, Bernard Blier, Romolo Valli

Two shirking soldiers (Gassman and Sordi) enjoy themselves with women in the town while a World War I battle rages. Learning that their company has been wiped out, they gain a sense of duty and return to the front, but are captured and shot for refusing to give information. Like *What Price Glory?*, which it resembles, this uneven film moves from low comedy to high drama, though not with the same ease. The two male leads, and Mangano as a prostitute, give likeable but predictable performances.

Best Film Venice 1959
Best Director Venice 1959

Green Mare, The see Green Mare's Nest, The

The Green Mare's Nest
(US: The Green Mare)
La Jument Verte

France 1959 105 mins col
Raimbourg/Star Presse/S.N.E.G./Sopac Films/Zebra Film

d **Claude Autant-Lara**
sc **Jean Aurenche, Pierre Bost**
ph **Jacques Natteau**
m **René Cloërec**
Bourvil, Sandra Milo, Francis Blanche, Yves Robert, Valérie Lagrange, Julien Carette

When Honoré (Bourvil) inherits the estate of his father, a horse dealer who became wealthy after a green filly was born to one of his mares, a jealous neighbour (Robert) plots against him. Honoré later takes his revenge by cuckolding him. Even if the French naughtiness has diminished for today's audiences, it is still an enjoyable, admirably performed, slightly silly romp. It was the film in which Bourvil (born André Raimbourg) first became widely known outside France.

The Green Ray
(US: Summer)
Le Rayon Vert

France 1986 92 mins col
Les Films Du Losange

d **Eric Rohmer**
sc **Eric Rohmer, Marie Rivière**
ph **Sophie Maintigneux**

m **Jean-Louis Valero**
Marie Rivière, Lisa Heredia, Vincent Gautier, Eric Hamm, Marc Vivas, Béatrice Romand

A Parisian secretary (Rivière) is let down at the last minute by a friend with whom she was going on holiday. Not knowing what to do, she takes herself off to Cherbourg, then to the mountains and, lastly, Biarritz, but is bored and depressed everywhere, until she meets the man of her dreams. Unlike Rohmer's previous films, the dialogue of this comedy of manners was entirely improvised, creating both the tedium and the fascination of real speech. How one reacts to the film may be greatly related to how one reacts to the overly fastidious girl. The title, taken from the Jules Verne novel, refers to the last ray of sunset, the green of which is supposed to make observers more aware of the feelings and perceptions of others. Rohmer's films have much the same effect.

Best Film Venice 1986

The Green Room
La Chambre Verte

France 1978 94 mins col
Les Films Du Carrosse/UA

d **François Truffaut**
sc **François Truffaut, Jean Gruault**
ph **Nestor Almendros**
m **Maurice Jaubert**
François Truffaut, Nathalie Baye, Jean Dasté, Jean-Pierre Moulin, Antoine Vitez

An obituary writer (Truffaut), obsessed with death, makes a shrine of his dead wife's bedroom and fills an old chapel with memento mori. A girl he meets (Baye) concludes that the only way he could love her would be if she were dead. Perhaps Truffaut's darkest film through which he himself walks in an expressionless and self-important manner, was an adaptation from two of Henry James's short stories, *Altar Of The Dead* with some ideas from *The Beast Of The Jungle*. It is to the director's credit that he created a morbid atmosphere without recourse to baroque or melodramatic methods.

The Green Wall
La Muralla Verde

Peru 1969 110 mins col
Amaru Producciones Cinematográficas Del Peru

d **Armando Robles Godoy**
sc **Armando Robles Godoy**
ph **Mario Robles Godoy**
m **Enrique Pinilla**
Julio Alemán, Sandra Riva, Raul Martin

An urban family—a father (Alemán), mother (Riva) and son (Martin)—try to make a home for themselves in the wilds, having to break down 'the green wall' of the jungle to do so. But a poisonous serpent invades their Garden of Eden. The first Peruvian film to gain attention in the USA interestingly demonstrates that pastoral bliss is threatened by civilization and nature itself. The Peruvian jungle makes a compelling background to the simple story which is rather spoiled by too much visual gimmickry.

Gribiche

France 1925 90 mins bw
Albatros

d **Jacques Feyder**
sc **Jacques Feyder**
ph **Maurice Forster, Maurice Desfassiaux**
m **Silent**
Jean Forest, Françoise Rosay, Rolla Norman, Cécile Guyon, Alice Tissot

When Gribiche (Forest), a young boy from a deprived background, returns a lost handbag to its wealthy owner (Rosay), she offers to adopt and educate him. Believing himself to be an obstacle to his widowed mother's remarriage, he accepts. An observant tale of social differences and human motivation—Gribiche's benefactress is more concerned with outward show than inner feelings, for example. Feyder has invested the story with an edge of satire that makes this film an ironic antidote to the Mary Pickford-style dramas about orphans saved by the kindly rich. As always, *grande dame* Rosay (Feyder's wife) is wonderful to watch, and Forest, who had played a not dissimilar role in the same director's *Visages D'Enfants* earlier that year, is excellent.

Gribouille
(US: Heart Of Paris)

France 1937 85 mins bw
André Davin

d **Marc Allégret**
sc **Marc Allégret, H.G. Lustig, Marcel Achard**
ph **G. Benoit, Armand Thirard, Michel Kelber**
m **Georges Auric**
Raimu, Michèle Morgan, Jeanne Provost, Gilbert Gilles, Jean Worms, Carette, Jacques Gretillat

While serving on a jury, the owner of a sports shop (Raimu) takes pity on a penniless young woman (Morgan) on trial for manslaughter. Knowing his wife (Provost) would object to employing someone on probation, he gets her a job in his shop by asking a friend to recommend her. Matters are complicated when the wife suspects her husband of falling for the girl. Although the plot has a melodramatic base, the film keeps a comic tone throughout, only occasionally tipping over into pathos. Except for the extraordinarily hammy court case that begins it, this comedy of behaviour has witty dialogue and perfect playing, notably from the imposing Raimu as the big lummox or *gribouille* of the title. The lovely 17-year-old, almond-eyed Morgan made an immediate impression in her screen debut. It was also the first film appearance of a young but already portly Bernard Blier in small role.

Grido, Il see Cry, The

The Grim Reaper
La Commare Secca
Italy 1962 100 mins bw
Cinematografica Cervi

d **Bernardo Bertolucci**
sc **Bernardo Bertolucci, Sergio Citti**
ph **Gianni Narzisi**
m **Carlo Rustichelli, Piero Piccioni**
Francesco Ruiu, Giancarlo De Rosa, Vincenzo Ciccora, Alvaro D'Ercole, Romano Labate

An investigation into the murder of a prostitute in Rome reveals different perspectives of different people on the events of her last day. Twenty-two-year-old Bertolucci's first film was based on a five-page outline by Pasolini, with whom the young man had worked as assistant on *Accatone*, and in whose style he attempted to make it. But Bertolucci was less engaged with the Roman proletariat that Pasolini loved, and the film became merely an interesting cinematic exercise. Each episode as told to the unseen investigator was filmed in a different style. It is, as the director admits, the film of 'someone who had never shot one foot of 35mm before but who had seen lots and lots of films'.

Grisbi
aka Honour Among Thieves
Touchez Pas Au Grisbi
France 1953 90 mins bw
Del Duca/Antares

d **Jacques Becker**
sc **Jacques Becker, Maurice Griffe**
ph **Pierre Montazel**
m **Jean Wiener**
Jean Gabin, Jeanne Moreau, Lino Ventura, Gaby Basset, Daniel Cauchy

After a bank robbery, the gangsters and their molls get involved in a fight to the death over the loot. What primarily interested Becker was not the cops and robbers plot based on a *série noire* novel by Albert Simonin, but the relationships of friendship and betrayal among the characters. It also gave the cast a chance to explore the depths of their roles, particularly Gabin in his poignant portrayal of a man afraid of growing old. Ventura, making his first screen appearance, was spotted in a wrestling ring by Becker.

Best Actor (Jean Gabin) Venice 1954

Grosse Liebespiel, Das see And So To Bed

Gruppo Di Famiglia In Un Interno see Conversation Piece

Guerre Des Boutons, La see War Of The Buttons, The

Guerre D'Un Seul Homme, La see One Man's War

Guerre Est Finie, La see War Is Over, The

Guichets Du Louvre, Les see Gates Of The Louvre, The

Güney's The Wall see Wall, The

The Guns

Os Fuzis

Brazil 1963 110 mins bw
Copacabana Films/Embracine/Daga Films

d **Ruy Guerra**
sc **Ruy Guerra**
ph **Ricardo Aronovich**
m **Moscir Santos**
Átila Iório, Nelson Xavier, Maria Gladys, Leonides Bayer, Hugo Carvana, Mauricio Loyola

A Holy Man exhorts starving peasants in North-east Brazil to follow a sacred ox which will bring rain. Meanwhile, soldiers occupy the nearby town to protect the Mayor's food supply, and senseless incidents of violence occur, culminating in an ex-soldier, infuriated by peasant apathy, firing on the troops. The peasants kill and devour the sacred ox. This is an early product from *Cinema Novo*, curiously static, yet quivering with the tension of underlying violence. A bleak and depressing illustration of a situation that requires revolution, the film offers no solutions as to how that might occur—except for the climactic killing of the ox which indicates the seeds of changed thinking as the peasants abandon the restrictive shibboleths of the church.

Special Jury Prize Berlin 1964

Gyakufunsha Kazoku see Crazy Family, The

Gycklarnas Afton see Sawdust And Tinsel

h

La Habañera

Germany 1937 95 mins bw
Bruno Duday/UFA

d **Detlef Sierck**
sc **Gerhard Menzel**
ph **Franz Weihmayr**
m **Lothar Brühne**
Zarah Leander, Karl Martell, Ferdinand Marian, Julia Serda, Boris Alekin

Swedish Astrée (Leander), on a visit to Puerto Rico, falls in love with the place and with a wealthy landowner (Marian) whom she marries. Ten years pass: the sultry island is in the grip of a fever epidemic and Astrée is desperately homesick. When her husband dies, she leaves for Sweden with her son and a Swedish scientist (Martell). An over-the-top melodrama, produced as a vehicle for Leander whom the Germans hoped would step into the departed Dietrich's shoes, the film has acquired added interest. Screenwriter Menzel went on to work for the Nazis and, even in this piece, insidiously favours Aryan notions of physical and mental health. The director, of course, is Douglas Sirk, who left Germany after this film which displays the characteristics his work would develop in Hollywood. Melodrama or no, Sirk views his subject with ironic detachment, and captures mood and atmosphere with skilfully deployed light play, mirror images, and a cleverly fluid camera which points to a vision at intelligent odds with the material.

Hadduta Misriya see Egyptian Story, An

Had No Shima see Island, The

Hail Mary

Je Vous Salue, Marie

France 1984 78 mins col
Pegase/JLG Films/Sara Films/TV Romande/Channel 4

d **Jean-Luc Godard**
sc **Jean-Luc Godard**
ph **Jean-Bernard Menoud, Jacques Firmann**
m **Bach, Dvořák, John Coltrane**
Myriem Roussel, Thierry Rode, Philippe Lacoste, Malachi Jara Kohan, Anne Gautier, Juliette Binoche

Marie (Roussel), the teenage daughter of a petrol station manager, dating Joseph (Rode), a cab driver, is told by her visiting Uncle Gabriel (Lacoste) that she is to have a child, although she's a virgin. Condemned by the Pope and some Church organizations, and acclaimed by some other Christians, Godard's updated reinterpretation of the Nativity is one of his most controversial films. The Virgin Birth is presented as a reality—the mystery for Godard is womanhood and birth in general. This he explores through stunning images of nature and the nude figure of his heroine, the latter photographed chastely without voyeurism or sexism. The ending has an irony and poetry that only Godard at the height of his powers could achieve. The film is generally shown with a short by Anne-Marie Miéville, Godard's long-time collaborator, called *The Book Of Mary.*

Hai Zi Wang see King Of The Children

Hakuchi see Idiot, The

Hal, El see Transes

Half-Truth

Ardh Satya

India 1983 130 mins col
Neo Films Associates

d **Govind Nihalani**
sc **Vijay Tendulkar**
ph **Govind Nihalani**
m **Ajit Verman**
0m Puri, Smita Patil, Amrish Puri, Naseeruddin Shah, Shafi Inamdar, Achyut Potdar, Sadashiv Amrapurkar

Anant (Om Puri), a young policeman with faith in law and justice, becomes depressed when he sees the ease with which a known criminal, whom he tries to apprehend, goes free. His disillusion drives him to drink and violence, causing pain to his girlfriend (Patil) and bringing him into conflict with his father (Amrish Puri). This is the second film (the first was *Aakrosh*, 1981) directed by one of India's finest colour cinematographers. *Half-Truth* exposes the corruption in the police force but, what distinguishes Nihilani's approach is his belief that the police themselves are victims of a larger corruption that rules the state. In Anant, he presents an individual coming into crisis with a system and having to make choices. How he makes them is the stuff of the drama in a well-made movie that startled and impressed the cinema-going public in India, where confidence in the police has been eroded and this kind of critique is rare. On the surface, the movie offers the entertainment of a good crime actioner more familiar in Hollywood.

Hamara Shaher see Bombay Our City

Ha Megjön József see When Joseph Returns...

Hamlet
Gamlet
USSR 1964 150 mins bw
Lenfilm

d **Grigori Kozintsev**
sc **Grigori Kozintsev (based on Boris Pasternak's translation of Shakespeare)**
ph **Jonas Gritsyus**
m **Shostakovich**
Innokenti Smoktunovsky (Hamlet), Michail Nazvanov (Claudius), Elza Radzin-Szolkonis (Gertrude), Yuri Tolubeyev (Polonius), Anastasia Vertinskaya (Ophelia), S. Oleksenko (Laertes)

The Russians filmed Shakespeare's most famous tragedy to commemorate the 400th anniversary of the playwright's birth. It is, of course, impossible for an English audience to judge the language, but Kozintsev's approach to the plot is clear. Smoktunovsky's Prince of Denmark is no vacillating dreamer but, like everything else in the film, muscular and volatile. The images, enriched by the dramatic Shostakovich music, are bold, sweeping and powerful with, for example, the Ghost a giant armour-clad figure who brings a palpable sense of terror with him. This *Hamlet* is a study in the sinister manipulations of medieval statecraft, played in an Elsinore that immures its inhabitants in a convincing fortress of stone and iron that requires large armies to penetrate it. Swift-moving, and with the text considerably cut, it is a memorable and exciting experience.

Hamnstad see Port Of Call

Hamsin see Eastern Wind

Handcuffs
Lisice
Yugoslavia 1970 80 mins bw
Jadran Film

d **Krsto Papić**
sc **Mirko Kovač, Krsto Papić**
ph **Vjenceslav Orešković**
m **Miljenko Prohaska, Boško Petrović, Silvije Glojnarić**
Fabijan Šovagović, Adem Čejvan, Jagodar Kaloper, Fahro Konjhodžić

During the celebrations at a Croatian village wedding in 1948, a decorated war hero (Čejvan) rapes the bride (Kaloper) and is then arrested for pro-Stalinist views. Despite the protestations of the groom (Šovagović), the drunken village men hunt down the deflowered bride. Set at the time of Stalin's attack on Yugoslavia for deviating from Soviet ideology, this powerful, pessimistic tale reflects the uncertainties of the period. Innuendo and double meanings pervade the narrative in which cruelty and repression contrast starkly, and in an original manner, with the gaiety of folkloric singing and dancing.

The Hand In The Trap
La Mano En La Trampa
Argentina 1961 90 mins bw
Angel(Buenos Aires)/UNINCI(Madrid)

d **Leopoldo Torre-Nilsson**
sc **Beatriz Guido, Leopoldo Torre-Nilsson, Ricardo Muñoz Suay, Ricardo Luna**
ph **Alberto Etchebehere, Juan Julio Baena**
m **Cristóbal Halffter, Atilio Stampone**
Elsa Daniel, Francisco Rabal, Leonardo Favio, Maria Rosa Gallo, Berta Ortegosa, Hilda Suarez

Laura (Daniel), a convent schoolgirl, comes to spend her summer holidays in her family's large old house, and discovers that her Aunt Inés (Gallo), whom she believed was dead, has been living on the top floor in solitary confinement since the rich and handsome Cristóbal (Rabal) broke off his engagement to her. Laura approaches Cristóbal and finds herself caught in an unforeseen relationship with him. Daniel again takes on the role of the unsmiling virgin in one of Torre-Nilsson's effective depictions of the narrowness of a crumbling Catholic *bourgeois* family, which lives by an empty code of 'honour'. At times too contrived, it does, nevertheless, tell the story vividly, and conveys, by fine camerawork, the mustiness of the house and the contrasting bright superficiality of the young people outside.

Händler Der Vier Jahreszeiten, Der see Merchant Of Four Seasons, The

---

The Hands Of Orlac
Orlacs Hände
Austria 1925 50 mins bw
Pan

d **Robert Wiene**
sc **Ludwig Nerz**
ph **Günther Krampf, Hans Andreschin**
m **Silent**
Conrad Veidt, Alexandra Sorina, Fritz Kortner

A pianist (Veidt) loses his hands in a railway accident and has new ones successfully grafted on. Because they are the hands of a convicted murderer, his character changes as he becomes afraid of succumbing to their evil influence. Wiene's *The Cabinet Of Dr Caligari* (1919) began the vogue for Expressionism in German cinema, of which this is a further example. All the elements are here: shadowy streets, dimly-lit rooms and characters on the verge of madness. The plot, based on Maurice Renard's novel, is melodramatic, and so is much of the acting. Better was the 1935 MGM version called *Mad Love* which introduced Peter Lorre to Hollywood; worse was a 1960 Franco-British effort.

Handsome Antonio
Il Bell'Antonio
Italy 1960 105 mins bw
Cina Del Duca/Arco/Lyre Cinematographique

d **Mauro Bolognini**
sc **Pier Paolo Pasolini, Gino Visentini**
ph **Armando Nannuzzi**
m **Piero Piccioni**
Marcello Mastroianni, Claudia Cardinale, Pierre Brasseur, Tomas Milian, Rina Morelli

Antonio (Mastroianni), a man with a reputation as a ladykiller, returns to his native Sicily to make an arranged marriage to a young woman (Cardinale). After he has proved impotent on his wedding night, the marriage is annulled and he is held up to public ridicule. The impotence of the Sicilian male in Vitaliano Brancati's novel was seen as a metaphor for Fascist Italy, a theme which is lost in this updating. Yet much of the satire on macho attitudes still holds true, despite Bolognini's tendency towards caricature. This is especially noticeable in Brasseur's performance as the father, but Mastroianni is perfect as the limp male.

Hands On The City see Hands Over The City

Hands Over The City
aka Hands On The City
Le Mani Sulla Citta
Italy 1963 105 mins bw
Galatea

d **Francesco Rosi**
sc **Enzo Provenzale, Enzo Forcella, Raffaele La Capria, Francesco Rosi**
ph **Gianni De Venanzo**

m **Piero Piccioni**
Rod Steiger, Salvo Randone, Guido Alberti, Angelo D'Alessandro, Guglielmo Metafora

When deaths result from the collapse of a building in a poor district of Naples, the disaster becomes an important factor in the forthcoming municipal elections. Rosi's sombre, realistic, and angry drama is an early example of his favourite theme—political corruption. Rod Steiger lent his name and weight to the role of a political boss in a cast that consisted mainly of non-professionals.

Best Film Venice 1963

Happiness
Schaste
USSR 1934 90 mins bw
Moskino Kombinat

d **Alexander Medvedkin**
sc **Alexander Medvedkin**
ph **Gleb Troianski**
m **Mussorgsky (re-issued version)**
Piotr Zinoviev, Elena Egorova, L. Nenascheva, W. Uspenski, G. Mirgoryan

Khmyr (Zinoviev), a poor peasant, and his wife Anna (Egorova) are dispossessed of their small farm for failing to pay their heavy taxes. He is sent off to the wars and returns after the Revolution to a collective farm where the couple finally find happiness. Two years before making this amusing satire, Medvedkin was in charge of the Ciné-Train that travelled all over the Soviet Union making films on the spot and showing them to the local people. In 1971, Chris Marker made *The Train Rolls On* about it, which included an interview with the director, as a prelude to the revelatory showing of this feature unknown in the West. Using burlesque, music-hall jokes, surrealism, masked figures and folk-tale images, it succeeds in producing what the title promises. Although finally orthodox in its praise for collectivization, it recalls the radical Soviet cinema of a decade earlier—surprising during the period of strict Socialist Realism.

Happiness see Bonheur, Le

Happy Day
Greece 1976 105 mins col
Greek Film Centre

d **Pantelis Voulgaris**
sc **Pantelis Voulgaris**
ph **George Panousopoulos**
m **Dionysis Savopoulos**
A large,unidentified cast

During the Greek civil war, the Government establishes concentration camps for political prisoners on a number of islands. In one such camp, the prisoners go about their meaningless tasks, such as killing flies and storing them in jars. Punishments include being bound to a pole in a tidal basin for days. At the climax, the prisoners put on a show for the visit of Queen Frederika. Voulgaris, who was incarcerated on an island during the junta of 1967-1974, adapted a book by a former inmate of the earlier repression, giving it the ironic English title, *Happy Day*. However, instead of filming a realistic portrayal of actual events, the director has opted for a symbolic, almost allegorical study of authority and resistance. But the daring decision not to characterize individuals—they are seen mostly in long shot—and to take a satiric rather than tragic tone is more often alienating than involving, even though the final vaudeville makes it point quite efficiently

---

Happy Gypsies
aka I Even Met Happy Gypsies
Sreo Sam Cak I Srecne Cigane
aka Skulpjaci Perja
Yugoslavia 1967 90 mins col
Avala

d **Aleksander Petrović**
sc **Aleksander Petrović**
ph **Tomislav Pinter**
m **Gypsy melodies**
Bekim Fehmiu, Olivera Vučo, Bata Zivojinović, Gordana Jovanović, Mija Aleksić

Bora (Fehmiu), a gypsy dealer in goose-feathers travels a great deal away from his wife and children. On one trip he meets a girl (Jovanović) whose lecherous stepfather he kills. These gypsies are far from happy (so is the screenplay), but the music and colour and the rare and authentic depiction of their life on the vast Yugoslavian plains, holds the attention. Among some of Yugoslavia's leading actors was Gordana Jovanović, an illiterate 16-year-old gypsy girl virtually playing herself. The film was nominated for the Best Foreign Film Oscar in 1967, as was Petrović's *Three* the previous year.

Special Jury Prize Cannes 1967

Happy New Year see Bonne Année, La

Harakiri
Seppuku
Japan 1962 135 mins bw
Shochiku

d **Masaki Kobayashi**
sc **Shinobu Hashimoto**
ph **Yoshio Miyajima**
m **Tohru Takemitsu**
Tatsuya Nakadai, Shima Iwashita, Akira Isahama, Rentaro Mikuni

The end of civil war in 1630 leaves many Samurai unemployed. One (Nakadai) visits a feudal lord and threatens harakiri in the hope that he will be taken on. When denied, he insists on carrying out the ritual suicide. While remaining true to the traditions of the Japanese period film, Kobayashi manages to criticize the rigid codes of honour which are basic to their subject. The brutal tale, beautifully composed on the wide screen, is skilfully told in flashbacks.

Special Jury Prize Cannes 1963

Här Börjar Äventyret see Adventure Starts Here

Harp Of Burma see Burmese Harp, The

Harry Munter
Sweden 1969 101 mins col
Sandrew

d **Kjell Grede**
sc **Kjell Grede**
ph **Lars Björne**
m **Dvořák, Johann Strauss, folk music**
Jan Nielsen, Carl-Gustaf Lindstedt, Gun Jönsson, Georg Adelly, Elina Salo

Harry Munter (Nielsen), a precociously brilliant schoolboy, is responsible for an electronic invention which an American company wants to market, thus offering his struggling parents a new start in the US. However, Harry is more concerned with a group of variously unhappy people who depend on him (Munter means happiness), causing a clash between his idealism and the demands of the real world. In his second film (*Hugo And Josephine* was first), Grede employs the same lyrical camera, and once again looks at the world through youthful eyes, but this time in a setting of oppressive and repressive urban wasteland. He deals with shifting planes of reality in an almost Fellini-esque manner that is only partially successful and is uncertain of his tone in charting Harry's journey to maturity. Nonetheless, his young hero as played by Nielsen, is interesting in an often appealing film.

Harvest
Regain
France 1937 122 mins bw
Marcel Pagnol

d **Marcel Pagnol**
sc **Marcel Pagnol**
ph **Willy**
m **Arthur Honegger**
Gabriel Gabrio, Fernandel, Orane Demazis, Edouard Delmont, Marguerite Moreno, Robert Le Vigan

A poacher (Gabrio), wishing for fatherhood, coaxes an itinerant girl (Demazis) away from her simple knifegrinder companion (Fernandel) and sets up house with her in a deserted village which they bring back to life. Filmed in the sunlight and space of Provence, Pagnol does justice to the Jean Giorno novel on which he based the film. Although the pantheism is a little overstrained—waving wheat and golden bread—it never detracts from the human comedy and the realism of the characters.

Harvest: 3000 Years
Mirt Sost Shi Amit
Ethiopia 1975 138 mins bw
Haile Gerima

d **Haile Gerima**
sc **Haile Gerima**
ph **Eliot Davis**
m **Tesfaye Lema**
Haregeweyn Tefferi, Melaku Mekonnen, Kasu Asfaw, Adane Melaku, Werke Abraha

A family of tenant farmers scratches a precarious living on the property of a ruthless landlord. The father (Mekonnen) dreams of a better life for his son (Melaku) and daughter (Abraha), but they are evicted from the land and the only hope is revolution. Gerima, an Ethiopian director trained at the University of California, has purposefully cast his characters as symbols of Third World exploitation. Nevertheless, although the particular situation is seen as a microcosm of Ethiopian peasant society, the people are still of flesh and blood. Music and song is used effectively to comment on the action, which gathers pace towards the optimistic conclusion.

Hasta Cierto Punto see Up To A Point

Hatred see Mollenard

Hatsukoi Jigoku-Hen see Inferno Of First Love, The

The Hatter's Ghosts

Les Fantômes Du Chapelier

France 1982 129 mins col
Horizon Productions/Films A2/SFPC

d **Claude Chabrol**
sc **Claude Chabrol**
ph **Jean Rabier**
m **Matthieu Chabrol**
Michel Serrault, Charles Aznavour, Monique Chaumette, Aurore Clément, Christine Paolini

In a small provincial town, a hatter (Serrault) murders his bed-ridden wife and other local women while continuing his life as a respected citizen who meets his tradesmen cronies nightly at a café. Though sticking quite closely to the particulars of the Georges Simenon story, Chabrol, in fine wry form, has made a film right up his own dark, provincial alley. The portrayal of the rainy town has the perfect, enclosed, semi-artificial atmosphere in which the mad hatter does his bad deeds. Michel Serrault, investing him with a walk that recalls Jean-Louis Barrault's in Renoir's *The Testament Of Dr Cordelier*, gives one of his quirkiest and finest performances.

The Haunted Castle

aka Castle Vogelöd

Schloss Vogelöd

Germany 1921 75 mins bw
Decla Bioscop

d **F.W. Murnau**
sc **Carl Mayer**
ph **Fritz Arno Wagner, Laszlo Scheffer**
m **Silent**
Arnold Korff, Lulu Keyser-Korff, Lothar Mehnert, Paul Bildt, Olga Tschechowa, Paul Hartmann

A group of people gathered for a hunting party at a mysterious castle are joined by a beautiful Baroness (Keyser-Korff) whose first husband died in suspicious circumstances. Certain strange goings-on eventually cause one of the guests to confess to the man's murder. Murnau's early, pre-*Nosferatu* chiller reveals some of the glories to come, especially in his handling of nightmares dreamt by the denizens of the castle and in the flashback scenes. However, the melodramatic story is rather complicated and is not much clarified by a surfeit of intertitles from a director who was to break new ground by using none in *The Last Laugh*, three years later.

Hauptmann Von Köpenick, Der see Captain From Kopenick, The

Havinck

Netherlands 1987 99 mins col
Riverside Pictures

d **Franz Weisz**
sc **Ger Thijs**
ph **Giuseppe Lanci**
m **Egisto Macchi**
Willem Nijholt, Will Van Kralingen, Anne Martien Lousberg, Carolien Van Den Berg, Coen Flink

Robert Havinck (Nijholt), a partner in a successful law firm, is married to Lydia (Van Kralingen) and has a 15-year-old daughter, Eva (Lousberg). When Lydia kills herself in a car crash, he begins to investigate why she acted as she did. This is a rather Bergmanesque tale in theme and character—

a godless world in which a man cut off from his feelings destroys a woman in touch with hers. Flashbacks are skilfully used to bridge past and present, and the Italian camera crew has caught the Dutch light to perfection. However, it is difficult to identify with such a cold fish of a hero.

The Hawks And The Sparrows

Uccellacci E Uccellini

Italy 1966 88 mins bw
Arco Film

d **Pier Paolo Pasolini**
sc **Pier Paolo Pasolini**
ph **Mario Bernardo, Tonino Delli Colli**
m **Ennio Morricone, Domenico Modugno**
Totò, Ninetto Davoli, Rossana Di Rocco, Renato Capogna, Pietro Davoli

A father (Totò) and son (Ninetto Davoli) become vagabonds and, accompanied by an intellectual talking bird, set out on a picaresque journey to emulate St Francis of Assisi's mission to the birds. Following his *The Gospel According To St Matthew*, Pasolini presents a tragicomic fable which shows two delightful innocents caught, like many Italians, between the Church and Marxism. A running (or rather walking) debate takes place in which the bird recounts left-wing parables, there are newsreels of the 1964 funeral of Togliatti, the Italian Communist leader, and quotations from a range of thinkers. This fairy story does not end happily ever after, but on a note of qualified optimism. The duo of the wizened Totò and the curly-haired simpleton Davoli, reappeared in another magic fable in the Pasolini episode from *The Witches* in the same year.

Häxan see Witchcraft Through The Ages

Heartbeat see Schpountz, Le

Heartbeat

La Chamade

France 1968 105 mins col
Les Films Ariane/Les Productions Artistes Associés(Paris)/P.E.A.(Rome)

d **Alain Cavalier**
sc **Françoise Sagan, Alain Cavalier**
ph **Pierre Lhomme**
m **Maurice Leroux**
Catherine Deneuve, Michel Piccoli, Roger Van Hool, Irène Tunc, Jacques Sereys

Lucile (Deneuve) lives luxuriously in the home of Charles (Piccoli), her middle-aged benefactor and occasional lover, moving in a dazzling social set until she meets Antoine (Van Hool), a comparatively penurious proof-reader. After much vacillation and a brief descent into the bottle, she enjoys an idyllic summer before recognizing her need for Charles. Working from her own book, Sagan and the director have come up with a slight romance that accurately catches the surface gloss of her once-fashionable work, but misses her novelist's nuances of character. A fragile entertainment that gets by on technical proficiency and accurate casting.

Heartbreakers, Die see Heartbreakers, The

The Heartbreakers

Die Heartbreakers

W. Germany 1983 113 mins col
Tura Film/Pro-Ject Film Produktion/ Filmverlag Der Autoren/WDR

d **Peter F. Bringmann**
sc **Matthias Seelig**
ph **Helge Weindler**
m **Lothar Meid**
Sascha Disselkamp, Mary Ketikidou, Uwe Enkelmann, Mark Eichenseher, Michael Klein

A group of teenage Rhine rockers set up a pop group in the mid-1960s to emulate British beat stars, but internal squabbles and inadequate talent lead to a disastrous first concert. An affectionate, often funny, nostalgic comedy, played by a likeable sextet of young actors, it is a refreshing change from the *angst* that dominates many of the films that come out of West Germany. However, the love interest between an aspiring German Mick Jagger (Disselkamp) and the female vocalist (Ketikidou) slows up the tempo and the running jokes are rather strained.

Heart Of A Mother

Serdtze Materi

USSR 1966 100 mins bw

Gorky Studio

d **Mark Donskoi**
sc **Zoya Voskhresenskaya, Irina Donskaya**
ph **Mikhail Yakovitch**
m **R. Khozac**
Elena Fadeyeva, Danili Sagal, Rodion Nakhapetov, Nina Menichkova, Gennady Tchertov

When the father of the Ulyanov family dies suddenly, mother (Fadeyeva) is left with the burden of caring for her six offspring. Subsequently, her eldest son and daughter are, respectively, executed and exiled to Siberia for their part in a plot to kill the Tsar, the family is uprooted from its contented life in a town on the Volga, and the second son, Vladimir Ilyich (Nakhapetov), much affected by events, commits himself to the Revolutionary cause, eventually taking the name Lenin. Donskoi's film, the first in his studies of the Russian leader's early life, is a work of impressive visual beauty, capturing landscape and period in sharp but lyrical images. If mother is portrayed as somewhat remote and enigmatic, the film as a whole opts for a warmth which humanizes this respectful and nostalgic journey into recent history.

Heart Of Glass

Herz Aus Glas

W. Germany 1976 94 mins col
Werner Herzog

d **Werner Herzog**
sc **Werner Herzog, Herbert Achternbusch**
ph **Jörg Schmidt-Reitwein**
m **Popul Vuh**
Josef Bierbichler, Stefan Guttler, Clemens Scheitz, Sepp Müller, Volker Prechtel

In a 19th-century Bavarian village, a mystical nomadic shepherd supplies a glass factory owner with the lost secret formula for a very precious glass and prophesies the coming of the industrial era. 'The film is meant to convey an atmosphere of hallucination, of prophecy, of the visionary and of collective madness,' quoth the director. Known for going to any lengths to make a film (vide *Fitzcarraldo*), Herzog had his actors perform under hypnosis to achieve the above effect. This impenetrable and hermetic film is pretty hypnotic for some of the time and soporific at others, but the landscapes are visually arresting.

Heart Of Paris see Gribouille

The Heat Line

La Ligne De Chaleur

Canada 1988 88 mins col
ACPAV

d **Hubert-Yves Rose**
sc **Micheline Lanctôt**
ph **Michel Caron**
m **Richard Grégoire**
Gabriel Arcand, Simon Gonzales, Gérard Parkes

Robert (Arcand), recently divorced and adjusting to life alone, takes his young son (Gonzales) from Montreal to Florida, where his father, whom he has not seen for years, has died. They drive the father's car back to Canada but very little goes smoothly on the way home. Like many road movies, from whatever country, this bleak, well-handled French Canadian example of the genre is about loneliness, alienation and loss, with the road leading towards some kind of illumination. Hubert-Yves Rose, who dedicated the picture to his own father, concentrates on the father-son relationships—Robert's with his dead father, and his own with his son. This develops skillfully thanks to the fine central performances and that of Parkes, who plays a loquacious dying stranger they meet. The climatic contrast between the cold of Canada and the heat of Florida is used to good effect.

Heaven Fell That Night

(US: The Night Heaven Fell)

Les Bijoutiers Du Claire De Lune

France 1957 91 mins col
Iena Productions/U.C.I.C.(Paris)/ C.E.I.A.P.(Rome)

d **Roger Vadim**
sc **Roger Vadim, Peter Viertel**
ph **Armand Thirard**
m **Georges Auric**
Brigitte Bardot, Stephen Boyd, Alida Valli, Pepé Nieto, José Marco Davo

Ursula (Bardot), a convent girl holidaying in Spain, runs off to the hills for an idyllic interlude of love and sex with handsome

Lamberto (Boyd). The trouble is that Lamberto is a criminal layabout who previously murdered Ursula's uncle and seduced her aunt (Valli) and the police are hot on his heels. A real piece of drivel and its only *raison d 'être* is to give audiences an eyeful (in CinemaScope) of Mrs Roger Vadim. Apparently, the filming was dogged with difficulties—unusually appalling weather for Spain, animosity between the leads—but one can't help feeling that a smooth ride would have made little difference.

Heaven Over The Marshes

Cielo Sulla Palude

Italy 1949 120 mins bw
Bassoli-Arx

d **Augusto Genina**
sc **Augusto Genina**
ph **G.R. Aldo**
m **Antonio Veretti**
Ines Orsini, Mauro Matteucci, Giovanni Martella, Assunta Radico, Francesco Tomalillo

Maria Goretti (Orsini), a poor peasant girl, resists a farmhand's repeated attempts to seduce her and he finally kills her. This is a true story of a religious girl who chose to be murdered rather than to be dishonoured by rape, became a folk heroine and was canonized 50 years later, soon after this film was made in tribute to her. Veteran director Genina, working on location in the desolate, malaria-infested Pontine marshes near Rome where the incident took place, has made a powerful and poignant film, drawing convincing performances from his cast of local farm people, and helped by the finely judged camera of the brilliant G.R. Aldo. Originally over-long, and at moments too slow, it is generally shown less 20 minutes, which is to its advantage. Genina, who entered films as a scriptwriter in 1913 and died in 1957, directed approximately 150 films during his career, ranging from early melodramas to Fascist propaganda.

Best Director Venice 1949

Heaven Sent

(US: Thank Heaven For Small Favors)

Un Drôle De Paroissien

France 1963 83 mins bw
Film D'Art/A.T.I.L.A.

d **Jean-Pierre Mocky**
sc **Michel Servin, Alain Moury, Jean-Pierre Mocky**
ph **L.H. Burel**
m **Joseph Kosma**
Bourvil, Francis Blanche, Jean Poiret, Jean Yonnel, Jean Tissier, Jean Galland

The Lachesnaye family, high-born aristocrats, have fallen on hard times and must resort to stripping off the doors and panelling of their Paris apartment for use as firewood. They are also threatened with eviction, but never waver from their conviction that they were not born to work. One of them, the ultra-religious Georges (Bourvil), takes the sound of coins dropping into the church offertory as a sign from the Lord and embarks on a project for removing money from poor-boxes to save his family... A thoroughly light-weight but delightfully irreverent comedy, which Mocky directs at a terrific pace. It errs on the side of predictability and superficiality, but the splendid performances, notably from Bourvil, Blanche and Galland, all in sparkling form, make for satisfying entertainment.

He Died With His Eyes Open

On Ne Meurt Que 2 Fois

France 1985 106 mins col
Swaine Productions/TFI Films

d **Jacques Deray**
sc **Jacques Deray, Michel Audiard**
ph **Jean Penzer**
m **Claude Bolling**
Michel Serrault, Charlotte Rampling, Elisabeth Depardieu, Xavier Deluc, Gérard Darmon, Jean-Pierre Bacri

When the body of a brutally murdered man, his eyes open, is found on a piece of waste ground in Paris, Inspector Staniland (Serrault) is called in. He discovers that the dead man was a pianist, and further investigations lead him to the victim's beautiful, mysterious and promiscuous mistress (Rampling), a photographic model. He develops a bizarre and obsessive relationship with her, and finds himself sucked into a morass of lies, eroticism and danger. The major attraction of this film is Serrault's superb performance which lends authority and flesh and blood—

characteristics conspicuously missing in everyone else—to his character. The ultra-chic sleaze of the film's milieu is well-captured, and there are a couple of intriguing ideas afloat in the screenplay, but it's all really rather silly and somewhat tasteless.

Heimat
aka Homeland

W. Germany 1983 924 mins bw/col
Edgar Reitz/WDR/SFB

d **Edgar Reitz**
sc **Edgar Reitz, Peter Steinbach**
ph **Gernot Roll**
m **Nicos Mamangakis**
Marita Breuer, Dieter Schaad, Kurt Wagner, Jörg Hube, Rüdiger Weigang, Karin Rasenack, Jörg Richter, Peter Harting

Life in a fictitious German village between 1919 and 1982, revolving around Maria (Breuer) and the Simon family into which she marries. An amusing, moving, absorbing and seldom boring high-class soap opera which mirrors modern German history through the eyes of ordinary people, and in which the characters age and develop convincingly. Particularly fascinating is the Nazi era as viewed from this standpoint. The film comes as close as any has to explaining how the evil of Hitler's ideology filtered down to taint otherwise decent citizens. The swastikas on buildings, frighteningly, lose their usual potency to become a natural feature of the decor; while the sudden shifting of former Party members to become American allies is dealt with satirically but subtly. The character of the composer who takes us through the modern era is Reitz's surrogate (he was himself a musician). The 2,000-page screenplay took five years and four months to shoot and lasts $15\frac{1}{2}$ hours. Although the director insists that it was made to be seen on the big screen, it is more practical and cheaper to see on TV with no great loss of impact. Only the constant change from monochrome to colour and back is often irritatingly arbitrary.

Hei Pao Shi Jian see Black Cannon Incident, The

Heir To Genghis Khan, The see Storm Over Asia

Helden see Arms And The Man

Heller Wahn see Friends And Husbands

Hell's Cargo
(US: S.O.S. Mediterranean)
Alerte En Méditeranée

France 1937 104 mins bw
Vega

d **Léo Joannon**
sc **Léo Joannon**
ph **Marcel Lucien**
m **Michel Michelet**
Pierre Fresnay, Rolf Wanka, Kim Peacock, Nadine Vogel

Three naval officers, French, German and English, are at odds, but combine to help each other after a murder is committed during a sailors' brawl in Tangier, where they are on leave. What ensues is an action-packed (if sometimes rather far-fetched) adventure, involving the pursuit of a freighter carrying illicit cargo, and the saving of passengers aboard a French liner whose lives are imperilled by poisonous, gas-filled seas. The acting is initially a little stiff and the continuity somewhat jumpy, but the movie—clearly calculated to involve the emotions of all the nationalities it represents—provides an exciting climax in Mediterranean waters, as well as some uplift about abandoning national prejudices.

The Herd
Sürü

Turkey 1978 118 mins col
Güney Film

d **Zeki Ökten**
sc **Yilmaz Güney**
ph **Izzet Akay**
m **Zülfü Livaneli**
Tarik Akan, Melike Demirag, Tuncel Kurtiz, Levent Inanir, Meral Niron

A nomadic herdsman (Akan) who has married a woman (Demirag) from a tribe with which his family has an ancient feud, takes a flock of sheep to sell in Ankara. On the way, some sheep die and others are stolen and in the big city, the man is paid much less by a dealer than he was promised. Finally, his wife dies. Like *The Enemy* and *Yol*, this abrasive, violent and lyrical film was supervised by Güney from prison. Apparently it was scripted in a room shared by 80 other prisoners. Without preaching or sentimentality, the film exposes the hardships and injustices of the society. The one cinema that dared show it in Turkey was closed down after a bomb attack. Güney's films are themselves bombshells.

Herkulesfürdöi Emlék see Improperly Dressed

The Heroes Are Tired

(US: Heros And Sinners)

Les Héros Sont Fatigués

France 1955 105 mins bw
Terra Film

d **Yves Ciampi**
sc **J.L. Bost, Yves Ciampi**
ph **Henri Alekan**
m **Louiguy**
Yves Montand, Maria Felix, Jean Servais, Curt Jurgens, Elisabeth Manet, Gérard Oury, Gert Fröbe

On the coast of the West African state of Liberia, a group of whites, mainly French, but including the odd German, play out a series of dramas that embrace diamond smuggling, marital discord, sensual affairs and strange political alliances. One can only assume that the title of this film is intended ironically, as the group are all on the verge of moral dereliction and do not appear to have any claim to heroism, past or present. Extravagantly overwritten and parading the art of coarse acting, the film offers every atmospheric cliché in the book to do with oppressive heat, insect-ridden interiors, rampant sexuality, booze-sodden verbosity, and 'the natives are restless tonight'. What a waste of the cast!

Heroism see Eroica

Heros And Sinners see Heros Are Tired, The

Héros Sont Fatigués, Les see Heroes Are Tired, The

Herr Arnes Pengar see Sir Arne's Treasure

Herrin Von Atlantis, Die see Atlantide, L'

Herr Puntila And His Servant Matti

Herr Puntila Und Sein Knecht Matti

Austria 1955 95 mins col
Bauerfilm

d **Alberto Cavalcanti**
sc **Alberto Cavalcanti, Vladimir Pozner, Ruth Wieden**
ph **André Bac, Arthur Hämmerer**
m **Hanns Eisler**
Curt Bois, Hans Engelmann, Maria Emo, Edith Prager

In Finland, Puntila (Bois), a well-to-do landowner, is generous, selfless and high-minded when under the influence of alcohol; sober, he is dictatorial, cruel, and exploitative. It is his chauffeur Matti (Engelmann) who has to bear the main brunt of his changing moods and who has to pacify the girls to whom Puntila proposes when he is drunk. Based on Bertolt Brecht's 1941 comedy of class, it is the only film adaptation of one of his plays that pleased him. In fact, Brecht gave Cavalcanti, that most cosmopolitan of directors, advice on the filming. The faithful screenplay and the performances are a delight, but considering that the original idea for the play came from a character in Chaplin's *City Lights*, it might have been more cinematically conceived.

Herr Puntila Und Sein Knecht Matti see Herr Puntila And His Servant Matti

Herz Aus Glas see Heart Of Glass

Hets see Frenzy

He Who Must Die

Celui Qui Doit Mourir

France 1957 126 mins bw
Indusfilms

d **Jules Dassin**
sc **Jules Dassin, Ben Barzman**
ph **Jacques Natteau**
m **Georges Auric**
Jean Servais, Carl Mohner, Pierre Vaneck, Melina Mercouri, Fernand Ledoux, Maurice Ronet, Gert Fröbe, Grégoire Aslan, Roger Hanin, Nicole Berger

In 1921, in a small Greek village under Turkish domination, the preparations for a Passion play are interrupted by the arrival of refugees from the mountains. Based on the Kazantzakis novel *Christ Recrucified*, Dassin's second film in France was one of his most ambitious. In spite of the obvious symbolism and some artiness, much of it succeeds because of the sincerity and passion of the direction and cast, including Melina Mercouri, Dassin's wife-to-be, in only her second film.

Hi see Sin, The

The Hidden Fortress

Kakushi Toride No San-Akunin

Japan 1958 123 mins bw
Toho

d **Akira Kurosawa**
sc **Akira Kurosawa, Ryuzo Kikushima, Hideo Oguni, Shinobu Hashimoto**
ph **Ichio Yamazaki**
m **Masaru Sato**
Toshiro Mifune, Misa Uehara, Minoru Chiaki

A Samurai leader (Mifune) offers his protection to the beautiful heiress (Uehara) of a feudal lord. She is fleeing with her treasure on a perilous journey to sanctuary during the civil wars in medieval Japan. Kurosawa embellishes a typical Japanese Western plot with a great deal of humour, excitement and magic. His use of the wide screen for the first time gives added visual sweep to the story.

Best Director Berlin 1959

Hideg Napok see Cold Days

Higan-Bana see Equinox Flower

High And Low

Tengoku To Jigoku

Japan 1963 142 mins bw
Toho

d **Akira Kurosawa**
sc **Hideo Oguni, Ryuzo Kikushima, Eijiro Hisaito, Akira Kurosawa**
ph **Asakazu Nakai, Takao Saito**
m **Masaru Satu**
Toshiro Mifune, Kyoko Kagawa, Tatsuya Nakadai, Tsutomu Yamakazi, Tatsuya Mihashi

Gondo (Mifune), a shoe manufacturer, faces a moral dilemma when the son of his chauffeur is mistaken for his own and kidnapped: if he pays the ransom, he will face financial ruin. The internationally-minded Kurosawa based this film on a detective novel by Ed McBain, but makes it very much his (and Japan's) own in tone and flavour. When Gondo decides to pay the ransom, the action moves into gripping high gear, wonderfully paced by the master director who invests his characters, notably the detectives, with a three-dimensional reality that lifts the piece above the Hollywood thriller formula which inspired it. The title refers to the social positions of the kidnapper, driven by envy, and his wealthy victim.

High Society Limited

Feine Gesellschaft Beschränkte Haftung

W. Germany 1982 100 mins col
Ottokar Runze Filmproduktion

d **Ottokar Runze**
sc **Uwe Dallmeier, Henning Gissel, Carlheinz Heitmann**

ph **Michael Epp**
m **Hans-Martin Majewski**
Lilli Palmer, Elisabeth Bergner, Hardy Kruger, Vadim Glowna, Gerhard Olschewski, Wolf Roth

Tenants of a building are evicted by developers. One of them, a poverty-stricken but saintly old lady (Bergner), unwittingly gets a ride with a couple of would-be bank robbers (Glowna and Olschewski) to a mansion on the banks of the Elbe. At that very moment, the mansion's owner, a glamorous multi-millionairess (Palmer), is being dispossessed of everything she owns by a bank consortium, thanks to the fraudulent actions of her manager. Old lady arrives with robbers, who hold everybody hostage, while we learn that the two women are sisters... A direr piece of drivel is difficult to imagine. The ludicrous plot and characters render this supposed comedy embarrassingly unfunny, while its vague attempts at substance—the poor will enter the kingdom of heaven, decent-minded citizens are driven to crime in order to pay the rent—are shapeless and clumsy. However, Lilli Palmer is exquisite even while being ridiculous, and it is interesting to see Bergner in the twilight of her years.

Hill Of Death

Kozara

Yugoslavia 1962 130 mins bw
Bosna Film

d **Veljko Bulajić**
sc **Ratko Djurović, Stevan Bulajić**
ph **Aleksander Sekulović**
m **Vladimir Kraus-Rajterić**
Bert Sotlar, Milena Dravić, Olivera Marković, Mihajlo Kostić, Bata Zinojinović

In 1942 the mighty German army descends on the mountain village of Kozara, bombing indiscriminately and executing all suspected Partisans. A band of the latter, led by Vuksha (Sotlar), fights back courageously, losing most of its number in the process. This is a conventional and predictable war film about the local heroes of Yugoslavia, with little of interest to offer in its depiction of characters and relationships. However, the battle scenes are extremely well done, sparing no details but avoiding sensationalism, and the images of men and machines against the landscape are very striking.

A Hill On The Dark Side Of The Moon

Berget Pa Manens Baksida

Sweden 1983 105 mins col
MovieMakers/Svenska Filminstitut/
SVT 1/Sandrew

d **Lennart Hjulström**
sc **Agneta Pleijel**
ph **Sten Holmberg, Rolf Lindström**
m **Lars-Erik Brossner**
Gunilla Nyroos, Thommy Berggren, Lina Pleijel, Bibi Andersson, Ingvar Hirdwall, Iwar Wiklander

The last years in the life of Sonya Kovalevsky (Nyroos), the brilliant Russian mathematician, who died of pneumonia in 1891 aged 41, after becoming Sweden's first woman professor. Her loveless marriage having ended in her husband's suicide, the lonely, rootless and work-obsessed Sonya finds her world upended by a cataclysmic love affair with her namesake and compatriot, Professor Maxim Kovalevsky (Berggren), who preaches doctrines of sexual equality and individual freedom, but is cruelly contained in his emotions. A film of ambitious intentions which attempts to air political and feminist issues, but degenerates into an *angst*-ridden account of sexual passion and destructive jealousy, accompanied by inappropriate music, and failing to develop its characters who languish in picturesque seasonal landscapes. Nyroos gives a brave performance as the academic whose rationality deserts her in the face of her feelings, while Berggren does his best in support. For all its flaws, though, the film has its compelling moments—not least in the silent commentary provided by the presence of Sonya's adoring but unhappy young daughter (Pleijel).

Himatsuri see Fire Festival

Himmel Über Berlin, Der see Wings Of Desire

Hintertreppe see Backstairs

Hiroshima Mon Amour

France 1959 91 mins bw
Argos/Comei/Pathé/Daiei

d **Alain Resnais**
sc **Marguerite Duras**
ph **Sacha Vierny, Takahashi Michio**
m **Giovanni Fusco, Georges Delerue**
Emmanuele Riva, Eiji Okada, Bernard Fresson, Stella Dassas, Pierre Barbaud

A French actress (Riva), filming in Hiroshima, has a brief affair with a Japanese architect (Okada). She tries to come to terms with the tragedy of his city while recalling her love for a German soldier in Nevers during the war. Resnais in his remarkable first feature, after 11 years of making short films, managed by a complex use of the flashback device to change the cinema's concept of subjective time. The past and present, personal and public anguish, Hiroshima and Nevers, intermingle in a masterly manner. It is also innovative in the use of sound (the past is silent), tracking shots and the literary but cinematic text by a leading modern novelist.

Histoire D'Adèle H, L' see Story Of Adèle H, The

Histoires Extraordinaires see Spirits Of The Dead

Histoire Simple, Un see Simple Story, A

Historia Official, La see Official Version, The

History Of The Burning Years see Flaming Years, The

Hitler, A Film From Germany
Hitler, Ein Film Aus Deutschland

W. Germany 1977 420 mins col
TMS/Solaris/Westdeutscher Rundfunk/Ina/BBC

d **Hans Jürgen Syberberg**
sc **Hans Jürgen Syberberg**
ph **Dietrich Lohmann**
m **Wagner, Mozart, Beethoven**
Harry Baer, Heinz Schubert, Peter Kern, Hellmut Lange, Rainer Von Artenfels, Martin Sperr, Johannes Buzalski

A phantasmagoric panorama of German history, culture and mythology, before, during and after Hitler, in four parts—'The Grail', 'A German Dream', 'The End Of A Winter's Tale' and 'We Children Of Hell'. Following his stimulating investigations into the German psyche in *Ludwig— Requiem For A Virgin King, Ludwig's Cook, Karl May* and *Winifred Wagner*, Germany's most original and eclectic director, opens his most copious Pandora's box of tricks to reveal 'the Hitler in us all'. An extensive use of puppets, back projection, visual quotes from *Caligari* and the German films of Fritz Lang, newsreels, interviews, narration, and burlesque, shows how Hitler was the great impresario/film director who mesmerized the masses. Syberberg's film does not seek to mesmerize, but to provoke audiences to thought and even anger.

Hitler, Ein Film Aus Deutschland see Hitler, A Film From Germany

Hoa-Binh

France 1970 90 mins col
Madeleine Films/Parc Film/Productions De La Guéville/C.A.P.A.C.

d **Raoul Coutard**
sc **Raoul Coutard**
ph **Georges Liron**
m **Michel Portal**
Phi San, Xvar Ha Moi, Le Qynh, Danièle Delorme, Huynh Cazenas, Xuan Ha

Tri (Qynh) goes to fight for the Vietcong, leaving behind his wife Thu (Ha Moi), 10-year-old son Hung (Phi San) and tiny daughter. Thu becomes ill, the village is razed by fire and the family takes refuge in the overcrowded and unwelcoming home of relatives. When Thu dies in hospital, Hung goes to Saigon with his baby sister, whom he eventually places in a nursery run by a sympathetic French nurse (Delorme) while he scratches a living from odd jobs. Coutard, the distinguished New Wave and combat photographer, lived in Vietnam for many years and made his directorial debut with this vivid evocation of an almost permanently war-torn society, seen through the eyes of a child. The title means 'Peace', and is implicitly ironic, since the children don't even know what peace is. The director's stance is determinedly neutral and even-handed—some would say wishy-washy—with both sides voicing more or less the same sentiments as a background to Hung's movingly impassive acceptance of his fate.

Hohenfeuer see Alpine Fire

The Hole
Le Trou

France 1959 123 mins bw
Play-Art/Filmsonor/Titanus

d **Jacques Becker**
sc **Jacques Becker, José Giovanni, Jean Aurel**
ph **Ghislain Cloquet**
Philippe Leroy, Marc Michel, Jean Keraudy, Michel Constantine, Raymond Meunier

Four long-term prisoners plan an escape which entails digging a tunnel through the prison vaults and into the Paris sewers. Doubts arise when a newcomer joins them in the cell. Becker, in his last film before his death in 1960 aged 54, seemed to be taking a new direction by using non- professional actors and a more austere camera style. With only natural noises on the sound track, he builds a meticulously detailed account of the characters' life in a small space and the preparations for escape.

Hole, The see Onibaba

Holiday For Henrietta
aka Henriette
La Fête À Henriette

France 1952 113 mins bw
Regina/Filmsonor

d **Julien Duvivier**
sc **Julien Duvivier, Henri Jeanson**
ph **Roger Hubert**
m **Georges Auric**
Dany Robin, Michel Auclair, Hildegard Knef, Michel Roux, Saturnin Fabre, Julien Carette, Henri Crémieux, Louis Seigner

Two screenwriters (Crémieux and Seigner) keep changing the adventures of a young shopgirl (Robin) in Paris on Bastille Day. They are finally soft-hearted enough to give her day out a happy, romantic ending. The evocation of Paris is reminiscent of René Clair's *The Fourteenth of July* (1932), more in atmosphere than in lightness of touch. The central idea of writers influencing the courses of the film is not fully explored, but the cast and plot make for pleasant entertainment. Its charm is more apparent when compared with the leaden Hollywood remake, *Paris When It Sizzles* (1963).

The Holy Innocents
Los Santos Inocentes

Spain 1984 105 mins col
Ganesh Producciones Cinematograficas/Televisí Española

d **Mario Camus**
sc **Antonio Larreta, Manuel Matji, Mario Camus**
ph **Hans Burmann**
m **Antón García Abril**
Alfredo Landa, Terele Pávez, Francisco Rabal, Augustín González, Juan Diego

Husband Paco (Landa), and wife, Régula (Pávez), exploited workers on the estate of a wealthy family in Franco's Spain in the 1960s, have to cope with a badly retarded child and Régula's mentally deficient and incontinent brother (Rabal). Their hopes rest in their son and elder daughter, but these are dashed by their feudal circumstance. It is difficult to be sure of Camus' intentions. His dark tale is lit with incidents of audacious black humour and is ravishingly filmed in a magnificent landscape, the only compensation for those who, he seems to be saying, are born to suffer. The story is told in the form of recollections by the suffering peasant couple's son and is formally, but rather oddly, divided into episodes. Religious parable or political fable—who knows? But it has some sharply original moments and a performance of outstanding dimensions from Rabal, simultaneously pathetic and repulsive.

Best Actor (Alfredo Landa and Francisco Rabal) Cannes 1984

Holy Terror, The see Bébert And The Train

The Home And The World

Ghare-Baire

India 1984 140 mins col
National Film Development Corporation Of India

d **Satyajit Ray**
sc **Satyajit Ray**
ph **Soumendou Roy**
m **Satyajit Ray**
Soumitra Chatterjee, Victor Banerjee, Swatilekha Chatterji, Gopa Aich, Jennifer Kapoor, Manoj Mitra

In 1907, Nikhil Choudhury (Banerjee), the wealthy and cultivated owner of a Bengali estate, decides that his wife (Chatterji) should leave the seclusion of the women's quarters. He introduces her to his friend Sandip (Chatterjee), a fiery and attractive leader of a nationalist movement. She falls in love with the man and and his cause, and he moves into the Choudhury home for a time, leaving political upheaval, personal betrayal and bloodshed in his wake. Ray adapted this dignified and poignant film from a novel by Tagore. At the centre of events is Nikhil, withdrawn from the world into the elegant refinements of his home, but eventually—and too late—deciding to act. This is the director in resigned mood, perhaps a little bitter in his sense of futility but, if it is not his most likeable or completely achieved work, it nonetheless holds the attention, and the three principals are superb.

Homeland see Heimat

Homme De Cendres, L' see Man Of Ashes

Homme De Nulle Part, L' see Late Mathias Pascal, The

Homme De Rio, L' see That Man From Rio

Homme Et Une Femme, Un see Man And A Woman, A

Homme Et Une Femme: Vingt Ans Déjà, Un see Man And A Woman: Twenty Years Later, A

Homme Qui Aimait Les Femmes, L' see Man Who Loved Women, The

Homme Sans Visage, L' see Shadowman

Hon Dansade En Sommar see One Summer Of Happiness

Honour Among Thieves see Grisbi

The Hooligans

Los Golfos

Spain 1959 90 mins bw
Films 59

d **Carlos Saura**
sc **Mario Camus, Carlos Saura, Daniel Sueiro**
ph **Juan Julio Baena**
m **Perico El Del Lunar**
Manuel Zarzo, Luis Marín, Oscar Cruz, Juanjo Losado, Ramón Rubio, Rafael Vargas, Maria Mayer

To finance their friend Juan (Cruz) in his ambition to become a bullfighter, a group of slum boys, living on the outskirts of Madrid, turn to crime and get one of their number killed. In spite of some uneven scripting and direction in the middle third of the film, Carlos Saura, making his feature debut, displays several of the gifts which would distinguish his later, better work. He portrays his chosen milieu with authenticity, his characters with objective sympathy, and achieves some visually poetic moments. However, it is with the final scenes in the bullring that the then young director most impresses with his energy and his uncompromising exposé of brutality to both man and beast.

Hora Da Estrela, A see Hour Of The Star

Hora De Los Hornos, La see Hour Of The Furnaces, The

Horizon

Horizont

Hungary 1971 87 mins bw
Mafilm Studio

d **Pál Gábor**
sc **Gyula Marosi, Pál Gábor**
ph **János Zsombolyai**
m **János Gonda**
Péter Fried, Lujza Orosz, Szilvia Marossy, Zoltán Vadász, József Madaras

Karesz (Fried), 16 years old, rebellious but aimless, drops out of school and, to please his factory-worker mother (Orosz) whose dream is to see him better himself, works as an office messenger. He gets himself the sack and, resisting all help and persuasion, abandons his half-hearted attempts to resume his education. Gábor gives an absorbing picture of dispossessed youth, a familiar problem seen here from the perspective of the particular difficulties which bedevil the Eastern Bloc. Script and director make no attempt to compromise Karesz's unsympathetic personality—his cavalier disregard for the older generation, for example. An honest approach, but one that alienates audience sympathy in a film which, aside from some unnecessary symbolism, is exemplary.

Horizont see Horizon

Horloger De St Paul, L' see Watchmaker Of St Paul, The

Hoří, Má Panenko see Firemen's Ball, The

Horror Chamber Of Doctor Faustus, The see Eyes Without A Face

---

Horse

Uma

Japan 1941 129 mins bw
Toho

d **Kajiro Yamamoto**
sc **Kajiro Yamamoto**
ph **Akira Mimura (summer), Hiroshi Suzuki (autumn), Hiromitsu Karasawa (spring), Takeo Ito (winter)**
m **Shigeaki Kitamura**
Hideko Takamine, Kahoru Futaba, Kamatari Fujiwara, Chieko Takehisa

The young daughter (Takamine) of a large, poor farming family lavishes her attention on her pet mare, much to her parents' disapproval. In spring, the horse gives birth to a colt, but debts force the heartbroken girl to sell it. The authenticity of this poignant, beautifully shot, bucolic tale of a girl and a horse was enhanced by the round-the-year shooting of the seasons and the documentation of horse-breeding in Japan. Akira Kurosawa, who was editor and assistant director, proposed marriage during the shooting to Takamine, the Japanese Shirley Temple, a veteran of 16 at the time. Her mother refused, as she did not feel he had much of a future. It was on the strength of Kurosawa's stunning second unit work that he was given his first film, *Judo Saga*, to direct.

Horse Thief

Daoma Zei

China 1986 88 mins col
Xi'an Film Studio

d **Tian Zhuangzhuang**
sc **Zhang Rui**
ph **Hou Yong, Zhao Fei**
m **Qu Xiaosong**
Tseshang Rigzin, Dan Jiji, Jayang Jamco, Daika, Drashi

In a remote and impoverished village in Tibet, Nordu (Rigzin), concerned for the welfare of his wife and son, takes to horse-stealing. After repenting in public at a religious ceremony, he kills a sacred ram, becomes a thief again,

and ends up a doomed outcast.
Zhuangzhuang is a member of an elite group of directors, known as the 'Fifth Generation', who have spearheaded the Chinese cinema's renaissance and *Horse Thief*, filmed on location in Tibet and western China, has been called both minimalist and expressionist. Its rich concentration of extraordinary imagery, filled with showy effects—camera angles, dissolves, superimposition, montage, slow fades—and its depiction of (sometimes incomprehensible) ritual observances, renders it memorable chiefly for its visual qualities. Awesomely mysterious, full of religious overtones, and haunted by images of death, the film nevertheless lacks any clearly discernible ideology or theme, but is an expansive and rewarding piece of pure cinematic art.

Hostsonaten see Autumn Sonata

L'Hôtel De La Plage

France 1977 111 mins col
Production 2000

d **Michel Lang**
sc **Michel Lang**
ph **Daniel Gaudry**
m **Mort Shuman**
Daniel Ceccaldi, Myriam Boyer, Francis Lemaire, Guy Marchand, Jean-Paul Muel, Anne Parillaud, Michel Robin

August, and the Hôtel De La Plage in Brittany is overflowing with holiday-makers. The guests include families with small children, families with teenagers, a divorced philanderer with his equally inconstant mistress, a bachelor and his elderly mother... To phrase it kindly, Michel Lang is no Jacques Tati. His first film, *À Nous Les Petites Anglaises*, was about English holiday-makers in Ramsgate; his second attempts a jolly romp about the French *en vacances*, but home ground hasn't helped. It is a clumsy, episodic and simpering collection of clichés, in which a lot of dreary people of all ages are preoccupied with romance, actual or longed-for. Awful, but a popular hit in France on its initial release.

Hôtel Du Nord

France 1938 110 mins bw
Sedif/Imperial

d **Marcel Carné**
sc **Henri Jeanson, Jean Aurenche**
ph **Armand Thirard**
m **Maurice Jaubert**
Annabella, Louis Jouvet, Jean-Pierre Aumont, Arletty, Jane Marken, Bernard Blier, François Périer

Among the residents of a rundown hotel on the Canal Saint-Martin in Paris, are a young couple (Aumont and Annabella) who make a suicide pact, and a bitter murderer on the run (Jouvet) with his lively mistress (Arletty). 'Atmosphere! Atmosphere!' cries Arletty, and we get plenty of it, mostly from Alexander Trauner's set and the subtle lighting. Though lacking the depth and irony of Jacques Prévert (Carné's collaborator on six films), the writers gave the director the opportunity to create a poetic bitter-sweet drama and the splendid cast a chance to shine.

Hot Winds

Garm Hava

India 1973 136 mins col
Unit 3 MM/Film Finance Corporation

d **M.S. Sathyu**
sc **Kaifi Azmi, Shama Zaidi**
ph **Ishan Arya**
m **Ustad Bahadur Khan, Aziz Ahmed, Khan Warsi**
Balraj Sahni, Gita, Jamal Hashmi, Badar Begum, Dinanath Zutshi, A.K. Hangal, Rajendra Raghuvanshi

In 1947, after independence and partition, Halim Mirza (Zutshi) and his son Kazim (Hashmi) join the Muslim exodus to Pakistan. Halim's brother Salim (Sahni), a prosperous manufacturer whose daughter is betrothed to Kazim, opts to remain in India. Gradually, anti-Muslim prejudice catches up with him and each member of his family, causing severe and escalating domestic and business problems. When Kazim returns to fetch his fiancée and is arrested, the result is tragedy. In an ambitious debut film, Sathyu has succeeded in creating a rich mosaic of the problems that dominated his country in a period of upheaval rarely dealt with in the Indian cinema. His portraits of Salim and his family unveil the customs, textures and temperaments of the individuals, revealing their differing responses to bewildering change. The character of the grandmother (Begum), rooted in the past, is particularly poignant. This is an absorbing human drama that culminates in the protagonists' growth to positive political involvement.

The Hour Of The Furnaces

La Hora De Los Hornos

Argentina 1968 260 mins col/bw
Grupo Cine Liberacion/Arger Film

d **Fernando E Solanas**
sc **Fernando E Solanas**
ph **Octavio Getino, Fernando E Solanas**
m **Various**

Part I: 'Neo-colonialism And Violence' deals with the history of Argentina. Part II: 'Act For Liberation' comprises notes and testimonies on the liberation struggles of the Argentinian people Part III: 'Violence And Liberation' considers the meaning and use of violence in the process of liberation. This masterpiece marks a way forward in didactic political documentaries. Solanas presents a dazzling array of newsreel material, extracts from films by Fernando Birri, Léon Hirszman, Joris Ivens and Humberto Rios, interviews, intertitles, songs, poems and new material with the camera zooming in on the faces of the people as evidence in his indictment and analysis of the effects of neo-colonialism on Argentina. This devastating film, made clandestinely, ends with a two minute close-up of the face of the dead Che Guevara, to whom the film is dedicated along with 'all who have died fighting to liberate Latin America'.

Hour Of The Star

A Hora Da Estrela

Brazil 1985 96 mins col
Raiz Producoes Cinematograficas

d **Suzana Amaral**
sc **Suzana Amaral, Alfredo Oroz**
ph **Edgar Moura**
m **Marcus Vinicius**
Marcelia Cartaxo, José Dumont, Tamara Taxman, Umberto Magnani, Denoy De Oliveira

Macabea (Cartaxo), a poor, naive, innocent and plain peasant girl, comes to Rio and labours inadequately as a typist, while dreaming of romance and of becoming a movie star. A novella by the renowned Brazilian novelist, Clarice Lispector, was the basis for this compassionate portrait of a deprived person whose fate is preordained by society. Macabea can break her chains only in death, which comes in circumstances both tragic and ironic. A poignant, intelligent and much acclaimed first feature from a director who began her career in her late thirties, after raising nine children.

Best Actress (Marcelia Cartaxo) Berlin 1986

Hour Of The Wolf

Vargtimmen

Sweden 1967 89 mins bw
Svensk Filmindustri

d **Ingmar Bergman**
sc **Ingmar Bergman**
ph **Sven Nykvist**
m **Lars Johan Werle**
Liv Ullmann, Max Von Sydow, Erland Josephson, Gertrud Fridh, Gudrun Brost, Ingrid Thulin

An artist (Von Sydow), living with his wife (Ullmann) at their summer island home, is subject to terrible nightmares and hallucinations. Bergman used the eerie landscape of the island of Fårö (where he himself lived) to reflect the descent into madness of his hero at odds with society. The gloom of one of his most haunting and frightening films is relieved by an enchanting extract from a puppet performance of *The Magic Flute*.

House Of Lovers

Pot Bouille

France 1957 118 mins bw
Paris/Panitalia

d **Julien Duvivier**
sc **Henri Jeanson**
ph **Michel Kelber**
m **Jean Wiener**
Gérard Philipe, Danielle Darrieux, Dany Carrel, Anouk Aimée, Jane Marken, Jacques Duby, Henri Vilbert, Claude Nollier

Penniless Octave Mouret (Philipe) arrives in Paris at the turn of the century to take up a job as assistant in a draper's shop run by Madame Hédouin (Darrieux). She takes a fancy to him, as do two girls (Carrel and Aimée) in the house where he lodges. A charming, often wickedly witty rendering of Zola's novel of snobbery and ambition among the *bourgeoisie*. An alert eye for the period, a stylish cast led by Philipe in his element, and a light erotic touch (the seduction scenes were considered quite naughty at the time) made it a return to form for Duvivier and his last film of merit.

House Of Pleasure see Plaisir, Le

The House Of The Angel

(US: End Of Innocence)

La Casa Del Angel

Argentina 1957 73 mins bw
Argentina Sono Film

d **Leopoldo Torre-Nilsson**
sc **Beatriz Guido, Leopoldo Torre-Nilsson, Martin Rodriguez Mentasti**
ph **Anibal Gonzalez Paz**
Elsa Daniel, Lautaro Murua, Giullermo Battaglia, Jordana Fain, Berta Ortegosa

In the 1920s, a sheltered young girl (Daniel) growing up in the repressive Catholic morality of a *bourgeois* family is made to feel shame for the rest of her life over her first love affair which turned horribly wrong. Although Torre-Nilsson had previously directed seven films (co- directing two with his father Leopoldo Torres-Rios), it was this claustrophobic Gothic drama that put him—and Argentina—on the cinematic map. Like the successes that followed, it was based on a novel by his wife, Beatriz Guido, and broke away from the then staple Argentinian product of superficial comedies and melodramas.

The House On Trubnaya Square

Dom Na Trubnoi

USSR 1928 64 mins bw
Mezhrabpom

d **Boris Barnet**
sc **B. Zoritch, Anatoly Marienhov, V. Cherchenievitch, V. Chklovski, Nikolai Erdman**
ph **E. Alekseyev**
m **Silent**
Vera Maretskaya, Vladimir Fogel, E. Tiapkina, S. Komarov, Boris Barnet, Anna Sten

A young country girl (Maretskaya) comes to Moscow and finds herself skivvying for a *petit-bourgeois* couple in a tenement on Trubnaya Square. But she is revitalized when she sees a play about Joan of Arc, and rebels when her employers refuse to let her go to a workers' co-operative stage show. At the very beginning the camera cranes down on the building of the title and we are introduced to the lovingly and sharply observed characters who inhabit it. A film jam-packed with delights includes an amusing scene of amateur theatricals, comically entangled relationships, a superb villain and some free- wheeling urban location shooting.

Hra O Jablko see Apple Game, The

Hrst Plna Vody see Adrift

Hsia Nu see Touch Of Zen, A

Huang Tudi see Yellow Earth

Hugo And Josephine

Hugo Och Josefin

Sweden 1967 82 mins col
Sandrew

d **Kjell Grede**
sc **Maria Gripe, Kjell Grede**
ph **Lars Björne**
m **Torbjörn Lundquist**
Maria Öhman, Fredrik Becklén, Beppe Wolgers, Inga Landgré, Helena Brodin

Lacking playmates, Josephine (Öhman) is lonely and unhappy until she meets Hugo (Becklén), whose conscientious-objector father is in prison, and who spends most of his time in the woods and fields. The children become close friends, sharing their thoughts and many adventures. Grede's debut feature enchants with its portrayal of the magic innocence of childhood, seen entirely from the children's point of view and conveyed quite unselfconsciously. The lyrical photography makes for overwhelming visual beauty and enhances a film that is free of sentimentality, a delight for children, and a poignant journey into the past for adults.

Hugo Och Josefin see Hugo And Josephine

Hugs And Kisses

Puss Och Kram

Sweden 1966 96 mins bw
Sandrews

d **Jonas Cornell**
sc **Jonas Cornell**
ph **Lars Swanberg**
m **Bengt Ernryd**
Sven-Bertil Taube, Agneta Ekmanner, Håkan Serner, Lina Granhagen, Rolf Larsson

A down-at-heel bohemian writer (Serner) is taken into the home of a rich friend (Taube) whose wife becomes torn between her vain but steady husband and the unpredictable carefree guest. The quality of this witty, sophisticated comedy of sexual manners was obscured by the fuss over one scene when the elegant heroine (played by the director's wife) looks at herself naked in the mirror. The British censor showed the film to the press before deciding whether to excise it. The reaction of the scribes was favourable, as they vociferously claimed that pubic hair was not in itself obscene. It was shown uncut and hailed as one of the most promising debuts of many a year. Unfortunately, Cornell has not fulfilled the promise, but the film can be enjoyed today without the attendant hullabaloo.

Huis Clos see No Exit

The Human Beast

La Bête Humaine

France 1938 99 mins bw
Paris Films

d **Jean Renoir**
sc **Jean Renoir**
ph **Curt Courant**
m **Joseph Cosma**
Jean Gabin, Simone Simon, Julien Carette, Fernand Ledoux, Jean Renoir

A train driver (Gabin) falls in love with the young wife (Simon) of a railwayman (Ledoux), whom the couple plan to kill. In this film, Renoir perhaps came closest to the dark mood of fatalistic 'poetic realism' that characterized the work of Marcel Carné and Julien Duvivier in the 1930s. The beautifully crafted screenplay, though updated, remained faithful to Zola's 1890 novel, and provided opportunities for the powerful brooding presence of Gabin, the enchanting pekinese profile of Simon, and at least two unforgettable sequences—the Paris-Le Havre run (actually filmed on a moving train) and the railwaymen's ball counterpointing a murder.

The Human Condition

Ningen No Joken

Japan 1958-1961 208 mins (No Greater Love), 181 mins (Road To Eternity), 190 mins (A Soldier's Prayer) bw
Shochiku

d **Masaki Kobayashi**
sc **Masaki Kobayashi, Zenzo Matsuyama**
ph **Yoshio Miyajima**
m **Chuji Kinoshita**
Tatsuya Nakadai, Michiyo Aratama, So Yamamura, Eitaro Ozawa, Akira Ishihama, Shinji Nambara, Ineko Arima

In 1943, with Japan at war, Kaji (Nakadai), a young pacifist, accepts a job as a mine supervisor in Manchuria, where he finds the workers exploited and ill-treated. For rebelling against the bosses, he is arrested and tortured, then sent to the army. The second film deals with Kaji's life there. He finds similar brutality in the barracks. When Japan is defeated, he is interned in a labour camp. The last episode follows his escape in the snow and his efforts to get back to his wife (Aratama). This impressive and harrowing trilogy, based on Gomika's monumental novel, conveys its humanist message through an almost documentary-like visual treatment. Despite the handsome, courageous hero being too good to be true, the rest of humanity so consistently awful and the structure of the films similar, the whole experience is moving and memorable.

The Hunchback Of Rome
Il Gobbo

Italy 1960 103 mins bw
Dino De Laurentiis Cinematografica/Orsay Films

d **Carlo Lizzani**
sc **Luciano Vincenzoni, Elio Petri, Tommaso Chiaretti**
ph **Aldo Tonti, Leonida Barboni**
m **Piero Piccioni**
Gérard Blain, Anna Maria Ferrero, Ivo Garrani, Bernard Blier, Pier Paolo Pasolini, Teresa Pellati

In Rome in 1944, the Hunchback (Blain), a senior figure in the Italian Resistance famed for his ruthless courage, rapes Ninetta (Ferrero), the daughter of a collaborator, but subsequently falls in love with her. This does not prevent him from killing her father. After the liberation, she refuses his offers of help and turns to prostitution. He, only able to function by violence, leads a gang of criminals, but uses the profits to attempt the reclamation of whores... Lizzani's intriguing film is based on the life and death of a real-life hunchback, who flourished as a bandit during the Occupation. Dramatically well-photographed, this account of a man who hits back at a society prejudiced against his deformity is very absorbing until the director allows the Robin Hood element to romanticize and weaken the tale.

Hunger
Sult

Denmark 1966 110 mins bw
Henning Carlsen (Copenhagen)/ABC Film (Oslo)/Sandrew/Svenska Filminstitutet (Stockholm)

d **Henning Carlsen**
sc **Henning Carlsen, Peter Seeberg**
ph **Henning Kristiansen**
m **Krzysztof Komeda**
Per Oscarsson, Gunnel Lindblom, Sigrid Horne-Rasmussen, Oswald Helmuth, Henki Kolstad

Norway 1890. Pontus (Oscarsson), a penniless and starving writer, unable to keep down food even if he can get it, is thrown out of his lodgings and wanders the streets. Offered money for an article, he struggles to write it by the light of a street lamp and, thus engaged, encounters a beautiful woman (Lindblom) who invites him home. Her attempted seduction ends in humilation for Pontus. In spite of a few misjudged moments—an unhappy use of distorted imagery, some unnecessary characteristics invented for Pontus—Carlsen has made an excellent screen adaptation of Knut Hamsen's famous first novel. Boasting some wonderfully atmospheric locations and a strong evocation of the squalor of poverty, the film triumphs above all in Oscarsson's complex, truthful portrayal of a man, ravaged by hunger, whose mind is on the verge of disintegration.
Best Actor (Per Oscarsson) Cannes 1966

Hungry For Love
(US: Love À La Carte)
Adua E Le Compagne

Italy 1960 150 mins bw
Zebra

d **Antonio Pietrangeli**
sc **Ruggero Maccari, Ettore Scola, Antonio Pietrangeli, Tullio Pinelli**
ph **Armando Nannuzzi**
m **Piero Piccioni**
Simone Signoret, Marcello Mastroianni, Sandra Milo, Emmanuele Riva, Gina Rovere, Claudio Gora

Following the official closing of brothels in Italy, four of the girls decide to pool their savings and open a restaurant. They make a go of it, until a wealthy former client causes problems. This is the sort of film that tries to give prostitutes a good name, but ends up giving Italian commercial cinema a bad one. Not that the acting of Signoret (as Adua) and company is anything but watchable, but the episodic plot is overstretched, clichés abound and it never gets to the heart, golden or otherwise, of the characters.

The Hunt
La Caza

Spain 1965 87 mins bw
Elias Querejeta

d **Carlos Saura**
sc **Angelino Fons, Carlos Saura**
ph **Luis Cuadrado**

m **Luis De Pablo**
Ismael Merlo, Alfredo Mayo, José Maria Prada, Fernando Sanchez Polack, Emilio Guiterrez Caba, Violeta Garcia

Four men go on a day's rabbit-hunting outside Madrid. José and Luis (Merlo and Prada), middle-aged business partners, are failing to prosper and are each locked into an unhappy marriage. Paco (Mayo), who has not seen his former associates for several years, brings his young brother-in-law (Caba) with him. He has married well and exudes well-being and success. As the day passes, hostilities and resentments build up amid memories of the Civil War that lurk in the scarred and barren landscape, and the outing ends in bloodshed. Made in the repressive climate of Franco's Spain, Saura's third feature, which made his name, is a finely wrought metaphor for its times, presented as a taut, spare psychological thriller. The violent and shocking denouement grows naturally out of the inner crises of the characters, generated by boredom, frustration and anxiety in the languid heat. Powerful and unhappy stuff.

Best Director Berlin 1966

Hunters, The see Huntsmen, The

Hunting Flies

Polowanie Na Muchy

Poland 1969 108 mins col
Zespoly

d **Andrzej Wajda**
sc **Janusz Glowacki**
ph **Zygmunt Samosiuk**
m **Andrzej Korzyński**
Malgorzata Braunek, Zygmunt Malanowicz, Ewa Skarzanta, Daniel Olbrychski, Joszef Pieracki

An ineffectual young translator (Malanowicz) is taken up by a glamorous, ambitious girl (Braunek) who tries to make him an artistic success by taking him away from his dull wife (Skarzanta) and introducing him to the right people. Wajda's first outright venture into comedy (few of his films find much to laugh at) is reminiscent of his compatriot Skolimowski's humour and milieu, but it is less focused and never exactly sure of its targets. For example, the film is plainly misogynistic while being dedicated to women, an unconvincing irony. Nevertheless, there are some fiercely satirical jibes at certain sectors of Polish society.

The Huntsmen

(US:The Hunters)

I Kynighi

Greece 1977 165 mins col
Angelopoulos/INA Production

d **Theo Angelopoulos**
sc **Theo Angelopoulos, Stratis Karras**
ph **Ghiorgios Arvanitis**
m **Loukianos Kilaidonis**
Vangelis Kazan, Georges Danis, Ilia Stamatiou, Stratos Pahis

A group of hunters in 1977, crossing a snowy mountainside in northern Greece, comes across the body of a Greek guerrilla fighter killed in 1949. At the subsequent inquest, each member of the hunting party, as well as various peasants and workers, speaks of his experiences during the civil war and the years that followed. Angelopoulos takes his time to unravel the various strands in this inquisition of the Right, using dream, memory and fantasy and the powerful symbol of the corpse as the silent accuser. The use of pastel shades, the deliberately languid pacing and the long takes are often justified in giving the spectator time to consider the issues—or to think of something else.

Hurdes, Las see Land Without Bread

Hustruer see Wives

Hustruer Ti Ar Etter see Wives (10 Years After)

Hypothèse Du Tableau Volé, L' see Hypothesis Of The Stolen Painting, The

---

The Hypothesis Of The Stolen Painting

L'Hypothèse Du Tableau Volé

France 1978 66 mins bw
L'Institut National De L'Audiovisuel

d **Râùl Ruiz**
sc **Râùl Ruiz**
ph **Sacha Vierny**
m **Jorge Arriagada**
Jean Rougeul, Gabriel Gascon, Chantal Paley, Jean Raynaud, Daniel Grimm

An art collector (Rougeul) guides an unseen interviewer around six paintings by Frédéric Tonnerre, an academic painter of the Second Empire, in an attempt to solve the mystery of a missing seventh painting, which provoked a major scandal. Ruiz's intriguing and singular meditation on the possibilities and limitations of the pictorial in the cinema, is also a detective story with clues and a solution. Based on the novel *Baphomet* by Pierre Klossowski, brother of the painter Balthus and himself an artist, the film presents the six paintings as *tableaux vivants* in which the actors hold poses as they are minutely examined. It forces a reappraisal of one's approach to static paintings and to the narrative flow of films. Vierny's exquisite black and white photography helped bring the paintings to life. The film made the director, a Chilean exile in Paris, the darling of the *avant-garde.*

I Accuse
J'Accuse

France 1919 150 mins bw
Pathé

d **Abel Gance**
sc **Abel Gance**
ph **L.H. Burel, Marc Bujart, Maurice Forster**
m **Silent**
Sevérin-Mars, Maryse Dauvray, Romuald Joubé, Maxime Des Jardine, Angèle Guys

The brutish François (Sevérin-Mars) seethes with jealousy because he knows his wife Edith (Dauvray) prefers his friend, the sensitive poet Jean (Joubé). But the war unites the men against a common enemy. Gance's biggest budget film to date, which he called 'a human cry against the bellicose din of armies,' begins with soldiers forming the letters of the title and ends with dead soldiers rising from their graves contrasted, in a split-screen sequence, with a victory parade to the Arc De Triomphe. This lengthy pacifist statement, depicting death, delusion and insanity in the trenches was actually shot during World War I with real soldiers under fire. However, much of its impact is weakened by the over-melodramatic triangular love story that takes up too much of the time. Gance remade this international success as a talkie in 1938, using many of the same techniques and sequences to less effect.

I Am Curious - Yellow
Jag Ar Nyfiken Gul

Sweden 1967 121 mins bw
Sandrews

d **Vilgot Sjöman**
sc **Vilgot Sjöman**
ph **Peter Wester**
m **Bengt Ernryd**
Lena Nyman, Peter Lindgren, Börje Ahlstedt, Vilgot Sjöman, Magnus Nilsson

A sociologist (Nyman) conducts a series of interviews with workers, trade unionists, women and young people about the Swedish class structure and their roles in it. Meanwhile, she has a passionate affair with a visitor (Ahlstedt) to her father's apartment. They copulate in her bedroom, in front of the Royal Palace, in a tree, on the grass and in a pond. This is the film that broke a number of sexual taboos, and was released in the USA (where it was a huge box-office hit) only in New York and New Jersey after a court battle, and cut by 11 minutes in Great Britain. The film's loose narrative structure and the use of *cinéma vérité* interviews and newsreel material reflect part of the changing political and sexual climate in Europe in the late 1960s, but much of it is now more heavy going than heavy breathing. This *succès de scandale* was followed up by *I Am Curious - Blue* (1968)—yellow and blue being the two colours of the Swedish flag reflecting the director's comments on aspects of life in Sweden.

I And My Lovers see Galia

Ich Bin Ein Elefant, Madame see I'm An Elephant, Madame

Ich War 19 see I Was 19

Ich Will Doch Nur, Dass Ihr Mich Liebt see I Only Want You To Love Me

Iconostasis
Ikonostasut

Bulgaria 1969 94 mins bw
Sofia Film Studios

d **Todor Dinov, Hristo Hristov**
sc **Todor Dinov, Hristo Hristov**

ph **Atanas Tassev**
m **Milcho Leviev**
Dimiter Tashev, Emilia Radeva, Violetta Gindeva, Nikolai Ouzounov, Annie Spassova

In a Bulgarian village, in the mid-19th century during the final years of the Ottoman rule, an itinerant master craftsman (Tashev) is hired to design and carve the iconostasis (a large screen set with icons) of a new church. The heavy-drinking, slovenly artist gets a girl (Gindeva) pregnant and is generally a disruptive force among a peasant population beginning to rebel against their Turkish masters. The complex historical background, the episodic structure and profusion of incident are likely to confuse the average Western viewer, but the different ways of life of the people are vividly captured by Dinov, a leading cartoon-maker, and Hristov, both making their first feature.

Idade Da Terra see Age Of The Earth

An Ideal Husband
Idealny Muzh
USSR 1981 92 mins col
Mosfilm

d **Viktor Georgiyev**
sc **Viktor Georgiyev, from the play by Oscar Wilde**
ph **Fyodor Dobronravov**
m **E. Denisov**
Yuri Yakovlev, Ludmila Gurchenko, Anna Tvelenyova, Eduard Martsevich, Pavel Kadochnikov

Mrs Cheveley (Gurchenko), an unprincipled upper-class schemer, attempts to blackmail Sir Robert Chiltern (Yakovlev) of the Foreign Office into protecting her business interests, and to bribe her former fiancé, Viscount Goring (Martsevich), into marrying her, but her chicanery backfires. Oscar Wilde's classic snipe at the morals of fashionable society works surprisingly well in the hands of a Russian director and cast, even though one is necessarily deprived of the pleasure of the Wildean language. There are one or two *faux-pas*—the view from a suite at Claridges, for example, discloses the Thames and the Houses of Parliament—but on the whole this is a creditable and pleasing entertainment from the USSR.

Idealny Muzh see Ideal Husband, An

Identification Marks: None
Rysopis
Poland 1964 76 mins bw
Panstwowa Wyzsza Szkola Filmowa w Lodzi

d **Jerzy Skolimowski**
sc **Jerzy Skolimowski**
ph **Witold Mickiewicz**
m **Krzysztof Sadowski**
Jerzy Skolimowski, Elzbieta Czyżewska, Tadeusz Mins, Andrzej Zarnecki, Jacek Szczek

A young man is drafted into military service for two years. On the day of his departure, he visits his estranged wife and meets various other people, including an old school colleague turned playboy and a disabled war veteran, before just making it to the train on time. Twenty-five-year-old Skolimowski plays the hero and his wife, Czyzewska, portrays four different women in his first feature (for which he was also the art director), which already has his identification marks all over it: the lively, episodic structure full of telling incidents, rather than a linear narrative, an off-centre humour, and non-conformism.

Identification Of A Woman
Identificazione Di Una Donna
Italy 1982 131 mins col
Iter Film(Rome)/Gaumont(Paris)

d **Michelangelo Antonioni**
sc **Michelangelo Antonioni, Gérard Brach**
ph **Carlo Di Palma**
m **John Foxx**
Tomas Milian, Daniela Silverio, Christine Boisson, Sandra Monteleoni, Giampaolo Saccarola

Niccolo (Milian), a 40-year-old divorced film director is searching for a particular female image for his next film. He and Mavi (Silverio), his aristocratic girlfriend, argue and he loses track of her. He then takes up with Ida (Boisson), a young actress, with whom he has an affair, but she also leaves him. After seven years of experimenting with video techniques, Antonioni, the former darling of the art circuit, returned to more familiar territory, but the film is a lugubrious exercise, like the thick fog that envelops Niccolo and Mavi on the road, and the hollow foundations of a villa referred to as 'the revenge of the void'. Every image, every aphorism is laden with a significance which the theme—the difficulty of loving someone fully in our times—cannot support. The picture has a plastic beauty, but it evoked the memory of Antonioni's past and the hope that, like the main character, he would find a more satisfying new project.

Identificazione Di Una Donna see Identification Of A Woman

Idi I Smotri see Come And See

Idiot, L' see Idiot, The

The Idiot
L'Idiot

France 1946 98 mins bw
Sacha Gordine/Lux

d **Georges Lampin**
sc **Charles Spaak**
ph **Christian Matras**
m **Maurice Thiriet**
Gérard Philipe, Edwige Feuillère, Lucien Coëdel, Nathalie Nattier, Marguerite Moreno

The attempts of the saintly Prince Mishkin (Philipe) to bring tranquillity into the life of the tormented Nastasia Filipovna (Feuillère) are fraught with difficulties. Watching this competently directed and smoothly acted film, it is difficult to believe that it was adapted from one of the world's great novels. Nevertheless, though more modest than the Japanese and Soviet versions, it is more pleasurable in many ways, not least in the fine performances from Philipe and Feuillère. It was the first feature, and possibly the best, from Lampin, former assistant to René Clair and Abel Gance. He returned less successfully to Dostoevsky in 1956 with *Crime And Punishment* starring Jean Gabin.

The Idiot
Hakuchi

Japan 1951 166 mins bw
Shochiku

d **Akira Kurosawa**
sc **Akira Kurosawa, Eijiro Hisaita**
ph **Toshio Ubukata**
m **Fumio Hayasaka**
Masayuki Mori, Setsuko Hara, Toshiro Mifune, Takashi Shimura

Prince Kameda (Mori), saintly and unworldly, falls in love with Taeko (Hara), a kept woman, who is also loved by Kameda's wild-living friend Akama (Mifune). As can be seen from the above, Dostoevsky's novel has been transposed to Japan and the names of Prince Mishkin, Natasha and Rogozhin changed. It was also updated to the post-World War II era. Otherwise, Kurosawa's attempts to follow his favourite literary work slavishly were undermined by large cuts made by the producers. Furthermore, the film that immediately followed on the heels of the international success of *Rashomon* suffered from some overacting, particularly from the miscast Hara. However, there are moments where the director manages to capture some of the original's greatness, filtered through his own sensibility.

The Idiot
Nastasia Filipovna

USSR 1957 122 mins col
Mosfilm

d **Ivan Pyriev**
sc **Ivan Pyriev**
ph **Valentin Pavlov**
m **Nikolai Kryukov**
Yuri Yakovlev, Julia Borisova, Nikita Podgorny, Leonid Parkhomenko, R. Maximova

Prince Mishkin (Yakovlev), a young and penniless nobleman, returns from Switzerland to St Petersburg and attempts to redeem Nastasia Filipovna (Borisova), a fallen woman. However, his Christ-like behaviour causes problems with her protector (Podgorny) and her passionate lover (Parkhomenko). Although much of the psychological and philosophical subtlety of the novel has been lost, a lot of its atmosphere and spirit have been retained. The first of Pyriev's lavish, rather academic Dostoevsky trilogy (*White Nights* and *The Brothers Karamazov* followed), it suffers from a somewhat operatic acting style.

Ieri, Oggi, Domani see Yesterday, Today And Tomorrow

I Even Met Happy Gypsies see Happy Gypsies

Igy Jöttem see My Way Home

I Had My Brother's Wife see Waterless Summer

I Have A New Master see Passion For Life

Ikimono No Kiroku see I Live In Fear

Ikiru see Living

Ikonostasut see Iconostasis

I Live In Fear

aka Record Of A Living Being

Ikimono No Kiroku

Japan 1955 113 mins bw
Toho

d **Akira Kurosawa**
sc **Shinobu Hashimoto, Akira Kurosawa, Hideo Oguni**
ph **Asakazu Nakai**
m **Fumio Hayasaka**
Toshiro Mifune, Eiko Miyoshi, Takashi Shimura, Haruko Togo, Masao Shimizu, Yutaka Sada

A prosperous owner of a foundry (Mifune) decides to emigrate to Brazil with his large family because he believes that the effects of a nuclear war will be less there. The family, wishing to remain in Japan and not lose their share of his father's wealth, apply to the court to have him committed to an insane asylum. This is another of Kurosawa's films in which Mifune is the dynamo of the picture. Playing a much older man, bespectacled and stooped, he is a quirky figure difficult to identify with in the less successful, satirical first half, but becomes a tragic, Lear-like figure towards the end. Despite Mifune, and other good performances, this sombre contemporary tale seldom gets to grips with the complexities of its vast subject.

Illicit Interlude see Summer Interlude

Ill Omen see Sign Of Disaster

Illuminacja see Illumination

Illumination

Illuminacja

Poland 1973 91 mins col
Tor

d **Krzysztof Zanussi**
sc **Krzysztof Zanussi**
ph **Edward Klosínski**
m **Wojciech Kilar**
Stanislaw Latallo, Monika Denisiewicz-Olbrzychska, Malgorzata Pritulak, Edward Zebrowski

A young scientist (Latallo), who believes that everything in life can be handled through rational analysis, has this conviction shattered by his difficult affair with an older woman (Denisiewicz-Olbrzychska) and the death of a close friend in a climbing accident. Zanussi, who studied physics and philosophy at Warsaw University, claimed that 'The scientist is more interesting than anyone else as he is more responsible for the world than the usual people one finds in movies'. Although this statement might not convince everybody, the first major Polish film-maker in the generation after Wajda's has certainly broken new ground in his cryptic, intelligent, ironic and ethical essays on the scientific mind. Non-scientists might be put off by the intercutting of documentary material, and non-Poles by the need to infer emotions hidden in the language.

Illustrious Corpses
Cadaveri Eccellenti
Italy 1976 120 mins col
PEA/UA

d **Francesco Rosi**
sc **Francesco Rosi, Tonino Guerra, Lino Jannuzzi**
ph **Pasqualino De Santis**
m **Piero Piccioni**
Lino Ventura, Alain Cuny, Charles Vanel, Paolo Bonacelli, Marcel Bozzuffi, Max Von Sydow, Fernando Rey, Tina Aumont

A police inspector (Ventura), attempting to solve the murders of judges, prosecutors and leading politicians, but instructed to uphold the *status quo*, slowly reveals a Right-wing conspiracy to arouse public outrage against the Left. The original title is a pun on the name of a game where the head, torso and legs of a body are drawn by different people in turn on a piece of paper, folded so that each player is unable to see the other's drawing. One of Rosi's most successful and acclaimed films resembles the drawing game, as each new fact is gradually revealed. Although the plot (in both senses) is unnerving, and the film is elegantly shot (except when Rosi can't resist strange camera angles and distortions), it is rather a cold exercise, and never seems quite equal to its subject.

Il Ne Faut Pas Mourir Pour Ça see Don't Let It Kill You

I Love You Rosa
Ani Ohev Otach Rosa
Israel 1971 91 mins col
Noah Film

d **Moshe Mizrahi**
sc **Moshe Mizrahi**
ph **Adam Grinberg**
m **Dov Seltzer**
Michal Bat-Adam, Gabi Otterman, Yossef Shiloah, Levana Finkelstein, Avner Hezkiahou, Moshe Tal

In 19th-century Jerusalem, Rosa (Bat-Adam), left widowed and childless at the age of 21, automatically belongs by Jewish law to the brother of her late husband. At the time, however, her brother-in-law, Nissim (Otterman), is only 11 years old, but his determination to do his duty does not waver, eventually maturing into love and desire... Rosa is clearly a name of resonances for Mizrahi whose *Madame Rosa* would win the Best Foreign Film Oscar six years later. This time he manages no more than a superficially charming exercise, generously laced with calculated doses of Jewish family comedy and sentimentality. The leads are controlled and appealing, but one is doubtful about the value of the flashback which has Rosa recounting her tale from the perspective of an ancient crone, now aged an amazing 107.

Il Suffit D'Aimer see Bernadette Of Lourdes

I'm An Elephant, Madame
Ich Bin Ein Elefant, Madame
W. Germany 1968 100 mins col
Iduna-Film

d **Peter Zadek**
sc **Robert Müller, Peter Zadek, Wolfgang Menge**
ph **Gerard Vandenberg**
m **Andy Warhol and The Velvet Underground**
Wolfgang Schneider, Günther Lüders, Tankred Dorst, Heinz Baumann, Peter Palitzsch, Robert Dietl

In 1968, the climate of student protest filters into a West Bremen school, causing disruption and a widening gap between pupils and teachers, the latter divided between dogged conservatives and bemused liberals. At the centre of events is Rull (Schneider), an anarchic pupil who plays by his own rules, insulting protesters and reactionaries alike, but often as attractive as his behaviour is appalling. This is an original, provocative and energetic film, bursting with the youth icons of its period and offering the perceptive and often wittily presented observation that rebellion is frequently an expression of personal rather than political anarchy. Zadek, who lived in England for many years, displays an eclectic style, and takes no sides here.

Imeres Tou 36 see Days Of 36

I'm Jumping Over Puddles Again

Už Zase Skáču Přes Kaluže

Czechoslovakia 1970 92 mins col
Barrandov Film Studios

d **Karel Kachyna**
sc **Ota Hofman, Karel Kachyna**
ph **Josef Illík**
m **Zdeněk Liška**
Vladimir Dlouhy, Karel Hlušička, Zdena Hadrbolcová, Vladimir Šmeral, Borivoj Navrátil, Božena Böhmová

Little Adam (Dlouhy), whose father trains and rides horses for the Imperial stables of the Austro-Hungarian Empire, dreams of the day when he will be old enough to participate, but contracts polio which paralyzes both his legs. Determined to ride, the boy fights his disability. Adapting and transposing an Australian autobiography by Allan Marshall to pre-World War I Moravia, Kachyna hymns a paean to courage, and to man's relationship with the noble horse, but the plot is thin and filled out with a deal of tediously repeated images, and some jarring tricks that disturb the beautiful photography. The film, largely seen through the eyes of the child, is best described as infuriatingly heart-warming.

Im Lauf Der Zeit see Kings Of The Road

Immoral Tales

Contes Immoraux

France 1974 103 mins col
Argos

d **Walerian Borowczyk**
sc **Walerian Borowczyk**
ph **Bernard Daillencourt, Guy Durban, Michel Zolat, Noël Véry**
m **Maurice Le Roux, Guillaume De Machaut, traditional Spanish and Hungarian music**
Lise Danvers, Fabrice Luchini, Charlotte Alexandra, Paloma Picasso, Pascal Christophe, Florence Bellamy, Jacopo Berinizi

1) 'The Tide'—In 1974, a young man (Luchini) takes his virginal 16-year-old cousin (Danvers) to the beach to teach her the joys of sex; 2) 'Thérèse, The Philosopher'—In 1890. Thérèse (Alexandra), locked in a lumber-room by her aunt as a punishment, finds a book with erotic engravings that lead her to discover masturbation; 3) 'Erzsebet Báthory'—In 1620, the Countess Báthory (Picasso) rounds up the pretty maids of the village for nefarious purposes; 4) 'Lucrezia Borgia'—In 1498, Lucrezia (Bellamy) makes love to Pope Alexander VI (Berinizi). Borowczyk's fascination with the iconography of erotica and the emotions that lie beneath is more interesting than the monotonously bawdy storytelling in itself. The pictorial provocation was enough to make the film a commercial success.

L'Immortelle

France 1962 100 mins bw
Como/Tamara/Cocinor (Paris)/Dino De Laurentiis (Rome)/Hamle (Istanbul)

d **Alain Robbe-Grillet**
sc **Alain Robbe-Grillet**
ph **Maurice Barry**
m **Georges Delerue, Tashin Kavalcioglu**
Françoise Brion, Jacques Doniol-Valcroze, Guido Celano, Catherine Carayon, Sezer Sezin

In Istanbul, a French lecturer (Doniol-Valcroze) meets a mysterious woman (Brion), also a foreigner, who shows him around the city and then abruptly vanishes. His attempts to find her prove fruitless, until she reappears only to be lost to him again. Robbe-Grillet's screenplay for *Last Year In Marienbad* revealed a preoccupation with the image of the labyrinth. In his first film as director, a foreign city is a labyrinth in which the un-named hero is lost linguistically, culturally, geographically and emotionally. The Turkish music, the threatening dogs, the incomprehensible language and the shrieking sirens emphasize his sense of alienation. 'The film is about a mythology which is that of the Orient, the Orient seen from Paris, a picture-postcard Orient,' Robbe-Grillet explained. This intriguing play on exotic and erotic stereotypes and the real and imaginary (the woman may only exist in the man's mind) is also a recognizable description of the nature of being uprooted.

Improperly Dressed

(US: Strange Masquerade)

Herkulesfürdöi Emlék

Hungary 1977 89 mins col
Hunnia Studio/Hungarofilm

d **Pál Sándor**
sc **Zsuzsa Tóth**
ph **Elemér Ragályi**
m **Zdenkó Tamássy**
Endre Holman, Margit Dayka, Ildikó Pécsi, Sándor Szabó, Irma Patkós, Carla Romanelli, Dezsö Garás

After the collapse of the Communist Republic in the winter of 1919, János (Holman), wanted by the police for political offences, disguises himself as a woman and takes a job as an orderly at an isolated female sanatorium from where a contact is to help him escape across the border. Slow-paced, carefully directed and almost distractingly beautiful to look at, Sándor's film manages to use cross-dressing effectively for dramatic purposes, but, in avoiding the comic pitfalls, he loses the sexual ambiguity implicit in the situation—even though his protagonist comes to a new awareness of both feminine and masculine behaviour during his enforced transvestism. Overall, the film, like the microcosmic sanatorium, seems cut off from the political reality (despite the intrusion of White soldiers, one of whom is killed by János for making amorous advances), and from genuine passion (despite the Italian woman who discovers the young man's secret and makes love to him). The piece benefits immeasurably from Holman—wide-eyed, angularly handsome, beguilingly androgynous and conveying a mixture of grace and uneasiness in his female garb.

Special Jury Prize Berlin 1977

An Impudent Girl

L'Effrontée

France 1985 97 mins col
Oliane Films/Films A2/Telema/Monthyon Films

d **Claude Miller**
sc **Claude Miller, Luc Beraud, Bernard Stora, Annie Miller**
ph **Dominique Chapuis**
m **Alain Jomy, and extracts from piano concertos by Beethoven, Mozart and Mendelssohn**
Charlotte Gainsbourg, Bernadette Lafont, Jean-Claude Brialy, Raoul Billerey, Clothilde Baudon, Julie Glenn, Jean-Philippe Ecoffey

Thirteen-year-old Charlotte (Gainsbourg) lives with her widowed father and older brother. Shy, withdrawn, and feeling unloved because she is gawky, she relies on the housekeeper (Lafont) and a sickly younger child (Glenn) for company. When her idol Clara (Baudon), a famous piano prodigy her own age, comes to town to give a concert, Charlotte devotedly pursues her, with a series of unexpected consequences. Miller's proficient, sensitive and beautifully constructed work is, in fact, a French extrapolation of Carson McCullers' *The Member Of The Wedding* although, curiously, the source is entirely uncredited. Brilliant as 27- year-old Julie Harris was in Fred Zinnemann's Hollywood version, this one has the advantage of a heroine who is the right age—and who gives a memorably delightful performance. Daughter of Jane Birkin and Serge Gainsbourg, the young star is admirably supported by a well-chosen cast. A charming, touching film.

In A Year With 13 Moons

In Einem Jahr Mit 13 Monden

W. Germany 1978 129 mins col
Tango Film/Pro-ject Film/Filmverlag Der Autoren

d **Rainer Werner Fassbinder**
sc **Rainer Werner Fassbinder**
ph **Rainer Werner Fassbinder**
m **Peer Raben**
Volker Spengler, Ingrid Caven, Gottfried John, Elisabeth Trissenaar, Eva Mattes, Günther Kaufmann

Erwin (Spengler), driven by love for his business partner Anton (John), has undergone a sex-change operation and is now called Elvira. However, Anton has gone off to further his ambitions, leaving unhappy Elvira to a series of brutal and humiliating relationships with men. Finally, helped by Zora (Caven), a prostitute who later betrays her, and by his/her former wife, Elvira delves into the past in an effort to resolve the present.

This tale is uncompromisingly pessimistic and told with the use of harsh colour, asymmetrical sets, shifting narrative techniques and a discordant sound-track to evoke the pain and ugliness of Erwin/Elvira's situation. In an introductory paragraph, the director explains that in a year of 13 moons—a planetary pattern which will have occurred six times in the 20th century—those vulnerable to depression often meet catastrophe. (The year here is 1978.) The film reflects Fassbinder's oft-expressed themes, but the images are elusive, contradictory, and quite unpleasant. Profound and disturbing, or flashy and pretentious? Make of it what you will.

Indagine Su Un Cittadino Al Di Sopra Di Ogni Sospetto see Investigation Of A Citizen Above Suspicion

---

India Song

France 1975 120 mins col
Sunchild Productions/Les Films Armorial

d **Marguerite Duras**
sc **Marguerite Duras**
ph **Bruno Nuytten**
m **Carlos D'Alessio**
Delphine Seyrig, Mathieu Carrière, Michel Lonsdale, Vernon Dobtcheff, Claude Mann

In Calcutta, Anne-Marie Stretter (Seyrig), a failed concert pianist and the pampered wife of the French vice-consul (Lonsdale) has numerous affairs to which her husband turns a blind eye. This evocation of heat and languor was filmed entirely in a house near Paris, the sounds as much as the camerawork giving the impression of India in the 1930s. The sound and images are often at variance, with a narrator commenting on a place and time other than that the camera is perceiving—generally in long, slow tracking shots. This 'Last Year In Calcutta' evolves like a repetitious and poetic dream, the characters going through a strange stylized ritual. Yet the physical distress of the beggar woman crying in the jungle and Anne-Marie's mental distress are palpable. The film was a follow-up to Duras' *Woman Of The Ganges* (1972), also set in a 'metaphorical India'.

In Einem Jahr Mit 13 Monden see In A Year With 13 Moons

The Inferno Of First Love
Hatsukoi Jigoku-Hen

Japan 1968 108 mins bw
Hani Productions/Japan Art Theatre Guild

d **Susumu Hani**
sc **Susumu Hani, Shuji Terayama**
ph **Yuji Okumura**
m **Akio Yashiro, Tohru Takemitsu**
Akio Takahashi, Kuniko Ishii, Koji Mitsui, Kazuko Fukuda

Shun (Takahashi), a young metalworker, finds difficulty in making love to Nanami (Ishii), a nude model. He tells her of his unhappy childhood and of how he was sexually molested by his foster father (Mitsui). Gradually the couple becomes entangled in sordid events, resulting in a tragic ending. In condemning child abuse and the sexual exploitation of women by men, the film is often in danger of becoming the very thing it is criticizing. There are scenes of women posing in the nude, sado-masochistic games and a young boy and a girl being sexually molested, although the director is ostensibly making a moral point. The censors didn't see it this way and 20 minutes was cut from the film on its first US release. Be that as it may, sharp camerawork and telling flashbacks, realistic locations and the excellent non-professional actors reveal Hani as a forceful and talented director.

Infidelity
(US: The Five-Day Lover)
L'Amant De Cinq Jours

France 1961 95 mins bw
Les Films Ariane/Filmsonor/Mondex Films/Cineriz

d **Philippe De Broca**
sc **Daniel Boulanger, Philippe De Broca**
ph **Jean-Bernard Penzer**
m **Georges Delerue**
Jean Seberg, Micheline Presle, Jean-Pierre Cassel, François Périer

Claire (Seberg), married to Georges (Périer), has an affair with bachelor Antoine (Cassel), who is being kept by her good friend Madeleine (Presle), a wealthy *couturière*. But the meetings at Antoine's apartment, five afternoons a week, come to a halt when their partners learn the truth. 'Love's a bubble. When it touches earth, it's over,' says Jean Seberg, and so is the film. De Broca's third film (Cassel also starred in *Playing At Love* and *The Joker*) is a classic sweet- and-sour *boudoir* comedy with a bored wife, staid husband, dashing young lover and the 'older' woman, done in a light and witty modern manner. It is well played by an excellent quartet, including the American Seberg, fresh from *Breathless*, as an English woman *(sic)* in Paris.

In For Treatment
Opname

Netherlands 1979 92 mins col
Het Werkteater/VARA TV/Fugitive Cinema

d **Erik Van Zuylen, Marja Kok**
sc **Het Werkteater (from a scenario devised by the cast)**
ph **Robby Müller**
Helmert Woudenberg, Frank Groothof, Hans Man In't Veld, Marja Kok, Daria Mohr, Herman Vinck

De Waal (Woudenberg), a middle-aged market gardener, is taken into hospital for extended exploratory treatment. The doctor tells his wife (Kok) that her husband has terminal cancer, but they conceal the information from him. Through his relationship with the young man (Groothof), himself a terminal patient, with whom he shares a room, De Waal realizes the truth and attempts to come to grips with it. In opening out its work for the screen, Het Werkteater retains the improvisational method of scripting that it uses for the stage, while employing the camera to create a convincing picture of hospital life. Restrained, accurate performances contribute to the veracity of the situation and the behaviour of the characters in a crisis of universal and ongoing interest. But the film loses its way towards the end, unsatisfactorily groping for philosophical expression instead of staying with the factual approach.

L'Ingénue Libertine
(US: Minne)

France 1950 88 mins bw
Codo Cinéma

d **Jacqueline Audry**
sc **Pierre Laroche**
ph **Grignon**
m **Vincent Scotto**
Danièle Delorme, Frank Villard, Jean Tissier, Claude Nicot

A romantic young woman (Delorme) is unable to make love to her possessive husband (Villard) who treats her like a child, until she gives into the advances of a philanderer (Nicot) and an old roué (Tissier). Following her successful adaptation of *Gigi*, starring Delorme, the year before, Audry tackled another Colette novel with the same sensitivity. Because of its hint of sexual misdemeanour, it was the first production released in Britain to gain the newly instigated 'X' certificate for films deemed suitable for adults only.

The Inheritance
L'Eredità Ferramonti

Italy 1976 103 mins col
Flag Productions

d **Mauro Bolognini**
sc **Ugo Pirro, Sergio Bazzini**
ph **Ennio Guarnieri**
m **Ennio Morricone**
Anthony Quinn, Fabio Testi, Dominique Sanda, Luigi Proietti, Adriana Asti, Paolo Bonacelli

Gregorio Ferramonti (Quinn) retires, having amassed a great fortune, and informs his family that they will inherit none of it. When his son Pippo (Proietti) marries Irene (Sanda), a local girl who works for him, she devotes herself to changing the *status quo*, eventually becoming Gregorio's mistress and his heir, while the rest of the family goes to pieces. Set in Rome in the 1880s, Bolognini's melodrama bears all the hallmarks of his painterly eye. It is a cornucopia of dazzlingly composed images and sumptuous period design which one should settle back and enjoy while its run-of-the-mill tale of greed, lust and the unworthiness of the rich plods along. The beautiful Sanda doesn't do much to justify her award.

Best Actress (Dominique Sanda) Cannes 1976

Innocence Unprotected

Nevinost Bez Zastite

Yugoslavia 1968 78 mins bw/col
Avala

d **Dušan Makavejev**
sc **Dušan Makavejev**
ph **Brank Perak, Stevan Miskovic**
m **Vojislav Dostić**
Dragolub Aleksić, Ana Milosavljević, Vera Jovanović, Bratoljub Gligorijević

Dragolub Aleksić, a circus strongman and the writer-star-director of *Innocence Unprotected*, a Serbian film of 1942, reminisces about the making of that picture and its confiscation by the occupying Germans. Other survivors of the original cast recall their roles, and much of the film itself is shown, as well as newreel footage. Although the extracts from the film under discussion prove it to have been a pretty awful melodrama, Makavejev is never snide about it. In fact, *his* title refers not to the orphan heroine rescued by the hero in the original film, but to the brave and innocent people who made the film, to whom he pays amusing and affectionate homage.

Special Jury Prize Berlin 1968

The Innocent

aka The Intruder

L'Innocente

Italy 1976 125 mins col
Rizzoli

d **Luchino Visconti**
sc **Suso Cecchi D'Amico, Luchino Visconti, Enrico Medioli**
ph **Pasqualino De Santis**
m **Chopin, Liszt, Mozart, Gluck**
Giancarlo Giannini, Laura Antonelli, Jennifer O'Neill, Didier Haudepin, Marc Porel

A wealthy Sicilian (Giannini) neglects his wife (Antonelli) for his mistress (O'Neill). When the wife tries to turn the tables on him by taking a lover (Porel), events take a tragic turn with the death of a child. Visconti's last film, directed when he was very ill, was a good example of Thomas Mann's expression, 'the voluptuousness of doom'. Adapted from the book by Gabriele D'Annunzio, the poignant tale of sexual double standards is told against sumptuous turn-of-the-century settings. Thankfully, there is little of the extravagant campness that mars much of Visconti's late work. Elegant and restrained, it might have been even better with a stronger cast. With *The Leopard*, it is perhaps the best of the 14 full-length films made by the Duke of Modrone (Visconti), who died in the year of its release.

Innocente, L' see Innocent, The

Innocent Sorcerers

Niewinni Czarodzieje

Poland 1960 91 mins bw
Film Polski

d **Andrzej Wajda**
sc **Andrzej Wajda, Jerzy Skolimowski**
ph **Krysztof Winiewicz**
m **Krysztof Komeda**
Tadeusz Lomnicki, Zbigniew Cybulski, Roman Polanski, Jerzy Skolimowski, Krystyna Stypulkowska

A young bachelor doctor (Lomnicki), who plays in a jazz band, finds difficulty in committing himself to his mannequin girlfriend (Stypulkowska) and in coping with the problems of his aimless friends. After his celebrated war trilogy, Wajda took the West by surprise with this ironic sex comedy which dealt uncompromisingly with cynical modern Polish youth. Although it is now as dated as many British and American films on the problems of young people in the newly-affluent societies, it still has interest as one of the first post-war Polish films to deal with contemporary issues, and as an influence on the films directed a few years later by co-scenarist Skolimowski and Roman Polanski, both important members of the cast.

The Inquisitor

Garde À Vue

France 1981 88 mins col
Les Films Ariane/T.F.1 Films

d **Claude Miller**
sc **Claude Miller, Jean Herman**

ph **Bruno Nuytten**
m **Georges Delerue**
Lino Ventura, Michel Serrault, Guy Marchand, Romy Schneider

A wealthy and successful lawyer becomes the prime suspect in a case of child rape and murder, and is detained by the police for questioning on New Year's Eve. In this taut *policier*, confined almost entirely to the interrogation room, Miller cunningly plays with truth and lies so that the pendulum of guilt and innocence swings continually back and forth, while the inquisitor (Ventura) and the suspect (Serrault) engage in an extraordinary and fascinating contest of cat and mouse. The parallel exposure of Serrault's appalling marriage (to Schneider in her last role before she committed suicide) is much less successful, although tantalizing. Ventura and Serrault are so mesmerizingly good that they render the holes in the plot almost invisible.

In Search Of Famine
Aakaler Sandhane

India 1981 125 mins col
DK Films Enterprise

d **Mrinal Sen**
sc **Mrinal Sen**
ph **K.K. Mahajan**
m **Salil Chowdhury**
Dhritiman Chatterjee, Smita Patil, Sreela Majumdar, Gita Sen, Dipankar Dey, Rajen Tarafder

When a film crew from Calcutta arrives in an isolated village to make a film about the disastrous famine of 1943, they encounter unexpected problems from the villagers who, caught in the grip of poverty and ignorance, are suspicious and hostile. Unable to bridge the terrible gap in understanding, the bewildered visitors return to the city without having achieved their object. One of the Indian cinema's most probing recorders of the country's social fabric, Sen has made a lively, truthful film, no less profound for perceiving the comedy in the situation of clashing worlds. An excellent piece, albeit somewhat too long and occasionally lacking clarity.

Special Jury Prize Berlin 1981

The Insect Woman
Nippon Konchuki

Japan 1963 123 mins bw
Nikkatsu Corporation

d **Shohei Imamura**
sc **Keije Hasebe, Shohei Imamura**
ph **Masahisa Himeda**
m **Toshiro Mayuzumi**
Sachiko Hidari, Yitsuko Yoshimura, Hiroyuki Nagato, Seizaburo Kawazu, Sumie Sasaki

An account of 45 years of the hard life of a woman (Hidari) who grafts with the industry of an ant to survive, be it as servant or whore. Her misfortunes begin when her foster father uses her as his mistress until, aged 20, she goes out into the world pregnant. Imamura's canvas is broad, crowded and extremely painful, reflecting the exploitation of women and the cruelty of human nature, as well as the problems brought to Japan by progress. Beautifully photographed, and with a superb performance from Hidari, aging from girlhood to late middle-age, it won 14 awards in its own country.

Best Actress (Sachiko Hidari) Berlin 1964

Insiang

The Philippines 1976 95 mins col
CineManila

d **Lino Brocka**
sc **Mario O'Hara, Lamberto E. Antonio**
ph **Conrado Baltazar**
m **Minda D. Azarcon**
Hilda Koronel, Mona Lisa, Ruel Vernel, Rez Cortéz

Insiang (Koronel), an adolescent girl living with her fishmonger mother (Lisa) and other relatives in the notorious Tondo slums of Manila, is raped by her mother's young lover (Vernal) and abandoned by the man (Cortéz) she hoped to marry. She plans a revenge which destroys them all. Shown at Cannes in 1978, this was the first commercially produced Filipino film to appear at a major European Festival for 26 years and established Brocka's international reputation. With an economy of means—the camera quickly establishes character and situations—and sparse dialogue (in a Filipino dialect), Brocka does not rub our noses in the degradation but gives us a good whiff of it nevertheless. Although the rape happens off screen, there are some pretty nasty things that happen on it—understandably, given the sordid settings and the melodramatic plot. The film pivots on the central mother-daughter clash, exceptionally well-played by Koronel who has appeared in over ten of Brocka's films, and the seldom-smiling Mona Lisa.

Inspecteur Lavardin

France 1986 103 mins col
MK2/Antenne2/Suisse Romande TV

d **Claude Chabrol**
sc **Claude Chabrol, Dominique Roulet**
ph **Jean Rabier**
m **Matthieu Chabrol**
Jean Poiret, Jean-Claude Brialy, Bernadette Lafont, Jacques Dacqmine, Hermine Claire, Jean-Luc Bideau

When a pillar of a French provincial community is found murdered, the renowned Inspecteur Lavardin arrives on the scene, only to find that the victim's widow (Lafont) is an old flame and that nothing in the case is what it appears to be. The redoubtable Lavardin (played with a nice dryness by Poiret) returns for a second neatly-scripted Chabrol detective tale after *Cop Au Vin.* It is full of surprises and an array of kinky characters, including a delightful Brialy (almost 30 years after appearing in Chabrol's first feature) as a gay uncle who paints glass eyes as a hobby. However, some may find the morality of the ending questionable.

Inspector Maigret see Maigret Sets A Trap

Intermezzo

Sweden 1937 88 mins bw
A.B. Svensk

d **Gustaf Molander**
sc **Gustaf Molander, Gösta Stevens**
ph **Äke Dahlquist**
m **Heinz Provost**
Ingrid Bergman, Gösta Ekman, Inge Tidblad, Britt Hagman, Hans Ekman

Anna Hoffman (Bergman), a promising young pianist, is hired to give lessons to the little daughter of a famous concert violinist (Ekman). He and Anna fall in love and, forsaking his family, they go on an extended European concert tour with her as his accompanist until he realizes that their idyll is an interlude—an intermezzo—which cannot last. Directed by one of Sweden's most distinguished film-makers and played by the country's veteran leading man teamed with a young girl at the beginning of her career, this three-handkerchief weepie is restrained and irresistible. David O. Selznick saw it, imported Bergman to Hollywood two years later, remade the film in English co-starring her with Leslie Howard and thus launched her international career.

Interviews On Personal Problems

aka Several Interviews On Personal Matters
Neskolko Intervyu Po Lichnyam Voprosam

USSR 1979 94 mins col
Gruziafilm

d **Lana Gogoberidze**
sc **Zaira Arsenishvili, Erlom Akhvlediani, Lana Gogoberidze**
ph **Nugzar Erkomaishvili**
m **Gia Kancheli**
Sofiko Chiaureli, Gia Badridze, Ketevan Orakhelashvili, Zhanri Lolashvili, Salome Kancheli

Sofiko (Chiaureli), a crusading journalist in her forties, travels extensively around the country interviewing women and getting involved in their problems. However, her career causes a conflict with her husband (Badridze), who would prefer her to pay more attention to her domestic duties. The theme of the dichotomy between a woman's career and her family obligations is a familiar one to Western audiences, but this first Georgian film to deal with feminist issues from a woman's perspective has an added interest. The interviews with various women—a librarian, a factory worker, a housewife etc—are ironically contrasted with the reality of their lives and that of the interviewee. This technically accomplished, emotionally involving film also touches on the Stalinist terror, during which the director herself lost both her parents.

Intervista

Italy 1987 105 mins col
Aljosha/RAI Uno/Cinecitta

d **Federico Fellini**
sc **Federico Fellini, Gianfranco Angelucci**
ph **Tonino Delli Colli**
m **Nino Rota**
Federico Fellini, Marcello Mastroianni, Anita Ekberg, Sergio Rubini, Tonino Delli Colli, Maurizio Mein, Antonio Cantafora, Lara Vendel

While making his next film at Cinecitta, 'Maestro' Fellini, interviewed by a Japanese TV crew, reminisces about his first visit to the studio as a young reporter and takes the Japanese, and Marcello Mastroianni, on a nostalgic visit to Anita Ekberg's house in the country. Conceived as a tribute to Cinecitta's 50th anniversary, this affectionate divertissement, lightly balancing illusion and reality, is more of a self-homage from a director who has earned such a right. The centrepiece is a moving reunion between Marcello and a now mammothly proportioned Anita, who watch a scene from *La Dolce Vita* together. There is some dead wood and reprises from earlier films, but it's a trip Felliniphiles will enjoy.

In The Name Of The Father

Nel Nome Del Padre

Italy 1971 107 mins col
Vides Cinematografica

d **Marco Bellocchio**
sc **Marco Bellocchio**
ph **Franco Di Giacomo**
m **Nicola Piovani**
Yves Beneyton, Renato Scarpa, Lou Castel, Piero Vida, Laura Betti, Aldo Sassi

Angelo (Beneyton), an aloof non-conformist, disrupts a private Jesuit college where his fellow pupils are 'unteachables' from rich families. Angelo links up with a rebellious student (Sassi) to turn the school play into a weapon of subversion and ends up taking control of the college. Bellocchio remembers his own school experience as 'a kind of intellectual degradation in atmosphere', and the film is a vigorous portrayal of a reactionary and moribund institution. Surreal images abound as the empty rituals become increasingly exaggerated and meaningless. Not content, however, merely to depict such a place, Bellocchio attempts to broaden it into an allegory of Italian society, when the 'Fascist' hero takes over. Derivative (Vigo, Buñuel), overheated and somewhat cloudy, it is yet powerful enough to disturb.

In The Realm Of The Senses

Ai No Corrida

Japan 1976 105 mins col
Argos/Oshima/Shibata

d **Nagisa Oshima**
sc **Nagisa Oshima**
ph **Hideo Ito**
m **Minoru Miki**
Tatsuya Fuji, Eiko Matsuda, Aoi Nakajima, Meika Seri

A married man (Fuji) and a geisha (Matsuda) retreat from the militarist Japan of 1936 into a world of their own where they obsessively act out their sexual fantasies. Finally, in a quest for the ultimate orgasm, she strangles and then castrates him. Oshima's first big commercial success was, for many, in the realm of pornography. For others, it was a serious treatment of the link between eroticism and death (a theme previously dealt with in *Last Tango In Paris*) and an artistic breakthrough in the representation of explicit sex on screen. No matter how powerful, passionate and stylish it is, the film takes some sitting through, unless watching more than an hour and a half of fornication appeals to you.

In The Town Of S

V Gorodye S

USSR 1966 105 mins bw
Lenfilm

d **Josef Heifits**
sc **Josef Heifits**
ph **Ghenrih Marandzhan**
m **Nadejda Simonian**
Anatoly Papanov, Nonna Terentieva, Lidia Stykan, Igor Gorbachov, Andrei Popov, Alexei Batalov

Dr Ionych Startsev (Papanov) arrives to practise in a stiflingly *bourgeois* provincial town, where the only distraction is the cripplingly boring soirées given by the Turkin family with whose daughter (Terentieva) Startsev falls in love. She rejects him and, over the years, he degenerates into a friendless money-grubber. The director of *The Lady With The Little Dog* (1960) has again turned to Chekhov for his material,using the playwright as a character to introduce the story. It is not as satisfying as the previous film, either in style or content, but the detailed evocation of the mood and period is superb and the few *longeurs* don't prevent enjoyment.

In The White City

Dans La Ville Blanche

Portugal/Switzerland 1983 108 mins col
Metro Filme(Lisbon)/Filmograph(Geneva)

d **Alain Tanner**
sc **Alain Tanner**
ph **Acácio De Almeida**
m **Jean-Luc Barbier**
Bruno Ganz, Teresa Madruga, Julia Vonderlinn, José Carvalho

Paul (Ganz), a ship's engineer, goes ashore at Lisbon and lodges in a little waterfront hotel where he falls in love with the maid (Madruga, excellent). He decides not to return to his ship, and wanders the city with a Super-8 camera, sending his wife the films as well as the news that he now loves two women. A compulsively watchable Bruno Ganz gives a marvellous portrayal of a man in crisis, alienated from his world and pursuing an elusive and ill-formulated freedom. Tanner reflects Paul's disjunction in his contrasting images of place—dazzling, sunbathed Lisbon on the sea, its evening backstreet shadows eerie and threatening; Switzerland where Paul's wife sits in ordered domesticity watching the films that reflect her husband's state of mind. Leisurely, complex, disturbing, the film is accompanied by a haunting saxophone score, while the pace and texture of the white city is tellingly caught by De Almeida's camera.

In The Wild Mountains

Ye Shan

China 1986 99 mins col
Xi'an Film Studio

d **Yan Xueshu**
sc **Yan Xueshu, Zhu Zi**
ph **Mi Jiaqing**
m **Xu Youfu**
Du Yuan, Yue Hong, Xin Ming, Xu Shouli, Tan Xihe

Two brothers and their wives farm in the mountains of Western China. One is lazy with a spirited, hard- working but infertile wife; the other, estranged from his wife and baby, lives with them and, encouraged by his admiring sister-in-law, is determined to make his fortune. Family differences escalate, causing break- up and scandal, until the women at last swap husbands. This is a leisurely, naturalistic and illuminating look at relationships and tradition in a simple Chinese community. Political statement is subtly implicit in gradual changes that we see taking place, but this is a human story, tender and funny, with just a hint of bitterness in its sweet resolution. The photography catches the countryside and the magnificent mountains in seductive, dewy textures and colours, the acting is first-class and the use of natural sound superb.

Intimate Lighting

Intimní Osvĕtleni

Czechoslovakia 1965 72 mins bw
Ceskoslovenský Film/Barrandov Studio

d **Ivan Passer**
sc **Ivan Passer, Jaroslav Papoušek, Václav Šašek**
ph **Miroslav Ondříček, Jan Střecha**
m **Oldřich Korte**
Věra Křesadlová, Zdeněk Bezušek, Jan Vostřcil, Karel Blažek, Jaroslava Stĕdrá, Vlastimila Vlková

A professional 'cello player (Bezušek) comes to a provincial town with his fiancée (Křesdalová, Miloš Forman's second wife) to visit old friends. They eat, drink, play music and reminisce. Passer's second and last film in his native country is a tender, well-observed comedy about the everyday pleasures of life, the gentle humour concealing regret. The director had previously co-scripted Miloš Forman's first films, and left with him in 1969 for the USA.

Intimní Osvesôbttleni see Intimate Lighting

Intruder, The see Innocent, The

Investigation Of A Citizen Above Suspicion

Indagine Su Un Cittadino Al Di Sopra Di Ogni Sospetto

Italy 1970 115 mins col
Vera

d **Elio Petri**
sc **Elio Petri, Ugo Pirro**
ph **Luigi Kuveiller**
m **Ennio Morricone**
Gian Maria Volonté, Florinda Bolkan, Salvo Randone, Gianni Santuccio

A top Rome police inspector (Volonté) slashes his girlfriend's throat and deliberately plants clues to see whether his own agents will be able to track him down. But he considers himself above suspicion. Flashy, rhetorical and emphatic when it needed more sobriety, subtlety and distance to score its political points, the film, nevertheless, created a furore in Italy on the Right (Petri is a Communist), and gained big box-office returns everywhere. Volonté is effective as the Fascist cop and the plot is gripping enough to overcome the stylistic weaknesses.

Best Foreign Film Oscar 1970
Special Jury Prize Cannes 1970

Invisible Adversaries

Unsichtbare Gegner

Austria 1978 109 mins col
Valie Export

d **Valie Export**
sc **Peter Weibel**
ph **Wolfgang Simon**
Susanne Widl, Peter Weibel, Dr Josef Plavee, Monika Helfer-Friedrich

Anna (Widl), a photographer and video artist, hears an announcement on the radio that invisible forces known as Hyksos are taking over the earth in the guise of human beings. During the day she makes love to her boyfriend (Weibel), develops erotic photographs, explores the streets of Vienna, interviews women on the topic of 'when is a human being a woman?' and visits her psychoanalyst. A film as curious as the name of its debutante director, it caused controversy wherever it was shown and became a cult in Vienna. Frank in its sexuality, mixing dream and reality, it's a kind of feminist *Invasion Of The Body Snatchers*. Much of it is original, amusing (most of it intentionally) and complex. A film not only from the city of Freud, but from his mind.

Invitation, L' see Invitation, The

The Invitation

L'Invitation

Switzerland 1973 100 mins col
Citel Films/Group 5/Swiss TV(Geneva)/Planfilm(Paris)

d **Claude Goretta**
sc **Claude Goretta, Michel Viala**
ph **Jean Zeller**
m **Patrick Moraz**
Michel Robin, Jean-Luc Bideau, Jean Champion, Pierre Collet, Corinne Coderey, François Simon, Rosine Rochette

When his mother dies Rémy (Robin), a mild-mannered, middle-aged bachelor, is given compassionate leave from his job. He buys a country house and gives his office colleagues a garden party where, as the afternoon wears on, social decorum wears off. This is a gentle session of eavesdropping on a group of recognizable types—loudmouthed joker, avuncular boss, giggly nymphet—who know each other well in one context, brought unfamiliarly together in another. Although Goretta has nothing new to say, the film is fluent and diverting and he and his excellent cast (notably Simon as the knowing and detached butler) offer some wry observations in attractive, well-photographed surroundings.

I Only Want You To Love Me

Ich Will Doch Nur, Dass Ihr Mich Liebt

W. Germany 1976 112 mins col
Bavaria Atelier/Westdeutscher Rundfunk

d **Rainer Werner Fassbinder**
sc **Rainer Werner Fassbinder**
ph **Michael Ballhaus**
m **Peer Raben**
Vitus Zeplichal, Elke Aberle, Alexander Allerson, Ernie Mangold, Johanna Hofer

Peter (Zeplichal), the only child of Bavarian innkeepers (Allerson and Mangold), tries in vain to please his parents. When he marries Erika (Aberle), he showers his wife with gifts he can ill afford. Rejection and hardship lead him to violence. Lack of parental love, a subject close to Fassbinder's own experience, is the theme of one of his most poignant and realist works, based on a true account from a book of interviews and originally made for television. The framing device of an interview (by real-life sociologist Erika Runge), with a number of flashbacks, gives us a deeper understanding of the protagonist than a straight narrative would have done.

Iphigenia

Greece 1976 129 mins col
Greek Film Centre

d **Michael Cacoyannis**
sc **Michael Cacoyannis**
ph **Ghiorgos Arvanitis**
m **Mikis Theodorakis**
Irene Papas (Clytemnestra), Costa Kazakos (Agamemnon), Costa Carras (Menelaus), Tatiana Papamosou (Iphigenia), Christos Tsangas (Odysseus), Dimitris Aronis (Calchas), Panos Michaopoulos (Achilles)

After the abduction of Helen of Troy, her husband Menelaus, his brother King Agamemnon and the Greek fleet and armies are camped at Aulis. The high priest Calchas, conspiring with Odysseus King of Ithaca, persuades Agamemnon that the Greeks will only sail to victory if he makes a human sacrifice of his daughter, Iphigenia... Basing his screenplay on *Iphigenia In Aulis*, Cacoyannis completed his trilogy of Euripidean drama after *Electra* and *The Trojan Women* with what is undoubtedly the weakest of the three. The play itself has only survived in a chopped about form, but the director has compounded the difficulties by going all out for cinematic effects that are excessive and often superfluous and that weaken the heart of the drama by diffusing it. There *are* some striking images, such as the approach of Clytemnestra's retinue bringing Iphigenia to the island, and the performances are of a high order, but it is a muddle.

Iskindirya - Leh? see Alexandria - Why?

The Island
Hadaka No Shima

Japan 1961 92 mins bw
Kindai Eiga Kyokai

d **Kaneto Shindo**
sc **Kaneto Shindo**
ph **Kiyoshi Kuroda**
m **Hikaru Hayashi**
Nobuko Otowa, Taiji Tonoyama, Shinji Tanaka, Masanori Horimoto

A man (Tonoyama) his wife (Otowa) and their two small sons are the only family on an island. Every day, year in and year out, the parents go to the mainland to fetch their only supply of water, and climb the hill to their home with the buckets on their backs. This human, moving, true and effective allegory unrolls beautifully on the wide screen, using no dialogue whatsoever. When the camera soars above the island in the end, we see it as the Earth on which humankind lives, works and dies. The performances, especially by Otowa, are stunning.

Isle Of Sinners
(US: God Needs Men)
Dieu A Besoin Des Hommes

France 1950 100 mins bw
Transcontinental

d **Jean Delannoy**
sc **Jean Aurenche, Pierre Bost**
ph **Robert Lefèbvre**
m **René Cloërec**
Pierre Fresnay, Madeleine Robinson, Daniel Gélin, Andrée Clément, Jean Brochard, Sylvie

The island of Sein is a rugged and barren tract off the Britanny coast. Its inhabitants rely on pickings from shipwrecks to augment their meagre subsistence. When the priest decides that his flock is beyond redemption and leaves, the islanders persuade the simple verger (Fresnay) to execute some of the church rituals. Initially reluctant and confused, he comes to assume the full role of priesthood, even eschewing his fiancée in pursuit of his 'calling'. Adapted from a novel, based in turn on an obscure fragment of French history, this film attempts to explore definitions of sacrilege and divinity while, at the same time, portraying the Sein community as a primitive and feckless lot. The result is thematically confusing although the plot, played against a realistically stark and dramatic background, does capture the attention. Fresnay, an old hand at religious roles, is splendid and helps lend the piece some conviction.

L'Isola Di Arturo see Arturo's Island

Israel Why?

Pourquoi Israel?

France 1973 185 mins col
Stephan Films/Parafrance/Compagnie D'Enterprise Et de Gestion

d **Claude Lanzmann**
sc **Claude Lanzmann**
ph **William Lubtchansky, Colin Mounier**

Three hours of travelogue and interviews with the citizens of Israel. They range from academics to lowly artisans, from the young to the old, and encompass native-born *sabras*, as well as long-time settled immigrants and tentative new arrivals of all nationalities. With the probing, incisive neutrality that would later inform his epic *Shoah*, Claude Lanzmann encourages his interviewees to reveal their hopes, fears, beliefs and, most tellingly, their differing viewpoints on vital and controversial issues. The film also reveals the challenge and beauty of the landscape and vividly captures incidents of daily life. With Israel becoming increasingly trapped in its political difficulties, this first-class piece of documentary film-making is of renewed interest.

The Italian Straw Hat

Un Chapeau De Paille D'Italie

France 1927 74 mins bw
Albatros

d **René Clair**
sc **René Clair**
ph **Maurice Desfassiaux, Nicolas Roudakoff**
m **Silent**
Albert Préjean, Olga Tschechowa, Marise Maia, Alice Tissot, Yvonneck

Fadinard (Préjean), on the way to his wedding, finds his horse eating the straw hat of an errant wife who happens to be in a mildly compromising situation with a cavalry officer. He cannot get to the wedding until he has found an identical replacement for the *chapeau*. Clair made this version of the Labiche-Michel 19th -century farce into a classic silent film comedy, substituting many of the play's verbal jokes with visual ones, such as using an object to introduce each character in the chain of events. Made with clockwork precision, it ticks along at a fine pace, culminating in the hilarious wedding scene.

It Happened At The Inn see Goupi-Mains-Rouges

It Happened In Broad Daylight see Assault In Broad Daylight

It Happened In Europe see Somewhere In Europe

It's In The Bag see Affaire Est Dans Le Sac, L'

It's My Life

(US: My Life To Live)

Vivre Sa Vie

France 1962 85 mins bw
Films De La Pléiade

d **Jean-Luc Godard**
sc **Jean-Luc Godard**
ph **Raoul Coutard**
m **Michel Legrand**
Anna Karina, Sady Rebbot, André Labarthe, Brice Parain

When she can't pay her rent, Nana S. (Karina), a girl from the provinces, is gradually initiated into prostitution in Paris, finally becoming experienced. Using interview techniques, direct sound, long takes, texts, quotations and statistics, Godard gives this probing and dazzling examination of prostitution (in 12 chapters) a documentary tone. But, above all, it is a passionate celluloid love letter to Karina, the director's then wife. Close-ups of her are reminiscent of Louise Brooks, Lillian Gish and Falconetti, the latter tearfully watched by Karina in Dreyer's *The Passion Of Joan Of Arc*.

Special Jury Prize Venice 1962

Ivan

USSR 1932 85 mins bw
Kiev Film Studio

d **Alexander Dovzhenko**
sc **Alexander Dovzhenko**
ph **Danylo Demutsky, Yuri Yekelchik, Mikhail Glider**
m **Igor Belza, Yuli Meitus, Boris Lyatoshinsky**
Pytor Masokha, Semyon Shagaida, D. Golubinsky, Stepan Shkurat

Three Ivans (a common Russian name) work on the construction of a hydro-electric dam on the Dnieper river in the Ukraine. Apart from the young peasant (Masokha) who is shaped into an ideal Soviet worker, the others are a worker killed in an accident and a youth who represents the future. Dovzhenko's first sound film opens with an explosion and continues with an array of aural experiments from the music to commentary via a loudspeaker. He brings the same lyricism to this industrial subject as he brought to the rural paradise of *Earth* two years previously. There are heroes and villains, slogans and speeches but, above all, there are powerful and poetic images that linger long after the noise has died away.

Ivan Groznyi see Ivan The Terrible

Ivanovo Detstvo see Ivan's Childhood

Ivan's Childhood

Ivanovo Detstvo

USSR 1962 97 mins bw
Mosfilm

d **Andrei Tarkovsky**
sc **Vladimir Bogomolov, Mikhail Papava**
ph **Vadim Yusov**
m **Vyacheslav Ovchinnikov**
Kolya Burlyaev, I. Tarkovskaya, Valentin Zubkov, E. Zharikov, Nikolai Grinko, V. Malyavina

When 12-year-old Ivan's family is wiped out by the Nazis, he is hell-bent on revenge and joins a detachment of Partisans who are able to use his size and agility for intelligence purposes. His superiors grow worried about him and send him to a safer area, but he rebels and is once again allowed dangerous assignments, with tragic results. Tarkovsky's film inevitably brings to mind Klimov's *Come And See* over two decades later but, where that film is determinedly grim and harrowing, its dazed protagonist wandering into the fight, this has a boy fully intent on his actions. Apart from a stark opening sequence where Ivan (Burlyaev) moves through swamp and forest near enemy lines, the director has opted for a plethora of cinematic effects, lyrically beautiful landscapes, and a treacly romantic sub-plot. This uncharacteristic softness from Tarkovsky is doubtless explained by the fact that this was his debut feature, and the first of several award-winning works.

Best Film Venice 1962

Ivan The Terrible

Ivan Groznyi

USSR 1944 (Part I), 1946 (Part II) 99 mins (Part I) 88 mins (Part II) bw (Part I), bw/col (Part II)
Mosfilm

d **Sergei Eisenstein**
sc **Sergei Eisenstein**
ph **Edouard Tissé**
m **Sergei Prokoviev**
Nikolai Cherkassov, Ludmila Tselikovskaya, Serafima Birman, Pavel Kadochnikov, Mikhail Nazvanov, Andrei Abrikosov, Vsevolod Pudovkin

The struggles of the 16th-century Tsar Ivan IV (Cherkassov) to establish himself, his love for the Tsarina Anastasia (Tselikovskaya), his political aims, and his conflict with the Boyars and the Church. Eisenstein began shooting his three-part epic (only two were completed) after more than two years of research, making sketches of every scene of the film. Stalin approved Part I, but as Ivan's character (in Cherkassov's powerful brooding central performance) became more complex he turned against it, and Part II (subtitled *The Boyars' Plot*) was not released until 1958. Taking its imagery from Grand Opera, the Japanese Kabuki Theatre and Russian icons, it is a slow-paced (the rapid montage of

Eisenstein's early films has disappeared), opulent and absorbing work. It was the great director's final film. He died of a heart attack in 1948 aged 50.

I Was Born, But...

Umarete Wa Mita Keredo

Japan 1932 100 mins bw
Shochiku/Kamata

d **Yasujiro Ozu**
sc **Akira Fushimi, Geibei Ibushiya**
ph **Hideo Shigehara**
m **Silent**
Tatsuo Saito, Hideo Sugahara, Tokkankozo, Mitsuko Yoshikawa, Takeshi Sakamoto

Two boys (Sugahara and Tokkankozo), aged 10 and eight, see their father (Saito), whom they love, kowtowing to his boss and playing the fool in order to ingratiate himself. Disgusted, they go on hunger strike until things become clearer to them. The first of Ozu's great films and a fine example of *shomin-geki*, or lower-middle-class domestic drama, of which he was to become a master. Although it reflects the melancholy theme of tainted innocence, the film is also wonderfully humorous, and the children a delight. Ozu was to use a similar plot in *Good Morning* in 1959.

I Was 19

Ich War 19

E. Germany 1968 121 mins bw
Deutsche Film Artien Gesellschaft

d **Konrad Wolf**
sc **Konrad Wolf, Wolfgang Kohlhaase**
ph **Werner Bergmann**
m **Songs: Am Ro Jarama**
Jaecki Schwarz, Wassili Liwanow, Alexei Ejboshenko, Galina Polskich, Jenny Gröllmann

In the last days of World War II, Gregor Hecker (Schwarz), a young bilingual German, works as an officer with the Red Army's propaganda team in the suburbs of Berlin, attempting to get German soldiers to surrender and to win over the population. There are still pockets of resistance, like the fortress of Spandau held by SS men, but these are overcome. 'I am German; I was nineteen,' says Hecker's offscreen voice at the end of the film, which is really Konrad Wolf's story. Yet, though autobiographical, the film is not very personal. With the aid of newsreels, including some featuring the concentration camps, and dialogues with a vast range of Germans, Wolf meticulously and a bit drily reconstructs the epoch that saw the beginning of the German Democratic Republic.

Iz Zhizni Otdikhayushchikh see Away From It All

Jaahyvaiset see Farewell, The

J'Accuse see I Accuse

The Jackal Of Nahueltoro
El Chacal De Nahueltoro

Chile 1969 95 mins bw
Cine Experimental De La Universidad De Chile/Cinematográfica Tercer Mundo

d **Miguel Littín**
sc **Miguel Littín**
ph **Héctor Ríos**
m **Sergio Ortega**
Nelson Villagra, Shenda Román, Marcelo Romo, Héctor Noguera, Luis Alarcón

An illiterate peasant (Villagra), who killed a widow and her five children, is hunted down and captured. In prison, he is taught to read and to understand social values. After being rehabilitated, he is executed by a firing squad. One of the best films to emerge from Chile in the creative period just before and during the presidency of Salvador Allende, it utilizes a real case to denounce injustices in the system. To create a raw and powerful authenticity, Littín shot in Nahueltoro and the prison where 'the jackal' was held and used dialogue taken directly from interviews with the prisoner himself. Most effective is the bitter irony that pervades the narrative, in which a man is taught to be literate in order to read and sign his death warrant, and to become a good Catholic in time to die within the faith. The film became a centre of discussion all over the country and was shown in prisons.

Jackboot Mutiny
Es Geschah Am 20 Juli

W. Germany 1955 77 mins bw
Arca/Ariston

d **G.W. Pabst**
sc **W.P. Zibaso, Gustav Machaty**
ph **Kurt Hasse**
m **Johannes Weissenbach**
Bernhard Wicki, Carl Ludwig Diehl, Carl Wery, Kurt Meisel, Erik Frey, Albert Hehn

A dramatic reconstruction of the 1944 attempt on Hitler's life by a group of army officers. One of Pabst's last films, it was neither more nor less distinguished than several other expiatory German films at the time. Hitler is seen as an evil monster, surrounded by weak and stupid sycophants, against whom opposition might have been possible with a few more Germans of the heroic character of the army conspirators. Simple, preachy and a little dull, it had much significance for German audiences.

Jacob The Liar
Jakob Der Lügner

E. Germany 1974 95 mins col
DEFA/East German TV

d **Frank Beyer**
sc **Gerd Gericke**
ph **Günther Marczinkowski**
m **Joachim Wetzlau**
Vlastimil Brodsky, Erwin Geschonneck, Manuela Simon, Henry Hübchen, Blanche Kommerell, Armin Müller-Stahl

A Jewish ghetto in Poland in 1943. Jacob Heym (Brodsky) is summoned to the Nazi guardhouse from which no one has ever been known to emerge, but he does, having overheard on the Gestapo radio that the Russians are advancing. He spreads the news but, frightened to say where he heard it, pretends that he has an illegal radio. He becomes a hero, pestered daily for news, and finds himself trapped in a cumulative series of lies which keep the hopes of his comrades alive. This is the nub of an extraordinary film which questions the value of truth in hopeless situations. Adapted from a novel by Jurek Becker, whose childhood was spent in a ghetto and a concentration camp, it's remarkable in wringing much full-blooded, absurdly funny comedy from a situation in which every resonance appals, and in doing so without giving offence. There is poignancy, too (Jacob's relationship with a small girl, wonderfully played by Manuela Simon), and horror (the cold-blooded shooting of a ghetto resident), and the film's successful amalgam of ingredients rests in the truthful writing, brought to life by a superb cast in which Czech star Brodsky shines.

Best Actor (Vlastimil Brodsky) Berlin 1975

Jag Ar Nyfiken Gul see I Am Curious - Yellow

Jakob Der Lügner see Jacob The Liar

Jalsaghar see Music Room, The

J.A. Martin Photographe

Canada 1976 101 mins col
National Film Board of Canada

d **Jean Baudin**
sc **Jean Baudin, Marcel Sabourin**
ph **Pierre Mignot**
m **Maurice Blackburn**
Marcel Sabourin, Monique Mercure, Marthe Nadeau, Marthe Thierry, Jean Lapointe, Germaine Lemyre

At the turn of the century, in the backwoods of French Canada, photographer Joseph-Albert (Sabourin) lives with his wife Rose-Aimée (Mercure), his mother, and his five children. Fifteen years of domestic drudgery for Rose-Aimée, and his having to grind out a living, has brought their marriage to an impasse of indifference which Rose-Aimée decides to cure by accompanying her husband on his annual cross-country business trip—a journey which proves to be packed with incident, both happy and sad. Baudin paints a portrait of a vanished era, nostalgic and affectionate, yet sympathetic to the difficulties of women. A little sentimental for some tastes, perhaps, but it's also a charming and sensitive love story, ravishing to look at, and making superb use of the period photographs 'taken' by its hero.

Best Actress (Monique Mercure) Cannes 1977

Jana-Aranya see Middle Man, The

Jänken see Yankee, The

A Japanese Tragedy

Nihon No Higeki

Japan 1953 116 mins bw
Shochiku

d **Keisuke Kinoshita**
sc **Keisuke Kinoshita**
ph **Hiroshi Kusuda**
m **Chuji Kinoshita**
Yuko Mochizuki, Yoko Katsuragi, Masami Taura, Keiji Sata, Ken Uehara

A war widow (Mochizuki) makes every sacrifice to bring up her son (Taura) and daughter (Katsuragi), but they reject her when they grow up. The daughter has an affair with her married English teacher (Uehara) and the son is adopted by a wealthy man whose own child has died. This moving personal story, is a *haha-mono*, or 'mother picture', a popular genre in Japan. It is placed in its historical context by Kinoshita's use of newsreel footage. Use is also made of rapid cutting to the past in order to give the present more resonance. The tragic performance of Mochizuki adds more handkerchiefs to the audience's laundry bills.

Jazz Comedy

Vesyolye Rebyata

USSR 1934 93 mins bw
Mosfilm

d **Grigori Alexandrov**
sc **Grigori Alexandrov, Nikolai Erdman, V. Mass**
ph **Vladimir Nilsen**
m **Isaac Dunayevsky**
Lyubov Orlova, Leonid Utyosov, Maria Strelkova

A shepherd boy comes to the city and becomes a jazz band leader. After having been Eisenstein's assistant for almost eight years, Alexandrov began his career as director by introducing the Hollywood-style musical to the USSR. He made four pleasantly anarchic musicals, using a pre-recorded music track, of which this is the best known. So popular was it at the time, that there were 5,000 copies of the film in circulation. Orlova, the pretty blonde female lead and later the director's wife, became the first popular star of the Soviet cinema.

Jealousy, Italian Style

(US: Drama Of Jealousy aka The Pizza Triangle)
Dramma Della Gelosia—Tutti I Particolare In Cronaca

Italy 1970 106 mins col
Dean Film/Jupiter Generale Cinematografica(Rome)/ Midega Film(Madrid)

d **Ettore Scola**
sc **Age, Furio Scarpelli, Ettore Scola**
ph **Carlo Di Palma**
m **Armando Trovaioli**
Marcello Mastroianni, Monica Vitti, Giancarlo Giannini, Manolo Zarzo, Marisa Merlini

Oreste (Mastroianni), a young Communist bricklayer, leaves his wife for gorgeous Adelaide (Vitti). All is bliss until she falls for his waiter friend Nello (Giannini). Plot complications increase, as does Adelaide's inability to choose. Finally she decides to marry Nello and disaster strikes. This contribution to that Italian genre which used dark, melodramatic plots to manufacture comedy, is moderately entertaining, with Scola managing—amid a characteristically Latin overdose of screaming and shouting—to achieve some delightful moments of political and social satire and a touch of pleasing parody (Fellini is one of his targets). The solid gold casting pays off.

Best Actor (Marcello Mastroianni) Cannes 1970

Jean De Florette

France 1986 122 mins col
Renn Productions/Films A2/RAI2/DD Productions

d **Claude Berri**
sc **Claude Berri, Gerard Brach**
ph **Bruno Nuytten**
m **Jean-Claude Petit**
Yves Montand, Gérard Depardieu, Daniel Auteuil, Elisabeth Depardieu, Ernestine Mazurowna, Marcel Champel

Jean (Depardieu), a hunchbacked tax collector from the city, with his wife (Elisabeth, Depardieu's real-life wife), and young daughter, Manon (Mazurowna), comes to farm some fertile land he has inherited. His neighbours, Ugolin (Auteuil) and his uncle César (Montand), covet the land so they plug up a half-buried spring with concrete to deprive Jean of water. The result is tragedy. In 1963, Marcel Pagnol turned the screenplay of his penultimate film, *Manon Des Sources* (1952) into a novel, adding a 'prequel' called *Jean De Florette*, which Berri turned into two highly successful separate movies. The director has been faithful to Pagnol's vision in the gorgeous sun-bleached Provençal settings, the narrative thrust and towering performances of the three male leads—Auteil, comic, simple and touching; Montand earthy, charming and cunning; and Depardieu indomitable, loving and tragic in the title role. There are few people who will not want to see how the story develops in *Manon Des Sources* of the same year.

Jeanne Dielman 23, Quai Du Commerce 1080 Bruxelles

Belgium 1975 225 mins col
Paradise Films(Brussels)/Unité Trois(Paris)

d **Chantal Akerman**
sc **Chantal Akerman**
ph **Babette Mangolte**
m **Beethoven (Bagatelle for Piano No 27)**
Delphine Seyrig, Jan Decorte, Henri Storck, Jacques Doniol-Valcroze, Yves Bical

Forty-eight hours, from Tuesday to Thursday, in the life of discreet prostitute Jeanne Dielman, begin with her receiving a caller—daily occurrence, different callers—in between shopping, chores, neighbourly acts and caring for Sylvain (Decorte), her teenage son. After servicing Thursday's caller, Jeanne stabs him to death with a pair of scissors. The individual sequences selected by Akerman for her sober, minimalist work are filmed in real time, which both accounts for its immense length and draws the viewer into directly experiencing the preparation of a dish or the making of a bed. Opening with its title printed in the form of an address, the contents do resemble the small events which might make up a letter. The focus of the feminist argument is clouded by Akerman's failure to reveal the root cause of Jeanne's final action, but this still, bleak film remains original and intriguing for those with the patience to engage with it—and, of course, there is Delphine Seyrig.

Jeder Fur Sich Und Gott Gegen Alle see Enigma Of Kaspar Hauser, The

---

Jenny

France 1936 105 mins bw
Réalisations Artistiques Cinématographique

d **Marcel Carné**
sc **Jacques Prévert, Jacques Constant**
ph **Roger Hubert**
m **Joseph Kosma, Lionel Cazeaux**
Françoise Rosay, Albert Préjean, Charles Vanel, Jean-Louis Barrault, Roland Toutain, Lisette Lanvin

Jenny (Rosay), the manager of a nightclub of dubious reputation, gets involved with Lucien (Préjean), a member of a gang of criminals. Benoît (Vanel), the crooked owner of the club, employs his hunchback accomplice (Barrault) to help put an end to their affair. Meanwhile, Jenny's daughter (Lanvin) falls in love with Lucien and becomes her mother's rival. Carné, who had been assistant to Jacques Feyder on four films, was given a rather conventional melodramatic plot, concocted for Feyder's wife, Françoise Rosay, for his first directorial effort. Thanks to the superior dialogue co- written by the poet Prévert, with whom Carné was to make six further pictures, the excellent use of locations, an innate narrative sense and a terrific cast (including the composer Kosma), it gave a taste of the Carné-Prévert masterpieces to come.

Jenny Lamour see Quai Des Orfèvres

A Jester's Tale

Bláznova Kronika

Czechoslovakia 1964 80 mins bw
Gottwaldov

d **Karel Zeman**
sc **Karel Zeman, Pavel Juráček**
ph **Václav Hunka**
m **Jan Novák**
Petr Kostka, Miroslav Holub, Emilie Vašáryová, Valentina Thielová

A young peasant (Kostka), forcibly conscripted during the Thirty Years War, is mistaken for a duke and accompanies a girl (Holub) who is disguised as a jester, on a search for a country without war. As in his *Baron Munchhausen*, Zeman wittily combines romantic fantasy, pacifist allegory and historical reconstruction by mixing live action, animation, stylized sets and real locations. The film won the Best Director's prize at the San Francisco Festival.

Je T'Aime, Je T'Aime

France 1968 94 mins col
Parc/Les Productions Fox Europa

d **Alain Resnais**
sc **Jacques Sternberg**
ph **Jean Boffety**
m **Krzysztof Penderecki**
Claude Rich, Olga Georges-Picot, Anouk Ferjac, Van Doude, Annie Fargue, Georges Jamin

A young man (Rich), saved from suicide, is invited by scientists to participate in an experiment that sends him back in time for short periods. Things go wrong and incidents from his past occur in disordered fragments. The main theme in Resnais' films is best expressed by the opening lines of T.S. Eliot's *Burnt Norton*: 'Time present and time past are both perhaps present in time future, and time future contained in time past'. This was brilliantly articulated in the director's first three features, in which correlatives of time were integral to the characters and structures of the films. Here, by using a time-exploring machine, it is rather like revealing the bare mechanics behind a magician's act. But there is not much in the hat. The man's past that we see in non-chronological segments, often dazzlingly conjured up, is not interesting enough to encourage us to make the effort to piece it together, and the leads lack presence.

Jeu De Massacre see Comic Strip Hero

Jeunes Loups, Les see Young Wolves, The

Jeux De L'Amour, Les see Playing At Love

Jeux Interdits see Forbidden Games

Les Jeux Sont Faits

(US: The Chips Are Down)

France 1947 91 mins bw
Les Films Gibe

d **Jean Delannoy**
sc **Jean-Paul Sartre**
ph **Christian Matras**
m **Georges Auric**
Micheline Presle, Michel Pagliero, Fernand Fabre, Colette Ripert

A Communist (Pagliero) who was killed in an uprising, and a woman (Presle) poisoned by her Fascist official husband meet in the afterlife and fall in love. They are sent back to earth with permission to remain there, provided they consummate their affair within 24 hours. They don't because they get caught up in political discussion and quarrels. The first of Sartre's attempts at an original screenplay is both an intellectually intriguing exercise, and a grim and depressing fable.

Je Vous Salue, Marie see Hail Mary

Jew Süss

Jud Süss

Germany 1940 85 mins bw
Terra

d **Veit Harlan**
sc **Veit Harlan, Ludwig Metzger, Eberhard Wolfgang Möller**
ph **Bruno Mundi**
m **Wolfgang Zeller**
Ferdinand Marian, Werner Krauss, Heinrich George, Kristina Söderbaum

Süss Oppenheimer (Marian), financial advisor and collector of taxes for the Duke of Württemburg, uses evil methods to gain power for himself and his people. Made with the personal encouragement of Josef Goebbels, this is one of the most notorious of the anti-Semitic films made by the Nazis during the war. The script is a travesty of Lion Feuchtwanger's famous pro-Jewish novel of 1925, filmed previously in Britain in 1934. Harlan, the leading director of propagandist fiction films for the Third Reich, was charged with war crimes by the Allies. The case was dropped due to lack of evidence, and he returned to making films in Germany until 1962, two years before his death.

Jigokumon see Gate of Hell

Jinruigaku Nyumon see Pornographer, The

The Job

(US: The Sound Of Trumpets)

Il Posto

Italy 1961 90 mins bw
24 Hores/Titanus

d **Ermanno Olmi**
sc **Ermanno Olmi**
ph **Lamberto Caimi**
Sandro Panzeri, Loredana Detto, Tullio Kezich

A shy young man (Panzeri) from a poor family gets his first job in a large office in Milan, progressing from office boy to clerk. The entire non-professional cast was made up of the employees at the Edison building in Milan, with the exceptions of Panzeri, who later got a job in an office, and Olmi's wife, Loredana Detto, as the girl who befriends him. The director's second feature film is a humorous, sad and astute study of white-collar workers, contrasting the dehumanization of the work with their humanity. A film of an uneventful life, rich in brilliantly observed incidents. It is not for nothing that the sad-faced boy wears a hat like Buster Keaton's at the office party.

Jób Lázadása see Revolt Of Job, The

Jofroi

France 1934 55 mins bw
Les Auteurs Associés

Joi Baba Felunath

d **Marcel Pagnol**
sc **Marcel Pagnol**
ph **Willy**
m **Vincent Scotto**
Vincent Scotto, Henri Poupon, André Robert, Annie Toinon, Charles Blavette

Jofroi (Scotto), an old peasant, sells some land to a neighbour (Poupon) and then objects to the new owner cutting down the trees. His protestations come in the form of various attempts at suicide. Pagnol's second film as sole director, and the first of the four works by Provençal writer Jean Giono to be made Pagnolian, came as a real breath of fresh air. The natural sound and settings gave this comic, ecological 'morality' tale an essential reality, though the performances, enjoyable as they are, are as broad as an oak.

Joi Baba Felunath see Elephant God, The

Joi-Uchi see Rebellion

The Joker

Le Farceur

France 1960 90 mins bw
A.J.Y.M.

d **Philippe De Broca**
sc **Daniel Boulanger, Philippe De Broca**
ph **Jean Penzer**
m **Georges Delerue**
Jean-Pierre Cassel, Anouk Aimée, Geneviève Cluny, Palau, Georges Wilson, Anne Tonietti, François Maistre

Dedicated philanderer Edouard (Cassel) searches for the perfect woman and thinks he's found her when he meets Hélène (Aimée), the bored and beautiful wife of a rich businessman. His rose-coloured spectacles, however, shatter when they go away together. De Broca's second film retains much of the charm and energy of his first, *Playing At Love*, as well as its eccentricity. (Edouard lives in a strange ménage that includes his illegitimate children, his elder brother who supports the family, a quaint old uncle—a gem from Palau—and several dogs.) Though there's much to enjoy, the joke is too thin to sustain, resulting in an overdose of frenzied vivacity from star and director in their efforts to keep up the momentum.

Le Joli Mai

France 1963 190 mins bw
Sofracima

d **Chris Marker**
sc **Chris Marker, Catherine Varlin**
ph **Pierre Lhomme**
m **Michel Legrand**

Interviews with ordinary people in the streets of Paris in May 1962 on the subjects of the day, including the Salan trial, the anti-OAS riots and current strikes. There is a linking commentary spoken by Yves Montand and sequences showing events and aspects of modern Paris. Compiled from 55 hours of interviews, this amusing, revealing and complex exercise in *cinéma vérité* has been boiled down to two-and-a-half hours (it lost 30 minutes in the English version narrated by Simone Signoret). Marker, whose three previous documentaries had been *Letter From Siberia, Description Of A Struggle (Israel), and Cuba Si!*, brought the same foreigner's eyeview to bear on his own city.

Jom

Jom: Ou, L'Histoire D'Un Peuple

Senegal 1982 80 mins col
Baobab Films/Zweites Deutschen Fernsehen

d **Ababacar Samb Makharam**
sc **Ababacar Samb Makharam, Babacar Sine**
ph **Peter Chappell, Orlando Lopez**
m **Lamine Konté**
Oumar Gueye, Amadou Lamine Camara, Zator Sarr, Ibou Camara, Oumar Seck, Oumi Sene

When the workers of a factory go on strike, the local sage (Gueye) encourages them with two stories that illustrate *jom* (the Wolof word for self-respect and integrity). One tells of a prince (Seck) who resisted the French colonizers, and the other relates how a dancer (Sene) defied her employers. This absorbing and brilliantly controlled mixture of socio-politics and African folk narrative is especially effective in its clever transitions from the past to the present. With the films of Ousmane Sembène and Makharam, the Senegalese film industry has plenty of *jom*.

Jom: Ou, L'Histoire D'Un Peuple see Jom

Jonah Who Will Be 25 In The Year 2000

Jonas Qui Aura 25 Ans En L'An 2000

Switzerland 1975 110 mins col
Citel/SSR/Action/SFP

d **Alain Tanner**
sc **Alain Tanner, John Berger**
ph **Renato Berta**
m **Jean-Marie Senia**
Jean-Luc Bideau, Myriam Boyer, Jacques Denis, Roger Jendly, Dominique Labourier, Myriam Mezières, Miou-Miou, Rufus

In Geneva, a copy editor, a secretary, a rural worker and his factory- worker wife, a farmer and his wife, a teacher and a supermarket cashier are all trying, in different ways, to maintain the ideals of May 1968 in Paris and find alternatives to capitalism. Tanner and the English Marxist writer John Berger have created that rare species—a polemical comedy whose eight protagonists are warmly and vividly portrayed. The sub-Brechtian interpolations in black and white are superfluous though.

Jonas Qui Aura 25 Ans En L'An 2000 see Jonah Who Will Be 25 In The Year 2000

Joseph Kilián

Postava K Podpírání

Czechoslovakia 1963 40 mins bw
Ceskoslovensky Film

d **Pavel Juráček, Jan Schmidt**
sc **Pavel Juráček, Jan Schmidt**
ph **Jan Curík**
m **Wiliam Bukovy**
Karel Vasícek, Consuela Morávková, Pavel Bártl, Zbynek Jirmar

Herold (Vasícek), searching old Prague for a vague acquaintance named Joseph Kilián, wanders into a jazz concert taking place inside an imposing building. Nobody there can help him but, on impulse, he hires a cat for the day from a neighbouring cat-lending office. When he tries to return the animal, the office has disappeared and he finds himself trapped in a web of bureaucratic stonewalling. With his cat, he continues looking for Kilián... Deliberately Kafkaesque in story, tone and style, this short but intriguing allegory criticizes the 'personality cult'—a huge portrait of Stalin dominates the political posters in the music room—and paints a vivid picture of isolation, confusion and bureaucratic pettiness in a totalitarian regime. It is well made and funny, as well as disturbing and elusive.

Joueur, Le see Gambler, The

Jour De Fête

France 1947 87 mins bw
Francinex

d **Jacques Tati**
sc **Jacques Tati, Henri Marquet**
ph **Jacques Mercanton**
m **Jean Yatove**
Jacques Tati, Guy Decomble, Paul Frankeur, Santa Relli, Maine Vallee, Roger Rafal, Beauvais

François (Tati), the postman in a small French village, decides to emulate the high-speed delivery of mail in the USA, something he witnessed in a documentary film shown at a travelling fair. It was as the vigorously cycling postman that Tati rode to everlasting comic fame in his first feature as director. Here we have the true descendant of the silent movie comedians, relying as he does on sight gags. What also emerges is his brilliant use of space—the tiny incident at the corner of the screen—an ability to create characters in a few revealing shots, and his slightly sentimental view of the old French values. *Jour De Fête* is an expanded version of Tati's short film *LÉcole Des Facteurs,* the success of which was responsible for the later feature. It was shot in an unsatisfactory new colour process, but was released in black and white. However, since the 1970s, a partly hand-coloured print has been shown successfully.

Journal D'Un Curé De Campagne see Diary Of A Country Priest

Journal D'Une Femme De Chambre see Diary Of A Chambermaid

Journal D'Une Femme En Blanc, Le see Woman In White

Journey Into Autumn

aka Dreams

Kvinnodröm

Sweden 1954 86 mins bw
Sandrew

d **Ingmar Bergman**
sc **Ingmar Bergman**
ph **Hilding Bladh**

Eva Dahlbeck, Harriet Andersson, Gunnar Björnstrand, Ulf Palme, Inga Landgré, Naima Wifstrand

Susanne (Dahlbeck), a fashion photographer, and Doris (Andersson), a model, go to Gothenburg where Susanne seeks to revive an affair with a married man (Palme), and Doris flirts with a wealthy, retired diplomat (Björnstrand). The gap between illusion and reality is pointedly demonstrated in 'Women's Dreams', the title's literal translation, and beautifully embodied by sophisticated Dahlbeck and pert Andersson. By turns sunny and dark, the film shows Bergman moving from his spring into his summer.

Journey To Italy

aka The Lonely Woman

(US: Strangers)

Viaggio In Italia

Italy 1953 79 mins bw
Italiafilm/Junior Film/Sveva Film

d **Roberto Rossellini**
sc **Roberto Rossellini, Vitaliano Brancati**
ph **Enzo Serafin**
m **Renzo Rossellini**

Ingrid Bergman, George Sanders, Natalia Ray, Leslie Daniels, Marie Mauban

An English couple (Bergman and Sanders) are travelling by car to Naples where they intend to sell a villa left to them by an uncle. Their marriage is going through a crisis, but certain significant events reunite them. This is an example of how a film can be buffeted around on the waves of fashion and critical opinion. With the appearance of this third Rossellini-Bergman picture, after both *Stromboli* and *Europa '51* had flopped, the reputations of the Italian director and his Swedish actress wife reached their lowest ebb. The film was attacked for being a clumsily made (the shadow of a camera crane is seen at the end), badly acted (Sanders and Bergman disliked making it), sentimental woman's picture. However, in the late 1950s, the directors of the *Nouvelle Vague* and young critics claimed it a masterpiece of narrative simplicity, a penetrating semi-documentary on a marriage, a camera's voyage into the Self. It happens to be all these things, good and bad.

Jour Se Lève, Le see Daybreak

Joyful Wisdom, The see Gai Savoir, Le

Joyless Street

(US: The Street Of Sorrow aka Street Of Sorrow)

Die Freudlose Gasse

Germany 1925 139 mins bw
Sofar Film

d **G.W. Pabst**
sc **Willi Haas**
ph **Guido Seeber, Kurt Oertel, Walter Robert Lach**
m **Silent**

Asta Nielsen, Werner Krauss, Greta Garbo, Valeska Gert, Agnes Esterhazy

In Vienna following World War I, the daughter (Garbo) of a middle-class father ruined by inflation, is faced with entering a brothel. In the course of her travails, she encounters a kept woman (Nielsen), a butcher (Krauss) and the brothel's Madame (Gert). Although obviously filmed on a studio set, the seedy view of post-war Vienna with its profiteers and poverty seemed to bring a change from Expressionism to Realism in the German cinema. The melodramatic tale is of little importance beside the performances of the lovely but plump 20-year- old Garbo (in her third and last film in Europe), contrasted with the 42-year-old Nielsen at the height of her fame and popular cabaret artist Gert. Note for buffs: Marlene Dietrich is to be spied in a small part.

Joyu Sumako No Koi see Love Of Sumako The Actress, The

Judex

France 1916 270 mins bw
Gaumont

d **Louis Feuillade**
sc **Louis Feuillade, Arthur Bernède**
ph **Klausse, A. Glattli**
m **Silent**
René Cresté, Musidora, Bout De Zan, Edouard Mathé, Gaston Michel, Yvonne Dario

Judex (Cresté), a mysterious cloaked crusader, battles against evil forces in order to destroy the empire of an arch criminal. After the Minister of Interior had criticized Feuillade's greatest serial, *Les Vampires*, for its immoral heroes, the director created the adventures of a handsome righter of wrongs in 12 episodes, and achieved his biggest success. More carefully structured, more sanctimonious and less frightening than its predecessors, it was still vastly entertaining and thrilling. It prompted an inferior sequel serial *La Nouvelle Mission De Judex*, and two features, one directed by Feuillade's son-in-law Maurice Champreux in 1933, and another by Georges Franju in 1963.

Judex

France 1963 95 mins bw
Comptoir Français Du Film

d **Georges Franju**
sc **Jacques Champreux, Francis Lacassin**
ph **Marcel Fradetal**
m **Maurice Jarre**
Channing Pollock, Francine Bergé, Edith Scob, Michel Vitold, Jacques Jouanneau, Sylva Koscina

Favraux (Vitold), a wicked banker, warned by Judex (Pollock), the righter of wrongs, that unless he reforms he will be punished, is apparently struck dead during a masked ball. Actually, he is held prisoner by Judex in his secret lair in order to trap Diana Monti (Bergé), a mistress of disguise, and prevent her from getting the inheritance of the banker's daughter (Scob). Louis Feuillade had been an influence on Franju's first films, now he was paid a direct homage in this remake of his 1916 serial. The casting of a real magician in the title role was an inspired idea, but the true magic came from Fradetal's re-creation of the starkly contrasting blacks and whites of Feuillade's surreal world. With Bergé in a cat suit and Pollock as the mysterious masked avenger bringing a dead dove back to life, Franju conjured up a lost era.

The Judge And The Assassin

Le Juge Et L'Assassin

France 1976 125 mins col
Lira Films

d **Bertrand Tavernier**
sc **Jean Aurenche, Pierre Bost, Bertrand Tavernier**
ph **Pierre William Glenn**
m **Philippe Sarde**
Philippe Noiret, Michel Galabru, Isabelle Huppert, Jean-Claude Brialy, Yves Robert, Renée Fauré

Judge Rousseau (Noiret) must decide whether an ex-army sergeant (Galabru), apprehended for a series of child murders, should be executed or whether he is insane. He develops a relationship with the man, a self-appointed holy avenger, and learns of the background that shaped his disturbed personality. For his third feature, Tavernier chose a complex subject, set in the 19th century against a background of political and economic unrest. The judge, well-played by Noiret, pursues the case with an energy that is part duty, part professional excitement and certainly part of a desire to achieve recognition and glory. An interesting and complex political parable that ultimately fails due to lack of clarity.

Judo Saga

aka Sanshiro Sugata

Sugata Sanshiro

Japan 1943 80 mins bw
Toho

d **Akira Kurosawa**
sc **Akira Kurosawa**
ph **Akira Mimura**
m **Seichi Suzuki**

Susumu Fujita, Denjiro Okochi, Takashi Shimura, Yukiko Todoroki

In the late 19th century, Sugata (Fujita) becomes a master of the new fighting style of Judo, gradually proving its superiority over the more established martial art of Ju-jitsu, and learns to gain spiritual peace at the same time. Thirty-three-year-old Kurosawa's first film immediately established him as a director to be reckoned with. Made at the height of World War II, it managed to avoid the patriotic and propagandistic aspects found in many Japanese films of the day, but told an exciting story of a young man's growth in a stylish manner. Xenophobia intrudes into the sequel, *Judo Saga, Part II (Zoku Sugata Sanshiro,* 1945), although it retains the pictorial and narrative strengths of the first.

Jud Süss see Jew Süss

Juge Et L'Assassin, Le see Judge And The Assassin, The

Jujiro see Crossways

Jules And Jim

Jules Et Jim

France 1961 105 mins bw
Films Du Carrosse/SEDIF

d **François Truffaut**
sc **François Truffaut, Jean Gruault**
ph **Raoul Coutard**
m **Georges Delerue**
Jeanne Moreau, Oskar Werner, Henri Serre, Marie Dubois, Vanna Urbino, Boris Bassiak, Sabine Haudepin

Close friends, the German Jules (Werner) and the Frenchman Jim (Serre) are both in love with Catherine (Moreau). However, Jules marries her and takes her back to Germany. World War I separates the two friends and when they meet again afterwards, Catherine changes partners. Although Truffaut's invigorating tale of friendship and love is full of cinematic allusions (one to Chaplin's *The Kid*), and is a homage to Jean Renoir, it is a unique piece of film-making. The director, while remaining true to Henri-Pierre Roché's first novel (another was used for the less successful *Anne And Muriel*), employs a wide range of cinematic devices to express the shifting moods of the characters and plot, including stills and newsreels. The three leads are a delight, and 'Le Tourbillon', the song sung so charmingly by Moreau, became a hit as did the film.

Jules Et Jim see Jules And Jim

Julia, Du Bist Zauberhaft see Adorable Julia

Juliet Of The Spirits

Giulietta Degli Spiriti

Italy 1965 145 mins col
Federiz/Francoriz

d **Federico Fellini**
sc **Federico Fellini, Tullio Pinnelli, Brunello Rondi, Ennio Flaiano**
ph **Gianni Di Venanzo**
m **Nino Rota**
Giulietta Masina, Mario Pisu, Sandra Milo, Valentina Cortese, Sylva Koscina, Caterina Boratto, Valeska Gert

While her husband (Pisu) philanders, a bored middle-aged, middle-class Roman housewife (Masina) consults clairvoyants and mediums, and escapes into a world of the imagination drawn from the 'spirits' of her past, present and future. Following the male fantasies of *8½* Fellini put his wife Masina under scrutiny in his first full-length colour feature. The brilliant photography by Venanzo and the opulent designs by Piero Gheradi can't alleviate the basic silliness of the character of the wife and her Vogueish dreams.

Juliette Or The Key Of Dreams

Juliette Ou La Clé Des Songes

France 1951 90 mins bw
Sacha Gordine

d **Marcel Carné**
sc **Marcel Carné, Jacques Viot**
ph **Henri Alekan**
m **Joseph Kosma**
Gérard Philipe, Suzanne Cloutier, Yves Robert, Jean Caussimon, Delmont

A young man (Philipe), sleeping in a prison cell, meets Juliette (Cloutier) in his dreams. He follows her far and wide, from a white village where the inhabitants have lost their memories to a mysterious Bluebeard's castle. Carné's attempt to return to the world of 1940s fantasy succeeds despite the whimsical and rather purposefully dated nature of the exercise. Weighing in its favour are the gentle performance of Philipe as the wide-eyed dreamer, the magical camera of Alekan and the sets by master designer Alexandre Trauner, who had worked with Carné over half a dozen times before. Against it was the playing of French- Canadian Cloutier (soon to become Mrs Peter Ustinov) and the imposed happy ending, neither of which did justice to the conception of Georges Neveux's play.

Juliette Ou La Clé Des Songes see Juliette Or The Key Of Dreams

---

July 14 see Fourteenth of July, The

Jument Verte, La see Green Mare's Nest, The

Junge Törless, Der see Young Törless

Jungfrukällan see Virgin Spring, The

Junoon

India 1978 141 mins col
Film-Valas

d **Shyam Benegal**
sc **Shyam Benegal**
ph **Govind Nihalani**
m **Vanraj Bhatia**
Shashi Kapoor, Jennifer Kendal, Nafisa Ali, Shabana Azmi, Naseeruddin Shah, Shushma Seth

During the Indian Mutiny, the congregation of a British church is attacked. Anglo-Indian Charles Labadoor is killed, leaving his wife, Mariam (Kendal), and daughter, Ruth (Ali), to fend for themselves. Jhavad Khan (Kapoor), a Pathan nobleman who desires Ruth, abducts the family to his palace where, to the jealous horror of his wife, he intends, as is his Muslim right, to marry her. Thus begins the conflict between Christian and Muslim and, for Jhavad, terrible confusion as his code of honour prevents him taking Ruth by force, and his passion keeps him from his duty as a fighting man. Shyam Benegal is one of a handful of directors who demonstrate that, if Ray set the precedent and remains the master in India, he is not without honorable competitors. *Junoon* is a complex and intricate work (adapted from a short story based on diaries of true events) drawing together the threads of love and war, and giving, to a Westerner, a new perspective on the Mutiny. Intelligent and moving, it's exquisite to look at and offers several memorable images and sequences.

Jury Of One see Verdict

Just Before Nightfall

Juste Avant La Nuit

France 1971 107 mins col
Films De La Boétie/Columbia(Paris)/
Cinégai(Rome)

d **Claude Chabrol**
sc **Claude Chabrol**
ph **Jean Rabier**
m **Pierre Jansen**
Stéphane Audran, Michel Bouquet, François Périer, Anna Douking, Marina Ninchi

Charles (Bouquet) murders his mistress, then confesses to his wife Hélène (Audran) and the victim's husband (Périer), neither of whom condemns him. In the final scene, Bouquet uses the word 'juste' 17 times in different ways, and Chabrol the moralist recognizes that justice has more than one interpretation. This classically photographed and structured picture is a reversal of *La Femme Infidèle*, being 'Le Mari Infidèle', but in both cases it is Bouquet married to Audran and living in Versailles, who does the killing and the confessing. The main ironic point is that murder must not be permitted to disturb the surface of the *bourgeois* marriage. Chabrol takes wicked delight in presenting his own wife as the adulterous or betrayed wives in his films, and their work makes for one of the most captivating husband-wife teams in cinema.

Juste Avant La Nuit see Just Before Nightfall

Justice Est Faite

aka Let Justice Be Done
(US: Justice Is Done)
France 1950 105 mins bw
Silver Films

d **André Cayatte**
sc **André Cayatte, Charles Spaak**
ph **Jean Bourgoin**
m **Raymond Legrand**
Claude Nollier, Michel Auclair, Valentine Tessier, Jean Debucourt, Balpêtre, Raymond Bussières

Elsa Lundenstein (Nollier) is brought to trial in the assize court at Versailles for the mercy killing of her lover. The proceedings are conducted with punctilious regard for the letter of the law by the court president (Balpêtre, intriguing and authoritative) before a jury of seven whose private lives and concerns are revealed to the movie audience. This is one of the most successful of ex-lawyer Cayatte's ironic examinations of French justice. Here,it is really the jury system itself that is on trial in a well-written (Spaak,too, was formerly a lawyer), tightly directed and beautifully acted film that could well have been titled, 'Has Justice Been Done?'

Best Film Venice 1950

Best film Berlin 1951

Justice Is Done see Justice Est Faite

Jutro see Morning

k

Kaadu see Forest, The

Kabinett Des Dr Caligari, Das see Cabinet Of Dr Caligari, The

Kaere Irene see Dear Irene

Kagemusha

Japan 1980 181 mins col
Toho/Kurosawa

d **Akira Kurosawa**
sc **Akira Kurosawa, Masato Ide**
ph **Kazuo Miyagawa, Asaichi Nakai, Takao Sato, Masaharu Ueda**
m **Shinichiro Ikebe**
Tatsuya Nakadai, Tsutomu Yamazaki, Kenichi Hagiwara, Kota Yui, Hideji Otaki, Hideo Murata

In 16th-century Japan, a thief (Nakadai) is employed as the double, or *kagemusha*, of a clan leader, who later dies, in order to confuse the enemy. When the deception is uncovered, he is thrown out and wanders the countryside like a pariah. Kurosawa's first film for five years was the most expensive Japanese movie ever made (with the assistance of executive producers Francis Coppola and George Lucas, and a Twentieth Century-Fox distribution deal). The screen is well used to frame the epic grandeur of the subject with red sunsets, vivid rainbows, the multi-coloured flags of soldiers, and the dream-like battle scenes with horses and men dying in slow motion. Yet there is something lifeless about the pictorial composition, the cutting and the camera angles, and the story never fulfils its Shakespearian promise. The export version lost 22 minutes.

Best Film Cannes 1980

Kagi see Odd Obsession

Kaiser Von Kalifornien, Der see Emperor Of California, The

Kak Molody My Byli see When We Were Young

Kakushi Toride No San-Akunin see Hidden Fortress, The

Kameradschaft

aka La Tragédie De La Mine
Germany 1931 92 mins bw
Nerofilm

d **G.W. Pabst**
sc **Laszlo Wajda, Karl Otten, Peter Martin Lampel**
ph **Fritz Arno Wagner, Robert Baberske**
Ernst Busch, Alexander Granach, Fritz Kampers, Gustav Puttjer, Daniel Mendaille, Elizabeth Wenst

French miners are trapped below ground near the Franco-German border, and the Germans burrow through the underground frontier to rescue their comrades. Pabst used a screen-play based on a real mining disaster to illustrate his plea for the international solidarity of workers. Although there was some outdoor location shooting, the mine galleries were built entirely in the studio, cleverly creating the utmost realism while allowing for effective lighting. The film's bilingualism was part of its didactic purpose, and like its pacifist companion piece, *Westfront 1918*, its commendable message is to be applauded, even though it seems naively optimistic from our cynical post-World War II standpoint.

Kamikaze 1989

W. Germany 1982 106 mins col
Regina Ziegler Filmproduktion/Trio Film/Oase Filmproduktion

d **Wolf Gremm**
sc **Wolf Gremm, Robert Katz**
ph **Xaver Schwarzenberger**
m **Tangerine Dream**
Rainer Werner Fassbinder, Günter Kaufmann, Boy Gobert, Arnold Marquis, Nicole Heesters, Brigitte Mira, Franco Nero

Inspector Jansen (Fassbinder) is sent to find out who sent a bomb threat to the president of a huge pop-media conglomerate known as The Combine. He tracks down suspects through slums, drug dens, mansions and the corrupt organization itself run by 'Blue Panther' (Gobert). The only excuse for seeing this bizarre version of the futuristic crime novel, *Murder On The Thirty-first Floor* by the Swedish writer Per Wahlöö, is the performance of the overweight Fassbinder, permitted to do as he pleased and enjoying himself in a phoney leopard-skin suit. (He kept the suit and wore it during the last year of his life.) Unfortunately, Gremm seems more dazzled by the brilliance of his vision of a society ruled by the most tawdry pop culture than critical of the values it represents. (Mind you, it looks good for a low-budget film shot in 25 days.)

Kanal

Poland 1957 97 mins bw
Film Polski

d **Andrzej Wajda**
sc **Jerzy Stefan Stawinski**
ph **Jerzy Lipman**
m **Jan Krenz**
Teresa Izewska, Tadeusz Janczar, Emil Kariewicz, Wienczylaw Glinski, Wladyslaw (later Vladek) Sheybal

During the 1944 Warsaw uprising, Polish partisans are pursued and trapped in the sewers by Nazi soldiers. The central film in Wajda's Resistance trilogy (between *A Generation* and *Ashes And Diamonds*) starkly re-creates the claustrophobic nightmare of an actual wartime incident. There are weaknesses in the characterization and in some of the dialogue (heavy-handed symbolic references to Dante's *Inferno*), but its powerful theme and imagery helped awaken the world to the new Polish cinema.

Special Jury Prize Cannes 1957

Kanojo To Kare see She And He

Kaos

Italy 1984 188 mins col
RAI/Filmtre

d **Paolo and Vittorio Taviani**
sc **Paolo and Vittorio Taviani**
ph **Giuseppe Lanci**
m **Nicola Piovani**
Margarita Lozano, Claudio Bigagli, Enrica Maria Modugno, Ciccio Ingrassia, Franco Franchi, Biagio Barone, Omero Antonutti

A group of four stories by Luigi Pirandello about peasant life in turn-of-the-century Sicily, concluding with an epilogue in which Pirandello (Antonutti) himself returns to his birthplace (Kaos). The ochre Sicilian landscape, stunningly photographed, is the main link between the peasant folk tales written and filmed without sentimentality or condescension by middle-class intellectuals. The film fully covers the gamut from tragedy to comedy, although the more serious narratives are more successful. As these—'The Other Son' and 'Moon Sickness'—are placed before the semi-humorous 'The Jar' and 'Requiem', there are slightly diminishing returns. But the frank performances and flamboyant imagery make this one of the Taviani brothers' best efforts.

Kapo

Italy/France 1960 115 mins bw
Vides/Zebra(Rome)/Francinex(Paris)

d **Gillo Pontecorvo**
sc **Franco Solinas, Gillo Pontecorvo**
ph **Goffredo Bellisario, Aleksandar Sekulović**
m **Carlo Rustichelli**
Susan Strasberg, Laurent Terzieff, Emmanuele Riva, Didi Perego, Gianni Garko

In a Nazi concentration camp, a doctor saves 14-year-old Parisian Jewess Edith (Strasberg) from extermination by giving her the identity of a non-Jewish political prisoner who has died. Sent to another camp, she becomes a

Kapo, or prisoner-guard, a role which takes her over and corrupts her into brutality, until she comes to her senses and sacrifices her life. What does one say about this effort? Pontecorvo has jam-packed his film with every kind of tear-jerking cliché on offer and entrusted the debasement and regeneration of his heroine to a sadly inept actress. The result is an overheated melodrama which does a grave disservice to the enormity of its subject, although the horrors of the camps are realistically portrayed.

Käpy Selän Alla see Skin Skin

Kare John see Dear John

Karin, Daughter Of Ingmar

Karin Ingmarsdotter

Sweden 1919 110 mins bw
Svenska Biographteatern

d **Victor Sjöström**
sc **Victor Sjöström, Esther Julin**
ph **Henrik Jaenzon, Gustav Boge**
m **Silent**
Victor Sjöström, Tora Teje, Bertil Malmstedt, Tor Weijden, Nils Lundell

Old Ingmar (Sjöström) thwarts the proposed marriage of his daughter Karin (Teje) to Halvor (Weijden), because he fears the young man may become an alcoholic like his father. Karin marries the sober and industrious Eljas (Lundell), who takes to drink. Karin and Halvor eventually make their future together. Sjöström followed up his two-part *The Ingmarssons*, taken from Selma Lagerlöf's epic novel *Jerusalem in Dalecarlia*, with a section that takes place several years later. Although the temperance tale is a plodding and puritanical one, made even longer by copious intertitles, the film is full of marvellous exterior and interior images, with the great pioneer director showing himself a master of framing people in their environment.

Karin Ingmarsdotter see Karin, Daughter Of Ingmar

Kärlek Och Journalistik see Love And Journalism

Kärlek 65 see Love 65

Karumen Kokyo Ni Kaeru see Carmen Comes Home

Katerina Ismailova see Lady Macbeth Of Mtsensk

Katzelmacher

W. Germany 1969 88 mins bw
Antiteater-X

d **Rainer Werner Fassbinder**
sc **Rainer Werner Fassbinder**
ph **Dietrich Lohmann**
m **Peer Raben**
Hanna Schygulla, Lilith Ungerer, Elga Sorbas, Doris Mattes, Rainer Werner Fassbinder, Harry Baer

In a bleak suburb of a big city, the lives of the bored young people who live there are disturbed by the arrival of a Greek 'guest worker' (Fassbinder). The girls, especially Maria (Schygulla), take a fancy to him, and the boys respond by beating him up. Fassbinder's second film, influenced by the work of Jean-Luc Godard, was based on the play he had written and staged successfully the year before. Using direct sound, limited dialogue and camera movements, he penetrates to the heart of xenophobia, an exploration developed later in films such as *Fear Eats The Soul.* Fassbinder himself plays the *Katzeimacher* (pejorative Bavarian slang for a foreigner) in a rare sympathetic role, while the rest of the cast effectively personifies ignorance.

Kazoku Geemu see Family Game

Kdo Hledá Zlaté Dno see Who Looks For Gold

Keep An Eye On Amelia

(US: Oh, Amelia!)

Occupe-Toi D'Amélie

France 1949 98 mins bw

Lux Film

d **Claude Autant-Lara**

sc **Jean Aurenche, Pierre Bost**

ph **André Bac**

m **René Cloërec**

Danielle Darrieux, André Bervil, Grégoire Aslan, Jean Desailly

Amelia (Darrieux), a Parisian cocotte, is dividing her favours between a Balkan prince (Aslan) and a slightly dim-witted officer (Bervil) who is her self-appointed protector. Away on army manouevres, the latter leaves her to the care of his best friend (Desailly) who persuades her into a mock marriage to ensure his inheritance. An extremely lively, sparkling and skilful adaptation of a Feydeau farce, imaginatively directed by Autant-Lara who retains the theatrical proscenium, but moves out into the audience, the streets, and back again, to maximum effect. On release, the movie incurred some local bans in Britain and enraged American critics who, in the moralistic climate of the times, considered it lewd and immoral.

The Keepers

La Tête Contre Les Murs

France 1958 98 mins bw

Attica/Sirius/Elpenor

d **Georges Franju**

sc **Jean-Pierre Mocky**

ph **Eugen Schüfftan**

m **Maurice Jarre**

Jean-Pierre Mocky, Pierre Brasseur, Paul Meurisse, Anouk Aimée, Charles Aznavour, Edith Scob

A rebellious and wealthy young man (Mocky) is committed by his father to a mental home, escapes to Paris, and is returned before he can prove his sanity. Much of Franju's first feature was shot in an actual asylum, the frightening reality of which sits uncomfortably with the fictional story (adapted from a 1949 Hervé Bazin novel about conditions in mental hospitals in the 1930s). Although there is some disturbing and poetic imagery, Franju's sense of a world hovering between sanity and madness, reality and fantasy was to be better developed in his next film, *Eyes Without A Face.*

Keep Walking see Camminacammina

Keetje Tippel

(US: Cathy Tippel)

Netherlands 1975 101 mins col

Rob Houwer Film

d **Paul Verhoeven**

sc **Gerard Soeteman**

ph **Jan De Bont**

m **Rogier Van Otterloo**

Monique Van De Ven, Rutger Hauer, Eddie Brugman, Hannah De Leeuwe, Andrea Domburg

In 1881, the adolescent Keetje (Van De Ven) leaves Friesland for Amsterdam with her impoverished family, who hope to improve their lot. They barely manage to earn a living and Keetje and her elder sister (De Leeuwe) are forced into prostitution. Keetje, however, manages to work her way out of it, becomes a socialist and marries a wealthy man (Brugman). The box-office success of films such as *Turkish Delight*, which also starred Van De Ven and Hauer (here as a snobbish clerk), enabled Verhoeven to make bigger budget commercial productions, a rarity in Dutch cinema. This attempt to paint a realistic picture of the harsh working class life in the 19th century (based on autobiographical stories by Neel Doff) is far too glossy and superficial to convince, but the performance of Van De Ven as a spirited girl shines through and there is a certain amount of wit.

Kermesse Héroïque, La see Carnival In Flanders

Key, The see Odd Obsession

Kiiroi Karasu see Behold Thy Son

Kilenc Hónap see Nine Months

Killer!
(US: This Man Must Die)
Que La Bête Meure

France 1969 110 mins col
Les Films La Boétie(Paris)/Rizzoli Films(Rome)

d **Claude Chabrol**
sc **Paul Gégauff**
ph **Jean Rabier**
m **Pierre Jansen, Brahms**
Michel Duchaussoy, Caroline Cellier, Jean Yanne, Anouk Ferjac, Marc Di Napoli, Maurice Pialat

The young and only son of Charles Thénier (Duchaussoy), a widower, is killed by a hit-and-run driver whom the police are unable to trace. Resolving to find and kill the killer, Charles becomes involved —at first cold-bloodedly, later genuinely—with Héléne (Cellier) whose brother-in-law, Paul (Yanne), he has reason to believe is the object of his pursuit. Complications multiply when the boorish Paul's adolescent son (Di Napoli), who detests his father, attaches himself to Charles. The intricate plot is based on a thriller by Nicholas Blake (alias the poet C. Day Lewis). Chabrol has constructed a remarkably complex film, finely shaded to diagnose the subtle shifts and contradictions in the balance of human motives and behaviour. Extremely well acted, notably by Yanne, it is further illuminated by Rabier's expressive camera and the effective use of a Brahms song. This is Chabrol at his masterly and gripping best.

Killing Game, The see Comic Strip Hero

King Lear
Korol Lir

USSR 1970 139 mins bw
Lenfilm

d **Grigori Kozintsev**
sc **Grigori Kozintsev (from Boris Pasternak's translation of the play by William Shakespeare)**
ph **Jonas Gritsyus**
m **Dmitri Shostakovich**
Yuri Yarvet (Lear), Elsa Radzinya (Goneril), Galina Volchek (Regan), Valentina Shendrikova (Cordelia), Karl Sebris (Gloucester), Oleg Dal (Fool)

Shakespeare's monumental late play about the King who, having misjudged his daughters and cast the youngest one out, is consigned to madness and grief in the wilderness, is here brought to the screen with a memorable magnificence of visual imagery. Unfortunately, however, the sureness of interpretation that marked the director's *Hamlet*, is missing here. This *Lear* (the king played as a merely irascible and neurotic old man, lacking the grandeur of kingship), is seen as an account of the collapse of a badly governed society. As such—and necessarily deprived of the original language—it fails to satisfy many English-speaking viewers.

King Of The Children
Hai Zi Wang

China 1988 107 mins col
Xi'an Film Studio

d **Chen Kaige**
sc **Chen Kaige, Wan Zhi**
ph **Gu Changwei**
m **Qu Xiaosong**
Xie Yuan, Yang Xuewen, Chen Shaohua, Zhang Caimei, Xu Guoqing

In a remote mountain district during the last stages of the Cultural Revolution, a labourer (Yuan), sent from the city to cultivate the fields alongside peasants, is suddenly asked to become a teacher although he is totally unqualified. He refuses to follow the official pedagogic line, and teaches his pupils not only the three 'R's', but also how to understand the world around them. He is eventually found out and incurs the wrath of the authorities. Dubbed affectionately as 'Goodbye Mr Chopsticks', the third film from the 30-year-old Kaige, visiting scholar at New York University in 1988, has a great deal of intelligence, freshness and charm, with attractively conceived locations. However, many of the elements of the education it attacks, such as the diligent copying of every character in a dictionary, may be lost on Occidental audiences; certain situations seem synthetic and the pace is rather slack at times.

Kings Of The Road

Im Lauf Der Zeit

W. Germany 1976 176 mins bw
Wim Wenders Produktion

d **Wim Wenders**
sc **Wim Wenders**
ph **Robby Müller, Martin Shäfer**
m **Improved Sound Ltd/Axel Linstädt**
Rüdiger Vogler, Hanns Zischler, Liza Kreuzer, Rudolf Schündler, Marquard Böhm

Robert (Zischler), fleeing his family, crashes his Volkswagen into the river where Bruno (Vogler), an itinerant film projector mechanic, has parked his pantechnicon. Bruno offers Robert a ride and they travel along the border between East and West Germany for over a week on the repair circuit. 'The Yanks have colonized our subconscious,' says one of the German friends in this leisurely (the original title translates as 'in the course of time'), complex, subtly comic, buddy-buddy road movie. American rock music dominates their listening and the image of the empty landscape as seen from the van recalls the wide open spaces of the USA. Taking a gloomy view of the present state of German cinema, the film makes direct references to the silent films of Fritz Lang and his exile in America. Exile and borders are used both literally and metaphorically throughout, effectively encapsulated by the use of the wide screen and the black and white images. But the two leads remain an enigma, because of the detached view the director takes of them.

The Kiss Of Mary Pickford

Potselui Meri Pikford

USSR 1927 70 mins bw
Mezhrabpom-RUS/Sovkino

d **Sergei Komarov**
sc **Sergei Komarov, V. Shershenevich**
ph **E. Alekseyev**
m **Silent**
Igor Ilinsky, Anna Sudakevich, E. Rozenstein

Dusya (Sudakevich), who works in a film studio, is loved by Hoha Palkin (Ilinsky), but only has eyes for the stars she idolizes. When Palkin receives a kiss from the visiting Mary Pickford, he becomes an object of worship. The movie, though no more than an extended sketch and light as air, is funny and charming, and boasts an outstanding comedy performance from Ilinsky. It is also of interest that Komarov was a disciple of Kuleshov, whose theories of montage are put into practice here in the use of newsreel footage. Contrary to popular belief, this footage was not culled from archives, but was specially shot by the makers of the film during the 1926 visit to Moscow of Mary and her husband Douglas Fairbanks Sr.

Klassenverhältnisse see Class Relations

Kleider Machen Leute see Clothes Make The Man

Knife In The Head

Messer Im Kopf

W. Germany 1978 113 mins col
Bioskop-Film/Hallelujah-Film/WDR

d **Reinhard Hauff**
sc **Peter Schneider**
ph **Frank Brühne**
m **Irmin Schmidt**
Bruno Ganz, Angela Winkler, Hans Hönig, Hans Brenner, Udo Samel, Carla Egerer

Biogeneticist Berthold Hoffman (Ganz) is calling for his estranged wife (Winkler) at a Left-wing youth centre when a police raid occurs and he is shot in the head. Waking in hospital, he has lost all memory and physical co-ordination. Against the odds, Hoffman determines to piece himself and his past together, but now has to battle against trumped-up charges of political subversion and murder. Hauff combines the elements of political thriller and psychodrama to explore the nature of human will and to warn against the dangers of a police state in West Germany. Ganz convinces, holding together a piece which, though intriguing, lacks depth and stylistic consistency, and leaves us to guess at the solution to its central mystery.

Knife In The Water

Noz W Wodzie

Poland 1962 94 mins bw
ZRF Kamera

d **Roman Polanski**
sc **Jerzy Skolimowski, Roman Polanski, Jajub Goldberg**

ph **Jerzy Lipman**
m **Krzysztof Komeda-Trzcinski**
Leon Niemczyk, Jolanta Umecka, Zygmunt Malanowicz

A married couple (Niemczyk and Umecka), on their way to their boat, pick up a handsome freewheeling young man (Malanowicz) and invite him to join them on a sailing trip. The man and the boy struggle for ascendency, competing for the attention of the woman. Polanski, in his only Polish feature, using a spare and subtle style, turns a simple tale of three people on a boat into an absurdist drama of sexual rivalry and the generation gap. The acting of the threesome (Polanski dubbed his own voice for the unprofessional Malanowicz) is excellent, and the film gained an Oscar nomination and the director immediate fame.

The Knife

Het Mes

Netherlands 1960 90 mins bw
Nederlandse Filmproductie Maatschappij(Rotterdam)

d **Fons Rademakers**
sc **Hugo Claus**
ph **Eduard J.R. Van Der Enden**
m **Pim Jacobs**
Reitze Van Der Linden, Ellen Vogel, Paul Cammermans, Marie-Louise Videc, Mia Goossen

During a school vacation, Thomas (Van Der Linden), 13 and fatherless, steals an oriental knife from an exhibition. His tutor, Oscar (Cammermans), confiscates it but Thomas steals it back, thus precipitating a series of emotional crises, particularly in his relationship with his mother (Vogel), whom he discovers to be locked into a degrading sexual relationship with Oscar. One of Rademakers' earliest films tells its story as a flashback recollection from Thomas, and entirely from his point of view. However, in spite of a convincing picture of Dutch small-town life, an interesting idea, and a startlingly mature and uncompromising central performance from the boy, the resulting film is somewhat plodding and pedestrian, and the director's attempts at the occasional Bergmanesque sequence tend to come unstuck.

Knights Of The Teutonic Order

Krzyzacy

Poland 1960 180 mins col
Studio Unit

d **Alexsander Ford**
sc **Alexsander Ford, Jerzy Stefan Stawinski**
ph **Mieczyslaw Jahoda**
m **Kazimierz Serocki**
Urszula Modrzynska, Grazyna Staniszewska, Andrzej Szalawski

In the middle ages, Poland is invaded by Teutonic knights wishing to convert the people to Christianity, but their cruelty causes the population to take up arms against them. In order to commemorate the 550th anniversary of the Battle of Grunwald, Ford, the distinguished Polish director, was given a large budget to make this epic, wide-screen, colour version of Henryk Sienkiewicz's classic novel. One of the very first Polish period films of the post-war years, it provided a stark contrast to the many intense examinations of the country's contemporary history. This no doubt contributed to its enormous success at home and abroad, apart from its obvious spectacular pictorial qualities.

Kocár Do Vidne see Coach To Vienna

Kohayagawa-Ke No Aki see End Of Summer, The

Koks I Kulissen see Ladies On The Rocks

Komödianten see Players, The

Kongress Tanzt, Der see Congress Dances

Konsequenz, Die see Consequence, The

Kontrakt see Contract, The

Konyets Sankt-Peterburga see End Of St Petersburg, The

Koritsi Me Ta Mavra, To see Girl In Black, The

Körkalen see Phantom Carriage, The

Korol Lir see King Lear

Korotkie Vstrechi see Short Encounters

Korpinpolska see Raven's Dance

Koshikei see Death By Hanging

Koto see Twin Sisters Of Kyoto

Ko To Tamo Peva see Who's That Singing Over There?

Kozara see Hill Of Death

Kradezat Na Praskovi see Peach Thief, The

Krajobraz Po Bitwie see Landscape After Battle

Krestyaniye see Peasants

Krik see Cry, The

Krótki Film O Zabijaniu see Short Film About Killing, A

Krzyzacy see Knights Of The Teutonic Order

Kühle Wampe

aka Whither Germany?

Germany 1932 90 mins bw
Praesens-Film

d **Slatan Dudow**
sc **Bertolt Brecht, Ernst Ottwald**
ph **Günther Krampf**
m **Hanns Eisler**
Hertha Thiele, Ernst Busch, Adolf Fischer, Martin Wolter

During a time of economic depression and unemployment, the Bönike family is dispossessed of its home, and moves to Kühle Wampe, a tent-city located outside Berlin. The son commits suicide and the daughter marries a chauffeur who later becomes a political activist. The only film that Brecht was involved in that did not distort his intentions, it was a cooperative venture using actors drawn from the theatre in the principal roles, supported by real workers. A passionate propaganda piece that included ballads in the manner of Brecht's plays, it pulled no punches. Thus the film fell foul of the censors who felt it 'endangered the safety of the state.' not realizing that the true danger was approaching with the emergence of the Nazi party. Eventually, after a court case, it was passed for showing in a cut version. A year later, Brecht and Dudow, both Communists, were in exile. The latter was killed in a car accident in East Germany in 1963 leaving an unfinished film.

Kukla S Millionami see Doll With Millions, The

Kumonosu-Jo see Throne Of Blood

Kurutta Ippeiji see Page Of Madness, A

Kvarteret Korpen see Raven's End

Kvinnas Ansikte, En see Woman's Face, A

Kvinnodröm see Journey Into Autumn

Kvinnors Väntan see Waiting Women

Kwaidan

Japan 1964 164 mins col
Ninjin Club/Bungei

d **Masaki Kobayashi**
sc **Yoko Mizuki**
ph **Yoshio Miyajima**
m **Tohru Takemitsu**
Rentaro Mikuni, Ganjiro Nakamura, Katsuo Nakamura, Michiyo Aratama, Misako Watanabe, Keiko Kishi

Four ghost stories—'The Black Hair', 'The Woman Of The Snow' (omitted in export prints on first release), 'Hoichi The Fearless' and 'In A Cup Of Tea'—based on tales by Lafcadio Hearn. Although taken from a Western writer, the tales ('kwaidan' means ghost story), peopled with samurais, Buddhist monks and lute players, are told in the haunting imagery derived from Japanese art. Eerie, beautifully composed using the wide screen shape, and somewhat overlong, the Oscar-nominated film took five years to prepare and one to shoot. It was the most expensive Japanese picture to date.

Special Jury Prize Cannes 1965

Kynighi, I see Huntsmen, The

Kyritiko Xyprima see Windfall In Athens

l

Lac Aux Dames

France 1934 90 mins bw
SOPRA

d **Marc Allégret**
sc **Colette**
ph **Jules Kruger**
m **Georges Auric**
Jean-Pierre Aumont, Simone Simon, Michel Simon, Illa Meery, Odette Joyeux, Rosine Déréan

An unemployed young engineer (Aumont) takes a job as a lifesaver and swimming instructor at a mountain lake resort. There he gets involved with a rich woman (Déréan), a mysterious child of nature called Puck (Simone Simon), and a former girlfriend (Meery) now turned crook. A Vicki Baum novel was the basis for this slight but satisfying romance set among attractive Tyrolean scenery. It displays Allégret's delicacy of touch and sense of fantasy, and it made stars of handsome Aumont and the kittenish Simone Simon, both in their early twenties.

The Lacemaker
La Dentellière

France 1977 107 mins col
Action/FR3/Citel/Janus

d **Claude Goretta**
sc **Claude Goretta, Pascal Lainé**
ph **Jean Boffety**
m **Pierre Jansen**
Isabelle Huppert, Yves Beneyton, Florence Giorgetti, Anne Marie Düringer

A reticent, young Parisian hairdresser (Huppert) is nicknamed 'Pomme' because she likes apples. While she is on holiday in Normandy, with an outgoing friend (Giorgetti), she has an affair with a university student (Beneyton). However, back in Paris the gap in class and education causes a rift and Pomme's breakdown. This discreet, observant study of an incompatible couple is, like their relationship, better in Normandy than in Paris, where the situations, though recognizable, become contrived. Huppert does well to retain our sympathy, despite the obvious loading of the film in her favour and the irritating passivity of the role.

Lacombe Lucien

France 1974 137 mins col
NEF/UPF/Vides/Hallelujah Films

d **Louis Malle**
sc **Louis Malle, Patrick Modiani**
ph **Tonino Delli Colli**
m **Performed by Django Reinhardt, André Claveau, Irène De Trebert**
Pierre Blaise, Aurore Clément, Holger Löwenadler, Gilberte Rivet, Jacques Rispal, Thérèse Giehse

Lucien (Blaise), a 17-year-old peasant of mean intelligence and dispossessed of family life, falls in with the Gestapo, and moves in on the Horns, a Jewish family in hiding. He becomes entangled with the daughter, provokes the father's death, saves the girl and her grandmother from execution and, after the liberation, is shot. Louis Malle's film was virtually the first French feature to air the thorny issue of collaboration without compromise and, while hailed as a masterpiece in certain circles, gave much offence in others. The director treats Lucien with cool objectivity, revealing the banality of his repellent actions. The wartime atmosphere of an occupied provincial town is authentic, and the terrifying dilemma of the Horns, at the mercy of their young captor, is expressed with the subtlety of understanding that distinguishes all Malle's best work. The acting is brilliant, notably from Holger Löwenadler as the once wealthy and fashionable Jewish Parisian tailor whose self-disgust drives him to give himself up to the Nazis.

Ladies Of The Park see Dames Du Bois De Boulogne, Les

Ladies On The Rocks
Koks I Kulissen

Denmark 1983 110 mins col
Kommune Film

d **Christian Braad Thomsen**
sc **Christian Braad Thomsen, Helle Ryslinge, Annemarie Helger**
ph **Dirk Brüel**
m **Helle Ryslinge**
Helle Ryslinge, Annemarie Helger, Flemming Quist Møller, Hans Henrik Clemmensen, Gyda Hansen, Aksel Erhardsen

Misse (Ryslinge), single and prone to falling for men who treat her like dirt, and Laura (Helger), married with two children, write and perform a provocative, self-mocking and somewhat risqué cabaret act. One winter, they find a certain personal liberation as they tour the show through Denmark, playing in small venues to bemused and occasionally outraged locals. A sometimes bleak, sometimes funny, and often charming film which clearly beats the feminist drum, while accepting its heroines' emotional dependency on men. The claustrophobia of the tacky life on the road is well caught, and the women's act is both good and bad enough to be believable.

Ladri Di Biciclette see Bicycle Thieves

The Lady From Constantinople
Sziget A Szárazföldön

Hungary 1968 76 mins bw
Mafilm Studio

d **Judit Elek**
sc **Iván Mándy**
ph **Elemér Ragályi**
Manyi Kiss (No further cast credits given)

An old lady, living on memories among the cluttered objects from her past, decides to exchange her apartment for a smaller one. She is thus temporarily brought into contact with other people until, resettled, she once again retreats into isolation. In this gem of a film Judit Elek, making her feature debut, builds up a character study and a picture of life in Budapest by the simplest of means: observation of small details. Unlike most Hungarian films seen abroad, it is not a political piece but a study of loneliness and human foibles, given truthful and unsentimental life by one of Hungary's leading stage actresses.

Ladykiller Of Rome, The see Assassin, The

Lady Macbeth Of Mtsensk
Katerina Ismailova

USSR 1966 116 mins col
Lenfilm

d **Mikhail Shapiro**
sc **Mikhail Shapiro (libretto: Dimitri Shostakovich, A. Preis)**
ph **Rostislav Davydov, V. Ponamarev**
m **Dimitri Shostakovich (conducted by Konstantin Simeonov)**
Galina Vishnevskaya (Katerina Ismailova), Artem Inozemtsev (Sergei, sung by V. Trepyak), Alexandrovich Sokolov (Boris, sung by A. Verdernikov), Nikolai Boyarksi (Zinovi, sung by V. Radziyevski), T. Gavirolova (Sonyetka, sung by V. Reka)

Katerina, a peasant who has married into the *petit bourgeoisie*, is bored by her dull husband, oppressed by the codes to which she must subscribe and ill-treated by her father-in-law, Boris, whose bullying conceals his lust for her. She takes Sergei, a workman, as her lover, but Boris discovers the affair and has him flogged almost to death. Katerina poisons the old man, the first of a series of violent deaths that culminates in her own. Shostakovich's powerful opera, blending passion and social critique (Wajda used the same story for his *Siberian Lady Macbeth)*, is given a gripping and naturalistic screen treatment by Shapiro, who capitalizes on its episodic structure to dramatic effect and utilizes outdoor locations that vividly capture the atmosphere. Vishnevskaya sings and acts superbly and the rest of the cast is well chosen and given appropriate vocal doubles. Only a periodic discrepancy in synchronization mars an otherwise excellent contribution to opera as film.

The Lady Of The Camellias
La Dame Aux Camélias

France 1981 121 mins col
Gaumont/Les Films Du Losange/FR3 Films Opera Films

d **Mauro Bolognini**
sc **Jean Aurenche, Vladimir Pozner**
ph **Ennio Guarnieri**
m **Ennio Morricone**
Isabelle Huppert, Gian Maria Volonté, Bruno Ganz, Fabrizio Bentivoglio, Fernando Rey, Yann Babilée

The rise and fall of Parisian courtesan Alphonsine Duplessis. This version (reputedly the 22nd), using flashback as Dumas *fils* rehearses his play, tells the story, not of tragic, romantic Marguerite Gauthier *à la* Garbo, but of the real-life woman on whom she was modelled. This Lady of The Camellias is conceived, and played by Huppert, as tough, ambitious and grasping. She comes complete with a drug-addicted father (Volonté) and a husband (Ganz), as well as a protector (Rey). The magnificent art direction and costumes recreate the lavishness of the Second Empire in all its decadent glory, and Bolognini directs with fluency and commendable lack of sentimentality.

The Lady Without Camellias
(US: Camille Without Camellias)
La Signora Senza Camelie

Italy 1953 105 mins bw
ENIC

d **Michelangelo Antonioni**
sc **Michelangelo Antonioni, Suso Cecchi D'Amico, Francesco Maselli, P.M. Pasinetti**
ph **Enzo Serafin**
m **Giovanni Fusco**
Lucia Bosé, Andrea Cecchi, Gino Cervi, Ivan Desny, Alain Cuny

A shopgirl (Bosé) becomes a starlet at Cinecittà, and marries her producer (Cecchi), who pushes her beyond her talent in the role of Joan of Arc. Her failure as a star reduces her again to playing ingénues in tatty films. Antonioni's third feature accurately evokes the less glamorous side of the Italian film industry. As in his following picture, *The Girl Friends*, he is concerned with the position of and pressures on women in society. The beautiful Lucia Bosé shows great sensitivity in a role originally intended for Gina Lollobrigida.

Lady With The Dog, The see Lady With The Little Dog, The

The Lady With The Little Dog
(US: The Lady With The Dog)
Dama S Sobachkoi

USSR 1959 90 mins bw
Lenfilm

d **Josef Heifits**
sc **Josef Heifits**
ph **Andrei Moskvin, D. Meschiev**
m **Jiří Sternwald**
Iya Savvina, Alexei Batalov, Ala Chostakova, N. Alisova

In the seaside resort of Yalta at the turn of the century, a married Moscow banker (Batalov) meets and falls in love with a beautiful woman (Savvina in an impressive debut), the unhappily married wife of a local petty official. She is on holiday alone, except for the company of her little dog. They continue their affair secretly in Moscow. The sensitive low-key direction subtly evokes the prose of Chekhov's short love story, and the contrast between Yalta in summer (brass bands, windy promenade *et al*), and Moscow in winter is vividly conveyed, reflecting the illicit lovers' psychology. This remains one of the most admired adaptations of Chekhov, although Heifits directed two others almost as good, *In The Town Of S* and *Duel*.

Special Jury Prize Cannes 1960

Lalka see Doll, The

Lancelot Du Lac see Lancelot Of The Lake

Lancelot Of The Lake
aka The Grail
Lancelot Du Lac
aka Le Graal

France 1974 85 mins col
Mara-Films/Laser Production/RTF

d **Robert Bresson**
sc **Robert Bresson**
ph **Pasquale De Santis**
m **Philippe Sarde**
Luc Simon, Laura Duke Condominas, Humbert Balsan, Vladimir Antolek-Oresek, Patrick Bernard

The Knights of the Round Table, their numbers heavily depleted by death, return to King Arthur's court (Antolek-Oresek) after a long, bloody and fruitless quest for the Holy Grail. Their rituals become debased as they are riven by jealousies and rivalries, with Lancelot (Simon) and his relationship with Guinevere (Condominas) at the centre of their strife. The film's rich and burnished colours often stand in for language to powerful effect, and there is little romance about these knights, who are viewed through Bresson's characteristically austere eye. The actors play with a flat detachment that is curiously compelling. This is a uniquely original and hypnotic study of the loss of spirituality, caught in distinctive images that are at once stark and sensuous, with arrestingly realistic sounds, such as the clanking of armour, to accompany them.

Land And Sons

Land Og Synir

Iceland 1980 94 mins col
Isfilm

d **Ágúst Gudmundsson**
sc **Ágúst Gudmundsson**
ph **Sigurdur Sverrir Pálsson**
m **Gunnar Reynir Sveinsson**
Sigurdur Sigurjónsson, Jón Sigurbjórnsson, Gudny Ragnarsdóttir, Jónas Tryggvason

In 1937, in a remote valley in northern Iceland, the rural landscape is glorious, but life is hard and lonely and the young are starting to drift south to Reykjavik. This leads to bitter conflict between a father and son, even though the latter (sensitively played by Sigurdur Sigurjónsson) is forcing himself to leave his beloved land and animals in the quest for future prospects. This is a rare opportunity to see a film from Iceland, a tiny country overshadowed by its better- known Scandinavian neighbours. Made for only $70,000, it was a tremendous success at home and recouped its costs in under two months—deservedly so, for it is refreshingly unsentimental, truthful and moving in its presentation of a real and painful problem and in its evocation of man's relationship with nature.

Land In Anguish

aka Earth Entranced

Terra Em Transe

Brazil 1967 115 mins bw
Spain 1932 27 mins bw
Ramon Acin
Mapa

d **Glauber Rocha**
sc **Glauber Rocha**
ph **Luiz Carlos Barreto**
m **Sergio Ricardo, Verdi, Carlos Gomes, Villa Lobos**
Jardel Filho, José Lewgoy, Glauce Rocha, Paulo Autran, Paulo Gracindo, Danuza Leão

A journalist and poet (Filho) is killed by the police as he and his mistress (Rocha) drive from the headquarters of Vieira (Lewgoy), the governor of a province of El Dorado. As he dies, he recalls his shifting political involvement from support of Diaz (Autran), a mystic and reactionary politician, to Vieira's popular cause. Rocha, the leading member of the Brazilian *Cinema Novo* movement, launched into a vigorous attack on the 'permanent state of madness' that his country seemed to be living in since the military *coup d'état* of 1964. In his denunciation, he calls on every cinematic weapon at his disposal—shock montage, jump cuts, an ironic use of the samba and other Brazilian rhythms and a film-within-a-film technique. Some of the cultural and political references may be obscure to non-Latin Americans, but there is no mistaking the power with which they are delivered. It comes as no surprise that the film was condemned in Brazil and banned outright for a period.

Land Of Desire, The see Ship Bound For India, A

Land Of Promise

Ziemia Obiecana

Poland 1974 178 mins col
Film Polski

d **Andrzej Wajda**
sc **Andrzej Wajda**
ph **Witold Sobociński, Waclaw Dybowski, Edward Klosinski**
m **Wojciech Kilar**
Daniel Olbrychski, Wojciech Pszoniak, Anna Nehrebecka, Andrzej Seweryn

Three industrialists representing different ethnic groups in Poland—a Pole (Olbrychski), a German (Seweryn) and a Jew (Pszoniak)—build a textile factory in Lodz at the turn of the century, but they encounter problems with the overworked, underpaid workers. Over-directed and under- characterized, this saga, based on a novel by Nobel Prize-winner Wladyslav Reymont, nevertheless vividly depicts a society on the edge of change. The portrayal of a ruthless Jew caused some Jewish groups in the USA mistakenly to accuse the film of anti-Semitism.

Land Og Synir see Land And Sons

Landru

aka Bluebeard

France 1962 115 mins col
CC Champion/Rome-Paris Films

d **Claude Chabrol**
sc **Claude Chabrol, Françoise Sagan**
ph **Jean Rabier**
m **Pierre Jansen**
Charles Denner, Michèle Morgan, Danielle Darrieux, Hildegard Knef, Juliette Mayniel, Stéphane Audran, Catherine Rouvel

The true story of the notorious Landru, who charmed a number of unsuspecting women, and then murdered them. After four flops in a row, Chabrol hoped that this period piece in colour, with a starry female cast, would be a commercial hit, but it failed to deliver the goods. No wonder! Although this stylized treatment of the same subject as Chaplin's *Monsieur Verdoux* (1947) had much of Chabrol's characteristic acid wit, Landru (Denner with bald dome, bushy eyebrows and black beard) was a cartoon figure, and the women were treated with neither sympathy nor depth.

Landscape After Battle

Krajobraz Po Bitwie

Poland 1970 11 mins col
Film Polski

d **Andrzej Wajda**
sc **Andrzej Wajda, Andrzej Brzozowski**
ph **Zygmunt Samosluk**
m **Zygmunt Konieczny**
Daniel Olbrychski, Stanislawa Celínska, Tadeusz Janczar

A group of concentration camp survivors await repatriation in a disused barracks in Germany in 1945. Two members of the group have a love affair until the Jewish girl is accidentally killed by an American guard. The first of Wajda's series of works based on Polish literary classics was taken from the stories of Tadeusz Borowski, an Auschwitz survivor who committed suicide in 1959 aged 29. The film, made in a non-realist, lyrical style using subdued colour, not only portrays a tender, fateful love story, but raises a polemical voice on the ambiguity of Polish behaviour during the war.

The Land

aka The Earth

El Ard

Egypt 1968 130 mins col
O.G.E.C.

d **Youssef Chahine**
sc **Hassan Fouad**
ph **Abdel Halim Nasr**
m **Ali Ismaïl**
Nagwa Ibrahim, Mahmoud El Meligui, Ezzat El Alaili, Yehia Chahine, Hamid Ahmed

A young peasant fights against rapacious property owners who are attempting to force him into the sale of his land. At first glance this would seem to be an old-fashioned tale of simple rural life, touching on the lure of urban attraction that threatens the peasants and featuring a pretty young girl who is much in demand. However, this impression is soon superseded by Chahine's mature and penetrating analysis of exploitation and social divisiveness, interpreted through powerful images and incidents that break the traditional view of the peasant as the 'eternal damned of the earth'. *The Land* subtly sows the seeds of a political thesis about the necessity for solidarity which Chahine would expand and develop in a trilogy composed of this film, *The Choice* (1970), and, most notably, *The Sparrow* (1973).

Land Without Bread

Las Hurdes

aka Terre Sans Pain

d **Luis Buñuel**
sc **Luis Buñuel**
ph **Eli Lotar**
m **Brahms**

The 8,000 inhabitants of Las Hurdes, a remote and poverty-stricken area of Spain, try to survive on the barren land. After his two surrealist masterpieces, *Un Chien Andalou* and *L'Âge D'Or*, Buñuel turned towards social realism with this stark documentary on the poverty of the peasants. The searing and sombre commentary and photography, eschewing any rhetoric, were so effective in revealing this festering social evil, that the film was banned in Spain. Buñuel did not make another in his native land until *Viridiana* 29 years later.

Lásky Jedné Plavovlásky see Blonde In Love, A

The Last Battle

Le Dernier Combat

France 1983 92 mins bw
Les Films Du Loup

d **Luc Besson**
sc **Luc Besson, Pierre Jolivet**
ph **Carlo Varini**
m **Eric Serra**
Pierre Jolivet, Jean Bouise, Fritz Wepper, Jean Reno

After a nuclear war, a man surviving on the top of a tower block buried by sand, makes contact with an aging doctor and a girl, and is set upon by a homicidal swordsman. Twenty-three-year-old Besson's impressive first feature is a fable of survival, played out against stark and striking black-and-white CinemaScope images of a wasteland of abandoned buildings and vehicles. However, it runs on lines familiar to apocalyptic films, and the decision to dispense with dialogue doesn't appear sufficiently justified.

The Last Bend

Le Dernier Tournant

France 1939 90 mins bw
Gladiator Films

d **Pierre Chenal**
sc **Charles Spaak, Henri Torres**
ph **Claude Renoir, Christian Matras**
m **Jean Wiener**
Michel Simon, Fernand Gravey, Corinne Luchaire, Florence Marly, Robert Le Vigan

A young woman (Luchaire), living an isolated existence in the French Alps, falls for a handsome stranger (Gravey) with whom she plots to kill her elderly husband (Simon). The first film adaptation of James M. Cain's novel *The Postman Always Rings Twice* is remarkably faithful to the original though transposed to France. Chenal directs with vigour, and there is excellent character work from Simon and from Le Vigan as the nasty blackmailer. Only the lovers lack the eroticism one finds in the other three versions (two from Hollywood, and Italy's *Ossessione*).

The Last Bridge

Die Letzte Brücke

Austria 1954 104 mins bw
Cosmopol Film

d **Helmut Käutner**
sc **Helmut Käutner, Norbert Kunze**
ph **Fred Kollhanek**
m **Carl De Groof**
Maria Schell, Bernhard Wicki, Barbara Rutting, Carl Mohner, Horst Haechler

Maria Schell portrays a German doctor who is captured by Yugoslav Partisans (led by Wicki) during World War II and forced to tend their wounded. Her initial resistance to co-operating is gradually overcome with her growing realization that a suffering Yugoslav is no different from a suffering German. A very simple plot, beautifully paced and carefully controlled, reveals a strong anti-war theme in this moving and intelligent, if slightly sanitized movie. Interestingly, in view of Yugoslav-German animosity, it was filmed on location in Yugoslavia with the co-operation of that country's film trades union.

Special Jury Prize Cannes 1954

Best Actress (Maria Schell) Cannes 1954

The Last Laugh
Der Letzte Mann
Germany 1924 73 mins bw
UFA

d **F.W. Murnau**
sc **Carl Mayer**
ph **Karl Freund**
m **Silent**
Emil Jannings, Max Hiller, Maly Delschaft, Hans Unterkirchen

An old doorman at a luxury hotel, proud of his work and uniform, is reduced to being a lavatory attendant. The film that made Murnau's international reputation is mainly remarkable for being told without any intertitles. The camera tracking through hotel corridors, the distortions, the subjective shots, the drunken dream sequence, and Jannings' expressive performance made words superfluous. The unconvincing happy ending was tacked on at the insistence of producer Eric Pommer to make the piece more commercial.

The Last Metro
Le Dernier Métro
France 1980 131 mins col
Les Films Du Carrosse/Andrea/SEDIF/TF1/SFP

d **François Truffaut**
sc **François Truffaut, Suzanne Schiffman, Jean-Claude Grumberg**
ph **Nestor Almendros**
m **Georges Delerue**
Catherine Deneuve, Gérard Depardieu, Jean Poiret, Heinz Bennent, Andréa Ferréol

In occupied Paris in 1942, a Jewish manager (Bennent) of a Montmartre theatre goes into hiding in the cellar of the building, while his wife (Deneuve) runs the company. This includes a member of the Resistance (Depardieu) and a homosexual director (Poiret), who are also in danger of being arrested by the Nazis. Truffaut stated that the film fulfilled three of his ambitions: to re-create on film the climate of the Occupation, to show the backstage life of the theatre, and to provide Deneuve with the role of a responsible woman. The film achieves all three, adeptly capturing the mood of the period and life in the theatre, although it could have delved deeper into the psychology of the characters, including that of the wife. There have certainly been better films about the time, but few more entertaining and exciting or with such a top-notch cast.

The Last Millionaire
La Dernière Milliardaire
France 1934 90 mins bw
Pathé Natan

d **René Clair**
sc **René Clair**
ph **Rudolph Maté**
m **Maurice Jaubert**
Max Dearly, Renée Saint-Cyr, Marthe Mellot, Raymond Cordy

A small European kingdom is saved from bankruptcy by the return of Banco (Dearly), a native-born millionaire who gets engaged to Princess Isabelle (Saint-Cyr) and runs the country, even though a knock on the head makes him temporarily insane. The last of Clair's features in France for 13 years was howled down by French Fascists at its first showing, presumably because they knew that the film had failed to get German financial backing. Although the comedy is a trifle strained and the decor rather airless, it is still an enjoyable Ruritanian fantasy, hardly more political than the Marx Brothers' *Duck Soup* the previous year.

The Last Stage
Ostatni Etap
Poland 1948 120 mins bw
Film Polski

d **Wanda Jakubowska**
sc **Wanda Jakubowska, Gerda Schneider**
ph **Borys Monastryrski**
m **Roman Palester**
Wanda Bartóvna, Huguette Faget, Barbara Drapinska, Stanislaw Zaczyk, Tatjana Gorecka

In the 'hospital' in the women's section of Auschwitz, Marta (Drapinska), a prisoner who acts as interpreter, sees others in the 'last stage', the final journey to the gas chambers and crematoria. As both Jakubowska and Schneider were former inmates of the notorious concentration camp, this searing, uncompromising testament has an immediacy and personal involvement missing from many later films on the subject. The documentary-like reconstruction of the day to day 'life' is even more affecting for being presented in a calm, almost matter-of-fact manner, rather than wallowing in degradation. The startling opening shots of the thinly-clad, shaven-haired barefoot women, the birth of a baby, sickness and death, and the prison orchestra playing Richard Strauss and Franz Lehar as the victims march to their fate, made an even greater impact when the film appeared in 1948. It also drew attention to a re-awakening Polish film industry.

The Last Supper

La Ultima Cena

Cuba 1976 110 mins col
Cuban Film Institute

d **Tomás Gutiérrez Alea**
sc **Tomás Gutiérrez Alea, Tomás Gonzalez, Maria Eugenia Haya**
ph **Mario Garcia Joya**
m **Leo Brouwer**
Nelson Villagra, Silvano Rey, Luis Alberto García, José Antonio Rodriguez

A plantation owner casts 12 of his slaves to play the apostles in a re-creation of The Last Supper during Holy Week, urging them momentarily to forget their shackles, but when they revolt all but one are beheaded. This 'allegory of Christian liberalism', as the director describes it, has much in common with Buñuel's *Viridiana* (1961) in its content and caustic wit. Filmed in muted colours with a powerful black cast, the picture belabours its message in the final sequence, a symbol of the coming Socialist Cuba.

Last Ten Days Of Adolf Hitler, The see Last Ten Days, The

The Last Ten Days

aka The Last Ten Days Of Adolf Hitler

Der Letzte Akt

Austria 1955 109 mins bw
Cosmopol

d **G.W. Pabst**
sc **Fritz Harbeck**
ph **Günther Anders, Hannes Staudinger**
m **Erwin Haletz**
Oskar Werner, Albin Skoda, Lotte Tobisch, Willy Krause, Helga Kennedy-Dohrn

In the bunker, Hitler (Skoda) and his staff await the end. As part of his atonement for having made three historical films under the Nazis, Pabst brought his jaundiced eye to bear on Erich Maria Remarque's account of Hitler's final hours. Much of it is as heavy as a jackboot, but there are glimmerings of the pre-war Expressionist master at work, particularly in the mad-dance orgy near the end.

Last Vacation, The see Dernières Vacances, Les

The Last Waltz

Der Letzte Walzer

Germany 1934 94 mins bw
Panorama

d **Georg Jacoby**
sc **Dr Max Wallner, Georg F. Weber**
ph **Carl Drews**
m **Oscar Straus**
Camilla Horn, Ivan Petrovitch, Ernst Dumcke, Adele Sandrock, Max Guelsdorf, Hans Junkermann

A young couple in 19th-century St Petersburg overcome the wicked machinations of a Grand Duke and find happiness together. Based on Oscar Straus's stage operetta, this Ruritanian-style romance, one of a plethora of German screen musicals of the 1930s, was notable for its rich portrayal of the lifestyle of the Russian nobility. Glamorous leads (Horn and Petrovitch) and well-paced direction resulted in entertaining escapist fare.

Last Will Of Dr Mabuse, The see Testament Of Dr Mabuse, The

The Last Woman

L'Ultima Donna

aka La Dernière Femme

Italy/France 1976 112 mins col
Jacques Roitfeld/Flaminia

d **Marco Ferreri**

sc **Marco Ferreri, Rafael Azcona**
ph **Luciano Tovoli**
m **Philippe Sarde**
Gérard Depardieu, Ornella Muti, Michel Piccoli, Renato Salvatori, Zouzou, Nathalie Baye, Carole Lepers

When the wife (Zouzou) of a young French engineer (Depardieu) walks out on him and their baby to join her friend (Lepers) in the feminist movement, he takes up with an unliberated woman (Muti), but feels threatened when she and the wife plot to take his son from him. For some of the time there is amusement to be had from the role reversal satire, and from Depardieu as the bemused phallocrat unable to deal with women asserting themselves. What, alas, is less pleasantly remembered, is the crude symbolism of the ending when the hero castrates himself with an electric carving knife.

Last Year At Marienbad

L'Année Dernière À Marienbad

France 1961 94 mins bw
Terra/Tamara/Cormoran/Precitel/Como/Argos/Cinetel/Silver/Cineriz

d **Alain Resnais**
sc **Alain Robbe-Grillet**
ph **Sacha Vierny**
m **Francis Seyrig**
Delphine Seyrig, Giorgio Albertazzi, Sacha Pitöeff, Françoise Bertin

In a vast baroque mansion with geometrically designed gardens, a man (Albertazzi) tries to convince a woman guest (Seyrig) that they had had an affair the year before, and that she should leave the man (Pitöeff) she is with. Rejecting a chronological structure, this mingling of memory and imagination, past and present, desire and fulfilment, can now be seen as one of the cinema's most haunting and erotic poems. The cryptic screenplay, the stylized playing, the organ music, the tracking shots down endless corridors, the dazzling decor by Jacques Saulnier, and the mysteriously beautiful Seyrig (in her first feature) in extravagant gowns and feathers, are all unforgettable.

Best Film Venice 1961

Late Autumn

Akibiyori

Japan 1960 125 mins col
Shochiku

d **Yasujiro Ozu**
sc **Yasujiro Ozu, Kogo Noda**
ph **Yushun Atsuta**
m **Kojun Saito**
Setsuko Hara, Yoko Tsukasa, Chishu Ryu, Mariko Okada

A widowed mother (Hara) attempts to find a husband for her daughter (Tsukasa), but the daughter mistakenly believes that her mother wishes to remarry. 'I wanted to show life, which seems complex, reveal itself as simple,' Ozu stated about his third film on the theme of arranged marriages. As always, Ozu has made a film of great formal beauty, rich in humour and emotion.

Late Chrysanthemums

Bangiku

Japan 1954 117 mins bw
Toho

d **Mikio Naruse**
sc **Sumie Tanaka, Toshiro Ide**
ph **Masao Tamai**
m **Ichiro Saito**
Haruko Sugimura, Yuko Mochizuki, Chikako Hosokawa, Ken Uehara, Sadako Sawamura

Four retired geishas contemplate their past lives and their continuing unequal relationships with men. One attempts suicide, and old lovers turn up. A subtle and detailed tragicomic character study adapted from three Fumiko Hayashi stories, the film gets its effects by using an unfussy camera style but with many set-ups per sequence. As in most of Naruse's films, the women (superbly played) suffer a kind of defeat but nevertheless continue to fight on.

The Late Mathias Pascal

(US: The Living Dead Man)

Feu Mathias Pascal

France 1924 169 mins bw
Albatros

d **Marcel L'Herbier**
sc **Marcel L'Herbier**

ph **René Guichard, Bourgassof, Jean Letort**
m **Silent**
Ivan Mosjoukine (Ivan Mozhukhin), Michel Simon, Marcelle Pradot, Pierre Batcheff, Douvan, Lois Moran

Reading about his own death in the newspaper, Mathias Pascal (Mosjoukine) decides to take advantage of the situation and leave his family to start a new life. When he tires of the deception, he returns to face his past. The great Russian emigré actor Mosjoukine (as he was known in France), gained his international reputation as the cynical observer of life at the centre of L'Herbier's lively, witty, expressionistic version of Pirandello's ironic story. It was the last major work as art director by Cavalcanti. Assisted by Lazare Meerson, he devised sets and lighting that were influenced by German films of the time. Michel Simon, in one of his very earliest films, puts in an amusing appearance.

The Late Mathias Pascal

L'Homme De Nulle Part

France 1937 98 mins bw
General Productions/Ala-Colosseum

d **Pierre Chenal**
sc **Roger Vitrac, Armand Salacrou, Pierre Chenal, Christian Stengel**
ph **Joseph-Louis Mundwiller, André Bac**
m **Jacques Ibert**
Pierre Blanchar, Isa Miranda, Ginette Leclerc, Robert Le Vigan, Palau

When a henpecked Italian provincial (Blanchar) is mistakenly believed to be dead, he moves to Rome, assumes a new identity and falls in love with his landlord's daughter (Miranda). Unlike Marcel L'Herbier's stylized, silent, studio-shot 1924 version of the Pirandello story, Chenal's was filmed on location in Italy. It turned out to be a delightful, ironic comedy with an excellent script (some of it reflecting the influence of surrealist writer Vitrac) and fine performances, especially from Blanchar, very different from his Raskolnikov in Chenal's *Crime And Punishment* two years previously.

Late Spring

Banshun

Japan 1949 108 mins bw
Ofuna

d **Yasujiro Ozu**
sc **Yasujiro Ozu, Kogo Noda**
ph **Yuharu Atsuta**
m **Senji Ito**
Setsuko Hara, Chisu Ryu, Haruko Sugimura, Jun Usami

A widowed father (Ryu) lives happily with his daughter (Hara), who is somewhat past the usual marrying age. Feeling he is keeping her from matrimony, he leads her to believe that he is to remarry in order to free her. This was one of Ozu's own favourites, and he would return to the theme again and again over the next decade. (He never married and lived with his mother all his life.) It also marked the return of his screenwriter Noda after 14 years, and the beginning of the director's mature style: a simplicity of story, structure and tempo, with short incisive exteriors punctuating the domestic scenes. There is a notable Noh theatre sequence that lasts about three minutes.

Lazarillo

El Lazarillo De Tormes

Spain 1959 109 mins bw
Hesperia Films

d **Cesar Ardavin**
sc **Cesar Ardavin**
ph **Manuel Berenguer**
m **Ruiz De Luna**
Marco Paoletti, Juan José Menendez, Carlos Casaravilla, Margarita Lozano

A fatherless boy (Paoletti), abandoned by his mother, finds a living with a series of employers who include a blind beggar, a miserly sacristan, a fake nobleman and a troupe of travelling players. He encounters vanity, cupidity and deception, and learns the skills of cunning and connivance in order to survive. A mildly satirical but otherwise stolid morality tale, enlivened by the young Italian actor's performance and an impeccable re-creation of 17th-century Castile.

Best Film Berlin 1960

Lazarillo De Tormes, El see Lazarillo

Leap Into The Void
Salto Nel Vuoto
Italy/France 1980 120 mins col
Clesi Cinematografica/M.K.2 Productions(Paris)

d **Marco Bellocchio**
sc **Marco Bellocchio, Piero Natoli, Vincenzo Cerami**
ph **Beppe Lanci**
m **Nicola Piovani**
Michel Piccoli, Anouk Aimée, Michele Placido, Gisella Burinato

Mauro (Piccoli), a middle-aged bachelor judge, and Marta (Aimée), his spinster sister, live together in the family house of their childhood. Marta's confined existence, cooking, washing and ironing for her brother with only a housemaid for company, has disturbed her mental balance until Mauro attempts to have her disposed of with unexpected results. Two decades on from *Fists In The Pocket* Bellocchio's vibrant, explosive anger has mellowed into moody introspection. Issues of family, dependency and feminism are here (incest is side-stepped but the hint hovers). It's played with the expertise one would expect, and the art direction and photography are broodingly atmospheric.However, like the lighting, the film's themes are shadowy and confused, making heavy weather of two hours.

Best Actor (Michel Piccoli) Cannes 1980
Best Actress (Anouk Aimée) Cannes 1980

Leather And Nylon see Action Man

Leaves From Satan's Book
Blade Of Satans Bog
Denmark 1919 133 mins bw
Nordisk

d **Carl Dreyer**
sc **Edgar Høyer, Carl Dreyer**
ph **George Schneevoigt**
m **Silent**
Helge Nissen, Halvard Hoff, Jacob Texiere, Hallander Hellemann, Ebon Strandin

Four episodes showing the activities of Satan (Nissen) through the ages: as a Pharisee at the time of Christ, as a Spanish Grand Inquisitor, as a police officer at work during the French Revolution and as a revolutionary monk in the Russo-Finnish war of 1918. Dreyer's second film was modelled on D. W. Griffith's *Intolerance* (1916), although he doesn't intercut the four stories. Pompous, preachy and patchy, it nevertheless displays the beginnings of Dreyer's thematic preoccupations and pictorial sense, as well as an accomplished style of montage.

Lebende Leichnam, Der see Living Corpse, The

Lebenszeichen see Signs Of Life

Leda see Web Of Passion

The Left-handed Woman
Die Linkshändige Frau
W. Germany 1977 119 mins col
Roadmovies

d **Peter Handke**
sc **Peter Handke**
ph **Robby Müller**
m **Bach**
Edith Clever, Marcus Muehleisen, Bruno Ganz, Michel Lonsdale, Gerard Dépardieu, Bernhard Wicki

A woman (Clever), living in the Paris suburbs, no longer loves her husband (Ganz) and does not relate to her young son, her father, or her friends. Novelist-playwright-screenwriter Peter Handke's directorial debut (produced by Wim Wenders) is a study of a suburban woman's boredom, apathy and non-communication. But as the film follows the almost wordless creature while she wanders aimlessly about her house, it not only presents *ennui* on screen but creates it in the audience.

Legenda Suramskoi Kreposti see Legend Of The Suram Fortress, The

---

Legend Of Gosta Berling, The see Atonement Of Gösta Berling, The

---

Legend Of Prague, The see Golem, The

The Legend Of The Suram Fortress

Legenda Suramskoi Kreposti

USSR 1985 87 mins col
Georgianfilm Studio

d **Sergo Paradjanov, Dodo Abashidze**
sc **Vazha Gigashvili**
ph **Sergo Sixarulidze**
m **Dzhansugh K'Axidze**
Levan Uchaneishvili, Zurab Kipshidze, Dodo Abashidze, Veriko Andzhaparidze

A mysterious force causes a medieval fortress to crumble and collapse as soon as it is built. In an attempt to solve the problem, the local soothsayer demands that the son of the lover who jilted her must brick himself up alive inside the wall of the fortress for it to remain standing and invincible. Based on a Georgian legend, the film is dedicated to 'Georgian warriors of all times who gave up their lives for the Motherland'. Yet this is no conventional patriotic pageant, but a poetic, pictorially breathtaking, personal celebration of the republic's history and folklore. Like Paradjanov's previous film, *The Colour Of Pomegranates*, the narrative is divided into chapters, each embodying a specific religious concept depicted in striking *tableaux vivants*, emblematic gestures or formalized movement. Specific meaning may be difficult to grasp, but the overall experience is a unique and sensuous one.

En Lektion I Karlek see Lesson In Love

Lenin In 1918

Lenin V 1918

USSR 1939 133 mins bw
Mosfilm

d **Mikhail Romm**
sc **Alexei Kapler, Tatiana Zlatogorova**
ph **Boris Volchok**
m **Nikolai Kryukov**
Boris Shchukin, Nikolai Okhlopkov, Vasily Vanin, Nikolai Cherkassov, Mikhail Gelovani

1918 sees Lenin (Shchukin) as head of the new Soviet state, struggling ceaselessly to bring order out of the chaos of war, revolution and famine. Aiding him in his task is the writer Maxim Gorky (Cherkassov) and Stalin (Gelovani). The tremendous success of *Lenin In October* led to the making of this sequel with virtually the same team. Given the deficiencies of hagiography and the obvious attempt to show Stalin as Lenin's heir, there is a good deal of warmth and depth in Shchukin's portrayal (he was to have starred in a third Lenin film, but it was cancelled because of his death) and, minor inaccuracies apart, it is a good reconstruction of the period.

Lenin In October

Lenin V Oktiabrye

USSR 1937 111 mins bw
Mosfilm

d **Mikhail Romm**
sc **Alexei Kapler**
ph **Boris Volchok**
m **Anatoli Alexandrov**
Boris Shchukin (Lenin), I. Golshtab (Stalin), Vasily Vanin, Nikolai Okhlopkov

Lenin's early political life, his exile and return to Russia to lead the October Revolution in 1917. Asked to make a film to celebrate the 25th anniversary of the October Revolution, Romm delivered, in a matter of months, this lively, human 'hagiopic', starring Lenin look-a-like Shchukin. The latter watched newsreels and studied Lenin's speech patterns in preparation for the role, which he played again in the sequel, *Lenin In 1918* (1939), and many more times.

Lenin V 1918 see Lenin In 1918

Lenin V Oktiabrye see Lenin In October

Leone Have Sept Cabecas, Der see Lion Has Seven Heads, The

Léon Morin, Prêtre see Léon Morin, Priest

Léon Morin, Priest

Léon Morin, Prêtre

France 1961 117 mins bw
Rome-Paris Films

Le Leçon Particulière

d **Jean-Pierre Melville**
sc **Jean-Pierre Melville**
ph **Henri Decaë**
m **Martial Solal, Albert Raisner**
Jean-Paul Belmondo, Emmanuele Riva, Irène Tunc, Marielle Gozzi

In rural France during the German Occupation, a young atheist widow falls in love with the priest who converts her to religion. Not as pious as it sounds, Melville's quietly polemical film explores the psychology and humanity of the priest (a restrained Belmondo) and the woman (Riva) through a series of discussions, set against the finely detailed background of the period.

Leçon Particulière, La see Private Lesson, The

The Leopard

Il Gattopardo

Italy 1963 205 mins col
GTCF/Titanus/SNPC/GPC

d **Luchino Visconti**
sc **Luchino Visconti**
ph **Giuseppe Rotunno**
m **Nino Rota**
Burt Lancaster, Claudia Cardinale, Alain Delon, Paolo Stoppa, Serge Reggiani, Leslie French

When his penniless nephew (Delon) marries Angelica (Cardinale), the daughter of a merchant (Stoppa), the Prince of Salina (Lancaster) reflects sadly on the death of the aristocratic world and the rise of the crass *bourgeoisie* during the Risorgimento. This gorgeous evocation of an era, faithfully adapted from Giuseppe De Lampedusa's novel, is full of superb set-pieces, particularly the final ball which takes up 40 minutes of screen time. In order to get the American Lancaster to play the dying 19th-century Sicilian prince, Visconti agreed to allow 20th Century-Fox to release the film internationally. Although it was overlong and somewhat lethargic, it didn't justify Fox's cutting (by about 44 minutes), dubbing, and reprocessing of it in CinemaScope and Deluxe Color. Visconti disowned this version, but Lancaster's mellow performance still shines through in both the maimed and original versions.

Best Film Cannes 1963

Lesson In Love

En Lektion I Karlek

Sweden 1954 95 mins bw
Svensk Filmindustri

d **Ingmar Bergman**
sc **Ingmar Bergman**
ph **Martin Bodin, Bengt Nordwal**
m **Dag Wirén**
Gunnar Björnstrand, Eva Dahlbeck, Harriet Andersson, Yvonne Lombard

A gynaecologist (Björnstrand) meets his estranged wife (Dahlbeck) on a train to Copenhagen where they relive their bumpy past. One of Bergman's few comedies is an entertaining if minor contribution to his despatches from the battle of the sexes. The lovely blonde Dahlbeck proved herself adept at sophisticated comedy, a talent even better used in the following year's *Smiles Of A Summer Night*.

Let Joy Reign Supreme

Que La Fête Commence

France 1975 120 mins col
Fildebroc

d **Bertrand Tavernier**
sc **Bertrand Tavernier, Jean Aurenche**
ph **Pierre William Glenn**
m **Philippe D'Orléans**
Philippe Noiret, Jean Rochefort, Marina Vlady, Jean-Pierre Marielle

The intellectual and atheistic Philippe D'Orléans (Noiret), aided by a power-hungry priest (Marielle), holds the reins of state for an under-age Louis XV, and keeps the populace in check, while his own life at court revolves around his mistresses. A rather glib and traditional look at the rottenness of the Baroque court and the horrors of life outside it, with the usual orgies and rompings in masks. Tavernier's favourite actor, Noiret, seems to relish the costumes, and the authentic music is by the character he plays.

Let Justice Be Done see Justice Est Faite

Let's Hope It's A Girl

Speriamo Che Sia Femmina

Italy 1985 119 mins col
Clemi Cinematografica/Producteurs Associés/ Soprofilms/Films A2(Paris)

d **Mario Monicelli**
sc **Leo Benvenuti, Piero De Bernardi, Suso Cecchi D'Amico, Tullio Pinelli, Mario Monicelli**
ph **Camillo Bazzoni**
m **Nicola Piovani**
Liv Ullmann, Catherine Deneuve, Philippe Noiret, Bernard Blier, Giuliana De Sio, Stefania Sandrelli, Athina Cenci

Elena (Ullmann), separated from her husband Leonardo (Noiret), an impoverished count, struggles to keep the family's crumbling country property and rules over its inhabitants who, but for daft old Uncle Gugo (Blier), are composed entirely of women. The spirits and resolve of the family are resurrected when Elena's daughter Franca (De Sio) becomes pregnant with the first (illegitimate) grandchild. After making comedies for 50 years, it is not surprising that Monicelli delivers a piece that is highly efficient, albeit one that suffers from an excess of plot and length. The tone is uncertain at times and the film tends to sprawl like the old family mansion in it, but the Tuscan settings are ravishing and there is a gentle and unexpected suggestion of pro-feminist bias. The expert Franco-Italian cast, led by Sweden's Ullmann, contribute to an appealing if light-weight movie.

Letter From Siberia

Lettre De Siberie

France 1958 60 mins col
Argos Films

d **Chris Marker**
sc **Chris Marker**
ph **Sacha Vierny**
m **Pierre Barbaud**

A personal documentary, filmed in Siberia, on various aspects of life there and attitudes towards it. 'I write to you from a far off country,' begins Marker's first full-length filmic letter, using texts, cartoons and a sequence repeated three times with a different commentary which brilliantly questions objectivity in non-fiction films. The humorous and poetic style tells us more about Marker than Siberia, but it beats all those boring travelogues.

Letter From The Wife

Stir Patra

India 1974 98 mins bw
Dhrupadi

d **Purnendu Pattrea**
sc **Purnendu Pattrea**
ph **Shakti Banerjee**
m **Ramkumar Chatterjee**
Madhabi Mukherjee, Ashim Chakrabarti, Smita Sinha, Nimu Bhowmick

Mrinal (Mukherjee) has married into a prosperous family that expects her to accept the traditional role of the Indian wife. However, by writing poetry secretly she gains a measure of personal freedom. When one of her husband's relatives is forced into marriage with a half-wit, she rejects all that his family represents. Because this is an adaptation of a story by Rabindranath Tagore and it stars the superb Madhabi Mukherjee of *The Big City* and *Charulata*, comparisons with the work of Satyajit Ray are inevitable. But Pattrea shows an individual visual talent and political sense and, although narrative and character are a little less assured than Ray's, it's a worthy addition to Tagore interpretations on screen.

Letters From A Dead Man

Pisma Myortvovo Chelovyeka

USSR 1986 87 mins col
Lenfilm

d **Konstantin Lopushansky**
sc **Konstantin Lopushansky, Vyacheslav Ribakov**
ph **Nikolai Pokoptsev**
m **Fauré, Giulio Gaccini**
Rolan Bykov, I. Riklin, V. Mikhailov, V. Sabinin, N. Gryakalova

A Soviet city is devastated by a nuclear holocaust that happened by mistake. A Nobel Prize-winning scientist (Bykov) tries to make sense of events in a series of imaginary letters to his missing son while his wife is dying of radiation sickness and, elsewhere, the young and healthy shelter in an overcrowded bunker to which a group of orphaned children are denied entry. Shot in a murky, tinted monochrome to capture the haunting rubble-strewn landscape of nuclear disaster, Lopushansky's film is a depressing document of the horror that awaits us if the button is pressed with, surprisingly, some underlying wry humour.

Letters From My Windmill

Lettres De Mon Moulin

France 1954 120 mins bw
Cie Mediterranéene De Films—Eminente

d **Marcel Pagnol**
sc **Marcel Pagnol**
ph **Willy**
m **Henri Tomasi**
Roger Crouzet, Henri Crémieux, Edouard Delmont, Henri Vilbert, Fernand Sardou

The author Alphonse Daudet (Crouzet) returns to Provence where he hears three tales—about monks who manufacture a new liqueur, how the Devil tricked a gourmand priest, and how a miller pretends his mill has been working for 18 years for a non-existent client. Originally three hours long, Pagnol's final film had a long prologue and epilogue cut on release. The loss was not severe, as this talkative and old-fashioned film could have done with even more pruning. But Daudet's tales, Pagnol's rich dialogue and the warm southern characters provide good rustic entertainment.

Lettre De Siberie see Letter From Siberia

Lettres De Mon Moulin see Letters From My Windmill

Letyat Zhuravli see Cranes Are Flying, The

Letzte Akt, Der see Last Ten Days, The

Letzte Brücke, Die see Last Bridge, The

Letzte Mann, Der see Last Laugh, The

Letzte Walzer, Der see Last Waltz, The

Les Liaisons Dangereuses 1960

France 1959 106 mins bw
Films Marceau

d **Roger Vadim**
sc **Roger Vadim, Roger Vailland, Claude Brûlé**
ph **Marcel Grignon**
m **Jack Murray, Thelonius Monk**
Gérard Philipe, Jeanne Moreau, Annette Vadim, Jeanne Valérie, Jean-Louis Trintignant

Valmont (Philipe) and his wife Juliette (Moreau) encourage each other's sexual conquests, until the wages of sin catch up with them. Good performances from Moreau and the dying Philipe, the display of Vadim's wife's body, and the cool ironic tone make this slickly directed updating of Laclos' 1782 epistolary novel one of the director's better efforts. The false denouement, with shooting, madness and fire, demonstrated that promiscuity doesn't pay—just in case audiences thought that it might from the tempting goings-on that preceded it.

Liebe Der Jeanne Ney, Die see Love Of Jeanne Ney, The

Liebe In Deutschland, Eine see Love In Germany, A

Liebe Ist Liebe see Love Is Love

Liebelei

Austria 1932 85 mins bw
Fred Lissa

d **Max Ophüls**
sc **Hans Wilhelm, Kurt Alexander**
ph **Franz Planer**
m **Theo Mackeben**
Magda Schneider, Wolfgang Liebeneiner, Luise Ullrich, Willy Eichberger

A young officer (Liebeneiner) and the daughter of a violinist (Schneider) have a brief love affair, until he is killed in a duel over a married woman, and she jumps to her death. Far less ironic and more romantic than Arthur Schnitzler's play—witness the invigorating sleigh ride—the film's emphasis is on music, sound and camera movement rather than dialogue. It was Max Ophüls' first big success and the most memorable performance from Magda Schneider, mother of Romy.

The Life And Loves Of Beethoven

Un Grand Amour De Beethoven

France 1937 135 mins bw
Générales

d **Abel Gance**
sc **Abel Gance**
ph **Robert Lefèbvre, Marc Fossard**
m **Beethoven**
Harry Baur, Annie Ducaux, Jany Holt, Jean-Louis Barrault

The great composer (Baur) has trouble with his hearing and with a girl who ignores him and prefers to marry a count, but another wins his heart. Gance was not at his best with dialogue as this rather leaden biopic demonstrates, but it does have the expected visual flourishes. The sequence when the hero loses his hearing, revealed by the silent shots of violins, bells and birds singing, is poignant and paradoxical. The loss of sound for Beethoven and the coming of sound for Gance were almost equally agonizing. Note that in the foreign release version Barrault, as the composer's nephew, has completely disappeared.

The Life And Music Of Giuseppe Verdi

Giuseppe Verdi

Italy 1938 123 mins bw
Grandi Film Storici

d **Carmine Gallone**
sc **Carmine Gallone, Lucio D'Ambra**
ph **Massimo Terzano**
m **Giuseppe Verdi**
Fosco Giachetti, Germana Paolieri, Gaby Morlay, Maria Cebotari, Beniamino Gigli, Pierre Brasseur

Verdi (Gachetti) comes to Milan, is rejected by the conservatory of music and marries. His young wife dies, his early operas flop and he falls in love with a singer (Paolieri).He later remarries, becomes a success and is then inspired to compose *Aida* by another young singer (Morlay). Apart from the chance to hear a liberal sprinkling of arias from the likes of Cebotari and Gigli, this biopic is really old opera hat. After 25 years in the business, veteran director Gallone made a second career out of workmanlike opera-related films such as *Manon Lescaut* (1939), *Rigoletto* (1947), *Il Trovatore* (1949), *Puccini* (1952), *Madame Butterfly* (1955) and *Tosca* (1956).

Life Dances On see Carnet De Bal, Un

Life Is A Bed Of Roses

La Vie Est Un Roman

France 1983 111 mins col
Soprofilms/Films A2/Fideline/Les Films Ariane/Filmedis

d **Alain Resnais**
sc **Jean Gruault**
ph **Bruno Nuytten**
m **M. Philippe-Gérard**
Vittorio Gassman, Ruggero Raimondi, Geraldine Chaplin, Fanny Ardant, Pierre Arditti, Sabine Azéma, Robert Manuel

In the early 1920s, at Count Forbek's château dedicated to happiness, his guests take a special drug to become 'reborn' and forget their pasts. In 1982, the building has been turned into a progressive school. During the summer vacation, a teachers' conference is held there, while the few remaining children imagine a world of knights and dragons. Despite its ostensibly complex structure—shifting seamlessly between the past, the present and the imagined—it is one of Resnais' lightest and most approachable films. It is a Feuillade-like drama, a satiric-comedy on intellectuals, a musical, and a children's fantasy all rolled into one, linked by the theme that happiness and imagination cannot be forced upon one, and that only children have the secret. Taken separately, the first episode is visually appealing, the second is rather unfunny, the music is slight, and the comic-book stuff (seen only in long shot) is fey. But, as a whole, the film is entertaining.

Life, Love, Death

La Vie, L'Amour, La Mort

France 1969 115 mins col/bw
Les Films 13/Les Films Ariane/Les Productions Artistes Associés (Paris)/P.E.A. (Rome)

d **Claude Lelouch**
sc **Claude Lelouch**
ph **Jean Collomb**
m **Francis Lai**
Amidou, Janine Magnan, Marcel Bozzufi, Caroline Cellier

A factory worker (Amidou) at Simca, with a wife (Magnan) and mistress (Cellier), is condemned to death for the murder of nine prostitutes. Lelouch, the incurable romantic, turned uneasily to the subject of sex crime and capital punishment, but managed to control some of his usual excesses with the camera. Based on a number of case histories, the film conveys the hapless man's last days in serious black and white, while the flashbacks are in colour. Amidou's touching performance helps to counteract the director's manipulation.

The Life Of Chikuzan

aka Chikuzan Travels Alone

Chikuzan Hitori Tabi

Japan 1977 122 mins col
Kindai Eiga Kyokai/Jean-Jean Productions

d **Kaneto Shindo**
sc **Kaneto Shindo**
ph **Kiyomi Kuroda**
m **Hikaru Hayashi**
Chikuzan Takahashi, Ryuzo Hayashi, Nobuko Otowa, Dai Kanai, Mitsuko Baisho

Chikuzan Takahashi, the blind singer and player of the Shamisen, a Japanese stringed instrument, has led the life of a vagabond for 50 years since he was apprenticed to a blind beggar as a child. Shindo discovered the virtuoso player and singing chronicler in a neglected corner of Tokyo where students flocked to hear his music, and re-created his life in a visually and aurally sublime semi-documentary. Actors play him as a child and as a young man, while the eponymous Chikuzan appears as himself, an old man, displaying no hint of self-pity.

The Life Of O-Haru

Saikaku Ichidai Onna

Japan 1952 133 mins bw
Shin Toho

d **Kenji Mizoguchi**
sc **Yoshitaka Yoda**
ph **Yoshimi Kono**
m **Ichiro Saito**
Kinuyo Tanaka, Toshiro Mifune, Ichiro Sugai, Toshiko Yanane, Ataro Shindo

O-Haru (Tanaka), the daughter of a samurai, falls in love with a man (Mifune) from a lower class. After he is beheaded, she is forced to become the mistress of the head of a great clan in order to bear him an heir. Her duty done, she is dismissed from the palace and descends from marriage to a poor merchant, who is later killed, to becoming a prostitute and beggar. Meanwhile, her son has become a lord. Against a meticulously realized background of 17th-century Japan (mostly filmed in a bombed out park), Mizoguchi, without sentimentality or moralizing, delineates the sufferings of a woman (Tanaka giving one of the greatest of screen performances). Like most of the women of the period, his camera watches the moments of crisis and violence from a discreet distance, deepening our sympathy for the characters. The 52-year-old director, a number of whose previous films had been flops, risked everything to make this adaptation from Saikaku's classic picaresque novel. Happily, it marked his recognition in the West and led to further masterpieces in the last four years of his life.

Life Size

aka Love Doll

Grandeur Nature

Spain/France 1973 100 mins col
Jet Film(Barcelona)/Uranus Productions/Fox Europa-Films 66 (Paris)/Verona(Rome)

d **Luis Garcia Berlanga**
sc **Rafael Azcona, Luis Garcia Berlanga**
ph **Alain Derobe**
m **Maurice Jarre, Johann Strauss**
Michel Piccoli, Valentine Tessier, Rada

Rassimov, Amparo Soler Leal, Manolo Alexandre

When Michel (Piccoli), a successful Parisian dentist, acquires a life-sized doll, he begins to treat it as human. He abandons his practice and his wife (Rassimov) to devote himself exclusively to life with the doll, whom he dresses and undresses, films in various positions and takes with him everywhere. His happy fantasy turns to horror when first the janitor, then his Spanish neighbours, make use of his precious possession... A bizarre portrait of fetishism which will shock some and amuse others. Piccoli carries off his role with aplomb and Berlanga, offering no explanations and delivering no judgement, directs with stylish expertise, rooting Michel's increasingly extreme behaviour in contexts of normalcy. (He provides several well-observed supporting characters.) However, its quality notwithstanding, the movie begins to pall by virtue of its simplicity.

Life Upside Down

La Vie A L'Envers

France 1964 92 mins bw
A.J. Films

d **Alain Jessua**
sc **Alain Jessua**
ph **Jacques Robin**
m **Jacques Loussier**
Charles Denner, Anna Gaylor, Guy Saint-Jean, Nicole Gueden, Jean Yanne

An ordinary young Paris office worker (Denner), suddenly decides to retreat into his own inner world, giving up his loquacious new wife (Gaylor), his friends, work and possessions. He ends contentedly staring at a blank wall in the bare room of a mental clinic. The theme of alienation, a prevalent one in the 1960s, has seldom been explored with such wry wit and sensitivity, although the film's attitude to its hero remains ambiguous. Audiences will have to make up their own minds whether he is to be admired, emulated, pitied or scorned. What is clear, however, is the subtle way in which the images in the film itself become more and more denuded, moving towards a blank screen. Inexplicably, the director never fulfilled the vast promise of this feature, which won the Best First Film award at Venice.

Lift To The Scaffold

(US: Frantic)

Ascenseur Pour L'Echafaud

France 1957 89 mins bw
Nouvelles Editions De Films

d **Louis Malle**
sc **Louis Malle, Roger Nimier**
ph **Henri Decaë**
m **Miles Davis**
Maurice Ronet, Jeanne Moreau, Georges Poujoly, Lino Ventura, Yori Bertin

A young man (Ronet) murders his boss with the complicity of the victim's wife (Moreau), but is nearly punished for another crime he did not commit. Twenty-five-year-old Malle's first solo feature overlaid a conventional, complicated and somewhat implausible plot with a dark atmosphere and psychological depth. Tension is also well built up, especially in the crucial scene in the lift of the title in which the hero is stuck. Decaë's vivid photography of the Paris locations would soon make him a favourite with the *Nouvelle Vague*, and the film launched Moreau into stardom after 10 years in pictures. The effective jazz score was improvised by Miles Davis and a group of European musicians while watching a screening of the film.

The Light Across The Street

La Lumière D'En Face

France 1955 99 mins bw
EGC/Fernand Rivers

d **Georges Lacombe**
sc **Louis Chavance, René Masson, René Lefèvre**
ph **Louis Page**
m **Norbert Glanzberg**
Brigitte Bardot, Raymond Pellegrin, Roger Pigaut, Claude Romain

When the sexy wife (Bardot) of a jealous truck driver (Pellegrin), who spends most of his time trying to make money, falls in love with a garage mechanic (Pigaut), the situation results in murder. There is not much light in this murky low-life melodrama, but Bardot's wanton gamine appeal manages to shine through for the first time. A year later, Roger Vadim, her husband since 1952, used that appeal to notorious effect in *And*

God Created Woman, thus creating the legendary sex kitten known as BB.

Lights Of Variety
(US: Variety Lights)
Luci Del Varieta'
Italy 1950 94 mins bw
Film Capitolium

d **Alberto Lattuada, Federico Fellini**
sc **Federico Fellini**
ph **Otello Martelli**
m **Felice Lattuada**
Peppino De Filippo, Carla Del Poggio, Giulietta Masina, John Kitzmiller

A stage-struck young girl (Del Poggio) joins a third-rate vaudeville troupe and casts her spell on the manager and principal comic (De Filippo), until she leaves for better things. Fellini, who wrote songs and sketches for the music hall in his youth, wonderfully re-creates the world of a tatty troupe of performers, while seeing the humanity behind their stage make-up. Already, in his first film as director (he handled the actors, Lattuada the camera and action), Fellini established his Chaplinesque style.

Ligne De Chaleur, La see Heat Line, The

La Ligne De Démarcation
France 1966 120 mins bw
Rome-Paris Films/SNC

d **Claude Chabrol**
sc **Claude Chabrol, Colonel Rémy**
ph **Jean Rabier**
m **Pierre Jansen**
Jean Seberg, Maurice Ronet, Daniel Gélin, Stéphane Audran, Jacques Perrin, Jean Yanne, Noël Roquevert

In a small provincial town in Occupied France, a group of inhabitants attempts to smuggle two spies and a pair of fugitive Allied airmen across the border into Vichy territory. This film holds few surprises, portraying the usual struggles of Resistance fighters and the treachery of collaborators and informers common to the genre. This is an unexpected piece from Chabrol, but displaying his usual intelligence and craftsmanship, together with his slightly ironic sense of detachment in looking at the individuals—heroes and traitors alike—of a troubled period.

Lika, Chekhov's Love
aka Subject For A Short Story
Siuzhet Dlya Nebloshova Rasskaza
aka Lika, Lyubov Chekhova
USSR 1968 90 mins col
Mosfilm/Telsia(France)

d **Sergei Yutkevich**
sc **Leonid Malyugin**
ph **Naum Ardashnikov**
m **Rodion Schedrin**
Nikolai Grinko, Marina Vlady, Iya Savvina, Yuri Yakovlev

Lika (Vlady), a beautiful singing teacher who was loved by Chekhov (Grinko), returns from Paris to St Petersburg in 1896 for the opening night of *The Seagull*, which turns out to be a scandalous flop. This sensitive, elegant and stylized episode from Chekhov's life could only have been made by a Russian director. Yutkevich and his performers, including French actress Marina Vlady (née Marina De Poliakoff-baidaroff), capture the nuances of language and tone necessary for the portrayal of real events and people. But this is really the material for a short story and should perhaps have been the subject for a shorter film.

Lika, Lyubov Chekhova see Lika, Chekhov's Love

Like Father, Like Son
(US: The Tailor's Maid)
Padri E Figli
Italy 1957 104 mins col
Royal Film/Filmel-Lyrica

d **Mario Monicelli**
sc **Age, Furio Scarpelli, Mario Monicelli, Leo Benvenuti, Luigi Emmanuele**
ph **Leonida Barboni**
m **Alessandro Cicognini**
Vittorio De Sica, Marcello Mastroianni, Antonella Lualdi, Marisa Merlini, Franco Interlenghi, Franco Di Trocchio

A tale of five families, all connected to each other by love and/or marriage, focuses particularly on the pregnant nurse with four children, her childless sister and brother-in-law to whom she gives her youngest boy, and on the tailor's amorous daughter who falls for the doctor's son. This typically Italianate romp of the sort at which Monicelli excels is somewhat overcrowded with characters, but extrovert, charming, and funny. The acting honours go to De Sica as the weak, rascally and lovable tailor, and Mastroianni as Cesare the mechanic, who shares some of the best scenes with the little nephew (Di Trocchio) whom he and his wife adopt.

Best Director Berlin 1957

Lili Marleen

W. Germany 1980 120 mins col
Roxy/CIP/Rialto/Bayerische Rundfunk

d **Rainer Werner Fassbinder**
sc **Rainer Werner Fassbinder, Manfred Purzer, Joshua Sinclair**
ph **Xaver Schwarzenberger**
m **Peer Raben**
Hanna Schygulla, Giancarlo Giannini, Mel Ferrer, Christine Kaufmann, Rainer Werner Fassbinder

A German singer (Schygulla) and a Swiss-Jewish composer (Giannini), in love with one another, are separated by World War II, but her song 'Lili Marleen', popular on both fronts, unites them forever. Fassbinder's attempt to ape a romantic Hollywood biopic, despite ironic touches, turns out even sillier than his model. The scene where the Gestapo tortures the hero with endless playings of a cracked record of the title song is pure Monty Python. Garish colour and campy back projection add to the artificiality.

Liliom

France 1934 120 mins bw
Erich Pommer/Fox Europa

d **Fritz Lang**
sc **Fritz Lang (uncredited), Robert Liebman**
ph **Rudolph Maté, Louis Née**
m **Jean Lenoir, Franz Waxman**
Charles Boyer, Madeleine Ozeray, Florelle, Pierre Alcover, Roland Toutain

A raffish carnival barker (Boyer) is killed in a knife fight, but is given one day to return to earth to see how his wife (Ozeray) and daughter are managing. Lang's adaptation of the Ferenc Molnar play, his only film made in France where he had fled the Nazis *en route* to the USA, was less sentimental and more amusing than the 1930 Hollywood version or the stage and screen musical *Carousel*. Particularly good were Boyer and the fantasy scenes in heaven.

Lina Braake

W. Germany 1975 85 mins col
Sinkel/WDF

d **Bernhard Sinkel**
sc **Bernhard Sinkel**
ph **Alf Brustellin**
m **Joe Haider**
Lina Carstens, Fritz Rasp, Herbert Botticher, Erica Schramm, Benno Hoffmann

Lina Braake (Carstens), a spry, 82-year-old woman has lost her house through the machinations of a bank. She meets a retired bankrupt gentleman (Rasp) in an old people's home and together they plot to defraud the bank of a large sum of money. Actually shot in an old people's home, with the inhabitants as extras, the film reveals a part of society rarely visited by film-makers. Thirty-five-year-old Sinkel's first feature shows a sensitivity towards its subject while managing to avoid sentimentality, before it moves unsteadily from reality into fairytale. Its principal attraction is the co-starring of two veterans of German cinema, Carstens and Rasp, the latter having appeared in *Metropolis* almost 50 years earlier.

Linea Del Cielo, La see Skyline

Linkshändige Frau, Die see Left-handed Woman, The

The Lion Has Seven Heads

Der Leone Have Sept Cabecas

Congo 1970 103 mins col
Claude Antoine/Polifilm

d **Glauber Rocha**
sc **Glauber Rocha, Gianni Amico**
ph **Guido Cosulich**
m **Congolese folk music**
Jean-Pierre Léaud, Rada Rassimov, Giulio Brogli, Gabriele Tinti

A CIA man, a Portuguese mercenary, a missionary priest, an ex-Nazi, puppet rulers, revolutionaries, and a blonde woman later crucified, act out Africa's colonial past and present. Rocha's first film abroad after his exile from Brazil is a highly symbolic, rhetorical, non-narrative cry for international revolution represented by the five languages that make up the original title—German, Italian, English, French and Portuguese. But this patchwork of protest theatre, carnival, caricature and political texts, moves in the direction of anarchy, madness and sado-masochism, only adding to the burdens of the Third World.

The Lipstick

Il Rossetto

Italy 1960 100 mins bw
Europa Cinematografica/Explorer/CFPC-Medallion

d **Damiano Damiani**
sc **Damiano Damiani, Cesare Zavattini**
ph **Pier Ludovico Pavoni**
m **Giovanni Fusco**
Laura Vivaldi, Pierre Brice, Giorgia Moll, Bella Darvi, Pietro Germi

A 13-year-old schoolgirl (Vivaldi) is infatuated with her handsome next door neighbour (Brice), leading to her involvement with a murder case in which he is heavily implicated. This is a competent and compact crime thriller in which suspense is well maintained, and to which added interest is given by the youthfulness of the heroine from whose point of view the action is observed. An excellent feature debut for former documentary-maker Damiani.

Lisice see Handcuffs

Liten Ida see Little Ida

Little Ida

Liten Ida

Norway 1981 79 mins col
Norsk Film A.S. Svensk Filminstituten

d **Laila Mikkelsen**
sc **Marit Paulsen, Laila Mikkelsen**
ph **Hans Welin, Kjell Vassdal**
m **Eyvind Solaas**
Sunniva Lindeklejv, Lise Fjeldstad, Howard Halvorsen, Arne Lindtner Ness, Ellen Westerfjell

During the Nazi occupation of Norway in 1944, seven-year-old Ida (Lindeklejv) has to endure an incomprehensible agony of loneliness and malicious abuse because her mother takes up with a German soldier. Based on writer Paulsen's own memoirs, this grim tale of survival is filmed in authentically chilly landscapes, and offers an astonishing performance from Lindeklejv. Director Mikkelsen, telling her dreadful tale with absolute fidelity to truth, avoids the pitfalls of maudlin sentimentality to achieve a moving document of childhood and of an aspect of World War II.

The Little Matchgirl

La Petite Marchande D'Allumettes

France 1928 29 mins bw
Jean Renoir & Jean Tedesco

d **Jean Renoir**
sc **Jean Renoir**
ph **Jean Bachelet**
m **Silent**
Catherine Hessling, Jean Storm, Manuel Raaby, Amy Wells

Unable to sell her matches, the destitute girl (Hessling) is reduced to striking them in a futile effort to keep warm, and comforts herself with dreams of a fantasy world. In the morning her tiny, frozen body is found dead in the snow. This poignant film was the last, and best, of the four silents Renoir made with his actress wife, noticeably drawing on her talent for mime. With the close collaboration of friends—Tedesco, Bachelet and Danish designer Eric Aës—the director devised an appropriate cinematic language for translating the world of Danish fairy tale writer Hans Christian Andersen to the screen, placing his actors in stylized sets, making use of double exposure and other tricks, and expanding the story to include themes from other well-known Andersen stories such as *The Tinder Box*, and *The Steadfast Tin Soldier* in which toys come to life.

The Little Nuns

Le Monachine

Italy 1963 100 mins bw

Ferruccio Brusarosco

d **Luciano Salce**
sc **Franco Castellano, Giuseppe Moccia**
ph **Erico Menczer**
m **Ennio Morricone**
Didi Perego, Catherine Spaak, Sylva Koscina, Amadeo Nazzari, Umberto Orsini

The sound waves of commercial jets flying overhead are destroying the treasured fresco of a humble convent. The Mother Superior (Perugo) and a naive young nun (Spaak) journey to Rome to plead with the airline's executive. Once they have accomplished their mission, they also save the executive's job and find him a wife. This is an easily digested comedy, liberally seasoned with charm and enhanced by convincing performances.

The Little Soldier

Le Petit Soldat

France 1960 88 mins bw

Georges De Beauregard/Société Nouvelle De Cinéma

d **Jean-Luc Godard**
sc **Jean-Luc Godard**
ph **Raoul Coutard**
m **Maurice Leroux**
Michel Subor, Anna Karina, Henri-Jacques Huet, Laszló Szábó, Paul Beauvais

In Geneva, at the time of the Algerian War, a French secret agent (Subor), on a mission to kill a top man in the FLN, finds himself used as a pawn by both sides. Godard's second feature was banned by the French Ministry of Information (it was released with minor cuts in 1963) because of its ambivalent attitude to the Algerian War, and its reflection of brutality on both sides which affronted both Left and Right opinion. Other reasons might have been its matter-of-fact filming of torture, and the treatment of the political crisis as a confusing gangster movie. This powerful reflection of the period saw the debut of Anna Karina, whom Godard married in 1961. They separated five years and eight films later.

The Little Theatre Of Jean Renoir

Le Petit Théâtre De Jean Renoir

France 1969 100 mins col

ORTF

d **Jean Renoir**
sc **Jean Renoir**
ph **Georges Leclerc**
m **Jean Wiener, Joseph Kosma, Octave Cremieux**
Jeanne Moreau, Fernand Sardou, Françoise Arnoul, Jean Carmet

A film in four parts: 1) two old tramps find freedom in dreams; 2) a housewife is obsessed with an electric floor polisher; 3) Jeanne Moreau, in Belle Époque costume, sings 'Quand L'Amour Meurt'; 4) a husband whose wife has betrayed him with his best friend, accepts the situation rather than be parted from either. Renoir's adieu to the cinema 'after seven years of unwilling inactivity', actually made for TV and released in 1971, is an uneven divertissement, looking back on some aspects of his art. There is the studio artifice of his silents in the whimsical first tale, the second is an unfunny sung satire, Moreau's song is charming, and the last episode reminds us of Renoir's great humanity.

The Little World Of Don Camillo

Il Piccolo Mondo Di Don Camillo

Italy 1952 106 mins bw

Rizzoli/Amato/Francinex

d **Julien Duvivier**
sc **Julien Duvivier, René Barjavel**
ph **Nicolas Hayer**
m **Alessandro Cicognini**
Fernandel, Gino Cervi, Sylvie, Franco Interlenghi, Vera Talqui

The parish priest (Fernandel) and the Communist mayor (Cervi) of an Italian village, usually at odds with each other, combine forces to help a modern Romeo and Juliet (Interlenghi and Talqui). Fernandel's portrayal of the scheming Camillo, who holds conversations with God, was so successful that it prompted several lesser sequels also based on the novels of Giovanni Guareschi.

Live For Life

Vivre Pour Vivre

France 1967 130 mins col
UA/Ariane/Vides

d **Claude Lelouch**
sc **Claude Lelouch, Pierre Uytterhoeven**
ph **Patrick Pouget**
m **Francis Lai**
Yves Montand, Candice Bergen, Annie Girardot, Irène Tunc

A globe-trotting TV news reporter (Montand) leaves his wife (Girardot) after their holiday in Amsterdam, has an affair with an American fashion model (Bergen) in Kenya, the Congo, and Paris, is taken prisoner in Vietnam, and is reconciled with his wife in the French Alps. For this follow-up to his vastly successful *A Man And A Woman* (1966), Lelouch was given the money to run around the world, but made specious use of the Vietnam War and other troublespots as backgrounds to Montand's marital problems. Put together with the expert eye of a smooth huckster, it was nominated for an Oscar.

Living

aka Doomed
(US: To Live)
Ikiru

Japan 1952 143 mins bw
Toho

d **Akira Kurosawa**
sc **Akira Kurosawa, Shinobu Hashimoto, Hideo Oguni**
ph **Asaichi Nakai**
m **Fumio Hayasaka**
Takashi Shimura, Nabuo Kaneko, Kyoko Seki, Miki Odagiri

Discovering he is in the terminal stages of cancer, an elderly civil servant (Shimura) spends his last months initially in self-absorption, but then devotes himself to forcing through the building of a children's playground in the slums. One of Kurosawa's rare looks at modern Japanese society is a bleak one. The low key photography and the regretful flashbacks build a picture of a sterile society, counteracted by the touching central character of a man who dies happily.

The Living Corpse

Der Lebende Leichnam
aka Zhivoi Trup

Germany/USSR 1928 108 mins bw
Prometheus/Mezhrabpomfilm

d **Fedor Ozep**
sc **B. Gusman, Anatoly Marienhof**
ph **Anatoli Golovnya**
m **Silent**
Vsevolod Pudovkin, Maria Jacobini, V. Garden, Gustav Diessl

A husband (Pudovkin), whose wife (Jacobini) is unfaithful to him and who is unable to get a divorce, decides to kill himself. The fine acting of the great Russian director Pudovkin and the splendid camerawork add considerably to the quality of this version of Leo Tolstoy's play, made in two languages in Germany. Much admired at the time, the content, but not the style, has lost much of its impact over the years.

Living Dead Man, The see Late Mathias Pascal, The

The Lizards

I Basilischi

Italy 1963 85 mins bw
Galatea

d **Lina Wertmüller**
sc **Lina Wertmüller**
ph **Gianni Di Venanzo**
m **Ennio Morricone**
Toni Petruzzi, Stefano Sattaflores, Sergio Ferrannino, Luigi Barbieri

In a sleepy southern Italian town a group of young men spend their time ogling the girls and vegetating in the sun. Not much happens in the film, nor to the aimless characters, but Wertmüller in her first feature displayed a sharp eye and a keen sense of humour, absent from most of her subsequent films.

Ljubavni Slucaj see Switchboard Operator, The

Loin De Vietnam see Far From Vietnam

Lola

France 1960 91 mins bw
Rome-Paris/Euro-International

d **Jacques Demy**
sc **Jacques Demy**
ph **Raoul Coutard**
m **Michel Legrand**
Anouk Aimée, Marc Michel, Jacques Harden, Elina Labourdette

Lola (Aimée), a cabaret singer and dancer in Nantes, tries to choose between three men, two of them sailors. Dedicated to Max Ophüls, Demy's first feature has the circular construction, long tracking shots and frothiness to remind one of the dedicatee, but it owes as much to *On The Town* (MGM, 1949) with its sailors on leave, chance encounters and fleeting love affairs. This modern fairytale brought Demy and the tall, brown-eyed enigmatic beauty, Anouk Aimée, international fame.

Lola

W. Germany 1981 114 mins col
Rialto Film/Trio Film

d **Rainer Werner Fassbinder**
sc **Rainer Werner Fassbinder, Peter Märthesheimer, Pea Fröhlich**
ph **Xaver Schwarzenberger**
m **Peer Raben**
Barbara Sukowa, Armin Müller-Stahl, Mario Adorf, Matthias Fuchs, Ivan Desny

A respectable middle-aged building commissioner (Müller-Stahl) falls helplessly in love with Lola (Sukowa), the star of a nightclub-cum-bordello and mistress of the owner, a sleazy building profiteer (Adorf). The flavour is of *The Blue Angel* updated (filled with 1950s kitsch) and revamped into a Douglas Sirkian melodrama, with Fassbinder's usual indictment of a corrupt, avaricious Germany. The garish pink and blue colours and non-naturalistic lighting helps create a heady atmosphere and consciously harks back to De Luxe Color of the late 1950s.

Lola Montès

France 1955 140 mins col
Gamma/Florida/Oska

d **Max Ophüls**
sc **Max Ophüls, Annette Wademant, Franz Geiger**
ph **Christian Matras**
m **Georges Auric**
Martine Carol, Anton Walbrook, Peter Ustinov, Oskar Werner, Will Quadflieg

The story of the famous courtesan Lola Montès (Carol), now become a circus attraction, including her love affairs with King Ludwig I (Walbrook), Liszt (Quadflieg) and a student (Werner), told by the ring master (Ustinov). Ophüls' final film, his only work in colour, treats the space of the CinemaScope screen (using masking and other devices) in an unprecedented and breathtaking manner. The crane shots and camera movements, plus a 360-degree revolve, have the virtuosity of a Liszt sonata. All this makes up for the discursive narrative and the deficiencies of the leading lady. The film, which lost a great deal of money and was shown in a heavily cut version for many years, should only be seen on the wide screen.

Lonely Wife, The see Charulata

Lonely Woman, The see Journey To Italy

Lone White Sail

Byeleyet Parus Odinoky

USSR 1937 92 mins bw
Soyuzdetfilm

d **Vladimir Legoshin**
sc **Valentin Katayev**
ph **Bentsion Monastirsky, G. Garibian**
m **M. Rauchberger**
Igor But, Boris Runge, A. Melnikov, Ivan Peltser, A. Chekayevsky

Two young boys (But and Runge) hide a mutinous sailor (Melnikov) from the battleship *Potemkin* and help him to make contact with fellow revolutionaries in Odessa in 1905. A children's tale, in the best tradition of *Kidnapped*, it is told by Legoshin (a pupil of Eisenstein's) in an exciting, humorous and highly attractive manner. No matter that the adults are stereotyped, the children are delightful, fully-rounded, splendidly played creations. This immensely enjoyable film was popular at home and abroad with audiences of all ages.

The Long Absence

Une Aussi Longue Absence

France 1961 96 mins bw
Procinex/Lyre/Galatea

d **Henri Colpi**
sc **Marguerite Duras, Gerald Jariot**
ph **Marcel Weiss**
m **Georges Delerue**
Alida Valli, Georges Wilson, Jacques Harden

A widow (Valli), who owns a café in a Paris suburb, meets a tramp (Wilson) who may or may not be her husband who disappeared 15 years before in a prison camp. Colpi, who worked as editor on Alain Resnais' first features, made his directorial debut with this poetic, poignant, beautifully underplayed and simple story. A quiet revolution in the cinema.

Best Film Cannes 1961

Longing For Love

aka The Thirst For Love

Ai No Kawaki

Japan 1967 105 mins bw
Nikkatsu

d **Koreyoshi Kurahara**
sc **Shigeo Fujita, Koreyoshi Kurahara**
ph **Yoshio Mamiya**
m **Toshiro Mayuzumi**
Ruriko Asaoko, Tetsuo Ishidate, Nobuo Nakamura, Chitose Kurenai, Akira Yamanouchi

A young widow (Asaoko), living with her husband's family and enduring the unwelcome attentions of her father-in-law (Nakamura), finds herself infatuated with the family's young gardener (Ishidate). Her growing obsession, although secret, gradually becomes obvious to everybody except the boy himself. When she learns that one of the servant girls (Kurenai) is pregnant by the gardener, she is precipitated into an emotional crisis that leads to violence. This extraordinarily disturbing film about loneliness and sexual frustration combines irony, absurdity and, ultimately, tragedy in a finely balanced mix. An intimate work that probes the depths of its central character, it is acted with uncompromising truth by Asaoko, and directed with subtlety, skill and an effective touch of black humour.

Lost Army, The see Ashes

The Lost Forest

aka The Forest Of The Hanged

aka Forest of Hanged Men

Padurea Spinzuratilor

Romania 1965 157 mins bw
Bucuresti Studios

d **Liviu Ciulei**
sc **Titus Popovici**
ph **Ovidiu Gologan**
m **Theodor Grigoriu**
Victor Rebengiuc, Liviu Ciulei, Anna Széles, György Kovács

During World War I, when Romanians, Czechs, and Serbians are forced by the Austro-Hungarian Empire to fight against their fellow countrymen, a Romanian lieutenant (Rebengiuc) suffers from divided loyalties. He finally makes a decision that leads to his execution. Romanian films were sparse until Ciulei made an international breakthrough with this rigorous, carefully composed, anti-war drama shot in 'Scope. The acting and writing have an understated quality, unlike the Romanian propaganda epics that preceded it.

Best Director Cannes 1965

The Lost Honour Of Katharina Blum

Die Verlorene Ehre Der Katharina Blum

W. Germany 1975 106 mins col
Paramount-Orion/WDR/Bioskop-Film(Munich)

d **Volker Schlöndorff, Margarethe Von Trotta**
sc **Volker Schlöndorff, Margarethe Von Trotta**
ph **Jöst Vacano, Peter Arnold**
m **Hans Werner Henze**
Angela Winkler, Mario Adorf, Dieter Laser, Jürgen Prochnow, Heinz Bennent, Hannelore Hoger, Karl Heinz Vosgerau

Katharina Blum (Winkler) spends the night with Ludwig Goetten (Prochnow), a new acquaintance who is, unknown to her, under police surveillance. The encounter has serious repercussions: taken in for questioning, she is released to find herself mercilessly hounded by the press who turn her into an object of public opprobrium. In adapting a novel by Heinrich Böll, Schlöndorff and his wife have shifted some of the emphases of the original to make a statement on modern terrorism and police methods in Germany. However, Böll's attack on the yellow press remains powerfully intact in this well-paced if over-literal film.

The Lost One

Der Verlorene

W. Germany 1951 90 mins bw
Arnold Pressburger

d **Peter Lorre**
sc **Peter Lorre, Benno Vigny, Axel Eggebrecht**
ph **Vaclav Vich**
m **Willi Schmidt-Gentner**
Peter Lorre, Karl John, Helmut Rudolph, Johanna Hofer, Richard Münch

A Nazi scientist (Lorre), who has murdered his fiancée and a woman who reminded him of her, changes his name and becomes a doctor in a refugee camp after the war. Nearly two decades after leaving Germany, Peter Lorre returned to direct his only film rather in the expressionistic manner of those that were being made there when he left. Although no Fritz Lang, Lorre does create a tangible atmosphere of evil which he manages to embody with his own hypnotic presence.

The Lost Son

Der Verlorene Sohn

Germany 1934 102 mins bw
Deutsche Universal Film

d **Luis Trenker**
sc **Luis Trenker, Reinhardt Steinbicker, Arnold Ulitz**
ph **Albert Benitz, Reimar Kuntze**
m **Giuseppe Becce**
Luis Trenker, Maria Andergast, Marian Marsh, Paul Henckels, Jimmie Fox

A mountain guide (Trenker) falls in love with an American girl (Marsh) he has rescued from death in the Alps. He then travels to the USA to find her, but only suffers in the Depression. They finally meet again by chance, but he returns to his girlfriend (Andergast) back home. With *The Emperor From California*, this film forms Trenker's American diptych, and gives a vivid and unforgettable picture of New York in the early 1930s, shot on location. The American section comes between some breathtaking mountain material (Trenker was an expert skier and alpinist), in the tradition of the popular *Bergfilm*, with their rather sentimental attitudes and idyllic images.

Lost Youth

Gioventu Perduta

Italy 1948 84 mins bw
Carlo Ponti/Lux Film

d **Pietro Germi**
sc **Pietro Germi, Mario Monicelli, Bruno Valeri, Leopoldo Trieste**
ph **Carlo Montuori**
m **Carlo Rustichelli**
Jacques Sernas, Massimo Girotti, Carla Del Poggio, Nando Bruno

A middle-class university student (Sernas) from a loving home stops at nothing, from big-time theft to the murder of his sweetheart when she stumbles on evidence against him. Directed with intelligent restraint by later comedy specialist Germi, the film—technically excellent in all departments—is a convincing character study of post-war delinquency. It was initially withheld by the Italian censors because of its suspected Left-wing bias, but the resultant publicity forced a release.

Lotna

Poland 1964 89 mins col
Film Polski

d **Andrzej Wajda**
sc **Andrzej Wajda, Wojciech Zukrowski**
ph **Jerzy Lipman**
m **Tadeusz Baird**
Božena Kurowska, Jerzy Pichelski, Jerzy Moes, Adam Pawlikowski

The history of the Polish cavalry in its fight against the Germans in World War II as symbolized by an off-white horse that passes to various people in the military until it breaks its leg and is shot. Wajda, son of a cavalry officer who was killed in the war, made his first colour film as a visually arresting and sweeping tribute to the heroic horsemen who faced German tanks. But the episodic screenplay leans too heavily on the *Black Beauty* formula.

Louise

Chère Louise

France 1972 105 mins col
Les Films Ariane/P.E.C.F.(Paris)/C.C.C.(Rome)

d **Philippe De Broca**
sc **Jean-Loup Dabadie**
ph **Ricardo Aronovitch**
m **Georges Delerue**
Jeanne Moreau, Julian Negulesco, Didi Perego, Yves Robert, Pippo Starnazza

After the death of her mother, divorcée Louise, grown somewhat spinsterish, starts a new life as a teacher in Annecy. There, she befriends Luigi (Negulesco), a destitute Italian many years her junior, who becomes her live-in lover. A tried and trusted formula is given new life by Louise's attitude to her affair and her attempts both to keep and to free Luigi, lent conviction by Moreau's beautifully balanced performance. However,in an obvious decision to avoid sugary sentiment, De Broca also succeeds in robbing his film of real depth.

Loulou

France 1980 105 mins col
Gaumont/Action Films

d **Maurice Pialat**
sc **Arlette Langmann**
ph **Pierre William Glenn, Jacques Loiseleux**
m **Philippe Sarde**
Isabelle Huppert, Gérard Depardieu, Guy Marchand, Humbert Balsan

A *bourgeois* businesswoman (Huppert) leaves her respectable lover (Marchand) to set up home with a working-class yobbo (Depardieu) who is solely preoccupied with booze and bed. Working within the naturalistic tradition, Pialat, with an unobtrusive camera, depicts a Zola-esque story about an incongruous couple drawn to each other by sex alone. One's attitude to the film might depend a great deal on one's reaction to the earthy Depardieu as Loulou—the name being a diminutive of Louis or, colloquially, meaning darling or lout.

Love

Szerelem

Hungary 1971 92 mins bw
Mafilm Studio/Ajay

d **Károly Makk**
sc **Tibor Déry**
ph **János Tóth**
m **András Mihály**
Lili Darvas, Mari Töröcsik, Iván Darvas, Erszi Orsolya

With her husband János in jail on a trumped up political charge, Luca (Töröcsik) is left to take care of her old and dying mother-in-law (Darvas). She writes letters purporting to come from János in America, telling of his glittering success as a Hollywood film director, and reads them to the old lady. Luca becomes ostracized for her political connections and loses her job. Makk has made an exquisitely wrought film about love, falsehood (political and personal) and illusion. Whether the old lady believes in the letters is left deliberately ambiguous, as is the truth of her extravagant memories of a Viennese girlhood. Ferenc Molnar's widow, Darvas made this—her second and last film—just before her death and gave a memorable performance, almost matched by that of Töröcsik.

Love Affair: Or The Case Of The Missing Switchboard Operator
see Switchboard Operator, The

Love À La Carte see Hungry For Love

Love And Anarchy

Film D'Amore E D'Anarchia

Italy 1973 108 Mins col
Euro International Films

d **Lina Wertmüller**
sc **Lina Wertmüller**
ph **Giuseppe Rotunno**
m **Nino Rota**
Giancarlo Giannini, Mariangela Melato, Lina Polito, Eros Pagni, Pina Cei

Tunin (Giannini), a simple farmer, commits himself to an anti-Fascist group that despatches him to assassinate Mussolini. He lodges in a whorehouse, the madame of which (Melato) became a political idealist when her lover was killed by the Fascists. Tunin falls in love with one of the prostitutes (Polito) and this, together with his oversensitive nature, impedes his mission and leads him to his own violent destruction. As is usual in her work, Wertmüller indulges in excess but, on this occasion, it comes into its own in creating a palpable sense of the period, with the Lautrec-like brothel and its anarchic inhabitants serving as a subtle metaphor for freedom.The film's thesis—romanticism is not a realistic basis for political activism—is a telling one, and director, cast and designers achieve an authentic evocation of the disturbed atmosphere and the look and feel of 1930s Italy while providing strong entertainment.

Best Actor (Giancarlo Giannini) Cannes 1973

Love And Anger
Amore E Rabbia

Italy 1969 102 mins col
Castoro Film (Rome)/Anouchka Film (Paris)

d **1) Carlo Lizzani 2) Bernardo Bertolucci 3) Pier Paolo Pasolini 4) Jean-Luc Godard**
sc **1) Carlo Lizzani 2) Bernardo Bertolucci 3) Pier Paolo Pasolini 4) Jean-Luc Godard**
ph **1) Sandro Mancori 2) Ugo Piccone 3) Giuseppe Ruzzolini 4) Alain Levent**
m **Giovanni Fusco**

1) Tom Baker 2) Julien Beck 3) Ninetto Davoli 4) Christine Guého, Nino Castelnuovo, Catherine Jourdan, Paolo Pozzesi

1) *Indifference*: In a high-rise New York housing estate nobody takes any notice of a murder, a car crash or a police chase. 2) *Agony*: A dying man sees visions in his final agony. 3) *The Sequence Of The Paper Flower*: God speaks to an innocent young man walking down a street in Rome, and then strikes him dead. 4) *Love*: One couple observes another couple in a garden. Of these modern interpretations of New Testament parables, only Pasolini's 12 minute gem can be considered a success, while Godard's is intellectually teasing, and Bertolucci's gives an indulgent and dated glimpse of the Living Theatre at work. A fifth episode by Marco Bellocchio about student militants was cut from the US and UK versions.

Love And Journalism
Kärlek Och Journalistik

Sweden 1916 60 mins bw
Svenska Bio

d **Mauritz Stiller**
sc **Harriet Bloch**
ph **Gustaf Boge**
m **Silent**

Richard Lund, Karin Molander, Jenny Tschernichin-Larsson, Stina Berg, Göran Cederberg

In search of a news story, young journalist Hertha (Molander) secures the post of maid in the household of Erik Bloome (Lund), a leading Antarctic explorer. She is unmasked and dismissed, but Bloome realizes he has fallen in love and sets out to find her... The picture is effectively stolen by the delightful Molander as the prototype of the intelligent, resourceful and emancipated 'modern' heroine of the day. This entertaining comedy was the first of many which Stiller directed in the late 'teens, and which clearly anticipate the work of Lubitsch in the 1920s. To those who identify the Swedish cinema (particularly Stiller's work) with more serious dramatic efforts, they come as a breath of fresh air.

Love And The Frenchwoman
La Française Et L'Amour

France 1960 135 mins bw
Metzger & Woog/Paris Elysée Film

d **1) Henri Decoin 2) Jean Delannoy 3) Michel Boisrond 4) René Clair 5) Henri Verneuil 6) Christian-Jaque 7) Jean-Paul Le Chanois**
sc **1) Felicien Marceau 2) Louise De Vilmorin, Jacques Robert 3) Annette Wademant 4) René Clair 5) France Roche, Michel Audiard 6) Charles Spaak 7) Jean-Paul Le Chanois**
ph **Robert Lefèbvre**
m **1) Joseph Kosma 2) Paul Misraki 3) Jean Constantin 4) Jacques Metehen 5) Norbert Glanzberg 6) Henri Crolla 7) Georges Delerue**

1) Martine Lambert, Pierre-Jean Vaillard, Jacqueline Porel 2) Annie Sinigalia, Roger Pierre, Sophie Desmarets, Pierre Mondy

3) Valérie Lagrange, Pierre Michael, Paul Bonifas, Nicole Chollet 4) Marie-José Nat, Claude Rich, Yves Robert 5) Dany Robin, Paul Meurisse, Jean-Paul Belmondo 6) Annie Girardot, François Périer, Jean Poiret, Michel Serrault 7) Robert Lamoureux, Martine Carol, Sylvia Montfort, Simone Renant

An anthology, taking a supposedly representative view of French women in relation to love at various stages of life, under the headings: 'Childhood', 'Adolescence', 'Virginity', 'Marriage', 'Adultery', 'Divorce', and 'A Woman Alone'. Inevitably light-weight, given the brevity of each episode, but the little stories are well written, directed and acted and the film has a lot of charm. Clair's episode, about a couple who are jolted by their first arguments *en route* to their honeymoon destination, is the most completely accomplished, but some might prefer the now engagingly old-fashioned 'Virginity' in which a young couple, forced to postpone their wedding, grapple with the problem of celibacy.

Love At Twenty

L'Amour À Vingt Ans

France/Italy/Japan/W. Germany/Poland 1962 123 mins bw
Ulysse-Unitec (Paris)/Cinesecolo (Rome)/Toho-Towa (Tokyo)/Beta Film (Munich)/Zespol Kamera (Warsaw)

d **1) François Truffaut 2) Renzo Rossellini 3) Shintaro Ishihara 4) Marcel Ophüls 5) Andrzej Wajda**
sc **1) François Truffaut 2) Renzo Rossellini 3) Shintaro Ishihara 4) Marcel Ophüls 5) Jerzy Stefan Stawinski**
ph **1) Raoul Coutard 2) Mario Montuori 3) Shigeo Hayashida 4) Wolfgang Wirth 5) Jerzy Lipman**
m **Georges Delerue, Tohru Takemitsu, Jerzy Matuszkiewicz**

1) Jean-Pierre Léaud, Marie-France Pisier 2) Eleanora Rossi Drago, Cristina Gajoni, Geronimo Meynier 3) Koji Furuhata, Nami Tamura 4) Christian Doermer, Barbara Frey 5) Barbara Lass, Zbigniew Cybulski, Wladyslaw Kowalski

1) Antoine Doinel falls for a music student, but spends an evening with her parents while she's out on a date. 2) The mistress of a young man warns off the innocent girl he thinks he loves. 3) A young factory worker murders a beautiful student. 4) A photographer falls in love with a woman after she has had his child. 5) Young people taunt a worker who lived through World War II. Three successes out of five is not bad for a sketch film—Truffaut's delightful vignette, Ishihara's perverted but powerful tale and Wajda's painful episode—all linked by Cartier-Bresson photographs.

A Love Bewitched

aka Love The Magician

El Amor Brujo

Spain 1985 98 mins col
Emiliano Piedra Prod.

d **Carlos Saura**
sc **Carlos Saura, Antonio Gades**
ph **Teo Escamilla**
m **Manuel De Falla**

Antonio Gades, Cristina Hoyos, Laura Del Sol, Juan Antonio Jimenez, Emma Penella

Two gipsy children, pledged in marriage by their fathers, grow up to fall in love elsewhere with tragic consequences. The culmination of the Saura-Gades Spanish dance trilogy (the others were *Blood Wedding*, 1981 and *Carmen*, 1983) is set in the splendidly stylized decor (by Gerardo Vera) of a studio with props representing a shanty town. Although the dancing is as passionate as ever, only enthusiasts of the genre will find it other than monotonous.

Love Doll see Life Size

Love Eternal

(US: The Eternal Return)

L'Eternel Retour

France 1943 111 mins bw
André Paulvé

d **Jean Delannoy**
sc **Jean Cocteau**
ph **Roger Hubert**
m **Georges Auric**

Jean Marais, Madeleine Sologne, Jean Murat, Yvonne De Bray, Piéral, Roland Toutain

Patrice (Marais) brings Nathalie (Sologne) to the château of his recently widowed friend Mark (Murat) in the hope they will marry.

However, Patrice and Nathalie fall hopelessly in love as a result of a love potion issued to them by Achille (Piéral), a vicious dwarf. They eventually find their apotheosis in death. Cocteau's updating of the Tristan and Iseult legend works on many levels and fails on others. Certainly, the presence of Cocteau, who was in constant attendance during the filming, is strongly felt in the dialogue and in the playing of the members of his stock company. But there is something a trifle ludicrous about the *liebestod* in the context of 'modern youth' in ski jerseys, apparel which became fashionable because of the film's huge success in France. Made during the Occupation, its Aryan lovers (Marais and Sologne lacking sexiness) were extremely pleasing to the Occupiers.

Love Game, The see Playing At Love

Love Hate see Albatross, The

A Love In Germany

Eine Liebe In Deutschland

W. Germany 1983 132 mins col
CCC/Filmkunst/Gaumont/TF1/Stand'art

d **Andrzej Wajda**
sc **Andrzej Wajda, Boleslaw Michalek, Agnieszka Holland**
ph **Igor Luther**
m **Michel Legrand**
Hanna Schygulla, Marie-Christine Barrault, Armin Müller-Stahl, Piotr Lysak, Daniel Olbrychski

In a small German town during World War II, a married woman shopkeeper (Schygulla) breaks Nazi law by having an affair with a young Polish POW (Lysak). She is sent to a work camp and he is executed. Wajda's second film outside Poland, like *Danton* of the same year, uses the past to make a forced comparison with his homeland today. Here, the shifts from past to present only detract and distance us from the interesting drama based on a true incident as documented in Rolf Hochhuth's bestseller.

Love In Question

L'Amour En Question

France 1978 100 mins col
Paris-Cannes-Alpes Cinema

d **André Cayatte**
sc **André Cayatte, Jean Laborde**
ph **Jean Badal**
m **Olivier Dassault**
Annie Girardot, Bibi Andersson, Michel Galabru, Michel Auclair

The Swedish wife (Andersson) of an elderly French architect is accused of plotting his murder with the aid of her English lover. Another of Cayatte's flat, didactic films dealing with aspects of the law, it throws up a few interesting sidelights on the contrast between the French and British legal systems. The casebook characters lack depth, though Annie Girardot does her best as an investigating judge.

Love In The Afternoon

(US: Chloë In The Afternoon)

L'Amour L'Après-Midi

France 1972 97 mins col
Films Du Losange

d **Eric Rohmer**
sc **Eric Rohmer**
ph **Nestor Almendros**
m **Arié Dzierlatka**
Bernard Verley, Zouzou, Françoise Verley, Daniel Ceccaldi, Malvina Penne, Babette Ferrier

Frédéric (Bernard Verley), a fairly young business executive, happily married to Hélène (Françoise Verley), meets up with Chloë (Zouzou), a friend from the past. They begin to see each other during his afternoon lunch breaks, but when Chloë offers herself to him, he returns to his wife. The last of Rohmer's Six Moral Tales is the first to present a married man with the choice between love and sex. The trouble is that, whereas the preceding films dealt with articulate, attractive, and interesting people, Frédéric is dull and unadmirable, representing rather unappealing *bourgeois* values which the director seems to uphold. (It was after seeing the Verleys' wedding photographs that Rohmer decided they should play a married couple in the film.)

Love In The City

Amore In Città

Italy 1953 110 mins bw
Faro

d **Dino Risi, Michelangelo Antonioni, Federico Fellini, Francesco Maselli, Cesare Zavattini, Alberto Lattuada, Carlo Lizzani**
sc **Aldo Buzzi, Luigi Malerba, Luigi Chiarini, Tullio Pinelli, Vittorio Vettroni**
ph **Gianni Di Venanzo**
m **Mario Nascimbene**
Antonio Cifariello, Livia Venturini, and non-professionals from the Centro Sperimentale Di Cinematografia, Rome

Six true episodes taken from newspaper reports were filmed in the locales where the events took place with the people involved in them. Screenwriter Zavattini, one of the major forces in the Neo-Realist movement, here as producer, tried to make an omnibus film that fulfilled his notions of objective reportage. It ends up being neither fish nor fowl. The only meat comes from Fellini, who subverted the whole venture by making an obviously fictional episode about a reporter at a matrimonial agency claiming to be a doctor representing a werewolf who thinks that marriage might cure him. Antonioni contributes a series of bleak interviews with young girls who survived suicide attempts, Zavattini and Maselli concentrate on a Sicilian girl seduced and abandoned in Rome, while Risi and Lattuada's subjects strain to be amusing. The Lizzani piece was cut from the print shown outside Italy because the authorities objected to its portrayal of prostitution.

Love Is Love

Liebe Ist Liebe

Germany 1932 88 mins bw
UFA

d **Paul Martin**
sc **Robert Gilbert, Robert Liebmann, Max Kolpe**
ph **Günther Rittau, Otto Baecker**
m **Werner R. Heymann**
Kaethe Von Nagy, Julius Falkenstein, Hans Albers, Frieda Richard, Hans Brausewetter

A young man quits his job after a big win on the horses, proceeds to lose both the money and his girl, and gets both back after a series of misunderstandings. A light-weight romantic comedy with the thinnest of plots, but boasting interesting Berlin locations, a charming and pretty leading lady in Von Nagy, and a dose of suitably pleasing waltz music.

Love Is My Profession

En Cas De Malheur

France 1958 120 mins bw
Iéna/UCIL/Incom

d **Claude Autant-Lara**
sc **Jean Aurenche, Pierre Bost**
ph **Jacques Natteau**
m **René Cloërec**
Jean Gabin, Edwige Feuillère, Brigitte Bardot, Franco Interlenghi, Nicole Berger

A wealthy middle-aged lawyer (Gabin) is smitten with a young client (Bardot) whom he is defending on a charge of theft. She steals him away from his long-suffering wife (Feuillère). The racy English title disguises a competent, well-acted melodrama, based on a Georges Simenon novel. It is fun to see the veteran Gabin being vamped by sex kitten BB. Although she has an obligatory nude scene, the film also gives her a chance to show some acting ability.

The Love Makers

La Viaccia

Italy 1961 106 mins bw
Titanus/Galatea/Arco(Rome)/S.G.C(Paris)

d **Mauro Bolognini**
sc **Vasco Pratolini, Pasquale Festa Campanile, Massimo Franciosa**
ph **Leonida Barboni**
m **Piero Piccioni, Debussy**
Jean-Paul Belmondo, Claudia Cardinale, Pietro Germi, Romolo Valli, Gabriella Pallotta, Paul Frankeur

When Ferdinando (Frankeur) takes control of the family farm, 'La Viaccia', he offers his nephew Amerigo (Belmondo) a job in his wine business. The young man takes up his position, but falls passionately in love with the première whore (Cardinale) in a Florentine brothel, thus ruining his prospects and his life. There are several intricacies to the plot, of course, but none of them matters over much. What impresses is the background against which this semi-dynastic melodrama is played—Florence in the 1880s filmed by Bolognini, one of the masters of visual beauty, atmosphere and period detail, all of which he evokes without any recourse to obvious glamour. Belmondo and Cardinale are good, but only as far as a slightly undernourished script allows.

Love Maker, The see Calle Mayor

Love Match see Partie De Plaisir, Une

The Love Of Jeanne Ney

aka Lusts Of The Flesh

Die Liebe Der Jeanne Ney

Germany 1927 120 mins bw
UFA

d **G.W. Pabst**
sc **Ladislas Vajda, Rudolf Leonhardt, Ilya Ehrenberg**
ph **Fritz Arno Wagner, Walter Robert Lach**
m **Silent**
Edith Jehanne, Uno Henning, Fritz Rasp, Brigitte Helm

Jeanne Ney (Jehanne) falls in love with the man (Henning) who killed her father in the Crimea during the Russian Revolution. The couple move to Paris, but are pursued by a sadistic political opportunist (Rasp) who schemes against them. Intended by UFA as a Hollywood-type romance set in rapidly changing locales, it was lighter and more naturalistically conceived than Pabst's other films of the period. Although the plot (from Ehrenberg's novel) is rather complicated, it is full of inventive sequences such as the officers' orgy reflected in a high mirror, and the shot of a bride weeping alone after a wedding, espied by lovers from a hotel bedroom.

The Love Of Sumako The Actress

Joyu Sumako No Koi

Japan 1947 96 mins bw
Shochiku

d **Kenji Mizoguchi**
sc **Hideo Nagata**
ph **Shigeto Miki**
m **Hisato Osawa**
Kinuyo Tanaka, So Yamamura, Eijiro Tono, Kikue Mori, Chiyeko Higashiyama

The noted stage director Hogetsu Shimamura (Yamamura) puts on the first Japanese production of Ibsen's *A Doll's House* with Sumako (Tanaka), a new young actress, with whom he falls in love. He leaves his wife and daughter to tour with her, but both are determined to dedicate their lives to their art. This true and fascinating account of the rise of Western theatre in Japan and of one of the country's first actresses, is also a rich melodrama with a mirror image of life and the stage. It was the third of 10 films the tender tragedienne Tanaka made for Mizoguchi.

Love On The Ground

L'Amour Par Terre

France 1984 125 mins col
La Cecilia

d **Jacques Rivette**
sc **Jacques Rivette, Pascal Bonitzer, Marilu Parolini, Suzanne Schiffman**
ph **William Lubtchansky**
Jane Birkin, Geraldine Chaplin, Jean-Pierre Kalfon, László Szabó, André Dussollier, Facundo Bo

Two foreign actresses (Chaplin and Birkin) in Paris are requested by a rich and enigmatic playwright (Kalfon) to appear in a special play he has written for a single performance at his château. When a director tries to return after a decade to the territory of his most popular film, watch out! This time, instead of *Céline And Julie Go Boating*, Rivette provides Charlotte And Emily (the Brontë names are typical of the archness of the exercise) Go Boring. Yet there is some intellectual pleasure to be had from the game-playing, the decor and performances. Though most critics found it soporific, there were a few who thought it superior to the earlier film.

Love On The Run

L'Amour En Fuite

France 1979 95 mins col

Les Films Du Carrosse

d **François Truffaut**
sc **François Truffaut, Marie-France Pisier, Jean Aurel, Suzanne Schiffman**
ph **Nestor Almendros**
m **Georges Delerue**
Jean-Pierre Léaud, Claude Jade, Marie-France Pisier, Rosy Varte, Dorothée

Antoine Doinel (Léaud), separated from his wife (Jade) and young son, is involved with Sabine (Dorothée), until he meets Colette (Pisier, who also played Colette in *Love At Twenty*), a childhood sweetheart now a lawyer. Encouraged by her, he decides to write a novel. This is the last of the five Truffaut films following the adventures of his alter-ego Antoine Doinel, alias Léaud, begun with *The Four Hundred Blows* almost 20 years previously. Although as lightweight as the others, it cannot hide the pain at the loss of youthful spontaneity and the difficulties of obtaining durable love. The film is really a look back in affection at the previous episodes, with some footage from them. When Truffaut died, Léaud suffered a breakdown and has never been the same again.

Lover Boy
L'Amant De Poche

France 1977 94 mins col
Progefi/S.F.P./Gaumont

d **Bernard Queysanne**
sc **Bernard Queysanne, Pierre Pelégri**
ph **Alain Levent**
m **Laurent Petitgirard**
Mimsy Farmer, Pascal Sellier, Stéphane Jobert, Bernard Fresson, Andréa Ferréol

Sixteen-year-old Julien (Sellier) is seduced by an American woman (Farmer) who buys him evening clothes and takes him to Tunisia for a weekend. After a last night together, she sends a message—via his father—that she loves him, and disappears. She is, in fact, a high-class whore, which leads to several plot complications. A light-hearted romp, verging on sexploitation, from the director of the much superior *Un Homme Qui Dort*.

The Lovers
Les Amants

France 1958 88 mins bw
Nouvelle Editions

d **Louis Malle**
sc **Louis Malle, Louise De Vilmorin**
ph **Henri Decaë**
m **Brahms**
Jeanne Moreau, Jean-Marc Bory, Alain Cuny, Judith Magre

A sensuous but bored provincial wife (Moreau), finds sexual gratification, a deeper love and a more meaningful life in an adulterous relationship with a young man (Bory), a house guest of her husband (Cuny). This chic, lyrical, erotic satire, which Truffaut called 'the first night of love in the cinema,' presumably because of its semi-nude love scenes to Brahms, caused a scandal in its day, made an international star of Moreau, and much money for the producers.

Special Jury Prize (Louis Malle) Venice 1958

Lovers And Thieves
Assassins Et Voleurs

France 1956 85 mins bw
CLM/SNEG

d **Sacha Guitry**
sc **Sacha Guitry**
ph **Paul Cotteret**
m **Jean Françaix**
Jean Poiret, Michel Serrault, Magali Noël, Clément Duhour

A middle-aged man about to commit suicide tells a burglar of how he shot the husband of his mistress and slipped the gun into the pocket of the very same burglar. Guitry, aged 72 and approaching death (he died a year later), had clearly run out of steam in this rather static, cynical boulevard comedy, but there were still some piquant lines and situations, and Poiret and Serrault always make an amusing team.

Lovers Like Us see Savage, The

Lovers' Net see Lovers Of Lisbon, The

The Lovers Of Lisbon
(US: Lovers' Net aka Port Of Shame)
Les Amants Du Tage

France 1954 123 mins bw
Enterprise Générale/Hoch/Fides

d **Henri Verneuil**
sc **Marcel Rivet, Jacques Companeez**
ph **Roger Hubert**
m **Lucien Legrand**
Daniel Gélin, Françoise Arnoul, Marcel Dalio, Trevor Howard, Amalia Rodrigues

Pierre (Gélin) kills his wife for infidelity. Acquitted, but distrustful of women, he settles in Lisbon and falls in love with Kathleen (Arnoul), the wealthy widow of an Englishman whose death she caused and which is under investigation by an English policeman (Howard). Romance is hardly a happy business in this lengthy film, which is a mixed bag of realism and pretension in which the actors don't seem entirely at ease.

Lovers Of Montparnasse, The see Montparnasse 19

The Lovers Of Teruel

Les Amants De Teruel

France 1962 90 mins col
Monarch/CD

d **Raymond Rouleau**
sc **Raymond Rouleau, René-Louis Laforgue**
ph **Claude Renoir**
m **Mikis Theodorakis, Henri Sauguet**
Ludmilla Tcherina, Milko Sparemblek, Milenko Banovitch, Antoine Marin

A gypsy dancer (Tcherina) stars in a ballet about a woman whose lover goes away for three years to prove his worth. When he fails to return she reluctantly marries, whereupon her lover reappears and kills himself. She follows suit. What lends the story interest is that the tragic heroine's life begins to mirror the Spanish legend she interprets. An attractive film, enhanced by the beauty and balletic gifts of Tcherina.

The Lovers Of Verona

Les Amants De Verone

France 1948 110 mins bw
CICC

d **André Cayatte**
sc **André Cayatte, Jacques Prévert**
ph **Henri Alekan**
m **Joseph Kosma**
Pierre Brasseur, Serge Reggiani, Anouk Aimée, Marcel Dalio, Martine Carol

Two young people (Reggiani and Aimée) understudying the roles of Romeo and Juliet in a film being shot in Italy, find their love, like that of the 'star-crossed lovers', blighted by their families. Although this romance of post-war gloom really needed Marcel Carné to bring all the nuances of Prévert's script to life, Cayatte, on the eve of his more didactic period, does a creditable job. It was Prévert who had the idea of writing the part of the modern-day Juliet for 16-year-old Anouk Aimée. Her glowing beauty and tender performance ensured that her first starring role was not her last.

Lovers On A Tightrope

La Corde Raide

France 1960 90 mins bw
Panda Film

d **Jean-Charles Dudrumet**
sc **Jean-Charles Dudrumet, Roland Laudenbach**
ph **Pierre Gueguen**
m **Maurice Jarre**
François Périer, Annie Girardot, Gérard Buhr

The bored wife (Girardot) of a wealthy businessman (Périer) has an affair with a motor mechanic who is after her money. He attempts to dispose of her husband by tampering with the latter's car, but the husband's brother is mistakenly killed instead. Dudrumet's first film is a humdrum effort, lacking both tension and credibility, despite good lead casting.

A Lover's Return

Un Revenant

France 1946 90 mins bw
C.F.C.C.

d **Christian-Jaque**
sc **Henri Jeanson, Louis Chavance, Christian-Jaque**
ph **Louis Page**
m **Arthur Honegger**
Louis Jouvet, Gaby Morlay, François Périer, Ludmilla Tcherina, Marguerite Moreno

A successful ballet impresario (Jouvet), returns to the provinces to exhume a love affair that went wrong. A basically static and rambling exercise in nostalgia offers some wry Gallic reflection on the nature of love, a characteristically polished performance from the leading man, and some lively—albeit brief—distraction provided by the lovely ballet dancer, Tcherina.

Love's Crucible

Vem Dömer?

Sweden 1921 88 mins bw
Svensk Filmindustri

d **Victor Sjöström**
sc **Hjalmar Bergman, Victor Sjöström**
ph **J. Julius Jaenzon**
m **Silent**
Jenny Hasselqvist, Ivan Hedkvist, Tore Svennberg, Gösta Ekman, Knut Lindroth

In Renaissance Florence, Ursula (Hasselqvist) is in love with Bertram (Ekman), but is married against her will to the elderly sculptor Anton (Hedkvist). When her husband dies, Ursula is accused of murder from which only an ordeal by fire can exonerate her. This large production, aiming for an international market with a subject away from a Scandinavian setting and themes, was a commercial flop. Now it can be seen as one of Sjöström's neglected masterpieces, full of bravura sequences and images derived from the great Italian painters of the period. Most famous is the final scene using superimpositions, rhythmic disolves and a tracking shot dramatically to represent Ursula at the stake.

Love 65

Kärlek 65

Sweden 1965 95 mins bw
Europa Film

d **Bo Widerberg**
sc **Bo Widerberg**
ph **Jan Lindeström**
m **Bill Evans, Vivaldi**
Keve Hjelm, Anne-Marie Gyllenspetz, Evabritt Strandberg, Ben Carruthers, Thommy Berggren

Keve (Hjelm), an established film director, is going through a difficult time in his marriage to Ann-Mari (Gyllenspetz), and is having problems with his leading man Thommy Berggren (playing himself). He takes up with Evabritt (Strandberg), the wife of a former student, but he can only find peace in flying kites. The reaction of most critics to this bleak, self-indulgent autobiography was to tell the director to 'go fly a kite'. Fragmented and fumbling, it has a morose, unsympathetic figure (a self-portrait?) at its centre. Some splendidly romantic images, and an interesting glimpse into the director's fantasies (a variation on Fellini's *8½*) are among the few things going for it.

Loves Of A Blonde see Blonde In Love, A

Loves Of Ariane

Ariane

Germany 1931 78 mins bw
Nero

d **Paul Czinner**
sc **Paul Czinner, Carl Mayer**
ph **Adolf Schlasy, Adolf Jansen**
m **Mozart, Richard Strauss**
Elisabeth Bergner, Rudolf Forster, Annemarie Steinsieck, Hertha Guthmar

When Ariane (Bergner), an innocent Russian girl studying in Berlin, falls for a man-of-the-world (Forster), she pretends to be a coquette because he dislikes inexperienced women. Billy Wilder remade this charming little sophisticated comedy as *Love In The Afternoon* with Audrey Hepburn and Gary Cooper in 1957, not one of his best. On the other hand, Czinner's film is above his own average, with his future wife, Bergner, in her first talkie, this time only adding half a spoon of sugar to her performance.

Loves Of Casanova

Aventures De Casanova

France 1947 101 mins bw
Sirius

d **Jean Boyer**
sc **Marc G. Sauvajon**
ph **Charles Suin**
m **René Sylvester**
Georges Guetary, Hélène Dassonville, Noelle Norman, Jacqueline Gauthier, Claudette Falco

Casanova (Guetary) journeys from Venice to Paris to seek his fortune. *En route*, and after his arrival, he engages in a succession of romantic affairs with various attractive women. Yet another replay of the Casanova legend, this time in the form of a musical. The boyish, engaging cabaret star essaying the great lover is too wholesome for the role by far and, aside from some picturesque duelling and horse-riding and frequent bursts of song, the movie is innocuous, insipid and forgettable.

Loves Of Pharaoh, The see Wife Of Pharaoh, The

Love Story see Douce

Love The Magician see Love Bewitched, A

The Love Trap
Un Couple
France 1960 84 mins bw
Balzac Films/La Société Discifilm

d **Jean-Pierre Mocky**
sc **Raymond Queneau, Jean-Pierre Mocky**
ph **Eugen Schüfftan**
m **Alain Romans**
Juliet Mayniel, Jean Kosta, Francis Blanche, Véronique Nordey, Christian Duvaleix

Pierre and Anne (Kosta and Mayniel) have been happily married for three years when they decide that their relationship has palled and they must part. Pierre, in any event attracted to his fellow employee Véronique (Nordey), spends the night at a hotel, but the next day he and Anne meet at a party. A reconciliation takes place but doesn't last, as each is overcome by fresh doubts. In his second film as director, actor Mocky deals frankly, sympathetically and sincerely with a realistic problem. Unfortunately, in spite of these promising ingredients and convincing performances from the leads, the director loses his grip and allows the piece to get out of hand. The supporting characters are unattractive stereotypes, and the external apparatus of his situations—the bizarre toy factory where Pierre works, for example—is crude and unhelpful. This lack of discipline would come to characterize Mocky's subsequent work.

Loving Couples
Älskande Pär
Sweden 1964 118 mins bw
Sandrew

d **Mai Zetterling**
sc **Mai Zetterling, David Hughes**
ph **Sven Nykvist**
m **Roger Wallis**
Harriet Andersson, Gunnel Lindblom, Anita Björk, Gunnar Björnstrand, Eva Dahlbeck, Gio Petre

In the early 1900s, three contrasting expectant mothers (Andersson, Lindblom, Petre) think over their past relationships with men and how they came to be pregnant. Mai Zetterling suddenly emerged from being an ingenue in a number of insipid British films of the 1950s into a far from insipid director with this ironically titled social comedy-drama, hugely influenced by Ingmar Bergman. In fact, the film's main strength is in the excellent acting and camerawork from members of the Bergman stable. Co-adapted with her then husband, a British novelist, from the *roman fleuve* by Agnes Von Krusentjerna, the film suffers somewhat from over-elaboration and a self-conscious desire to shock.

Loving In The Rain
Un Amour De Pluie
France 1974 90 mins col
Lira Films/Claudia Cinematografica/Terra Film

d **Jean-Claude Brialy**
sc **Jean-Claude Brialy, Jean-Claude Carrière**
ph **Andreas Winding**
m **Francis Lai**
Romy Schneider, Nino Castelnuovo, Bénédicte Boucher, Suzanne Flon, Alain David

A still young and glamorous woman (Schneider) takes a holiday with her 15-year-old daughter. Two romantic episodes ensue as mother has an affair with a mysterious Italian (Castelnuovo), and daughter her first adolescent flirtation with a youth, before they return home to their mundane existences. Competent, but superficial and forgettable, with Brialy—although himself a polished and experienced actor—missing the opportunity to draw real feeling from his protagonists.

The Lower Depths
Les Bas Fonds

France 1936 92 mins bw
Albatros

d **Jean Renoir**
sc **Jean Renoir, Charles Spaak**
ph **Jean Bachelet**
m **Jean Wiener**
Jean Gabin, Louis Jouvet, Vladimir Sokoloff, Jany Holt, Robert Le Vigan, Suzy Prim

A ruined Baron (Jouvet) befriends a thief (Gabin) and goes to live with him and other assorted losers in a doss house. 'I was not trying to make a Russian film. I wanted to make a human drama based on the play by Gorky,' stated Renoir about his very French, very free adaptation of a classic play. In fact, it differed so much from the original that the director sought and gained Gorky's approval before embarking on it. Less profound in tone, it still has two splendid performances from Gabin and Jouvet, the latter telling a tale while a snail climbs up his finger.

The Lower Depths
Donzoko

Japan 1957 124 mins bw
Toho

d **Akira Kurosawa**
sc **Akira Kurosawa, Hideo Oguni**
ph **Kazuo Yamasaki**
m **Masaru Sato**
Toshiro Mifune, Isuzu Yamada, Kyoko Kagawa, Bokuzen Hidari

A pedlar (Mifune) wanted by the police goes to live in a hovel filled with human derelicts. Among these is an aging woman who loves a thief who loves a young girl. Kurosawa's version of Gorky's play is as Japanese as Renoir's was French, demonstrating the universality of the Russian original. Although most of the action takes place in one large room—effectively filmed with multiple cameras (witness the 180 degree camera reversals)— the visual fluidity and the extraordinary characterizations keep the picture alive.

Lowland
Tiefland

W. Germany 1954 98 mins bw
Leni Riefenstahl

d **Leni Riefenstahl**
sc **Leni Riefenstahl**
ph **Albert Benitz**
m **Eugen D'Albert, Herbert Windt**
Leni Riefenstahl, Franz Eichberger, Bernhard Minetti, Aribert Wäscher, Maria Kappenhöfer

Don Sebastian (Minetti), an impoverished Spanish nobleman, marries the wealthy mayor's daughter (Kappenhöfer), but will not give up his mistress Marta (Riefenstahl), a flamenco dancer. She marries Pedro (Eichberger), a shepherd, but when Sebastian tries to take her back, Pedro kills him. Riefenstahl started filming this melodrama, based on D'Albert's *verismo* opera, in 1935, but was constantly interrupted during the war. The French confiscated the unfinished film after the war, but Riefenstahl regained, completed, edited and released it in 1954. Despite the picture's chequered history, it makes (except for the ending) an aesthetic whole. The pictorial beauty (1930s black-and-white textures) and spectacular mountain set-pieces compensate for some of the deficiencies of plot and performance. Rumours still abound that gypsies from the concentration camps were used as extras, a charge of which the director was officially cleared in 1949.

The Loyal 47 Ronin
Genroku Chushingura

Japan 1941-1942 222 mins bw
Koa (Part I), Shochiku (Part II)

d **Kenji Mizoguchi**
sc **Kenichiro Hara, Yoshitaka Yoda**
ph **Kohei Sugiyama**
m **Shiro Fukai**
Chojuro Kawarazaki, Yoshizaburo Arashi, Mantoyo Mimasu, Kenemon Nakamura

Following the forced harikari of Lord Asano, 47 of his ronin (disbanded samurai) avenge his death by trapping the court ruler who caused it. They are then condemned to death, but allowed the honour of taking their own lives. One of the most famous incidents in early 18th-century Japanese history became a success of the Kabuki theatre and the basis for some 20 screen adaptations, notably Inagaki's wide-screen and colour version of 1962, and Mizoguchi's, both in two parts. It started off being made under a new independent company, but Mizoguchi overshot the budget and Shochiku took over. One does not usually turn to Mizoguchi for such epic tales, but he avoids the excesses of the genre and creates a noble ritualistic tragedy.

Luch Smerti see Death Ray, The

Lucia

Cuba 1969 155 mins bw
Cuban Institute of Art and Cinema

d **Humberto Solas**
sc **Humberto Solas, Julio Garcia Espinosa, Nelson Rodriguez**
ph **Jorge Herrera**
m **Leo Brouwer**
Raquel Revuelta, Eslinda Nuñez, Adela Legra, Adolfo Liaurado, Ramon Brito

Three episodes about three women called Lucia: 1) in 1895, the aristocratic Lucia (Revuelta) kills the married man who abandoned her; 2) in 1932, the middle-class divorced mother Lucia (Nuñez) takes up with a young revolutionary; 3) in 1969, the agricultural worker Lucia (Legra) meets a teacher who will make her literate, but her truck-driver husband objects. One of Cuba's most ambitious films since the Revolution, it manages admirably to tell three stories in different styles while making sharp points about women's changing role in a 'macho' society.

Luci Del Varieta' see Lights Of Variety

Ludwig

Italy/France/W. Germany 1972
186 mins col
Mega/Cinetel/Dieter Gessler/Divina

d **Luchino Visconti**
sc **Luchino Visconti, Enrico Medioli**
ph **Armando Nannuzzi**
m **Richard Wagner**
Helmut Berger, Romy Schneider, Trevor Howard, Silvana Mangano, Helmut Griem, Gert Fröbe

The young Ludwig (Berger) ascends the throne of Bavaria, is forced to marry, becomes obsessed with the music of Wagner (Howard), indulges in homosexual orgies, goes mad, and is drowned. The poorest of Visconti's love-hate epics about a decaying European society is an extremely slow, long, rambling, academic and superficial soap opera. But the usually ham Berger is good and looks the part, and the locations, castles, costumes and manners are depicted in loving detail.

Ludwig: Requiem For A Virgin King

Ludwig II: Requiem Fur Einen Jungfräulichen König

W. Germany 1972 139 mins col
TMS Film

d **Hans Jürgen Syberberg**
sc **Hans Jürgen Syberberg**
ph **Dietrich Lohmann**
m **Richard Wagner, Franz Lehar, Kurt Weill**
Harry Baer, Balthasar Thomas, Peter Kern, Peter Moland, Günter Kaufmann

The inner and outer life, real and imagined, of the mad castle-building King of Bavaria (Baer), told in 28 chapters, or *tableaux-vivants*. Cheaply made, and using a blend of theatrical techniques such as backdrops and back projections, this collage of German history, culture and psychology—at different moments puerile, fatuous, stimulating, amusing and over-extended—says far more about Ludwig than Visconti's plodding film on the same subject. Among the *dramatis personae* are a dwarf Wagner, Hitler dancing a tango with Röhm, and Bismarck on a bicycle.

Ludwig II: Requiem Fur Einen Jungfräulichen König see Ludwig: Requiem For A Virgin King

---

Lulu see Pandora's Box

Lulu The Tool see Working Class Go To Heaven, The

Lumière D'En Face, La see Light Across The Street, The

Lumière D'Été

(US: Summer Light)

France 1943 112 mins bw

Discina

d **Jean Grémillon**

sc **Jacques Prévert, Pierre Laroche**

ph **Louis Page**

m **Roland Manuel**

Madeleine Renaud, Pierre Brasseur, Madeleine Robinson, Paul Bernard, Jane Marken, Georges Marchal

An ex-dancer (Renaud) runs an isolated mountain hotel where the guests include a number of people with problems. This melancholy allegory about characters living on the edge of a figurative and literal abyss, was made under the restrictions of Vichy France. Nevertheless, Grémillon managed a personal statement and the script and performances are first rate. Madeleine Renaud is outstanding, making the third of four wartime films in a row for the director.

La Luna

Italy 1979 142 mins col

TCF/Fiction Cinematografica

d **Bernardo Bertolucci**

sc **Bernardo Bertolucci, Giuseppe Bertolucci, Clare Peploe**

ph **Vittorio Storaro**

m **Verdi**

Jill Clayburgh, Matthew Barry, Laura Betti, Renato Salvatori, Alida Valli

An internationally renowned opera singer (Clayburgh) has an almost incestuous relationship with her spoiled teenage son (Barry), who is searching for his (a) father. The film, paying homage to Verdi, threads together a series of splendid scenes (or arias and duets) on the string of an opaque, operatic and Oedipal plot which doesn't really hang together. The virtuosity, however, is undeniable.

Lunch On The Grass

(US: Picnic On The Grass)

Le Déjeuner Sur L'Herbe

France 1959 91 mins col

Compagnie Jean Renoir

d **Jean Renoir**

sc **Jean Renoir**

ph **Georges Leclerc**

m **Joseph Kosma**

Paul Meurisse, Catherine Rouvel, Fernand Sardou, Ingrid Nordine

A pompous Parisian professor (Meurisse), concerned with artificial insemination, finds himself seduced by the mysteries of the countryside and the farmer's daughter (Rouvel, her debut). At 65, Jean Renoir wished to pay his most direct homage to his painter father in this hymn to nature. Shot almost entirely at Les Collettes, the Renoir family home near Cannes, its sensuous colours and sunlit images derive from the Impressionists. But the satire is sour, the plot ponderous and the characters mere cardboard.

Lune Dans Le Caniveau, La see Moon In The Gutter, The

Lupa, La see She-Wolf, The

Lusts Of The Flesh see Love Of Jeanne Ney, The

Lyckliga Skitar see Blushing Charlie

m

M

Germany 1931 118 mins bw
Nero Film

d **Fritz Lang**
sc **Thea Von Harbou, Paul Falkenberg, Adolf Jansen, Karl Vash**
ph **Fritz Arno Wagner**
m **Karl Vollbrecht, Emil Hasler**
Peter Lorre, Otto Wernicke, Gustav Gründgens, Theodore Loos, Ellen Widmann, George John

A psychopathic child murderer on the loose in Berlin creates panic among mothers, and in the underworld whose members are hounded by the police in their search for the killer. Fritz Lang's first sound film is a masterpiece of low-keyed expressionism, in which fear permeates every brick of the dark alleys and crumbling buildings which form its background. If Lang's choice of images and his uncompromising examination of his subject were both penetrating and progressive, he had, in Peter Lorre, the ideal actor. His bulbous eyes reflecting terror and self-loathing in equal measure, Lorre made of *M* an unforgettable figure which brought him international fame, but doomed him to playing a succession of criminals in Hollywood.

Macht Der Männer Ist Die Geduld Der Frauen, Die see Power Of Men Is The Patience Of Women, The

---

Macskajaték see Cats' Play

Mad Adventures Of Rabbi Jacob, The see Adventures Of Rabbi Jacob, The

---

Madame Bovary

France 1934 117 mins bw
Nouvelle Société De Film

d **Jean Renoir**
sc **Jean Renoir**
ph **Jean Bachelet**
m **Darius Milhaud, Donizetti**
Valentine Tessier, Pierre Renoir, Fernand Fabre, Daniel Lecourtois

A romantic young woman (Tessier), soon bored with marriage to a dull country doctor, has affairs with other men, gets deeply into debt, and finally poisons herself. Renoir originally made a three-hour film of Flaubert's great 19th-century novel, but was forced to release it in a much shorter version. A further hour would have given the picture more breadth and, perhaps, depth, but the fatal miscasting of the title role would still have remained. Tessier, a close friend of the director, was too much the 'grande dame' in the part, too emotional, and not young enough. Neither the fine use of Normandy landscapes nor Pierre Renoir's well-judged performance as Dr Bovary compensate.

Madame Bovary

Germany 1937 94 mins bw
Terra Film

d **Gerhard Lamprecht**
sc **Hans Neumann, Erich Ebermayer**
ph **Karl Hasselmann**
m **Giuseppe Becce**
Pola Negri, Aribert Wäscher, Ferdinand Marian, Werner Scharf

Emma Bovary (Negri), young and beautiful, marries a dull, middle-aged doctor in a French provincial town during the 19th century. Growing bored and restless, and the victim of an over-romantic nature, she runs up debts and has a couple of affairs, most cataclysmically with Léon (Scharf), a handsome friend of her husband with whom she falls in love. Gustave Flaubert's classic novel has fallen prey to three screen versions—Renoir's in French (1934), this one, and Hollywood (1949). Curiously, the last, directed by Vincente Minnelli with Jennifer Jones, is the most successful. Lamprecht's effort is competent, although the look and flavour retain a distinctly German air, but the film is mainly interesting as an opportunity to see the legendary and flamboyant Pola Negri, abandoned by Hollywood when the talkies came and here attempting (with Hitler's approval) to remake her career in Germany. As Emma, she's okay—no more, no less.

Madame Butterfly

Italy/Japan 1955 114 mins col
Rizzoli/Toho

d **Carmine Gallone**
sc **Illica & Giacosa (libretto)**
ph **Claude Renoir**
m **Giacomo Puccini (conducted by Oliviere De Fabritiis)**
Karuo Yachigusa (Ci-Cio-San, sung by Orietta Moscucci), Nicola Filacuridi (Pinkerton, sung by Giuseppe Campora), Michiko Tanaka (Suzuki, sung by Anna Maria Canali), Ferdinando Lidonni (Sharpless), Satoshi Nakamura (Yamadori, sung by Adelio Zagonara)

Made before the fashion for opera *as* film, this is very much opera *on* film, and thus somewhat stagy and static. However, it was notable as the first attempt to bring one of the most popular, famous and accessible works of the romantic repertoire to the screen, and the Japanese-Italian collaboration is a happy one. With Japanese-designed sets (ravishingly photographed by Renoir) and Japanese actors, the film offers a sense of authenticity while, musically, it is served by an excellent cast of Italian voices under a fine conductor.

Madame De ...

(US: The Earrings Of Madame De ...)
France 1953 102 mins bw
Franco London/Indus/Rizzoli

d **Max Ophüls**
sc **Max Ophüls, Marcel Achard, Annette Wademant**
ph **Christian Matras**
m **Oscar Straus, Georges Van Parys**
Charles Boyer, Danielle Darrieux, Vittorio De Sica, Jean Debucourt, Lea Di Lea

A fickle society woman (Darrieux) sells her diamond earrings. They are acquired by her husband (Boyer) who gives them to his mistress (Di Lea) who loses them gambling. They are then bought by an Italian diplomat (De Sica) who gives them to *his* mistress—the society woman. Ophüls' penultimate film was another of his witty merry-go-round confections, where both the camera and the plot make giddy circles. Based on the novel by Louise De Vilmorin it has, like Viennese coffee, much whipped cream above the bitterness. The surface covering to the theme of the transitory nature of love consists of the elaborate period designs by Jean D'Eaubonne.

Madame Dubarry

(US: Passion)
Germany 1919 85 mins bw
Union/UFA

d **Ernst Lubitsch**
sc **Fred Orbing (pseudonym of Norbert Falk), Hans Kräly**
ph **Théodor Sparkühl**
m **Silent**
Pola Negri, Emil Jannings, Harry Liedtke, Reinhold Schünzel, Edouard Von Winterstein

The rise and fall of Jeanne (Negri), a woman of the people, who became the Countess Dubarry and mistress to King Louis XV (Jannings). The first of Lubitsch's ironical historical romances really established his own reputation and that of the German film industry abroad. The director's intentions were 'to humanize my historical characters. I treated the intimate nuances just as importantly as the mass movements and tried to blend them both together.' In this he succeeded, and with Negri and Jannings, and the lavish costumes and designs, the film was welcomed by British and American audiences as the height of European sophistication—an essence Lubitsch bottled and brought to Hollywood in 1923.

Madame Rosa

La Vie Devant Soi

France 1977 105 mins col
Lira Films

d **Moshe Mizrahi**
sc **Moshe Mizrahi**
ph **Nestor Almendros**
m **Philippe Sarde**
Simone Signoret, Claude Dauphin, Samy Ben Youb, Michal Bat Adam, Costa-Gavras

Rosa, a survivor of Auschwitz and an ex-prostitute, has run an unofficial nursery for the children of her colleagues. Now aging, ill, and tormented by failing memory, she is cared for by her sole remaining ward, Mohammed. When a doctor friend comes to persuade her that she must be moved, Mohammed carries out his promise to hide her, and she dies. Signoret, fat and herself aging, is charismatic as a big-hearted woman haunted by the ghosts of the Holocaust, and Ben Youb is enchanting as the young Arab orphan. However, Mizrahi's film, while unavoidably moving, is a heavily sentimentalized version of the racy and much tougher prize-winning novel by Emil Ajar (a pseudonym for Romain Gary) from which it was adapted, and which gave a more vibrant and truthful account of life in the Arab- Jewish *quartier* of Paris than the somewhat deodorized view here.

Best Foreign Film Oscar 1977

Mädchen In Uniform

aka Girls In Uniform

Germany 1931 110 mins bw
Deutsche Film-Gemeinschaft

d **Leontine Sagan**
sc **Christa Winsloe (based on her novel), F.D. Andam**
ph **Reimar Kuntze**
m **Hansen Milde-Meissner**
Dorothea Wieck, Hertha Thiele, Emilia Unda, Hedwig Schlichter

Manuela (Thiele), sent to boarding school, is away from home for the first time. A highly strung girl, she reacts badly to the school's aggressively authoritarian atmosphere, and finds solace only in the company of a sympathetic teacher (Wieck). The consequences of the relationship lead to the girl's attempted suicide. An all-female enterprise, this is a powerful film the Lesbian undertones of which lend it a strange, subtle eroticism. This, however, is secondary to the warning against the rigidity of austere and oppressive regimes. The very uniforms worn by the girls, and the methods by which the headmistress imposes her disciplines, prefigure the already looming Third Reich. An interesting political, as well as emotional, document.

Mädchen In Uniform

aka Children In Uniform

W. Germany 1958 91 mins col
Les Films Modernes/S.N.C./CCC/Filmkunst

d **Géza Radványi**
sc **Franz Hollering, F.D. Andam**
ph **Werner Krien**
m **Peter Sandloff**
Lilli Palmer, Romy Schneider, Thérèse Giehse, Christine Kaufmann

A remake of Leontine Sagan's 1931 classic, with Lilli Palmer as the teacher and Romy Schneider as the tormented student who falls in love with her. This version is lacking in the weapons with which to hurt politically, and the Lesbian aspect is more explicit. With its two Technicolored international beauties in the lead, it is an artfully manicured copy of its predecessor, but retains the power to move.

Mädchen Rosemarie, Das see Girl Rosemarie, The

Made In Italy

Italy 1965 102 mins col
Documento Film

d **Nanni Loy**
sc **Ettore Scola, Ruggero Maccari, Nanni Loy**
ph **Ennio Guarnieri**
m **Carlo Rustichelli**
Anna Magnani, Sylva Koscina, Jean Sorel, Virna Lisi, Alberto Sordi, Catherine Spaak, Nino Manfredi, Lea Massari, Walter Chiari, Giulio Bosetti, Rosella Falk

A group of boisterous Italian workmen is travelling to Stockholm on a plane which, *en route*, touches down at destinations throughout the length of Italy, including Rome,

Naples, Sicily, Amalfi, Venice, Florence and Turin. The format is an excuse, and a good one at that, for a series of vignettes about Italian life. Employing a large star cast, together with an army of uncredited players, Loy presents a wry, sympathetic and loving look at his land and his compatriots which embodies social criticism, particularly of the Church, and is, by turns, funny and sad. Though the film crams in too much and is sometimes off-course, it is enjoyable, with Guarnieri's contrasting urban and rural photography not the least of its pleasures.

Made In Sweden

Sweden 1969 86 mins col
AB Svensk Filmindustri

d **John Bergenstrahle**
sc **Sven Fagenberg, John Bergenstrahle**
ph **Gunnar Fischer**
m **Bengt Ernryd**
Lina Granhagen, Per Myrberg, Karl-Birger Blomdahl, Börje Ahlstedt, Ingvar Kjellson, Max Von Sydow

A committed journalist (Myrberg) who refuses to conform to the dictates of officialdom, follows up a rumour that a major Swedish financial organization is involved in gun-running on the Vietnam border. He secures the evidence to support the accusation. A promising debut by the director, who uses the relationship between his hero and girlfriend (Granhagen) to air intellectual issues, juxtaposes horrific documentary footage with telling irony, and defines the chasm between rich and poor, as well as commenting on war and corruption. Fresh insights, and good acting—the ubiquitous Von Sydow scores in a cameo as the industrialist villain—contribute to an intelligent, thought-provoking and interesting socio-political film.

Special Jury Award Berlin 1969

Made In USA

France 1966 85 col
Rome-Paris Films/Anouchka Films/Sepic

d **Jean-Luc Godard**
sc **Jean-Luc Godard**
ph **Raoul Coutard**
m **Schumann, Beethoven**
Anna Karina, Jean-Pierre Léaud, László Szabó, Yves Alfonso, Ernest Menzer

A young woman (Karina), in trying to discover the identity of her lover's killer, comes across agents of corruption and intrigue. Any attempt by the spectator to understand the plot in a conventional sense will be frustrated by Godard's elliptical style in which he continually breaks the narrative up with quotes, slogans, a song by a Japanese girl, a sound track that is often purposefully distorted and an attempt to make the audible visual with a long take of a tape-recorder. The film also makes references to the Ben Barka and Kennedy assassinations. This is Godard, in brilliant colours, continually redefining image in a spontaneous, topical, pop art manner.

Maestro I Margarita see Master And Margarita, The

Magasiskola see Falcons, The

The Magic Donkey

(US: Donkey Skin)

Peau D'Âne

France 1970 90 mins col
Mag Bodard/Marianne

d **Jacques Demy**
sc **Jacques Demy**
ph **Ghislain Cloquet**
m **Michel Legrand**
Catherine Deneuve, Jacques Perrin, Delphine Seyrig, Jean Marais, Micheline Presle

In a fairytale kingdom, the King (Marais) swore to his wife on her death bed that he would not remarry unless his new wife was as beautiful as she. There seems to be only one person who fits this description—his daughter (Deneuve). However, with the magic aid of her fairy godmother (Seyrig), the Princess finally marries the handsome prince (Perrin) of a neighbouring kingdom and they all live happily ever after. Demy's tribute to Walt Disney's *Snow White* (there is some animation), and Jean Cocteau's *Beauty And The Beast* (more than just the presence of Marais) has much charm and pleasant songs. However, its airy-fairy storytelling makes only tolerable enough kiddie fare, despite the Freudian side to Perrault's tale. Adults might enjoy Seyrig's witty Lilac Fairy most.

The Magic Flute

Trollflöjten

Sweden 1975 135 mins col
TV2

d **Ingmar Bergman**
sc **Ingmar Bergman, (libretto by Emanuel Schikeneder)**
ph **Sven Nykvist**
m **Mozart (conducted by Erik Ericson)**
Josef Köstlinger (Tamino), Irma Urrila (Pamina), Håkan Hagegård (Papageno), Ulrik Cold (Sarastro), Birgit Nordin (Queen of the Night)

Tamino and his bird-catcher friend Papageno are sent to rescue Pamina, the Queen of the Night's daughter from the clutches of Sarastro. But Sarastro is a wise priest who unites the lovers, Tamino and Pamina, after various ordeals. The darkness and gloom of Bergman's films suddenly gave way to the light and joy of Mozart's last operatic masterpiece. Shot in a studio reconstruction of the interior of the exquisite 18th-century Drottningholm Theatre, Bergman's production (sung in Swedish) is a paradigm of opera films, respecting the theatrical conventions yet making the experience cinematic. He also demystifies the enterprise by showing the singers backstage at the interval, playing chess, reading a comic and smoking. Pity, therefore, that the overture is used like a Coca-Cola commercial (faces in the audience of all ages and races), and that there are some perverse liberties taken with the text.

Magician, The see Face, The

Magnificent Tramp, The see Archimède The Tramp

Mahanagar see Big City, The

Maigret Sets A Trap

(US: Inspector Maigret)
Maigret Tend Un Piège

France 1957 120 mins bw
Intermondia/J.P. Guibert/Jolly Film

d **Jean Delannoy**
sc **Michel Audiard**
ph **Louis Page**
m **Paul Misraki**
Jean Gabin, Annie Girardot, Jean Desailly, Olivier Hussenot, Lino Ventura

Inspector Maigret (Gabin) tries to trap a killer, and discovers why a happily married, wealthy, talented man should want to bump off women at night. Gabin is perfect as Georges Simenon's secure and steady sleuth, and old-hand Delannoy expertly keeps up the pace and suspense. Although a trifle extended and not exactly living up to its opening sequence of the killer choosing his weapon from a butcher's shop, it is an enjoyable whodunnit.

Maigret Tend Un Piège see Maigret Sets A Trap

Les Mains Sales

aka Dirty Hands

France 1951 103 mins bw
Fernand Rivers/Eden Production

d **Fernand Rivers**
sc **Jacques Bost, Fernand Rivers, Jean-Paul Sartre**
ph **Jean Bachelet**
m **Paul Misraki**
Pierre Brasseur, Daniel Gélin, Claude Nollier, Monique Artur, Marcel André, Jacques Castelot

A young Communist (Gélin), fighting the Nazis in a nameless country, is despatched by his fellows to kill the boss of their faction, who is considering selling out the cause by compromise. Taking his wife (Artur) with him, he finds himself unable to do the deed, engaging, instead, in philosophical discussion, until he finds his wife in the man's arms. This is a screen adaptation of a successful and controversial play by Sartre, which originally starred Charles Boyer. Unfortunately, as a film, it is very static and too wordy by half, betraying its honorable origins while failing to hold one's interest in spite of competent actors who do their best.

Making It

(US: Going Places)

Les Valseuses

France 1974 118 mins col
CAPAC/UPF/SN

d **Bertrand Blier**
sc **Bertrand Blier, Philippe Dumarçay**
ph **Bruno Nuytten**
m **Stéphane Grappelli**
Gérard Depardieu, Miou-Miou, Patrick Dewaere, Jeanne Moreau, Jacques Chailleux, Brigitte Fossey, Isabelle Huppert, Jacques Rispal

Jean-Claude (Depardieu) and Pierrot (Dewaere) steal cars and break into houses, but largely as a prelude to abducting, seducing and otherwise exploiting women. No moral, no judgement and no retribution interferes with the unfolding of events in Blier's film, adapted from his own novel, the original title of which is French slang for 'testicles'. The purpose of this slick caper, the high point of which is the boys' encounter with Jeanne Moreau as a just-released jailbird, is not evident. By turns revolting, funny, and tedious, it cleverly utilizes Grappelli's score to counterpoint the action but, when all is said and done, it's a nasty shocker in chic dress.

Malevil

France 1981 119 mins col
NEF Diffusion/Stella Film(Munich)/ Antenne 2/Les Films Gibe/Télécip

d **Christian De Chalonge**
sc **Christian De Chalonge, Pierre Dumayet**
ph **Jean Penzer**
m **Gabriel Lared**
Michel Serrault, Jacques Dutronc, Robert Dhéry, Jean-Louis Trintignant, Jacques Villeret

Malevil is a country château, in the wine cellars of which the owner (Serrault) and a small group of companions take refuge during a nuclear attack on the village. In due course, they emerge and begin to reclaim and cultivate some land, encountering another band of survivors, led by a rabid Fascist (Trintignant). A timely and disturbing subject, in which the burnt-out devastation of a futuristic holocaust is brilliantly photographed in telling contrast to the rustic idyll that precedes it. Unfortunately, when the two groups of survivors meet, action, dialogue and plot topple over into some obvious melodramatics that reduce the the overall impact and quality of the film.

Malou

W. Germany 1980 93 mins col
Regina Ziegler

d **Jeanine Meerapfel**
sc **Jeanine Meerapfel**
ph **Michael Ballhaus**
m **Peer Raben**
Ingrid Caven, Grischa Huber, Helmut Griem, Ivan Desny, Marie Colbin, Peter Chatel

A young German schoolteacher (Huber), in the midst of spiritual crisis, attempts to come to terms with the memory of her dead mother, Malou (Caven), by travelling to Argentina where Malou had lived a tragic existence. This autobiographical journey of self-discovery has many interesting aspects, particularly the way in which the two women of different generations take different roads to reach a feminist awareness through suffering. But the director often sacrifices our sympathy by ponderously stating the obvious and striving to make the women representative rather than individual. The presence of the splendid Caven and other Fassbinder regulars in this worthy movie makes unfavourable comparison with the latter's work inevitable.

Malu Tianshi see Street Angel

Malva

USSR 1957 85 mins col
Kiev Film Studio

d **Vladimir Braun**
sc **Nikolai Kovarski**
ph **Vladimir Voitenko**
m **Igor Sciamo**
Zidra Ritenberg, Pavel Usovicenko, Anatoli Ignatiev, A. Tolbuzin, G. Yukhtin

Malva (Ritenberg), a lusty girl who lives in a small fishing village, doesn't wish to tie herself down to one man and, consequently, finds herself involved with four of them. Braun's film (he died shortly after completing it) is adapted from a story by Maxim Gorky and emerges as an extremely static conversation piece, although it takes place largely outdoors on beaches and similar locations. Thus, in spite of excellent performances, notably from the strapping and lively leading lady, and exquisite colour photography in attractive settings, it's rather dreary.

Best Actress (Zidra Ritenberg) Venice 1957

Maman Et La Putain, La see Mother And The Whore, The

Mamma Roma

Italy 1962 110 mins bw
Arco/Cineriz

d **Pier Paolo Pasolini**
sc **Pier Paolo Pasolini**
ph **Tonino Delli Colli**
m **Vivaldi**

Anna Magnani, Franco Citti, Ettore Garofolo, Silvana Corsini, Luisa Loiano

A woman, trying to escape her past as a prostitute, harbours middle- class ambitions for her teenage son. However, her former pimp threatens to tell the boy of his mother's profession unless she goes back 'on the game'. Pasolini's second film, like *Accatone* (1961), is a study of the sub- proletariat of Rome but, though it has a certain rude vigour derived from the volcanic Magnani and the location shooting, it lacks the debut picture's freshness and vitality.

Man About Town see Silence Est D'Or, Le

A Man And A Woman

Un Homme Et Une Femme

France 1966 102 mins col
Les Films 13

d **Claude Lelouch**
sc **Claude Lelouch, Pierre Uytterhoeven**
ph **Claude Lelouch**
m **Francis Lai**

Jean-Louis Trintignant, Anouk Aimée, Pierre Barouh, Valérie Lagrange, Simone Paris

A racing driver widower (Trintignant) and a script-girl widow (Aimée) fall in love while visiting their children at the seaside resort of Deauville. Should they, shouldn't they, do they, don't they make it together? An ultra-chic love story told in glossy advertising images, with a certain freewheeling charm and attractive performers, is backed by the popular 'daba-daba-da' musical theme. The 'artistic' device of using colour and sepia came about because the director ran out of funds and couldn't afford any more colour stock. The film's huge success made Lelouch's international reputation.

Best Film Cannes 1966,
Best Foreign Film Oscar 1966

A Man And A Woman: Twenty Years Later

Un Homme Et Une Femme: Vingt Ans Déjà

France 1986 120 mins col
Les Films 13/Sofica Cinergie/Sofimage

d **Claude Lelouch**
sc **Claude Lelouch, Pierre Uytterhoeven, Monique Lange, Jérôme Tonnerre**
ph **Jean-Yves Le Mener**
m **Francis Lai**

Anouk Aimée, Jean-Louis Trintignant, Richard Berry, Evelyne Bouix, Marie-Sophie Pochat

When a former script-girl-turned-producer (Aimée) and a now middle-aged racing driver (Trintignant) decide to make a film about their affair of 20 years ago, they fall in love all over again. When Lelouch made *A Man And A Woman* on a shoestring budget in the 1960s and found himself with an unexpected mega-hit on his hands, he remarked that, all things being equal, the team would make a sequel in 20 years' time. And they did—complete with Francis Lai's music, the formula as before, and its two stars as attractive as ever.

Mandabi see Money Order, The

Mandat, Le see Money Order, The

Manden I Maanen see Dark Side Of The Moon, The

Man Die Zijn Haar Kort Liet Knippen, De see Man Who Had His Hair Cut Short, The

---

Mandragola, La see Mandrake, The

The Mandrake

La Mandragola

Italy 1965 99 mins bw
Arco Film (Rome)/Lux (Paris)

d **Alberto Lattuada**
sc **Alberto Lattuada, Luigi Magni, Stefano Strucchi**
ph **Tonino Delli Colli**
m **Gino Marinuzzi Jr**
Rosanna Schiaffino, Philippe Leroy, Totò, Jean-Claude Brialy, Romolo Valli, Nilla Pizzi

Callimaco (Leroy), a rich Florentine, determines to possess Lucrezia (Schiaffino), the strikingly beautiful wife of the notary, Nicia (Valli), who is desperately seeking a cure for her barrenness. Callimaco poses as a doctor and, by a series of cunning ploys, gets himself successfully into Lucrezia's bed. With style, wit and attention to detail, Lattuada has made an entertaining filmed version of the play by Machiavelli which, while still very much of a stage work, strikes just the right note of bawdiness and cynicism.

Manèges see Wanton, The

A Man Escaped, Or The Wind Bloweth Where It Listeth

Un Condamné À Mort S'est Échappé, Ou Le Vent Souffle Où Il Vent

France 1956 102 mins bw
GAU/SNE

d **Robert Bresson**
sc **Robert Bresson**
ph **L.H. Burel**
m **Mozart**
François Leterrier, Charles Le Clainche, Roland Monot, Maurice Beerblock, Jacques Ertand

Fontaine (Leterrier) of the French Resistance, imprisoned by the Nazis, plans his escape. When condemned to death, he puts the plan into action, accompanied by a newly acquired teenage cell-mate. André Devigny, on whose account of his own experiences the story was based, acted as technical adviser, and the film reconstructed his actual cell at Montluc, the fortress which would house Klaus Barbie in the 1980s. Bresson's camera stripped the action of all but the bare essentials, allowing the viewer to become totally involved with Fontaine's painstaking and ingenious preparations. A testament to courage and faith, all the more authentic for its use of non-professional actors and the director's spare, matter-of-fact style.

Best Director Cannes 1957

The Man From Majorca

Mannen Fran Mallorca

Sweden 1984 105 mins col
Drakfilm/Svensk Filmindustri/Svenska Filminstitutet/SV2/Filmhuset KB/Crone Film Sales

d **Bo Widerberg**
sc **Bo Widerberg**
ph **Thomas Wahlberg, Gunnar Nilsson, Hans Welin**
m **Björn Jason Lindh**
Sven Wollter, Tomas Von Brömssen, Håkan Serner, Ernst Gunther, Margreth Weivers, Nina Gunke

While two plainclothes policemen keep watch on a call-girl's flat, a lone masked gunman robs a neighbouring post office. The detectives give chase, thus becoming involved in a case which grows in complexity and drags the special squad and the Minister of Justice into the web of suspicion. Widerberg, in tune with his liberal voice, points a finger at police methods and political corruption in a well-acted, well-scripted film. However, the director over-indulges in too many supposedly significant close-ups in a piece which, for all its professional excellence, is really little more than a conventional *policier*.

Manila: In The Claws Of Neon

Maynila Sa Mga Kuko Ng Liwanag

The Philippines 1975 125 mins col
Cinema Artists

d **Lino Brocka**
sc **Clodualdo Del Mundo Jr**
ph **Miguel Del Leon**
m **Max Jocson**
Rafael Roco Jr, Hilda Koronel, Tommy Abuel, Lou Salvador Jr, Jojo Abella, Joonee Gamboa

Julio (Roco Jr), a provincial fisherman, comes to Manila to look for his childhood sweetheart Ligaya (Koronel) who has disappeared. Before coming across Ligaya in sordid circumstances, Julio works under gruelling conditions on a building site and becomes an unwilling and ineffective male prostitute. Lino Brocka's film stood out among the 200 or so trashy pictures the Filipino cinema produced every year, mainly soap operas and kung fu-type adventures. While using elements of these popular films—sex, sentiment and violence—Brocka has tried to inject some social consciousness. The director wanted 'to put a mirror before the audience'. Most effective are the depictions of the urban squalour of Chinatown and the waterside slums, but they are without any political context, not surprising as it was made some years into the martial law imposed by Marcos.

Man In The Moon, The see Dark Side Of The Moon, The

Man Is Not A Bird

Čovek Nije Tica

Yugoslavia 1965 80 mins bw
Avala Film

d **Dušan Makavejev**
sc **Dušan Makavejev**
ph **Aleksandar Petković**
m **Petar Bergamo**
Milena Dravić, Janez Vrhovec, Eva Ras, Stojan Arandelović, Boris Dvornik, Roko

In a bleak industrial town in Slovenia, a visiting engineer (Vrhovec) has an affair with a young and carefree hairdresser (Dravić), which does not prevent her making love to a truckdriver (Dvornik) she had known previously. With its guiltless eroticism, vertiginous images from hand-held cameras, and satiric attitude to authority, Makavejev's first feature came as a revelation from Eastern Europe. Its light side is balanced by its portrayal of the noisy, dirty, dehumanizing work done by industrial workers. The provocative ending cross-cuts between a performance of Beethoven's Ninth Symphony as a special event for local dignitaries at a factory, and the lovemaking of the heroine, finding her own 'Ode To Joy'.

Mani Sulla Citta, Le see Hands Over The City

Manji see Passion

A Man Like Eva

Ein Mann Wie Eva

W. Germany 1983 89 mins col
Schier-Straub/Trio/Impuls/Maran

d **Radu Gabrea**
sc **Radu Gabrea, Laurens Straub**
ph **Horst Schier**
m **Verdi (***La Traviata* with Maria Callas)
Eva Mattes, Liza Kreuzer, Werner Stocker, Charles Regnier, Carola Regnier, Charly Muhamed Huber

The relationships of the film director Eva (Mattes) with various people during the shooting of his version of *The Lady Of The Camellias* in a large mansion. He repulses his ex-lover Ali (Huber), marries the leading lady (Kreuzer) and seduces the leading man (Stocker). Although Rainer Werner Fassbinder (1946-1982) is not mentioned by name, this bizarre and dubious enterprise is an apochryphal portrait of him, played in a beard by his erstwhile star Eva Mattes. Gabrea directs in Fassbinder's own most Sirkian manner, but without his control of excess. Many of the bare facts of the director's life are here telescoped, trivialized and turned into melodrama. As Fassbinder did the same with his life, fans might not object.

Mannen Fran Mallorca see Man From Majorca, The

Mannen Pasòbt Taket see Man On The Roof, The

Männer see Men

Mann Wie Eva, Ein see Man Like Eva, A

Mano En La Trampa, La see Hand In The Trap, The

Man Of Ashes

Rih Essed

aka L'Homme De Cendres

Tunisia 1986 109 mins col
SATPEK/Ciné-Télé Films

d **Nouri Bouzid**
sc **Nouri Bouzid**
ph **Youssef Ben-Youssef**
m **Salah Mahdi**
Imed Malaal, Khaled Ksouri, Habib Belhadi, Mohamed Dhrif, Mouna Noureddine, Mahmoud Bel-Hassen

Hachemi (Malaal), a young furniture maker in the Tunisian town of Sfax and about to be married, is haunted by childhood memories of being sodomized. Unlike his friend Farfat (Ksouri), who had the same experience and is publicly known (and ridiculed) as homosexual, Hachemi suffers privately, giving in to destructive introspection until a sympathetic prostitute initiates him into heterosexual sex. Bouzid's controversial first film is not so much about the pros and cons of homosexuality as about the power of masculinity in Tunisian society which is judged in relation to women. Efficiently filmed to give the flavour of a community where Muslim, Christian and Jew co-exist peacably, it's also an immature work, focusing on the surface hysteria rather than the inner character of its protagonists. Consequently, what should provoke and move merely irritates—rather in the manner of an over-intense and tedious first novel.

Man Of Iron see Railroad Man, The

Man Of Iron

Czlowiek Z Zelaza

Poland 1981 152 mins col/bw
PRF/Filmowy

d **Andrzej Wajda**
sc **Aleksander Scibor-Rylski**
ph **Edward Klosínski**
m **Andrzej Korzyński**
Jerzy Radziwilowicz, Krystyna Janda, Marian Opania

A radio reporter (Opania), expected to cover the 1980 shipyard strike at Gdansk from the official point of view, meets the son of 1950s worker hero Birkut (*Man Of Marble*) now married to a dissident film-maker (Janda). Wajda's sequel to *Man Of Marble* (1972), filmed under enormous pressure during the actual events, leaped off the screen like the day's headlines. The personal story is linked with the wider struggle for the recognition of Solidarity, thus making the film dependent to a large extent on its political topicality. As Wajda uses an unfussy narrative technique, it might soon seem as dated as yesterday's headlines.

Best Film Cannes 1981

Man Of Marble

Czlowiek Z Marmur

Poland 1972 165 mins col
PRF/Zespol

d **Andrzej Wajda**
sc **Aleksander Scibor-Rylski**
ph **Edward Klosínski**
m **Andrzej Korzyński**
Jerzy Radziwilowicz, Krystyna Janda, Michael Tarkowski, Tadeusz Lomnicki

As a basis for her graduation film project, a student (Janda) investigating the life of a bricklayer hero of the 1950s who has since been discredited, finds obstacles in getting at the truth. This bold, no-frills, no-holds-barred political tale is Wajda's reflection on Poland's immediate past, whereas the sequel, *Man Of Iron* (1981), looked at the present. Most effective are the black and white reconstructions of the newsreels of the time, and Radziwilowicz's convincing performance as Birkut, the worker who stepped out of line. Wajda, too, was thought to have gone over the official limits, and the film's release was held up for four years. Although good polemical cinema, the nervous chain-smoking portrayal by Janda acts as an irritant.

Man Of Straw

L'Uomo Di Paglia

Italy 1958 95 mins bw
Vides/Lux Film

d **Pietro Germi**
sc **Alfredo Giannetti, Leo Benvenuti, Piero**

De Bernardi, Pietro Germi
ph **Leonida Barboni**
m **Carlo Rustichelli**
Pietro Germi, Luisa Della Noce, Franca Bettoja, Edoardo Nevola, Saro Urzi

A married man (Germi), father to a little son, falls in love with a young girl (Bettoja) and neglects his family in pursuit of the affair. Both he and the girl are painfully aware that their relationship cannot last but, when the parting comes, the effect on her is unexpected and tragic. Using many of the team, both in front of and behind the camera, from his previous film, *The Railroad Man*, Germi, working from an excellent screenplay, has delivered an honest, downbeat and perceptive tale of adultery, subtly conveying how life can never again be the same for the protagonist after this poignant interlude. The rest of the cast also give confident performances.

Manon

France 1949 100 mins bw
Alcina

d **Henri-Georges Clouzot**
sc **Henri-Georges Clouzot, Jean Ferry**
ph **Armand Thirard**
m **Paul Misraki**
Cecile Aubrey, Michel Auclair, Serge Reggiani, Gabrielle Dorziat

After the liberation, a former Resistance fighter (Auclair) rescues Manon (Aubrey), a collaborator, from the avenging villagers. They flee to Paris where Manon drives her lover to jealous rage by her involvement with profiteering and prostitution but, when he commits a murder, she leaves France with him, and ends up dying in the desert. A curious reworking of the Abbé Prévost's 18th-century novel, *Manon Lescaut*, the film fails to convince, due to sketchy characterization and underpowered casting. Not one of Clouzot's better efforts, his style is nonetheless evident in capturing the atmosphere of post-war, low-life Paris— sufficiently so to have made an impression on the Festival jury at Venice.

Best Film Venice 1949

Manon Des Sources

France 1952 190 mins bw
Films Marcel Pagnol

d **Marcel Pagnol**
sc **Marcel Pagnol**
sc **Willy**
m **Raymond Legrand**
Jacqueline Pagnol, Raymond Pellegrin, Henri Vibert, Rellys, Henri Poupon

Manon (Pagnol), a wild girl who lives in the hills, takes her revenge on the villagers, particularly Ugolin (Rellys) and his uncle Papet (Poupon), who indirectly caused her father's death. 'If water plays an important role in my work, it's because it is a major problem in Provence which is so often deprived of it,' Pagnol commented. The theme of water flows like a stream through his penultimate film, which originally ran almost five hours (when it was released commercially it lost two hours). Despite the pastoral beauty, the narrative suffered cruelly, and it flopped. Jacqueline Pagnol (formerly Bouvier), the director's wife, was unconvincing in the title role, and some of the other performances were too caricatured. An exception is Rellys, whose desperate declaration of love for Manon is one of the highlights. Claude Berri's 1986 remake (plus the 'prequel *Jean De Florette*) kept most of the wonderful dialogue, but rectified many of the acting and structural weaknesses.

Manon Des Sources

France 1986 114 mins col
Renn Productions/A2/RAI 2/DD

d **Claude Berri**
sc **Claude Berri, Gérard Brach**
ph **Bruno Nuytten**
m **Jean-Claude Petit**
Yves Montand, Daniel Auteuil, Emmanuelle Béart, Hippolyte Girardot, Elisabeth Depardieu

Ten years after watching her father die as a result of the plugging up of the spring on his land by two malicious neighbours, Manon (Béart) wreaks revenge on the whole community by depriving them of water. Of the two films, this continuation of *Jean De Florette* is the more pantheistic and, as the title suggests, more operatic. In fact, the film should not be approached as naturalistic drama: the Marcel Pagnol story (filmed by him in 1952) was conceived as an updated Greek tragedy transposed to Provence. Against the sensuous settings are rich portrayals from a mellow Montand and the unforgettable tragicomic Auteuil.

The Man On The Roof

Mannen På Taket

Sweden 1976 109 mins col
Svensk Filmindustri

d **Bo Widerberg**
sc **Bo Widerberg**
ph **Odd Geir Saether, Per Källberg and others**
m **Björn Jason Lindh**
Carl-Gustaf Lindstedt, Gunnel Wadner, Håkan Serner, Sven Wollter

When a tough policeman is killed by a sniper in Stockholm, a vast manhunt is put into operation. Based on a popular crime novel by Maj Sjöwall and Per Wahlöö, Widerberg's stylish and suspenseful thriller is divided into two distinct sections—detection and chase. Both parts are familiar from Hollywood and TV cop dramas, but unfamiliar in settings and attitudes. A little less significance-searching might have made it even better entertainment.

Man's Hope

aka Days Of Hope

Espoir

aka Sierra De Teruel

France-Spain 1939 73 mins bw
Corniglion/Molinier

d **André Malraux**
sc **André Malraux**
ph **Louis Page**
m **Darius Milhaud**
Mejuto, Nicolas Rodriguez, José Lado

A small group of ill-equipped Republican fighters in the Spanish Civil War attempts to blow up a bridge to prevent arms and supplies reaching Franco's troops. The only feature directed by the esteemed French writer Malraux, based on his novel *L'Espoir*, was begun in 1938, but shooting was interrupted when General Franco took Barcelona. It was completed in Paris, but not shown until after World War II with altered editing and a prologue by Government minister Maurice Schumann. The film is remarkable for the feeling it gives of the actual war, although most of it was shot in a studio. The climax of the villagers carrying their dead down a mountainside is truly memorable.

Manthan see Churning, The

Ma Nuit Chez Maud see My Night With Maud

The Man Who Had His Hair Cut Short

De Man Die Zijn Haar Kort Liet Knippen

Belgium 1966 95 mins bw
Belgium Ministry of Culture/Belgian TV

d **André Delvaux**
sc **André Delvaux, Anna De Pagter**
ph **Ghislain Cloquet**
m **Frédéric Devreese**
Senne Rouffaer, Beata Tyszkiewicz, Hector Camerlynck

A married middle-aged lawyer (Rouffaer) falls idealistically in love with a pupil (Tyszkiewicz) at a girls' school where he teaches. When he meets her again years later, she has become a famous actress while he gradually loses his sanity. Delvaux's first feature already reveals a firm grip on grim material that veers between beauty and ugliness, illusion and reality, with a self-conscious reference to Flemish old masters. The title refers to the hero's compulsive visits to the barber which vividly symbolize his encroaching madness.

The Man Who Loved Women

L'Homme Qui Aimait Les Femmes

France 1977 119 mins col
Les Films Du Carrosse/Les Productions Artistes Associés

d **François Truffaut**
sc **François Truffaut, Michel Fermaud, Suzanne Schiffman**
ph **Nestor Almendros**
m **Maurice Jaubert**
Charles Denner, Brigitte Fossey, Leslie Caron, Nelly Borgeaud, Geneviève Fontanel, Nathalie Baye

Bertrand (Denner) dedicates his life to the indefatigable pursuit of women, for whom he has a limitless passion, until his obsession involves him in an accident and leads to his death. Truffaut attempts to examine what drives his protagonist by using the device of flashback as Bertrand writes his memoirs, but his tone is that of romantic comedy, the structure lacks shape, and the film obstinately refuses to cast light on its characters, making it no more than a superficial and sporadically entertaining exercise.

Man Without A Face, The see Shadowman

The Man With The Movie Camera

Chelovek S Kinoapparatom

USSR 1928 90 mins bw
VUFKU

d **Dziga Vertov**
sc **Dziga Vertov**
ph **Mikhail Kaufman**
m **Silent**

A montage of Moscow life showing the inhabitants—workers, shoppers, holiday-makers—and the machines that keep the city moving. The first full length film by Vertov (real name Denis Kaufman, whose brother was the photographer) is a joyous and spectacular constructivist celluloid poem displaying all the techniques of cinema at his disposal: split screen, dissolves, slow motion, and freeze frames. Yet the pyrotechnics are mostly entertaining and seldom abstract. Documentary and experimental film-makers still acknowledge its influence and Jean-Luc Godard formed the Group Dziga Vertov to produce his movies between 1968 and 1972.

Marcelino

Marcelino Pan Y Vino

Spain 1955 90 mins bw
Charmartin Production

d **Ladislao Vajda**
sc **José Maria Sanchez-Silva, Ladislao Vajda**
ph **Enrique Guerner**
m **Pablo Sarosabal**
Pablito Calvo, Rafael Rivelles, Juan Calvo, Antonio Vico, Isabel De Pomes, Fernando Rey

Abandoned at birth on the steps of a humble monastery, Marcelino (Pablito Calvo) is brought up by the gentle monks who impart a purity and compassion of spirit to the boy without curbing his high spirits. Finding a life-sized crucifix in the attic where he has been forbidden to go, he thinks the Christ figure is real and brings it food. Christ reaches out for it and thanks the boy... Made when audiences were less jaded and cynical, this Spanish fantasy is a gem and a delight. Although undeniably sentimental even in its day, it has been directed, photographed and acted with great finesse and charm and Calvo, no more than six or seven, is irresistible.

Marcelino Pan Y Vino see Marcelino

Il Mare

aka The Sea

Italy 1962 110 mins bw
Gianni Buffardi

d **Giuseppe Patroni Griffi**
sc **Giuseppe Patroni Griffi, Alfio Valdarini**
ph **Ennio Guarnieri**
m **Giovanni Fusco**
Umberto Orsini, Françoise Prévost, Dino Mele

An actor (Orsini), visiting Capri in winter, meets a moody boy (Mele) who drinks heavily. In due course, they befriend a woman (Prévost) who has come to sell her house, and whose presence causes complications. Patroni Griffi's film is a beautifully constructed study of lonely and insecure people seeking, and failing to find, reassurance and comfort in one another. The director tells us little about his protagonists (they don't even have names), but doesn't need to because it is their particular circumstance— that of finding themselves in a cold, deserted place where unseasonal deadness triggers off their needs and emotions—with which the film is concerned. Beautifully photographed and acted with finesse, it is laced with ironic humour that keeps it from becoming either maudlin or overweighted with *angst*.

Marguerite De La Nuit

France 1955 126 mins col
SNEG/Gaumont Actualités/Cino Del Duca

d **Claude Autant-Lara**

sc **Ghislaine Autant-Lara, Gabriel Arout**
ph **Jacques Natteau**
m **René Cloërec**
Michèle Morgan, Yves Montand, Jean-François Calvé, Massimo Girotti, Fernand Sardou, Palau

Old Dr Faust (Palau) signs away his soul to Mephistopheles (Montand), disguised as the drug-trafficking owner of a Pigalle night-club, in return for his lost youth. He wakes next morning as a handsome young man (Calvé) with whom Marguerite (Morgan) falls in love. Autant-Lara's rather limp updating of the Faust legend suffers from miscasting, garish lighting and mechanical tricks. It's only *raison d'être* seems to be the *art déco* settings by Max Douy (the action takes place in the 1920s), and some flashes of humour.

Maria Candelaria

Mexico 1943 102 mins bw
Films Mundiales

d **Emilio Fernández**
sc **Emilio Fernández, Mauricio Magdaleno**
ph **Gabriel Figueroa**
m **Francisco Dominguez**
Dolores Del Rio, Pedro Armendáriz, Alberto Galan, Margarita Cortes, Manuel Inclan

Maria (Del Rio), an Indian peasant girl, lives in a primitive community whose members stoned her mother to death after she had posed nude for an artist (Galan). Maria and her fiancé (Armendariz) are poverty-stricken, and he is jailed for stealing quinine for her malaria. To obtain funds, she poses for Galan, head only, but the locals make assumptions and history repeats itself. The exquisite Dolores Del Rio, showing few signs of age (at 38, she had been a star of the Hollywood silents), is excellent, and Figueroa's photography of the Mexican landscape is impressive. Although verbose and sometimes lacking in action, the film has surprising flashes of humour embedded in its sad tale.

Best Film Cannes 1946

Maria Chapdelaine

aka The Naked Heart

France 1934 120 mins bw
Société Nouvelle De Cinématographie

d **Julien Duvivier**
sc **Julien Duvivier, Gabrielle Boissy**
ph **Jules Kruger, Georges Périnal**
m **Jean Wiener**
Madeleine Renaud, Suzanne Despres, Jean Gabin, Jean-Pierre Aumont, André Bac, Alexandre Rignault

The Chapdelaines are a French Canadian family battling with the hardships of pioneer life in the icy wilderness, but determined to preserve their French custom and heritage. Both Maria's mother and her adored fiancé (Gabin), a fur trapper, die during a cruel winter, but she resists the temptation to escape to the city with a new suitor. Duvivier brought the full mastery of his poetic realism to bear on this sensitive adaptation of Louis Hemon's best-seller. Impeccably acted by all the cast, particularly Renaud in the title role, the film also benefits from some spectacular location photography, shot amid the Canadian snowscapes.

María De Mi Corazón see Mary My Dearest

Marie—A Hungarian Legend

(US: Spring Shower)

Tavaszi Zapor

Hungary 1932 66 mins bw
Adolphe Osso

d **Pál Fejós**
sc **Ilona Fülöp, Pál Fejós**
ph **István Eiban, Pawerel Marley**
m **László Angyal, Vincent Scotto**
Annabella, István Gyergyai, Karola Zala, Ilona Dajbukát, Erzsi Bársony

Maria Szabó (Annabella), a maid working for a rich family, is seduced by the fiancé (Gyergyai) of the daughter (Bársony) of the house. Turned out by the family, she gets a job as a waitress in an unsavoury tavern. When her baby is born, a group of local women take the child away from her, she becomes a drunk and dies. Fejós' first film in his native Hungary for nine years (after his sojourn in Hollywood and a couple of pictures in France) could reasonably be considered the best Hungarian film of the 1930s. Paradoxically, its strength is also its weakness. The trite melodramatic tale of woe, with a climax of gooey religiosity, is filmed in such a glowing way as to be reminiscent of the magical silent pictures of Sjöström and Murnau, and the ravishing Annabella puts one in mind of Gish and Pickford. The influence of Hollywood is seen in the amusing coda when Annabella, installed in 'Heaven's kitchen', saves her daughter from a fate similar to her own.

La Marie Du Port

France 1949 100 mins bw
Films Corona/Sacha Gordine

d **Marcel Carné**
sc **Marcel Carné, Louis Chavance**
ph **Henri Alekan**
m **Joseph Kosma**
Jean Gabin, Nicole Courcel, Blanchette Brunoy, Carette, Claude Romain

Chatelard (Gabin), a world-weary restaurant owner from Cherbourg, escorts his mistress to the funeral of her father, a poor fisherman, in a little Breton port town. Once there, he becomes involved with her younger sister (Courcel). Director and cameraman capture the life and atmosphere of the port with realistic exactitude, while Gabin and Courcel convince as the couple—he sophisticated and cynical, she a willing novice in the game of love. Shades of irony lend an intriguing ambiguity to the romance but it is Carné (working from a novel by Georges Simenon) past his best.

Mariée Était En Noir, La see Bride Wore Black, The

Marie Octobre

France 1958 102 mins bw
Orex/SF/Abbey/Doxa

d **Julien Duvivier**
sc **Julien Duvivier, Jacques Robert**
ph **Robert Le Fèbvre**
m **Jean Yatove**
Danielle Darrieux, Serge Reggiani, Bernard Blier, Paul Meurisse, Noël Roquevert, Lino Ventura, Paul Guers, Paul Frankeur

A group of ex-Resistance fighters meets some years after the war for a reunion dinner. During the course of the evening one of their number is exposed as a traitor, and the obligatory consequence follows. An experiment on the lines of Hitchcock's *Rope*, the action takes place in one set, the director using long takes. Although verbose and rather stifling, the dramatic possibilities are fully exploited by the excellent cast.

Mariés De L'An Deux, Les see Scoundrel, The

Marius

France 1931 125 mins bw
Marcel Pagnol/Paramount

d **Alexander Korda**
sc **Marcel Pagnol**
ph **Ted Pahle**
m **Francis Grammon**
Raimu, Pierre Fresnay, Orane Demazis, Charpin, Alida Rouffe, Robert Vathier

Marius (Fresnay), who works in his father's dockside café in Marseilles, is set to marry Fanny (Demazis) his childhood sweetheart, but the call of the sea is too strong for him, and he joins the merchant navy, unaware that Fanny is pregnant. Pagnol's entry into cinema was as producer, adviser, and screenwriter on the film of his successful play of the same name with almost the same cast. The warm atmosphere of the trilogy (*Fanny* and *César* followed) was immediately established, although it is the least cinematic of the three and rather crude when trying to expand the location, which is largely confined to César's café. No matter. The interest lies in character, the wisdom of the writing and the wonderful performances, especially from the great Raimu as the crabby but lovable César.

Marlene

W. Germany 1983 94 mins col
OKO-Filmproduktion/Karel Dirka

d **Maximilian Schell**
sc **Meir Dohnal, Maximilian Schell**
ph **Ivan Slapeta, Pavel Hispler, Henry Hauck**
m **Nicholas Economou**
Annie Albers, Bernard Hall, Marta Rakosnik, Patricia Schell, Ivana Spinell, William Von Stranz, Maximilian Schell, and the voice of Marlene Dietrich

A still from *Marlene* in the British Film Institute's monthly bulletin is captioned 'interview with an absent subject', which would seem to sum up Maximilian Schell's documentary. Having agreed to be interviewed for a film, the legendary German star then refused point blank to appear before the camera. Undaunted, Schell pressed on, giving us the star's (mostly ill-tempered) views on her art and those who helped to elevate her in it. What we look at is a detailed reconstruction of her Paris apartment, with the director's crew and producer trying to make the best of a bad job, a handful of interviews and a good selection of clips from her best-known movies. The high point is a disagreement between star and director where he walks out and provokes her wrath. Overall, in spite of some understandably chaotic fill-in material—editing machines and the like—this is a fascinating documentary, part homage, part critique from which, frankly, the great Dietrich emerges as an unpleasantly perverse and difficult woman, but with an appealing forthrightness that cuts through the cult of idolatry. By her absence, her presence is the stronger.

The Marquise Of O

Die Marquise Von O

W. Germany 1976 107 mins col
Janus/Films Du Losange

d **Eric Rohmer**
sc **Eric Rohmer**
ph **Nestor Almendros**
m **Roger Delmotte**
Edith Clever, Volker Frächtel, Bruno Ganz, Peter Lühr, Edda Seippel, Eric Rohmer

A highly moral Marquise (Clever), a widow with two children, is drugged and then raped by Count F (Ganz), a lieutenant-colonel in the invading Russian army of Lombardy in the early 18th century. When she finds herself pregnant, the Marquise gets the Count to marry her, and they separate immediately after the ceremony. Shooting in Germany, in German and with a German cast, the typically French Rohmer conjured up a restrained, ironic and touching version of Heinrich Von Kleist's classic novella. It is also intentionally funny in some of the more melodramatic moments. The film's pictorial beauty was inspired by painters such as Caspar David Friedrich.

Special Jury Prize Cannes 1976

Marquise Von O, Die see Marquise Of O, The

Marriage Italian Style

Matrimonio All'Italiana

Italy 1964 102 mins col
C.C. Champion (Rome)/Films Concordia (Paris)

d **Vittorio De Sica**
sc **Eduardo De Filippo, Renato Castellani, Tonino Guerra, Leo Benvenuto, Piero De Bernardi**
ph **Roberto Gerardi**
m **Armando Trovaioli**
Sophia Loren, Marcello Mastroianni, Aldo Puglisi, Giovanni Ridolfi, Vito Moriconi, Generoso Cortini

Filomena (Loren) who met Domenico (Mastroianni) in a brothel, has been his mistress for 20 years but he now intends to marry a young girl. However, on hearing she is mortally ill, he rushes to her bedside and marries her as a last gesture, whereupon she 'miraculously' recovers, and reveals three grown-up sons. . . . The plot of this comedy, based on De Filippo's play *Filomena*, contains elements of both the erotically vulgar and the ludicrously silly, but is always extremely funny. Loren— sexy, uninhibited and cunning—is a delight and Mastroianni—vain, egotistical and bemused—is marvellous, while De Sica directs with inventiveness and the lightest of touches.

The Marriage Of Maria Braun

Die Ehe Der Maria Braun

W. Germany 1978 119 mins col
Albatros/Trio/WDR/FDA

d **Rainer Werner Fassbinder**
sc **Peter Märthesheimer, Pea Fröhlich**
ph **Michael Ballhaus**
m **Peer Raben**
Hanna Schygulla, Klaus Löwitsch, Ivan Desny, Gottfried John, George Byrd

Maria Braun (Schygulla) survives in Berlin through the war years while her husband

(Löwitsch) is at the Russian front. On his return, he is imprisoned for killing a black GI who befriended her. She takes up with an industrialist (Desny) and rises to wealth and power. Fassbinder's biggest international box-office success is a dramatic and subtle picture of an indomitable woman and his most effective metaphorical onslaught on Germany's 'Economic Miracle' of the 1950s. Framed between photographs of Hitler and Helmut Schmidt, the story is filled with superbly conceived comic and soap opera incidents, giving Schygulla one of her best roles. The producers had wanted Romy Schneider for the part, but a meeting between the director and star ended up with him calling her a 'dumb cow', and she declaring she would never work with such a 'beast'.

Best Actress (Hanna Schygulla) Berlin 1979

A Married Woman
(US: The Married Woman)
Une Femme Mariée

France 1964 98 mins bw
Anouchka/Orsay

d **Jean-Luc Godard**
sc **Jean-Luc Godard**
ph **Raoul Coutard**
m **Beethoven, Claude Nougaro**
Macha Meril, Philippe Leroy, Bernard Noël, Roger Leenhardt, Rita Maiden

A young Parisian wife (Mercil) who moves between her airline pilot husband (Leroy) and her lover (Noël), is overly influenced by advertising and women's magazines. General De Gaulle objected greatly to this humorously erotic portrayal of French womanhood, no doubt thus contributing to its considerable box-office takings. Godard's depiction of the sex act by showing patterned portions of the anatomy has been much imitated and so has his feminist theme. But his use of sexuality for polemical purposes was far more effective in his films of the 1980s.

Married Woman, The see Married Woman, A

Marry Me! Marry Me!
Mazel Tov Ou Le Mariage

France 1968 90 mins col
Renn Productions/Parafrance Films/Madeleine Films

d **Claude Berri**
sc **Claude Berri**
ph **Ghislain Cloquet**
m **Emile Stern**
Claude Berri, Elizabeth Wiener, Grégoire Aslan, Luisa Colpeyn, Prudence Harrington

When Isabelle (Wiener), daughter of a rich Antwerp diamond merchant, becomes pregnant by her lover Claude (Berri), he decides to marry her. Meanwhile, however, he becomes infatuated with his English teacher Helen (Harrington), rushes back to Paris from Belgium, and breaks off his engagement. Soon disillusioned with Helen, he is reunited with Isabelle and her family. Berri, playing the lead as well as writing and directing, has drawn on his own background to create a detailed portrait of Jewish family life, climaxing with the colourful wedding. It is an endearing film, presenting very real characters and a deal of wry light comedy, free of sugary sentiment or Jewish clichés.

Marseillaise, La see Marseillaise, The

The Marseillaise
La Marseillaise

France 1938 135 mins bw
CGT

d **Jean Renoir**
sc **Jean Renoir**
ph **Jean Bourgoin**
m **Joseph Kosma, Lalande Rameau, Mozart, Bach, Rouget L'Isle, Sauveplane**
Pierre Renoir, Lise Delamare, Louis Jouvet, Julien Carette, Gaston Modot, Léon Larive

A group of volunteers march from Marseilles to Paris to take part in the downfall of the French monarchy in 1789. One of Renoir's favourite movies was also one of his least successful. His affection for it might have attached more to the comradely manner in which it was made rather than to its actual consummation. The collective production, financed by the French trades unions, was 'the film of the union of the French nation against a minority of exploiters, the film of the rights of man and of the citizen'. These were great claims for an episodic picture which lacked a grand design. Although there are some stirring moments with the people, it is, ironically, the aristos—led by a touching Pierre Renoir as Louis XVI— who come off best.

Martha

W. Germany 1974 95 mins col
WDR

d **Rainer Werner Fassbinder**
sc **Rainer Werner Fassbinder**
ph **Michael Ballhaus**
m **Archive music**
Margit Carstensen, Karl-Heinz Böhm, Gisela Fackeldey, Barbara Valentin, Adrian Hoven

Martha (Carstensen), a wealthy and selfish woman, marries a stranger (Böhm) whom she gradually discovers is a sadist. He tries to subdue her, but it is not until she is paralyzed in an accident that he becomes the dominant partner. If Fassbinder's previous film, *Fear Eats The Soul*, was his tribute to the Douglas Sirk of *All That Heaven Allows*, then this baroque extravagance is a homage to Sirk's *Written On The Wind*. Over the top it may be, and full of cinematic and private allusions, but there is no discounting the virtuosity of the direction, the bold use of colour, lighting and decor—and all shot on 16mm at a cost of the coffee break at Universal Studios.

Martin Roumagnac

(US: The Room Upstairs)
France 1946 115 mins bw
Alcina

d **Georges Lacombe**
sc **Pierre Véry**
ph **Roger Hubert**
m **Marcel Mirouze**
Jean Gabin, Marlene Dietrich, Margo Lion, Daniel Gélin, Marcel André

Martin (Gabin), a builder in a dusty French provincial town, is hired to construct a house for Blanche (Dietrich), a sophisticated, cosmopolitan newcomer to the district. They have a passionate affair until he discovers that she is a high-class whore, whereupon he kills her and is tried for murder. Played as flashback from the courtroom, the film lost 16 minutes on release in Britain and 27 in the US where the Catholic Legion of Decency raised moral objections. In the event, the promise of so electric and starry a pairing as Gabin and Dietrich resulted in no more than a disappointingly old-fashioned, superficial and mediocre drama.

Marusa No Onna see Taxing Woman, A

Mary My Dearest

María De Mi Corazón
Mexico 1983 100 mins col
Azteca Films/Universidad Veracruzana

d **Jaime Humberto Hermosillo**
sc **Gabriel García Márquez, Jaime Humberto Hermosillo**
ph **Angel Goded**
m **Joaquin Gutiérrez Heras**
Héctor Bonilla, María Rojo, Ana Ofelia Murguia, Blanca Torres, Salvador Sánchez

Héctor (Bonilla), a small-time crook, is reunited with his former girlfriend María (Rojo) who persuades him to give up crime and join her in a touring magic show. One day, the van in which she is travelling breaks down and, in her frantic search for a telephone, she finds herself in a sanatorium for the mentally ill from which she cannot escape. One of Mexico's best-known directors, Hermosillo gathered together a dedicated group of actors, technicians, intellectuals and artists and engineered this independent production on a miniscule budget, free from the traditional constraints of the industry, thus starting a new trend. The film combines a naturalistic view of everyday *bourgeois* life with the fantastical and bizarre and does it well, building up inexorably to a horrifying conclusion. But the mixture of styles often undercuts the clarity of the piece and minimizes one's involvement with the characters.

Masculin-Féminin see Masculine-Feminine

Masculine-Feminine

Masculin-Féminin
France 1966 104 mins bw
Anouchka/Argos/Svensk Filmindustri/Sandrews

d **Jean-Luc Godard**
sc **Jean-Luc Godard**
ph **Willy Kurant**
m **Francis Lai**
Jean-Pierre Léaud, Chantal Goya, Michel Debord, Marlène Jobert, Catherine-Isabelle Duport

Paul (Léaud), fresh from military service, meets Madeleine (Goya), who gets him a job on the magazine where she works. But he is more interested in spending his time in Left-wing political activity and his relationship with the two girls (Duport and Jobert) with whom he shares an apartment. Godard's view of the generation of 'the children of Marx and Coca Cola' is represented by Léaud at the start of his six-film collaboration with the director in the late 1960s. (In fact, Léaud has made as many films with Godard as he did with his mentor, Truffaut.) Less engaging here than as Truffaut's Antoine Doinel, Léaud was able to create the right anarchic, questioning image of French youth typical of the attitude that led to the 'events' of May 1968 in Paris. The fragmented techniques and seemingly improvised style reflect the character, but disguise a firm structure. Brigitte Bardot can be glimpsed briefly on the Métro.

Best Actor (Jean-Pierre Léaud) Berlin 1966

Maskerade
(US: Masquerade In Vienna)

Austria 1934 101 mins bw
Tobis/Sascha

d **Willi Forst**
sc **Willi Forst, Walter Reisch**
ph **Franz Planer**
m **Willi Schmidt-Gentner**
Anton Walbrook, Paula Wessely, Olga Tschechowa, Peter Petersen, Walter Janssen, Hilde Von Stolz

A ladies' man and celebrated artist (Walbrook) is the love object of an unsophisticated young woman (Wessely), whom his friends suspect of being the model in his painting of a female nude in a ball-mask. A delightful bitter-sweet comedy set in the favourite era of pre-war romantic escapism—Vienna at the turn of the century. The adult script, the waltzing camera, and two fine leads in the vulnerable Wessely and the suave Walbrook, made it justifiably actor-singer Willi Forst's most famous film as a director, and presented an image of the Austria that most people had before the *Anschluss*.

Masquerade In Vienna see Maskerade

Masques

France 1987 100 mins col
MK2 Productions/Films A2

d **Claude Chabrol**
sc **Odile Barski, Claude Chabrol**
ph **Jean Rabier**
m **Matthieu Chabrol**
Philippe Noiret, Robin Renucci, Bernadette Lafont, Anne Brochet, Monique Chaumette, Pierre-François Duméniaud

Writer Roland Woolf (Renucci) arrives to stay at the country house of Christian Legagneur (Noiret), a famous TV game-show host whom he is to interview. Woolf, in fact, is really there to seek clues to the disappearance of his sister, and soon discovers that his host's niece-cum- ward (Brochet), is confined to bed in the grip of a mysterious malady, and that the affable Legagneur is, to put it mildly, not what he seems. Directing with his customary flair and efficiency—and with a couple of obvious nods towards Hitchcock—Chabrol unfolds a tale of murderous duplicity, with Noiret immensely entertaining as the ambiguous centre of the action, but the enterprise is pretty thin under its thick coating of style.

The Master And Margarita
Maestro I Margarita

Yugoslavia/Italy 1972 101 mins col
Dunav Film (Belgrade)/Euro International Film (Rome)/Tzigane Film Productions

d **Aleksander Petrović**
sc **Aleksander Petrović, Barbara Alberti, Amedeo Pagani**
ph **Roberto Gerardi**
m **Ennio Morricone**
Ugo Tognazzi, Mimsy Farmer, Alain Cuny, Tasko Nacić, Danilo Stojković, Zlatko Madunić

The brilliant playwright Nikolai Maksudov (Tognazzi), known as The Master, attends the dress rehearsal of his new play, 'Pontius Pilate', at a Moscow theatre during the 1920s.

The theatre manager and others object to the play on ideological grounds but The Master, supported by his girlfriend Margarita (Farmer) and a mysterious Professor Woland (Cuny), refuses to withdraw the piece. The Master then discovers that the professor is the Devil but, when he tries to alert people, he is committed to a madhouse. Petrović based his film on 'ideas' from Bulgakov's novel, and has presented it as an explicit plea on behalf of so-called 'dissident' artists, whose plight he exposes in a mixture of formal restraint, special effects and animation. It is all expertly achieved, but an ambiguous ending which implies that the action has been a hallucination suffered by the mad Nikolai, dilutes the central theme and begs its questions.

Mat see Mother

Mata-Hari, Agent H.21

France 1964 99 mins bw
Filmel/Les Films Du Carrosse/ Simar(Paris)/Fida Cinematografica(Rome) Cinematografica(Rome)

d **Jean-Louis Richard**
sc **Jean-Louis Richard, François Truffaut**
ph **Michel Kelber**
m **Georges Delerue**
Jeanne Moreau, Jean-Louis Trintignant, Claude Rich, Frank Villard, Albert Rémy, Henri Garcin

Spying for the Germans in Paris during World War I, Mata-Hari (Moreau) is ordered to seduce a young captain (Trintignant) in order to keep him occupied while certain important documents are stolen by her masters. Everything goes according to plan except that spy and soldier fall in love, thus sealing their doom. This account of the absurd Mata-Hari legend offers a superbly sophisticated and versatile performance from Jeanne Moreau, as well as some amusement early on while she masquerades as a Javanese nightclub dancer. However, the love affair is clichéd and the film lacks credibility, succeeding neither as espionage thriller nor as melodrama. An improvement, though, on the ghastly Garbo version.

La Maternelle

France 1932 89 mins bw
Photosonor

d **Jean Benoît-Lévy, Marie Epstein**
sc **Jean Benoît-Lévy**
ph **Georges Asselin**
m **Edouard Flament**
Madeleine Renaud, Paulette Elambert, Alice Tissot, Mady Berry, Henri Debain

Rose (Renaud), a teacher at a *maternelle* (nursery school) is devoted to the children, particularly a little girl abandoned by her prostitute mother. However, the child becomes distraught when Rose considers marrying. Benoît-Lévy and Marie Epstein (the sister of the distinguished director Jean Epstein) made a number of features in the 1920s and early 1930s about the plight of children, of which this is the most famous and widely seen. Deeply felt and wonderfully acted, it is still worth seeing, despite the inherent sentimentality and well-meant ending.

Matka Joanna Od Aniolów see Devil And The Nun, The

Matrimonio All'Italiana see Marriage Italian Style

The Mattei Affair

Il Caso Mattei

Italy 1972 118 mins col
Vides Verona

d **Francesco Rosi, Tonino Guerra**
sc **Francesco Rosi**
ph **Pasqualino De Santis**
m **Piero Piccioni**
Gian Maria Volonté, Luigi Squarzina, Peter Baldwin, Renato Romano, Franco Graziosi

The life and death in a mysterious plane crash in 1962 of Enrico Mattei (Volonté), the socialist oil magnate, the 'most powerful Italian since Augustus Caesar', is examined in flashback. Using a bold, semi-documentary cinematic style, Rosi in another of his incisive studies of corrupt post-war Italian power games, leaves the audience to choose from the hypotheses offered as to the cause of Mattei's death. Volonté has enough charisma to carry off the role of the man whose public behaviour interests Rosi far more than his private life.

Best Film Cannes 1972

A Matter of Dignity
To Telefteo Psemma

Greece 1957 104 mins bw
Finos

d **Michael Cacoyannis**
sc **Michael Cacoyannis**
ph **Walter Lassally**
m **Manos Hadjidakis**
Ellie Lambetti, Athena Michaelidou, Georges Pappas, Eleni Zafiriou, Minas Christides, Michel Nikolinakas

Chloe (Lambetti), daughter of a once-wealthy family on the brink of ruin, tries to save their situation by agreeing to marry a millionaire whose dullness she can barely tolerate. Photographed with graphic clarity and acted with expertise, this is one of the director's best melodramas, focusing with powerful truth and accuracy on its issues. The hollow values of the idle rich are ruthlessly exposed in the character of Chloe's mother (Michaelidou), obsessed with keeping up appearances even to the point of sacrificing her daughter; the gulf between rich and poor is made manifest in the tragic plight of the family servant. Chloe's painful journey to self-discovery carries moving conviction, thanks particularly to the beautiful Lambetti's striking mobility of expression.

Maudits, Les see Damned, The

Mauvaise Graine

France 1933 80 mins bw
Compagnie Nouvelle Cinématographique

d **Alexander Esway, Billy Wilder**
sc **Alexander Esway, H.G. Lustig, Billy Wilder**
ph **Paul Cotteret, Maurice Delattre**
m **Walter Gray, Franz Waxman**
Danielle Darrieux, Pierre Mingand, Raymond Galle, Jean Wall, Michel Duran, Paul Escoffier

Henri Pasquier (Mingand), charming but idle, has his smart car removed and sold by his stern doctor father (Escoffier). The loss lands him in an awkward situation which he takes care of by impulsively stealing another vehicle, but is seen doing so by members of a professional gang who give chase. One thing leads to another and Henri becomes a member of the gang, falling in love with Jeanette (Darrieux), their attractive decoy. Filmed on location in Paris and Marseilles, this slight but appealing comedy-drama marks the first film Billy Wilder made outside Germany, prior to his great Hollywood career. Although it's a collaborative effort, the Wilder touch can be discerned in moments of imaginatively wry humour and the moral ambiguities of the characters and situation. The movie was a superb showcase for the beautiful and talented 17-year-old Danielle Darrieux.

Mauvais Fils, Un see Bad Son, A

Mauvais Sang see Night Is Young, The

Max see Max Et Les Ferrailleurs

Max Et Les Ferrailleurs
aka Max

France 1971 110 mins col
Lira Films/Sonocam

d **Claude Sautet**
sc **Claude Neron, Claude Sautet**
ph **René Mathelin**
m **Philippe Sarde**
Michel Piccoli, Romy Schneider, Bernard Fresson, François Périer, Georges Wilson

Max (Piccoli), a former magistrate-turned-police inspector, is obsessed by the fact that known gangsters go free for lack of evidence. Determined to redress the balance, he invests his time, skill and private income in schemes to push small-time crooks into big-time activities in order to nail them. His bizarre plans come unstuck when he falls in love with a prostitute (Schneider) who is the companion of Max's latest target, a petty junk thief. Sautet has come up with a nice idea for an unusual cop-and-gangster film, to which he brings the right wry tone. However, it falls apart because Max's behaviour loses credibility, there is insufficient action and Romy Schneider is uncomfortably miscast.

Max Havelaar

Netherlands 1976 170 mins col
Fons Rademakers Productie/PT Mondial Motion Pictures

d **Fons Rademakers**
sc **Gerard Soeteman**
ph **Jan De Bont**
Peter Faber, Sacha Bulthuis, Lerry Iantho, Elang Mohamad Adenan Soesilaningrat

Civil servant Max Havelaar (Faber) is sent to Dutch colonial Java to try to reform a corrupt local system, but he is thwarted in his efforts by his own government and by mercantile interests. Rademakers' eighth film, his most expensive and expansive, was adapted from an 1859 novel by 'Multatuli' (Edouard Douwes Dekker), which attacked the colonial rule in the Dutch East Indies (now Indonesia). The film takes a less astringent approach than the book, and the portrayal of the idealistic Havelaar lacks nuance. However, the contrast between the scenes in Amsterdam and Java is effective and the recreation of the era is compelling. The best performances come from the Indonesian actors in a film which switches between Dutch and a Malay dialect.

Max, Mon Amour see Max, My Love

Max, My Love

Max, Mon Amour

France 1986 94 mins col
Greenwich Film Production/Films A2

d **Nagisa Oshima**
sc **Nagisa Oshima, Jean-Claude Carrière**
ph **Raoul Coutard**
m **Michel Portal**
Charlotte Rampling, Anthony Higgins, Christopher Hovik, Victoria Abril, Anne-Marie Besse, Pierre Etaix

When a British diplomat (Higgins) in Paris discovers that his bored wife (Rampling) has rented an apartment where she can visit her lover Max, a chimpanzee (!), he invites the ape to come and live with them. The shade of Buñuel hovers over this witty, black comedy of manners that judiciously avoids the vulgarity inherent in the subject. In fact, this *menagérie à trois* is often tender and sensitive, thanks mainly to the enigmatic and sensuous performance by Rampling, and is often hilarious, such as during the dinner party scene. The only problem is that Max's character is not sufficiently developed.

Mayerling

France 1935 96 mins bw
Concordia Cinématographique/Nero

d **Anatole Litvak**
sc **Joseph Kessel, Irmgard Von Cube**
ph **Armand Thirard**
m **Arthur Honegger**
Charles Boyer, Danielle Darrieux, Suzy Prim, Jean Debucourt, Vladimir Sokoloff

Crown Prince Rudolph (Boyer), heir to the Austro-Hungarian Empire, is forced into a loveless marriage, but subsequently falls passionately for 17-year-old Marie Vetsera (Darrieux), a girl of good family. When the Pope refuses Rudolph's request to annul his marriage, the lovers flee to Mayerling, the prince's hunting lodge, where they spend an idyllic 24 hours before he shoots her, and then himself, in a death pact. One of the most famous and poignant of romantic tragedies in history, *Mayerling* was impeccably cast and directed with taste and discretion. It made Boyer an idol of women the world over and led to a Hollywood contract for Litvak. Another French version (Max Ophüls' *Mayerling To Sarajevo*) was made in the 1940s, and Terence Young directed it with Omar Sharif and Catherine Deneuve in 1968, but this remains the definitive version. Sad footnote: A few days after the death of his beloved wife in 1978, Boyer committed suicide, thus echoing the fate of Rudolph.

Mayerling To Sarajevo see Sarajevo

Maynila Sa Mga Kuko Ng Liwanag see Manila: In The Claws Of Neon

Mazel Tov Ou Le Mariage see Marry Me! Marry Me!

Me see Naked Childhood

Me'Achorei Hasoragim see Beyond The Walls

The Meadow

Il Prato

Italy 1979 120 mins col
Filmtre/RAI

d **Paolo and Vittorio Taviani**
sc **Paolo and Vittorio Taviani**
ph **Franco Di Giacomo**
m **Ennio Morricone**
Isabella Rossellini, Michele Placido, Saverio Marconi, Giulio Brogi, Ermanno Taviani, Angela Goodwin

Anthropology graduate Eugenia (Rossellini) earns a dull living in a Florence tax office; her long-standing lover Enzo (Placido) is an agronomist who dreams of reclaiming idle land; Giovanni(Marconi), a young Milanese magistrate, longs to be a film-maker. In Tuscany on business, Giovanni meets Eugenia, falls in love with her and they have an affair, but she has no intention of leaving Enzo. The Taviani brothers' portrait of three young professional people searching for fulfilment and wrestling with notions of happiness is a disappointment. Overlong and containing a gaudy Pied Piper story sequence that could happily be excised, the film is a blend of dreams and reality, of the over-intellectual and the over-emotional, in which the protagonists' behaviour grows increasingly irrational. The redeeming features are the exquisitely photographed Tuscan landscape, the excellent performances and the beautiful presence of Ingrid Bergman's and Roberto Rossellini's daughter.

Mechanical Man

aka Pathetic Fallacy

Ajantrik

India 1958 102 mins bw
West Bengal Government

d **Ritwik Ghatak**
sc **Ritwik Ghatak**
ph **Dinen Gupta**
m **Ali Akbar Khan**
Kali Bandyopadhyay, Gyanesh Mukhopadhyay, Satindra Bhattacharya, Gangapada Basu

The greatest friend of Bimal (Bandyopadhyay) is his ancient, broken-down taxi, the object of ridicule to the people of the small country town where he scrapes a living. This is a satirical comment on the attitude to machinery in a traditional society, as well as being an entertaining episodic tale, expertly told with humour and pathos. Ghatak, who died an alcoholic aged 49 in 1975, made only eight feature films, few of them known outside India until after his death. He has since been recognized as a key figure in the development of modern Indian cinema.

Medea

Italy 1969 118 mins col
San Marco/Number One/Janus

d **Pier Paolo Pasolini**
sc **Pier Paolo Pasolini**
ph **Ennio Guarnieri**
m **Pier Paolo Pasolini, Che Ringrazia, Elsa Morante**
Maria Callas, Giuseppe Gentile, Laurent Terzieff, Massimo Girotti, Margareth Clementi

Jason (Gentile) arrives back in Corinth with Medea (Callas), the daughter of the King of Colchis and a high priestess with magical powers. After some years living with their two children, Jason tires of his 'barbarian' princess, but she wreaks a terrible revenge. It might have seemed a good idea to cast the fieriest of actresses from the operatic stage in the 'straight' part of Euripides' Medea, but the result was a damp squib. Much of the blame for the diva's disappointing (dubbed) performance must be laid at the door of Pasolini's wayward direction. At least this turgid mythological mish-mash contained some scenic splendour.

Meetings Of Anna, The see Rendezvous D'Anna, Les

Megalexandros, O see Alexander The Great

Megáll Az Idó see Time Stands Still

Még Kér A Nép see Red Psalm

Meilleure Façon De Marcher see Best Way to Walk, The

Meisje Met Het Rode Haar, Het see Girl With The Red Hair, The

Melissokomos, O see Beekeeper, The

Melo

Der Träumende Mund

France/Germany 1932 95 mins bw
Pathé/Nathan/Matador

d **Paul Czinner**
sc **Paul Czinner, Carl Mayer**
ph **Jules Kruger, René Ribault**
m **Beethoven, Wagner**
Elisabeth Bergner, Anton Edthofor, Rudolf Forster, Margarete Hruby

The wife (Bergner) of an orchestra musician falls in love with her husband's best friend, a concert violinist. All three are tormented by the situation, which she finally resolves by killing herself. Adapted from a mediocre play by Henri Bernstein, it is a sad and romantic, if rather tedious piece, of interest chiefly because it introduced the famous German star to American audiences and critics who gave due adulation to her transcendental qualities. This version was simultaneously shot in French, starring Gaby Morlay; then, in 1937, Czinner remade it in English in Britain, again starring his wife Miss Bergner, and calling it *Dreaming Lips*. The German director Josef Von Baky had another go at the story in the 1950s, eliminating the suicide, among other changes, and casting Maria Schell as the wife, and it resurfaced yet again in a much better light in 1987 in Alain Resnais' version.

Mélo

France 1986 112 mins col
MK2/Films A2/CNC

d **Alain Resnais**
sc **Alain Resnais**
ph **Charlie Van Damme**
m **Philippe-Gérard**
Sabine Azéma, Fanny Ardant, Pierre Arditi, André Dussollier, Jacques Dacqmine, Hubert Gignoux

Marcel (Dussollier), a celebrated violinist, falls in love with Romaine (Azéma), the wife of Pierre (Arditi), an old friend. But Marcel's loyalty to Pierre is stronger than his love for Romaine, and she commits suicide. Henri Bernstein's boulevard drama of the 1920s had already served as vehicles for the fragile talents of Elisabeth Bergner (1932, 1937) and for Maria Schell (1953) before Resnais used it as a consciously theatrical ensemble piece. Yet, despite its being set behind a proscenium arch, the brilliant camerawork and editing make it a curiously satisfying cinematic experience. Every nuance is caught in the expert performances by the same four leads as in his previous film, *L'Amour À Mort*, giving the old-fashioned plot (it is set in the 1940s) a depth and resonance it lacked previously.

Mélodie En Sous-Sol see Big Snatch, The

Melody Haunts My Memory, The see You Only Love Once

Memorias Del Subdesarrollo see Memories Of Underdevelopment

Memórias Do Cárcere see Memories Of Prison

Memories Of Prison

Memórias Do Cárcere

Brazil 1984 187 mins col
Produçoes L. C. Barreto

d **Nelson Pereira Dos Santos**
sc **Nelson Pereira Dos Santos**
ph **José Medeiros**
m **Giya Kancheli**
Carlos Vereza, Glória Pires, Jofre Soares, José Dumont, Wilson Grey

In 1936, the Brazilian author Graciliano Ramos became a political prisoner, first in a prison in Rio and then in a penal colony together with 900 other convicts. He managed to write down his experiences and published his *Memoirs Of Prison* when he was finally released. The extraordinary book was the inspiration behind an almost equally extraordinary film. Set in the 1930s, it can also be taken as a metaphor for Brazilian society in the 1980s and, although most of the cast are men, lead by Vereza as Ramos, it also shows his wife (Pires) gaining her independence. This is the second film by Pereira Dos Santos to be based on a work by Ramos, the first being the acclaimed *Barren Lives*.

Memories Of Underdevelopment

Memorias Del Subdesarrollo

Cuba 1968 104 mins bw
ICAIC

d **Tomás Gutiérrez Alea**
sc **Tomás Gutiérrez Alea, Edmundo Desnoes**
ph **Ramón Suárez**
m **Leo Brower**
Sergio Corrieri, Daisy Granádos, Eslinda Nuñez, Beatriz Ponchora

A wealthy *bourgeois* intellectual (Corrieri) whose family flees to Miami when Castro comes to power, elects to stay and come to terms with the revolution. This most subtle and ironical investigation into the role of the intellectual in the new Cuba, proved—if proof were needed—that Third World cinema could hold its own in sophistication with that of European films. Edmundo Desnoes, on whose book it was based, appears as himself in a scene at a writers' conference.

Men

Männer

W. Germany 1985 99 mins col
Olga Film/ZDF

d **Doris Dörrie**
sc **Doris Dörrie**
ph **Helge Weindler**
m **Claus Bantzer**
Heiner Lauterbach, Uwe Ochsenknecht, Ulrike Kriener, Janna Marangosoff, Dietmar Bär

When Julius (Lauterbach), a successful, happily married advertising executive, discovers that his wife (Kriener) is having an affair with Stefan (Ochsenknecht), a hippy aritist, he rents a room in Stefan's apartment in order to spy on the unsuspecting couple, meanwhile developing a friendship with his rival. Doris Dörrie may have little new to say about the childish insecurities, double standards and reactionary prejudices of men, but she presents her material as a well-written, well- constructed comedy, bringing a fresh, detached, razor-sharp eye and a touch of surreal fantasy to bear on a thoroughly entertaining and intelligent film.

Ménilmontant

France 1924 50 mins bw
Dimitri Kirsanov

d **Dimitri Kirsanov**
sc **Dimitri Kirsanov**
ph **Léonce Crovan**
m **Silent**
Nadia Sibirskaïa, Yolande Beaulieu, Guy Belmont, Jean Pasquier

Two sisters, left alone and poor after their father has savagely murdered their mother, quarrel and part. They meet some years later, by which time one (Sibirskaïa) has become a prostitute and the other (Beaulieu) has had a child by a lover killed in a street fight. One of the most famous experimental films of the 1920s, it is a ciné poem which combines several styles—ultra-rapid montage, static compositions, hand-held camera movements, flashbacks and superimpositions. Yet its series of visual impressions makes narrative sense and has an emotional impact, and Sibirskaïa is remarkable.

Menschen Am Sonntag see People On Sunday

Mephisto

Hungary 1981 144 mins col
Mafilm Studio Objectiv/Manfred Durniok Productions

d **István Szabó**
sc **Peter Dobai, István Szabó**
ph **Lajos Koltai**
m **Karl Millöcker, Mendelssohn, Reinitz, Liszt, Johann Strauss, Franz Meissner, Aldar Pege**

Klaus Maria Brandauer, Ildikó Bánsági, Krystyna Janda, Rolf Hoppe, György Cserhalmi, Peter Andorai, Karin Boyd

Högen, an acclaimed actor in pre-war Germany, famous for his interpretation of Mephistopheles, is a man of Left-wing leanings, hoping to establish a workers' theatre. When, however, the Nazis take power, his hunger for fame supersedes his political and moral principles and silences his conscience and he sells out to the oppressors, betraying his colleagues and his family. Szabó's chilling study of compromise, expertly directed and edited, was based on the novel by Klaus Mann (son of Thomas), itself drawing on the life of his uncle, actor Gustav Grundgens. A gripping story of overweening ambition, steeped in creeping political corruption, the film is beautifully cast, but it is Brandauer's monumental performance—explosively committed and energetic—that makes the film an unforgettable experience.

Best Foreign Film Oscar 1982

Mépris, Le see Contempt

The Merchant Of Four Seasons
Der Händler Der Vier Jahreszeiten

W. Germany 1971 89 mins col
Tango Film

d **Rainer Werner Fassbinder**
sc **Rainer Werner Fassbinder**
ph **Dietrich Lohmann**
m **Rocco Granata plus archive material**
Hans Hirschmüller, Irm Hermann, Hanna Schygulla, Andrea Schober, Klaus Löwitsch, Karl Scheydt

Hans Epp (Hirschmüller), unable to achieve any of his ambitions, which included joining the Foreign Legion, embarks on a loveless marriage and becomes a trader in fruit and vegetables. He drinks heavily, beats his wife and, finally, drinks himself deliberately to death. The first of Fassbinder's works to demonstrate the development of a schematic and unambiguous style, it was also the first to gain general praise and recognition in Germany. Hans is the product of stifling *petit bourgeois* values, and his disillusionment and disintegration constitute the director's pointed attack on those values. Well-acted, and encompassing a measure of black humour, the film is both bleak in its vision and enthralling in its presentation, and retains sympathy for its hopeless chief protagonist.

Merlusse

France 1935 75 mins bw
Les Films Marcel Pagnol

d **Marcel Pagnol**
sc **Marcel Pagnol**
ph **A. Assouad**
m **Vincent Scotto**
Henri Poupon, André Pollack, Thommeray, André Robert, Rellys

Merlusse (Poupon), a schoolteacher hated by his pupils, reveals an unsuspected warmth to the boys left behind in the boarding school during the Christmas holidays. It transpires that the teacher frightened the boys because he was afraid of them. Pagnol filmed this sensitive story in the lycée in Marseilles where he had been both pupil and teacher. Any sentimentality is avoided by the disarming playing and the ironic edge to the dialogue. Unhappy with the technical aspects of the first filming, Pagnol had the whole film reshot.

Mes, Het see Knife, The

Meshi see Repast

Messer Im Kopf see Knife In The Head

Messidor

Switzerland 1977 120 mins col
Action/Gaumont/Citel

d **Alain Tanner**
sc **Alain Tanner**
ph **Renato Berta**
m **Arié Dzierlatka**
Clémentine Amouroux, Catherine Rétoré, Franziskus Abgottspon, Gérald Battiaz, Hansjorg Bedschard

Jeanne (Amouroux), a university student, and Marie (Rétoré), a shop assistant, meet at the roadside while hitch-hiking. Both are bored with their lives and decide to escape. When they run out of money they begin to hold up stores and become wanted criminals. Tanner observes his repellent, amoral heroines (convincingly played by two young newcomers) with a cold but fascinated eye as they travel across Switzerland—not the country of the tourist brochures, but one of crowded motorways, and roadside cafés. He may have given the lie to those who say the Swiss only produce cuckoo-clocks and chocolate, but chocolate is easier to digest than this controversial film.

Metello

Italy 1970 112 mins col
Documento Film

d **Mauro Bolognini**
sc **Luigi Bazzoni, Ugo Pirro, Suso Cecchi D'Amico, Mauro Bolognini**
ph **Ennio Guarnieri**
m **Ennio Morricone**

Massimo Ranieri, Lucia Bosé, Ottavia Piccolo, Tina Aumont, Frank Wolff

Metello (Ranieri), a young workman, becomes involved with the rise of the Italian labour movement towards the end of the 19th century. Over the years, he has affairs, marries, enjoys political triumph as a successful strike leader, and is twice imprisoned. In this film Bolognini combined his bent for 19th-century subjects with a later sense of political commitment. The result is a story that is somewhat well-worn, and overcrowded with scenes of riot and anarchy, but a film that is nonetheless authentic in flavour, very well cast and exceedingly handsome to look at.

Best Actress (Ottavia Piccolo) Cannes 1970

Metropolis

Germany 1926 153 mins bw
UFA

d **Fritz Lang**
sc **Thea Von Harbou**
ph **Karl Freund, Günther Rittau**
m **Silent**

Brigitte Helm, Alfred Abel, Gustav Frölich, Rudolf Klein-Rogge, Fritz Rasp

The down-trodden factory workers in a futuristic city are confused by a malign robot made in the image of the saintly girl (Helm) who tried to lead them towards justice. Lang was given an unprecedented budget to create the still impressive huge sets inspired by the New York skyline, such as flying machines moving between skyscrapers, and Eugen Schüfftan introduced a new special effects process combining life-size action with models. Despite its ridiculously naive ending—Capital and Labour reconciled by love—and a soppy romantic hero (Frölich), the film is a potent allegory of totalitarianism. In 1984, Giorgio Moroder added a rock music score, tinted sequences, and edited it down to 83 minutes with less disastrous results than anticipated.

Mexican Bus Ride

aka Ascent To Heaven

Subida Al Cielo

Mexico 1951 85 mins bw
Producciones Isla

d **Luis Buñuel**
sc **Juan De La Cabada, Manuel Altolaguirre, Luis Buñuel**
ph **Alex Phillips**
m **Gustavo Pittaluga**

Lilia Prado, Carmelita González, Esteban Márquez, Manuel Dondé, Roberto Cobo

A young man (Márquez) is hauled away on his wedding night by his grasping elder brothers, anxious to get him to the next town to ratify their dying mother's will. On the hazardous bus journey over the mountains, the bus gets stuck in a flooded river, a woman has a premature delivery, the young man is pursued by the local tart and there is an unscheduled banquet. Buñuel was particularly fond of this sardonic, quickly-made comedy, based on a real-life trip made by the director's friend, the poet Altolaguirre. It is one of his lightest films, while retaining the deeper themes of birth, copulation and death, and a delightful self-parodic dream sequence.

The Middle Man

Jana-Aranya

India 1975 131 mins bw
Indus

d **Satyajit Ray**
sc **Satyajit Ray**
ph **Soumendou Roy**
m **Satyajit Ray**

Pradip Mukherjee, Satya Banerjee, Dipankar Dey, Lily Chakravarty, Aparna Sen

A young university graduate (Mukherjee) cannot find work in Calcutta after eight months of trying. In desperation, he takes a job as a middle man in a corrupt business that traffics in goods and prostitutes. One of Ray's most astringent comments on contemporary Indian society cleverly pinpoints the dilemma of choice between ethics and survival. His principal characters are viewed with less warmth than usual and the ending is rather contrived, but the depiction of the 'order-supply' business is enthralling.

The Middle Of The World

Le Milieu Du Monde

Switzerland 1974 115 mins col
Action/Citel

d **Alain Tanner**
sc **John Berger, Alain Tanner**
ph **Renato Berta**
m **Patrick Moraz**
Olympia Carlisi, Philippe Léotard, Juliet Berto, Jacques Denis

Adriana (Carlisi) comes from Italy to a small Swiss town to work as a waitress at a railway café. There she has an affair with Paul (Léotard), a married engineer. He tries to make her enter his *bourgeois* world, but she finally rejects it and him. Although a simple love story on the surface, it has a parable of the conflict between rich and poor, male and female and North and South embedded in it. Tanner spoke of its structure as 'a hundred little short films, each done in one take'. The title refers to a posh restaurant and also to Switzerland. The film, too, whatever its Left-wing objectives, comes out as neutral, because the characters are not well enough defined and the message is too elusive.

Mikaël

(US:Chained)

Germany 1924 74 mins bw
Decla Bioskop

d **Carl Dreyer**
sc **Carl Dreyer, Thea Von Harbou**
ph **Karl Freund, Rudolph Maté**
m **Silent**
Benjamin Christensen, Walter Slezak, Nora Gregor, Robert Garrison

Zoret (Danish director Christensen), a renowned and elderly artist, is driven to despair when Mikaël (Slezak), his model and pupil whom he loves more than a son, is taken from him by Princess Zamikoff (Gregor). Dreyer's study of passion and loneliness could be considered the first film of his mature period. The *fin de siècle* sets, the expressionistic lighting and the 'decadent' subject of latent homosexuality show the work's German provenence, but Dreyer keeps a steady hand on the helm, quietly penetrating into the deeper recesses of the artist's psychology. (Sigmund Freud himself makes an appearance.) Gregor became more widely known for her role in Renoir's *The Rules Of The Game*, and the handsome, 22-year-old Slezak would gain weight, lose his looks and become a favourite Hollywood villain.

Mikres Aphrodites see Young Aphrodites

Milieu Du Monde, Le see Middle Of The World, The

The Milky Way

La Voie Lactée

France 1968 102 mins col
Greenwich/Medusa

d **Luis Buñuel**
sc **Luis Buñuel, Jean-Claude Carrière**
ph **Christian Matras**
m **Luis Buñuel**
Laurent Terzieff, Paul Frankeur, Delphine Seyrig, Bernard Verley, Pierre Clémenti, Georges Marchal, Edith Scob, Michel Piccoli, Alain Cuny

Two tramps (Terzieff and Frankeur) set off from Paris to make a pilgrimage to the Spanish shrine of Santiago De Compostella. *En route* they meet various characters who expound in different ways on the six central 'mysteries' of Catholic dogma: the nature of God, Christ, the Virgin Mary, the Eucharist, divine grace, and evil. The first of Buñuel's four anecdotal French films of his last years (*The Discreet Charm Of The Bourgeoisie, The Phantom Of Liberty,* and *That Obscure Object Of Desire* followed) is the fervent atheist director's most direct treatment of Catholicism. Many of the arguments may seem somewhat obscure to non-Catholic audiences, but it is as wryly amusing and mischievously anti-clerical and anti-Establishment as the other films, although Buñuel stated that it 'is neither for nor against anything at all'. Only Christian fundamentalists might take offence at some of the episodes, including the depiction of Christ (Verley) being dissuaded by the Virgin Mary (Scob) from shaving off his beard.

Le Million

France 1931 89 mins bw
Tobis

d **René Clair**
sc **René Clair**
ph **Georges Perinal**
m **Georges Van Parys**
Annabella, René Lefèvre, Paul Olivier, Louis Allibert, Vanda Gréville, Raymond Cordy

A young painter (Lefèvre) wins a large lottery prize but loses the ticket. His search for it takes him across Paris, where he ends up on the stage of the opera house. In his second sound film, with dialogue, music and sound effects recorded on a single track while it was being shot, Clair retained the ease of movement of his best silent work, with the added joy of integrated musical numbers. In fact, this funny, charming cinematic operetta had a great influence on the film musical.

The Mill On The Po

Il Mulino Del Po

Italy 1949 105 mins bw
Lux Film

d **Alberto Lattuada**
sc **Federico Fellini, Tullio Pinelli**
ph **Aldo Tonti**
m **Ildebrando Pizzetti**
Jacques Sernas, Carla Del Poggio, Giacomo Giuradei, Isabella Riva, Mario Besesti

A young farmer (Sernas) and the daughter (Del Poggio) of a small mill owner wish to marry, but public events overtake private concerns when the farmers' demands for agrarian reform lead to social unrest and revolt in which the young man is a leading participant. The film was adapted from Ricardo Bachelli's epic novel about the events in 1876 depicted here, and Lattuada has delivered an account that is both graphic and epic, if a little too episodic and crowded with incident. The panoramas of the Po valley are authentic and effective, and the performances—particularly from real-life farmer and first-time actor Giuradei—excellent.

Mimi Metallurgico Ferito Nell'Onore see Seduction Of Mimi, The

---

Minne see Ingénue Libertine, L'

Miquette

Miquette Et Sa Mère

France 1950 95 mins bw
Alcina

d **Henri-Georges Clouzot**
sc **Henri-Georges Clouzot, Jules Ferry**
ph **Louis Née**
m **Albert Lasry**
Louis Jouvet, Danièle Delorme, Bourvil, Saturnin Fabre, Pauline Carton

Miquette (Delorme), confined to a strict girls' school, is courted by a naive and maladroit young man (Bourvil). The lovers are separated by her mother (Carton) and his uncle (Fabre), who sends him off to work in a travelling theatre run by a ham actor (Jouvet). But love finds a way. A surprisingly bright entry into the gloom of Clouzot's *oeuvre*, this version of an old boulevard comedy is treated with a delightfully light touch. In his cinematic use of the theatre, Clouzot puts one in mind of Renoir. However, the main joy comes from the choice cast and the hilariously disastrous climactic theatrical performance.

Miquette Et Sa Mère see Miquette

Miracle In Milan

Miracolo A Milano

Italy 1950 101 mins bw
ENIC

d **Vittorio De Sica**
sc **Cesare Zavattini, Vittorio De Sica**
ph **G.R. Aldo**
m **Alessandro Cicognini**
Francesco Golisano, Brunella Bovo, Emmo

Gramatica, Paolo Stoppa

Toto (Golisano), a foundling rescued from a cabbage patch, grows into an optimist who loves his fellow men, thanks to the old lady who adopted him. Through force of circumstance, he becomes the youthful leader of a colony of homeless poor in Milan, and fights injustice with the help of a magic dove given to him by the ghost of his long-dead guardian. Following De Sica's starkly realistic *Bicycle Thieves*, this one is best described as a Neo-Realist fairytale. The plot is allegorical, the characters a mix of real and caricature, the exposition pure fable, and the background harsh. It is an imaginative film, very well received in its day, but nearly 40 years on it is a sentimental, whimsical and sometimes tedious hotchpotch.

Best Film Cannes 1951

The Miracle Of Malachias

Das Wunder Des Malachias

W. Germany 1961 122 mins bw
Bernhard Wicki

d **Bernhard Wicki**
sc **Heinz Pauck, Bernhard Wicki**
ph **Klaus Von Rautenfeld, Gerd Von Bonin**
m **Hans-Martin Majewski**

Horst Bollmann, Richard Munch, Christiane Nielsen, Günter Pfitzmann, Karin Moorbach, Kurt Ehrhardt

When a huge gambling casino opens near his monastery, attracting bad elements, Father Malachias prays for its destruction. God obliges with a miracle, but the cure becomes worse than the disease, when the press, advertising agencies, big business and the Church begin to profit from the event. A serious, funny and very sharp satire on Germany's post-war 'economic miracle'. (Notice the banker who resembles Adenauer.) What makes it more effective is that Wicki, whose *The Bridge* was one of the best German films in the 1950s on World War II, shoots this allegory in a realistic manner. Only its frightening ending, hinting at a nuclear holocaust, unbalances the tale somewhat. The gentle monk, through whose large eyes we see the corruption, is beautifully played by Bollmann.

Best Director Berlin 1961

Miracolo A Milano see Miracle In Milan

Miris Poljs Kog Svecca see Fragrance of Wild Flowers, The

Miroir A Deux Faces, Le see Mirror Has Two Faces, The

Mirror

aka A White White Boy . . .

Zerkalo

USSR 1974 106 mins col/bw
Mosfilm Unit 4

d **Andrei Tarkovsky**
sc **Andrei Tarkovsky, Aleksandr Misharin**
ph **Georgy Rerberg**
m **Eduard Artemyev, Pergolesi, Bach, Purcell**

Margarita Terekhova, L. Tarkovskaya, Philip Yankovsky, Ignat Danilisev, Oleg Yankovsky, Innokenti Smoktunovsky (narrator)

An artist (heard but not seen) reflects on three generations of his family, and his relationships—as both child and adult—with his mother and father, and those with his wife and small son. This intensely personal and somewhat impenetrable multi-layered film is best approached without searching too hard for specific meaning. It is full of haunting dream-like images, evoking memories and fantasies of Tarkovsky's private and public life in the form of a visual poem. The poems in the film were written and read by his own father, and his mother (Tarkovskaya) plays the old mother on screen. The mother as a young woman and the wife are played by the same actress (Terekhova), with her hair pinned up and let down.

The Mirror Has Two Faces

Le Miroir A Deux Faces

France 1958 98 mins bw
Paris/Union

d **André Cayatte**
sc **André Cayatte, Gérard Oury**
ph **Christian Matras**
m **Louiguy**

Michèle Morgan, Bourvil, Ivan Desny, Elisabeth Manet, Gérard Oury, Sandra Milo, Sylvie, Jane Marken

A sober, unambitious schoolmaster (Bourvil), living with his mother (Sylvie), marries a very plain woman (Morgan). After six dreary years of marriage, the wife is transformed into a beauty by plastic surgery and her husband's indifference to her is transformed into jealousy. Credit must be given to make-up man Charles Parker for doing the opposite of what the plastic surgeon (Oury) does in the film, by transforming Michèle Morgan into an ugly duckling. Unsurprisingly, however, there is no suspense while her 'new face' is being revealed. As usual, Cayatte raises some interesting issues, but the script and direction are only skin deep.

Mirt Sost Shi Amit see Harvest: 3000 Years

Les Misérables

France 1934 305 mins bw
Pathé Natan

d **Raymond Bernard**
sc **Raymond Bernard, André Lang**
ph **Jules Kruger**
m **Arthur Honegger**
Harry Baur, Charles Vanel, Henry Krauss, Charles Dullin, Odette Florel, Jean Servais, Josseline Gaël, Orane Demazis

Jean Valjean (Baur), sentenced to 10 years hard labour for stealing a loaf of bread, escapes from jail an embittered man. Helped by a bishop, he regains his sense of compassion and forgiveness, adopting an orphaned child as his own daughter. Changing his identity, he rises in the world but is haunted by his Nemesis, Inspector Javert, who is determined to recapture him. This version of Victor Hugo's classic benefits from the best of Valjeans (Fredric March is a close contender) and an unrivalled Javert (Vanel),and is probably the most detailed and faithful adaptation of the original. If Bernard's respectful direction is a little short of energy, the film is nevertheless a must for lovers of the material. It is generally shown in two parts, titled *Jean Valjean* and *Cosette*, and is the best of the six French versions of the film; the most recent one, made in 1982, stars Lino Ventura.

The Mission

Ferestadeh

USA/W. Germany 1983 108 mins col
The New Film Group(Michigan)/Aria Film Produktion(Munich)

d **Parviz Sayyad**
sc **Parviz Sayyad**
ph **Reza Aria**
Houshang Touzie, Parviz Sayyad, Mohammed B. Gaffari, Mary Apick, Hedyeh Anvar, Hatam Anvar, Kamran Nozad

Douad (Touzie), a religious young Iranian, arrives in New York on a mission to assassinate an opponent of Ayatollah Khomeini, only to learn that the man has already been murdered. He is given another target, a former colonel in the Shah's army, but a series of accidental happenings push him into a personal relationship with the man and his family, and unmask the corruption of His Eminence, a Muslim clergyman from whom Douad is taking his orders. Parviz Sayyad's previous film was the last made in Iran before the Revolution and the director, one of his country's finest, and his New Film Group were forced into exile in the US, in spite of having always courted trouble with the Shah's authorities. *The Mission* is a marvellous piece of work, well made and beautifully acted, notably by Sayyad himself as the reluctant assassin's ebullient quarry. Tense, ironic and moving, the film understands and exposes the contradictions on both sides of the conflict.

The Mississippi Mermaid

La Sirène Du Mississippi

France 1969 123 mins col
Les Films Du Carrosse

d **François Truffaut**
sc **François Truffaut**
ph **Denys Clerval**
m **Antoine Duhamel**
Jean-Paul Belmondo, Catherine Deneuve, Michel Bouquet, Nelly Borgeaud, Marcel Berbert

The mail-order bride (Deneuve) of a tobacco planter (Belmondo) on the island of Réunion turns out to be a dangerous imposter and a thief. Taking his plot from a William Irish mystery novel, Truffaut, while exploring the possibilities of the thriller genre, has also tried to make a love story. Unfortunately, though it looks good on the wide screen, it is far too allusive and knowing to be either exciting or moving. There are homages to *Johnny Guitar, Vertigo,* and the work of Renoir and Cocteau, while the private eye featured in the plot is named after the editor of *Cahiers Du Cinéma* for which Truffaut was once a critic. Belmondo and Deneuve, both at the height of their popularity, play the game rather than their roles.

Miss Julie
Fröken Julie

Sweden 1951 87 mins bw
Sandrew

d **Alf Sjöberg**
sc **Alf Sjöberg**
ph **Göran Strindberg**
m **Dag Wirén**

Anita Björk, Ulf Palme, Max Von Sydow, Märta Dorff, Anders Henrikson

Miss Julie (Björk), the daughter in a wealthy 19th-century household, chooses the highly charged atmosphere of the Midsummer Night revels to humiliate the valet, Jean (Palme), and to attempt to will him to seduce her. Although August Strindberg's famous play about repression, both sexual and class, loses some of its claustrophobia in this adaptation—the action has moved from one room to take in other areas of the mansion and the estate—it gains by the complex flashback and flash forward technique in which characters from the past appear in scenes with those of the present. Björk gives a remarkable performance as the neurotically defiant Julie.

Best Film Cannes 1951

Miss Oyu
Oyusama

Japan 1951 96 mins bw
Daiei

d **Kenji Mizoguchi**
sc **Yoshitaka Yoda**
ph **Kazuo Miyagawa**
m **Fumio Hayasaka**

Kinuyo Tanaka, Nobuko Otowa, Yuji Hori, Kiyoko Hirai, Reiko Kongo

In the Meiji period (1867-1912), a wealthy bachelor (Hori) falls in love with Oyu (Tanaka), a widow whose young son will lose his inheritance if she remarries. Oyu's younger sister (Otowa) agrees to marry him in name only in order to form a bridge between the two lovers. But the triangular arrangement leads to jealousy and tragedy. *Miss Oyu* is another fine vehicle for Tanaka, made and played with great delicacy, style and emotion. The long takes give the characters and relationships time to breathe and deepen the audience's experience.

Mistero Di Oberwald, Il see Oberwald Mystery, The

Mistress, The see Swedish Mistress, The

Mit Liv Som Hund see My Life As A Dog

Mitsou

France 1957 95 mins col
Ardennes Films

d **Jacqueline Audry**
sc **Pierre Laroche**
ph **Marcel Grignon**
m **Georges Van Parys**

Danièle Delorme, Fernand Gravey, François Guérin, Claude Rich, Odette Laure, Gaby Morlay

In Paris during World War I, Mitsou (Delorme), a chorus girl, is in love with a handsome young lieutenant (Guérin) who throws her over because she lacks refined taste, social finesse and a knowledge of food and wine. Mitsou confesses all to her sugar-daddy (a suave and sophisticated Gravey) who generously gives her a crash course in becoming a lady. With its suggestion of *Gigi*, it's easy to tell that the plot came from Colette, but the emaciated screenplay is devoid of the novelist's piquancy. What we get is a feeble romance that, in spite of some frank moments, remains bland and lifeless. On the credit side, Delorme looks gorgeous, as do the sets and clothes, photographed in pleasing pastels.

Mitten Ins Herz see Straight Through The Heart

Mitt Hem Är Copacabana see My Home Is Copacabana

Miyamoto Musashi see Samurai

Moderato Cantabile

France 1960 95 mins bw
Raoul J. Levy/Iena Production(Paris)/Documento Films(Rome)

d **Peter Brook**
sc **Marguerite Duras, Gérard Jariot, Peter Brook**
ph **Armand Thirard**
m **Antonio Diabelli**
Jeanne Moreau, Jean-Paul Belmondo, Didier Haudepin, Valerie Dobuzinsky, Pascale De Boysson

The desperately bored and frustrated wife (Moreau) of a wealthy industrialist in the Gironde, who accompanies her son (Haudepin) to his piano lessons, one day hears a woman's scream from a nearby café, then sees her dead body. Obsessed with the murder, she frequents the café, becoming acquainted with a man (Belmondo) who purports to give her the information for which she hungers and to whom she grows increasingly attracted. Adapted from a novella by Duras and directed by international theatre guru Peter Brook with a spare, bleak style, this is very much a mood piece where words are used in place of action. A study of boredom and emotional sterility, in which Moreau expressively captures the despair of the woman and Belmondo the ambiguity of the man. Unfortunately, although the atmosphere and performances cast a certain spell, this is a rather airless and arty film.

Best Actress (Jeanne Moreau) Cannes 1960

A Modern Dubarry

Eine Dubarry Von Heute

Germany 1927 110 mins bw
Felsom/UFA

d **Alexander Korda**
sc **Lajos Biro**
ph **Fritz Arno Wagner**
m **Silent**
Maria Corda, Hans Albers, Alfred Abel, Jean Bradin, Julia Serda, Alfred Gerasch, Friedrich Kayssler

Toinette (Corda), a young Parisian coquette, is helped by one of her male friends to become a fashion model. She meets and falls in love with a man (Bradin) who, unbeknown to her, is the King of Astoria. Circumstance separates them and she continues to work her way up the ladder of success via a series of influential lovers until she and her king are reunited. A combination of frothy Gallic 'society' picture and Ruritanian romance—it comes complete with a revolution—this is an uneven piece in which the action grows over-complicated and then flags. The director's wife is well-showcased— part of the film's aim and object, as the Kordas were leaving to take up a contract with First National in Hollywood, prior to the producer-director becoming a key figure in the growth of the British film industry. Look out for Marlene Dietrich, passing through as a coquette.

Modigliani Of Montparnesse see Montparnasse 19

Moglie Del Prete, La see Priest's Wife, The

Moi Drug Ivan Lapshin see My Friend Ivan Lapshin

Moi Universiteti see My Universities

Mole, The see Topo, El

Molière

France 1978 188 mins col
Les Films Du Soleil Et De La Nuit/Les Films 13/Antenne 2/RAI

d **Ariane Mnouchkine**
sc **Ariane Mnouchkine**
ph **Bernard Zitzermann**
m **René Clemencic**

Philippe Caubère, Joséphine Derenne, Brigitte Catillon, Claude Merlin, Roger Planchon

The life story of the great 17th-century French playwright Molière (Caubère), born Jean-Baptiste Poquelin, from his childhood and schooling, through his years with a troupe of travelling players until he gains the patronage of King Louis XIV, up to his death while playing the title role in *Le Malade Imaginaire*. Mnouchkine, founder-director of the Théâtre Du Soleil, has reconceived her epic stage production for the cinema, framing much of it in the manner of the master painters of the epoch. Some of the exciting theatrical quality of the original is dissipated, but the evocation of the theatre of the day and the unequal society—the contrast between the extreme poverty of the people and the opulence of the court—comes through strongly in this sprawling pageant. However, some of the sequences outstay their welcome, a mistake Molière, played with splendid conviction by Caubère, would not have made. It was initially made as 4¼ hours of television, to be shown in episodes, and was later cut for the cinema.

Mollenard

(US: Hatred)

France 1937 89 mins bw
Corniglion/Molinier

d **Robert Siodmak**
sc **Charles Spaak**
ph **Eugen Schüfftan**
m **Darius Milhaud**

Harry Baur, Gabrielle Dorziat, Albert Préjean, Dalio, Pierre Renoir, Jacques Baumer, Walter Rilla

Dunkirk-based Captain Mollenard (Baur), whose arms-trafficking activities cause the disruption of his ship and family, and earn him the enmity of his cold and spiteful wife (Dorziat), finds his happiness in the brothels of Shanghai. This curious but intriguing drama mixes realistic Dunkirk locations with Alexandre Trauner's artificial atmospheric sets of murky ports. The two contrasting halves of the story are dominated by the wonderful Baur, given splendid support from an array of the most talented performers around.

Moment D'Égarement, Un see Summer Affair, A

Momento Della Verità, Il see Moment Of Truth, The

The Moment Of Truth

Il Momento Della Verità

Italy/Spain 1964 110 mins col
Federiz/AS Films (Madrid)

d **Francesco Rosi**
sc **Francesco Rosi**
ph **Gianni Di Venanzo, Aiace Parolin, Pasquale De Santis**
m **Piero Piccioni**

Miguel Mateo Miguelin, José Gomez Sevillano, Linda Christian, Pedro Basauri

A peasant boy (Miguelin) comes from Andalucia to Barcelona to seek his fortune in the bullring. Considered by many to be the greatest of all bullfighting movies, it stars one of Spain's most famous matadors. By the use of a telephoto lens, Rosi was able to show in close-up the unremitting slaughter of the bulls in a sacrificial ceremony to appease a savage god. Between the killings of the bulls, there is a story of sorts in which the young hero falls for Linda Christian playing herself.

Monachine, Le see Little Nuns, The

Monde Du Silence, La see Silent World, The

Mondo Cane

aka A Dog's Life

Italy 1961 105 mins col
Cineriz

d **Gualtiero Jacopetti**
sc **Gualtiero Jacopetti (commentary)**
ph **Antonio Climati, Benito Frattari**
m **Nino Oliviero, Riz Ortolani**

A documentary made up of approximately 30 episodes in the life of man and beast, filmed all over the world—New Guinea, Germany, Singapore, Portugal, Australia, America, and beyond. Admittedly it is well made, but the sole motive behind it seems to be to show us to ourselves in the worst possible light. Apart from a couple of sequences in which humans are made to look merely ridiculous, most of the material is concerned with cruelty, debasement and revolting carnage. One dignifies it with inclusion here because it was unique at the time (unhappily spawning some successors) and, terrifyingly, a massive box-office hit worldwide. Even the theme music became popular. Called by one critic, 'a hymn to death and mutilation embellished with a shrug and a giggle,' it is not for the sensitive.

The Money Order
Le Mandat
aka Mandabi

Senegal 1968 90 mins col
Films Domirêve (Dakar)/Comptoir Français Du Film (Paris)

d **Ousmane Sembène**
sc **Ousmane Sembène**
ph **Paul Soulignac**
m **Ousmane Sembène and traditional music**
Makourédia Gueye, Younousse N'diaye, Issa Niang, Moustapha Touré, Farba Sarr, Serigne Sow

Ibrahima (Gueye), an unemployed man living with his two wives and seven children in a poor suburb of Dakar, receives a letter from his nephew in Paris containing a money order for 250 francs. The news spreads through the neighbourhood and Ibrahima's troubles begin. Although France gave three million francs towards the production, this superb Senegalese satire was the first feature ever made by an all-African crew in a native African language, in this case, Wolof. Already in his second film (after the medium-length *Black Girl* of 1966), Sembène reveals his favourite theme—the hangover his country is suffering after nearly 400 years of colonial rule—through wry humour and pathos. It works not only as political allegory but as a social comedy, rooted in the African experience.

Monika see Summer With Monika

Mon Oncle see My Uncle

Mon Oncle Antoine see My Uncle Antoine

Mon Oncle D'Amérique see My American Uncle

Monsieur Hawarden

Belgium 1968 106 mins bw
Sofidoc(Brussels)/Parkfilm(Amsterdam)

d **Harry Kümel**
sc **Jan Blokker, Harry Kümel**
ph **Eduard J.R. Van Der Enden**
m **Pierre Bartholomée**
Ellen Vogel, Hilde Uitterlinden, Johan Remmelts, Dora Van Der Groen, Xander Fisher

Monsieur Hawarden, accompanied by his beautiful maid Victorine (Uitterlinden), arrives to stay at a remote farmhouse in the Ardennes. The household retainers gossip about the newcomers and develop rivalries over Victorine which end in her death. Hawarden leaves for Spa and resumes 'his' true identity, that of Meriora Gillibrand, daughter of Viennese aristocrats, has a brief affair with an officer, and returns—as Hawarden again—to the French farm... Filmed with a cool, stylish elegance and an eye for period detail, this deliberately slow-paced film unfolds in the manner of a mystery story. Based on a Flemish novel which took its inspiration from a true case, it made an impressive debut for Kümel, who only occasionally lapses into self-conscious or melodramatic effects. Vogel is powerfully convincing in the tragic title role.

Monsieur Hulot's Holiday
Les Vacances De Monsieur Hulot

France 1953 91 mins bw
Cady/Discina

d **Jacques Tati**
sc **Jacques Tati, Henri Marquet**
ph **Jacques Mercanton, Jean Mousselle**
m **Alain Romans**
Jacques Tati, Nathalie Pascaud, Michèle Rolla, Valentine Camax

Monsieur Hulot (Tati), an amiable bachelor, spends his summer holidays at a small Breton seaside resort where he inadvertently triggers off a series of mishaps. Inspired by a sergeant he had known in the army and a clumsy architect called Hulot, Tati introduced his endearing, maladroit character in the first of four comic gems. Hulot, invariably wearing a hat, overcoat and rather too short trousers, smoking a pipe and walking as if against a strong wind, is not only an instigator of incidents but an observer of the idiosyncracies of the French middle class at the seaside. There is very little dialogue, the gentle humour residing in the body language and the eloquently organized sound track.

Monsieur Vincent

France 1947 113 mins bw
EDIC/UGC

d **Maurice Cloche**
sc **Jean Anouilh, Jean-Bernard Luc**
ph **Claude Renoir**
m **Jean-Jacques Grünewald**
Pierre Fresnay, Aimé Clairiond, Jean Debucourt, Lise Delamare, Gabrielle Dorziat, Michel Bouquet

The life and work of the 17th-century Saint Vincent De Paul (Fresnay), who was in conflict with the rich and powerful because of his pioneer work among the poor. Although the film had some financial backing from the Catholic Church, this inspiring depiction of saintliness contains only a modicum of sermonizing. The beauty of the photography does not exclude the starkness of the poverty or the brutality of the age. Fresnay, growing from a young man to old age, carries even atheists along with him.

Best Foreign Film Oscar 1948
Best Actor (Pierre Fresnay) Venice 1947

Montparnasse 19

aka The Lovers Of Montparnasse
(US: Modigliani Of Montparnesse)

France 1958 110 mins bw
Franco London Films/Astra

d **Jacques Becker**
sc **Jacques Becker, Max Ophüls, Henri Jeanson**
ph **Christian Matras**
m **Georges Van Parys, Paul Misraki, Bach**
Gérard Philipe, Lilli Palmer, Anouk Aimée, Gérard Séty, Lino Ventura, Lila Kedrova, Lea Padovani

The tubercular and alcoholic painter Modigliani (Philipe) leads a wild and dissolute life in Paris with his mistress (Palmer). He falls in love with Jeanne (Aimée), who follows him to the South of France. She becomes his mistress and his model and commits suicide before his untimely death. The twelfth of Becker's 13 films provides a vivid glimpse of the milieu and period of Modigliani's life but does not rank with the director's best work. The performance of his stellar lead was lacklustre, but the women were excellent and the action reasonably convincing. It was a troubled project: Ophüls, who was meant to direct the film, died, Becker quarrelled with co-writer Jeanson, and the artist's daughter was on the set to add to Becker's problems. Nonetheless, it is quite entertaining and occasionally moving.

The Moon In The Gutter

La Lune Dans Le Caniveau

France 1983 130 mins col
Gaumont/TF1 Productions/SFPC (Paris)/Opera Film Produzione (Rome)

d **Jean-Jacques Beineix**
sc **Jean-Jacques Beineix**
ph **Philippe Rousselot**
m **Gabriel Yared**
Gérard Depardieu, Nastassja Kinski, Victoria Abril, Bertice Reading, Vittorio Mezzogiorno, Dominique Piñon

In his search for the rapist of his sister, who has since killed herself in despair, a stevedore (Depardieu) becomes involved with a wealthy girl (Kinski) whose alcoholic brother (Mezzogiorno) he suspects of the crime. Depardieu himself suggested Jean-Jacques (*Diva*) Beineix's second feature be called 'Film In The Gutter'. Based on a 1953 American crime novel by David Goodis, it was shot at Cinecitta among elaborate sets which give it an airless, stagey atmosphere steeped in the aesthetics of pop record sleeves. The film works as neither fantasy nor reality, and was rightly rounded on by the critics. However, it is the sort of bad arty movie that could easily become a cult in a few years.

Mörder Sind Unter Uns, Die see Murderers Are Among Us, The

Mord Und Totschlag see Degree Of Murder, A

More Than A Miracle see Cinderella—Italian Style

Morning

Jutro

Yugoslavia 1967 104 mins bw
Dunav Film

d **Purisa Djordjević**
sc **Purisa Djordjević**
ph **Mika Popović**
m **Miodrag Ilić-Beli**
Milena Dravić, Ljubisa Samardzić, Mija Aleksić, Neda Arnerić, Ljuba Tadić, Olga Jancevecka

Events in the Serbian town of Cacak during the last day of war and the first of peace, involving the reactions of a diverse collection of characters including victorious Partisans, captured Germans, a Red Army officer, collaborators and, of course, the townspeople. Djordjević, who himself left school at 17 to join the Partisans, claims that there was both more brutality and more tenderness during 1945 than he has succeeded in showing. Nonetheless, it is an affecting piece, the third and most acclaimed of a quartet of films the director has made on the war years.
Best Actress (Ljubisa Samardzić) Venice 1967

Mort De Mario Ricci, La see Death Of Mario Ricci, The

Morte A Venezia see Death In Venice

Morte Di Un Amico see Death Of A Friend

Mort En Ce Jardin, La see Evil Eden

Morte Risale A Ieri Sera, La see Death Occurred Last Night

Morte-Saison Des Amours, La see Season For Love, The

Moscow Distrusts Tears

(US: Moscow Does Not Believe In Tears)

Moskava Slezam Ne Verit

USSR 1979 148 mins col
Mosfilm

d **Vladimir Menshov**
sc **Valentin Chernykh**
ph **Igor Slabnevich**
m **Sergei Nikitin**
Vera Alentova, Alexei Batalov, Irina Muraveva, Alexander Fatiushin, Raisa Ryazanova, Boris Smorchkov

Three young Russian girls share a room in a Moscow workers' dormitory during 1958, pursuing their careers and their love affairs. Tonya (Ryazanova) achieves a happy and settled marriage, Ludmila (Muraveva) an unhappy marriage, and Katerina (Alentova), the central protagonist, is abandoned with an illegitimate child. Twenty years later—denoted on screen by the ticking of a clock—we meet them again. This is a competent, well-acted diversion of a kind that would be termed 'a woman's picture' in the West. The film is chiefly interesting for being a good old Hollywood romantic comedy-drama, with all its familiar clichés and conventions transported to an unfamiliar—and unexpected—setting.

Best Foreign Film Oscar 1980

Moscow Does Not Believe In Tears see Moscow Distrusts Tears

Moses And Aaron

Moses Und Aron

Austria 1975 col
Janus Films/Austrian TV/ARD

d **Jean-Marie Straub**
sc **Jean-Marie Straub, Danièle Huillet (Text Arnold Schönberg)**

ph **Ugo Piccone**
m **Arnold Schönberg (Conductor Michael Gielen)**
Guenther Reich, Louis Devos, Eva Csapo, Roger Lucas, Richard Salter, Werner Mann

Moses (Reich), through his brother Aaron (Devos), tries to communicate God's message to his people. In the wilderness, while waiting for Moses to return from Sinai, the people make a Golden Calf to worship as a god. Moses returns and smashes the tablets bearing the Commandments. By shooting this Biblical opera in a Roman amphitheatre (in Italy) and using direct sound, Straub avoided the awkward technique of dubbing. The singers could hear the orchestra through earphones, conveniently concealed under their head-dresses, and see the conductor on closed circuit TV screens. The result is a remarkably faithful and musically exciting rendering of Schönberg's religious and philosophical opera. He allows the work to unravel and flow, with few cuts per sequence, keeping the camera either fixed or continuously revolving. Only the Act II orgy is unconvincing and disappointing, represented as it is by one nude couple. The spoken Act III, for which Schönberg never got to write music, is staged in one long take.

Moses Und Aron see Moses And Aaron

Moskava Slezam Ne Verit see Moscow Distrusts Tears

Mother
Mat

USSR 1926 90 mins bw
Mezhrabpom-Russ

d **Vsevolod Pudovkin**
sc **Nathan Zarkhi, Vsevolod Pudovkin**
ph **Anatoli Golovnya**
m **Silent**
Vera Baranovskaya, A.P. Khristiakov, Nikolai Batalov, Ivan Koval-Samborski, Anna Zemtsova, Vsevolod Pudovkin

At the time of the abortive revolution of 1905, Pavel (Batalov), the son of a drunken father (Khristiakov) and an overworked mother (Baranovskaya), leads an illegal strike. The mother inadvertently gives her son away to the police, but gradually turns to Communism through her experience of injustice and suffering. Pudovkin's first feature turns Maxim Gorky's rambling novel into a tightly constructed narrative. The film's emotional and visual impact has not diminished with time, nor has Baranovskaya's performance. The remarkable montage—water is a constant visual metaphor, as in the scene of blocks of ice flowing rapidly in the river as the May Day demonstrators run through the streets—is never allowed to usurp the human factor. Mark Donskoi remade it in 1956, and Brecht's version for the Berliner Ensemble was filmed two years later.

The Mother And The Whore
La Maman Et La Putain

France 1973 215 mins bw
Films Du Losange/Elites Films/Ciné Qua Non/Simar/V.M.

d **Jean Eustache**
sc **Jean Eustache**
ph **Pierre Lhomme, Jacques Renard, Michel Cenet**
m **Mozart, Offenbach**
Jean-Pierre Léaud, Bernadette Lafont, Françoise Lebrun, Isabelle Weingarten, Jacques Renard

Alexandre (Léaud), who lives with the slightly older Marie (Lafont), picks up Veronika (Lebrun), a sexually liberated nurse. They set up a *ménage-à-trois*, until tensions and stresses within it force them to face themselves and discuss possible options. Funny, irritating, obsessive, verbose, witty, provocative and erotic, this long film consists mainly of conversations, stories, confessions and monologues delivered by the three brilliant players. It might be described as the summation of the French New Wave. Eustache shot the film economically in his own apartment and in local bistros. The film's success led on to his last film, the bigger budgeted *Mes Petites Amoureuses*. He committed suicide in 1981 aged 43.

Special Jury Prize Cannes 1973

Mother Joan Of The Angels see Devil And The Nun, The

Mother Kuster Goes To Heaven

Mutter Küsters Fahrt Zum Himmel

W. Germany 1975 120 mins col
Tango Film

d **Rainer Werner Fassbinder**
sc **Rainer Werner Fassbinder**
ph **Michael Ballhaus**
m **Peer Raben**
Brigitte Mira, Margit Carstensen, Karl-Heinz Böhm, Ingrid Caven, Armin Meier

When Frau Kuster (Mira) learns that her husband has killed one of his bosses and committed suicide in protest against dismissals at his factory, she becomes politicized, and finally joins a Left-wing urban guerrilla movement. Like *Fear Eats The Soul*, also starring the remarkable Brigitte Mira, this bitterly ironic film (the woman is exploited by Left and Right) depicts a lonely, aging woman liberating herself. One of Fassbinder's most cohesive narratives, it continues and improves upon the theme of the pressures of industrial society on the individual as expounded in *Why Does Herr R Run Amok?*.

Mouchette

France 1967 90 mins bw
Parc/Argos

d **Robert Bresson**
sc **Robert Bresson**
ph **Ghislain Cloquet**
m **Monteverdi, Jean Wiener**
Nadine Nortier, Jean-Claude Guilbert, Marie Cardinal, Paul Hébert, Jean Vimenet

Mouchette (Nortier), a 14-year-old village schoolgirl, the loveless, abused and humiliated daughter of an alcoholic father and a dying mother, drowns herself. Bresson returned to the work of Georges Bernanos, the author of *Diary Of A Country Priest* (1951). He changed the locale from the north to Provence for the sake of better weather for shooting, but there is little warmth in the film itself—a relentlessly oppressive detailing of a wasted young life. There is something almost sadistic in the way the girl is used, in the same manner as the donkey in his previous film *Balthazar*.

Moul Le Ya, Moul Le Ya see Wheel, The

The Mountain Cat

(US: The Wildcat)

Die Bergkatze

Germany 1921 80 mins bw
Union/UFA

d **Ernst Lubitsch**
sc **Hans Kräly, Ernst Lubitsch**
ph **Théodor Sparkühl**
m **Silent**
Pola Negri, Viktor Janson, Paul Heidemann, Wilhelm Diegelmann, Hermann Thimig

Rischka (Negri), the strong-willed and outspoken daughter of the chief of a comical band of mountain brigands, is attracted to Lieutenant Alexis (Heidemann) and demonstrates her affection by stealing his clothes and pelting him with snowballs. Rischka's father, however, wants her to marry a member of his gang... In this delightfully stylized and offbeat comedy, Lubitsch succeeded in satirizing the military while creating a bizarre imaginary world for which he drew on surrealism, expressionism and everything in between. The extraordinary sets are by stage designer Ernst Stern, but it is Negri, the cat of the title, who steals the show, giving one of her liveliest comedy performances in the days before she became a big star of costume pictures, none of which could hold a candle to this little gem.

Mourir À Madrid see To Die In Madrid

Mourir À Tue-Tête see Primal Fear

Mrigaya see Royal Hunt, The

Mr Klein

France 1976 123 mins col
Lira Films/Adel Productions/Nova Films (Paris)/Mondial Te-Fi (Rome)

d **Joseph Losey**
sc **Franco Solinas**
ph **Gerry Fisher**
m **Egisto Macchi, Pierre Porte**

Alain Delon, Jeanne Moreau, Suzanne Flon, Michel Lonsdale, Juliet Berto, Louis Seigner, Francine Racette, Massimo Girotti

In 1942, Robert Klein, a womanizing antique dealer, remains untouched by the German occupation of Paris and indifferent to the fate of Jews under Nazi rule—until he is confused with another Robert Klein, a wanted man and a Jew. As he gets caught in the web of mistaken identity, Klein grows obsessed with finding his *doppelgänger*, and eventually assumes his identity. Co-produced by Alain Delon, excellent in the title role, this film is a blend of Kafkaesque mightmare and glossy thriller. Made with Losey's customary expertise and feel for atmosphere, it is a complex and absorbing examination of identity crisis, moral ambivalence, and the implications of French reaction to Hitler's invasion.

Muddy River

Doro No Kawa

Japan 1981 105 mins bw
Kimura Productions

d **Kohei Oguri**
sc **Takako Shigemori**
ph **Shohei Ando**
m **Kurato Mori**

Nobutaka Asahara, Takahiro Tamura, Yumiko Fujita, Minoru Sakurai, Mariko Kaga, Makiko Shibata

Nine-year-old Nobuo (Asahara) makes friends with Kiichi (Sakurai), a boy of his own age who lives on a barge with his sister (Shibata) and their widowed mother (Kaga). When Nobuo's parents (Tamura and Fujita) learn that the widow is a prostitute, they warn him not to visit the barge at night. The theme of friendship between children has been extensively covered in the Japanese cinema over the years, including works by Ozu and Shimizu, so this extremely promising first feature suffered somewhat from comparisons. The main flaws occur in the latter sequences, when Nobuo witnesses the sexual activities of his friend's mother. Nevetheless, most of the film minutely builds up a loving picture of children and their relationship with adults (all excellently played) against a well-observed background of riverside life in Osaka in 1956. The film received an Oscar nomination.

Müde Tod, Der see Destiny

Muerte De Un Burocrata, La see Death Of A Bureaucrat

Muerte De Un Ciclista see Death Of A Cyclist

Muerte En Esta Jardin, La see Evil Eden

Mulino Del Po, Il see Mill On The Po, The

Mumia, El see Night Of Counting The Years, The

Münchhausen see Adventures Of Baron Münchhausen, The

Mura Di Malapaga, Le see Walls of Malapaga, The

Muralla Verde, La see Green Wall, The

Murder À La Carte

(US: Deadlier Than The Male)

Voici Les Temps Des Assassins

France 1955 113 mins bw
C.I.C.C./Agiman

d **Julien Duvivier**
sc **Julien Duvivier, Maurice Bessy, Charles Dorat**
ph **Armand Thirard**
m **Jean Wiener**

Jean Gabin, Danièle Delorme, Gérard Blain, Germaine Kerjean, Lucienne Bogaërt, Robert Manuel, Gabrielle Fontan

Chatelin (Gabin),a good-hearted and elderly Paris restaurateur, is visited by a girl (Delorme) who claims to be the daughter of his ex-wife (Bogaërt). She tells him that her mother has died, leaving her alone and helpless, and he takes her in, in spite of the misgivings of his possessive mother (Kerjean). As time goes by, it turns out that her mother is alive, albeit half-crazed by drugs, and that she herself is a ruthless gold-digger. This film firmly belongs to the period of Duvivier's decline. The whole farrago is implausible and rather squalid, but nonetheless fairly compulsive thanks to the uninhibited and skilful performances of the women who surround an uncharacteristically docile Gabin—a quartet of vipers, completed by Chatelin's horribly vindictive housekeeper (Fontan).

Murder Czech Style

Vrazda Po Cesky

Czechoslovakia 1966 87 mins bw (part col)
Ceskoslovensky Film

d **Jiří Weiss**
sc **Jan Otcenašek, Jiří Weiss**
ph **Jan Nemeček**
m **Zdeněk Liška**
Rudolf Hrušínsky, Kveta Fialová, Vaclav Voska, Vladimír Menšík, Vera Uzelacova, Libuse Svormová

František (Hrušínsky), a dull, overweight, middle-aged clerk in a provincial city, leads a boring and loveless existence until he meets Alice (Fialová), a beautiful colleague from Prague and, surprisingly, marries her. At her behest, the marriage is not consummated for some time and he discovers that she has a married lover in Prague. František plans several increasingly unlikely methods of revenge... Jiří Weiss's last Czech- made film before he moved to the West is an awful disappointment, particularly as it begins so promisingly. Hrušínsky's nondescript inadequate is beautifully played, and the details of his daily life are expertly observed by director and cameraman. However, halfway through, the story degenerates into a silly and pointless fantasy.

The Murderer Lives At No. 21

L'Assassin Habite Au 21

France 1942 90 mins bw
Continental

d **Henri-Georges Clouzot**
sc **Henri-Georges Clouzot**
ph **Armand Thirard**
m **Maurice Yvain**
Pierre Fresnay, Suzy Delair, Noël Roquevert, Pierre Larquey, Jean Tissier

A murder takes place in a boarding house full of eccentrics, each one a likely suspect. Clouzot, whose films are generally dark in character, made his feature debut with this delightful comedy-thriller of the *Thin Man* type. Fresnay is witty as the detective, but Delair as his bubble-headed assistant is irritating enough to drive anyone to murder.

Murderers Among Us see Murderers Are Among Us, The

The Murderers Are Among Us

(US: Murderers Among Us)

Die Mörder Sind Unter Uns

W. Germany 1946 87 mins bw
Defa

d **Wolfgang Staudte**
sc **Wolfgang Staudte**
ph **Friedl Behn-Grund, Eugen Klagemann**
m **Ernst Roters**
Hildegard Knef, Ernst Borchert, Arno Paulsen, Erna Sellmer, Robert Forsch

In the ruins of immediate post-war Germany, a doctor (Borchert) who has witnessed the atrocities in a death camp is tormented by guilt. His former captain (Paulsen), by contrast, lives a contented family life, untroubled by the mass executions he carried out. Encouraged by his girlfriend (Knef), the doctor denounces the captain to the war crime investigators. Although a heavy-handed, plodding piece of bleak introspection, this film raises questions that compel attention, and is also interesting as one of the first productions to come out of Germany itself which faced the question of responsibility for the crimes of the Nazi era.

Murder Of Dmitri Karamazov, The see Brothers Karamazov, The

Muriel

Muriel, Ou Le Temps D'Un Retour

France 1963 116 mins col
Argos/Alpha/Eclair/Les Films De La

Muriel, Ou Le Temps D'Un Retour

Pléiade/Dear Films

d **Alain Resnais**
sc **Jean Cayrol**
ph **Sacha Vierny**
m **Hans Werner Henze**

Delphine Seyrig, Jean-Pierre Kérien, Nita Klein, Jean-Baptiste Thierrée, Laurence Badie, Martine Vatel

A middle-aged woman (Seyrig) invites her lover (Kérien) of 20 years earlier and his niece (Klein) to stay with her and her stepson (Thierrée) in Boulogne. The latter, just returned from military service in Algeria, is haunted by the memory of a girl called Muriel, just as the ex-lovers are haunted by their past. Seemingly more realistic on the surface than Renais' previous film, *Last Year At Marienbad*, it is almost as stylized and metaphysical. The rhythmic dialogue and overlapping sounds, the ethereal Henze music, Boulogne shot in visionary colour, and the fragmented narrative technique give a resonance to the actions of a group of characters placed in mundane situations and surroundings but tortured by their memories. Arguably Resnais' last great film until *Providence* 14 years later.

Best Actress (Delphine Seyrig) Venice 1963

Muriel, Ou Le Temps D'Un Retour see Muriel

Mur, Le see Wall, The

Murmur Of The Heart see Dearest Love

Music In The Dark see Night Is My Future

The Music Room

Jalsaghar

India 1958 100 mins bw
Satyajit Ray

d **Satyajit Ray**
sc **Satyajit Ray**
ph **Subrata Mitra**
m **Satyajit Ray**

Chabi Biswas, Padma Devi, Tulsi Lahin, Pinaki Sen Gupta, Kali Sarkar

An aristocratic provincial landowner (Biswas), forced to sell his crumbling mansion because of his extravagances, decides to spend the remains of his dwindling fortune on a last concert of classical Indian music. As a composer himself, music has always played an important role in Ray's films but never more so than in this exquisite early chamber work. The performance of Biswas as the declining reclining nobleman is as formalized as the elegiac concert finale, interrupted by a sudden storm.

Musik I Mörker see Night Is My Future

Mustaa Valkoisella see Black On White

Mutter Küsters Fahrt Zum Himmel see Mother Kuster Goes To Heaven

---

My American Uncle

Mon Oncle D'Amérique

France 1980 126 mins col
Andrea Films/TF1

d **Alain Resnais**
sc **Jean Gruault**
ph **Sacha Vierny**
m **Arié Dzierlatka**

Gérard Depardieu, Nicole Garcia, Roger Pierre, Henri Laborit

The lives of the manager of a small manufacturing plant (Depardieu), a committed actress (Garcia), and a TV executive (Pierre) are analysed in terms of the animal behaviourist theories of Dr Henri Laborit. From the peak of *Providence*, Resnais plunged into the numbing banality of this semi-satire on modern French life which comes to the hardly original conclusion that we are only what society makes us. This is reached through the stories of three unappealing characters compared mostly with laboratory rats by what seems a parody professor who happens to be playing himself. It is all put together with Resnais' usual brilliant cutting technique.

Special Jury Prize Cannes 1980

My Apprenticeship

aka Out In The World

(US: Among People)

Vlyudyakh

USSR 1939 98 mins bw
Soyezdetfilm

d **Mark Donskoi**
sc **Mark Donskoi, Ilya Grouzdez**
ph **Piotr Ermolov**
m **Lev Schwartz**
Alexei Lyarsky, Varvara Massalitinova, Mikhail Troianovski, V. Novikov

The teenage Maxim Gorky (Lyarsky) gets work on a ferry on the river Volga, becomes a servant in a large household and an apprentice to ikon painters. He also begins to read of and to observe the hardships of the society around him. As in the first of Donskoi's trilogy, *The Childhood Of Maxim Gorky*, there is a rich gallery of characters, particularly Massalitinova's wonderful old grandmother, and a vivid depiction of the bustling riverside life. It culminates with the heart-rending and uplifting scene when the young man leaves his grandparents for the first time. His adventures are followed in *My Universities*, the following year.

My Best Friend's Girl

La Femme De Mon Pote

France 1983 100 mins col
Renn Productions/Sara Films

d **Bertrand Blier**
sc **Bertrand Blier, Gérard Brach**
ph **Jean Penzer**
m **J. J. Cale, Mozart Serenade No 5, and 11 pop songs**
Coluche, Isabelle Huppert, Thierry Lhermitte, Farid Chopel, François Perrot

While on holiday in the ski resort of Courchevel, Pascal (Lhermitte) acquires a new flame, Viviane (Huppert), whom he leaves in the care of his best friend Micky (Coluche). When Viviane throws herself at Micky, who can't resist her, the friendship of the boys is threatened. Blier's film is expertly played, naturistically directed, has much charm and attractive locations. However, the director seems unsure whether he is making a boulevard comedy or taking a profound look at the motivations and morality of his characters. The result is a superficial entertainment, larded with vague pretensions. Interesting footnote: Coluche stood for the French presidency, and was killed in an accident.

My Friend Ivan Lapshin

Moi Drug Ivan Lapshin

USSR 1986 99 mins bw/col
Lenfilm

d **Alexei Gherman**
sc **Eduard Volodarsky**
ph **Valery Fedosov**
m **Arkady Gagulashvili**
Andrei Boltnev, Nina Ruslanova, Andrei Mironov, Alexei Zharkov, Yu. Kuznetsov

Ivan Lapshin (Boltnev), a police chief in a provincial Russian town, shares an apartment with his self-important immediate subordinate (Zharkov), and with a man who has a nine-year-old son. Lapshin's main activity in the cold winter of 1935 is to track down a notorious gang of criminals, but he finds time to make a clumsy attempt at romance with an actress (Ruslanova) and to take care of his best friend (Mironov) whose wife has died. The film opens in the present (in colour) and reverts to the past (black and white) via an unseen narrator who, it would seem, was the little boy living with Lapshin. Gherman based his third feature on stories written by his father Yuri, a well-known literary figure. It is a densely packed and richly detailed tapestry of life and conditions in the period just prior to the Stalin purges, made with perception and a naturalistic style, and offering performances as good as one could wish for.

My Girlfriend's Boyfriend

L'Ami De Mon Amie

France 1987 102 mins col
Les Films Du Losange

d **Eric Rohmer**
sc **Eric Rohmer**
ph **Bernard Lutic**
m **Jean-Louis Valero**
Emmanuelle Chaulet, Sophie Renoir, Eric Viellard, François-Eric Gendron, Anne-Laure Meury

In a new town outside Paris, Blanche (Chaulet) becomes friends with Lea (Renoir).

They meet Alexandre (Gendron), an engineer, to whom Blanche is attracted. While Lea is on holiday, Blanche gets to know Lea's boyfriend Fabien (Viellard). Lea and Alexandre get together, and Blanche and Fabien... Like the preceding five of Rohmer's 'Comedies and Proverbs', the film involves rather trivial, egoistic young people, concerned only with their love lives. But Rohmer has proved (perhaps a little too often) that it is possible to make an interesting film about uninteresting people. His model for his pastel comedies of manners is the 18th-century playwright Marivaux. The main pleasure comes from watching modern youth indulging in the amorous games people have always played. Rohmer, as hedonistic as ever, provides his characters with good food, wine and sunshine, the camera lapping up the artificial lake, the woods and the futuristic buildings of Cergy-Pointoise.

My Home Is Copacabana
Mitt Hem Är Copacabana

Sweden 1965 88 mins bw
Svensk Filmindustri

d **Arne Sucksdorff**
sc **Arne Sucksdorff, Flavio Migliaccio, Joâo Bethecourt**
ph **Arne Sucksdorff**
m **Radamés Gnatalli, Luciano Perrone, Luis Antonio**
Leila Santos De Sousa, Cosme Dos Santos, Antonio Carlos De Lima, Josafa Da Silva Santos

Four child outcasts from the underbelly of Rio make a home for themselves in a clifftop shelter and eke out an existence by begging, pilfering and executing a number of ingenious con-tricks. Documentary-maker Sucksdorff is a superior visual artist with a gift for judging the effect of a moment. However, in this feature he has constructed a semi-fictionalized tale in which the young protagonists are all angelic to look at and both calm and worldly-wise in accepting their lot. This is salutary, but somewhat hard to swallow. In short, the film is a half revealing, half romanticized view of grinding poverty and underprivilege, which raises questions, stretches credibility and is yet affecting.

My Life As A Dog
Mit Liv Som Hund

Sweden 1985 100 mins col
AB Filmteknik/Svensk Filmindustri

d **Lasse Hallström**
sc **Lasse Hallström, Reidar Jønsson, Brasse Brännstrom, Pelle Berglund**
ph **Jörgen Persson, Rolf Lindström**
m **Björn Isfält**
Anton Glanzelius, Manfred Serner, Anki Liden, Tomas Von Brömssen, Melinda Kinnamen

Twelve-year-old Ingemar lives with his dog, elder brother and sick mother until he is sent away to stay with relatives in a small country village where he leads an eventful life. The depiction of a village that seems populated entirely by eccentrics, a boy's love for his dog from whom he is parted, and the death of his beloved mother may signal cuteness and sentimentality, but Hallström's enchanting film of childhood, set in the 1950s, nimbly avoids such traps. That it is so amusing and moving can be put down to the unaffected playing of Glanzelius as the young hero, and to the magical camerawork.

My Life To Live see It's My Life

My Love Has Been Burning
(US: Flame Of My Love)
Waga Koi Wa Moenu

Japan 1949 84 mins bw
Shochiku

d **Kenji Mizoguchi**
sc **Yoshitaka Yoda, Kaneto Shindo**
ph **Kohei Sugiyama**
m **Senji Ito**
Kinuyo Tanaka, Mitsuko Mito, Kuniko Miyabe, Ichiro Sugai, Koreya Senda

Eiko (Tanaka), a feminist in a Japanese province in 1884, has her school closed because of her politics and is distraught when Chiyo (Mito), a servant girl, is sold into slavery. She goes to Tokyo, where she becomes a Liberal Party activist and is imprisoned. On her release, heavily disillusioned by her experiences, she decides to go home and open another school, this time for the purpose of educating women to understand their role in society. Released in the West some three decades after it was made, this film reflects Mizoguchi's ongoing concern with the nature and position of women, and points to the flowering of his best work in the 1950s. Made quckly and cheaply, it is highly critical of society and politics in Japan, and sometimes brutal in its imagery. It was ill-received in his own country, where one critic accused it of being made 'by a wild animal' but, apart from tending to treat the characters as mouthpieces for ideas rather than as flesh and blood beings, it is an absorbing piece.

My Night At Maud's see My Night With Maud

My Night With Maud
(US: My Night At Maud's)
Ma Nuit Chez Maud

France 1968 110 mins bw
Films Du Losange /Les Films Du Carrosse/ Les Films De La Pléiade

d **Eric Rohmer**
sc **Eric Rohmer**
ph **Nestor Almendros, Emmanuel Machuel**
m **Classical selections**
François Fabian, Jean-Louis Trintignant, Marie-Christine Barrault, Antoine Vitez

An engineer and devout Catholic (Trintignant), determined to marry the blonde girl (Barrault) he has noticed in church, spends a chaste night with the beautiful, dark, free-thinking Maud (Fabian), although they are mutually attracted. The film that made Rohmer's international name, set in a snowy Clermont Ferrand, proved that long intellectual discussions could be as cinematic as more obviously visual material. As Rohmer has stated, 'The people in my films are not expressing abstract ideas . . . but revealing what they think about relationships between men and women, about friendship, love, desire . . .'. Witty, erotic, profound and deliciously performed, this fourth released of his Six Moral Tales, was Oscar- nominated.

My Sister, My Love
Syskonbädd 1782

Sweden 1966 96 mins bw
Sandrew

d **Vilgot Sjöman**
sc **Vilgot Sjöman**
ph **Lars Björne**
Bibi Andersson, Per Oscarsson, Jarl Kulle, Gunnar Björnstrand, Tina Hedstrom, Berta Hall

When Jacob (Oscarsson) returns home after several years' absence to learn that his sister Charlotte (Andersson) is about to marry, he is beset by jealousy. Brother and sister realize they are in love and, by the time of her wedding night—which he spends in a brothel—she is carrying his child. The story climaxes in both violence and regeneration. Although played with dignity and restraint by the two leads, and filmed with a Bergmanesque eye for bleak and dramatic landscape, Sjöman's study of incest suffers from a lack of cohesive style or structure, is heavy-handed, and overloaded with neurotic incident. Like all of this director's work, it fails to live up to its aspirations, in spite of having drawn its inspiration from John Ford's Jacobean classic, *'Tis Pity She's A Whore.*

Mystère Alexina see Mystery Of Alexina, The

Mystère De La Chambre Jaune, Le see Mystery Of The Yellow Room, The

---

Mystère Picasso, Le see Picasso Mystery, The

The Mystery Of Alexina
Mystère Alexina

France 1985 90 mins col
Les Cinéastes Associés/TF1 Films

d **René Ferét**
sc **Jean Gruault, René Ferét**
ph **Bernard Zitzermann**
m **Anne-Marie Deschamps**
Vuillemin, Valérie Stroh, Véronique Silver, Bernard Freyd, Pierre Vial

In the year 1858 Alexina (Vuillemin), fresh from a convent, goes to teach in a small boarding school where the owner's daughter,

Sara (Stroh), becomes her friend. Sexual desire grows between them, whereupon they discover that Alexina is really a young man. Unperturbed, Sara rechristens him Camille and he determines to marry her. René Ferét based his film on the diary, edited by Michel Foucault, of Herculine Barbin, a real-life 19th-century hermaphrodite, but the film doesn't quite do justice to its poignant, intriguing and ultimately tragic subject matter. The love affair is over-romanticized, and insufficient attention is paid to psychological and emotional processes, but Ferét tries hard and, despite its shortcomings, the piece is affecting.

Mystery of Kaspar Hauser, The see Enigma Of Kaspar Hauser, The

---

Mystery Of Picasso, The see Picasso Mystery, The

The Mystery Of The Yellow Room

Le Mystère De La Chambre Jaune

France 1930 108 mins bw
Film Osso

d **Marcel L'Herbier**
sc **Marcel L'Herbier**
ph **L.H. Burel**
m **Edouard Flament**
Huguette Duflos, Kissa Kouprine, Roland Toutain, Belières

A journalist (Toutain), investigating a series of attacks on a professor's daughter (Duflos) by an unknown assailant, finds himself in some curious situations, not least in an 'old dark house'. One of the most effective of L'Herbier's sound films (second only to its sequel *The Perfume Of The Woman In Black*), this pacy, semi-serious yarn is based on the famous detective thriller by Gaston Leroux. Bringing with him some of his marvellous technical tricks from the silent days, the director adds the dimension of chilling sound effects and overlapping dialogue, while Burel's camerawork creates a sinister shadowy world.

My Sweet Little Village

Vesničkó Má Středisková

Czechoslovakia 1985 100 mins col
Barrandov Film Studio

d **Jiří Menzel**
sc **Zdeněk Sverak**
ph **Jaromír Šofr**
m **Jiří Šust**
János Bán, Marian Labuda, Rudolf Hrušínsky, Milena Dvorska, Ladislav Zupanic, Petr Cepek

The everyday events in a rural village, among them an adulterous affair, a teenager's crush on a schoolmistress, an accident-prone doctor's unorthodox methods, and the uneasy partnership between a small, fat truck driver and his tall, thin mentally-retarded workmate. Menzel, who made an international reputation in the 1960s with such films as the Oscar-winning *Closely Observed Trains* (1966) returned to favour with this sweet little Oscar-nominated movie. Edging on cuteness and without much bite, it is full of gentle comic touches and a real feel for a living community.

My Uncle

Mon Oncle

France 1958 116 mins col
Spectra/Gray/Alterdel/Centaure

d **Jacques Tati**
sc **Jacques Tati, Jacques Lagrange**
ph **Jean Bourgoin**
m **Alain Romans, Franck Borcellini**
Jacques Tati, Jean-Pierre Zola, Adrienne Servatie, Alain Becourt

Monsieur Hulot (Tati) cannot come to terms with the job he has at his brother-in-law's factory, nor with the ultra-modern gadget-filled home where his small nephew lives unhappily, so different from the shabby old boarding house where he resides. Despite the simplistic, sentimental nostalgia for the picturesque Paris of the corner bistro and accordian music, Tati depicts a mechanized house in which the *bourgeois* inhabitants have become dehumanized in a series of brilliant and original sight and sound gags. Hulot's second screen appearance was enough to put him among the immortals.

Best Foreign Film Oscar 1958
Special Jury Prize Cannes 1958

My Uncle Antoine

Mon Oncle Antoine

Canada 1971 110 mins col
National Film Board Of Canada

d **Claude Jutra**
sc **Clément Perron**
ph **Michel Brault**
m **Jean Cousineau**
Jean Duceppe, Jacques Gagnon, Lyne Champagne, Olivette Thibault, Claude Jutra, Hélène Loiselle

Fourteen-year-old orphan Benoit (Gagnon) lives with his Uncle Antoine (Duceppe) and family in a small provincial mining town where Antoine keeps the local store, as well as being the town's undertaker. One Christmas Eve, during the 1940s, Uncle Antoine is called away from the festivities to fetch a body, and takes Benoit with him. Antoine gets drunk and, on their return home, Benoit observes many incidents, including his aunt in the embrace of the store clerk. This is a rites-of-passage essay, both tender and funny and, aside from some over-indulgence with a zoom lens which disturbs the balance of mood, it is a finely observed portrait of family life in Quebec, made with a feeling for the contrast between intimate interiors and open winter landscape.

My Universities

Moi Universiteti

USSR 1940 104 mins bw
Soyezdetfilm

d **Mark Donskoi**
sc **Mark Donskoi**
ph **Piotr Ermolov**
m **Lev Schwartz**
Nilolai Valbert, Stepan Kaioukov, Nicolas Dorokhine, Plotnikov

Having left home, Maxim Gorky (Valbert) goes from job to job witnessing the exploitation of the workers, which makes him more and more politically aware. There is a slight falling off in the third part of Donskoi's Gorky trilogy as it becomes more episodic and didactic, but it is still packed with memorable sequences. One of them takes place in a bakery where the wily boss talks all through the night. The film ends symbolically with the great Russian writer-to-be seeing the coming of a better future. The three films, *The Childhood Of Maxim Gorky*, *My Apprenticeship* and this one, based on Gorky's autobiography, are shot through with the author's observation, humanism and patriotism, adding up to one of the masterpieces of Socialist Realism in the cinema.

My Way Home

Igy Jöttem

Hungary 1964 109 mins bw
Studio IV, Mafilm

d **Miklós Jancsó**
sc **Gyula Hernádi**
ph **Tamás Somló**
m **Zoltán Jenei**
András Kozák, Sergei Nikonenko

Joská (Kozák), a Hungarian youth making his way home across Russian- occupied countryside near the end of World War II, is arrested, interned, released, arrested again, and sent to tend a herd of cows together with Kolya (Nikonenko), a young Russian soldier. The two transcend barriers of language as well as nationality, to become close friends, but Kolya becomes ill and dies while Joská is fetching help. This stark and moving film, eloquently conveying the dislocation of an occupied country, was Jancsó's third solo feature. It affirms his uniquely individual style— choreographed camera work, interplay of figures and landscape—as well as treating the themes that would mark all his best work: man alienated from himself and others by the cruelty of war, the harshness of nature and the unreliability of allegiances.

n

Nachalo see Beginning, The

Nachts Wenn Der Teufel Kamm see Devil Strikes At Night, The

Nackt Unter Wölfen see Naked Among Wolves

Nada

France 1974 134 mins col
Films De La Boétie(Paris)/Verona Film(Rome)

d **Claude Chabrol**
sc **Jean-Patrick Manchette**
ph **Jean Rabier**
m **Pierre Jansen**
Fabio Testi, Michel Duchaussoy, Maurice Garrel, Michel Aumont, Lou Castel, Viviane Romance, Mariangela Melato, Katia Romanoff

Nada (the Spanish for 'nothing') is the name of a small and disparate group of terrorists who decide to kidnap the American ambassador in Paris during his regular weekly visit to a brothel. The plan unleashes conflicts within the group and within the police, with the former coming into uncompromisingly bloody contact with the latter. In this articulation of the view that the destroyers of the state and its protectors are two sides of the same coin, Chabrol, while eliciting occasional sympathy for the courage of his anarchists, offers no comfort to the viewer. Very violent, but punctuated with black humour and subtle observation, this superlatively cynical exercise is realized with expertise in all departments.

Nagarik see Citizen, The

Naked Among Wolves

Nackt Unter Wölfen

E. Germany 1963 125 mins bw
DEFA

d **Frank Beyer**
sc **Bruno Apitz**
ph **Günther Marczinowski**
Erwin Geschonneck, Gerry Wolff, Fred Delmare, Armin Müller-Stahl, Boleslaw Plotnicki, Krystyn Wójcik

As the Americans draw near to the notorious Buchenwald concentration camp in 1945, the prison resistance group decides to revolt rather than face elimination by the Nazi guards. An unexpected and dangerous problem confronts them when a new prisoner arrives, bringing a small boy hidden in a suitcase... The negative qualities of the film include two-dimensional characters and the suggestion that all good men and true in the camps were Communists. However, the subject is compelling and, if the direction is a little flat, it is nonetheless dignified and there is much authentic detail—partly, no doubt, because writer Apitz was himself an inmate.

Naked Childhood

(US: Me)

L'Enfance Nue

France 1968 80 mins col
Parc Film/Stephan Films/Renn Productions/Les Films Du Carrosse

d **Maurice Pialat**
sc **Maurice Pialat, Arlette Langman**
ph **Claude Beausoleil**
Michel Terrazon, Marie-Louise Thierry, René Thierry, Marie Marc, Henri Puff, Pierrette Deplanque

Ten-year-old François (Terrazon), abandoned by his mother, is sent to a working-class foster family where his behaviour is disturbed. After several incidents, including his throwing a cat down a stairwell to prove it can land on its feet, he is removed. The second family, where the parents (Marie-Louise and René Thierry) are elderly, the grandmother (Marc) ancient and a foster brother (Puff) awkward and shy, proves a success, although François' tendency to uncontrollable behaviour leads to a crisis. Making his first full-length feature, Pialat exhibits superb control of his subject, an examination of childhood, which is never allowed to become sentimental. The film tells a simple and touching story with warmth and directness, offering some splendid performances, notably from Marie Marc as the grandmother with whom François forms a deep bond. As a distant cousin to both *The Four Hundred Blows* and *The Two Of Us*, it is no surprise to notice that François Truffaut and Claude Berri were two of the producers.

Naked Heart, The see Maria Chapdelaine

Naked Hearts
Les Coeurs Verts
France 1966 105 mins bw
Films Raoul Ploquin/Sodor Films

d **Edouard Luntz**
sc **Edouard Luntz**
ph **Jean Badal**
m **Serge Gainsbourg, Henri Renaud**
Gérard Zimmerman. Erick Penet, Marise Mair, Françoise Bonneau, Arlette Thomas

Two juvenile offenders, Zim (Zimmerman) and Jean-Pierre (Penet), meet in prison and are released on the same day. Zim decides to go straight and becomes a labourer, but Jean-Pierre's efforts to do likewise peter out. Set in the conurbations of outer Paris, Luntz's first full-length feature is a triumph of *cinéma vérité*, with non-professional actors communicating an authentic sense of truth. A detached study of aimless youth in incoherent revolt, revealing their haunts, lifestyles and insecurities without comment, the film has the authority of a documentary with the added impact of Luntz's gift for the unexpected situation and Badal's for the imaginative image.

Naked Night, The see Sawdust And Tinsel

Nana
France 1926 98 mins bw
Jean Renoir

d **Jean Renoir**
sc **Pierre Lestringuez**
ph **Jean Bachelet, Edmund Corwin**
m **Silent**
Catherine Hessling, Werner Krauss, Jean Angelo, Raymond Guerin-Catelain, Pierre Champagne, Valeska Gert, Pierre Philippe

Nana has a fleeting triumph as a third-rate actress, and briefly enjoys the life of an admired courtesan before dying a horrible death. Zola's celebrated novel provided Renoir with the greatest challenge of his early career. The film offers a hint of pleasures to come, touching on the director's love of artifice and theatrical spectacle, his fascination with class relations, the exploration of character within a wide social setting, the mixing of comedy with tragedy. Hessling's Nana is light-weight and doll-like, but Renoir subtly undercuts her performance by his sympathetic treatment of the male characters. The relatively lavish production (it flopped at the box-office) was designed by future director Claude Autant-Lara.

Nana
France 1955 100 mins col
Cigno Films

d **Christian-Jaque**
sc **Henri Jeanson, Jean Ferry, Albert Valentin**
ph **Christian Matras**
m **Georges Van Parys**
Martine Carol, Charles Boyer, Jacques Castelot, Elisa Cegani, Noël Roquevert, Jean Debucourt

Nana (Carol), a luxury-loving girl from the slums, becomes a small-time actress-cum-courtesan at the height of the Second Empire. Involved with a man of substance (Boyer), she decides to run away with his rival, thus provoking fatal consequences. Emile Zola, on the whole, doesn't fare too well with film-makers. The best attempt at *Nana* was probably Renoir's silent version in 1926, while

Hollywood made a watchable but cleaned-up version with Anna Sten in 1934, and the Swedes took the liberty of turning it into a sexploitation film in 1971. Here, Christian-Jaque concentrates on spotlighting his beautiful wife (a mediocre performance) in authentic period settings of sumptuous opulence, into which Debucourt wanders as Napoleon III. The political implications of Zola's novel have, however, been ignored.

Naniwa Hika see Osaka Elegy

Napló Gyermekeimnek see Diary For My Children

Napoleon

France 1927 270 mins bw
WESTI/Société Générale De Films

d **Abel Gance**
sc **Abel Gance**
ph **Jules Kruger**
m **Silent**
Albert Dieudonné, Wladimir Roudenko, Gina Manès, Nicolas Koline, Annabella, Antonin Artaud, Van Daële, Koubitsky, Abel Gance, Pierre Batcheff

The life of Napoleon: his childhood, military schooling, and rise to power. Abel Gance's unhistorical but historic film was first shown at the Paris Opera in a five-hour version. After its poor reception, it was released in various truncated forms until filmologist (*sic*) Kevin Brownlow's reconstruction as close to the original as possible, was shown in 1980 complete with the triptychs—a triple screen process that anticipated Cinerama by 30 years. The film is a pyrotechnical display of almost every device of the silent screen and beyond, using hand-held cameras and one strapped to a horse's back, wide-angle lenses, superimposition and rapid cutting. The most famous set-piece is the symbolic sequence in which Napoleon (Dieudonné) sails back from Corsica in a storm, as the storm in the Convention rages. But Gance's view of Napoleon as a Nietzschean superman and the rhetorical devices with which he expresses it, makes the film, notwithstanding its greatness, as demagogic as its hero.

Napoleon

France 1955 190 mins col
Filmsonor/CLM/Francinex

d **Sacha Guitry**
sc **Sacha Guitry**
ph **Pierre Montazel**
m **Jean Françaix**
Daniel Gélin, Raymond Pellegrin, Sacha Guitry, Michèle Morgan, Danielle Darrieux, Orson Welles, Jean Marais, Yves Montand, Maria Schell, Jean Gabin, Erich Von Stroheim, Gianna-Maria Canale

Talleyrand (Guitry) recounts a series of anecdotes about the life and loves of Napoleon which develop into dramatized illustration of the tales, with the little Corsican rebel who became Emperor of France played first by Gélin, then by Pellegrin. The film is a series of vignettes which act as the excuse for one of Guitry's witty all-star extravaganzas (only about half the mouth-watering cast is listed above!). The lovely Michèle Morgan is Josephine, and Von Stroheim's cameo has him impersonating Ludwig Van Beethoven. Expensively made—it was reputed to have cost a record $1.8 million—it looks good, and is three hours of light entertainment that casts no serious light on its huge subject.

Nara Livet see So Close To Life

Narayama-Bushi-Ko see Ballad Of Narayama, The

Nastasia Filipovna see Idiot, The

Nattlek see Night Games

Nattvardsgasterna see Winter Light

Nazarín

Mexico 1958 94 mins bw
Manuel Barbachano Ponce

d **Luis Buñuel**
sc **Luis Buñuel, Julio Alejandro**

ph **Gabriel Figueroa**
Francisco Rabal, Marga López, Rita Macedo, Jesús Fernández, Noe Murayama

Nazarín (Rabal), a humble and unworldly priest, attempts to live by the precepts of Christianity but is despised for his pains, finding compassion only in a prostitute. One of Buñuel's most astringent and forceful attacks on formal religion, told in the manner of a Christian parable, the film was ambiguous enough for it to win the International Catholic Cinema Office award—a supreme irony for the cinema's most famous anti-Catholic atheist. The theme of the impossibility of leading a pure Christian life was further explored in *Viridiana*.

Nazi Terror At Night see Devil Strikes At Night, The

Nejkrasnejsí Vek see Best Age, The

Nella Citta L'Inferno see Caged

Nel Nome Del Padre see In The Name Of The Father

Neobychainiye Priklucheniya Mistera Vesta V Stranya Bolshevikov see Extraordinary Adventures Of Mr West In The Land Of The Bolsheviks, The

---

Neokonchennaya Pyesa Dlya Mekhanicheskogo Pianin see Unfinished Piece For Mechanical Piano

---

Neskolko Dnei Iz Zhizni I. I. Oblomov see Oblomov

Neskolko Intervyu Po Lichnyam Voprosam see Interviews On Personal Problems

---

The Nest
El Nido

Spain 1980 97 mins col
A-Punto ELSA

d **Jaime De Armiñán**
sc **Jaime De Armiñán**
ph **Teo Escamilla**
m **Joseph Haydn, anon 17th century**
Héctor Alterio, Ana Torrent, Luis Politti, Agustín González, Patricia Adriani

A wealthy old widower (Alterio) becomes enthralled by a 13-year-old girl. His priest, his maid, the girl's teacher, her father and a police sergeant all try to dissuade them both from the liaison which ends in death. This is a gentle, intriguing film on a taboo subject that manages to avoid prurience. Beautifully acted by Alterio and Torrent (the marvellous little girl in *The Spirit Of The Beehive* seven years before) and luminously photographed, it might have been even better had it been less literary and explored the subject with more irony.

A Nest Of Gentlefolk
Dvorianskoe Gnezdo

USSR 1969 106 mins col
Mosfilm

d **Andrei Mikhalkov-Konchalovsky**
sc **Valentin Yezhov, Andrei Mikhalkov-Konchalovsy**
ph **Georgy Rerberg**
m **Vyacheslav Ovchinnikov**
Leonid Kulagin, Irina Kupchenko, Beata Tyszkiewicz, A. Kostomolotsky, V. Sergachov, Nikita Mikhalkov

Disenchanted with the superficial glitter of Parisian society and with his frivolous wife (Tyszkiewicz), Fyodor Lavretsky (Kulagin) returns to his long-neglected estate in Russia, reflects on his past while sorting through the cobweb-covered *objets* of a lifetime, and falls unrequitedly in love with his neighbour's young daughter (Kupchenko). In adapting a work by Turgenev, Konchalovsky has focused on his central character, narrowing the novelist's range of observation, and creating a mood piece. He does so with superb visual sensitivity, evoking the atmosphere of lethargy and decay that has come to signify the texture of Russian *bourgeois* life just before the Revolution. Occasionally bordering on the monotonous, the film is nonetheless full of good things, not least the performance of Kupchenko.

Never On Sunday
Pote Tin Kyriaki

Greece 1959 97 mins bw
Lopert/Melinafilm

d **Jules Dassin**
sc **Jules Dassin**
ph **Jacques Natteau**
m **Manos Hadjidakis**
Melina Mercouri, Jules Dassin, Georges Foundas, Tito Vandis, Despo Diamantidou

An exuberant and contented waterfront prostitute (Mercouri) meets an earnest American (Dassin) who falls for her and, in Professor Higgins fashion, attempts to educate her to literature and a higher strain of music than *bouzouki*. A low-budget movie, that manages some wonderful views of Piraeus and a lot of Greek atmosphere, offers a mediocre performance from Dassin and a high-octane one from Mercouri which brought her international fame. A thoroughly good-natured romp which, in its day, seemed invitingly shocking and became a world-wide hit, as did the catchy but rather repetitive Oscar-winning title song.

Best Actress (Melina Mercouri) Cannes 1960

Never Strike A Woman—Even With A Flower
Zénu Ani Kvêtinou Neuhodis

Czechoslovakia 1966 100 mins bw
Barrandov Film Studio

d **Zdeněk Podskalsky**
sc **Jaroslav Dietl, Zdeněk Podskalsky**
ph **František Valert**
m **Evzen Illín**
Vlastimil Brodsky, Hana Brejchová, Slávka Budínová, Jirina Bohdalová, Kveta Fialová

Ludvík (Brodsky), a middle-aged and married musician, is diffident and obliging, especially to women, wherein lies the secret of his charm. His several attempts at affairs all go awry, belying his reputation as an enviable philanderer, but result in his wife throwing him out, whereupon he has a surprise love affair with an innocent girl (Brejchová). Popular in his own country since 1958, Podskalsky's work has been virtually unknown in the West. This example is a comedy, filled with the kind of charmingly ridiculous situations which point to the silent cinema or the films of Lubitsch and Billy Wilder. If the story itself is unoriginal, the treatment is fresh and Brodsky's performance as the bewildered hero is a delight.

Nevinost Bez Zastite see Innocence Unprotected

The New Angels
I Nuovi Angeli

Italy 1961 105 mins bw
Titanus/Galatea/Arco

d **Ugo Gregoretti**
sc **Mino Guerrini, Ugo Gregoretti**
ph **Tonino Delli Colli, Mario Bernardi**
m **Piero Umiliani**
Non-professionals from Chianti, Milan, Naples, Agrigento, Riccione and Rome

In a series of eight episodes occurring across the length and breadth of the country, the attitudes and behaviour of contemporary Italian youth are demonstrated. The tales feature young people of differing classes and backgrounds, revealing their contrasting attitudes to progress, ambition, social mores and sexual ethics. Gregoretti's first film adopts a documentary style and approach and comes across as factual and informative, although the stories themselves are fictional. Utilizing some gentle irony and black humour, the director points up the contradictions that co-exist in the society of his time—the cowherd, for example, who would rather have his wife and baby starve than suffer the 'disgrace' of her taking a job as a waitress—in a pleasing if ephemeral exercise.

The New Babylon
Novyi Vavilon

USSR 1929 80 mins bw
Sovkino

d **Grigori Kozintsev, Leonid Trauberg**
sc **Grigori Kozintsev, Leonid Trauberg**
ph **Andrei Moskvin**
m **Silent**

Elena Kuzmina, Pyotr Sobelevsky, Sophie Magarill, D. Gutman, Vsevolod Pudovkin, Sergei Gerasimov

Louise (Kuzmina), a shop assistant in a luxury store (The New Babylon), sees the effects of the German advance on Paris on the cowardly *bourgeoisie* and the patriotic working class, and the collapse of the Commune of 1871. Kozintsev's and Trauberg's great silent period culminated with this dazzlingly inventive satire. Despite the symbolic intentions and episodic structure, there is a warmth in the performances of the proletarian characters and a realism in some of the sequences. But it is in the montage and the lighting used to contrast the rich and the poor that the film is at its best.

The Newcomer

Le Nouveau Venu

Benin 1979 87 mins col
Iris Films/International Tropic Films

d **Richard De Meideros**
sc **Richard De Meideros, René Ewagnion, Bouraima Lawani**
ph **Maxime Lefevre, Bouraima Lawani**
Michel Djondo, Sikirou Ogoujobi, Ages Capo-Cichi, Sebastien De Souza

A young administrator of the new order is appointed to run a government office. His determination to increase output and efficiency brings him into conflict with the old-fashioned workers' leader who resents the challenge to his status and methods. The latter even resorts to putting an ancient spell on the new boss but undergoes a change of heart and mind. Yet another expression of the conflict between independence and the hangover of colonialism which characterizes many of the films from the Third World (Benin was formerly the French colony of Dahomey), this particular film is somewhat naive and simplistic, with a pat and unconvincing resolution. Nonetheless, it offers a slant on African custom and the problems of progress, doing so at an acceptable level of efficiency and with some warmth and humour.

New Gentlemen, The see Nouveaux Messieurs, Les

The New Gulliver

Novyi Gulliver

USSR 1935 85 mins bw
Mosfilm

d **Alexander Ptoushko**
sc **Alexander Ptoushko, B. Roshal**
ph **N. Renkov**
m **Lev Schwartz**

A reading of Swift's *Gulliver's Travels* to a group of Young Pioneers at a camp gives them dreams in which they see updated episodes from the book. Among the imaginings are a newsreel cameraman filming Gulliver being hauled into the Lilliputian capital, modern engineering techniques used to feed the 'giant' and the hero helping the oppressed in a class war. The world's first feature-length puppet film took Ptoushko three exhausting years to make; he had already shot a number of short puppet films and been responsible for the special effects for Dovzhenko's *Aerograd*. The manipulation of the wax dolls as caricature humans worked wonderfully as satire not far removed from Swift's own, and the Lilliput chapter lends itself easily to the Soviet ideology of the time.

The New Land

Nybyggarna

Sweden 1972 205 mins col
Svensk Filmindustri

d **Jan Troell**
sc **Jan Troell, Bengt Forslund**
ph **Jan Troell**
m **Bengt Ernryd, George Oddner**
Max Von Sydow, Liv Ullmann, Eddie Axberg, Monica Zetterlund, Pierre Lindstedt

Karl Oskar Nillson (Von Sydow) and his wife Kristina (Ullmann), Swedish immigrants to Minnesota in the 19th century, struggle to build a home, to farm their land and bring up a family, against all odds. Although the ending of this sequel to *The Emigrants*, even longer than the previous film, shows a third generation of Nillsons happy and assimilated in America, it does reveal a darker side to the saga. The hardships caused by nature are more brutally depicted, from a blizzard to a scorching desert, yet Troell still visualizes things from an idealized perspective. There are moving moments, but historical events such as the Civil War and the Indian wars are dragged in unconvincingly. The dyptich was the most expensive Swedish cinematic project to date.

New Tales Of The Taira Clan
Shin Heike Monogatari

Japan 1955 113 mins col
Daiei

d **Kenji Mizoguchi**
sc **Yoshitaka Yoda, Masashige Narusawa, Hisakazu Tsuji**
ph **Kazuo Miyagawa**
m **Fumio Hayasaka, Masaru Sato**
Raizo Ichikawa, Yoshiko Kuga, Narutoshi Hayashi, Michiyo Kogure, Ichijiro Oya, Eitaro Shindo, Ichiro Sugai

In 12th-century Japan, the soldier monks of the rich and powerful monasteries clash with the families of the samurai. When the young samurai Kiyomori Taira hears of a plot to assassinate Tadamori, the head of the Taira clan, he comes to the clan's rescue. After Tadamori's death, he assumes leadership, facing the monks and destroying their idols. One of Mizoguchi's last films shows a remarkable use of colour, ranging from pastel blues to deep red. Working closely with Miyagawa, the great cinematographer, the director decided on the colours which were to predominate in each scene. He also manages to keep the main characters in the complex plot in focus with a never-slacking narrative. The film is marginally less successful than his other late films, because it moved away from his 'woman' pictures into the more familiar and predictable samurai territory of Japanese cinema.

Nibelungen, Die see Nibelungen, The

Nibelungen, Die see Whom The Gods Wish To Destroy

The Nibelungen
Die Nibelungen

Germany 1924 118 mins (Part I—Siegfried); 131 mins (Part II—Kriemhild's Revenge) bw
Decla Bioskop/UFA

d **Fritz Lang**
sc **Fritz Lang, Thea Von Harbou**
ph **Carl Hoffman, Günther Rittau, Walter Ruttmann**
m **Silent**
Paul Richter, Margarete Schon, Hanna Ralph, Bernhard Goetzke, Theodore Loos, Hans Adalbert Von Schlettow, Rudolf Klein-Rogge

Siegfried (Richter), married to Kriemhild (Schon), journeys from Iceland to Burgundy with Brunhild (Ralph) as a bride for his brother-in-law Gunther (Loos). After many adventures, magical and otherwise, Brunhild has Siegfried killed by Hagen (Von Schlettow). Kriemhild gets her revenge on the Burgundians. Lang's adaptation of the 13th-century German saga is a superb example of the craftsmanship at the UFA studios. The stylized set designs by Otto Hunte, Erich Kettelhut and Karl Vollbrecht create a mysterious beauty, especially the misty forest (constructed in a Zeppelin hangar) and the romantic castles. There is also a wonderful dragon that the hero slays early in Part I and a massively staged battle to end Part II. The characters are deliberately one-dimensional as befits the epic mode.

Nicht Versöhnt, Oder Es Hilft Nur ... see Not Reconciled, Or Only Violence ...

Nido, El see Nest, The

Niewinni Czarodzieje see Innocent Sorcerers

Night, The see Notte, La

Night And Fog
Nuit Et Brouillard

France 1955 31 mins bw/col
Argos/Como/Cocinor

d **Alain Resnais**
sc **Jean Cayrol**
ph **Ghislain Cloquet, Sacha Vierny**
m **Hanns Eisler**

This is a tour of the ruins of Auschwitz in the mid-1950s, filmed in colour but intercut with black-and-white archive material of the horrors that took place there not too many years before. The peak of Resnais' eight short films prior to his feature debut *Hiroshima, Mon Amour* (1959), was reached with this moving and thought-provoking documentary. The carefully controlled commentary, narrated by Michel Bouquet and written by ex-deportee Cayrol, (later the screenwriter of *Muriel*), as well as the gentle music, contrast starkly with the newsreels of the concentration camp victims—the past intrudes upon the present, memory precludes forgetting. The theme and the long exploratory tracking shots were to become characteristics of Resnais' feature films.

Night Beauties

(US: Beauties Of The Night)

Les Belles De Nuit

France 1952 89 mins bw

Franco-London/Film Rizzoli

d **René Clair**

sc **René Clair**

ph **Armand Thirard**

m **Georges Van Parys**

Gérard Philipe, Gina Lollobrigida, Martine Carol, Magali Vendeuil, Paolo Stoppa, Raymond Bussières, Raymond Cordy

A shy young music teacher (Philipe) escapes from his drab life into dreams of romantic adventures in different epochs and places where he encounters beautiful women derived from acquaintances he meets in his waking hours. Most of Clair's films have a dreamlike atmosphere, so he was naturally at home when creating dreams more overtly. The film is not only an entertaining fantasy, but makes an ironic comment on the interaction between fact and fiction.

Night Games

Nattlek

Sweden 1966 105 mins bw

Sandrews

d **Mai Zetterling**

sc **Mai Zetterling**

ph **Rune Ericson**

m **Jan Johansson, George Riedel**

Ingrid Thulin, Keve Hjelm, Lena Brundin, Naima Wifstrand, Jörgen Lindström

A sexually inhibited and disturbed man (Hjelm), unable to come to terms with adult life, recalls his mother-dominated childhood. Mai Zetterling's second feature, adapted from her own novel, caused a furore among moralists who objected to its frank treatment of sex. It is, in fact, a wickedly sensuous Strindbergian drama, handled with maturity and a sharp eye for decadent details. However, the theme, together with the presence of Thulin, caused critics to compare the director unfavourably with Bergman.

Night Heat

(US: On Any Street aka Bad Girls Don't Cry)

La Notte Brava

Italy 1959 93 mins bw

AJACE/Franco-London

d **Mauro Bolognini**

sc **Pier Paolo Pasolini**

ph **Armando Nannuzzi**

m **Piero Piccioni**

Laurent Terzieff, Jean-Claude Brialy, Franco Interlenghi, Rosanna Schiaffino, Mylène Demongeot, Elsa Martinelli, Antonella Lualdi, Tomas Milian

Twenty-four hours in the life of three young working-class Romans, on the make for money and girls. Their activities include selling stolen firearms, trafficking with prostitutes and petty theft. The day ends with a fight between them. Bella-Bella (Interlenghi) is left unconscious, Scintillone (Brialy) is arrested for causing a fracas in a nightclub and Ruggeretto (Terzieff), after a night of carousal with a girl, ends up forlorn and penniless. Pasolini's screenplay, albeit a little repetitive, is a cynical and sharply observant dissection of the amorality to which the hopelessly underprivileged Italian poor are driven in their desire for a better life. Things have changed somewhat since the film was made, of course, but it is still reasonably interesting and entertaining, if a little slow at times. It is a pity that Bolognini undercuts the impact of the piece by glamourizing the fundamentally sleazy lives and locales that are presented.

Night Heaven Fell, The see Heaven Fell That Night

Night Is My Future

aka Music In The Dark
Musik I Mörker
Sweden 1948 87 mins bw
Terra Film

d **Ingmar Bergman**
sc **Dagmar Edqvist**
ph **Göran Strindberg**
m **Erland Von Koch**
Birger Malmsten, Mai Zetterling, Bengt Eklund, Naima Wifstrand, Gunnar Björnstrand

A young man (Malmsten) who has been blinded determines to adjust to his affliction and to live and work as an equal of the sighted. He takes up the piano, and hires a housekeeper-companion (Zetterling) to whom he acts as a sort of Professor Higgins. After several set-backs in the outside world, the couple find love and fulfilment together. Bergman's fourth film, only released outside Sweden many years after he had found his form and his fame, is mainly interesting in demonstrating how far he progressed. There are clear hints of the powerful imagery to come, and a pointed picture of provincial life but, overall, it is an over-earnest, sentimental and clichéd romantic melodrama—although one would hesitate to join the *New York Times* in calling it 'cinematic juvenilia'.

The Night Is Young

Mauvais Sang
France 1986 119 mins col
Les Films Plain Chant/Soprofilms/FR3 Films

d **Leos Carax**
sc **Leos Carax**
ph **Jean-Yves Escoffier**
m **Prokofiev, Britten, Charlie Chaplin, David Bowie, Charles Aznavour, Serge Reggiani**
Denis Lavant, Juliette Binoche, Michel Piccoli, Hans Meyer, Carroll Brooks, Julie Delphy

Alex (Lavant), a petty thief, joins two crooks (Piccoli and Mayer) in a plan to rob a laboratory of the drug to stop the spread of STBO (a disease which attacks only insincere lovers), but he is more interested in Anna (Binoche), the girlfriend of one of the crooks. Carax's second feature is almost a sequel to his debut film, *Boy Meets Girl*, in sharing a central character called Alex played by the glowering, antipathetic Lavant. They also share a soulful, passive, short-haired heroine and a visual flair. But, unlike the previous picture which had some resemblance to real life, this is filtered through other movies and pulp literature. Godard did it with more style and conviction in the 1960s.

The Night Of Counting The Years

El Mumia
Egypt 1969 102 mins col
Egyptian Cinema General Organisation

d **Shadi Abdelsalam**
sc **Shadi Abdelsalam**
ph **Abdel Aziz Fahmy**
m **Mario Nascimbene**
Ahmed Marei, Zouzou El Hakim, Ahmad Hegazi, Nadia Loutfy, Gaby Karraz

In Thebes in 1881, Wanniss (Marei), the younger son of the chief of the Horrabat tribe, shocked to learn that the tribe has been robbing the mummies' tombs and selling the trophies to mercenary dealers, reveals the whereabouts of the tombs to a team of archeologists trying to discover the source of the valuable objects. Towering like a pyramid over the commercial dross of the Egyptian film industry, this first feature from former art director Abdelsalam is notable for its startling visual beauty. The brooding story evolves slowly against the glories of Ancient Egypt, captured in deep-focus photography and vividly contrasting colours.

The Night Of San Lorenzo

(US: Night Of The Shooting Stars)
La Notte Di San Lorenzo
Italy 1981 107 mins col
RAI/Ager Cinematografica

d **Paolo and Vittorio Taviani**
sc **Paolo and Vittorio Taviani, Giuliani De Negri**
ph **Franco Di Giacomo**
m **Nicola Piovani**
Omero Antonutti, Margarita Lozano, Claudio

Bigagli, Massimo Bonetti, Norma Martelli, Enrica Maria Modugno

The Tuscan town of San Martino is threatened with destruction by the Nazis as the Americans advance in August 1944. Many flee and join up with a resistance group. A bloody battle between them and the Fascists takes place on the eve of Liberation. The Taviani brothers have used all the rhetorical devices at their disposal to illustrate an important moment in modern Italian history and in their own lives—the Tuscan-born directors were 13 and 15 respectively at the time. Many of the events in the film are seen through the eyes of a six-year-old girl. There are enough bravura and inspiring sequences in the rambling structure and among the simplistic gestures to make it worthwhile.

Special Jury Prize Cannes 1982

Night Of The Shooting Stars see Night Of San Lorenzo, The

The Night Of Varennes

La Nuit De Varennes

France 1982 155 mins col
Gaumont/Opéra Film/FR3

d **Ettore Scola**
sc **Sergio Amedei, Ettore Scola**
ph **Armando Nannuzzi**
m **Armando Trovaioli**

Marcello Mastroianni, Jean-Louis Barrault, Hanna Schygulla, Daniel Gélin, Harvey Keitel, Jean-Claude Brialy, Laura Betti, Andréa Ferréol, Michel Vitold

During 1791, the French King and Queen flee across their country in a coach that is finally captured by the people of Varennes. Following and observing them is a collection of people who include the writer Restif De Bretonne (Barrault), Casanova (Mastroianni), well past his prime, and American revolutionary Tom Paine (Keitel). They have been joined by a countess (Schygulla) travelling with her hairdresser (Brialy), an Italian opera singer (Betti), a rich widow, an industrialist and a magistrate. The group spends the journey engaged in philosophical discussion and commentary on life, love, politics and history—which is about to sweep several of them away in the Revolution. On the credit side, it is a handsome film, glitteringly cast, mounted in the style of an ambitious pageant and directed with evident finesse. However, it becomes an overlong and rather tedious exercise. The characters fail to come to life and the screenplay sheds little light on the period. One very nice touch is that all that is seen of the ill-fated Louis and Marie Antoinette are their lower legs and feet.

Night Paths

(US: Ways In The Night)

Wege In Der Nacht

W. Germany 1979 98 mins col
Westdeutscher Rundfunk

d **Krzysztof Zanussi**
sc **Krzysztof Zanussi**
ph **Witold Sobociński**
m **Wojciech Kilar**

Mathieu Carrière, Maja Komorowska, Horst Frank, Zbigniew Zapasiewicz, Irmgard Forst

A cultivated German officer (Carrière), billeted in a small Polish town in 1943, is bewitched by an older Polish baroness (Komorowska). She uses their relationship in order to obtain information and give it to the local partisans. The director, too, uses this romance for his own ends in order to analyse, in a series of dialogues, the nature of aesthetics, the difficulties of remaining civilized while in the uniform of a 'barbarian' and to cast doubt on whether people with similar backgrounds can transcend the historical circumstances that divide them. Dry as much of it is, the use of small but significant events, such as the stripping of a Jew to 'determine' his race, effectively brings the greater horror into focus.

Nights Of Cabiria

Le Notti Di Cabiria

Italy 1956 110 mins bw
Dino De Laurentiis/Les Films Marceau

d **Federico Fellini**
sc **Federico Fellini, Ennio Flaiano, Tullio Pinelli, Pier Paolo Pasolini**
ph **Otello Martelli**
m **Nino Rota**

Giulietta Masina, Amadeo Nazzari, François Périer, Franca Marzi, Mario Passante, Dorian Gray

Cabiria (Masina) is a prostitute living on the outskirts of Rome. Life is hard, but she never loses her sunny smile or her faith in human nature, even when she is cruelly dumped by a glamorous film star (Nazzari) and —worse— the respectable man (Périer) who is going to marry her disappears with her life savings. The perennially attractive idea of the whore with the heart of gold is given the full Fellini treatment in its wonderful observation of detail, and the narrative is veined with humour as well as sadness. However, it's difficult to escape memories of *La Strada* with funny, Chaplinesque Masina on display, fighting unkind fate but hardly anyone's idea of a woman of the streets. It was made into the hit American musical *Sweet Charity* directed by Bob Fosse, with Gwen Verdon on Broadway and Shirley MacLaine on film.

Best Foreign Film Oscar 1957

Nights When The Devil Came see Devil Strikes At Night, The

Night Train

Pociag

Poland 1959 100 mins bw
Kadr Unit, Film Polski

d **Jerzy Kawalerowicz**
sc **Jerzy Lutowski, Jerzy Kawalerowicz**
ph **Jan Laskowski**
m **Andrzej Trzaskowski**
Lucyna Winnicka, Leon Niemczyk, Zbigniew Cybulski, Teresa Szmigielowna, Roland Glowacki

Suffering an inner crisis, Marthe (Winnicka) buys a ticket from a stranger for a crowded holiday train, and finds herself in a 'Men Only' sleeper with an unhappy doctor (Niemczyk). The police board the train in search of a killer... Some interesting and compassionate images are insufficient to hold this film together. Kawalerowicz seems uncertain as to whether he's making a psychological study of loneliness or a thriller and doesn't really succeed in either direction.

Nihon No Higeki see Japanese Tragedy, A

Nilouhe, Nuer see Daughter Of The Nile

Nine Days Of One Year

Devyat Dnei Odnogo Goda

USSR 1961 110 mins bw
Mosfilm

d **Mikhail Romm**
sc **Mikhail Romm, Daniel Khrabrovitsky**
ph **German Lavrov**
m **D. Ter-Tatevosyan**
Alexei Batalov, Innokenti Smoktunovsky, Tamara Lavrova, Nikolai Plotnikov

Nine separate days of a year in the life of a young scientist (Batalov), whose work has exposed him to radiation. Neither his neglected wife (Lavrova) nor his colleague (Smoktunovsky) can persuade him to give up his dangerous experiments. The years of Stalinism began to hang heavily on the films of Romm, but after the 'thaw' he emerged from mediocrity with this revealing and realistic glimpse into the world of Soviet science. It was not only the subject matter that was unusual, but the placing of discussion rather than action at its dramatic centre. The plot, which sometimes approaches Hollywood's idealistic view of the man of science, is elevated by the fine performances from the three leads and the craftsmanship of the direction.

Nine Months

Kilenc Hónap

Hungary 1976 93 mins col
Hunnia Filmstudió

d **Márta Mészáros**
sc **Gyula Hernádi, Ildikó Kóródy, Márta Mészáros**
ph **János Kende**
m **György Kovács**
Lili Monori, Jan Nowicki, Djoko Rodič

Juli (Monori), a worker in an iron foundry, has a passionate affair with János (Polish actor Nowicki), the foreman. When he discovers that she has had a child by a married professor (Rodič), he becomes insanely jealous. But Juli retains her independence, despite having János's baby. As in most of the low-key films of Mészáros, the central figure is a woman who, without being a rebel, refuses to bow to convention and who values her freedom. The fact that the heroine is squat and plain is relevant only because it is rare in films where women are more likely to be attractive. Most of the plot is taken up by the slow and largely uneventful relationship between Juli and János, against a nicely observed background of a small industrial town. Monori, who was pregnant at the start of shooting, allowed herself to be photographed in childbirth for the film's conclusion.

Nineteen Hundred

Novecento

Italy 1976 175 mins (Part I); 165 mins (Part II) col
PEA/Artistes Associés/Artemis

d **Bernardo Bertolucci**
sc **Bernardo Bertolucci, Franco Arcalli, Giuseppe Bertolucci**
ph **Vittorio Storaro**
m **Ennio Morricone**
Burt Lancaster, Robert De Niro, Gérard Depardieu, Dominique Sanda, Donald Sutherland, Sterling Hayden, Alida Valli, Laura Betti, Stefania Sandrelli

Italian history as seen through the lives of Olmo (Depardieu) and Alfredo (De Niro) born on January 27, 1901 (novecento means the 20th century), until Liberation Day on April 25, 1945. Olmo, the son of a peasant woman, and Alfredo, the son of the lord of the manor (Lancaster) grow up together as friends until differences in class and politics separate them. Bertolucci, turning away from the introspection of his previous films, tried to make a popular movie of the class struggle using the style of both American epics and the lyrical Soviet cinema of the 1930s. It is operatic (it opens with a clown announcing the death of Verdi), didactic, bombastic, mean, moody and magnificent to look at. The second part gets rather over-Baroque and violent (a cat and a boy's head being smashed against a wall is not for the squeamish), and Sutherland and Betti are ludicrously caricatured Fascists. But, with the last 30 minutes—symbolic of revolution and post-revolution—it enters greatness.

Ningen No Joken see Human Condition, The

The Ninth Circle

Deveti Krug

Yugoslavia 1960 108 mins bw
Jadran Film

d **France Štiglic**
sc **Zora Dirnbach**
ph **Ivan Marinček**
m **Branimir Sakač**
Dušica Žegarac, Boris Dvornik, Desanka Lončar, Branko Tatić

In Croatia in the early 1940s, Ruth (Žegarac), the young, upper middle-class daughter of a Jewish family, marries a Catholic boy (Dvornik) to avoid being sent to a concentration camp. like her father. The pretence is maintained with difficulty, until Ruth can no longer bear to hide her true identity. The first Yugoslavian film to deal with the concentration camps and the atrocities committed by the Uštaše, the Croatian Nationalists who collaborated with the Nazis, opened up the way for other films in the 1960s to deal with the Occupation. Štiglic, in a taut and classical style, avoids melodrama while boldly and movingly shifting from the lighter first part about the lives of the young people and the marriage of convenience towards the inferno of the camps.

Nippon Konchuki see Insect Woman, The

Nobi see Fires On The Plain

Noces Rouges, Les see Blood Wedding

No End

Bez Konca

Poland 1984 108 mins col
Zespoly Filmowe

d **Krzysztof Kieslowski**
sc **Krzysztof Kieslowski, Krzysztof Piesiewicz**
ph **Jacek Petrycki**
m **Zbigniew Preisner**
Grazyna Szapolowska, Maria Pakulnis, Aleksander Bardini, Jerzy Radziwilowicz, Artur Barcis, Michal Bajor

The ghost of a dead lawyer (Radziwilowicz)

watches his wife (Szapolowska) and young son (Bajor) as they struggle to survive without him. He also sees the way the case of a young worker, charged with organizing a strike, is handled by another lawyer (Bardini) with a different approach. Set during Poland's martial law in 1982, Kieslowski's film was not shown outside Poland until 1986. While plainly deeply felt, it is far too schematic, studied, slow and solemn to create the desired effect. Intensely acted by the two female leads—Pakulnis plays the wife of the accused worker—the film, like the solid ghost that wanders through it, resides in a kind of creative limbo.

No Exit

Huis Clos

France 1955 99 mins bw
Les Films Marceau

d **Jacqueline Audry**
sc **Pierre Laroche**
ph **Robert Juillard**
m **Joseph Kosma**
Arletty, Frank Villard, Gaby Sylvia, Nicole Courcel, Yves Deniaud, Danièle Delorme

A weak man (Villard), a sexy woman (Sylvia) and an embittered Lesbian (Arletty), strangers to one another and each with a dark past, find themselves walled up together in a hotel room where, since they are all actually dead, they are condemned to a vile eternity of dislike, wrangling and rivalry. Jean-Paul Sartre's famous play, the theme of which is 'hell is other people', travels badly to the screen. Wordy and static, it is neither particularly well photographed nor well acted, although Arletty remains an attraction. Audry attempts to buck things up by introducing cinema screens on which the characters can visualize incidents in their lives, and there are some new characters, but none of it really helps. The film initially ran into some censorship problems—uncharacteristically for France.

No Good To Die For That see Don't Let It Kill You

No Habra Mas Penas Ni Olvido see Funny Dirty Little War, A

Noia, La see Empty Canvas, The

Noir Et Blanc

France 1986 80 mins bw
Les Films Du Volcan

d **Claire Devers**
sc **Claire Devers**
ph **Daniel Desbois**
m **Sung by Chorale Rhapsodes**
Francis Frappat, Jacques Martial, Josephine Fresson, Marc Berman, Claire Rigollier

Antoine (Frappat), a shy, conventional, young accountant, takes a job at a health club and is persuaded to avail himself of the facilities. Gradually, a strange sado-masochistic relationship develops between him and his black masseur, Jacques (Martial), as each explores the attraction of pain in their increasingly violent massage sessions which lead to an inevitably horrifying conclusion. Winner of the 1986 *Camera D'Or* prize for a first film at Cannes, Devers' astonishingly accomplished debut movie (suggested by a Tennessee Williams story) is, in turn, enigmatic, droll, sickening and illuminating. Dispassionately observing the development of the relationship, the director eschews the actual depiction of violence, but succeeds in conveying it. Kinky, certainly, but skilful and imaginative.

No Mercy No Future

Die Berührte

W. Germany 1981 108 mins col
Helma Sanders-Brahms Filmproduktion

d **Helma Sanders-Brahms**
sc **Helma Sanders-Brahms, Rita G.**
ph **Thomas Mauch**
m **Manfred Opitz, Harald Grosskopf**
Elisabeth Stepanek, Hubertus Von Weyrauch, Irmgard Mellinger, Nguyen Chi Danh, Jorge Reis, Erich Koitzsch-Koltzack

The daughter of wealthy middle-class parents, Veronika Christoph (Stepanek), between bouts of enforced hospitalization and repeated attempts to kill herself, wanders Berlin searching for a Christ figure and giving herself to men on the fringes of society. She sleeps with a Ghanaian (Reis) and believes she has found her Christ. Back in hospital she has visions of her father burning on the Cross. Sanders-Brahms, one of Germany's most radical and adventurous directors, based this film on a letter she received from her co-credited screenwriter, Rita G., about the latter's life as a schizophrenic. Directed and acted with passionate commitment and conviction, this study of modern madness caused an outrage at Cannes and split critical opinion. Is it merely a farrago of sexual and hallucinatory sensationalism, conveyed in shocking images of great skill, or is it a work of multi-layered complexity, crowded with religious emblems, politico-historical allegory, scathing social attack and compassion?

Non Uccidere see Thou Shalt Not Kill

Nora Inu see Stray Dog

The Northern Star

L'Étoile Du Nord

France 1982 124 mins col
Sara Films/Antenne 2

d **Pierre Granier-Deferre**
sc **Jean Aurenche, Michel Grisolia, Pierre Granier-Deferre**
ph **Pierre-William Glenn**
m **Philippe Sarde**
Simone Signoret, Philippe Noiret, Fanny Cottençon, Julie Jezequel, Jean Rougerie

In a Belgian boarding house in the 1930s, world-weary Edouard (Noiret) fascinates the landlady (Signoret) with his tales of Egypt, but he has blanked out the memory of his murder of an Egyptian millionaire aboard L'Étoile du Nord, the Paris to Amsterdam express. Despite some bizarre alterations to Georges Simenon's novel *Le Locataire*, previously filmed in 1939 (destroyed) and 1947, this is good old-fashioned story-telling, assured by the contribution of veteran screenwriter Aurenche. But most of the pleasure is provided by the Signoret-Noiret duet and the careful period detail.

Nosferatu

Nosferatu, Eine Symphonie Des Grauens

Germany 1921 72 mins bw
Prana

d **F.W. Murnau**
sc **Henrik Galeen**
ph **Fritz Arno Wagner**
m **Silent**
Max Schreck, Gustav Von Wangenheim, Greta Schroeder-Matray, Alexander Granach, Georg H. Schnell, Ruth Landshoff

Hutter (Wangenheim), a newly married clerk, travels to Transylvania to complete some business with Count Orlock alias Nosferatu, a vampire (Schreck). When the Count's secret is discovered, he is forced to leave his castle. He travels to Bremen (via a ship stricken by the 'plague') in order to take up residence there because he desires Ellen (Schroeder), Hutter's young wife whose picture he had seen. But the sacrifice of Ellen finally vanquishes the vampire. This film marked the first appearance on screen of Bram Stoker's Dracula. In fact, it was pirated from the 1897 novel and the characters' names were changed. (Recent prints restored Stoker's original names.) But the author's widow brought a successful action for breach of copyright and official prints of the film were destroyed, leaving only a few of poor quality. Later, longer and better prints were discovered. It remains arguably the eeriest and most magical of all the multitude of film versions of the famous supernatural tale. The use of real locations to create atmosphere instead of the usual stylized studio sets, the special effects—negative film and speeded-up motion to suggest a ghostly ride—and the spectral gaunt figure of Schreck's Dracula make the first work of Murnau's maturity also one of his best.

Nosferatu, Eine Symphonie Des Grauens see Nosferatu

Nosferatu: Phantom Der Nacht see Nosferatu The Vampire

Nosferatu The Vampire

Nosferatu: Phantom Der Nacht

W. Germany 1979 107 mins col
Werner Herzog Filmproduktion/Gaumont(Paris)

d **Werner Herzog**
sc **Werner Herzog**
ph **Jörg Schmidt-Reitwein**
m **Popul Vuh, Florian Fricke, Wagner, Gounod**
Klaus Kinski, Isabelle Adjani, Bruno Ganz, Walter Ladengast, Roland Topor, Dan Van Husen

Jonathan Harker (Ganz) is sent from Wismar to Transylvania to complete a property deal with Count Dracula (Kinski). Dracula, who has shown an interest in Harker's wife, Lucy (Adjani), comes to Wismar, coffins and all. Lucy gives herself up to him, hoping that the vampire will linger beyond cock-crow and thus be destroyed. Herzog's attraction to bizarre characters (*Aguirre, Kaspar Hauser, Stroszek*) led him naturally into the horror genre. Although the director claimed that he went back to the Bram Stoker novel for inspiration, many of the sequences—as well as Kinski's make-up—indicate a somewhat slavish attempt to remake Murnau's 1922 classic version of the Dracula tale. In truth, colour and sound have subtracted from, rather than added to, the quality of this rather irrelevant exercise. The film was released in the USA with an English soundtrack, but audiences found it so risible that the original German was reinstated. There still remains much to laugh (and shiver) at in the camp Gothic proceedings and in Kinski's kinky performance.

Nostalghia see Nostalgia

Nostalgia

Nostalghia

Italy 1983 126 mins col/bw
Opera Film/Sovin Film/RAI

d **Andrei Tarkovsky**
sc **Andrei Tarkovsky, Tonino Guerra**
ph **Giuseppe Lanci**
m **Verdi, Beethoven, Russian folk music**
Oleg Jankovsky, Erland Josephson, Domiziana Giordano, Patrizia Terreno, Delia Boccardo

At a spa in the Tuscan hills, a Russian poet and musicologist (Jankovsky), researching the life of an 18th-century composer, meets a mysterious man (Josephson) who is convinced that the end of the world is nigh. The Russian is asked to cross an ancient sulphur pool from side to side carrying a lighted candle as an act of faith. Tarkovsky's first film outside the USSR expresses, through his hero *in extremis*, great homesickness. This enclosed, melancholy and poetic film is full of personal and Christian symbols, such as birds bursting forth from the breast of a statue of the Madonna. Monochrome is used for the past in Russia and desaturated colour for the present. The extremely long takes, the camera moving almost imperceptibly at times, create an intense concentration on the many extraordinary images. But there are scenes of an almost perverse obscurity and the final sequence is tedious beyond belief.

No Tomorrow

Sans Lendemain

France 1939 82 mins bw
Gray Film/Ciné Alliance

d **Max Ophüls**
sc **Hans Wilhelm (billed as Jean Villeme), Jacot**
ph **Eugen Schüfftan**
m **Allan Gray**
Edwige Feuillère, Georges Rigaud, Daniel Lecourtois, Paul Azais, Gabriello, Georges Lannes

A stripper (Feuillère) in a Montmartre nightclub meets her ex-lover (Rigaud) whom she hasn't seen for ten years. She wishes him to bring up her son, but in trying to keep the truth of her profession from him and in pretending she is wealthy, she gets involved with a racketeer (Lannes). As usual Ophüls, by an elegant sleight of hand, has transformed a novelettish story into a tragic romance. Edwige Feuillère suffers beautifully as the misused mother who becomes a *poule de luxe* in spite of herself, while the men are rather unsympathetic—whether by design or by accident one cannot be sure.

Not On Your Life see Executioner, The

Not Reconciled, Or Only Violence Helps Where Violence Rules

Nicht Versöhnt, Oder Es Hilft Nur Gerwalt, Wo Gewalt Herrscht

W. Germany 1965 53 mins bw
Straub-Huillet

d **Jean-Marie Straub**
sc **Jean-Marie Straub, Danièle Huillet**
ph **Wendelin Sachtler, Gerhard Ries, Christian Schwarzwald (Christian Blackwood), Jean-Marie Straub**
m **Bartok, Bach**
Heinrich Hargesheimer, Carlheinz Hargesheimer, Martha Ständer, Danièle Straub (Danièle Huillet), Henning Harmssen, Ulrich Hopmann

A half-century (1910-1960) in the lives of the middle-class Fähmel family, headed by the architect Heinrich (Heinrich Hargesheimer at 80, Carlheinz Hargesheimer at 35), and his wife Joanna (Ständer at 70, Straub as young woman). In less than an hour, Straub deconstructs Heinrich Böll's *Billiards At Half-Past Nine*, a long novel about three generations, by, as he says, 'eliminating as much as possible any historical aura in both costumes and sets, thus giving the images a kind of atonal character'. The film also leaps backwards and forwards in time, giving the impression of the co-existence of past and present, thus making the point that Nazism didn't begin in 1933 or end in 1945. It may not convince those not reconciled to experimental cinema, but to others this first feature will astonish.

Notre Histoire see Our Story

Notte Brava, La see Night Heat

Notte Di San Lorenzo, La see Night Of San Lorenzo, The

La Notte

aka The Night

Italy 1961 121 mins bw
Nepi Film/Silva Film (Rome)/Sofitepid (Paris)

d **Michelangelo Antonioni**
sc **Michelangelo Antonioni, Ennio Flaiano, Tonino Guerra**
ph **Gianni Di Venanzo**
m **Giorgio Gaslini**
Marcello Mastroianni, Jeanne Moreau, Monica Vitti, Bernhard Wicki, Rosy Mazzacurati

Twenty-four hours in the life of a Milanese novelist (Mastroianni) and his wife (Moreau), during which they visit a dying friend (Wicki) in hospital, go to a nightclub, meet a rich industrialist's daughter (Vitti) at a party, and face the emptiness of their lives and marriage. Following *L'Avventura*, Antonioni further explored an alienated couple placed in an unresponsive environment. Here, the background is the cold beauty of Milan's modern architecture, and the streets through which Moreau (in a role she detested) wanders in the longest and most impressive sequence.

Best Film Berlin 1961

Notti Bianche, Le see White Nights

Notti Di Cabiria, Le see Nights Of Cabiria

Nous Étions Un Seul Homme see We Were One Man

Nous Ne Vieillerons Pas Ensemble see We Will Not Grow Old Together

Nous Sommes Tous Les Assassins see Are We All Murderers?

Nouveau Venu, Le see Newcomer, The

Les Nouveaux Messieurs

(US: The New Gentlemen)

France 1928 135 mins bw
Albatros/Séquence

d **Jacques Feyder**
sc **Charles Spaak, Jacques Feyder,**
ph **Georges Périnal**
m **Silent**
Albert Préjean, Gaby Morlay, Henri Roussel

An electrician (Préjean) at the Paris Opera is enamoured of a ballerina (Morlay) who has an elderly and wealthy protector whom she decides to leave. The electrician, who is a politically ambitious trade unionist, decides to become a deputé. It was following a French ban on this lively satirical comedy that Feyder accepted MGM's invitation to direct Garbo in *The Kiss* in Hollywood. The film, which pokes fun at rival politicians, was officially felt to undermine 'the dignity of Parliament and its ministers', a decision more farcical than anything the screenplay dreamed up. The contributions of Préjean, Périnal, and the designer Lazare Meerson, are a reminder that it doesn't quite have the *joie de vivre* of René Clair's comedies of the period.

Novecento see Nineteen Hundred

Novembermond see Novembermoon

Novembermoon

Novembermond

W. Germany 1984 107 mins col
Ottokar Runze Filmproduktion(West Berlin)/ Sun 7 Productions(Paris)

d **Alexandra Von Grote**
sc **Alexandra Von Grote**
ph **Bernard Zitzermann**
m **Egisto Macchi**
Gabriele Osburg, Christiane Millet, Danièle Delorme, Stéphane Garcin, Bruno Pradal

In 1939, a Jewish girl by the somewhat unlikely name of November (Osburg), leaves Hitler's Germany for Paris. Courted by Laurent (Garcin), she falls in love with his sister Férial (Millet) and they enjoy an idyllic affair until the Nazi invasion. November ends up in hiding with Férial and her mother (the veteran Delorme) in Paris. Férial, to avoid suspicion, takes a job with a pro-Nazi sympathizer and, at the liberation, is shot for her pains. Von Grote joins the formidable list of Berlin's female *auteurs* and made this film under the auspices of Basis Film, the independent company which has encouraged the work of Helke Sander, Helma Sanders-Brahms, Jutta Bruckner, and several others. All the more disappointing, therefore, that *Novembermoon* has so little insight to offer. In taking her story to France, the director fashions clichés of character and situation, and the only real interest of her heroine lies in the casting of Osburg who is sympathetically gauche.

Novyi Gulliver see New Gulliver, The

Novyi Vavilon see New Babylon, The

Now About These Women

(US: All These Women)

För Att Inte Tala Om Alla Dessa Kvinnor

Sweden 1964 80 mins col
Svensk Filmindustri

d **Ingmar Bergman**
sc **Ingmar Bergman, Erland Josephson**
ph **Sven Nykvist**
m **Eric Nordgren**
Jarl Kulle, Georg Funkquist, Eva Dahlbeck, Karen Kavli, Harriet Andersson, Bibi Andersson, Gertrud Fridh

A pompous music critic (Kulle), attempting a biography of a famous cellist, is hampered in his efforts by a flock of the maestro's female companions. Bergman responded to the mixed critical reaction to his recent 'morbid' films by making a farce that pokes fun at critics. Also, to get away from any accusations of darkness, he decided to use colour for the first time to bring out the prettiness of the ornate sets and flamboyant 1920s costumes. Unfortunately, though well-played, it is a strained, airless and unfunny film. The critics were unamused, and Bergman returned to drama.

Noz W Wodzie see Knife In The Water

Nuit Americaine, La see Day For Night

La Nuit De Carrefour

France 1932 80 mins bw
Europa Films

d **Jean Renoir**
sc **Jean Renoir**
ph **Marcel Lucien, Asselin**
Pierre Renoir, Winna Winfried, Georges Koudria, Georges Térof, Dignimont, G.A. Martin, Jean Mitry

When the body of an Amsterdam diamond dealer is found in mysterious circumstances in a small town north of Paris, Inspector Maigret (Renoir) is sent to investigate. Holding each member of the small community suspect in turn, he discovers a link with the Parisian underworld before finally solving the case. The first Simenon thriller to be adapted to the screen, this is a sadly neglected masterpiece of the early sound cinema, largely filmed on location and using direct sound. It effectively captures the atmosphere of the crossroads community with its dank fields, speeding cars, and mysterious inhabitants: the slightly sleazy garage owner, the sinister Dane with a black monocle, the latter's young sister (or wife?) who is attracted to Maigret—a remarkable erotic performance from Winna Winfried. In his first major film role, the director's elder brother convincingly portrays the famous detective.

Nuit De Varennes, La see Night Of Varennes, The

Nuit Et Brouillard see Night And Fog

Nuit Fantastique, La see Fantastic Night, The

Nuits De La Pleine Lune, Les see Full Moon In Paris

Nuits Rouges see Shadowman

Numéro Deux

France 1975 90 mins col
Sonimage/Bela/SNC

d **Jean-Luc Godard**
sc **Jean-Luc Godard, Anne-Marie Miéville**
ph **William Lubtchansky**
m **Léo Ferré**
Sandrine Battistella, Pierre Oudry, Alexandre Rignault, Rachel Stefanopol

The daily lives of a young couple (Battistella and Oudry), their two children and two grandparents (Rignault and Stefanopol). The wife feels imprisoned in the home, the husband is exhausted at work; she has chronic constipation, he cannot achieve an erection. Godard's 'home movie of family life' is an astonishing experiment in the use of video on to film. For nine-tenths of the duration, only part of the screen is used—two rectangles placed top-left and bottom-right—where different images are seen simultaneously. As always, Godard's manipulation of the medium cannot be separated from the message it contains. Here the relationship between the social, political and sexual is also tied up with how they are portrayed on the part-screen. It does take rather an effort to adjust to the method and it is even more frustrating on TV where the two images are reduced in size. Only at the end is there the relief of a full-screen image, like an orgasm or the end to constipation (number two/numéro deux?).

Nunta De Pietra see Stone Wedding

Nun, The see Religieuse, La

Nuovi Angeli, I see New Angels, The

Nybyggarna see New Land, The

O

Obchod Od Na Korze see Shop On The High Street, The

The Oberwald Mystery

Il Mistero Di Oberwald

Italy 1980 129 mins col
RAI

d **Michelangelo Antonioni**
sc **Michelangelo Antonioni, Tonino Guerra**
ph **Luciano Tovoli**
m **Richard Strauss, Schoenberg, Brahms**
Monica Vitti, Franco Branciaroli, Luigi Diberti, Elisabetta Pozzi, Paolo Bonacelli

The Queen (Vitti) of a middle European country at the turn of the century, in hiding for ten years after the assasination of the King, gives refuge to a fleeing anarchist poet (Branciaroli) who resembles her dead husband and who becomes her 'angel of death' lover. Returning to Italy after some years, and to Monica Vitti with whom he had last worked in 1964 on *The Red Desert*, Antonioni made the flawed but interesting experiment of shooting a film with a video camera, then transferring it on to 35mm. Some of the colours evoke the early two-tone colour processes, and others are decidedly muddy. But the most evident problem lies in the fact that the restrained, ascetic Antonioni is temperamentally at the opposite pole to the flamboyant, aesthetic Cocteau, upon whose *The Eagle Has Two Heads* the film is based. This fustian melodrama seems no less silly when played in such a muted manner by the splendid looking leads, than it did in the hammier method the piece requires (see Cocteau's own screen version).

Oblomok Imperii see Fragment Of An Empire

Oblomov

Neskolko Dnei Iz Zhizni I. I. Oblomov

USSR 1979 140 mins col
Mosfilm

d **Nikita Mikhalkov**
sc **Nikita Mikhalkov, Aleksander Adabashyan**
ph **Pavel Lebechev**
m **Eduard Artemyev**
Oleg Tabakov, Elena Solovei, Andrei Popov, Yuri Bogatyrev

Oblomov (Tabakov), a civil servant in his thirties, decides to take to his bed for the foreseeable future. There he stays, looked after by his servant Zakhar (Popov), until Andrei (Bogatyrev) gets him up and introduces him to the lovely Olga (Solovei), whom the slothful Oblomov marries. As Goncharov's great 1859 satire on the Russian aristocracy is as static as its indolent and infuriating hero, Mikhalkov has tricked out the narrative with copious flashbacks and dreams. Adapted from only a section of the novel, it has some scenes that do justice to the original. Overall, however, it lacks bite and, as played by Tabakov, Oblomov is not a harmful parasite, but an enviable charmer. At over two hours, it might produce an Oblomovist effect on the spectator.

The Occupation In 26 Pictures

Okupacija U 26 Slika

Yugoslavia 1978 116 mins col
Jadran Film/Croatia Film

d **Lordan Zafranovic**
sc **Mirko Kovač, Lordan Zafranovic**
ph **Karpo Godina**
m **Alfi Kabiljo**
Frano Lasic, Milan Strljic, Ivan Klemenc, Boris Kralj

Twenty-six events that take place in the first

days of the Italian occupation of the coastal town of Dubrovnik during World War II and their effect on three friends from different backgrounds. Brilliantly contrasting the beauties of the medieval town with the nastiness of the Occupation, Zafranovic also reveals how much of the war is fought in the salons of powerful civilians. Some of these pictures are far from pretty, one in particular is as gruesome as any to be found in a modern horror film, but their purpose was part of a serious and uncompromising attempt to understand the reality of the events.

Occupe-Toi D'Amélie see Keep An Eye On Amelia

Ochazuke No Aji see Flavour Of Green Tea Over Rice, The

Oci Ciornie see Dark Eyes

October

aka Ten Days That Shook The World

Oktyabr

USSR 1928 164 mins bw

Sovkino

d **Sergei Eisenstein**

sc **Sergei Eisenstein, Grigori Alexandrov**

ph **Edouard Tissé**

m **Silent**

Nikandrov, Vladimir Popov, Boris Livanov, soldiers of the Red Army, sailors of the Red Navy, and citizens of Leningrad

The 10 days in October 1917 when the Bolsheviks brought down the Kerensky government, showing the dismantling of the statue of Alexander III and the storming of the Winter Palace. The best of a number of films commissioned by the Soviet government to celebrate the tenth anniversary of the Revolution, it was also the most unpopular. Firstly, the official rejection of Trotsky, who had figured prominently in the film, necessitated his being expunged from it. Audiences were disorientated by its dynamic montage, the constantly contrasting images, its visual metaphors (Kerensky is seen as a mechanical peacock) and ambiguous attitude to religious relics— everything that makes the film such a rich experience today. A new print was released in 1967 with music by Shostakovitch on the sound track.

Odd Obsession

aka The Key

Kagi

Japan 1959 107 mins col

Daiei

d **Kon Ichikawa**

sc **Natto Wada, Keiji Hasebe, Kon Ichikawa**

ph **Kazuo Miyagawa**

m **Yasushi Akutagawa**

Ganjiro Nakamura, Machiko Kyo, Tatsuya Nakadai, Junko Kano, Tanie Kitabayashi, Ichiro Sugai, Jun Hamamura

Elderly Mr Kenmochi (Nakamura), obsessed and frightened by his growing impotence, encourages his daughter's fiancé (Nakadai) to show interest in his beautiful young wife in the hope that jealousy will restore his virility. His machinations lead to increasingly bizarre sexual situations, ending in the death of all concerned. Stylishly shot in appropriately muted colours and essentially exposing the unrewarding nature of lust and perversion, Ichikawa's film is an amalgam of morbidity and black farce. The denouement is frankly silly, but executed with the confident sense of tension and perverse air of normalcy which prevails throughout. An undeniably skilful and absorbing excursion into degeneracy, beautifully acted by Nakamura and Kyo, but a bleak and ugly tale which might offend the sensitive.

Special Jury Prize Cannes 1960

Oedipus Rex

Edipo Re

Italy 1967 110 mins col

Arco

d **Pier Paolo Pasolini**

sc **Pier Paolo Pasolini**

ph **Giuseppe Ruzzolini**

m **Pasolini, Mozart, popular Roman songs, ancient Japaneses music**

Franco Citti, Silvana Mangano, Carmelo Bene, Julian Beck, Pier Paolo Pasolini, Alida Valli

Despite the warnings of the blind soothsayer Tiresias (Beck), Oedipus (Citti) unknowingly kills his father and marries his mother Jocasta (Mangano). When the truth is revealed, she kills herself and he puts out his eyes. Pasolini's splendid version of the great Greek tragedy was ravishingly filmed in Morocco, using the desert landscapes and Moorish architecture as backgrounds. Although faithful to Sophocles, it has a surprising prologue and epilogue set in modern times. This Oedipus ends up on the arm of his daughter Antigone, a common blind beggar walking through the streets of 1960s Rome. Perhaps this is an unnessary straining after a universality the work already has, but it is cinematically effective. The interesting cast includes *avant-garde* film and theatre director Carmelo Bene as Creon, Julian Beck from New York's Living Theater, and Pasolini himself (typecast?) as the High Priest.

Oeil Du Malin, L' see Third Lover, The

Oeuvre Au Noir, L' see Abyss, The

Of A Thousand Delights

(US: Sandra)

Vaghe Stelle Dell'Orsa

Italy 1965 100 mins bw
Vides/Royal

d **Luchino Visconti**
sc **Luchino Visconti, Suso Cecchi D'Amico**
ph **Armando Nannuzzi**
m **César Franck**
Claudia Cardinale, Jean Sorel, Michael Craig, Marie Bell, Renzo Ricci

Sandra (Cardinale), returning to Italy from America with her husband (Craig) to attend a memorial ceremony for her Jewish scientist father killed by the Nazis, has to face her mother (Bell), whom she believes responsible for his death, and her brother (Sorel) who has incestuous longings for her. Vivid black and white images and strong performances from the women are the main qualities of this operatic tale of guilt, betrayal and incest derived from the Electra myth. But the men are anaemic and the melodramatics override any characterization. The literal translation of the title is 'misty stars of the great bear', the opening line of a poem by Leopardi.

Best Film Venice 1965

Official Story, The see Official Version, The

The Official Version

(US: The Official Story)

La Historia Official

Argentina 1985 115 mins col
Historias Cinematograficas/Progress Communications

d **Luis Puenzo**
sc **Aida Bortnik, Luis Puenzo**
ph **Felix Monti**
m **Atilio Stampone**
Héctor Alterio, Norma Aleandro, Chela Ruiz, Chunchuna Villafane, Hugo Arana

Roberto (Alterio), a businessman, and his wife Alicia (Aleandro), a history teacher, live comfortably in a suburb of Buenos Aires with their adopted little daughter. Alicia, decent but complacent and intellectually moribund, is gradually made aware of the facts about children removed from detained and tortured parents and then given away. She comes to suspect that her own child might be one of them. Puenzo's film, both unbearably moving (a towering performance from Aleandro) and highly intelligent, weaves several interlocking themes into the centre of what he calls an 'intimate' film. The main focus is Alicia's gradual politicization and recognition of her own unwitting complicity. Her journey of self-discovery, however, exposes the horrors and the imminent collapse of the corrupt military regime under Galtieri.

Best Foreign Film Oscar 1985
Best Actress (Norma Aleandro) Cannes 1985

Of Flesh And Blood

Les Grands Chemins

France 1963 95 mins col
Films Du Saphrène/Films Copernic(Paris)/ Dear Film(Rome)

d **Christian Marquand**
sc **Christian Marquand, Paul Gégauff, Pierre La Salle**
ph **Andreas Winding**
m **Michel Magne**
Robert Hossein, Renato Salvatori, Anouk Aimée, André Bervil, Jean Lefèvre, Andrée Turcy

En route to deliver a jeep in Grenoble, Francis (Salvatori) gives a ride to Samuel (Hossein), a conman and card-sharp, and Anna (Aimée), a young widow. The jeep breaks down near to a hotel owned by Anna and repairs take a week, during which time Francis works on a farm and has an affair with Anna. Samuel, however, cons the locals, who retaliate by crushing his hands in a barn door, thus triggering off a series of bizarre events that end in terrible bloodshed. For his directorial debut, actor Marquand turned to a novel by Jean Giono. The film is strong on mood and beautifully photographed in attractive colour, and there is an attempt to penetrate the depths of Giono's abstract themes about strange loyalties. However, the movie fails to get to the heart of the matter, partly because the casting is not ideal, while new characters—notably Anna—are introduced, along with extraneous sex and violence. (Could it be the hand of Roger Vadim, who 'supervised'?) Marquand's second career foundered forever on one more film, the notoriously awful *Candy* (1968).

Offret see Sacrifice, The

Oh, Amelia! see Keep An Eye On Amelia

Ohayo see Good Morning

Ohm Krüger

Germany 1941 135 mins bw
Tobis

d **Hans Steinhoff**
sc **Harold Bratt, Kurt Heuser**
ph **Fritz Arno Wagner**
m **Theo Mackeben**
Emil Jannings, Franz Schafheitlin, Ferdinand Marian, Gustav Gründgens, Hedwig Wangel

Heroic Boers led by Paul Kruger (Jannings) fight against the brutal British in South Africa. British missionaries incite the natives to attack the Boers, many of whom are put into concentration camps. But there are victories and Kruger goes to London to negotiate with a whisky-swigging Queen Victoria (Wangel). One of the Nazi regime's biggest propaganda hits was made on a lavish scale with fine photography. Some of the crudities of the message in the long-winded screenplay were somewhat ameliorated by the impressive avuncular performance of Jannings (who also directed a few sequences) as the first president of South Africa. The film would probably be welcomed by the present South African regime. Steinhoff, Goebbels pet propagandist, died in a plane crash in 1945.

Oh, Sun see Soleil Ô

Oiseaux Vont Mourir Au Pérou, Les see Birds Come To Die In Peru, The

---

Oka Oorie Katha see Outsiders, The

Oktyabr see October

Okupacija U 26 Slika see Occupation In 26 Pictures, The

Old And New see General Line, The

Old Capital, The see Twin Sisters Of Kyoto

The Old Country Where Rimbaud Died

Le Vieux Pays Où Rimbaud Est Mort

Canada/France 1977 113 mins col
Cinak/Filmoblic/Institut National De L'Audiovisuel

d **Jean Pierre Lefèbvre**
sc **Mireille Amiel, Jean Pierre Lefèbvre**
ph **Guy Dufaux**

m **Claude Fonfrède**
Marcel Sabourin, Anouk Ferjac, Myriam Boyer, Mark Lesser, Germaine Delbat

Québecois Abel (Sabourin) records his impressions of visiting France, 'the Old Country'. He stays in Paris, then goes to Charleville, the home town of the woman (Boyer) with whom he is having an affair, and then on to the Côte D'Azur where he meets a probation officer (Ferjac) who gains his affection. Abel then decides to return to Canada. This episodic exploration of the relationship between France and French Canada, takes the form of a letter home by the film's taciturn hero, who observes and listens 'to see if there were still Frenchmen in France—to see if they resembled me'. Much of what he (and Lefèbvre, the most renowned of Québecois directors) observes is amusing, touching and surprising, despite the often self-conscious use of long takes, a static camera and quotes from Rimbaud on the sound track.

The Oldest Profession

Le Plus Vieux Métier Du Monde

France/Italy/W. Germany 1967
115 mins col
Gibé/Francoriz/Rialto/Rizzoli

d **Franco Indovini, Mauro Bolognini, Philippe De Broca, Michel Pfleghar, Claude Autant-Lara, Jean-Luc Godard**
sc **Ennio Flaiano, Daniel Boulanger, Georges and André Tabet, Jean Aurenche, Jean-Luc Godard**
ph **Pierre Lhomme**
m **Michel Legrand**
Michèle Mercier, Elsa Martinelli, Gastone Moschin, Jean-Claude Brialy, Jeanne Moreau, Raquel Welch, Martin Held, France Anglade, Jacques Charrier, Anna Karina, Jean-Pierre Léaud

Five episodes illustrate prostitution through the ages—prehistoric times, Ancient Rome, the French Revolution, *La Belle Époque*, and Paris in the year 2,000. Movie directors, one of the newest professions, pay tribute to the oldest profession, no doubt recognizing certain similarities—certainly in this commercial venture. One has to sit through four sketches ranging from the mildly amusing to the completely unfunny before coming to the Godard chapter, the only one with artistic merit. Until 1968, prostitution was a major theme in his films, and here he elaborates on it through the eyes of a visitor from outer space.

Old Maid, The see Vieille Fille, La

Ole Dole Doff see Who Saw Him Die?

Olivia

France 1950 96 mins bw
Memnon Films

d **Jacqueline Audry**
sc **Colette Audry, Pierre Laroche**
ph **Christian Matras**
m **Pierre Sancan**
Edwige Feuillère, Simone Simon, Claire Olivia, Yvonne De Bray, Suzanne Dehelly, Lesly Meynard, Rita Roanda

In the 1880s Olivia (Olivia), an English girl, attends a French boarding school run by two sisters, Mademoiselle Julie (Feuillère) and Mademoiselle Cara (Simon). She is enchanted by the frivolous atmosphere, but it transpires that staff and pupils are split into two factions, and Olivia's gravitation towards Julie precipitates a severe crisis. This film is based on the autobiographical novel by Lytton Strachey's sister, Dorothy Bussy. A colourful character, she too, subscribed to *Olivia's* epigraph—'Love has always been the chief business of my life'. Like *Mädchen In Uniform*, this story of hothouse emotions with Lesbian undercurrents is richly dramatic, but also contains humour and presents the teachers as willing participants in the relationships. Audry has brought this material to the screen with tremendous style and period authenticity and with a superbly well-chosen cast, but it slightly disappoints in lacking the required depths of passion.

Oltre Il Bene E Il Male see Beyond Good And Evil

Olvidados, Los see Young And The Damned, The

Olympia see Olympiad

Olympiad
(US: Olympia)
Olympische Spiele 1936

Germany 1938 118 mins (Part I—Festival Of The Nations)—107 mins (Part II—Festival Of Beauty) bw
Tobis

d **Leni Riefenstahl**
sc **Leni Riefenstahl**
ph **Hans Ertl and others**
m **Herbert Windt**

A documentary on the 1936 Berlin Olympics attended by Hitler. A prologue links the ideals of beauty in Greek antiquity with those of the Third Reich. Part I concentrates on the track events inside the stadium; Part II takes in events around the stadium and in the Olympic village. Riefenstahl was commissioned to film the Games 'as a song of praise to the ideals of National Socialism'. As there could be no retakes of the great moments, the film was organized with Nazi efficiency. The director had over 30 cameramen as well as planes and airships at her disposal, and spent two years in the cutting room. Slow and reverse motion make the diving sequence a *tour de force*, the Marathon becomes an 'epic hymn to endurance'; the yacht racing under a darkened sky, and the screen filling with thousands of girls swinging clubs are some of the other remarkable sequences. But it is easy for the audience to be seduced by the exceptional beauty and grace of many of the images into ignoring the sinister significance of the swastikas, and to forget the persecution of the Jews that was taking place outside the walls of the stadium.

Olympische Spiele 1936 see Olympiad

On Any Street see Night Heat

One Deadly Summer
L'Été Meurtrier

France 1983 133 mins col
SNC/CAPAC/T.F.1 Films

d **Jean Becker**
sc **Sébastien Japrisot**
ph **Etienne Becker**
m **Georges Delerue**
Isabelle Adjani, Alain Souchon, Jenny Clève, Suzanne Flon, François Cluzet, Manuel Gélin, Maria Machado

Elle (Adjani) comes to live in a small Provençal village with her crippled father and German mother. Nineteen, beautiful, sexually provocative and extraordinarily moody, she captivates Pin Pon (Souchon), moves in with his family, and traps him into marrying her as part of a plan to avenge her mother's rape (which led to her birth). Japrisot, adapting his own novel, has constructed an intricate psychosexual mystery, using voice-over narrative which shifts from Pin Pon to Elle and, in so doing, subtly and shockingly reveals Elle's obsessions. Dialogue, action, and Adjani's mercurial performance gradually unfold a tale of mental derangement, the roots of which are explained in well-judged flashbacks. If the film is a mite too long and occasionally inclined to melodrama, it is nonetheless directed with care and conviction, its village life beautifully caught, and it provides an extra pleasure in the veteran Suzanne Flon's portrayal of a stone deaf but perceptive family aunt.

One Fine Day
Un Certo Giorno

Italy 1969 105 mins col
Cinema s.p.a./Italnoleggio/Istituto Luce

d **Ermanno Olmi**
sc **Ermanno Olmi**
ph **Lamberto Caimi**
m **Gino Negri**
Brunetto Del Vita, Maria Crosignani, Vitaliano Damioli, Lidia Fuortes, Raffaele Modugno

A middle-aged philandering advertising executive (Del Vita) runs down a workman on the day he is offered the managing directorship of his company. On trial for dangerous driving, he reassesses his job and marriage. The first of Olmi's films to deal with the middle classes is less moving and original than his studies of the lower echelons of society, although he applies the same perception and brings the same humanity to bear on his characters, avoiding easy satire on the advertising industry. This is achieved by his continuing use of non-professionals. The dialogue and events were based on conversations Olmi had with Del Vita, an advertising executive in real life.

One Life

Une Vie

France 1958 88 mins col
Agnès Delahaie Production/Nepi Film

d **Alexandre Astruc**
sc **Roland Laudenbach, Alexandre Astruc**
ph **Claude Renoir**
m **Roman Vlad**
Maria Schell, Christian Marquand, Ivan Desny, Antonella Lualdi, Pascale Petit, Marie-Hélène Dasté

Young, innocent and aristocratic Jeanne (Schell) marries Julien (Marquand), unaware that her handsome husband is a womanizer, but gradually comes to realize that he has no desire to be with her. Julien's affair with a friend's wife (Lualdi) leads to his death, leaving Jeanne and her son to face life alone. Astruc's refined treatment of De Maupassant's story catches the sexual tensions of the original, but otherwise misses its depths. Schell's cloying sweetness is no help, but Marquand, Lualdi and Petit are excellent, and the 19th-century country milieu is beautifully caught by Renoir's richly textured, almost impressionistic camerawork.

One Man's War

La Guerre D'Un Seul Homme

France 1981 106 mins bw
Marion Films/INA/ZDF(W. Germany)

d **Edgardo Cozarinsky**
sc **Edgardo Cozarinsky with text by Ernst Junger**
ph **Newsreel cameramen**
m **Hans Pfitzner, Richard Strauss, Schönberg, Franz Schreker**

French newsreels during the German occupation of 1940-1944 show the life in Paris: the theatre, fashions and sport, as well as propaganda on the progress of the war and the benevolence of the Third Reich. Counterpointing these bland commentaries of half-truths is a linking narration from the Paris diaries of Ernst Junger, a German officer critical of Nazism, and a superb use of music. Cozarinsky, a Jewish Argentinian exile living in Paris, uses a method that goes beyond the mere documentary into the realms of a meditation on history, disinformation, and the inability of people to see their own times with any clarity.

1 + 1 = 3

W. Germany 1979 85 mins col
Peter Genée & Von Fürstenberg Produktion/Heidi Genée Filmproduktion

d **Heidi Genée**
sc **Heidi Genée**
ph **Gernot Roll**
m **Andreas Köbner**
Adelheid Arndt, Dominik Graf, Christoph Quest, Helga Storck, Dietrich Leiding

Katarina (Arndt), an unmarried actress in Munich becomes pregnant. Initially shocked at the news, her boyfriend Bernhard (Graf) later offers a proposal, and money for an abortion. Both are refused, since Katarina is determined to have her child while avoiding the pitfalls of marriage as exemplified by her sister's unhappy situation. Katarina takes a holiday, meets divorced Jürgen (Quest) and ends up living with him. It becomes clear that his major enthusiasm is for the forthcoming baby to whom Bernhard also continues to lay claim... This committedly feminist film is, in fact, played with much gentle comedy and offers a heroine who is warm, wry and attractive, as well as steadfastly independent. Involved in the chaos of her sister's life, Katarina is constantly surrounded by children, and Genée sketches in the domestic detail of life with an eye both caring and sharp, while her male characters are bemused inadequates rather than reactionary heavies. The pacy narrative reveals a world that, even when turbulent, is charmingly familiar.

One Sings, The Other Doesn't

L'Une Chante, L'Autre Pas

France 1976 120 mins col
Ciné Tamaris/Société Française De Production/Institut National De L'Audiovisuel/Contrechamp(Paris)/Paradise Films(Brussels)/Population Films(Curaçao)

d **Agnès Varda**
sc **Agnès Varda**
ph **Charlie Van Damme**
m **François Wertheimer**
Valérie Mairesse, Thérèse Liotard, Robert Dadiès, Gisèle Halimi, Ali Raffi, Jean-Pierre Pellegrin, Rosalie Varda, Mathieu Demy

Pauline (Mairesse), aged 17, helps her friend Suzanne (Liotard), 22 and the unmarried mother of two children, to procure an abortion. Pauline becomes a singer, travels the world, and has children by her Iranian lover; Suzanne returns to her parents' farm, educates herself, and runs a family planning clinic. They meet 10 years later at an anti-abortion demonstration, and again 12 years after that, this time having kept in touch. After a nine-year absence from features, Varda made a triumphant return with this irrefutably feminist film, which is somewhat marred by the softness of its glossy, romantic approach. Taking Simone De Beauvoir's maxim that 'Women are made, not born,' as her theme, the director presents two friends of different temperaments and backgrounds who both face adversity but achieve independence and fulfilment. Mairesse and Liotard are stunning.

One Summer Of Happiness

Hon Dansade En Sommar

Sweden 1952 103 mins bw
Nordisk Tonefilm/Lennart Landheim

d **Arne Mattsson**
sc **W. Semitjov**
ph **Göran Strindberg**
m **Sven Skjöld**
Folke Sundqvist, Ulla Jacobsson, Edvin Adolphson, John Elfstrom, Irma Christensson

Göran (Sundqvist), having recently finished his studies, spends a summer in the country with his uncle (Adolphson). He meets Kerstin (Jacobsson), the innocent daughter of the neighbouring farmer, and they fall in love. The puritanical atmosphere and the opposition of the rigid pastor (Elfstrom) impose constraints, but they manage to find some happiness until their affair is destroyed by tragedy. With the help of an excellent cast, Mattsson gives a fresh and moving account of young love, strengthened by the lyrical photography of nature and landscape. This is contrasted with the stark, low-angle shooting of the sequences with the pastor designed to project the harsh religion which he represents. But the director's moral point remains unclear due to an unsatisfactory ending. The film's shimmering nude bathing/love scene caused much controversy at the time.

One Way Or Another

De Cierta Manera

Cuba 1974 79 mins bw
Instituto Cubano Del Arte E Industria Cinematográficos

d **Sara Gómez**
sc **Sara Gómez, Tomás González Pérez**
ph **Luis García**
m **Sergio Vitier**
Mario Balmaseda, Yolanda Cuéllar, Mario Limonta, Guillermo Díaz

Two young lovers, a mulatto worker (Balmaseda) in a bus assembly factory and a middle-class schoolteacher (Cuéllar), learn about each other's backgrounds and the class prejudices they grew up with before embracing the revolution. Sara Gómez, who made a number of impressive short documentaries before her only feature, died from an asthma attack while it was being completed. The first Cuban film to be directed by a woman confronts the problems of being both black and female in the Third World. This is brilliantly done by Gómez (also known as Sara Gómez Yera), subverting a conventional love story by interjecting documentary footage, interviews and voice over and with the characters occasionally speaking directly to the camera.

One Wild Moment see Summer Affair, A

Onibaba

aka The Hole

Japan 1964 104 mins bw
Kindai Eiga Kyokai/Tokyo Eiga

d **Kaneto Shindo**
sc **Kaneto Shindo**
ph **Kiyomi Juroda**
m **Hikaru Hayashi**
Nobuko Otowa, Yitsuko Yoshimura, Kei Sato

In medieval times, on a remote plain, a widow (Yoshimura) and her mother-in-law (Otowa) kill wandering Samurai, put their bodies in a hole in the ground and sell their armour and valuables, until the daughter-in-law falls in love with one of them. This strange and violent folk-tale is marred by a penchant for sensationalism and sentimentality. But the strong performances, notably from Otowa Shindo's regular star, and the eerie atmosphere were partly responsible for its popularity in the West.

Only The French Can see French Cancan

Onna No Rekishi see Woman's Life, A

On Ne Meurt Que 2 Fois see He Died With His Eyes Open

Onorevole Angelina, L' see Angelina

On Purge Bébé

France 1931 62 mins bw
Braunberger-Richebé

d **Jean Renoir**
sc **Jean Renoir**
ph **Théodor Sparkühl, Roger Hubert**
Michel Simon, Louvigny, Marguerite Pierry, Olga Valéry, Fernandel

Monsieur Follavoine (Louvigny), a porcelain manufacturer, attempts to clinch a deal with Monsieur Chouilloux (Simon) to supply the French army with 200,000 unbreakable chamber pots. Meanwhile, Follavoine's wife, obsessed with their baby's constipation, inflicts the purge on the hapless Chouilloux. Renoir's first sound picture, adapted from a Feydeau farce, is little more than a piece of filmed theatre. Shot quickly and cheaply, and using long takes on an artificial-looking set, with most of the action staged in front of a stationary camera, it nonetheless swiftly earned a substantial profit, thus enabling Renoir to make the Michel Simon picture he really wanted—*La Chienne*.

Open City see Rome, Open City

Opera Do Malandro

Brazil 1986 108 mins col
MK2 Productions (Paris)/Austra (Brazil)/T.F.1. Films

d **Ruy Guerra**
sc **Chico Buarque, Orlando Senna, Ruy Guerra**
ph **Antonio Luis Mendes**
m **Chico Buarque**
Edson Celulari, Claudia Ohana, Elba Ramalho, Ney Latorraca, Fabio Sabag

Max (Celulari) is a pimp and profiteer, but passionately anti-Nazi and pro-American. During the period between Pearl Harbor and Brazil's declaration of war on Germany, his complicated activities involve him heavily with two women—his regular girlfriend who is a whore, and the criminally minded daughter of a wealthy German club owner—as well as with his friend, the corrupt police chief. Guerra's musical film is an eclectic, indeed, somewhat chaotic affair, being a loose attempt at a Brazilian version of *The Threepenny Opera*, combined with images and assumptions drawn from the Hollywood musical. Its political and social messages are somewhat hazy, but there is enjoyment to be had from some imaginative dance sequences and from the sheer ebullience of the piece.

Ophelia

France 1962 105 mins bw
Boreal

d **Claude Chabrol**
sc **Claude Chabrol, Martial Matthieu**
ph **Jean Rabier**
m **Pierre Jansen**
André Jocelyn, Alida Valli, Claude Cerval, Juliette Mayniel, Robert Burnier

Yvan Lesurf (Jocelyn), son of a wealthy industrialist, is grief-stricken at his father's death and disturbed by the swift remarriage of his mother (Valli) to his uncle (Cerval). He behaves badly towards them and, on seeing Olivier's film of *Hamlet*, draws parallels with Gertrude and Claudius, and plots revenge. Chabrol plays an inventive, if not altogether successful, game in this film, delighting in the bizarre notions of his eccentric hero and upending the Shakespearian details to suit himself. Set in a gloomy mansion and its appropriate surroundings, the film is photographed with flair and cool detachment, well played, and enhanced by acid wit as well as some brilliant set-pieces.

Opname see In For Treatment

Orage

France 1938 85 mins bw
André Daven

d **Marc Allégret**
sc **Marcel Achard, H.G. Lustig**
ph **Armand Thirard**
m **Georges Auric**
Charles Boyer, Michèle Morgan, Lisette Lanvin, Robert Manuel, Jean-Louis Barrault

André Pascaud (Boyer) is indifferent to the wife (Lanvin) who adores him, while his brother-in-law Gilbert (Manuel) loves Françoise (Morgan) who doesn't reciprocate his feelings. At Gilbert's behest, André looks up Françoise in Paris and they fall passionately for one another, enjoying a brief idyll before his wife reclaims him and tragedy ensues. Adapted from a play by the popular Henri Bernstein, this triangular tale starts out well but ends up drowning in its own repetitive intensity. In one of her first major roles, Morgan's personality and looks make an impact, though her acting abilities were to improve substantially with experience. Boyer is as smooth, attractive and skilful as always, and Barrault lends the colour of his unique personality to a small role. A competently directed but disappointing romance.

Orchestra Rehearsal

Prova D'Orchestra

Italy 1978 72 mins col
Daimo Cinematografica(Rome)/Albatros Produktion(Munich)

d **Federico Fellini**
sc **Federico Fellini, Brunello Rondi**
ph **Giuseppe Rotunno**
m **Nino Rota**
Balduin Baas, Clara Colosimo, Elisabeth Labi, Ronaldo Bonacchi, Ferdinando Villella, Giovanni Javarone, David Mauhsell, Francesco Aluigi, Andy Miller, Sibyl Mostert, Franco Mazzieri, Daniele Pagani, Filippo Trincia, Claudio Ciocca, Cesare Martignoni

Orchestral musicians argue the merits of their respective instruments while waiting for a rehearsal that is to be filmed as a television documentary. When the German conductor (Baas) arrives, the ancient building is shaken by rumblings, the electricity fails and a demolition crew gets to work. Meanwhile, the musicians stage a revolt against the conductor's authoritarianism. However, by employing increasingly Hitlerian techniques and tone, he finally persuades them that to play together is their only salvation. This is clearly intended as an allegory about totalitarianism, but that's about all that *is* clear in this lumbering, banal and simplistic exercise. The music doesn't pass muster as a symphony, but is nonetheless beguiling and, sadly, Nino Rota's last score before his death.

Ordet

aka The Word

Denmark 1955 125 mins bw
Palladium

d **Carl Dreyer**
sc **Carl Dreyer**
ph **Henning Bendtsen**
m **Poul Schierbeck**
Henrik Malberg, Emil Hass Christensen, Preben Lerdorff Rye, Caj Kristiansen, Birgitte Federspiel, Ejner Federspiel

In a remote, West Jutland farming community, a severe father (Malberg) of three sons refuses to let one of them, Anders (Kristiansen), marry the daughter of a man with whom he has religious differences. When Inge (Birgitte Federspiel), his daughter-in-law, married to Mikkel (Christensen), dies in childbirth, Johannes (Rye), the visionary son, prays for her resurrection. Dreyer's penultimate work, based on a famous play by Kai Munk (already filmed by Gustaf Molander in 1943), is an extraordinary expression of spiritual optimism. Dreyer achieves the powerful effects by deceptively simple means. A tale of a miraculous resurrection brought about by human love could have been pious, sentimental and even risible—Dreyer makes it into an enriching experience.

Best Film Venice 1955

Ordnung see All In Order

Orfeu Negro see Black Orpheus

The Organizer
I Compagni

Italy 1963 130 mins bw
Lux/Vides/Mediteranée/Cinema/Avala

d **Mario Monicelli**
sc **Age, Scarpelli, Mario Monicelli**
ph **Giuseppe Rotunno**
m **Carlo Rustichelli**
Marcello Mastroianni, Renato Salvatori, Annie Girardot, Gabriella Giorgelli, Bernard Blier, François Périer, Folco Lulli

In turn-of-the-century Turin, the factory workers are on strike for better pay and conditions. They are helped to form a union by an impoverished aristocratic professor (Mastroianni). Monicelli, renowned for comedies tinged with a social purpose, successfully handles this poignant social drama tinged with humour. Although its relevance to present-day labour conditions is somewhat lessened by the rather picturesque and detailed period setting (often filmed in the style of contemporary daguerrotypes), the film still packs a reasonable punch. The entire cast give well-rounded characterizations, particularly a myopic Mastroianni as the eponymous organizer, although the Italian title, 'Comrades', is closer to the plot's communal nature.

Orgueilleux, Les see Proud Ones, The

Orion's Belt
Orions Belte

Norway 1985 105 mins col
Filmeffekt

d **Ola Solum**
sc **Richard Harris**
ph **Harald Paalgard**
m **Geir Bøhren, Bent Åserud**
Helge Jordal, Sverre Anker Ousdal, Hans Ola Sørlie, Kjersti Holmen, Vidar Sandem, Jon Eikemo

Three sailors earn a living running tours in the North Sea and simultaneously practising minor thefts and fiddles on the side, until their old freighter puts ashore at the site of a Soviet spy installation and they become fatally involved in international politics and violence. A notably big-budget production by Norwegian standards, the film is strikingly located in the isolated Arctic reaches of Spitzbergen, but its content veers unevenly between serious ideology and over-the-top spy thriller. Efficiently made, it is often enjoyably gripping, but it has some rather ponderous stretches during which only the atmosphere and visual detail hold the audience's wandering attention.

Orions Belte see Orion's Belt

Orlacs Hände see Hands Of Orlac, The

Oro Di Napoli, L' see Gold Of Naples

Orökbefogadás see Adoption

Oro, Plata, Mata see Gold, Silver, Bad Luck

Orphée see Orpheus

Orpheus
Orphée

France 1950 112 mins bw
André Paulvé/Films Du Palais Royal

d **Jean Cocteau**
sc **Jean Cocteau**
ph **Nicolas Hayer**
m **Georges Auric**
Jean Marais, François Périer, Maria Casarès, Marie Déa, Edouard Dermithe, Juliette Greco

The poet Orpheus (Marais) falls in love with the Princess of Death (Casarès), while her chauffeur, the angel Heurtebise (Périer), falls in love with the poet's wife Eurydice (Déa). When Heurtebise takes Eurydice to the Underworld through the looking-glass, Orpheus follows to get her back. Probably Cocteau's finest film, this is a perfect marriage between Greek legend and his own personal mythology. Although he uses reverse slow-motion and negative images to suggest the Underworld, the modern-day, ordinary domestic life of Mr and Mrs Orpheus is filmed 'realistically', effectively elaborating the theme of the poet caught between the worlds of the real and the imaginary. This witty and haunting film can be considered the centrepiece of Cocteau's entire *oeuvre,* and of his Orphic trilogy (it comes between *The Blood Of The Poet* and *The Testament Of Orpheus*), in particular.

Osaka Elegy

Naniwa Hika

Japan 1936 66 mins bw
Daiichi

d **Kenji Mizoguchi**
sc **Yoshitaka Yoda**
ph **Minoru Miki**
m **Koichi Takagi**
Isuzu Yamada, Seiichi Takegawa, Chiyoko Okura, Shinpachiro Asaka, Benkei Shiganoya

A young telephonist (Yamada) in a pharmaceutical company allows herself to be set up as the mistress of her married boss (Shiganoya) in order to resolve the debts of her drunken father (Takegawa) and put her brother (Okura) through school. When turned out by the boss, she resorts to prostitution. The title explains the tone, an elegy for the heroine and others like her. Yamada, the great actress who starred 20 years later in Kurosawa's *Throne Of Blood* and Ozu's *Tokyo Twilight*, is wonderful at the centre of the film, finally looking accusingly at the camera and, by implication, the audience. The film, with its twin masterpiece, *Sisters Of The Gion*, of the same year, brought fame to Mizoguchi and began his creative partnership with the unknown writer Yoshitaka Yoda, which lasted through more than 20 pictures.

Osenny Marafon see Autumn Marathon

Ososhiki see Funeral, The

Oss Emellan see Close To The Wind

Ossessione

Italy 1942 135 mins bw
Industria Cinematografica Italiana

d **Luchino Visconti**
sc **Antonio Pietrangeli, Mario Alicata, Gianni Puccini, Giuseppe De Santis, Luchino Visconti**
ph **Aldo Tonti, Domenico Scala**
m **Giuseppe Rosati**
Massimo Girotti, Clara Calamai, Juan De Landa, Elia Marcuzzo, Dhia Christiani

Gino (Girotti), a handsome drifter, and Giovanna (Calamai), the beautiful and desperately unhappy wife of Bragana (De Landa), an elderly and boorish innkeeper, have an affair which leads them to kill Bragana, whereupon their relationship drifts to inevitable tragedy. Significant both as the first film to be labelled Neo-Realist (by writer Pietrangeli) and the first to be directed by Visconti, *Ossessione* displays control, assurance, and the director's eye for detail. However, James M. Cain's study of fatal lust in rural America, *The Postman Always Rings Twice*, did not travel well to provincial Italy. Realistic it certainly is, but the reworking of the story's context, the addition of new characters, and Visconti's coolly distanced vision resulted, in spite of a couple of inspired moments, in a film that is curiously devoid of passion. The French had already attempted it as *Le Dernier Tournant* in 1939, but Hollywood would do it best in 1945 and again in 1981, under its original title.

Ostatni Etap see Last Stage, The

Ostře Sledované Vlaky see Closely Observed Trains

Otac Na Sluzsŏbtbenom Putu see When Father Was Away On Business

Otello

Italy 1986 123 mins col
Cannon Productions (Rome)/Italian International Film

d **Franco Zeffirelli**

sc **Franco Zeffirelli (libretto by Arrigo Boito)**
ph **Ennio Guarnieri**
m **Giuseppe Verdi (conducted by Lorin Maazel)**
Placido Domingo (Otello), Katia Ricciarelli (Desdemona), Justino Díaz (Iago), Petra Malakova (Emilia), Urbano Barberini (Cassio)

Otello the Moor, military governor of Cyprus, is deceived by Iago into believing that his wife, Desdemona, is unfaithful, and murders her. Verdi's late, great Shakespearian tragedy is given the full panoply of cinematic embellishment: wonderful Greek locations, magnificent colour alternately vivid, burnished and white, a superb re-creation of a Renaissance world after the manner of its paintings. The principals, too, are cast from the best available, and there are thus moments to admire and enjoy. However, in an effort to popularize the work and highlight its most overtly passionate elements, Zeffirelli has over-reached himself in an enterprise that is, alas, hindered by a series of technical imperfections. Worse, the director has tampered with Verdi's (and Shakespeare's) nuances, the score has suffered unacceptable excisions, notably that of Desdemona's famous 'Willow Song', and the camera has run riot with close-ups and histrionic flourishes that serve finally, to obscure the painful impact of both Shakespeare *and* Verdi.

Othello

USSR 1955 109 mins col
Mosfilm

d **Sergei Yutkevitch**
sc **Sergei Yutkevitch**
ph **Yevgeny Andrikanis**
m **Aram Khachaturian**
Sergei Bondarchuk, Irina Skobotseva, Andrei Popov, A. Maximova, Vladimir Soshalsky, Evgeny Vesnik

Othello (Bondarchuk) is led by his ensign Iago (Popov) to believe that his wife Desdemona (Skobtseva) has been unfaithful to him with his lieutenant Cassio (Soshalsky). Bondarchuk, following in the footsteps of Emil Jannings and Orson Welles in the role of the Moor on celluloid, gives an admirable but rather passionless performance, concentrating more on the character's nobility and bafflement than on his rage and power. Skobotseva (subsequently Bondarchuk's wife) is touching as the doomed Desdemona. The faithful, often academic adaptation (ironically marred by the initial release in the UK and USA in a dubbed English version with the songs remaining in Russian), is filmed in striking colours (except for an unfortunate moment when Othello's face literally turns into a green-eyed monster), with splendid costumes, and has some inventive sequences, such as the swearing of vengeance on the sea shore.

Best Director Cannes 1956.

Otto E Mezzo see 8½

Our Story

Notre Histoire

France 1984 111 mins col
Adel Productions/Sara Films/A2

d **Bertrand Blier**
sc **Bertrand Blier**
ph **Jean Penzer**
m **Martinu, Beethoven, Schubert, Laurent Rossi**
Alain Delon, Nathalie Baye, Michel Galabru, Geneviève Fontanel, Gérard Darmon, Sabine Haudepin

Robert (Delon), befuddled with beer and feeling morose, encounters Donatienne (Baye) on a train. She tells him a 'story' about a girl who picks up a man on a train for a quick, never-to-be-repeated sexual encounter. Her story becomes a real incident between them, but Robert, believing he has found the love of his life, follows her...Blier, adopting methods clearly—and no doubt deliberately—culled from Buñuel, has delivered a mystifying muddle which veers back and forth between the surreal and the farcical, until the ending reveals the mystery. Ludicrous, irritating and seemingly interminable, it offers gold in the dross in the shape of the two leads, and some very inventive and funny sequences, but nothing keeps the tedium at bay(e)!

Outcast, The see Sin, The

Outcry, The see Cry, The

Out In The World see My Apprenticeship

The Outlaw And His Wife

Berg-Ejvind Och Hans Hustru

Sweden 1917 136 mins bw
Svenska Biografteatern

d **Victor Sjöström**
sc **Victor Sjöström, Sam Ask**
ph **J. Julius Jaenzon**
m **Silent**
Victor Sjöström, Edith Erastoff, John Ekman, Nils Aréhn

Berg-Ejvind (Sjöström), wanted for stealing sheep to feed his starving family, falls in love with a rich land-owning widow (Erastoff, Sjöström's third wife) in mid-18th century Iceland. She abandons her estate and they flee to the mountains. After an idyllic summer together, winter brings tragedy. Although filmed in northern Sweden, Sjöström has suggested the grandeur of the Icelandic mountain landscape, the primitive setting for this tempestuous, passionately performed melodrama. Here can be seen the beginnings of the fatalism and animism that run through Swedish films to the present day, and the equating of summer with hope and winter with despair.

Out Of Order

Abwärts

W. Germany 1984 88 mins col
Laura Film/Mutoskop Film/Maran Film/Dieter Geissler Film-production

d **Carl Schenkel**
sc **Carl Schenkel**
m **Jacques Zwart**
Götz George, Renée Soutendijk, Wolfgang Kieling, Hannes Jaenicke, Klaus Wennemann

The lift of an office block jams between two floors. Trapped within are an executive (George) and his seductive former mistress (Soutendijk), a punk youth (Jaenicke), and a nondescript accountant (Kieling) clutching a briefcase filled with cash that he has embezzled. The predictable inter-relationships, as tempers fray in tandem with the lift cables, cannot avoid engendering a certain tension, particularly as Schenkel uses all the effective, if clichéd, devices of cut-aways and close-ups with maximum efficiency, but it is essentially a re-tread of a well-worn formula.

The Outsiders

aka Band of Outsiders

Bande A Part

France 1964 95 mins bw
Anouchka/Orsay

d **Jean-Luc Godard**
sc **Jean-Luc Godard**
ph **Raoul Coutard**
m **Michel Legrand**
Anna Karina, Sami Frey, Claude Brasseur, Luisa Colpeyn

Two young men (Brasseur and Frey) and a woman (Karina) plan to steal a great deal of money hidden in the house where the latter works, but things go awry and murder is the result. Godard transposes a Hollywood thriller format to a grey suburb of Paris where his three protagonists act out their fantasies. Needless to say, the director's concerns are less with the plot than with the isolation of the characters as seen lounging in cafés, for example, or on the Métro. It makes for a touching, refreshing and illuminating film.

The Outsiders

Oka Oorie Katha

India 1977 114 mins col
Chandrodaya Art Films

d **Mrinal Sen**
sc **Mrinal Sen, Mohit Chattopadhyaya**
ph **K.K. Mahajan**
m **Vijay Raghava Rao**
Vasudeva Rao, Narayana Rao, Mamata Shankar, A.R. Krishna, Pradeep Kumar

Venkaiah (Vasudeva Rao), an anarchic old man opposed to work, lives with his son Kistaiah (Narayana Rao) on the outskirts of a village in conditions of grinding poverty. Kistaiah marries Nilamma (Shankar), who brings some order to the house and encourages a more ambitious attitude in her husband, infuriating the old man who later denies her a midwife on the grounds of expense, thus causing her death. Set in a virtually feudal context where the only power resides with the landlords, Sen's film, devoid of the analysis and irony which informs much of his work, does no more than present, without embellishment, a picture of the consequences of poverty. It is unrelievedly and appallingly bleak and depressing, with a compelling central performance from Vasudeva Rao.

The Overcoat
aka The Cloak
Shinel

USSR 1959 78 mins bw
Lenfilm

d **Aleksei Batalov**
sc **L. Solovyov**
ph **Ghenrih Marandzhan**
m **N. Sidelnikov**
Rolan Bykov, Yuri Tolubeyev, A. Yezhkina, Y. Ponsova, T. Teykh

An insignificant and ill-paid clerk (Bykov) spends his Christmas bonus on a necessary—and tailormade—overcoat which becomes his pride and joy. One night he is set upon in the snow and robbed of the garment. Receiving no help from the police, he tramps out into the cold, catches a chill and dies. There's more to it than that, but why spoil the tale? Adapted from the story by Gogol, this poignant little parable is very watchable. It had been made as a Russian silent in 1926, even shorter at 65 minutes, and less persuasive, but visually superb where this is perfectly adequate.

Overgreppet see Question Of Rape, A

The Oyster Princess
Die Austernprinzessin

Germany 1919 70 mins bw
Union Film/UFA

d **Ernst Lubitsch**
sc **Hans Kräly, Ernst Lubitsch**
ph **Théodor Sparkühl**
m **Silent**
Ossi Oswalda, Harry Liedtke, Viktor Janson, Curt Bois, Julius Falkenstein

A 'dollar princess' (Oswalda), daughter of Mr Quaker (Janson) the American 'oyster king', hopes to gain a real title by marrying an impoverished prince (Falkenstein) from an old aristocratic Prussian family. Lubitsch's first major satirical comedy (a genre in which he would become a master) successfully opened UFA's first large theatre. In just over an hour, the 27-year- old director delivers plenty of juicy jibes at the parvenu Yankees and the decadent blue-bloods. Lubitsch-discovery Oswalda, one of Germany's most popular stars of the 1920s, gives a delightful Mary Pickford-like performance.

Oyusama see Miss Oyu

P

Paciorki Jednego Różańca see Beads Of One Rosary, The

Padre Padrone

aka Father Master
Italy 1977 113 mins col
RAI

d **Paolo and Vittorio Taviani**
sc **Paolo and Vittorio Taviani**
ph **Mario Masini**
m **Egisto Macchi**
Fabrizio Forte, Omero Antonutti, Saverio Marconi, Marcella Michelangeli, Gavino Ledda

In Sardinia, a father sends his small peasant son (Forte) to the mountains to look after the sheep all by himself. He is deprived of company and language throughout his teens, until education during military service enables him (now played by Marconi) to break away from his domineering father. This potentially fascinating story was based on the autobiography of Gavino Ledda, who appears at the beginning and end of the film. If the Taviani brothers had approached it in a more sober and detached manner, instead of overstating their case and allowing music to supply much of the emotion, the story might have been a moving one as well. However, there are interesting sidelights into primitive patriarchal Sardinian life.

Best Film Cannes 1977

Padri E Figli see Like Father, Like Son

Padurea Spinzuratilor see Lost Forest, The

Pagador De Promessas, O see Given Word, The

A Page Of Madness

Kurutta Ippeiji
Japan 1926 60 mins bw
Shin Kankaku-ha Eiga Renmei

d **Teinosuke Kinugasa**
sc **Yasunari Kawabata**
ph **Kohei Sugiyama**
m **Minoru Muraoka, Toru Kurashima**
Masao Inoue, Yoshie Nakagawa, Ayako Iijima, Hiroshi Nemoto, Misao Seki, Eiko Minami

An elderly man (Inoue) works voluntarily at odd jobs in the lunatic asylum where his wife (Nakagawa) is confined (having attempted to drown her baby son in a fit of madness many years earlier), and hopes to set her free. Kinugasa rediscovered this film in his storeroom during the early 1970s, and made it available for release with a musical sound-track added. It is a remarkable work of concentrated emotional power, seeking to understand the nature of insanity while offering a straight narrative (the wife's story) in flashback. Relying on its images, the film uses no inter-titles, displaying breathtaking technical virtuosity: the director employs every available camera device, in the style of German Expressionism which was unknown to him at the time. A masterpiece of imagination and control, it has not dated in 60-odd years.

Pai Mao Nu see White-Haired Girl, The

Paisa

(US: Paisan)
Italy 1946 115 mins bw
OFI/Foreign Film Productions/Capitani

d **Roberto Rossellini**
sc **Roberto Rossellini, Federico Fellini, Sergio Amedei**
ph **Otello Martelli**
m **Renzo Rossellini**
William Tubbs, Gar Moore, Maria Michi, Carmelo Sazio, Robert Van Loon, Dots Johnson, Dale Edmonds

Six episodes which take place from the first Allied landings in Sicily to the day of victory, concentrating on the encounters between the Italian people and their liberators. They include the meeting of a black American soldier and an urchin boy who steals his boots, a soldier who tries to communicate with a Sardinian peasant girl, a nurse who risks her life to join her partisan-leader lover and the rounding up and execution of partisans. The second of Rossellini's post-war films, following *Rome, Open City*, uses mainly non-professional actors in often deliberately undramatic anecdotes. There are some weaknesses in the playing and partly improvised dialogue, but the film has a passion and immediacy that is difficult to deny and is a document of historical importance.

Paisan see Paisa

Palava Enkeli see Burning Angel

Palermo Oder Wolfsburg see Palermo Or Wolfsburg

Palermo Or Wolfsburg
Palermo Oder Wolfsburg

W. Germany 1980 175 mins col
Thomas Mauch Film Produktion/Eric Franck

d **Werner Schroeter**
sc **Werner Schroeter, Giuseppe Fava**
ph **Thomas Mauch**
m **Alban Berg, folk music**
Nicola Zarbo, Calogero Arancio, Padre Face, Cavaliere Comparato, Magdalena Montezuma

A naive young Sicilian (Zarbo), who leaves his poverty-stricken family in Palermo to take a job at the Volkswagen factory at Wolfsburg in Germany, is tried for manslaughter after he has stabbed two Germans for impugning his honour. The low-key beginning is an unexpected one from such a flamboyant director, but as the film moves along its three hours (it was edited down from eight hours), it becomes more and more extravagant and operatic, which in some way diminishes its plea for the oppressed. There are some sharply observed episodes and the non-professional Zarbo lends conviction to the central role.

Best Film Berlin 1980

Paltoquet

France 1986 92 mins col
Elefilm/Erato Films

d **Michel Deville**
sc **Michel Deville**
ph **André Diot**
m **Dvořák, Janáček**
Fanny Ardant, Daniel Auteuil, Richard Bohringer, Philippe Léotard, Jeanne Moreau, Michel Piccoli, Claude Piéplu, Jean Yanne

Five card players and a prostitute (Ardant) gather each night in a bar run by The Bar Owner (Moreau) assisted by a barman (Piccoli) who is a paltoquet or simpleton. A man is murdered in a nearby hotel, and The Detective (Yanne) investigates. Shot virtually in one set—what looks like a disused warehouse pretends to be a sleazy bar—the film has the air of a dated *avant-garde* drama of the 1930s. Actually, the six client suspects are six characters in search of an *auteur*—waiting for Godard. The cast is good enough to convince that they believed in this pointless exercise in deconstructing the cheap crime thriller genre.

Pandemonium
Shura

Japan 1970 134 mins bw
Matsumoto Productions/Art Theatre Guild

d **Toshio Matsumoto**
sc **Shuji Ishizawa, Toshio Matsumoto**
ph **Tatsuo Suzuki**
m **Nishimatsu Fumikazu**
Katsuo Nakamura, Yasuko Sanjo, Juro Kira, Masao Imafuku, Tamotsu Tamura

Gengobe (Nakamura), a samurai in love with a geisha (Sanjo), finds out she has been promised to a rival samurai and he must buy her if he wishes to keep her. But when Gengobe discovers that he has been tricked and that she is already married with a child, he carries out a bloody vendetta. Matsumoto, in his second film, has been entirely faithful to the gruesome spirit of the original 18th-century Kabuki play upon which the screenplay is based. Apart from the opening shot of the setting sun in colour, the rest of the film is shot in stark black-and-white as the characters move through the nocturnal plot and counterplot, reminiscent of English Jacobean tragedy. The static compositions, interrupted by some surreal sequences, give the film a formal beauty, while tension is maintained by a tightly constructed script.

Pandora's Box

aka Lulu

Die Büchse Der Pandora

Germany 1929 97 mins bw
Nero Film

d **G.W. Pabst**
sc **G.W. Pabst, Laszlo Wajda**
ph **Günther Krampf**
m **Silent**
Louise Brooks, Fritz Kortner, Franz Lederer, Gustav Diessl, Alice Roberts, Carl Goetz

Lulu (Brooks), a *femme fatale*, wreaks emotional and physical havoc on Dr Schön (Kortner), his son Alva (Lederer) and the Lesbian Countess Geschwitz (Roberts) before meeting her death at the hands of Jack the Ripper (Diess). It was after seeing Louise Brooks in Howard Hawks' *A Girl In Every Port*, that Pabst asked her to play Lulu in his adaptation of two of Frank Wedekind's plays. The black, bobbed hair framing a pale kittenish face, the intense eroticism of each expression and gesture, has made Brooks one of the icons of the cinema and inspired Pabst to his greatest film. But it was many years before the performance and the picture were appreciated. The Germans objected to an American in the lead, and the film was heavily cut around the world. One print omitted Jack the Ripper and showed Lulu joining the Salvation Army.

Pane, Amore, E Fantasia see Bread, Love, And Dreams

Pane, Amore E Gelosia see Bread, Love And Jealousy

Pane E Cioccolata see Bread And Chocolate

Panic

Panique

France 1946 98 mins bw
Filmsonor

d **Julien Duvivier**
sc **Charles Spaak, Julien Duvivier**
ph **Nicolas Hayer**
m **Jacques Ibert**
Michel Simon, Viviane Romance, Paul Bernard, Charles Dorat, Max Dalban

The blame for a woman's murder is shifted on to a respectable man (Simon) by the real culprit (Bernard) and his girlfriend (Romance). Duvivier marked his return to his homeland after his wartime sojourn in Hollywood with a taut thriller based on a Georges Simenon novel. Freed from the sex-code restrictions imposed on him in the USA, he managed to get some 'oomph' into the love scenes. It was also a reminder of what a master of atmosphere Duvivier had been in films like *Pépé Le Moko* (1937).

Panique see Panic

Panny Z Wilka see Young Ladies Of Wilko, The

Paracelsus

Germany 1943 104 mins bw
Bavaria-Filmkunst

d **G. W. Pabst**
sc **Kurt Heuser, G. W. Pabst**
ph **Bruno Stephan**
m **Herbert Windt**
Werner Krauss, Mathias Wieman, Harald Kreutzberg, Martin Urtel, Harry Langewisch

Paracelsus, (Krauss) appointed town physician of medieval Basle, fights traditional medicine, reactionary academics and greedy merchants in an attempt to keep plague from the city. The second of the three films directed by Pabst for the Third Reich was shot at the Barrandov studios outside occupied Prague with a German crew. The script has all the elements which appealed to his Nazi masters—a rebel hero cleansing Germany of ancient practices, anti-intellectualism ('Resolute imagination can accomplish all things,' states Paracelsus) and the replacement of Latin (foreign influences) with the German language. Most of it is a stagey, plodding costume drama, with one or two scenes involving the dancer Harald Kreutzberg to wake one up.

Parade

France/Sweden 1974 85 mins col
Gray Film/Sveriges Radio

d **Jacques Tati**
sc **Jacques Tati**
ph **Jean Badal, Gunnar Fischer**
m **Charles Dumont**
Jacques Tati, Karl Kossmayer, Pia Colombo, Les 'Williams', Les 'Veterans', Les 'Sipolo', Bertilo

Jacques Tati does a number of his famous music-hall mimes of sportsmen, in between various circus acts—a magician, acrobats, clowns—in a circus tent in front of an audience in Sweden. In every way it was sad that this co-production was Tati's last film. He used video techniques to record a series of dismal and repetitive provincial circus acts, occasionally enlivened by his own presence. He also attempted to demonstrate his whimsical philosophy that everyone is a natural clown by showing some comical members of the audience and, rather in the manner of Bergman's *The Magic Flute*, cutting to the reactions of two children, with whom the film finishes as they play endlessly with props in an empty circus tent.

Parade Of The Planets

Parad Planyet

USSR 1984 96 mins col
Mosfilm

d **Vadim Abdrashitov**
sc **Alexander Mindadze**
ph **Vladimir Shevtsik**
m **Vyacheslav Ganin, and extracts from Beethoven and Shostakovich**
Oleg Borisov, Sergei Nikonenko, Sergei Shakurov, Alexei Zharkov, Pyotr Zaichenko, Aleksander Pashutin

Five territorial army comrades, called up on an exercise discover they are now considered too old to be useful, so mark their last meeting by journeying to the village where they would have been detailed to go, and experience a series of strange encounters. Abdrashitov's study of human beings who no longer fit into a world of masculine-orientated values—and those, such as women, who never did—is not without some interest, but it is an unyieldingly cryptic piece of which the dreamlike atmosphere and shadowy images serve only to obscure the director's intentions even further.

Paradise Place see Summer Paradise

Paradistorg see Summer Paradise

Parad Planyet see Parade Of The Planets

Paraguelia

Greece 1980 95 mins col
Greca Film

d **Pavlos Tassios**
sc **Pavlos Tassios**
ph **Sakis Maniatis**
m **Kyriakos Sfetsas**
Antonis Antoniou, Katerina Gogou, Sophia Roubou, Nikitis Tsakiroglou, Antonis Kafetzopoulos

Two brothers and their girlfriends are spending an evening at a *bouzouki* house. One of the boys pays the musicians for a 'paraguelia'—a session of music to which the customer dances solo and during which it is taboo for anyone else to take the floor. When somebody from another party insists on joining in, a fight breaks out, a man is killed and the elder brother (Antoniou) is tried for murder. Tassios, one of the most popular and successful of the current crop of Greek directors, has delivered a drama redolent with passion and violence and enough *bouzouki* to enthral fans and discourage anyone who can't bear it. Characterization is pretty sketchy and there is some ill-judged voice-over poetry used as a narrative link, but it's crisply directed, efficiently acted and the fight scene is terrific.

Parapluies De Cherbourg, Les see Umbrellas Of Cherbourg, The

Pardon Mon Affaire

Un Eléphant Ça Trompe Enormément

France 1976 108 mins col
Les Films De La Guéville/Gaumont International

d **Yves Robert**
sc **Jean-Loup Dabadie, Yves Robert**
ph **René Mathelin**
m **Vladimir Cosma**
Jean Rochefort, Claude Brasseur, Guy Bedos, Victor Lanoux, Danièle Delorme, Annie Duperey, Martine Sarcey

Middle-aged Etienne (Rochefort), although happily married to Marthe (Delorme), decides to pursue Charlotte (Duperey), the girl on an advertising poster. Numerous mix-ups later, he spends a night with her which ends in a farcical public exposure of his dalliance. Evidently drawing on *The Seven Year Itch* for some much-needed inspiration—Duperey's skirt being blown over her head by a hot-air grille is the most obvious pointer—Robert has come up with a rather meandering and unsubtle farce, full of sub-plots involving Etienne's three friends (Brasseur, Bedos and Lanoux). However, the mediocre enterprise is rescued by some superlative comedy performances, notably from Brasseur, who carries off some outrageous set-pieces with expertise, and Rochefort, whose versatile range of facial expressions is a delight. A sequel the following year, *Pardon Mon Affaire, Too*, was in some respects even more witless, but with the same cast again proving effective and Delorme's Marthe pivotal to the action. The original was remade by Gene Wilder in 1984 as *The Woman In Red*.

Les Parents Terribles

(US: The Storm Within)

France 1948 98 mins bw
Sirius

d **Jean Cocteau**
sc **Jean Cocteau**
ph **Michel Kelber**
m **Georges Auric**
Jean Marais, Yvonne De Bray, Gabrielle Dorziat, Marcel André, Josette Day

When the son (Marais) of a middle-class Parisian family announces his love for a young woman (Day), neither he nor his domineering mother (De Bray), who cannot accept his adulthood, knows that the girl is the mistress of his father (André). Making few cuts in his play of the same name, using only two settings, and keeping camera movement to a minimum, Cocteau retained the theatricality of his over-ripe melodrama. But the use of close-ups—witness the mouth of Marais and the eyes of De Bray as he tells her of his love—enabled the director 'to catch my wild beasts unawares with my tele-lens'. Although it enables us to appreciate the superb performances, excepting the 35-year-old Marais as the *maman*'s boy, it would have been happier kept behind a proscenium arch.

Parfum De La Dame En Noir, Le see Perfume Of The Lady In Black, The

---

Paris Au Mois D'Août see Paris In August

Paris Belongs To Us

Paris Nous Appartient

France 1960 140 mins bw
AJYM/Les Films Du Carrosse

d **Jacques Rivette**
sc **Jacques Rivette, Jean Gruault**
ph **Charles Bitsch**
m **Philippe Arthuys**
Betty Schneider, Gianni Esposito, Françoise Prévost, Daniel Crohem, François Maistre, Jean-Claude Brialy

A group of young amateurs come together in the deserted Paris of summer to stage a performance of Shakespeare's *Pericles*, but there are sexual and political tensions; their composer dies and the producer kills himself. Because of lack of funds, Rivette's first feature was made over a period of two years, and strangely reflects its subject in the struggles of creation against all odds. Despite some of its aural and visual inadequacy and slackness, its austere style builds up an atmosphere of doom against a vividly realized Paris. Fellow *nouvelle vague* directors Chabrol, Demy and Godard make appearances.

Paris Does Strange Things see Eléna Et Les Hommes

Paris Frills see Falbalas

Paris In August

Paris Au Mois D'Août

France 1965 98 mins bw
Sirius

d **Pierre Granier-Deferre**
sc **R.M. Arlaud, Pierre Granier-Deferre**
ph **Claude Renoir**
m **Georges Garvarentz, Charles Aznavour**
Charles Aznavour, Susan Hampshire, Daniel Ivernel, Michel De Ré, Alan Scott, Jacques Marin

Department store salesman Henri (Aznavour), alone in Paris while his wife and children are away, meets an English girl (Hampshire) and shows her Paris. He pretends to be an artist, she a famous model, and they enjoy an idyllic affair. Granier-Deferre uses this run-of-the-mill romance as an excuse to explore Paris, so beguilingly photographed by Renoir that it transcends the selection of myths and clichés on offer. The combination of tiny Gallic Aznavour and English rose Hampshire (who married the director) is unusual, but whether it appeals is a matter of taste. A sweet, inconsequential outing.

Paris Nous Appartient see Paris Belongs To Us

Paris Vu Par... see Six In Paris

Par Le Sang Des Autres see By The Blood Of Others

Parsifal

W. Germany 1982 255 mins col
TMS Film(Munich)/Gaumont(Paris)

d **Hans Jürgen Syberberg**
sc **Hans Jürgen Syberberg (after Wagner's text)**
ph **Igor Luther**
m **Richard Wagner (Conductor: Armin Jordan)**
Michael Kutter and Karin Krick (Parsifal I and II, sung by Rainer Goldberg), Edith Clever (Kundry, sung by Yvonne Minton), Armin Jordan (Amfortas, sung by Wolfgang Schöne), Robert Lloyd (Gurnemanz), Aage Haugland (Klingsor)

The tale of the redemption of the wounded Amfortas, Leader of the Knights of the Grail, by Parsifal, 'the innocent fool enlightened by pity'. It was inevitable that Syberberg, that chronicler of the German soul, should tackle Wagner's last opera, the synthesis of the composer's own religious and mystic beliefs. Syberberg's film, while demystifying the work, also presents it as an unassailable masterpiece. The action takes place on and around a gigantic death mask of Wagner and embraces a wide range of startling images, associations and film techniques—long takes, back projections, puppets, and *tableaux vivants.* The most daring device has Parsifal played both by a boy, who represents the 'fool', and a girl as the asexual symbol of purity he becomes after Kundry's kiss. This splendidly sung and acted kitsch celebration, is the most personal of opera films.

Partie De Campagne, Une see Day In The Country, A

Une Partie De Plaisir

aka Love Match
(US: Pleasure Party)

France 1975 100 mins col
Films De La Boétie/Sunchild/Gerico

d **Claude Chabrol**
sc **Paul Gégauff**
ph **Jean Rabier**
m **Beethoven, Brahms, Schubert**
Paul Gégauff, Danielle Gégauff, Clémence Gégauff, Paula Moore, Michel Valette, Pierre Santini

The anatomy of the breakdown of the marriage between an unfaithful husband and a wife he has subjected to his will. When she follows his suggestion that she take a lover, he is furious. Paul Gégauff, screenwriter on over a dozen of Chabrol's films, plays the monstrous husband opposite his real ex-wife and daughter. The director is obviously fascinated and disgusted by his friend's behaviour—Gégauff slaps his wife and forces her to kiss his foot—and the audience might feel the same. Finally, the loathsomeness of the man and the exhibitionism of the whole enterprise outweigh the interest. Gégauff, in fact, was stabbed to death in 1983 by his second wife.

Partner

Italy 1968 105 mins col
Red Film

d **Bernardo Bertolucci**
sc **Bernardo Bertolucci, Gianni Amico**
ph **Ugo Piccone**
m **Ennio Morricone**
Pierre Clémenti, Stefania Sandrelli, Tina Aumont, Sergio Tofano, Giulio Cesare Castello

Jacob (Clémenti), a confused and shy young man, is ejected from the birthday party given for Clara (Sandrelli), whom he loves. He therefore creates Jacob II, his more confident double. Based loosely on Dostoevsky's short novel, *The Double*, it was updated to the Rome of 1968, with the central character played by Clémenti speaking French while all the rest speak Italian. The young man, divided into two, seems to represent Respectability/ Rebellion—Bertolucci/Godard. It is, in fact, incoherent, undigested Godard, interesting as a typical product of 1968, that year of student revolt.

The Party And The Guests

(US: A Report On The Party And The Guests)

O Slavnosti A Hostech

Czechoslovakia 1966 71 mins bw
Ceskoslovensky Films, Barrandov Studio

d **Jan Němec**
sc **Jan Němec, Ester Krumbachová**
ph **Jaromír Šofr**
m **Karel Mares**
Ivan Vyskocil, Jan Klusák, Jiří Němec, Zdenka Skvorecká, Helena Pejsková, Karel Mares, Jana Pracharová

Everybody at a large *al fresco* party seems to be enjoying themselves and they constantly reassure each other that they are. Only one man refuses to be happy and, when he leaves, he is pursued by the other guests with tracker dogs. This bitter political allegory, made by a group of friends, was denounced in the National Assembly and had to wait for the Prague Spring before it could be released. Although many of the references are obscure to non-Czechs, the script (co-written by Němec's then wife, Krumbachová) and the visual conception carry a clear enough message.

Pasazerka see Passenger

Pasqualino Settebellezze see Seven Beauties

Passage Du Rhin, Le see Crossing Of the Rhine, The

Les Passagers

aka Shattered

France 1976 103 mins col
Viaduc Productions/Trianon Productions(Paris)/ PIC(Rome)

d **Serge Leroy**
sc **Christopher Frank, Serge Leroy**
ph **Walter Wottitz, Jacques Assuérus, Patrick Morin**
m **Claude Bolling**
Jean-Louis Trintignant, Mireille Darc, Bernard Fresson, Richard Constantini, Adolfo Celi

While air stewardess Nicole (Darc) sorts out their new Paris apartment, her husband Alex (Trintignant) goes to fetch his 11-year-old stepson Marc (Constantini) from school in Rome. Soon after their journey commences, Marc disconcerts a sceptical Alex by insisting that they are being followed by a van. And, indeed, they are. The driver, Fabio (Fresson), is a disbarred airline pilot and a former lover of Nicole's, now grown seriously disturbed and violent. This is an extremely well-crafted film which, on the surface, is a first cousin to Spielberg's *Duel*, with its overtones of elusive menace on the highway. However, the thriller elements are neatly interwoven into the central 'father-son' relationship and, with the aid of a skilfully used tracking camera, Leroy contrives constantly shifting balances of atmosphere, locale and emotion that hold one's interest right through to the brutal and gripping climax. Trintignant and Constantini make an excellent and appealing pair.

Passenger
Pasazerka

Poland 1963 63 mins bw
WFF Lódź/Kadr

d **Andrzej Munk**
sc **Andrzej Munk, Zofia Posmysz-Piasecka**
ph **Krzysztof Winiewicz**
m **Tadeusz Baird**
Aleksandra Slaska, Anna Ciepielewska, Marek Walczewski, Jan Kreczmer, Irena Malkiewicz

In the 1960s, a coincidental meeting on board a liner between a former female guard (Slaska) at Auschwitz and one of the prisoners (Ciepielewska), who had been in her charge, triggers off a series of bitter memories. Munk, one of Poland's most promising directors, was killed in a car crash, at the age of 40, during the shooting. Three of the completed episodes were put together, plus a montage of stills with music and commentary. The powerful and haunting sequences in Auschwitz, and the play of past and present, guilt and expiation, show every sign that it would have been his best film.

Passe Ton Bac D'Abord
aka Graduate First
aka Pass Your Exam First

France 1978 90 mins col
Livardois Films/Renn Productions/FR3/I.N.A.

d **Maurice Pialat**
sc **Maurice Pialat**
ph **Pierre William Glenn**
m **Patrick Juvet**
Sabine Haudepin, Philippe Marland, Valérie Chassigneux, Annick Alane, Michel Caron

In a provincial city in the mining region of Northern France, a group of disillusioned students with no prospects other than dead-end jobs or unemployment, see little point in doing any work for their *baccalauréat*. Ignoring the futile dissertations of their teachers, they drift aimlessly round the local bistro or down to the coast; some engage in hollow sexual encounters; others go to Paris. Pialat's minutely detailed observation of dispossessed youth is made with an admirable combination of objectivity and compassion. The director's youthful cast is remarkable for a naturalness so complete as to become almost tedious, but which gives this rather dispiriting film the ring of truth. Shooting was interrupted and later resumed with a different crew and this, no doubt, accounts for certain technical discrepancies.

Pas Si Méchant Que Ça see This Wonderful Crook

Passion see Madame Dubarry

Passion
Manji

Japan 1964 90 mins col
Daiei

d **Yasuzo Masumura**
sc **Kaneto Shindo**
ph **Setsuo Kobayashi**
m **Tadashi Yamauchi**
Ayako Wakao, Kyoko Kishida, Yusuke Kawazu, Eiji Funakoshi

Sonoko (Kishida) falls in love with Mitsuko (Wakao), and the two girls have an affair. Sonoko's husband (Funakoshi) is tolerant of the situation, but she is herself thrown by the discovery that Mitsuko has a male lover. From then on, complications proliferate among the foursome, ending in a bizarre and ambiguous death pact. A film that often borders on the ludicrous and sometimes hints at sexploitation, it is also redolent of absurdist black comedy and never boring. Difficult as it is to be sure of the director's intentions, his control over the curious goings-on is undeniably skilled.

Passion

aka Godard's Passion

France 1982 88 mins col

Sara Films/Sonimage/Films A2/Film et Video Productions/SSR

d **Jean-Luc Godard**
sc **Jean-Luc Godard**
ph **Raoul Coutard**
m **Mozart, Dvořák, Beethoven, Fauré**

Jerzy Radziwilowicz, Hanna Schygulla, Michel Piccoli, Isabelle Huppert, László Szabó

A Polish film director (Radziwilowicz), trying to make a movie called *Passion*, has an affair with the owner (Schygulla) of the French motel where he and the crew are staying. Her husband (Piccoli) has to cope with a labour dispute at his factory led by a woman worker (Huppert). Meanwhile, money for the film is beginning to run out. The first and best of a number of films in the 1980s in which Godard directly confronted the nature of his own art—*First Name Carmen*, the made-for-TV *Rise And Fall Of A Little Film Company* (1986), and *King Lear* (1987) are principally about the making of a film. But the passion of the title does not apply only to film-making, it also has a sexual and religious (or blasphemous) sense. Through *tableaux vivants* based on the Old Masters, great music contrasted with traffic noise, and verbal dialectic, Godard continues to astonish, and annoy, those who want films to tell a story.

A Passion

(US: The Passion Of Anna)

En Passion

Sweden 1969 100 mins col

Svensk Filmindustri

d **Ingmar Bergman**
sc **Ingmar Bergman**
ph **Sven Nykvist**
m **Allan Gray, Bach**

Max Von Sydow, Liv Ullmann, Erland Josephson, Bibi Andersson, Erik Hell, Hjördis Petterson

A man with a past (Von Sydow) has found peace living in remote seclusion, but is disturbed one day by a crippled woman (Ullmann) asking to use the telephone. In due course this chance encounter results in his becoming embroiled with the woman and her friends, a married couple (Josephson and Andersson) with problems. A homicidal maniac is at large, exacerbating the tensions of the foursome. Bergman's second excursion into colour, filmed, on the bleak island of Fårö, is widely considered one of his best works. It is a penetrating examination of personal pain, bearing all the hallmarks of the director's unique style of expression— and those of his cast and cameraman—and is never less than interesting.

Passion, En see Passion, A

Passion De Jeanne D'Arc, La see Passion Of Joan Of Arc, The

Passione D'Amore

Italy 1981 119 mins col

Massfilm(Rome)/Marceau/Cocinor(Paris)

d **Ettore Scola**
sc **Ruggero Maccari, Ettore Scola**
ph **Claudio Ragona**
m **Armando Trovaioli**

Bernard Giraudeau, Valeria D'Obici, Laura Antonelli, Jean-Louis Trintignant, Massimo Girotti, Bernard Blier

Army captain Giorgio (Giraudeau) is parted from his mistress Clara (Antonelli) when he is transferred to a frontier post. There, he is intrigued by the empty place set at dinner each evening for the indisposed Fosca (D'Obici), ward and cousin to the Colonel (Girotti). When Fosca does appear, Giorgio is shocked by her appalling ugliness, apparently aggravated by a neurotic illness. To Giorgio's horror, Fosca conceives a hopeless passion for him and, when he takes leave to visit Clara, she falls dangerously ill, thus drawing him into a fatal web of pity and obligation... Set in 1862 and making a reasonable attempt at period opulence *à la* Visconti, Scola's simplistic study in contrasts fails to make full use of the rich possibilities of the story. Thus, with its lack of characterization and a plethora of high emotional dramatics, it comes across as no more than a mildly entertaining and minor psycho-sexual excursion into *Grand Guignol*.

Passion For Life

aka I Have A New Master

L'École Buissonière

France 1949 94 mins bw

Cooperative Générale Du Cinématographie Français

d **Jean-Paul Le Chanois**

sc **Elise Freinet, Jean-Paul Le Chanois**

ph **André Dumaître, Marc Fossard, Maurice Pecqueux**

m **Joseph Kosma**

Bernard Blier, Juliette Faber, Edouard Delmont, Pierre Coste, Jean-Louis Allibert, Danny Caron

Pascal Laurent (Blier) is a dedicated schoolteacher of rare enthusiasm who brings new ideas and a modern approach into the classroom. His methods meet with opposition from the parents as well as from the old-guard staff, but the pupils are responsive. One of the great stalwarts of the French cinema, Bernard Blier can usually be relied upon to raise the level of a film. Not that there's much to raise here. It's a simple, old-fashioned and slightly sentimental story, competently executed and sometimes touching.

Passion Of Anna, The see Passion, A

The Passion Of Joan Of Arc

La Passion De Jeanne D'Arc

France 1928 114 min bw

Société Générale Des Films

d **Carl Dreyer**

sc **Carl Dreyer, Joseph Delteil**

ph **Rudolph Maté**

m **Silent**

Renée Falconetti, Eugène Silvain, Maurice Schutz, Michel Simon, Antonin Artaud

The 29 examinations of Joan of Arc (Falconetti) on her last day before she was burned at the stake. Based on transcripts of the 18-month long trial, the screenplay telescopes the events into one day, thus providing the film with more formal intensity. Dreyer's constant and unforgettable use of long-held close-ups has led some critics to describe it as a film consisting entirely of close-ups. The faces of Joan's judges, wearing no make-up, are cruelly exposed to Maté's camera, but it is the agonized face of Falconetti, in her only film, that burns itself on the mind. It was said that Dreyer bullied her unmercifully to draw out the suffering he required. Since the nature of the material is intrinsically verbal, the images are frequently interrupted by long titles. Dreyer was given a free hand by his French producers. He took 18 months—as long as Joan's 15th-century trial—to shoot in costly sets. Like most of the director's work, his first masterpiece was a critical but not a commercial success.

Pass Your Exam First see Passe Ton Bac D'Abord

Pather Panchali

India 1955 122 mins bw

Government of West Bengal

d **Satyajit Ray**

sc **Satyajit Ray**

ph **Subrata Mitra**

m **Ravi Shankar**

Subir Bannerjee, Kanu Bannerjee, Karuna Bannerjee, Uma Das Gupta, Chunibala

Apu (Subir Bannerjee), a young boy lives in a small Bengal village with his parents, his sister and aged aunt (Chunibala) on the borderline of poverty. Out of an industry almost entirely dominated by formula, escapist musical films in Hindi, Ray suddenly appeared on the international scene with this masterpiece about Apu's childhood in the minority language of Bengali, and entirely altered notions of Indian cinema. He had great difficulty in raising funds for his debut film, the first of a trilogy based on a popular book by Bhibuti Bashan Bannerjee. He was about to abandon shooting after 18 months when he was rescued by the West Bengal government. The title means 'little song of the road', and the motif throughout is one of travel, of something beyond the confines of the tiny rural community. There are the travelling players viewed with wonder and delight by the child, and the lyrical sequence when Apu and his sister run through the long grass towards the railway line to see a train taking people to the big cities. The boy was to take this journey himself in the following film, *Aparajito*.

Pathetic Fallacy see Mechanical Man

The Patriot
Die Patriotin

W. Germany 1979 120 mins bw/col
Kairos Film

d **Alexander Kluge**
sc **Alexander Kluge**
ph **Thomas Mauch, Jörg Schmidt-Reitwein, Werner Lüring, Günther Hörmann**
m **Beethoven, Mahler, Haydn, Sibelius and others**
Hannelore Hoger, Dieter Mainka, Alfred Edel, Alexander Von Eschwege, Beate Holle

Gabi Teichert (Hoger), a history teacher in Frankfurt, investigates new ways of presenting Germany's past to a new generation. The teacher's investigation into the historical process becomes part of Kluge's own dialectical method of film- making. The film is a kaleidoscopic commentary on Germany's relationship to its past, starting with the statement that it is wrong to assume 'the dead are somehow dead'. In the process, use is made of newsreel material, interviews, speeded up takes of life in Frankfurt, fairy tales illustrated by magic lantern scenes and inserts into real events such as the SPD party conference. Kluge's own voice is heard on the soundtrack in the role of a knee *(sic)* that belonged to a corporal killed at Stalingrad. Much of it is as illuminating as it is puzzling, enriching as it is irritating.

Patriotin, Die see Patriot, The

Patsy, The see Addition, L'

Pauline À La Plage see Pauline At The Beach

Pauline At The Beach
Pauline À La Plage

France 1983 95 mins col
Les Films Du Losange/Les Films Ariane

d **Eric Rohmer**
sc **Eric Rohmer**
ph **Nestor Almendros**
m **Jean-Louis Valero**
Arielle Dombasle, Amanda Langlet, Pascal Greggory, Féodor Atkine, Simon De La Brosse, Rosette

Pauline (Langlet) and her older, recently divorced cousin Marion (Dombasle) arrive to spend two weeks at the family's holiday cottage on the Normandy coast. Both of them get entangled with Pierre (Greggory), Marion's former lover, Henri (Atkine), a divorced anthropologist, and Sylvain (De La Brosse), a teenage boy. In the third of his 'Comedies and Proverbs', Rohmer shows his unique and witty way of placing an 18th-century plot of mistaken identity, sentimental subterfuge and an interplay of couples in a modern setting. As Rohmer is a summer director (few of his films take place in another season), he uses the beach setting and the warm evenings sensuously, and continues his obsession with '*les jeunes filles en fleur*'. He also manages to laugh with and at his rather empty and vain characters, all impeccably and realistically played.

Best Director Berlin 1983

Paura, La see Fear

The Peach Thief
Kradezat Na Praskovi

Bulgaria 1964 84 mins bw
Bulgaria State Films

d **Vulo Radev**
sc **Vulo Radev**
ph **Todor Stoyanov**
m **Simeon Pironkov**
Nevena Kokanova, Rade Markovich, Mikhail Mikhailov, Vassil Vachev

Towards the end of World War I in Turnovo, the medieval capital of Bulgaria, attractive Lisa (Kokanova) spends lonely days in her garden with its beautiful peach orchard while her husband, the colonel, supervises the local garrisons and POW camp. Lisa's life changes when Ivo (Markovich), a Serbian officer prisoner, breaks into her garden to steal peaches, an incident that leads to the couple's falling in love. A sensitively realized love story and beguilingly atmospheric, but the later stages of the film lose focus when the action overbalances into a *mélange* of political and military incident that weakens the impact of the ending. Acting and photography achieve a level of respectable competence, while the period reconstruction is notably fine.

The Pearls Of The Crown
Les Perles De La Couronne

France 1937 120 mins bw
Tobis

d **Sacha Guitry, Christian-Jaque**
sc **Sacha Guitry**
ph **Jules Kruger, Marc Fossard**
m **Jean Françaix**
Sacha Guitry, Renée Saint-Cyr, Lyn Harding, Percy Marmont, Arletty, Raimu, Claude Dauphin, Jean-Louis Barrault, Jacqueline Delubac, Marguerite Moreno

The history of seven pearls given to a range of famous personages over the ages, and a number of contemporary people of different nationalities in search of them. Guitry's trilingual movie—French, English and Italian—was meant as a celebration of the coronation of Edward VIII. It happens to be more of a celebration of Guitry's style and wit. (He plays four parts, including François I and Napoleon III.) There is also an enjoyable string of cameos, among them Barrault as Bonaparte, Harding as Henry VIII and Guitry's wife, Delubac, as Mary, Queen of Scots and the Empress Josephine. However, most of the pearls are to be found in the dialogue rather than in the plot.

Peasants
Krestyaniye

USSR 1935 120 mins bw
Lenfilm

d **Friedrich Ermler**
sc **Friedrich Ermler, Mikhail Bolshintsov, V. Portnov**
ph **Alexander Gintzburg**
m **Venedikt Pushkov**
A. Petrov, Ekaterina Korchagina-Alexandrovskaya, Nikolai Bogolyubov, Yelena Yunger

A dispossessed kulak (Petrov) tries to sabotage a collective by sowing suspicion among the peasants. After beating his pregnant wife (Yunger) to death when she declares she will dedicate her future child to the Revolution, his schemes are finally revealed. A fine, and neglected, example of the Soviet cinema of the mid-1930s, full of earthy humour and passion in its realistic depiction of peasant life. Memorable sequences are an eating contest and the murder scene. The narrative drive and human touches transcend its simple propagandist ending.

Peau D'Âne see Magic Donkey, The

Peau Douce, La see Silken Skin

The Pedestrian
Der Fussgänger

W. Germany 1974 97 mins col
ALFA/MFG

d **Maximilian Schell**
sc **Maximilian Schell**
ph **Wolfgang Treu, Klaus König**
m **Manos Hadjidakis**
Gustav Rudolf Sellner, Ruth Hausmeister, Maximilian Schell, Alexander May, Manuel Sellner, Gila Von Weitershausen

The past begins to catch up with a wealthy and respectable West German industrialist (Gustav Rudolf Sellner), when a newspaper editor (May) reveals that, as a Nazi officer, he participated in the burning of an occupied building in Greece in 1943. The issues are explored in a TV debate in which the industrialist and what he represents are condemned. One of the many guilt-ridden German films over the last few decades says very little new, but says it reasonably well. An effective use is made of flashbacks to link the horror of the past with the present—references are made to Vietnam—and the Weimar Republic with the Germany of today. More predictable than pedestrian, it does have a surprising sequence of a tea party at which Peggy Ashcroft, Lil Dagover, Elisabeth Bergner and Françoise Rosay make cameo appearances.

Peek-A-Boo see Femmes De Paris

Pelle Erobreren see Pelle The Conqueror

Pelle The Conqueror
Pelle Erobreren

Denmark 1987 160 mins col
Per Holst Filmproduktion Aps/Danish Film Institute/Svensk Filmindustri

d **Bille August**
sc **Bille August**
ph **Jörgen Persson**
m **Stefan Nilsson**

Max Von Sydow, Pelle Hvenegaard, Erik Paaske, Björn Granath, Axel Strøbye, Astrid Villaume

At the turn-of-the century, Lasse (Max Von Sydow), a widowed farmer, and his nine-year-old son Pelle (Hvenegaard), leave poverty-stricken Sweden for what they hope will be a better life on the Danish Baltic Island of Bornholm. But the father finds himself little more than a slave as a cowherd, while his son suffers at the rural school. Pelle decides to leave and conquer the world. Director August, refusing American money and the offer to make the film in English, settled for making only the first part (in Danish) of Nobel-Prizewinner Martin Andersen Nexoe's best-selling four-volume novel. The result is a stylistically old-fashioned, beautiful-to-look-at, unsentimental but moving epic of exploitation, with a cast of characters that includes the staples of period soap—the farm owner's alcoholic wife, a cruel foreman and a seduced and abandoned servant girl. The performances from Von Sydow and Hvenegaard are outstanding.

Best Film Cannes 1988

Pension Mimosas

France 1935 110 mins bw
Tobis

d **Jacques Feyder**
sc **Charles Spaak, Jacques Feyder**
ph **Roger Hubert**
m **Louis Beydts**

Françoise Rosay, Paul Bernard, Alermé, Lise Delamare

Louise (Rosay), the proprietor of the Pension Mimosas on the French Riviera, which caters for *habitués* of the Nice casinos, carries out a desperate ploy to save her shiftless godson (Bernard) from gambling and women. Like *Le Grand Jeu*, the year before, which concentrated on the inhabitants of a café, this comedy-drama centres on a small community, the hotel of the title. In the midst of the flow of well-defined characters stands Rosay's rich portrait of a woman whose passion for her 'son' is more than maternal. Lazare Meerson's vivid sets add to Feyder's splendid sense of place.

People Of France, The see Vie Est À Nous, La

People On Sunday
Menschen Am Sonntag

Germany 1929 72 mins bw
Studiofilm

d **Robert Siodmak, Edgar Ulmer**
sc **Billy Wilder, Curt Siodmak**
ph **Eugen Schüfftan**
m **Silent**

Brigitte Borchert, Christl Ehlers, Annie Schreyer, Wolfgang Von Waltershausen, Erwin Splettstösser

Twenty-four hours in the lives of a group of Berliners on a day's outing, including a taxi driver, a salesman, a shopgirl and a model. This fresh, humorous and romantic semi-documentary (the people involved re-enact their real-life roles), shot in a freewheeling style on location, launched the careers of a number of film-makers who would all make it big in Hollywood. These are the first credits for the Siodmak brothers, Ulmer and Wilder. In addition, Schüfftan's photographic assistant was Fred Zinnemann.

Pépé Le Moko

France 1936 90 mins bw
Paris Film

d **Julien Duvivier**
sc **Henri Jeanson, Roger D'Ashelbe, Julien Duvivier**
ph **Jules Kruger**
m **Vincent Scotto**

Jean Gabin, Mireille Balin, Gabriel Gabrio, Lucas Gridoux, Line Noro, Gilbert-Gil, Saturnin Fabre

Pépé Le Moko, high-powered jewel thief and bank robber forced to flee from his beloved Paris, lives in the Algerian Casbah as his only means of avoiding arrest. When he falls in love with a beautiful visiting Parisienne, he leaves the Casbah to seek her, and is caught. The quintessential loner at his most attractively roguish, Gabin created one of the cinema's best loved anti-heroes in a film teeming with life, romance, suspense and humour. Under Duvivier's direction, the film is immaculately acted, and beautifully lit and photographed. It remains a classic of the genre, which Hollywood was swift to plunder, giving us *Algiers* with Charles Boyer and Hedy Lamarr in 1938 (rather good), and a semi-musical, *Casbah*, in 1948 with Tony Martin and Yvonne De Carlo (rather poor).

Peppermint Frappé

Spain 1968 94 mins col
Elias Querejeta Productions

d **Carlos Saura**
sc **Carlos Saura, Angelino Fons, Rafael Azcona**
ph **Luis Cuadrado**
m **Luis De Pablo**
José Luis Lopez Vasquez, Geraldine Chaplin, Alfredo Mayo

Julian (Lopez Vasquez), a doctor, becomes obsessively infatuated with his brother's lively and attractive wife, Elena. Since she is unattainable, he sets out to transform Ana, his shy, plain nurse, into a replica of Elena, and seduces her with tragic consequences. The director dedicates his film to Buñuel, whose influence is evident in this treatment of a disturbed mind as Julian falls prey to illusions, dreams and memories, focused on his repressed religious upbringing. Geraldine Chaplin impresses in the dual roles of Elena and Ana in this controlled suspense story, illuminated by Saura's insight and imagination.

Peppermint Freedom

Peppermint Frieden

W. Germany 1982 112 mins bw/part col
Nourfilm Produktion

d **Marianne S.W. Rosenbaum**
sc **Marianne S.W. Rosenbaum**
ph **Alfred Tichawsky**
m **Konstantin Wecker**
Peter Fonda, Saskia Tyroller, Gesine Strempel, Hans Peter Korff, Cleo Kretschmer

After the war Marianne (Tyroller) and her family go to live in a small village in Germany's American zone. There, the little girl and her friends try to make sense of the war and of the peace through imaginary games and the hero-worship of an American soldier (Fonda) whom they call 'Mr Freedom'. In her play- acting, and in a series of vivid dreams, Marianne tries to understand the contradictions, concealments and repressive teachings of the adult world. Working from a pacifist and feminist perspective, and drawing inspiration from her own childhood memories, the director defines her imaginative anti-war film as being about 'the birth of guilt'. A serious piece that is dense in content and surreal in style, it also encompasses a measure of humour.

Peppermint Frieden see Peppermint Freedom

Peppermint Soda

Diabolo Menthe

France 1977 101 mins col
Les Films De L'Alma/Alexandre Films

d **Diane Kurys**
sc **Diane Kurys**
ph **Philippe Rousselot**
m **Yves Simon**
Eléonore Klarwein, Odile Michel, Anouk Ferjac, Michel Puterflam, Yves Renier

Thirteen-year-old Anne (Klarwein), withdrawn and a non-achiever, and her sister Frédérique (Michel), extrovert and into her first adolescent love affairs, are the daughters of a divorced Jewish couple. They live with their mother, attend a joyless and authoritarian school, and spend holiday time with their father with whom they are ill at ease. Kurys' debut feature is a gentle, observant and nostalgic piece, drawn from experiences of her own adolescence, and with the action occupying a year from the time of Kennedy's assassination. If the director betrays inexperience in her somewhat clumsy handling of the social and political climate of the times, she has an admirable command of her excellent cast—notably Klarwein—and is sensitive to the school milieu.

Perceval

Perceval Le Gallois

France 1978 140 mins col
Les Films Du Losange/
FR3/A.R.D./Gaumont/RAI(Italy)

d **Eric Rohmer**
sc **Eric Rohmer**
ph **Nestor Almendros**
m **Guy Robert**
Fabrice Luchini, André Dussollier, Arielle Dombasle, Marc Eyraud, Marie-Christine Barrault

The young Welsh knight Perceval (Luchini) comes in his wanderings to a mysterious castle in which he sees the Holy Grail. In the morning, the castle is deserted and he rides away, only realizing too late what he had seen. He cannot find the place again and continues his quest for the Grail. Following his other excursion into the past in *The Marquise Of O*, Rohmer went even further back, almost to the beginning of French literature, for the inspiration of what is also a decidedly moral tale. Based on the unfinished 12th-century poem by Chrétien De Troyes, the film retains the verse form in a translation of the original Old French. Shot entirely on stylized painted sets, it gives the impression of being an animated medieval miniature. However, despite many incidental aural and visual pleasures, it takes a bit of sitting through at over two hours.

Perceval Le Gallois see Perceval

The Perfume Of The Lady In Black

Le Parfum De La Dame En Noir

France 1931 109 mins bw
Film Osso

d **Marcel L'Herbier**
sc **Marcel L'Herbier**
ph **Georges Périnal**
Huguette Duflos, Roland Toutain, Kissa Kouprine, Belières

After solving *The Mystery Of The Yellow Room* for the professor's daughter (Duflos), the intrepid journalist (Toutain) comes once more to her rescue when she is haunted by the presence of her first husband whom she believes is dead. Even better than the previous film based on Gaston Leroux's novel, this sequel shows L'Herbier at his delirious best, revealing a marvellous mosaic of film techniques to serve the purposes of this labyrinthine thriller—mirror images, *trompe l'oeil* sets, fragmented cutting and inventive sound. Sadly, L'Herbier never reached this height again and was forced to 'accept forms of cinema which were the very ones I'd always avoided'.

Péril En La Demeure see Death In A French Garden

Per Le Antiche Scale see Down The Ancient Stairs

Perles De La Couronne, Les see Pearls Of The Crown, The

Persona

Sweden 1966 81 mins bw
Svensk Filmindustri

d **Ingmar Bergman**
sc **Ingmar Bergman**
ph **Sven Nykvist**
m **Lars Johan Werle**
Liv Ullmann, Bibi Andersson, Gunnar Björnstrand, Margaretha Krook, Jörgen Lindström

Elisabeth Vogler (Ullmann), a famous actress, is stricken with psychosomatic loss of speech and is placed in the care of Nurse Alma (Andersson) at a remote seaside cottage. The woman who has renounced language and the other, who talks incessantly, begin to understand one another and exchange identities. With *Persona*, the female face in close-up became Bergman's main field of vision. In this virtual two-hander, everything is written on the features of the superb female leads, including the spiritual anguish from which most Bergman characters suffer. The poetic and tragic face-to-face encounter is only cluttered by an extraneous prologue of brutal images, a strange young boy, and an ending of film burning in a projector.

Personal Column see Snares

Persons Unknown

(US: Big Deal On Madonna Street aka The Usual Unidentified Thieves)

I Soliti Ignoti

Italy 1958 105 mins bw
Lux/Vides/Cinecitta

d **Mario Monicelli**
sc **Age, Scarpelli, Suso Cecchi D'Amico, Mario Monicelli**
ph **Gianni Di Venanzo**
m **Piero Umiliani**
Vittorio Gassman, Renato Salvatori, Marcello Mastroianni, Totò, Memmo Carotenuto, Claudia Cardinale, Rosanna Rory

A group of incompetent amateur crooks plan an elaborate robbery of a pawn shop through an empty apartment next door, but end up merely stealing pasta and peas. This delightful comedy of errors, spoofing *Rififi*, is no less funny for being firmly rooted in social conditions of deprivation. The impeccable cast, the comic silent-film intertitles and the jaunty jazz score added to its popularity. It was remade by Louis Malle as *Crackers* in 1984 and given a San Francisco setting.

Pervy Uchitel see First Teacher, The

Peter And Pavla

(US: Black Peter)

Cerny Petr

Czechoslovakia 1964 85 mins bw
Czechoslovak State

d **Milŏs Forman**
sc **Milŏs Forman, Ivan Passer, Jaroslav Papoušek**
ph **Miroslav Ondříček**
m **Jiří Šlitr**
Ladislav Jakim, Pavla Martínková, Jan Ostrčil, Božena Matušková, Vladimír Pucholt

Teenage Peter (Jakim), finds his first job as a trainee store detective not to his liking, has problems of communication with his conservative father (Ostrčil) and makes little headway with carefree Pavla (Martínková) whom he takes dancing. After two shorts in which he gave documentary material fictional form—they were about talent and brass band contests—Forman, in his first feature, gave his fictional material documentary form. Using non-professional actors, improvised dialogue and shooting in the streets, the film brought a new vitality into the Czech cinema. This sharply observed, satiric, affectionate and humorous movie, with a smattering of a plot, was the launch of a career that led Forman to bigger things and Hollywood.

Petite Marchande D'Allumettes, La see Little Matchgirl, The

Petit Soldat, Le see Little Soldier, The

Petit Théâtre De Jean Renoir, Le see Little Theatre Of Jean Renoir, The

---

Petomane, Il see Windbreaker, The

The Phantom Baron

Le Baron Fantôme

France 1943 100 mins bw
Consortium De Productions De Films

d **Serge De Poligny**
sc **Serge De Poligny**
ph **Roger Hubert**
m **Louis Beydts**
Jany Holt, Odette Joyeux, Alain Cuny, Gabrielle Dorziat, Claude Sainval, André Lefauer, Jean Cocteau

In 1826 a Countess (Dorziat), her daughter, Elfy (Joyeux), and the latter's friend (Holt) arrive at the castle of the Countess's uncle, the Baron Carol (Cocteau), to learn that, during one of his sleepwalking fits, he has spirited himself and his possessions away. The trio moves into the manor next door where the girls pass their childhood. Ten years later, romantic love and its attendant problems enter their lives and the discovery of the crumbling Baron in a crypt brings revelations. On the face of it, this is an escapist period romance with an immensely complicated plot, tailor-made for wartime audiences. However, the hand of Cocteau, who wrote the effervescent dialogue, is everywhere evident in the fairytale elements that abound. A magical flavour, prefiguring *Beauty And The Beast*, clings to much of it, but credit must go, too, to Poligny and Hubert for the atmosphere and striking visuals, by turns bleak, mysterious, frightening, pretty and poetic. The fantasy is realistically acted by a highly professional cast.

The Phantom Carriage

aka Thy Soul Shall Bear Witness

aka The Stroke of Midnight

Körkalen

Sweden 1921 70 mins bw
Svenska Bio

d **Victor Sjöström**
sc **Victor Sjöström**
ph **J. Julius Jaenzon**
m **Silent**

Victor Sjöström, Hilda Borgström, Tore Svennberg Astrid Holm

The drunkard David Holm (Sjöström) has an accident on New Year's Eve, and relives the upright life he led before drink ruined him. He is finally reformed after seeing the carriage of death. Sjöström tells this simple moralistic folk tale with a brilliant array of flashbacks and eerie special effects. Shot mainly outdoors, with a fine lead performance by the director himself, it is widely considered to be his greatest Swedish film. It was mainly due to its success (and the decline of the Swedish cinema industry) that he found himself working in Hollywood as Victor Seastrom a few years later. The film was remade in France in 1939 and in Sweden in 1958.

Phantom Love see Empire Of Passion

The Phantom Of Liberty

Le Fantôme De La Liberté

France 1974 104 mins col
Greenwich/20th Century-Fox

d **Luis Buñuel**
sc **Luis Buñuel, Jean-Claude Carrière**
ph **Edmond Richard**

Monica Vitti, Michel Piccoli, Jean-Claude Brialy, Jean Rochefort, Adolfo Celi, Bernard Verley

A series of casually linked episodes moving from Toledo in 1808 and Goya's painting of *The Executions Of 3 May* to contemporary Paris, where various people try to grasp or shun, in Karl Marx's phrase, 'the phantom of liberty'. Buñuel's penultimate film is as mordantly comic, fluent and subversive as one would expect, but the loose, episodic structure and some easy jokes and targets betray a certain laziness. The best remembered sequence has elegant guests seated on individual lavatories around a table from which they excuse themselves to go and have a meal in a little room behind a locked door. The film ends with a close-up of the eye of an ostrich, the most unlikely bird to represent Buñuel's view of the world.

Pharaoh

Faraon

Poland 1965 183 mins col
Film Polski, Kadr Unit

d **Jerzy Kawalerowicz**
sc **Tadeusz Konwicki, Jerzy Kawalerowicz**
ph **Jerzy Wójcik**
m **Adam Walacinski**

George Zelnik, Barbara Bryl, Krystyna Mikolajewska, Piotr Pawlowski, Andrzej Girtler, Leszek Herdegen

Young Prince Rameses (Zelnik) incurs the disfavour of the powerful high priest Herihor (Pawlowski) when he takes a Jewish girl (Mikolajewska) as his mistress. Further conflict with the hierarchy results from his liberal and aggressive efforts to solve Egypt's severe economic and military problems. When his father the Pharaoh dies, he succeeds him and, as Rameses III, his battle with Herihor escalates, leading to duplicity and violence. An historical epic, complete with battle scenes, but more restrained and realistic than, say, its Hollywood counterparts, this visually striking film, marked by a fine sense of historical veracity, is also a fascinating dissection of the nature of power. Regrettably, it is sometimes shown in a severely cut version which distorts the scale and leaves gaps in the narrative. In any version, Zelnik is not up to his task.

Piaf see Sparrow Of Pigalle, The

Piatka Z Ulicy Barskiej see Five Boys From Barska Street

The Picasso Mystery

aka The Mystery Of Picasso

Le Mystère Picasso

France 1956 78 mins col
Filmsonor

d **Henri-Georges Clouzot**
sc **Henri-Georges Clouzot, Pablo Picasso**
ph **Claude Renoir**
m **Georges Auric**
Henri-Georges Clouzot, Pablo Picasso

Pablo Picasso, the 75-year-old modern master, talks to the film director Clouzot about his work and inspiration and creates paintings in front of the camera. An intriguing documentary and a valuable record of arguably the greatest artist of the 20th century at work, brilliantly captured by Claude Renoir, the grandson of August Renoir. Special transparent 'canvases' were prepared so that Renoir could film the paintings from behind. It is also an odd meeting between the passionate Spaniard, executing his paintings with furious rapidity, and the cool, punctilious French film-maker.

Piccolo Mondo Di Don Camillo, Il see Little World Of Don Camillo, The

Pickpocket

France 1959 80 mins bw
Lux Films

d **Robert Bresson**
sc **Robert Bresson**
ph **L.H. Burel**
m **Lully**
Martin La Salle, Marika Green, Kassagi, Pierre Leymarie, Jean Pelegri, Pierre Etaix, Dolly Scal

A lonely young man (La Salle) embarks on a career as a pickpocket. Arrested, he reflects on the morality of a life of crime but, although temporarily deterred, returns to it, taking lessons from a master (Kassagi). 'With theft I entered by the back door into the kingdom of morality,' stated Bresson on this Jansenist tale (inspired by *Crime And Punishment*) of a sinner who finds redemption through the love of a woman (Green). The protagonist is deliberately kept blank and representational as he moves through the dark, untextured photography which concentrates on his hands, the tools of his trade. The first person narrative technique is used, as in *Diary Of A Country Priest* and *A Man Escaped*, and the visual economy is matched by the spare dialogue. A typical Bressonian exercise, it may be too stoical for those who prefer something less thin-blooded, but its final sequence was copied by Paul Schrader, an admirer of Bresson, in his own *American Gigolo*.

Picnic On The Grass see Lunch On The Grass

Piège Pour Cendrillon see Trap For Cinderella, A

Pièges see Snares

Pierrot-Le-Fou

France 1965 110 mins col
Rome-Paris Films/Dino De Laurentiis/Georges De Beauregard

d **Jean-Luc Godard**
sc **Jean-Luc Godard**
ph **Raoul Coutard**
m **Antoine Duhamel**
Anna Karina, Jean-Pierre Belmondo, Dirk Sanders, Raymond Devos, Graziella Galvani, Sam Fuller

Ferdinand (Belmondo), dissatisfied with his Parisian life and his wife, sets off on a picaresque journey across France to the South with Marianne (Karina), getting involved with her criminal activities along the way. Godard's stunning study of personal and global violence (there are references to Angola, Vietnam etc) uses colour in a dramatic and symbolic manner. Asked why there was so much blood in the film, Godard replied, 'It is not blood but red'. But most of all it is a tragedy about the transience of love. It is not difficult to see the Belmondo-Karina love-hate relationship as a reflection of the

Godard-Karina marriage, then reaching its end. As American director Sam Fuller reflects in the picture, 'The film is like a battleground, love, hate, action, violence, death...in one word, Emotion'.

A Pig Across Paris

(US: Four Bags Full)

La Traversée De Paris

France 1956 90 mins bw
Franco London/Continentale

d **Claude Autant-Lara**
sc **Jean Aurenche, Pierre Bost**
ph **Jacques Natteau**
m **René Cloërec**
Jean Gabin, Bourvil, Jeanette Batti, Louis De Funès, Georgette Anys

A wealthy artist (Gabin) and a simple cab driver (Bourvil) join up to transport four suitcases of blackmarket pork across Paris during the Occupation, avoiding German roadblocks, hungry dogs and collaborators. Although one of the first Occupation therapy French films to recognize that there was cowardice, stupidity, apathy and hypocrisy among the populace during the period, the movie is principally a competent comedy-thriller with two rattlingly good performances from the well-contrasted male leads.

Best Actor (Bourvil) Venice 1956

Pigs And Battleships

Buta To Gunkan

Japan 1961 108 mins bw
Nikkatsu

d **Shohei Imamura**
sc **Hisashi Yamanouchi**
ph **Shinsaku Himeda**
m **Toshiro Mayuzumi**
Hiroyuki Nagato, Yitsuko Yoshimura, Tetsuro Tamba, Sanae Nakahara

When a brothel, which services American sailors from a naval base at Yokosuka, is forced to close down, the owner (Nakahara) sets up a pig farm and places a former pimp (Nagato) in charge. A gang tries to steal the pigs, and chaos and death ensue. This is a splendid mix of melodrama, satire and black comedy, even though it somewhat labours the metaphor of prostitution in US-Japanese relationships. However, the American connection is triumphantly used in the climactic pig stampede, plainly a reference to the Western. At the film's centre is a quintessential Imamura heroine, played by Yoshimura, who retains her decency in the midst of corruption.

Pigsty

Il Porcile

Italy 1969 90 mins col
Film Dell'Orso/Idi Cinematografica/INDIEF/CAPAC(Paris)

d **Pier Paolo Pasolini**
sc **Pier Paolo Pasolini**
ph **Tonino Delli Colli**
m **C.A.M. Ghiglia**
Pierre Clementi, Franco Citti, Jean-Pierre Léaud, Anne Wiazemsky, Ugo Tognazzi, Alberto Lionello

The story of a soldier cannibal (Clementi) in a medieval wasteland is interwoven with that of the son (Léaud) of an ex-Nazi industrialist (Tognazzi) in modern-day Germany. The young German, who is more attracted to pigs than to his fiancée (Wiazemsky), and the cannibal become sacrificial victims of their different societies. This strange, grotesque and rather silly parable is filmed with such calm beauty and underlying disgust that it seems to gain significance. *Theorem* and *Pigsty* were the only films in which Pasolini dealt directly with the hated middle classes; thereafter he was to leave the 20th century behind until his final film, *Salo*.

Pillars Of Society

Stützen Der Gesellschaft

Germany 1935 82 mins bw
Krüger-Ulrich/UFA

d **Detlef Sierck**
sc **Dr Georg C. Klaren, Peter Gillmann**
ph **Carl Drews**
m **Franz R. Friedl**
Heinrich George, Maria Krahn, Horst Teetzmann, Albrecht Schönhals, Suse Graf

Johann Tönnessen (Schönhals), having left Norway 20 years previously, is a successful rancher in America. Homesickness prompts him to accompany his circus-owner friend on a tour to his native land where he has a reunion with his ex-business associate

Bernick (George), now his brother-in-law. Johann's presence reopens old wounds and triggers off new tensions, particularly as he attracts the hero-worship of Bernick's son (Teetzmann) and falls in love with his ward (Graf) who, it transpires, is actually his illegitimate daughter... This screen version of Ibsen's play is only partially successful. It comes across as standard melodrama, a genre on which Sierck (Douglas Sirk) would, of course, capitalize, and benefits from images which demonstrate the director's imaginative visual skills. However, apart from those sequences where he has opened the material out (the horses in the prologue and, again, at the circus and the climactic storm that spells destruction to Bernick), the piece remains obstinately and detrimentally rooted in its stage origins.

The Pink Telephone

Le Téléphone Rose

France 1975 93 mins col
Gaumont

d **Edouard Molinaro**
sc **Francis Véber**
ph **Gérard Hameline**
m **Vladimir Cosma**
Mireille Darc, Pierre Mondy, Michel Lonsdale, Daniel Ceccaldi, Françoise Prévost, Gérard Hérold

Naive, middle-aged provincial industrialist Mondy is harassed by threatened strikes at his factory, as well as tax difficulties, leading him to consider a takeover by an American company. The latter instals him in the luxury of the Hôtel Georges V in Paris, and introduces him to Darc with whom he falls in love, only to discover that she is a high-class call-girl. He nevertheless abandons his wife (Prévost) to pursue a future with her. This film offers some impeccable acting, Mlle Darc's fair looks, and the suggestion of insight into ruthless business methods. Unfortunately, neither writer nor director seems certain whether this is a comedy, and Molinaro's crude direction only helps to wreck the enterprise.

Pirosmani

USSR 1971 84 mins col
Gruziafilm

d **Georgy Shengelaya**
sc **Georgy Shengelaya, Erlom Akhvlediani**
ph **Konstantin Apryatin**
m **V. Kukhianidze**
Avtandil Varazi, David Abashidze, Zurab Kapianidze, Teimuraz Beridze, Boris Tsipuria

The Georgian artist Niko Pirosmani (born 1863) roams the taverns of his native land, paying for his keep with his paintings, and finding solace in alcohol. Shengelaya, the son of pioneer Georgian film-maker Nikolai Shengelaya, has vividly captured the qualities of Pirosmani's art—the soft and subtle colours, the primitive forms, the wide-ranging subjects from animals and birds to ordinary people and historical figures. As not much is known about Pirosmani, who is played by the film's art director (Varazi), his life is recounted in a fragmented but naturalistic manner. An original and imaginative work.

Pisma Myortvovo Chelovyeka see Letters From A Dead Man

Pixote

Brazil 1981 125 mins col
Embrafilme/Hector Babenco

d **Hector Babenco**
sc **Hector Babenco, Jorge Duran**
ph **Rodolfo Sanches**
m **John Neschling**
Marilia Pera, Fernando Ramos De Silva, Jorge Juliao, Gilberto Moura, Jose Nilson Dos Santos

During a routine police sweep of the squalid streets of São Paulo, Pixote (De Silva), an abandoned 10-year-old boy, the effeminate 17-year-old Lilica (Juliao) and another youth (Dos Santos) are taken to a detention centre. The three boys escape, aided by Lilica's lover (Moura) and get involved with a homosexual drug dealer and an aging alcoholic prostitute (Pera) ... The plight of the three million homeless children in Brazil needs to be exposed and Babenco, who introduces the film, plainly has his heart in the right place. However, any political or social purpose the movie might have had gets lost in sensationalism. Unlike Güney's *The Wall* or Buñuel's *The Young And The Damned*, it creates disgust rather than outrage. The performances by actual street kids are horrifyingly natural; in fact, the child in the title role returned to his life of crime after making the film and was shot and killed by the police in 1987.

Le Plaisir

(US: House Of Pleasure)

France 1952 97 mins bw
Stera/CCFC

d **Max Ophüls**
sc **Jacques Natanson, Max Ophüls**
ph **Christian Matras, Philippe Agostini**
m **Joe Hajos (adapted from Offenbach)**
Claude Dauphin, Gaby Morlay, Madeleine Renaud, Danielle Darrieux, Ginette Leclerc, Jean Gabin, Pierre Brasseur, Simone Simon, Daniel Gélin, Jean Servais, Jean Galland

Three tales based on stories by Guy de Maupassant. 1) 'Le Masque'—an old man (Galland) finds his youth again by wearing a magic mask. 2) 'La Maison Tellier'—a group of prostitutes pays an annual holiday visit to the country. 3) 'La Modèle'—an artist (Gélin) in the habit of making mistresses of his models has to marry one (Simone) out of sympathy when she cripples herself during a suicide attempt. Each of the three complementary stories has memorable sequences which ensure that the film lives up to its title: the exhilarated camera moving with the masked dancer as he whirls and whirls until he falls, the contrast between the brothel and the country, between shadow and light in the second story, and the trapped painter wheeling his wife along the beach in the last. Pleasure comes too from performances such as Renaud's Madame and Gabin as her lecherous peasant brother.

The Players

aka The Actors

Komödianten

Germany 1941 110 mins bw
Bavaria Filmkunst

d **G. W. Pabst**
sc **Axel Eggebrecht, Walter Von Hollander, G. W. Pabst**
ph **Bruno Stephan**
m **Lothar Brühne**
Käthe Dorsch, Hilde Krahl, Henny Porten, Gustav Diessl, Richard Häussler

In mid-18th century Germany, Philine Schröder (Krahl) runs away from home to find refuge with a company of players run by Carolina Neuber (Dorsch). After the troupe suffers many artistic and financial problems, Philine gets the Duchess of Weisenfels (Porten), the aunt of the man she has married, to build a theatre for Carolina. This was the first of three films Pabst made in Germany during the war, the other two being the equally ponderous *Paracelcus* and *Der Fall Molander.* Two were biopics about German geniuses, this one being about the establishment of the first German national theatre and the need to put on German plays rather than foreign 'muck'. Mechanical, melodramatic and platitudinous, it is an example of how a once-great director could be manipulated by the needs of the State. It must be remembered that Pabst's award was given by the then Fascist-controlled Venice Festival.

Best Director Venice 1941

Playing At Love

(US: The Love Game)

Les Jeux De L'Amour

France 1960 87 mins bw
AJYM

d **Philippe De Broca**
sc **Philippe De Broca, Daniel Boulanger**
ph **Jean Penzer**
m **Georges Delerue**
Jean-Pierre Cassel, Geneviève Cluny, Jean-Louis Maury, Robert Vathier

A feckless young painter (Cassel) will not give in to his live-in girlfriend's (Cluny) desire for marriage and/or a child, but when his best friend (Maury) makes her an offer, he finally promises a wedding. This effervescent sex comedy, De Broca's first film, is dominated by the running, jumping and gesticulating Cassel, giving a performance as maddening as it is charming.

Playtime

La Recréation

France 1961 87 mins bw
General-Élite/Audubon

d **François Moreuil**
sc **Daniel Boulanger, François Moreuil**
ph **Jean Penzer**

m **Georges Delerue**
Jean Seberg, Christian Marquand, Françoise Prévost, Evelyn Ker

An American student (Seberg), studying at a college in Versailles, becomes fascinated to the point of obsession with the couple who live in the house next door. He (Marquand) is a sculptor, she (Prévost) his glamorous older mistress and wealthy patron. Eventually, she meets the man and they have an affair, until she recognizes his car as the vehicle that was involved in a fatal hit-and-run accident which she witnessed... The debut film of Moreuil, who was married to Seberg at the time, is not a particularly distinguished effort. Adapted from a story by Françoise Sagan, it meanders along much in the diffuse manner of that novelist, managing a little comedy, some intriguing drama and much tedium. Seberg and Marquand are somewhat bland, leaving such honours as there are to the cool Prévost.

Playtime

France 1967 152 mins col
Specta Films

d **Jacques Tati**
sc **Jacques Tati, Jacques Lagrange**
ph **Jean Badal, Andreas Winding**
m **Francis Lemarque**
Jacques Tati, Barbara Dennek, Jacqueline Lecomte, Henri Piccoli, Valérie Camille, France Romilly, Jack Gautier

Monsieur Hulot (Tati), doing battle with objects, observes a group of American tourists on their perigrinations around the Paris of modern office blocks and skyscrapers. They end up at the opening of a nightclub which is far from ready. The only glimpse of old Paris the tourists get as they scurry through the extraordinary metropolis of glass and concrete, designed by Eugène Roman, is on postcards. Tati's use of space and the possibilities of the 70mm screen have probably never been equalled. As the critic Noël Burch has written, it is the only film which must be seen 'not only several times, but at different distances from the screen'. Unfortunately, Tati's masterpiece (which appeared nine years after his previous film) did not get the recognition it deserved and was shown mainly only in versions reduced in time and space.

Pleasure Party see Partie de Plaisir, Une

Plein Soleil see Purple Noon

Pleure Pas La Bouche Pleine see Spring Into Summer

Plot
L'Attentat

France 1972 124 mins col
Transinter(Paris)/Terza(Rome)/Corona-Filmproduktion(Munich)

d **Yves Boisset**
sc **Ben Barzman, Basilio Franchini**
ph **Ricardo Aronovich**
m **Ennio Morricone**
Jean-Louis Trintignant, Michel Piccoli, Gian Maria Volonté, Jean Seberg, François Périer, Philippe Noiret, Michel Bouquet, Bruno Cremer, Roy Scheider

Sadiel (Volonté), exiled leader of a progressive political party in a North African state, is a continuing threat to the government of his country, as well as to French and American interests. The CIA and the French Secret Service concoct an elaborate plan to get rid of Sadiel, duping Darien (Trintignant), a seedy Left-wing journalist, into luring him to Paris. When Darien discovers the betrayal, his efforts to expose the affair lead to his brutal murder. In setting out to make one film, Boisset has succeeded in making quite another. Drawing his material from such facts as are known about the notorious Ben Barka affair in 1965—for which he suffered much harassment during and after filming—the director has failed in his ambition to create a truly realistic political document. On the level of a tough, hard-hitting and thoroughly gripping thriller, however, it works wonderfully well.

Plötzliche Reichtum Der Armen Leute Von Kombach, Der see Sudden Fortune Of The Poor People Of Kombach, The

Plovec see Swimmer, The

Plumbum Ili Opasnaya Igra see Plumbum, Or A Dangerous Game

Plumbum, Or A Dangerous Game

Plumbum Ili Opasnaya Igra

USSR 1986 96 mins col
Mosfilm

d **Vadim Abdrashitov**
sc **Aleksander Mindadze**
ph **Georgi Rerberg**
m **Vladimir Dashkevich**
Anton Adrosov (Ruslan, alias Plumbum), Elena Dmitrieva, Elena Yakovleva, Zoya Lirova, Aleksander Feklistov, Vladimir Steklov, Aleksander Pashutin

Plumbum (Latin for lead) is the self-chosen *nom-de-guerre* of 16- year-old Ruslan, a schoolboy obsessed with stamping out crime. He worms his way into acting as an informer for a special police squad with bizarre results, such as arresting his own father for poaching. Based on a controversial best-selling novel, this movie has provoked fierce debate in Russia: some argue that Ruslan is an unacceptable product of a repressive regime which allows power to reside in hands not yet fit to exercise it, while others see him as a paragon of virtue. An extraordinarily interesting film that offers a picture of day-to-day life in a Russian city but, to a Western view, the moral focus is less perplexing than its sometimes unbelievable context. Ruslan (very well acted), whose doting parents don't appear to notice when he stays out all night, is obnoxious, a ghastly child whose immaturity distorts the lens of his own vision and leads, finally, to disaster.

Plus Belles Escroqueries Du Monde, Les see Beautiful Swindlers, The

Plus Vieux Métier Du Monde, Le see Oldest Profession, The

Pociag see Night Train

Poema O Morye see Poem Of The Sea

Poem Of The Sea

Poema O Morye

USSR 1958 110 mins col
Mosfilm

d **Julia Solntseva**
sc **Alexander Dovzhenko**
ph **Gavril Yegiazarov**
m **Gavril Popov**
Boris Livanov, Boris Andreyev, Mikhail Tsaryov, M. Romanov, Zinaida Kiriyenko

The construction of an artificial sea in the midst of the Ukraine is about to take place, necessitating the flooding of a village. Villagers past and present gather to bid farewell to their home, among them a veteran General (Livanov), his lifelong friend and the chairman of the farm collective (Andreyev), an elderly carpenter and a young boy and girl (Tsaryov and Kiriyenko). Assembling from all corners of the country, the gathering acknowledges that the past must make way for a better future. Alexander Dovzhenko died in 1956, the night before he was to begin shooting the film he had prepared for two years. Working from his detailed script, his widow fulfilled his dream. The finished product is an extremely bold venture, painted in bold colours, which attempts to marry the past, the present and the future in the form of a visual poem. Sometimes bombastic and confusing, often static, the film—which begins the vast and unique Dovzhenko- Solntseva 70mm triptych with *The Flaming Years* and *The Enchanted Desna*—is nonetheless remarkable for its confidence, grandeur and glowing beauty.

Poil De Carotte

(US: Redhead)

France 1932 94 mins bw
Film D'Art

d **Julien Duvivier**
sc **Jules Rénard**
ph **Armand Thirard, Emil Monniot**
m **Alexandre Tansman**
Harry Baur, Robert Lynen, Catherine Fonteney, Louis Gauthier, Christiane Dor

In rural France, 'Carrot Top' (Lynen), an undernourished and unloved young boy, is badly treated by his aging mother (Fonteney), but his often absent father (Baur) is unaware of this. Everything comes to a head when the child attempts suicide. Duvivier's second attempt to make Jules Rénard's classic novella of childhood (the first was a silent version in 1925), turned out to be a classic film of childhood. This was thanks to the author's own screenplay, the fine photography and the wonderful key performance by the great Harry Baur. The colour remake of 1973 could not equal it.

Poison
Gift
Denmark 1966 98 mins bw
Nordisk Films/Morten Schyberg

d **Knud Leif Thomsen**
sc **Knud Leif Thomsen**
ph **Claus Loof**
m **Niels Viggo Bentzon**
Søren Strømberg, Sisse Reingard, Poul Reichhardt, Astrid Villaume, Judy Gringer

Henrik Steen (Reichhardt), middle-aged, comfortably off, and married with a teenage daughter, indulges in affairs with the maid, his secretary and other available girls. His double standards receive a jolt when his daughter's boyfriend (Strømberg) moves in, preaching and acting out an unashamed gospel of sexual liberation. An interesting and amusing idea which Thomsen renders lifeless by directing with deathly earnestness, while ignoring all but unintentional humour.

Pokjaniye, Monanieba see Repentance

Pokolenie see Generation, A

Police
France 1985 113 mins col
Gaumont/TFI

d **Maurice Pialat**
sc **Catherine Breillat, Sylvie Danton, Jacques Fieschi, Maurice Pialat**
ph **Luciano Tovoli**
m **Henryk Mikolaj Gorecki**
Gérard Depardieu, Sophie Marceau, Richard Anconina, Pascale Rocard, Sandrine Bonnaire, Franck Karoui

A Parisian police inspector (Depardieu), investigating a drug ring operating out of Marseilles, becomes passionately involved with a girl (Marceau) at its centre. Pialat's first big budget film, a tremendous hit in France, is a tough *policier* that unintentionally (?) seems to collude with the rascist, sexist cop played by Depardieu with his usual compelling power. Equally forceful is the direction, especially in the documentary-type realism of police procedure in the first half. But when the film moves away from the genre into the central erotic relationship between Depardieu and Marceau, it resounds with the familiar ring of the 'cops and crooks are alike' plot. Marceau declared Pialat a 'sado-masochistic pervert' in his treatment of her during the shooting, and he called her 'a young bitch'. Charmant!

Polioty Vo Sne Naiavou see Dream Flights

Polowanie Na Muchy see Hunting Flies

Ponirah
Ponirah Terpidana
Indonesia 1983 105 mins col
Sukma Putra Film

d **Slamet Rahardjo**
sc **Slamet Rahardjo**
ph **Tantra Suryadi**
m **Eros Djarot**
Nani Vidya, Christine Hakim, Ray Sahetapy, Slamet Rahardjo, Bambang Hermanto, Lina Budiarti, Teguh Karya

Ponirah (Vidya), whose mother died giving birth to her, has grown up in the care of her loving nurse (Hakim) but rejected by her father. This denial has scarred her emotionally and, harbouring feelings of both guilt and resentment, she sets out to take a bitter revenge on her past and on a society that exploits her. Made by a well-known actor and one of Indonesia's foremost theatre directors, Rahardjo's third excursion into film-making demonstrates the emergence of an original and maturing talent. What could so easily have been a melodrama develops as a profound tragedy, thanks to the director's accomplished and disciplined approach which lends the piece a grand dimension. The performances, too, are convincingly on target. It's interesting to note that Rahardjo has tackled Japanese Noh, a Czech play and Brecht's *The Good Woman Of Szechuan* in the theatre, all of which has no doubt contributed to his experimental yet formal sense of style and structure.

Ponirah Terpidana see Ponirah

Popiol I Diament see Ashes And Diamonds

Popioly see Ashes

Porcile, Il see Pigsty

The Pornographer
Jinruigaku Nyumon

Japan 1966 128 mins bw
Nikkatsu

d **Shohei Imamura**
sc **Koji Numata, Shohei Imamura**
ph **Shinsaku Himeda**
m **Toshiro Mayuzumi**
Shoichi Ozawa, Sumiko Sakamoto, Masaomi Kondo, Keiko Sagawa, Ganjiro Nakamura

Mr Ogata (Ozawa), officially a medical instruments salesman, in fact devotes his energies to the purveyance of sex aids in the committed belief that he is spreading happiness. He lives with the widowed Haru (Sakamoto), towards whose daughter he feels both guilt (for an accident she suffered) and lust. Harassed and put-upon, he goes to pieces when Haru, ill and mad, kills herself, and decides that man's happiness must lie in satisfying his physical needs free of women. Moving into a dilapidated houseboat, he begins work on his most dedicated pornographic project—the construction of an artificial but physically authentic woman... Imamura's film, generally shown cut by 35 minutes, borders on the bizarre but is played and photographed in a matter-of-fact style, neither prurient nor judgemental in tone. Depressing and discomfiting, it is also riveting.

Porte Des Lilas see Gates Of Paris

Portes De La Nuit, Les see Gates Of The Night

Port Of Call
Hamnstad

Sweden 1948 100 mins bw
Svensk Filmindustri

d **Ingmar Bergman**
sc **Ingmar Bergman**
ph **Gunnar Fischer**
m **Erland Von Koch**
Nine-Christine Jönsson, Bengt Eklund, Mimi Nelson, Berta Hall, Birgitta Valberg

A tormented girl (Jönsson), caught between her reformatory past and the rigid puritanism of the social workers, turns to an honest, slow-thinking young sailor (Eklund) for love. The film, belonging to Bergman's short 'realist' period, was largely shot on location in the Göteborg docks in a rare attempt to strike an almost documentary note. Against this coherent background is a bleak tale, tinged with elements of melodrama that often verge on hysteria. But Fischer's photography and Jönsson's performance hold this early work together.

Port Of Shadows see Quai Des Brumes

Port Of Shame see Lovers Of Lisbon, The

Portrait Of A Life
Ekti Jiban

India 1988 130 mins col
Chalchitra Productions

d **Raja Mitra**
sc **Raja Mitra**
ph **Kamal Nayak**
m **Raja Mitra**
Soumitra Chatterjee, Madhavi Chakrabarty, Avory Dutta, Munna Chakrabarty

In the 1930s, Gurudas (Chatterjee), a humble teacher of Sanskrit in a poor country school, becomes fascinated by the origin of Bengali words and decides to write the first Bengali dictionary. This he does by dedicating the rest of his life to the task, only winning official recognition on his death bed in a hovel. Not a subject to catch the film publicist's eye—'See the Writing of the First Bengali Dictionary!' 'Thrill to the Academic Quest for Knowledge!'—nevertheless, it does make enthralling viewing. Although Mitra plainly views Gurudas as saintly, the film avoids the pitfalls of hagiography by showing him to be a very human but obsessive man (beautifully played by Satyajit Ray's favourite actor) who neglects his family as he goes about his huge undertaking. It also proves that there is no subject that cannot be turned into something cinematic when done with artistry.

Portrait Of Chieko

Chieko-Sho

Japan 1967 125 mins col
Shochiku

d **Noboru Nakamura**
sc **Minoru Hirose, Noboru Nakamura**
ph **Hiroshi Takamura**
m **Masaru Sato**
Tetsuro Tamba, Shima Iwashita, Eiji Okada, Takamura Sasaki, Jin Nakayama

Chieko (Iwashita), the wife of poet and sculptor Kotaro Takamura (Tamba), is passionately dedicated to the creation of beauty. Her gifts, however, are unable to match her inspiration and, when her paintings come in for criticism, she withdraws, attempts suicide and finally, in spite of her husband's devoted care, becomes incurably insane. This detailed and intensely moving document of human suffering is based on the true story of Takamura, one of Japan's major artists. Directed at an appropriately measured pace, exquisitely photographed and acted at the highest level (notably by Iwashita as the tormented Chieko), the film is a profound mood piece, enhanced by the music and the use of Takamura's poetry to annotate events.

Portrait Of Teresa

Retrato De Teresa

Cuba 1979 103 mins col
Instituto Cubano De Arte E Industria

d **Pastor Vega**
sc **Pastor Vega, Ambrosio Fornet**
ph **Livio Delgado**
m **Carlos Fariñas**
Daisy Granádos, Adolfo Llauradó, Raúl Pomares, Alina Sánchez

Teresa (Granádos), a textile worker and mother of three, spends time after work as factory cultural secretary, much to the displeasure of her macho husband (Llauradó), who resents the household duties that fall on him. After he has an affair with a younger woman (Sánchez), Teresa resolves to make a life of her own. Part of the reconstruction of post-revolutionary Cuba was legislation for sexual equality and Vega's first feature (after making documentaries) was an effective instrument in the re-education of the Cuban male. Using his own wife (an exuberant Granádos) and sons, the director intended to 'drop a bomb' into every Cuban household. Despite being a step forward, the film still defines its heroine in terms of men, but is technically assured and benefits from Vega's attention to authenticity. Granádos, for example, spent some months working in a textile factory before shooting began.

A Portuguese Goodbye

Um Adeus Português

Portugal 1985 85 mins col/bw
Um Adeus Português/João Botelho

d **João Botelho**
sc **Leonor Pinhão, João Botelho**
ph **Acácio De Almeida**
m **Messiaen, Domingos Bomtempo, Frei Manuel Cardoso, Música Popular Angolana, Conjunto Monte Cara, Anamar**
Rui Furtado, Isabel De Castro, Maria Cabral, Fernando Heitor, Cristina Hauser

Fatigued soldiers trek through the jungle of a Portuguese African colony in 1973, embroiled in the last stages of war against the native inhabitants. In Lisbon in 1985, an elderly couple visit their bachelor son, and their daughter-in-law who is the widow of their other son, killed in action in Africa. Botelho's unusual film deals with the necessity of coming to terms with the past in order to live in the present. The effect of recent history on individuals who are unaware of the full implications of their country's/brother's/son's engagement in colonial warfare is delicately suggested, and the resolution of the family relationships realistic and unsentimental. The director's fluid juxtaposition of past and present help point the way to his themes.

Poseban Tretman see Special Treatment

Poshchyochina see Slap In The Face, A

Possessors, The see Grandes Familles, Les

Postava K Podpírání see Joseph Kilián

Posto, Il see Job, The

Postriziny see Short Cut

Pot Bouille see House Of Lovers

Potemkin see Battleship Potemkin, The

Pote Tin Kyriaki see Never On Sunday

Potomok Chingis-Khana see Storm Over Asia

Potselui Meri Pikford see Kiss Of Mary Pickford, The

Poulet Au Vinaigre see Cop Au Vin

Poupées De Roseau see Reed Dolls

Pourquoi Israel? see Israel Why?

Poussière D'Ange see Angel Dust

Povest' Plamennykh Let see Flaming Years, The

The Power Of Men Is The Patience Of Women

Die Macht Der Männer Ist Die Geduld Der Frauen

W. Germany 1978 80 mins col
Sphinx Filmproduktion

d **Cristina Perincioli**
sc **Cristina Perincioli**
ph **Katia Forbert Petersen, Henrietta Loch**
m **Flying Lesbians**
Elisabeth Walinski, Eberhard Feik, Dora Kürten, Christa Gehrmann, Ulrich Thiel, Barbara Stanek

Addi Flemming (Walinski) sells clothes at a market stall to help support her young son, and suffers beatings at the hands of her husband (Feik), a boorish, womanizing and violent drunk. She finally leaves him, but economics force her return and the whole cycle starts again until she finds refuge in a shelter for battered wives. This is a feminist film, certainly, but one which is even-handed in its judgement, identifying the contribution of women's passivity to the retention of male power. Filmed naturalistically with much hand-held camerawork, and beginning deceptively as a tale of deprivation and underprivilege, this is a bitter, salutary and clever attack on social structures and institutions, interpreted by actresses who wrote much of their own dialogue.

Po Zakonu see By The Law

Pratidwandi see Adversary, The

Prato, Il see Meadow, The

Prénom Carmen see First Name Carmen

Préparez Vos Mouchoirs see Get Out Your Handkerchiefs

Prestupleniye I Nzaniye see Crime And Punishment

The Price Of Love

I Timi Tis Agapis

Greece 1984 110 mins col
Andromeda/Greek Film Centre/ERTI

d **Tonia Marketaki**
sc **Tonia Marketaki**
ph **Stavros Hassapis**
m **Helen Karaindrou**
Toula Stathopolou, Anny Loulou, Stratis Tsopanellis, Spyros Antiochos

Andreas (Tsopanellis), the son of a formerly wealthy family, falls in love with Rini (Loulou), the poor working-class daughter of Epistimi (Stathopolou), who works in a factory to support her children and alcoholic husband. Andreas wants to marry Rini, but demands the price of his mortgage as a dowry. Epistimi's refusal begins a chain of events that ends in dishonour, betrayal and violence. The talented and intelligent Marketaki, who spent the years of the Colonels in exile in Algeria, has set her film in Corfu at the turn of the century. A well-constructed, well-acted drama of romance and revenge, played in glorious settings. However, in unfolding her tale, the director also lays bare a society where past and present overlap and clash, with modernization ruining the fabric of tradition, and women are trapped between the demands of subservience and progress.

The Priest's Wife

La Moglie Del Prete

Italy 1970 103 mins col
Carlo Ponti

d **Dino Risi**
sc **Ruggero Maccari, Bernardino Zapponi**
ph **Alfio Contini**
m **Armando Trovaioli**
Sophia Loren, Marcello Mastroianni, Venantino Venantini, Pippo Starnazza, Miranda Campa, Augusto Mastrantoni

Poor, embarrassed by her height, and longing to marry, Valeria (Loren) suffers a suicidal depression on learning that her boyfriend has a wife. Seeking guidance through a telephone help line, she falls for her therapist (Mastroianni), only to discover later that he is a priest, but pursues him nevertheless until they become lovers, and he promises to leave the Church. At the heart of this film lies the primary dilemma of the Catholic priesthood: what to do about celibacy. However, as written and directed, it is a slightly tasteless hotch-potch of comedy and melodrama, its leads too glamorous by half, and its plot resolution barely credible. Valeria is really quite an irritating and stupid character and Marcello's tormented cleric is a wooden bore.

Prima Angelica, La see Cousin Angelica

Prima Della Rivoluzione see Before The Revolution

Primal Fear

aka A Scream From Silence

Mourir À Tue-Tête

Canada 1979 96 mins col
National Film Board Of Canada

d **Anne Claire Poirier**
sc **Marthe Blackburn, Anne Claire Poirier**
ph **Michel Brault**
m **Maurice Blackburn**
Julie Vincent, Germain Houde, Paul Savoie, Monique Miller, Micheline Lanctôt

While walking home from work one night, a young nurse (Vincent) is attacked from behind, forced at knife point into a truck and raped. She never recovers from the experience and, finding herself unable to make love again with her boyfriend (Savoie), she commits suicide. The central story takes less than half the running time of this analytical and provocative study of the nature and consequences, but not causes, of rape. By prefacing the narrative with the camera 'tracking' down the rapist (Houde) in the guise of ostensibly respectable different men, Poirier makes the contentious point that all men are potential rapists. The rape itself is filmed subjectively through the victim's eyes and then commented on by a director (Miller) and her editor (Lanctôt). More 'alienation' techniques are added to the argument, such as documentary footage of women collaborators having their hair shaved and a clitoridectomy being performed in Africa. The analogies are intellectually shaky, but the film does offer a springboard for further debate.

Princes, Les see Princes, The

The Princes

Les Princes

France 1982 100 mins col
ACC/Babylone Films

d **Tony Gatlif**
sc **Tony Gatlif**
ph **Jacques Loiseleux**
m **Tony Gatlif**
Gérard Darmon, Muse Dalbray, Céline Militon, Concha Tavora, Marie-Hélène Rudel

Nara (Darmon) is a gypsy who, having thrown his wife out because she took the pill, lives with his old mother and young daughter in derelict circumstances. A series of misfortunes resulting from his own volatile temperament, drives them to a nomadic existence. Gatlif's intended study of the gypsy plight in urban France has lost sight of its objectives. Technically, the film is part *vérité* (lots of hand-held camera) and part stylishly photographed. In content it swings all over the place, juxtaposing comedy and drama at ill-chosen moments, and obscuring its message by making Nara destructive and reactionary while caricaturing its non-gypsy participants. A well-meaning muddle.

Princess Yang Kwei Fei see Empress Yang Kwei Fei, The

Prise De Pouvoir Par Louis XIV, La see Rise Of Louis XIV, The

Prisonnière, La see Woman In Chains

A Private Conversation

aka Without Witnesses

Bez Svidetelei

USSR 1983 96 mins col
Mosfilm

d **Nikita Mikhalkov**
sc **Nikita Mikhalkov, Sofia Prokofyeva, Ramiz Fataliyev**
ph **Pavel Lebeshev**
m **Eduard Artemyev**
Michael Ulyanov, Irina Kupchenko

A man visits his ex-wife one winter evening and old wounds are reopened. They argue. He tries to make love to her again. She reveals she is about to remarry. A film with only two characters, which takes place entirely in one setting, is easily open to accusations of being 'too theatrical' (an accusation springing from a limited definition of 'cinematic'). The impact of the film derives as much from the discreet camerawork and cutting as from the intensity of the performances and the brillant dialogue. The whole is a fascinating, Strindberg-flavoured war of words, as the protagonists continually shift position, nor is it without humour.

The Private Lesson

La Leçon Particulière

France 1968 82 mins col
Mannic Films/Francos Films/C.I.C.C.

d **Michel Boisrond**
sc **Claude Brûlé, Annette Wademant**
ph **Michel Boisrond**
m **Francis Lai**
Nathalie Delon, Renaud Verley, Robert Hossein, Bernard Le Coq, Katia Cristina, Martine Sarcey

Olivier (Verley), a senior student at a Paris lycée, becomes infatuated with beautiful, 25-year-old Frédérique (Delon), who turns out to be the mistress of a famous racing driver (Hossein) whom the boy much admires. He nonetheless pursues Frédérique and, in time, circumstances conspire to bring them together in an idyllic affair. A formula French romance, glossy, slick, trendy and superficial. However, there is some genuine tenderness and humour on offer, and a cheeky, engaging performance from Verley as the schoolboy already acquainted with sex but learning the lessons of love.

Private Life

Chastnaya Zhizn

USSR 1982 104 mins col
Mosfilm

d **Yuli Raizman**
sc **Anatoly Grebnyev, Yuli Raizman**
ph **Nikolai Olonovsky**
Michael Ulyanov, Iya Savvina, Irina Gubanova, Tatyana Dogileva, Aleksei Blokhin, Elena Sanayeva

Sergei Abrikosov (Ulyanov), a businessman in his fifties, is not given the company directorship he expects, and resigns. At home, angry and idle, he gradually perceives the distance that has grown up between him and his wife (Savvina) and children due to his long preoccupation with his career. He turns to his former secretary (Gubanova) for sympathy but she grows impatient with him. At last, helped by a series of unforeseen events, Sergei and his family begin to communicate again. Precise and formal in its composition, striking in its images, the veteran Raizman's much admired film is at once a universally recognizable drama of mid-life crisis and a metaphor for certain Socialist ideals that have outlived their usefulness. The screenplay is let down by contrivances that have no logic or sense, but this is still an intelligent and provocative movie.

Private Vices And Public Virtues

(US: Vices And Pleasures)

Vizi Privati, Pubbliche Virtù

Italy/Yugoslavia 1976 104 mins col
Filmes (Rome)/Jadran Film (Zagreb)

d **Miklós Jancsó**
sc **Giovanna Gagliardo**
ph **Tomislav Pinter**
m **Francesco De Masi**
Lajos Balázsovits, Pamela Villoresi, Franco Branciaroli, Teresa Ann Savoy, Laura Betti, Ivica Pajer

The young heir (Balázsovits) to the throne of a Central European kingdom at the turn of the century spends his time in wild orgies a a country estate. After ignoring the King's request to return to the capital, the Prince, his friends and his lovers are faced with troops. From 1970, Jancsó made films in his native Hungary and inferior ones in Italy. Because of its soft-porn elements, this erotico-political version of the Mayerling story gained a wider audience than his previous ritualistic and revolutionary pictures using a minimal number of shots. Ritual and revolutionary sentiments are still present, but they have been subsumed by the nudity of most of the romping protagonists in this playful, often childishly shocking, representation of history in terms of an orgy.

Prix Du Danger, Le see Prize Of Peril, The

The Prize Of Peril

Le Prix Du Danger

France 1983 93 mins col
Swanie/TF1/UGC/Top 1/Avala/Brent Walker

d **Yves Boisset**
sc **Yves Boisset, Jean Curtelin**
ph **Pierre William Glenn**
m **Vladimir Cosma**
Gérard Lanvin, Michel Piccoli, Marie-France Pisier, Bruno Cremer, Andréa Ferréol

Contestants on a TV game show, hosted by a smarmy MC (Piccoli), are invited to be chased around Paris for four hours by paid assassins. If they survive, they will receive a million dollars. Robert Sheckley's black comic novel might have made a fascinating thriller set in a psychotic society. Alas, after a promising build-up, Boisset has gone for the usual violent metropolitan chase movie so that, instead of observing and commenting on the bloodthirsty TV audience, the cinema audience is asked to share its perverse pleasure.

Procès De Jeanne D'Arc see Trial Of Joan Of Arc

Professor Mamlock

USSR 1938 100 mins bw
Lenfilm

d **Adolph Minkin, Herbert Rappaport**
sc **Adolph Minkin, Herbert Rappaport, Friedrich Wolf**
ph **G. Filatov**
m **Y. Kochurov, N. Timofeyev**
S. Mezhinski, E. Nikitina, Otto Zhakov, V. Chesnokov, B. Svetlov, N. Shaternikova

A brilliant surgeon (Mezhinski) at a Berlin hospital in 1933 is publicly degraded because he is a Jew. He makes an impassioned speech against the Nazi regime and is shot down. Carefully recreating the Berlin setting, it was one of the rare Soviet films of the period to deal with a foreign subject and was initially banned in Britain because of its anti-German stance. The irony and understatement of the direction make it a far more pungent work than more rhetorical efforts. In 1961, it was remade in East Germany by Konrad Wolf, the son of the co-screenwriter and author of the original play

---

Profumo Di Donna see Scent Of A Woman

Proie Pour L'Ombre, La see Shadow Of Adultery

Proshchanie see Farewell

Prostoi Sluchai see Simple Case, A

The Proud Ones

Les Orgueilleux

France 1953 105 mins bw
C.I.C.C./Reforma/Chrysaor/Iena

d **Yves Allégret**
sc **Jean Aurenche, Pierre Bost, Jean Clouzot, Yves Allégret**
ph **Alex Phillips**
m **Paul Misraki**
Michèle Morgan, Gérard Philipe, Carlos Moctezuma, Victor Mendoza, Michèle Cardone

A young Frenchwoman (Morgan), holidaying with her husband in the Gulf of Mexico, finds herself stranded and penniless in a grubby harbour town after he dies of a contagious fever. She falls in love with a local doctor (Philipe) who has taken to the bottle since the death of his wife and, when her feelings are eventually reciprocated, she stays to help him in his work. Although adapted from a novel by Sartre (*L'Amour Redempteur*), the screenplay reeks of banality and cliché. All the more credit then to Allégret for riveting the attention with his oppressively realistic evocation of a filthy, fly-blown tropical milieu—riveting, that is, if you can stand looking at the uncompromising details of the sordid and unpleasant. Morgan and Philipe do their best with their unworthy roles.

The Proud Ones

Le Cheval D'Orgueil

France 1980 118 mins col
Bela/TF1

d **Claude Chabrol**
sc **Claude Chabrol, Daniel Boulanger**
ph **Jean Rabier**
m **Pierre Jansen**
Jacques Dufilho, Bernadette Lesache, François Cluzet, Ronan Hubert, Arnel Hubert

A young boy grows up in a poor but independent community in Brittany in the first decade of the century, playing pranks, seeing the villagers suffer economic deprivation and his father go off to war, and witnessing the struggle to maintain their Breton language and customs. Chabrol's first film, *Le Beau Serge*, was a rural melodrama and he has returned to the theme of village life from time to time, most powerfully in *Le Boucher*, most unconvincingly in this *faux naïf* peasant romp. Chabrol's method is that of a museum curator meticulously and lovingly recreating the regional costumes, decoration and artefacts of the period, without an overall political or social perspective. Even the question of Breton pride in their own language is fudged by having the actors speak French (presumably for commercial reasons).

Prova D'Orchestra see Orchestra Rehearsal

Proverka Na Dorogakh see Trial On The Road

Provinciale, La see Girl From Lorraine, A

Prozess, Der see Trial, The

Pugni In Tasca, I see Fists In The Pocket

Puritain, Le see Puritan, The

The Puritan

Le Puritain

France 1937 87 mins bw
Derby

d **Jeff Musso**
sc **Jeff Musso**
ph **Curt Courant, Charles Bauer**
m **Jeff Musso, Jacques Dallin**
Jean-Louis Barrault, Pierre Fresnay, Viviane Romance, Mady Berry, Jean Tissier

Francis Ferriter (Barrault) believes that 'God is dead,' and belongs to a secret society dedicated to cleansing society of its moral impurities. When a fellow member refuses to denounce his own son's affair, Ferriter kills the girl in question, only realizing much later that he was motivated by his own repressed sexual desire. In its day, Musso's film, transposed from an Irish story by Liam O'Flaherty, was considered shocking and was banned in the Irish Free State and also in the State of New York. Now it is dated, but provides a wonderful opportunity to watch the unique Barrault at work, and is interesting, too, in implying criticism of Ferriter's dangerous puritanism rather than an attack on the values of society, here represented by the probing and perceptive police chief (Fresnay).

Purple Noon

Plein Soleil

France 1959 115 mins col
Paris/Panitalia/Titanus

d **René Clément**
sc **René Clément, Paul Gégauff**
ph **Henri Decaë**
m **Nino Rota**
Alain Delon, Maurice Ronet, Marie Laforêt, Elvire Popesco, Erno Crisa, Bill Kearns

Ripley (Delon), indolent and impecunious friend of a rich playboy (Ronet), schemes to take his friend's clothes, yacht, girlfriend (Laforêt) and life. Although the plot, taken from Patricia Highsmith's *The Talented Mr Ripley*, is pure *film noir*, the picture glows with the warm hedonism of the Mediterranean, courtesy of Decaë's camera. But it's not only gorgeous to look at, it's entertainingly suspenseful as well. The film also launched the 24-year-old Delon into stardom, his beautiful face accurately reflecting both the charm and the coldness of the ambiguous character in this perverse tale. *Purple Noon*, crassly retitled *Lust For Evil* for TV in the USA, was the last ray of warmth in Clément's prestigious career.

Pursuit see Tragic Pursuit, The

Puss Och Kram see Hugs And Kisses

Putyovka V Zhizn see Road To Life, The

Pyat' Vecherov see Five Evenings

Pyshka see Boule De Suif

q

Quai Des Brumes

(US: Port Of Shadows)

France 1938 89 mins bw
Ciné Alliance/Pathé

d **Marcel Carné**
sc **Jacques Prévert**
ph **Eugen Schüfftan**
m **Maurice Jaubert**
Jean Gabin, Michèle Morgan, Michel Simon, Pierre Brasseur, Aimos, Delmont

An army deserter (Gabin) commits murder and flees to Le Havre where he meets and falls in love with Nelly (Morgan), but their plan to escape together is foiled by her guardian (Simon). This is the first film in which the distinctive melancholy poetic realism of Carné and Prévert expressed itself. The slant-eyed 18-year-old Morgan, in trench coat and beret, together with the doomed Gabin trying to grab some happiness in a sombre fog-bound port (superb sets by Alexandre Trauner) are quintessential images associated with the world-weariness prevalent in pre-war France.

Quai Des Orfèvres

(US: Jenny Lamour)

France 1947 105 mins bw
Productions Majestic

d **Henri-Georges Clouzot**
sc **Henri-Georges Clouzot, Jean Ferry**
ph **Armand Thirard**
m **Francis Lopez**
Louis Jouvet, Suzy Delair, Bernard Blier, Simone Renant

A music hall entertainer (Delair) believes she has killed a lascivious old man. Her husband, (Blier) who *intended* to kill him, arrives to find him already dead. Each conceals the experience from the other, and the husband becomes the prime suspect. An accomplished thriller is the outer casing for an exposure of relationships and a wonderfully atmospheric portrait of a milieu. Clouzot's observation of human frailty, made with a mixture of wit and compassion, and shot with an extraordinarily fine sense of composition and lighting and use of chiaroscuro, renders the piece a classic of its kind. The great Louis Jouvet is memorable as the worldly-wise policeman—part cynic, part sentimentalist—determined to wrap up the last case before his retirement and take care of his motherless, half-caste son.

Best Director Venice 1947

Quarterly Balance see Woman's Decision, A

Quatorze Juillet see Fourteenth Of July, The

Quatre Aventures De Reinette Et Mirabelle see Four Adventures Of Reinette And Mirabelle

Quatre Cents Coups, Les see Four Hundred Blows, The

Quatre Nuits D'Un Reveur see Four Nights Of A Dreamer

Quattro Giornate Di Napoli, Le see Four Days Of Naples, The

Quattro Passi Fra Le Nuvole see Four Steps In The Clouds

Queda, A see Fall, The

Queen Bee

(US: The Conjugal Bed)

Una Storia Moderna: L'Ape Regina

Italy 1963 90 mins bw
Sancro Film/Fair Film/Les Films Marceau

d **Marco Ferreri**
sc **Goffredo Parise, Massimo Franciosa, Diego Fabbri, Rafael Azcona, Pasquale Festa Campanile, Marco Ferreri**
ph **Ennio Guarnieri**
m **Teo Usuelli**
Ugo Tognazzi, Marina Vlady, Walter Giller, Linda Sini, Achille Maieroni

A middle-aged car dealer (Tognazzi) marries a young girl (Vlady) who not only wants to have a baby as quickly as possible, but has a voracious sexual appetite which wears him out to the point of suffering an ultimately fatal heart attack after his final—and successful—attempt to make her pregnant. The plot belies an eventful entertainment, characteristic of the Italian sex comedies that were all the rage in the 1960s. Vlady is good to look at while Tognazzi, of course, is a dab hand at this sort of thing. Not to be taken seriously for a moment, it's funny and enjoyable.

Best Actress (Marina Vlady) Cannes 1963

Queen Of Atlantis see Atlantide, L'

Que La Bête Meure see Killer!

Que La Fête Commence see Let Joy Reign Supreme

Querelle

W. Germany 1982 105 mins col
Planet/Gaumont(Paris)

d **Rainer Werner Fassbinder**
sc **Rainer Werner Fassbinder**
ph **Xaver Schwarzenberger**
m **Peer Raben**
Brad Davis, Franco Nero, Jeanne Moreau, Laurent Malet, Hanno Pöschl, Günther Kaufmann

The crew of a marine destroyer takes its leave of each other at the port of Brest. The captain (Nero) worships Querelle (Davis), a handsome young sailor, from afar. Querelle, involved in drug smuggling, murders a fellow seaman and then goes to a famous brothel where he meets the rapacious Madame (Moreau) and other habitués of the place who all succumb to his fatal allure. Jean Genet's classic 1947 homoerotic novel *Querelle De Brest* seemed a perfect subject for the innovative and imaginative gifts of the openly gay Fassbinder. He opted to shoot it in a garish, stylized studio set in which a collection of gay icons—macho clones, sailors and men in leather—pose against a permanently orange sky, fight and philosophize. This is punctuated by quotes from Plutarch and an unbelievably monotonous song warbled by a ludicrous Moreau. Sadly, this was to be the 36-year-old Fassbinder's last film. He died soon after its completion. At least he left behind 41 better films—an astonishing output—to be remembered by.

Questione D'Onore, Una see Question Of Honour, A

A Question Of Honour

Una Questione D'Onore

Italy 1965 110 mins col
Mega Film(Rome)/Orphée Productions(Paris)

d **Luigi Zampa**
sc **Piero De Bernardi, Leo Benvenuti, Luigi Zampa, Ennio Gicca Palli**
ph **Carlo Di Palma, Luciano Trasatti**
m **Luis Bacalov**
Ugo Tognazzi, Nicoletta Machiavelli, Bernard Blier, Franco Fabrizi, Tecla Scarano, Lucien Raimbourg

A thick-headed, in both senses, salt-mine worker (Tognazzi) finds himself caught in the crossfire of a vendetta between the Sannas (headed by Blier) and the Porcus (leader Fabrizi), and eventually has to kill his own wife in order to preserve his honour and hers. On the credit side, Zampa offers some dramatic locations, the effortless talents of Tognazzi and a few unexpected twists in the plot. For the rest, this is an Italian comedy utilizing the ingredients of high drama without drawing too much mirth from the spectator.

A Question Of Rape
(US: The Rape)
Le Viol
aka Overgreppet

France/Sweden 1967 84 mins col
Sandrew(Stockholm)/Parc Film/Argos(Paris)

d **Jacques Doniol-Valcroze**
sc **Jacques Doniol-Valcroze**
ph **Rune Ericson**
m **Michel Portal**
Bibi Andersson, Bruno Cremer, Frédéric De Pasquale, Katerina Larsson

At home alone one Sunday, Marianne (Andersson) is disturbed by a stranger (Cremer) who holds her hostage at gun point. In the event, he is cultivated and sympathetic and, eventually, they make love. That night, one of her husband's dinner guests is the stranger... An absorbing film, directed with a precise, formal elegance in geometrically designed interiors that reflect its abstract nature. The Swedish Andersson, speaking her own French, is, as usual, first-class, and is well-matched by Cremer. Doniol-Valcroze's intentions remain ambiguous: is Marianne's experience the acting out of a desirable fantasy or the delusory by-product of sexual repression? More significantly, did the encounter with the stranger actually take place? A provocative exploration of illusion and reality, recalling elements of *Last Year In Marienbad*.

A Question Of Silence
De Stilte Rond Christine M.

Netherlands 1982 96 mins col
Sigma Films

d **Marleen Gorris**
sc **Marleen Gorris**
ph **Frans Bromet**
m **Lodewijk De Boer, Martijn Hasebos**
Edda Barends, Nelly Frijda, Henriette Tol, Cox Habbema, Eddy Brugman, Hans Croiset

Three women, entirely unknown to each other, and of differing backgrounds and occupations, brutally murder the male owner of a boutique. Dr Janine Van Den Bos (Habbema) is called in to assess their mental capacity and finds Christine (Barends) wedded to catatonic silence and Annie (Frijda) garrulous and cheerful, while Andrea (Tol), the most intelligent of the three, attacks Van Den Bos's motives and line of questioning. The eventual court hearing disintegrates as Van Den Bos maintains that the women are sane and walks out of the proceedings. In constructing an uncompromising feminist polemic, Gorris has made an original and powerful film, gripping in its story and in its technique. Indeed, the latter—a formalized pattern of flashback and cross-cutting both to contrast and link the protagonists—creates a world of absolute reality which overcomes the fundamental, almost surreal irrationality of the plot. The piece has its weaknesses, but is a well-written, well-acted examination of women in a men's world, taking an oblique approach to achieve a transparent and convincing thesis.

A Quiet Duel
aka A Silent Duel
Shizuka Naru Ketto

Japan 1949 95 mins bw
Daiei

d **Akira Kurosawa**
sc **Senkichi Taniguchi, Akira Kurosawa**
ph **Shoichi Aisaka**
m **Akira Ifukube**
Toshiro Mifune, Takashi Shimura, Miki Sanjo, Kenjiro Uemura, Chieko Nakakita, Noriko Sengoku

Kyoji (Mifune), a young and idealistic doctor and still a virgin, has an understanding to marry Misao (Sanjo), who works devotedly for him and his father (Shimura) in the small hospital they run. During the war he becomes an army surgeon and contracts syphilis from the blood of a patient when he cuts himself during an operation. Six years later, treating himself in secret and tormented by his conscience and his celibacy, he rejects the heartbroken Misao without explanation and throws himself into his work. Again demonstrating another aspect of his affinity to the cinematic conventions of the West, Kurosawa has constructed an out-and-out Hollywood melodrama, tear-stained and replete with noble self-sacrifice; as well as a sub-plot concerning the moral reclamation of a trainee nurse (Sengoku), and a low-life villain in the syphilitic soldier who contaminates Kyoji. However, acting and atmosphere are both of a high standard and, ironically, the film has acquired special interest today in its unmistakable parallel with AIDS which gives it a meaningful contemporary resonance.

A Quiet Place In The Country

Un Tranquillo Posto Di Compagna

Italy 1969 106 mins col
PEA(Rome)/Les Artistes Associés(Paris)

d **Elio Petri**
sc **Luciano Vincenzoni, Elio Petri**
ph **Luigi Kuveiller**
m **Ennio Morricone**
Franco Nero, Vanessa Redgrave, Georges Géret, Gabriella Grimaldi, Madeleine Damien, Renato Menegotto

A successful modern artist (Nero), needful of a change, goes off to a country house rented for him by his mistress-cum-agent (Redgrave). Troubled by mysterious happenings, he learns that the ghost of the former owner's daughter supposedly haunts the place. He becomes increasingly obsessed with the vision of the girl, who materializes as Gabriella Grimaldi, transfers his affections to her and brutally murders Miss Redgrave. Or does he?... Nero performs with suitable taciturnity, Redgrave is fine, Grimaldi is a convincingly erotic nymphomaniac ghost. However, the honours belong firmly to the director and the photographer, with Kuveiller stunningly capturing the kaleidoscope of bizarre images intended by Petri. On the surface this is a carefully constructed, coldly calculated Gothic horror creepy; beneath, it is a terrifying visual realization of the onset and progress of insanity. A little pretentious, perhaps, but mysterious and chilling.

Special Jury Prize Berlin 1969

---

r

Raba Lubvi see Slave Of Love, A

Racconti Di Canterbury, I see Canterbury Tales, The

Raduga see Rainbow, The

Ragazza Con La Valigia, La see Girl With A Suitcase, The

Ragazza Di Bube, La see Bebo's Girl

The Railroad Man

aka Man Of Iron

Il Ferroviere

Italy 1956 110 mins bw
Carlo Ponti/ENIC

d **Pietro Germi**
sc **Alfredo Giannetti, Luciano Vincenzoni, Pietro Germi**
ph **Leonida Barboni**
m **Carlo Rustichelli**
Pietro Germi, Luisa Della Noce, Sylva Koscina, Saro Urzi, Giulia, Edoardo Nevola

The relationships and problems of an Italian railway worker (Germi) and his unruly family during a period when life and the world seem to be turning against him. The misfortunes begin with the pregnancy of his daughter (Koscina), who refuses to marry the baby's father and runs off with another man, and continue with setbacks in his working life which lead him to seek solace in wine with old friends. One of the last films made during actor-director-writer Germi's Neo-Realist period, this is a well-observed, warm and detailed slice of Italian domestic drama. There are uniformly excellent performances from the cast, including Saro Urzi—who would win the Best Actor award at Cannes eight years later in Germi's *Seduced And Abandoned*—in a supporting role.

The Rainbow

Raduga

USSR 1944 92 mins bw
Kiev Studios

d **Mark Donskoi**
sc **Wanda Wasilevska**
ph **Bentsion Monastirsky**
m **Lev Schwartz**
Natalia Uschvy, Nina Alisova, Yelena Tyapkina, B. Ivashova

In 1943, during the German invasion of the Soviet Union, a peasant woman Olena (Uschvy), pregnant and lightly clad, flees from the Nazis across the snow-covered wastes of the Ukrainian countryside. Everywhere there is hardship and brutality, but in the end a rainbow appears as a symbol of hope. Although Donskoi's reputation rests on the enriching *Gorky Trilogy*, this inspirational wartime drama is no less remarkable. What gives it extra poignancy and power is that it was filmed in the winter of 1943, during the horrifying events it depicts. In fact, Yelena Tyapkina, who plays a mother who sees her son shot, lost her own son in the war and others among the cast and crew suffered similar losses. The simplicity and realism of the film made it an overwhelming success in the Allied countries.

Raise Ravens

aka Cria!

Cria Cuervos

Spain 1975 115 mins col
Elias Querejeta

d **Carlos Saura**

sc **Carlos Saura**
ph **Teo Escamilla**
m **Federico Mompoll**
Ana Torrent, Geraldine Chaplin, Conchita Perez, Maite Sanchez

Nine-year-old Ana (Torrent) is a serious-minded child desperately seeking to understand the world she inhabits. Having watched her mother die a terrible death of cancer a few years earlier, and blaming her father for this tragedy, she then holds herself responsible for his subsequent death. Saura's almost dreamlike attempt to enter the mind of a deeply unhappy child moves across three periods in Ana's life and the result is a bit of a curate's egg. Agony is piled on to the point where it becomes difficult to believe and the motive force is not clear. There are some magic moments, though, with Torrent superb and Chaplin, doubling as the dying mother and Ana as an adult, terrific.

Special Jury Prize Cannes 1976

Ran

Japan 1985 162 mins col
Herald Ace/Nippon Herald/Greenwich Films(France)

d **Akira Kurosawa**
sc **Akira Kurosawa, Hideo Oguni, Masato Ide**
ph **Takao Saito, Masaharu Ueda**
Tatsuya Nakadai, Satoshi Terao, Jinpachi Nezu, Daisuke Ryu, Mieko Harada, Yoshiko Miyazaki, Peter

The aged Lord Hidetora (Nakadai) abdicates power in favour of his eldest son Taro (Terao), but finds himself driven out of his own kingdom which then is torn apart by greed and rivalry. Seventy-five-year-old Kurosawa's epic version of *King Lear* keeps many of the main themes and the thrust of Shakespeare's play, while turning the daughters into sons and transposing the action to 16th-century Japan. The powerful performances of Nakadai, Terao, and Harada as an evil encapsulation of Goneril and Regan, burst from the screen. There is, too, an effective rendering of the Fool by a transvestite called merely Peter. The battles are visually stunning, far more involving than in *Kagemusha*, Kurosawa's previous film made five years before. *Ran*, which means 'chaos', cost $11½ million.

Rape, The see Question Of Rape, A

Rape Of Love see Violated Love

Rashomon

Japan 1950 83 mins bw
Daiei

d **Akira Kurosawa**
sc **Akira Kurosawa, Shinobu Hashimoto**
ph **Kazuo Miyagawa**
m **Takashi Matsuyama**
Toshiro Mifune, Machiko Kyo, Masayuki Mori, Takashi Shimura, Minoru Chiaki

In feudal times a samurai (Mori), travels through the woods with his wife (Kyo). She is raped and then he is killed by a bandit (Mifune). At the trial, the incident is described in conflicting versions by the bandit, the wife, a priest (Chiaki) and a woodcutter (Shimura), demonstrating the subjective nature of truth. The first Japanese film to be widely shown in the West is significant beyond its indubitable qualities because it opened the way for greater works by Mizoguchi and Ozu. Its popularity was due to its intriguing story and the forceful performances, as much as to its then unfamiliar background. It was ineffectively remade in Hollywood as a Western entitled *The Outrage*, in 1964.

Best Film Venice 1951

Raskolnikov

Germany 1923 116 mins bw
Lionardi-Film

d **Robert Wiene**
sc **Robert Wiene**
ph **Willy Goldberger**
Gregory Khmara, Michael Tarkhanov, Maria Guermanova, Maria Kryjanovskaya, Pavel Pavlov

Raskolnikov (Khmara), an impecunious student, has written a dissertation on the relationship between the individual and the law. However, he murders an elderly pawnbroker and her sister to obtain money for the Marmeladovs, whose daughter Sonia (Kryjanovskaya) has been driven to prostitution to save the family from destitution.

Making his first film since *The Cabinet Of Dr Caligari* four years earlier, Wiene again utilizes Expressionist design techniques but, overall, it is much more naturalistic. Unfortunately, this leads to a clash of styles that disturbs one's involvement, and the adaptation of Dostoevsky's *Crime And Punishment* has been limited to the narrative outline, dispensing with the psychology. Thus Porfiry, the sinister chief-of-police of the original who traps Raskolnikov into a cat-and-mouse game of unbearable tension, is here reduced to a conventional character known as The Coroner. Nonetheless, enough of the imaginative qualities of both Russian novelist and German film-maker remain to give it some interest.

The Rats
Die Ratten

W. Germany 1955 91 mins bw
CCC/Herzog

d **Robert Siodmak**
sc **Jochen Huth**
ph **Göran Strindberg**
m **Werner Eisbrenner**
Maria Schell, Heidemarie Hatheyer, Curt Jurgens, Gustav Knuth, Ilse Steppat

A pregnant refugee from East Germany (Schell) is abandoned by her lover. When her baby is born, she gives it to a woman (Hatheyer) who has always longed for a child but been unable to conceive. Inevitably, a bitter conflict between the two ensues. Adapted from a stage play by Gèrhard Hauptmann, with considerable changes to the material that serve only to complicate and weaken the plot, this is nonetheless a gripping movie. Siodmak has brought all his expertise to constructing a realistic picture of the bleak underside of life in post-war West Berlin, well served by absolutely first-class performances.

Best Film Berlin 1955

Ratten, Die see Rats, The

Rat-Trap
Elippathayam

India 1981 121 mins col
General Pictures

d **Adoor Gopalakrishnan**
sc **Adoor Gopalakrishnan**
ph **Ravi Varma**
m **M.B. Srinivasan**
Karamana, Sarada, Jalaja, Rajam K. Nair, Prakash, Sonan, John Samuel

Unni (Karamana), middle-aged and bad-tempered, lives on the family estate in a remote village with two of his sisters, Rajamma (Sarada) and teenaged Sridevi (Jalaja). The former looks after him without complaint, even though he deprives her of marriage, but the latter longs for escape. Eventually, Sridevi disappears, Rajamma falls ill and Unni, grown reclusive, allows the estate to collapse. This film is about the inev.,ability of change and the price to be paid for failing to adapt to it. Its social critique is conveyed through formal, symbolic images which gradually unfold the extent of Unni's social displacement, ending in his death in the river where Rajamma used to drown the rats. Made with a sharp feeling for atmosphere, the film suffers from excessive length and some rather muddled narrative detail, but Gopalakrishnan is clearly talented.

The Raven
Le Corbeau

France 1943 92 mins bw
L'Atelier Français

d **Henri-Georges Clouzot**
sc **Louis Chavance**
ph **Nicolas Hayer**
m **Tony Aubain**
Pierre Fresnay, Pierre Larquey, Ginette Leclerc, Hélène Manson, Micheline Francey

The effect on the inhabitants of a small French provincial town of a spate of poison pen letters from someone who seems to know the secrets of many of the recipients. Among the latter is a doctor (Fresnay), torn between two women (Leclerc and Francey). Clouzot's second film—an effective but sour view of French provincial life—was accused of being anti-French Nazi propaganda at the time. In fact, although made under the Occupation by a German-run company, the excellent script had been written by Chavance six years previously. Both Clouzot and the film were temporarily banned after the Liberation. As well as tight direction, it is full of telling character studies. Otto Preminger remade it, less memorably, under the title *The Thirteenth Letter* in 1951.

Raven's Dance

Korpinpolska

Finland 1980 80 mins col
Suomi/Filmi Oy/SFI/Television Lulla

d **Markku Lehmuskallio**
sc **Markku Lehmuskallio**
ph **Bekka Martevo, Markku Lehmuskallio**
Pertti Kalinainen, Paavo Katajsaari, Hilka Matikainen, Eero Kemila

In an unspoiled region of Northern Finland, an old man (Katajsaari), formerly a hunter, his young son (Kalinainen) and his daughter-in-law (Matikainen) live a challenging but simple life. The young man hunts, but with respect for the animals, and all three are in harmony with nature. When 'progress' comes with the building of a road, the young hunter is arrested and his gun confiscated. The raven, traditionally a dark omen, occupies a symbolic place in this hauntingly beautiful film, which opens with a silent half-hour prologue revealing the lakes and forests, the reindeer and elk, the birds and flowers, in images of breathtaking beauty. The dialogue is minimal, the acting thoroughly convincing in the service of a story in which little happens—until the climax in which so-called civilization heralds the destruction of nature and of the lives of the protagonists who symbolize its value. Lehmuskallio's message is poignant, painful and salutary.

Raven's End

Kvarteret Korpen

Sweden 1963 100 mins bw
Europa Film/Svensk Filminstitutet

d **Bo Widerberg**
sc **Bo Widerberg**
ph **Jan Lindeström**
m **Giusepe Torelli, Arthur Hedström, Karl Jularbo, Hermann Gellin, Edvard Persson**
Thommy Berggren, Keve Hjelm, Emy Storm, Ingvar Hirdwall, Christina Frambäck,

Anders (Berggren), a young would-be writer, lives with his drunken father (Hjelm) and worn-out mother (Storm) in a dingy apartment in Malmö in 1936 during the Depression. Each believes they can better their conditions. Widerberg's second feature, one of the first to benefit from funds given by Svenska Filminstitutet, was rather too lyrical and the poverty too picturesque to carry much of its political message. But it does have a freshness and an autobiographical feel (Widerberg was born in 1930) that is hard to resist. The film was overpraised at the time because its social realism seemed to mark a new trend away from the cerebral and visceral works of Ingmar Bergman that had dominated Swedish cinema for over a decade.

A Ray Of Sunshine

Sonnenstrahl

Austria 1933 85 mins bw
Serge Otzoup Filmproduktion/Tobis-Sascha

d **Pál Fejós**
sc **Pál Fejós, Adolf Lantz**
ph **Adolf Weith**
m **Ferenc Farkas**
Annabella, Gustav Frölich, Paul Otto, Hans Marr

A young couple (Annabella and Frölich) tries to survive in the harsh world of the Depression in Vienna in the early 1930s. Some of the jobs they manage to find—and lose—are at a fairground, cleaning a department store and working for a hairdresser. Finally, after many ups and downs, they are able to buy a taxi. Very much in the tradition and tone of Murnau's *Sunrise* (1927) and Fejós's most celebrated Hollywood film, *Lonesome* (1928), this is an endearing urban romance, charmingly played by the two leads. As a statement of economic exploitation it lacks substance and its fairy-tale Capraesque ending, when the inhabitants of a tenement shower Annabella with money to pay the rent, is only for the sweet of tooth. Yet, the director's imaginative use of sound and free-flowing location shooting compensates for the deficiencies.

Rayon Vert, Le see Green Ray, The

Rebellion

Joi-Uchi

Japan 1967 121 mins bw
Toho/Mifune

d **Masaki Kobayashi**
sc **Shinobu Hashimoto**
ph **Kazuo Yamada**
m **Tohru Takemitsu**
Toshiro Mifune, Takeshi Kata, Michiko Otsuka, Yoko Tsukasa, Tatsuya Nakadai

Yogoro (Kata), a young man forced to marry his overlord's mistress (Tsukasa), is ordered to give her up when her son becomes the overlord's heir. He refuses to part with his wife and, supported by his father (Mifune), rebels against the feudal lord and his men. Kobayashi composes his shots beautifully on the Tohoscope screen, as the complex manoeuverings of early 18th-century Japanese politics are detailed. The measured pace often explodes with action, such as the intricately choreographed swordfights. As in *Harakiri*, Kobayashi shows his ability to extend the limits of the Japanese period film.

Record Of A Living Being see I Live In Fear

Recréation, La see Playtime

The Red And The Black

aka Scarlet And Black

Le Rouge Et Le Noir

France 1954 170 mins col
Franco London/Documento

d **Claude Autant-Lara**
sc **Jean Aurenche, Pierre Bost, Claude Autant-Lara**
ph **Michel Kelber**
m **René Cloërec**
Gérard Philipe, Danielle Darrieux, Antonella Lualdi, Jean Martinelli

The ambitious Julien Sorel (Philipe), a carpenter's son, chooses the black robe of the priest rather than the scarlet of the soldier to make his way up the social ladder. In his first post as tutor, he seduces Madame De Renal (Darrieux), the mother of his pupils. He then courts and wins Mademoiselle De La Mole (Lualdi), the daughter of an aristocrat whose secretary he has become. Gérard Philipe, who had six years previously played Fabrice in *The Charterhouse At Parma*, embodied another Stendhal hero admirably in a sumptuous but rather superficial rendering of the great 1831 novel. Lacking much of the irony and psychology of the original, it is merely a prettily illustrated tale of a handsome opportunist.

The Red And The White

Csillagosok, Katonák

Hungary/USSR 1967 90 mins bw
Mafilm/Mosfilm

d **Miklós Jancsó**
sc **Georgy Mdivani, Gyula Hernádi, Miklós Jancsó**
ph **Tamás Somló**
Tatyana Konyukova, Krystyna Mikolajewska, Mikhail Kasakov, Viktor Ardyushko, Bolot Beyshenaliyev

In central Russia in 1918, Hungarians fighting in the International Brigade of the Red Army are hunted by White Russian troops. Only a small group of them escapes death. The first Russian-Hungarian co-production, made to celebrate the fiftieth anniversary of the Revolution, has all the Jancsó stylistic flourishes first recognized in *The Round-Up*, his preceding film. Using the possibilities of the large screen, he orchestrates an enthralling, sweeping, large-scale drama of domination and submission with a minimum of dialogue. The original title translates as 'Stars, Soldiers'.

The Red Balloon

Le Ballon Rouge

France 1956 36 mins col
Montsouris

d **Albert Lamorisse**
sc **Albert Lamorisse**
ph **Edmond Séchan**
m **Maurice Le Roux**
Pascal Lamorisse

On his way to school one morning, a little boy comes upon a balloon hanging round a lamp-post. The balloon seems to have almost human powers of communication, takes a fancy to the child and attaches itself to him until the sad event that ends its life. A whimsical, imaginative and thoroughly delightful fantasy which received a standing ovation at Cannes when it was first seen. It passed into the small and select canon of well-remembered and much-loved short features, continuing to enchant adults and children alike ever since. There is no dialogue as such, only random voices, street sounds and music, and the film was shot in an old quarter of Paris in soft hues of blue and grey against which the bright red balloon shines—a symbol of dreams and a poignant reminder of the cruelty of those who thoughtlessly destroy them.

Red Beard

Akahige

Japan 1965 185 mins bw
Toho

d **Akira Kurosawa**
sc **Akira Kurosawa, Ryuzo Kukishima, Hideo Oguni, Masato Ide**
ph **Asaichi Nakai, Takao Saito**
m **Masaru Sato**
Toshiro Mifune, Yuzo Kayama, Kamatari Fujiwara, Tsutomu Yamakazi, Terumi Niki

Under the guidance of an aging, autocratic doctor (Mifune), an idle and socially ambitious new intern (Kayama) learns the rewards of healing the poor clinic patients in 19th-century Japan. This very long, discursive, complex, often sentimental social drama, yields rewards in its detailed reconstruction of a feudal era, its humanitarian message, and in the powerhouse performance of Mifune in the title role.

The Red Desert

Il Deserto Rosso

Italy 1964 116 mins col
Duemila/Francoriz

d **Michelangelo Antonioni**
sc **Michelangelo Antonioni, Tonino Guerra**
ph **Carlo Di Palma**
m **Giovanni Fusco**
Monical Vitti, Richard Harris, Carlo Chionetti, Xenia Valderi

Giuliana (Vitti), the wife of an electronics engineer (Chionetti) in Ravenna has an affair with her husband's best friend (Harris), but becomes increasingly alienated from the souless industrial environment around her. The main interest in this rather banal exercise in modern *angst* is Antonioni's meticulous and creative use of colour for the first time. He even had buildings painted to serve the film's mood. Deep reds and greens reflect the wife's neurosis, while brighter colours appear during her flights into fantasy. Vitti struggles to convince in the part, and Harris merely looks lost.

Best Film Venice 1964

Redhead see Poil De Carotte

The Red Inn

L'Auberge Rouge

France 1951 110 mins bw
Memnon/Cocinor

d **Claude Autant-Lara**
sc **Jean Aurenche, Pierre Bost**
ph **André Bac**
m **René Cloërec**
Fernandel, Françoise Rosay, Julien Carette, Grégoire Aslan, Marie-Claire Olivia, Lud Germain

In 1833, a monk (Fernandel), discovers that stage-coach travellers staying at a desolate inn are robbed and murdered by the proprietor (Carette) and his wife (Rosay). He tries to save a coachload of stupid unsuspecting people from the same fate. This is an extremely amusing macabre comedy, but its 'blasphemous' aspects have now dated somewhat. (It took the British censor six years to pass it uncut.) Although it is inclined to get too hectically farcical at times, as Fernandel finds himself in more and more difficult situations, the almost ballad-like structure contains it. Yves Montand introduces the tale and the moral in song on the sound-track.

Redl Ezredes see Colonel Redl

The Red Mantle

Den Røde Kappe

Denmark 1967 100 mins col
Asa Film(Denmark)/Movie Art Of Europe(Sweden)/ Edda Film(Iceland)

d **Gabriel Axel**
sc **Gabriel Axel, Frank Jaeger**
ph **Henning Bendtsen**
m **Per Norgaard**
Gitte Haenning, Oleg Vidov, Gunnar

Björnstrand, Eva Dahlbeck, Birgitte Federspiel, Johannes Meyer

After King Hamund is killed by King Sigvor (Björnstrand), his three sons, following the demands of custom, ride off to take vengeance on the victor's sons. After a day's fighting, Sigvor brings about a truce, which is just as well, since his daughter (Haenning) and Hamund's eldest son (Vidov) have fallen in love. However, due to the machinations of an evil German who covets the girl himself, everything ends in bloodshed and tragedy. The dramatically brooding and impressive Icelandic landscape against which this 11th-century saga is unfolded, soon palls in the face of the simplistic drivel of the script. It's marginally amusing to watch Gunnar Björnstrand and Eva Dahlbeck (as his Queen) making fools of themselves, and interesting to note that director Axel would put his spare approach to rather better use 20 years later in creating the Oscar-winning *Babette's Feast*.

Red Psalm

Még Kér A Nép

Hungary 1971 88 mins col
Mafilm

d **Miklós Jancsó**
sc **Gyula Hernádi**
ph **János Kende**
m **Folk music and revolutionary songs (arranged Ferenc Sebo)**
Lajos Balázsovits, András Bálint, Gyöngyi Bürös, Andrea Drahota

In the 1890s, on a large Hungarian estate owned by a wealthy count (Bálint), a group of striking farm workers wait for a reply to their demands. The army moves in, but there is a temporary respite from hostilities when they all join in a festive dance. Then the strikers are fired upon. Moving even further in the direction of balletic cinema (Ferenc Pesovár is credited with the choreography), Jancsó has become even more master of his inimitable style. Only 28 shots are used in the entire film to convey, almost exclusively in symbols, a pattern of tyranny and revolution. Colour, too, takes on emblematic meaning, especially red. A hand wound is turned into a red rosette, a river runs red with blood, and a woman in a red shift shoots down soldiers with a pistol wrapped in a red ribbon. Jancsó's cinema does not conform to narrative or psychological conventions, but opens up other areas which are usually only found in the screen musical.

Red Wedding see Blood Wedding

Reed Dolls

Poupées De Roseau

Morocco 1981 88 mins col
Herakles Productions

d **Jillali Ferhati**
sc **Farida Belyazid**
ph **Abdelkrim M. De Kaoui**
Chaiba Adraoui, Bisiam, Sand Thami, Ahmed Ferhati, Jillali Ferhati, Ahmed Boudouadi

Aicha (Bisiam), a poor country girl, is sent to live with her aunt in town and is married to her cousin when she is old enough (i.e. when she begins menstruating). Her husband dies suddenly, leaving her a victim of the severe social and economic difficulties of an unprotected woman with children in a traditionalist Arab community. The film is a riveting and detailed insight into Moroccan culture, and a rare exposé of the oppression of Muslim women. Brilliantly well-acted by two Aichas (Bisiam the girl, Thami the woman) and Adraoui, outstanding as the supportive aunt battling to ward off catastrophe, the film is also visually exquisite, displaying a superb sense of both colour and composition, and directed with authority and understanding.

The Refusal

Die Verweigerung

aka Der Fall Jägerstätter

Austria 1972 94 mins bw
Neue Thalia-Film

d **Axel Corti**
sc **Hellmut Andics**
ph **Walter Kindler**
Kurt Weinzierl, Julia Gschnitzer, Hugo Gottschlich, Helmut Wlasak, Fritz Schmiedl

In the Upper Austrian village of St Radegund in 1943, Franz Jägerstätter (Weinzierl), an anti-Nazi farmer, family man and devout Catholic, refused conscription on the grounds of conscience. Ignoring exhortations from the Church, his wife and even the sympathetic army Major who offered him a non-combatant unit as a way out, he was guillotined in Brandenburg prison. From these true facts about a remarkable man, Corti has made a restrained and dignified film in which the dramatic reconstruction is intercut with film of the survivors of the place and period who were involved with or witnessed the events. Truthful, balanced and unmelodramatic, it is a monument to a man of uncompromising integrity, though it ends on a salutary note: an old man in the village remarks that 'Wars are always unjust. When another one comes along, it will be unjust too,' implying that Jägerstätter's self-sacrifice was pointless.

Regain see Harvest

Règle Du Jeu, La see Rules Of The Game, The

Rehearsal For A Crime see Criminal Life Of Archibaldo De La Cruz, The

---

Rekopis Znaleziony W Saragossie see Saragossa Manuscript, The

---

La Religieuse

aka Suzanne Simonin, La Religieuse De Diderot

(US: The Nun)

France 1965 140 mins col

Rome-Paris Films/Société Nouvelle De Cinématographie

d **Jacques Rivette**
sc **Jacques Rivette, Jean Gruault**
ph **Alain Levent**
m **Jean-Claude Eloy**

Anna Karina, Liselotte Pulver, Micheline Presle, Christine Lenier, Francine Bergé, Francisco Rabal

Suzanne Simonin (Karina) is forced, through lack of a dowry, to enter a convent where she is subjected to semi-starvation and beatings. Her efforts to annul her vows fail, but she is transferred to another convent where the Mother Superior makes Lesbian overtures to her until she escapes with the help of a priest (Rabal), who then attempts to rape her, and she has to endure new sufferings on the outside. Taken from a novel by Diderot written in 1760, this film was initially banned in France on grounds of anti-clericalism, although it was shown at Cannes in the interim. It is directed with austere detachment and an authentic sense of claustrophobia and pain, with the suggestion that the corruption and cruelty lurking behind the façades of religion is a metaphor for the world at large. If one can sit out the heavy-handed and repetitive sequences, there is much of interest, and the attractive Karina is adequate.

Remedy

Derman

Turkey 1984 90 mins col

Gülsah Film

d **Serif Gören**
sc **Ahmet Soner**
ph **Erdogan Engin**
m **Yeni Türkü Gurubu**

Hülya Koçyigit, Tarik Akan, Talat Bulut, Nur Sürer

Mürüvett (Koçyigit), a midwife, journeys to a post in Anatolia. On the way, she is trapped in a snowstorm in a nearby village and, the place becoming entirely snowbound, is forced to spend four months there. Before long, she is tending the sick children and delivering the babies, while two men, one of them (Akan) on the run from the police, become dependent on her. Serif Gören was responsible for directing Güney's *Yol* while Güney was in prison, and it is quite clear from this film that he must share in the credit for *Yol's* success. Working on his own account here, he not only draws good performances from his cast, but creates a palpable sense of the atmosphere and daily life in a small and remote Anatolian village. Above all, however, it is his outstanding visual flair that distinguishes this movie, with the ever-present and constraining snow extraordinarily photographed as both reality and as an emblem of hardship.

Rémorques see Stormy Waters

Le Rempart Des Béguines

aka The Beguines

France 1972 90 mins col

Paris Film/Antheo Film(Rome)

d **Guy Casaril**
sc **Guy Casaril, Françoise Mallet-Joris**
ph **Andreas Winding**
m **Michel Delpech, Roland Vincent**
Nicole Courcel, Anicée Alvina, Venantino Venantini, Jean Martin, Ginette Leclerc

Schoolgirl Hélène (Alvina) is seduced by her father's mistress Tamara (Courcel) and a passionate affair develops, marred only by demands of submission and a touch of violence from Tamara. When Tamara agrees to marry Hélène's father, the girl overcomes her jealousy through the realization that her lover is doing it for material security and that she herself will now have the upper hand. This sounds like a piece of typical Lesbian sexploitation but, in fact, Mallet-Joris' successful first novel has been brought to the screen with a touch of class. Directed with elegance, restraint and sensuality, and offering convincing performances from the women, its weakest element is the absence of any social or domestic context, thus robbing it of genuine conflict. Casaril places us, together with his protagonists, in a hothouse of sexual emotion which becomes a little too humid and enervating for comfort.

Rendez-Vous

France 1985 83 mins col
T. Films/Films A2

d **André Téchiné**
sc **André Téchiné, Olivier Assayas**
ph **Renato Berta**
m **Philippe Sarde**
Juliette Binoche, Lambert Wilson, Wadeck Stanczak, Jean-Louis Trintignant, Dominique Lavanant

Naive Nina (Binoche), just 18, arrives in Paris from the provinces, seeking independence and a theatrical career. She becomes enmeshed with over-idealistic Paulot (Stanczak) and destructive Quentin (Wilson), loses both of them, but gains the lead in *Romeo And Juliet.* It masquerades as a study of opposing forces in life and fate and Téchiné delivers a chic, well-cast, and certainly eventful, drama that rises above the level of drivel only because of the expertise with which it is put together.

Best Director Cannes 1985

Rendezvous At Midnight

Le Rendez-Vous De Minuit

France 1961 90 mins bw
Editions Cinégraphiques/Argos/Films Roger Leenhardt

d **Roger Leenhardt**
sc **Roger Leenhardt, Jean-Pierre Vivet**
ph **Jean Badal**
m **Georges Auric**
Lilli Palmer, Michel Auclair, Jean Galland, Maurice Ronet, Michel De Ré, France Anglade

At the cinema Jacques (Auclair) is watching a film called *Rendez-vous De Minuit* starring Lilli Palmer and Maurice Ronet. Eva, a young woman next to him, becomes emotional and rushes out of the cinema. Concerned, he goes after her and she explains that her life is following the pattern of the film's heroine and that she is about to commit suicide as the latter does on screen. Eva is the image of Lilli Palmer... Leenhardt, in the second of his two features (the first was *The Last Vacation*) has constructed an intricate study of illusion versus reality that is difficult to describe. He constantly intercuts the film-within-a-film to contrast two different 'realities' and complicates the issue further when a third Lilli Palmer, presumably as herself, makes a brief appearance at the end. Although it's not difficult to follow the action, the director's aim and object is somewhat obscure. No matter. It's inventive and funny, with Palmer splendid in her multiple roles.

Les Rendezvous D'Anna

aka The Meetings Of Anna

Belgium/France/W. Germany 1978
122 mins col
Hélène Films/Paradise Films/Zweites Deutsches Fernsehen

d **Chantal Akerman**
sc **Chantal Akerman**
ph **Jean Penzer**
Aurore Clément, Helmut Griem, Magali Noël, Hans Zieschler, Lea Massari, Jean-Pierre Cassel

Anna Silver (Clément), a Belgian film director in her twenties (like Chantal Akerman at the time), travels to several European cities to publicize her latest film. In Essen, she meets a

German journalist (Griem), with whom she goes to bed; in Paris, she visits her mother (Massari) and goes out with an ex-lover (Cassel). She returns to her apartment alone. For those who are willing to enter Akerman's world—static camera, medium long shots, mournful monologues and solemn silences—it does bring some rewards. The cryptic style and dislocated characters, existing in impersonal hotel rooms and railway stations, get close to the heart of a modern malaise in cool and understated images.

Rendezvous De Juillet

France 1949 120 mins bw
UGC/SNEG

d **Jacques Becker**
sc **Jacques Becker, Maurice Griffe**
ph **Claude Renoir**
m **Jean Wiener, Mezzmezzrow**
Daniel Gélin, Bernard Lajarrige, Brigitte Auber, Nicole Courcel, Maurice Ronet

A group of young people planning to make an anthropological film in Africa, attempt to find maturity and happiness through love, theatre, and jazz in post-war St-Germain-des-Prés. Although very much a film of its day, the performances still have a rare freshness and the interplay of the characters is more interesting than the thin plot and sociological angles.

Rendez-Vous De Minuit, Le see Rendezvous At Midnight

Renegade Priest see Defroqué, Le

Repast

Meshi

Japan 1951 101 mins bw
Toho

d **Mikio Naruse**
sc **Toshiro Ide, Sumie Tanaka**
ph **Masao Tamai**
m **Fumio Hayasaka**
Setsuko Hara, Ken Uehara, Yukiko Shimazaki, Kan Nihonyanagi, Keiju Kobayashi

The empty, unfulfilled five-year marriage of Michiyo (Hara) and her husband Hatsunosuke (Uehara) is brought to a head when their flirt of a niece (Shimazaki) comes to stay. Michiyo tries to become independent, but returns to her husband in the end. The first of six works that Naruse adapted from the novels of Fumiko Hayashi, all of which deal with women who are trying to redefine their lives, but who are ultimately defeated. The ambiguous ending of *Repast* is often seen as a compromise, but it is more truthful than most happy conclusions to melodramas. The whole delicate, minutely-observed work is greatly enriched by the playing of the two leads.

Repentance

Pokjaniyeaka, Monanieba

USSR 1984 150 mins col
Gruziafilm/Georgian State TV

d **Tengiz Abuladze**
sc **Tengiz Abuladze, Nana Djanelidze, Rezo Kveselava**
ph **Mikhail Agranovich**
m **Nana Djanelidze**
Avtandil Makharadze, Zeynab Botsvzadze, Edisher Giorgobiani, Katevan Abuladze, Iya Ninidze, Merab Ninidze

When Varlam Avaridze (Makharadze), the mayor of a small Georgian town, dies, he is buried with full pomp. But the attractive Guliko (Iya Ninidze), who had been persecuted by him, continually digs up his corpse. During her trial, the full extent of Varlam's crimes emerges. There are few Soviet films that so epitomize *glasnost* as this searing exposé of Stalinism and the 'cult of personality'. Shot in Georgian in Stalin's own republic, it was cleared for mass distribution two years after its completion. A dark, and, paradoxically, lucid, bitter film, laced with black humour, it unfolds in a series of nightmarish flashbacks and meaningful symbols.

Report On The Party And The Guests, A see Party And The Guests, The

---

Repos Du Guerrier, Le see Warrior's Rest

Republic Of Sin

La Fièvre Monte À El Pao

France/Mexico 1960 100 mins bw

Groupe Des Quatre(Paris)/Cinematografica Filmex(Mexico)

d **Luis Buñuel**
sc **Louis Sapin, Luis Buñuel**
ph **Gabriel Figueroa**
m **Paul Misraki**
Gérard Philipe, Jean Servais, Maria Felix, Raoul Dantes, M.A. Ferriz, Domingo Soler

A satellite island off the coast of a Latin-American Republic has a large population of jailbirds and political prisoners from the mainland. The administration is corrupt and callous, and the governor is assassinated. Vasquez (Philipe), his former secretary and a man of ideals, takes care of matters—and falls in love with the dead man's widow (Felix)—until a new governor (Servais) is appointed. The two men do not see eye to eye, mutiny breaks out and, eventually, Vasquez becomes governor, only to find that power forces him to betray his humane principles. Buñuel here has come up with part potboiler, part acute political analysis. There is a splendid villain from Servais, and Maria Felix's sexy beauty is given rein in some well-shot bedroom scenes. However, the cruel cynicism of the director's message—that individuals are forced to bow to systems—comes through loud and clear. Gérard Philipe, making his last film before his early death, seems unable to inject life into his somewhat vaguely characterized role. A disappointing exit for the French superstar.

Restless Night see All Night Through

Retour De Martin Guerre, Le see Return Of Martin Guerre, The

Retrato De Teresa see Portrait Of Teresa

The Return Of Martin Guerre
Le Retour De Martin Guerre

France 1982 123 mins col
SFP/France Region 3/Marcel Dassault/Roissi Films

d **Daniel Vigne**
sc **Jean-Claude Carrière, Daniel Vigne**
ph **André Neau**
m **Michel Portal**
Gérard Depardieu, Stéphane Peau, Nathalie Baye, Bernard-Pierre Donnadieu, Sylvie Meda, Maurice Barrier

In the 16th century, a man (Depardieu) comes to a French village claiming to be Martin Guerre, a youth who left his child-bride (Baye) pregnant eight years earlier. A trial is held to establish whether he is an imposter. The main strength of Vigne's 'who is it?' medieval mystery is the extraordinary re-creation of a cruel, ignorant and suspicious society. But the plot is never as intriguing as it promises and takes quite a time to get to the point. Depardieu's calm presence holds the film together.

The Return Of Maxim
Vozvrashcheniye Maksima

USSR 1937 114 mins bw
Lenfilm

d **Grigori Kozintsev, Leonid Trauberg**
sc **Grigori Kozintsev, Leonid Trauberg, Lev Slavin**
ph **Andrei Moskvin**
m **Dmitri Shostakovitch**
Boris Chirkov, Valentina Kibardina, A. Kuznetsov, Alexander Zrazhevsky, Mikhail Zharov

In 1914, Maxim (Chirkov), his girlfriend Natasha (Kibardina) and their comrades take part in the workers' demonstrations against the war and the operations to discover an armaments factory. With the dramatist Slavin, brought in to enliven the complicated political scenes, Kozintsev and Trauberg continued the mood of *The Youth Of Maxim* (1935), although tinged with more seriousness as the hero becomes a full-blown revolutionary. The introduction of a new character, Dimba (Zharov), St Petersburg's billiards king, good enough to worry Paul Newman, the stirring crowd scenes and the stirring music, make an impressive second part of *The Maxim Trilogy*, to be concluded by *The Vyborg Side*.

Revenant, Un see Lover's Return, A

The Revolt Of Job
Jób Lázadása

Hungary 1983 98 mins col
Mafilm Tarsulás Studio/Hungarian TV(Budapest)/ ZDF(Mainz)

d **Imre Gyöngyössi, Barna Kabay**
sc **Katalin Petényi, Imre Gyöngyössi, Barna Kabay**
ph **Gábor Szabó**
m **Zoltán Jeney**
Ferenc Zenthe, Hédi Temessy, Gábor Fehér, Péter Rudolf, Leticia Caro

By 1943, Job and Rosa (Zenthe and Temessy), an elderly Jewish couple in an East Hungarian farming community, have outlived their seven children. Eager to hand on their heritage before they die, they adopt Lacko (Fehér), a seven-year-old orphan. The period of adjustment is difficult, with the boy rebellious and distrustful. He comes to love his adoptive parents, whereupon the Nazi round-up of the Jews begins and Job must find a way to protect Lacko... This story is told from the boy's point of view, much in the same manner as Kusturica's *When Father Was Away On Business.* Screenplay, direction and cast are workmanlike, but it's the superbly natural and committed performance of young Gábor Fehér that lends it special poignancy and distinction.

Richard Tauber Story, The see You Are The World For Me

Rideau Cramoisi, Le see Crimson Curtain, The

Rififi

Du Rififi Chez Les Hommes

France 1955 116 mins bw
Indus/Pathé/Prima

d **Jules Dassin**
sc **Jules Dassin, René Wheeler, Auguste Le Breton**
ph **Philippe Agostini**
m **Georges Auric**
Jean Servais, Carl Mohner, Robert Manuel, Marie Sabouret, Perlo Vita (Jules Dassin), Magali Noël

A group of criminals plan and execute a jewel robbery and then fall out over the loot. After being forced out of Hollywood by the McCarthy blacklist, Dassin settled in France where he made this clever and much imitated (in films and life) heist movie, originally assigned to Jean-Pierre Melville. The film's reputation rests on the meticulously enacted and tense 22-minute robbery sequence played in total silence, and the sleazy view of the Montmartre underworld.

Best Director Cannes 1955

Riflemen, The see Carabiniers, Les

Rih Essed see Man Of Ashes

The Ripening Seed

(US: The Game Of Love)

Le Blé En Herbe

France 1953 105 mins bw
Franco London

d **Claude Autant-Lara**
sc **Claude Autant-Lara, Jean Aurenche, Pierre Bost**
ph **Robert Lefèbvre**
m **René Cloërec**
Nicole Berger, Pierre-Michel Beck, Edwige Feuillère

While on holiday at the seaside with his childhood sweetheart (Berger), an adolescent boy (Beck) is seduced by a mysterious, attractive, much older woman (Feuillère). This tender triangular tale, intelligently adapted from Colette's novel, was condemned as 'immoral and obscene' by the Church and banned in Nice and Chicago, no doubt a contributing factor to its success. However, the grace and glamour of Feuillère was the clincher.

Ripoux, Les see Cop, Le

Riptide see Such A Pretty Little Beach

The Rise Of Louis XIV

aka The Rise To Power Of Louis XIV

La Prise De Pouvoir Par Louis XIV

France 1966 100 mins bw
ORTF

d **Roberto Rossellini**
sc **Philippe Erlanger**

ph **Georges Leclerc**
m **Betty Willemetz**
Jean-Marie Patte, Raymond Jourdan, Silvagni, Katharina Renn

The early life of Louis XIV (Patte) under the domination of the regents, his later taking over of power for himself, the building of Versailles and the centralized court life. From the mid-1960s to his death in 1977, Rossellini turned his attention almost exclusively to the making of historical and religious features for TV. This was one of the few of them to escape the confines of the small screen and obtain a wide theatrical release. His method here was not only to approach his subject in a direct and realistic manner, to reveal the man beneath the wig, but also to show that power resides in routine and ritual. Impressive is the central documentary-like section detailing life at the court, and the ending, when the little king is divested of his robes.

Rise To Power Of Louis XIV, The see Rise Of Louis XIV, The

Riso Amaro see Bitter Rice

The Rite
Riten

Sweden 1969 74 mins bw
Svensk Filmindustri/Sveriges TV/A.B. Cinematograph

d **Ingmar Bergman**
sc **Ingmar Bergman**
ph **Sven Nykvist**
Ingrid Thulin, Anders Ek, Gunnar Björnstrand, Erik Hell

An internationally famous theatrical troupe consisting of husband (Björnstrand), wife (Thulin) and wife's lover (Ek), have their show stopped because an item, 'The Rite', is considered obscene. Summoned by a Judge, they are subjected to provocative and sadistic examinations of their private lives which ruthlessly expose their serious neuroses and misdemeanours. This was the first film that Bergman made specifically for television, but it soon received cinema release. Dealing with one of the director's major and recurring themes—the relationship of the artist to society and the dislocation between his private and public self—it shows no compromise for the small screen. A complex, disturbing, and deeply pessimistic film, with a brilliant performance from Thulin as the unhappy, alcoholic actress.

Riten see Rite, The

Road, The see Strada, La

The Road To Corinth
La Route De Corinthe

France 1967 90 mins col
Les Films De La Boétie(Paris)/ CGFC(Rome)/Orion Films(Athens)

d **Claude Chabrol**
sc **Claude Brûlé, Daniel Boulanger**
ph **Jean Rabier**
m **Pierre Jansen**
Jean Seberg, Maurice Ronet, Christian Marquand, Michel Bouquet, Saro Urzi, Claude Chabrol

Robert Ford (Marquand), a NATO security officer, is shot while investigating mysterious electronic boxes that are jamming US radar installations in Greece. His wife Shanny (Seberg), falsely convicted of his murder and ordered to leave the country, sets out to find the killer, giving the slip to Dex (Ronet), whom Robert's superior (Bouquet) has detailed to chaperone her. Complications multiply as Dex becomes Shanny's ally... High-class escapist hokum with a wry undertone and magnificent Greek locations that could equally well have served Hitchcock or the James Bond team. That said, Chabrol has used his light-hearted caper as the basis for a witty, bizarre and sumptuous exercise in style, expertly photographed by Rabier.

The Road To Life
Putyovka V Zhizn

USSR 1931 121 mins bw
Mezhrabpomfilm

d **Nicolai Ekk**
sc **Nikolai Ekk**
ph **Vaslli Pronin**
m **Yakov Stollyar**
Maria Gonfa, Tsifan Kyria, Nikolai Batalov

In the early 1920s, during the chaotic aftermath of the Civil War, thousands of homeless orphans roam the countryside as vagabonds and petty criminals. At a children's collective, they are rehabilitated and taught a trade. The first Soviet film to be conceived and made as a talkie showed an impressive grasp of the potential of sound, while still using intertitles. Although there were also some remnants of the montage techniques Ekk had learnt from his teacher Eisenstein, the film moved towards a more personalized kind of Soviet cinema. Praised technically and dramatically at home and abroad, today it needs to be seen in its historical context to be fully appreciated.

Rocco And His Brothers

Rocco E I Suoi Fratelli

Italy 1960 180 mins bw
Titanus/Les Films Marceau

d **Luchino Visconti**
sc **Luchino Visconti, Suso Cecchi D'Amico, Vasco Pratolini**
ph **Giuseppe Rotunno**
m **Nino Rota**
Alain Delon, Renato Salvatori, Annie Girardot, Katina Paxinou, Roger Hanin, Paolo Stoppa, Suzy Delair, Claudia Cardinale, Spiros Focas, Rocco Vidolazzi

Rosaria Pafundi (Paxinou) and her four sons, Rocco (Delon), Simone (Salvatori), Vincenza (Focas), and Luca (Vidolazzi), come to Milan to escape the poverty of the South, but find that the streets of the unfeeling metropolis are not exactly paved with gold. Visconti's long family saga, told in four episodes bearing the name of each of the brothers, was an attempt to return to Neo-Realism, but the melodramatics and the star cast put it nearer the world of Hollywood soap. Delon as a 'wise fool' is unconvincing, especially as a boxer who wouldn't harm a flyweight. Salvatori and Girardot bring the necessary weight to their tragic roles, although placed in an operatic finale. 'Rococo And His Brothers'? Yet there is much to admire in the scale of the enterprise, the scenes of the family's arrival and the Milanese locations.

Best Director Venice 1960

Rocco E I Suoi Fratelli see Rocco And His Brothers

Røde Kappe, Den see Red Mantle, The

RoGoPaG

Italy 1962 125 mins bw/col
Arco/Cineriz/Lyre

d **Roberto Rossellini, Jean-Luc Godard, Pier Paolo Pasolini, Ugo Gregoretti**
sc **Roberto Rossellini, Jean-Luc Godard, Pier Paolo Pasolini, Ugo Gregoretti**
ph **Luciano Trasatti, Jean Rabier, Tonino Delli Colli, Mario Bernardo**
m **Carlo Rustichelli**
Orson Welles, Ugo Tognazzi, Rosanna Schiaffino, Alexandra Stewart, Jean-Marc Bory, Renato Salvatori, Lisa Gastoni, Bruce Balabin

Rossellini (Ro): An airline hostess (Schiaffino) has to fend off an American passenger (Balabin). Godard (Go): A couple (Stewart and Bory) has an unsatisfactory love affair in a post-nuclear world. Pasolini (Pa): A man dies on the cross while acting in a religious epic directed by Orson Welles. Gregoretti (G): A couple (Tognazzi and Gastoni) comes up against modern selling techniques. 'Ragbag' might have been a better title for this quartet of sketches on the horrors of contemporary life. The most effective is Pasolini's view of the contrast between the Christian message and those who propagate it, which got him four months suspended sentence for 'public defamation'. Godard's is a disturbing and sharp premonitory essay, Gregoretti offers a familiar satire, and the first feeble sketch is unworthy of its director.

Rok Spokojnego Słońca see Year Of The Quiet Sun, A

The Role

Bhumika

India 1977 142 mins col
Blaze Film Enterprises

d **Shyam Benegal**
sc **Girish Karnad, Pandit Satyadev Dubey, Shyam Benegal**
ph **Govind Nihalani**
m **Vanraj Bhatia**

Smita Patil, Anant Nag, Amrish Puri, Naseeruddin Shah, Amol Palekar

Keshav (Palekar) gets Usha (Patil), the young daughter of his mistress, into films as a singer. She falls in love with her regular co-star Rajan (Nag), but his attitude to her is ambivalent and, eventually, she finds herself marrying Keshav, who plays on a multitude of her emotions, including her sense of obligation, to get her to do so. She becomes the family breadwinner, forced to continue working against her desires. Benegal's deceptively simple seventh film, with its narrative echoes of a Hollywood-style 'woman's picture' is, in fact, a multi-layered, complex affair which reveals the difficulties and contradictions of a woman's role in India. The director cunningly combines past and present, drawing skilful correspondences between Usha's screen roles and her life, in an absorbing and excellent story.

Roma see Fellini's Roma

Roma, Città Aperta see Rome, Open City

Roman D'Un Tricheur, Le see Story Of A Cheat, The

Romeo, Julie A Tma see Romeo, Juliet And Darkness

Romeo, Juliet And Darkness

Romeo, Julie A Tma

Czechoslovakia 1959 96 mins bw
Ceskoslovensky Film

d **Jiří Weiss**
sc **Jiří Weiss, Jan Otčenásek**
ph **Václav Hanus**
m **Jiří Srnka**
Ivan Mistrik, Dana Smutná, František Smolik, Blanka Bohdanová, Jiří Koder, Vladimir Ráž

In 1942, during the Nazi occupation of Czechkoslovakia, Hana (Smutná), a Jewish schoolgirl, escapes the ghetto round-up and is given refuge by Pavel (Mistrik), a boy who hides her in his mother's attic and keeps her going as best he can until the inevitable bleak outcome. A restrained and atmospheric film in which Weiss admirably captures the daily stress and consequence of living in fear. The close relationship that grows between the two young people, and sparks off the climax of the plot, relies for its credibility on Mistrik's depth of performance. (Smutná is beautiful but blank.) The film is affecting and authentic; its director, interestingly, escaped the Occupation and spent the war years in Britain.

Rome, Open City

(US: Open City)

Roma, Città Aperta

Italy 1945 101 mins bw
Minerva/Excelsa

d **Roberto Rossellini**
sc **Sergio Amedei, Federico Fellini**
ph **Ubaldo Arata**
m **Renzo Rossellini**
Aldo Fabrizi, Anna Magnani, Marcel Pagliero, Maria Michi, Harry Feist

In 1944, in the last days of the German occupation of Italy, Resistance leader Manfredi (Pagliero), fleeing the Gestapo, is given refuge by the pregnant Pina (Magnani). When she is shot, he takes shelter with a good-time girl (Michi) who betrays him. Manfredi and a priest (Fabrizzi) are arrested and executed. The film that brought the Italian Neo-Realist movement to fruition was concerned with capturing, as directly as possible, the experiences of ordinary people caught in political events. Using a documentary approach and filming with minimum resources in the streets and apartments of Rome, Rossellini achieved an immediacy and intensity that audiences had never previously witnessed. Two of the few professionals in the cast, Magnani and Fabrizzi, give extremely moving performances.

Best Film Cannes 1946

La Ronde

France 1950 97 mins bw
Sacha Gordine

d **Max Ophüls**
sc **Jacques Natanson, Max Ophüls (from Arthur Schnitzler's play)**
ph **Christian Matras**
m **Oscar Straus**

Anton Walbrook, Simone Signoret, Serge Reggiani, Daniel Gélin, Danielle Darrieux, Simone Simon, Fernand Gravey, Odette Joyeux, Jean-Louis Barrault, Isa Miranda, Gérard Philipe

Ten episodes, linked by a puppet master/narrator (Walbrook), in which the protagonists ride a sexual merry-go-round in 19th-century Vienna, with one partner always connecting to the next story eg the whore and the soldier, the soldier and the maid, the maid and the master, and so forth. Schnitzler's mordant comment on sexual mores and the illusion of love, never seems to come off in performance, emerging, for the most part, as whimsical rather than piquant. Here, Ophüls has assembled a glittering cast, and the opening credits are classy, elegant and full of promise. In the event, although wonderfully photographed with a camera that, itself, acts as a carousel, and exquisitely dressed and mounted, this exercise in artifice is a soufflé that takes a long time to rise, and is distressingly quick to collapse. Gélin, Darrieux and Miranda are outstanding and almost worth the price of admission, but it is difficult, three decades on, to appreciate the rapturous reception originally accorded to the film, including the story and screenplay prize at Venice, two Oscar nominations and the British Academy's Best Film award.

La Ronde

France 1964 110 mins col
Paris Film Production/Interopa Film(Rome)

d **Roger Vadim**
sc **Jean Anouilh**
ph **Henri Decaë**
m **Michel Magne**
Marie Dubois, Claude Giraud, Anna Karina, Jean-Claude Brialy, Jane Fonda, Maurice Ronet, Catherine Spaak, Bernard Noël, Francine Bergé, Jean Sorel

A merry-go-round of lovers, for the plot of which see Ophüls' *La Ronde*, with which comparison is inevitable. Vadim and his distinguished writer, Anouilh, have left Schnitzler even further behind than did Ophüls, updating the material to the eve of World War I, transferring the Viennese setting to Paris, bringing sexual explicitness to the bedroom(s), and substituting simplistic comedy for elegant wit. The big gain is Henri Decaë's colour and 'Scope photography, but almost everything else can be counted a loss. Catherine Spaak and Francine Bergé, midinette and actress respectively, are first-class, but Fonda is too young, Brialy too gauche and the rest simply not as good as their glittering predecessors. The general tenor of the movie is uneven, but the women, and the sets, look ravishing.

Rondo

Yugoslavia 1966 94 mins bw
Jadran Film(Zagreb)

d **Zvonimír Berković**
sc **Zvonimír Berković**
ph **Tomislav Pinter**
m **Mozart**
Stevo Zigon, Relja Basić, Milena Dravić

Fedja (Basić), a young, married man, encounters the older Mladen (Zigon) playing chess in a café and invites him home. Observed by Fedja's wife, Neda (Dravić), the two men meet regularly each week to play chess; their games echo the developing relationships as Neda grows apart from her husband and is finally seduced by Mladen. The simplicity of a synopsis gives no clue to the formal brilliance of Berković's debut film. The constantly recurring situation—the weekly chess game—undergoes subtle changes with each repetition (as do the audience's shifting sympathies), and deliberately echoes Mozart's *Rondo in A Minor* which gives this finely acted film its title.

The Roof

Il Tetto

Italy 1957 101 mins bw
Titanus/Les Films Marceau

d **Vittorio De Sica**
sc **Cesare Zavattini**
ph **Carlo Montuori**
m **Alessandro Cicognini**
Gabriella Pallotta, Giorgio Listuzzi, Gastone Renzelli, Maria Di Rollo, Giuseppe Martini

A newly-wed humble bricklayer (Listuzzi) and his bride (Pallotta) have to live with his relations in their already overcrowded quarters. A family quarrel results in his sleeping in the toolshed, while she shares with a servant-girl friend. Finally, in the course of a single night and with the help of some friends, they set about constructing a meagre dwelling that will serve as a home of their own. Apparently, by Italian law, once the roof is on a building, the occupants cannot be evicted. This fact allowed De Sica to film a race against time and the police from which he has extracted a maximum of gentle comedy, while retaining a sense of the seriousness of the young couple's plight. Unpretentious and well played, this is one of the last of the director's quality Neo-Realist films. It is no *Bicycle Thieves* or *Umberto D*, being much lighter-weight, but it manifests the same sense of compassion for the poor.

Room Upstairs, The see Martin Roumagnac

Rosa Luxemburg

W. Germany 1986 120 mins col
Bioskop Film

d **Margarethe Von Trotta**
sc **Margarethe Von Trotta**
ph **Franz Rath**
m **Nicolas Economou**
Barbara Sukowa, Daniel Olbrychski, Otto Sander, Adelheid Arndt, Jurgen Holtz, Doris Schade

Rosa Luxemburg (Sukowa), the Polish-born Jewish revolutionary, falls under the spell of activist Leo Jogiches (Olbrychski), involves herself with the German Social Democratic Party, undergoes a series of imprisonments and is murdered in January 1919 by members of the Freikorps, her body thrown into a canal. Although basing the film primarily on Rosa's letters and speeches, thus somewhat limiting the perspective, Von Trotta falls into the trap of seeing the widely influential radical from a modern feminist angle. However, the material is potent enough, and Sukowa's passionate rendition of the great speeches drives the film forward.

Best Actress (Barbara Sukowa) Cannes 1986

Rosemary see Girl Rosemarie, The

Rossetto, Il see Lipstick, The

La Roue

aka The Wheel

France 1922 144 mins (see text) bw
Pathé

d **Abel Gance**
sc **Abel Gance**
ph **L.H. Burel, Bujard, Duverger**
m **Silent**
Séverin-Mars, Ivy Close, Gabriel De Gravone

Sisif (Séverin-Mars), a railwayman, and his son (De Gravone), both fall in love with Norma (Close), with tragic results. This film was originally of epic time proportions, running for eight hours, until Gance spent several months cutting it down to the practical length of approximately 144 minutes. In the 1980s, however, Marie Epstein has come up with a restored version lasting 303 mins and it's impossible to know which version one is most likely to see. As to the film itself: its interest lies not in its cheap, melodramatic plot, but in the authentic location work in the railway milieu and Gance's innovative rapid montage techniques. The most celebrated section is a rhythmic sequence on a train as Sisif drives Norma away to the big city at full speed. Jean Cocteau pronounced that, 'There is cinema before and after *La Roue*, as there is painting before and after Picasso'.

Rouge Baiser

France 1985 112 mins col
Stephan Films

d **Vera Belmont**
sc **Vera Belmont**
ph **Ramón Suárez**
m **Jean-Marie Senia**
Charlotte Valandrey, Lambert Wilson, Marthe Keller, Laurent Terzieff, Günther Lamprecht

In Paris in 1952, 15-year-old Nadia (Valandrey), ardently championing Left-wing causes, falls for an older, cynical *Paris Match* photographer (Wilson) with a taste for decadent night life. She finds she must choose between politics and her passion for him. Belmont's semi- autobiographical film convincingly conjures up the world of Communist meetings and of the girl's Stalinist Polish-Jewish parents (Terzieff and Keller), and the atmosphere of jazz clubs in the Paris of the 1950s. But the director can't leave well alone. Each scene is invested with fussy camera movements and staccato editing, and the young heroine is not interesting enough to transcend the style.

Rouge Et Le Noir, Le see Red And The Black, The

Rough Treatment

aka Without Anaesthesia

Bez Znieczulenia

Poland 1978 131 mins col

Group X/Film Polski

d **Andrzej Wajda**
sc **Andrzej Wajda, Agnieszka Holland**
ph **Edward Klosinski**
m **Piotr Derfel, Wojciech Mlynarski**
Zbigniew Zapasiewicz, Ewa Dalkowska, Andrzej Seweryn, Krystyna Janda

A middle-aged TV personality and journalist (Zapasiewicz), returning home from yet another trip abroad, finds that his wife (Dalkowska) is leaving him for a younger man (Seweryn) whose political and cultural attitudes are diametrically opposed to his own. Wajda, in a functional and uncluttered style, charts the man's disintegration, 'without anaesthesia'. Together with *Ashes And Diamonds* and *Man Of Marble*, Wajda considers that this film most clearly mirrors the concerns and interests of the majority of Polish film audiences. The ambiguity of the characters and the understated relationship between the personal and political may make it less clear to other audiences, but the grim humour and mental agony come across.

The Round-Up

Szegénylegények

Hungary 1965 94 mins bw

Mafilm Studio IV

d **Miklós Jancsó**
sc **Gyula Hernádi**
ph **Tamás Somló**
m **Popular songs**
János Görbe, Tibor Molnár, András Kozák, Gábor Agárdy, Zoltán Latinovits

On a bleak plain, a group of peasants is rounded up by Austro-Hungarian troops, who, by means of torture, interrogations and killings, attempt to weed out the leader of a partisan group in the Kossuth revolution 20 years before in 1848. In this film, Jancsó's very personal style blossomed, giving the tracking shot a new meaning. The camera weaves in and out like an invisible observer, as groups of people split up and realign, sometimes moving with them, sometimes tracking them down and shooting them. There is little dialogue, the characters are depersonalized, the setting is timeless. The film's hypnotic beauty and the daring technique launched Jancsó as a leading director on the international scene.

Route De Corinthe, La see Road To Corinth, The

The Royal Hunt

Mrigaya

India 1976 112 mins col

Uday Bhaskar International

d **Mrinal Sen**
sc **Mrinal Sen, Mohit Chattopadhya**
ph **K.K. Mahajan**
m **Salil Chowdhury**
Mithun Chakraborty, Mamata Shankar, Robert Wright, Ann Wright, Sadhu Meher

In a remote village in British India, a curious friendship is struck up between Ghenua (Chakraborty), a young tribesman, and the English District Commissioner (Robert Wright). But when Ghenua kills the moneylender (Meher) who kidnapped his wife (Shankar) in lieu of an unpaid debt, the Englishman condemns him to death and riots ensue. Sen's first film in colour is also a return to more narrative concerns after the rigour of his agit-prop 'Calcutta Trilogy'— *Interview, Calcutta '71,* and *The Guerrilla Fighter*— though it is no less political. Based on the Santhal Revolt of 1901, it is a devastating attack on colonialism, paternalism and *bourgeois* justice. But the beautifully shot tale, drawing upon local storytelling traditions and strong on generalities, fails to penetrate beneath the surface of the characters.

Rozmarné Léto see Capricious Summer

Rue Cases Nègres see Black Shack Alley

Rue De L'Estrapade see Françoise Steps Out

The Rules Of The Game

La Règle Du Jeu

France 1939 113 mins bw
La Nouvelle Edition Française

d **Jean Renoir**
sc **Jean Renoir, Carl Koch**
ph **Jean Bachelet**
m **Joseph Kosma, Mozart, Monsigny, Saint-Saëns, Johann Strauss**
Marcel Dalio, Nora Gregor, Jean Renoir, Mila Parély, Julien Carette, Gaston Modot, Roland Toutain, Paulette Dubost

The Count and Countess La Chesnaye (Dalio and Gregor) organize a lavish weekend party at their country château, where there are sexual tensions among the hosts, guests and servants. Renoir's most archetypal and perfect film, made on the eve of the outbreak of war, shows modern French society being disrupted from within. The structure, setting and plot was inspired by the works of Marivaux, Beaumarchais and Musset, and this dynamic juxtaposition of past, present, comedy, tragedy, melodrama, farce and realism gives the film its uniqueness. Apart from the wonderful performances, especially Renoir's own central one, there are two outstanding set pieces—the after-dinner entertainment and the rabbit shoot. It was a commercial disaster on its initial release and was cut to 85 minutes before being banned as 'too demoralizing'. It was only in 1956, when restored to its original length, that the film was acclaimed the masterpiece it undoubtedly is.

The Runaway

Atithi

India 1966 103 mins bw
New Theatres(Exhibitors)Pvt

d **Tapan Sinha**
sc **Tapan Sinha**
ph **Dilip Ranjan Mukherjee**
m **Tapan Sinha**
Partha Mukherji, Basabi Banerji, Samita Biswa, Salil Dutta, Smita Sinha, Mita Mukherji

Tarapada (Partha Mukherji) is an exceptionally engaging teenager who, to the despair of his mother and brothers, is possessed of a wanderlust which takes him on several adventures—among other things, he becomes a fairground acrobat and a musician with a group of strolling players—and finally brings him into contact with a wealthy family who take him in, educate him, and arrange for his marriage to their daughter. But that's not all... Tapan Sinha, working from a story by Rabindranath Tagore and treading territory in the tradition of Satyajit Ray, has made a leisurely, detailed film, rich in nostalgic and beautiful visual resonances, full of charm and humour.

La Rupture

(US: The Breakup)

France 1970 124 mins col
Films De La Boétie/Euro International/Cinévog

d **Claude Chabrol**
sc **Claude Chabrol**
ph **Jean Rabier**
m **Pierre Jansen**
Stéphane Audran, Jean-Claude Drouot, Michel Bouquet, Jean-Pierre Cassel, Catherine Rouvel, Jean Carmet, Annie Cordy

When a man on LSD (Drouot) attacks his wife (Audran) and child, she retaliates and he ends up in hospital. Wanting to gain custody of the child, her father-in-law (Bouquet) hires a seedy detective (Cassel) to spy on her activities. Chabrol's terse and suspenseful style works to great advantage in this neat thriller based on a Charlotte Armstrong novel. *Bourgeois* evil is well represented by Bouquet, while Audran is at her best as an innocent woman fighting to keep her son.

Rysopis see Identification Marks: None

The Sacrifice

Offret

Sweden 1986 145 mins col/bw
Swedish Film Institute/SVT2/Film Four International/Argos/Sandrew/Josephson and Nykvist

d **Andrei Tarkovsky**
sc **Andrei Tarkovsky**
ph **Sven Nykvist**
m **Bach, Swedish and Japanese folk music**
Erland Josephson, Susan Fleetwood, Allan Edwall, Valérie Mairesse, Sven Wollter, Gudrún Gísladóttir

At the start of a nuclear war, a distinguished writer (Josephson), isolated on a Swedish island with his wife (Fleetwood), two small children and friends, makes a pact with God that he will renounce his family, self and possessions if the world is allowed to return to normal. The opening six-minute take of a man and child planting a tree prepares the audience to be patient. By the time the film reaches its brilliant climax—an unbroken 10-minute take of a burning house seen from a distantly-placed camera, many might have lost that patience. In between, the mixture of Swedish and Russian post-nuclear *angst* is heavy going, despite the mastery of the camerawork and some impressive set pieces. It was Tarkovsky's final film. He died of cancer in 1987, at the age of 54.

Special Jury Prize Cannes 1986

Saiehaien Bolan De Bad see Tall Shadows Of The Wind

Saikaku Ichidai Onna see Life Of O-Haru, The

Salaire De La Peur, Le see Wages Of Fear, The

The Salamander

La Salamandre

Switzerland 1971 129 mins bw
Svociné

d **Alain Tanner**
sc **John Berger, Alain Tanner**
ph **Renato Berta**
m **Patrick Moraz**
Jean Luc Bideau, Jacques Denis, Bulle Ogier

A novelist and a journalist constantly interview a working-class girl suspected of shooting her guardian. This wordy, worthy study of a non- conformist seen from different angles appealed greatly to the conformist population of Switzerland who made the film into one of the country's first native box-office hits. It also enjoyed a certain success elsewhere, awakening the world to the existence of Swiss cinema. Bulle Ogier, as the focus of the investigation, helps flesh out Berger and Tanner's rather theoretical character.

Salamandre, La see Salamander, The

Sallah

Israel 1964 105 mins bw
Sallah Ltd(Tel Aviv)

d **Ephraim Kishon**
sc **Ephraim Kishon**
ph **Floyd Crosby**
m **Yohanan Zarai**
Haym Topol, Geula Noni, Gila Almagor, Arik Einstein, Esther Greenberg, Shraga Friedman, Shaika Levy

Sallah, a likeable, ebullient but bone-idle

Oriental Jew, arrives in Israel with his wife and seven children in 1948. The family finds itself housed unhappily in a transit camp near the local kibbutz, and when Sallah's son (Levi) and daughter (Noni) each fall in love with a kibbutz resident, dowry difficulties result. Managing to lose all the jobs he gets, Sallah finally solves the family's problems by devious cunning. A rough-hewn, folksy, syrupy tale which tries for satire, and in one of its best scenes —some American tourists come to check on 'their' trees being planted—succeeds. The leading man, who would drop his first name to become internationally known as Topol, displays the charismatic energy that would bring him stardom (in *Fiddler On The Roof*), but is hammy in his efforts to appear at least 25 years older than he actually was. As a glimpse of the then newly created State of Israel, this early Menachem 'Cannon' Golan production is not without interest but, overall, it's naive and rambling.

Salo O Le Centiventi Giornate Di Sodoma see Salo Or The 120 Days Of Sodom

---

Salo Or The 120 Days Of Sodom
Salo O Le Centiventi Giornate Di Sodoma

Italy 1975 117 mins col
PEA/UA

d **Pier Paolo Pasolini**
sc **Sergio Citti**
ph **Tonino Delli Colli**
m **Ennio Morricone**
Paolo Bonacelli, Giorgio Cataldi, Umberto Paolo Quintavalle, Caterina Boratto, Elsa De Giorgi, Hélène Surgère

During the days of Mussolini's Italy, in a vast mansion, a party of Fascists have rounded up a group of attractive young people to satisfy their depraved desires. Pasolini's last film before he was murdered, is an astute updating of the Marquis De Sade's novel—'nothing more than a cinematic transposition,' the director claimed. An almost unbearable film to watch (if it weren't there'd be something wrong with both spectator and picture), it never sets out to titillate, neither does it relish its horrors while clinically exposing the exploitation of human beings by their fellow men. The last 10 minutes of executions are among the most revolting, memorable and beautiful (the camerawork, the music, the poignancy) in all cinema.

Salto Nel Vuoto see Leap Into The Void

Salut L'Artiste

France 1973 96 mins col
Gaumont/Productions De La Guéville Euro International

d **Yves Robert**
sc **Jean-Loup Dabadie**
ph **Jean Penzer**
m **Vladimir Cosma**
Marcello Mastroianni, Françoise Fabian, Jean Rochefort, Carla Gravina

Nicholas (Mastroianni), a bit part actor in plays, films and commercials, is separated from his wife (Gravina) and two children. He lives with his jealous mistress (Fabian), but when she leaves him, he tries to return to his wife, now pregnant by another man. Robert's bitter-sweet comedy, revealing the less glamorous side of show business, takes its tone from Mastroianni's amusing and melancholy performance. Sentimentalized though the character is—and actor-director Robert's view of the acting profession—there are enough sardonic sequences to balance it. Jean Rochefort as Nicholas's friend and fellow actor gives good support, and the women do their best with their underwritten roles of wife and mistress. The bit part players aren't bad either.

Salvatore Giuliano

Italy 1961 125 mins bw
Lux/Vides/Galatea

d **Francesco Rosi**
sc **Francesco Rosi, Suso Cecchi D'Amico, Enzo Provenzale, Franco Solinas**
ph **Gianni Di Venanzo**
m **Piero Piccioni**
Frank Wolff, Salvo Randone, Federico Zardi, Pietro Cammarata (Salvatore), Fernando Cicero

The true story of how a Sicilian outlaw, whose

bullet-ridden body was found in a courtyard on 5 July, 1950, had risen to become a Mafia boss. Filmed in the heart of Mafia country, with a mixed cast of amateur and professional actors, it was the first of Rosi's 'reconstructed documentaries'. Using a probing camera, flashbacks and interviews, he builds an intricate, sometimes obscure, maze of facts in an objective, uncompromising manner. The film was instrumental in getting the government in Palermo to set up an inquiry into Mafia activities. Michael Cimino remade it in 1987 as *The Sicilian*.

Best Director Berlin 1962

Samma No Aji see Autumn Afternoon, An

Samo Jednom Se Ljubi see You Only Love Once

Samourai, Le see Samurai, The

Samurai

Miyamoto Musashi

Japan 1954-1955 92 mins (Part I), 104 mins (Part II), 105 mins (Part III) col
Toho

d **Hiroshi Inagaki**
sc **Hiroshi Inagaki, Tokuhei Wakao**
ph **Jun Yasumoto (Parts I and II), Kazuo Yamada (Part III)**
m **Ikuma Dan**
Toshiro Mifune , Rentaro Mikuni, Karuo Yashigusa, Koji Tsurata, Sachio Sakai, Akihiko Hirata

Takezo (Mifune) joins an army, lives as an outlaw, is nearly hanged but is freed by a widow (Yashigusa) who loves him, is imprisoned in a castle, studies the ways of the sword and becomes the legendary samurai Miyamoto Musashi. Of the 100 or so films turned out by Inagaki, (mostly *jidai-geki* or period pictures) only a few have reached the West. This most ambitious and renowned of his works (a colour remake of his 1941 trilogy of the same name) came in on the first wave of Japanese samurai films to leave the country after the war. Much of the action is splendidly staged and impressive looking, but the style is slow and the spiritual quest for the Way may seem rather simplistic. It was some years before Western audiences could compare such epics with the masterpieces of Mizoguchi. It won an honorary Oscar as Best Foreign Film in 1955 (competitive Foreign Oscars were not instituted by the Academy until 1956, when *La Strada* was the first winner).

The Samurai

Le Samourai

France 1967 95 mins col
Filmel/CICC/Fida

d **Jean-Pierre Melville**
sc **Jean-Pierre Melville, Georges Pellegrin**
ph **Henri Decaë**
m **François De Roubaix**
Alain Delon, François Périer, Nathalie Delon, Cathy Rosier, Jacques Le Roy

A hired killer (Alain Delon) goes about his fatal business with a watertight alibi, but makes the mistake of falling in love with a girl (Rosier) who inadvertently betrays him. With little dialogue, muted colours, a meticulous eye for atmospheric detail—the killer's dingy room, the chromium night club, the Paris Métro—Melville reached the peak of his romantic and ritualistic gangster movies. Alain Delon's expressionless but riveting performance is the focus of each formal scene.

Sandakan-8

Sandakan Hachiban Shokan: Bokyo

Japan 1975 120 mins col
Toho

d **Kei Kumai**
sc **Kei Kumai, Sakae Hirosawa**
ph **Mitsuji Kaneo**
m **Akira Ifukube**
Kinuyo Tanaka (Saki as old woman), Yoko Takahashi (Saki as young woman), Komaki Kurihara, Eitaro Ozawa

This impressive Oscar-nominated film on the exploitation of women is told in the framework of an old woman telling her story to a woman journalist (Kurihara). Sandakan-8 is the brothel in Borneo where the young Saki works so that she can send money back to her relatives in Japan. After many years and much hardship, she marries and has a son. She now lives as a poor widow in Japan. The flashback within a flashback technique, and the juxtaposition with modern Japan allows Kumai, one of the most political of the younger Japanese directors, to set the story in context and gives ideological reasons for Saki's suffering. More intellectually than emotionally involving, the film has the advantage of Tanaka, perhaps Japan's greatest screen actress, in the central role.

Best Actress (Kinuyo Tanaka) Berlin 1975

Sandakan Hachiban Shokan: Bokyo see Sandakan-8

Sandra see Of A Thousand Delights

Sang Des Bêtes, Le see Blood Of The Beasts

Sang D'Un Poète, Le see Blood Of The Poet, The

Sangen Om Den Røde Rubin see Song Of The Red Ruby, The

Sanjuro

Tsubaki Sanjuro

Japan 1962 96 mins bw
Toho

d **Akira Kurosawa**
sc **Akira Kurosawa, Ryuzu Kikushima, Hideo Oguni**
ph **Fukuzo Koizumi, Kozo Saito**
m **Masaru Sato**
Toshiro Mifune, Tatsuya Nakadai, Masao Shimizu, Yunosuke Ito, Takako Irie

Sanjuro (Mifune), an unwashed, lonely wandering samurai, joins up with eight young warriors to fight corruption and treachery, and rescue a kidnapped chancellor from a wicked war lord. Virtually a sequel to the previous year's *Yojimbo* (on which *A Fistful Of Dollars* was based), this Eastern-Western is the nearest Kurosawa came to spoofing the samurai genre. Apart from the humour, there is plenty of sparkling sword-play and an exciting final duel ending with a fountain of gushing blood.

Sans Famille see Adventures of Rémi, The

Sanshiro Sugata see Judo Saga

Sansho Dayu see Sansho The Bailiff

Sansho The Bailiff

Sansho Dayu

Japan 1954 125 mins bw
Daiei

d **Kenji Mizoguchi**
sc **Yahiro Fuji, Yoshikata Yoda**
ph **Kazuo Miyagawa**
m **Fumio Hayasaka, Kanahichi Odera, Tamekichi Mochizuki**
Kinuyo Tanaka, Yoshiaki Hanayagi, Kyoko Kagawa, Masao Shimizu, Eitaro Shindo, Akitare Kawano

The son (Hanayagi) and daughter (Kagawa) of a noble family in feudal Japan are kidnapped and sold as slaves to a tyrannical bailiff (Shindo). Years later, the son escapes and is reunited with his mother (Tanaka), now blind, crippled and living in abject poverty. Set in a barbaric period, authentically re-created, Mizoguchi's sublime work transforms the ancient Japanese legend, as related by the novelist Ogai Mori, into a timeless, humanist statement of injustice and suffering. The long takes, lingering long shots and the weaving camera create an elegiac mood and a deep involvement in the unfolding tale, making it often unbearably moving and yet never sentimental. This is one of the director's most awesome achievements.

Sans Lendemain see No Tomorrow

Sans Soleil see Sunless

Sans Toit Ni Loi see Vagabonde

Santos Inocentes, Los see Holy Innocents, The

São Bernardo

Brazil 1972 110 mins col
Saga Filmes

d **Leon Hirszman**
sc **Leon Hirszman**
ph **Lauro Escorel**
m **Caetano Veloso**
Othon Bastos, Isabel Ribeiro, Nildo Parente, Vande Lacerda, Mario Lago

An old plantation owner (Bastos), who started life as a humble labourer, sits alone in his decaying mansion reflecting on his acquisition of wealth, property and a wife (Ribiero) who later committed suicide. Based on a novel by Graciliano Ramos (*Barren Lives, Memories Of Prison*), the film tries to retain the book's first person perspective, organized as it is around the old man at his desk writing and narrating. However, Hirszman has cleverly rendered a literary mode into a cinematic experience, shot with a painterly sense of colour and composition, evolving in long shots and lengthy takes. Despite its stylization and slightly hermetic atmosphere, the military dictatorship in Brazil still saw it as a criticism of the regime and delayed its release for seven months—enough time to bankrupt the independent company that financed it.

The Saragossa Manuscript

Rekopis Znaleziony W Saragossie

Poland 1964 175 mins bw
Kamera Film Unit/Film Polski

d **Wojciech Has**
sc **Tadeusz Kwiatkowski**
ph **Mieczyslaw Jahoda**
m **Krzysztof Penderecki**
Zbigniew Cybulski, Iga Cembrzynska, Joanna Jedryka, Slawomir Linder

Early in the 19th century, a Belgian army officer (Cybulski) travelling to Madrid meets two beautiful princesses who send him on a fantastic journey to prove himself worthy of them. Probably the Chinese-box effect (a story within a story within a story) worked better in the 1813 Polish novel written in French by Jan Potocki, who thereafter committed suicide. However, the adept use of the wide screen, and the amiable performance by Cybulski, looking rather like Bob Hope on the road to somewhere or other, made this ambitious undertaking watchable.

Sarajevo

(US: Mayerling To Sarajevo)

De Mayerling À Sarajevo

France 1940 89 mins bw
B.U.P. Française

d **Max Ophüls**
sc **Kurt Alexander**
ph **Curt Courant, Otto Heller**
m **Oscar Straus**
Edwige Feuillère, John Lodge, Aimé Clariond, Jean Worms, Gabrielle Dorziat, Aimos

A morganatic marriage takes place between the Countess Sophie (Feuillère) and the Archduke Franz-Ferdinand (Lodge), despite opposition from the Austro-Hungarian court. They lead a happy and uneventful married life until their assassination in Sarajevo that led to the outbreak of World War I. Ophüls' last completed film before his departure for the USA (he had begun *L'École Des Femmes*) found him relishing the sort of thing he did best—casting an ironic eye on the extravagances and absurdities of the aristocracy and portraying a bitter-sweet romance against a background of operas, balls, and rides through the woods. However, the film has rather a jaded air about it, and neither Feuillère nor Lodge (rhymes with stodge) are at ease, but Dorziat as the Archduchess Maria Theresa reigns supreme.

Sarraounia

Burkino Faso 1986 121 mins col
Films Soleil Ô

d **Med Hondo**
sc **Med Hondo, Abdoulaye Mamani**
ph **Guy Famechon**
m **Pierre Akendengué, Abdoulaye Cissé, Issouf Compaore**
Aï Keïta, Jean-Roger Milo, Féodor Atkine, Jean Edmond, Roger Mirmont, Aboubacar Traoré, Tidjani Ouedraogo

Sarraounia (Keïta), Queen of the Aznas of Lugu and well-schooled in the arts of herbalism and warfare, leads her people to victory against a neighbouring tribe. However, she loses her valued general and former lover, Baka (Traoré), who is jealous of the poet-musician with whom she is involved. Now the Queen must defend her territory against the advancing French army, led by Captain Voulet (Milo), as well as combat the hostility of certain neighbouring tribes who consider her a 'witch and an infidel'. Med Hondo's fluid and visually striking film, with its echoes of the classic Japanese cinema in its treatment of tradition and custom, is a jewel in the expanding crown of Third World cinema. The story, which can be enjoyed at the level of a superior war epic, unfolds on a foundation of strong themes which juxtapose resistance and resignation, the colonial expansionist oppression against the contradictions in tribal society, the differing roles and attitudes between men and women in the African tribes. Sarraounia herself, played with awe-inspiring dignity and presence, is a symbol of courage.

Sasòbtsom I En Spegel see Through A Glass Darkly

Satansbraten see Satan's Brew

Satan's Brew

Satansbraten

W. Germany 1976 100 mins col
Albatros/Trio

d **Rainer Werner Fassbinder**
sc **Rainer Werner Fassbinder**
ph **Michael Ballhaus, Jürgen Jürgens**
m **Peer Raben**
Kurt Raab, Margit Carstensen, Helen Vita, Volker Spengler, Ingrid Caven, Y Sa Lo

A written-out poet (Raab) murders his mistress, then plagiarizes and takes on the identity of the symbolist poet Stefan George, even down to his idol's homosexual tastes. The title well describes this diabolical mixture of the Theatre of the Absurd, Hollywood screwball comedy, German Expressionism and Fassbinder's own sexual politics. It is all rather difficult to swallow, but there is some amusement to be had in the excess, and Raab and company hold the attention.

Satyricon see Fellini Satyricon

Sauvage, Le see Savage, The

The Savage

(US: Lovers Like Us)

Le Sauvage

France 1978 110 mins col
Lira/PAI

d **Jean-Paul Rappeneau**
sc **Jean-Paul and Elizabeth Rappeneau, Jean-Loup Dabadie**
ph **Pierre Lhomme**
m **Michel Legrand**
Yves Montand, Catherine Deneuve, Luigi Vannucchi, Dana Wynter, Tony Roberts

A businessman (Montand), who is fleeing from his wife (Wynter), ends up on a small tropical South American island alone with a runaway heiress (Deneuve). A strained French attempt to make a romantic comedy on the lines of those made in Hollywood in the 1930s. Despite their attractiveness and talent, Montand and Deneuve are not Cary Grant and Carole Lombard but, even so, they help to make it reasonable escapist fare.

Savage Princess see Aan

Sawdust And Tinsel

aka The Naked Night

Gycklarnas Afton

Sweden 1953 95 mins bw
Sandrew/Svensk Filmindustri

d **Ingmar Bergman**
sc **Ingmar Bergman**
ph **Sven Nykvist, Hilding Bladh**
m **Karl-Birger Blomdahl**
Harriet Andersson, Åke Grönberg, Hasse Ekman, Anders Ek, Annika Tretow, Gudrun Brost

The owner and ring master (Grönberg) of a circus troupe passing through a provincial town, tries to make up with his wife (Tretow) who left him years before, and has his jealousy aroused when his mistress (Andersson) is seduced by a suave actor

(Ekman). Reviled by both Swedish and foreign critics at the time, the film is now seen as a *tour de force*, a landmark in Bergman's *oeuvre*. Perhaps the Baroque style is rather too self-conscious, purposefully based on the Expressionism of German silent cinema (particularly the 1925 *Variety* with Emil Jannings), but the technique is masterful. The silent dream sequence in which the clown (Ek) is humiliated by his wife (Brost), is one of the director's most brilliant moments.

Sayat Nova see Colour Of Pomegranates, The

Scandal

Shuban

Japan 1950 105 mins bw
Shochiku

d **Akira Kurosawa**
sc **Akira Kurosawa, Ryuzo Kikushima**
ph **Toshio Ubukata**
m **Fumio Hayasaka**
Toshiro Mifune, Yoshiko Yamaguchi, Takashi Shimura

A handsome young artist (Mifune) and a beautiful concert singer (Yamaguchi) become the innocent victims of a libellous article in a scandal magazine. He decides to sue but, being a soft touch, hires a questionable lawyer (Shimura) because the man's small daughter has TB. Made just before *Rashomon*, which established his international reputation, but only released in the West 30 years later, this is a fascinating movie for Kurosawa collectors. Borrowing, as he frequently has, from the American model, the director has made, at one level, a soap opera from which every last tear is shamelessly wrung by his accomplished cast. Look more closely, however, and you'll detect a caustic parody of the genre it appears to ape and a satire on the Japanese willingness to accept the alien culture thrust upon them by America. All the iconography is there, from the hero's motorbike, to the elaborately decorated Christmas tree the lovers take the dying child, and Yamaguchi warbles a collection of Western songs, including 'Auld Lang Syne' and 'Silent Night' (in Japanese).

Scandale, Le see Champagne Murders, The

The Scandalous Adventures Of Buraikan

Buraikan

Japan 1970 104 mins col
Ninjin Club/Toho

d **Masahiro Shinoda**
sc **Shuji Terayama**
ph **Kozo Okazaki**
m **Masaru Sato**
Tatsuya Nakadai, Tetsuro Tamba, Shima Iwashita, Suisen Ichikawa, Shoichi Ozawa

In 1842, in Tokyo's pleasure district of Edo, the lives of three people cross: a good-for-nothing layabout (Nakadai) who dreams of becoming a Kabuki actor, a man (Ozawa) who has left his wife and child and the shogun's tea master (Tamba), who is really the notorious outlaw Buraikan. Shinoda and Terayama (a year before his first feature as director) have plainly made a political parallel between the Tempo Reformation, when the long established shogunate was threatened by rebellion, and the student movements of the 1960s. This is done in a boisterous, erotic and blackly humorous manner, aided by wide screen, lavish colour, and an anachronistic jazz score, capturing some of the subversive spirit of the earliest Kabuki.

Scandals of Clochemerle, The see Clochemerle

Scarlet And Black see Red And The Black, The

The Scarlet Letter

Der Scharlachrote Buchstabe

W. Germany 1972 89 mins col
Filmverlag Der Autoren/WDR/Elias Querejeta (Madrid)

d **Wim Wenders**
sc **Wim Wenders, Bernardo Fernández**
ph **Robby Müller**
m **Jürgen Knieper**

Senta Berger, Hans Christian Blech, Lou Castel, Yelena Samarina, Yella Rottländer

When Dr Roger Prynne (Blech) arrives in New England after two years of captivity by Indians, he finds that his wife Hester (Berger) is the object of public scorn, forced to display a scarlet letter 'A' for adulteress on her dress. Prynne, who changes his name, becomes obsessed with proving that the Reverend Arthur Dimmesdale (Castel) is the father of his wife's child (Rottländer). Wenders' version of Nathaniel Hawthorne's classic was not as authentic as the director had wished. Budget limitations forced him to film in Spain with rather artificial New England sets, Senta Berger was not his choice for the lead and he was asked to truncate his extended takes and go for a snappier editing style. These retrictions tell on the finished product, and yet there is a fascination in the way Wenders has brought a modern sensibility to bear on the puritanism in the novel. Still, Victor Sjöström's silent 1926 version, starring Lillian Gish, gives more satisfaction.

Sceicco Bianco, Lo see White Sheik, The

Scener Ur Ett Aktenskap see Scenes From A Marriage

Scenes From A Marriage

Scener Ur Ett Aktenskap

Sweden 1974 168 mins col
Cinematograph AB Sweden

d **Ingmar Bergman**
sc **Ingmar Bergman**
ph **Sven Nykvist**
Liv Ullmann, Erland Josephson, Bibi Andersson, Jan Malmsjö, Gunnel Lindblom

Marianne (Ullmann) has to cope with the infidelity of her husband (Josephson) who is seriously involved with a younger woman (Andersson). The trauma of a beleaguered marriage is played largely in close-up, creating a claustrophobic, hermetically sealed atmosphere, while the terse exchanges and bitter silences convey a sense of bleak aridity. Originally conceived as a six-part television series running 300 minutes (and subsequently shown in that form and medium), Bergman himself edited the film for cinematic release. It is undeniably absorbing, with the hand of the director everywhere evident, especially in the use of his uniquely accomplished actresses, but it is, finally, sterile and unrewarding.

Scent Of A Woman

Profumo Di Donna

Italy 1974 103 mins col
Dean

d **Dino Risi**
sc **Dino Risi, Ruggero Maccari**
ph **Claudio Cirillo**
m **Armando Trovaioli**
Vittorio Gassman, Alessandro Momo, Agostina Belli, Moira Orsei

A blind, one-armed ex-Army captain (Gassman), who is a proud and arrogant ladies' man, travels to Naples with a young army cadet (Momo) who acts as his eyes, describing beautiful women, but the officer cannot declare his love for the woman (Belli) whose portrait he keeps beside a pistol. For a great deal of the film there is a sharp serio-comic interplay between the aristocratic soldier and his naive guide, but sentimentality, melodrama and a dubious attitude to women encroach upon the latter part of the plot.

Best Actor (Vittorio Gassman) Cannes 1975

Scharlachrote Buchstabe, Der see Scarlet Letter, The

Schaste see Happiness

Schatten see Warning Shadows

Schaukel, Die see Swing, The

Scherben see Shattered

Schloss Vogelöd see Haunted Castle, The

Schlussakkord see Final Chord

Le Schpountz
(US: Heartbeat)
France 1938 140 mins bw
Marcel Pagnol

d **Marcel Pagnol**
sc **Marcel Pagnol**
ph **Willy**
m **Casimir Oberfeld**
Fernandel, Charpin, Odette Roger, Jean Castan, Orane Demazis, Léon Bélières, Maupi

A film-fan grocer (Fernandel) is a victim of a practical joke played on him by a film crew touring his district of Provence. He arrives at the studio in Paris on their false promises, but reveals himself as a successful comic. The title of this ironic, very amusing, self-mocking satire is Slav argot used by the photographer Willy (Faktorovitch) meaning a simple or screwy person. Fernandel is wonderfully 'Schpountzy', surrounded by a rich gathering of movie characters. When accusations of anti-Semitism were levelled at Pagnol for his depiction of the producer Meyerboom (Bélières), he cut a whole scene from the film, which had already been in the cinemas for a few weeks.

Schweizermacher, Die see Swissmakers, The

Schwestern Oder Die Balance Des Glücks see Sisters Or The Balance Of Happiness

Sciuscia see Shoeshine

The Scoundrel
Les Mariés De L'An Deux
France 1971 100 mins col
Gaumont International(Paris)/Rizzoli Film(Rome)/ Bucuresti Film(Bucharest)

d **Jean-Paul Rappeneau**
sc **Jean-Paul Rappeneau, Daniel Boulanger**
ph **Claude Renoir**
m **Michel Legrand**
Jean-Paul Belmondo, Marlène Jobert, Michel Auclair, Sami Frey, Laura Antonelli, Pierre Brasseur

Nicolas Philibert (Belmondo), an 18th-century anti-Royalist who fled to America, returns to France some years later to seek out his wife Charlotte (Jobert) and obtain a divorce. He finds her living with a Marquis (Frey) while being wooed by a Prince (Auclair) but, after numerous complications and adventures, she and Nicolas are reunited and live happily as titled aristocrats of Napoleon's Empire. Rappenau's swashbuckling comedy, very Gallic, very tongue-in-cheek, is loaded with high-spirited action, charm and plenty of laughs. It is also polished in execution with an appealing performance by Belmondo. The film even survives the American dubbed version.

Scream From Silence, A see Primal Fear

The Seagull
Chaika
USSR 1971 98 mins col
Mosfilm

d **Yuli Karasik**
sc **Yuli Karasik, from the play by Anton Chekhov**
ph **Mikhail Suslov**
m **A. Schnitke**
Ludmila Savelyeva, Vladimir Tchetverikov, Alla Demidova, Yuri Yakovlev, Nikolai Plotnikov, Valentina Telichkina, Armen Djigarkhanyan, Sofia Pavlova, S. Torchachevsky

Guests at a country house party include the actress Arkadina (Demidova) and her lover Trigorin (Yakovlev), a famous writer. They gather to watch a play by Arkadina's son, Konstantin (Tchetverikov), starring Nina (Savelyeva) whom Konstantin loves, but who loves Trigorin. Three years later, the unhappy group reassembles, its members having undergone certain changes in their lives. A synopsis cannot do justice to the complexities and subtleties of Chekhov's famous play. Alas, neither does this film. Karasik directs with respectful restraint, utilizing a skilful ensemble cast, but his tone is so hushed and his pace so uniform as to deprive the piece of its essential drama. There are one or two moments when he frees himself to take advantage of the medium, thus demonstrating the missed opportunities.

The Seashell And The Clergyman

La Coquille Et Le Clergyman

France 1928 45 mins bw
Germaine Dulac

d **Germaine Dulac**
sc **Antonin Artaud**
ph **Paul Guichard**
m **Silent**
Alex Allin, Gerica Athanasiou, Bataille

The dream imagery of a frustrated celibate clergyman (Allin). 'This film is so cryptic as to be almost meaningless. If there is a meaning, it is doubtless objectionable,' commented the British censor on the film's being refused a certificate. It is now considered to be the first surrealist film, just as Dulac's *The Smiling Madame Beudet* (1923), is recognized as the first feminist film. Artaud had intended to direct it and play the lead, but he later withdrew and repudiated it. It would have been fascinating to see how he would have managed the automatic associations and the projection of his hypnotic personality into the role of the priest, but he might not have had the extraordinary technical skill that Dulac brought to this pioneering *avant-garde* classic.

The Season For Love

La Morte-Saison Des Amours

France 1960 100 mins bw
Jad Film/Europa/Beaux Arts/Gaston Hakim

d **Pierre Kast**
sc **Pierre Kast, Alain Aptekman**
ph **Sacha Vierny**
m **Georges Delerue**
Daniel Gélin, Françoise Arnoul, Pierre Vaneck, Françoise Prévost

Sylvain (Vaneck), a writer, and his young wife Geneviève (Arnoul) leave Paris to seek idyllic fulfilment in the (actual) beautiful village of La Saline Des Chaux. Once there, Sylvain's creativity dries up and Geneviève, feeling betrayed, becomes involved with the local lord of the manor (Gélin), a libertine who falls genuinely in love with her, while Sylvain has an affair with his wife (Prévost). Kast has made a penetratingly observant film about crisis of self and crisis in relationships, to which he brings the surface glitter of a comedy of manners while allowing a compassionate examination of his characters to emerge. The cast is skilful and polished, and the haunting locations are exquisitely caught by Vierny's camera.

Sea, The see Mare, Il

The Second Awakening Of Christa Klages

Das Zweite Erwachen Der Christa Klages

W. Germany 1977 93 mins col
Bioskop-Film/West Deutsches Rundfunk

d **Margarethe Von Trotta**
sc **Margarethe Von Trotta, Luise Francia**
ph **Franz Rath**
m **Klaus Doldinger**
Tina Engel, Sylvia Reize, Katharina Thalbach, Marius Müller-Westernhagen, Peter Schneider

Christa Klages (Engel), deeply comitted to the progressive nursery she opened three years previously and which is now threatened by lack of funds, robs a bank, together with her lover Werner (Müller-Westernhagen). This desperate act turns them into fugitives, leads to Werner's violent death and drives Christa temporarily out of the country with her friend Ingrid (Reize) who has harboured her. The first of Von Trotta's non-collaborative works but, confusingly, not shown abroad until after her maturer works, this film presages all the themes to come: the limitations of the German *bourgeoisie*, the struggles of the socially aware, the bonding of women and the catastrophic consequences of misguided acts. It is a film which conjoins despair with comic irony, and is jam-packed with plot, within which is buried the director's characteristic needle-sharp observation.

Second Breath

Le Deuxième Souffle

France 1966 150 mins bw
Productions Montaigne

d **Jean-Pierre Melville**
sc **Jean-Pierre Melville**

ph **Marcel Combes**
m **Bernard Gérard**
Lino Ventura, Paul Meurisse, Raymond Pellegrin, Christine Fabrega, Marcel Bozzufi

A gangster (Ventura) breaks out of jail and joins a gang that carries out a daring robbery outside Marseilles, but he is trapped by a police inspector (Meurisse) into betraying his partners in crime and his honour. The key to Melville's attitude to his gangster heroes lies in a reference to the character played by Ventura: 'He is a danger to society, but he has preserved a sort of purity'. Underneath the surface thrills of the realistic crime movie is a romantic meditation on the nature of friendship and betrayal told in images of almost Bressonian restraint. (The pre-credit sequence is a homage to *A Man Escaped*.) But perhaps it was the exciting execution of the hold-up on a winding mountain road and the power of the trench-coated figure of Ventura that were major factors in making it Melville's biggest box-office success.

Second Chance
Si C'Était À Refaire
France 1976 99 mins col
Les Films 13

d **Claude Lelouch**
sc **Claude Lelouch**
ph **Jacques Lefrançois**
m **Francis Lai, Pierre Barouh**
Catherine Deneuve, Anouk Aimée, Charles Denner, Francis Huster, Jean-Jacques Briot

Catherine (Deneuve) has a baby son, whom she calls Simon, while she is in prison on a charge of being an accessory to murder. On her release 18 years later she and Simon (Briot) are reunited, he falls in love with her friend from the prison (Aimée), and engineers a happy match for his mother with his history teacher. Typical Lelouch tosh, redolent with 'meaningful' musings which lead nowhere, woven into a woman's magazine story filmed with a largesse of gloss and glamour.

The Secret
Le Secret
France 1974 102 mins col
President/Euro International

d **Robert Enrico**
sc **Pascal Jardin**
ph **Etienne Becker**
m **Ennio Morricone**
Jean-Louis Trintignant, Marlène Jobert, Philippe Noiret, Jean-François Adam, Solange Pradel

Escaping from prison, David (Trintignant) goes on the run and finds refuge with Thomas and Julia (Noiret and Jobert), a couple living in seclusion in the mountains. He tells them that he has been tortured in a mysterious asylum and is under threat of death because he is in possession of a state secret. Thomas believes him, Julia has her doubts, and the audience is kept in suspense wondering whether he is a dangerous maniac or a victim of ruthless chicanery. This thriller, with its political overtones, may occasionally strain credibility, but it's full of incident and surprise, is well acted, and ties up its sinister loose ends with satisfying clarity.

Secret, Le see Secret, The

Secret Game, The see Forbidden Games

Secrets Of A Soul
Geheimnisse Einer Seele
Germany 1926 95 mins bw
UFA/Hans Neumann

d **G.W. Pabst**
sc **G.W. Pabst, Hans Neumann, Colin Ross**
ph **Guido Seeber, Kurt Oertel, Walter Robert Lach**
m **Silent**
Werner Krauss, Jack Trevor, Ruth Weyher, Pawel Pawlow

A professor (Krauss) consults a psychoanalyst (Pawlow) because he has nightmares whenever he sees or thinks of a knife, a phobia which leads to an attempt to stab his wife (Weyher). The film's reputation rests not on its uninteresting surface domestic drama, but on the stunning depiction of the dreams told to the analyst, fine examples of Expressionist cinema. They contain multi-layer superimpositions, cut-out figures against blank backgrounds, and menacing images of razors and knives. Werner Krauss, the face of German Expressionism, gives another powerful performance. Although Pabst was assisted in the script by two of Freud's collaborators, the Viennese doctor repudiated the final film.

Secrets Of Women see Waiting Women

Section Spéciale

aka Special Section

France 1975 118 mins col

Reggane Films/Les Productions Artistes Associés (Paris)/Goriz Films(Rome)/Janus Film(Frankfurt)

d **Costa-Gavras**
sc **Jorge Semprun**
ph **Andreas Winding**
m **Eric De Marsan, Takis**

Louis Seigner, Michel Lonsdale, Ivo Garrani, François Maistre, Pierre Dux, Claude Piéplu, Heinz Bennent, Michel Galabru, Jacques Rispal, Julien Bertheau

When a group of young Communists shot a German naval officer in Paris in 1941, the Vichy government placated the Nazis by offering the execution of six Frenchmen. Costa-Gavras, continuing his interest in the poisonous effects of State complicity in the perversion of justice, records the setting up of the Special Section which was detailed to select the victims from already imprisoned Jews, Communists and anarchists, and follows the bizarre legal entanglements, compromises and protests that marked the ensuing trials. This is an unavoidably sober and salutary tale, but characterization, motivation and conflict are all rather superficial and academic, leaving one with little more than a grand display of the mechanics of power, enacted by a vast, proficient and well-directed cast.

Best Director Cannes 1975

Sedmikrásky see Daisies

Sedotta E Abbandonata see Seduced And Abandoned

Seduced And Abandoned

Sedotta E Abbandonata

Italy 1963 123 mins bw

Lux/Ultra/Vides/Lux C.C. De France

d **Pietro Germi**
sc **Pietro Germi, Luciano Vincenzoni, Age, Furio Scarpelli**
ph **Aiace Parolin**
m **Carlo Rustichelli**

Stefania Sandrelli, Aldo Puglisi, Saro Urzi, Lando Buzzanca, Leopoldo Trieste

Fifteen-year-old Agnese (Sandrelli) is seduced by her sister's fiancé (Puglisi) and becomes pregnant. His engagement is broken off, but he abandons Agnese because she is no longer a virgin. Germi's follow-up to *Divorce—Italian Style* is a somewhat frenzied farce in which genuine wit and pointed satire only occasionally surface. The director has concocted an efficient farrago of authentic Sicilian passions, but it lacks the appeal of its predecessor.

Best Actor (Saro Urzi) Cannes 1964

Seduction Of Julia, The see Adorable Julia

The Seduction Of Mimi

Mimi Metallurgico Ferito Nell'Onore

Italy 1972 120 mins col

Vera Film

d **Lina Wertmüller**
sc **Lina Wertmüller**
ph **Blasco Giurato**
m **Piero Piccioni**

Giancarlo Giannini, Mariangela Melato, Agostina Belli, Elena Fiore, Turri Ferro

Mimi (Giannini), a simple labourer in Southern Italy, finds himself caught between the local Mafia on the one hand and the Communist party on the other. All he wants is a decent living for his family and a contented personal life, but manages to sabotage himself on both counts: he offends the Mafia and has an affair with a liberated and anarchic girl (Melato), thus driving his wife into the arms of another man and himself to some grotesquely ill-judged behaviour. Cooking up her usual stew of sex and politics, Wertmüller here seasons it with humour to come up with a comment on Sicilian society that is both bitter and funny. Some sequences demonstrate the director's penchant for the erotic, but unfortunately serve to undercut the suggestion of feminist argument, and there are several longeurs. Giannini delivers a terrific performance, well matched by Melato, and by Turri Ferro, who plays six different characters—all Mafia men.

The Seedling
Ankur

India 1974 131 mins col
Blaze

d **Shyam Benegal**
sc **Shyam Benegal**
ph **Govind Nihalani, Kamath Ghanekar**
m **Vanraj Ram Mohan**
Anant Nag, Shabana Azmi, Sudhu Meher, Priya Tendulkar, Mirza Qadir Ali Baig

A servant girl (Azmi) with a deaf-mute husband (Meher) is seduced by an arrogant young man (Nag), sent by his father to manage a remote farm on the family estate. The landlord's son leaves her pregnant and beats her husband out of fear, an act which only plants the seed of revolution. This brilliantly assured feature film debut by former documentary-director Benegal was based on a story he had written when he was 16, revolving around an incident of which he had first-hand knowledge. Made in Hindi, the dominant language of Indian commercial cinema, it succeeds in being accessible to a mass audience while carrying a political message. The beautiful images contrast vividly with the exposure of the brutal feudalism still prevalent in some parts of India today.

See Here My Love
Écoute Voir...

France 1978 110 mins col
Prospectacle

d **Hugo Santiago**
sc **Claude Ollier, Hugo Santiago**
ph **Ricardo Aronovitch**
m **Edgardo Canton, Michel Portal**
Catherine Deneuve, Sami Frey, Florence Delay, Anne Parillaud, Didier Haudepin, Antoine Vitez, Gilbert Adair

A bisexual private eye (Deneuve) is hired by the mysterious owner of a château (Frey) to investigate a break-in. She discovers a strange Right-wing sect operating from the château, using a machine that interferes with radio waves to brainwash the population. The film starts out as a parody of Raymond Chandler, with a female Philip Marlowe, but gradually moves away from the thriller into more metaphysical, sexual and political preoccupations, none of which is particularly engaging. The film's quality lies in the stereo soundtrack (écoute), which contains clues to the mystery (if one cares), the photography and creative use of the 'Scope screen (voir). The ending, an expert telescoping of time and space, is merely further obfuscation.

Seemabaddha see Company Limited

See You Tomorrow
Do Widzenia Do Jutra

Poland 1960 85 mins bw
Film Polski-Kadr Film Unit

d **Janusz Morgenstern**
sc **Zbigniew Cybulski, Bogumil Kobiela, Wilhelm Mach**
ph **Jan Laskowski**
m **Krzysztof T. Komeda**
Zbigniew Cybulski, Teresa Tuszynska, Grazyna Muszynska, Jacek Fedorowicz, Roman Polanski

Jacek (Cybulski), who runs a student theatre in Gdansk, falls in love with Marguerite (Tuszynska), the daughter of a foreign diplomat. He neglects his work to court her, although they can barely communicate because of language difficulties, and she is unreceptive to the seriousness of his intentions. The slightest of interludes, this film offers a series of incidental pleasures—the sharply evoked sense of a sleepy summer, fine photography, an exuberantly youthful Polanski as one of Jacek's friends—but there's not enough material to support a full-length film.

Sehnsucht Der Veronika Voss, Die see Veronika Voss

Semaine De Vacances, Une see Week's Holiday, A

Senilità

Italy 1961 110 mins bw
Zebra (Rome)/Aera (Paris)

d **Mauro Bolognini**
sc **Mauro Bolognini, Tullio Pinelli, Goffredo Parise**
ph **Armando Nannuzzi**
m **Piero Piccioni**
Anthony Franciosa, Claudia Cardinale, Betsy Blair, Philippe Leroy, Raimondo Magni

Emilio (Franciosa), a mild-mannered, middle-aged clerk whose intellect controls his passions, lives with his lonely spinster sister, Amalia (Blair). He becomes infatuated with the beautiful but amoral Angiolina (Cardinale, sporting a Louise Brooks hair-do), who humiliates and destroys him. Based on a novel by Italo Svevo and set in a graphically well- reproduced, rain-drenched Trieste in the 1920s, Bolognini's low-keyed film accurately conveys the stultifying atmosphere of lives lived in a state of repression (Amalia) and frustration (Emilio), but finally misses the mark. The acting is not quite good enough, and there is a failure of clarity on the part of both screenplay and leading man in expressing the degree of Emilio's intellectual arrogance which reduces him to the one condition he is determined to avoid—that of emotional slavery.

Senso

aka The Wanton Contessa

Italy 1954 115 mins col
Lux

d **Luchino Visconti**
sc **Luchino Visconti, Suso Cecchi D'Amico, Giorgio Prosperi, Carl Alianello, Giorgio Bassani**
ph **G.R. Aldo, Robert Krasker**
m **Bruckner, Verdi**
Alida Valli, Farley Granger, Massimo Girotti, Heinz Moog, Rina Morelli, Christian Marquand

In 1866 in Venice, a married Italian noblewoman (Valli), working for the cause of independence, falls in love with an Austrian officer (Granger) in the army of occupation, but she denounces him for desertion after he has been unfaithful to her. Working through the conventions of Italian grand opera—the film opens sumptuously at the opera house at a performance of *Il Trovatore*—Visconti creates a lush melodramatic historical romance. Inferior to *The Leopard* (1963), the other of his films set during the Risorgimento, the colour photography is no less stunning. A cut version with dubbed dialogue by Tennessee Williams and Paul Bowles was inflicted on American audiences.

Sensualita

aka Barefoot Savage

Italy 1952 93 mins bw
Ponti/DD

d **Clemente Fracassi**
sc **Alberto Moravia, Ennio De Concini**
ph **Aldo Tonti**
m **Enzio Masetti**
Eleonora Rossi Drago, Amedeo Nazzari, Marcello Mastroianni, Francesca Liddi

Franca (Rossi Drago), a seductive Slav immigrant in Italy, is tired of working in the fields and marries the owner (Nazzari) of the farm although she actually prefers his brother (Mastroianni). Desirable as the smouldering Rossi Drago is, this steamy melodrama still leaves a lot to be desired. The hand of co-writer Moravia is sometimes in evidence, and the settings are convincing even if the plot triangle is not.

Senza Pietà see Without Pity

Seppuku see Harakiri

Septième Juré, Le see Seventh Juror, The

Sept Péchés Capitaux, Les see Seven Deadly Sins, The

Serdtze Materi see Heart Of A Mother

Seryozha see Splendid Days, The

Seven Beauties
Pasqualino Settebellezze
Italy 1975 115 mins col
Medusa

d **Lina Wertmüller**
sc **Lina Wertmüller**
ph **Tonino Delli Colli**
m **Enzo Iannacci**
Giancarlo Giannini, Fernando Rey, Shirley Stoler, Enzo Vitale, Piero Di Iorio

Pasqualino (Giannini), a small-time crook and ladykiller, lives in Naples with his mother and seven fat sisters (the 'beauties' of the title). After killing a pimp while defending the honour of the eldest of them, he is put into an insane asylum where he rapes an inmate, then joins the Italian army, deserts, is captured by the Germans and sent to a concentration camp where he seduces a large and sadistic female commandant... *The New York Times* called this extraordinary, grotesque, cacophonous comic-strip 'Miss Wertmüller's *King Kong*, her *Nashville*, her *8½*, her *Navigator*, her *City Lights*', Another—and equally just—comparison might be with the vat of excrement in which a Spanish anarchist (Rey) drowns himself.

The Seven Deadly Sins
Les Sept Péchés Capitaux
France/Italy 1952 150 mins bw
Franco London/Costellazione

d **Eduardo De Filippo, Jean Dréville, Yves Allégret, Roberto Rossellini, Carlo Rim, Claude Autant-Lara, Georges Lacombe**
sc **Charles Spaak, Carlo Rim, Pierre Bost, Jean Aurenche, Roberto Rossellini, Claude Autant-Lara**
ph **Enzo Serafin, André Thomas, Roger Hubert, Robert Le Fevre, André Bac**
m **Yves Baudrier, René Cloërec**
Eduardo De Filippo, Isa Miranda, Paolo Stoppa, Louis De Funès, Jean Richard, Françoise Rosay, Gérard Philipe, Noël-Noël, Viviane Romance, Michèle Morgan

Sketches illustrating 'Avarice and Anger', 'Sloth', 'Lust', 'Envy', 'Gluttony', 'Pride' and 'The Eighth Sin'. Gérard Philipe introduces each of the sinful tales, or collection of dirty jokes, which reveal a lot about attitudes to sex in the early 1950s. Because of its irreverence towards subjects which, at that time, were taboo in English-speaking films, it was a tremendous hit. A few of the sketches still survive in their own right, especially Rossellini's 'Lust' and Rim's 'Envy'. The latter was based on a story by Colette about a wife who was jealous of her husband's cat. The stellar cast also reaps rewards. A number of *Nouvelle Vague* directors had a go at interpreting the seven sins in a similar, multi-episode format in 1961 (see below).

The Seven Deadly Sins
Les Sept Péchés Capitaux
France 1961 113 mins bw
Franco London/Gibe/Titanus

d **Sylvain Dhomme, Eugene Ionesco, Max Douy, Edouard Molinaro, Philippe De Broca, Jacques Demy, Jean-Luc Godard, Roger Vadim, Claude Chabrol**
sc **Eugene Ionesco, Claude Mauriac, Roger Peyrefitte, Daniel Boulanger, Jacques Demy, Jean-Luc Godard, Roger Vadim, Felicien Marceau**
ph **Jean Penzer, Louis Miaille, Henri Decaë, Jean Rabier**
m **Michel Legrand, Sacha Distel, Pierre Jansen**
Marie-José Nat, Claude Brasseur, Georges Wilson, Laurent Terzieff, Jean-Louis Trintignant, Micheline Presle, Corinne Marchand, Jean-Pierre Aumont, Sami Frey, Jean-Claude Brialy, Claude Rich, Claude Berri, Eddie Constantine

'Gluttony'—a family stops to eat once too often on the way to a funeral, 'Pride'—a cheating wife finds her husband having an affair, 'Envy'—a chambermaid falls in love with a millionaire, 'Sloth'—a movie star is too lazy to undress for sex, 'Lust'—a man finds he can see through girls' clothes, 'Anger'—flies pop up in bowls of soup around town, 'Greed'—25 students pool their money to buy one of their number some time with a high-class prostitute. An inconsequential collection of modern parables, unworthy of the names involved, the best being Godard's 'Sloth'. The eighth sin was making the film in the first place.

Seven Samurai

Shichinin No Samurai

Japan 1954 200 mins bw
Toho

d **Akira Kurosawa**
sc **Shinobu Hashimoto, Hideo Oguni, Akira Kurosawa**
ph **Asaichi Nakai**
m **Fumio Hayasaka**
Takashi Shimura, Yoshio Inaba, Isao Kimura, Seiji Miyaguchi, Toshiro Mifune, Minoru Chiaki, Daisuke Kato, Keiko Tsushima, Ko Kimura, Kuniniri Kodo

A farming community of meagre resources decides to hire samurai to fight off the annual incursion of brutal bandits who steal the harvest. After many travails, they persuade one warrior (Shimura) to take it on, and he sets about recruiting his chosen minimum of six more men—with the greatest difficulty, since the job offers neither money nor glory, but only the challenge of the fight. The samurai band moves into the village with the inept and frightened inhabitants to plan their strategy, and finally routs the 40 bandits. On this simple framework, Kurosawa has constructed a superb narrative, bursting with incident that is by turns exciting, absorbing, moving and funny. Carefully and lovingly reconstructing medieval Japan, he reveals the entire spectrum of human strength and weakness with absolute clarity of vision. The warrior heroes are seen as a shabby, lonely band of outcasts, retaining dignity, courage and good humour, but no glamour. Shimura's wise leader and Mifune's half-crazed, self-appointed samurai dominate a brilliant cast, while the lighting and photography are unforgettable. The film, on which Hollywood based the Western *The Magnificent Seven* (1960), remains one of the greatest achievements in cinema history.

Seventeen

Sytten

Denmark 1965 88 mins col
Palladium

d **Annelise Meineche**
sc **Bob Ramsing**
ph **Øle Lytken**
m **Øle Hoyer**
Øle Soltøft, Ghita Norby, Hass Christensen, Øle Monty, Bodil Steen, Lise Rosendahl

In the summer of 1913, a 17-year-old schoolboy (Soltøft) loses his virginity with his pretty cousin (Norby) and learns the art of love-making from the maid (Rosendahl). This predictable, heavy-humoured piece was popular when Scandinavia still had a sexy reputation. Only 17-year-old virgins, if any still exist in the world, would find anything to entertain them in this piece.

The Seventh Juror

Le Septième Juré

France 1964 90 mins bw
Orex/Trans-Lux

d **Georges Lautner**
sc **Jacques Robert, Pierre Laroche**
ph **Maurice Fellous**
m **Jean Yatove**
Bernard Blier, Danièle Delorme, Francis Blanche, Jacques Riberolles

A middle-aged, married, and popular pillar of the community, Grégoire Duval (Blier) kills a provocative girl who spurns his advances. When her disreputable boyfriend is charged with the crime, Duval finds himself on the jury and, troubled by conscience, engineers an acquittal. Later, he confesses his guilt, but nobody will believe him. . . . Full of nice twists and turns of plot, and with a splendidly ironic ending, this makes a diverting little film for addicts of the genre, and for admirers of the excellent Blier.

The Seventh Seal

Det Sjunde Inseglet

Sweden 1957 90 mins bw
Svensk Filmindustri

d **Ingmar Bergman**
sc **Ingmar Bergman**
ph **Gunnar Fischer**
m **Erik Nordgren**
Max Von Sydow, Gunnar Björnstrand, Bengt Ekerot, Nils Poppe, Bibi Andersson

A knight (Von Sydow) returns from the Crusades to find Sweden ravaged by plague. In his search for God he meets a group of strolling players, suffering peasants and Death (Ekerot), with whom he plays a deadly game of chess. Shot in only 35 days, this powerful morality tale depicts the cruelty of medieval life—witch burning, flagellation—as well as the joys and noble aspirations of people in luminous images derived from early church paintings. Bergman's seventeenth film set him firmly in the pantheon of great directors.

Special Jury Prize Cannes 1957

Several Interviews On Personal Matters

see Interviews On Personal Problems

Sex Shop

France 1972 105 mins col
Renn Productions/Les Artistes Associés(Paris)/ P.E.A. Cinematografica(Rome)/Regina Films(Munich)

d **Claude Berri**
sc **Claude Berri**
ph **Pierre Lhomme**
m **Serge Gainsbourg**
Juliet Berto, Claude Berri, Nathalie Delon, Jacques Martin, Grégoire Aslan, Jean-Pierre Marielle, Béatrice Romand

Business is bad for Paris bookseller Claude (Berri). With an extravagant wife (Berto) and two children to support, he follows a friend's suggestion and turns the premises into a sex shop stocking erotic literature, movies and gadgets. The enterprise leads him to try and inject some experimental excitement into his marriage and complications proliferate until the police close the shop and he and his wife settle back into their comfortable routine. Berri here makes a comic excursion into fantasy and permissiveness that is harmless and also pointless. The action takes place in prettified exteriors and Art Deco interiors and is overlaid with excessively lush music, the cast lacks vitality and the director's usual commitment to subject and gift for observation are missing.

Shadowman

aka The Man Without A Face
L'Homme Sans Visage
aka Nuits Rouges

France 1974 105 mins col
Terra/SOAT

d **Georges Franju**
sc **Jacques Champreux**
ph **Guido Renzo Bertoni**
m **Georges Franju, Berlioz**
Jacques Champreux, Gayle Hunnicutt, Gert Fröbe, Josephine Chaplin, Ugo Pagliai

A sinister masked criminal attempts to mastermind the stealing of the treasure of the Knights' Templar, but he has to overcome members of the 12th-century sect that still guards it. Franju's first film for four years was a pitiful return to the shadowy serial world of his magical *Judex* (1963). However, whereas the earlier film was a remake of a Feuillade serial, this is cod Feuillade which, lacking in visual flair and atmosphere, and offering only listless performances, is diabolical in both senses.

Shadow Of Adultery

La Proie Pour L'Ombre

France 1960 99 mins bw
Marceau/Cocinor

d **Alexandre Astruc**
sc **Alexandre Astruc**
ph **Marcel Grignon**
m **Bach, Richard Cornu**
Annie Girardot, Daniel Gélin, Christian Marquand, Anne Caprile, Michèle Gerbier

The wife (Girardot) of a rich building contractor (Gélin), beginning to tire of being merely a social asset to her husband, finds an outlet by running an art gallery and taking a lover (Marquand). In the end, she sacrifices both men for her independence. White sports cars, cocktail parties, an art gallery, a recording studio, modern skyscapers, jazz and Bach on the soundtrack and quick, slick cross-cutting, give Astruc's contribution to the *Nouvelle Vague* an over-riding air of chic. The main interest of the film lies in the conflict of the woman (superbly played by Girardot) and her place in a man's world.

Shadows Of Our Forgotten Ancestors

Teni Zabytykh Predkov

USSR 1964 100 mins col
Dovzhenko Studio

d **Sergo Paradjanov**
sc **Sergo Paradjanov, Ivan Chendei**

ph **Viktor Bestayeva**
m **Y. Shorik**
Ivan Nikolaychuk, Larisa Kadochnilova, Tatiana Bestayeva, Spartak Bagashvili

In a primitive community in the Carpathian mountains at the turn of the century, a young peasant falls in love with the daughter of the man responsible for the death of his father, but marries a woman who indulges in sorcery. Paradjanov's first film to be shown in the West (UK 1968, USA 1967) revealed his remarkable talent for lyrical extravagance which reached its peak five years later with *The Colour Of Pomegranates*. Perhaps the latter story of a poet and his works lent itself better to his swirling, kaleidoscopic camera style than this rural folk tale. However, it exerts a greater fascination than most Soviet films of the period.

Shadows Of The Yoshiwara, The see Crossways

The Shame

Skammen

Sweden 1968 103 mins bw
Svensk Filmindustri

d **Ingmar Bergman**
sc **Ingmar Bergman**
ph **Sven Nykvist**
Liv Ullmann, Max Von Sydow, Gunnar Björnstrand, Birgitta Valberg, Sigge Furst

In the year 1971, on an island off an unnamed country, an apolitical couple are unwillingly caught up in, and gradually corrupted by, a bitter civil war. 'Sometimes it's like a dream. Not mine. I'm forced into someone else's dream,' says Ullmann, exactly describing the spectators' experience in entering Bergman's powerful parable illustrated in stark, realistic, black and white images, static camera movements, and sharp sounds (interestingly, there is no music, although the couple are, in fact, musicians). The two leads, especially Von Sydow's big gangling baby forced to face reality, are superb, having been allowed by the director for the first time to improvise some of their dialogue.

The Shameless Old Lady

La Vieille Dame Indigne

France 1965 94 mins bw
SPAC

d **René Allio**
sc **René Allio**
ph **Denys Clerval**
m **Jean Ferrat**
Sylvie, Malka Ribovska, Victor Lanoux, Etienne Bierry

A septuagenarian grandmother has lived a quiet life devoted to her large family but, on becoming a widow, she begins a new life by buying a *Deux Chevaux*, joining a political group, befriending a prostitute, and going on holiday, before dying happy. Sylvie, a character actress in the cinema for over 50 years, grasped her first starring role brilliantly before her death in 1970 aged 87. She is the principal reason for seeing this tale based on a story by Bertolt Brecht about his grandmother, but Allio's approach is more traditional, laying on both the charm and the message rather thickly.

The Shanghai Drama

Le Drame De Shanghai

France 1938 100 mins bw
Marc Sorkin

d **G.W. Pabst**
sc **Leo Laniz, Alexandre Arnoux**
ph **Eugen Schüfftan**
m **Ralph Erwin**
Louis Jouvet, Christiane Mardayne, Raymond Rouleau, Dorville, Elina Labourdette

A group of White Russian refugees in Shanghai, just prior to the Sino-Japanese war, are drawn into the network of a terrorist society promoting the Japanese cause. One of them, a cabaret singer (Mardayne), wants to get out because she fears for her daughter's safety which, in the end, is secured with the help of a journalist (Rouleau). More a character study than an action drama, Pabst made this stylized film during his brief sojourn in Paris before returning to work in Nazi Germany. It was vividly photographed by Schüfftan—later a leading Hollywood cinematographer and Oscar-winner for *The Hustler*—but the top-billed Jouvet was wasted in a minor role as a villainous member of a spy ring.

Shatranj Ke Khilari see Chess Players, The

Shattered

Scherben

Germany 1921 62 mins bw

Rex Film

d **Lupu Pick**
sc **Carl Mayer**
ph **Friedrich Weimann**
m **Silent**
Werner Krauss, Edith Posca, Paul Otto

A railway worker's daughter (Posca) is seduced by her father's superior. The couple are discovered by the girl's mother who, shocked and distraught, runs out into the cold and freezes to death. Further destruction comes when the girl's seducer abandons her and is killed by her father. This grim, small-scale film is one of the important works of Lupu Pick, a theatre director who rose to prominence as the chief exponent of *kammerspiel* (chamber play) on the screen—sparse, naturalistic, dealing in a minimum number of characters and observing the unities of time, place and action. After this, Pick quarrelled with Mayer whose *The Last Laugh* he was due to direct, and his work deteriorated over the years. He died of poisoning in 1931, aged 45.

Shattered see Passagers, Les

Shchors

aka Shors

USSR 1939 140 mins bw

Kiev Film Studio

d **Alexander Dovzhenko**
sc **Alexander Dovzhenko**
ph **Yuri Ekelchik**
m **Dmitri Kabalevsky**
Evgeni Samailov, Ivan Skuratov, F. Ishchenko, L. Liashenko, O. Khvylia

Under the leadership of the young Nikolai Shchors (Samailov), a regiment of pro-Bolshevik Ukrainian partisans liberate Kiev from the Germans in 1918. After reversals and victories, Shchors founds a school for Red Army officers. Stalin asked Dovzhenko to make a 'Ukrainian *Chapayev*' and the director came up with a vivid, heroic epic of the regiment in which he had served for a short while as a young man. In the tradition of 'the cult of personality' Soviet films of the period, which extolled the achievements of one man, the idealized title character is seldom off the screen. Discursive, episodic and, at times, wordily didactic, it contains some of Dovzhenko's renowned poetic imagery, and shows his ability to use characters to embody ideas without taking away their humanity.

She And He

Kanojo To Kare

Japan 1963 115 mins bw

Iwanami

d **Susumu Hani**
sc **Susumu Hani, Kunio Shimizu**
ph **Juichi Nagano**
m **Tohru Takemitsu**
Sachiko Hidari, Eiji Okada, Kikuji Yamashita, Mariko Igarashi

Fire destroys rag-pickers' shacks next to the comfortable apartment block where Naoko (Hidari) and her husband Eiichi (Okada) live. They encounter Ikona (Yamashita), one of the victims, who was once at the university with Eiichi, but now lives in poverty with his dog and a blind orphan. Fascinated by Ikona's world, Naoko encourages a friendship which only leads to terrible discord. A minutely observed, intimate and unsentimental drama of social consciousness that uncovers the spiritual wasteland of suburbia, and explores the barriers erected by differences of class, money and, above all, aspiration. Naoko (sensitively played by Hidari) is perceived as a woman drawn to wider human contact, but deprived of it by virtue of her social position.

Best Actress (Sachiko Hidari) Berlin 1964

Shestoe Iulya see Sixth Of July, The

The She-Wolf

La Lupa

Italy 1953 90 mins bw

Ponti/De Laurentiis

d **Alberto Lattuada**
sc **Alberto Lattuada, Luigi Malerba, Antonio Pietrangeli, Ivo Perilli, Ennio Concini**
ph **Aldo Tonti**
m **Felice Lattuada**
Kerima, Ettore Manni, Maj Britt, Mario Passante, Maresa Gallo

Although kept by her rich, factory-owning lover, a woman with a passionate hunger for men has an affair with a young soldier. He then falls in love with and marries her daughter. When the couple has a baby, mother moves in and seduces her son-in-law all over again, creating havoc and destruction. Another offering from the lust-obsessed end of the Neo-Realist spectrum, with Lattuada expertly capturing the heat and dust of a Sicilian village. Whether the swarthy Kerima convinces in the title role is a matter of opinion but, like several similar Italian offerings of the period, it caused some excitement at the time.

Shichinin No Samurai see Seven Samurai

Shina Ningyo see Fruits Of Passion, The

Shinel see Overcoat, The

Shin Heike Monogatari see New Tales Of The Taira Clan

Shinjo Ten No Amijima see Double Suicide

Shinjuko Dorobo Nikki see Diary Of A Shinjuku Thief

A Ship Bound For India

aka The Land Of Desire
(US: Frustration)
Skepp Till Indialand
Sweden 1947 102 mins bw
Sveriges Folkbiografer

d **Ingmar Bergman**
sc **Ingmar Bergman**
ph **Göran Strindberg**
m **Erland Von Koch**
Holger Löwenadler, Anna Lindahl, Birger Malmsten, Gertrud Fridh, Lasse Krantz, Jan Molander, Erik Hell,

Alexander Blom (Löwenadler), the captain of a salvage ship, treats his hunchback son Johannes (Malmsten) with cruelty and contempt. The enmity between them comes to a head when Blom brings Sally (Fridh), a backstreet dancer, to the ship and Johannes falls in love with her, provoking his father to an attempt on his life. Bergman's third film as director has, in fact, a complicated plot, and a melodramatic one at that—a tone which is emphasized by the high-pitched direction and playing (although Löwenadler is first-class in a difficult role). The murky events are unfolded in one long flashback as Johannes, reunited with Sally after seven years, recalls past events. It is an interesting movie for Bergman followers because it sows so many seeds of the concerns and techniques that would flower later—human beings battling with illness, emotional isolation and frustration, the fascination of the theatre, and a magic moment of release from inner and outer claustrophobia, as when Johannes and Sally temporarily escape the oppressive confines of the ship.

Shivers see Dreszcze

Shizuka Naru Ketto see Quiet Duel, A

Shlosha Yamim Ve Yeled see Three Days And A Child

Shoah

France 1985 9 hrs 43 mins col
Les Films Aleph/Historia Films

d **Claude Lanzmann**
ph **Dominique Chapuis, Jimmy Glasberg, William Lubtchansky**

Survivors of the Nazi extermination camps at Treblinka, Auschwitz and elsewhere, plus witnesses, Polish bystanders and a handful of German officials, recall the Holocaust. Under Lanzmann's unwavering and detailed questioning they reveal the inconceivable horror and obscenity of the atrocities, and the minutiae of the detached planning that was the Final Solution. Lanzmann spent 10 years travelling and visiting the scenes of humanity's greatest crime to amass his towering document edited from 350 hours of film. Marcel Ophüls terms *Shoah* (meaning annihilation) 'the greatest documentary about contemporary history ever made, bar none'; Lanzmann maintains that it is neither a documentary nor a historical film. Be that as it may, it is certainly a work of art as well as a unique and disturbing testament. The images are made manifest without using a single frame of archive material, and are all the more powerful for that: the Jewish barbers sent to cut the hair of their own wives and daughters at the entrance to the gas chambers; the Jews of the *sonderkommando* forced to shovel the crushed bodies of their fellows into ovens as the price of their own survival; the nightmarish conditions of the Warsaw ghetto. This landmark in film-making is, perhaps, most significant of all in reminding us that anti-Semitism is still alive and well.

Shoeshine
Sciuscia

Italy 1946 93 mins bw
Alfa/ENIC

d **Vittorio De Sica**
sc **Vittorio De Sica, Cesare Zavattini, Sergio Amedei, Adolfo Franci, Cesare Giulio Viola**
ph **Anchise Brizzi**
m **Alessandro Cicognini**
Rinaldo Smordoni, Franco Interlenghi, Anielo Mele, Bruno Ortensi, Pacifico Astrologo

In post-war Rome, Giuseppe (Smordoni) and Pasquale (Interlenghi), two shoeshine boys, dream of buying a horse with the little extra money they make out of dealing in black market goods, but they end up in reform school. One of the first pictures to come out of Italy after the war, it created an international sensation. It was also the first foreign-language movie to win an honorary Academy Award for proving 'to the world that the creative spirit can triumph over adversity'. (Until 1956, foreign films were given special, non-competitive awards.) Its impact was due to the powerful and touching semi-documentary treatment of poverty in post-war Italy, the main theme of the Neo-Realists.

Shokutaku No Nai Ie see Empty Table, The

Shonen see Boy

Shoot The Pianist
(US: Shoot The Piano Player)
Tirez Sur Le Pianiste

France 1960 80 mins bw
Films De La Pléiade

d **François Truffaut**
sc **François Truffaut, Marcel Moussy**
ph **Raoul Coutard**
m **Georges Delerue**
Charles Aznavour, Marie Dubois, Nicole Berger, Michèle Mercier, Albert Rémy

An ex-concert pianist (Aznavour), working in a seedy bar in the outskirts of Paris, gets involved with gangsters when he helps his two petty-crook brothers escape from them, an action culminating in the death of his girlfriend (Dubois). 'A pastiche of the Hollywood B film,' said Truffaut of his second picture. The plot, derived from a pulp novel by David Goodis, has the elements of American *film noir*, but the style is pure *Nouvelle Vague* with its mobile camera, mood changes and visual gags. Aznavour's sad-eyed figure at the centre gives depth to the light-hearted proceedings.

Shoot The Piano Player see Shoot The Pianist

Shop On Main Street, The see Shop On The High Street, The

The Shop On The High Street
aka The Shop On Main Street
Obchod Od Na Korze

Czechoslovakia 1965 128 mins bw
Barrandov

d **Jan Kadar**
sc **Jan Kadar, Elmar Klos**

ph **Vladimir Novotny**
m **Zdeněk Liška**
Jožef Kroner, Ida Kaminska, Hana Slivková, František Zvarik

In Nazi-occupied Czechoslovakia, a lowly carpenter (Kroner) becomes the 'Aryan comptroller' of a button shop owned by an old Jewish lady (Kaminska). She turns out to be stone deaf, unaware there's a war on, and has barely a button in the place. Caught between self-interest and his growing affection for her, his bungled attempts to protect her lead to tragedy for them both. Kadar conveys the political climate with absolute clarity (and comedy) and Kaminska's performance is a miracle that shouldn't be missed.

Best Foreign Film Oscar 1965

Shors see Shchors

Short Cut
Postriziny
Czechoslovakia 1981 98 mins col
Barrandov Studios

d **Jiří Menzel**
sc **Bohumil Hrabal, Jiří Menzel**
ph **Jaromír Šofr**
m **Jiří Šust**
Jiří Schmitzer, Magda Vašáryová, Jaromír Hanzlík, Rudolf Hrušinsky, František Rehák, Oldřich Vlach

Francin (Schmitzer), shy and serious, manages the local brewery in a small provicial town prior to World War I and attempts to cope with the high spirits of his beautiful and extrovert wife, Marja (Vašáryová), who is universally adored by the locals. The coming of sound radio is the 'short cut' that projects the lifestyle of the village into the present. On this flimsy foundation, popular Czech novelist Bohumil Hrabal, drawing on the life of his parents in the days of the Austro-Hungarian empire, has constructed a funny and affectionate exercise in nostalgia to which Jiří Menzel brings the full measure of his gifts for warmth, humour, and satirical observation. The period is evoked with atmosphere, enhanced by a lyrical camera, and the townsfolk are given authentic life by cast and director.

Short Encounters
aka Short Meetings
aka Brief Encounters
Korotkie Vstrechi
USSR 1967 88 mins bw
Odessa Feature Film Studio

d **Kira Muratova**
sc **Kira Muratova, Leonid Zhukovitsy**
ph **G. Kariuk**
m **Oleg Karavaichuk**
Nina Ruslanova, Kira Muratova, Vladimir Vysotsky

A young village girl and her employer, the latter the dedicated organizer of the town's housing committee, are in love with the same man, a free-wheeling, guitar-strumming geologist. A simple love story, simply shot in unglamourized black-and-white and utilizing flashback techniques, it gives a picture of daily life in the Russian provinces, revealing the existence of free love, bureaucratic inefficiency and fiddling the system. These facts, coupled with the presence of Vysotsky, theatre idol and composer of protest songs who was regarded as a dissident, resulted in the multi-talented Muratova's film being suppressed for 20 years. Vysotsky, who died at the age of 42, and the stunning Ruslanova, were both making their screen debuts.

A Short Film About Killing
aka Thou Shalt Not Kill
Krótki Film O Zabijaniu
Poland 1988 84 mins col
Film Polski, Tor Unit

d **Krzysztof Kieslowski**
sc **Krzysztof Piesiewicz, Krzysztof Kieslowski**
ph **Slawomir Idziak**
m **Zbigniew Preisner**
Miroslaw Baka, Krzysztof Globisz, Jan Tesarz

A young and aimless drifter (Baka) kills an ill-natured taxi driver by repeatedly bashing in his head with a stone. He is caught, arrested and condemned to death, and the authorized killing is as horribly disturbing as the senseless and brutal crime. Kieslowski's powerful and purposefully shocking film was made as part of a TV series based on the Ten Commandments. It differs from most other anti-capital punishment films in that its treatment of the subject starkly refuses to sentimentalize the situation, with the director determined to show both killings in the most graphic detail. Shot in bleached out greenish-browns, utilizing eerie camera angles and sudden cuts to discomforting images, it's made with a masterly hand that cannot fail to shake any sense of audience complacency. Whether it will make conversions, either to its cause or the style of its director, is another matter entirely.

Special Jury Prize Cannes 1988

Short Meetings see Short Encounters

Shuban see Scandal

Shura see Pandemonium

Siberiada see Siberiade

Siberiade

Siberiada

USSR 1979 190 mins col

Mosfilm

d **Andrei Mikhalkov-Konchalovsky**

sc **Valentin Yezhov, Andrei Mikhalkov-Konchalovsky**

ph **Levan Paatashvili**

m **Eduard Artemyev**

Vladimir Samoilov, Vitaly Solomin, Nikita Mikhalkov, Ludmila Gurchenko, Nathalia Andretchenko

The lives of the wealthy Solomins and the poor Ustyuzhanins in a Siberian village from 1909 to 1969, and how the many changes in Soviet society affect them. There are certain parallels between the wastes of Siberia and those of the wide open spaces of the American West, and this saga showing the republic's 'progress' from forests to oil rigs has similarities to an Edna Ferber epic. However, Konchalovsky's sometimes confusing and rambling narrative is far more symbolic and concerned with how individuals are the tools of history. Forceful performances by Samoilov as the woodsman grandfather Solomin, Nikita Mikhalkov (the director's actor-director brother) as a flamboyant oilman, and Gurchenko, the girl he loves from the other family, shine in a fine cast that brings the characters sharply into focus.

Special Jury Prize Cannes 1979

Siberian Lady Macbeth

Sibirska Ledi Magbet

Yugoslavia 1962 95 mins bw

Avala

d **Andrzej Wajda**

sc **Sveta Lukić**

ph **Aleksandar Sekulović**

m **Dušan Radić adapted from Dimitri Shostakovitch**

Olivera Marković, Ljuba Tadić, Miodrag Lazarvić, Bojan Stupica

The bored wife (Marković) of a merchant takes an itinerant workman (Tadić) as a lover while her husband is away. She then gives her father-in-law rat poison and, aided by her lover, strangles the husband on his return. Wajda, working outside Poland for the first time, went uncharacteristically for a passionate melodrama based on Nikolai Leskow's 1865 story, which also served for Shostakovitch's opera *Lady Macbeth Of Mtsensk*. Much of the film is operatic, as well as being influenced by the work of Kurosawa whose 'Japanese Lady Macbeth' (*Throne Of Blood*) had appeared a few years before. Wajda then returned to Poland and sobriety.

Sibirska Ledi Magbet see Siberian Lady Macbeth

Si C'Était À Refaire see Second Chance

The Sicilian Clan

Le Clan Des Siciliens

France 1968 120 mins col

Fox-Europa/Les Films Du Siècle

d **Henri Verneuil**

sc **Henri Verneuil, José Giovanni, Pierre Pelégri**

ph **Henri Decaë**

m **Ennio Morricone**

Jean Gabin, Alain Delon, Lino Ventura, Irina Demick, Amedeo Nazzari, Sydney Chaplin

Roger Sartet (Delon) escapes from a French jail and joins forces with Manalese (Gabin), an aging Sicilian looking for a last coup which Sartet proposes in the form of an audacious jewel robbery in Venice. All goes well until Manalese discovers that Sartet has been having an affair with his daughter-in-law. The pairing of Delon and Gabin was obviously intended to spark off an atmosphere of dramatic conflict. In the event, the stars give mechanical performances in what is no more than a competent, routine crime thriller, enlivened by a couple of first-class action sequences and lent a touch of class by Decaë's atmospheric photography.

Siddharta And The City see Adversary, The

Sierra De Teruel see Man's Hope

Signe Du Lion, Le see Sign Of Leo, The

Sign Of Disaster

aka Ill Omen

Znak Bedy

USSR 1986 145 mins col
Byelerus Film

d **Mikhail Ptashuk**
sc **Yevgeni Grigoryev, Oskai Nikich**
ph **Tatyana Loganova**
m **Oleg Yanchenko**
Nina Ruslanova, Gennady Garbuk, Vladimir Ilin, Aleksandr Timoshkin, Kaspar Putse, Slava Soldatenko

A troop of Germans is billeted on the little farm of Stepanida (Ruslanova) and Petrok (Garbuk) but, finally, it is the hatred and brutality of the local collaborators that destroys them. Based on Vasil Bykov's best-selling novel, this controversial and relentlessly harrowing work depicts the chilling injustices that arose from the collectivization programme as well as the horrors of the Nazi occupation, and amply demonstrates the pervasive influence of fear that leads to corruption. At the centre is Stepanida who remains courageously and defiantly committed to the original principles of Bolshevism. Filmed in the vast spaces of Byelorussia, and moving skilfully back and forth in time, *Sign Of Disaster* is a political landmark in Soviet cinema—a clear indication that *glasnost* is no myth. In spite of an unconvincing and melodramatic ending, it is also a moving and powerful document, wonderfully well acted, particularly by Ruslanova.

The Sign Of Leo

Le Signe Du Lion

France 1959 90 mins bw
AJYM Productions

d **Eric Rohmer**
sc **Eric Rohmer**
ph **Nicolas Hayer**
m **Louis Saguer**
Jess Hahn, Van Doude, Michèle Girardon, Jean Le Poulain, Stéphane Audran, Françoise Prévost

An impoverished 40-year-old American composer (Hahn) lives on the Left Bank in Paris. Hearing that he has inherited a fortune, he borrows money to hold a party, only to learn that the money has gone to a cousin. The ensuing crises lead him by subtle degrees into becoming a tramp, begging outside cafés, until an unexpected turn of events brings rescue. Rohmer (born Maurice Schérer) was the editor of the influential *Cahiers Du Cinéma* when he made this, his modest first full-length feature, a perceptive portrait of a good-natured but hopelessly irresponsible man slowly disintegrating in the face of reality. Only the pat ending strikes a false note. However, what makes the film particularly watchable is the detailed and vivid evocation—brilliantly captured by Nicolas Hayer's camera—of a sweltering Paris in August, deserted by its regular inhabitants. Rohmer would not make another feature for eight years, when his style would develop in another direction.

La Signora Di Tutti

Italy 1934 89 mins bw
Novella

d **Max Ophüls**
sc **Max Ophüls, Hans Wilhelm, Kurt Alexander**
ph **Ubaldo Arata**
m **Daniele Amfitheatrof**

Isa Miranda, Memo Benassi, Tatiana Pavlova, Federico Benfer, Nelly Corradi, Franco Coop

A famous Italian film star (Miranda) recalls the events leading up to her suicide attempt. Expelled from school because of a scandal involving the music teacher, she becomes the mistress of a banker (Benfer), whose son (Benassi) really loves her, but she only learns of this too late. Shooting in Italy on a contemporary subject, Ophüls retained the hallmarks of his style—extensive use of flashbacks, flowing camera movements, stunning cross-cuts and lilting music—which suited the romantic tale admirably. Like *Lola Montes*, the heroine is a *femme fatale* and an innocent victim, a woman who publicly has everything and privately nothing. These ambiguities are securely handled by the director and by Miranda in her first leading role.

Signora Senza Camelie, La see Lady Without Camellias, The

Signore E Signori see Birds, The Bees And The Italians, The

Signs Of Life
Lebenszeichen

W. Germany 1968 90 mins bw
Werner Herzog Filmproduktion

d **Werner Herzog**
sc **Werner Herzog**
ph **Thomas Mauch**
m **Stavros Xarchakos**

Peter Brogle, Wolfgang Reichmann, Athina Zacharopoulou, Wolfgang Von Ungern-Sternberg, Wolfgang Stumpf

Stroszek (Brogle), a German soldier wounded during the Occupation of Crete, is sent with two other soldiers and his Greek wife to the peaceful island of Kos to recuperate. Once there, the men have nothing to do other than guard a deserted fortress and a store of redundant Greek ammunition, and the enforced idleness and isolation drive Stroszek to inner reflections which finally result in madness. Herzog's first feature foreshadows his later preoccupation with outsiders unable to conform to a prescribed structure. Photographed with an impressive feel for the hot and dusty landscape, the film employs images as narrative and as emblems of inner states of being, and does so with remarkable command.

Special Prize Berlin 1968

Si Jolie Petite Plage, Une see Such A Pretty Little Beach

The Silence
Tystnaden

Sweden 1963 96 mins bw
Svensk/Janus

d **Ingmar Bergman**
sc **Ingmar Bergman**
ph **Sven Nykvist**
m **Bo Nilsson, Bach**

Ingrid Thulin, Gunnel Lindblom, Jörgen Lindström, Eduardo Futierrez, Haken Jahnberg

Ester (Thulin), a Lesbian intellectual, is physically attracted to her sister Anna (Lindblom), herself the sexually vibrant mother of a 10-year-old boy. While the carefree Anna indulges in casual sex, her son briefly falls in with a troupe of dwarfs, and Ester wastes away from alcohol and tuberculosis. Bleak, dense, puzzling, and heavy with symbolism, the film is explicitly erotic. Certain scenes (Thulin masturbating, a couple copulating in a cinema) were profoundly shocking at the time—all the more so, perhaps, for the unadorned frankness with which they were presented. Impeccably interpreted by two of the best actresses in Bergman's impressive stable, this is a dark, passionate, elusive and disturbing work.

Silence And Cry
Csend Es Kiáltás

Hungary 1968 79 mins bw
Mafilm

d **Miklós Jancsó**
sc **Gyula Hernádi**
ph **János Kende**

A. Kozák, Zoltán Latinovits, Mari Töröcsik, Andrea Drahota, József Madaras

After the defeat of the first Hungarian Communist regime in 1919, Istvan (Kozák), a fugitive from the White terror of Admiral Horthy's regime, is sheltered on a farm among peasants demoralized by the cruelty of the police. Photographed in a series of long sequences, with each cut representing a time lapse, the film depicts the cruelty, dehumanization and claustrophobia that comes from oppression. Jancsó's ritualistic style manages to make the particular Hungarian situation into a universal parable of evil, ending with a cry of hope.

Le Silence De La Mer

France 1947 86 mins bw
Melville

d **Jean-Pierre Melville**
sc **Jean-Pierre Melville**
ph **Henri Decaë**
m **Edgar Bischoff**
Howard Vernon, Jean-Marie Robian, Nicole Stéphane

During the Occupation, a German officer (Vernon), a musician and an intellectual, is billeted in the countryside in the home of an old French farmer (Robian) and his niece (Stéphane). They have sworn never to speak to the invader and listen in silence as the German pours out his ideas and feelings about music, the war and his love of France. Melville's first feature succeeds in transposing Vercors' almost unfilmable parable of the Resistance to the screen. 'I wanted to attempt a language composed entirely of images and sounds, and from which movement and action would be more or less banished,' commented the director. The film is virtually a monologue by the German officer, but a great deal of what is going on beneath the surface is suggested by look and gesture. This sensitive and intense film on the Occupation, a theme the director would return to in *Léon Morin, Priest* and *The Army In The Shadows*, was an influence on the style of Robert Bresson.

Le Silence Est D'Or

aka Silence Is Golden
(US: Man About Town)
France 1947 100 mins bw
Pathé/RKO

d **René Clair**
sc **René Clair**
ph **Armand Thirard**
m **Georges Van Parys**
Maurice Chevalier, François Périer, Marcelle Derrien

In 1906 a middle-aged ex-comedian, now a film-maker (Chevalier), tutors his young assistant (Périer) in the arts of seduction, unaware that they are both in love with the same girl (Derrien). Clair's first French film for over a decade was a bitter-sweet regretful look at the silent cinema in which he began his career. It also reunited him with Chevalier (showing rare depth) with whom he had worked on *Break The News* in 1937. The re-creation of the era is more entertaining than the rather strained, leisurely plot.

Silence Is Golden see Silence Est D'Or, Le

Silencieux, Le see Silent One, The

Silent Duel, A see Quiet Duel, A

The Silent One

(US: Escape To Nowhere)
Le Silencieux
France 1973 113 mins col
S.N.E.G./Trianon (Paris)/Medusa (Rome)

d **Claude Pinoteau**
sc **Jean-Loup Dabadie, Claude Pinoteau**
ph **Jean Collomb**
m **Jacques Datin, Alain Goraguer**
Lino Ventura, Leo Genn, Robert Hardy, Lea Massari, Suzanne Flon, Pierre-Michel Le Conte, Bernard Dhéran

Russian nuclear scientist Haliakov (Ventura) arrives in London, is involved in a car accident, and hospitalized. In fact, it's a put-up job by MI5 who know that he is really Frenchman Clément Tibère, kidnapped by the Russians some years before. The British offer him a new identity in exchange for certain information. . . This plot seems so familiar as to make it appear redundant, but don't be fooled. If spy thrillers are to your taste, you'll enjoy this one for its taut building of suspense, its intelligent exposé of the illusory nature of freedom and, of course, the immaculate Lino Ventura who brings nuances of depth to the character of a man trapped by both past and present circumstances.

The Silent World

Le Monde Du Silence

France 1956 86 mins col
Filmad/F.S.J.Y.C.

d **Jacques-Yves Cousteau, Louis Malle**
sc **Jacques-Yves Cousteau, Louis Malle**
ph **Edmond Séchan**
m **Yves Baudrier**
Frédéric Duman, Albert Falco, Jacques-Yves Cousteau

The exploration of the fauna and flora of the oceans' depths by Jacques-Yves Cousteau, the famous French oceanographer, diver and documentary film-maker. This extraordinary voyage into an unknown (before all those TV programmes of which Cousteau's were the best), silent (except for music and commentary by Cousteau) world, had no less than four underwater cameramen (including the co-directors) to frighten the most frightening fish. Although 24-year-old Louis Malle had worked with Bresson as assistant on *A Man Escaped* and had participated on Cousteau's voyages for some years, this was his first credit as director. Apart from the boardwalk in *Atlantic City*, he never seemed to go near the sea again in his own films. The film won the documentary Oscar in 1956.

Best Film Cannes 1956

Silken Skin

(US: The Soft Skin)

La Peau Douce

France 1964 118 mins bw
Films Du Carrosse/SEDIF

d **François Truffaut**
sc **François Truffaut, Jean-Louis Richard**
ph **Raoul Coutard**
m **Georges Delerue**
Jean Desailly, Françoise Dorléac, Nelly Benedetti, Daniel Ceccaldi, Laurence Bady

A married, middle-aged literature professor (Desailly) falls in love with an air stewardess (Dorléac) after a trip to Lisbon and leaves home for her. When she rejects him, he seeks reconciliation with his wife (Benedetti) who shoots him in a restaurant. After the triumph of *Jules And Jim* (1961), Truffaut followed with another triangle story, this time, as he stated, 'a truly modern love; it takes place in planes, elevators, it has all the harassments of modern life'. Like the title, it has a brilliant surface, but, despite patches of warmth and wit, is uncharacteristically cool with rather remote characters.

Simón Del Desierto see Simon Of The Desert

Simon Of The Desert

Simón Del Desierto

Mexico 1965 45 mins bw
Gustavo Alatriste

d **Luis Buñuel**
sc **Luis Buñuel**
ph **Gabriel Figueroa**
m **Raúl Lavista**
Claudio Brook, Silvia Pinal, Hortensia Santovena, Enrique Alvarez Felix

For six years, six weeks and six days, Simon (Brook), emulating St Simon Stylites, has stood on a pillar in the Mexican desert as an inspiration and example to the peasants who crowd below. The Devil tries to tempt him down, first in the guise of a young woman (Pinal) and then disguised as Jesus, but Simon will not be moved. Originally conceived as a full-length feature, the film had to be truncated when the money ran out. What another hour might have done to this economical, pointed and wry anecdote can only be surmised, but it stands, like its hero, high above most films with a theological theme. It makes a good companion piece to *Nazarín*, also about the impossibility of absolute piety.

Special Jury Prize Venice 1965

Simon The Swiss

(US: The Crook)

Le Voyou

France 1970 120 mins col
Les Films Ariane/Les Films 13/Artistes Associés

d **Claude Lelouch**
sc **Claude Lelouch, Pierre Uytterhoeven, Claude Pinoteau**
ph **Jean Collomb**

m **Francis Lai**
Jean-Louis Trintignant, Danièle Delorme, Charles Gérard, Christine Lelouch, Yves Robert, Charles Denner

A crooked lawyer (Trintignant), imprisoned for 20 years for stealing $1 million, escapes, hides in the apartment of a girl (Delorme) he meets at the movies, and leads the police a merry chase through Europe. The antithesis of the sombre gangster films being made in France at the time by Jean-Pierre Melville, this slick caper offers colourful locations, a plug for Simca cars, contrived plot twists, and an appearance by Sacha Distel.

A Simple Case
Prostoi Sluchai

USSR 1932 96 mins bw
Mezhrabpom

d **Vsevolod Pudovkin**
sc **Alexander Rzheshevsky**
ph **G. Bobrov, G. Kabalov**
m **Silent**
Aleksandr Baturin, Yevgeniya Rogulina, A. Gorchilin, A. Chekulaeva, I. Novoseltsev, Alexander Chistyakov

A Red Army commander (Baturin) and his wife (Rogulina) endure the danger and deprivation of the Russian Civil War together. Afterwards, while his wife is away recuperating in the country, he meets and falls in love with another woman. He is condemned by his friends for betraying their 'comrade citizen' and returns to her. In the early 1930s, the great classics of the Russian cinema, including those by Pudovkin, were condemned as élitist. This may explain why the director's last silent film contains such a banal triangular love conflict, lacking depth or development. Yet it was criticized as 'overly abstract and pseudo- significant'. Despite the restrictions placed on him, Pudovkin achieved much visual poetry and some virtuoso montage sequences, including a powerful and passionate battle scene and an impressionistic vision of nature erupting.

A Simple Story
Un Histoire Simple

France 1978 110 mins col
Renn Productions/Sara Films/FR3(Paris)/ Rialto-Film(Berlin)

d **Claude Sautet**
sc **Claude Sautet, Jean-Loup Dabadie**
ph **Jean Boffety**
m **Philippe Sarde**
Romy Schneider, Bruno Cremer, Claude Brasseur, Arlette Bonnard, Sophie Daumier, Roger Pigaut

Marie (Schneider), divorced and with a teenage son, a lover (Brasseur), a high-powered job and a circle of women friends, seems successful and content but is, in fact, questioning the meaning of her life as she approaches the big Four-0. Her self-examination leads her to break off with her lover and abort his child, whereupon she has a reunion of sorts with her ex-husband (Cremer) and becomes pregnant by him. Pursuing his preoccupation with the 'things of life' as they affect the fashionable French middle classes, Sautet has made a fashionable French middle-class film, in which attractive people prepare and eat a lot of attractive food, while grappling with life and love. It's all superficially agreeable, particularly if you're a fan of Romy Schneider who gives a convincing performance, but the director's aim and object remain rather vague and the film fails to live up to its pretensions.

The Sin
aka The Outcast
aka The Broken Commandment
Hakai

Japan 1961 119 mins bw
Daiei

d **Kon Ichikawa**
sc **Natto Wada**
ph **Kazuo Miyagawa**
m **Yasushi Akutagawa**
Raizo Ichikawa, Rentaro Mikune, Hiroyuki Nagato, Eiji Fujimura, Ganjiro Nakamura

Segawa (Ichikawa, no relation to the director), born of an *eta* family (the very bottom of the social scale in 19th-century Japan) and educated far from his roots, promises his dying father to hide his class origins forever. A popular teacher, Segawa finds the strain of living a lie too much and follows in the footsteps of the murdered *eta* writer Rentaro Inoko (Mikune) in campaigning for the rights of the social outcasts. Although the nuances of the social background may elude most Western audiences, there is no escaping the impact of the situation in which the hero finds himself, nor the beauty and passion with which it is expressed. There are dollops of sentimentality, but fewer than to be found in Keisuke Kinoshita's 1948 version of the same novel by Toson Shimazaki.

Sinbad see Sindbad

Sindbad

aka Sinbad

Szindbád

Hungary 1971 98 mins col
Mafilm

d **Zoltán Huszárik**
sc **Zoltán Huszárik**
ph **Sándor Sára**
m **Zoltán Jeney**
Zoltán Latinovits, Margit Dayka, Éva Ruttkai, Erika Szegedi, Bella Tanay

The dying Sindbad (Latinovits), a lifelong hedonist, thinks back over all the beautiful women he has loved and all the wonderful food and drink he has consumed. This startlingly original, impressionistic work, based on Gyula Krúdy's classic stories in Hungarian literature, owes a great deal to the director's recreation of sensuality, aided by Sára's superb camerawork and Latinovits' performance. The parade of female pulchritude, gastronomic delights, rich costumes and colour tends to cloy after a while, but that is, after all, the thematic point of the film.

The Sin Of Father Mouret

(US: The Demise Of Father Mouret)

La Faute De L'Abbé Mouret

France 1970 93 mins col
Stéphan/Valoria/Les Films Du Carrosse/New Films Production (Rome)

d **Georges Franju**
sc **Georges Franju, Jean Ferry**
ph **Marcel Fradetal**
m **Jean Wiener**
Francis Huster, Gillian Hills, Tino Carrero, André Lacombe, Hugo Fausto

Father Mouret (Huster), a young parish priest in a remote area of France, devotes his life to the worship of the Virgin Mary. But when he meets a wild young girl (Hills), the priest gives in to lust with tragic consequences. The purple prose of Zola's novel is matched by the lush colour photography of the floral landscape of Provence—the girl dies smothered by the fragrance of flowers—a sensuous contrast to the self-abnegatory nature of the tale. In fact, the overheated erotic sections work less well than the harshness and violence of the religious scenes loomed over by Lacombe's fanatic Friar. Huster and Hills make a pretty pair in Franju's first colour feature, made near the end of his career.

Sir Arne's Treasure

aka The Three Who Were Doomed

Herr Arnes Pengar

Sweden 1919 114 mins bw
Svensk Biografteatern

d **Mauritz Stiller**
sc **Mauritz Stiller, Gustaf Molander**
ph **J. Julius Jaenzon**
m **Silent**
Hjalmar Selander, Richard Lund, Mary Johnson

In 16th-century Denmark, three Scottish mercenaries steal Pastor Arne's treasure, massacre everyone in the household except his adopted daughter Elsalill (Johnson) and burn it to the ground. Later she unwittingly falls in love with the gang's leader Sir Archie (Lund), but betrays him when she discovers the truth. Under the influence of his friend Victor Sjöström, Stiller moved from sophisticated comedies nearer the more sombre Swedish literary tradition with the first of his films based on the novels of Selma Lagerlöf, in which the close relation between the landscape and the characters is explored. Particularly impressive in this regard is the climax, when a procession of black-robed figures follow a coffin across a frozen lake.

Sirène Du Mississippi, La see Mississippi Mermaid, The

Sissi see Forever My Love

Sissi-Die Junge Kaiserin see Forever My Love

Sissi-Schicksalsjahre Einer Kaiserin see Forever My Love

Sisters Of The Gion

Gion No Shimai

Japan 1936 69 mins bw
Daiichi Eiga

d **Kenji Mizoguchi**
sc **Kenji Mizoguchi, Yoshitaka Yoda**
ph **Minoru Miki**
Isuzu Yamada, Yoko Umemura, Benkei Shiganoya, Eitaro Shindo, Taizo Fukami, Fumio Okura

Two Geisha sisters, the elder (Umemura) faithful to the old traditions, the younger (Yamada) more modern in her attitudes, both end up being hurt, the one injured by a jealous ex-lover and the other deserted by a man to whom she had given her love. Mizoguchi's most famous pre-war film, made at the time when realism was entering Japanese cinema, is full of beautifully composed contrasting scenes, gentle humour and pathos. The director condemns neither woman but the society that exploits them.

Sisters Or The Balance Of Happiness

Schwestern Oder Die Balance Des Glücks

W. Germany 1979 95 mins col
Bioskop-Film/Westdeutscher Rundfunk

d **Margarethe Von Trotta**
sc **Margarethe Von Trotta, with Luise Francia, Martje Grohmann**
ph **Franz Rath, Thomas Schwan**
m **Konstantin Wecker**
Jutta Lampe, Gudrun Gabriel, Jessica Früh, Konstantin Wecker, Heinz Bennent, Agnes Fink

Efficient, high-powered secretary Maria (Lampe) shares a comfortable flat with dreamy, introspective Anna (Gabriel), her younger biology-student sister whom she is supporting—and encouraging, controlling and dominating. When the emotionally fragile Anna can no longer bear her dependency on Maria, she kills herself. Maria takes up with Miriam (Früh), a girl at her office, and starts repeating the pattern of her disastrous sibling relationship. Made two years earlier than Von Trotta's *The German Sisters* (but released later in Britain and the US), this is, in fact, a more coherent and finely controlled work. An intimate study—very well acted—of sibling and 'mother-daughter' relationships, the film also explores the implications of the materialistic society of post- war Germany and the suffocating stranglehold of family guilt. The director's eye for detail and her sensitivity to the psychology of her characters, make for some telling and visually brilliant moments.

Siuzhet Dlya Nebloshova Rasskaza see Lika, Chekhov's Love

Six In Paris

Paris Vu Par...

France 1965 98 mins col
Films Du Losange/Barbet Schroeder

d **1) Jean Douchet 2) Jean Rouch 3) Jean-Daniel Pollet 4) Eric Rohmer 5) Jean-Luc Godard 6) Claude Chabrol**
sc **1) Jean Douchet, Georges Keller 2) Jean Rouch 3) Jean-Daniel Pollet 4) Eric Rohmer 5) Jean-Luc Godard 6) Claude Chabrol**
ph **1) Nestor Almendros 2) Etienne Becker 3) and 4) Alain Levent 5) Albert Maysles 6) Jean Rabier**
1) Barbara Wilkind 2) Nadine Ballot, Barbet Schroeder 3) Micheline Dax, Claude Melki 4) Jean- Michel Rouzière, Marcel Gallon 5) Joanna Shimkus 6) Claude Chabrol, Stéphane Audran

1) A American girl is dropped by one French boy only to be picked up by another. 2) After quarrelling with her husband, a wife encounters a wealthy stranger who intends to kill himself. 3) A timid dishwasher brings a prostitute back to his room. 4) A salesman hits a tramp with his umbrella and imagines he has killed him. 5) A girl fears she has mixed up letters to her two lovers. 6) A small boy is so tired of hearing his parents arguing that he buys earplugs and, later, cannot hear his

mother's cries for help. These slight but entertaining sketches, of which the one by Chabrol is the best, were shot in 16 mm in different parts of the city.

The Sixth Of July

Shestoe Iulya

USSR 1968 112 mins bw
Mosfilm

d **Yuli Karasik**
sc **Mikhail Shatrov**
ph **Mikhail Suslov**
m **A. Shnitke**
Yuri Kayurov, Alla Demidova, Vladimir Tatosov, Vassily Lanovoi, Vyacheslav Shalevich, B. Rizhukhin

In July 1918 (about 10 days before the assassination of the Tsar), under the Treaty of Brest-Litovsk, the newly-born Soviet Republic under the leadership of Lenin (Kayurov) ceded the Ukraine and the Baltic States to Germany in return for peace. An opposing Russian faction, led by Maria Spiridovna (Demidova), opposed the move without success, murdered the German ambassador in Moscow and attempted to overthrow the Bolsheviks. Lenin quelled this uprising by force. Resuscitating an incident little-known or remembered in the West, Karasik has combined a political thriller with a somewhat sketchy history lesson that ignores the welter of political complications surrounding the period, and fails to make clear just how strong Spiridovna's Left Socialist-Revolutionaries were and how close they came to overthrowing Lenin. The film is, nonetheless, well paced and absorbing, notably in the second half when events gather momentum.

Sjecas Li Se Dolly Bell see Do You Remember Dolly Bell?

Sjunde Inseglet, Det see Seventh Seal, The

Skammen see Shame, The

Skepp Till Indialand see Ship Bound For India, A

Skin Skin

Käpy Selän Alla

Finland 1967 88 mins bw
Mikko Niskanen

d **Mikko Niskanen**
sc **Marja-Leena Mikkola**
ph **Esko Nevalainen**
m **Kaj Chydenius**
Kristina Halkola, Eero Melasniemi, Kirsti Wallasväära, Pekka Autiovuori

Four Helsinki students take a camping holiday together. Leena (Wallasväära), hoping to become a writer, is hungry for experience but frightened of sex and not helped by the timidity of her boyfriend (Autiovuori); for Rita, sex is no problem, but she's looking for marriage, which doesn't suit *her* boyfriend. The four learn something of themselves and return home a little sadder and wiser. A light-weight offering, it still has much charm and insight. Niskanen paints an accurate picture of young people searching, often painfully, for identity, the atmosphere of the beautiful Finnish lakes is well caught and the performances are convincing.

Skønheden Og Udyret see Beauty And The Beast, The

Skulpjaci Perja see Happy Gypsies

Skyline

La Linea Del Cielo

Spain 1983 90 mins col
La Salamandra

d **Fernando Colomo**
sc **Fernando Colomo**
ph **Angel Luis Fernandez**
m **Miguel Angel Santamaria**
Antonio Resines, Beatriz Perez-Porro, Patricia Cisarano, Jaime Nos, Roy Hoffman

Gustavo (Resines), a Spanish photographer, arrives in New York hoping to make it as a photo-journalist. He rents a sumptuous loft, but is short of professional contacts and speaks virtually no English. He goes to English classes, acquires an agent, battles with enforced idleness and, being a bit of a wet, goes home. The movie is not without interest as a bird's eye view of a foreigner's difficulties in the Big Apple, but it is really no more than a vignette suitable for a TV documentary. Shot almost entirely in the small streets and large lofts of Manhattan, the skyline of the title is barely in evidence, and the lack of visual interpretation of the world's most famous modern city is doubly bizarre in a movie concerned with a photographer of buildings.

A Slap In The Face

Poshchyochina

USSR 1980 col 90 mins
Armenfilm Studio

d **Genrikh Malyan**
sc **Stepan Aldzhadzhyan**
ph **Sergei Israelyan**
m **Tigran Mansurian**
Ashot Adamian, Mger Mkrtchyan, Sofico Chiaureli, Galina Belyaeva, Tigran Voskonyan

A simple Armenian saddlemaker (Mkrtchyan) and his wife (Chiaureli) adopt a young orphan, Torik (Adamian). The boy, shy and slightly slow-witted, finally masters his foster father's trade, but marrying him off proves insurmountable until three prostitutes come to town... Malyan's film is reminiscent of the best French rural comedies of the 1930s. It is beautifully acted; the efforts of the concerned mother (now widowed) to find a wife for her boy are both hilarious and moving. The exposure of *bourgeois* hypocrisy in the village folk's outraged reaction when Torik weds a pretty, orphaned whore (Belyaeva), lends an added dimension to this thoroughly charming romance.

A Slave Of Love

Raba Lubvi

USSR 1976 94 mins col
Mosfilm

d **Nikita Milhalkov**
sc **Andrei Mikhalkov-Konchalovsky, Friedrich Gorenstein**
ph **Pavel Lebeshev**
m **Eduard Artemyev**
Elena Solovei, Rodion Nakhapetov, Alexander Kalyagin, Oleg Basilashvili

In Odessa in 1917, an impoverished film crew is attempting to complete a dreadful melodrama. They are only dimly aware that the government has fallen to the Revolution in Moscow, but distant events become meaningful when the cameraman who has secretly filmed White Guard atrocities is shot before the eyes of his lover, the leading actress. Milhalkov, who had acted in other people's pictures for 10 years before directing, brought his knowledge of both sides of the camera to bear on this bitter-sweet, atmospheric, rather self-conscious film about filming. The director's obvious affection for his feckless characters is realized in the performances, notably those of Solovei and Kalyagin as bitchy actress and batty director respectively.

Slavnosti A Hostech, O see Party And The Guests, The

The Sleeping Car Murders

Compartiment Tueurs

France 1965 95 mins bw
PECF

d **Costa-Gavras**
sc **Costa-Gavras**
ph **Jean Tournier**
m **Michel Magne**
Yves Montand, Simone Signoret, Pierre Mondy, Catherine Allégret, Jacques Perrin, Jean-Louis Trintignant, Michel Piccoli, Charles Denner, Daniel Gélin, Claude Dauphin, Claude Mann

During the investigation of the murder of a woman on the overnight express from Marseilles to Paris, some of the suspects are killed. Costa-Gavras, the maker of distinguished political thrillers such as *Z* (1969), started his career with this commercially successful, non-political thriller on the Hollywood model of the 1940s. Its entertainment value lies mainly in the starry cast headed by Montand, his wife Signoret, and her daughter by director Yves Allégret.

Slingrevalsen see Stepping Out

Slow Attack

Endstation Freiheit

W. Germany 1980 112 mins col
Bioskop-Film/Planet Film (Munich)/ZDF(Mainz)

d **Reinhard Hauff**
sc **Burkhard Driest**
ph **Frank Brühne**
m **Irmin Schmidt**
Burkhard Driest, Rolf Zacher, Katja Rupé, Carla Egerer, Kurt Raab, Eckehard Ahrens, Irm Hermann

Nik Dellman (Driest), released after eight years in prison for robbery, decides to write a novel. As his girlfriend Eva (Rupé) has acquired another man and a child, he takes refuge with a friend (Egerer) and, when his prison mate (Zacher) turns up and proposes a heist, Nik refuses, planning a huge crime on paper instead of in fact—until the manuscript is repeatedly turned down... Reinhard Hauff's concern with outsiders and violence surfaces in an imaginative plot, set in a world of subways, bunkers, hermetic rooms and night streets, crisply and atmospherically photographed. A penetrating and absorbing study of character and morals, the film is often strongly reminiscent of Hollywood *film noir* in tone and style.

Slow Motion

(US: Every Man For Himself)

Sauve Qui Peut (La Vie)

France 1980 87 mins col
Sonimage/Sara/MK2/Saga/Zoetrope

d **Jean-Luc Godard**
sc **Jean-Claude Carrière, Anne Marie Miéville**
ph **William Lubtchansky, Renato Berta**
m **Gabriel Yared**
Isabelle Huppert, Jacques Dutronc, Nathalie Baye, Roland Amstutz, Anna Baldaccini

Three different characters move between the city and the countryside: Isabelle (Huppert), a country girl, comes to the city and becomes a prostitute, Denise (Baye) seeks out an idyllic pastoral life, and Paul (Dutronc) finds it difficult either to exist in or escape from urban life. 'My second first film,' Godard called it after 12 years away from 'commercial' film-making. Using stars, a narrative of sorts, and a somewhat banal theme of the role of sexuality in the consumer society, he retains his artistic integrity by the masterful manipulation of his material, continually re-educating the audience to see and hear differently.

Smaak Van Water, De see Taste Of Water, The

Small Change

L'Argent De Poche

France 1976 105 mins col
Films Du Carrosse/Artistes Associés

d **François Truffaut**
sc **François Truffaut, Suzanne Schiffman**
ph **Pierre William Glenn**
m **Maurice Jaubert**
Geory Desmouceaux, Philippe Goldman, Claudio and Franck Deluca, Jean-François Stevenin

A series of happenings in the lives of a group of young schoolchildren in a small provincial town, revolving around their wise, protective teacher (Stevenin). Truffaut's way with children was proven in *The Four Hundred Blows* (1959) and *Wild Child* (1970), neither of which sentimentalized or idealized childhood. In contrast, *Small Change*, the English title suggested by Steven Spielberg, tends to lean towards cuteness. Not that there aren't some amusing vignettes such as the boy telling his first dirty joke, and the girl, who has been locked up as punishment, using a loud-hailer to procure food.

Smiles Of A Summer's Night

Sommarnattens Leende

Sweden 1955 105 mins bw
Svensk Filmindustri

d **Ingmar Bergman**
sc **Ingmar Bergman**
ph **Gunnar Fischer**
m **Erik Nordgren**
Gunnar Björnstrand, Eva Dahlbeck, Ulla Jacobsson, Harriet Andersson, Margit Carlquist, Jarl Kulle, Björn Bjelvenstam

A middle-aged lawyer (Björnstrand), his still-virgin, young wife (Jacobsson) and her stepson (Bjelvenstam) are invited to a country mansion for a summer weekend. Also invited are a beautiful actress (Dahlbeck) who is the lawyer's ex-mistress and the current lover of another guest, and a count (Kulle), there with his wife (Carlquist). During the course of the weekend, couples meet, separate and exchange partners. Beneath the bubbly surface and behind the sensuous light of the Swedish summer of this charmed and charming comedy of manners, the illusions and pretentions of the turn-of-the-century *haute bourgeois* are sharply exposed. The plot, in the tradition of Marivaux, formed the basis of Stephen Sondheim's musical *A Little Night Music*, and was the inspiration behind Woody Allen's *A Midsummer Night's Sex Comedy* (1982). The film was a milestone in Bergman's career, bringing him the prestige and independence to do virtually anything he desired.

The Smiling Madame Beudet

La Souriante Madame Beudet

France 1923 32 mins bw
Film D'Art/Vandal/Dulac-Aubert

d **Germaine Dulac**
sc **André Obey**
ph **A. Morrin**
m **Silent**
Germaine Dermoz, Alexandre C. Arquillière, Madeleine Guitty, Jean D'Yd

The bored wife (Dermoz) of a pompous, bullying merchant (Arquillière), always teasing her by putting a gun to his head, decides to take her revenge. One of the first woman directors in French films (and elsewhere for that matter), Dulac could lay claim to having made the first feminist film with this little gem with an ironic title—Madame Beudet, in fact, only ever smiles in her daydreams. Based on a one-act play by Denys Amiel and André Obey, it uses imaginative techniques such as superimposition, distorted close-ups, and dream images. *The Seashell And The Clergyman* was the other short masterpiece by Dulac, who gave up directing with the coming of sound.

Smultronstället see Wild Strawberries

Snares

(US: Personal Column)

Pièges

France 1939 115 mins bw
Speva

d **Robert Siodmak**
sc **Jacques Companeez, Ernst Neubach, Jacques Gantillon**
ph **R. Voinquel, Ted Pahle, Michel Kelber**
m **Michel Michelet**
Maurice Chevalier, Marie Déa, Pierre Renoir, Erich Von Stroheim

When a series of young women go missing after replying to advertisements in the personal column of a newspaper, the police enlist the aid of the latest victim's roommate (Déa) to act as a decoy. She meets and falls in love with a prime suspect (Chevalier), but he is arrested. All, however, ends happily. Siodmak's last French-made film before his departure for Hollywood is not his best, but prefigures his American period. With Chevalier cast as a nightclub owner and given a couple of songs to deliver, the piece is an unsatisfying mixture of crime chiller and love story, and somewhat run-of-the-mill in both directions. It is also overlong, but was not improved by 26 minutes of cuts made by the American censors on its first release. The film was remade by Douglas Sirk as *Lured* in 1947.

Snobs

France 1961 90 mins bw
UFA Comacico/Investissements Overseas Service

d **Jean-Pierre Mocky**
sc **Jean-Pierre Mocky**
ph **Marcel Weiss**
m **Joseph Kosma**
Michel Lonsdale, Gérard Hoffman, Véronique Nordy, Noël Roquevert, Francis Blanche

The president of a milk co-operative is drowned in a vat of milk while inspecting a dairy plant. Four directors become rivals for his post, each playing on the snobbery and foibles of the electors. Mocky continued to live up to his name in his third film, an iconoclastic comedy which he milks unmercifully for laughs. Some good gags can be salvaged from the bawdy slapstick, but not enough.

Few of Mocky's later comedies have made it to the English-speaking world.

So Close To Life
(US: Brink Of Life)
Nara Livet

Sweden 1957 84 mins bw
Nordisk Tonefilm

d **Ingmar Bergman**
sc **Ingmar Bergman, Ulla Isaksson**
ph **Max Wilen**
Ingrid Thulin, Eva Dahlbeck, Bibi Andersson, Max Von Sydow, Erland Josephson, Barbro Hiort Af Ornäs

Three women in a maternity ward: one (Thulin) has had a miscarriage and feels it's a punishment for her marriage break-up; the second (Dahlbeck) is happily married and desperately wanting a child, but loses it; the youngest (Andersson), unmarried, decides to keep her baby after trying an abortion. Mothers-to-be or not to be, that is the question in Bergman's clinical, pessimistic film that hardly strays outside the maternity ward. Although the treatment of birth is realistic, the script is over-literary at times and two of the stories have too-neatly tied endings. However, there are three good reasons for seeing the film—the female leads.

Best Actress (Collective Prize—Thulin, Dahlbeck, Andersson, Ornäs) Cannes 1958

Sodrásban see Current

Soeurs Brontë, Les see Brontë Sisters, The

Soft Skin, The see Silken Skin

Soir Sur La Plage, Un see Violent Summer

Un Soir, Un Train

Belgium 1968 90 mins col
Fox Europa/Films Du Siècle/Parc

d **André Delvaux**
sc **André Delvaux**
ph **Ghislain Cloquet**
m **Frédéric Devreese**
Yves Montand, Anouk Aimée, Adriana Bogdan, Hector Camerlynck, François Beukelaers

Mathias (Montand), a rationalist Flemish professor living with Anne (Aimée), a French-speaking theatrical designer, seldom questions his way of life or their relationship. One autumn evening, on a train journey, Anne disappears, and Mathias, set down in an unknown region, begins to look for her while being forced to come to terms with himself. Delvaux's second film is a sensitively photographed and melancholy story of lost love, intermingling past and present, reality and fantasy. As in most of his films, there is an elusive image of womanhood, here ideally embodied by the beautiful Anouk Aimée. Montand drifts enigmatically through the symbol-cluttered screenplay.

Solaris

USSR 1972 165 mins col
Mosfilm/Magna

d **Andrei Tarkovsky**
sc **Andrei Tarkovsky, Friedrich Gorenstein**
ph **Vadim Yusov**
m **Eduard Artemyev**
Natalya Bondarchuk, Donatas Banionis, Yuri Yarvet, Anatoly Solonitsin

An astronaut travels to a distant space station orbiting the planet of Solaris, to investigate the many deaths occuring there, and the phenomenon whereby people in the thoughts of the space travellers materialize. This visually striking Soviet sci-fi film, based on a novel by Stanislav Lem, manages to convince technologically without reliance on special effects. However, Tarkovsky does take his time in space, and weighs the movie down with somewhat turgid philosophical discussions as the cosmonauts are forced into self-examination.

Soldiers, The see Carabiniers, Les

Soleil Des Voyous, Le see Action Man

Soleil Ô

aka Oh, Sun

Mauritania 1970 105 mins bw
Shango Production

d **Med Hondo**
sc **Med Hondo**
ph **François Catonne**
m **Georges Anderson**

Robert Liensol, Theo Legitimus, Yane Barry, Bernard Fresson, Gabriel Glissand, Ambroise M'Bia, Jean Baptiste Tiemele

In an unnamed French colony in West Africa, black men line up before a white priest for baptism and re-naming—the first step in a process which simultaneously deracinates and subjugates them. In France, encouraged by propaganda, colonial blacks arrive to seek a better life. What they find is unemployment but for a handful of 'dirty' jobs, unacceptable living conditions, naked racism and bureaucratic indifference. Searching for a new form, Med Hondo has eschewed all conventional narrative. From the stylized and surreal opening sequences to the episodic adventures of a particular man (Liensol) —an educated black who conducts dialogues with a Frenchman (Fresson) and who functions as a collective emblem for the immigrant—the director presents a series of imaginative set-pieces, linked by voice-over narrative, to investigate and dramatize a complex web of inter-related themes. A scathing attack on colonialism, the film is also a shocking exposé of racism and a brutal indictment of Western capitalist values. If the imagery and sentiments are sometimes crude, it is nonetheless a gripping and original work.

Soliti Ignoti, I see Persons Unknown

Solo Sunny

E. Germany 1979 102 mins col
Deutsche Film Aktien Gesellschaft/Babelsberg Group

d **Konrad Wolf, Wolfgang Kohlhaase**
sc **Wolfgang Kohlhaase**
ph **Eberhard Geick**
m **Günther Fischer**

Renate Krössner, Alexander Lang, Dieter Montag, Heide Kipp, Klaus Brasch

Ex-factory worker Sunny (Krössner) sings and travels with a pop group called The Tornadoes, but wants to go solo. She also has trouble with the men in her life—a saxophone player (Brasch), a taxi-driver (Montag) and a musician-philosopher (Lang). An interesting, perceptive and sometimes amusing portrait of a young woman trying to find independence against the uncaptivating background of East German bars and cabarets. It greatly appealed to East German youth, the theme song became a hit and it seemed to steer the cinema of the GDR into a less restricted direction. The film's main strength lies in the terse script and the vibrant performance from the pretty and petite Krössner.

Best Actress (Renate Krössner) Berlin 1980

Somewhere In Europe

(US: It Happened In Europe)

Valahol Európában

Hungary 1947 90 mins bw
Mafirt-Radványi

d **Géza Radványi**
sc **Géza Radványi, Béla Bálazs, Judit Fejér, Félix Máriássy**
ph **Barnabás Hegyi**
m **Dénes Buday**

Arthur Somlay, Zsuzsa Bánki, Miklós Gábor, Laci Horváth, György Bárdy

A band of thieving and begging orphans takes refuge in a castle inhabited by an orchestra conductor (Somlay), and find a new way of life in contrast to the bitter realities of post-war Hungary. Hungary's first international success for many years led to the cinema becoming a nationalized industry, and marked the return to creative work in his homeland (after wartime exile in the USSR) of Béla Bálazs, the great film theorist and author. The Neo-Realist-influenced film addresses the problems facing a new generation with directness and optimism.

Sommaren Med Monika see Summer With Monika

Sommarlek see Summer Interlude

Sommarnattens Leende see Smiles Of A Summer's Night

Söndag I September, En see Sunday In September, A

Song of Bwana Toshi, The see Bwana Toshi

The Song Of The Red Ruby

Sangen Om Den Røde Rubin

aka Den Røde Rubin

Denmark 1970 106 mins col
Palladium

d **Annelise Meineche**
sc **Annelise Meineche, John Hilbard**
ph **Erik Wittrup Willumsen**
m **Øle Hoyer**
Øle Soltøft, Ghita Norby, Lotte Horn, Annie Birgit Garde, Gertie Jung, Lizzi Varencke, Eva Weinreich

Ash Burlefoot (Soltøft) dreams of becoming a great musician but is constantly waylaid by his insatiable appetite for women, two of whom he makes pregnant. Eventually, he falls in love with a teacher (Norby), settles down, and realizes his ambitions. Trumpeted as a frank account of a young man's journey to maturity, and taken from a best-selling novel by Agnar Mykle, this film is, in fact, a series of sexual and romantic clichés. Mediocre acting and pedestrian direction fail to improve matters.

Sonnenstrahl see Ray Of Sunshine, A

Sorcières De Salem, Les see Witches of Salem, The

Sorok Pervyi see Forty First, The

The Sorrow And The Pity

Le Chagrin Et La Pitié France 1971
270 mins bw
Télévision Rencontre (France)/Norddeutscher Rundfunk (Hamburg)/S.S.R.(Lausanne)

d **Marcel Ophüls**
sc **Marcel Ophüls, André Harris**
ph **André Gazut, Jürgen Thieme**
m **Popular songs of the period**

Four-and-a-half hours of footage largely consists of interviews with inhabitants of the city of Clermont-Ferrand who lived through World War II. A probing, incisive and fluent interviewer, as well as a brilliantly accomplished documentary director, Ophüls (son of Max) ruthlessly exposes the degree of collaboration among the French citizenry. He also talks to former members of the Resistance and some of the Nazi occupiers, inter-cutting archive material of Hitler in Paris and famous figures of the day going about their business—for example, Danielle Darrieux blithely setting of to tour Germany. The soundtrack, featuring Maurice Chevalier, is a masterstroke in setting period and ironically counterpointing the realities of the subject. Made for French TV which then refused to show it, it went on cinema release where its ugly revelations courted both acclaim and bitter controversy. In finally uncovering and probing the still unwelcome topic of collaboration, Ophüls opened the way for feature film-makers to re-examine the war, beginning notably with Louis Malle's *Lacombe Lucien*.

Soshun see Early Spring

S.O.S. Mediterranean see Hell's Cargo

Souffle Au Coeur, Le see Dearest Love

Sound Of Trumpets, The see Job, The

Soupirant, Le see Suitor, The

Souriante Madame Beudet, La see Smiling Madame Beudet, The

Sous Le Soleil De Satan see Under Satan's Sun

Sous Les Toits De Paris

aka Under The Roofs Of Paris

France 1929 92 mins bw
Tobis

d **René Clair**
sc **René Clair**
ph **Georges Périnal**
m **Armand Bernard**

Albert Préjean, Pola Illery, Gaston Modot, Edmond Gréville

A street singer (Préjean) falls for a pretty Romanian girl (Illery) whom he protects from her lecherous lover (Modot), but he is accused of theft. Although this is one of the very first French talkies, it doesn't have a great deal of talk. What it has is a wisp of a story with sound effects and street noises (studio created), sometimes purposefully drowning out the dialogue for effect, and a number of pleasant songs. The title song is rendered by various Parisians, with the camera moving from singer to singer, from house to house. Creaky as much of it seems today, it still retains considerable charm and is a good example of the more fluent, early French sound films.

South

Sur

Argentina 1988 127 mins col
Cinesur(Buenos Aires)/Pacific/Canal Plus(Paris)

d **Fernando E Solanas**
sc **Fernando E Solanas**
ph **Felix Monti**
m **Astor Piazzola**

Miguel Angel Sola, Susu Pecoraro, Philippe Léotard, Lito Cruz, Ulises Dumont

In 1983, after five years in prison on charges of subversion, Floreal (Sola) is released, but finds he must reckon with the past before he can find the strength to return home and face the future. His wife (Pecoraro), meanwhile, has her own adjustments to make, having endured the nightmare of his absence, with the help of his best friend (Léotard) who, in her loneliness, she allowed to become her lover. Following on *Tangos, The Exile Of Gardel*, Solanas (himself a former exile) again deals with the theme but, this time, it's the exile of imprisonment which tears life and relationships apart, and it's a far more sombre film than its predecessor. The lead performances are beautifully controlled and the film is magnificent to look at as Floreal wanders through dreams and memories in the neighbourhood from which he was cruelly removed. As with *Tangos*, the music once again plays a cardinal role in the evocation of emotion and atmosphere but the piece suffers from a profusion of incidental characters and occurrences that serve only to confuse.

Best Director Cannes 1988

The South

El Sur

Spain 1983 94 mins col
Elias Querejeta/Chloe/Spanish Radio Television

d **Victor Erice**
sc **José Luis Lopez Linares**
ph **José Luis Alcaine**

Omero Antonutti, Lola Cardona, Sonsoles Aranguren, Iciar Bollan, Rafaela Aparicio

A young girl grows up in the 1950s away from her enigmatic Republican father, imagining things about him, including an affair with a famous actress, and the South where he lives. Erice's second film came an astonishing 10 years after the much-acclaimed *The Spirit Of The Beehive*. It was worth the wait. Like the previous film, the world is seen through the sensibility of a child—poetic, elusive and mysterious. There is also a wonderful rapport between the director and the two young actresses (Aranguren aged eight, Bollan aged 15) who play the daughter. Unfortunately, because of a disagreement with the producer, a second part was abandoned.

Sparkling Winds see Confrontation, The

The Sparrow

Al Asfour

Egypt 1973 120 mins col
Misr-International(Cairo)/ONCIC(Algeria)

d **Youssef Chahine**
sc **Lofti El Kholly, Youssef Chahine**
ph **Mustapha Imam**
m **Sheikh Imam, Ali Ismaïl, N. Bahgat**

Mahmoud El Miligui, Habiba, Mohsena Tewfik,

Meriam Fakhreddine, Salah Kabil, Aly El Sharif, Seif El Dine

It is 1967 and the Arabs have lost the war with Israel. Several parallel stories bring their Left- wing protagonists together at the house of Bahiah who releases a sparrow—symbol of the Egyptian people— from its cage and leads his fellow men into the streets of Cairo in a surge of proud defiance. Stylistically adventurous and politically explosive, Chahine's uncompromising attack on corruption and weakness among the ruling classes was banned for several years in most Arab countries. This film is a cry for solidarity, not just among oppressed classes but among Arab nations, and attempts to show how the war was lost from within. Chahine's pleas, first made in the narrower context of *The Land* (1969), are couched in dramatic, powerful and imaginative cinematic language that grips the attention and makes this one of the most acclaimed works in the Arab cinema.

The Sparrow Of Pigalle

Piaf

France 1974 105 mins col
Films Feuer/Ernie Martin Films

d **Guy Casaril**
sc **Françoise Ferley, Guy Casaril**
ph **Edmond Séchan**
m **Ralph Burns plus the Piaf song repertoire**
Brigitte Ariel, Pascale Christophe, Guy Tréjean, Pierre Vernier, Jacques Duby, Anouk Ferjac

In the first 20 years of her life, Edith Piaf, born in the gutter, faced poverty, illness and degradation, before her magical voice, extraordinary presence and spirited determination hauled her up to stardom. Based on the book by Piaf's half-sister Simone Berteaut, Casaril's film does little either to illumine or enhance the Piaf legend, being an absolutely superficial account of the disasters that dogged her young life. Musically, too, it's a mishmash, using stills of the real Piaf with her voice over, Ariel miming to some of the songs, and with yet others sung by Betty Mars. On the credit side, the colourful sleaze of pre-war Pigalle is very well caught, Ariel looks suitably waif-like and Christophe is excellent as Momone (otherwise Berteaut), Edith's self-appointed protector.

A Special Day

Una Giornata Particolare

Italy 1977 105 mins col
Champion/Canafox

d **Ettore Scola**
sc **Ettore Scola, Ruggero Maccari, Maurizio Costanzo**
ph **Pasqualino De Santis**
m **Armando Trovaioli**
Sophia Loren, Marcello Mastroianni, John Vernon, Françoise Berd, Nicole Magny

Two lonely residents of a seedy apartment building—the weary mother of six children and a homosexual radio announcer—are drawn together on a day in 1938 while the populace is in the streets cheering Hitler's visit to Mussolini in Rome. Some of the minor appeal of this depressing, contrived piece is in the casting against type of Loren as a frumpish housewife, and Mastroianni as a gay man. The political background is merely an excuse to show that repression is a common bond between two differing people, even to the point of making love.

Special Section see Section Spéciale

Special Treatment

Poseban Tretman

Yugoslavia 1980 93 mins col
Centar Film

d **Goran Paskaljević**
sc **Dušan Kovačević, Filip David, Goran Paskaljević**
ph **Aleksandar Petković**
m **Vojislav Kostić, Wagner, Dvořák**
Ljuba Tadić, Dušica Žegarac, Milena Dravić, Danilo Stojković, Petar Kralj, Milan Srdoć

Dr Ilich (Tadić) runs a sanatorium for alcoholics where his cure consists of strict diet and exercise, extensive playing of Wagner's music and, above all, the use of psychodrama. His supposedly progressive methods, however, mask his own moral decline and disaster strikes his group during a visit to a brewery. This is a well-made and expertly acted allegory about authoritarianism and the imprisonment of the individual will, but a lot of heavy-handed symbolism is tacked on to a somewhat meagre plot. It remains in the memory more because it is so depressing than for any other reason.

Speriamo Che Sia Femmina see Let's Hope It's A Girl

Spetters

Holland 1983 109 mins col
VSE

d **Paul Verhoeven**
sc **Gerard Soeteman**
ph **Jöst Vacano**
m **Ton Scherpenzeel, Kayak**
Toon Agterberg, Maarten Spanjer, Hans Van Tongeren, Renée Soutendijk, Marianne Boyer

Three young men, involved with a scheming blonde who runs a hot-dog stand, dream of winning the motor-cross championships, but disillusion sets in after one is beaten up and another is crippled in an accident. Despite the explicit sex, gay and straight, graphic violence and motor-bike action, *Spetters*, which means grease spots or whizz-kids, is not your average teen exploitation movie. Using its elements and delirious visuals, Holland's leading director pulls out all the stops but also peels off the leather-jacketed characters to reveal the hollowness of their dreams.

Spicy Rice
aka Dragon's Food
Drachenfutter

W. Germany 1987 75 mins bw
Novoskop Film Jan Schütte (West Germany)/Probst Film (Switzerland)

d **Jan Schütte**
sc **Jan Schütte, Thomas Strittmatter**
ph **Lutz Konermann**
m **Claus Bantzer**
Bhaskar, Ric Young, Buddy Uzzaman, Wolf-Dieter Sprenger, Ulrich Wildgruber, Peter Fitz

Two young immigrants in Germany, a Pakistani (Bhaskar) without a work permit, and a Chinese waiter (Ric Young), decide to start their own restaurant where they employ a mixture of struggling immigrants like themselves. Thirty-year-old Schütte manages a delightful new slant on the oft-treated immigrant problem in Germany through affectionate observation of his melting pot of characters. The fact that very few of them can understand each other—they communicate in Urdu, Swahili, Mandarin, Gujarati and pidgin German—puts the spectator in their position, yet doesn't obscure what is happening. A film that enriches and entertains, and possibly creates more tolerance than more strident projects—and all the more praiseworthy for succeeding at an unfashionably short length and in black-and-white.

The Spiders
Die Spinnen

Germany 1919-1920 80 mins (Part I); 94 mins (Part II) bw
Decla-Bioskop

d **Fritz Lang**
sc **Fritz Lang**
ph **Emil Schünemann (Part I), Karl Freund (Part II)**
m **Silent**
Carl De Vogt, Lil Dagover, Ressel Orla, Paul Morgan, Georg John, Rudolf Lettinger, Thea Zander

I. 'The Golden Lake': Hoog (De Vogt) is pitted against Lio-Shah (Orla) and the criminal gang, The Spiders, all rivals in a search for Inca treasure in a subterranean city. II. 'The Diamond Ships': Hoog, Lio-Shah and The Spiders are after a diamond, shaped like the head of Buddha, the wearer of which will rule Asia. One of Fritz Lang's earliest works seems to have been inspired by the German pulp writer Karl May and the serials of Louis Feuillade, but Langian elements are already implanted—the use of mirrors, hypnosis, underground chambers and arch criminals—that would reappear frequently throughout his *oeuvre*. 'I simply wanted to film adventurous subjects...I loved everything that was exuberant and exotic', Lang stated. The two stories, broken up into many episodes in the serial structure, are certainly exuberant and exotic, filmed against gigantic architectural sets with ordinary German sunshine providing the lighting effects.

The Spider's Stratagem
Strategia Del Ragno

Italy 1970 110 mins col
Radiotelevisione Italiana

d **Bernardo Bertolucci**
sc **Bernardo Bertolucci, Eduardo De Gregorio, Marilu Parolini**
ph **Vittorio Storaro, Franco Di Giacomo**
m **Verdi, Schoenberg**
Alida Valli, Giulio Brogi, Tino Scotti, Pino Campanini

A young man (Brogi) revisits the village in the Po valley where his father was murdered by the Fascists in 1936, but gradually discovers that the hero he thought his father to be, was really a traitor. Jorge Luis Borges' story, *Theme Of The Traitor And The Hero*, transposes easily from Ireland to Italy, though it comes across on screen as an over-elaborate piece of Oedipal plotting. However, much of it is intriguing and the photography, sometimes evoking the paintings of De Chirico, is memorable.

The Spies
Les Espions

France 1957 120 mins bw
Filmsonor/Vera Films

d **Henri-Georges Clouzot**
sc **Henri-Georges Clouzot, Jérôme Jeronimi**
ph **Christian Matras**
m **Georges Auric**
Curt Jurgens, Gérard Séty, Peter Ustinov, Sam Jaffe, Vera Clouzot, O.E. Hasse

A second-rate psychiatrist (Séty), running a shabby sanatorium with only a couple of patients in residence, is offered a generous sum of money by the American military to harbour a mystery personage. The bemused doctor accepts and a stranger (Jurgens)—purportedly a top-level German physicist—arrives, followed by a bevy of international spies and some rather curious replacements for the hospital staff... Leaving the ingenuity of *Les Diaboliques* behind him, Clouzot ventured into the formula territory of the espionage thriller and came up with a formula entertainment. The director's command of atmosphere and gift for suspense is laid on a bit too thickly, but there is some good acting, especially from Vera Clouzot.

Spinnen, Die see Spiders, The

The Spirit Of The Beehive
El Espiritu De La Colmene

Spain 1973 98 mins col
Elias Querejeta

d **Victor Erice**
sc **Francisco J. Querejeta**
ph **Luis Cuadrado**
m **Luis De Pablo**
Ana Torrent, Isabel Telleria, Fernando Fernan Gomez, Teresa Gimpera

In a remote Castilian village in 1940, eight-year-old Ana (Torrent) becomes obsessed with Boris Karloff's good-bad monster in *Frankenstein* seen at a travelling film show, and believes that a fugitive whom she befriends is the spirit of the monster. Most of what happens in this sensitive, cryptic film is reflected in the wide, brown eyes of the lonely little girl, creating the world of a child's imagination to perfection. This is all the more effective for being shot realistically. A profoundly impressive first film by Erice, it drew beautifully underplayed performances from the non-professional cast. For those willing to look, it also says something about Franco's Spain.

Spirits Of The Dead
Histoires Extraordinaires
aka Tre Passi Nel Delirio

France/Italy 1968 117 mins col
Les Films Marceau/Cocinor/P.E.A.

d **1) Roger Vadim** (*Metzengerstein*), **2) Louis Malle** (*William Wilson*), **3) Federico Fellini** (*Toby Dammit*)
sc **1) Roger Vadim, Pascal Cousin, Clement Biddle Wood 2) Louis Malle, Daniel Boulanger, Clement Biddle Wood 3) Federico Fellini, Bernardino Zapponi, Clement Biddle Wood**
ph **1) Claude Renoir 2) Tonino Delli Colli 3) Giuseppe Rotunno**
m **1) Jean Prodromidès 2) Diego Masson 3) Nino Rota**
1) Jane and Peter Fonda, Carla Marlier, James Robertson Justice 2) Alain Delon, Brigitte Bardot, Katia Christina 3) Terence Stamp, Salvo Randone

1) In the Middle Ages, a young woman believes that the spirit of the cousin she loved,

killed in a stable fire that she had ignited, was transferred to a horse that escaped. 2) A mean-spirited, gambling Austrian officer murders his *doppelgänger*, confesses and kills himself. 3) A famous British film star, after making a movie in Rome, gets very drunk at the end-of-shooting party and is beheaded while speeding in his Maserati. All three episodes are based on the grotesque and macabre tales of the 19th-century American author, Edgar Allan Poe; the third, the only one updated, is far and away the best, though pretty familiar Fellini territory. Malle's telling is handsome and straightforward and the detail gruesome; while Vadim saw to it that his wife (Fonda) wore revealing clothes, and caused an incestuous *frisson* by casting her brother as her lover.

The Splendid Days

Seryozha

USSR 1960 80 mins bw
Mosfilm

d **G. Danieli, Igor Talankin**
sc **Vera Panova, G. Danieli, Igor Talankin**
ph **A. Nitochkin**
m **B. Chaikovsky**
Boria Barchatov, Sergei Bondarchuk, Irina Skobotseva, Natasha Chechetkina, Seryosha Metelitsin, Yura Kozlov

Five-year-old Seryozha (Barchatov) lives on a farm with his widowed mother (Skobtseva). One summer's day, she brings home the burly Korostelyov (Bondarchuk) and introduces him as the boy's new father. The summer passes in the typical activities of childhood but, as Seryozha rides his bicycle or plays with his friends, he is constantly under a cloud of unease. Two young directors, working from a story by Panova, a well-known Russian children's novelist, have come up with an intimate, detailed and often charming observation of childhood and a child's psychology. Seryozha's gradual perception of his stepfather's sterling qualities and the way in which the family becomes a welded and loving whole is conveyed with simplicity and truth. Unfortunately, it is also heavily garnished with sentimentality and 'poetic' effects and, nowadays, has an even more curiously old-fashioned air than it already suffered from on its original release.

Spoiled Children

Des Enfants Gâtés

France 1977 113 mins bw
Films 66/Little Bear/Sara Film/Gaumont

d **Bertrand Tavernier**
sc **Christine Pascal, Charlotte Dubreuil, Bertrand Tavernier**
ph **Alain Levent**
m **Philippe Sarde**
Michel Piccoli, Christine Pascal, Michel Aumont, Gérard Jugnot, Arlette Bonnard

A famous film director (Piccoli), unable to concentrate on his new script at home with his family, rents a high rise apartment. Instead of finding peace and quiet, he gets involved in the tenants' fight against an exploitative landlord, and with a girl (Pascal) half his age. Tavernier, staunch defender of *Le Cinéma De Papa*, the more traditional style of narrative in pre- *Nouvelle Vague* days, has come up with another of his own examples. This 'dramatic comedy' of a 'blocked' artist exchanging an ivory tower for a tower block never goes much below the surface of the issues it raises—feminism, art vs life, modern Paris vs the Paris of the past—but Piccoli brings credence to the central role.

Spring Into Summer

Pleure Pas La Bouche Pleine

France 1973 117 mins col
Renn Productions/Les Films Du Chef-Lieu/ORTF

d **Pascal Thomas**
sc **Pascal Thomas, Roland Duval, Suzanne Schiffman**
ph **Colin Monnier**
m **Vladimir Cosma**
Annie Cole, Frédéric Duru, Jean Carmet, Christiane Chamaret, Bernard Menez, Daniel Ceccaldi

Annie (Cole) and Frédéric (Duru), aged 16 and 19 respectively, are courting during the summer in Poitou where they live. Secretly, Annie yearns for some excitement and when Alexandre (Menez), superficially more sophisticated than the local boys, comes to Poitou, she gets it. Fragile and charming, this is, refreshingly, a female rites of passage film, played in the context of happy family relationships and everyday people doing everyday things. Annie's sexual initiation, the centre of a story in which nothing much happens, is handled with matter-of-fact truth, and Thomas brings to the whole enterprise an observant eye for the details of village life.

Spring River Flows East
Yijiang Chunshui Xiang Dong Liu

China 1947 188 mins bw
LinHua Film Company

d **Cai Chusheng, Zheng Junli**
sc **Cai Chusheng, Zheng Junli**
ph **Zhu Jimming**
m **Zhang Zhengfan**
Tao Jin, Pai Yang, Wu Yin, Yan Gongshang, Shu Xiuwen

An initially idealistic schoolteacher (Jin), leaves his father and mother (Gongshang and Yin), his young wife (Yang) and his child to join the Red cross and take part in the struggle against the Japanese in 1931. He is captured, but escapes to the Kuomintang capital Chongqing, where he is seduced by *bourgeois* life and bigamously marries a high-society woman (Xiuwen), while his family suffers extreme deprivation in occupied Shanghai. Made in two parts, titled 'Wartime Separation' and 'Darkness And Dawn', this is one of Chinese cinema's greatest pre-Revolutionary achievements. Sprawling, often sentimental and simplistic, it is also richly entertaining, illuminating the whole tumultuous era it covers, and immensely involving. The cross-cutting between parallel stories not only demonstrates the social contradictions in the country, but allows Junli (the director of *Crows And Sparrows*) and the veteran Chusheng (who apparently worked mainly on the script) to present both powerful drama and sophisticated comedy sequences.

Spring Shower see Marie—A Hungarian Legend

Spring Symphony
Frühlingssinfonie

W. Germany/E. Germany 1983
103 mins col
Allianz/Peter Schamoni/ZDF/DEFA/Greentree

d **Peter Schamoni**
sc **Peter Schamoni**
ph **Gerard Vandenberg**
m **Schumann**
Nastassja Kinski, Herbert Grönemeyer, Rolf Hoppe, Anja-Christine Preussler, Bernhard Wicki, Edda Seipel, André Heller, Gideon Kremer

The love affair of composer Robert Schumann (Grönemeyer) and the gifted pianist Clara Wieck (Kinski), from their meeting in adolescence (the younger Clara played by Preussler) when Wieck's father (Hoppe) taught Schumann the piano, until their wedding. Schamoni's film is an ambitious failure. It paints a vivid picture of Clara's relationship with her over-possessive father who tries to prevent the marriage; it wanders, in typical biopic fashion, through the concert halls of Europe with Clara as she is hailed a virtuoso by everybody from Goethe to Chopin. What Schamoni fails to do is bring the complexities, excitement and difficulty of genius to life. The movie is dull, reverent and superficial, leaving little besides the glorious outpouring of music, interpreted by several great artists such as Dietrich Fischer-Dieskau, Wilhelm Kempff and Ivo Pogorelich.

Sreo Sam Cak I Srecne Cigane see Happy Gypsies

Stachka see Strike

Stalker

USSR 1979 161 mins col/bw
Mosfilm

d **Andrei Tarkovsky**
sc **Boris and Arkady Strugatsky**
ph **Aleksandr Knyazhinsky**
m **Eduard Artemyev**
Aleksandr Kaidanovsky, Anatoly Solonitsin, Nikolai Grinko

The stalker (Kaidanovsky) guides a writer (Solonitsin) and a scientist (Grinko) to the centre of a dangerous, overgrown, forbidden area called the Zone where a room is said to contain the Truth. One wonders if the long (almost three hours of screen time) journey was really necessary when the writer and scientist, on reaching their destination, discuss their differing viewpoints in terms of bad didactic drama reminiscent of the 1930s, and little truth is revealed to them or to the spectator. But Tarkovsky's strength lies in startling images and the creation of mystical *milieux* rather than in narrative, and the nightmarish trip undertaken by the shaven-headed stalker and his companions, shot in eerie sepia colour, haunts the memory.

Stammheim

W. Germany 1986 107 mins col
Bioskop-Film/Thalia Theater/Filmverlag Der Autoren

d **Reinhard Hauff**
sc **Stefan Aust**
ph **Frank Brühne**
m **Marcel Wengler**
Ulrich Tukur, Therese Affolter, Sabine Wagner, Hans Kremer, Ulrich Pleitgen, Marina Wandruszka, Hans Christian Rudolph, Gunther Flesch, Horst Mendroch

A dramatized account of the notorious Baader-Meinhof trial that shook Germany from 1975 to 1977. One of the defendants dies at the outset as a result of a hunger strike; during the trial Ulrike Meinhof (Affolter) is found dead in her cell, an apparent suicide; the chief prosecutor is murdered before the end of the proceedings at which Andreas Baader (Tukur) and the other two defendants are sentenced to life imprisonment, only to be found dead shortly afterwards. Director Hauff, who had already demonstrated his concern with man's relationship to authority in *Knife In The Head* and *Slow Attack*, has brought this most controversial of political trials to the screen with gripping and powerful conviction. That the screenplay is largely taken from the trial transcript and the action confined mainly to the courtroom at Stammheim prison (recreated in an old Hamburg warehouse), does not limit the sense of action. Made on a tiny budget with the help of the Thalia Theater Ensemble, the film caused a major furore at the Berlin Festival.

Best Film Berlin 1986

Stärker Als Die Nacht see Stronger Than The Night

Staroye I Novoye see General Line, The

Stars
Sterne

E. Germany/Bulgaria 1959 95 mins bw
DEFA(Berlin)/Studiya Za Igralni Filmi(Sofia)

d **Konrad Wolf**
sc **Anzhel Wagenstein**
ph **Werner Bergmann**
m **Simeon Pironkov**
Sascha Kruscharska, Jürgen Frohriep, Erik S. Klein, Stefan Pejtschew, Milka Tujkowa

A small Bulgarian town in 1943. In the schoolyard, now a barbed-wire prison, a consignment of Greek Jews awaits deportation to the death camps. A young Jewess (Kruscharska) and a German soldier (Frohriep) fall in love and he determines to save her. When he fails, his new awareness of his country's atrocities and his guilt at his own complicity fuel his decision to join the Partisans and fight the Nazi regime. Written by a Bulgarian Jew and directed by a former Red Army officer, *Stars*—the badge of the doomed Jewish fate as well as the romantic canopy for the lovers—is a convincing re-creation of a specific time and place. Wolf, one of East Germany's finest directors, has admirably avoided the pitfalls of melodrama and maudlin sentimentality, offering instead haunting and graphically realistic images of despair in a film that is both moving and thought provoking.

Special Jury Prize Cannes 1959

State Of Siege
État De Siège

France 1973 120 mins col
Reggana/Cinema 10/Unidis/Euro International/Dieter Geissler/Cinema 5

d **Costa-Gavras**
sc **Costa-Gavras, Franco Solinas**
ph **Pierre William Glenn**
m **Mikis Theodorakis**
Yves Montand, Renato Salvatori, O.E. Hasse, Jacques Weber, Jean Luc Bideau

In an unnamed repressive South American country, an American CIA agent (Montand) is held hostage by a Left-wing guerrilla group demanding the release of 150 political prisoners. Using the manipulatively skilful cinematic techniques of *Z* (1969) and *The Confession* (1970), Costa-Gavras convincingly indicts the USA's clandestine involvement with dictatorships in Latin America, which caused the film to be withdrawn from Washington D.C.'s American Film Institute Theater in 1973. Filmed in Chile under Allende, the setting for the same director's *Missing* (1982) after the coup, it was also criticized by the Left for representing the CIA in the sympathetic guise of Montand.

A Station For Two

Vokzal Dlya Dvoikh

USSR 1983 133 mins col
Mosfilm

d **Eldar Ryazanov**
sc **Emil Braginsky, Eldar Ryazanov**
ph **Vadim Alisov**
m **Andrei Petrov**
Ludmila Gurchenko, Oleg Basilashvili, Nikita Mikhalkov, Nonna Mordinkova, Mikhail Kononov

A former concert pianist (Basilashvili), held in a Siberian labour camp on a manslaughter charge, is sent off to visit his wife by the kindly (*sic*) commandant. During the journey he is delayed at a stopover by an argument with a waitress, misses his train, falls in love with the waitress (Gurchenko) and finds her waiting for him when he returns to the camp. Although made by one of the USSR's best-known satirical directors, this film adds up to no more than a gently amusing and oddly incoherent romantic comedy.

Stavisky

France 1974 117 mins col
Cerito Films/Les Films Ariane/Euro International

d **Alain Resnais**
sc **Jorge Semprun**
ph **Sacha Vierny**
m **Stephen Sondheim**
Jean-Paul Belmondo, Charles Boyer, François Périer, Anny Duperey, Michel Lonsdale, Claude Rich, Silvia Badesco

Serge Alexandre (Belmondo), born Sacha Stavisky, a Russian Jew, is a financier and swindler whose powerful allies and connections include politicians and police. These desert him when a major fraud is unmasked, and he dies in mysterious circumstances. Basing his film on the real-life Stavisky who provoked a scandal which almost toppled the French government in 1934, Resnais has combined fact and fiction into what one critic aptly described as 'a tone poem to the 1930s'. The director's first feature after a six-year break, of which he himself said, 'It is not a political or historical document but rather an entertainment,' it is, in spite of its political context, an empty exercise beneath its glittering exterior. Resnais' characteristic approach is evident in the symbolic use of colour—white as a romantic emblem of death—and in his employment of shifting time scales. *Stavisky* is visually breathtaking in its evocation of period and expertly acted but, coming from Resnais, a disappointment.

Stella

Greece 1955 94 mins bw
Millas Films

d **Michael Cacoyannis**
sc **Michael Cacoyannis**
ph **Costa Theodorides**
m **Manos Hadjidakis**
Melina Mercouri, Yiorgo Fountas, Alekos Alexandrikis, Sophia Vembo

Men are wild about Stella (Mercouri), singer in a *bouzouki* hall and a free spirit who will not be caged. Her involvement with a middle-class writer and a football hero leads to tragedy for all three. Only the second film made by Cacoyannis, it hints at his particular talent for capturing a sense of pre-ordained doom and is characterized by effective low-key photography, punctuated with some lively set-pieces. Mercouri, Greece's Minister of Culture in the 1980s, was here making her screen debut, and holds nothing back in exhibiting her narrow range of gifts: sex appeal, a generous smile, a captivating wink, uninhibited earthiness and an ouzo-soaked singing voice. All of which makes for a reasonably entertaining melodrama of uneven quality.

Stem Van Het Water, De see Voice Of The Water, The

Stepfather
Beau-Père
France 1981 120 mins col
Sara Films/Antenne 2

d **Bertrand Blier**
sc **Bertrand Blier**
ph **Sacha Vierny**
m **Philippe Sarde**
Patrick Dewaere, Ariel Besse, Maurice Ronet, Nicole Garcia, Nathalie Baye, Maurice Risch

A bar pianist (Dewaere), widowed when his wife is killed in a motor accident, is left with his adolescent stepdaughter (Besse), who decides that he should be her first lover. Further complications arise when her real father (Ronet) comes to claim her. Working from his own novel, Blier's overlong and *Lolita*-like tale is played largely for comedy. It manages to stay just this side of tastelessness thanks to a strand of tenderness and the performances of the leads, notably newcomer Besse, who conveys an appealing mixture of childlike qualities and sensuality.

Stepping Out
Slingrevalsen
Denmark 1981 104 mins col
Metronome Productions A/S

d **Esben Høilund Carlsen**
sc **Nils Schou**
ph **Dirk Brüel**
m **Bent Fabricius-Bjerre**
Solbjørg Højfeldt, Kurt Dreyer, Ole Ernst, Ulf Pilgaard, Lisbeth Lundquist, Nikolaj Harris, Anne- Stine Lier

Karen (Højfeldt) leaves Soren (Ernst) for Jens (Dreyer) who leaves Lis (Lundquist) who is married to Blom (Pilgaard) who...'How many combinations do you think are left—mathematically speaking?' asks a puzzled guest at a party attended by all the various couples in this 'Divorce Danish Style' comedy. There is a lot in it that compares favourably with serious American films such as *Kramer Vs Kramer*, plus some Scandinavian sexual insights. The humour in the marital discords may escape many—cornflakes are emptied over a husband's head—but the innumerable plot complications are well-handled, and the playing is amiable, especially by the two children (Harris and Lier) caught up in the battle of the sexes.

Sterne see Stars

Stilte Rond Christine M., De see Question Of Silence, A

Stir Patra see Letter From The Wife

Stolen Kisses
Baisers Volés
France 1968 91 mins col
Films Du Carrosse/Artistes Associés

d **François Truffaut**
sc **François Truffaut, Claude De Givray, Bernard Revon**
ph **Denys Clerval**
m **Antoine Duhamel**
Jean-Pierre Léaud, Delphine Seyrig, Michel Lonsdale, Claude Jade, Harry-Max

Antoine Doinel (Léaud), aged 20 and discharged from the army, returns to Paris where he is employed variously as a hotel clerk, private detective, salesman in a shoe store, where he has a brief affair with the owner's wife (Seyrig), and TV repair man, before proposing to his long-time girlfriend (Jade). The light tone of 1930s romantic comedies is set immediately by Charles Trenet singing 'Que Reste T'Il De Nos Amours?' on the sound track at the start of this third episode in the life of Doinel, Truffaut's alter-ego. It is difficult to believe that while Truffaut was being true to the spirit of the endearing Paris of the films of René Clair and Jacques Becker, the city was in turmoil with the student riots of May 1968.

Stone Wedding
Nunta De Pietra
Romania 1973 83 mins bw
Bucuresti Studios

d **1) Mircea Veroiu 2) Dan Piţa**
sc **1) Mircea Veroiu 2) Dan Piţa**
ph **Iosif Demian**
m **Dorin Liviu Zaharia, Dan Andrei**
1)Leopoldina Bălănută, Nina Domiga

2) Mircea Dianconu, Radu Boruzescu, Ursula Nussbächer

Two tales of peasant life in the Carpathian Mountains. In the first, a poor widow (Bălănută) sells everything to buy a wedding dress for the burial of her teenage daughter (Domiga), her last remaining child, who never lived to marry. In the second, an itinerant fiddler (Boruzescu), playing at a village wedding, runs off with the bride (Nussbächer). Both stories, one dark, the other lighter in tone, take place against a spectacular mountain setting captured in elegant and atmospheric black and white images. A successful blend of the realistic peasant life with Romanian folk myth, this unusual and striking film debut by two young directors helped launch a new wave in Romanian cinema.

Stora Aventyret, Det see Great Adventure, The

Storia Moderna: L'Ape Regina, Una see Queen Bee

Storm Over Asia

aka The Heir To Genghis Khan

Potomok Chingis-Khana

USSR 1928 93 mins bw
Mezhrabpom

d **Vsevolod Pudovkin**
sc **Osip Brik**
ph **Anatoli Golovnya**
m **Silent**
Valeri Inkizhinov, A. Dedintsev, V. Tzoppi, Paulina Belinskaya

Bair (Inkizhinov) a nomadic fur-trapper claiming to be the heir to Genghis Khan, is set up as a puppet monarch by the occupying British interventionist forces in Mongolia in 1918 but, realizing his national identity, he rouses the Asian hordes against their oppressors. A film of great visual beauty, dynamic montage, humour and compassion, it was banned in the UK for some years because the British are portrayed as the baddies. It was the last great silent film by Pudovkin, who was never really happy in the sound era, but a new version with a sound track added under his supervision was released in 1950.

Storm Within, The see Parents Terribles, Les

Stormy Waters

Rémorques

France 1941 80 mins bw
Sedis

d **Jean Grémillon**
sc **Jacques Prévert, André Cayatte**
ph **Armand Thirard, Louis Née**
m **Roland Manuel**
Jean Gabin, Michèle Morgan, Madeleine Renaud, Jean Marchat

The captain of a tugboat (Gabin) is happily married but, when he rescues a boat from stormy waters, he falls in love with the wife (Morgan) of its captain, a hateful boor. He leaves her to keep a vigil at the bedside of his own wife (Renaud) who is mortally ill. An intimate and perceptive study of passion and the nature of fidelity which benefits from a Prévert script and a trio of France's top stars. Filmed partly on location at Brest—Grémillon wanted only authentic sea and storm footage—work began in 1939, was hampered by the restrictions imposed by the Nazis, and was completed two years later in a Paris studio.

The Story Of A Cheat

Le Roman D'Un Tricheur

France 1936 85 mins bw
Cinéas

d **Sacha Guitry**
sc **Sacha Guitry**
ph **Marcel Lucien**
m **Adolphe Borchard**
Sacha Guitry, Jacqueline Delubac, Rosine Déréan, Marguerite Moreno, Pauline Carton, Serge Grave, Pierre Assy

An aging gentleman (Guitry) settles himself at a table of a pavement café and commences writing his memoirs. As he scribbles, his voice-over narrates the tale which begins when, as a young boy (Grave, later Assy), he is sent to bed without supper as punishment for stealing a few sous. That evening, his whole family dines on poisonous mushrooms and dies, thus setting him on a dishonest course on the basis that cheating pays. Guitry's most internationally celebrated film is a masterpiece of wit, style and invention in which we see the events acted out without dialogue, except for one scene in which a countess (Moreno) joins The Cheat at the café and is permitted a few words which reveal that he had been a passing lover of hers in his youth. Amoral to be sure and slightly repetitious, but charm and cleverness keep it constantly entertaining. With its masterly cutting back and forth between past and present, the film influenced such directors as Truffaut, Godard and Alain Resnais.

The Story Of Adèle H
L'Histoire D'Adèle H

France 1975 98 mins col
Films Du Carrosse/Artistes Associés

d **François Truffaut**
sc **François Truffaut, Jean Gruault, Suzanne Schiffman**
ph **Nestor Almendros**
m **Maurice Jaubert**
Isabelle Adjani, Bruce Robinson, Sylvia Marriott, Reubin Dorey, Joseph Blatchley

Adèle (Adjani), Victor Hugo's daughter, falls madly in love with a young English lieutenant (Robinson) in Guernsey and, despite his indifference to her, follows him to Nova Scotia and then to Barbados where she becomes a vagrant. Based on Adèle's diary written in code and decoded in 1955, the film is 'a musical composition for one instrument,' as Truffaut called it. That instrument is the exquisite 19-year-old Adjani (Adèle was in her thirties at the time) seldom off the screen and having to portray a passionate woman in the throes of *amour fou*. But because of the director's ironic detachment, both she and the film are muted and uninvolving. It was finely shot, partly in English, on location in Guernsey and Dakar.

Story Of A Love Affair see Chronicle of A Love

The Story Of Sin
Dzieje Grezechu

Poland 1975 128 mins col
TOR

d **Walerian Borowczyk**
sc **Walerian Borowczyk**
ph **Zygmunt Samosiuk**
m **Mendelssohn**
Grazyna Dlugolecka, Jerzy Zelnik, Olgierd Lukaszewicz

In turn-of-the-century Poland, a teenage girl of strict upbringing falls in love with a married man. When he leaves her pregnant, she drowns the child and sinks into degradation and prostitution. Borowczyk's brief return to his homeland from France produced a creaky period melodrama, based on a popular sentimental novel by Stefan Zeromski and overlaid with his usual highly decorative style (art direction by Teresa Barska), erotic fetishism and narrative sluggishness.

The Story Of The Late Chrysanthemums
Zangiku Monogatari

Japan 1939 142 mins bw
Shochiku

d **Kenji Mizoguchi**
sc **Yoshitaka Yoda**
ph **Shigeto Miki**
m **Senji Ito**
Shotaro Hanayagi, Kakuko Mori, Gonjuro Kawarazaki, Kokichi Takada, Ryotaro Kawanami

The actor Kikunosuke (Hanayagi) is criticized for ineptitude by the other members of a Kabuki troupe. Despondent, he returns home and starts an affair with Otoku (Mori), one of his family's maids. They marry and live in poverty, until Kikunosuke, with the help and sacrifices of his wife, becomes a successful actor. The only obstacle to Western audiences' appreciating one of Mizoguchi's finest middle-period films is the need to distinguish between good and bad acting in the Japanese theatrical traditions of *kabuki* and *shinpa* (popular melodrama), but the poignant tale of a woman's sacrifice for the man she loves can be appreciated in any language. The successful film, made up mostly of a single, long, mobile take per sequence, was originally shown in the West in a cut version running 115 minutes.

La Strada
aka The Road
Italy 1954 115 mins bw
Trans-Lux

d **Federico Fellini**
sc **Federico Fellini, Tullio Pinelli, Ennio Flaiano**
ph **Otello Martelli**
m **Nino Rota**
Giulietta Masina, Anthony Quinn, Richard Basehart, Aldo Silvani, Marcella Rovere, Livia Venturini

Gelsomina (Masina), a simple-minded girl, loves the whoring, drunken itinerant circus strong-man, Zampano (Quinn), who bought her for a few lire, put her to work as a clown, and ignores her. When Zampano fights and kills the gentle tightrope-walker (Basehart) who befriended her, she dies of a broken heart. Simplicity itself, *La Strada* is a magical tale and an unbearably painful account of loneliness which will always be associated with the sublimely Chaplinesque Masina (here given her first starring role by her husband, Fellini), but Quinn, too, is superb, particularly in the final revelation of his own heartbreak and isolation. The inherent sentimentality of the plot is off-set by the realistically desolate provincial towns in which it is played out.

Best Foreign Film Oscar 1956

Straight Through The Heart
Mitten Ins Herz
W. Germany 1983 91 mins col
WDR (Cologne)/Olga Film (Munich)

d **Doris Dörrie**
sc **Jelena Kristl**
ph **Michael Goebel**
m **Paul Shigihara**
Beata Jensen, Sepp Bierbichler, Gabrielle Litty, Jens-Muller Rastede, Joachim Hoepner

Anna (Jensen), a lonely 20-year-old whose attempts to assert herself have gone no further than dying her hair blue, attracts the attention of Armin (Bierbichler), a middle-aged and reclusive dentist. He persuades her to live with him in return for money, but turns out to want absolutely nothing from her other than her presence. Her increasingly determined efforts to involve him with her emotionally inevitably doom them both. Essentially a two-hander, best described as Absurdist in style, this drama explores the themes of role-play in male-female relationships. An original, imaginative and commendably assured first feature from a director who would lighten her tone, if not the weight of her meaning, with the highly successful *Men* two years later.

Straits Of Love And Hate
Aien Kyo
Japan 1937 88 mins bw
Shinko Kinema

d **Kenji Mizoguchi**
sc **Yoshitaka Yoda**
ph **Minoru Miki**
Fumiko Yamaji, Seizaburo Kawazu, Masao Shimizu, Haruo Tanaka

A servant (Yamaji) is seduced by the weak son (Shimizu) of the household and becomes pregnant. She parts with her baby, takes to the streets, and then joins a theatrical troupe. Some years later, the man tries to make amends. Mizoguchi, forced for commercial reasons, since 1922, to make many films in which he had little interest, now began to develop his own style and subject matter, although ostensibly the idea for this story came from Tolstoy's *Resurrection*. The melodrama is continually undercut by realism and humour. There is also a tragicomic rendering of 'My Blue Heaven' by the heroine.

Strange Adventure Of David Gray, The
see Vampyr

Strange Masquerade see Improperly Dressed

The Strange Ones
Les Enfants Terribles
France 1949 100 mins bw
Gaumont/Continentale/Concord

d **Jean-Pierre Melville**
sc **Jean-Pierre Melville, Jean Cocteau**
ph **Henri Decaë**
m **Vivaldi, Bach**

Nicole Stéphane, Edouard Dermithe, Renée Cosima, Jacques Bernard

Paul (Dermithe) and Elisabeth (Stéphane), a teenage brother and sister unhealthily obsessed with each other, create a private enclosed world in their untidy, shared single room, but the intrusion of others leads to suicide. Written in the late 1920s, Cocteau's strange novel would have seemed unfilmable except by the author himself. (Not that he is not overly present as narrator.) But Melville's severe style and craftsmanship combined with the bejewelled prose of the screenplay retains much of the claustrophobic spirit of the original. Made on a small budget, it was shot almost entirely on the stage of the Théâtre Pigalle with the then unusual use of baroque music on the sound track. The passionate performance of Stéphane makes up for the deficiencies in that of Dermithe, Cocteau's adopted son.

The Stranger

Lo Straniero

Italy 1967 104 mins col
DD/Master/Marianne/Casbah

d **Luchino Visconti**
sc **Luchino Visconti, Suso Cecchi D'Amico, Georges Conchon, Emmanuel Robles**
ph **Giuseppe Rotunno**
m **Piero Piccioni**
Marcello Mastroianni, Anna Karina, Bernard Blier, Georges Wilson, Bruno Cremer

Meursault (Mastroianni), a French clerk living in Algiers who shot and killed a young Algerian for no apparent reason, reflects on his existence while awaiting the guillotine. The flamboyant Visconti was particularly unsuited to the astringency of Albert Camus' psychological and philosophical modern classic novel about an outsider and, though Mastroianni approached this role intelligently, it really needed a Gérard Philipe to carry it off. The steamy atmosphere of 1938 Algeria is quite well caught, but the film was one of the director's biggest flops.

The Stranger And The Fog

Gharibeh-Va-Meh

Iran 1974 140 mins col
Rex Cinema Theater Company

d **Bahram Beyzai**
sc **Bahram Beyzai**
ph **Mehrdad Fakhimi**
m **Bahram Beyzai**
Khosrow Shojazadeh, Parvaneh Ma'soumi, Esmat Safavi, Manuchehr Farid

One day, a stranger (Shojazadeh) arrives out of the fog at a small, tightly-knit fishing community. He cannot recall where he came from and the villagers are suspicious of him. Gradually he is accepted and marries a young widow (Ma'soumi) whose husband presumably died a year earlier. But the 'dead' husband returns and a group of men come in search of the stranger. The film is heavily infused with symbolic elements and themes (intolerance, injustice, martyrdom) from traditional Persian theatre, of which the director is a major scholar. This may prove an obstacle to Western audiences, since the film only occasionally manages to go beyond the specific culture in its allegorical depiction of the oppression of the innocent. Certainly the atmosphere comes across potently in Beyzai's economical visual style, and the enigmas are the more haunting for not being understood. There is no problem, though, with the expertly staged, ten-minute, brutal climactic battle in the woods.

Strangers see Journey To Italy

Straniero, Lo see Stranger, The

Strategia Del Ragno see Spider's Stratagem, The

Stray Dog

Nora Inu

Japan 1949 122 mins bw
Shin Toho

d **Akira Kurosawa**
sc **Akira Kurosawa, Ryuzo Kikushima**
ph **Asakazu Kakai**
m **Fumio Hayasaka**
Toshiro Mifune, Takashi Shimura, Ko Kimura, Keiko Awaji

A young policeman (Mifune) has his gun stolen from him in a bus, resulting in a long search for the thief (Kimura) through the underworld, during which the cop has to face his own criminal impulses. Kurosawa, always the most Western-influenced of older generation Japanese directors, made this atmospheric thriller on location with the contemporary Hollywood model in mind, but the pace is slower due to some of the techniques such as slow dissolves and double exposures. However, an interesting picture of post-war Japan emerges.

Street Angel
Malu Tianshi

China 1937 100 mins bw
Mingxing

d **Yuan Muzhi**
sc **Yugu Muzhi**
ph **Wu Yinxiang**
m **He Luting**
Zhao Dan, Wei Heling, Qian Qianli, Zhou Xuan

In one of the poorest areas of Shanghai in the 1930s, the owners of a teahouse have pressed two women into prostitution. A young man (Dan) from the run-down lodgings opposite carries on a chaste affair with the younger woman (Xuan). Around them life is hard, money and work are short and street violence prevails. One of the last and most celebrated of pre-war Chinese films (Shanghai fell to the Japanese in the same year) derives its title and much of its sentimental urban poetic style from Frank Borzage's Hollywood movie of 1928 starring Janet Gaynor. But it has a tragicomic vein of its own, is more firmly rooted in reality and more explicit in its social criticism. The 28-year-old director's only subsequent film was a war documentary.

Street Of Shame
Akasen Chitai

Japan 1956 88 mins bw
Daiei Kyoto

d **Kenji Mizoguchi**
sc **Masashige Narusawa**
ph **Kazuo Miyagawa**
m **Toshiro Mayazumi**
Machiko Kyo, Ayako Wakao, Aiko Mimasu, Michiyo Kogure

The night-by-night existence of a group of prostitutes working in a bordello called Dreamland in the red light district of Tokyo. In his last completed film, Mizoguchi returned to an earlier contemporary subject to illustrate his major theme—the exploitation of women throughout the ages. Perhaps commercial pressure influenced some of the melodramatic and vulgar lapses, but the insight, humour and humanity still shine through. The greatest of all Japanese directors died of leukemia at the age of 58 in the year of the film's release.

Street of Sorrow see Joyless Street

Streghe, Le see Witches, The

Strike
Stachka

USSR 1924 82 mins bw
Goskino

d **Sergei Eisenstein**
sc **Sergei Eisenstein, Valeri Pletniov, I. Kravchinovski**
ph **Edouard Tissé**
m **Silent**
Maxim Shtraukh, Grigori Alexandrov, Mikhail Gomorov, I. Ivanov, I. Klukvin

In 1912, after peaceful efforts to settle a strike caused by the suicide of a sacked worker fail, strikers and their families are brutally slaughtered by cavalrymen sent by the state. Made with members of the Proletkult theatre, Eisenstein's first feature was a vital part of the *avant-garde* Constructivist art movement in the Soviet Union of the 1920s. Already much in evidence was his 'dialectic montage' *viz* the use of caricature, visual metaphor and shock cutting. For example, a factory boss uses a lemon squeezer as police move in on the striking workers, and shots of a slaughterhouse are cut in as they are mown down.

Strohfeuer see Summer Lightning

Stroke of Midnight, The see Phantom Carriage, The

Stromboli

Stromboli, Terra Di Dio

Italy 1950 107 mins bw
Be-Ro/RKO

d **Roberto Rossellini**
sc **Roberto Rossellini, Art Cohen, Renzo Cesana, Sergio Amedei, C.P. Callegari**
ph **Otello Martelli**
m **Renzo Rossellini**
Ingrid Bergman, Mario Vitale, Renzo Cesana, Mario Sponza

A Lithuanian refugee (Bergman), interned in Italy after the war, gains her freedom by marrying a simple fisherman (Vitale), but finds only loneliness and hostility on his barren, volcanic island. When she becomes pregnant, she flees as the volcano erupts. Moral indignation erupted from puritan groups in the USA who boycotted the film because of Bergman's 'wanton ways' in leaving her husband for Rossellini. But more harm was done to the film by the indifferent narration, sloppy pace and the uneasy teaming of Bergman (although stripped of the trappings of Hollywood stardom) with non-actors. Further damage was perpetrated by routine director Alfred Werker who edited the English version down to 81 minutes and changed the ending for RKO.

Stromboli, Terra Di Dio see Stromboli

Stronger Than The Night

Stärker Als Die Nacht

E. Germany 1954 117 mins bw
Deutsche Film

d **Slatan Dudow**
sc **Jeanne Stern, Kurt Stern**
ph **Karl Plintzner, Horst Brandt**
m **Ernst Roters**
Wilhelm Koch-Hooge, Helga Göring, Kurt Oligmüller, Rita Gödikmeier

When Hitler comes to power in Germany, Hans Löning (Koch-Hooge) is imprisoned for seven years for his Communist activities. Released in 1940, he immediately forms an underground group, but is informed upon and executed. One of the best East German films of the 1950s was based on an original script by Communist party activists Jeanne and Kurt Stern, who participated in the Spanish Civil War and worked for the French Resistance. Although it has its share of rhetorical gestures, especially in the closing paean to its martyr hero, and a slight bending of history to suit the argument, Dudow, who worked with Fritz Lang, G. W. Pabst and Bertolt Brecht, is too sophisticated a director to be content with simplistics. The characters are finely nuanced, and the bitter denunciation of Nazism is forcefully expressed by some expressionist techniques, voice-over interventions and newsreel shots.

Stroszek

W. Germany 1977 108 mins col
Werner Herzog

d **Werner Herzog**
sc **Werner Herzog**
ph **Thomas Mauch**
m **Tom Paxton, Chet Atkins, Sonny Terry**
Eva Mattes, Bruno S, Clemens Scheitz

An ex-con (Bruno S), his unemployed neighbour (Scheitz) and a prostitute (Mattes) leave Germany for America where they settle in Wisconsin in a mobile home bought on credit. After a bungled robbery, they split up. Another of Herzog's ventures off the beaten track finds him in Middle America with Bruno S, his curious lead from *The Enigma Of Kaspar Hauser* (1974), virtually playing himself. Unhappily, though the location shooting is interesting, the acting is stilted and the outsider's view of the barrenness of American life is obvious.

The Structure Of Crystals

Struktura Krysztalu

Poland 1969 137 mins bw
Tor Film Unit

d **Krzysztof Zanussi**
sc **Krzysztof Zanussi, Edward Zebrowski**
ph **Stefan Matjaszkiewicz**
m **Wojciech Kilar**
Barbara Wrzesińska, Andrzej Żarnecki, Jan Myslowicz, Wladyslaw Jarema, Daniel Olbrychski

A metropolitan member of the scientific élite (Zarnecki) visits an old friend and colleague (Myslowicz) who has retreated with his wife

(Wrzesinska) to a remote meteorological station, and tries to persuade him to return to the city. Zanussi's first feature, after a number of documentaries, showed considerable intelligence and maturity. It was the first of a series of films that looked at the scientific community, (mainly uncharted territory in the cinema except for science fiction) to make general philosophical points. Rather too long and cerebral, despite the sex scenes, it might not seem as clear as the title suggests.

Struktura Krysztalu see Structure Of Crystals, The

Stubby

Fimpen

Sweden 1974 87 mins col
Bo Widerberg Film

d **Bo Widerberg**
sc **Bo Widerberg**
ph **John Olsson, Hanno Fuchs, Roland Sterner, Åke Åstrand**
m **Prokofiev**

Johan Bergman (Stubby), Monica Zetterlund, Ernst-Hugo Jaeregard

An amazing six-year-old soccer wizard becomes a national hero as anchor man on the senior Swedish team in the World Cup series, but he quits when his school work suffers and he still can't even sign autographs. Little Johan's soccer skills were spotted by Widerberg while the director was waiting to play in a match between two teams of film technicians, and he resolved to make a film around him. This reasonable family entertainment, with the boy's real-life parents and top international players as themselves, basically has only one visual joke.

The Student Of Prague

Der Student Von Prag

Germany 1913 56 mins bw
Bioskop

d **Stellan Rye**
sc **Hanns Heinz Ewers**
ph **Guido Seeber**
m **Silent**

Paul Wegener, John Gottowt, Grete Berger, Lyda Salmonova, Lothar Körner

A penniless student (Wegener), sells his reflection to the mysterious Scapinelli (Gottowt) to obtain the means to woo the girl of his choice. The reflection, however, haunts him, driving him to kill it and, eventually, himself. This film lit the early spark which flamed into the German cinema's love of supernatural subjects, leading in turn to the making of classics in the Expressionist tradition. Filmed on location, it capitalized on the medieval quarters of the city and it has been suggested that it was there that Wegener (one of whose five wives was Salmonova) first heard the legend of *The Golem* which he would film three times.

The Student Of Prague

Der Student Von Prag

Germany 1926 116 mins bw
H.R. Sokal-Film

d **Henrik Galeen**
sc **Henrik Galeen, Hanns Heinz Ewers**
ph **Günther Krampf, Erich Nitzschmann**
m **Silent**

Conrad Veidt, Werner Krauss, Agnes Esterhazy, Elizza La Porta, Ferdinand Von Alten

In return for a large sum of money, Balduin (Veidt), an impoverished student, agrees that the sinister Scapinelli (Krauss) may remove an item of his choice from his room, Scapinelli chooses, and takes Balduin's reflection, which dogs the young man until he and it meet their end. If the 1913 version of this tale is a landmark and effective in its own right, this studio-bound version, reflecting the full flowering of German Expressionism, is certainly the more accomplished. It is rich in atmosphere and includes some striking and memorable images—such as Scapinelli's shadow looming over a tryst between the doomed lovers—and both leads, who had made so strong an impact in *The Cabinet Of Dr Caligari*, do their roles full justice.

The Student Of Prague

Der Student Von Prag

Germany 1935 87 mins bw
Cine-Allianz

d **Arthur Robison**
sc **Arthur Robison, Hans Kyser**

ph **Bruno Mondi**
m **Theo Mackeben**
Adolf Wohlbrück, Dorothea Wieck, Theodor Loos, Erich Fiedler, Edna Greyff

As in previous versions, Balduin (Wohlbrück) sells his reflection. This time the buyer is Dr Carpis (Loos) and Balduin uses the cash to pursue Julia (Wieck), a beautiful singer. Here, Balduin discovers that he has sold his better half and, deprived of it, he grows unscrupulous, becomes a murderer and finally goes insane. This sound production, though packed with plot, is the weakest of the three attempts. The Chicago-born German director died before its completion, and the star (to become internationally known as Anton Walbrook) lacked the intensity of his predecessors, especially Conrad Veidt. Quite simply, the film fails to frighten. But it has been acknowledged as the last of the pre-Nazi period films in style, of interest as a kind of throwback to the great era of the German silent cinema.

Student Von Prag, Der see Student Of Prague, The

Stützen Der Gesellschaft see Pillars Of Society

Subida Al Cielo see Mexican Bus Ride

Subject For A Short Story see Lika, Chekhov's Love

Subway

France 1985 102 mins col
Films Du Loup/TSF/TF1

d **Luc Besson**
sc **Luc Besson, Alain Le Henry, Pierre Jolivet, Sophie Schmit, Marc Perrier**
ph **Carlo Varini**
m **Eric Serra**
Christopher Lambert, Isabelle Adjani, Richard Bohringer, Michel Galabru, Jean-Hugues Anglade

Fred (Lambert) steals some important documents from the crooked businessman-husband of Helena (Adjani), and flees to the Paris Métro where he lives in the labyrinthine passages with various other outcasts. Twenty-six-year-old Besson's underground film (only in the sense of its setting) has the advantage of high-tech art work from the veteran Alexander Trauner, and an audacious use of 'Scope and Dolby. But not even the intensity of Lambert in dinner-jacket and yellow hair (Sting was the first choice for the role of Fred), and the beauty of Adjani (in her first film for two years) could make the characters and situations seem anything other than absolutely preposterous. Breathless and flashy and wholly superficial, it is a film for the pop video generation.

Such A Gorgeous Kid Like Me see Gorgeous Bird Like Me, A

Such A Pretty Little Beach

(US: Riptide)
Une Si Jolie Petite Plage

France 1949 97 mins bw
CICC/Dormer/Films Corona

d **Yves Allégret**
sc **Jacques Sigurd**
ph **Henri Alekan**
m **Maurice Thiriet, Jacques Sigurd**
Madeleine Robinson, Gérard Philipe, Jane Marken, Jean Servais, Julien Carette, Mona Dol

A young man (Philipe) registers at a dismal hotel at a desolate seaside resort in Normandy in winter. He had worked here as a kitchen boy some years before and run off with a famous singer, recently murdered. He is suspected by a mysterious fellow guest (Servais) of committing the *crime passionel*. Rain falls incessantly in this archetypal romantic, fatalistic post-war French drama, dominated by the boyish, sensitive, intense face of Philipe, perfectly cast as the melancholy fugitive. Far too schematically doom-laden, the film does have superb photography and wonderful all-round performances.

Sudba Cheloveka see Destiny Of A Man

The Sudden Fortune Of The Poor People Of Kombach

Der Plötzliche Reichtum Der Armen Leute Von Kombach

W. Germany 1971 102 mins bw
Hessischer Rundfunk/Hallelujah

d **Volker Schlöndorff**
sc **Volker Schlöndorff, Margarethe Von Trotta**
ph **Franz Rath**
m **Klaus Doldinger**
Reinhard Hauff, Georg Lehn, Karl Joseph Cramer, Wolfgang Bachler, Margarethe Von Trotta, Rainer Werner Fassbinder

In 1821, seven poor peasants rob the monthly tax-money cart. They are arrested and executed after they have spent much of their ill-gotten fortune. One of Schlöndorff's most forceful films, this is a stark, analytical depiction of 19th-century social irrationalism without any period embellishments. The accomplished narrative reaches a pessimistic conclusion about the nature of rebellion that fits modern times. Rainer Werner Fassbinder, then beginning to make a name for himself as a director of a very different type of film, plays a peasant.

Sugarbaby

Zuckerbaby

W. Germany 1984 86 mins col
Pelemele Film/BMI/Bayerischen Rundfunks

d **Percy Adlon**
sc **Percy Adlon**
ph **Johanna Heer**
m **Dreier, Franz Erlmeier, Fritz Köstler, the Paul-Würges Combo**
Marianne Sägebrecht, Eisi Gulp, Manuela Denz, Toni Berger

An overweight, plain woman in her late thirties, leading a boring existence as a mortician's assistant, is smitten with a handsome young subway train driver. She tracks him down and takes advantage of his wife's absence to draw him into a brief but rewarding encounter. A boost for fat women, this idiosyncratic romantic comedy is full of mischievous wit, cleverly avoiding both mockery and pathos. Sometimes Adlon decorates the slight story with too many stylistic devices, but Sägebrecht's gently nuanced performance holds the picture together.

Sugata Sanshiro see Judo Saga

The Suitor

Le Soupirant

France 1962 85 mins bw
CAPAC/Cocinor

d **Pierre Etaix**
sc **Pierre Etaix, Jean-Claude Carrière**
ph **Pierre Levant**
m **Jean Paillaud**
Pierre Etaix, Laurence Lignères, France Arnell, Karin Vesely

A shy and studious young man (Etaix), urged by his mother to marry, proposes to a Swedish girl who fails to understand him, meets a drunken beauty, becomes obsessed with a music-hall star, and returns to the Swede—who accepts him. This first, and most successful, feature by Etaix, who had been an assistant to Jacques Tati on *Mon Oncle* (1958), relies almost exclusively on physical humour and is constructed, like all his films (and Tati's), around a series of comic set-pieces. Yet, though often amusing, his comedy is too derivative, similar jokes having been better executed by Buster Keaton, and Max Linder whom Etaix resembles.

Sult see Hunger

Summer see Green Ray, The

A Summer Affair

(US: One Wild Moment)

Un Moment D'Égarement

France 1977 100 mins col
Renn Productions/Société Française De Production

d **Claude Berri**
sc **Claude Berri**
ph **André Neau**
m **Michel Stelio**
Jean-Pierre Marielle, Victor Lanoux, Christine Dejoux, Agnes Soral, Martine Sarcey

Divorced Pierre (Marielle), his friend Jacques (Lanoux) and their 17-year-old daughters holiday on the Côte D'Azur. Pierre, and Jacques' daughter Françoise (Soral) have an affair, with initially comic results as Jacques tries to discover the identity of his daughter's seducer and assaults the wrong man. The ending is more sober as Jacques learns the truth, and Pierre must face both the damage to their friendship and unresolved problems posed for himself by his relationship with Françoise. Berri's film, although it has its excellent moments, the glamour of the Riviera and polished performances from the two lead men, seems uncertain of its intention. It comes out as a confused mix of love story, moral tale, exploration of the generation gap and exposé of the dangers beneath the surface of the holiday mood. It was remade by Stanley Donen in 1984 as *Blame It On Rio*, starring Michael Caine.

A Summer At Grandpa's

Dongdong De Jiaqui

Taiwan 1984 102 mins col
Marble Road Productions

d **Hou Hsiao-hsien**
sc **Zhu Tianwen**
ph **Chen Kunhou**
m **Edward Yang**
Wang Qiguang, Zhou Shengli, Gu Jun, Mei Fang, Lin Xiuling

When the mother of a 12-year-old boy (Qiguang) and his little sister (Shengli), who live in Taipei, has surgery, the children are sent, escorted by an irresponsible uncle, to spend the summer with their grandfather (Jun) who is an old-fashioned country doctor. Once there, a variety of experiences and adventures, from the amusing to the frightening, befall them. It is rare to see a quality film from Taiwan, which this is in terms of charm, good performances and a story that provides some delightful moments. Gentle and enjoyable, but lightweight.

Summer Interlude

aka Illicit Interlude

Sommarlek

Sweden 1950 97 mins bw
Svensk Filmindustri

d **Ingmar Bergman**
sc **Ingmar Bergman, Herbert Grevenius**
ph **Gunnar Fischer, Bengt Järnmark**
m **Erik Nordgren**
Maj-Britt Nilsson, Birger Malmsten, Alf Kjellin, Stig Olin

A prima ballerina (Nilsson) looks back on the idyllic summer she spent several years before on an island near Stockholm with the boy (Malmsten) she loved. But the affair comes to an abrupt and tragic end when he is killed in an accident. This heartbreaking loss leaves her bitter and without emotion until she meets a young journalist (Kjellin). Bergman's first mature film deals with adolescent love, the subject of much of his early work, also revealing the emotional and psychological dangers of dwelling on the past. The limpid Swedish summer is wonderfully captured in the early, lyrical love scenes.

Summer Light see Lumière D'Été

Summer Lightning

Strohfeuer

W. Germany 1972 100 mins col
Hallelujah Films

d **Volker Schlöndorff**
sc **Volker Schlöndorff, Margarethe Von Trotta**
ph **Sven Nykvist**
m **Stanley Myers**
Margarethe Von Trotta, Friedhelm Ptok, Martin Lüttge, Walter Sedlmayer

Elisabeth (Von Trotta) feels wonderfully free after her divorce from her husband (Ptok), although a legal decision on the custody of their five-year-old son is still pending. But the feeling of relief does not last as she struggles from one job to another and attempts to regain her child. This portrait of a woman trying to make her way in a male world in the early days of the women's liberation movement seems pretty loaded over a decade later, though, it must be said, many of the problems raised have yet to be solved. Schlöndorff's wife, Von Trotta, who would become a director herself a few years later, gives a performance that sometimes transforms the political tract into human drama.

Summer Manoeuvres

(US: The Grand Maneuver)

Les Grandes Manoeuvres

France 1955 106 mins col
Filmsonor/Rizzoli

d **René Clair**
sc **René Clair**
ph **Robert Lefèbvre**
m **Georges Van Parys**
Gérard Philipe, Michèle Morgan, Yves Robert, Brigitte Bardot, Jean Desailly, Pierre Dux

In a pre-World War I garrison town, a handsome dragoon (Philipe) wagers he can seduce a stand-offish divorcée (Morgan). In the process, he falls in love with her, but his reputation as a Don Juan has destroyed his credibility. Clair stated that 'love is the only concern of the film . . . a very serious matter'. This gently ironic romantic comedy, Clair's first in colour, has more genuine emotion than any of his previous work. The leads play with charm and intelligence.

Summer Paradise

aka Paradise Place

Paradistorg

Sweden 1977 113 mins col
Cinematograph AB/Swedish Film Institute/Svensk Filmindustri

d **Gunnel Lindblom**
sc **Ulla Isaksson, Gunnel Lindblom**
ph **Tony Forsberg**
m **Georg Riedel**
Birgitta Valberg, Sif Ruud, Solveig Ternström, Per Myrberg, Margareta Byström, Holger Löwenadler, Pontus Gustafson, Göran Stangertz, Agneta Ekmanner

Katha Wilk (Valberg), a doctor and divorced grandmother, is the centre of a large family group and assorted friends of all ages, who gather at her lakeside house to enjoy the Midsummer holiday. Once there, tensions mount, particularly between the generations, and the sojourn ends in tragedy. No surprise that the producer was Ingmar Bergman, whose protegée, Gunnel Lindblom, was making her debut film as director. The title is ironic: scenery aside, here is no paradise but a focal point for the meeting of unhappiness, futility, frustration and madness. Intended to expose the underside of 'progressive' Swedish society, this is a depressing and all-too-convincing film.

Summer Soldiers

Japan 1971 103 mins col
Teshigahara Productions

d **Hiroshi Teshigahara**
sc **John Nathan**
ph **Hiroshi Teshigahara**
m **Tohru Takemitsu**
Keith Sykes, Lee Reisen, Kazuo Kitamura, Toshiko Kobayashi, Shoichi Ozawa, Greg Antonacci

An American GI (Sykes), stationed in Japan, deserts in order to avoid being sent to Vietnam. He and other American deserters hide out with Japanese families, constantly moving from one household to the next to avoid arrest. John Nathan, screenwriter and scholar of Japanese literature, and Teshigahara, have created an interesting culture-clash drama out of a topical situation. Questions about the American action in Vietnam are raised that were ignored by American films of the time. In *cinéma vérité* style, its cast of amateurs includes members of the Tokyo Deserters Aid Committee and Japanese host families. The film's main weakness lies in the passive, bland performance of Sykes, a folk-rock singer from Kentucky, in the main role.

Summer With Monika

(US: Monika)

Sommaren Med Monika

Sweden 1952 97 mins bw
Svensk Filmindustri

d **Ingmar Bergman**
sc **Ingmar Bergman, Per-Anders Fogelström**
ph **Gunnar Fischer**
m **Erik Nordgren**
Harriet Andersson, Lars Ekborg, Åke Grönberg, Naemi Briese, Åke Fridell

An irresponsible teenage girl (Andersson) spends a summer island holiday with a young clerk (Ekborg), but she gets pregnant and later literally leaves him holding the baby. Bergman sees little hope for these adolescents in the winter of their discontent after a summer made glorious by Fischer's camera. The two young leads give this simple tale a remarkable veracity. Thereafter, until *Fanny And Alexander* (1982), adults, principally women, took centre stage in the director's work.

Suna No Onna see Woman Of The Dunes

Sunday Daughters

Vasárnapi Szülok

Hungary 1979 100 mins col
Mafilm

d **János Rósza**
sc **István Kardos**
ph **Elemér Ragályi**
m **Levente Szorényi**
Julianna Nyakó, Julianna Balogh, Andrea Blizik, Melinda Szakács, Erzsi Pásztor, Agnes Kakassy, Sergei Elistratov

Teenage girls in a reformatory dream of, and attempt, escape. Eventually one of them, Juli (Nyakó), makes it to her sister's distant home, but is forced to leave. She finds refuge with Aranka (Pásztor), her one-day (Sunday) foster mother appointed by the institution, where she makes love with Aranka's son, but must leave there, too ... In common with Yugoslavia's *Special Treatment*, this film looks at the methods and consequences of repressive, bureaucratic correctional institutions where no attempt is made to understand the inmates. Rósza directs with exemplary judgement of action and character, allowing the natural and high spirits of the girls to emerge in the otherwise bleak atmosphere: in a memorable sequence, a dormitory party spills over into hysteria and a suicide attempt. Both engaging and salutary, the film ends with recaptured Juli and the others watching *The Four Hundred Blows*, the final scenes of which are a poignant echo of their plight.

Sunday In August

Domenica D'Agosto

Italy 1950 75 mins bw
Colonna

d **Luciano Emmer**
sc **Franco Brusati, Luciano Emmer, Cesare Zavattini, Giulio Macchi**
ph **Domenica Scala, Leonida Barboni, Ubaldo Marelli**
m **Roman Vlad**
Anna Baldini, Franco Interlenghi, Elvy Lissia, Massimo Serato, Correda Verga, Marcello Mastroianni, Ave Ninchi

One August Sunday, five groups of ordinary people leave Rome to spend the day at the beach resort of Ostia. Former documentary film-maker Emmer's first and most successful feature was a gentle, perceptive and humorous look at Italian *petit bourgeois* mores, made on location in the Neo-Realist vein. The script was purposefully diffuse—there is little or no connection between the five groups—but is given form by skilful editing. The little-known, 26-year-old Mastroianni appeared in Emmer's next two films.

A Sunday In September

En Söndag I September

Sweden 1963 113 mins bw
Europa Film

d **Jörn Donner**
sc **Jörn Donner**
ph **Tony Forsberg**
m **Bo Nilsson**
Harriet Andersson, Thommy Berggren, Barbro Kollberg, Harry Ahlin, Axel Düberg, Jan-Erik Lindqvist

Stig and Birgitta (Berggren and Andersson) fall in love, marry—by which time she is pregnant—survive her miscarriage and gradually drift apart. Within this framework, the debut film of Finnish writer, political reporter and critic Donner, highlights the incompatabilities of his young couple, while attempting a serious examination of the social background to marriage and relationships, concluding on a downbeat note. The piece is divided into four distinct segments—romance, marriage, estrangement and divorce—each one introduced by a montage of shots of landscape and life in contemporary Sweden. The leads are excellent (the gifted Andersson would become the director's wife) and the film won the Opera Prima at Venice. There are definite echoes of Bergman, particularly in Donner's treatment of Birgitta—fascinating in view of his public criticism of the Swedish master's work as irrelevant to contemporary society.

Sunday In The Country
Un Dimanche À La Campagne
France 1984 94 mins col
Sara Films/Films A2/Little Bear

d **Bertrand Tavernier**
sc **Bertrand Tavernier, Colo Tavernier**
ph **Bruno De Keyzer**
m **Fauré**
Louis Ducreux, Sabine Azéma, Michel Aumont, Geneviève Mnich, Monique Chaumette, Claude Winter, Thomas Duval

On a Sunday in 1912, the widowed, 76-year-old artist, Monsieur Ladmiral (Ducreux), who lives in the country looked after by his housekeeper (Chaumette), awaits a visit from his son Edouard (Aumont), daughter-in-law and grandchildren. They arrive, later joined by Ladmiral's unattentive but adored daughter Irène (Azéma) of whom Edouard, feeling cheated of his father's love, is jealous. The day passes, the family leaves, and Ladmiral returns to his easel... The film is stylish, good-looking and beautifully played, dealing in nuances and thoroughly beguiling. However, its deeper themes are dealt with superficially and, like so much of Tavernier's work, there is more show than substance, making for ephemeral pleasure.

Best Director Cannes 1984

The Sunday Of Life
Le Dimanche De La Vie
France 1965 100 mins bw
Sofracima/Doxa(Paris)Taurus(Munich)/Schermi(Rome)

d **Jean Herman**
sc **Olivier Hussenot, Georges Richard, Raymond Queneau**
ph **Jean-Jacques Tarbes**
m **Georges Delerue**
Danielle Darrieux, Jean-Pierre Moulin, Françoise Arnoul, Olivier Hussenot, Berthe Bovy, Jean Rochefort

Julia (Darrieux) and her sister (Arnoul) run a hat shop in provincial France during the 1930s. On his discharge from the army, Valentin (Moulin) marries Julia but goes off and becomes a picture framer in Paris. Julia joins him and, discovering that she can foresee events, sets herself up as Madame Saphir, clairvoyant. Her success is laced with sadness as the threat of war grows and begins to affect the future.... This first feature is a gently satirical series of vignettes revealing the life in a Parisian *quartier* between two world wars, when time seems to be standing still. Director, writer and actors achieve an authentic and nostalgic atmosphere and some vivid and witty characterization through imaginative moments that speak volumes. However, these moments are fleeting, leaving an impression of contrivance that begins to pall and reduces the film to a forgettable exercise in charm.

A Sunday Romance
Bakaruhaban
Hungary 1957 92 mins bw
Hunnia Studio

d **Imre Fehér**
sc **Miklós Hubay**
ph **János Badal**
m **Tibor Polgár**
Margit Bara, Iván Darvas, Sándor Pécsi, Maria Lázár, Vali Korompai, Adám Szirtes

World War I has just begun. In a small Hungarian town, Sándor (Darvas), a comfortably off journalist and gentleman, dons a humble private's uniform every Sunday and goes out walking. He meets Vilma (Bara), a delightful and naive girl who falls in love with him. It turns out that she works as a maid for the lawyer whose daughter Sándor is courting but, by the time he finds the courage to admit to his feelings for Vilma, it is too late. A beautifully controlled first film from a director who has a fine sense of irony, a gift for intimacy and an eye for detail. The bitter-sweet love story is told in a well-observed social context in which the character of provincial life is beautifully delineated. Well-acted and splendidly photographed, its weakness is that the narrative intermittently runs out of steam.

Sundays And Cybèle
Cybèle Ou Les Dimanches De Ville D'Avray
France 1962 110 mins bw

Terra/Fides/Orsay/Trocadero

d **Serge Bourgignon**
sc **Serge Bourgignon, Antoine Tudal**
ph **Henri Decaë**
m **Maurice Jarre**
Hardy Kruger, Patricia Gozzi, Nicole Courcel, Daniel Ivernel

In a small town near Paris, a former German pilot, now suffering from amnesia, forges a friendship with a 12-year-old girl from the convent orphanage, but when they innocently spend Christmas together in the woods, he is suspected of assaulting her. The warm playing of Kruger and Gozzi as the odd couple helps to counteract some of the self-conscious charm and aesthetics of the direction. Bourgignon, who won an Oscar with this debut film, has done nothing to merit much attention since.

Best Foreign Film Oscar 1962

Sunflower

I Girasoli

Italy 1970 107 mins col
Champion/Concordia/Mosfilm

d **Vittorio De Sica**
sc **Tonino Guerra, Cesare Zavattini, Georgy Mdivani**
ph **Giuseppe Rotunno**
m **Henry Mancini**
Sophia Loren, Marcello Mastroianni, Ludmila Savelyeva, Galina Andreyeva, Germano Longo

An Italian couple, married for 12 days, are separated when the husband is sent to the Russian front and reported missing, but they find each other again after the war. A sad example of how much De Sica's work had declined since the 1950s. The sentimentality incipient in his earlier films has here taken over, and any social message is wrapped in a glossy package containing a predictable plot and lifeless characters. Interesting sidelight: this was the first Italian film to be shot mainly in Russia, and Loren's child in the film was her own by producer Carlo Ponti, her husband.

Sunless

Sans Soleil

France 1982 100 mins col
Argos

d **Chris Marker**
sc **Chris Marker**
ph **Chris Marker, Sana Na N'Hada, Jean-Michel Humeau, Mario Marret, Eugenio Bentivoglio, Daniel Tessier, Haroun Tazieff**
m **Moussorgsky, Sibelius**

A fictional cameraman tries to make sense of the cultural dislocation he sees and feels in Japan, West Africa and Iceland. Using diverse images, letters, quotes and musings, Marker continues to extend the limits of the 'documentary'. Here, he makes use of new video technology and image-processing provided by Hayao Yamaneko, credited with special effects. The result is a poetic, philosphical and political collage, which Marker describes as like 'a musical composition, with recurrent themes, counterpoints and mirror-like fugues'.

Sur see South

Sur, El see South, The

Sürü see Herd, The

Susana

(US: The Devil And The Flesh)

Demonio Y Carne

Mexico 1951 82 mins bw
Internacional Cinematografica/Oscar Dancigers

d **Luis Buñuel**
sc **Jaime Salvador**
ph **José Órtiz Ramos**
m **Raúl Lavista**
Rosita Quintana, Fernando Soler, Victor Manuel Mendoza, Matilde Palau

Susana (Quintana) begs God to work a miracle and free her from prison. He does so. After wandering over the mountains, she is taken in by a kindly rich family that employs her as a maid on its ranch, but she repays her benefactors by seducing every man in sight. 'A perfectly routine film,' Buñuel called this rehearsal for his more mature excursions into the world of sex and power games and, despite an inspired opening scene, his estimation is about right. Yet no film by the Spanish master is without interest and this cheaply-made melodrama contains many of his anything-but-routine trademarks, including the amoral vamp and an ironic anti-religious ending.

Susuz Yaz see Waterless Summer

Suzanne Simonin, La Religieuse De Diderot see Religieuse, La

Swann In Love

Un Amour De Swann

France 1983 110 mins col

Gaumont/Bioskop/FR3/SFPC

d **Volker Schlöndorff**
sc **Peter Brook, Jean-Claude Carrière, Marie-Héléne Estienne**
ph **Sven Nykvist**
m **Hans-Werner Henze**
Jeremy Irons, Ornella Muti, Alain Delon, Fanny Ardant, Marie-Christine Barrault, Anne Bennent

Charles Swann (Irons), received into aristocratic circles despite the fact that he is a Jew, has a passionate affair with Odette (Muti), a beautiful demi-mondaine over whom he is racked with insane jealousy. Elegant, refined and well played—especially, and unexpectedly, by Delon as the decadent Baron Charlus—with turn-of-the-century Paris exquisitely caught by Nykvist's camera, the film nonetheless cannot begin to approach the richness of *Swann's Way*, the first volume of Marcel Proust's great novel. The elimination of the narrator is only one essential dimension that is lost.

The Swedish Mistress

aka The Mistress

Älskar Innan

Sweden 1962 77 mins bw

Svensk Filmindustri/Janus

d **Vilgot Sjöman**
sc **Vilgot Sjöman**
ph **Lasse Björne**
Bibi Andersson, Max Von Sydow, Per Myrberg, Ølegard Welton, Birgitta Valberg

A young woman (Andersson), who already has a regular boyfriend (Myrberg), meets an older married man (Von Sydow) at a scientific conference. They have an involved affair, but his refusal to leave his wife causes her much pain and leads to a reassessment of her life. This was the first feature from Ingmar Bergman's former assistant, who would make his own mark by causing a sensation with *I Am Curious—Yellow* five years later. It is conventional in both subject and treatment, but helped no end by the high-powered lead casting.

Best Actress (Bibi Andersson) Berlin 1963

The Sweet Body Of Deborah

Il Dolce Corpo Di Deborah

Italy 1967 95 mins col

Zenith Cinematografica/Flora Film (Rome)/Lux (Paris)

d **Romolo Guerrieri**
sc **Ernesto Gastaldi**
ph **Marcello Masiocchi**
m **Nora Orlandini**
Carroll Baker, Jean Sorel, George Hilton, Ida Galli, Luigi Pistilli

Returning to Geneva from their honeymoon, Deborah (Baker) and Marcel (Sorel) encounter unpleasant accusations from Marcel's friend Philip (Pistelli) concerning the death of his former fiancée, and are hounded by threatening phone calls. They seek respite in Nice, but things go from bad to worse, culminating in murder. The title of this film, together with its erotic opening sequence of lovemaking in the shower, suggests a salacious sex movie. In fact, it is a superior and ingenious suspense thriller, full of surprise twists in the tradition of *Les Diaboliques*.

Sweet Hours

Dulces Horas

Spain 1981 103 mins col

Elias Querejeta Productions

d **Carlos Saura**
sc **Carlos Saura**
ph **Teo Escamilla**
Assumpta Serna, Iñaki Aierra, Alvaro De Luna, Jacques Lalande, Luisa Rodrigo, Pedro Samson

A playwright (Aierra), rehearsing a play about his own childhood during the Franco era, finds himself falling in love with the actress (Serna) who is playing his beloved mother, a vivacious woman whose sudden death shocked him profoundly. Using his favourite (and now rather worn) device of the melding of memories, dreams, fantasies, the past and the present, Saura adds the more interesting Pirandellian twist of breaking down the boundaries of reality and the theatre. We are seldom sure whether we are watching the play, the playwright's memories, or both. What is certain and rather banal is that, having the sensuous and attractive Assumpta Serna (an impressive debut) playing both the mother and actress, the shade of Oedipus is not far away.

Sweet Life, The see Dolce Vita, La

Swept Away...By An Unusual Destiny In The Blue Sea Of August

Travolti Da Un Insolito Destino Nell'Azzurro Mare D'Agosto

Italy 1975 120 mins col
Medusa Cinematografica

d **Lina Wertmüller**
sc **Lina Wertmüller**
m **Ennio Guarnieri**
m **Piero Piccioni**
Giancarlo Giannini, Mariangela Melato, Riccardo Salvino, Aldo Puglisi, Isa Danieli

A Sicilian deck-hand (Giannini), working on a yacht, and his boss's wife (Melato) find themselves adrift on a dinghy. After two nights, they reach an island on which they carry out a series of sexual and class strategies. Reality intrudes when the castaways are rescued. Wertmüller's twee title and desert island plot disguise a simple-minded determinist parable. If the message is that people's sexual attitudes are governed by economics and class, then the medium shows a director working in gender stereotypes. The two leads play the puppet characters with as much conviction as is possible in the circumstances, and there are successful moments of bitter irony.

The Swimmer

Plovec

USSR 1981 105mins bw/sepia/col
Gruzia Film

d **Irakli Kvirikadze**
sc **Irakli Kvirikadze**
ph **Turam Tugushi**
m **Teimuraz Bakuradze**
Elgudzha Burduli, Ruslan Mikaberidze, Baadur Tsuladze, Guram Pirtskhalava, Nana Kvachantiradze, Gia Lezhava

Three generations of a family—grandfather, father, grandson—are obsessed with swimming. This passion destroys the first two, while the middle-aged surviving member tries to keep it at bay. Made in Georgia, this is an original piece of work, constructed as a film within a film, and shot as distinct segments intercut with the activities of the crew which is supposed to be making it. Grandfather's tale is photographed in sepia, intriguingly beautiful and lyrical; son's episode is black and white, and redolent with the atmosphere of the post-war Stalinist period; grandson's story takes place on the contemporary film set and is in colour. There is little dialogue, voice-over commentary being largely used, and it is difficult to appreciate why the film's release was withheld for a few years. An interesting, often absorbing curiosity, that falls apart in the third segment.

Swindle, The see Swindlers, The

The Swindlers

(US: The Swindle)

Il Bidone

Italy 1955 114 mins bw
Titanus/SGC

d **Federico Fellini**
sc **Federico Fellini, Ennio Flaiano, Tullio Pinelli**
ph **Otello Martelli**
m **Nino Rota**
Broderick Crawford, Richard Basehart, Franco Fabrizi, Giulietta Masina

Three small-time crooks fleece the poor by disguising themselves as priests, but when one of them tries to double-cross the others, he is beaten up and left to die alone on a stony hillside. In answer to criticism from the Left about his betrayal of Neo-Realist principles in *La Strada* (1954), Fellini made his starkest and most bitter social drama, but failed to please the general public. Seriously lacking his natural exuberance, the film does reach tragic dimensions in the remarkable final scene when Crawford finds salvation prior to his death.

The Swing

Die Schaukel

W. Germany 1983 133 mins col
Pelemele Film/Pro-ject Film/Roxy Film

d **Percy Adlon**
sc **Percy Adlon**
ph **Jürgen Martin**
m **Peer Raben, Johann Strauss**
Anja Jaenicke, Lena Stolze, Joachim Bernhard, Rolf Illig, Suzanne Herlet, Christine Kaufmann

In Munich during the 1880s, the Lautenschlag family—singing teacher mother (Kaufmann), father (Illig) who is the Royal Bavarian landscape gardener, four teenage children—lives a madcap existence, pawning antiques and entertaining the Crown Prince at a musical recital in its shabby home. In contrast to the stuffy Prussian Von Zwingers who frown upon them, the Lautenschlags are short of money, enthusiastic about art, high-spirited and unconventional. This is an affectionate, charming, nostalgic and humorous portrait of a madcap family, one of whose daughters (Jaenicke) records the events in her diary and, in later years, becomes a novelist who writes the story we see. As in his earlier *Céleste*, Adlon reveals a striking gift for evoking period through authentic visual detail.

The Swissmakers

Die Schweizermacher

Switzerland 1978 108 mins col
Lyssy/Rex/Willora/Schoch/Ecco

d **Rolf Lyssy**
sc **Rolf Lyssy, Beatrice Kessler**
ph **Fritz E. Maeder**
m **Jonas C. Haefeli**
Walo Lüond, Emil Steinberger, Beatrice Kessler, Wolfgang Stendar, Hilde Ziegler, Claudio Caramaschi

A pair of policemen (Lüond and Steinberger) in the naturalization section of the government have to investigate the suitability of three candidates who have applied for Swiss citizenship—an Italian baker (Caramaschi), a German doctor (Stendar) and a Yugoslavian ballet dancer (Kessler), whom one of the policeman falls for. An amusing and trenchant social comedy on 'How To Be A Swiss', it is realized with a much lighter touch than many of the other satires by Swiss directors on their 'clean, conservative and complacent' country. The opening lecture is influenced by the Swiss-born Jean-Luc Godard.

The Switchboard Operator

aka The Tragedy Of A Switchboard Operator
(US: Love Affair: Or The Case of The Missing Switchboard Operator aka An Affair Of The Heart)
Ljubavni Slucaj
aka Tragedija Sluzbenice P.T.T.

Yugoslavia 1967 69 mins bw
Avala

d **Dušan Makavejev**
sc **Dušan Makavejev**
ph **Aleksandar Petković**
Eva Ras, Slobodan Aligrudić, Ruzica Sokic, Miodrag Andrić

A young independent switchboard operator (Ras) sets up house with a Turkish ratcatcher (Aligrudić), who becomes jealous and accidentally kills her after she is seduced by a postman (Andrić). Using hand-held cameras in the streets, newsreels, asides, and ironic juxtapositions between traditional and modern Yugoslavia, Makavejev invests his second feature with vitality and an anarchic spirit. However, the interruptions of the narrative by a criminologist and a sexologist have dated, as has the director's obvious attempt to affront a conservative audience.

Swords Of Blood see Cartouche

Sylvia And The Ghost

(US: Sylvia And The Phantom)
Sylvie Et Le Fantôme

France 1945 93 mins bw

Écran Français/André Paulve

d **Claude Autant-Lara**
sc **Jean Aurenche**
ph **Philippe Agostini**
m **René Clöerec**
Odette Joyeux, François Périer, Jean Desailly, Jacques Tati, Louis Salou

Sixteen-year-old Sylvia (Joyeux) is enamoured of a nobleman in a portrait which hangs in her castle home. Her father pays someone to impersonate the dead man, but two of her suitors have the same idea until the real ghost pops up. Less whimsical than it sounds, the film is an entertaining light comedy romance with a chance to see Jacques Tati as the ghost making his first appearance—and disappearance—in a feature. The 28-year-old Joyeux was made to look younger by her husband, photographer Agostini.

Sylvia And The Phantom see Sylvia And The Ghost

Sylvie Et Le Fantôme see Sylvia And The Ghost

Symphonie Fantastique

France 1947 90 mins bw
L'Atelier Français

d **Christian-Jaque**
sc **J.P. Feydeau, H.A. Legrand**
ph **Armand Thirard**
m **Berlioz**
Jean-Louis Barrault, Renée Saint-Cyr, Lise Delamare, Bernard Blier, Gilbert-Gil

The struggles of French composer Hector Berlioz as he climbs from obscurity to fame. *En route*, domestic discord drives him to leave his wife for a more understanding woman, whereupon he creates his masterpieces. As this romantic hero of a romantic age, Jean-Louis Barrault, agonized and posturing, is not very sympathetic in a biopic which, while meticulously reproducing the elegance of the age, fails to capture its excitement, remaining tedious and pedestrian. The film does, however, provide a feast of musical extracts from some of Berlioz's most famous works, 'conducted' by Barrault, sometimes to the accompaniment of quite dramatic effects, such as storms raging without.

La Symphonie Pastorale

France 1946 110 mins bw
Pathé/Les Films Gibe

d **Jean Delannoy**
sc **Jean Aurenche, Jean Delannoy**
ph **Armand Thirard**
m **Georges Auric, Beethoven**
Michèle Morgan, Pierre Blanchar, Jean Desailly, Line Noro, Louvigny, Andrée Clément, Rosine Luguet

Gertrude (Morgan), a blind orphan girl, is taken in and raised by Pastor Martin (Blanchar) and his wife. He imbues her with a sense of the world as a place of beauty and harmony and eventually falls in love with her, as does his son Jean (Desailly). Jean wants to marry Gertrude and arranges an operation to restore her sight but, although this is successful, disillusion and tragedy follow. This is a sensitive if sombre adaptation of André Gide's heartbreaking novella, capturing the ironically beautiful and serene atmosphere of the mountain village where it is set. Delannoy directs with taste and discretion and Morgan, her beautiful and expressive eyes communicating Gertrude's innermost thoughts, is superb.

Best Film Cannes 1946
Best Actress (Michèle Morgan) Cannes 1946

Symphony Of The Don Basin see Enthusiasm

Syskonbädd 1782 see My Sister, My Love

Sytten see Seventeen

Szegénylegények see Round-Up, The

Szerelem see Love

Szerelmem, Elektra see Elektreia

Szerencsés Daniel see Daniel Takes A Train

Sziget A Szárazföldön see Lady From Constantinople, The

Szindbád see Sindbad

t

Tagenbuch Einer Verloren see Diary Of A Lost Girl

Taiheiyo Hitoribochi see Alone On The Pacific

Tailor's Maid, The see Like Father, Like Son

The Tall Blond Man With One Black Shoe

Le Grand Blond Avec Une Chaussure Noire

France 1972 89 mins col
Gaumont International/Productions De La Guéville/ Madeleine Films

d **Yves Robert**
sc **Yves Robert, Francis Véber**
ph **René Mathelin**
m **Vladimir Cosma**
Pierre Richard, Bernard Blier, Jean Rochefort, Mireille Darc, Jean Carmet, Colette Castel

When secret service agency chief Toulouse (Rochefort) suspects that Milan (Blier) is after his job, he sets him up by sending him to tail a dangerous agent who, in reality, is somebody picked at random from a crowd. The innocent victim, a naive and clumsy violinist (Richard), is engaged in an affair with his friend's wife, whose apartment is bugged by Milan's men. The idea is brilliantly ironic but the story muddled in its realization. Everything points to a wild comedy but the humour is only sporadically injected into what is played as a straight spy thriller. The acting, particularly from new comic discovery Richard, is accomplished, and there are a number of clever elements, but the sum of the parts is greater than the whole, even though it spawned a sequel, *The Return Of The Tall Blond*, in 1974.

Special Jury Prize Berlin 1973

Tall Shadows Of The Wind

Saiehaien Bolan De Bad

Iran 1978 110 mins col
Telfilm/Iran Biograph Film Centre

d **Bahman Farmanara**
sc **Hushang Golshiri, Bahman Farmanara**
ph **Alireza Zarindast**
m **Ahmad Pejman**
Faramaz Gharibian, Saiid Nikpour, Nadia Khalilpur

A bus driver (Gharibian), plying a route between remote villages, draws a face on a scarecrow and puts his own hat on its head. Various mysterious events take place thereafter, and the villagers, believing the scarecrow to be an evil deity, blame the bus driver. Working through visually striking symbols in a folk tale format, Farmanara and the short story writer Golshiri, have created an arresting film which implicitly attacks superstition and authoritarianism. The film came into disfavour under the Shah and then under Khomeini, each regime seeing itself represented by the scarecrow. The vivid colours and the lush musical score add to the atmosphere of the piece, and there is a memorable dream sequence.

Tampopo

Japan 1986 117 mins col
Itami Productions/New Century Producers

d **Juzo Itami**
sc **Juzo Itami**
ph **Masaki Tamura**

m **Kinihiko Murai**
Tsutomu Yamazaki, Nobuko Miyamoto, Koji Yakusho, Ken Watanabe, Rikiya Yasuoka

An all-night truck driver (Yamazaki) pulls in for a snack at a wayside noodle shop run by the widowed Tampopo (Miyamoto, Itami's wife). Finding the food uneatable, he stays to help her turn the place into one of the best restaurants in the country. This gorgeous gastronomic comedy of table manners satirizes Japanese social mores in a series of vignettes, mostly set in the *ramen* (noodle) shop. The director calls it a '*ramen* western', due to some similarities to such films as *Shane*, not to mention spaghetti westerns—wandering trouble shooter rides into town and then rides off alone. The film satisfies like a good meal, although it should not be seen on an empty stomach.

Tangos, L'Exil De Gardel see Tangos, The Exile Of Gardel

Tangos, The Exile Of Gardel
Tangos, L'Exil De Gardel

Argentina/France 1985 130 mins col
Cinesur(Buenos Aires)/Terciné(Paris)

d **Fernando E Solanas**
sc **Fernando E Solanas**
ph **Felix Monti**
m **Astor Piazzola**
Marie Laforêt, Philippe Léotard, Miguel Angel Sola, Marina Vlady, Georges Wilson, Lautaro Murua, Anna Maria Picchio

A group of Argentinian exiles in Paris must battle with nostalgia, problems of national identity and the practicalities of making ends meet. They decide to stage a tango ballet inspired by the memory and music of Carlos Gardel, the legendary Argentinian tango star who was killed in 1935. Coming from the radically politicized director of, among other things, *The Hour Of The Furnaces*, this movie is something of a surprise. Solanas displays humour and a gift for the staging of dance numbers, unfolding a tale about the pain of exile through the relationships and incidents that attend the rehearsals and production of the show. The movie is marred by its undisciplined structure and inordinate length, but the lighting photography, music and dance are a triumph.
Special Jury Prize Venice 1985

Tanin No Kao see Face Of Another, The

Tant Qu'on A La Santé see As Long As You're Healthy

Tanu, A see Witness, The

Tartüff see Tartuffe

Tartuffe
Tartüff

Germany 1925 70 mins bw
UFA

d **F.W. Murnau**
sc **Carl Mayer**
ph **Karl Freund**
m **Silent**
Emil Jannings, Werner Krauss, Lil Dagover, Lucie Höflich

Having ingratiated himself with the wealthy Orgon (Krauss), the rascally and hypocritical Tartuffe (Jannings) comes to dominate the man's household. Orgon's eyes are finally opened when he catches Tartuffe trying to make love to his attractive young wife (Dagover). This heavily Germanic adaptation of Molière's classical French comedy, ridiculing 17th-century society, was turned into a chamber film, eliminating the secondary characters in order to concentrate on the central triangle of relationships. Murnau also added a superfluous prologue to introduce the story. Stylishly made, the picture benefited from an outstanding team behind the camera which included top art directors Walter Röhrig and Robert Herlth, but it is best remembered for the performances of its stellar cast.

The Taste Of Water
De Smaak Van Water

Netherlands 1982 100 mins col
Maya Film

d **Orlow Seunke**
sc **Orlow Seunke, Dirk Ayelt Kooiman**

ph **Albert Van Der Wildt**
m **Jan Musch**
Gerard Thoolen, Dorijn Curvers, Joop Admiraal, Hans Van Tongeren, Olga Zuiderhoek

A social worker (Thoolen), efficient, but seemingly indifferent after years of dealing with poverty and suffering, dedicates himself to the education and rehabilitation of a neglected, dirty, animal-like 14-year-old girl (Curvers), who hardly leaves the cupboard in which she was raised. In the tradition of *The Miracle Worker* and Truffaut's *Wild Child*, Seunke's film deals with the civilizing process while, at the same time, attacking Dutch bureaucracy. Directed in a straightforward manner, without seeking sympathy, the film gains its emotional impact both from the subject matter and from the extraordinary performance from Dorijn Curvers, who worked on the material with the director for over four years before shooting began.

Tausend Augen Des Dr Mabuse, Die see Thousand Eyes Of Dr Mabuse, The

---

Tavaszi Zapor see Marie—A Hungarian Legend

Taxidi Sta Kithira see Voyage To Cythera

A Taxing Woman
Marusa No Onna

Japan 1987 127 mins col
Itami Productions/New Century Producers

d **Juzo Itami**
sc **Juzo Itami**
ph **Yoneza Maeda**
m **Toshiyuki Honda**
Nobuko Miyamoto, Tsutomu Yamazaki, Masahiko Tsugawa, Hideko Murota

The day-to-day life of an eager-beaver female tax inspector (Miyamoto, Itami's wife) determined to track down every small-scale tax fraud, despite being harassed, humiliated and harmed by the people she pursues, although a certain sympathy develops between her and a petty criminal (Yamazaki). The bright new meteor of the Japanese cinema followed up his 'noodle Western' *Tampopo* with an equally successful comedy on the unlikely subject of tax returns (to be followed by *A Taxing Woman 2*, dealing with million-dollar tax evasions). The detailed observation of the heroine's profession is as obsessive as that of Bresson's *Pickpocket*, but to more satiric ends. Itami's legerdemain allows him to shift easily from comedy to the realism of the gangster movie, ending in a tender, tense and surprising manner.

Taxi Zum Klo

W. Germany 1981 92 mins col
Frank Ripploh, Horst Schier, Laurens Straub

d **Frank Ripploh**
sc **Frank Ripploh**
ph **Horst Schier**
m **Hans Wittstadt**
Frank Ripploh, Bernd Broaderup, Magdalena Montezuma, Tabea Blumenschein, Gitte Lederer

A gay teacher (Ripploh), having a bad time with his jealous, home-making lover (Broaderup), spends his nights looking for pick-ups at public lavatories and loses his job. The director, whose debut film this is, plays himself as an amusing, randy and lovable rogue, supported by real-life friends and lovers. Despite the self-indulgence, some misogyny, and scenes 'of an explicit nature that might offend', it is a touching, humorous and generally positive view of homosexual life on the eve of the AIDS scare. Especially good are Ripploh in front of his class, and a tragicomic fancy dress party. The title could be translated as 'Taxi To The Loo'.

Tchaikovsky

USSR 1970 191 mins col
Mosfilm(Moscow)/Warner Bros.-7 Arts (Hollywood)

d **Igor Talankin**
sc **Budimir Metalnikov, Yuri Nagibin, Igor Talankin**
ph **Margarita Pilikhina**
m **Tchaikovsky**
Innokenti Smoktunovsky, Antonina Shuranova, Evgeni Leonov, Maya Plisetskaya, Vladislav Strzeltchik, Alla Demidova, Kirill Lavrov, Bruno Friendlikh, Evgeni Evstigneev, Lidiya Yudina

The childhood memories, adult struggles, loneliness and despair of Peter Ilyich Tchaikovsky (Smoktunovsky), culminating in his death a week after conducting the first performance of the Sixth symphony *(Pathétique)*. The making of this film realized a long-cherished dream of the celebrated Russian-born composer, Dimitri Tiomkin, who served as executive producer. However, all he came up with was a respectable and dull biopic, which ignores the composer's homosexuality and puts the collapse of his marriage down to a trivial social incident. Made with an eye to the West, where it is generally shown cut by about an hour-and-a-half and with an English commentary spoken by Laurence Harvey, the film offers a few splendid visuals, and the great Smoktunovsky manages to rise above the generally static script. The music, of course, is glorious.

Teen Kanya see Two Daughters

Telefteo Psemma, To see Matter Of Dignity, A

Téléphone Rose, Le see Pink Telephone, The

Tema see Theme, The

Tempo Si E Fermato, Il see Time Stood Still

Ten Days That Shook The World see October

The Tender Age

aka Adolphe Or The Awkward Age

Adolphe Ou L'Âge Tendre

France 1968 103 mins col
Prisma Films/Oceanic

d **Bernard T. Michel**
sc **Bernard T. Michel, Jean Moal**
ph **Jean Charvein**
m **Michel Damase**

Ulla Jacobsson, Philippe Noiret, Jean-Claude Dauphin, Claude Giraud, Nathalie Nell

A young man (Dauphin), making a film of Benjamin Constant's 19th-century novel about an older woman's love for a youth, finds a parallel situation between himself and Hélène (Jacobsson), the mistress of the count (Noiret), whose château is being used for the film. The attractive location photography does not make up for this misconceived, miscast film-within-a-film. Constant's classic novel has subtlety and grace, two qualities lacking in this pointless updating.

The Tender Enemy

La Tendre Ennemie

France 1936 69 mins bw
Eden/SELF

d **Max Ophüls**
sc **Max Ophüls, Kurt Alexander**
ph **Eugen Schüfftan, Lucien Colas**
m **Albert Wolff**

Simone Berriau, Georges Vitray, Jacqueline Daix, Maurice Devienne, Catherine Fonteney, Valbel

Three men meet for the first time after death and discuss the woman (Berriau) who had cheated them in life. It is revealed that she destroyed their lives because her mother (Fonteney) had refused to allow her to elope with the only man she ever loved. Ophüls' sweet tooth makes him sugar the sour play by André-Paul Antoine, while still retaining some of its bite. Not one of his better romances, but there are enough gags and nicely executed camera movements to give pleasure.

Tenderness Of Wolves

Zärtlichkeit Der Wölfe

W. Germany 1973 83 mins col
Tango Film

d **Ulli Lommel**
sc **Kurt Raab**
ph **Jürgen Jürges**
m **Peer Raben**

Kurt Raab, Jeff Roden, Margit Carstensen, Hannelore Tiefenbrunner, Tanara Schanzara, Wolfgang Schenk, Rainer Werner Fassbinder, Brigitte Mira

During the depression in Germany in the 1920s, Fritz Haarman (Raab), apparently a charming, friendly, inoffensive man, works as a police informer. Actually, he is the 'Vampire of Düsseldorf'—the murderer of at least 25 young boys, whose remains he sells as meat on the black market. The actual case depicted had been the basis of Fritz Lang's *M* (in which Peter Lorre killed young girls) and other German horror films, but it had never been so explicitly or chillingly portrayed. The film has the mark of its producer, Fassbinder, all over it; many of the cast and the technical crew belong to the Fassbinder 'family' and he was also one of the editors. Despite its nasty subject, there is a certain tongue-in-cheek humour and a distancing stylization that prevents it from becoming too distasteful. Raab gives quite a good imitation of Peter Lorre.

Tendre Ennemie, La see Tender Enemy, The

Tendre Poulet see Dear Inspector

Tengoku To Jigoku see High And Low

Teni Zabytykh Predkov see Shadows Of Our Forgotten Ancestors

The Ten Thousand Suns

Tízezer Nap

Hungary 1967 112 mins bw
Mafilm Studio

d **Ferenc Kosá**
sc **Sándor Csoóri, Imre Gyöngyössi, Ferenc Kosá**
ph **Sándor Sárá**
m **András Szöllösy**
Tibor Molnár, Gyöngyi Bürös, János Koltai, András Kozák, Ida Simenfalvi

István Széles (Molnár), a successful landowning farmer who started life as a poverty-stricken peasant, is prompted by his son's optimistic departure from home, and his own necessity to adapt to the new Communist society, to look back over the past 30 years of his life. Director Kosá made his feature debut with this startlingly mature and expert piece of film-making. His themes embrace the clash of ideologies as personified by the serious disagreement between István and his one-time friend Fulop (Koltai), and he gives a detailed view of 20th-century Hungarian history. The exemplary camerawork is out of the school of Jancsó, but Kosá's choice of surprise images is very much his own. If the subtleties of argument elude the English-speaking viewer, this fine, well-acted film is nonetheless richly rewarding.

Best Director Cannes 1967

Tenue De Soirée see Evening Dress

Teorema see Theorem

Terminus

France 1986 83 mins col
Les Films Du Cheval De Fer/Cat Production/Initial Group/CBL/Films A2

d **Pierre William Glenn**
sc **Pierre William Glenn**
ph **Jean-Claude Vicquery**
m **Stan Ridgeway**
Johnny Hallyday, Jürgen Prochnow, Karen Allen, Gabriel Damon, Julie Glenn, Louise Vincent

A computer-guided juggernaut zig-zags across country in an elaborate race where the losers forfeit their lives. The players include a tough jailbird (Hallyday), an American woman truck-driver (Allen) and an evil doctor (Prochnow) who wants to take over the world. Pierre William Glenn's disappointing directorial debut confirmed the general rule that fine cinematographers, of whom he is one of France's best, seldom make fine directors. This tortuous science fiction road-race movie has an impassive performance from Hallyday and three ham ones from Prochnow as a mad doctor in black leather, a mad scientist and a mad driver. *Terminus* is the end.

Terra Em Transe see Land In Anguish

La Terra Trema

Italy 1948 160 mins bw
Universalia

d **Luchino Visconti**

sc **Luchino Visconti**
ph **G.R. Aldo**
m **Luchino Visconti, Willy Ferrero**
The inhabitants of Aci Trezza, Sicily

An account of the hard life of a group of Sicilian fishermen, in particular the young 'Ntoni Valastro, who have to struggle not only against nature, but against unscrupulous middlemen. Visconti originally intended an epic trilogy about the exploitation of Sicilian fishermen, peasants and miners, but only the first part (inspired by Verga's 1881 novel) was made. Visconti himself speaks the commentary in standard Italian (added after the film had flopped) because the population, playing themselves, speak in their own Sicilian dialect. Although Visconti initially gained his reputation as a Neo-Realist—the term coined to describe his first film, *Ossessione*— only this film comes close to the movement's ideals. It is difficult to remain unmoved by this human document, shot entirely on location, despite some operatic notions on the part of the director and the beautiful camera compositions at odds with the harsh world depicted. It won a special prize at Venice for its 'choral qualities and style'.

Terre Sans Pain see Land Without Bread

Testament, Le see Verdict

Testament Des Dr Mabuse, Das see Testament Of Dr Mabuse, The

Testament D'Orphée, Le see Testament Of Orpheus, The

Testament Du Dr Cordelier, Le see Testament Of Dr Cordelier, The

---

The Testament Of Dr Cordelier

(US: Experiment In Evil)
Le Testament Du Dr Cordelier
France 1959 100 mins bw
ORTF/Sofirad/Renoir

d **Jean Renoir**
sc **Jean Renoir**
ph **Georges Leclerc**
m **Joseph Kosma**
Jean-Louis Barrault, Michel Vitold, Teddy Billis, Jean Topart, Micheline Gary

A series of brutal attacks, mainly on women and children, are traced to a mysterious Monsieur Opale, whom the respected Dr Cordelier (Barrault) claims as a friend. One day, the doctor's lawyer (Billis) discovers that his client and Opale are one and the same, the doctor having created an evil alter ego by means of a drug. Renoir's reworking of *The Strange Case Of Dr Jekyll And Mr Hyde*, gave him a wonderful opportunity to return to the anarchy and freedom of the eponymous tramp hero of *Boudu Saved From Drowning*. Renoir, using up to eight cameras and 12 microphones, which gives the film a fluid, rough-edged, spontaneous appeal, first conceived it as a live TV play. The director's method of cutting only after each sequence and allowing the actors to determine their own speed was completely vindicated by the wonderfully unique performance by Barrault as the jaunty, twitching, shaggy, prancing Opale, his finest film work since *Les Enfants Du Paradis*.

The Testament Of Dr Mabuse

aka The Last Will Of Dr Mabuse
Das Testament Des Dr Mabuse
Germany 1932 122 mins bw
Nero

d **Fritz Lang**
sc **Thea Von Harbou, Fritz Lang**
ph **Fritz Arno Wagner**
m **Hans Erdmann**
Rudolf Klein-Rogge, Otto Wernicke, Gustav Diessl, Oscar Beregi, Vera Liessem

The arch-criminal Dr Mabuse (Klein-Rogge), confined to a lunatic asylum, uses his hypnotic powers—and the asylum director as the agent of those powers—to operate his plan to master the world. But he is finally foiled by Inspector Lohmann (Wernicke). Or is he? Lang continued the *pfennig* dreadful adventures of *Dr Mabuse, The Gambler*, saturating the film with the same atmosphere of decadence and evil, but with the added layer of sound which he uses forcefully. The mad villain expressed sentiments too close for Nazi comfort, provoking Goebbels to ask Lang politely to change the last reel. The director realized that the monster he had created could now control him, so he fled to France and then to the USA for a second career, leaving behind his wife, Thea Von Harbou, who had joined the Nazi party.

The Testament Of Orpheus

Le Testament D'Orphée

France 1960 83 mins bw

Les Éditions Cinégraphiques

d **Jean Cocteau**
sc **Jean Cocteau**
ph **Roland Pointoizeau**
m **Georges Auric**

Jean Cocteau, Edouard Dermithe, Maria Casarès, François Périer, Yul Brynner, Jean Marais, Pablo Picasso, Jean-Pierre Léaud, Charles Aznavour

Jean Cocteau as The Poet wanders weightlessly through a dream landscape peopled by his friends, and the characters and images from his works, including The Princess (Casarès), Heurtebise (Périer) and Cégeste (Dermithe) from his *Orpheus*. Made on a shoestring, Cocteau's valedictory film is a self-indulgent, self-mocking self-portrait, mystifying but intriguing to those who have no previous knowledge of his films, plays, poems and novels, fascinating and illuminating to those who have. Yet the whole of his unique *oeuvre* is allusive and personal. As he says, 'A film, whatever it may be, is always its director's portrait'. In this film, he is penetrated by a sword, but pops up from his grave uttering the words, 'A poet can never die'. Cocteau's body died in 1963, but his art lives on.

Tête Contre Les Murs, La see Keepers, The

Tetto, Il see Roof, The

Teufel's General, Des see Devil's General, The

Thank Heaven For Small Favors see Heaven Sent

Thank You, Aunt see Grazie Zia

That Cat see When The Cat Comes

That Man From Rio

L'Homme De Rio

France 1964 120 mins col

Ariane/ Artistes Associés/Dear/Vides

d **Philippe De Broca**
sc **Jean-Paul Rappeneau, Ariane Mnouchkine, Daniel Boulanger, Philippe De Broca**
ph **Edmond Séchan**
ph **Georges Delerue**

Jean-Paul Belmondo, Françoise Dorléac, Jean Servais, Adolfo Celi, Simone Renant

An airline pilot (Belmondo) becomes involved in a wild adventure that takes him from Paris to Rio, Brasília and the Amazon in order to help his archeologist fiancée (Dorleac) search for stolen treasures. Since 007 hit the screens in 1962, a deluge of spy spoofs followed in the USA and Europe, many of them rating double zero. This is one of the best in that it uses the cheeky, bouncy persona of Belmondo, the beauty of Dorléac and exotic Brazilian locations to good effect. De Broca directs in his early frenetic style, not always sharing his fun with the audience.

That Obscure Object Of Desire

Cet Obscur Objet Du Désir

France 1977 103 mins col

Greenwich/Galaxie/In Ciné

d **Luis Buñuel**
sc **Luis Buñuel, Jean-Claude Carrière**
ph **Edmond Richard**
m **Wagner**

Fernando Rey, Carole Bouquet, Angela Molina, Julien Bertheau, André Weber, Piéral

A rich businessman (Rey) falls under the spell of his maid Conchita, who refuses to give herself to him, although she continues to feed his hopes. He, therefore, does everything in his power to persuade her. When Maria Schneider left the project after three weeks' shooting, Buñuel, with the surreal logic that runs through his career, decided to cast two actresses (Bouquet and Molina) to alternate the role of Conchita. At first, the dual casting is disconcerting, but it gradually becomes strangely normal—revealing two different sides of the same woman which the man fails to notice. In the background to the activities of this discreetly charming *bourgeois* (Rey perfect), are those of a revolutionary group. Buñuel's last film (based like the Sternberg-Dietrich 1935 movie, *The Devil Is A Woman*, on Pierre Loüys' novel *La Femme Et Le Pantin*) is another sly and witty bomb placed under the privileged classes. The great Spanish-born director died in 1983, the same age as the century.

The Theme

Tema

USSR 1979 98 mins col
Mosfilm

d **Gleb Panfilov**
sc **Gleb Panfilov, Aleksander Cervinski**
ph **Leonid Kalashnikov**
m **Vadim Bibergan**
Inna Churikova, Michael Ulyanov, Stanislav Lyubshin, Evgeny Vesnik, Sergei Nikonenko, Natalya Selezneva

Esenin (Ulyanov) is a successful but mediocre Moscow writer, having sold out to the easy plaudits and privileges that come from kow-towing to the regime. In need of fresh inspiration, he visits his native village where he meets Sasa Nikolaeva (Churikova) and falls in love with her. An artist who has refused to compromise, she is involved with a poet with the same views, rebuffs Esenin, and is frank in expressing her low opinion of him. The Berlin award for Panfilov's film was also a tacit honour conferred upon *glasnost*, which allowed *The Theme* to come off the shelf where it had been languishing for eight years. Unlike some other Soviet films, the reasons why this one was repressed are not hard to discern, for Panfilov airs the two very thorny themes of artistic freedom and emigration. The latter arises with the determination of Sasa's lover, reduced by his refusal to compromise his artistic integrity to digging graves, to settle in Israel. Aside, however, from the didactic worthiness of the enterprise, it is well made, intelligent and—thanks to the director's skilful sense of irony and two wonderful performances from Churikova and Ulyanov—entertaining.

Best Film Berlin 1987

Themroc

France 1972 110 mins col
Filmanthrope/FDL Productions

d **Claude Faraldo**
sc **Claude Faraldo**
ph **Jean-Marc Ripert**
Michel Piccoli, Béatrice Romand, Marilù Tolo, Francesca R. Coluzzi, Mme Herviale, Members of the Café De La Gare Théâtre Troupe

Factory worker Themroc (Piccoli) lives in a squalid flat with his mother and sister and pursues an existence of repetitive routine and urban grind. He suddenly rebels, causing havoc in the factory, making love to his sister, smashing down the apartment walls and drawing all comers into his web of anarchy. Faraldo's controversial film has its roots in the French tradition of comedy as a social weapon, but his approach is uniquely original in abandoning language and having his characters communicate in a series of formless noises (their meaning is clear). Initially using the hand-held cameras of *cinéma vérité* to evoke the nightmare of city life, he switches techniques to unfold the bizarre goings-on that result from Themroc's rebellion. Faraldo's attack on robot-like conformity is surreal, absurdist and funny, holding up to ridicule our pitiful rituals, our authority figures and the passivity of the workers.

Theorem

Teorema

Italy 1968 98 mins col
Aetos Film

d **Pier Paolo Pasolini**
sc **Pier Paolo Pasolini**
ph **Giuseppe Ruzzolini**
m **Ennio Morricone**
Terence Stamp, Silvana Mangano, Massimo Girotti, Anne Wiazemsky, Laura Betti, Andrés José Cruz

A handsome young man (Stamp) ingratiates himself into the home of a rich industrialist (Girotti) and sleeps with every member of the family—the father, the mother (Mangano), the daughter (Wiazemsky), the son (Cruz) and the maid (Betti)—completely changing their lives. This fable on the middle classes was banned and Pasolini charged with obscenity by the Italian government (he was acquitted), although it contains no recognizable human beings. The director sets out to prove that, once the family was liberated from its *bourgeois* existence by the young stranger (long-haired English actors were very fashionable in European films of the 1960s), it goes mad because sex is the one thing it cannot control.The QED of Pasolini's theorem may be unconvincing, but there is a certain mathematical beauty in his efforts to reach it.

Best Actress (Laura Betti) Venice 1968

Thérèse see Thérèse Desqueyroux

Thérèse

France 1986 90 mins col
AFC/Films A2/CNC

d **Alain Cavalier**
sc **Alain Cavalier, Camille De Casabianca**
ph **Isabelle Dedieu**
Catherine Mouchet, Hélène Alexanderis, Aurore Prieto, Sylvia Habault, Clémence Massart, Ghislaine Mona

Fifteen-year-old Thérèse (Mouchet), at her own request, leaves her father to enter the strict Carmelite Order at Lisieux. Her love of life and God help her to endure the deprivations and inspire those around her. She contracts TB and dies aged 24 in 1897. She was canonized 27 years later. A series of tableaux of convent life containing little drama and less dialogue sounds as if the film might be a chastening experience in itself. But each scene has much to tell about the simple faith of Thérèse, beautifully played by stage actress Mouchet, and the various other nuns. What comes through is not religiosity but an almost mundane domesticity and humanity, and an underlying eroticism.

Thérèse Desqueyroux

aka Thérèse

France 1962 109 mins bw
Filmel

d **Georges Franju**
sc **François Mauriac, Claude Mauriac, Georges Franju**
ph **Christian Matras**
m **Maurice Jarre**
Emmanuele Riva, Philippe Noiret, Edith Scob, Sami Frey

Thérèse (Riva), finding herself stifled by provincial life and a dull marriage, decides to poison her boring but gentle and inoffensive husband (Noiret). Emanuele Riva was at the height of her film career when she took on the role of the dissatisfied heroine in this updated version of François Mauriac's novel. She subtly portrays the psychological and physical deterioration of Thérèse, while director Franju succeeds in capturing the oppressiveness of the natural world around her.

Best Actress (Emanuele Riva) Venice 1962

Thérèse Raquin

(US: The Adulteress)

France 1953 110 mins bw
Paris Films/Lux Films

d **Marcel Carné**
sc **Charles Spaak, Marcel Carné**
ph **Roger Hubert**
m **Maurice Thiriet**
Simone Signoret, Raf Vallone, Jacques Duby, Sylvie, Roland Lesaffre

Thérèse Raquin (Signoret), the bored, unhappy and love-starved wife of a weak, flabby and petulant railway worker (Duby), becomes involved with a handsome Italian truck driver (Vallone), an affair that leads to murder and blackmail. For what was his last notable film, Carné updated Émile Zola's famous novel of destructive sensual passion, and set it in the bleak provincial back streets of Lyons. It is redolent with brooding atmosphere but, somehow, it is a cold film in which the leads are efficient rather than passionate, leaving the acting honours to Sylvie as Thérèse's crippled, unpleasant and vigilant mother-in-law. The famous version of this tale, made in 1928 by Jacques Feyder is, alas, no longer extant.

There Was A Father
Chichi Ariki

Japan 1942 94 mins bw
Shochiku/Ofuna

d **Yasujiro Ozu**
sc **Tadao Ikeda, Takao Yanai, Yasujiro Ozu**
ph **Yushun Atsuta**
m **Gyoichi Saiki**
Chishu Ryu, Shuji Sano, Haruhiko Tsuda, Mitsuko Mito, Takeshi Sakamoto, Shin Saburi

A widowed schoolteacher (Ryu) is very close to his son (Tsuda young, Sano older), but circumstances make them live separate lives with the son at boarding school and then university. However, the father has the pleasure of seeing him married to the daughter (Mito) of his best friend (Sakamoto) before he dies. Although made at the height of World War II, and subject to a range of restrictions, among them the necessity to include some propaganda, Ozu managed to make one of his most affecting films. Chishu Ryu, Ozu's favourite actor, is outstanding, giving a sensitive and appealing performance. Unusual for Ozu are the many locations and the long time span of the plot, but his special insights into the parent-child relationship and the attention to the details of ordinary existence remain intact.

They Don't Wear Black Tie
Eles Nao Usam Black Tie

Brazil 1981 120 mins col
Embrafilme

d **Leon Hirszman**
sc **Leon Hirszman, Gianfrancesco Guarnieri**
ph **Lauro Escorel**
m **Radamés Gnatelli, Adoniram Barbosa**
Fernanda Montenegro, Gianfrancesco Guarnieri, Carlos Alberto Ricelli, Bete Mendes

In São Paulo, a working-class family is deeply divided over a strike at the factory in which father (Guarnieri), son (Ricelli), and the latter's pregnant fiancée (Mendes) work. The father resists the police and is sent to prison, but the son crosses the picket line. Scrupulously avoiding stereotypes, Hirszman, with the help of exceptional ensemble playing, gives an unidealized and wide-ranging view of the working classes. Unlike his earlier more Brechtian approach, the director has gone for a more popular style which he calls 'democratic realism'. A little too glossy for the subject, the film nevertheless gets its point across effectively.

Special Jury Prize Venice 1981

They Were Five see Belle Équipe, La

Thiassos, O see Travelling Players, The

The Thief Of Paris
Le Voleur

France 1967 120 mins col
Nouvelles Éditions/Compania Cinematografica

d **Louis Malle**
sc **Jean-Claude Carrière, Daniel Boulanger, Louis Malle**
ph **Henri Decaë**
Jean-Paul Belmondo, Geneviève Bujold, Marie Dubois, Julien Guiomar, Françoise Fabian, Charles Denner

A young man (Belmondo), taught to despise poverty by his guardian uncle who then fleeces him of his inheritance, takes to crime as an act of revenge. By the time he is a fully-fledged thief, he knows no other way of earning a living. After the frivolity of *Viva Maria*, Malle, for his seventh film, turns his attention to a solid period thriller-cum-romance, which also contains an incisive comment on hypocrisy, injustice, anarchy and corruption, examining the causes of crime without condoning it. If the director's stance is a little cold and detached, he has nonetheless lovingly and in lavish detail re-created the glory and the squalor of turn-of-the-century Paris. Flashback is effectively used to reveal the thief's past and Belmondo, carrying an aura of suppressed violence which occasionally erupts, is excellent; so is Guiomar's criminal priest, while Bujold makes a suitably fragile and pretty object of the protagonist's affections.

The Things Of Life
Les Choses De La Vie

France 1969 89 mins col
Lira Films(Paris)/Fida

Cinematografica(Rome)

d **Claude Sautet**

sc **Paul Guimard, Jean-Loup Dabadie, Claude Sautet**

ph **Jean Boffety**

m **Philippe Sarde**

Michel Piccoli, Romy Schneider, Lea Massari, Gérard Lartigau, Jean Bouise

Pierre (Piccoli), separated from his wife (Massari) and having an affair with Hélène (Schneider), still retains an attachment to, and an interest in, his wife, his son, his friends, the places he has known—in short, the 'things' of life—and consequently finds it difficult to make the absolute commitment that Hélène requires. Sautet and his cast bring fluent expertise to a subtle and universally interesting subject. However, too much weight is given to the details of Pierre's car accident, which is the fulcrum of an essentially plotless film, and the characters are insufficiently explored, leaving an impression of coldness and superficiality.

The Third Generation

Die Dritte Generation

W. Germany 1979 111 mins col
Tango Film (Berlin)/Pro-ject Filmproduktion/Filmverlag Der Autoren

d **Rainer Werner Fassbinder**

sc **Rainer Werner Fassbinder**

ph **Rainer Werner Fassbinder, Hans Günther Bücking**

m **Peer Raben**

Volker Spengler, Bulle Ogier, Hanna Schygulla, Margit Carstensen, Harry Baer, Udo Kier, Hark Bohm, Eddie Constantine

The cell of a Berlin terrorist group includes Suzanne (Schygulla), who is secretary to international computer dealer Lurz (Constantine), and Petra (Carstensen), a banker's wife. Step by step the group is destroyed by a combination of internal tensions and betrayal by August (Spengler), leader of the group. Fassbinder's terrorists, however, are largely middle-class radical chic individuals, far from the usual stereotype, although the introduction of a hardened professional to the group triggers the chain of disasters. The effect of the director's approach results in an intriguing, semi-satirical thriller, but the political clues are oblique and the message blunted for all but the most acute viewer.

The Third Lover

L'Oeil Du Malin

France 1962 80 mins bw
Rome-Paris Films/Lux Films

d **Claude Chabrol**

sc **Martial Matthieu, Claude Chabrol**

ph **Jean Rabier**

m **Pierre Jansen**

Jacques Charrier, Stéphane Audran, Walther Reyer, Daniel Boulanger, Badri

A second-rate French journalist (Charrier), visiting West Germany to write a series of articles, meets a successful author (Reyer) and his French wife (Audran), who appear to be an exceptionally happy couple. He insinuates himself into their lives, becomes obsessed with their relationship and attempts to seduce the wife, thereby causing destruction. One of the most elegant of Chabrol's early works, the film presents an intriguing situation that develops with Hitchcockian undertones, even though the warped behaviour of the journalist remains somewhat of a puzzle. However, Chabrol's Peeping Tom camera is effectively used to suggest a study in voyeurism.

Thirst

aka Three Strange Loves

Törst

Sweden 1949 88 mins bw
Svensk Filmindustri

d **Ingmar Bergman**

sc **Herbert Grevenius**

ph **Gunnar Fischer**

m **Erik Nordgren**

Eva Henning, Birger Malmsten, Birgit Tengroth, Mimi Nelson, Hasse Ekman

Rut (Henning) and Bertil (Malmsten) are locked into a badly disintegrating marriage, exacerbated by her inability to bear children because of a botched abortion after an earlier affair. We follow them on a journey to Stockholm, trapped in the claustrophobic confines of a train compartment where they reach the nadir of their disillusion and misery. Taking its material from stories by Birgit Tengroth, Rut and Bertil's tale is intercut with the story of Bertil's ex-wife Viola (Tengroth), whose own desperation drives her to consult a psychiatrist (Ekman) and to turn to a sympathetic female ballet dancer (Nelson) for friendship, both with disastrous consequences. The two stories are unfolded in parallel time, together with a lot of flashback. This approach leads to a measure of confusion, while some of the connections made between the protagonists are tenuous and the arm of coincidence occasionally stretches too far. That said, this ambitious but uneven work brilliantly reflects the inner desolation of the married couple in powerful exterior images.

Thirst For Love, The see Longing For Love

37°2 Le Matin see Betty Blue

This Man Must Die see Killer!

This Special Friendship

Les Amitiés Particulières

France 1964 105 mins bw
Christine Gouze Renal

d **Jean Delannoy**
sc **Jean Aurenche, Pierre Bost**
ph **Christian Matras**
m **Jean Prodromidès**
Michel Bouquet, Didier Haudepin, Louis Seigner, Lucien Nat, Francis Lacombrade

In a boys' Catholic boarding school, the 'special friendship' between an older boy (Lacombrade) and a young cherub (Haudepin) is discouraged in a heavy-handed manner by most of the priest-teachers, which inevitably leads to tragedy. Roger Peyrefitte's sensitive novel of youthful homo-eroticism has become rather sentimental and pussy-footing under Delannoy's pedestrian direction. Among the adults, Bouquet is best as a more tolerant priest, but the elder boy is poorly played. Nevertheless, it has its affecting moments and the well-worn subject is reasonably explored.

This Strange Passion see El

This Sweet Sicknees

Dîtes-Lui Que Je L'Aime

France 1977 107 mins col
Prospectacle/Filmoblic/FR3(Paris)

d **Claude Miller**
sc **Claude Miller, Luc Béraud**
ph **Pierre Lhomme**
m **Alain Jomy, Mozart, Schubert**
Gérard Depardieu, Miou-Miou, Dominique Laffin, Claude Piéplu, Christian Clavier

On the surface, David Martinaud (Depardieu) is a hardworking, solitary man who visits his ailing parents every weekend. Juliette (Miou-Miou) falls in love with him and discovers he has no parents but goes to a mountain chalet he has built for Lise (Laffin),the object of his obsessional love who is married to someone else, but whom he deludes himself will one day be his. Ensuing events lead to tragedy. Miller, in his second film, evokes several deliberate, well-chosen echoes of Hitchcock (and a direct reference in the use of a clip from *Rebecca*) in his approach to the suspense elements but, overall, this is a study of the destructive possibilities of sexual passion and contradictory faces of love to which the title refers. Well-photographed on location in the French Alps and with superb leads, it's an uncomfortable but gripping movie, adapted from Patricia Highsmith's novel.

The Thistles Of Baragan

Ciulinii Baraganului

Romania 1957 140 mins bw
Bucuresti Studios

d **Louis Daquin**
sc **Louis Daquin, Antoine Tudal, Alexandru Struteanu**
ph **André Dumaître**
m **Radu Palade**
Nuta Chirlea, Ana Vladescu, Florin Piersic, Ruxandra Ionescu

In 1907, a poor orphan boy (Chirlea), unofficially adopted by a young peasant girl (Vladescu), witnesses poverty and violence in a small village on the harsh plain of the Baragan. After a bitter winter, the peasants rise up against the repressive village boyar, but are slaughtered by soldiers. To commemorate the 50th anniversary of the peasants' uprisings, the ten-year-old Romanian film industry invited the French director, known principally for his *Nous Les Gosses* (1941) about children, to direct this adaptation of a well-known novel by the proletarian writer Panait Istrati. With telling camerawork and an imaginative use of sound and music, Daquin captures the atmosphere of the dusty and windy Baragan and vividly re-creates the life of the Romanian peasant at the beginning of the century. Pity about the cardboard characters and some weak acting.

This Wonderful Crook

Pas Si Méchant Que Ça

Switzerland 1974 110 mins col

Citel-Films/Artco Films (Geneva)/Action Films/M.J. Productions (Paris)

d **Claude Goretta**
sc **Claude Goretta**
ph **Renato Berta**
m **Arié Dzierlatka, Patrick Moraz**
Gérard Depardieu, Marlène Jobert, Dominique Labourier, Philippe Léotard

When his father, the owner of a small craftsmanship furniture factory, has a stroke, hitherto carefree Paul (Depardieu) takes over the running of the business, only to discover that it is in dire financial straits. In an effort to rescue the situation, he takes to holding up banks and post- offices and, although happily married, becomes romantically involved with one of his victims, a postmistress (Jobert). Filmed in a Swiss locale of flat fields and provincial towns, Goretta's tale begins with a clever idea but steadily loses both credibility and focus, leaving the ever ebullient Depardieu as the only real attraction.

Thomas Graals Bästa Film see Thomas Graal's Best Film

Thomas Graal's Best Film

Thomas Graals Bästa Film

Sweden 1917 62 mins bw

Svenska Bio

d **Mauritz Stiller**
sc **Harald B. Harald (pseudonym for Stiller & Gustaf Molander)**
ph **Henrik Jaenzon**
m **Silent**
Victor Sjöström, Karen Molander, Albin Laven, Jenny Tschernichin-Larsson

Scriptwriter Thomas Graal (Sjöström) is suffering from writer's block and decides to invent a story about his secretary (Molander) with whom he is infatuated. These imagined events, fantasies and flashbacks intermingle with the reality of Graal's romantic involvement. This relatively early and extremely inventive use of the film-within-a-film format is a witty pastiche of early film-making, with a charming performance from actor-director Sjöström, a close friend and associate of Stiller's at the time. It was so successful that Stiller reassembled the same cast and production team for an equally entertaining sequel, *Thomas Graal's Best Child*, the following year.

Thomas L'Imposteur see Thomas The Imposter

Thomas The Imposter

Thomas L'Imposteur

France 1965 93 mins bw

Filmel

d **Georges Franju**
sc **Jean Cocteau, Michel Worms, Georges Franju**
ph **Marcel Fradetal**
m **Georges Auric**
Emmanuele Riva, Fabrice Rouleau, Jean Servais, Edith Scob, Michel Vitold, Gabrielle Dorziat, Edouard Dermithe

Guillaume (Rouleau), a romantic adolescent calling himself Thomas, sets off happily for the battle front in World War I and meets up with a princess (Riva) who is helping the wounded. But the horror of war begins to intrude on his dreams. 'In him, fiction and reality became one,' is Cocteau's epitaph on his young hero (derived from his novel). It might well apply to the visual style which Franju uses to interpret Cocteau's last work for the cinema—the often surreal depiction of the war (a horse with its mane on fire) and the realism of mutilated men and corpses. But the characters lack substance and the film is too cold and decorative to be moving.

Those Wonderful Men With A Crank
see Those Wonderful Movie Cranks

Those Wonderful Movie Cranks

(US: Those Wonderful Men With A Crank)

Báječni Muži S Klikou

Czechoslovakia 1978 90 mins col
Studio Barrandov

d **Jiří Menzel**
sc **Jiří Menzel, Oldřich Vlček**
ph **Jaromír Šofr**
m **Jiří Šust**
Rudolf Hrušinský, Jiří Menzel, Blažena Holišová, Vlasta Fabiánová, Vladimír Menšík

In 1907, an itinerant showman (Hrušinský) goes around the country towns of Czechoslovakia, screening one-reel films, before returning to Prague where he obtains funds to set up the city's first real film theatre. Menzel's noted charm, wit and melancholy are all in abundant evidence in this affectionate re-creation of the early days of his country's cinema. Despite some anachronisms, the period atmosphere is well created, particularly in the sepia hues that conjure up early photography. The director must have found it easy to play the role of the showman's enthusiastic assistant.

Thousand And One Nights, A see Arabian Nights, The

The Thousand Eyes Of Dr Mabuse

Die Tausend Augen Des Dr Mabuse

W. Germany 1960 103 mins bw
CCC/CEI/Criterion

d **Fritz Lang**
sc **Fritz Lang, Heinz Oskar Wutting**
ph **Karl Löb**
m **Bert Grund**
Wolfgang Preiss, Gert Fröbe, Peter Van Eyck, Dawn Addams, Andrea Checchi, Werner Peters

A police detective (Fröbe) investigates a series of crimes that all seem to be connected with the Luxor Hotel, particularly a murder which bears the mark of arch criminal Dr Mabuse, thought to be dead. In his last film, Fritz Lang returned to the villain he created over 30 years earlier in *Dr Mabuse, The Gambler*, now using TV monitors (the 'thousand eyes' of the title) to aid him in his heinous crimes. However, although Mabuse is up-to-date, the cheaply made, badly acted film seems a trifle old-fashioned. There are elements from the earlier Mabuse films, such as a two-way mirror and a séance, but the sense of evil is less strong and much of the plot is a whodunnit. Some fun can be got from the improbable goings-on, but Lang's memory is best served by his films of the 1920s and early 1930s.

Thou Shalt Not Kill

Non Uccidere

aka Tu Ne Tueras Point

France/Yugoslavia/Italy 1961
129 mins bw
Moris Ergas/Lovcen Film (Belgrade)/Gold Film Anstalt (Vaduz)

d **Claude Autant-Lara**
sc **Jean Aurenche, Pierre Bost, Claude Autant-Lara**
ph **Jacques Natteau**
m **Charles Aznavour**
Laurent Terzieff, Horst Frank, Suzanne Flon, Mica Orlović, Majan Lovrić

Cordier (Terzieff), a French conscientious objector, and Adler (Frank), a German priest who killed a Resistance fighter during the war, are both put on trial. Cordier is found guilty under French law of evading his duty, while Adler is acquitted because his action was part of his duty. The story takes place in 1949, the year Autant-Lara (inspired by a newspaper article) set up the production but lost his finance because of his controversial theme. The project suffered similarly in Italy, was finally made 12 years later in Yugoslavia, and was denied commercial release in France and Italy for some time. In spite of the director's dedication to the material, the finished product is disappointing. Although the arguments are intriguing and the situation occasionally comes to life, the schematic and rambling narrative is unexciting and the characters lack depth which the actors largely fail to supply.

Best Actress (Suzanne Flon) Venice 1961

Thou Shalt Not Kill see Short Film About Killing, A

Three Brothers

Tre Fratelli

Italy 1981 111 mins col
Iter/Gaumont(Paris)

d **Francesco Rosi**
sc **Francesco Rosi, Tonino Guerra**
ph **Pasqualino De Santis**
m **Piero Piccioni**
Philippe Noiret, Vittorio Mezzogiorno, Michele Placido, Charles Vanel, Andréa Ferréol

Three very different brothers return to their rural childhood home to attend their mother's funeral and to comfort their aged father (Vanel). Each brother represents a contrasting social and geographical strain in Italian society—a judge (Noiret) from Rome, a teacher (Mezzogiorno) of maladjusted children in Naples, and a factory worker (Placido) in Turin. Rosi's film is no mere family chronicle, but a symbolic meditation on the cultural split between northern and southern Italy. Some ponderous political points are made and no conclusion is reached. The most successful moments are those that take on a more elegiac tone and concentrate on the relationship of the teacher, Rocco, and his brothers with the father, movingly played by Vanel.

Three Crowns Of The Sailor

Les Trois Couronnes Du Matelot

France 1982 117 mins col/bw
Société Du Cinéma Du Panthéon/INA/ Antenne 2

d **Râúl Ruiz**
sc **Râúl Ruiz, Emilio De Solar, François Ede**
ph **Sacha Vierny**
m **Jorge Arriagada**
Jean-Bernard Guillard, Philippe Deplanche, Jean Badin, Nadège Clair, Lisa Lyon

A student, after committing a brutal murder, is persuaded to spend the night listening to a drunken sailor's tales of brothels, Latin American ports and a ship with a ghost crew. Râúl Ruiz, a Chilean exile living in Paris, is one of the most prolific (he makes about four features a year) and exciting of new directors, yet this was one of his first films to get a theatrical release outside France. Ruiz is a storyteller who conjures up a series of vivid surreal images out of the slender movie resources at his disposal. This mixture of *The Ancient Mariner*, Orson Welles and his own distinctive modern voice makes for a film that takes one, like the haunted sailor, off the beaten track.

Three Days And A Child

Shlosha Yamim Ve Yeled

Israel 1967 87 mins bw
S.Y.V. Tel Aviv

d **Uri Zohar**
sc **Uri Zohar**
ph **David Gurfinkel**
Oded Kottler, Germaine Unikovski, Illy Gorlitzky, Judith Soleh, Misha Asherov

Eli (Kottler), has left the kibbutz to become a student in Jerusalem where he is involved in a triangular relationship with his best friend's girl (Unikovski). He is visited by Noa (Soleh), a girl with whom he had the briefest of liaisons on the kibbutz, who asks him to look after her three-year-old son for three days. Uri Zohar's film, while displaying a hotch-potch of influences, including some rather well-done Scandinavian-style sex scenes, is nevertheless one of Israel's better efforts. The story has charm, the action energy, and the characters and situations carry conviction. The flavour of Israeli life is well caught and, as Eli is led a merry dance by the child with whom he develops a love-hate relationship, we are left to join him in wondering whether he is, in fact, the boy's father. An ending that both intrigues and irritates.

Best Actor (Oded Kottler) Cannes 1967

Three From The Gas Station see Three Men And Lilian

Three Men And A Cradle

Trois Hommes Et Un Couffin

France 1985 106 mins col
Floch Film/Soprofilm/T.F.1 Films

d **Coline Serreau**
sc **Coline Serreau**

ph **Jean-Yves Éscoffier, Jean-Jacques Bouhon**
m **Schubert**
Roland Gireaud, Michel Boujenah, André Dussollier, Philippine Leroy Beaulieu, Dominique Lavanant

Three outwardly macho men-about-town who share an apartment have a baby thrust upon them. Initial panic turns to 'maternal' devotion as they school themselves in child care and grow genuinely attached to the tiny girl. An efficient, enjoyable and well-acted comedy, the film has added interest in that it subverts traditional notions of role playing. Serreau presents events from the male point of view and, in so doing, she throws up some provocative observations as to how men view women and parenthood.

Three Men And Lilian

(US: Three From The Gas Station)

Die Drei Von Der Tankstelle

Germany 1930 80 mins bw
UFA

d **Wilhelm Thiele**
sc **Frantz Schultz, Paul Frank**
ph **Franz Planer**
m **Werner R. Heymann**
Willy Fritsch, Lilian Harvey, Oskar Karlweis, Heinz Rühmann, Olga Tschechowa

Into the lives of three young petrol station attendants (Fritsch, Karlweis and Rühmann) comes the enchanting Lilian (Harvey), but three into one won't go. This is one of the best examples of the type of frothy, sentimental musical romance, with lilting songs and lively dances, with which Germany delighted the world in the early 1930s. It also shows Lilian Harvey at the peak of her popularity, although she might seem a trifle too ingratiating for today's tastes.

The Threepenny Opera

Die Dreigroschenoper

Germany 1931 114 mins bw
Tobis/Nero/Warner Bros.

d **G.W. Pabst**
sc **Leo Lania, Béla Balázs, Laszlo Wajda**
ph **Fritz Arno Wagner**
m **Kurt Weill**
Rudolf Forster, Lotte Lenya, Carola Neher, Valeska Gert, Fritz Rasp, Ernst Busch, Vladimir Sokoloff

In Victorian London, Mack the Knife (Forster), ladies' man, gentleman and thief, is loved by Jenny (Lenya), his favourite whore, Polly Peachum (Neher), daughter of the Beggar King (Rasp), and Lucy the jailor's daughter, but comes to a bad end. Bertold Brecht and Kurt Weill were engaged in 1929 to adapt their successful transposition of John Gay's *The Beggar's Opera* to the screen. Brecht, however, wanting to give his libretto even more anti-*bourgeois* bite than in the stage version, changed Mackie into a banker. This proved too strong for the capitalist producers. Brecht sued them and lost. Also lost were some of the songs and the disenchanted irony which was replaced by charm. The mixture of realism with stylized settings (an effectively foggy and decadent Soho designed by André Andreiev), doesn't really work either, but the performances, particularly from the inimitable Lenya (Weill's wife), and the wonderful score and lyrics retain much of the pungency of the original. The film, using a substantially different cast, was simultaneously shot in French. It was also remade in colour with an international cast in 1963.

Three Strange Loves see Thirst

Three Who Were Doomed, The see Sir Arne's Treasure

Throne Of Blood

(US: Castle Of The Spider's Web aka Cobweb Castle)

Kumonosu-Jo

Japan 1957 110 mins bw
Toho

d **Akira Kurosawa**
sc **Hideo Oguni, Shinobu Hashimoto, Ryuzo Kikushima, Akira Kurosawa**
ph **Asaichi Nakai**
m **Masaru Sato**
Toshiro Mifune, Isuzu Yamada, Minoru Chiaki, Akira Kubo, Takamaru Sasaki, Yoichi Tachikawa, Takashi Shimura, Chieko Namira

In medieval Japan, a samurai (Mifune) is spurred on by his wife (Yamada) and a spirit

(Namira) to murder his friend (Chiaki) and his lord (Shimura). Kurosawa found close parallels between feudal Japan and feudal Scotland in the first of two versions of Shakespearian plays—*Ran* (based on *King Lear*) came 28 years later. Although *Macbeth* is reduced mainly to action, images and gestures—many elements deriving from the Noh theatre—the film retains much of the original's power and momentum. An eerie mood is created, especially in the mist-shrouded forests and the castle. The climactic moments as Mifune is pierced with arrows is startlingly effective. Incidentally, it was said to have been T. S. Eliot's favourite film.

Through A Glass Darkly

Såsom I En Spegel

Sweden 1961 91 mins bw
Svensk Filmindustri

d **Ingmar Bergman**
sc **Ingmar Bergman**
ph **Sven Nykvist**
m **Bach**

Harriet Andersson, Gunnar Björnstrand, Max Von Sydow, Lars Passgård

On a remote island live a coldly detached novelist (Björnstrand), his son (Passgård) repulsed by women, his daughter (Andersson) lapsing into insanity, and her anguished husband (Von Sydow). Happy Families this isn't! Bergman moved into a more *angst*-ridden and intimate world with the first (and least good) of his uncompromising trilogy—*Winter Light* and *The Silence* were to follow. Where this fails, despite the intense performances and probing camerawork, is in the almost parodic piling up of symbols and suffering. There is a danger that the emptiness that the characters feel communicates itself only too well to the audience.

Best Foreign Film Oscar 1961

Thy Soul Shall Bear Witness see Phantom Carriage, The

Tiefland see Lowland

Tiempo De Morir see Time To Die, A

Tiempo De Revancha see Time For Revenge, A

The Tiger Of Eschnapur/ The Indian Tomb

Der Tiger Von Eschnapur/ Das Indische Grabmal

W. Germany 1958 101 mins (Part I), 95 mins (Part II) col
CCC Film (West Berlin)/Rizzoli Film (Rome)/Régina/Critérion Film (Paris)

d **Fritz Lang**
sc **Werner Jörg Lüddecke, Fritz Lang**
ph **Richard Angst**
m **Michel Michelet (Part I), Gerhard Becker (Part II)**

Debra Paget, Walther Reyer, Paul Hubschmid, Claus Holm, Sabine Bethmann

1) An architect (Hubschmid), on his way to act as adviser to Chandra, the Maharajah of Eschnapur (Reyer), recues Seeta (Paget), a dancer, from a tiger. They become lovers, despite the fact that the Maharajah has proposed to her, and escape the palace together. 2) Chandra recaptures Seeta and threatens to bury her alive in a massive tomb but, after a revolt against him is put down, he allows the lovers to leave. Lang, in his penultimate film and after over 20 years in Hollywood, returned to the exotic pulp serial he scripted for Joe May in 1921 and the world of his own earliest works like *The Spiders*. The authentic Indian settings, fine decor and colour, the use of 'Scope, and a refusal to send up this comic strip material compensate for some of the stiff acting. The two parts played as a double bill in Europe, but were dubbed and shown as one film of 94 minutes under the titles *Tigress Of Bengal* in Britain, and *Journey To The Lost City* in the USA.

Tiger Von Eschnapur, Der see Tiger Of Eschnapur, The

Tikhi Don see And Quiet Flows The Don

Till Glädje see To Joy

A Time For Revenge

Tiempo De Revancha

Argentina 1981 112 mins col
ARIES Cinematografica Argentina

d **Adolfo Aristarain**
sc **Adolfo Aristarain**
ph **Horacio Maira**
m **Enrique Kauderer**
Federico Luppi, Haydée Padilla, Julio De Grazia, Rudolfo Ranni, Ulises Dumont

A demolition expert (Luppi), who has been blacklisted because of his radical union work, adopts a new identity and gets a job in a multi-national company. Confronted with exploitation, he decides to fight back. Good political thrillers in the style of *Z* are rare, particularly when produced under a repressive regime, so it is all the more remarkable that Aristarain carried it off under the noses of the Junta. A rapidly moving, but somewhat over-contrived, *film noir* plot, a surprise ending and a splendid leading performance from Luppi (Best Actor at the Chicago Film Festival) make the film work on the purely entertainment level; the theme of an idealist fighting a corrupt system works on the political plane.

Time Stands Still

Megáll Az Idó

Hungary 1982 99 mins col
Mafilm/Budapest Studio Production

d **Péter Gothár**
sc **Péter Gothár, Géza Bereményi**
ph **Lajos Koltai**
m **György Selmeczi**
István Znamenák, Henrik Pauer, Sándor Sóth, Péter Galfy

In 1963, Gabor (Pauer) and Denes (Znamenák), two teenage brothers and the sons of a man who escaped Hungary only steps ahead of the Russians in 1956, try to adjust to the restrictions imposed upon them. Gabor, the elder brother, is the more conventional, concerned that his father's past will prevent his going to medical school, but Denes finds escape in rock music. Time may stand still for these energetic adolescents trying to find expression through American music, but the camera is continually on the move in an attempt to keep up with them. But this is no youth movie on the Western model. It is given a political context by being topped and tailed by newsreel footage of the 1956 uprising, and the return of the father in 1967 to what he hopes is a better society. Athough an interesting and entertaining blend of themes, the film, like its young heroes, also seems to be searching for an identity.

Time Stood Still

Il Tempo Si E Fermato

Italy 1959 80 mins bw
22 Dicembre

d **Ermanno Olmi**
sc **Ermanno Olmi**
ph **Carlo Bellero**
m **Pier Emilio Bassi**
Natale Rossi, Roberto Seveso, Paolo Quadrubbi

Isolated high in the mountains, a taciturn older man (Rossi) and a raw boy (Seveso) live out the long winter months, guarding an unfinished hydro-electric dam until the workers can return to complete it in the spring. Gradually their initial mutual mistrust turns to respect and affection. Olmi had shot over 40 industrial shorts for the Edison-Volta company (for which he worked) before making his first feature, partly financed by the firm. Using non-professionals, and filming in winter in the mountains, he meticulously describes the routine job of the two men with warmth and humour, managing the trick of portraying tedium without being tedious.

Time To Die, A see Amelia Or The Time For Love

A Time To Die

Tiempo De Morir

Colombia 1985 94 mins col
FOCINE (Colombia)/ICAIC (Cuba)

d **Jorge Ali Triana**
sc **Gabriel García Márquez**
ph **Mario García Joya**
m **Leo Brouwer, Nafer Duran**
Gustavo Angarita, Sebastian Ospina, Jorge Emilio Salazar, Maria Eugenia Davila, Lina Botero

After serving 18 years in jail for killing a man in a gunfight, Juan Sayago (Angarita) returns to his native Colombian village hoping to resume his once peaceful life as a horse breeder. Unfortunately, his victim's sons seek to avenge their father's death. Using a traditional revenge tragedy plot and the theme from countless Westerns, Triana, in his debut film as director, builds in a criticism of Latin American *machismo*. Although familiar and less impressive than one would have expected from Nobel Prize-winning author Gabriel García Márquez's first screenplay, it is intelligently paced, finely photographed and well acted.

Time To Live And A Time To Die, A see Feu Follet, Le

The Time To Live And The Time To Die

Tongnian Wangshi

Taiwan 1985 137 mins col
Central Motion Picture Corporation,Taipei

d **Hou Hsiao-hsien**
sc **Zhu Tianwen**
ph **Li Pingbin**
m **Wu Chuchu**
You Anshun, Tian Feng, Mei Fang, Tang Ruyun, Xiao Ai, Xin Shufen, Hu Xiangping

In 1947, seeking fresh opportunities, Femming (Tian Feng), his wife, children and elderly mother leave the Chinese mainland for a village in Taiwan. The sojourn is intended as temporary, but the revolution comes and they remain. With this autobiographical piece, the director of *A Summer At Grandpa's* has enhanced and expanded his international reputation. It is an understated, intimate family saga which spans several years of everyday life, recalled through the childhood memories of Ah-Ha-Gu (Anshun), otherwise Hou Hsiao-hsien himself. The quiet ordinariness of content and the spare simplicity of style make this an eloquent, sometimes humorous document, memorable for the discrete detail with which illness and several deaths are movingly chronicled. The tone and approach is reminiscent of the early films of Satyajit Ray, creating a world of small events into which we are irresistibly drawn.

Timi Tis Agapis, I see Price Of Love, The

The Tin Drum

Die Blechtrommel

W. Germany 1979 142 mins col
UA/Franz Seitz/Bioskop/GGB 14 KG/Hallelujah/ Artemis/Argos/Jadran/Film Polski

d **Volker Schlöndorff**
sc **Jean-Claude Carrière, Franz Seitz, Volker Schlöndorff**
ph **Igor Luther**
m **Maurice Jarre**
David Bennent, Mario Adorf, Angela Winkler, Daniel Olbrychski, Katharina Thalbach, Berta Drews, Tina Engel, Heinz Bennent, Charles Aznavour, Andréa Ferréol

The teenage Oskar (David Bennent), stopped growing at the age of three by an act of will. Naturally, he is a concern to his parents (Adorf and Winkler) because he has tantrums, constantly bangs a toy tin drum and has a scream that shatters glass. He acts as a sort of conscience to the inhabitants of Danzig when the Nazis come to power and the war rages. The film is often a disturbing look at German history through the relentless gaze of a weird child—an amazing performance from 12-year-old David Bennent, son of the actor Heinz Bennent. However, although much of the complexity of Günther Grass's allegorical novel has been lost, it hasn't gained in clarity.

Best Foreign Film Oscar 1979
Best Film Cannes 1979

Tire-Au-Flanc

France 1928 80 mins bw
Néo-Film

d **Jean Renoir**
sc **Jean Renoir, Claude Heymann**
ph **Jean Bachelet**
m **Silent**
Georges Pomiés, Michel Simon, Félix Oudart, Jeanne Helbling, Jean Storm, Paul Velsa, Manuel Raaby

Jean (Pomiés), an aristocratic, absent-minded and bungling poet, lives a sheltered life with his wealthy mother and his faithful valet and companion, Joseph (Simon). The men are called up for national service during which Jean, ill-prepared for life in the barracks, constantly finds himself in trouble. There have been four screen versions of this stage farce by Mouézy-Eon and Sylvane, the most recent directed by Claude De Givray in 1961. Filmed with refreshing spontaneity, Renoir's loose adaptation avoids any suggestion of theatricality, and links the silent comedy tradition of Chaplin and Keaton with the early sound films of Vigo *(Zéro De Conduite)* and his own *Boudu Saved From Drowning.* While satirizing *bourgeois* life and institutions, the film is perhaps most worth watching for its fine ensemble acting.

Tirez Sur Le Pianiste see Shoot The Pianist

Tízezer Nap see Ten Thousand Suns, The

To Bed... Or Not To Bed see Devil, The

To Begin Again

Volver A Empezar
Spain 1981 92 mins col
Nickel Odéon

d **José Luis Garci**
sc **José Luis Garci, Angel Llorente**
ph **Manuel Rojas**
m **Pachelbel's 'Canon', Cole Porter's 'Begin The Beguine'**

Antonio Ferrándis, Encarna Paso, José Bódalo, Agustín González, Pablo Hoyos, Marta Fernandez Muro

Antonio Albajara (Ferrándis), one-time Republican soldier in the Spanish Civil War and now a professor at a Californian university, wins the Nobel Prize for Literature and visits his birthplace at Gijon. There, he relives the past, reminiscing with his great love (Paso), and his best friend (Bódalo) to whom he confides that he is dying. After receiving many honours, he returns to unhappy exile. Spain's first Oscar winner is lushly sentimental and self-consciously poetical, and it's difficult to understand—or care—why Albajara keeps abandoning all that is dearest to him. The director has made much of his choice of music, and perhaps the curious idea that Pachelbel and Porter make comfortable and significant bedfellows best sums up the confused thinking that bedevils this well-meant film.

Best Foreign Film Oscar 1983

Toda Nudez Sera Castigada see All Nudity Shall Be Punished

Tod Der Maria Malibran, Der see Death Of Maria Malibran, The

To Die In Madrid

Mourir À Madrid
France 1962 87 mins bw
Ancinex

d **Frédéric Rossif**
sc **Madeleine Chapsal**
ph **Georges Barsky**
m **Maurice Jarre**

Newsreel and documentary footage of the Spanish Civil War from the archives of six countries is combined with more recent sequences shot in contemporary Spain. This often facile, but still forceful, emotive and subjective compilation film generally won great praise, but also opened up old wounds. East Germany replied with *Untameable Spain* in the same year, attacking the Allied governments' apathy, and *Morir En España* (1965) gave Franco's side of the story. Rossif's film, some footage of which was used at the opening of Fred Zinnemann's *Behold A Pale Horse*, had a commentary spoken in English by John Gielgud and Irene Worth for the original British and American releases.

To Homa Vaftike Kokkino see Blood On The Land

To Joy

Till Glädje
Sweden 1949 98 mins bw
Svensk Filmindustri

d **Ingmar Bergman**
sc **Ingmar Bergman**
ph **Gunnar Fischer**

m **Beethoven, Mozart, Mendelssohn, Smetana**
Victor Sjöström, Maj-Britt Nilsson, Stig Olin, Margit Carlquist, Birger Malmsten

Two young musicians (Olin and Nilsson) in a provincial orchestra get married and dream of becoming soloists. Years later, the husband carries on an affair with a married woman (Carlquist) which leads to disaster. Students of Bergman's *oeuvre* will find plenty of clues to his more mature work in this early minor drama—married couples devouring one another, the duties of an artist and music as a unifying force, while the avuncular appearance of Victor Sjöström as the conductor looks forward to his commanding role in *Wild Strawberries*. The title derives from the choral movement of Beethoven's Ninth Symphony that ends the film on a note of hope.

Tokyo Boshoku see Tokyo Twilight

Tokyo Chorus
Tokyo No Gassho

Japan 1931 91 mins bw
Shochiku/Kamata

d **Yasujiro Ozu**
sc **Kogo Noda**
ph **Hideo Shigehara**
m **Silent**
Tokihiko Okada, Hideo Sugawara, Emiko Yagumo, Mitsuo Ichimura, Takeshi Sakamoto

A married man (Okada) loses his job when he objects to the unfair dismissal of a fellow worker. After many misadventures while searching for work, he gets into the restaurant business. Although Ozu seldom criticized social conditions directly, this Depression-set satire says a lot about the pettiness of certain aspects of society. It is done with a deft comic touch—and what the director called 'his darker side' in the second half. Ozu here uses a great deal of camera movement and several exteriors, not prevalent in his more mature work. The film contains two of his funniest sequences, focusing, in turn, on the workers on a parade ground, and the office clerks in a washroom.

Tokyo Monogatari see Tokyo Story

Tokyo No Gassho see Tokyo Chorus

Tokyo Olympiad
Tokyo Orinpikku

Japan 1965 130 mins col
Toho

d **Kon Ichikawa**
sc **Natto Wada, Yoshio Shirasaka, Shuntaro Tanikawa, Kon Ichikawa**
ph **Shigeo Hayashida, Kazuo Miyagawa, Juichi Nagano, Kinji Nakamura, Tadashi Tanaka, plus 159 more**
m **Toshiro Mayuzumi**

A documentary on the 1964 Olympic Games in Tokyo. 'I have attempted to capture the solemnity of the moment when man defies his limits...I have tried to penetrate human nature not through fiction, but in the truth of the Games.' Unlike Leni Riefenstahl's view of the 1936 Berlin Games, Ichikawa presents the human rather than the god-like qualities of the participants, although they are no less heroic. Not much factual information is given—TV and the Press were there for that— but it does get nearer the body and soul of the athlete than any previous attempt. This the director achieved with the help of 164 cameramen who used 232 different lenses. The result was a crystallization of Japanese technical wizardry and creative genius.

Tokyo Orinpikku see Tokyo Olympiad

Tokyo Story
Tokyo Monogatari

Japan 1953 136 mins bw
Shochiku

d **Yasujiro Ozu**
sc **Yasujiro Ozu, Kogo Noda**
ph **Yushun Atsuta**
m **Senji Ito**
Chishu Ryu, Chiyeko Higashiyama, Setsuko Hara, Satoshi Yamamura, Haruko Sugimura

An elderly married couple (Ryu and Higashiyama), paying a visit to their children and grandchildren in Tokyo, begin to feel that they are a burden on them. They return home where the woman dies. Ozu claimed this was his most melodramatic film, yet in Western terms, this radiant, gentle, heartbreaking, perceptive investigation into the tensions within the generations of a family is far from our definition of melodrama. As usual, there are remarkable performances all round, and a unique use of sound and exteriors punctuating the subtle interior sequences. One of the finest films of Ozu's last decade, it was the one that belatedly made his reputation in the West.

Tokyo Twilight

Tokyo Boshoku

Japan 1957 141 mins bw
Shochiku/Ofuna

d **Yasujiro Ozu**
sc **Yasujiro Ozu, Koga Noda**
ph **Yuharu Atsuta**
m **Takanobu Saito**
Setsuko Hara, Isuzu Yamada, Ineko Arima, Chishu Ryu, Masami Taura

Two daughters, the elder (Hara) having left her husband and the younger (Arima) having an affair that results in an abortion, live with their father (Ryu). But they are shattered when they discover that the mother (Yamada) they thought dead is still alive and living with another man. This is the nearest that Ozu ventured towards Western ideas of melodrama, although he is still more restrained than the plot suggests. His last black-and-white film is also one of his darkest and most intense. The dialogue and acting are superb and it's interesting to note the difference between the subtle performance Isuzu Yamada gives for Ozu, and the stylized one she gives as 'Lady Macbeth' for Kurosawa in *Throne Of Blood*.

To Live see Living

To Love

Att Älska

Sweden 1964 95 mins bw
Sandrew

d **Jörn Donner**
sc **Jörn Donner**
ph **Sven Nykvist**
m **Bo Nilsson, and Eje Thelin's Jazz Quintet**
Harriet Andersson, Zbigniew Cybulski, Isa Quensel, Tomas Svanfeldt, Jane Friedmann, Nils Eklund

Louise (Andersson), the attractive mother of a young son, is suddenly widowed. At her late husband's funeral she meets Frederik (Cybulski), a foreigner working in Stockholm and, before long, they embark on a relationship and he moves in with her. In his second film, Donner paints an observant portrait of a developing relationship in which the temperamental balance of the partners subtly shifts so that serious Louise is infected by Frederik's insouciance, whereas he becomes sober and wants stability and permanence. The director is helped immeasurably by his expert actors but, for all this, the film disappoints because a slight story has been padded out with generalizations about life in Sweden, which are no doubt meant to be illuminating but serve only to jar.

Best Actress (Harriet Andersson) Venice 1964

Tomorrow Is My Turn see Crossing Of the Rhine, The

Tomorrow's Warrior

Avrianos Polemistis

Cyprus 1981 95 mins col
Cyprian(MP)Films

d **Michael Papas**
sc **Michael Papas**
ph **John McCallum**
m **Nicos Mamangakis**
Christos Zannides, Aristodemos Fessas, Dimitri Andreas, Jenny Lipman, Joanna Shafkali, Antonis Katsaris

Orestes (Zannides), a young Greek Cypriot, and his parents, flee their mountain village to escape the Turkish invasion of July 1974, but are caught and imprisoned in a dispiriting refugee camp. Months later, Orestes escapes and begins to make his way back to the mountains where his grandfather (Fessas), a former guerrilla fighter, has remained and where he will, presumably, become 'tomorrow's warrior'. Papas begins imaginatively, using flashback and fantasy to recall the history of Cyprus since independence, and the personal memories of the freedom fighters, as Orestes' grandfather recounts his experiences. A chronicle of the cruel fate suffered by Greeks at the hands of the Turks, the film contains a couple of sequences of real power. However, the uncompromisingly pro-Greek, anti-Turk bias, while perhaps understandable, succeeds in turning it into a piece of blatant and sentimental nationalistic propaganda, thereby reducing its impact.

Tongnian Wangshi see Time To Live And The Time To Die, The

Toni

France 1935 95 mins bw
Films D'Aujourd'hui

d **Jean Renoir**
sc **Jean Renoir, Carl Einstein**
ph **Claude Renoir**
m **Paul Bozzi**
Charles Blavette, Jenny Hélia, Célia Montalvan, Edouard Delmont, Andrex, Max Dalban

Toni (Blavette), an immigrant Italian worker in Provence, falls in love with Joséphа (Montalvan) but is unable to marry her. They meet up years later, each unhappily married. The result is a *crime passionnel*. Following the example of Marcel Pagnol, Renoir completely abandoned the studio and filmed exclusively outdoors and in genuine interiors in the Midi, using authentic sound and actors drawn from the region. The film is remarkable for its avoidance of the melodramatic, the depth and fluidity of the camerawork and the feeling for figures in a landscape. This important film was not appreciated in its time.

Ton Kero Ton Hellinon see When The Greeks

To Our Loves

À Nos Amours

France 1983 102 mins col
Les Films Du Livradois/Gaumont/FR3

d **Maurice Pialat**
sc **Arlette Langmann, Maurice Pialat**
ph **Jacques Loiseleux**
m **Purcell**
Sandrine Bonnaire, Dominique Besnehard, Maurice Pialat, Christophe Odent, Cyr Boitard, Maïté Maillé

Suzanne (Bonnaire), aged 15, leaves her gentle boyfriend (Boitard) because she is unable to feel love and becomes increasingly promiscuous in her quest for it. Meanwhile, her father (Pialat), to whom she is attached, leaves home, where her hysterical mother (Ker) and camp, ambitious brother (Besnehard) vent their own frustrations on her in the form of physical blows. At 17, she marries a man she doesn't love, and leaves him only days later for yet another lover (Odent). Brilliantly well acted by a mixed cast of professionals and amateurs, it is directed with style, commitment and compassion. Albeit that Pialat's incessant pursuit of naturalism becomes self-defeating at moments, his film is a painful and perceptive study of fragmented psyches. Suzanne, played with vitality and intensity by Bonnaire, is the focus of a screenplay that deals with the chasm between romantic yearnings and the ability to realize them; it is not about aimless youth or adolescent growing pains. If the movie tends to end somewhat vaguely, it is nonetheless thoroughly absorbing and good to look at.

Topaze

France 1933 103 mins bw
Paramount

d **Louis Gasnier**
sc **Marcel Pagnol**
ph **Fred Langenfeld**
Louis Jouvet, Edwige Feuillère, Pauley, Simone Heliard, Pierre Larquey

Monsieur Topaze (Jouvet), a shy and idealistic provincial schoolteacher, is hired as a front by a disreputable financier (Pauley) to sign cheques and take the rap if necessary. But he catches on fast, and ends up by appropriating both his boss's organization and his mistress (Feuillère). The combination of Jouvet's magisterial performance and the pungent dialogue of the play that made Pagnol famous is irresistible. Pagnol himself would direct it, with Arnoudy in 1936 and Fernandel in 1951 in the title role, and in 1961, Peter Sellers directed himself disastrously in *Mr Topaz*. Gasnier, who made this first and choicest of the versions, gained his reputation in America directing *Pearl White* serials.

Topaze

France 1936 110 mins bw
Films Marcel Pagnol

d **Marcel Pagnol**
sc **Marcel Pagnol**
ph **Willy**
m **Vincent Scotto**
Arnaudy, André Pollack, Sylvie Bataille, Pierre Asso, Jean Arbuleau, Henri Poupon

Topaze (Arnaudy), a naive schoolmaster, discovers that he is being manipulated by a crooked businessman (Pollack). This revelation leads him to quit his post and enter into dubious business deals himself. Pagnol was disappointed that the 1933 French film version of his hit play, starring the incomparable Louis Jouvet, had cut much of his dialogue and rearranged some of his scenes, nor was he happy with the John Barrymore Hollywood adaptation of the same year. Therefore, after he had directed a number of films, he decided to remake it himself in 1936 (and again in 1951) restoring most of the original text. But the memory of Jouvet was too strong in the public mind and it flopped, despite its having the more authentic Pagnol touch.

Topaze

France 1951 135 mins bw
Les Films Marcel Pagnol

d **Marcel Pagnol**
sc **Marcel Pagnol**
ph **Philippe Agostini**
m **Raymond Legrand**
Fernandel, Marcel Vallée, Jacqueline Pagnol, Pierre Larquey, Jacques Morel

Topaze (Fernandel), an idealistic schoolmaster, soon learns from his boss (Vallée) that there are more profitable (and less legal) ways of making a living. The third French version of the popular and still topical satire gave Fernandel the chance to follow in the footsteps of Jouvet, Arnaudy and John Barrymore (in the 1933 RKO production), bringing more affection to the role. Of the string of Topazes, this one pleased Pagnol most, as it is nearest to his original play and is technically superior to the others.

El Topo

aka The Mole
Mexico 1971 124 mins col
Producciones Panicas

d **Alexandro Jodorowsky**
sc **Alexandro Jodorowsky**
ph **Raphael Corkidi**
m **Alexandro Jodorowsky**
Alexandro Jodorowsky, Mara Lorenzio, Brontis Jodorowsky, Paula Romo, Robert John, David Silva

Gunfighter El Topo (Alexandro Jodorowsky), accompanied by his seven-year-old son, sets out on an avenging journey, massacring a group of murderers and going on to defeat rival master gunfighters in the desert. All is achieved by means of deception, which leads him to seek redemption. Jodorowsky's epic is divided into four sections, subtitled Genesis, Prophets, Psalms and Apocalypse, and is top-heavy with allegory and symbolism, both Christian and Pagan. Crudely derivative—Fellini, Buñuel and Sergio Leone are the more obvious influences—it gathered a hysterically enthusiastic and youthful cult following its release in New York but, to more considered critics, it is a pretentious philosophical mess, liberally spattered with blood and violence. There are, however, one or two highly original sequences, and it is strikingly photographed against a dramatically beautiful landscape.

Torment see Frenzy

Törst see Thirst

La Tosca

Italy 1940 91 mins bw
Scalera

d **Carl Koch**
sc **Jean Renoir,**
ph **Ubaldo Arata**
m **Puccini**
Imperio Argentina, Michel Simon, Massimo Girotti, Rossano Brazzi

In Rome in 1800, the opera singer Floria Tosca (Argentina) is in love with the painter Cavaradossi (Brazzi), who has helped her rebel brother Angelotti (Girotti) to escape the clutches of Scarpia (Simon), the dreaded chief of police. When Cavaradossi is taken prisoner, Tosca is prepared to give herself up to Scarpia in exchange for his release. Jean Renoir, invited to Rome by Mussolini, a fan of *La Grande Illusion*, to lecture on film-direction, started shooting this version of the Sardou play— best known as Puccini's opera version— at the same time. But he only got to film a few scenes (two horsemen galloping through the night) before war was declared and he had to leave Italy. Koch, Renoir's German assistant, completed it with the Italian cast and the Swiss Simon. The latter's contribution is virtually the sole reason for seeing this uninspired 'nasty little shocker', although there are some well-used views of the Eternal City.

Tosen Fran Stormytorpet see Girl From Stormycroft, The

Touchez Pas Au Grisbi see Grisbi

A Touch Of Zen
Hsia Nu

Taiwan 1969 180 mins col
International Film

d **King Hu**
sc **King Hu**
ph **Hua Hui-Ying, Chou Yeh-Hsing**
m **Wu Ta-Chiang**
Hsu Feng, Shih Chun, Pai Ying, Hseuh Han, Roy Chiao

A young woman (Feng), fleeing the army of her father's enemies, takes refuge in an old fort and seeks the aid of a young scholar (Chun) who loves her. They frighten the troops away by making the fort appear to be haunted. Some months later, the adversaries meet again in a bamboo forest. Because of the 'chop-socky' films of Bruce Lee in the 1970s, martial arts films have been devalued. Hu's ravishing and exciting three-hour epic, set during the Ming dynasty, is in a higher realm altogether, being the finest example of the genre. Much of the choreographic art of the Peking Opera has been brought to bear on the breathtaking sword fights, stunningly filmed in 'Scope using zooms, pans and tracks. The director has also succeeded in showing the philosophy of Zen in practice rather than in theory.

Toute Une Nuit see All Night Long

Toute Une Vie see And Now My Love

Tout L'Or Du Monde see All The Gold In The World

Tout Va Bien

France 1972 95 mins col
Anouchka/Vicco/Empire

d **Jean-Luc Godard, Jean-Pierre Gorin**
sc **Jean-Luc Godard, Jean-Pierre Gorin**
ph **Armand Marco**
Jane Fonda, Yves Montand, Vittorio Caprioli, Jean Pignol, Anne Wiazemsky

During a strike, the workers occupy the factory and hold the bosses prisoner. An American journalist (Fonda) and her lover (Montand), a film director now forced to make TV ads for a living, come to report the sit-in, but are themselves held. In an attempt to get their Marxist ideas across to a wider public, the team of Godard and Gorin returned to 'commercial' cinema after four years making 16mm and video movies to be shown in work places and youth clubs. During that period, Godard had made TV ads for *Dim* stockings, as the Montand character does here. The film comments directly on the need to sign up stars in order to raise money from producers and cleverly plays on Fonda's radical image. The message of the film is also radical, but the medium is more conservative than Godard's previous work. Now it seems a marvellous monument to the revolutionary spirit of 1968. The composite set is used as brilliantly as in Jerry Lewis's *The Ladies' Man*, although for a vastly different purpose.

Traffic
Trafic

France 1970 96 mins col
Corona/Gibe/Selenia

d **Jacques Tati**
sc **Jacques Tati, Jacques Lagrange**

ph **Eduard J.R. Van Der Enden, Marcel Weiss**
m **Charles Dumont**
Jacques Tati, Maria Kimberley, Marcel Fraval, Honoré Bostel, François Maisongrosse, Tony Kneppers

Monsieur Hulot (Tati), entrusted with taking a newly invented camping car from Paris to a motor show in Amsterdam, encounters a multitude of problems on the way. In Tati's deeply suspicious view of the motorcar, many of the gags go beautifully, some run out of gas or stall and others come a cropper. Both during the production of his masterpiece, *Playtime*, and since, Tati suffered great financial difficulties, and *Traffic*, a Dutch co-production, did not give him the amount of time and freedom he needed. Nevertheless, Tati's last feature (leaving aside the dismal *Parade* made for TV) is a fond farewell to the incomparable Monsieur Hulot.

Trafic see Traffic

Tragedia Di Un Uomo Ridicolo, La see Tragedy Of A Ridiculous Man, The

---

Tragédie De La Mine, La see Kameradschaft

Tragedija Sluzbenice P.T.T. see Switchboard Operator, The

The Tragedy Of A Ridiculous Man

La Tragedia Di Un Uomo Ridicolo

Italy 1981 116 mins col
Fiction Cinematographica

d **Bernardo Bertolucci**
sc **Bernardo Bertolucci**
ph **Carlo Di Palma**
m **Ennio Morricone**
Ugo Tognazzi, Anouk Aimée, Laura Morante, Victor Cavallo, Olympia Carlisi, Ricardo Tognazzi

Primo Spaggiari (Ugo Tognazzi), a factory owner and a self-made man, sees his son being forcibly hustled into a car. The police suspect the victim of colluding in his own kidnapping because of his far-Left sympathies, Primo's wife (Aimée) determines to pay the ransom demand, and he begins to realize he never knew his own son. This elliptical, elegantly shot semi-thriller, the reverse of *The Spider's Stratagem* in which a son investigates his father's life , was Bertolucci's first film for many years to deal with contemporary Italy. Its ambiguous view of terrorism suggests that in politics he prefers to be lost in a maze than find his way out. It is more interesting on the psychological level, but it failed critically and commercially, mainly because the crime remains unsolved.

Best Actor (Ugo Tognazzi) Cannes 1981

Tragedy Of A Switchboard Operator, The see Switchboard Operator, The

---

Tragic Hunt see Tragic Pursuit, The

The Tragic Pursuit

aka Pursuit (US: Tragic Hunt)

Caccia Tragica

Italy 1947 89 mins bw
Lux/ANPI

d **Giuseppe De Santis**
sc **Giuseppe De Santis, Michelangelo Antonioni, Cesare Zavattini, Carlo Lizzani, Umberto Barbaro**
ph **Otello Martelli**
m **Giuseppe Rosati**
Massimo Girotti, Andrea Checci, Vivi Gioi, Carla Del Paggio, Vittorio Duse, Checcho Rissone, Guido Della Valle

After the Liberation, a young couple (Girotti and Del Paggio) get involved with two bandits (Checci and Gioi) who steal money that was to be used to buy farming implements for a collective farm in the Po Valley. The peasants unite to hunt them down. The frequent crane shots, expressionist lighting and echoes of pre-war Marcel Carné with whom Antonioni, one of the quintet of screenwriters, had worked, hardly qualify De Santis's debut feature as Neo-Realist. It does have elements of the latter in its social concerns but topples too often into melodrama and sentimentality to be entirely convincing. It was voted Best Italian Film at Venice in 1947.

Trances see Transes

Tranquillo Posto Di Compagna, Un see Quiet Place In The Country, A

Transes
aka Trances
El Hal
Morocco 1981 87 mins col
SOGEAV/Interfilms(France)

d **Ahmed El Maanouni**
sc **Ahmed El Maanouni**
ph **Ahmed El Maanouni**
m **Nass El Ghiwane**
Boujema Hgour, Omar Sayed, Allal Yaala, Aberrahman Paco, Larbi Batma

Nass El Ghiwane (People of Song), a group of five singing musicians are idolized and mobbed by the young of the Maghreb. Here they are interviewed and seen in concert, cross-cut with historical and ethnological material and views of the reality of life in Morocco. An unusual musical documentary to Western eyes and ears, it shows not only a Third World Beatlemania, but analyses the group's appeal and sets them in a historical and cultural context. Their aim to bring modern electronic techniques to bear on traditional Moroccan music is brought home in a scene where the folk tradition of trance dancers merges into that of the contemporary musicians. However, to the untutored spectator, much of the music and lyrics are as banal as the images illustrating the songs.

Trans-Europ Express
France 1966 90 mins bw
Como

ph **Alain Robbe-Grillet**
sc **Alain Robbe-Grillet**
ph **Willy Kurant**
m **Verdi**
Jean-Louis Trintignant, Marie-France Pisier, Nadine Verdier, Christian Barbier, Alain Robbe- Grillet, Catherine Robbe-Grillet

A film director (Alain Robbe-Grillet), on the Trans-Europ Express from Paris to Antwerp, decides to write a script about a sadistic drug smuggler (Trintignant) on his way to Antwerp to collect a shipment of cocaine. There, the character gets involved with a prostitute (Pisier) and is caught up in a series of perilous situations. To an extent, Robbe-Grillet prepared audiences for the kind of film he was to direct with his screenplay for *Last Year At Marienbad*, in that they were asked, in a certain sense, to participate in the films, which could take any number of paths and be open to any number of interpretations. In his second film, he plays the creator in the course of creation, far more concerned with form than content. Everything has a double perspective—a film-within-a-film about double-crossing, double agents, and a double murder. It is a game with a serious purpose—reinventing stereotypes—which excludes those who don't know the rules.

A Trap For Cinderella
Piège Pour Cendrillon
France 1965 118 mins bw
S.N.E.G.(Paris)/Jolly Film(Rome)

d **André Cayatte**
sc **André Cayatte, Jean-Baptiste Rossi, Jean Anouilh**
ph **Armand Thirard**
m **Louiguy**
Dany Carrel, Madeleine Robinson, Hubert Noël, Jean Gaven, Francis Nani, René Dary

A girl burnt in a fire undergoes plastic surgery and finds herself suffering from amnesia. Determined to trace her identity, she learns that her name is Michèle, that she lived with her cousin Dominique in the South of France in a house that exploded and that the orphaned Dominique was cared for by Jeanne, an older companion. On meeting Jeanne, Michèle uncovers revelations that lead her to suicide. Leaving the French judicial system behind him for a while, Cayatte delivers a quest-for-identity mystery that is neat and ingenious until it plunges into absurdity. However, like most of his films it is, even at its most melodramatically idiotic, entertaining—not least in Madeleine Robinson's delicious over-the-top portrayal of the sinister Jeanne, and the clever use of Dany Carrel doubling as Michèle and Dominique.

Träumende Mund, Der see Melo

The Travelling Players

O Thiassos

Greece 1975 230 mins col
George Papalios

d **Theo Angelopoulos**
sc **Theo Angelopoulos**
ph **Ghiorgos Arvanitis**
m **Loukianos Kilaidonis**
Eva Kotamandiou, Petros Zarkadis, Maria Vassiliou, Statos Pachis, Aliki Georgoulis

In Egion in 1952, on the eve of the election of Papagos, the field marshal who won the Civil War against Left-wing forces, a troupe of travelling players recall Greek political history and their own personal histories since they last visited the place in 1939. Angelopoulos emerged on to the international scene after the seven years of military dictatorship in Greece with one of the most ambitious Greek films to date, partly filmed during the last months of the colonels' regime. Knowledge of Greek history, politics and culture—allusions are made to the *Oresteia*—and plenty of patience are required to appreciate this extremely slow but ultimately impressive epic drama.

Traversée De Paris, La see Pig Across Paris, A

La Traviata

Italy 1982 105 mins col
Accent Films B.V./R.A.I./UNIV

d **Franco Zeffirelli**
sc **Franco Zeffirelli (Libretto by Francesco Maria Piave)**
ph **Ennio Guarnieri**
m **Guiseppe Verdi (conducted by James Levine)**
Teresa Stratas (Violetta), Placido Domingo (Alfredo), Cornell MacNeil (Germont), Alan Monk (The Baron), Axelle Gall (Flora)

Dumas' novel, *The Lady Of The Camellias*, in its operatic incarnation by Verdi. The ill-fated lovers, Marguerite and Armand, were rechristened Violetta and Alfredo by the great composer, but the story of the consumptive courtesan who sacrifices her happiness to protect her lover's reputation is intact. Zeffirelli adds an imaginative prologue and epilogue and skilfully opens out the action away from stagy confines, while his collaboration with designer and cameraman, though sometimes over-prettified, is ravishing to the eye, as is the music to the ear. The beautiful and gifted Teresa Stratas delivers a moving Violetta, well-matched by Domingo's attractively mature Alfredo. Opera-goers, however, will be disconcerted by cuts in the score.

Travolti Da Un Insolito Destino Nell'Azzurro Mare D'Agosto see Swept Away...By An Unusual Destiny In The Blue Sea Of August

The Tree Of Wooden Clogs

Albero Degli Zoccoli

Italy 1978 186 mins col
RAI/Italnoleggio Cinematografica/GPC(Milan)

d **Ermanno Olmi**
sc **Ermanno Olmi**
ph **Ermanno Olmi**
m **Bach, Mozart**
Luigi Ornaghi, Francesca Morrigi, Omar Brignoli, Antonio Ferrari, Teresa Brescianini, and the peasants and people of the Bergamo countryside

The lives of four peasant families, all living in the same Lombardy farmhouse at the end of the 19th century, are slowly revealed in a mosaic of small incidents: the cultivation of prize tomatoes, the sending of a child to school, a wedding, the recovery of a sick cow. Almost documentary in style (shot in 16mm with non-professional players), this lovingly constructed work is perfectly paced, deeply spiritual, and a moving tribute to the enduring relationship between the earth and those who work it. Using the simplest of narratives, the film re-established the international reputation of Olmi, who brilliantly sustains the Biblical symbolism of the expulsion from Eden, as well as his political and religious sub-texts.

Best Film Cannes 1978

Tre Fratelli see Three Brothers

Tre Passi Nel Delirio see Spirits Of The Dead

Tretia Mecht Chanskaya see Bed And Sofa

Trêve, La see Truce, The

The Trial

Der Prozess

Austria 1948 108 mins bw
Oesterricheische Wecheschau/Filmproduktion A.G.

d **G.W. Pabst**
sc **Rudolf Braungraber, Kurt Heuser, Emmerich Roboz**
ph **Oscar Schnirch**
m **Alois Melichar**
Ewald Balser, Ernst Deutsch, Albert Truby, Heinz Moog, Gustav Diessl, Maria Eis, Aglaja Schmid

In a Hungarian village in 1882, the disappearance and suicide of a young servant girl is construed as a Jewish-organized ritual murder, and several Jews are arrested and tried. The defending lawyer (Balser), dedicated to religious freedom, eloquently proves their innocence. Presumably attempting to atone for his work with the Nazis, Pabst here made a telling case against anti-Semitism, drawing the material from an actual incident that was something of a *cause célèbre.* The skilled director creates some powerful moments, and the use of traditional Jewish music—notably in a synagogue scene where it is sung by the famous cantor Ladislaus Morgenstern—is affecting. However, the film is weakened by needless sentimentality, flashy effects, emotional manipulation and the outrageously caricatured anti-Semites, led by a virulent Baron (Moog). The portrayals of the Jewish defendants, notably Deutsch, are much better handled.

Best Director Venice 1948
Best Actor (Ernst Deutsch) Venice 1948

Trial Of Joan Of Arc

Procès De Jeanne D'Arc

France 1962 65 mins bw
Agnès Delahaie

d **Robert Bresson**
sc **Robert Bresson**
ph **L.H. Burel**
m **Francis Seyrig**
Florence Carrez, Jean-Claude Fourneau, Marc Jacquier, Roger Honorat, Jean Gillibert, André Régnier, Philippe Dreux, E.R. Pratt, Harry Sommers

The period of Joan of Arc's imprisonment and trial, during which she is relentlessly interrogated by the court and persecuted by her gaolers. Eventually shaken, she recants, but only briefly, and is burned at the stake. In theory, Bresson would appear the ideal film-maker to undertake this subject with its medieval context and religious themes. However, he carries his austerity and detachment to such an extreme that the whole business is actually rather a bore, its restraint interrupted only by the regular English shouts of 'Burn the Witch'. With Bresson drawing the trial scenes from the actual transcripts, Joan herself, especially as impersonated by Florence Carrez, is no more than a one-dimensional mouthpiece for the utterance of her faith. There are details to admire, notably the sombre opening and the dramatic and horrifying closing images of the charred stake, but perhaps the subject needs dramatic licence after all. The Cannes Festival jury clearly held a different opinion.

Special Jury Prize Cannes 1962

Trial On The Road

Proverka Na Dorogakh

USSR 1971 98 mins bw
Lenfilm

d **Alexei Gherman**
sc **Eduard Volodarsky**
ph **L. Kolganov, B. Aleksandrovsky**
m **Isaak Shvarts**
Rolan Bykov, Anatoly Solinitsin, Vladimir Zamansky, Oleg Borisov, Fyodor Odinokov, Anda Zaitse

Lazarev (Zamansky), a German soldier, is captured by Russian partisans but reveals that he is a former Red Army sergeant who was forced to serve the Nazis. Major Petushkov (Solinitsin) wants Lazarev shot, but Lieutenant Erofeyich (Odinokov) prevails on him to take the man into the fighting unit. There, he is treated with suspicion and, from Petushkov, vindictiveness, but distinguishes himself by bravery. Gherman's first film, restrained and assured, was banned for 15 years for reasons which are not at all evident—indeed, even difficult to guess at. The director's choice of monochrome, effectively evoking the atmosphere of the landscape, together with his focus on individuals who are committed to their own course (Lazarev, Erofeyich), set both the style and the theme for his future work. Here, the context is that of an excellent combat movie.

Tribulations D'Un Chinois En Chine, Les see Up To His Ears

Tricheurs, Les see Youthful Sinners

Trip To The Moon
Le Voyage Dans La Lune

France 1902 14 mins bw or tinted
Châtelet Productions

d **Georges Méliès**
sc **Georges Méliès**
ph **Georges Méliès**
m **Silent**
Georges Méliès, Bluette Bernon, Victor André, Henri Delannoy, Farjaux, Kelm, Brunnet

Six members of the Astronomers' Club take off in a rocket to the moon. They land in the Plain of Craters, are attacked by an army of creatures, but manage to get back to the spaceship in time to return to Earth. 'A film that people will talk about for 30 years. It made a deep impression, being the first of its kind. In brief, it was considered a masterpiece—I don't agree with that,' said Méliès, conjuror, cartoonist, mechanic and pioneer film-maker about one of the most famous of his 100 or so innovative short films. Based partly on Alfred De Neuville's illustrations for the Jules Verne novel of the same name and Méliès' own inventions, such as the rocket landing in the right eye on the face of the moon causing it to shed a tear, it still astonishes and amuses. The film was available at a higher price in the hand-tinted version, as were almost all of his later works, including another Verne adaptation, *20,000 Leagues Under The Sea* (1907).

Tristana

Spain 1970 105 mins col
Epoca/Talia/Selenia Cinematografica/Les Films Corona(Paris)

d **Luis Buñuel**
sc **Luis Buñuel, Julio Alejandro**
ph **José F. Aguayo**
Catherine Deneuve, Fernando Rey, Franco Nero, Lola Gaos, Antonio Casas

Don Lope (Rey), a progressive, liberal, agnostic Spanish gentleman, is laid low by his reactionary and hedonistic code towards women and the lust he feels for his ward, the gentle and innocent Tristana (Deneuve). By transferring the story—by Benito Pérez Galdós, the author of *Nazarín*—to the Spain of the 1920s and from Madrid to provincial Toledo, Buñuel was able to relate to the time of his youth and create a stifling provincial atmosphere that traps the two main characters. One of the least complicated and symbolic of the director's films, it is also one of his most assured. Without wasting a single shot, he goes to the heart of his subject, while keeping a sly and ironic distance. Both Rey and Deneuve give their finest performances—he the volcano, she the iceberg.

Triumph Des Willens see Triumph Of The Will

Triumph Of The Will
Triumph Des Willens

Germany 1934 120 mins bw
NSDAP

d **Leni Riefenstahl**
sc **Leni Riefenstahl**
ph **Sepp Allgeier (supervisor)**
m **Herbert Windt**

The preparations for the 1934 Nuremberg Rally, the arrival of Hitler, the marches and the speeches. Riefenstahl was given over 40 cameramen and many technicians by the Nazi Party to make this documentary under a title suggested by Hitler. Despite her later protestations that it was merely a record of an historical event and not a propaganda film, the rally was shaped into a great, mythic spectacle, with the Führer as a Wagnerian hero descending upon the medieval town to save *das volk*. Ecstatic faces stare up at him as the sun catches his head like a halo. Using dramatic editing, the people become a dehumanized mass moving through Busby Berkeley routines in a 'Springtime for Hitler' show.

Trois Couronnes Du Matelot, Les see Three Crowns Of The Sailor

Trois Hommes Et Un Couffin see Three Men And A Cradle

Trollflöjten see Magic Flute, The

Trou, Le see Hole, The

The Truce

La Trêve

France 1968 90 mins col

T.E.C.

d **Claude Guillemot**

sc **Claude Guillemot**

ph **Denys Clerval**

m **Jorge Milchberg, Armand Mijiani**

Daniel Gélin, Charles Denner, Caroline Car, Virginie Vignon, Marc Lamole, Jean Mondain, Eric Husberg

Paris nightclub owner Arno (Gélin) is invited to an exclusive high-stakes gambling party at a country manor one weekend. He decides to enjoy some fishing *en route*, accompanied by Laura, the club's stripper (Car). They bump into Julien (Denner), an old underworld rival of Arno's, and his girlfriend Fifine (Vignon) and team up with them, but fall into arguments and one-upmanship while, at the same time, being tailed by a gangster and his henchmen. An energetic and unusual treatment of the popular French gangster genre, featuring beguilingly 'ordinary' protagonists in Arno and Julien. The tale zips along, combining tension with comedy in an appealing mix.

The Truth

La Vérité

France 1960 130 mins bw

Iéna/C.E.L.A.P

d **Henri-Georges Clouzot**

sc **Henri-Georges Clouzot, Jérôme Géronimi, Simone Drieu, Michèle Perrein, Christiane Rochefort**

ph **Armand Thirard**

m **Beethoven, Stravinsky**

Brigitte Bardot, Marie-José Nat, Sami Frey, Charles Vanel, Paul Meurisse

Dominique (Bardot) and her sister Annie (Nat) arrive in Paris where Annie settles in at the music conservatoire and falls in love with Gilbert (Frey). Dominique, however, finds it impossible to settle to anything other than a tempestuous affair with her sister's lover, which ends in her shooting him when he's had enough. Set in the court during Dominique's trial, the events that brought her there are told in flashback, but it is the court scenes themselves (shades of Cayatte) that work best. For the rest, this meeting of H-G and BB, the Old Guard and the New Wave, is a disappointment. Working from an undistinguished script, Clouzot seems lost in his wanderings through the new generation, and Bardot, trying hard, despite having to cha-cha in the nude, portrays a character so two-dimensional and tedious as to be hardly worth the bother.

Tsubaki Sanjuro see Sanjuro

Tsuma Yo Bara No Yo Ni see Wife, Be Like A Rose

Tsvet Granata see Colour Of Pomegranates, The

Tulipää see Flame Top

Tulipe Noir, La see Black Tulip, The

Tu Ne Tueras Point see Thou Shalt Not Kill

Turbulent Years, The see Flaming Years, The

Turkish Delight

Turks Fruit

Netherlands 1973 106 mins col
Rob Houwer Film Holland

d **Paul Verhoeven**
sc **Gerard Soeteman**
ph **Jan De Bont**
m **Rogier Van Otterloo**
Monique Van De Ven, Rutger Hauer, Tonny Huurdeman, Wim Van Den Brink

Eric (Hauer), a young sculptor and rebel, marries Olga (Van De Ven), a girl from a *bourgeois* family. When the pressures of married life drive them apart, he tries to forget her by sleeping with as many girls as he can, but they meet again in sad circumstances. Paul Verhoeven burst on to the tranquil and somewhat sparse Dutch cinema scene with this aggressive, juvenile, alienating, emetic and erotic movie, based on a 1969 bestseller by Jan Wolkers. The box-office success at home and abroad for this 'love story for today' must be attributable to the full-frontal sex and not to its heavy-handed attempts to satirize Dutch middle-class mores.

Turks Fruit see Turkish Delight

Turksib

USSR 1929 60 mins bw
Vostok Kino

d **Victor Turin**
sc **Victor Turin, Alexander Macheret, Viktor Shklovsky, Y. Aron**
ph **E. Slavinski, B. Frantzisson**
m **Silent**

A documentary following the building of the Turkestan-Siberian Railway, a tremendous engineering feat, climaxing with the men hastening to lay the last tracks to meet the first Five Year Plan. This exuberant, splendidly pictorial morale-booster was, in fact, completed before the railway. It made a great impact on documentary film-makers in Britain, such as John Grierson.

Tutto A Posto see All Screwed Up

Tuzolto Utca 25 see 25 Fireman's Street

Twenty Days Without War

Dvadtsat Dnei Bez Voini

USSR 1976 100 mins bw
Lenfilm

d **Alexei Gherman**
sc **Konstantin Simonov**
ph **Valery Fedosov**
m **V. Lavrov**
Yuri Nikulin, Ludmila Gurchenko, R. Sadykov, Nikolai Grinko, A. Stepanova

Major Lopatin (Nikulin), novelist and war correspondent, has 20 days leave after the Battle of Stalingrad and visits his home town in Tashkent where a film based on his articles is being made. Once there, he visits his ex-wife and her new husband, addresses the workers at an armaments factory and, above all, spends time with the film unit, only to discover that their perceptions of the war are very different from what he has tried to convey. Gherman's second film, like his first (*Trial On The Road*, 1971), was banned for several years, and for reasons almost as obscure. The director's assurance and eye for detail displayed in his debut is confirmed in this study of people's attitudes to war: Lopatin learns that those who stayed at home need romantic and heroic illusions, and the film's subject broadens into an examination of the nature of truth.

25 Fireman's Street

Tuzolto Utca 25

Hungary 1973 97 mins col
Budapest Studio

d **István Szabó**
sc **István Szabó**
ph **Sándor Sára**

m **Zdenkó Tamássy**
Rita Békés, Lucyna Winnicka, Péter Müller, András Bálint, Mari Szémes

The dreams and memories of the inhabitants of an old house on the eve of its demolition, particularly those of the baker's wife (Békés), who helped shelter fugitives from the Nazis in her attic, and Mária (Winnicka), who was arrested during World War II. The memories move through the socialization in the late 1940s and the 1956 uprising to the relative stability of the present day. Szabó was born in 1938 and most of his restrained and reflective films are concerned with the German occupation of Hungary and the events of 1956 from the perspective of his own generation. By using one specific location circumscribing a small group of characters and a fragmentary, non-chronological structure, he has successfully protrayed public and private events stretching over 40 years. At the haunting climax, the director's alter ego, András Bálint who plays Mária's son, looks back at the house and sees the previous inhabitants, alive and dead, arrayed as if for a photograph.

Twenty-Four Hours In A Woman's Life

Vingt-Quatre Heures De La Vie D'Une Femme

France 1968 84 mins col
Progefi/Consortium Pathé(Paris)/Roxy Film(Munich)

d **Dominique Delouche**
sc **Dominique Delouche, Albert Valentin, Marie-France Rivière**
ph **Walter Wottitz**
m **Brahms, Jean Podromidès**
Danielle Darrieux, Robert Hoffman, Romina Power, Marthe Alycia, Lena Skerla

During 1914, a society widow (Darrieux) encounters a handsome young man (Hoffman) losing heavily in the casino of an Italian resort. In spite of their age difference, they become lovers for that night, during which she learns that he is a deserter from the Austrian army who has become a compulsive gambler. Delouche began life as a painter, moved into film as Fellini's assistant, and much admired Max Ophüls, three facts which exercised a clear influence on his first feature: Ophüls had intended to make Stefan Zweig's short story (originally set in 1890) with Darrieux, and Delouche strives to achieve the composition and camera style of the great director. Some bedroom scenes are redolent of Fellini at his worst, but the overall look of the film glows with the exquisite painterly colours and textures of the Impressionists. In all, a period romance which doesn't fulfil its promise, but with the advantage of Darrieux's always magical and dignified presence in a role played by Merle Oberon in English in 1952.

Twenty Six Days In The Life Of Dostoevsky

Dwadzat Schest Dnej Is Shisni Dostojewskogo

USSR 1981 87 mins col
Mosfilm

d **Alexander Zarkhi**
sc **Vladimir Vladimirov, Pavel Finn**
ph **Vladimir Klimov**
m **Irakli Gabeli**
Anatoly Solinitsin, Evgenia Simonova, Eva Szykulska

In the winter of 1866, Dostoevsky (Solinitsin), his genius as yet unrecognized, has just suffered the death of his first wife and that of his beloved brother and collaborator. He has family dependants, is a compulsive gambler and badly in debt. When his publisher sends the police chief to pressure him for repayment of a loan, he hires a stenographer (Simonova) and dictates a novel to her in 26 days. It is *The Gambler*, drawing on his own experiences during a European trip four years earlier. The film brings these to life and traces the growing bond between the writer and the stenographer, who became his second wife. An intriguing idea with a complex structure and much of interest, but screenplay and direction are erratic, and it is left to the power of Solinitsin's performance to carry it through.

Best Actor (Anatoly Solinitsin) Berlin 1981

Twin Sisters Of Kyoto

aka The Old Capital

Koto

Japan 1963 107 mins col
Shochiko

d **Noboru Nakamura**

sc **Toshihide Gondo**
ph **Toshiro Narushima**
m **Tohru Takemitsu**
Shima Iwashita, Seiji Miyaguchi, Teruo Yoshida, Tamotsu Hayakawa, Hiroyuki Nagato, Michiyo Tamaki

Chieko, the adopted daughter of a comfortably off Kyoto merchant, suspects that her parents are concealing something of her history. In fact, she is one of a pair of twins, abandoned at birth because twins are considered an omen of ill-fortune, and, for the twin, it is a shame and disgrace to be so born. In due course, Chieko meets a poor village girl who is her double and, gradually, they both have to face the traumatic truth that they are twin sisters. A splendid film, boasting breathtaking photography, and a *tour de force* of acting from Iwashita in the dual roles of both girls. Nakamura brings much sensitivity to handling the conflicts and eventual resolution of feelings in the sisters. He also contrasts the lifestyles between rich and poor and vividly evokes Kyoto, an ancient city where custom dies hard.

Two Cents Worth Of Hope see Two Pennyworth Of Hope

Two Daughters

Teen Kanya

India 1961 114 mins bw
Satyajit Ray productions

d **Satyajit Ray**
sc **Satyajit Ray**
ph **Soumendou Roy**
m **Satyajit Ray**
1) Anil Chatterji, Chandana Banerji, Nriparti Chatterji, Kagen Rathak, Gopal Roy
2) Soumitra Chatterjee, Aparna Das Gupta, Sita Mukherji, Gita Dey, Santosh Dutt, Mihir Chakravarty

Two separate episodes, based on stories by Tagore, made as Ray's salute to the centenary of the author's birth. In 'The Postmaster', a new postmaster (Anil Chatterji) in an isolated village is taken care of by a little orphan girl (Banerji). He begins to give her the basics of the education she longs for; she nurses him through a malaria bout. But the life is too dull for him and he leaves. In 'Samapti', a student (Soumitra Chatterjee) returns home to his village to find his mother has arranged a marriage for him. Rejecting her choice, he marries the local tomboy (Das Gupta) who causes a scandal by running away on her wedding night. These gentle, graceful and observant tales owe as much to the eye and ear of the director and the gifts of his actors as to their distinguished literary origins. Combining humour and pathos, Ray's rich tapestry of the emotions and behaviour of ordinary people is revealed at a leisurely pace, drawing us into their world. *Teen Kanya*, in fact, means 'Three Daughters', but Ray cut the third story 'Monihara', when the film was sent abroad for release.

Two English Girls see Anne And Muriel

Two Lions In The Sun

Deux Lions Au Soleil

France 1980 110 mins col
Asta Films/F.R.3

d **Claude Faraldo**
sc **Claude Faraldo**
ph **Bernard Lutic**
m **Albert Marcoeur, François Ovide**
Jean-François Stevenin, Jean-Pierre Sentier, Catherine Lachens, Jean-Pierre Tailhade, Martine Sarcey, Michel Robin

Paul (Stevenin) and René (Sentier) are two middle-aged factory workers, respectively divorced and widowed. Fed up with their low pay and humdrum routine, and convinced that life should hold excitement and pleasure, they temporarily become conmen until they have enough ill-gotten gains to run away from Paris and enjoy a final fling. The director of *Themroc* (1972) has come up with an uneven entertainment, often interesting, sometimes poignant, but occasionally teetering on the edge of crassness. What makes it unmistakably off-beat and original is that the heroes, beautifully played by both actors, are bisexual live-in lovers who, in the most charming sequence, share the favours of a love-starved barmaid.

The Two Of Us

Le Vieil Homme Et L'Enfant

France 1966 90 mins bw

P.A.C./Valoria/Renn Productions

d **Claude Berri**
sc **Claude Berri**
ph **Jean Penzer**
m **Georges Delerue**
Michel Simon, Alain Cohen, Charles Denner, Luce Fabiole, Roger Carol, Paul Préboist, Zorica Lozice

During the Nazi occupation of Paris, an irrepressible eight-year-old Jewish boy, Claude (Cohen), is sent to stay with an elderly couple in the country. Since Pepé, the old man (Simon), is a rabid anti-Semite, the boy is instructed to conceal his origins (and his circumcision) and is taught the Lord's prayer. Once there, Claude and Pepé forge a close relationship—beautifully realized in the playing—in which the boy is amused by the old man's bigoted outbursts and delights in provoking him, while Pepé comes to dote on the child. The complex situation is sensitively and charmingly handled and made simple by being seen through a child's eyes. Berri's film is a reconstruction of his own childhood experience and he described it as 'a love affair between a Jew and an anti-Semite'. Made with warmth, humour and an accurate eye for the atmosphere of the period, it does occasionally lapse into sentimentality and overstatement. However, this can be forgiven in a debut feature, particularly from the director who, 20 years later and rather more ambitiously, would tackle *Jean De Florette* and *Manon Des Sources*.

Best Actor (Michel Simon) Berlin 1967

Two Or Three Things I Know About Her

Deux Ou Trois Choses Que Je Sais D'Elle

France 1966 95 mins col
Anouchka/Argos/Les Films Du Carrosse/Parc Film

d **Jean-Luc Godard**
sc **Jean-Luc Godard**
ph **Raoul Coutard**
m **Beethoven**
Marina Vlady, Anny Duperey, Roger Montsoret, Jean Narboni, Raoul Lévy

Juliette (Vlady) lives with her husband (Montsoret) and young child in a new high-rise building in the suburbs of Paris. She spends one day a week in the city centre where she prostitutes herself to obtain consumer durables. Godard makes it clear that the '*Elle*' or 'Her' of the title of his 'sociological essay' refers to Paris and not to his practical heroine. Inspired by a magazine article on housewife prostitutes, the film moves into the wider political sphere, at the same time Godard's voice on the soundtrack questions his own choice of images. The film is an important milestone on the way to Godard's total political commitment and his attempt to find an alternative to *'bourgeois* cinema'. For those who care, this is a particularly stimulating exercise.

Two Pennyworth Of Hope

(US: Two Cents Worth Of Hope)

Due Soldi Di Speranza

Italy 1952 98 mins bw
Universalcine

d **Renato Castellani**
sc **Renato Castellani, Titina De Filippo**
ph **Arturo Gallea**
m **Alessandro Cicognini**
Vincenzo Musolino, Maria Fiore, Filumena Russo, Luigi Astarita

A young man (Musolino) returns from the war to his village on the slopes of Vesuvius. Here he tries his hand at a number of jobs while trying to impress his future father-in-law who dislikes him. The rest of the villagers seem to be divided between the Church and Communism, and spend their time squabbling. Castellani, a minor figure in the Neo-Realist movement, brought a great deal of humour and vivacity to this comedy-drama, making it one of his best films. It completes an optimistic post-war trilogy of Italian life, following *Under The Sun Of Rome* and *It's Forever Springtime.*

Best Film Cannes 1952

Two Stage Sisters

Wutai Jiemei

China 1964 114 mins col
Tianma Film Studio(Shanghai)

d **Xie Jin**
sc **Lin Gu, Xu Jin, Xie Jin**

ph **Zhou Daming**
m **Huang Zhun**
Xie Fang, Cao Yindi, Feng Ji, Li Wei, Deng Nan, Wu Baifang, Shangguan Yunzhu, Shen Hao, Gao Yuansheng

Chunhua (Fang), a runaway, finds refuge with a travelling opera troupe and grows very close to Yuehong (Yindi). Life on the road is cruel, and the two girls are in bondage to Ax'in (Nan), the troupe's owner, who takes them to Shanghai. There, they impress manager Tang (Wei) and become stars, but Yuehong, seduced by materialism, gives up singing, marries Tang and drifts into misery. The distraught Chunhua commits herself to the Revolution and forms a women's co-operative opera company. This is a marvellous film. One of the last made before the Cultural Revolution, it was suppressed for reasons that can only be put down to extreme and irrational puritanism, since its political bias—anti-Capitalist corruption, pro-Feminist—is of the correct hue. However, while putting its revolutionary message across forcefully, it takes the form of theatrical melodrama with which the West is totally familiar, doing so at the highest level of skill. An involved and involving story, spanning the years 1935-50, it is superbly well acted (Xie Fang gives an outstanding performance), and photographed with a breathtaking sense of colour, composition, and inventive camera angles. The music beguiles, too, particulary the sung melodies that form part of the narration.

Two Women
La Ciociara

Italy 1960 110 mins bw
Champion/Marceau/Cocinor/SGC

d **Vittorio De Sica**
sc **Cesare Zavattini, Vittorio De Sica**
ph **Gabor Pogany**
m **Armando Trovaioli**
Sophia Loren, Eleonora Brown, Jean-Paul Belmondo, Raf Vallone, Renato Salvatori

A widow (Loren) and her 13-year-old daughter (Brown), fleeing south after the Allied bombing of Rome in 1943, survive dangers, deprivation and ultimately rape by soldiers. The title refers to mother and daughter, but it was Loren's all-stops-out performance which gained her the rare distinction of being the first (and last?) actress (or actor) to win an Oscar for a foreign-language film, proving that Hollywood never knew how to make use of her dramatic talents. The film itself, based on a story by Alberto Moravia, was greeted, in the main, with less rapture by the critics, although it was a commercial success. De Sica's usual warmth and insight gave way too often to melodrama, but it has its touching and harrowing moments.

Best Actress (Sophia Loren) Oscar 1961
Best Actress (Sophia Loren) Cannes 1961

Tystnaden see Silence, The

U

Uccellacci E Uccellini see Hawks And The Sparrows, The

Udienza, L' see Audience, The

Ugetsu see Ugetsu Monogatari

Ugetsu Monogatari
(US: Ugetsu)

Japan 1953 96 mins bw
Daiei

d **Kenji Mizoguchi**
sc **Matsutaro Kawaguchi, Yoshitaka Yoda**
ph **Kazuo Miyagawa**
m **Fumio Hayasaka**
Masayuki Mori, Kinuyo Tanaka, Sakae Ozawa, Machiko Kyo

Genjuro (Mori), a poor potter trying to make a living in a war-torn medieval village, is lured away from his devoted wife (Tanaka) and young son by the mysterious Lady Wasaka (Kyo) who turns out to be a ghost. When Genjuro returns home repentant, his wife, too, has become a ghost. The first film to introduce Mizoguchi to the West (translated as *Tales Of The Pale And Silvery Moon After The Rain*, but known under its original title), it was immediately acclaimed as one of the masterpieces of world cinema. Based on two 18th-century ghost stories by Akinari Veda and one by Guy De Maupassant, it is told in lyrical, haunting and intense images which never ignore the human element. Mizoguchi's artistry is best demonstrated by the trip across the lake as the boat emerges from the mist, hinting at the supernatural; Genjuro and Wasaka on the grass beside a shimmering lake, and the final sequence, when the potter see the phantom of his dead wife where there was emptiness before, giving the film an emotional impact that has seldom been equalled.

Ugly, Dirty and Mean see Down And Dirty

Ukigumo see Floating Clouds

Ukigusa see Floating Weeds

Ulica Graniczna see Border Street

Ultima Cena, La see Last Supper, The

Ultima Donna, L' see Last Woman, The

Uma see Horse

Umarete Wa Mita Keredo see I Was Born, But...

Umberto D

Italy 1952 89 mins bw
Dear Films

d **Vittorio De Sica**
sc **Cesare Zavattini, Vittorio De Sica**
ph **G.R. Aldo**
m **Alessandro Cicognini**
Carlo Battisti, Maria Pia Casilio, Lina Gennari

An old-age pensioner (Battisti), unable to pay his rent, has only his dog and a pregnant housemaid (Casilio) for friends. He is forced to consider begging and suicide. Dedicated to his father, the film marked the end of De Sica's great Neo-Realist period. Using non-professionals in real locations—Umberto was played by an elderly professor of philology—one of the director's most affecting films avoids sentimentality by its truth, harshness and accuracy. From child neglect in *Shoeshine* to discarded old age in *Umberto D*, De Sica's films showed, in his own words, 'the indifference of society towards suffering. They are a word in favour of the poor and unhappy.'

The Umbrellas Of Cherbourg

Les Parapluies De Cherbourg

France 1964 92 mins col
Parc/Madeleine/Beta(Munich)

d **Jacques Demy**
sc **Jacques Demy**
ph **Jean Rabier**
m **Michel Legrand**
Catherine Deneuve, Anne Vernon, Nino Castelnuovo, Ellen Farner, Marc Michel

Geneviève (Deneuve), who works in the umbrella shop of her widowed mother (Vernon), loves Guy (Castelnuovo), a garage mechanic. She discovers that she is pregnant after he has gone on military service, so she marries a young diamond merchant (Michel) for security. Demy, a lover of the Hollywood musical (his first feature *Lola* owed much to *On The Town*), attempted to distil the genre through his own French sensibility. The originality of the film lies in the fact that all the dialogue is sung (the cast is dubbed) in a kind of recitative. Filming in colour for the first time, Demy had both the exterior and interior of houses in Cherbourg painted in an array of colours, matching the clothes of the characters. It's all very pretty-pretty and Legrand's tinkly music makes it more chanting than enchanting. The film's immense popularity proves how much tastes differ.

Best Film Cannes 1964

Under Satan's Sun

Sous Le Soleil De Satan

France 1987 98 mins col
Erato/Films A2/Flach/Action

d **Maurice Pialat**
sc **Sylvie Danton**
ph **Willy Kurant**
m **Henri Dutilleux**
Gérard Depardieu, Sandrine Bonnaire, Maurice Pialat, Alain Artur, Yann Dedet, Brigitte Legendre

Father Donissan (Depardieu), a simple and devout priest, senses Satan everywhere, especially in the heart of Mouchette (Bonnaire), a wild young woman who has killed a man. She cuts her throat when he declares that she is possessed. In another village, he gains the reputation of a saint. Pialat, who also plays Donissan's superior, has constructed this uncompromisingly bleak, claustrophobic and humourless film as a series of long duologues. Obviously influenced by Bresson's method—based, like *Diary Of A Country Priest* and *Mouchette*, on a novel by Georges Bernanos—the narrative suffers from a number of ellipses that provoke unanswered questions. The performances of Depardieu and Bonnaire (both of whom had worked with Pialat before) are riveting, but it might leave one agreeing with Buñuel's statement: 'Thank God, I'm an atheist'.

Best Film Cannes 1987

Under The Roofs Of Paris see Sous Les Toits De Paris

Une Chante, L'Autre Pas, L' see One Sings, The Other Doesn't

Unfaithful Wife, The see Femme Infidèle, La

Unfinished Piece For Mechanical Piano

(US: An Unfinished Piece For Player Piano)

Neokonchennaya Pyesa Dlya Mekhanicheskogo Pianin

USSR 1977 100 mins col
Mosfilm

d **Nikita Mikhalkov**
sc **Aleksander Adabashyan, Nikita Mikhalkov**
ph **Pavel Lebeshev**
m **Eduard Artemyev**
Alexander Kalyagin, Elena Solovei, Eugenia

Glushenko, Antonina Shuranova, Yuri Bogatyrev, Nikita Mikhalkov

Schoolteacher Platanov (Kalyagin), is married to the unintellectual Sasha (Glushenko). At the country estate of the widow Anna Petrovna (Shuranova), he again meets Sophia (Solovei), a girlfriend of seven years previously, just married to Sergei (Bogatyrev), a complete fool. Their attempt to recapture their past only leads to tragic farce. Mikhalkov (who plays the drunken doctor) has splendidly adapted *Platanov*, Chekhov's rambling first play, to give his stock company ample opportunity to display its acting skills. The atmosphere of the lazy summer's day is beautifully caught by Lebeshev's cinematography, although there are times when the pictorial distracts from the text and the sweet takes over too often from the bitter.

Unfinished Piece For Player Piano, An see Unfinished Piece For Mechanical Piano

---

Unholy Love see Alraune

Unruhige Nacht see All Night Through

Unsichtbare Gegner see Invisible Adversaries

Unvanquished, The see Aparajito

Uomo A Meta, Un see Almost A Man

Uomo Di Paglia, L' see Man Of Straw

The Uprising

Der Aufstand

W. Germany 1980 96 mins col
Joachim Von Vietinghoff

d **Peter Lilienthal**
sc **Peter Lilienthal, Antonio Skármeta**
ph **Michael Ballhaus**
m **Claus Bantzer**
Agustin Pereira, Carlos Catanía, María Lourdes Centano De Zelaya, Oscar Castillo

Nicaragua in the last days of the dictator Somoza and his brutal National Guard. In the university town of Léon, a young man (Pereira) in the Guard, sides with the Sandinistas, to which his father (Catanía) belongs, participates in the taking of the government stockade. The West German director, who spent his adolescence in Uruguay and lived in Allende's Chile, shot the film in Léon four months after the Sandinista victory, using the people themselves in place of actors. As a result, this is a simple, direct, hot-off-the- press document, re-enacted with fervour by the participants. Given the youth of the revolution, it would have been too much to expect that Lilienthal and the exiled Chilean novelist Skármeta should go deeper into the political and economic questions rather than deal on the level of the undoubted solidarity and heroics of the people.

Up To A Point

Hasta Cierto Punto

Cuba 1983 68 mins col
ICAIC

d **Tomás Gutiérrez Alea**
sc **Juan Carlos Tabío, Serafin Quiñones, Tomás Gutiérrez Alea**
ph **Mario García Joya**
m **Leo Brouwer**
Oscar Alvarez, Mirta Ibarra, Omar Valdés, Coralia Veloz, Rogelio Blaín, Ana Viña

Oscar (Alvarez), a writer married to an actress, is researching a film about Latin-American *machismo*. While interviewing workers of both sexes at the Havana docks, he falls in love with one of them, the attractive Lina (Ibarra). As their involvement deepens, it becomes clear that under his veneer of acquired liberated views, Oscar is as much trapped in notions of maleness as the workers he talks to. Juxtaposing video interviews with workers—one of whom says that women should be free 'up to a point'—with artistic and working-class life, the film demonstrates the difficulties of resolving those traditional sexual and social conflicts that are at odds with the political ideology by which the characters are governed and to which they willingly subscribe. As an account of a dead-end love affair, the story is banal, but is lent conviction by the well-chosen cast.

Up To His Ears
Les Tribulations D'Un Chinois En Chine

France 1965 110 mins col
Les Films Ariane/Artistes Associés(Paris)/Vides(Rome)

d **Philippe De Broca**
sc **Daniel Boulanger, Philippe De Broca**
ph **Edmond Séchan**
m **Georges Delerue**
Jean-Paul Belmondo, Ursula Andress, Valérie Lagrange, Maria Pacôme, Valery Inkijinoff, Jean Rochefort

Arthur Lempereur (Belmondo) is so bored by his colossal wealth that he wants to die. His Chinese advisor Mr Goh (Inkijinoff) persuades him to suspend his suicide attempts for insurance purposes, and rather have himself killed after a suitable interval. Arthur embarks on a yacht trip round the world with an entourage that includes his fiancée (Lagrange), meets an alluring striptease dancer (Andress) in Hong Kong and decides he doesn't want to die after all... So far, so good, in a plot derived from a novel by Jules Verne, the film offers attractive Far Eastern locations, Belmondo's unique charm and a splendidly inscrutable performance from Inkijinoff. However, when Arthur sets off to look for Mr Goh and intercept the plans for his own assassination, we get an inferior re-run of *That Man From Rio*, so jam-packed with comic-book escapades played at a frenzied pace, that the film grows very tiresome well before its ironic resolution.

U Samovo Sinyevo Morya see By The Bluest Of Seas

Usual Unidentified Thieves, The see Persons Unknown

Utamaro And His Five Women see Five Women Around Utamaro

Utamaro O Meguru Gonin No Onna see Five Women Around Utamaro

Utvandrarna see Emigrants, The

Už Zase Skáču Přes Kaluže see I'm Jumping Over Puddles Again

V

Vacances De Monsieur Hulot, Les see Monsieur Hulot's Holiday

Vache Et Le Prisonnier, La see Cow And I, The

Vagabonde

Sans Toit Ni Loi

France 1985 104 mins col
Cine-Tamaris/Films A2/Ministère De La Culture

d **Agnès Varda**
sc **Agnès Varda**
ph **Patrick Blossier**
m **Joanna Bruzdowicz**
Sandrine Bonnaire, Macha Meril, Stéphane Freiss, Eliane Cortadellas, Marthe Jarnias, Joel Fosse

The body of a young woman, Mona, is found frozen to death in a ditch. Various 'witnesses' tell of their encounters with her and of how she threw up an office job for life on the open road. Varda's first feature for nine years is also one of her best. It is a telling study of an aimless existence upon which the director imposes a rigorous form. It is to the credit of both Varda and the magnificent Bonnaire that such an unsympathetic character manages to reach tragic stature as she moves further and further into degradation.
Best Film Venice 1985

Vaghe Stelle Dell'Orsa see Of A Thousand Delights

Valahol Európában see Somewhere In Europe

Valerie And Her Week Of Wonders

Valerie A Tyden Divu

Czechoslovakia 1970 77 mins col
Barrandov Studio

d **Jaromil Jires**
sc **Jaromil Jires, Ester Krumbachová**
ph **Jan Curík**
m **Jan Klusák**
Jaroslava Schallerová, Helena Anýzková, Petr Kopriva, Jiři Prymek, Jan Klusák

Innocent Valerie (Schallerová), aged 13, lives in small town with her young-looking grandma (Anýzková), who becomes a vampire and is tried for witchcraft. However, the magic earrings given to Valerie by a young man called the Eagle—who turns out to be her brother—and which have protected her from the Weasel and from rape by a priest, save granny from the stake. These are, in fact, Valerie's baroque, Gothic fairytale dreams, in which images mystical, religious, sexual, brutal and romantic, jostle for position. Jires has moved a great distance from his simple early narratives (e.g. *The Cry*, 1963), to join that school of Czech film- makers with a penchant for the bizarre and fantastical. Unfortunately, although the form of this one is visually spectacular, the content is an irritating jumble.

Valerie A Tyden Divu see Valerie And Her Week Of Wonders

Valseuses, Les see Making It

Vámmentes Házasság see Duty Free Marriage

Les Vampires

France 1915-1916 420 mins bw
Gaumont

d **Louis Feuillade**
sc **Louis Feuillade**
ph **Manichoux**
m **Silent**
Musidora, Edouard Mathé, Marcel Lesque, Jean Aymé, Jacques Feyder

'The Vampires', a gang of brilliant jewel thieves led by The Grand Vampire (Aymé) and the anagrammatically named Irma Vep (Musidora), are tracked down by a crusading journalist (Mathé). This visually compelling, 10-part serial is generally considered Feuillade's best work. It's certainly the most typical, with its strange combination of fantasy, realism, thrills and comedy. And at its centre the electrifying Musidora in black tights and cloak as the arch-villainess. Although the gang is finally vanquished, the Ministry Of the Interior temporarily banned a couple of episodes for what it deemed the glamorization of crime.

Vampyr

aka The Strange Adventure Of David Gray
France/Germany 1932 83 mins bw
Tobis Klangfilm/Carl Dreyer

d **Carl Dreyer**
sc **Carl Dreyer, Christen Jul**
ph **Rudolph Maté, Louis Née**
m **Wolfgang Zeller**
Julian West, Henriette Gérard, Sybille Schmitz, Maurice Schutz, Jan Hieronimko

David Gray (West), a young traveller, witnesses the effects of vampires on the lord of a remote castle and on his two daughters. Financed by the Baron Nicolas De Gunzberg, a Dutch amateur actor (it shows), on condition that he should play the leading role under a pseudonym, Dreyer's first sound film was shot entirely on location near Paris in French, German and English. Despite or because of the necessity of keeping dialogue to a minimum, the shooting restrictions and the money limitations, Dreyer went far beyond the purely Gothic, creating a horror film that makes most others pale into insignificance. The eerie mood was partly due to the luminous photography, achieved by reflecting light off gauze. The supernatural gives way to the magnificent 'natural' climax when the villain is buried alive by flour in a mill. The disturbing tale was based on a short story by Sheridan Le Fanu.

Vangelo Secondo Matteo, Il see Gospel According To Saint Matthew, The

Vanina Vanini

aka The Betrayer
Italy 1961 130 mins col
Zebra Film(Rome)/Orsay Film(Paris)

d **Roberto Rossellini**
sc **Roberto Rossellini, Diego Fabbri, Franco Solinas, Antonello Trombadori**
ph **Luciano Trasatti**
m **Renzo Rossellini**
Sandra Milo, Laurent Terzieff, Martine Carol, Paolo Stoppa, Isabelle Corey, Fernando Cicero

Pietro Missirilli (Terzieff), a Carbonari revolutionary, travels to Rome to kill a traitor and is given refuge by a sympathetic Countess (Carol). She passes him on to her lover, Prince Vanini (Stoppa), who places him in hiding where he is discovered by the prince's daughter Vanina (Milo). The couple fall in love and, when Pietro leaves to rejoin his comrades, Vanina secretly accompanies him, beginning a chain of events whereby, in her efforts to hold him, she ends up betraying him. This excursion into period politics and romance richly evokes the conflicts and contradictions of the time. Rossellini uses colour to brilliant effect and his handling of several different interlocking strands of action is admirable. Social inequality, religious and political corruption, intrigue, guilt and betrayal are everywhere palpable in this high romance of the Risorgimento. Only some mediocre acting lets it down.

The Vanishing Corporal

Le Caporal Épinglé
France 1962 110 mins bw
Les Films Cyclope

d **Jean Renoir**
sc **Jean Renoir, Guy Lefranc**
ph **Georges Leclerc**
m **Joseph Kosma**

Jean-Pierre Cassel, Claude Brasseur, O.E. Hasse, Claude Rich, Jacques Jouanneau, Mario David

The majority of French soldiers in a German P.O.W camp adjust to the life in spite of their homesickness and grumbles, but one young corporal (Cassel), good-looking, educated and off-beat, dedicates himself to escape. Although his repeated attempts fail, he keeps trying, even managing a romantic interlude with the receptionist daughter of a female German dentist. It is an unusual film in which Renoir treats his subject from a perspective of gentle comedy and with great charm, yet manages to suggest, by a series of subtle shifts of mood, the rather grimmer reality beneath the surface of the situation. Cassel is perfectly cast, supported by a gallery of sharply observed characters who demonstrate the melting pot of backgrounds that characterize any army. Finely photographed in misty winter landscapes that are evocative without being depressing, it's wry, touching and entertaining, while suggesting echoes of Renoir's World War I masterpiece, *La Grande Illusion.*

Vargtimmen see Hour Of The Wolf

Variété see Variety

Variety

aka Vaudeville

Variété

Germany 1925 104 mins bw
UFA

d **E.A. Dupont**
sc **E.A. Dupont, Leo Birinsky**
ph **Karl Freund**
m **Silent**

Emil Jannings, Lya De Putti, Maly Delschaft, Warwick Ward

An aging trapeze artist (Jannings) kills the newcomer (Ward) who seduced his wife and partner (De Putti). This trite and conventional melodrama of heated passion and seething jealousy was notable for its unconventional impressionistic use of swirling light and movement and spectacular camera effects. It was a tremendous success, stylistically influential, and brought Dupont to the attention of Hollywood, where, rather sadly, he ended up making mostly B-movie trash.

Variety Lights see Lights Of Variety

Vasárnapi Szülok see Sunday Daughters

Vassa

USSR 1983 136 mins col
Mosfilm

d **Gleb Panfilov**
sc **Gleb Panfilov**
ph **Leonid Kalashnikov**
m **Vadim Bibergan**

Inna Churikova, Vadim Medvedev, Nikolai Skorobogatov, Valentina Yukeninia, Valentina Telichkina, Vyacheslav Bogachov

Vassa (Churikova) rules both her family and its shipping empire with a rod of iron, but when her efforts to save her husband from prosecution for molesting young girls fail, she persuades him to commit suicide. But even the formidable Vassa, locked in mortal combat with her political-activist daughter-in-law (Yukeninia), cannot stay the gathering forces of revolution. In adapting Maxim Gorky's mainstay of Soviet repertory theatre, *Vassa Zhelevnova*, as a vehicle for his wife and regular leading lady, Panfilov has shifted the work's emphasis to make the eponymous heroine a reasonably sympathetic character. He brings the story to life as an accessible domestic drama, but with an overlay of fascinating political ambiguity. The splendid Churikova convinces, as does the richly detailed re-creation of the life lived by the Russian provincial *bourgeoisie* in 1913, when the Bolsheviks began to beat at the door of the merchant classes.

Vaudeville see Variety

Velikii Uteshitel see Great Consoler, The

Vem Dömer? see Love's Crucible

Verdict

aka Jury Of One

Le Testament

France 1974 97 mins col
Les Films Concordia/P.E.C.F./Champion Cinematografica

d **André Cayatte**
sc **André Cayatte, Henri Pierre Dumayet, Paul Andreota**
ph **Jean Badal**
m **Louiguy**
Sophia Loren, Jean Gabin, Henri Garcin, Michel Albertini, Gisèle Casadessus, Muriel Catala

A young law student is charged with rape and murder, but his adoring mother (Loren), the wealthy widow of a gangster, is convinced of his innocence. To secure his acquittal, she intimidates the trial judge (Gabin) by kidnapping his seriously ill wife. What starts out as a respectable courtroom drama quickly degenerates into a salacious, lurid, ugly and fanciful melodrama of confused and questionable moral focus. One keeps watching, though, held by the *gravitas* of the aged Gabin in the penultimate film before his death, and the irresistible sight of the beautiful Loren as a ruthless tigress protecting her less than endearing cub.

Verdugo, El see Executioner, The

Vérité, La see Truth, The

Verkaufte Braut, Die see Bartered Bride, The

Verlorene, Der see Lost One, The

Verlorene Ehre Der Katharina Blum, Die see Lost Honour Of Katharina Blum, The

---

Verlorene Sohn, Der see Lost Son, The

Veronika Voss

Die Sehnsucht Der Veronika Voss

W. Germany 1981 104 mins bw
Maura/Tango/Rialto/Trio/Maran

d **Rainer Werner Fassbinder**
sc **Peter Märthesheimer, Pea Frölich**
ph **Xaver Schwarzenberger**
m **Peer Raben**
Rosel Zech, Hilmar Thate, Anne Marie Düringer, Cornelia Froeboess, Doris Schade, Armin Müller-Stahl

In the 1950s, a journalist (Thate) becomes involved in the life of Veronika Voss (Zech), a screen idol of the previous decade but now at the end of her career and under the influence of a doctor (Düringer) who supplies her with drugs. Fassbinder's striking use of black and white evokes in different ways the atmosphere of Germany in the dour post-war years and—in dreams—the brashness of the Nazi era. One of the director's last films, it is a flamboyant tribute to the UFA Studios with a nod towards *Sunset Boulevard* by the great Billy Wilder.

Best Film Berlin 1982

Verweigerung, Die see Refusal, The

Very Curious Girl, A see Dirty Mary

Very Happy Alexandre see Alexandre

A Very Moral Night

Egy Erkölcsös Éjszaka

Hungary 1979 99 mins col
Dialög Filmstudio

d **Károly Makk**
sc **István Örkény, Péter Bacsó**
ph **János Tóth**
m **Chopin, Offenbach, Délibes, Johann Strauss, Leo Fall, Ferenc Erkel, György Forrai, István Major, Béla Radics**
Margit Makay, Irén Psota, Carla Romanelli, Györgyi Tarján, György Cserhalmi

Kelepey (Cserhalmi), a young student in a small Hungarian town early in the century, frequents the local brothel where he is a great favourite of the girls, particularly Darinka (Tarján), with whom he shares a chaste bed. Eventually, he moves into the brothel. When his mother turns up to visit him, Madame and the girls encourage her assumption that the place is a boarding house. A pleasant enough film, sweet, gentle and rather old- fashioned, but missing out on its obvious comic potential. Well-acted and directed, and boasting photography of outstanding quality, it is nonetheless disappointing coming, as it does, from the distinguished Károly Makk whose usual sense of commitment to painful situations has been abandoned here.

A Very Private Affair

Vie Privée

France 1961 103 mins col
Progefi/Cipra(Paris)/CCM(Rome)

d **Louis Malle**
sc **Jean-Paul Rappeneau, Louis Malle**
ph **Henri Decaë**
m **Fiorenzo Carpi**
Brigitte Bardot, Marcello Mastroianni, Grégoire Von Rizzori, Ursula Kubler, Dirk Sanders

In love with Fabio (Mastroianni), her best friend's husband, Jill (Bardot) goes to Paris where she becomes a film actress. Ill from the pressures of stardom, she returns to Geneva, meets the now separated Fabio again and enjoys an idyllic affair with him until her life ends in tragedy. Louis Malle's fifth feature is one of his least distinguished. Bardot is called upon to give a sort of parody of herself, while Mastroianni battles with his two-dimensional role as a soulful theatre director straight out of magazine fiction—as is the story, which never reaches a seriously credible level. However, what the director lacks in material, he compensates for in detailed visuals, breathtakingly photographed by Decaë, particularly the final dramatic sequences at Spoleto.

Vesničkó Má Střediskowá see My Sweet Little Village

Vesyolye Rebyata see Jazz Comedy

V Gorodye S see In The Town Of S

Viaccia, La see Love Makers, The

Viaggio In Italia see Journey To Italy

Vice And Virtue

Le Vice Et La Vertu

France 1963 100 mins bw
SNE/Gaumont/Trianon

d **Roger Vadim**
sc **Roger Vailland, Claude Choublier, Roger Vadim**
ph **Marcel Grignon**
m **Michel Magne**
Annie Girardot, Catherine Deneuve, Robert Hossein, O.E. Hasse, Philippe Lemaire, Serge Marquand, Luciana Paluzzi

In Nazi-occupied France, sisters Juliette (Girardot) and Justine (Deneuve) are arrested. At the opulent German headquarters in Paris they are ordered to dispense their sexual favours to the High Command. Justine, a Resistance worker, somehow manages to keep her honour intact, while Juliette becomes the mistress of an SS officer, and thus they exemplify the 'vice' and 'virtue' of the title. Vadim has drawn his material from two novels of the Marquis De Sade, updating them in an attempt to give an impression of contemporary relevance. However, this intention is but a thin veneer overlaying a wallow in decadence, torture and hysteria, occasionally relieved by a measure of stylish eroticism. The classy leading ladies, some wildly baroque sets and a pseudo-Wagnerian score cannot disguise that this is a superficial exercise in sensationalism, albeit quite cleverly manipulated by the director.

Vice Et La Vertu, Le see Vice And Virtue

Vices And Pleasures see Private Vices And Public Virtues

Victoire En Chantant, La see Black And White In Colour

Vidãs Sêcas see Barren Lives

Vie A L'Envers, La see Life Upside Down

Vie Conjugale, La see Anatomy Of A Marriage

Vie, Une see One Life

La Vie De Château

France 1965 93 mins bw
Ancinex/Cobela/Films De La Guéville

d **Jean-Paul Rappeneau**
sc **Jean-Paul Rappeneau, Alain Cavalier, Claude Sautet**
ph **Pierre Lhomme**
m **Michel Legrand**
Catherine Deneuve, Pierre Brasseur, Philippe Noiret, Henri Garcin, Carlos Thompson

World War II is raging but the Normandy château of Jérôme (Noiret) and Marie (Deneuve) is a haven of peace—if not of marital bliss. When Marie discovers Julien (Garcin), a mysterious stranger who claims to be in love with her but who is, in fact, a Free French agent on a mission, hiding in the château, events take a complicated turn. In his debut directorial effort, Rappenau manages a dose of charm and a sense of the comic which he would seldom repeat in his later films. There is the odd lapse in pace and, indeed, in credibility, but director, writers (would it, perhaps, be more appropriate to call them co-directors?) and the accomplished Lhomme create a good-natured, good-looking fairy story in which even Klopstock (Thompson), the German C.O., is not noticeably villainous. Garcin and Noiret give superior performances.

Vie Devant Soi, La see Madame Rosa

La Vie Est À Nous

(US: The People Of France)
France 1936 66 mins bw
Partie Communiste Français

d **Jean Renoir, Jean-Paul Le Chanois, Jacques Becker, André Zwoboda, Pierre Unik, Henri Cartier-Bresson**
sc **Jean Renoir, Jean-Paul Le Chanois, Pierre Unik, Paul Vaillant-Couturier**
ph **Claude Renoir, Jean-Serge Bourgoin, Jean Isnard, Alain Douarinou**
m **Songs of the Front Populaire**
Gaston Modot, Jean Dasté, Julien Berthot, Madeleine Sologne, Jacques Brunius, Roger Blin, Charles Blavette, Madeleine Dax, Jean Renoir, Jacques Becker, Vladimir Sokoloff

A number of sketches, newsreels and political speeches put forward the policies of the French Communist Party. The staged scenes include a bailiff being driven off a farm by peasants, an unemployed intellectual joining the Party and a newspaper vendor selling *L'Humanité* being beaten up by Fascist thugs. Asked by the Communist Party to make a propaganda work, Renoir merely supervised the film, which was shot and edited principally by his youthful assistants. Given that it was a collaborative effort, filmed in a few weeks in order to be ready in time for the 1936 election, Renoir's warm-hearted realism comes flooding through much of it, especially, it must be said, in the less directly political scenes. Later forbidden by the censors and then thought lost, it resurfaced again after May 1968.

Vie Est Un Roman, La see Life Is A Bed Of Roses

Vieil Homme Et L'Enfant, Le see Two Of Us, The

Vieille Dame Indigne, La see Shameless Old Lady, The

La Vieille Fille

aka The Old Maid
France 1972 85 mins col
Lira Films(Paris)/Praesidens SPA(Rome)

d **Jean-Pierre Blanc**
sc **Jean-Pierre Blanc**
ph **Pierre Lhomme**
m **Michel Legrand**
Annie Girardot, Philippe Noiret, Michel Lonsdale, Edith Scob, Jean-Pierre Darras, Marthe Keller

Gabriel (Noiret), a carefree, womanizing bachelor, is on his way to Spain when his car breaks down, forcing him to put up at a small seaside hotel on the French border. Taking the only available chair at dinner, he finds himself sitting with Muriel (Girardot), a shy, self-effacing single woman in her thirties. Both are ill-at-ease but, as the days pass, a sympathetic relationship develops between them. This charming vignette slyly and comically observes the idiosyncracies of life in this kind of establishment—man-eating maids, skirt-chasing waiters, highly eccentric guests—while gently delineating the fragile central relationship, which ends on a note of hope, but not certainty, for Muriel. The stars are excellent, the supporting cast superior.

Best Director Berlin 1972

Vie, L'Amour, La Mort, La see Life, Love, Death

Vie Privée see Very Private Affair, A

Vierde Man, Die see Fourth Man, The

Une Vie Sans Joie

aka Catherine

France 1924 75 mins bw
Jean Renoir

d **Albert Dieudonné**
sc **Jean Renoir**
ph **Jean Bachelet, Gibory**
m **Silent**
Catherine Hessling, Albert Dieudonné, Louis Gauthier, Pierre Philippe, Eugénie Naud, Oléo, Pierre Champagne

Catherine, a young servant girl (Hessling), accompanies the tubercular Maurice (Dieudonné) and his family when they move from their village to Nice for the sake of Maurice's health. After his dramatic death, Catherine is forced to fend for herself, helped by a sympathetic prostitute and her pimp. She returns to the village and her former employer, M. Mallet (Gauthier) the Mayor, but when he is vilified for employing a fallen women she runs away. Caught in a storm, Catherine is forced to shelter in a deserted tram car which breaks loose...
Unimaginatively directed by Dieudonné (remembered as Gance's Napoleon), the picture nonetheless offers a climactic romantic rescue in the vein of D.W. Griffith and some outstanding location photography by Bachelet, who would become Renoir's regular cameraman. It is noteworthy as Renoir's first venture into film-making, with a script that anticipates such films as *Nana, La Chienne and Diary Of A Chambermaid* (made in Hollywood) in its sympathetic treatment of low-life characters, contrasted with the hypocrisy of the *bourgeoisie*.

Vieux Pays Où Rimbaud Est Mort, Le see Old Country Where Rimbaud Died, The

---

Viktor Und Viktoria

Germany 1933 101 mins bw
UFA

d **Reinhold Schünzel**
sc **Reinhold Schünzel**
ph **Konstantin Irmen-Tschet**
m **Franz Doelle**
Renate Müller, Hermann Thimig, Adolf Wohlbrück, Hilde Hildebrand, Fritz Odemar, Aribert Wäscher

Viktor (Thimig), a would-be tragedian down on his luck, is reduced to performing in vaudeville as a female impersonator. He meets Susanne (Müller), an equally hapless aspiring singer, and, feeling unwell, persuades her to don drag and appear for him. She is a huge hit, Viktor becomes her manager and they tour their star act through Europe. Needless to say, complications multiply due to the constant switches of gender and wreak havoc with their personal lives. An extremely well-paced and funny comedy, directed with a light touch and lots of *echt* backstage atmosphere. The performances are excellent and Renate Müller, wonderfully relaxed and confident in drag, also has a pleasing singing voice. It was simultaneously made in French as *Georges Et Georgette* with Julien Carette and Meg Lemonnier. Of several subsequent remakes, the best known is Blake Edwards's *Victor/Victoria*, starring his wife Julie Andrews.

Village In The Mist

Angemaeul

South Korea 1983 90 mins col
Hwa-Chun Trading Co

d **Lim Kwon-Taek**
sc **Song Kil-Han**
ph **Jong Il-Song**
m **Kim Jong-Kil**
Ahn Song-Ki, Chong Yun-Hee, Lee Yea-Min, Kim Ji-Yung, Choi Dong-Jun, Jin Bong-Jin

Su-ok (Yun-Hee), a graduate teacher engaged to be married, takes up her first post in a village far from her fiancé and the urban custom and comfort of her home town. She learns that the villagers comprise one large clan, the only outsider being Kae-chol (Song-Ki), a mysterious layabout whose presence disturbs her. Lim Kwon-Taek made his reputation with *Mandala*, a controversial film about Buddhist monks, that was shown at Berlin in 1982. Here he deals with the hidden emotional behaviour and sexual problems that arise in a closed and inbred community. Filming in 'Scope, he calls on a dazzling array of camera and editing effects to give a compelling picture of a way of life that is vanishing in Korea, as well as drawing a perceptive portrait of his young schoolteacher, through whose eyes the life is observed. The movie was made on location in a picturesque village, detailed to be swallowed up by the construction of a dam.

Ville Des Pirates, La see City Of Pirates

Vincent, François, Paul And The Others

Vincent, François, Paul...Et Les Autres

France 1974 118 mins col
Lira Films/President Produzione

d **Claude Sautet**
sc **Jean-Loup Dabadie, Claude Neron, Claude Sautet**
ph **Jean Boffety**
m **Philippe Sarde**
Yves Montand, Michel Piccoli, Serge Reggiani, Gérard Depardieu, Stéphane Audran, Marie Dubois, Antonella Lualdi, Umberto Orsini, Catherine Allégret, Ludmilla Mikael

Machine-shop owner, Vincent (Montand), successful doctor, Francøis (Piccoli), and failed novelist, Paul (Reggiani), are old friends who are pushing fifty; the 'others' are Vincent's young protegé (Depardieu), a boxer and the men's assorted wives and mistresses, most of whom are leaving or have left their partners. The story, if such it can be termed, deals with a period of mid-life crisis for the protagonists, during which they fall back on one another for emotional support. This movie is a paradigm of all that is best and worst about the work of Claude Sautet. It looks very good, boasts clever performances and chronicles middle-class Parisian lifestyle with deft accuracy, but it is overwhelmed by its superficial perfection and the powerful glamour of its all-star cast. The real issues of pain, fear and failure are thus left to lie buried in the hollow at its centre.

Vincent, François, Paul...Et Les Autres see Vincent, François, Paul And The Others

Vingt-Quatre Heures De La Vie D'Une Femme see Twenty-Four Hours In A Woman's Life

Viol, Le see Question Of Rape, A

Violated Love

(US: Rape Of Love)

L'Amour Violé

France 1977 110 mins col
Equinoxe/Dragon/MK2

d **Yannick Bellon**
sc **Yannick Bellon**
ph **Georges Barsky, Pierre William Glenn**
m **Aram Sedefian**
Nathalie Nell, Alain Fourès, Michèle

Simonnet, Pierre Arditi, Daniel Auteuil, Bernard Granger

After the initial trauma of being brutally raped by four young men, a nurse (Nell) starts to ask questions of herself and others, and tries to find a meaning to the crime. The film can be accused of predictability and didacticism, but not of pussyfooting, and it effectively emphasizes the banality of evil.

Violent Summer

Un Soir Sur La Plage

France 1961 85 mins bw
Francos/Mannic/Cocinor/Marceau

d **Michel Boisrond**
sc **Annette Wademant**
ph **L.H. Burel**
m **Michel Durand**
Martine Carol, Jean Desailly, Daliah Lavi, Henri-Jacques Huet, Michel Galabru

Successful author Michel (Huet) goes to stay with rich widow Georgina (Carol) on the Riviera, where she lives with her doctor lover (Desailly) and two children. His visit is marked by strange and sinister happenings, culminating in the beach murder of a retarded girl with whom he has had a fleeting and anonymous sexual encounter. Some intriguing ideas, atmospherically presented, together with an attractive cast, promise a good entertainment. However, both style and content depart a third of the way through, leaving a disappointingly flaccid and unconvincing thriller, foundering on its lost opportunities.

Violette see Violette Nozière

Violette Et François

France 1977 99 mins col
Président Films/FR3

d **Jacques Ruffio**
sc **Jean-Loup Dabadie**
ph **Andreas Winding**
m **Philippe Sarde**
Isabelle Adjani, Jacques Dutronc, Serge Reggiani, Lea Massari, Françoise Arnoul

Violette (Adjani), François (Dutronc) and their baby son live together in a highly unsuitable liaison given their extreme differences of background and, more seriously, of temperament. François, a drifter and a dreamer, shoplifts—first for fun, then seriously, then compulsively. They marry, but nothing changes and, for a while, Violette becomes his accomplice... Goodness only knows what the point of this film is. Half delighting in the youthful high spirits of its protagonists and half aspiring to a moral tale, it's best viewed as a slick, superficial romance, worth watching for the ever-delightful Adjani.

Violette Nozière

(US: Violette)

France 1977 122 mins col
Filmel/Cinevideo/FR3

d **Claude Chabrol**
sc **Odile Barski, Herve Bromberger, Frédéric Grendel**
ph **Jean Rabier**
m **Pierre Jansen**
Isabelle Huppert, Jean Carmet, Stéphane Audran, Bernadette Lafont, Jean-François Garreaud

In 1933, 18-year-old Violette (Huppert), a lower-middle-class Parisian girl, leads a promiscuous life, contracts syphilis, and poisons her mother (Audran) and putative father (Carmet). The mother survives to accuse her daughter of murder. After another bad spell, Chabrol popped back into critical and box-office favour with his sordid but excellently crafted and acted tale based on a true case history. Huppert is particularly impressive in expressing Violette's mixture of innocence and evil. The backgrounds— the parents' small apartment and the Left Bank cafés—are well delineated. It is, however, one of Chabrol's most impersonal films.

Best Actress (Isabelle Huppert) Cannes 1978

Les Violons Du Bal

France 1974 108 mins col/bw
Port Royal/Planfilm

d **Michel Drach**
sc **Michel Drach**
ph **William Lubtchansky (col) Yan Le Masson (bw)**
m **Jean Manuel De Scareno, Jacques Monty**
Michel Drach, Jean-Louis Trintignant, Marie-

José Nat, David Drach, Christian Rist, Nathalie Roussel, Gabrielle Doulcet

Michel Drach attempts to persuade producers to back a film about his own childhood as a Jewish boy in Nazi-occupied France. They demand a star name, whereupon Trintignant materializes as both Drach and his father, while Drach's real-life wife, Nat, plays his wife and his mother, and his son David plays him as a child. Action shifts constantly between past and present in a complex pattern of filmic tricks which, combined with the doubling, make the film at times difficult to follow (or swallow). However, Drach has a firm grasp of his technical manoeuvres as well as drawing a winning performance from his son. For the rest, it's rather old- fashioned—the climactic escape of young Michel, his mother and grandmother on foot to Switzerland the kind of thing that has been done countless times before—but it is sometimes amusing and occasionally inspired, as in the beautifully handled sequences where schoolboy Michel learns that to be Jewish is to invite insult and assault.

Best Actress (Marie-José Nat) Cannes 1974

The Virgin Spring

Jungfrukällan

Sweden 1960 88 mins bw
Svensk Filmindustri

d **Ingmar Bergman**
sc **Ulla Isaksson**
ph **Sven Nykvist**
m **Erik Nordgren**
Max Von Sydow, Brigitta Valberg, Gunnel Lindblom, Brigitta Pettersson

In 14th-century Sweden, a young virgin (Pettersson) is raped and murdered by three swineherds after her half-sister (Lindblom) has invoked a pagan curse. When her father (Von Sydow) avenges his daughter's death, a spring bubbles up from the spot where she died. As in *The Seventh Seal*, Bergman meticulously conjures up a cruel and superstitious medieval world, but with heavier symbols and more unrelieved gloom than in the previous film. The performers, too, have less room to breathe, but there are some haunting visual images created by Nykvist (replacing Gunnar Fischer as Bergman's constant cameraman). Although the film won the International Critics Prize at Cannes, it was, curiously, announced as too good to be judged for the Best Film award.

Best Foreign Film Oscar 1960

Viridiana

Spain 1961 91 mins bw
Uninci/Films 59/Gustavo Alatriste

d **Luis Buñuel**
sc **Luis Buñuel, Julio Alajandro**
ph **José Agayo**
m **Handel**
Silvia Pinal, Fernando Rey, Francisco Rabal, Margarita Lozano, Victoria Zinny

Out of Christian charity, Viridiana (Pinal), a novice about to take her vows who has been abused and cheated by her uncle (Rey) and his bastard son (Rabal), opens up the former's house to a collection of cripples and beggars. As Buñuel's first film made in his native land for 29 years is a savage attack on Catholic mentality and rituals, it was also his last in Spain for many years. Although the script had been unaccountably passed by Franco's censors, the film itself was banned outright in Spain. The notorious set-piece of The Last Supper being enacted by the scum of the earth also caused the Vatican to condemn it. In general, however, the public and critics enjoyed the mordant humour and anti-clericalism, and welcomed Buñuel back to the centre stage of world cinema.

Best Film Cannes 1961

Les Visiteurs Du Soir

(US: The Devil's Envoys)

France 1942 120 mins bw
André Paulvé

d **Marcel Carné**
sc **Jacques Prévert, Pierre Laroche**
ph **Roger Hubert**
m **Joseph Kosma, Maurice Thiriet**
Arletty, Jules Berry, Marie Déa, Alain Cuny, Fernand Ledoux, Marcel Herrand

In 1485, Gilles (Cuny) and Dominique (Arletty), two minstrels, arrive during the celebrations of the betrothal of a baron's daughter (Déa) to a knight (Herrand). But they are really servants of the devil (Berry). Gilles seduces the bride, but forgetting the devil's work, falls in love with her. The first of the two 'escapist' films that Carné and Prévert made during the Occupation (the other was *Les Enfants Du Paradis*) was seen by the French at the time as an allegory of their situation, with the devil as Hitler. None of this comes through today in this stilted, whimsical, medieval fairytale. But there are pleasures in the art design (Alexandre Trauner and Georges Wakhevitch), the photography and (the too long in arriving) Berry in another of his ingratiating villain roles.

Viskingar Och Rop see Cries And Whispers

Visszaesök see Forbidden Relations

I Vitelloni

(US: The Young And The Passionate)
Italy 1953 109 mins bw
Peg/Cité

d **Federico Fellini**
sc **Federico Fellini, Ennio Flaiano, Tullio Pinelli**
ph **Otello Martelli**
m **Nino Rota**
Franco Fabrizi, Franco Interlenghi, Eleonora Ruffo, Alberto Sordi, Leopoldo Trieste, Riccardo Fellini

A group of five layabouts in their late twenties hang around a small Italian seaport, playing pool, drinking, getting up to mischief and day-dreaming. Only Moraldo (Interlenghi) manages to break away and go to Rome. In his second film as solo director, Fellini revisited and re-created, with acute observation and ambivalence, the place and friends he grew up with. (His brother Riccardo plays one of them.) Although critical of these 'overgrown calves' (vitelloni), Fellini and the inseparable music of Rota, lend the whole film an aura of nostalgia, regret and loss of innocence. The director would follow his alter-ego Moraldo (who becomes Marcello) to the big city in *La Dolce Vita*.

Viva La Muerte

Tunisia/France 1971 90 mins col
Isabelle Films/SATPEC

d **Fernando Arrabal**
sc **Fernando Arrabal, Claudine Lagrive**
ph **Jean-Marc Ripert**
m **Jean-Yves Bosseur**
Mahdi Chaouch, Nuria Espert, Anouk Ferjac, Ivan Henriques, Jazia Klibi

Fando (Chaouch), a 12-year-old boy living with his mother (Spanish stage director Espert) and aunt (Ferjac), tries to discover the fate of his gentle father (Henriques) who disappeared. Memories and visions intrude upon his mind as he finds out that his mother betrayed his father to Franco's police for being a 'Red' and an atheist. The *avant-garde* Spanish novelist and playwright Arrabal's first film might have had a serious intent, presenting an indictment of tyranny, but, in reality, it is drowned in an excessive flow of grotesque, ugly, visceral and perverse images. Among these are a priest being forced to eat his own genitals, a city drowned in urine, female masturbation, the biting off of a lizard's head... The film, therefore, can only be recommended to those who find such activities appealing, such metaphors illuminating or who are interested in the outer reaches of the Surrealist movement. There were enough of them to make it a cult midnight movie in New York at the time.

Viva Maria!

France 1965 120 mins col
Nouvelles Éditions/Artistes Associés/Vides

d **Louis Malle**
sc **Louis Malle, Jean-Claude Carrière**
ph **Henri Decaë**
m **Georges Delerue**
Jeanne Moreau, Brigitte Bardot, George Hamilton, Paulette Dubost, Claudio Brook

The Two Marias (Moreau and Bardot), a double song 'n' dance act working in an un-specified Central American state, both fall in love with a revolutionary leader (Hamilton) whom they help in the struggle to overthrow the country's dictator. The gaiety of this large scale extravaganza was in complete contrast to the solemnity of *Le Feu Follet* (1963). Filmed in colour and on location in mexico, it wittily takes off the kind of big production it is. France's two top female stars seemed to relish the zestful occasion and their partnership, as did the public. A great many critics enjoyed it less.

Vivement Dimanche see Finally Sunday

Vivre Pour Vivre see Live For Life

Vivre Sa Vie see It's My Life

Vizi Privati, Pubbliche Virtù see Private Vices And Public Virtues

Vlyudyakh see My Apprenticeship

The Voice Of The Water

De Stem Van Het Water

Netherlands 1966 82 mins col
Haanstra's Filmproductie

d **Bert Haanstra**
sc **Bert Haanstra**
ph **Anton Von Munster**
m **Robert Heppener**

Haanstra's acclaimed film, three years in the making, observes the relationship of the Dutch people with the water that is their main ally and their greatest threat. Using a simple, clear-cut approach, matched by vivid and unpretentious camerawork, the director shows us all manner of ordinary people engaged in all manner of activities connected with water: eel fishermen, brave tugboat sailors, children skating. The people are viewed with affection, the water with respect, and not all the incidents are happy ones. A little gem of documentary film-making, accompanied by an economical and charming English commentary, it is alas, sometimes screened shorn of a good half-hour.

Voici Les Temps Des Assassins see Murder À La Carte

Voie Lactée, La see Milky Way, The

Voile Bleu, Le see Blue Veil, The

Voina I Mir see War And Peace

Vokzal Dlya Dvoikh see Station For Two, A

Voleur, Le see Thief Of Paris, The

Volpone

France 1940 98 mins bw
Ile de France Productions

d **Maurice Tourneur**
sc **Jules Romains, Stefan Zweig**
ph **Armand Thirard**
m **Marcel Delannoy**
Harry Baur, Louis Jouvet, Fernand Ledoux, Marion Dorian

Volpone (Baur), a wealthy Venetian merchant, with the aid of his servant Mosca (Jouvet), decides to pretend to be dying in order to watch the reactions of his 'friends' as they jostle to inherit his money. One of the few of Maurice Tourneur's sound films of interest, this Gallic version of Ben Jonson's classic comedy boasts two memorable performances from Baur and Jouvet. The director's eye for pictorial composition and décor that so suited his Hollywood fantasies, such as *The Blue Bird* (1918), and his taste for literature are fairly well satisfied in this lavishly presented production.

Volver A Empezar see To Begin Again

Voskhozhdenie see Ascent, The

Voyage Dans La Lune, Le see Trip To The Moon

Voyage Surprise

France 1946 85 mins bw
Pathé-Consortium Cinema

d **Pierre Prévert**
sc **Jacques Prévert, Pierre Prévert**
ph **Sinoël**
m **Joseph Kosma**

Jean Bourgoin, Maurice Baquet, Brevant, Pierre Prévert, Piéral, Martine Carol

The life-long dream of an old man (Bourgoin) is to organize a 'voyage surprise' or mystery tour by coach. In spite of the machinations of wicked competitors, he is finally able to carry it off with results that neither he nor his eccentric passengers could ever have imagined. The third and final feature made by the Brothers Prévert is a fast and furious fantasy, a delightful *voyage surprise* in itself, featuring anarchists, evil Grand Duchesses and comic cops. Pierre Prévert died in his 82nd year in 1988, eleven years after his writer brother.

Voyage To Cythera

Taxidi Sta Kithira

Greece 1984 149 mins col

Cinema Centre of Greece/RAI/Channel 4/ Greek TV/ZDF/Angelopoulos Productions

d **Theo Angelopoulos**
sc **Theo Angelopoulos, Theo Valtinos, Tonino Guerra**
ph **Giorgios Triantafyllou**
m **Helen Karapiperis**

Manos Katrakis, Giulio Brogi, Mary Chronopoulou, Dionyssis Papayannopoulos, Dora Volanaki

An old man (Katrakis), a Communist fighter in the Civil War, returns to Greece after more than 30 years' exile in the Soviet Union. He attempts to come to terms with his country and the wife and family he hardly knows. A knowledge of Greek politics would be a help in understanding this lengthy, oblique and taciturn drama. In fact, it is so understated that the spectator has to fill in a great deal. Yet the long takes against urban landscapes have a mesmeric effect and the man's plight is genuinely moving. The last impressive long shot of him and his wife adrift on a raft has a strong symbolic impact.

Voyou, Le see Simon The Swiss

Vozvrashcheniye Maksima see Return Of Maxim, The

Vrazda Po Cesky see Murder Czech Style

Vredens Dag see Day Of Wrath

Všichni Dobří Rodaci see All My Good Countrymen

The Vyborg Side

Vyborgskaya Storona

USSR 1939 120 mins bw

Lenfilm

d **Grigori Kozintsev, Leonid Trauberg**
sc **Grigori Kozintsev, Leonid Trauberg**
ph **Andrei Moskvin, G. Filatov**
m **Dmitri Shostakovitch**

Boris Chirkov, Valentina Kibardina, Mikhail Zharov, Natalia Uzhvi, Maxim Strauch, Mikhail Gelovani

After the Revolution in 1917 and the capture of the Winter Palace, Maxim (Chirkov) is put in charge of the State Bank as political commissar and has meetings with Lenin (Strauch) and Stalin (Gelovani). His comrade Natasha (Kirbardina) becomes a judge and Dimba (Zharov), the billiards-playing clerk, an 'anarchist activist.' The responsibilities of the characters in the new state also seemed to weigh more heavily on the shoulders of Kozintsev and Trauberg, whose direction lost some of the sparkle of *The Youth Of Maxim* and *The Return Of Maxim*. However, there are still some memorable scenes—Maxim's embarrassment when offered his position—fine pictorial compositions and the finely etched portraits of Lenin and Stalin. The character of Maxim became so popular that Chirkov was called upon to play him in further pictures.

Vyborgskaya Storona see Vyborg Side, The

Vzlomshchik see Burglar

W

Wachsfigurenkabinett, Das see Waxworks

Waga Ai see When A Woman Loves

Waga Koi Wa Moenu see My Love Has Been Burning

The Wages Of Fear
Le Salaire De La Peur

France 1953 140 mins bw
Filmsonor/CICC/Vera

d **Henri-Georges Clouzot**
sc **Henri-Georges Clouzot**
ph **Armand Thirard**
m **Georges Auric**
Yves Montand, Folco Lulli, Peter Van Eyck, Charles Vanel, Vera Clouzot, William Tubbs

Four down-and-outs in a sleazy South American town agree to risk their lives transporting two truckloads of highly dangerous nitro-glycerine over treacherous roads to an oil field 300 miles away. One of the most successful French films of all time, it is also one of the most suspenseful ever made. Clouzot, shooting on location in the South of France, brilliantly creates the sweaty atmosphere of the tropics where his disenchanted and greedy characters are put through the mill. A high-octane thriller in every sense.

Best Film Cannes 1953
Best Actor (Charles Vanel) Cannes 1953
Best Film Berlin 1953

Waiting Women
(US: Secrets Of Women)
Kvinnors Väntan

Sweden 1952 107 mins bw
Svensk Filmindustri

d **Ingmar Bergman**
sc **Ingmar Bergman**
ph **Gunnar Fischer**
m **Erik Nordgren**
Anita Björk, Maj-Britt Nilsson, Eva Dahlbeck, Gerd Andersson, Aino Taube, Jarl Kulle, Birger Malmsten, Gunnar Björnstrand

While a group of women wait for their husbands to join them for the summer, three of them relate decisive incidents in their married lives. Rakel (Björk) recalls a friend who wanted to seduce her while her husband was away; Marta (Nilsson) remembers a Swedish artist she met in Paris; and Karin (Dahlbeck) recounts the time she was stuck in a lift with her husband. A good example of Bergman's early concern with relations between the sexes, particularly from a woman's point of view. The first two tales belong on the dark side, but the last episode is a sardonic comedy, beautifully written and delightfully played by Dahlbeck and Björnstrand.

Walking, Walking see Camminacammina

Walkover
Walkower

Poland 1965 78 mins bw
Syrena/Film Polski

d **Jerzy Skolimowski**
sc **Jerzy Skolimowski**
ph **Antoni Nurzynski**
m **Andrzej Trzaskowski**
Aleksandra Zawieruszanka, Jerzy Skolimowski, Krzystof Chamiec, Elzbieta Czyżewska, Andrzej Herder

On the eve of his thirtieth birthday, rootless

amateur boxer Andrzej (Skolimowski) meets Teresa (Zawieruszanka), a girl he had known at university before he was expelled. After spending the night with her, he enters a boxing tournament at a factory, winning it by a walkover. Skolimowski, a former amateur boxer himself, had made a documentary called *Boxing* (1961). Following his first feature, *Identification Marks: None*, he presents here another picture of an equivocal outsider. Making use of a moving camera and long takes, the entire film consists of only 29 shots. The film has a brittle energy, creates a feeling for the industrial locale and poses questions about competition and aging.

Walkower see Walkover

The Wall
aka Güney's The Wall
Duvar
aka Le Mur

France 1983 117 mins col
Güney Productions/MK2 Productions/TF1 Films/Ministère De La Culture

d **Yilmaz Güney**
sc **Yilmaz Güney**
ph **İzzet Akay**
m **Ozan Garip Şahin, Setrak Bakirel**
Tuncel Kurtiz, Ayse Emel Mesci, Selahattin Kuzuoğlu, Şaban, Şişo, Ziya, Garip, Zapata, Mankafa, Malik Berrichi, Nicolas Hossein

A Turkish prison is full of both criminal and political prisoners. In Dormitory 4 the young boys are treated like slaves by the sadistic guards. When they revolt, the riot is brutally quelled. This searing, almost unbearably powerful film was the first directed by Güney in person since 1974 when he was imprisoned. It was made in Turkish in France where Güney lived in exile until his death in 1984. He based his screenplay on an actual revolt of children in Ankara prison in March 1976, and claimed to have softened the facts. 'In blood, fire and tears, walled in, they sought water and light. I dedicate this film to these young friends in this quest'—Yilmaz Güney.

The Walls Of Malapaga
Au Dela Des Grilles
aka Le Mura Di Malapaga

France/Italy 1949 91 mins bw
Francinex

d **René Clément**
sc **Jean Aurenche, Pierre Bost**
ph **Louis Page**
m **Roman Vlad**
Jean Gabin, Isa Miranda, Vera Talchi, Andrea Checchi, Robert Dalban

Having killed his mistress, a Frenchman (Gabin) stows away aboard a ship to Italy. Suffering from toothache, he gets off in Genoa only to have his money and papers stolen. He meets up with a lonely waitress (Miranda) and her young daughter (Talchi) and realizes he loves her—too late, for the authorities catch up with him. Clément's almost plotless, bilingual film with its understated script that nonetheless speaks volumes, is a simple and honest slice of life in which two lost and lonely people find temporary solace together—in this instance, complicated by the bewildered jealousy of the little girl, played with remarkable expressiveness by Talchi. Gabin, trading in his familiar mix of tenderness and cynicism, is perfectly cast, while Miranda brings subtlety and complexity to the waitress. It is a sad film, played against the awful reality of the war-torn Genoese slums and ending on a note of hopelessness.

Best Director Cannes 1949
Best Actress (Isa Miranda) Cannes 1949

The Wanderer
Le Grand Meaulnes

France 1967 104 mins col
Madeleine

d **Jean-Gabriel Albicocco**
sc **Jean-Gabriel Albicocco, Isabelle Rivière**
ph **Quinto Albicocco**
m **Jean-Pierre Bourtayre**
Jean Blaise, Alain Libolt, Brigitte Fossey, Alain Noury, Juliette Villard

In the small town of Sologne at the turn of the century, the young Augustin Meaulnes (Blaise) falls deeply in love with Yvonne De Galais (Fossey), a beautiful and mysterious girl whom he meets at a strange house party. When she disappears, he searches for her and for his lost adolescence. Alain Fournier's popular young people's classic waited 30 years before Isabelle Rivière agreed to allow her brother's work to be filmed. Despite her participation in the screenplay, it is a far too frenetic and flashy attempt to re-create the fairy-tale atmosphere of the novel in visual terms, but it remains the director's only film to make an impact outside France.

Wanderers, The see Gens Du Voyage, Les

The Wandering Jew

L'Ebreo Errante

Italy 1948 97 mins bw
Distributori Indipendenti

d **Goffredo Alessandrini**
sc **Goffredo Alessandrini, Ennio De Concini, Anton Giulio Majano**
ph **Vaclav Vich**
m **Enzio Masetti**
Vittorio Gassman, Valentina Cortese, Noelle Norman, Pietro Sharoff

A young and wealthy Jew (Gassman) collaborates with the Nazis when they take over Paris but, realizing his treachery, allows himself to be sent to a concentration camp. He escapes with the girl he loves (Cortese), but returns in order to save others from execution. Director Alessandrini had made several award-winning propaganda films for Mussolini and must here have been exorcising his guilt. In so doing, he came up with a poignant film, well acted and using a big budget to good effect. However, the symbol of the Wandering Jew is clumsily and not too coherently woven into the plot.

The Wanton

(US: The Cheat)

Manèges

France 1950 90 mins bw
Films Modernes/Discina

d **Yves Allégret**
sc **Jacques Sigurd**
ph **Jean Bourgoin**
m **Paul Misraki**
Simone Signoret, Bernard Blier, Frank Villard, Jane Marken

A dull middle-aged owner of a riding school (Blier) marries a much younger woman (Signoret), and is bled dry by her and her greedy mother (Marken). When she is paralyzed in an accident, both her husband and lover (Villard) desert her. A moody, glum but accomplished little melodrama, it finally fails to involve because of its lack of any sympathetic characters. The flashback is quite cleverly used to reveal the truth after we first see the minx (Signoret, languorous) through the eyes of her devoted husband (Blier, dogged). Signoret's subsequent divorce from first husband Allégret made this their last film together.

Wanton Contessa, The see Senso

War And Peace

Voina I Mir

USSR 1966-1967 507 mins col
Mosfilm

d **Sergei Bondarchuk**
sc **Sergei Bondarchuk, Vasily Solovyov**
ph **Anatoli Petritsky**
m **Vyacheslav Ovchinnikov**
Ludmila Savelyeva, Sergei Bondarchuk, Vyacheslav Tikhonov, Anastasia Vertinskaya, Vasily Lanovoi, Irina Skobotseva

How Napoleon's invasion of Russia in 1812 affected the lives of two upper-class families, centering on the love of clumsy, myopic Pierre (Bondarchuk) for his vivacious young cousin Natasha (Savelyeva), and her marriage to army officer Andrei (Tikhonov). This four-part, eight-hour, 70mm, $100 million epic is a remarkable achievement. Never just content to use the vast resources at his disposal to illustrate the literary masterpiece, Bondarchuk attempts to find visual equivalents of Tolstoy's prose. The Battle of Borodino, is not only a breathtaking spectacle, but Pierre becomes the spectator's surrogate in the midst of the horror. The film's frequent lapses into grandiloquence and its reliance on the dissolve don't detract from the stunning use of overhead tracking shots, split- screen techniques and the subjective camera.

Best Foreign Film Oscar 1968

The War Is Over

La Guerre Est Finie

France 1966 122 mins col
Sofracima/Europa Film

d **Alain Resnais**
sc **Jorge Semprun**

ph **Sacha Vierny**
m **Giovanni Fusco**
Yves Montand, Ingrid Thulin, Geneviève Bujold, Michel Piccoli, Paul Crauchet, Jean Bouise, Jean Dasté

An aging and tired Spanish revolutionary exile in Paris (Montand) remembers his experiences during the Civil War but has to face the fact that his 25 years of struggle against Franco have achieved nothing. Resnais' masterly technique of shifting between temporal and mental states does not disguise the fact that this portrait of a man imprisoned by his past is simplistic and monotonous. The sensual sex scenes seem to have been influenced by Godard's *A Married Woman* (1964). The screenplay by Spanish exile Semprun received an Oscar nomination.

Warning Shadows

Schatten

Germany 1923 62 mins bw
Pan Film/Dafu Film Verleih

d **Arthur Robison**
sc **Rudolf Schneider, Arthur Robison**
ph **Fritz Arno Wagner**
m **Silent**
Fritz Kortner, Ruth Weyher, Alexander Granach, Gustav Von Wangenheim, Fritz Rasp

A travelling showman (Granach) enters a country mansion and introduces himself to the host (Kortner), his wife (Weyher) and their four guests, one of them the wife's effete young lover (Von Wangenheim). He puts them all under hypnosis so that they can act out their subconscious desires, which has a beneficial effect on the marriage. One of the most celebrated of the films of the period of German Expressionism called Caligarism (after the first manifestation of the genre, *The Cabinet Of Dr Caligari*), was subtitled 'A Nocturnal Hallucination'. The shadowy camerawork and the strange settings by Albin Grau (credited with the 'idea' for the film) create an atmosphere in which the highly erotic pschyodrama takes place.

Warnung Vor Einer Heiligen Nutte see Beware Of A Holy Whore

The War Of The Buttons

La Guerre Des Boutons

France 1962 95 mins bw
Productions De La Guéville

d **Yves Robert**
sc **Yves Robert, François Boyer**
ph **André Bac**
m **José Berghmans**
André Treton, Michel Isella, Martin Lartigue, Jean Richard, Yvette Etievant, Jacques Dufilho

Two rival gangs of small boys wage a daily battle in a sandpit between their two villages, taking prisoners whose belts, braces and buttons are cut off. Lebrac (Treton), leader of one gang, conceives the idea of surprising the other side by going into battle naked and chalks up a victory. As the war games become more elaborate, the parents have to intervene and Lebrac and his rival counterpart (Isella) end up in a reformatory. Robert's film, inarguably picturesque, occasionally satirical and sometimes humorous, is also cutesy-cutesy and a little insipid (which didn't stop the British censor X-rating it on the grounds of some mild bad language), although the director coaxes good performances from the boys. The movie was a huge commercial success on initial release, but it's unlikely to appeal much to those more interested in the infinitely complex and unequivocally nasty *The Lord Of The Flies.*

Warrior's Rest

Le Repos Du Guerrier

France 1962 101 mins col
Francos Films(Paris)/Incei(Rome)

d **Roger Vadim**
sc **Claude Choublier, Roger Vadim**
ph **Armand Thirard**
m **Michel Magne**
Brigitte Bardot, Robert Hossein, James Robertson Justice, Jean-Marc Bory, Jacqueline Porel

Geneviève (Bardot), young, beautiful and wealthy, is suitably engaged to Pierre (Bory). In Dijon on business, she wanders into the wrong hotel room by mistake and finds Renaud (Hossein), an alcoholic, collapsed after attempting suicide. The encounter leads to a passionate affair in which he initiates her into the joys of uninhibited sex and the pain of abuse and degradation. Eschewing the subtleties of the novel by Christiane Rochefort on which this is based, Vadim and Choublier have come up with a superficial screenplay which, while allowing Bardot to flex her acting muscles a little and casting her in the unusual role of emotional and moral redeemer, offers more than its fair share of titillation and nudity. The resolution is both mawkish and ludicrous. Nevertheless, it was a huge hit in Paris on release.

Warui Yatsu Yoku Nemuru see Bad Sleep Well, The

Warum Läuft Herr R Amok see Why Does Herr R Run Amok?

The Watchmaker Of St Paul

L'Horloger De St Paul

France 1973 105 mins col
Lira

d **Bertrand Tavernier**
sc **Jean Aurenche, Pierre Bost, Bertrand Tavernier**
ph **Pierre William Glenn**
m **Philippe Sarde**
Philippe Noiret, Jean Rochefort, Sylvain Rougerie, Christine Pascal

A watchmaker (Noiret), living a quiet life in a suburb of Lyons, is stunned when he learns that his son is wanted for the murder of a factory owner. He is then forced to reconsider his life as a man and father. Former critic Tavernier made his name with this well-crafted, intelligent debut feature based on a story by Georges Simenon, transferred from the USA to the director's home town. The social detail and the interplay between Noiret and Rochefort, as a police inspector, are the best parts of the rather clockwork plot.

Special Jury Prize Berlin 1974

Waterless Summer

aka I Had My Brother's Wife
(US: Dry Summer)
Susuz Yaz

Turkey 1964 84 mins bw
Hitit Film

d **Ismail Metin**
sc **Jim Lehner**
ph **Ali Ugur**
m **Manos Hadjidakis**
Ulvi Dogan, Errol Tash (Erol Tas), Julie Kotch (Hülya Kocyigit), members of the Jerusalem Theatre Arts Players, The Athens Hellenic Theatre, The Istanbul Theatre Of Performing Arts

During a drought, tyrannical landowner Osman (Tash) shuts off the water supply to neighbouring farmers, in opposition to his brother Hassan (Dogan). He spies on Hassan and his wife making love. Violent protest springs up in the district, in the course of which Osman kills a farmer, but Hassan takes the blame. While he is in prison, Osman tries to alienate Hassan's wife after whom he lusts. Metin's film is, overwhelmingly, about sexual frustration, for which the drought and its consequences become an extended metaphor. The action and images are deliberately repetitive and the music insistent, but it is a hypnotic rather than a monotonous experience.

Best Film Berlin 1964

Waxworks

Das Wachsfigurenkabinett

Germany 1924 93 mins bw
Neptun-Film

d **Paul Leni**
sc **Henrik Galeen**
ph **Helmar Lerski**
m **Silent**
Wilhelm Dieterle, Emil Jannings, Conrad Veidt, Werner Krauss, Olga Belajeff

A young poet (Dieterle) in a fairground wax museum tells the story of three of the exhibits—Haroun-al-Raschid (Jannings), Ivan the Terrible (Veidt) and Jack the Ripper (Krauss). 'I have tried to create sets so stylized that they evince no ideas of reality,' wrote Paul Leni, the director of one of the best examples of German Expressionism on film. The lighting and the remarkable designs by Leni, Alfred Junge and Ernst Stern are symbolic of character and plot, creating a sinister atmosphere. It was Leni's last film as a director in Germany (he continued to design) before continuing his contribution to the horror genre at Universal Studios in Hollywood. He died of blood poisoning in 1929 aged 44.

The Way To Bresson

De Weg Naar Bresson

Netherlands 1984 54 mins col/bw
Frans Rasker

d **Jurrien Rood, Leo De Boer**
sc **Jurrien Rood, Leo De Boer**
ph **Deen Van Der Zaken**
Robert Bresson, Louis Malle, Dominique Sanda, Paul Schrader, Andrei Tarkovsky

A series of interviews, interspersed with short illustrative clips from his films, on the work of the highly individualistic French director, Robert Bresson. It is divided, not altogether satisfactorily, into segments with subtitles such as 'camera', 'actors', 'theory', and so forth, which tend to disturb the flow and, on occasion grow a little portentous. Unsurprisingly, perhaps, the tone is one of undiluted veneration and the film frustrates in being too short to explore its subject with sufficient thoroughness. However, the documentary's great triumph is the rare presence of the great director himself, an elusive man who, by 1984, had made just 13 films in a 40-year long career.

Ways In The Night see Night Paths

Ways Of Love see Amore, L'

We All Loved Each Other So Much

C'Eravamo Tanto Amati

Italy 1975 136 mins col/bw
Dean Cinematografica/Delta

d **Ettore Scola**
sc **Age, Furio Scarpelli, Ettore Scola**
ph **Claudio Cirillo**
m **Armando Trovaioli**
Nino Manfredi, Vittorio Gassman, Stefania Sandrelli, Stefano Satta Flores, Giovanna Ralli, Aldo Fabrizi

Three men from different backgrounds have been bound by their friendship for 30 years since they met as partisans in World War II, and through their love for the beautiful Luciana (Sandrelli). The lives of Antonio (Manfredi), a good-natured, politically active proletarian, Gianni (Gassman), a *bourgeois* opportunist, and Nicola (Flores), a radical intellectual film buff, are paralleled by the history of Italian cinema over the years. This often moving, sometimes sentimental, amusing and humanistic study of friendship also offers an added pleasure to the film fan. There are extracts from films by directors Michelangelo Antonioni, Roberto Rossellini, Luchino Visconti, Vittorio De Sica (to whom the film is dedicated) and Federico Fellini, the last two appearing as themselves, and there are film pastiches, some good, some crass.

We Are All Murderers see Are We All Murderers?

Web Of Passion

aka Leda

À Double Tour

France 1959 110 mins col
Paris/Panitalia

d **Claude Chabrol**
sc **Paul Gégauff**
ph **Henri Decaë**
m **Paul Misraki**
Jacques Dacqmine, Madeleine Robinson, Jean-Paul Belmondo, Bernadette Lafont, Antonella Lualdi, André Joselyn

When the beautiful mistress (Lualdi) of a wealthy wine merchant (Dacqmine) is murdered, tensions grow in the man's Provençal house among his neurotic wife (Robinson), mother-fixated son (Joselyn), wilful daughter (Lafont) and her uncouth Hungarian fiancé (Belmondo). Chabrol, using colour for the first time, seems dazzled by its decorative possibilities, particularly in the Japanese style of the mistress' home. Beneath the gloss is a gimmicky second-rate thriller, told in a banal flashback form with a Hollywood ending. Only a glimpse of Belmondo's *Breathless* character of the following year holds the interest.
Best Actress (Madeleine Robinson) Venice 1959

The Wedding

Wesele

Poland 1972 110 mins col

Film Polski/Plan Film Unit

d **Andrzej Wajda**
sc **Andrzej Kijowski**
ph **Witold Sobocinski**
m **Stanislaw Radwan**
Ewa Zietek, Daniel Olbrychski, Andrzej Lapícki, Wojciech Pszoniak, Franciszek Pieczka, Maya Komorowska

When a girl (Zietek) in a small village near Cracow marries a poet (Olbrychski), her painter brother-in-law gives a wedding party to which he invites artists, intellectuals, a city journalist, a priest, and a mystically 'possessed' Jewish girl (Komorowska). The celebrations give way to rumours of border war, the headman arms the peasants, and the wedding guests fall prey to visions. Wajda, working from a famous stage play by Stanislaw Wyspianski, made this film during his 'literary' period when censorship threatened his contemporary political dramas. Here, he deliberately fuses fantasy and reality, dreams and legends, bringing some 20 years of experience to his masterly control of changing pace and mood, but failing to avoid a certain confusion.

Wedding In Blood see Blood Wedding

Weekend

France 1967 105 mins col

Lira/Comacico/Copernic/Ascot Cineraid

d **Jean-Luc Godard**
sc **Jean-Luc Godard**
ph **Raoul Coutard**
m **Mozart, Antoine Duhamel**
Mireille Darc, Jean Yanne, Jean-Pierre Léaud, Juliet Berto, Anne Wiazemsky

A *bourgeois* couple (Darc and Yanne), driving into the country from Paris, find themselves in a nightmare of traffic jams, car crashes, murder, destruction and cannibalism. A virtuoso piece of film-making and the most devastating of attacks on modern society and the motor car. This is best captured in the famous 10-minute tracking shot along miles of immobile vehicles, irate drivers, and the injured and dead victims of accidents. The impact is occasionally lessened when Godard decides to explore some of the byways of the main theme.

Weekend At Dunkirk

Week-End À Zuydcoote

France 1964 119 mins col

Paris Film(Paris)/Interopa(Rome)

d **Henri Verneuil**
sc **François Boyer**
ph **Henri Decaë**
m **Maurice Jarre**
Jean-Paul Belmondo, Catherine Spaak, Georges Géret, Jean-Pierre Marielle, Pierre Mondy, Marie Dubois, François Périer, Kenneth Haigh, Ronald Howard

In June 1940, thousands of French and English troops are trapped on the Dunkirk beaches as the Germans advance. Four Frenchman camp in an abandoned ambulance: a courageous sergeant (Belmondo), a man only interested in saving his own skin (Mondy), a chaplain (Marielle) and a resourceful fellow who finds them supplies (Périer). What befalls them and the sergeant's efforts to save a local girl (Spaak) in danger form the substance of the action. This French view of a famous episode in World War II which has provided so much film fodder for Britain and America, is distinguished by the truthfulness of the battle scenes and the exceptional photography by Decaë. The personal stories, however, in spite of the cast's best efforts, are banal and melodramatic.

Week-End À Zuydcoote see Weekend At Dunkirk

A Week's Holiday

Une Semaine De Vacances

France 1980 103 mins col

Sara Films/Antenne 2/Little Bear

d **Bertrand Tavernier**
sc **Bertrand Tavernier, Marie-Françoise Hans, Colo Tavernier**
ph **Pierre William Glenn**
m **Pierre Papadiamandis**

Nathalie Baye, Michel Galabru, Flore Fitzgerald, Gérard Lanvin

A Lyons schoolteacher (Baye) in her early thirties suffers from severe depression as a result of a crisis of faith in her work and unresolved differences in her relationship with her lover. On doctor's orders she takes a week's holiday, during which she visits her parents and has several encounters, notably with the father of one of her pupils, and decides to return to teaching. Placed specifically in time—winter, 1980—and place—Lyons, its landscapes filmed with loving detail—this is a somewhat glib and self-satisfied comment on the life it reveals, with everything sliding rather too neatly into place. Nonetheless, it is reasonably entertaining and intelligent.

Wege In Der Nacht see Night Paths

Weg Naar Bresson, De see Way To Bresson, The

Weib Des Pharao, Das see Wife Of Pharaoh, The

Weisse Hölle Vom Piz Palü, Die see White Hell Of Pitz Palu, The

---

Welcome, Mr Marshall

Bienvenido, Mr Marshall

Spain 1952 75 mins bw
UNINCI

d **Luis Berlanga**
sc **Luis Berlanga, Juan Antonio Bardem**
ph **Manuel Berenguer**
m **Jesús García Leoz**
Lolita Sevilla, Manolo Moran, José Isbert, Alberto Romea, Elvira Quintilla

The news that a Marshall Plan commission intends to visit a poor village in Castille causes the inhabitants to make what they can of their surroundings in order to create a good impression on the visiting Americans in the hope of getting financial aid. American diplomats and Edward G. Robinson, a member of the Cannes Festival jury, mistakenly denounced the film for its anti-American bias, for it is far more a sardonic look at Spanish foibles and greed. Pointedly written and observed, the film is an example of 'Spanish Neo-Realism', taking the style from the Italians but without the freedom to criticize the system directly. It was one of Spain's biggest international successes during the Franco years.

The Well-Digger's Daughter

La Fille Du Puisatier

France 1940 131 mins bw
Marcel Pagnol

d **Marcel Pagnol**
sc **Marcel Pagnol**
ph **Willy**
m **Vincent Scotto**
Raimu, Fernandel, Charpin, Josette Day

A crusty old well-digger (Raimu) is shocked to discover that his daughter (Day) has been seduced and abandoned. His simple assistant (Fernandel) agrees to marry her and accept the child as his own. 'The subjects of my films are simple, for I find there is no art outside ordinary places and people,' stated Pagnol. But one of his achievements was to show that the subjects and forms of *bourgeois* drama could be transposed to peasant life. Melodrama it may be, but it is laced through with piquant dialogue, heady Provençal settings, and towering performances from his single-named male stars. The film originally ended with father and daughter being reconciled by listening to a speech by Pétain on the radio. After the Liberation, Pagnol substituted the voice of De Gaulle.

Wend Kuuni see Gift Of God, The

Werther

France 1938 85 mins bw
Nero Film

d **Max Ophüls**
sc **Hans Wilhelm**
ph **Eugen Schüfftan**
m **Henri Herblay (on classical themes)**
Pierre-Richard Willm, Annie Vernay, Jean Galland, Paulette Pax, Henri Guisol

Young Werther (Willm) falls in love with

Charlotte (Vernay), whom he discovers is to be married to his best friend Albert (Galland). He leaves her and begins to lead a dissipated life. Seeing Charlotte again gradually forces him to suicide. Ophüls seemed unsympathetic towards Goethe's *Sorrows Of Young Werther*, as witness his turning of the pre-Romantic 18th-century drama into a wild 19th-century romance, shifting the tragedy from the hero to the heroine and also adding a comic-relief aunt (Pax). There are some pretty country scenes, moments of bravura with the camera and some good acting from Vernay.

Wesele see Wedding, The

Westfront 1918

aka Comrades Of 1918

Germany 1930 96 mins bw
Nero-Film

d **G.W. Pabst**
sc **Laszlo Wajda, Peter Martin Lampel**
ph **Fritz Arno Wagner, Charles Métain**
Gustav Diessl, H.J. Moebis, Fritz Kampers, Claus Clausen, Jackie Monnier

The horror and futility of life in the trenches in general, and for four soldiers in particular, and the ignorance at home of the reality at the Front. Released in the same year as the superior *All Quiet On The Western Front*, Pabst's film also caught the anti-war mood of the times. It captures the monotony and chaos of trench warfare through a series of short scenes and long tracking shots over the battleground. Much of it is now too familiar and the plea for universal brotherhood is expressed in a naive manner.

We Were One Man

Nous Étions Un Seul Homme

France 1978 90 mins col
Sou Mau

d **Philippe Vallois**
sc **Philippe Vallois**
ph **François About**
m **Jean Jacques Ruhlmann**
Serge Avédikian, Piotr Stanislas, Catherine Albin

Guy (Avédikian), a patient escaped from a mental hospital, lives in an isolated cottage during 1943. When he discovers Rolf, a wounded German soldier, in the woods, he takes him home and a complex friendship develops through which Rolf becomes a deserter since Guy prevents him leaving. Their relationship develops into a homosexual affair until Rolf is captured. Vallois has created an unnerving study of isolation, madness, passion, guilt and betrayal. He eloquently conveys the claustrophobic emotions of his characters, and draws a superb performance from Avédikian, but he presents gay men as a doomed species, here represented by a disturbed neurotic and a Nazi.

We Will Not Grow Old Together

Nous Ne Vieillerons Pas Ensemble

France 1972 107 mins col
Lido Film

d **Maurice Pialat**
sc **Maurice Pialat**
ph **Luciano Tovoli**
m **Haydn**
Marlène Jobert, Jean Yanne, Macha Meril, Jacques Galland, Christine Fabrega, Muse Dalbray

A selfish and domineering married man (Yanne), estranged from his wife (Meril) but still living with her, has been having an affair for six years with a much younger woman (Jobert). Now, inevitably, the relationship is disintegrating, causing pain and confusion to the girl and involving her distressed friends and parents. Pialat's disturbing and truthful film unfolds in a series of perceptive episodes in which the couple alternately indulges in damaging recriminations and tearful reconciliations before finally breaking off the liaison. Script and direction probe and reveal the intricacies of the dying days of a long love affair, lent extra conviction by the uncompromising performances of forceful Yanne and wistful Jobert.

Best Actor (Jean Yanne) Cannes 1972

The Wheelchair

El Cochecito

Spain 1959 81 mins bw
Films 59

d **Marco Ferreri**

sc **Marco Ferreri, Rafael Azcona**
ph **Juan Julio Baena**
m **Miguel Asins Arbó**
José Isbert, Pedro Porcel, José Luis Lopez Vázquez, Maria Luisa Ponte, Lepe, Antonio Gavilán, Angel Alvarez

Don Anselmo (Isbert) lives with his lawyer son and the latter's family. Elderly but fit, he spends much of his time going on outings with a group of cripples in motorized wheelchairs, of whom his best friend is one. He becomes obsessed by the desire to own such a contraption himself and, to this end, does some very strange things. This grotesque and perverse one-joke farce wears very thin very quickly. On the credit side, a couple of scenes are of such absurdity as to become funny in spite of themselves, Isbert plays his ridiculous role with dignity and the evocation of Spanish life, particularly in a middle-class home, is interesting.

Wheel, The see Roue, La

The Wheel

Moul Le Ya, Moul Le Ya

South Korea 1983 105 mins col
Han Lim Cinema Corp

d **Lee Doo-Yong**
sc **Lim Chung**
ph **Lee Sung-Choon**
m **Chung Yun-Ju**
Won Mi-Kyung, Shin Il-Yong, Choi Sung-Kwan, Mun Chung-Sook, Choi Sung-Ha, Mun Mi-Bong

Gil-rye (Won Mi-Kyung), the beautiful daughter of an impoverished scholar, is sold to the wealthy and aristocratic Kim family. They marry her posthumously to their dead son, remind her to protect her chastity and set her to work at a spinning wheel. One day she sees her brother-in-law Han making love with his wife and her own dormant sexual needs are awakened. Han subsequently rapes her and forces her into a regular illicit relationship, the discovery of which leads to his execution and her banishment... The tragedy of Gil-rye is carefully detailed, echoing the style of Mizoguchi. With a perfectly judged central performance from the victim-heroine, it is a period piece which exposes the appalling subjugation of women in a society dominated by men and by rigid social codes and traditions. The title is well-chosen, for Gil-rye is literally broken by the wheel of unhappy fortune on which her fate relentlessly turns.

When A Woman Loves

Waga Ai

Japan 1959 97 mins col
Shochiku

d **Heinosuke Gosho**
sc **Toshio Yasumi**
ph **Haruo Takeno**
m **Yasushi Akutagawa**
Ineko Arima, Shin Saburi, Yatsuko Tan-ami, Nobuko Otowa

At the funeral wake of a renowned journalist and war correspondent (Saburi), a mysterious young girl briefly appears, offering prayers and incense. Afterwards. she reflects on her relationship with the dead man which we see in flashback—a meeting before the war when she is too young for him, another during the war and, several years later, a few months of happiness together in a mountain retreat before he returns to his family. Firmly in the popular tradition of Japanese 'women's pictures', this is a full-blooded weepie romance, backed by a lush Western-style score that would do justice to Hollywood. However, within its genre, it's a superior piece of film-making in every department, displaying the skills of Gosho who, having reached his peak in the mid-1950s, notably with *Where Chimneys Are Seen*, entered a period of unashamed commercial film-making.

When Father Was Away On Business

Otac Na Službenom Putu

Yugoslavia 1985 136 mins col
Forum/Sarajevo Film

d **Emir Kusturica**
sc **Abdulah Sidran**
ph **Vilko Filač**
m **Zoran Simjanović**
Manolo De Bartoli, Miki Manojlović, Mirjana Karanović, Mustafa Nadarević, Mira Furlan, Predrag Laković

In 1950, six-year-old Malik (De Bartoli) lives a normal family life in Sarajevo until Mešac (Manojlović), his womanizing father, is denounced by his mistress as a Stalinist and sentenced to three years' exile. Kusturica's surprise Festival winner gets off to an intolerably slow start. However, once underway, it lives up to its reputation, offering an absorbing, absolutely naturalistic portrait of Yugoslavian customs and politics of the period. Key incidents—among them circumcision, one of Měsac's whoring expeditions, and his avenging rape of his ex-mistress—are seen largely through Malik's young eyes (and reported through his voice-over narrative), lending freshness, poignancy and a deal of comedy to the proceedings. The performances are terrific, especially from Mirjana Karanović as Malik's struggling mother, and the photography first rate.

Best Film Cannes 1985

When Joseph Returns...

Ha Megjön József

Hungary 1975 88 mins col
Hungarofilm

d **Zsolt Kézdi Kovács**
sc **Zsolt Kézdi Kovács**
ph **János Kende**
György Pogány, Lili Monori, Éva Ruttkai, Gábor Koncz, Mária Ronyecz

Mária (Monori), a newly-wed country girl working in a Budapest factory, is left with her mother-in-law Agnes (Ruttkai) when her sailor husband returns to his ship. Agnes takes casual lovers in an attempt to get over her broken marriage while Mária, insecure and lonely, becomes involved in an affair, leaves her job, becomes pregnant and miscarries. Her plight moves Agnes to awareness and concern and, strengthened, the women await Joseph's return. This story of personal suffering and recovery is observed with an unsentimental and accurate eye. Acted with an almost documentary-like veracity, particularly by Monori, it's well photographed, detailing the unhappy life in the women's small flat and the landscape without, with atmospheric precision.

When Moscow Laughs see Girl With The Hatbox

When The Cat Comes

aka That Cat

Až Přijde Kocour

Czechoslovakia 1963 110 mins col
Czech State Film

d **Vojtěch Jasný**
sc **Jiří Brdečka, Vojtěch Jasný**
ph **Jaroslav Kučera**
m **Svatopluk Havelka**
Jan Werich, Vlastimil Brodský, Jiří Sovák, Emilie Vašáryová

A magician (Werich) comes to a small town, bringing his bespectacled cat who is able to see people in their true colours. Thus, cheats appear grey, adulterers yellow, and so forth, while those with nothing to hide remain the same. This inventive film is humorous Czech fantasy at its best (notwithstanding some repetitive sequences), made with lightness and charm by one of Prague's favourite directors of the period. Song, dance and sentiment are adroitly woven into the tale, making it appealing to children, while, for adults, it cocks a cleverly veiled snook at the politics of totalitarianism.

Special Jury Prize Cannes 1963

When The Greeks

Ton Kero Ton Hellinon

Greece 1981 100 mins col
Cinetic/Greek Film Centre

d **Lakis Papastathis**
sc **Lakis Papastathis**
ph **Theodoros Margas**
m **Georges Papadakis**
Alexis Damianos, Kostas Arzoglou, George Sampanis, Stavros Mermighis

A rich, young landowner (Damianos) is kidnapped by a gang of nationalist bandits at the turn of the century. For the first time, he sees the ancient landscape and culture of his own country, and learns to identify with his captors, who seem to be like ancient Greek warriors. Papastathis's debut feature is a poetic meditation on class and culture but, most of all, on what it is to be Greek. Stunningly filmed against splendid landscapes, its highpoints are two beautifully staged rituals—a wedding and a funeral.

When We Were Young

Kak Molody My Byli

USSR 1985 92 mins col

Dovzhenko Studio

d **Mikhail Belikov**

sc **Mikhail Belikov**

ph **Vasily Trushkovsky**

m **Chopin, Gershwin, Y. Vinnik**

Taras Denisenko, Elena Shkurpelo, N. Sharolapova, Aleksander Pashutin, A. Sviridovsky

Teenage Sasha (Denisenko) training as a sanitary engineer while doing a part-time labouring job, is sexually initiated by an older woman, and then marries his childhood friend Yulka (Shkurpelo) who is suffering from a rare blood disease. Spanning a few years from sometime in the 1950s to the day of Gagarin's space flight in 1961, Belikov's film is a muddled exercise in nostalgia which suggests that the protagonists are the 'lost' generation, bridging the gap between the old Russia and the new, whose children will ignite the society of the 1980s. Quite touching, but it suffers from anachronisms and, to a non-Russian viewer, domestic references that are meaningless.

Where Chimneys Are Seen

aka Four Chimneys

Entotsu No Mieru Basho

Japan 1953 108 mins bw

Studio 8 Productions/Shin Toho

d **Heinosuke Gosho**

sc **Hideo Oguni**

ph **Mitsuo Miura**

m **Yasushi Akutagawa**

Ken Uehara, Kinuyo Tanaka, Hiroshi Akutagawa, Hideko Takamine

A struggling, childless, middle-aged couple (Uehara and Tanaka) find themselves having to look after an abandoned baby. The responsibility and the effort required puts a great strain on them and their upstairs neighbours (Akutagawa and Takamine). The baby, however, becomes a positive force in their lives. One of the best surviving examples of 'Goshoism', a distinctive blend of comedy and pathos among a wide range of characters in *shomin-geki*, stories of everyday life. Unlike the other great masters of the genre, Ozu and Naruse, Gosho uses a swift cutting style and mobile camera. In this 'tenement' film, beginning with shots of the chimneys of a smoggy Tokyo, the interior scenes are always resourceful and the ensemble playing is perfect.

The White-Haired Girl

Pai Mao Nu

China 1970 90 mins col

Shanghai Film Studio

d **Sang Hu**

sc **Shanghai Dance School, 'White-Haired Girl' Unit**

ph **Shen Xilin**

m **Revolutionary music and songs**

Mao Huifang, Ling Jiaming, Wang Guojun, Dong Xilin

Xi'er (Huifang), the daughter of a peasant (Xilin) beaten to death by the henchmen of a wicked landlord, is now held prisoner by the landlord. She escapes to the mountains where hardship turns her hair white (the symbol of purity and righteousness). Her boyfriend (Jiaming), who is in the army, comes with his battalion to the town, liberates the peasants, hangs the landlord and is reunited with Xi'er. She joins him in the army to take part in the class struggle. This ballet version of the celebrated Chinese opera of 1944, filmed previously as a realistic drama in 1950, was supervised by Mao Tse-tung's wife, the former film actress and dancer Chiang Ching, at the height of the Cultural Revolution. It was typical of film ballets such as *The Red Detachment Of Women* (1960) and *The East Is Red* (1964), influenced by Western classical choreography, but instilled with revolutionary fervour. Although much of it is naive and monotonous, the heavily made-up faces, the heroic gestures, the distinctive goodies and the baddies have the visual appeal of pop art as well as being able to inspire.

The White Hell Of Pitz Palu

Die Weisse Hölle Vom Piz Palü

Germany 1929 121 mins bw

UFA

d **Arnold Fanck, G.W. Pabst**

sc **Arnold Fanck, G.W. Pabst**

ph **Sepp Allgeier, Richard Angst, Ladislaus Vajda, Hans Schneeberger**

m **Silent**
Gustav Diessl, Leni Riefenstahl, Ernst Petersen, B. Spring

A famous mountain climber (Diessl) returns every year to the place on the 12,000 ft Pitz Palu in the Alps where his wife disappeared on their honeymoon. One day, caught in a storm, he finds himself reunited with his young bride. This most celebrated of 'Mountain Films'—a popular German genre in the 1920s and early 1930s—was both a vivid documentary and a symbolic melodrama. It was shot in conditions of extreme cold by technicians who were expert alpinists and skiers over five months of location work in the Alps. Universal, who bought it for release in the United States, later used much of the footage in many B-movies and serials.

White Nights
Le Notti Bianche

Italy 1957 107 mins bw
Vides/Intermondia/CIAS

d **Luchino Visconti**
sc **Suso Cecchi D'Amico, Luchino Visconti**
ph **Giuseppe Rotunno**
m **Nino Rota**
Maria Schell, Marcello Mastroianni, Jean Marais, Clara Calamai

A young man of slender means (Mastroianni) falls in love with a mysterious girl (Schell) who spends her days dreaming of the lover (Marais) who will one day return to her. In contrast to his first two 'Neo- Realist' films and the operatic-style colour spectacle of *Senso*, Visconti here moved into the misty, dreamlike world of the Dostoevsky story also tackled by Pyriev in 1959 and Bresson in 1971. Whereas those versions were set in 19th-century St Petersburg and modern-day Paris respectively, Visconti's takes place in what passes for contemporary Livorno. But an emphasis on the artificiality of the theatrical settings and the soft-textured photography, gives it an air of feyness despite some magic moments. Only Calamai injects some reality into the proceedings.

White Nights
Beliye Nochi

USSR 1959 97 mins col
Mosfilm

d **Ivan Pyriev**
sc **Ivan Pyriev**
ph **Valentin Pavlov**
m **Rachmaninov, Glazounov, Rossini, Scriabin**
Oleg Strizhenov, Ludmila Marchenko, U.N. Popova

A poor young man (Strizhenov) in love with an enigmatic, gullible girl (Marchenko), dreams every night that he is a romantic hero fighting single-handedly against tyrants and villains and winning the heroine. This was the second of Pyriev's three adaptations from the works of Dostoevsky, the others being *The Idiot* and *The Brothers Karamazov*. It comes off better than the other two because the original is more suited to transference to the screen; it is more compact, and has fewer characters. Unlike Visconti's and Bresson's updating to modern Italy and France respectively, Pyryev has retained the 19th-century St Petersburg setting, recreating Dostoevsky's visionary view of the city. The tragicomic dreams themselves tend towards the fey but the performances of the two leads are admirable.

The White Sheik
Lo Sceicco Bianco

Italy 1952 88 mins bw
Luigi Rovere/PDC/OFI

d **Federico Fellini**
sc **Federico Fellini, Ennio Flaiano, Tullio Pinelli**
ph **Arturo Gallea**
m **Nino Rota**
Alberto Sordi, Brunella Bovo, Leopoldo Trieste, Giulietta Masina, Lilia Landi, Ernesto Almirante

A *petit-bourgeois* couple (Trieste and Bovo) arrive in Rome on their honeymoon, but the bride spends most of the time with her idol (Sordi), an egocentric, womanizing star of *fumetti*, romantic magazine picture stories. Fellini's first solo film, based on a story by Michelangelo Antonioni, is an ironic and touching satire on marriage, illusions, and popular culture. It is already recognizably a Fellini work, although he might have deepened the one-dimensional characters later in his career. It is interesting to note his wife Masina in the small role of the prostitute

Cabiria, the subject of *Nights of Cabiria* four years later.

White White Boy . . ., A see Mirror

Whither Germany? see Kühle Wampe

Whity

W. Germany 1970 95 mins col
Antiteater-X Film

d **Rainer Werner Fassbinder**
sc **Rainer Werner Fassbinder**
ph **Michael Ballhaus**
m **Peer Raben**
Günter Kaufmann, Hanna Schygulla, Ulli Lommel, Harry Baer, Katrin Schaake, Rainer Werner Fassbinder, Ron Randall

Half-black Whity (Kaufmann) is overworked by the Nicholson family until Hanna (Schygulla), a sexually exploited barmaid, incites him to murder his white masters. They end up together in the desert. After putting his new boyfriend Kaufmann in *Gods Of The Plague*, Fassbinder wrote a Western with his 'Bavarian Negro' in the misspelt title role. The tensions and tantrums during the 20-day shoot in Spain became the basis for the director's *Beware The Holy Whore* the following year. Some of this spills over into the atmosphere of this bizarre, sadistic and playful pastiche. However, there are so many personal obsessions on display that audiences may feel quite excluded at times.

Who Looks For Gold

Kdo Hledá Zlaté Dno

Czechoslovakia 1975 98 mins col
Barrandov Studio

d **Jiří Menzel**
sc **Vojtěch Měštan, Rudolf Ráž, Jiří Menzel**
ph **Jaromír Šofr**
m **Jiří Šust, Angelo Michajlov**
Jan Hrušínsky, Jana Giergielová, Julius Pántik, František Husák, Míla Mystíková, Otakar Dadák

Returning to Prague after completing his military service, Lada (Hrušínsky) finds it difficult to adjust to civilian society. Gifted with his hands and able to repair more or less anything from a wristwatch to a motor car, he is put in the way of easy-money jobs by his knowing girlfriend Petra (Giergielová). But Lada is an idealist and, although he loses both Petra and his illusions as a result, he takes a job out in the country with a dam construction outfit. Jiří Menzel's first film after a six-year break has little plot to speak of. However, the director's gift for the telling nuance, his perceptive control of the performances which touch subtle depths of character, and the impact of Šofr's swirling camera (particularly in the dam sequences) make this an absorbing experience.

Whom The Gods Wish To Destroy

Die Nibelungen (Part I: Siegfried Von Xanten Part II: Kriemhild's Rache)

W. Germany 1966 Part I: 91 mins
Part II: 104 mins col
CCC/Avala

d **Harald Reinl**
sc **Harald G. Petersson**
ph **Ernst W. Kalinke**
m **Rolf Wilhelm**
Uwe Beyer (Siegfried), Maria Marlow (Kriemhild), Karin Dor (Brunhild), Rolf Henninger (Gunther), Herbert Lom (Attila), Siegfried Wischnewski (Hagen)

After killing a dragon, Siegfried gains magic powers, undergoes many trials and adventures in winning the hand of Brunhild on behalf of Gunther, and bringing tragedy to his wife Kriemhild. Director Reinl, whose previous claim to fame rested in the odd Karl May Western and cheap Dr Mabuse spin-offs, has gone to town with this colour version of the 13th-century poem which boasts the use of 8,000 extras in one battle scene alone. Slick, spectacular and offering an impressive dragon, it is nonetheless a fairly ludicrous enterprise which will either amuse or offend fans of Fritz Lang's 1920s epic (and scholars of German literature). It is generally shown in Britain and America as one film lasting a total of 53 mins.

Who Saw Him Die?

aka Eeny Meeny Miny Moe

Ole Dole Doff

Sweden 1967 110 mins bw
Svensk Filmindustri

d **Jan Troell**
sc **Claes Engström, Bengt Forslund, Jan Troell**
ph **Jan Troell**
m **Erik Nordgren**
Per Oscarsson, Kerstin Tidelius, Anne-Marie Gyllenspetz, Bengt Ekerot, Harriet Forssell

Martensson (Oscarsson), a schoolteacher at odds with the education system, is able neither to communicate with nor discipline his pupils. Sensing his weakness, they torment him cruelly and highlight his sense of failure, which extends to his unhappy marriage. Inevitably, events terminate his career in a tragic climax. Former schoolteacher Troell shot his second film entirely on location in a Malmö school, using the actual pupils and a fluid 16mm camera, thus lending it a documentary veracity. Although the root causes of Martensson's problems remain unexplored and his point of view is left one-sided, this is an accurate picture of a bleak life in bleak surroundings, lent weight by Oscarsson's powerfully truthful and understated performance.

Best Film Berlin 1968

Who's That Singing Over There?
Ko To Tamo Peva
Yugoslavia 1980 83 mins col
Centar Film

d **Slobodan Šijan**
sc **Dušan Kovačević**
ph **Božidar Nikolić**
m **Vojislav Kostić**
Pavle Vuisić, Aleksandar Berček, Dragan Nikolić, Danilo Stojković, Miodrag and Nenad Kostić

'Somewhere in Serbia, April 5, 1941', a rickety old bus, crammed with a motley group of passengers, tries to make it to Belgrade before the Nazis arrive. This stylish, manic, picaresque, black comedy is an impressive debut feature by director Šijan. The answer to the question of the title is two Gypsies (Miodrag and Nenad Kostić) who act as a chorus by singing the narration. The rest of the travellers are seen purposefully as comic stereotypes, which the splendid cast, nevertheless, present as fully-rounded personages.

Why?
Detenuto In Attesa Di Giudizio
Italy 1971 102 mins col
Documento

d **Nanni Loy**
sc **Sergio Amedei, Amilio Sanna**
ph **Sergio D'Offizi**
m **Carlo Rustichelli**
Alberto Sordi, Elga Andersen, Lino Banfi, Giuseppe Anatrelli, Tano Cimarosa

Giuseppe Di Noi (Sordi), Italian head of a Swedish civil engineering firm, returns to Italy for a holiday with his Swedish wife (Andersen) and two children, but he is arrested at the border by the Italian police for an unspecified crime. He goes from one tough jail to another, suffering physically and mentally, until his case finally comes up. With the popular comic actor Sordi in the lead and the jaunty opening, it comes as a shock when the film moves into the harsh area of a prison exposé. Loy builds up a relentless, rather over-emphatic indictment of a horrific system and cleverly uses Sordi's persona to gain sympathy.

Best Actor (Alberto Sordi) Berlin 1972

Why Does Herr R Run Amok?
Warum Läuft Herr R Amok
W. Germany 1970 88 mins col
Antiteater-Produktion for Maran-Film

d **Rainer Werner Fassbinder, Michael Fengler**
sc **Rainer Werner Fassbinder, Michael Fengler (improvised)**
ph **Dietrich Lohmann**
m **'Geh' Nicht Vorbei' by Christian Anders**
Kurt Raab, Lilith Ungerer, Amadeus Fengler, Franz Maron, Hanna Schygulla

Middle-class and comfortably married with one child, Kurt Raab represents a typical urban species. He has his share of domestic problems, and mars his chances of promotion with an ill-judged speech at the office Christmas party, but no matter. One night, watching TV while his wife chatters to a visiting neighbour, he suddenly picks up a heavy candelabrum, smashes in the women's skulls, and similarly kills his son. A favourite Fassbinder theme—ordinary man destroyed by his inability to cope with modern life—is here based on a case history. The film calls its characters by the actors' names, thus further distancing the audience from any sense of artifice in what is a painfully realistic study. Close examination, however, reveals the characters as stereotypes, and it is a matter of opinion whether Raab's outbreak of violence and subsequent suicide have a valid cause.

Why Not?

Eijanaika

Japan 1981 151 mins col
Shochiku

d **Shohei Imamura**
sc **Shohei Imamura, Ken Miyamoto**
ph **Masahisa Himeda**
m **Shinichiro Ikebe**
Kaori Momoi, Shigeru Izumiya, Ken Ogata, Shigeru Tsuyuguchi, Masao Kusakari

Genji (Japanese rock star Izumiya) returns to 19th-century Japan from a six-year absence in the USA to find his wife (Momoi) has become the mistress of a gangster(Tsuyuguchi). The population around them consists of wandering samurai, murderers, entertainers, whores and gamblers who rise up in revolt against the ruling shogunate screaming the anarchist slogan 'Why not?'. Imamura isn't one to do things by halves and this period film is full of bustling energy, sexuality and violence, captured in bright colours and with a mobile camera—a style that suits the subject.

Wife, Be Like A Rose

Tsuma Yo Bara No Yo Ni

Japan 1935 83 mins bw
PCL/Toho

d **Mikio Naruse**
sc **Mikio Naruse**
ph **Hiroshi Suzuki**
m **Noburu Itoh**
Sachiko Chiba, Sadao Maruyama, Yuriko Hanabusa, Kamatari Fujiwara

On the eve of her marriage, an office worker (Chiba), hoping to reunite her father (Maruyama) with her poet mother (Hanabusa) whom he had left some time before, finds he is perfectly happy with his mistress (Fujiwara) and second family in the country. The 1930s and 1950s were Naruse's two great creative periods and this is a masterwork from the first epoch. The framing, editing and playing are all elegantly controlled in this poignant yet humorous study of a disrupted family, which leads to a shattering climax. Many of Naruse's best films, such as *Repast* (1951), are about marriage break-ups.

The Wife Of Pharaoh

(US: The Loves Of Pharaoh)

Das Weib Des Pharao

Germany 1921 115 mins bw
EFA/UFA/Ernst Lubitsch

d **Ernst Lubitsch**
sc **Norbert Falk, Hans Kräly**
ph **Théodor Sparkühl, Alfred Hansen**
m **Silent**
Emil Jannings, Harry Liedtke, Dagny Servaes, Paul Wegener, Lyda Salmonova

War between Egypt and Ethiopia ensues when the tyrannical Pharaoh Amenes (Jannings) falls in love with Theonis (Servaes), the Greek serving girl of the Ethiopian Princess (Salmonova) he had arranged to marry. Theonis, in turn, loves Ramphis (Liedtke), who eventually becomes Pharaoh. Made on a huge scale, it had 126,000 extras and took ten months to shoot. Considering that the narrative is somewhat confused and the lavish sets tend to overwhelm the players, Lubitsch managed to sustain the atmosphere throughout. The only weak link in the cast was Dagny Servaes who got the part because Pola Negri was unavailable.

Wildcat, The see Mountain Cat, The

The Wild Child

L'Enfant Sauvage

France 1970 84 mins bw
Films Du Carrosse/Artistes Associés

d **François Truffaut**
sc **François Truffaut, Jean Gruault**
ph **Nestor Almendros**
m **Vivaldi**
Jean-Pierre Cargol, Jean Dasté, François Truffaut, Françoise Seigner, Paul Ville

In 1798, a boy (Cargol) who resembles a wild beast is discovered in the woods in central France. He is sent to the Institute for the Deaf and Dumb in Paris where Dr Jean Itard

(Truffaut) struggles to make him walk upright, wear clothes and give him speech. Dedicated to Jean-Pierre Léaud, the remarkable child in Truffaut's first feature *The Four Hundred Blows*, this coolly made but very moving film has another extraordinary performance from a young boy. Cargol, of gypsy parentage, is directed by Truffaut (playing the doctor without any emotion) from in front of the camera instead of behind it. Based on a true case, the film meticulously charts each fascinating step in the boy's education, making an interesting comparison with *The Miracle Worker.*

The Wild Duck

Die Wildente

Austria 1976 100 mins col
Solaris

d **Hans W. Geissendörfer**
sc **Hans W. Geissendörfer**
ph **Robby Müller**
m **Nils Janette Walen**
Jean Seberg, Peter Kern, Bruno Ganz, Anne Bennent, Heinz Moog

Hjalmar (Kern), a dreaming egoist who can barely feed his wife, Gina (Seberg), and 14-year-old daughter, Hedwig (Bennent), attempts in vain to better his situation with the Consul Werle (Moog). Geissendörfer's faithful adaptation of the first of Ibsen's symbolist plays was shot in seven weeks in a studio in Vienna. In as much as the play can be made cinematic, and without being *The Quintessence Of Ibsenism* in Shaw's terms, it is a well-acted, satisfactory version. It was Jean Seberg's last film before her suicide three years later. *The Wild Duck* was filmed in a silent German version in 1925, and was made again in Norway in 1963—astonishingly, the first indigenous screen adaptation of an Ibsen work.

Wildente, Die see Wild Duck, The

Wild Flowers see Fleurs Sauvages, Les

Wild Game

Wildwechsel

W. Germany 1972 102 mins col
Intertel

d **Rainer Werner Fassbinder**
sc **Rainer Werner Fassbinder**
ph **Dietrich Lohmann**
m **Beethoven**
Jörge Von Liebenfels, Ruth Drexel, Eva Mattes, Kurt Raab, Harry Baer

Although 19-year-old Franz (Baer) and 14-year-old Hanni (Mattes) are in love, he is sent to prison for seducing an under-age girl. When he is released a few months later, Hanni goads him into killing her repressive father (Liebenfels). Franz Kroetz protested violently against Fassbinder's interpretation of his play, but by playing up the Nazism and incipient incestuousness of the girl's father, the director-writer gives an extra dimension to this depiction of distorted social values. The cool distance from which Fassbinder views his subject, and the somewhat stylized performances, allow the spectator to assess the rather melodramatic tale with a certain objectivity.

Wild Strawberries

Smultronstället

Sweden 1957 93 mins bw
Svensk Filmindustri

d **Ingmar Bergman**
sc **Ingmar Bergman**
ph **Gunnar Fischer**
m **Erik Nordgren**
Victor Sjöström, Ingrid Thulin, Gunnar Björnstrand, Bibi Andersson, Naima Wifstrand, Max Von Sydow

An aged professor (Sjöström) travels by car with his daughter-in-law (Thulin) to Lund to receive an honorary doctorate. A visit to the family home and various encounters on the way inspire reminiscences, insights into his own shortcomings and intimations of mortality. Bergman's smiles and tears on a summer's day make for a mellow modern morality, with the action shifting skilfully between past and present, dream and reality. Most memorable of all is the extraordinary farewell performance of 78-year-old Victor Sjöström, Bergman's predecessor as the greatest Swedish film director.

Best Film Berlin 1958

Wildwechsel see Wild Game

Will O' The Wisp see Feu Follet, Le

The Wind

Finyé

Mali 1982 100 mins col
Les Films Cissé

d **Souleymane Cissé**
sc **Souleymane Cissé**
ph **Etienne Carton De Grammont**
m **Pierre Gorse, Mali folk music**
Fousseyni Sissoko, Goundo Guisse, Balla Moussa Keïta, Ismaïla Sarr, Oumou Diarra

Two university students from very different backgrounds fall in love, to the chagrin of their families. He fails his exams because of his poor background, and she passes hers because she is the daughter of the repressive military governor. Together they join other students in a fight for equality. Although Cissé's third feature (in seven years) is a bitter attack on the 'haves' on behalf of the 'have nots' in his country, he demonstrates subtlety, perception and humour. Sissoko and Guisse, as the young couple, are a delight.

The Windbreaker

Il Petomane

Italy 1983 101 mins col
Filmauro

d **Pasquale Festa Campanile**
sc **Leo Benvenuti, Piero De Bernardi, Enrico Medioli**
ph **Alfio Contini**
m **Carlo Rustichelli, Paolo Rustichelli**
Ugo Tognazzi, Mariangela Melato, Vittorio Caprioli, Anna Maria Gherardi, Ricardo Tognazzi

Joseph Pujol, or Le Petomane, is famous for his music hall act which consists of farting in an amazing variety of sounds and styles, and to music. Slighted by some deprecating remarks from Paris society, he determines to present a Haydn symphony to the accompaniment of his farts and, after a period in the wilderness and some complications in a love affair, achieves his ambition. The film, inspired by the existence of the actual Pujol, is a tiresome imbroglio of fact, fiction and caricature, somewhat redeemed by Tognazzi's courtly, comic and touching performance in the title role.

Windfall In Athens

Kyriakatiko Xyprima

Greece 1956 112 mins bw
Millas Film

d **Michael Cacoyannis**
sc **Michael Cacoyannis**
ph **Alvize Orphanelli**
m **André Ryder**
Elli Lambetti, George Pappas, Dimitri Horn, Tasso Kavadia, Chris Pateraki, Margarita Georgiou

A pretty Athens salesgirl (Lambetti) has a lottery ticket stolen and, in her distress, is befriended by a middle-aged lawyer (Pappas) who becomes infatuated with her. When the lottery is drawn, the stolen ticket wins and turns out to be in the possession of a penniless young musician (Horn) who bought it from the thieves. Needless to say, the ensuing battle between him and the girl leads to romance. Overlong for its featherweight subject and utterly predictable, this is nonetheless a good-natured and pleasant little entertainment. Of note as Cacoyannis' debut feature and, although moderately successful outside Greece, it does not really point to the particular gifts of the former English-educated lawyer and actor which would soon show in more substantial and interesting films.

Wings Of Desire

Der Himmel Über Berlin

W. Germany 1987 127 mins bw/col
Road Movies (Berlin)/Argos Films(Paris)

d **Wim Wenders**
sc **Wim Wenders in collaboration with Peter Handke**
ph **Henri Alekan**
m **Jürgen Knieper**
Bruno Ganz, Solveig Dommartin, Otto Sander, Curt Bois, Peter Falk

Two angels, Damiel (Ganz) and Cassiel (Sander) descend to earth to observe and minister to the people of Berlin, but Damiel falls in love with a trapeze artist (Dommartin) and decides to give up his immortality and become human. For the first hour, this angel's eye view of a modern and crumbling Berlin inhabited by a melancholy population in need of hope holds the attention. Gradually, the enterprise becomes more spurious as Damiel, benignly smiling throughout, is drawn towards life in the shape of a performer at a tatty circus. It also ludicrously turns out that Peter Falk, making a film in Berlin, is himself a fallen angel. The only real magic comes from the masterful, mostly black-and-white photography of the great 78-year-old Henri Alekan. It is to be noted that the Circus in the film is called the Cirque Alekan.

Best Director Cannes 1987

Winifred Wagner Und Die Geschichte

see Confessions Of Winifred Wagner, The

Winter Light

aka The Communicants

Nattvardsgasterna

Sweden 1962 80 mins bw
Svensk Filmindustri

d **Ingmar Bergman**
sc **Ingmar Bergman**
ph **Sven Nykvist**
m **Extracts from Swedish psalms**
Max Von Sydow, Ingrid Thulin, Gunnar Björnstrand, Gunnel Lindblom

A village pastor (Björnstrand) begins to doubt his beliefs, and his sermons fail to give comfort to his mistress (Thulin), a widow (Lindblom), and a man (Von Sydow) afraid of nuclear annihilation. The central drama in Bergman's despairing trilogy of the 1960s, between *Through A Glass Darkly* and *The Silence*, is probably his most austere and solemn film on the silence of God. The opening church service brilliantly suggests the hollowness behind the ritual and the joylessness of the congregation by a juxtaposition of stark images. The excellent cast expose the characters' suffering in revealing close-ups.

Wir Wunderkinder see Aren't We Wonderful?

The Wishing Tree

Drevo Zhelanya

USSR 1976 107 mins col
Grusiafilm (Georgia)

d **Tengiz Abuladze**
sc **Revaz Inanishvili, Tengiz Abuladze**
ph **Lomer Ahvlediani**
m **Bidzina Kvernadze, Yakov Bobohidze**
Lika Kavzharadze, Soso Dzachvliani, Zaza Kolelishvili, Kote Daushvili, Sofiko Chiaureli

An account of life in a Georgian village at the beginning of the century where the village elder decrees rules which, in the case of two young lovers, leads to tragedy. Among the gallery of village eccentrics is a man who, in the process of searching for the legendary wishing tree, freezes to death. A curious film, visually elaborate and employing a primitive camera style to capture its *faux-naïf* approach to colour and composition, but unfolding a series of somewhat random incidents at too leisurely a pace to hold one's interest.

Witchcraft Through The Ages

Häxan

Sweden 1922 83 mins bw
Svensk Filmindustri

d **Benjamin Christensen**
sc **Benjamin Christensen**
ph **Johan Ankarstjerne**
m **Silent**
Oscar Stribolt, Clara Pontoppidan, Karen Winther, Maren Pedersen, Elith Pio, Benjamin Christensen

Christensen conducts a documentary-style investigation into the practice of witchcraft from medieval times using etchings, manuscripts and re- enacted episodes, in which he also plays the Devil. His most famous film, three years in the making, sees the witch as the victim of a superstitious and repressive Church. An array of cinematic devices creates a film that is illuminating, frightening and amusing. In 1968, an unnecessary sound version was released with a commentary by William Burroughs and a jazz score.

The Witches

Le Streghe

Italy 1966 104 mins col
Dino De Laurentiis Cinematografica (Rome)/
Les Productions Artistes Associés (Paris)

d **1) Luchino Visconti 2) Mauro Bolognini 3) Franco Rossi 4) Pier Paolo Pasolini 5) Vittorio De Sica**
sc **1) Guiseppe Patroni Griffi 2) Age, Scarpelli, Bernardino Zapponi 3) Franco Rossi, Luigi Mani 4) Pier Paolo Pasolini 5) Cesare Zavattini**
ph **Giuseppe Rotunno**
m **Piero Piccioni, Ennio Morricone**
Silvana Mangano and 1) Annie Girardot 2) Alberto Sordi 3) Pietro Tordi 4) Totò, Ninetto Davoli 5) Clint Eastwood

1) A film star, on holiday in the Swiss Alps, is miserable and lonely despite being surrounded by many people. 2) A woman drives an injured truckdriver to hospital, but makes a fatal detour. 3) When a Sicilian woman cannot marry the man of her choice, her father starts a civil war. 4) Two tramps invent a maid servant. 5) The bored wife of a banker imagines her husband competing for her favours with comic-book heroes. This not uninteresting portmanteau picture displays the undoubted versatility of La Mangano (Mrs De Laurentiis) in five different roles. Pasolini's wonderful little wordless fable emerges the winner, with Visconti, among the others, riding the clichés best. Look out for a young Helmut Berger (then Steinberger), playing his first movie role in the first story.

The Witches Of Salem

aka The Crucible

Les Sorcières De Salem

France 1957 143 mins bw
Borderie/CICC/Pathé/DEFA (E. Germany)

d **Raymond Rouleau**
sc **Jean-Paul Sartre**
ph **Claude Renoir**
m **Georges Auric**
Simone Signoret, Yves Montand, Mylène Demongeot, Jean Debucourt

In Massachusetts in 1692, a servant girl (Demongeot) accuses her mistress Elizabeth Proctor (Signoret) of witchcraft to hide her guilt for having slept with her master (Montand), thus leading to multiple trials and executions. It is a pity that the McCarthy witch-hunt prevented this adaptation of *The Crucible* from being filmed in America because its author Arthur Miller was blacklisted at the time. It is a pity, too, that his superb play was not given less lethargic direction or a less plodding screenplay. It was the first co-starring of Montand and Signoret, who had played the Proctors on stage the previous year.

Witch Hunt

Forfolgelsen

Norway 1981 93 mins col
Norsk Film AS/Svensk Filminstitutet

d **Anja Breien**
sc **Anja Breien**
ph **Erling Thurmann-Andersen**
m **Arne Nordheim**
Lil Terselius, Björn Skagestad, Anita Björk, Erik Mørk, Ella Hval

During the 17th-century, a Swedish woman (Terselius), who has left her husband, comes to a remote mountain community in Norway in search of work. Her arrival coincides with a witch hunt and, soon, her foreignness, her independence and her frankness (she openly has an affair with a farmhand) place her under suspicion of being a witch. Anja Breien made Norway's biggest international success, *Wives*, and returns here, albeit in a very different context, to the theme of non-conformist women and their place in society. It's a fascinating piece, superbly photographed on location, and with a persuasively strong central performance from Terselius.

Without Anaesthesia see Rough Treatment

Without Pity

Senza Pietà

Italy 1949 94 mins bw
Lux Films

d **Alberto Lattuada**
sc **Tullio Pinelli, Federico Fellini, Alberto Lattuada**
ph **Aldo Tonti**
m **Nino Rota**
Carla Del Poggio, John Kitzmiller, Pierre Claudé, Giulietta Masina, Folco Lulli

Without Witnesses

A prostitute (Del Poggio), working for a ruthless bootlegger (Claudé), falls in love with a black American soldier (Kitzmiller) on the run from the military police. They arrange to hold up the bootlegger in order to get enough money to go to America, but things go wrong. While the film seems to be part of the Neo-Realist movement then at its peak—an almost documentary view of post-war Livorno—it draws its inspiration from American *film noir*. The stylistic balance is well struck, and it looks forward to the early films of Fellini (here a co-writer).

Without Witnesses see Private Conversation, A

The Witness

A Tanu

Hungary 1968 108 mins col
Mafilm Studio One

d **Péter Bacsó**
sc **Péter Bacsó**
ph **János Zsombolyai**
m **György Yukán**
Ferenc Kállai, Lajos Öze, Zoltán Fabri, Béla Both, Lili Monori

Loyal Party member József Pelikán (Kállai) illegally slaughters the family pig and is imprisoned, but swiftly released. He puts it down to his long friendship with Zoltán Daniel (Fabri), a government minister who has, in fact, disappeared. His successor takes an interest in József, constantly promoting and protecting him, and finally grooming him to be a prosecution witness at Zoltán's trial on a trumped-up treason charge. The Hungarian authorities withheld *The Witness* for nine years, a compliment to its ability to wound official political sensibilities. Bacsó has opted to transmit his message through comedy but, although the film, set in 1949, is an interesting and often funny document, it suffers from a clash of styles—farce, satire, the odd dash of symbolism—which leaves it ultimately less satisfying than it ought to be.

Wives

Hustruer

Norway 1975 84 mins col
Norsk Film

d **Anja Breien**
sc **Anja Breien (with the cast)**
ph **Halvor Naess**
m **Finn Ludt**
Anne Marie Ottersen, Frøydis Armand, Katja Medbøe, Nøste Schwab, Helge Jordal, Sverre Anker Ousdal

Former schoolmates Mie, Heidrun and Kaja (Ottersen, Armand and Medbøe), married and in their late twenties, meet for the first time since leaving school. The occasion is an all-night reunion party for their former teacher, at which they indulge in heady reminiscence and decide to go off and kick over the traces together. After sobering up in a sauna, they pool resources, send postcards to their husbands and embark on a series of irresponsible adventures that include getting themselves picked up. Breien's episodic and improvisational film, very well photographed and appealingly acted, is pro-feminist in its sympathies, accurate in its portrait of female companionship and quite clever in asking questions about responsibility. It's a good-natured escapade, too, but one in which the women's behaviour sometimes seems contrived and irritatingly immature.

Wives (10 Years After)

Hustruer Ti Ar Etter

Norway 1985 88 mins col
Norsk Film

d **Anja Breien**
sc **Anja Breien, Knut Faldbakken**
ph **Erling Thurmann-Andersen**
Anne Marie Ottersen, Frøydis Armand, Katja Medbøe, Henrik Scheele, Per Frisch, Jon Eikemo, Nøste Schwab

Ten years after their reckless spree together (see *Wives* above), the three friends meet again, this time at a fancy dress party just before Christmas, and decide to repeat history. Times, however, have changed. Heidrun (Armand) is divorced and involved with Jens (Scheele), himself estranged from his wife but not ready for another commitment; Kaja (Medbøe) is still married to Kristian (Frisch), who comes after her in a rage at having been abandoned; Mie's husband is remarried and she (Ottersen), too, has a lover (Eikemo). Using the same narrative structure as the previous film,

Breien uncompromisingly exposes the changes that age and failure in marriage have made to her protagonists. This time, their friendship almost founders as the result of the tensions each is suffering in relation to her need for men. The three end up spending Christmas in a deserted hotel in Malmö where the manager waits on them hand and foot, but this time there is little joy to be had. If the atmosphere of female *angst* grows a little hard to take, the film is undeniably truthful and the return of the same actresses is a bonus.

Woman see Amore, L'

Woman From Nowhere, The see Femme De Nulle Part, La

Woman In Chains
(US: The Female Prisoner)
La Prisonnière

France 1968 110 mins col
Films Corona/Vera Films(Paris)/Fono Roma(Rome)

d **Henri-Georges Clouzot**
sc **Henri-Georges Clouzot, Monique Lange, Marcel Moussy**
ph **Andreas Winding**
m **Gilbert Amy, various classical pieces**
Laurent Terzieff, Elizabeth Wiener, Bernard Fresson, Dany Carrel, Dario Moreno

Film editor José (Wiener) and her artist husband Gilbert (Fresson) are frank about their extra-marital affairs, although they don't seem too happy about it. When José becomes involved with gallery-owner Stan (Terzieff), seemingly a morose loner but who turns out to indulge in photographing women in poses of masochistic submission, Gilbert's equilibrium deserts him. After his only half successful attempt to climb on the bandwagon of modernity with *The Truth* some 10 years earlier, Clouzot did not make another film until this one. (Ill-health prevented him from completing *L'Enfer* in 1964). Here, the French master of the dark-toned thriller has left all his familiar ground behind him and the result is an uncomfortable, unconvincing and rather tawdry sex drama which serves no purpose.

Woman In The Dunes see Woman Of The Dunes

The Woman In The Moon
(US: By Rocket To The Moon)
Die Frau Im Mond

Germany 1929 107 mins bw
UFA

d **Fritz Lang**
sc **Thea Von Harbou, Fritz Lang**
ph **Curt Courant, Oskar Fischinger, Otto Kanturek**
m **Silent**
Willy Fritsch, Klaus Pohl, Gustav Von Wangenheim, Gerda Maurus, Fritz Rasp

A scientist (Pohl), who believes the moon is rich in gold, has a rocket flight financed by a group of five capitalists hoping to corner the gold market. The other passengers include a young rocket designer (Fritsch), the woman he loves (Maurus), and her fiancé (Von Wangenheim). Films made about moon landings long before the actual event are often quaint and misguided. Lang's comic-strip fantasy is no exception, and the plot is both melodramatic and farcical. However, the best moments come from the few elements of clairvoyance, such as the take-off, portrayed in dramatic montage and camera angles. Later, the Nazis thought the film authentic enough to take it out of distribution because the rocket design seems to have been close to one they were working on at the time. One of the film's technical advisors, Professor Hermann Oberth, was, in fact, a contributor to the V2 programme.

Woman In White
Le Journal D'Une Femme En Blanc

France 1965 110 mins bw
Sopac/S.N.E.G. (Paris)/Arco Film (Rome)

d **Claude Autant-Lara**
sc **Jean Aurenche, René Wheeler**
ph **Michel Kelber**
m **Michel Magne**
Marie-José Nat, Jean Valmont, Claude Gensac, Robert Benoît, Paloma Matta, Jean-Pierre Dorat

Claude Sauvage (Nat) is a senior medical

student specializing in gynaecology. She becomes especially involved in the plight of an unmarried patient, ill from a self-induced abortion, and fights, side by side with resident specialist Pascal (Valmont) to save the girl's life, but to no avail. Claude herself ends up pregnant by Pascal and determines to have the baby out of wedlock. Another controversial piece of didacticism from Autant-Lara, this time arguing for the rights of women, particularly the right to contraception. The thematic focus is, however, slightly befuddled and the points are made by implication rather than directly. The film's professional gloss is high and the world of the hospital is portrayed with clinical realism, but the plot and surface characterization is pure *Dr Kildare*.

A Woman Is A Woman

Une Femme Est Une Femme

France 1961 85 mins col
Rome Paris

d **Jean-Luc Godard**
sc **Jean-Luc Godard**
ph **Raoul Coutard**
m **Michel Legrand**
Jean-Paul Belmondo, Jean-Claude Brialy, Anna Karina, Marie Dubois

A nightclub stripper (Karina) wants to have a baby and settle down with her lover (Brialy). When he refuses, she turns to his best friend (Belmondo). Godard's third film is also one of his lightest hearted, his first in colour and 'Scope, and the first in which Karina played a dominant role. In fact, the camera is so besotted by her that it's no surprise that the director behind it married her soon after. There are the usual literary references, jump cuts and film quotes, but it seems to be Godard's homage to the MGM musical, set mainly in a Paris apartment with three characters. Jeanne Moreau appears briefly.

Best Actress (Anna Karina) Cannes 1961

The Woman Next Door

La Femme D'Á Côté

France 1981 106 mins col
Les Films Du Carrosse/T.F.1 Films Production

d **François Truffaut**
sc **François Truffaut, Suzanne Schiffman, Jean Aurel**
ph **William Lubtchansky**
m **Georges Delerue**
Gérard Depardieu, Fanny Ardant, Henri Garcin, Michèle Baumgartner, Véronique Silver, Roger Van Hool

Bernard Coudray (Depardieu), a marine engineer, lives with his wife and child in a village near Grenoble where social life revolves round the tennis club. When the Bauchards move in next door, Bernard discovers that Mathilde (Ardant) is none other than the old flame of his youth. The pair resurrect their affair with disastrous and, finally, fatal consequences. Doubtless intended as a sophisticated study of an *amour fou* among the professional middle classes, Truffaut's film emerges as an old-fashioned, lazy and somewhat boring soap opera. The protagonists are sketchy and superficial, and Depardieu (wooden) and Ardant (petulant) walk through their roles, failing to lend them any interest or to arouse any sympathy. Sad to see Truffaut's special gifts as badly tarnished as this.

Woman Of Antwerp see Dédée

Woman Of Darkness

Yngsjömordet

Sweden 1966 120 mins bw
Svensk Filmindustri

d **Arne Mattsson**
sc **Eva Dahlbeck**
ph **Lasse Björne**
Gunnel Lindblom, Gösta Ekman, Christina Schollin, Rune Lindström, Heinz Hopf

On a chilly morning in 1890, Anna Mansdotter (Lindblom) is taken from her prison cell to the executioner's yard where she is to be decapitated for committing incest and murder. As she awaits the axe, Anna recalls the trial where, in the face of local outrage but lack of evidence, she and her son and lover Per (Ekman) were found guilty of the murder of his wife. Her recollections then move further back to the events that led up to the crime. One of Sweden's most prolific directors of thrillers (and the romantic *One Summer Of Happiness*) here turned his attention to the notorious real-life case of the last woman to suffer the death penalty in Sweden. Not surprisingly, the film is grimly doom-laden, but superbly photographed and with a powerful central performance from Lindblom. A bit overloaded with gloomy visual clichés, it is nonetheless absorbing and disturbing.

Woman Of The Dunes

(US: Woman In The Dunes)

Suna No Onna

Japan 1964 127 mins bw
Teshigahara

d **Hiroshi Teshigahara**
sc **Kobo Abe**
ph **Hiroshi Segawa**
m **Tohru Takemitsu**
Eiji Okada, Kyoto Koshoda

An entomologist (Okada) finds an attractive young widow (Kishoda) living at the bottom of an enormous sandpit on a deserted beach. He becomes her prisoner, endlessly shovelling sand to avoid being engulfed. Teshigahara's best known film is a heavily symbolic erotic drama which effectively uses extreme close-ups until the characters almost become part of the landscape. Produced independently and made for a mere $100,000, it made a great impression on Western audiences.

Special Jury Prize Cannes 1964

Woman Of The River

La Donna Del Fiume

Italy 1954 95 mins col
Les Films De Centaur

d **Mario Soldati**
sc **Basilio Franchini, Giorgio Bassani, Pier Paolo Pasolini, Florestano Vancini, Antonio Altoviti, Mario Soldati**
ph **Otello Martelli**
m **Angelo Lavagnino**
Sophia Loren, Gérard Oury, Rik Battaglia, Lise Bourdin, Enrico Olivieri

A girl (Loren) working in a village factory is loved by the local policeman (Oury), but her heart belongs to a handsome smuggler (Battaglia). When he deserts her, refusing to believe she is carrying his child, she betrays him. Years pass, bringing only disaster to all concerned. The usual excess of screenwriters so beloved of the Italian cinema—working from a story by no less than Alberto Moravia and Ennio Flaiano—dreamed up no more than a familiar potboiler, reminiscent in particular of *Bitter Rice*. What it's got going for it, of course, is sexy, smouldering Sophia, showcased by producer Carlo Ponti whom she would soon marry. Interesting, too, to note the first screenplay credit of Pasolini, who would move on to more profound topics.

A Woman Or Two

Une Femme Ou Deux

France 1985 97 mins col
Hachette Première/Philippe Dussart/FR3 Films/DD Productions

d **Daniel Vigne**
sc **Daniel Vigne, Elizabeth Rappenau**
ph **Carlo Varini**
m **Kevin Mulligan, Evert Verhees, Toots Thielemans**
Gérard Depardieu, Sigourney Weaver, Ruth Westheimer, Michel Aumont, Zabou, Jean-Pierre Bisson

Archeologist Julien (Depardieu) unearths the two million-year-old remains of the 'first Frenchwoman' and, as a result becomes embroiled with American advertising executive Jessica (Weaver) and follows her to New York. What starts out as a latter day French-flavoured screwball comedy, in which Jessica and Julien meet only because she's pretending to be somebody else, steadily disintegrates into a contrived and irritating farce without much point or purpose. One would have expected more from the director of *The Return Of Martin Guerre.*

A Woman's Decision

aka Quarterly Balance

Bilans Kwartalny

Poland 1974 99 mins col
Film Polski

d **Krzysztof Zanussi**
sc **Krzysztof Zanussi**
ph **Slawomir Idziak**
m **Wojciech Kilar**
Maya Komorowska, Piotr Franczewski, Marek Piwowski

Marta (Komorowska) combines marriage and motherhood with a career as an accountant. She is the union representative at her office, and a reliable friend in solving other people's problems. Her strengths desert her, however, in facing difficulties in her own marriage which crystallize in having to decide whether to leave with her lover (Piwowski). This is an accessible and straightforward exercise from Zanussi, dealing perceptively and sympathetically with its subject. An enjoyable film, enhanced by a marvellous performance from Komorowska, but it reduces the sharpness of its impact by its intrusively lush and over-romantic photography.

A Woman's Face

En Kvinnas Ansikte

Sweden 1937 100 mins bw
Svensk Filmindustri

d **Gustaf Molander**
sc **Gösta Stevens**
ph **Äke Dahlquist**
m **Eric Bengtson, Chopin**
Ingrid Bergman, Anders Henrikson, Georg Rydeberg, Karin Carlsson-Kavil, Goran Bernhard, Tore Svennberg

Anna Holm(Bergman), hideously disfigured since childhood by a facial scar received in an accident, has become an embittered and remorseless woman. A successful operation transforms her into a beauty and softens her nature, so that she shoots the man she loves rather than commit a murder on his behalf. Bergman working, as in *Intermezzo*, with Molander, is breathtaking in what is essentially high melodrama, adapted from a French play by De Croisset and here given effectively solemn and well-controlled treatment. An extremely entertaining piece of hokum, it surfaced again in Hollywood in 1941 and became a hit for Joan Crawford, directed by George Cukor.

A Woman's Life

aka A Woman's Story

Onna No Rekishi

Japan 1964 120 mins bw
Toho

d **Mikio Naruse**
sc **Ryozo Kasahara**
ph **Asaichi Nakai**
m **Ichiro Saito**
Hideko Takamine, Tatsuya Nakadai, Akira Takarada, Yuriko Hoshio

Nobuko (Takamine) is widowed when her husband is killed in the war. Later, her beloved son marries a girl of whom she disapproves, and is then killed in a car accident. She comes to terms with her grief only when she learns to accept her daughter-in-law, pregnant with the dead husband's child. This moving film has been directed and acted with sensitivity, perception, and a delicacy that is characteristic of the Japanese cinema when it deals with intimate subjects on a small canvas. Nobuko's struggle with her inner self is timeless and universal.

Woman's Story, A see Woman's Life, A

Woman Who Dared, The see Ciel Est À Vous, Le

Word, The see Ordet

The Working Class Go To Heaven

(US: Lulu The Tool)

La Classe Operaia Va In Paradiso

Italy 1972 126 mins col
Euro International Films

d **Elio Petri**
sc **Elio Petri, Ugo Pirro**
ph **Ubaldo Terzano**
m **Ennio Morricone**
Gian Maria Volonté, Mariangela Melato, Salvo Randone, Gino Pernice, Luigi Diberti, Donato Castellaneta

Lulu Massa (Volonté), a factory piece-worker, is obsessed with achieving the highest daily output, thus arousing the resentment of his fellow-workers, inviting exploitation by the shop stewards and frustrating his mistress (Melato) with whom he lives. Crisis and change come when he is temporarily laid off as a result of an accident at work and he visits a retired worker (Randone), now in a mental hospital, who gives him a different perspective. Returning to work, he attempts to become a leader in the Left's fight for better conditions. A plot synopsis cannot possibly convey the complex layers of Petri's film. He explores the corruption of capitalism with ingenuity and imagination, at the same time revealing the innate weaknesses of Lulu the man, whose working and domestic lives become destructively reversed. The film has its flaws, particularly in failing to flesh out anybody who represents the system that is under attack, but it's an intelligent and provocative work, boasting a magnificent performance from Volonté, and from Melato as the person who appears the quickest to grasp reality.

Best Film Cannes 1972

The World Of Apu

Apu Sansar

India 1959 117 mins bw
Satyajit Ray-West Bengal Government

d **Satyajit Ray**
sc **Satyajit Ray**
ph **Subrata Mitra**
m **Ravi Shankar**
Soumitra Chatterjee, Sharmila Tagore, Shapan Mukerjee

Apu (Chatterjee), a young man in Calcutta, comes to love his wife of an arranged marriage, but when she dies in childbirth, he refuses to see his son. They are reconciled some years later. The final part of the 'Apu Trilogy' is taken at a less leisurely pace and is more conventionally structured than the previous two (*Pather Panchali*, 1955 and *Aparajito*, 1956), but it is still imbued with the same keen observation, beautiful playing, and memorable scenes such as Apu's scattering of the pages of his novel over a mountain at dawn. The triptych, a humanist masterpiece of cinema begun in Ray's mind almost 10 years before, ends on a note of hope.

Woyzeck

W. Germany 1978 80 mins col
Herzog/ZDF

d **Werner Herzog**
sc **Werner Herzog**
ph **Jörg Schmidt-Reitwein**
m **Vivaldi, Benedetto Marcello**
Klaus Kinski, Eva Mattes, Wolfgang Reichmann, Willy Semmelrogge, Josef Bierbichler, Paul Burian

Franz Woyzeck (Kinski), a poor, simple-minded, brow-beaten soldier, takes on a variety of jobs in order to support his common-law wife Maria (Mattes) and their young child. When he suspects Marie of betraying him with the handsome Drum Major (Bierbichler), Woyzek stabs her to death. Although prettily shot in Czechoslovakia, and sticking as closely as possible to the 27 short scenes of Georg Büchner's remarkable 1836 play, the film rings hollow, and Kinski, in his third role for Herzog, fails to elicit sympathy for the character. It was filmed more imaginatively in 1947 by Georg Klaren.

Best Supporting Actress (Eva Mattes) Cannes 1979

WR—Misterije Organizma see WR—Mysteries Of The Organism

WR—Mysteries Of The Organism

WR—Misterije Organizma

Yugoslavia 1971 86 mins col
Neoplanta (Yugoslavia)/Telepool (W. Germany)

d **Dušan Makavejev**
sc **Dušan Makavejev**
ph **Pega Popović, Aleksandar Petković**
m **Bojana Makavejev**
Milena Dravić, Jagodar Kaloper, Zoran Radmilović, Ivica Vidović, Miodrag Andrić, Tuli Kupferberg

A documentary and fictional examination of the theories of sexologist Wilhelm Reich and the actions of two of his Yugoslav disciples (Dravić and Kaloper). Using a fusion of styles, the anarchic Makavejev ambiguously compares the West with the Eastern bloc countries and Reich with Stalin. While seeming to admire Reich, he gives him and his followers, including porn merchants, enough rope to beat each other with. This shocking, amusing and exasperating movie caused offence wherever it was shown and made a lot of money.

Wrong Movement

Falsche Bewegung

W. Germany 1975 103 mins col
Solaris Film/Peter Genée-Bernd Eichinger

d **Wim Wenders**
sc **Peter Handke**

ph **Robby Müller**
m **Jürgen Knieper**
Rüdiger Vogler, Hanna Schygulla, Ivan Desny, Marianne Hoppe, Hans-Christian Blech, Peter Kern, Nastassja Nakszynski (Nastassja Kinski)

Wilhelm (Vogler), a discontented writer, leaves on a journey through Germany. On his travels he gets involved with Laertes (Blech), an old singer, Therese Farmer (Schygulla), an actress, a suicidal industrialist (Desny) and a poet (Kern). Inspired by *Wilhelm Meister's Apprenticeship,* Goethe's renowned *Bildungsroman*, Wenders and Handke derived a typically bleak and cryptic road movie which set Rüdiger Vogler in melancholy motion again. (It is the second of a trilogy between *Alice In The Cities* and *Kings Of The Road.*) The vision of a figurative and literal wasteland that is Germany and its suggestions of the Nazi past are effective, if rather obvious, milestones on the journey. Nastassja Kinski makes a non-speaking screen debut in the role of an adolescent mute juggler.

Wszystko Na Sprzedaz see Everything For Sale

Wunder Des Malachias, Das see Miracle Of Malachias, The

Wutai Jiemei see Two Stage Sisters

Wuthering Heights
Abismos De Pasión

Mexico 1953 90 mins bw
Producciones Tepeyac

d **Luis Buñuel**
sc **Luis Buñuel**
ph **Augustín Jiménez**
m **Raúl Lavista**
Jorge Mistral, Irasema Dilian, Lilia Prado, Ernesto Alonso

Having been adopted by his master when a young orphaned servant boy, the adult Alexandro (Mistral), returns to the family home having made his fortune. He resumes his close, passionate and almost mystical relationship with his adopted sister Cataline (Dilian), to the discomfort of her husband whose sister Isabelle (Prado) falls in love with him. Driven by motives of revenge, he marries her, while Cataline, now desperately ill, dies, and Alexandro is killed by Isabelle's brother. Played in harsh, white light against a dry and stony Mexican landscape which bears little resemblance to the murky Yorkshire moors of Emily Brontë's celebrated novel, Buñuel's adaptation nonetheless successfully and imaginatively captures the dark heart of the original. This is a skilfully made and intimate melodrama with deeper resonances than the surface would suggest. Although remaining true to the spirit of the novel, a favourite of the Surrealists, the director makes the work very much his own: a relentless celebration of *l'amour fou*, combined with a strongly implied critique of class differences. Mistral, an utterly ruthless Alexandro/Heathcliffe, is, together with the rest of the cast, adequate.

Wuya Yu Maque see Crows And Sparrows

---

x

Xala

aka The Curse

Senegal 1974 123 mins col
Filmi Domireew/Société Nationale De Cinématographie

d **Ousmane Sembène**
sc **Ousmane Sembène**
ph **Georges Caristan**
m **Samba Diabara Samb**
Tierno Leye, Seune Samb, Miriam Niang, Younouss Seye, Dieynaba Niang, Fatim Diagne

A rich and powerful businessman (Leye) is about to take a third wife (Dieynaba Niang). Neither of his other two wives (Samb and Seye) nor his daughter (Miriam Niang) is happy with the situation. On his wedding night, his usual prowess lets him down. Someone has evidently bestowed a Xala on him—a curse rendering the victim impotent. It is only a matter of time before his financial affairs start to crumble. Sembène sees the impotence of the man as the impotence of Senegal, a country that has failed to remove class injustices and has 'formed new classes that only know how to imitate Western *bourgeoisies*'. Based on the director's own widely praised novel, this savage and funny satirical film was equally extolled, except by the Senegalese government which cut the last 10 minutes.

Xiaozi Bei see Bus Number Three

The Yankee
Jänken

Sweden 1970 95 mins bw
Svensk Filminstitutet

d **Lars Forsberg**
sc **Lars Forsberg**
ph **Petter Davidson**
Anita Ekström, Lars Green, Mona Dan-Bergman, Louise Hedberg, Inger Ekström, Tommy Sernling

Inger (Anita Ekström) has grown up in a slum, is bored by her factory job and ill-equipped to deal with the pregnancy that results from an affair with a boy visiting from America. She moves in with Mascot (Green), an old friend and small-time crook, and lands in all kinds of uninvited trouble. Lars Forsberg's debut film is assured in execution, well photographed, sympathetic and secures an excellent performance from Ekström. However, the story of an underprivileged girl as society's victim is numbingly familiar.

Yawar Mallku see Blood Of The Condor

A Year Of The Quiet Sun
Rok Spokojnego Słońca

Poland 1984 108 mins col
Tor Film Unit(Warsaw)/Teleculture(New York)/ Regina Ziegler(W.Berlin)

d **Krzysztof Zanussi**
sc **Krzysztof Zanussi**
ph **Slawomir Idziak**
m **Wojciech Kilar**
Maja Komorowska, Scott Wilson, Hanna Skarżanka, Ewa Dalkowska, Vadim Glowna

In the Poland of 1946, an American soldier (Wilson) and a Polish widow (Komorowska) strike up a relationship, even though neither speaks the other's language. He is under orders to go to Berlin where he hopes she will join him, but he waits in vain. The drab and bitter aftermath of the war in East Europe is visited once again and so is the story of unfulfilled love in Zanussi's circumspect, stoical and rather conventional film. Yet there are interesting details—Polish profiteers, the problems of crossing the border—and two tender performances from Wilson and Zanussi's favourite actress, Komorowska.

Best Film Venice 1984

Yeelen see Brightness

Yellow Earth
Huang Tudi

China 1984 89 mins col
Guangxi Film Studio

d **Chen Kaige**
sc **Zhang Ziliang**
ph **Zhang Yimou**
m **Zhao Jiping**
Xue Bai, Wang Xueqi, Tan Tuo, Liu Qiang

In the spring of 1939, a soldier arrives in a small community to research folk songs. He becomes involved in the life of one family—an old man, his 14-year-old daughter about to make an arranged marriage, and the younger son—and finds himself unable to alter their traditional, superstitious ways. Yellow Earth came like a bolt from the blue in the West, altering received ideas of Chinese cinema. A heady mixture of music, poetry, dance and drama, it is set against the vividly evoked dusty, barren landscape of the title. Although it has a rather pessimistic ending—the people do not heed the soldier's exhortation that 'all of China must change'—audiences know that it finally did.

Ye Shan see In The Wild Mountains

Yesterday Girl
Abschied Von Gestern
W. Germany 1966 90 mins bw
Kairos Film/Alexander Kluge/Independent

d **Alexander Kluge**
sc **Alexander Kluge**
ph **Edgar Reitz, Thomas Mauch**
Alexandra Kluge, Günther Mack, Hans Korte, Eva Marie Meinecke

Anita G. (Kluge), a completely amoral and rebellious East German girl, escapes to West Germany only to find herself still at odds with a different but equally conservative society. Alexander Kluge's first feature was based on the case of a woman he encountered during his work as a lawyer. Greatly influenced by Godard, he uses documentary-style interviews, combined with jump cuts, inserts, and other fragmenting techniques, to get to the heart of his subject. It came as a breath of fresh air to the moribund German film industry. Kluge was instrumental in setting up the Young German Film Fund which would help finance quality productions, and *Yesterday Girl* received over 60 per cent of its budget from it. The director's sister made a superb film debut as Anita G.

Special Jury Prize Venice 1966

Yesterday, Today And Tomorrow
Ieri, Oggi, Domani
Italy 1963 119 mins col
CCC(Rome)/Les Films Concordia(Paris)

d **Vittorio de Sica**
sc **1)Eduardo De Filippo, Isabella Quarantotti**
2) Cesare Zavattini, Billa Billa Zanuso
3) Cesare Zavattini
ph **Giuseppe Rotunno**
m **Armando Trovaioli**
Sophia Loren, Marcello Mastroianni, Aldo Guiffre, Agostino Salvietta, Tina Pica, Armando Trovaioli, Giovanni Ridolfi, Gennaro Di Gregorio

Three separate stories, 'Adelina Of Naples', 'Anna Of Milan', and 'Mara Of Rome', utilize the services of a distinguished director, two superstars, a leading dramatist (De Filippo), a highly skilled screenwriter (Zavattini), and one of the world's best colour cameramen. What a waste! The threadbare and slightly vulgar content is neither especially romantic nor particularly amusing, though the film looks handsome. The best segment is the first, in which Loren plays Adelina, a wife who avoids imprisonment for black-marketeering by keeping herself continuously pregnant by Mastroianni's sexy husband. It was clearly thought more highly of at the time (see below).

Best Foreign Film Oscar 1964

Yeux Sans Visage, Les see Eyes Without A Face

Yiddle With His Fiddle
Yidl Mitn Fidl
Poland 1936 92 mins bw
Greenfilm

d **Joseph Green, Jan Nowina-Przybylski**
sc **Joseph Green**
ph **Seweryn Steinwurzel**
m **Abraham Ellstein, Itzik Manger**
Molly Picon, Simche Fostel, Max Bozyk, Leon Liebgold, Dora Fakiel

A young woman (Picon) disguises herself as a boy and travels with a group of itinerant musicians in order to help support her aging father (Fostel). She falls in love with one of them (Liebgold). but must keep her real identity a secret. The first international Yiddish hit had all the essential ingredients. Technically superior to many of the cheap Yiddish films made in the USA at the time, it was full of well-known Jewish songs, comic vaudeville routines, a dose of tears, a wedding scene and a strong-willed heroine. The popular Yiddish comedienne, Molly Picon, at the height of her career, made the most of this role. The charming film also offers a glimpse of Jewish society in Poland before it was tragically destroyed.

Yidl Mitn Fidl see Yiddle With His Fiddle

Yijiang Chunshui Xiang Dong Liu see Spring River Flows East

Yngsjömordet see Woman Of Darkness

Yoidore Tenshi see Drunken Angel

Yojimbo

Japan 1961 110 mins bw
Toho

d **Akira Kurosawa**
sc **Ryuzo Kikushima, Akira Kurosawa**
ph **Kazuo Miyagawa**
m **Masaru Sato**
Toshiro Mifune, Eijiro Tono, Kamatari Fujiwara, Takashi Shimura, Seizaburo Kawazu, Isuzu Yamada, Hiroshi Tachikawa

Yojimbo (Mifune), a masterless samurai, wanders into a town to find it terrorized by two rival factions. He offers his services to the highest bidder but, uncovering treachery, he arranges events so that both sides will destroy each other. Kurosawa's love of the Western shows itself in the plot and in some of the set-ups (the small town with its wide street) and effective use of the wide 'Scope image—a compliment that was repaid by Sergio Leone's 'Spaghetti Western' remake, *A Fistful Of Dollars* (1964). Yet the film is also in the tradition of the *jidai-geki* (samurai action film), although the graphic violence and black humour tend to subvert the more stylized and serious examples of the genre. The big scenes leading up to the showdown between the cynical hero and villain are well staged, despite the over-use of the telephoto lens. *Sanjuro*,a semi- sequel of this popular film, was released the following year.

Yokihi see Empress Yang Kwei Fei, The

Yol

Turkey 1982 114 mins col
Güney/Cactus/Maran/Antenne 2/Swiss Television

d **Serif Gören**
sc **Yilmaz Güney**
ph **Erdogan Engin**
m **Sebastian Argol, Kendal**
Tarik Akan, Halil Ergün, Necmettin Cobanoglu, Serif Sezer, Meral Orhonsoy, Semra Ucar, Tuncay Akca, Hikmet Celik

The story of five prisoners on a week's parole. Yusuf (Akca) is arrested at the outset because he has lost his papers; Mevlut (Celik) is kept from his fiancée by patriarchal customs; Mehmit (Ergün) flees with his wife from her vengeful family; Omer (Cobanoglu), a Kurd, returns to his village to find it devastated by the Turkish army ; and Seyit (Akan) is required by tradition to kill his wife (Sezer) for having been unfaithful to him during his absence. *Yol* ('the road of life' being the nearest translation) was based on an extremely detailed script written by Güney, when he was in jail and directed in Turkey by his long-time assistant. The negatives were smuggled out to Europe where Güney, following his 1981 escape from prison, edited it. Acted with great conviction, against vividly realized landscapes, the film is an exceptionally powerful condemnation of an oppressive society.

Best Film Cannes 1982

You Are The World For Me

aka The Richard Tauber Story

Du Bist Die Welt Für Mich

Austria 1953 107 mins bw
Erma

d **Ernst Marischka**
sc **Ernst Marischka**
ph **Sepp Ketterer**
m **The Tauber Repertoire (Musical director Anton Profes)**
Rudolf Schock, Anne Marie Düringer, Richard Romanowsky, Fritz Imhof, Dagny Servaes

An account of the rise to fame of the world-famous tenor and operetta star, Richard Tauber (Schock). On his way to the top, he neglects the ballerina (Düringer) he loves and so loses her. And that is about as eventful as this conventional biopic ever gets. Efficiently made by Marischka, the doyen writer-producer-director of German musicals, Schock's singing is dubbed by recordings of Tauber himself (he died in 1948), making this a good bet for any extant fans, but rather dull and old-fashioned for anybody else.

The Young And The Damned

Los Olvidados

Mexico 1950 88 mins bw
Ultramar/Oscar Dancigers

d **Luis Buñuel**
sc **Luis Buñuel, Luis Alcoriza, Oscar Dancigers**

ph **Gabriel Figueroa**
m **Gustavo Pittaluga**
Alfonso Mejía, Miguel Inclán, Estela Inda, Roberto Cobo

Pedro (Mejía), a pure young boy, becomes corrupted and destroyed by Jaibo (Cobo) and a group of juvenile delinquents living a violent life in the slums of Mexico City. After making a couple of trashy commercial films in his first years of exile in Mexico, Buñuel was able to return to serious film-making. His last great film had been *Land Without Bread*, the stark documentary on the contrast between the poverty of the Spanish peasants and the wealth of the church. He continued where he had left off 18 years before and became famous once more. This powerful yet detached view of slum conditions and their effect on children was made in only 21 days but 'for several months I toured the slums...I came to know these people and much of what I saw went unchanged into the film'. The harsh realism—note the beating up of the blind musician (Inclán)—is mixed with Buñuel's surrealism in the dream sequences.

Best Director Cannes 1951

Young And The Passionate, The see Vitelloni, I

Young Aphrodites
Mikres Aphrodites
Greece 1962 98 mins bw
Minos Films/Anzervos Studios

d **Nikos Koundouros**
sc **Costas Sphikas, Vassilis Vassilikos**
ph **Giovanni Variano**
m **Yiannis Markopoulos**
Takis Emmanouel, Vangelis Joannides, Cleopatra Rota, Eleni Prokopiou, C. Papaconstantinou

In Ancient Greece, a group of mountain shepherds in search of pasture come upon a fishing village where the inhabitants are all women. Skymnos (Joannides), fascinated by this strange world, strikes up a tentative friendship with Chloë (Rota), a young girl he sees fishing in a rock pool. Meanwhile, Tsakalos (Emmanouel), seduces Arta (Prokopiou). Skymnos's dreams are shattered when Lykas (Papaconstantinou), a dumb shepherd boy, ravishes the innocent Chloë. Koundouros drew his material from the tale of *Daphnis And Chloë* and the *Idylls* of Theocritus. The result is a film of magical, mythological atmosphere, quite breathtaking in its settings and photography, primitive and poetic in tone. Nonetheless, although it was well received on release and won prizes, it is, frankly, very thin in content, sometimes slow and often twee.

Best Director Berlin 1963

The Young Have No Morals
(US: The Chasers)
Les Dragueurs
France 1959 78 mins bw
Lisbon Films/Films Fernand Rivers

d **Jean-Pierre Mocky**
sc **Jean-Pierre Mocky**
ph **Edmond Séchan**
m **Maurice Jarre**
Jacques Charrier, Charles Aznavour, Dany Robin, Anouk Aimée, Nicole Berger, Belinda Lee, Margit Saad, Inge Schoener, Dany Carrel

Freddy (Charrier), aged 20 and experienced, and Joseph (Aznavour), 25 but shy and green, spend an evening in Paris searching for their ideal girl. Before ending up at a society orgy where Freddy has a disillusioning encounter with an aimless beauty (Lee) while Joseph finds a sympathetic nurse (Berger), they encounter a string of women who include a cripple (Aimée) and a couple of Swedish Lesbians. In making his first film, actor Mocky adopts a New Wave approach and a subject reminiscent of Carné's *The Cheaters* (1958) but does so with more conviction. It is efficiently made and very well photographed, but both character development and moral centre are left underdeveloped and vague, leaving only surface attractions—pleasing ironies, a noticeably good score, and some lively acting.

The Young Ladies Of Wilko
Panny Z Wilka
Poland 1979 116 mins col
Zespól Filmowy(Warsaw)/Les Films Molière(Paris)

d **Andrzej Wajda**
sc **Zbigniew Kamínski**

ph **Edward Klosínski**
m **Szymanowski (First Violin Concerto)**
Daniel Olbrychski, Anna Seniuk, Christine Pascal, Maja Komorowska, Stanislawa Celinska, Krystyna Zachwatowicz, Zofia Jaroszewska, Tadeusz Bialoszczynski

Viktor Ruben (Olbrychski), a solitary bachelor who saw service in World War I, is advised by his doctor to take a vacation. He visits his aunt and uncle in Wilko where the neighbouring estate belongs to five sisters (six until one died), in all of whose lives Viktor once featured as a romantic fantasy. The reunion rekindles new hopes in each now disillusioned breast, but they fade with the collective realization that all of them have changed. Wajda, temporarily deserting topical political statement, has made an exquisite period piece which lays bare the futility of attempting to resurrect the past. Wonderfully photographed and perfectly cast, the film has an engaging theatrical charm, but is overloaded with wearisome Chekhovian yearning.

Young Törless

Der Junge Törless

W. Germany 1966 85 mins bw
Franz Seitz/Nouvelles Éditions De Film

d **Volker Schlöndorff**
sc **Volker Schlöndorff**
ph **Franz Rath**
m **Hans Werner Henze**
Matthieu Carrière, Bernd Fischer, Marian Seidowsky, Alfred Dietz, Barbara Steele

At a semi-military boarding school, Törless (Carrière), an intelligent pupil, is the silent witness to the dreadful bullying of his friend Basini (Seidowsky) by the sadistic Beineberg (Fischer) and Reiting (Dietz). By the time he realizes his moral responsibility it is too late. Twenty-seven-year-old Schlöndorff's first feature, which won the International Critics award at Cannes, is an accomplished transposition of the Robert Musil novel of embryonic Nazis at the turn of the century. It marks the beginning of the director's obsession with modern German history. Among the excellent young actors, is Barbara Steele, English queen of Italian horror movies, as a waitress who teaches the boys things that are not on the school curriculum.

The Young Wolves

Les Jeunes Loups

France 1968 111 mins col
S.N.C.(Paris)/West Film(Rome)

d **Marcel Carné**
sc **Marcel Carné, Claude Accursi**
ph **Jacques Robin**
m **Jack Arel, Guy Magenta, Cyril**
Haydée Politoff, Christian Hay, Roland Lesaffre, Yves Benyeton, Maurice Garrel, Bernard Dhéran

Alain Langlois (Hay), good-looking and ruthlessly ambitious, exploits the affections of wealthy older women, at the same time becoming involved with Sylvie (Politoff), a girl of his own age. When Ugo (Garrel), a wealthy property owner in a position to employ Alain, is attracted to Sylvie, the young man passes her off as his sister and they move in to Ugo's mansion, until Sylvie grows jealous of Alain's ambiguous relationship with his employer. There is little in this clichéd, determinedly 'with it' account of youthful amorality to link it with Marcel Carné other than its technical competence. The characters are superficial stereotypes and the director lacks a point of view, failing even to inject the energy of his first disappointing attempt to move with the times, *The Young Have No Morals* (1958).

You Only Love Once

(US: The Melody Haunts My Memory)

Samo Jednom Se Ljubi

Yugoslavia 1980 103 mins col
Jadran Film

d **Rajko Grlić**
sc **Rajko Grlić, Branko Šömen, Srdjan Karanović**
ph **Tomislav Pinter**
m **Branislav Živković**
Predrag Manojlović, Vladica Milosavljević, Zijah Sokolović, Mladen Budiščak, Erland Josephson

Just after World War II, Tomislav (Manojlović), a Partisan hero with Communist ideals, becomes obsessed with and marries Baby (Milosavljević), a middle-class ballerina with traditional views. The tempestuous relationship leads him to prison and a mental hospital. On one level, the film reflects the difficult and complex post-war period when Yugoslavia was searching for a new identity—the class conflict is compellingly revealed—and on another level, it can be seen as a study of a destructive relationship. However, the hero's macho behaviour and the woman's shallow passivity—only she is seen nude in the graphic sex scenes—reveal a rather dubious ambiguity of purpose.

Youthful Sinners
aka The Cheats
Les Tricheurs

France 1958 117 mins bw
Silver Films/Cinétel/Zebra Film/CD

d **Marcel Carné**
sc **Marcel Carné, Jacques Sigurd**
ph **Claude Renoir**
Jacques Charrier, Pascale Petit, Andrea Parisy, Jean-Paul Belmondo

A middle-class Parisian student (Charrier) becomes involved with a crowd dedicated to defying social and moral convention. Nonetheless, he and one of the young crowd (Petit) fall in love, until blackmail, infidelity and group pressures sabotage the relationship which ends in tragedy. Carné, who had reached the peak of his creativity with *Les Enfants Du Paradis* in 1945, was making a bid to keep up with the youth movement by dealing with contemporary subject matter. Alas, in spite of some good moments and the introduction of some new stars, his efforts resulted in an overlong and somewhat tedious film.

The Youth Of Maxim
Yunost Maksima

USSR 1935 97 mins bw
Lenfilm

d **Grigori Kozintsev, Leonid Trauberg**
sc **Grigori Kozintsev, Leonid Trauberg**
ph **Andrei Moskvin**
m **Dmitri Shostakovitch**
Boris Chirkov, Stepan Kayukov, Valentina Kibardina, Michael Tarkhanov

In 1910, Maxim (Chirkov), a young worker, falls in love with Natasha (Kibardina) and through a militant Bolshevik (Kayukov) becomes a revolutionary. He is drawn into the struggle against workers' exploitation and is arrested. The team of Kozintsev and Trauberg, dissatisfied with contemporary representations of the Bolsheviks as 'heroes of adventure fiction', created the most human of revolutionary films, a study of a flesh-and-blood unromanticized individual caught up in the struggle. There is plenty of humour mixed with the message and Maxim is no mean accordian player (his theme tune is still a favourite in the Soviet Union). The lively episodic structure, Chirkov's natural performance (he spent months working in a factory and talking to old Bolsheviks prior to filming) and Moskvin's photographic compositions are at their best in the first of what became *The Maxim Trilogy*, followed by *The Return Of Maxim* and *The Vyborg Side*.

Yoyo

France 1965 97 mins bw
C.A.P.A.C(Paris)

d **Pierre Etaix**
sc **Pierre Etaix, Jean-Claude Carrière**
ph **Jean Boffety**
m **Jean Paillaud**
Pierre Etaix, Luce Klein, Philippe Dionnet, Claudine Auger

A millionaire, bored by the solitude and idle luxury of his life, yearns for his former sweetheart (Klein). Later, he recognizes her as the equestrienne in a visiting circus and, when the Wall Street crash robs him of his wealth, he joins her and her clown child, Yoyo, who is his son. Yoyo grows up to be a star and takes steps to restore his father's now decaying château, but... In his second feature, Etaix pays tribute to the tone and technique of the silent cinema with a nostalgic and enchanting comedy romance, filming the first half-hour or so without dialogue (but with splendid sound effects, such as the creaking of the vast château doors). As both the adult Yoyo and the millionaire, Etaix brings the same control and individual sense of style to his performance as to his direction.

Yukinojo Henge see Actor's Revenge, An

Yunost Maksima see Youth Of Maxim, The

Z

France 1968 125 mins col
Reggane Films/ONCIC(Algiers)

d **Costa-Gavras**
sc **Jorge Semprun, Costa-Gavras**
ph **Raoul Coutard**
m **Mikis Theodorakis**
Yves Montand, Irene Papas, Jean-Louis Trintignant, Jacques Perrin, François Périer, Charles Denner, Bernard Fresson, Jean Bouise

In an unidentified Mediterranean country, support is growing for 'Z' (Montand), the leader of the pacifist opposition party. Following a meeting, 'Z' is knocked down by a van and dies after undergoing brain surgery. An investigating magistrate (Trintignant) assigned to the case, treats the death as murder when he uncovers a secret organization supported by the government and police. Based on a novel by Vassili Vassilikos, this very slick and effective political thriller, shot in Algeria by the Greek-born Costa-Gavras, plainly points its finger at the Colonels' regime in Greece. Despite the topicality, and the simple treatment of complicated issues, the film's message and passion still communicate to an audience because, though the specifics have altered, the generality of totalitarian regimes has not. Its popularity and awards rocketed the director into world prominence and enabled him to continue making the kind of political thrillers which were his speciality.

Best Foreign Film Oscar 1969
Best Actor (Jean-Louis Trintignant) Cannes 1969

Zacharovannaya Desna see Enchanted Desna, The

Zamach see Answer To Violence

Zangiku Monogatari see Story Of The Late Chrysanthemums, The

Zärtlichkeit Der Wölfe see Tenderness Of Wolves

Zazie
Zazie Dans Le Métro

France 1960 88 mins col
Nouvelles Éditions

d **Louis Malle**
sc **Louis Malle, Jean-Paul Rappeneau**
ph **Henri Raichi**
m **Fiorenzo Carpi**
Catherine Demongeot, Philippe Noiret, Carla Marlier, Vittorio Caprioli, Hubert Deschamps, Annie Fratellini, Yvonne Clech

Precocious, foul-mouthed pre-teen Zazie (Demongeot) spends 36 hours with her female impersonator uncle Gabriel (Noiret) in Paris with the sole intention of going for a ride on the Métro, but everything seems to conspire to prevent this. Malle's brave attempt to find visual equivalents to the eccentric syntax of Raymond Queneau's novel by using a series of cinematic tricks, quotes from other movies and silent comedy techniques, was more frenetic than funny. The surreal view of Paris in bright colours gives much pleasure, but even that burns itself out.

Zazie Dans Le Métro see Zazie

Zbehovia A Poutníci see Deserter And The Nomads, The

Zemlya see Earth

Zénu Ani Kvêtinou Neuhodis see Never Strike A Woman—Even With A Flower

Zerkalo see Mirror

Zéro De Conduite

France 1933 45 mins bw
Gaumont/Franco/Aubert

d **Jean Vigo**
sc **Jean Vigo**
ph **Boris Kaufman**
m **Maurice Jaubert**
Jean Dasté, Louis Lefèvre, Gilbert Pruchon, Robert Le Flon, Delphin, Coco Goldstein

At a dreadful and repressive boarding school in a Paris suburb, four schoolboys organize an uprising because of the petty restrictions imposed on them. Little money and not much experience account for the rough edges of Vigo's iconoclastic masterpiece, but these only add to its strange, anarchic poetry. It has a fresh, child's-eye view of authority from which adults are seen as hypocritical, oppressive and corrupt. The headmaster, played by the long-bearded dwarf Delphin (who killed himself in 1938), is looked down upon by the boys, whereas the only likeable teacher (Dasté) does handstands and imitations of Chaplin. The most celebrated sequences are the dormitory pillow fight that becomes a snow-covered wonderland of feathers and a mock Catholic procession. After its first showing, the film was banned on political grounds until 1945. Its influence on François Truffaut and Jean-Luc Godard is noticeable, and it was the direct inspiration behind Lindsay Anderson's highly-acclaimed *If*... (1968).

Zezowate Szczescie see Bad Luck

Zhivoi Trup see Living Corpse, The

Zhonghua Nuer see Daughters Of China

Ziemia Obiecana see Land Of Promise

Znak Bedy see Sign Of Disaster

Zouzou

France 1934 100 mins bw
Arys Films

d **Marc Allégret**
sc **Carlo Rim**
ph **Michel Kelber**
m **George Van Parys, Vincent Scotto**
Josephine Baker, Jean Gabin, Pierre Larquey, Yvette Lebon, Palau, Madeleine Guitry

Zouzou (Baker) adores her foster-brother (Gabin), a womanizing sailor. They go to Paris and find work in a music hall where Zouzou, given an opportunity to step into the star's shoes, becomes one herself. This stock yarn is an unashamed showcase for the considerable gifts of the legendary black American entertainer who became the toast of Paris, and includes her memorable rendition of 'Pour Moi Y'a Qu'un Homme Dans Paris'. Incidental pleasures include a good evocation of the backstage atmosphere at the music hall and a clutch of showy production numbers which are best described as Busby Berkeley out of *Folies Bergère*. But it is the extraordinary dynamism of singer-dancer Baker that holds everything together.

Zuckerbaby see Sugarbaby

Zur Chronik Von Grieshuus see Chronicles Of The Grey House, The

Zvenigora

USSR 1927 66 mins approx bw
VUFKU

d **Alexander Dovzhenko**
sc **Alexander Dovzhenko**
ph **Boris Zavelev**
m **Silent**

Das Zweite Erwachen Der Christa Klages

Mikola Nademsky, Polina Otava, Semyon Svashenko, Alexander Podorozhin, Mikhail Barbe, Astafiev

An old man (Nademsky) and his two grandsons, one revolutionary (Svashenko), one reactionary (Podorozhin), go in search of treasure buried in the hill of Zvenigora. On the way, the grandfather dreams of early Ukrainian history, and the reactionary grandson advertises his own suicide at a theatre to raise money. The first of Dovzhenko's films in which he had total freedom was experimental and allegorical, changing from dream to reality, past to present, an example of the last flowering of the exciting *avant-garde* Soviet cinema of the 1920s, the product of a young, revolutionary society. When Eisenstein and Pudovkin saw it, they gave 'a joyful welcome to our new colleague,' and the three directors celebrated with an all-night drinking session.

Zweite Erwachen Der Christa Klages, Das see Second Awakening Of Christa Klages, The

---

Zwischen Zeit Und Ewigkeit see Between Time And Eternity

Zwischen Zwei Kriegen see Between Two Wars

Zycie Rodzinne see Family Life